SMALL CRAFT ALMANAC 2005

EDITORS
Neville Featherstone & Peter Lambie

**THE UNITED KINGDOM & IRELAND
AND DENMARK TO GIBRALTAR**

REEDS PRACTICAL BoatOwner
SMALL CRAFT ALMANAC 2005

Editors: Neville Featherstone & Peter Lambie

The Editors would like to thank the many official bodies who have kindly provided essential information in the preparation of this Almanac. They include the UK Hydrographic Office, Trinity House, Northern Lighthouse Board, Irish Lights, HM Nautical Almanac Office, HM Stationery Office, HM Customs, Meteorological Office and the Maritime and Coastguard Agency.

Information from the Admiralty List of Lights, Admiralty Tide Tables and the Admiralty List of Radio Signals is reproduced with the permission of the UK Hydrographic Office and the Controller of HMSO. Extracts from the following are published by permission of the Controller of HM Stationery Office: International Code of Signals, 1969; Meteorological Office Weather Services for Shipping. Phases of the Moon and Sun/Moon rising and setting times are derived from the current editions of the Channel and Eastern Almanacs, and are included by permission of HM Nautical Almanac Office. UK and Foreign tidal predictions are supplied by the UK Hydrographic Office, Taunton TA1 2DN. Acknowledgment is also made to the following authorities for permission to use tidal predictions stated: Royal Danish Administration of Navigation and Hydrography, Farvandsvæsnet: Esbjerg. SHOM, France: Dunkerque, Dieppe, Le Havre, Cherbourg, St Malo, Brest, Pointe de Grave, Authorisation (No. 81/2004). Rijkswaterstaat, The Netherlands: Vlissingen, and Hoek van Holland. BSH, Hamburg and Rostock: Helgoland, Wilhelmshaven and Cuxhaven (BSH 8095·02/99-Z1102). Marina Institute Hidrográfico, Portugal: Lisboa, Authorisation (No. 3/2004). **Warning:** The UK Hydrographic Office has not verified the reproduced data and does not accept any liability for the accuracy of reproduction or any modifications made thereafter.

Corrections Any necessary corrections will be published on the website www.reedsalmanac.co.uk. Data in this almanac is corrected up to Edition 24/2004 of the *Admiralty Notices to Mariners*.

Important note The information, charts, maps and diagrams in this Almanac should not be relied on for navigational purposes as this Almanac is intended as an aid to navigation only. The information contained within should be used in conjunction with official hydrographic data. Whilst every care has been taken in its compilation, this Almanac may contain inaccuracies and is no substitute for the relevant official hydrographic charts and data, which should always be consulted in advance of, and whilst, navigating in the area.

The publishers, editors and their agents accept no responsibility for any errors or omissions, or for any accidents or mishaps which may arise from its use.

Before using any waypoint or coordinate listed in this Almanac it must first be plotted on an appropriate official hydrographic chart to check its usefulness, accuracy and appropriateness for the prevailing weather and tidal conditions.

The decision to use and rely on any of the data in this Almanac is entirely at the discretion of, and is the sole responsibility of, the Captain of the vessel employing it.

Correspondence Letters on nautical matters should be addressed to: The Editor, Reeds PBO Small Craft Almanac, 37 Soho Square, London W1D 3QZ.

Practical Boat Owner is published monthly by IPC Magazines Ltd, Kings Reach Tower, Stamford Street, London SE1 9LS. For subscription enquiries and overseas orders call 0845 676 7778 (fax: 01444 445599).

Copyright © Adlard Coles Nautical 2004 All rights reserved. No reproduction, copy or transmission of this publication may be made without written permission. No paragraph of this publication may be reproduced, copied or transmitted save with permission or in accordance with the provisions of the Copyright, Designs and Patents Act 1988 (as amended). Any person who does any unauthorised act in relation to this publication may be liable to criminal prosecution and civil claims for damages. Printed in the UK.
ISBN 0 7136 7059 2. A CIP catalogue record for this book is available from the British Library.

Production manager: Chris Stevens
Cartography & production: Jamie Russell, Chris Stevens

Adlard Coles Nautical
37 Soho Square, London W1D 3QZ
Tel: +44 (0)207 758 0200 Fax: +44 (0)207 758 0222
www.reedsalmanac.co.uk

FOREWORD

Welcome to the almanac that's designed especially for skippers and crew of yachts large and small. Brought to you by *Practical Boat Owner*, Britain's biggest-selling boating magazine, and the team of editors at publishers Adlard Coles, it contains all the information that you need at your fingertips.

Whether you are looking for the time of high water, the VHF channel for your next port of call, or where to find a weather forecast, all this and more are contained within the compact, handy-sized *PBO Almanac*.

Twenty specially designed geographical sections for selected lights, buoys and waypoints will help you plan your passages, from short coastal hops, to Channel crossings, as far north as Denmark, or south to Gibraltar.

We hope you find the large-format tidal curves easy to use. We also aim to please with the full-colour fold-out covers with information that all skippers need close at hand for quick reference: lights and shapes, Mayday, buoyage, code flags and chart symbols.

Our aim each year is to make the almanac even better, so please let us know if there are any further changes or additions which you would like to see included in the 2006 edition.

Enjoy your cruising in 2005.

Sarah Norbury
Editor
Practical Boat Owner
Britain's biggest selling boating magazine

NAVIGATION
CONTENTS

Abbreviations 5
General language glossary 6

CHAPTER 1 - NAVIGATION
Contents 8
Lights, buoys and waypoints by Areas .... 9 to 52
Marinas: Access, VHF, Tel .... 53 to 58
Sunrise/set, moonrise/set .... 59 to 62
Speed, time & distance table 63
Distance off dipping/rising lights 64
Conversions table 65

CHAPTER 2 - WEATHER
Contents 66
Beaufort scale & Met terminology 67
UK shipping forecast areas/record .... 68 to 69
Weather sources in the UK .... 70 to 80
Weather sources abroad .... 81 to 92
Weather glossary .... 92 to 93

CHAPTER 3 - COMMUNICATIONS
Contents 94
Radio operation .... 95 to 96
Radio data .... 97 to 98
Port radio .... 99 to 107
VTS charts .... 108 to 111
Coast radio .... 112 to 114
Sound signals & Shapes 115

CHAPTER 4 - SAFETY
Contents 116
Think about safety 117
Mayday .... 118 to 119
First aid .... 120 to 123
Coastguard services .... 124 to 131
Emergency VHF Direction Finding Service .... 132 to 134
Naval exercise areas .... 135 to 138
GMDSS .... 139 to 140

CHAPTER 5 - TIDES
Contents 141
Dover tidal ranges 142
Brest tidal coefficients 143
Tidal calculations .... 144 to 147
Calculations/curves, Bournemouth to Selsey .... 148 to 151
Secondary ports: time/height differences .... 152 to 170
Tidal gates .... 171 to 179
Tidal stream charts .... 180 to 217
Tidal curves & predictions .... 218 to 413

Index .... 414 to 415

ABBREVIATIONS

AC, ACA	Admiralty Chart, Admiralty Chart Agent	Lt F	Light float
		Lt Ho	Lighthouse
ALL	Admiralty List of Lights	Lt V	Light vessel
ALRS	Admiralty List of Radio Signals	LW	Low Water
Bcst	Broadcast	M	Sea mile(s)
BST	British Summer Time	m	Metre(s)
By(s)	Buoy(s)	Météo	Météorologie/Weather
CD	Chart Datum	MF	Medium Frequency
CG	Coastguard	MHWN	Mean High Water Neaps
Ch	Channel (VHF)	MHWS	Mean High Water Springs
chan.	Channel (navigational)	MHz	Megahertz
cm	Centimetre(s)	MLWN	Mean Low Water Neaps
CROSS	Centre Régional Opérationnel de Surveillance et Sauvetage (MRCC)	MLWS	Mean Low Water Springs
		MMSI	Maritime Mobile Service Identity
CRS	Coast Radio Station(s)	MRCC	Maritime Rescue Co-ordination Centre
DF	Direction Finding		
Dir Lt	Directional light	MRSC	Maritime Rescue Sub-Centre
DSC	Digital Selective Calling	MSI	Maritime Safety Information
DST	Daylight Saving Time	N	North
E	East	NCM	North Cardinal Mark (buoy/beacon)
ECM	East Cardinal Mark (buoy/beacon)		
		Oc	Occulting light
ED	European Datum	PHM	Port-hand Mark (buoy/beacon)
EPIRB	Emergency Position Indicating Radio Beacon		
		Pt(e)	Point(e)
F	Fixed light/ force	R	Red
Fl	Flashing light	R	River
FM	Frequency Modulation	Ra	Coast Radar Station
G	Green	Racon	Radar Transponder Beacon
GMDSS	Global Maritime Distress and Safety System	RCC	Rescue Coordination Centre
		RG	Emergency RDF Station
H, Hrs, h	Hour(s)	R/T	Radiotelephony
H24	Continuous	S	South
Hbr	Harbour	s	second(s) of time
Hd	Head, headland	SAR	Search and Rescue
HF	High Frequency	SCM	South Cardinal Mark (buoy/beacon)
HJ	Day service only, Sunrise to Sunset		
		SHM	Starboard-hand Mark (buoy/beacon)
ht	Height		
HW	High Water	Sig	Signal
HX	No fixed hours	Sig Stn	Signal Station
Hz	Hertz	SMS	Short Message Service
IALA	Intl Association of Lt Ho authorities	SOG	Speed over the ground
IDM	Isolated Danger Mark (buoy/beacon)	SOLAS	Safety of Life at Sea (IMO Convention)
IMO	International Maritime Organisation	SSB	Single Sideband (Radio)
		SRR	Search & Rescue Region
Inmarsat	International Maritime Satellite System	Stn	Station
		Tfc	Traffic
Is, I	Island, Islet	TSS	Traffic Separation Scheme
Iso	Isophase light	UT	Universal Time
K/Kn	Knot(s)	VHF	Very High Frequency
kHz	Kilohertz	VTS	Vessel Traffic Service
km	Kilometre(s)	W	West
Lat	Latitude	W	White
Ldg	Leading	WCM	West Cardinal Mark (buoy/beacon)
LMT	Local Mean Time		
Long	Longitude	WGS	World Geodetic System (datum)
LT	Local Time		
Lt(s)	Light(s)	WPT	Waypoint
Lt by	Light buoy	Y	Yellow, orange, amber

Chapter 1

NAVIGATION

GENERAL LANGUAGE GLOSSARY. See also Weather Glossary in Chapter 2

ENGLISH	GERMAN	FRENCH	SPANISH	DUTCH
ASHORE				
Ashore	An Land	A terre	A tierra	Aan land
Airport	Flughafen	Aéroport	Aeropuerto	Vliegveld
Bank	Bank	Banque	Banco	Bank
Boathoist	Bootskran	Travelift	Travelift	Botenlift
Boatyard	Bootswerft	Chantier naval	Astilleros	Jachtwerf
Bureau de change	Wechselstelle	Bureau de change	Cambio	Geldwisselkantoor
Bus	Bus	Autobus	Autobús	Bus
Chandlery	Yachtausrüster	Shipchandler	Efectos navales	Scheepswinkel
Chemist	Apotheke	Pharmacie	Farmacia	Apotheek
Dentist	Zahnarzt	Dentiste	Dentista	Tandarts
Doctor	Arzt	Médecin	Médico	Dokter
Engineer	Motorenservice	Ingénieur/mécanique	Mecánico	Ingenieur
Ferry	Fähre	Ferry/transbordeur	Ferry	Veer/Pont
Garage	Autowerkstatt	Station service	Garage	Garage
Harbour	Hafen	Port	Puerto	Haven
Hospital	Krankenhaus	Hôpital	Hospital	Ziekenhuis
Mast crane	Mastenkran	Grue	Grúa	Masten kraan
Post office	Postamt	Bureau de poste/PTT	Correos	Postkantoor
Railway station	Bahnhof	Gare de chemin de fer	Estación de ferrocanil	Station
Sailmaker	Segelmacher	Voilier	Velero	Zeilmaker
Shops	Geschäfte	Boutiques	Tiendas	Winkels
Slip	Slip	Cale	Varadero	Helling
Supermarket	Supermarkt	Supermarché	Supermercado	Supermarkt
Taxi	Taxi	Taxi	Taxis	Taxi
Village	Ort	Village	Pueblo	Dorp
Yacht club	Yachtclub	Club nautique	Club náutico	Jacht club
NAVIGATION				
Abeam	Querab	A côté	Por el través	Naast
Ahead	Voraus	Avant	Avante	Voor
Astern	Achteraus	Arrière	Atrás	Achter
Bearing	Peilung	Cap	Maración	Peiling
Buoy	Tonne	Bouée	Boya	Boei
Binoculars	Fernglas	Jumelles	Prismáticos	Verrekijker
Channel	Kanal	Chenal	Canal	Kanaal
Chart	Seekarte	Carte	Carta náutica	Zeekaart
Compass	Kompass	Compas	Compás	Kompas
Compass course	Kompass Kurs	Cap du compas	Rumbo de aguja	Kompas koers
Current	Strömung	Courant	Coriente	Stroom
Dead reckoning	Koppelnavigation	Estime	Estimación	Gegist bestek
Degree	Grad	Degré	Grado	Graden
Deviation	Deviation	Déviation	Desvio	Deviatie
Distance	Entfernung	Distance	Distancia	Afstand
Downstream	Flußabwärts	En aval	Río abajo	Stroom afwaards
East	Ost	Est	Este	Oost
Ebb	Ebbe	Jusant	Marea menguante	Eb
Echosounder	Echolot	Sondeur	Sonda	Dieptemeter
Estimated position	Gegißte Position	Point estimé	Posición estimado	Gegiste positie
Fathom	Faden	Une brasse	Braza	Vadem

Chapter 1

ENGLISH	GERMAN	FRENCH	SPANISH	DUTCH
Feet	Fuß	Pieds	Pie	Voet
Flood	Flut	Flot	Flujo de marea	Vloed
Handbearing compass	Handpeilkompass	Compas de relèvement	Compás de marcaciones	Handpeil kompas
Harbour guide	Hafenhandbuch	Guide du port	Guia del Puerto	Havengids
High water	Hochwasser	Peine mer	Altamer	Hoog water
Latitude	Geographische Breite	Latitude	Latitud	Breedte
Leading lights	Feuer in Linie	Alignement	Luz de enfilación	Geleide lichten
Leeway	Abdrift	Dérive	Hacia sotavento	Drift
Lighthouse	Leuchtturm	Phare	Faro	Vuurtoren
List of lights	Leuchtfeuer Verzeichnis	Liste des feux	Listude de Luces	Lichtenlijst
Log	Logge	Loch	Corredera	Log
Longitude	Geographische Länge	Longitude	Longitud	Lengte
Low water	Niedrigwasser	Basse mer	Bajamar	Laag water
Metre	Meter	Mètre	Metro	Meter
Minute	Minute	Minute	Minuto	Minuut
Nautical almanac	Nautischer Almanach	Almanach nautique	Almanaque náutico	Almanak
Nautical mile	Seemeile	Mille nautique	Milla marina	Zeemijl
Neap tide	Nipptide	Morte-eau	Marea muerta	Dood tij
North	Nord	Nord	Norte	Noord
Pilot	Lotse	Pilote	Práctico	Loods/Gids
Pilotage book	Handbuch	Instructions nautiques	Derrotero	Vaarwijzer
RDF	Funkpeiler	Radio gonio	Radio-gonió	Radio richtingzoeker
Radar	Radar	Radar	Radar	Radar
Radio receiver	Radio, Empfänger	Récepteur radio	Receptor de radio	Radio ontvanger
Radio transmitter	Sender	Emetteur radio	Radio-transmisor	Radio zender
River outlet	Flußmündung	Embouchure	Embocadura	Riviermond
South	Süd	Sud	Sud, Sur	Zuid
Spring tide	Springtide	Vive-eau	Marea viva	Springtij/springvloed
Tide	Tide, Gezeit	Marée	Marea	Getijde
Tide tables	Tidenkalender	Annuaire des marées	Anuario de mareas	Getijdetafel
True course	Wahrer Kurs	Vrai cap	Rumbo	Ware Koers
Upstream	Flußaufwärts	En amont	Río arriba	Stroom opwaarts
VHF	UKW	VHF	VHF	Marifoon
Variation	Mißweisung	Variation	Variación	Variatie
Waypoint	Wegpunkt	Point de rapport	Waypoint	Waypoint/Route punt
West	West	Ouest	Oeste	West

OFFICIALDOM

ENGLISH	GERMAN	FRENCH	SPANISH	DUTCH
Certificate of registry	Schiffszertifikat	Acte de franchisation	Documentos de matrícuia	Zeebrief
Check in	Einklarieren	Enregistrement	Registrar	Check-in
Customs	Zoll	Douanes	Aduana	Douane
Declare	Verzollen	Déclarer	Declarar	Aangeven
Harbour master	Hafenmeister	Capitaine du port	Capitán del puerto	Havenmeester
Insurance	Versicherung	Assurance	Seguro	Verzekering
Insurance certificate	Versicherungspolice	Certificat d'assurance	Certificado deseguro	Verzekeringsbewijs
Passport	Paß	Passeport	Pasaporte	Paspoort
Police	Polizei	Police	Policía	Politie
Pratique	Verkehrserlaubnis	Pratique	Prático	Verlof tot ontscheping
Prohibited area	Sperrgebiet	Zone interdite	Zona de prohibida	Verboden gebied
Register	Register	Liste de passagers	Lista de tripulantes/rol	Register
Ship's log	Logbuch	Livre de bord	Cuaderno de bitácora	Logboek
Ship's papers	Schiffspapiere	Papiers de bateau	Documentos del barco	Scheepspapieren
Surveyor	Gutachter	Expert maritime	Inspector	Opzichter

NAVIGATION

CHAPTER 1 - NAVIGATION

CONTENTS

Selected lights, buoys and waypoints by Areas
- Area 1 - SW England 9
- Area 2 - S Central England 11
- Area 3 - SE England 13
- Area 4 - E England 14
- Area 5 - E Scotland 17
- Area 6 - NW Scotland 20
- Area 7 - SW Scotland 22
- Area 8 - NW England, Wales & E Ireland 24
- Area 9 - SW England, S Wales & S Ireland 26
- Area 10 - Ireland 28
- Area 11 - Denmark 31
- Area 12 - Germany 33
- Area 13 - Netherlands & Belgium 35
- Area 14 - N France 38
- Area 15 - N Central France & Channel Is 40
- Area 16 - NW France & N Biscay 42
- Area 17 - S Biscay 45
- Area 18 - N & NW Spain 47
- Area 19 - Portugal 49
- Area 20 - SW Spain & Gibraltar 51

Charts showing Marina access times, telephone and VHF
- England - South East 53
- Scotland & East England 54
- Ireland & West UK 55
- Germany, Netherlands & Belgium 56
- France 57
- Spain, Portugal & Gibraltar 58

Tables
- Sunrise/set times 59
- Moonrise/set times 61
- Speed, time and distance 63
- Distance off dipping/rising lights 64
- Conversions 65

AREA 1 South West England - *Isles of Scilly to Anvil Point*
SELECTED LIGHTS, BUOYS & WAYPOINTS | Positions are referenced to WGS84

▶ ISLES OF SCILLY
Bishop Rock ☆ 49°52'·37N 06°26'·74W, Fl (2) 15s 44m **24M**; part obsc 204°-211°, obsc 211°-233°, 236°-259°; Gy ○ twr with helo platform; *Horn Mo (N) 90s;* **Racon T, 18M, 254°-215°**.
Peninnis Hd ☆ 49°54'·28N 06°18'·22W, Fl 20s 36m **17M**; 231°-117° but part obsc 048°-083° within 5M; W ○ twr on B frame, B cupola.
Spanish Ledge ⚓ 49°53'·94N 06°18'·86W, Q (3) 10s; *Bell*.
N Bartholomew ⚓ 49°54'·49N 06°19'·99W, Fl R 5s.
Spencers Ledge ⚓ 49°54'·78N 06°22'·06W, Q (6) + L Fl 15s.
Steeple Rock ⚓ 49°55'·46N 06°24'·24W, Q (9) 15s.
Round Island ☆ 49°58'·74N 06°19'·40W, Fl 10s 55m **18M**, shown during periods of reduced vis only; 021°-288°; *Horn (4) 60s;* **Racon M, 10M**.

▶ SCILLY TO LAND'S END
Seven Stones ⚓ 50°03'·62N 06°04'·34W, Fl (3) 30s 12m **25M**; H24; R hull; *Horn (3) 60s;* **Racon O, 15M**.
Wolf Rock ☆ 49°56'·72N 05°48'·57W, Fl 15s 34m **16M**; H24; *Horn 30s;* **Racon T, 10M**.
Longships ☆ 50°04'·01N 05°44'·81W, Iso WR 10s 35m **W16M, R15**/13M; R189°-208°, R (unintens) 208°-307°, R307°-327°, W327°-189°; *Horn 10s*.
Runnel Stone ⚓ 50°01'·19N 05°40'·36W, Q (6) + L Fl 15s; *Whis*.
Tater-du ☆ 50°03'·14N 05°34'·68W, Fl (3) 15s 34m **20M**; 241°-074°; W ○ twr. Also FR 31m 13M, 060°-074° over Runnel stone and in places 074°-077° within 4M; *Horn (2) 30s*.

▶ NEWLYN AND PENZANCE
S Pier ☆ 50°06'·19N 05°32'·57W, Fl 5s 10m 9M.
Penzance S Pier ☆ 50°07'·07N 05°31'·68W, Fl WR 5s 11m **W17M, R**12M; R (unintens) 159°-224°, R224°-268°, W268°-344·5°, R344·5°-shore.
Lizard ☆ 49°57'·61N 05°12'·13W, Fl 3s 70m **26M**; H24; 250°-120°, partly visible 235°-250°; W 8-sided twr; *Horn 30s*.

▶ FALMOUTH
St Anthony Head ☆ 50°08'·47N 05°00'·96W, Iso WR 15s 22m, **W16M, R**14M, H24; W295°-004°, R004°-022° over Manacles, W022°-172°; *Horn 30s*.
Black Rock ⚓ 50°08'·68N 05°01'·74W, Q (3) 10s.
The Governor ⚓ 50°09'·15N 05°02'·40W, VQ (3) 5s.

▶ MEVAGISSEY
Victoria Pier ☆ 50°16'·15N 04°46'·93W, Fl (2) 10s 9m 12M; *Dia 30s*.

▶ FOWEY
Fowey ☆ 50°19'·62N 04°38'·84W, L Fl WR 5s 28m **W**11M, **R**9M; R284°-295°, W295°-028°, R028°-054°; W 8-sided twr, R lantern.
Whitehouse Pt ☆ 50°19'·98N 04°38'·24W, Iso WRG 3s 11m **W**11M, R/G8M; G017°-022°, W022°-032°, R032°-037°; R col.

▶ POLPERRO
Spy House Pt ☆ 50°19'·81N 04°30'·70W, Iso WR 6s 30m 7M; W288°-060°, R060°-288°.

▶ LOOE, EDDYSTONE
Banjo Pier ☆ 50°21'·05N 04°27'·06W, Oc WR 3s 8m **W15M**, R12M; R207°-267°, W267°-313°, R313°-332°.
Eddystone ☆ 50°10'·85N 04°15'·94W, Fl (2) 10s 41m **17M**. Same twr, Iso R 10s 28m 8M; 110·5°-130·5° over Hand Deeps; Gy twr, helicopter platform; *Horn 30s;* **Racon T, 10M**.

▶ PLYMOUTH
Draystone ⚓ 50°18'·85N 04°11'·07W, Fl (2) R 5s.
Plymouth bkwtr W ☆ 50°20'·07N 04°09'·53W, Fl WR 10s 19m **W**12M, **R**9M; W262°-208°, R208°-262°; W ○ twr. Same twr, Iso 4s 12m 10M; 033°-037°; *Horn 15s*.
Bridge Chan, No 1, ⚓ QG 4m; 50°21'·03N 04°09'·53W. No 2, ⚓ QR 4m.
Bkwtr E ⚓ 50°20'·01N 04°08'·25W, L Fl WR 10s 9m W8M, R6M; R190°-353°, W353°-001°, R001°-018°, W018°-190°.
Ldg lts 349°. Front, Mallard Shoal ⚓ 50°21'·60N 04°08'·33W, Q WRG 5m W10M, R/G3M; W △, Or bands; G233°-043°, R043°-067°, G067°-087°, W087°-099°, R099°-108° ldg sector. Rear, 396m from front, Hoe ⚓ Oc G 1·3s 11m 3M, 310°-040°; W ▽, Or bands.
QAB (Queen Anne's Battery) ldg lts ☆048·5°. Front, 50°21'·84N 04°07'·84W, FR, Or/W bcn. Rear, Dir Oc WRG 7.5s 14m 3M; G038°-047·2°, W047·2°-049·7°, R049·7°-060·5°.
Sutton Hbr, lock 50°21'·98N 04°07'·96W; IPTS.
PYH (Plymouth Yacht Haven), 2 FG (vert).
Mayflower marina, outer bkwtr, E end, 2 FR.

NAVIGATION

▶ RIVER YEALM
Sand Bar ≈ 50°18'·59N 04°04'·12W, Fl R 5s.

▶ SALCOMBE
Sandhill Point Dir ☆ 000°. 50°13'·77N 03°46'·67W, Fl WRG 2s 27m W10M, R/G7M; G182·5°-357·5°, W357·5°-002·5°; R002·5°-182·5°; R/W ◇ on W mast. Pound Stone, 230m S, R/W ⬇ in line 000°. Ldg lts 042·5°. Front 50°14'·53N 03°45'·31W, Q 5m 8M. Rear, 180m from front, Q 45m 8M.

Start Pt ☆ 50°13'·33N 03°38'·54W, Fl (3) 10s 62m **25M**; 184°-068°. Same twr: FR 55m 12M ; 210°-255° over Skerries Bank; *Horn 60s*.

▶ DARTMOUTH
Kingswear Dir ☆ 328°. 50°20'·81N 03°34'·10W, Iso WRG 3s 9m 8M; G318°-325°, W325°-331°, R331°-340°; W ○ twr.
Homestone ≈ 50°19'·60N 03°33'·56W, QR.
Castle Ledge ⬆ 50°19'·99N 03°33'·12W, Fl G 5s.

▶ BRIXHAM
Berry Head ☆ 50°23'·97N 03°29'·01W, Fl (2) 15s 58m 14M; 100°-023°; W twr. R lts on radio mast 5·7M NW.
Victoria bkwtr ☆ 50°24'·33N 03°30'·78W, Oc R 15s 9m 6M; W twr.
Fairway ☆ 159°. 50°23'·83N 03°30'·57W, Iso WRG 5s 4m 6M; G145°-157°, W157°-161°, R161°-173°.

▶ TORQUAY
⬆ 50°27'·42N 03°31'·80W, QG (May-Sep).

▶ TEIGNMOUTH
Outfall ≈ 50°31'·95N 03°27'·78W, Fl Y 5s; 288°/ 1·3M to hbr ent.
The Point ⬆ 50°32'·42N 03°30'·05W, Oc G 6s 3M & FG (vert).

▶ RIVER EXE
E Exe ⬆ 50°36'·00N 03°22'·38W, Q (3) 10s.
Ldg lts 305°. Front, 50°36'·99N 03°25'·34W, Iso 2s 6m 7M. Rear, 57m from front, Q 12m 7M.
No. 10 ≈ 50°36'·73N 03°24'·77W, Fl R 3s.
No. 12 Warren Pt ≈ 50°36'·91N 03°25'·40W.
Straight Pt ☆ 50°36'·49N 03°21'·76W, Fl R 10s 34m 7M; 246°-071°.

▶ LYME REGIS
Ldg lts 296°. Front, Victoria Pier ☆ 50°43'·19N 02°56'·17W, Oc WR 8s 6m, W9M, R7M; R296°-116°, W116°-296°; Bu col. Rear, 240m from front, FG 8m 9M.

▶ PORTLAND
Portland Bill lt ho ☆ 50°30'·85N 02°27'·38W, Fl (4) 20s 43m **25M**. 221°-244°, gradu changes from 1 Fl to 4 Fl; 244°-117°, shows 4 Fl; 117°-141°, gradu changes from 4 Fl to 1 Fl; W ○ twr; *Dia 30s*. Same twr, FR 19m 13M; 271°-291° over The Shambles. W Shambles ⬆ 50°29'·78N 02°24'·40W, Q (9) 15s; *Bell*.
E Shambles ⬆ 50°30'·78N 02°20'·08W, Q (3) 10s.
Portland Hbr, Outer Breakwater (N end) ☆ QR 14m 5M; 50°35'·11N 02°24'·87W,.
NE Bkwtr (A Hd) ☆ 50°35'·16N 02°25'·07W, Fl 10s 22m **20M**.
NE Bkwtr (B Hd) ☆ 50°35'·65N 02°25'·88W, Oc R 15s 11m 5M.

▶ WEYMOUTH
Ldg lts 239·6°: both FR 5/7m 7M; R ♦ on W posts; Front 50°36'·46N 02°26'·87W.
S Pier hd ☆ 50°36'·57N 02°26'·49W, Q 10m 9M.

▶ LULWORTH COVE TO ANVIL POINT
Lulworth Cove ent, E point 50°37'·00N 02°14'·78W.

Anvil Pt ☆ 50°35'·51N 01°57'·60W, Fl 10s 45m **19M**; vis 237°-076° (H24); W ○ twr and dwelling.

1	Longships	**1**														
2	Scilly (Crow Rock)	22	**2**													
3	Penzance	15	35	**3**												
4	Lizard Point	23	42	16	**4**											
5	Falmouth	39	60	32	16	**5**										
6	Mevagissey	52	69	46	28	17	**6**									
7	Fowey	57	76	49	34	22	7	**7**								
8	Looe	63	80	57	39	29	16	11	**8**							
9	Plymouth (bkwtr)	70	92	64	49	39	25	22	11	**9**						
10	R. Yealm (ent)	72	89	66	49	39	28	23	16	4	**10**					
11	Salcombe	81	102	74	59	50	40	36	29	22	17	**11**				
12	Start Point	86	103	80	63	55	45	40	33	24	22	7	**12**			
13	Dartmouth	95	116	88	72	63	54	48	42	35	31	14	9	**13**		
14	Torbay	101	118	96	78	70	62	55	50	39	38	24	15	11	**14**	
15	Exmouth	113	131	107	90	82	73	67	61	51	49	33	27	24	12	**15**	
16	Lyme Regis	126	144	120	104	96	86	81	74	63	62	48	41	35	30	21	**16**
17	Portland Bill	135	151	128	112	104	93	89	81	73	70	55	49	45	42	36	22	**17**

AREA 2 South Central England - *Anvil Point to Selsey Bill*
SELECTED LIGHTS, BUOYS & WAYPOINTS

Positions are referenced to WGS84

SWANAGE TO ISLE OF WIGHT
▶ **SWANAGE**
Peveril Ledge 50°36'·41N 01°56'·10W QR.

POOLE HARBOUR AND APPROACHES
Bar (No. 1) 50°39·32N 01°55'·16W QG; *Bell*.

▶ **SWASH AND E. LOOE CHANNELS**
South Hook 50°39'·70N 01°55'·20W..
No. 3 50°39'·76N 01°55'·49W Fl G 3s.
Training Bk 50°39'·84N 01°55'·92W 2 FR (vert).
No. 12 (Ch) 50°40'·45N 01°56'·26W Fl R 2s.
No. 13 Swash 50°48'·88N 01°56'·70W Q (9) 15s.
East Looe 50°41'·34N 01°55'·97W QR.
South Deep. Marked by lit and unlit Bns from ent South of Brownsea Castle to Furzey Is.

▶ **BROWNSEA ROADS**
N Haven 50°41'·15N 01°57'·17W Q (9) 15s 5m.
Brownsea (No. 42) 50°41'·16N 01°57'·41W Q (3) 10s.

▶ **MIDDLE SHIP AND N. CHANNELS**
No. 20 50°41'·38N 01°57'·10W Q (6) + L Fl 15s; *Bell*.
Aunt Betty (No. 50) 50°41'·96N 01°57'·39W Q (3)10s.
Diver (No. 51) 50°42'·28N 01°58'·34W Q (9) 15s. 01°57'·10W 2 FR (vert) 2M; Tfc sigs.
Stakes No. 55 50°42'·43N 01°59'·01W Q (6) + L Fl 15s.

▶ **WAREHAM CHANNEL**
Wareham Chan initially marked by and , and then by stakes.

W. APPROACHES TO THE SOLENT
▶ **NEEDLES AND NORTH CHANNELS**
Needles Fairway 50°38'·24N 01°38'·98W L Fl 10s; *Whis*.
Bridge 50°39'·63N 01°36'·88W VQ (9) 10s; **Racon (T) 10M**.
Needles ☆ 50°39'·73N 01°35'·50W Oc (2) WRG 20s 24m **W17M**, R14M, R13M G14M; ○ Twr, R band and lantern; vis: Rshore- W300°-R (unintens) 083°- W212°- G217°-224°. *Horn (2) 30s*; H24.
NE Shingles 50°41'·96N 01°33'·41W Q (3) 10s.
Hurst Point Ldg Lts 042°. Front 50°42'·48N 01°33'·03W Fl (4) WR 15s 23m W13M, R11M; W ○ Twr; vis: W(unintens) 080°-104°, W234°-

R244°- W250°-053°.Same Twr, Iso WRG 4s 19m **W21M, R18M, G17M**; vis: G038·8°-W040·8°- R041·8°-043·8°; By day W7M, R/G5M,
N. Head 50°42'·69N 01°35'·52W Fl (3) G 10s.

▶**YARMOUTH/LYMINGTON**
Sconce 50°42'·53N 01°31'·43W Q; *Bell*.
Black Rock 50°42'·58N 01°30'·64W Fl G 5s.
Yarmouth E. Fairway 50°42'·64N 01°29'·88W Fl R 2s.
Jack in the Basket 50°44'·27N 01°30'·57W Fl R 2s 9m.

▶ **SOLENT MARKS**
Newtown River 50°43'·75N 01°24'·91W Fl R 4s.
Gurnard Ledge 50°45'·51N 01°20'·59W Fl (4) G 15s.
Lepe Spit 50°46'·78N 01°20'·64W Q (6) + L Fl 15s.
W Bramble 50°47'·20N 01°18'·65W VQ (9) 10s; *Bell*; **Racon (T) 3M**.
W. Knoll 50°47'·43N 01°17'·84W Fl Y 2·5s.
Beaulieu Spit, E end 50°46'·85N 01°21'·76W Fl R 5s 3M; R dolphin; vis: 277°-037°.

▶ **SOUTHAMPTON WATER/ R.HAMBLE**
CALSHOT SPIT 50°48'·35N 01°17'·64W Fl 5s 12m 11M; R hull, Lt Twr amidships; *Horn (2) 60s*.
Calshot 50°48'·44N 01°17'·03W VQ; *Bell*.
Hook 50°49'·52N 01°18'·30W QG; *Horn (1) 15s*.
Hamble Pt 50°50'·15N 01°18'·66W Q (6) + L Fl 15s.
No. 1 50°50'·34N 01°18'·65W QG 2m 2M.
Greenland 50°51'·11N 01°20'·38W IQ G 10s.
Weston Shelf 50°52'·71N 01°23'·26W Fl (3) G 15s.
Hythe Pier Hd 50°52'·49N 01°23'·61W 2 FR (vert) 12m 5M.

▶ **SOUTHAMPTON/ITCHEN/TEST**
Swinging Ground No. 1 50°53'·00N 01°23'·44W Oc G 4s.

NAVIGATION

Queen Elizabeth II Terminal, S end ☆ 50°53'·00N 01°23'·71W 4 FG (vert) 16m 3M.
Gymp ≈ 50°53'·17N 01°24'·30W QR.

▶ THE E. SOLENT
▶ NORTH CHANNEL/HILLHEAD
Hillhead ≈ 50°48'·07N 01°16'·00W Fl R 2·5s.
E Bramble ≰ 50°47'·23N 01°13'·64W VQ (3) 5s.

▶ COWES
Gurnard ≰ 50°46'·22N 01°18'·84W Q.
P. Consort ≰ 50°46'·42N 01°17'·55W VQ.
No. 1 ▲ 50°46'·07N 01°18'·03W Fl G 3s.
No. 2 ≈ 50°46'·07N 01°17'·87W QR.

▶ E. SOLENT MARKS/WOOTTON
W. Ryde Middle ≰ 50°46'·48N 01°15'·79W Q (9) 15s.
Norris ≈ 50°45'·97N 01°15'·51W Fl (3) R 10s.
SE Ryde Middle ≰ 50°45'·93N 01°12'·10W VQ (6)+L Fl 10s.
N Sturbridge ≰ 50°45'·33N 01°08'·23W VQ.
Wootton Beacon ≰ 50°44'·53N 01°12'·13W 1M; (NB).s.

▶ PORTSMOUTH AND APPROACHES
Horse Sand Ft ☆ 50°45'·01N 01°04'·34W Iso G 2s 21m 8M.
Outer Spit ≰ 50°45'·58N 01°05'·50W Q (6) + L Fl 15s.
No. 1 Bar (NB) ▲ 50°46'·77N 01°05'·81W Fl (3) G 10s.15s 1M.
Fort Blockhouse ☆ 50°47'·37N 01°06'·74W Dir lt 320°; WRG 6m W13M, R/G5M; vis: Oc G 310°- Al WG 316°- (W phase incr with brg), Oc 318·5°- Al WR 321·5°-(R phase incr with brg), Oc R 324°-330°. 2 FR (vert) 20m E.
Ballast ≈ 50°47'·62N 01°06'·84W Fl R 2·5s.

▶ E. APPROACHES TO THE SOLENT
Outer Nab 1 ≰ 50°38'·18N 00°56'·88W VQ (9) 10s.
Outer Nab 2 ≰ 50°38'·43N 00°57'·70W VQ (3) 5s.
Nab Tower ☆ 50°40'·08N 00°57'·15W Fl 10s 27m **16M**,
Horn (2) 30s; **Racon (T) 10M**.
N 7 ≰ 50°42'·35N 00°57'·20W Fl Y 5s.
Nab End ≰ 50°42'·63N 00°59'·49W Fl R 5s; *Whis*.
Dean Tail S ≰ 50°43'·04N 00°59'·57W Q (6) + L Fl 10s.
Horse Elbow ▲ 50°44'·26N 01°03'·88W QG.
Warner ≰ 50°43'·87N 01°03'·99W QR; *Whis*.
No Man's Land Ft ☆ 50°44'·40N 01°05'·70W Iso R 2s 21m 8M.

▶ BEMBRIDGE
St Helen's Fort ☆ (IOW) 50°42'·30N 01°05'·05W Fl (3) 10s 16m 8M; large ○ stone structure.

SE COAST OF THE ISLE OF WIGHT
St Catherine's Point ☆ 50°34'·54N 01°17'·87W Fl 5s 41m **27M**; vis: 257°-117°; FR 35m **17M** (same Twr) vis: 099°-116°.
Bembridge Ledge ≰ 50°41'·15N 01°02'·81W Q (3) 10s.

▶ LANGSTONE AND APPROACHES
Langstone Fairway ≰ 50°46'·32N 01°01'·36W L Fl 10s.

▶ CHICHESTER ENTRANCE
West Pole ≰ 50°45'·71N 00°56'·50W Fl WR 5s W7M, R5M; vis: W321°- R081°-321°.
Chichester Bar ≰ 50°45'·92N 00°56'·46W Fl (2) R 10s 14m 2M; Tide gauge.

		1	2	3	4	5	6	7	8	9	10	11	12	13	14	15	16	17	18
1	Portland Bill	**1**																	
2	Weymouth	8	**2**																
3	Swanage	22	22	**3**															
4	Poole Hbr ent	28	26	6	**4**														
5	Needles Lt Ho	35	34	14	14	**5**													
6	Lymington	42	40	20	24	6	**6**												
7	Yarmouth (IOW)	40	39	18	22	4	2	**7**											
8	Beaulieu R. ent	46	45	25	29	11	7	7	**8**										
9	Cowes	49	46	28	27	14	10	9	2	**9**									
10	Southampton	55	54	34	34	20	16	16	9	9	**10**								
11	R. Hamble (ent)	53	51	32	34	18	12	13	6	5	**11**								
12	Portsmouth	58	57	37	35	23	19	19	12	10	18	13	**12**						
13	Langstone Hbr	61	59	39	39	25	21	21	14	12	21	18	5	**13**					
14	Chichester Bar	63	62	42	42	28	23	24	17	15	23	18	8	5	**14**				
15	Bembridge	59	58	38	39	24	18	19	13	10	18	15	5	6	8	**15**			
16	Nab Tower	64	63	43	44	29	23	24	18	15	24	19	10	7	6	6	**16**		
17	St Catherine's Pt	45	44	25	25	12	19	21	27	15	36	29	20	20	19	17	15	**17**	
18	Littlehampton	79	79	60	61	46	44	45	38	36	45	42	31	28	25	28	22	35	**18**

AREA 3 South East England - *Selsey Bill to North Foreland*
SELECTED LIGHTS, BUOYS & WAYPOINTS | Positions are referenced to WGS84

▶ SELSEY BILL/THE OWERS
Boulder ▲ 50°41'·56N 00°49'·09W Fl G 2·5s
Owers ⚓ 50°38'·63N 00°41'·19W Q (6) + L Fl 15s; *Whis*; **Racon (O) 10M**.
E Borough Hd ⚓ 50°41'·54N 00°39'·09W Q (3) 10s *Bell*.

▶ LITTLEHAMPTON/SHOREHAM
W.Pier Hd ⚓ 50°47'·88N 00°32'·46W QR 7m 6M.
Shoreham E Bkwtr Head ☆ 50°49'·54N 00°14'·80W Fl G 5s 8M; *Siren 120s*.

▶ BRIGHTON MARINA
W Bkwtr Hd ☆ 50°48'·50N 00°06'·38W QR 10m 7M; W ○ structure, R bands; *Horn (2) 30s*.

NEWHAVEN TO DUNGENESS
Newhaven Bkwtr Head ☆ 50°46'·56N 00°03'·50E Oc (2) 10s 17m 12M.
GREENWICH ⚓ 50°24'·54N 00°00'·10 Fl 5s 12m **15M**; Riding light FW; R hull; **Racon (M) 10M**; *Horn 30s*.
Beachy Head ☆ 50°44'·03N 00°14'·49E Fl (2) 20s 31m **20M**; W round twr, R band and lantern; vis: 248°-101°; (H24); *Horn 30s*.
Royal Sovereign ☆ 50°43'·45N 00°26'·09E Fl 20s 28m 12M; W ○ twr, R band on W cabin on col; *Horn (2) 30s*.
Sovereign Hr Marina ☆ 50°47'·24N 00°19'·83E Fl (3) 15s 12m 7M.
Rye Fairway ⚓ 50°54'·04N 00°48'·04E L Fl 10s.
Dungeness ☆ 50°54'·81N 00°58'·56E Fl 10s 40m **21M**; B ○ twr, W bands and lantern, f/lit; Part obsc 078°-shore; (H24). F RG 37m 10M (same twr); vis: R057°- G073°-078°, R196°-216°; *Horn (3) 60s*.

DUNGENESS - DOVER STRAIT
VARNE ⚓ 51°01'·29N 01°23'·90E Fl R 20s 12m **19M**; **Racon (T) 10M**; *Horn 30s*.
CS 4 ⚓ 51°08'·67N 01°34'·02E Fl (4)Y 15s; *Whis*.
S GOODWIN ⚓ 51°07'·97N 01°28'·49E Fl (2) 20s 12m **15M**; R hull; *Horn (2) 60s*.
E GOODWIN ⚓ 51°13'·26N 01°36'·37E Fl 15s 12m **23M**; R hull with lt twr amidships; **Racon (T) 10M**; *Horn 30s*.
NE Goodwin ⚓ 51°20'·31N 01°34'·16E Q (3) 10s; **Racon (M) 10M**.
Folkestone Breakwater Head ☆ 51°04'·56N 01°11'·69E Fl (2) 10s 14m **22M**; *Dia (4) 60s*. In fog Fl 2s; vis: 246°-306°, intens 271·5°-280·5°.

DOVER TO NORTH FORELAND
Dover Admiralty Pier Extension Head ☆ 51°06'·69N 01°19'·66E Fl 7·5s 21m **20M**; W twr; vis: 096°-090°, obsc in The Downs by S Foreland inshore of 226°; *Horn 10s*; Int Port Tfc sigs.
Knuckle ☆ 51°07'·04N 01°20'·49E Fl (4) WR 10s 15m **W15M**, R13M; W twr; vis: R059°-W239°-059°.
Goodwin Fork ⚓ 51°14'·33N 01°26'·86E Q (6) + L Fl 15s; *Bell*.
NW Goodwin ⚓ 51°16'·57N 01°28'·57E Q (9) 15s; *Bell*.
Gull ⚓ 51°19'·57N 01°31'·30E VQ (3) 5s.

▶ RAMSGATE/BROADSTAIRS
RA ⚓ 51°19'·60N 01°30'·13E Q(6) + L Fl 15s.
B'stairs Knoll ⚓ 51°20'·88N 01°29'·48E FR 2·5s.
North Foreland ☆ 51°22'·49N 01°26'·70E Fl (5) WR 20s 57m **W19M**, **R16M**, **R15M**; W twr; vis: W shore-150°, R(**16M**)150°- R(**15M**) 181°- W200°-011°; H24.

		1															
1	Nab Tower	1															
2	Boulder Lt Buoy	5	2														
3	Owers Lt Buoy	11	8	3													
4	Littlehampton	19	13	12	4												
5	Shoreham	32	24	21	13	5											
6	Brighton	35	28	24	17	5	6										
7	Newhaven	40	34	29	24	12	7	7									
8	Beachy Head Lt	46	41	36	30	20	14	8	8								
9	Eastbourne	51	45	40	34	24	19	12	7	9							
10	Rye	72	67	62	56	46	41	34	25	23	10						
11	Dungeness Lt	76	71	66	60	50	44	38	30	26	9	11					
12	Folkestone	92	84	81	76	65	60	53	43	40	23	13	12				
13	Dover	97	89	86	81	70	65	58	48	45	28	18	5	13			
14	Ramsgate	112	104	101	96	85	80	73	63	60	43	33	20	15	14		
15	N Foreland Lt	115	107	104	99	88	83	76	66	63	46	36	23	18	3	15	
16	Sheerness	146	139	135	132	119	114	107	97	96	79	67	54	49	34	31	16
17	London Bridge	188	184	177	177	161	156	149	139	141	124	109	96	91	76	73	45	17

NAVIGATION

AREA 4 East England - *North Foreland to Berwick-upon-Tweed*
SELECTED LIGHTS, BUOYS & WAYPOINTS | Positions are referenced to WGS84

THAMES ESTUARY
(Direction of buoyage generally East to West)
Changes are regularly made to buoyage in the Thames Estuary. Check Notices to Mariners for the latest information.

▶ **OUTER APPROACHES**
Outer Tongue ⚓ 51°30'·73N 01°26'·40E L Fl 10s; *Racon (T) 10M*; *Whis*.

▶ **N.KENT COAST/MEDWAY**
Foreness Pt Outfall ⚓ 51°24'·61N 01°26'·02E Fl R 5s.
SE Margate ⚓ 51°24'·05N 01°20'·40E Q (3) 10s.
E Last ⚓ 51°24'·06N 01°11'·84E QR.
Spaniard ⚓ 51°26'·23N 01°04'·00E Q (3) 10s.
Spile ⚓ 51°26'·43N 00°55'·70E Fl G 2·5s.
Whitstable Street ⚓ 51°23'·85N 01°01'·59E Q.

▶ **PRINCES CHANNEL/MEDWAY**
Princes ⚓ 51°28'·74N 01°18'·26E VQ R.
Medway ⚓ 51°28'·83N 00°52'·81E Mo (A) 6s.
No. 1 ⚓ 51°28'·55N 00°50'·50E Fl G 2·5s..
Queenborough Spit ⚓ 51°25'·81N 00°43'·93E Q (3) 10s.

▶ **FOULGER'S - FISHERMAN'S GATS**
Long Sand Inner* ⚓ 51°38'·77N 01°26'·00E Mo 'A' 15s.
Long Sand Outer* ⚓ 51°35'·87N 01°26'·58E L Fl 10s.
Outer Outer Fisherman ⚓ 51°33'·89N 01°25'·01E Q (3) 10s.
Inner Fisherman ⚓ 51°36'·07N 01°19'·87E Q R.

THAMES ESTUARY – NORTHERN
▶ **KENTISH KNOCK**
Kentish Knock ⚓ 51°38'·53N 01°40·39E Q (3) 10s; *Whis*.
S Knock ⚓ 51°34'·13N 01°34'·29E Q (6) + L Fl 15s; *Bell*.

▶ **BLACK DEEP**
No. 10 ⚓ 51°34'·74N 01°15'·60E Fl (3) R 10s.
No. 8 ⚓ 51°36'·36N 01°20'·43E Q (9) 15s. Fl R 2·5s.
Sunk Head Tower ⚓ 51°46'·63N 01°30'·51E Q; *Whis*.
Long Sand Head ⚓ 51°47'·90N 01°39'·42E VQ; *Bell*.

▶ **BARROW DEEP**
SW Barrow ⚓ 51°32'·29N 01°00'·31E Q (6) + L Fl 15s; *Bell*.
Barrow No. 3 ⚓ 51°42'·02N 01°20'·24E Q (3) 10s; *Racon (M)10M*.

▶ **WEST SWIN AND MIDDLE DEEP**
Maplin ⚓ 51°34'·03N 01°02'·30E Q (3) 10s; *Bell*.
W Swin ⚓ 51°33'·40N 01°01'·97E QR.
Maplin Bk ⚓ 51°35'·50N 01°04'·70E Fl (3) R 10s.

▶ **EAST SWIN (KING'S) CHANNEL**
NE Maplin ⚓ 51°37'·43N 01°04'·90E Fl G 5s; *Bell*.
S Whitaker ⚓ 51°40'·23N 01°09'·05E Fl (2) G 10s.
W Sunk ⚓ 51°44'·33N 01°25'·80E Q (9) 15s.
Gunfleet Spit ⚓ 51°45'·33N 01°21'·70E Q (6) + L Fl 15s; *Bell*.

▶ **WHITAKER CHANNEL/R. CROUCH/ BURNHAM-ON-CROUCH**
Whitaker ⚓ 51°41'·43N 01°10'·51E Q (3) 10s; *Bell*.
Swin Spitway ⚓ 51°41'·95N 01°08'·35E Iso 10s; *Bell*.
Sunken Buxey ⚓ 51°39'·54N 01°00'·59E Q.
Outer Crouch ⚓ 51°38'·38N 00°58'·48E Q (6) + L Fl 15s.

▶ **GOLDMER GAT/WALLET**
NE Gunfleet ⚓ 51°49'·93N 01°27'·79E Q (3) 10s.
Wallet No. 2 ⚓ 51°48'·88N 01°22'·99E Fl R 5s.
Wallet Spitway ⚓ 51°42'·86N 01°07'·30E L Fl 10s; *Bell*.
Knoll ⚓ 51°43'·88N 01°05'·07E Q.

▶ **RIVER COLNE/BRIGHTLINGSEA**
Colne Bar ⚓ 51°44'·61N 01°02'·57E Fl (2) G 5s.
Brightlingsea Spit ⚓ 51°48'·08N 01°00'·70E Q (6) + L Fl 15s.

▶ **WALTON BACKWATERS**
Pye End ⚓ 51°55'·03N 01°17'·90E L Fl 10s.

HARWICH APPROACHES
▶ **MEDUSA CHANNEL/CORK SAND**
Medusa ⚓ 51°51'·23N 01°20'·35E Fl G 5s.

Stone Banks 51°53'·19N 01°19'·23E. Fl R 5s.
S Cork 51°51'·33N 01°24'·09E Q (6) + L Fl 15s.
SUNK 51°51'·03N 01°34'·89E Fl (2) 20s 12m **16M**; R hull with lt twr; *Racon (T)*; *Horn (2) 60s*.
S Shipwash 2 By(s) 51°52'·71N 01°33'·97E Q (6) + L Fl 15s.
Harwich Chan No. 1 51°56'·13N 01°27'·06E Fl Y 2·5s; *Racon (T)10M*.
S Bawdsey 51°57'·23N 01°30'·22E Q (6) + L Fl 15s; *Whis*.
Wadgate Ledge 51°56'·16N 01°21'·99E Fl (4)
Cork Sand Yacht Bn 51°55'·21N 01°25'·20E VQ 2M.
Landguard 51°55'·45N 01°18'·84E Q.

HARWICH TO GREAT YARMOUTH
▶ OFFSHORE MARKS

S Galloper 51°43'·98N 01°56'·39E Q (6) L Fl 15s; *Racon (T)10M*; *Whis*.
Outer Gabbard 51°57'·83N 02°04'·19E Q (3) 10s; *Racon (O)10M*; *Whis*.

▶ DEBEN/ORE/SUFFOLK COAST

Woodbridge Haven 51°58'·55N 01°24'·25E Mo(A)15s.
Orford Haven 52°01'·85N 01°28'·28E L Fl 10s; *Bell*.
N Shipwash 52°01'·73N 01°38'·27E Q 7M; *Racon (M) 10M*; *Bell*.
S Bawdsey 51°57'·23N 01°30'·22E Q (6) + L Fl 15s; *Whis*.
NE Bawdsey 52°01'·73N 01°36'·09E Fl G 10s.
SW Whiting 52°00'·96N 01°30'·69E Q (6) + L Fl 10s.

ORFORDNESS TO GT YARMOUTH
Direction of buoyage becomes S to N

Orford Ness ☆ 52°05'·03N 01°34'·46E Fl 5s 28m **20M**; W twr, R bands. F WRG 14m **W17M**, R13M, **G15M** (same twr). vis: R shore-210°, R038°-047°, G047°-shore; *Racon (T) 18M*.FR 13m 12M vis: 026°-038° over Whiting Bank.
Southwold ☆ 52°19'·63N 01°40'·89E Fl (4) WR 20s 37m **W16M, R12M**, R14M; vis R (intens) 204°-W215°-001°.

▶ LOWESTOFT/GREAT YARMOUTH/ GORLESTON APPROACHES

E Barnard 52°25'·14N 01°46'·38E Q (3) 10s.
Newcome Sand 52°26'·28N 01°46'·97E QR.
Lowestoft ☆ 52°29'·22N 01°45'·35E Fl 15s 37m **23M**; W twr; part obscd 347°-shore.
E Newcome 52°28'·51N 01°49'·21E Fl (2) R 5s.

Corton 52°31'·13N 01°51'·39E Q (3) 10s; *Whis*.
S Corton 52°32'·47N 01°49'·36E Q (6) + L Fl 15s; *Bell*.
Gorleston South Pier Hd ☆ 52°34'·33N 01°44'·28E Fl R 3s 11m 11M; *Horn (3) 60s*.

GT YARMOUTH TO THE WASH
▶ GT YARMOUTH/COCKLE GATEWAY AND OFFSHORE

N Scroby 52°41'·58N 01°46'·40E VQ; *Whis*.
Cockle 52°44'·03N 01°43'·59E VQ (3) 5s; *Bell*.
Cross Sand 52°37'·03N 01°59'·14E L Fl 10s 6m 5M; *Racon (T)10M*.
Newarp 52°48'·37N 01°55'·69E L Fl 10s 7M; *Racon (O) 10M*.
N Haisbro 53°00'·22N 01°32'·29E Q; *Racon (T) 10M*; *Bell*.

▶ N. NORFOLK COAST/THE WASH

Cromer ☆ 52°55'·45N 01°19'·01E Fl 5s 84m **21M**; W 8-sided twr; vis: 102°-307° H24; *Racon (O) 25M*. .
Blakeney Overfalls 53°03'·01N 01°01'·37E Fl (2) R 5s; *Bell*.
Wells Fairway 52°59'·81N 00°50'·49E Q.
S Race 53°07'·81N 00°57'·34E Q (6) + L Fl 15s; *Bell*.
S Inner Dowsing 53°12'·12N 00°33'·69E Q (6) + L Fl 15s; *Bell*.
Burnham Flats 53°07'·53N 00°34'·89E Q (9) 15s; *Bell*.
N Well 53°03'·02N 00°27'·90E L Fl 10s; *Whis*; *Racon (T) 10M*.
Roaring Middle 52°58'·64N 00°21'·08E L Fl 10s 7m 8M.

▶ THE WASH TO THE HUMBER

Dudgeon 53°16'·62N 01°16'·90E Q (9) 15s 7M; *Racon (O) 10M*; *Whis*.
B.1D Platform Dowsing 53°33'·68N 00°52'·63E Fl (2) 10s 28m **22M**; Morse (U) R 15s 28m 3M; *Horn (2) 60s*; *Racon (T) 10M*.
Humber 53°38'·83N 00°20'·17E L Fl 10s 7M; *Horn (2) 30s*; *Racon (T) 7M*.
SPURN 53°33'·56N 00°14'·20E Q (3) 10s 8M; *Horn 20s*; *Racon (M) 5M*.

RIVER HUMBER TO WHITBY
▶ BRIDLINGTON/SCARBOROUGH/ WHITBY

SW Smithic 54°02'·41N 00°09'·21W Q (9) 15s.
Flamborough Hd ☆ 54°06'·98N 00°04'·96W Fl (4) 15s 65m **24M**; W twr; *Horn (2) 90s*.

NAVIGATION

THE WASH TO THE HUMBER

Dudgeon ⚓ 53°16'·62N 01°16'·90E Q (9) 15s 7M; *Racon (O) 10M; Whis*.

B.1D Platform Dowsing ⚓ 53°33'·68N 00°52'·63E Fl (2) 10s 28m **22M**; Morse (U) R 15s 28m 3M; *Horn (2) 60s*; *Racon (T) 10M*.

Humber ⚓ 53°38'·83N 00°20'·17E L Fl 10s 7M; *Horn (2) 30s*; *Racon (T) 7M*.

SPURN ⚓ 53°33'·56N 00°14'·20E Q (3) 10s 8M; *Horn 20s; Racon (M) 5M*.

RIVER HUMBER TO WHITBY
▶ **BRIDLINGTON/FILEY/ SCARBOROUGH/WHITBY**

SW Smithic ⚓ 54°02'·41N 00°09'·21W Q (9) 15s.
Flamborough Hd ☆ 54°06'·98N 00°04'·96W Fl (4) 15s 65m **24M**; W ○ twr; *Horn (2) 90s*.
Filey Brigg ⚓ 54°12'·74N 00°14'·60W Q (3) 10s;
Scarborough Pier 54°16'·91N 00°23'·40W Iso 5s 17m 9M; W ○ twr; (tide sigs); *Dia 60s*.
Whitby ⚓ 54°30'·33N 00°36'·58W Q; *Bell*.
Whitby High ☆ Ling Hill 54°28'·67N 00°34'·10W Fl WR 5s 73m **18M**, R16M; W 8-sided twr and dwellings; vis: R128°- W143°-319°.

WHITBY TO RIVER TYNE
▶ **TEES/HARTLEPOOL/SUNDERLAND**

Tees Fairway ⚓ 54°40'·94N 01°06'·48W Iso 4s 8m 8M; *Racon (B) unknown range*; *Horn (1) 5s*.
Bkwtr Hd S Gare ☆ 54°38'·85N 01°08'·27W Fl WR 12s 16m **W20M**, **R17M**; W ○ twr; vis: W020°- R274°-357°; Sig Stn; *Horn 30s*.
Longscar ⚓ 54°40'·86N 01°09'·89W Q (3) 10s; *Bell*.
The Heugh ☆ 54°40'·09N 01°47'·98W Fl (2) 10s 19m **19M** ; W twr.
Sunderland Roker Pier Hd ☆ 54°55'·28N 01°21'·15W Fl 5s 25m **23M**; W ☐ twr, 3 R bands and cupola: vis: 211°-357°; S*iren 20s*.

▶ **TYNE ENTRANCE**

Ent North Pier Hd ☆ 55°00'·88N 01°24'·18W Fl (3) 10s 26m **26M**; Gy ☐ twr, W lantern; *Horn 10s*.

RIVER TYNE TO BERWICK-ON-TWEED
▶ **BLYTH**

Blyth Fairway ⚓ 55°06'·59N 01°28'·60W Fl G 3s; *Bell*. .

▶ **COQUET ISLAND**

Coquet ☆ 55°20'·03N 01°32'·39W Fl (3) WR 30s 25m **W23M, R19M**; W ☐ twr, turreted parapet, lower half Gy; vis: R330°-140°, W140°-163°, R163°-180°, W180°-330°; sector boundaries are indeterminate and may appear as Alt WR; *Horn 30s*.

▶ **BAMBURGH/ FARNE ISLANDS**

The Falls ⚓ 55°34'·61N 01°37'·12W Fl R 2·5s.
Shoreston Outcars ⚓ 55°35'·88N 01°39'·34W QR.
Bamburgh Black Rocks Point ☆ 55°36'·99N 01°43'·45W Oc (2) WRG 8s 12m **W14M**, R11M, G11M; W bldg; vis: G122°- W165°- R175°- W191°- R238°- W275°- G289°-300°.
Inner Farne ⚓ 55°36'·92N 01°39'·35W Fl (2) WR 15s 27m W10M, R7M; W ○ twr.
Longstone ☆ **W side** 55°38'·62N 01°36'·65W Fl 20s 23m **24M**; R twr, W band; *Horn (2) 60s*.

▶ **HOLY ISLAND**

Ridge ⚓ 55°39'·70N 01°45'·97W Q (3) 10s.
Triton Shoal ⚓ 55°39'·61N 01°46'·59W QG.

▶ **BERWICK-ON-TWEED**

Bkwtr Hd ⚓ 55°45'·88N 01°59'·06W Fl 5s 15m 6M; vis: 201°-009°, (obscured 155°-201°); W ○ twr, R cupola and base; FG (same twr) 8m 1M; vis G009°-155°.

1	Ramsgate	1		11	31	61	78	91	107	126	189	205	205	232	Berwick-upon-Tweed	11
2	Sheerness	34	2		10	27	42	65	81	102	157	176	185	203	Amble	10
3	Gravesend	56	22	3		9	16	36	51	70	138	149	156	180	Sunderland	9
4	London Bridge	76	45	23	4		8	24	39	58	122	137	140	169	Hartlepool	8
5	Burnham-on-Crouch	44	34	53	76	5		7	16	35	88	114	121	143	Whitby	7
6	Brightlingsea	41	28	47	71	22	6		6	20	81	98	105	130	Scarborough	6
7	Harwich	40	50	65	83	31	24	7		5	58	83	87	114	Bridlington	5
8	River Deben (ent)	45	55	71	89	35	38	6	8		4	72	75	113	Hull	4
9	Southwold	62	80	95	113	58	63	30	23	9		3	34	83	Boston	3
10	Lowestoft	72	90	105	123	68	73	40	33	10	10		2	85	King's Lynn	2
11	Great Yarmouth	79	97	112	130	76	80	52	41	18	7	11		1	Great Yarmouth	1

AREA 5 E. Scotland - *Berwick-upon-Tweed to C Wrath & N Isles*
SELECTED LIGHTS, BUOYS & WAYPOINTS | Positions are referenced to WGS84

BERWICK-UPON-TWEED TO BASS RK
▶ EYEMOUTH/ST ABB'S/DUNBAR
Blind Buss 55°52'·80N 02°05'·25E Q.
St Abb's Hd ☆ 55°54'·96N 02°08'·29W Fl 10s 68m **26M**; W twr; *Racon (T) 18M*.
Bass Rock, S side, ☆ 56°04'·61N 02°38'·48W Fl (3) 20s 46m 10M; W twr; vis: 241°-107°.

FIRTH OF FORTH
▶ SOUTH CHANNEL
Fidra ☆ 56°04'·39N 02°47'·13W Fl (4) 30s 34m **24M**; W twr; obsc by Bass Rock, Craig Leith and Lamb Island.
Craigh Waugh 56°00'·26N 03°04'·47W Q.

▶ LEITH
Leith Approach 55°59'·95N 03°11'·51W Fl R 3s.

▶ NORTH CHANNEL/MIDDLE BANK
Inchkeith Fairway 56°03'·49N 03°00'·10W Iso 2s; *Racon (T) 5M*.
Inchkeith ☆ 56°02'·01N 03°08'·17W Fl 15s 67m **22M**; stone twr.
No. 7 56°02'·80N 03°10'·97W QG; *Bell*; *Racon (T) 5M*.

▶ MORTIMER'S DEEP
Hawkcraig Point Ldg Lts 292°. Front, 56°03'·03N 03°17'·07W Iso 5s 12m 14M; W twr; vis: 282°-302°. Rear, 96m from front. Iso 5s 16m 14M; W twr; vis: 282°-302°.
No. 2 56°02'·70N 03°15'·83W QR.
No. 14 56°01'·55N 03°19'·04W Q (9) 15s.

▶ ELIE/ANSTRUTHER/MAY ISLAND
Thill Rock 56°10'·87N 02°49'·70W Fl (4) R 10s.
Elie Ness ☆ 56°11'·04N 02°48'·77W Fl 6s 15m **18M**; W twr.
Anstruther Easter, W Pier Hd ☆ 56°13'·18N 02°41'·84W 2 FR (vert) 5m 4M; Gy mast; *Horn (3) 60s (occas)*.
Isle of May ☆, Summit 56°11'·12N 02°33'·46W Fl (2) 15s 73m **22M**; ☐ twr on stone dwelling.
Fife Ness ☆ 56°16'·74N 02°35'·19W Iso WR 10s 2m **W21M, R20M**; W bldg; vis: W143°-R197°-W217°-023°.

FIFE NESS TO ARBROATH
N Carr 56°18'·05N 02°32'·94W Q (3) 10s 3m 5M.
Bell Rk ☆ 56°26'·08N 02°23'·21W Fl 5s 28m **18M**; *Racon (M) 18M*.

▶ RIVER TAY/TAYPORT/DUNDEE
Tay Fairway 56°29'·24N 02°38'·26W L Fl 10s; *Bell*.
Abertay N 56°27'·39N 02°40'·36W Q (3) 10s; *Racon (T) 8M*.
Inner 56°27'·09N 02°44'·33W Fl (2) R 12s.
N Lady 56°27'·39N 02°46'·85W Fl (2) G 20s.
.Tayport High Lt Ho ☆ Dir lt 269°, 56°27'·17N 02°53'·96W Iso WRG 3s 24m **W22M, R17M, G16M**; W twr; vis: G267°- W268°- R270°-271°.

ARBROATH TO RATTRAY HEAD
▶ ARBROATH/MONTROSE
Arbroath E Pier S Elbow ☆ 56°33'·25N 02°34'·97W Fl G 3s 8m 5M; W twr; shows FR when hbr closed; *Siren (3) 60s (occas)*.
Scurdie Ness ☆ 56°42'·10N 02°26'·24W Fl (3) 20s 38m **23M**; W twr; *Racon (T) 14-16M*.
Montrose, Ldg Lts 271·5°. Front 56°42'·21N 02°27'·41W, FR 11m 5M; W twin pillars, R bands. Rear, FR 18m 5M; W twr, R cupola.
Annat 56°42'·23N 02°25'·95W Fl G 3s.
Todhead ☆ 56°53'·00N 02°12'·97W Fl (4) 30s 41m **18M**; W twr.
Stonehaven, Outer Pier Hd ☆ 56°57'·59N 02°12'·00W Iso WRG 4s 7m W11M, R7M, G8M; vis: G214°- W246°- R268°-280°.
Girdle Ness ☆ 57°08'·34N 02°02'·91W Fl (2) 20s 56m **22M**; obsc by Greg Ness when brg more than about 020°; *Racon (G) 25M*.

▶ ABERDEEN
Fairway 57°09'·31N 02°01'·95W Mo (A) 5s; *Racon (T) 7M*.
Aberdeen N Pier Hd ☆ 57°08'·74N 02°03'·69W Oc WR 6s 11m 9M; W twr; vis: W145°-055°, R055°-145°. In fog FY 10m (same twr) vis: 136°-336°; *Bell (3) 12s*.
Buchan Ness ☆ 57°28'·23N 01°46'·51W Fl 5s 40m **28M**; W twr, R bands; *Racon (O) 14-16M*.
Cruden Skares 57°23'·17N 01°50'·36W Fl R 10s; *Bell*.

▶ PETERHEAD
N Bkwtr Hd ☆ 57°29'·84N 01°46'·32W Iso RG 6s 19m 11M; W tripod; vis: R171°- G236°-171°; *Horn 30s*.
Rattray Hd ☆ 57°36'·61N 01°49'·03W Fl (3) 30s 28m **24M**; W twr; *Racon (M) 15M*.

NAVIGATION

RATTRAY HEAD TO INVERNESS

Rattray Hd ☆ 57°36'·61N 01°49'·03W Fl (3) 30s 28m 24M; W twr; *Racon (M) 15M*; *Horn (2) 45s*.

▶ **FRASERBURGH**

Balaclava Bkwtr Head ⚓ 57°41'·51N 01°59'·70W Fl (2) G 8s 26m 6M; dome on W twr; vis: 178°-326°.

Kinnaird Hd ☆ 57°41'·87N 02°00'·26W Fl 5s 25m 22M; vis: 092°-297°.

▶ **MACDUFF/BANFF/WHITEHILLS**

Macduff Pier Hd ⚓ 57°40'·25N 02°30'·02W Fl (2) WRG 6s 12m W9M, R7M; W twr; vis: G shore-W115°-R174°-210°.

Banff N Pier Head ⚓ 57°40'·22N 02°31'·27W Fl 4s.

Whitehills Pier Head ⚓ 57°40'·80N 02°34'·88W Fl WR 3s 7m W9M, R6M; W twr; vis: R132°-W212°-245°.

▶ **LOSSIEMOUTH/HOPEMAN/ BURGHEAD/FINDHORN/NAIRN**

Lossiemouth S Pier Hd ⚓ 57°43'·42N 03°16'·69W Fl R 6s 11m 5M; *Siren 60s*.

Covesea Skerries ☆ 57°43'·47N 03°20'·45W Fl WR 20s 49m **W24M, R20M**; W twr; vis: W076°- R267°-282°.

Hopeman W Pier Head ⚓ 57°42'·69N 03°26'·29W Oc G 4s 8m 4M.

Burghead N Bkwtr Hd ⚓ 57°42'·09N 03°30'·03W Oc 8s 7m 5M.

Findhorn Landfall ⌁ 57°40'·33N 03°38'·76W.

Nairn E Pier Head ⚓ 57°35'·62N 03°51'·65W Oc WRG 4s 6m 5M.

▶ **INVERNESS FIRTH**

Navity Bank ▲ 57°38'·16N 04°01'·18W Fl (3) G 15s 3m 4M.

Riff Bank S ⌁ 57°36'·73N 04°00'·97W Q (6) + L Fl 15s.

Chanonry ☆ 57°34'·44N 04°05'·57W Oc 6s 12m 15M; W twr; vis: 148°-073°.

INVERNESS TO DUNCANSBY HEAD
▶ **CROMARTY FIRTH**

Fairway ⊙ 57°39'·96N 03°54'·19W L Fl 10s; *Racon (M) 5M*.

The Ness ☆ 57°40'·98N 04°02'·20W Oc WR 10s 18m **W15M**, R11M; W twr; vis: R079°- W088°-275°, obsc by N Sutor when brg less than 253°

▶ **DORNOCH FIRTH**

Tarbat Ness ☆ 57°51'·88N 03°46'·76W Fl (4) 30s 53m **24M**; W twr, R bands; *Racon (T) 14-16M*.

Clyth Ness ☆ 58°18'·64N 03°12'·74W Fl (2) 30s 45m 14M.

▶ **WICK**

S Pier Head ⚓ 58°26'·34N 03°04'·73W Fl WRG 3s 12m W12M, R/G9M; W twr; vis: G253°- W270°-R286°-329°; *Bell (2) 10s* (occas).

Noss Head ☆ 58°28'·71N 03°03'·09W Fl WR 20s 53m **W25M, R 21M**; W twr; vis: R shore-W191°-shore.

DUNCANSBY HEAD TO CAPE WRATH

Duncansby Head ☆ 58°38'·65N 03°01'·58W Fl 12s 67m **22M**; W twr; *Racon (T)*.

Pentland Skerries ☆ 58°41'·41N 02°55'·49W Fl (3) 30s 52m **23M**; W twr; *Horn 45s*.

Lother Rock ⚓ 58°43'·80N 02°58'·68W Q 13m 6M; *Racon (M) 10M*.

Stroma ☆, Swilkie Point 58°41'·75N 03°07'·01W Fl (2) 20s 32m **26M**; W twr; *Horn (2) 60s*.

Dunnet Head ☆ 58°40'·28N 03°22'·60W Fl (4) 30s 105m **23M**.

Scrabster Queen Elizabeth Pier Hd 58°36'·66N 03°32'·31W Fl(2)4s 8m 8M.

Strathy Point ☆ 58°36'·04N 04°01'·12W Fl 20s 45m **26M**; W twr on W dwelling. F.R. on chimney 100° 8·5M.

Sule Skerry ☆ 59°05'·09N 04°24'·38W Fl (2) 15s 34m **21M**; W twr; *Racon (T)*.

North Rona ☆ 59°07'·27N 05°48'·91W Fl (3) 20s 114m **24M**.

Cape Wrath ☆ 58°37'·54N 04°59'·94W Fl (4) 30s 122m **22M**; W twr.

ORKNEY ISLANDS

Tor Ness ☆ 58°46'·78N 03°17'·86W Fl 5s 21m **17M**; W twr.

Cantick Head (S Walls, SE end) ☆ 58°47'·23N 03°07'·88W Fl 20s 35m **18M**; W twr.

▶ **CLESTRAN SOUND**

Peter Skerry ▲ 58°55'·25N 03°13'·51W Fl G 6s.

Riddock Shoal ⌁ 58°55'·86N 03°15'·15W Fl (2) R 12s.

▶ **HOY SOUND**

Graemsay Is Hoy Sound Low ☆ Ldg Lts 104°. **Front**, 58°56'·42N 03°18'·60W Iso 3s 17m **15M**; W twr; vis: 070°-255°. **High Rear**, 1·2M from front, Oc WR 8s 35m **W20M, R16M**; W twr; vis: R097°- W112°-R163°- W178°-332°; obsc on Ldg line within 0·5M.

▶ STROMNESS
Stromness 58°57'·25N 03°17'·61W QR.
N Pier Head 58°57'·75N 03°17'·71W Fl R 3s 8m 5M.

▶ AUSKERRY
Copinsay ☆ 58°53'·77N 02°40'·35W Fl (5) 30s 79m **21M**; W twr;
Auskerry ☆ 59°01'·51N 02°34'·34W Fl 20s 34m **20M**; W twr.

▶ KIRKWALL/WIDE FIRTH
Scargun Shoal 59°00'·69N 02°58'·58W.
Pier N end ☆ 58°59'·29N 02°57'·72W Iso WRG 5s 8m **W15M**, R13M, G13M; W twr; vis: G153°-W183°-R192°-210°.
Galt Skerry 59°05'·21N 02°54'·20W Q.
Brough of Birsay ☆ 59°08'·19N 03°20'·41W Fl (3) 25s 52m **18M**.
Papa Stronsay NE end, The Ness 59°09'·34N 02°34'·93W Fl(4)20s 8m 9M; W twr.

▶ STRONSAY, PAPA SOUND
Quiabow 59°09'·82N 02°36'·30W Fl (2) G 12s.
No. 1 (off Jacks Reef) 59°09'·16N 02°36'·51W Fl G 5s.
Whitehall Pier Hd 50°08'·61N 02°35'·96W 2 FG (vert) 8m 4M.

▶ SANDAY ISLAND/NORTH RONALDSAY
Start Point ☆ 59°16'·69N 02°22'·71W Fl (2) 20s 24m **18M**.
N Ronaldsay ☆ NE end, 59°23'·37N 02°23'·03W Fl 10s 43m **24M**; R twr, W bands; *Racon (T) 14-17M*; *Horn 60s*.

▶ WESTRAY/PIEROWALL
Noup Head ☆ 59°19'·86N 03°04'·23W Fl 30s 79m **20M**; W twr; vis: about 335°-282° but partially obsc 240°-275°.
Pierowall E Pier Head 59°19'·35N 02°58'·53W Fl WRG 3s 7m W11M, R7M, G7M; vis: G254°-W276°-R291°-G308°-215°.
Papa Westray, Moclett Bay Pier Head 59°19'·60N 02°53'·52W Fl WRG 5s 7m W5M, R3M, G3M; vis: G306°-W341°-R040°-074°.

SHETLAND ISLES
▶ FAIR ISLE
Skadan South ☆, 59°30'·84N 01°39'·16W Fl (4) 30s 32m **22M**; W twr; vis: 260°-146°, obsc inshore 260°-282°; *Horn (2) 60s*.
Skroo ☆ N end 59°33'·13N 01°36'·58W Fl (2) 30s 80m **22M**; W twr; vis: 086·7°-358°.

▶ MAINLAND, SOUTH
Sumburgh Head ☆ 59°51'·21N 01°16'·58W Fl (3) 30s 91m **23M**.
Pool of Virkie, Marina E Bkwtr Head 59°53'·01N 01°17'·16W 2 FG (vert) 6m 5M.

▶ BRESSAY/LERWICK
Bressay, Kirkabister Ness ☆ 60°07'·20N 01°07'·29W Fl (2) 20s 32m **23M**.
Soldian Rock 60°12'·51N 01°04'·73W Q (6) + L Fl 15s.
Gremista Marina S Hd 60°10'·20N 01°09'·61W Iso R 4s 3m 2M.
Rova Hd 60°11'·46N 01°08'·60W Fl (3) WRG 18s 12m W12M, R9M, G9M; W twr; vis: R 090°-W182°-G191°-R213°-W241°-G261·5°-R009°-040°. Same structure/synchronised: Fl (3) WRG 18s 14m **W16M**, R13M, G13M; vis: R176·5°-W182°-G191°-196·5°.

1	Berwick-upon-Tweed	1		11	155	79	47	76	104	144	126	120	125	145	Cape Wrath	11
2	Eyemouth	10	2		10	95	124	120	148	190	170	162	156	160	Lerwick	10
3	Dunbar	26	17	3		9	50	46	74	114	104	90	95	115	Kirkwall	9
4	Port Edgar	58	50	34	4		8	31	59	99	89	75	80	100	Scrabster	8
5	Methil	45	36	20	20	5		7	29	69	58	44	50	72	Wick	7
6	Fife Ness	38	29	17	34	16	6		6	43	32	26	44	74	Helmsdale	6
7	Dundee	58	49	37	54	36	20	7		5	13	34	59	90	Inverness	5
8	Montrose	59	51	43	61	43	27	27	8		4	23	48	79	Nairn	4
9	Stonehaven	72	66	60	78	60	44	45	20	9		3	25	56	Lossiemouth	3
10	Aberdeen	82	78	73	90	72	56	57	32	13	10		2	33	Banff/Macduff	2
11	Peterhead	105	98	93	108	94	78	80	54	35	25	11		1	Peterhead	1

NAVIGATION

AREA 6 NW Scotland - *C. Wrath to Oban including The Western Isles*
SELECTED LIGHTS, BUOYS & WAYPOINTS | Positions are referenced to WGS84

CAPE WRATH TO LOCH TORRIDON
Cape Wrath ☆ 58°37'·54N 04°59'·99W Fl (4) 30s 122m **22M**; W twr.

► LOCH INCHARD/LOCH LAXFORD
Kinlochbervie Dir lt 327° ☆. 58°27'·49N 05°03'·08W WRG 15m **16M**; vis: FG326°- Al GW326·5°- FW326·75°-327·25°, Al RW327·25°- FR327·5°-328°.

Stoer Head ☆ 58°14'·43N 05°24'·07W Fl 15s 59m **24M**; W twr.

► LOCH INVER
Soyea I ⚓ 58°08'·56N 05°19'·67W Fl (2) 10s 34m 6M.
Glas Leac ⚓ 58°08'·68N 05°16'·36W FlWRG 3s 7m 5M; vis: .

► ULLAPOOL
Rubha Cadail ⚓ 57°55'·51N 05°13'·40W FlWRG 6s 11m W9M, R/G6M; W twr; vis: G311°- W320°- R325°- W103°- G111°- W118°- R127°- W157°-199°.
Ullapool Pt ⚓ 57°53'·70N 05°10'·68W QR.

► LOCH EWE/LOCH GAIRLOCH
Fairway ⚓ 57°51'·98N 05°40'·09W L Fl 10s.
Rubha Reidh ☆ 57°51'·52N 05°48'·72W Fl (4) 15s 37m **24M**.
Gairloch Pier ⚓ 57°42'·59N 05°41'·03W QR 6m 2M.

OUTER HEBRIDES – EAST SIDE
► LEWIS
Butt of Lewis ☆ 58°30'·89N 06°15'·84W Fl 5s 52m **25M**; R twr; vis: 056°-320°.
Tiumpan Head ☆ 58°15'·66N 06°08'·29W Fl (2) 15s 55m **25M**; W twr.
Arnish Point ☆ 58°11'·50N 06°22'·16W FlWR 10s 17m W9M, R7M; W ○ twr; vis: W088°- R198°- W302°-013°.
Rubh' Uisenis ⚓ 57°56'·25N 06°28'·36W Fl 5s 24m 11M; W twr.
Shiants ⚓ 57°54'·57N 06°25'·70W QG.
Sgeir Inoe ⚓ 57°50'·93N 06°33'·93W Fl G 6s.
Scalpay, **Eilean Glas** ☆ 57°51'·41N 06°38'·55W Fl (3) 20s 43m **23M**; W twr, R bands; *Racon (T) 16-18M.*
Sgeir Bràigh Mòr ⚓ 57°51'·51N 06°43'·84W Fl G 6s.
Sgeir Graidach ⚓ 57°50'·36N 06°41'·37W Q (6) + L Fl 15s.
Tarbert ⚓ 57°53'·82N 06°47'·93W Oc WRG 6s 10m 5M

► LOCH MADDY
Weaver's Pt ⚓ 57°36'·49N 07°06'·00W Fl 3s 24m 7M; W hut.
Glas Eilean Mòr ⚓ 57°35'·95N 07°06'·70W Fl (2) G 4s 8m 5M.

► SOUTH UIST, LOCH CARNAN
Landfall ⚓ 57°22'·27N 07°11'·52W L Fl 10s.
Ushenish ☆ (S Uist) 57°17'·89N 07°11'·58W Fl WR 20s 54m **W19M, R15M**; W twr; vis: W193°- 356°, R356°-018°.

► LOCH BOISDALE
MacKenzie Rk ⚓ 57°08'·24N 07°13'·71W Fl (3) R 15s 3m 4M.
Calvay E End ⚓ 57°08'·53N 07°15'·38W Fl (2) WRG 10s 16m W7M, R/G4M; W twr; vis: W111°- G190°- W202°- R286°-111°.

► BARRA/CASTLEBAY
Binch Rock ⚓ 57°01'·71N 07°17'·16W Q (6) + L Fl 15s.
Castle Bay S ⚓ 56°56'·09N 07°27'·21W Fl (2) R 8s; *Racon (T) 7M.*
Barra Hd ☆ 56°47'·11N 07°39'·26W Fl 15s 208m **18M**; W twr; obsc by islands to NE.

OUTER HEBRIDES – WEST SIDE
Flannan I ☆, Eilean Mór 58°17'·32N 07°35'·23W Fl (2) 30s 101m **20M**; W twr; obsc in places by Is to W of Eilean Mór.
Haskeir I ☆ 57°41'·98N 07°41·36W Fl 20s 44m **23M**; W twr.

LOCH TORRIDON TO MULL
► SKYE
Eilean Trodday ⚓ 57°43'·64N 06°17'·89W Fl (2) WRG 10s 52m W12M, R/G9M; W Bn; vis: W062°- R088°- W130°- G322°-062°.
Comet Rock ⚓ 57°44'·60N 06°20'·50W Fl R 6s.

► RONA/INNER SOUND
Rona NE Point ☆ 57°34'·68N 05°57'·56W Fl 12s 69m **19M**; W twr; vis: 050°-358°.

► CROWLIN ISLANDS/RAASAY
Eilean Beag ⚓ 57°21'·21N 05°51'·42W Fl 6s 32m 6M; W Bn.
Eyre Point ⚓ 57°20'·01N 06°01'·29W Fl WR 3s 6m W9M, R6M; W twr; vis: W215°- R266-W288°- 063°.

▶ KYLE AKIN AND KYLE OF LOCH ALSH
Carragh Rk 57°17'·18N 05°45'·36W Fl (2) G 12s; **Racon (T) 5M**.
String Rock 57°16'·50N 05°42'·89W Fl R 6s.
Sgeir-na-Caillich 57°15'·59N 05°38'·90W Fl (2) R 6s 3m 4M.

▶ SOUND OF SLEAT
Kyle Rhea 57°14'·22N 05°39'·93W Fl WRG 3s 7m W11M, R9M, G8M; W Bn; vis: Rshore-W219- G228°- W338°- R346°-shore.
Ornsay, SE end 57°08'·59N 05°46'·88W Oc 8s 18m **15M**; W twr; vis: 157°-030°.
Pt. of Sleat 57°01'·08N 06°01'·08W Fl 3s 20m 9M; W twr.

▶ MALLAIG
Sgeir Dhearg 57°00'·74N 05°49'·50W QG.
Northern Pier E end 57°00'·47N 05°49'·50W Iso WRG 4s 6m W9M, R/G6M; Gy twr; vis: G181°- W185°- R197°-201°. Fl G 3s 14m 6M; same structure.

▶ NW SKYE
Neist Point 57°25'·41N 06°47'·30W Fl 5s 43m **16M**; W twr. .

WEST OF MULL
Hyskeir 56°58'·14N 06°40'·87W Fl (3) 30s 41m **24M**; W twr. N end Horn 30s; **Racon (T) 14-17M**.
Bogha Ruadh 56°49'·56N 06°13'·05W Fl G 5s 4m 3M
Ardnamurchan 56°43'·63N 06°13'·58W Fl (2) 20s 55m **24M**; Gy twr; vis: 002°-217°; Horn (2) 20s.

▶ TIREE
Roan Bogha 56°32'·23N 06°40'·18W Q (6) + L Fl 15s 3m 5M.
Placaid Bogha 56°33'·22N 06°44'·06W Fl G 4s.

Scarinish, S side of ent 56°30'·01N 06°48'·27W Fl 3s 11m **16M**; W twr; vis: 210°- 030°.
Skerryvore 56°19'·36N 07°06'·88W Fl 10s 46m **23M**; Gy twr; **Racon (M) 18M**; Horn 60s.

▶ LOCH NA LÀTHAICH (LOCH LATHAICH)
Dubh Artach 56°07'·94N 06°38'·08W Fl (2) 30s 44m **20M**; Gy twr, R band.

SOUND OF MULL
▶ LOCH SUNART/TOBERMORY/LOCH ALINE
Ardmore Pt 56°39'·37N 06°07'·70W Fl (2) 10s 18m 13M.
New Rks 56°39'·05N 06°03'·30W Fl G 6s.
Rubha nan Gall 56°38'·33N 06°04'·00W Fl 3s 17m **15M**, W twr.
Avon Rock 56°30'·78N 05°46'·80W Fl (4) R 12s.
Yule Rocks 56°30'·01N 05°43'·96W Fl R 15s.

MULL TO OBAN
Lismore, SW end 56°27'·34N 05°36'·45W Fl 10s 31m **17M**; W twr; vis: 237°-208°.
Lady's Rk 56°26'·92N 05°37'·05W Fl 6s 12m 5M.
Duart Pt 56°26'·84N 05°38'·77W Fl (3) WR 18s 14m W5M, R3M; vis: W162°- R261°- W275°- R353°-shore.

▶ OBAN
N spit of Kerrera 56°25'·49N 05°29'·56W Fl R 3s 9m 5M; W col, R bands.
Dunollie 56°25'·37N 05°29'·05W Fl (2) WRG 6s 7m W5M, G/R4M; vis: G351°-W009°- R047°- W120°- G138°-143°.
Corran Ledge 56°25'·19N 05°29'·11W VQ (9) 10s.

		1	2	3	4	5	6	7	8	9	10	11	12	13	14	15	16	17
1	Cape Wrath	**1**																
2	Ullapool	54	**2**															
3	Stornoway	53	45	**3**														
4	East Loch Tarbert	75	56	33	**4**													
5	Portree	83	57	53	42	**5**												
6	Kyle of Lochalsh	91	63	62	63	21	**6**											
7	Mallaig	112	82	83	84	42	21	**7**										
8	Eigg	123	98	97	75	54	35	14	**8**									
9	Castlebay (Barra)	133	105	92	69	97	76	59	46	**9**								
10	Tobermory	144	114	115	87	74	53	32	20	53	**10**							
11	Loch Aline	157	127	128	100	87	66	45	33	66	13	**11**						
12	Fort William	198	161	162	134	121	98	75	63	96	43	34	**12**					
13	Oban	169	138	139	111	100	77	56	44	77	24	13	29	**13**				
14	Loch Melfort	184	154	155	117	114	93	69	61	92	40	27	45	18	**14**			
15	Craobh Haven	184	155	155	117	114	92	70	60	93	40	27	50	21	5	**15**		
16	Crinan	187	157	158	129	112	95	74	63	97	42	30	54	25	14	9	**16**	
17	Mull of Kintyre	232	203	189	175	159	143	121	105	120	89	87	98	72	62	57	51	**17**

NAVIGATION

AREA 7 SW. Scotland - *Oban to Kirkudbright*
SELECTED LIGHTS, BUOYS & WAYPOINTS | Positions are referenced to WGS84

OBAN TO LOCH CRAIGNISH
Bogha Nuadh ⚓ 56°21'·69N 05°37'·88W Q (6) + LFl 15s

Fladda ☆ 56°14'·89N 05°40'·83W Fl (2) WRG 9s 13m W11M, R/G9M; W twr; vis: R169°- W186°- G337°- W344°- R356°-026°.

Dubh Sgeir (Luing) ☆ 56°14'·76N 05°40'·20W Fl WRG 6s 9m W6M, R4M. G4M; W twr; vis: W000°- R010°- W025°- G199°-000°; *Racon (M) 5M*.

▶ LOCH MELFORT/CRAOBH HAVEN
Melfort Pier ☆ 56°16'·14N 05°30'·19W Dir FR 6m 3M; (Private shown 1/4 to 31/10).

Craobh Marina Bkwtr Hd ☆ 56°12'·78N 05°33'·52W Iso WRG 5s.

COLONSAY TO ISLAY
▶ COLONSAY/SOUND OF ISLAY/ PORT ELLEN
Scalasaig, Rubha Dubh ☆ 56°04'·01N 06°10'·90W Fl (2) WR 10s 8m W8M, R6M; W bldg; vis: R shore- W230°- R337°-354°.

Rhubh' a Mháil (Ruvaal) ☆ 55°56'·18N 06°07'·46W Fl (3) WR 15s 45m **W24M, R21M**; W twr; vis: R075°- W180°-075°.

Black Rocks ⚓ 55°47'·50N 06°04'·09W Fl G 6s.

McArthur's Hd ☆ 55°45'·84N 06°02'·90W Fl (2) WR 10s 39m W14M, R11M; W twr; W in Sound of Islay from NE coast- R159°-W244°-E coast of Islay.

Eilean a Chùirn ☆ 55°40'·12N 06°01'·22W Fl (3) 18s 26m 8M; W Bn; obsc when brg more than 040°.

Otter Rock ⚓ 55°33'·86N 06°07'·92W Q (6) + LFl 15s.

Port Ellen ⚓ 55°37'·00N 06°12'·27W QG.

Orsay Is, **Rhinns of Islay** ☆ 55°40'·40N 06°30'·84W Fl 5s 46m **24M**; W twr; vis: 256°-184°.

JURA TO MULL OF KINTYRE
▶ SOUND OF JURA/CRAIGHOUSE/ LOCH SWEEN/GIGHA
Reisa an t-Struith, S end of Is ☆ 56°07'·77N 05°38'·91W Fl (2) 12s 12m 7M; W col.

Ruadh Sgeir ☆ 56°04'·32N 05°39'·77W Fl 6s 15m 9M; W ○ twr.

Skervuile ☆ 55°52'·46N 05°49'·85W Fl 15s 22m 9M; W twr.

Eilean nan Gabhar ☆ 55°50'·04N 05°56'·25W Fl 5s 7m 8M; framework twr; vis: 225°-010°.

Sgeir Gigalum ⚓ 55°39'·96N 05°42'·67W Fl G 6s 3m 4M.

Cath Sgeir ⚓ 55°39'·66N 05°47'·50W Q (9) 15s.

▶ WEST LOCH TARBERT
Eileen Tráighe (off S side) ⚓ 55°45'·37N 05°35'·75W Fl (2) R 5s 5m 3M; R post.

Corran Pt ⚓ 55°46'·12N 05°34'·35W QG 3m 3M; G post.

Mull of Kintyre ☆ 55°18'·64N 05°48'·25W Fl (2) 20s 91m **24M**; W twr on W bldg; vis: 347°-178°; *Horn Mo (N) 90s*.

▶ CRINAN CANAL/ARDRISHAIG
E of lock ent ☆ 56°05'·48N 05°33'·37W Fl WG 3s 8m 4M; W twr, R band; vis: W shore- G146°- shore.

Adrishaig Breakwater Hd ☆ 56°00'·76N 05°26'·59W L Fl WRG 6s 9m 4M; vis: G287°- W339°-R350°-035°.

Sgeir Sgalag No. 49 ⚓ 56°00'·36N 05°26'·30W Fl G 5s

LOCH FYNE TO SANDA ISLAND
▶ EAST LOCH TARBERT
Madadh Maol ☆ 55°52'·02N 05°24'·25W Fl R 2·5s 4m 3M..

▶ KILBRANNAN SOUND/ CARRADALE BAY
Crubon Rock ⚓ 55°34'·48N 05°27'·07W Fl (2) R 12s.

Otterard Rock ⚓ 55°27'·07N 05°31'·11W Q (3) 10s.

▶ CAMPBELTOWN LOCH
Davaar N Pt ☆ 55°25'·69N 05°32'·42W Fl (2) 10s 37m **23M**; W twr; vis: 073°-330°; *Horn (2) 20s*.

Arranman's Barrels ⚓ 55°19'·40N 05°32'·87W Fl (2) R 12s.

Sanda Island ☆ 55°16'·50N 05°35'·01W Fl 10s 50m **15M**; W twr.

Patersons Rock ⚓ 55°16'·90N 05°32'·48W Fl (3) R 18s.

KYLES OF BUTE TO RIVER CLYDE
▶ KYLES OF BUTE/CALADH
Rubha Ban ⚓ 55°54'·95N 05°12'·40W Fl R 4s.

Burnt I No. 42 ⚓ (S of Eilean Buidhe) 55°55'·76N 05°10'·39W Fl R 2s.

Rubha á Bhodaich ⚓ 55°55'·38N 05°09'·59W Fl G.

Ardmaleish Point No. 41 ⚓ 55°53'·02N 05°04'·70W Q.

▶ FIRTH OF CLYDE
Toward Pt ☆ 55°51'·73N 04°58'·79W Fl 10s 21m **22M**; W twr.

Skelmorlie 55°51'·65N 04°56'·34W Iso 5s.

▶ **WEMYSS/INVERKIP/HOLYLOCH**
Kip 55°54'·49N 04°52'·98W QG.
Warden Bank 55°54'·77N 04°54'·54W Fl G 2s.
Cowal 55°56'·00N 04°54'·83W L Fl 10s.
Cloch Point 55°56'·55N 04°52'·74W Fl 3s 24m 8M; W ○ twr, B band, W dwellings.
Holy Loch Marina 55°59'·00N 04°56'·80W 2 FR (vert) 4m 1M.

▶ **LOCH LONG/LOCH GOIL/GOUROCK**
Loch Long 55°59'·15N 04°52'·42W Oc 6s.
Ashton 55°58'·10N 04°50'·65W Iso 5s.
Whiteforeland 55°58'·11N 04°47'·28W L Fl 10s.
Rosneath Patch 55°58'·52N 04°47'·45W Fl (2) 10s 5m 10M.

▶ **ROSNEATH/RHU NARROWS**
Ldg Lts 356°. **Front, No. 7N** 56°00'·05N 04°45'·36W Dir lt 356°. WRG 5m **W16M**, R/G13M; vis: Al WG 353°- FW 355°- Al WR 357°- FR 000°- 002°.
Row 55°59'·84N 04°45'·13W Fl G 5s.
Cairndhu 56°00'·35N 04°46'·00W Fl G 2·5s. .
Rhu SE 56°00'·64N 04°47'·17W Fl G 3s.
Rhu NE 56°01'·02N 04°47'·58W QG.
Rhu Spit 56°00'·84N 04°47'·34W Fl 3s 6m 6M. 9m 4M.

CLYDE TO MULL OF GALLOWAY
▶ **LARGS AND FAIRLIE QUAY**
Approach 55°46'·40N 04°51'·85W L Fl 10s.
Fairlie Quay Pier Hd N 55°46'·06N 04°51'·78W 2 FG (vert).

▶ **MILLPORT, GREAT CUMBRAE**
The Eileans, W end 55°44'·89N 04°55'·59W QG 5m 2M.
Mountstuart 55°48'·00N 04°57'·57W L Fl 10s.
Portachur 55°44'·35N 04°58'·52W Fl G 3s.

Little Cumbrae I Cumbrae Elbow 55°43'·22N 04°58'·06W Fl 6s 28m 14M; W twr; vis: 334°-193°.

▶ **ARDROSSAN/TROON**
N Bkwtr Hd 55°38'·53N 04°49'·64W Fl R 5s 7m 5M; R gantry.
W Crinan Rk 55°38'·47N 04°49'·89W Fl R 4s.
Eagle Rock 55°38'·21N 04°49'·69W Fl G 5s.
Troon 55°33'·06N 04°41'·35W Fl G 4s.
West Pier Head 55°33'·07N 04°41'·02W Fl (2) WG 5s 11m 9M; W twr; vis: G036°- W090°-036°.

▶ **ARRAN/RANZA/LAMLASH**
Hamilton Rk 55°32'·63N 05°04'·90W Fl R 6s.
Pillar Rk Pt (Holy Island), 55°31'·04N 05°03'·67W Fl (2) 20s 38m **25M**; W ☐ twr.
Pladda 55°25'·50N 05°07'·12W Fl (3) 30s 40m **17M**; W twr.

▶ **AYR**
S. Nicholas 55°28'·12N 04°39'·44W Fl G 2s.
Ayr N Breakwater Head 55°28'·21N 04°38'·78W QR 9m 5M.
Turnberry Point , near castle ruins 55°19'·56N 04°50'·71W Fl 15s 29m **24M**; W twr.
Ailsa Craig 55°15'·12N 05°06'·52W Fl 4s 18m **17M**; W twr; vis: 145°-028°.

LOCH RYAN TO MULL OF GALLOWAY AND KIRKUDBRIGHT
Milleur Point 54°01'·28N 05°05'·66W Q.
Cairn Pt 54°58'·46N 05°01'·85W Fl (2) R 10s 14m 12M; W twr.
Corsewall Point 55°00'·41N 05°09'·58W Fl (5) 30s 34m **22M**; W twr; vis: 027°-257°.
Killantringan Black Head 54°51'·70N 05°08'·85W Fl (2) 15s 49m **25M**; W twr.
Crammag Hd 54°39'·90N 04°57'·92W Fl 10s 35m **18M**; W twr.
Mull of Galloway , SE end 54°38'·08N 04°51'·45W Fl 20s 99m **28M**; W twr; vis: 182°-105°.
Hestan I, E end 54°49'·95N 03°48'·53W Fl (2) 10s 42m 9M.

1	Loch Craignish	**1**												
2	Crinan	5	**2**											
3	Ardrishaig	14	9	**3**										
6	East Loch Tarbert	24	19	10	**4**									
5	Campbeltown	55	50	39	31	**5**								
6	Lamlash	48	43	34	25	24	**6**							
7	Largs	48	43	34	24	39	17	**7**						
8	Kip Marina	53	48	39	28	50	25	10	**8**					
9	Greenock	59	54	45	36	53	31	16	6	**9**				
10	Rhu (Helensburgh)	62	57	48	37	59	33	19	9	4	**10**			
11	Troon	54	49	40	33	33	16	20	29	34	38	**11**		
12	Girvan	67	62	53	43	29	20	33	46	49	51	21	**12**	
13	Stranraer	89	84	75	65	34	39	56	69	65	74	44	23	**13**
14	Kirkcudbright	136	131	122	114	88	92	110	116	124	125	97	94	71	**14**

NAVIGATION

AREA 8 NW. England & Wales - *Kirkudbright and I.o.Man to Swansea*
SELECTED LIGHTS, BUOYS & WAYPOINTS | Positions are referenced to WGS84

SOLWAY FIRTH TO BARROW-IN-FURNESS APPROACHES
Two Feet Bank ↙ 54°42'·40N 03°44'·46W Q (9) 15s.
Solway ▲ 54°46'·80N 03°30'·14W Fl G 4s.
S Workington ↙ 54°37'·01N 03°38'·58W VQ (6) + L Fl 10s.
Saint Bees Hd ☆ 54°30'·81N 03°38'·23W Fl (2) 20s 102m **18M**; W○ twr; obsc shore-340°.
Selker ▲ 54°16'·14N 03°29'·58W Fl (3) G 10s; *Bell.*
Lightning Knoll ⬡ 53°59'·83N 03°14'·28W L Fl 10s; *Bell.*
Isle of Walney ☆ 54°02'·92N 03°10'·64W Fl 15s 21m **23M**; stone twr; obsc 122°-127° within 3M of shore.

WALNEY IS. TO RIVERS MERSEY & DEE
▶ **MORECAMBE**
Morecambe ↙ 53°51'·99N 03°24'·10W Q (9) 15s; *Whis.*
Lune Deep ↙ 53°55'·81N 03°11'·08W Q (6) + L Fl 15s; *Whis*; *Racon (T).*

▶ **FLEETWOOD/RIVER RIBBLE**
Fairway No. 1 ↙ 53°57'·67N 03°02'·03W Q; *Bell.*
Gut ⬡ 53°41'·74N 03°08'·98W L Fl 10s.
Jordan's Spit ↙ 53°35'·76N 03°19'·28W Q (9) 15s.

▶ **RIVER MERSEY APPROACHES**
BAR ⚓ 53°32'·01N 03°20'·98W Fl 5s 10m 12M; *Horn (2) 20s*; *Racon (T) 10M.*
Q1 ⚓ 53°31'·00N 03°16'·72W VQ. R hull, W stripes.

▶ **R. DEE/N. WALES COAST & INNER PASSAGE**
HE1 ↙ 53°26'·33N 03°18'·08W Q (9) 15s.
Hilbre I ☆ 53°22'·99N 03°13'·72W Fl R 3s 14m 5M; W twr.
Dee ↙ 53°21'·99N 03°18'·68W Q (6) + L Fl 15s.
N Hoyle ↙ 53°26'·68N 03°30'·58W VQ.
South Hoyle Outer ⬡ 53°21'·47N 03°24'·70W Fl R 2·5s.
N Rhyl ↙ 53°22'·76N 03°34'·58W Q.
W Constable ↙ 53°23'·14N 03°49'·26W Q (9) 15s; *Racon (M) 10*

ISLE OF MAN
Point of Ayre ☆ 54°24'·94N 04°22'·13W Fl (4) 20s 32m **19M**; W twr, two R bands; *Horn (3) 60s*, *Racon (M) 13-15M.*
Low Lt ☆ 54°25'·03N 04°21'·86W Fl 3s 10m 8M; R twr, lower part W, on B Base; part obsc 335°-341°.

Thousla Rock ☆ 54°03'·73N 04°48'·05W Fl R 3s 9m 4M.
Calf of Man ☆ W Pt 54°03'·19N 04°49'·78W Fl 15s 93m **26M**; W 8-sided twr; vis 274°-190°; *Horn 45s.*
Chicken Rock ☆ 54°02'·26N 04°50'·32W Fl 5s 38m 13M; twr; *Horn 60s.*
Douglas Head ☆ 54°08'·60N 04°27'·95W Fl 10s 32m **24M**; W twr; obsc brg more than 037°. FR Lts on radio masts 1 and 3M West.
Maughold Head ☆ 54°17'·72N 04°18'·58W Fl (3) 30s 65m **21M**.
Bahama ↙ 54°20'·01N 04°08'·57W VQ (6) + L Fl 10s; *Bell.*
King William Bank ↙ 54°26'·01N 04°00'·08W Q (3) 10s.

N. & NW. WALES COAST/ANGLESEY
Conwy Fairway ⬡ 53°17'·95N 03°55'·58W L Fl 10s.

▶ **MENAI STRAIT - N. APPROACHES**
Trwyn-Du ☆ 53°18'·77N 04°02'·44W Fl 5s 19m 12M; W ○ castellated twr, B bands; vis: 101°-023°; *Bell (1) 30s*, sounded continuously. FR on radio mast 2M SW.
Ten Feet Bank ⬡ 53°19'·47N 04°02'·82W QR.

▶ **ANGLESEY**
Point Lynas ☆ 53°24'·98N 04°17'·35W Oc 10s 39m **18M**; W castellated twr; vis: 109°-315°; *Horn 45s*; H24.
Archdeacon Rock ↙ 53°26'·71N 04°30'·87W Q.
The Skerries ☆ 53°25'·27N 04°36'·55W Fl (2) 10s 36m **22M**; W ○ twr, R band; *Racon (T) 25M.* FR 26m **16M**; same twr; vis: 231°-254°; *Horn (2) 20s*; H24.
Langdon ↙ 53°22'·74N 04°38'·74W Q (9) 15s.

▶ **HOLYHEAD**
Bkwtr Head ☆ 53°19'·86N 04°37'·16W Fl (3) G 10s 21m 14M; W □ twr, B band; Fl Y vis: 174°-226°; *Siren 20s.*
South Stack ☆ 53°19'·31N 04°41'·98W Fl 10s 60m **24M**; (H24); W ○ twr; obsc to N by N Stack and part obsc in Penrhos bay; *Horn 30s.* Fog Det lt vis: 145°-325°. 27m 3M, one either side (shown Apr-Sep). SE end of bridge, FR 21m 3M either side, NW end of bridge section FG 21m 3M either side.

▶ **CAERNARFON APPROACHES**
Mussel Bank ⬡ 53°07'·27N 04°20'·81W Fl (2) 5s.
Llanddwyn I ☆ 53°08'·05N 04°24'·79W Fl WR

2·5s 12m W7M, R4M; W twr; vis: R280°- W015°- 120°.

CARDIGAN BAY

Bardsey I ☆ 52°45'·00N 04°47'·98W Fl (5) 15s 39m 26M; W ☐ twr; R bands; obsc by Bardsey I 198°-250° and in Tremadoc B when brg less than 260°; *Horn Mo(N) 45s.*
St Tudwal's ⚓ 52°47'·92N 04°28'·30W Fl WR 15s 46m W14, R10M; vis: W349°- R169°- W221°- R243°- W259°- R293°- 349°; obsc by East I 211°-231°.

▶ **PWLLHELI/PORTHMADOG/ BARMOUTH/ABERDOVEY**

Pwllheli App ⚓ 52°53'·02N 04°23'·07W Iso 2s.
Porthmadog Fairway ⚓ 52°52'·97N 04°11'·18W L Fl 10s.
Barmouth Outer ⚓ 52°42'·62N 04°04'·83W L Fl 10s.
Sarn Badrig Causeway ⚓ 52°41'·19N 04°25'·36W Q (9) 15s; *Bell.*
Sarn-y-Bwch ⚓ 52°34'·81N 04°13'·58W VQ (9) 10s.
Aberdovey Outer ⚓ 52°32'·00N 04°05'·56W; Iso 4s.
Patches ⚓ 52°25'·83N 04°16'·41W Q (9) 15s.

▶ **ABERYSTWYTH/FISHGUARD**

Aberystwyth S Breakwater Head ☆ 52°24'·40N 04°05'·52W Fl (2) WG 10s 12m 10M; vis: G030°-W053°-210°.
Fishguard N Bkwtr Hd ☆ 52°00'·76N 04°58'·23W Fl G 4·5s 18m 13M; *Bell (1) 8s.* 5M.
Strumble Head ☆ 52°01'·79N 05°04'·43W Fl (4) 15s 45m **26M**; vis: 038°-257°; (H24).

BISHOPS AND SMALLS

South Bishop ☆ 51°51'·14N 05°24'·74W Fl 5s 44m **16M**; W ○ twr; *Horn(3) 45s; Racon(O) 10M;* (H24).
The Smalls ☆ 51°43'·28N 05°40'·19W Fl (3) 15s 36m **25M**; *Racon (T) 25M; Horn (2) 60s.* Same twr, FR 33m 13M; vis: 253°-285° over Hats and Barrels Rk; both Lts shown H24.

Skokholm I ☆, 51°41'·64N 05°17'·22W Fl WR 10s 54m **W18M, R15M;** vis: 301°- R154°-129°; part obsc 226°-258°; (H24).

WALES SOUTH COAST – BRISTOL CHANNEL
▶ **MILFORD HAVEN**

St Ann's Head ☆ 51°40'·87N 05°10'·42W Fl WR 5s 48m **W18M, R17M,** R14M; W 8-sided twr; vis: W233°-R247°- R(intens)285°- R314°- W332°-131°, partially obscured between 124°-129°; *Horn (2) 60s.*
W Blockhouse Point ⚓ Ldg Lts 022·5°. Front, 51°41'·31N 05°09'·56W F 54m 13M; B stripe on W twr; vis: 004·5°-040·5°; intens on lead. By day 10M; vis: 004·5°-040·5°; *Racon (Q).*
Watwick Point Common Rear ☆, 0·5M from front, F 80m **15M**; vis: 013·5°-031·5°. By day 10M; vis: 013·5°-031·5°; *Racon (Y).*
St Ann's ⚓ 51°40'·25N 05°10'·51W Fl R 2·5s.
Sheep ⚓ 51°40'·06N 05°08'·31W QG.
Dakotian ⚓ 51°42'·15N 05°08'·29W Q (3) 10s.
Turbot Bank ⚓ 51°37'·41N 05°10'·08W VQ (9) 10s.
St Gowan ⚓ 51°31'·93N 04°59'·77W Q (6) + L Fl 15s, *Whis, Racon (T) 10M.*

▶ **CALDEY I/TENBY/CARMARTHEN BAY/ BURRY INLET**

Caldey I ☆ 51°37'·90N 04°41'·08W Fl (3) WR 20s 65m W13M, R9M; vis: R173°- W212°- R088°-102°.
Spaniel ⚓ 51°38'·06N 04°39'·75W.
Tenby Pier Head ☆ 51°40'·40N 04°41'·89W FR 7m 7M.
Burry Port Inlet ☆ 51°40'·62N 04°15'·06W Fl 5s 7m **15M**.
W. Helwick (W HWK) ⚓ 51°31'·40N 04°23'·65W Q (9) 15s; *Racon (T) 10M; Whis.*
East Helwick ⚓ 51°31'·80N 04°12'·68W VQ (3) 5s; *Bell.*
Ledge ⚓ 51°29'·93N 03°58'·77W VQ (6) + L Fl 10s.

		1	2	3	4	5	6	7	8	9	10	11	12	13	14	15	16	17
1	Portpatrick	**1**																
2	Mull of Galloway	16	**2**															
3	Kirkcudbright	48	32	**3**														
4	Maryport	65	49	26	**4**													
5	Workington	63	47	25	6	**5**												
6	Ravenglass	70	54	40	30	23	**6**											
7	Point of Ayre	38	22	28	37	31	34	**7**										
8	Peel	41	26	46	55	49	52	18	**8**									
9	Douglas	60	42	46	50	44	39	19	30	**9**								
10	Glasson Dock	101	85	74	66	60	37	64	85	63	**10**							
11	Fleetwood	95	79	68	59	53	30	58	80	57	10	**11**						
12	Liverpool	118	102	97	89	83	60	80	86	70	52	46	**12**					
13	Conwy	111	95	95	92	86	58	72	72	59	62	56	46	**13**				
14	Beaumaris	109	93	94	95	89	72	71	73	58	60	49	72	14	**14**			
15	Caernarfon	117	103	104	105	99	82	81	73	68	76	70	59	22	10	**15**		
16	Holyhead	93	81	94	96	90	69	68	62	50	79	73	68	36	32	26	**16**	
17	Fishguard	171	158	175	175	169	160	153	140	134	153	147	136	100	88	78	89	**17**

NAVIGATION

AREA 9 S.Wales & SW. England - *Swansea to Padstow*
SELECTED LIGHTS, BUOYS & WAYPOINTS | Positions are referenced to WGS84

▶ SWANSEA BAY/SWANSEA
Grounds ↓ 51°32′·81N 03°53′·47W VQ (3) 5s.
Mumbles ☆ 51°34′·01N 03°58′·27W Fl (4) 20s 35m **15M**; W twr; *Horn (3) 60s*.
SW Inner Green Grounds ↓ 51°34′·06N 03°57′·03W Q (6) + L Fl 15s; *Bell*.

▶ SWANSEA BAY/PORT TALBOT
Cabenda ↓ 51°33′·36N 03°52′·23W VQ (6) + L Fl 10s; *Racon (Q)*.
P Talbot N Outer ⚓ 51°33′·78N 03°51′·38W Fl R 5s.

BRISTOL CHANNEL – EASTERN PART (NORTH SHORE)
Kenfig ↓ 51°29′·44N 03°46′·06W VQ (3) 5s.
W Scar ↓ 51°28′·31N 03°55′·57W Q (9) 15s, *Bell*, *Racon (T) 10M*.
East Scarweather ↓ 51°27′·98N 03°46′·76W Q (3) 10s; *Bell*.
Fairy ↓ 51°27′·86N 03°42′·07W Q (9) 15s; *Bell*.
Tusker ⚓ 51°26′·85N 03°40′·74W Fl (2) R 5s *Bell*.
W Nash ↓ 51°25′·99N 03°45′·95W VQ (9) 10s; *Bell*.
East Nash ↓ 51°24′·06N 03°34′·10W Q (3) 10s.
Nash ☆ 51°24′·03N 03°33′·06W Fl (2) WR 15s 56m **W21M, R16M**; vis: R280°- W290°- R100°- W120°- 128°.
BREAKSEA ⚓ 51°19′·88N 03°19′·08W Fl 15s 11m 12M; *Racon (T) 10M*; *Horn (2) 30s*.
Merkur ⚓ 51°21′·88N 03°15′·95W QR.
Lavernock Spit ↓ 51°23′·02N 03°10′·82W VQ (6) + L Fl 10s.
Mackenzie ⚓ 51°21′·75N 03°08′·24W QR.
Wolves ↓ 51°23′·13N 03°08′·88W VQ.
Flat Holm ☆, SE Pt 51°22′·54N 03°07′·14W Fl (3) WR 10s 50m **W15M**, R12M; W ○ twr; vis: R106°- W140°- R151°- W203°- 106°.
Weston ⚓ 51°22′·60N 03°05′·75W Fl (2) R 5s.
Monkstone Rock ⚓ 51°24′·89N 03°06′·02W Fl 5s 13m 12M.

▶ CARDIFF/PENARTH/NEWPORT DEEP
S Cardiff ↓ 51°24′·18N 03°08′·57W Q (6) + L Fl 15s; *Bell*.
N Cardiff ⚓ 51°26′·52N 03°07′·19W QG. 2 FR (vert) 8/6m 3M;
Outer Wrach ↓ 51°26′·20N 03°09′·46W Q (9) 15s.
EW Grounds ↓ 51°27′·12N 02°59′·95W L Fl 10s 7M, *Whis*, *Racon (T) 7M*.
Newport Deep ⚓ 51°29′·36N 02°59′·12W Fl (3) G 10s; *Bell*.

East Usk ☆ 51°32′·40N 02°58′·01W Fl (2) WRG 10s 11m **W15M** R/G11M; vis: W284°- R290°- W017°- G037°- W115°-120°. Also Oc WRG 10s 10m W11M, R/G9M.

BRISTOL CHANNEL E PART(S SHORE)
▶ BRISTOL DEEP
N Elbow ⚓ 51°26′·97N 02°58′·65W QG; *Bell*.
S Mid Grounds ↓ 51°27′·62N 02°58′·68W VQ (6) + L Fl 10s.
E Mid Grounds ⚓ 51°28′·14N 02°53′·56W Fl R 5s.
Clevedon ↓ 51°27′·39N 02°54′·93W VQ.
Welsh Hook ↓ 51°28′·53N 02°51′·86W Q (6) + L Fl 15s; *Bell*.
Avon ⚓ 51°27′·92N 02°51′·73W Fl G 2·5s.
Black Nore Point ☆ 51°29′·09N 02°48′·05W Fl (2) 10s 11m **17M**; obsc by Sand Pt when brg less than 049°; vis: 044°-243°.
Firefly ⚓ 51°29′·96N 02°45′·35W Fl (2) G 5s.
Cockburn ⚓ 51°30′·46N 02°44′·07W Fl R 2·5s.
Portishead Point ☆ 51°29′·68N 02°46′·42W Q (3) 10s 9m **16M**; B twr, W base; vis: 060°-262°; *Horn 20s*.

▶ AVONMOUTH
Royal Edward Dock N Pier Head ⚓ 51°30′·49N 02°43′·09W Fl 4s 15m 10M; vis: 060°-228·5°.

SEVERN ESTUARY
▶ THE SHOOTS
Second Severn Crossing, Centre span ☆ 51°34′·45N 02°42′·03W Q Bu 5M; *Racon (O) (3cm) range unknown*.
Old Man's Hd ↓ 51°34′·74N 02°41′·69W VQ (9) W 10s 6m 7M.
Lady Bench (Lts in line 234°) ↓ 51°34′·85N 02°42′·20W QR 6m 6M. Rear, Oc R 5s 38m 3M.
Charston Rock ⚓ 51°35′·35N 02°41′·68W Fl 3s 5m 8M.
Chapel Rock ⚓ 51°36′·44N 02°39′·21W Fl WRG 2·6s 6m 8M.

▶ SEVERN BRIDGE TO SHARPNESS
Aust ⚓ 51°36′·16N 02°38′·00W 2 QG (vert) 11m 6M.
Centre of span ⚓ 51°36′·59N 02°38′·43W Q Bu, each side.
Lyde Rock ⚓ 51°36′·89N 02°38′·67W Q WR 5m 5M.
COUNTS ⚓ 51°39′·48N 02°35′·84W.

LEDGES ⚓ 51°39'·77N 02°34'·15W Fl (3) G 10s.
Bull Rock ☆ 51°41'·80N 02°29'·89W Fl 3s 6m 8M.
Sharpness S Pier Hd ☆ 51°42'·97N 02°29'·12W 2 FG (vert) 6m 3M; Siren 20s.

BRISTOL CHANNEL (SOUTH SHORE)
▶ WESTON-SUPER-MARE

E Culver ⚓ 51°18'·00N 03°15'·44W Q (3) 10s.
W Culver ⚓ 51°17'·37N 03°18'·68W VQ (9) 10s.

▶ BURNHAM-ON-SEA/RIVER PARRET

Gore ⚓ 51°13'·94N 03°09'·79W Iso 5s; Bell.
Bridgewater Bar No. 1 ⚓ 51°14'·53N 03°03'·75W QR.

▶ WATCHET/MINEHEAD

Watchet W Bkwtr Head ☆ 51°11'·03N 03°19'·74W Oc G 3s 9m 9M.
Minehead Bkwtr Hd ☆ 51°12'·81N 03°28'·36W Fl (2) G 5s 4M; vis: 127°-262°.
Lynmouth Foreland ☆ 51°14'·73N 03°47'·21W Fl (4) 15s 67m **18M**; W ○ twr; vis: 083°-275°; (H24).

▶ LYNMOUTH/WATERMOUTH

Harbour Arm ☆ 51°13'·92N 03°49'·84W 2 FG (vert) 6m 5M.
Sand Ridge ⚓ 51°15'·01N 03°49'·78W.
Copperas Rock ⚓ 51°13'·78N 04°00'·60W.
Watermouth ☆ 51°12'·93N 04°04'·60W Oc WRG 5s 1m 3M; W △.

▶ ILFRACOMBE

Lantern Hill ☆ 51°12'·66N 04°06'·78W Fl G 2·5s 39m 6M.
Horseshoe ⚓ 51°15'·02N 04°12'·96W Q.
Bull Point ☆ 51°11'·94N 04°12'·09W Fl (3) 10s 54m **20M**; W ○ twr, obscd shore-056°. Same twr; FR 48m 12M; vis: 058°-096°.
Morte Stone ⚓ 51°11'·30N 04°14'·95W.
Baggy Leap ⚓ 51°08'·92N 04°16'·97W.

▶ BIDEFORD/R.TAW/R.TORRIDGE/ CLOVELLY

Bideford Fairway ⚓ 51°05'·25N 04°16'·25W L Fl 10s; Bell.
Instow ☆ Ldg Lts 118°. **Front**, 51°03'·62N 04°10'·67W Oc 6s 22m **15M**; vis: 104·5°-131·5°. **Rear**, 427m from front, Oc 10s 38m **15M**; vis: 104°-132°; (H24).
Crow Pt ☆ 51°03'·96N 04°11'·40W Fl WR 5s 8m W6M R5M.
Clovelly Hbr Quay Hd ☆ 50°59'·92N 04°23'·83W Fl G 5s 5m 5M.

▶ LUNDY

Near North Point ☆ 51°12'·10N 04°40'·65W Fl 15s 48m **17M**; vis: 009°-285°.
South East Point ☆ 51°09'·72N 04°39'·37W Fl 5s 53m **15M**; vis: 170°-073°; Horn 25s.
Hartland Point ☆ 51°01'·29N 04°31'·59W Fl (6) 15s 37m **25M**; (H24); Horn 60s.

NORTH CORNWALL
▶ PADSTOW

Stepper Point ☆ 50°34'·12N 04°56'·72W L Fl 10s 12m 4M.
Greenaway ⚓ 50°33'·78N 04°56'·06W Fl (2) R 10s.
Bar ⚓ 50°33'·46N 04°56'·12W Fl G 5s.
Trevose Head ☆ 50°32'·94N 05°02'·13W Fl 7·5s 62m **21M**; Horn (2) 30s.

▶ ST IVES

The Stones ⚓ 50°15'·64N 05°25'·51W Q.
Godrevy I ☆ 50°14'·54N 05°24'·04W Fl WR 10s 37m W12M, R9M; vis: W022°-R101°-W145°-272°.
East Pier Head ☆ 50°12'·80N 05°28'·61W 2 FG (vert) 8m 5M.
Pendeen ☆ 50°09'·90N 05°40'·32W Fl (4) 15s 59m **16M**; vis: 042°-240°; in bay between Gurnard Hd and Pendeen it shows to coast; Horn 20s.

1	Aberystwyth	1		12	64	66	122	164	192	224	254	286	299	318	361		Kilrush	12
2	Fishguard	40	2		11	13	69	111	139	171	201	233	246	265	308		Dingle	11
3	Milford Haven	84	48	3		10	56	102	131	165	188	227	242	252	295		Valentia	10
4	Tenby	107	71	28	4		9	42	70	102	132	164	177	196	239		Baltimore	9
5	Swansea	130	94	55	36	5		8	35	69	95	135	150	168	202		Kinsale	8
6	Cardiff	161	125	86	66	46	6		7	34	65	100	115	133	172		Youghal	7
7	Sharpness	192	156	117	106	75	33	7		6	32	69	84	102	139		Dunmore East	6
8	Avonmouth	175	139	100	89	58	20	18	8		5	34	47	66	108		Rosslare	5
9	Burnham-on-Sea	169	133	94	70	48	53	50	33	9		4	15	36	75		Arklow	4
10	Ilfracombe	128	92	53	35	25	44	74	57	45	10		3	21	63		Wicklow	3
11	Padstow	142	106	70	70	76	97	127	110	98	55	11		2	48		Dun Laoghaire	2
12	Longships	169	133	105	110	120	139	169	152	140	95	50	12		1		Carlingford Lough	1

NAVIGATION

AREA 10 Ireland - *South and Westwards from Rockabill to Inisheer*
SELECTED LIGHTS, BUOYS & WAYPOINTS | Positions are referenced to WGS84

LAMBAY ISLAND TO TUSKAR ROCK

▶ **LAMBAY ISLAND/HOWTH**
Rowan Rocks ₄ 53°23'·88N 06°03'·27W Q (3) 10s.
Howth E Pier Head ☆ 53°23'·66N 06°04'·03W Fl (2) WR 7·5s 13m W12M, R9M; W twr.
Baily ☆ 53°21'·70N 06°03'·14W Fl 15s 41m **26M**; twr.
Rosbeg E ₄ 53°21'·02N 06°03'·45W Q (3) 10s.
Rosbeg S ₄ 53°20'·22N 06°04'·17W Q (6) + L Fl 15s.
S Burford ₄ 53°18'·07N 06°01'·27W VQ (6) + L Fl 10s; *Whis*.

▶ **PORT OF DUBLIN/DUN LAOGHAIRE**
Dublin Bay ₄ 53°19'·92N 06°04'·64W Mo (A) 10s; *Racon (M) range unknown*.
Great S Wall Hd Poolbeg ☆ 53°20'·53N 06°09'·08W Oc (2) R 20s 20m **15M**; R O twr; *Horn (2) 60s*.
Dun Laoghaire E Bkwtr Head ☆ 53°18'·15N 06°07'·62W Fl (2) R 10s 16m **17M**; twr, R lantern; *Horn 30s* (or *Bell (1) 6s*).
Muglins ☆ 53°16'·55N 06°04'·58W Fl 5s 14m 11M.
Bennett Bank ₄ 53°20'·17N 05°55'·11W Q (6) + L Fl 15s; *Whis*.
Kish Bank ☆ 53°18'·64N 05°55'·48W Fl (2) 20s 29m **22M**; W twr, R band; *Racon (T) 15M*; *Horn (2) 30s*.
S Codling ₄ 53°04'·74N 05°49'·76W VQ (6) + L Fl 10s.
S India ₄ 53°00'·36N 05°53'·31W Q (6) + L Fl 15s.
CODLING LANBY ⚓ 53°03'·02N 05°40'·76W Fl 4s 12m **15M**; tubular structure on By; *Racon (G) 10M*; *Horn 20s*.

▶ **WICKLOW/ARKLOW**
Wicklow Head ☆ 52°57'·95N 05°59'·89W Fl (3) 15s 37m **23M**; W twr.
N Arklow ₄ 52°53'·86N 05°55'·21W Q; *Whis*.
S Arklow ₄ 52°40'·82N 05°59'·21W VQ (6) + L Fl 10s.
ARKLOW LANBY ⚓ 52°39'·52N 05°58'·16W Fl (2) 12s 12m **15M**; *Racon (O) 10M*; *Horn Mo (A) 30s*.
No. 2 Glassgorman ⚓ 52°44'·52N 06°05'·36W Fl (4) R 10s.
S Blackwater ₄ 52°22'·76N 06°12'·86W Q (6) + L Fl 15s; *Whis*.

▶ **WEXFORD/ROSSLARE**
S Long ₄ 52°14'·84N 06°15'·64W VQ (6) + L Fl 10s; *Whis*.
Splaugh ⚓ 52°14'·37N 06°16'·76W Fl R 6s.

Tuskar ☆ 52°12'·17N 06°12'·42W Q (2) 7·5s 33m **24M**; W twr; *Horn (4) 45s*, *Racon (T) 18M*.

TUSKAR ROCK TO OLD HEAD OF KINSALE

Barrels ₄ 52°08'·32N 06°22'·05W Q (3) 10s; *Whis*.
CONINGBEG ⚓ 52°02'·40N 06°39'·49W Fl (3) 30s 12m **24M**; R hull, and twr, *Racon (M) 13M*; *Horn (3) 60s*.

▶ **WATERFORD**
Hook Head ☆ 52°07'·32N 06°55'·85W Fl 3s 46m **23M**; W twr, two B bands; *Racon (K) 10M vis 237°-177°*; *Horn (2) 45s*.
Waterford ₄ 52°08'·95N 06°57'·00W Fl R 3s. Fl (3) R 10s.
Dunmore East Pier Head ☆ 52°08'·93N 06°59'·37W Fl WR 8s 13m **W17M**, R13M; Gy twr, vis: W225°-310°, R310°-004°.

▶ **DUNGARVAN**
Helvick ₄ 52°03'·61N 07°32'·25W Q (3) 10s.
Mine Head ☆ 51°59'·52N 07°35'·25W Fl (4) 20s 87m **20M**; W twr, B band; vis: 228°-052°.

▶ **YOUGHAL**
W side of ent ☆ 51°56'·57N 07°50'·53W Fl WR 2·5s 24m **W17M**, R13M; W twr; vis: W183°- R273°- W295°- R305½°- W351°-003°.

▶ **BALLYCOTTON**
Ballycotton ☆ 51°49'·52N 07° 59'·09W Fl WR 10s 59m **W21M, R17M**; B twr/W walls, B lantern; vis: W238°- R048°-238°; *Horn (4) 90s*.

▶ **CORK**
Cork ₄ 51°42'·92N 08°15'·60W L Fl 10s; *Racon (T) 7M*.
Fort Davis Ldg lts 354·1°. Front, 51°48'·82N 08°15'·80W Dir WRG 29m **17M**; vis: FG351·5°- AIWG352·25°- FW353°- AIWR355°- FR355·75°- 356·5°. Rear, Dognose Quay, Oc 5s 37m 10M; Or 3, synch with front.
Roche's Point ☆ 51°47'·59N 08°15'·29W Fl WR 3s 30m **W20M, R16M**; vis: Rshore- W292°- R016°- W(unintens) 033°- R159°-shore.

▶ **KINSALE/OYSTER HAVEN**
Bulman ₄ 51°40'·14N 08°29'·74W Q (6) + L Fl 15s.
Charle's Fort ☆ 51°41'·74N 08°29'·97W Fl WRG 5s 18m W9M, R6M, G7M; vis: G348°- W358°- R004°-168°; H24.

OLD HEAD OF KINSALE TO MIZEN HEAD

Old Head of Kinsale ☆, S point 51°36'·28N 08°32'·03W Fl (2) 10s 72m **25M**; B twr, two W bands; *Horn (3) 45s*.

Galley Head ☆ summit 51°31'·80N 08°57'·19W Fl (5) 20s 53m **23M**; W twr; vis: 256°-065°.

▶ BALTIMORE/SCHULL/CROOKHAVEN

Barrack Point ☆ 51°28'·33N 09°23'·65W Fl (2) WR 6s 40m W6M, R3M; vis: R168°- W294°-038°.

Fastnet ☆, W end 51°23'·35N 09°36'·19W Fl 5s 49m **27M**; Gy twr, *Horn (4) 60s*, *Racon (G) 18M*

Mizen Head ☆ 51°27'·00N 09°49'·24W Iso 4s 55m **15M**; vis: 313°-133°.

MIZEN HEAD TO DINGLE BAY

Sheep's Head ☆ 51°32'·60N 09°50'·95W Fl (3) WR 15s 83m **W18M, R15M**; W bldg; vis: R007°-W017°-212°.

▶ BANTRY BAY/KENARE RIVER

Roancarrigmore ☆ 51°39'·19N 09°44'·83W Fl WR 3s 18m **W18M**, R14M; W ☐ twr, B band; vis: W312°- R050°- R(unintens) 122°- R242°-312°. Reserve lt W8M, R6M obsc 140°-220°.

Ardnakinna Pt ☆ 51°37'·11N 09°55'·08W Fl (2) WR 10s 62m **W17M**, R14M; W ○ twr; vis: R319°- W348°-R066°-shore.

Bull Rock ☆ 51°35'·51N 10°18'·08W Fl 15s 83m **21M**; W twr; vis: 220°-186°.

Skelligs Rock ☆ 51°46'·12N 10°32'·51W Fl (3) 15s 53m **19M**; W twr; vis: 262°-115°; part obsc within 6M 110°-115°.

▶ VALENTIA/PORTMAGEE

Fort (Cromwell) Point ☆ 51°56'·02N 10°19'·27W Fl WR 2s 16m **W17M, R15M**; W twr; vis: R304°-351°, W102°-304°; obsc from seaward by Doulus Head when brg more than 180°.

DINGLE BAY TO LOOP HEAD

Inishtearaght ☆, W end Blasket Islands 52°04'·55N 10°39'·68W Fl (2) 20s 84m **19M**; W twr; vis: 318°-221°; *Racon (O)*.

Little Samphire I ☆ 52°16'·26N 09°52'·91W Fl WRG 5s 17m **W16M**, R/G13M; Bu ○ twr; vis: R262°-275°, R280°- G090°- W140°- R152°-172°.

▶ SHANNON ESTUARY

Loop Head ☆ 52°33'·68N 09°55'·96W Fl (4) 20s 84m **23M**.

Ballybunnion ↙ 52°32'·52N 09°46'·93W VQ; *Racon (M) 6M*.

Kilstiffin ⚓ 52°33'·80N 09°43'·83W Fl R 3s.

> Positions are referenced to WGS84

North and Westwards from Rockabill to Inisheer

LAMBAY ISLAND TO DONAGHADEE

Rockabill ☆ 53°35'·82N 06°00'·25W Fl WR 12s 45m **W22M, R18M**; W twr, B band; vis: W178°-R329°-178°; *Horn (4) 60s*.

▶ R. BOYNE/DROGHEDA

Port Approach Dir lt 53°43'·30N 06°14'·73W WRG 10m **W19M, R15M, G15M**; vis: FG268°- Al WG269°- FW269·5°- Al WR270·5°- FR271°-272°; H24.

▶ DUNDALK/CARLINGFORD LOUGH

Dundalk Pile Light ☆ 53°58'·56N 06°17'·70W Fl WR 15s 10m **W21M, R18M**; W Ho; vis: W124°-R151°- W284°- R313°-124°. Fog Det lt VQ 7m, vis: when brg 358°; *Horn (3) 60s*.

Hellyhunter ↙ 54°00'·35N 06°02'·10W Q (6) + L Fl 15s; *Racon* .

Haulbowline ☆ 54°01'·19N 06°04'·74W Fl (3) 10s 32m **17M**; Gy twr; reserve lt 15M; Fog Det lt VQ 26m; vis: 330°. Turning lt ⚓ FR 21m 9M; same twr; vis: 196°-208°; *Horn 30s*.

▶ DUNDRUM BAY

St John's Point ☆ 54°13'·61N 05°39'·30W Q (2) 7·5s 37m **25M**; B twr, Y bands; H24 when horn is operating. **Aux'y Light** ☆ Fl WR 3s 14m **W15M**, R11M; same twr, vis: W064°-078°, R078°-shore; Fog Det lt VQ 14m vis: 270°; *Horn (2) 60s*.

▶ STRANGFORD/ARDS PENINSULA

Strangford ⚓ 54°18'·61N 05°28'·67W L Fl 10s. *SOUTH ROCK* ⚓ 54°24'·49N 05°22'·02W Fl (3) R 30s 12m **20M**; R hull and lt twr, W Mast, *Horn (3) 45s*, *Racon (T) 13M*.

▶ BALLYWATER/DONAGHADEE

Skulmartin ⚓ 54°31'·82N 05°24'·80W L Fl 10s; *Whis*.

Donaghadee ☆, S Pier Head 54°38'·70N 05°31'·86W Iso WR 4s 17m **W18M**, R14M; W twr; vis: W shore- R326°-shore; *Siren 12s*.

DONAGHADEE TO RATHLIN ISLAND
▶ BELFAST LOUGH

Mew I ☆ NE end 54°41'·91N 05°30'·79W Fl (4) 30s 37m; B twr, W band; *Racon (O) 14M*.

Belfast Fairway ↙ 54°41'·71N 05°46'·24W L Fl 10s; *Horn (1) 16s*; *Racon (G) range unknown*.

Black Hd ☆ 54°45'·99N 05°41'·33W Fl 3s 45m **27M**; W 8-sided twr.

29

NAVIGATION

▶ LARNE/GLENARM
East Maiden ☆ 54°55'·74N 05°43'·65W Fl (3) 20s 29m **24M**; W twr, B band; *Racon (M) 11-21M*. Aux'y lt Fl R 5s 15m 8M; same twr; vis:142°-182° over Russel and Highland Rks.

RATHLIN ISLAND TO INISHTRAHULL
Altacarry Head Rathlin East ☆ 55°18'·06N 06°10'·30W Fl (4) 20s 74m **26M**; W twr, B band; vis: 110°-006° and 036°-058°; *Racon (G) 15-27M*.
Rathlin W 0·5M NE of Bull Pt ☆ 55°18'·05N 06°16'·82W Fl R 5s 62m **22M**; W twr, lantern at base; vis: 015°-225°; H24.

▶ LOUGH FOYLE
<u>Foyle</u> ⚓ 55°15'·32N 06°52'·60W L Fl 10s; *Whis..*.
Inishowen ☆ 55°13'·56N 06°55'·75W Fl (2) WRG 10s 28m **W18M**, R14M, G14M; W twr, 2 B bands; vis: G197°-W211°-R249°-000°; *Horn (2) 30s*. Fog Det lt VQ 16m vis: 270°.

INISHTRAHUL TO BLOODY FORELAND
Inishtrahull ☆ 55°25'·86N 07°14'·62W Fl (3) 15s 59m **19M**; W twr; obscd 256°-261° within 3M; *Racon (T) 24M 060°-310°*.

▶ LOUGH SWILLY/SHEEPHAVEN
Fanad Head ☆ 55°16'·57N 07°37'·91W Fl (5) WR 20s 39m **W18M**, R14M; W twr; vis R100°-110°, W110°-313°, R313°-345°, W345°-100°.
Tory Island ☆ 55°16'·36N 08°14'·97W Fl (4) 30s 40m **27M**; B twr, W band; vis: 302°-277°; *Racon (M) 12-23M*; H24.
Bloody Foreland ☆ 55°09'·51N 08°17'·03W Fl WG 7·5s 14m W6M, G4M; vis: W062°-G232°-062°.

BLOODY FORELAND TO RATHLIN O'BIRNE
Aranmore, Rinrawros Pt ☆ 55°00'·90N 08°33'·66W Fl (2) 20s 71m **29M**; W twr; obsc by land about 234°-007° and about 013°. Auxiliary lt Fl R 3s 61m 13M, same twr; vis: 203°-234°.
Rathlin O'Birne, W side ☆ 54°39'·80N 08°49'·94 W Fl WR 15s 35m **W18M**, R14M; W twr; vis: R195°-W307°-195°; *Racon (O) 13M, vis 284°-203°*.

RATHLIN O'BIRNE TO EAGLE ISLAND
St John's Pt ☆ 54°34'·16N 08°27'·64W Fl 6s 30m 14M; W twr.
Rotten I ☆ 54°36'·97N 08°26'·41W Fl WR 4s 20m **W15M**, R11M; W twr; vis: W255°-R008°-W039°-208°.

▶ SLIGO
Black Rock ☆ 54°18'·45N 08°37'·06W Fl 5s 24m 13M; W twr, B band. Aux'y lt Fl R 3s 12m 5M; same twr; vis: 107°-130° over Wheat and Seal rks.

▶ BROAD HAVEN BAY
Gubacashel Point ☆ 54°16'·06N 09°53'·33W Iso WR 4s 27m **W17M**, R12M; R110°-W133°-R355°-021° W twr.

EAGLE ISLAND TO SLYNE HEAD
Eagle I, W end ☆ 54°17'·02N 10°05'·56W Fl (3) 15s 67m **19M**; W twr.
Black Rock ☆ 54°04'·03N 10°19'·25W Fl WR 12s 86m **W20M**, R16M; W twr; vis: W276°- R212°-276°.

▶ BLACKSOD BAY/CLEW BAY
Blacksod ⚓ 54°05'·89N 10°03'·01W Q (3) 10s.
Achillbeg I S Point ☆ 53°51'·51N 09°56'·85W Fl WR 5s 56m **W18M, R18M, R15M**; W ▢ twr on ▢ building; vis: R262°- W281°- R342°- W060°-R(intens) 092°-W099° -118°.
Inishgort S Point ☆ 53°49'·61N 09°40'·25W L Fl 10s 11m 10M; W twr. Shown H24.
Slyne Head, North twr, Illaunamid ☆ 53°23'·99N 10°14'·06W Fl (2) 15s 35m **19M**; B twr.

SLYNE HEAD TO BLACK HEAD
▶ GALWAY BAY/INISHMORE
Eeragh, Rock Is ☆ 53°08'·10N 09°51'·39W Fl 15s 35m **23M**; W twr, two B bands; vis: 297°-262°.
Straw Is ☆ 53°07'·06N 09°37'·85W Fl (2) 5s 11m **15M**; W twr.
Black Head ☆ 53°09'·26N 09°15'·83W Fl WR 5s 20m W11M, R8M, W ▢ twr; vis: 045°- R268°-276°.
Inisheer ☆ 53°02'·78N 09°31'·58W Iso WR 12s 34m **W20M, R16M**; vis: 225°- W231°- R245°- W269°-115°; *Racon (K) 13M*.

See table on page 27 for distances anticlockwise between Kilrush and Carlingford Lough

1	Strangford Lough	1												
2	Bangor	34	2											
3	Carrickfergus	39	6	3										
4	Larne	45	16	16	4									
5	Carnlough	50	25	26	11	5								
6	Portrush	87	58	60	48	35	6							
7	Lough Foyle	92	72	73	55	47	11	7						
8	L Swilly (Fahan)	138	109	104	96	81	48	42	8					
9	Burtonport	153	130	130	116	108	74	68	49	9				
10	Killybegs	204	175	171	163	148	115	109	93	43	10			
11	Sligo	218	189	179	177	156	123	117	107	51	30	11		
12	Eagle Island	234	205	198	193	175	147	136	123	72	62	59	12	
13	Westport	295	266	249	240	226	193	187	168	120	108	100	57	13	
14	Galway	338	309	307	297	284	253	245	227	178	166	163	104	94	14
15	Kilrush	364	335	332	323	309	276	270	251	203	191	183	142	119	76	15

AREA 11 West Denmark - *Skagen to Rømø*
SELECTED LIGHTS, BUOYS & WAYPOINTS
Positions are referenced to WGS84

▶ SKAGEN
Skagen W ☆ 57°44'·92N 10°35·66E, Fl (3) WR 10s 31m **W17M**/R12M; W053°-248°, R248°-323°.
Skagen ☆ 57°44'·11N 10°37'·76E, Fl 4s 44m **23M**; Gy ○ twr; **Racon G, 20M**.
Skagen No 1A ⚓ 57°43'·42N 10°53'·51E, L Fl 10s; **Racon N**.
Ldg lts 334·5°, both Iso R 4s 13/22m 8M. Front 57°43'·06N 10°35'·45E; mast. Rear, 57°43'·2N 10°35'·4E.
E bkwtr ☆ 57°42'·88N 10°35'·66E, Fl G 3s 8m 5M; G twr; *Horn (2) 30s*.

▶ HIRTSHALS
Hirtshals ☆ 57°35'·07N 09°56'·45E, F Fl 30s 57m **F 18M; Fl 25M**; W ○ twr, approx 1M SSW of hbr.
Ldg lts 166°, both 156°-176°. Front 57°35'·69N 09°57'·64E, Iso R 2s 10m 11M; R △ on twr; Rear, Iso R 4s 18m 11M; R ▽ on twr.
Outer W mole ☆ 57°35'·97N 09°57'·36E, Fl G 3s 14m 6M; G mast; *Horn 15s*.

▶ HANSTHOLM
Hanstholm ☆ 57°06'·65N 08°35'·74E, Fl (3) 20s 65m **26M**; shown by day in poor vis.
Ldg lts 142·6, both Iso 2s 37/45m 13M; synch. Front 57°07'·12N 08°36'·15E; R △ on mast.
W outer mole ☆ 57°07'·54N 08°35'·46E, Fl G 3s 11m 9M; G pillar. E outer mole ☆ Fl R 3s 11m 9M; R pillar.

▶ THYBORØN
Landfall ⚓ 56°42'·55N 08°08'·70E, L Fl 10s; **Racon T, 10m**.
Agger Tange ldg lts 082°. Front 56°42'·97N 08°14'·11E, Oc WRG 4s 8m W11M, R/G8M. Rear, Iso 4s 17m 11M; 080°-084°; R ▽ on Gy twr.
☆ 56°42'·49N 08°12'·90E Fl (3) 10s 24m 12M.
Langholm ldg lts 120°, both Iso 2s 7/13m 11M.
Yderhavn, N mole ☆ 56°42'·02N 08°13'·52E, Fl G 3s 6m 4M; G pedestal. S mole ☆ 56°41'·97N 08°13'·53E, Fl R 3s 6m 4M; R pedestal.

Bovbjerg ☆ 56°30'·74N 08°07'·13E, L Fl (2) 15s 62m **16M**.

▶ TORSMINDE HAVN (Positions approx)
Lt ho ☆ 56°22'·34N 08°06'·99E, F 30m 13M; Gy twr.
N mole ☆ 56°22'·36N 08°06'·62E, Iso R 2s 9m 4M.

▶ HVIDE SANDE
Lyngvig ☆ 56°02'·95N 08°06'·17E, Fl 5s 53m **22M**.
N outer bkwtr ☆ 55°59'·94N 08°06'·55E, Fl R 3s.
Lt ho ☆ 56°00'·00N 08°07'·35E, F 27m 14M; Gy twr.

▶ HORNS REV
Blåvands Huk ☆ 55°33'·46N 08°04'·95E Fl (3) 20s 55m **23M**; W ☐ twr.

Slugen Channel (N to S)
▲ 55°33'·99N 07°49'·38E, L Fl G 10s.
▲ 55°32'·26N 07°53'·65E, Fl G 3s.
▱ 55°31'·46N 07°52'·88E, Fl (2) R 5s.
▲ 55°30'·52N 07°59'·20E, Fl (2) G 5s.
▱ 55°29'·42N 08°02'·56E, Fl (3) R 10s.

Horns Rev is ringed clockwise by:
Tuxen ⚓ 55°34'·22N 07°41'·92E, Q.
Vyl ⚓ 55°26'·22N 07°49'·99E, Q (6) + L Fl 15s.
No. 2 ⚓ 55°28'·74N 07°36'·49E, L Fl 10s.
Horns Rev W ⚓ 55°34'·47N 07°26'·05E, Q (9) 15s; 22M offshore.

Wind farm in ☐, 2·7M x 2·5M, centred on 55°29'·22N 07°50'·21E: 80 turbines, the 12 perimeter turbines marked by Fl (3) Y 10s.
NE turbine (55°30'·28N 07°52'·63E), Racon (U); transformer platform, 55°30'·52N 07°52'·53E, 2 Mo (U) 15s 15m 5M.
SW turbine (55°28'·11N 07°48'·26E), Racon (U).
7 recording stations each marked by SPM buoy Fl (5) Y 20s.
Met mast (60m) ☆ 55°31'·32N 07°47'·33E, 2 Mo (U) 15s 8m 3M.
Met masts 151B (55°29'·21N 07°54'·72E) and 151C (55°29'·24N 07°58'·52E): both 70m, ☆ 2 Mo (U) 15s `12m 5M and Aero QR.

▶ ESBJERG
Grådyb ⚓ 55°24'·63N 08°11'·59E, L Fl 10s; **Racon G, 10M**.
Sædding Strand ldg lts 053·8°; H24. **Front** 55°29'·74N 08°23'·87E, Iso 2s 13m **21M**.
Middle, 55°29'·94N 08°24'·33E, Iso 4s 26m **21M**; 051°-057°; R twr, W bands. **Rear**, 55°30'·18N 08°24'·92E, F 37m **18M**, 052°-056°; R twr.
Strandby, shelter mole, NW corner ☆ 55°28'·76N 08°24'·63E, Oc WRG 5s 6m W13M.
No. 1 ⚓ 55°25'·49N 08°13'·89E, Q.

NAVIGATION

No. 2 ⌐ 55°25'·62N 08°13'·73E, Fl (3) R 10s.
No. 3 ▲ 55°25'·93N 08°14'·84E, Fl G 3s.
No. 4 ⌐ 55°26'·02N 08°14'·72E, Fl R 3s.
Tide Gauge ☆ 55°26'·05N 08°15'·93E, Fl (5) Y 20s 8m 4M.
No. 5 ▲ 55°26'·32N 08°15'·83E, Fl G 5s.
No. 6 ⌐ 55°26'·44N 08°15'·70E, Fl R 5s.
No. 7 ↕ 55°26'·76N 08°16'·91E, Q.
No. 8 ⌐ 55°26'·89N 08°16'·81E, Fl (2) R 5s.
Ldg lts 067°, valid as far as Nos 9/10 buoys. Both FG 10/25m **16M**, H24. Front, 55°28'·76N 08°24'·70E, Gy tripod; rear, Gy twr.
Ldg lts 049°, valid as far as No 16 buoy/Jerg. Both FR 16/27m **16M**, H24. Front, 55°29'·92N 08°23'·75E, W twr; rear, Gy twr.
Konsumfiskerihavn, W mole ☆ 55°28'·31N 08°25'·33E, Fl R 3s 6m; 203°-119°; R tr. Yacht hbr in Basin II, N part.
Aero ☆ 55°27'·27N 08°27'·32E, 3 x Fl 1·5s (vert, 82m apart) 251m 12M, H24; on chimney.

▶ FANØ

Slunden outer ldg lts 242°, both Iso 2s 5/8m 3M; 227°-257°. Front 55°27'·20N 08°24'·53E; twr. Rear, 106m from front; twr.
Nordby ldg lts 214°, both FR 7/9m 4M; 123·7°-303·7°. Front 55°26'·94N 08°24'·44E; W mast. Rear, 84m from front; Gy twr. Kremer Sand ☆ 55°27'·3N 08°24'·9E, FG 5m 3M; G dolphin.
Næs Søjord ☆ 55°27'·27N 08°24'·86E, FR 5m 3M; R pile.
Nordby marina 55°26'·65N 08°24'·53E.

▶ KNUDEDYB

G ↕ 55°20'·50N 08°24'·28E.
K ↕ 55°18'·92N 08°20'·06E.
No. 2 ⌐ 55°18'·82N 08°21'·33E.
No. 4 ⌐ 55°18'·81N 08°22'·21E.
No. 6 ⌐ 55°18'·38N 08°24'·63E.
No. 10 ⌐ 55°18'·68N 08°28'·50E.
Knoben ⌐ 55°18'·71N 08°30'·60E.

▶ JUVRE DYB

No. 4 ⌐ 55°13'·76N 08°24'·73E.
No. 6 ⌐ 55°13'·41N 08°26'·60E.
No. 8 ⌐ 55°12'·69N 08°26'·83E.
No. 10 ⌐ 55°12'·55N 08°28'·72E.
Rejsby Stjært ↕ 55°13'·15N 08°30'·55E.

LISTER TIEF (Outer appr to RØMØ)

Rode Klit Sand ↕ 55°11'·11N 08°04'·88E, Q (9) 15s, (130°/9M to Lister Tief ↕).
Lister Tief ↕ 55°05'·32N 08°16'·80E, Iso 8s, Whis.
No. 1 ▲ 55°05'·21N 08°18'·20E.
No. 3 ↕ 55°04'·75E 08°18'·73E, Fl G 4s.
No. 2 ⌐ 55°04'·23N 08°22'·32E, Fl (3) R 10s.
No. 9 ↕ 55°03'·76N 08°23'·05E, Fl (2) G 9s.
Lister Landtief No 5 ▲ 55°03'·68N 08°24'·73E.
No. 4 ⌐ 55°03'·84N 08°25'·29E, FL (2) R 5s.
G1 ↕ 55°03'·27N 08°28'·32E, Fl Y 4s.

▶ RØMØ DYB and HAVN

No. 1 ▲ 55°03'·23N 08°30'·30E, Fl (2) G 10s.
No. 10 ☆ 55°03'·50N 08°31'·10E, Fl (2) R 10s 5m 3M; R pole.
No. 14 ☆ 55°03'·85N 08°32'·55E, Fl R 3s 6m 2M; R pole.
No. 20 ☆ 55°04'·79N 08°34'·13E, Fl R 5s 5m 2M; R pole.
No. 9 ▲ 55°04'·79N 08°34'·63E.
No. 11 ▲ 55°05'·17N 08°34'·69E.
Rømø Hbr:
S mole ☆ 55°05'·19N 08°34'·31E, Fl R 3s 7m 2M; Gy twr.
N mole ☆ 55°05'·23N 08°34'·30E, Fl G 3s 7m 2M; Gy twr.

1	Skagen	**1**																
2	Hirtshals	33	**2**															
3	Hanstholm	85	52	**3**														
4	Thyborøn	114	84	32	**4**													
5	Torsminde	141	108	56	24	**5**												
6	Hvide Sande	162	179	77	45	24	**6**											
7	Esbjerg	200	174	122	90	76	54	**7**										
8	Fanø	210	177	125	93	79	57	3	**8**									
9	Rømø	233	200	148	116	94	73	30	33	**9**								
10	Hörnum	248	215	163	131	108	86	70	73	29	**10**							
11	Husum	275	247	195	163	152	131	95	98	68	45	**11**						
12	Kiel/Holtenau	261	233	281	249	232	208	180	183	189	126	129	**12**					
13	Bremerhaven	306	285	233	201	185	163	127	129	107	83	82	123	**13**				
14	Wilhelmshaven	414	296	242	310	184	162	125	128	106	82	82	123	45	**14**			
15	Helgoland	259	238	186	154	141	119	83	85	63	39	47	104	44	43	**15**		
16	Cuxhaven	304	284	232	200	162	138	110	113	85	56	66	70	58	56	38	**16**	
17	Wangerooge	283	262	210	178	168	147	109	112	94	68	52	108	38	27	24	42	**17**
18	Hamburg	338	317	265	233	216	192	163	167	139	99	113	90	81	110	88	54	61	**18**

AREA 12 Germany (North Sea coast) - *List to Emden*
SELECTED LIGHTS, BUOYS & WAYPOINTS
Positions are referenced to WGS84

▶ SYLT
Lister Tief 55°05'·33N 08°16'·79E, Iso 8s; *Whis*.
List West ☆ 55°03'·15N 08°24'·00E, Oc WRG 6s 19m W14M, R11M, G10M; R040°-133°, W133°-227°, R227°-266·4°, W266·4°-268°, G268°-285°, W285°-040°.
List Ost, ☆ 55°02'·93N 08°26'·58E, Iso WRG 6s 22m W14M, R11M, G10M; W010·5°-262°, R262°-278°, W278°-296°, R296°-323·3°, W323·3°-324·5°, G324·5°-350°, W350°-010·5°.
List Hafen, N mole ☆ 55°01'·03N 08°26'·52E, FG 8m 4M; 218°-038°; G mast.
Kampen, ☆ 54°56'·76N 08°20'·38E, L Fl WR 10s 62m **W20M**, **R16M**; W193°-339°, W339°-165°, R165°-193°; W twr, B band.
Hörnum It ho ☆ 54°45'·23N 08°17'·47E, Fl (2) 9s 48m **20M**. Hbr N pier ☆ FG 6m 4M, 024°-260°.
Vortrapptief 54°34'·88N 08°12'·97E, Iso 4s.

▶ AMRUM ISLAND
Norddorf ☆ 54°40'·13N 08°18'·46E, Oc WRG 6s 22m **W15M**, R12M, G11M; W031°-097°, R097°-176·5°, W176·5°-178·5°, G178·5°-188°.
Amrum ☆ 54°37'·84N 08°21'·23E, Fl 7·5s 63m **23M**.

▶ FÖHR ISLAND
Nieblum ☆ 54°41'·10N 08°29'·20E, Oc (2) WRG 10s 11m **W19M**, **R/G15M**; G028°-031°, W031°-032·5°, R032·5°-035·5°; R twr, W band.

▶ DAGEBÜLL
Dagebüll 54°43'·82N 08°41'·43E, Iso WRG 8s 23m **W18M**, **R/G15M**; G042°-043°, W043°-044·5°, R044·5°-047°; G mast. FW lts on N and S moles.

▶ RIVER HEVER
Hever 54°20'·41N 08°18'·82E, Iso 4s; *Whis*.
Westerheversand, 54°22'·37N 08°38'·36E, Oc (3) WRG 15s 41m; W012·2°-069°, G069°-079·5°, W 079·5°-080·5°, R080·5°-107°, W107°-233°, R233°-248°.

▶ RIVER EIDER
Eider 54°14'·54N 08°27'·61E, Iso 4s.
St Peter ☆ 54°17'·24N 08°39'·10E, L Fl (2) WR 15s 23m **W15M**, R12M; R271°-280·5°, W280·5°-035°, R035°-055°, W055°-068°, R068°-091°, W091°-120°.

▶ BÜSUM
Süderpiep 54°05'·82N 08°25'·70E, Iso 8s; *Whis*.
Büsum ☆ 54°07'·60N 08°51'·48E, Iso WR 6s 22m **W19M**, R12M; W248°-317°, R317°-024°, W024°-148°.

▶
GB LightV 54°10'·80N 07°27'·60E, Iso 8s 12m **17M**; *Horn Mo (R) 30s*; *RaconT, 8M*.

▶ HELGOLAND
Helgoland ☆ 54°10'·91N 07°52'·93E, Fl 5s 82m **28M**. Vorhafen. Ostmole, S elbow ☆ 54°10'·31N 07°53'·94E, Oc WG 6s 5m W6M, G3M; W203°-250°, G250°-109°; G post; fog det lt.
Düne. Ldg lts 020°. Front 54°10'·87N 07°54'·80E, ☆ Iso 4s 11m 8M. Rear, Iso WRG 4s 17m W11M, R/G10M; G010°-018·5°, W018·5°-021°, R021°-030, G106°-125°, W125°-130°, R130°144°.

▶ RIVER ELBE APPROACHES
Elbe 53°59'·95N 08°06'·49E, Iso 10s; *Racon T, 8M*. No.1 53°59'·21N 08°13'·20E, QG.
Neuwerk ☆ 53°54'·92N 08°29'·73E, L Fl (3) WRG 20s 38m **W16M**, R12M, G11M; G165·3°-215·3°, W215·3°-238·8°, R238·8°-321°, R343°-100°.

▶ CUXHAVEN/OTTERNDORF
Yacht hbr ent, 53°52'·43N 08°42'·49E, ☆ F WR & F WG. Medem 53°50'·15N 08°53'·85E, Fl (3) 12s.

▶ BRUNSBÜTTEL
Ldg lts 065·5°, both Iso 3s 24/46m **16/21M**; Front, ☆ 53°53'·32N 09°08'·47E.
Alter Vorhafen ☆ 53°53'·27N 09°08'·59E, F WG 14m W10M, G6M; G273·9°-088·8°.

▶ HAMBURG, WEDEL YACHT HAFEN
E ent, ☆ 53°34'·25N 09°40'·79E, FG 5m 3M.
City Sport Hafen Ent ☆ 53°32'·52N 09°58'·81E.

▶ RIVER WESER APPROACHES
ALTE WESER
Schlüsseltonne 53°56'·25N 07°54'·76E, Iso 8s.
Alte Weser ☆ 53°51'·79N 08°07'·65E, F WRG 33m **W23M**, **R19M**, **G18M**; W288°-352°, R352°-003°, W003°-017°, G017°-045°, W045°-074°, G074°-118°, W118°-123°, R123°-140°, W140°-175°, W175°-183°, R183°-196°, W196°-238°; *Horn Mo (AL) 60s*.

NEUE WESER
3/Jade 2 53°52'·40N 07°44'·00E, Fl (2+1) G 15s; *Racon T, 8M*.
Tegeler Plate ☆, 53°47'·87N 08°11'·45E, Oc (3) WRG 12s 21m **W21M**, **R17M**, **G16M**; W329°-340°, R340°-014°, W014°-100°, G100°-116°, W116°-119°, R119°-123°, G123°-144°, W144°-147°, R147°-264°.

NAVIGATION

▶ BREMERHAVEN
No. 61 ⚓ 53°32'·26N 08°33'·93E, QG; (Km 66·0).
Vorhafen S pier hd ☆ 53°32'·09N 08°34'·50E FG 15m 5M; 355°-265°.

▶ BREMEN
Hasenbüren Sporthafen ☆ 53°07'·51N 08°40'·03E, 2 FY (vert).

▶ RIVER JADE APPROACHES
Jade-Weser ⚓, 53°58'·33N 07°38'·83E, Oc 4s; *Racon T, 8M*.
Mellumplate ☆ 53°46'·28N 08°05'·51E, F 28m **24M**; 116·1°-116·4°; R □ twr, W band.

▶ HOOKSIEL
No. 37 ⚓ 53°39'·37N 08°06'·58E, IQ G 13s.
Vorhafen ent ☆ 53°38'·63N 08°05'·25E, L FI R 6s 9m 3M.

▶ WILHELMSHAVEN
Fluthafen N mole ☆ 53°30'·86N 08°09'·32E, F WG 9m; W6M, G3M; W216°-280°, G280°-010°, W010°-020°, G020°-130°.

▶ WANGEROOGE
Harle ⚓ 53°49'·24N 07°48'·92E, Iso 8s.
Buhne W bkwtr ☆ 53°46'·33N 07°51'·93E, FR 3m.

▶ SPIEKEROOG
Otzumer Balje ⚓ 53°47'·98N 07°37'·12E, Iso 4s.
Spiekeroog ☆ 53°45'·0N 07°41'·3E, FR 6m 4M.

▶ LANGEOOG
Accumer Ee ⚓ 53°46·81N 07°26·12E, Iso 8s.
W mole head ☆ 53°43'·42N 07°30'·13E, Oc WRG 6s 8m; *Horn Mo (L) 30s* (0730-1800LT).

▶ NORDERNEY
Dovetief ⚓ 53°45'·25N 07°09'·13E, Iso 4s.
Schluchter ⚓ 53°44'·45N 07°02'·23E, Iso 8s.

W mole ☆ 53°41'·9N 07°09'·9E, Oc (2) R 9s 13m 4M.
Norderney ☆ 53°42'·58N 07°13'·83E, FI (3) 12s 59m **23M**; R 8-sided twr.

▶ BENSERSIEL
E training wall ☆ 53°41'·80N 07°32'·84E, Oc WRG 6s 6m W5M, R3M, G2M; G110°-119°, W119°-121°, R121°-110°.

▶ DORNUMER-ACCUMERSIEL
W bkwtr head ☆ 53°41'·25N 07°29'·40E.

▶ NESSMERSIEL
N mole head ☆ 53°41'·9N 07°21'·7E, Oc 4s 6m 5M.

▶ NORDDEICH
Outer ldg lts 144°, both B masts. Front, Iso WR 6s 6m W6M, R5M; R078°-122°, W122°-150°. Rear, Iso 6s 9m 6M; synch.

▶ RIVER EMS APPROACHES
GW/EMS 🛥 54°09'·96N 06°20'·72E, Iso 8s 12m **17M**; *Horn Mo (R) 30s (H24)*; *Racon T, 8M*.
Borkumriff ⚓ 53°47'·44N 06°22'·05E, Oc 4s; *Racon T, 8M*.
Osterems ⚓ 53°41'·91N 06°36'·17E, Iso 4s.
Riffgat ⚓ 53°38'·96N 06°27'·07E, Iso 8s.
Westerems ⚓ 53°36'·9N 06°19'·41E, Iso 4s; *Racon T, 8M*.
H1 ⚓ 53°34'·91N 06°17'·97E.

▶ BORKUM
Borkum Grosser ☆ 53°35'·32N 06°39'·64E, FI (2) 12s 63m **24M**. Same lt ho, F WRG 46m **W19M**.
Fischerbalje ☆ 53°33'·16N 06°42'·86E, Oc (2) WRG 16s.

▶ EMDEN
Outer hbr, E pier ☆ 53°20'·05N 07°10'·84E, FG 7m 5M; R twr, B band.

1	Esbjerg	**1**																	
2	Hörnum Lt (Sylt)	47	**2**																
3	Husum	95	48	**3**															
4	Hamburg	163	112	113	**4**														
5	Kiel/Holtenau	179	128	129	90	**5**													
6	Brunsbüttel	126	75	76	37	53	**6**												
7	Cuxhaven	110	63	66	54	70	17	**7**											
8	Bremerhaven	127	80	82	81	131	78	58	**8**										
9	Wilhelmshaven	125	78	82	110	123	70	56	45	**9**									
10	Hooksiel	116	69	73	101	117	64	47	36	9	**10**								
11	Helgoland	83	38	47	88	104	51	38	44	43	35	**11**							
12	Wangerooge	109	60	52	61	108	55	42	38	27	19	24	**12**						
13	Langeoog	119	72	77	114	130	77	60	47	43	34	35	21	**13**					
14	Norderney	123	77	85	81	137	84	69	62	53	44	44	29	18	**14**				
15	Emden	165	129	137	174	190	137	120	115	106	97	85	80	63	47	**15**			
16	Borkum	133	97	105	104	163	110	95	88	80	71	67	55	46	31	32	**16**		
17	Delfzijl	155	119	127	159	173	120	105	100	89	83	81	65	56	41	10	22	**17**	
18	Den Helder	187	192	198	229	245	192	175	180	159	150	153	148	130	115	125	95	115	**18**

AREA 13 Netherlands & Belgium - *Delfzijl to Nieuwpoort*
SELECTED LIGHTS, BUOYS & WAYPOINTS | Positions are referenced to WGS84

▶ DELFZIJL
W mole ☆ 53°19'·01N 07°00'·26E, FG.
Ldg lts 203° both Iso 4s. Front, 53°18'·62N 07°00'·16E. Rear, 310m from front.

▶ LAUWERSOOG
Lauwersoog W mole ☆ 53°24'·68N 06°12'·00E, FG 3M; *Horn (2) 30s*.

▶ KORNWERDERZAND
Buitenhaven, W mole ☆ 53°04'·76N 05°20'·03E, FG 9m 7M; *Horn Mo(N) 30s*.

▶ HARLINGEN
P9/BO44 ⚓ 53°10'·59N 05°23'·88E VQ.
Pollendam ldg lts 112°, both Iso 6s 8/19m 13M (H24); B masts, W bands. Front, 53°10'·51N 05°24'·18E. Rear, 500m from front, vis 104·5°-119·5°.
N mole hd ☆ 53°10'·59N 05°24'·32E, FR 9m 4M; R/W pedestal.

▶ SCHIERMONNIKOOG TO AMELAND
WG (Westgat) ⚓ 53°32'·57N 06°10'·70E, Iso 8s; **Racon N**.
Schiermonnikoog ☆ 53°29'·19N 06°08'·76E, Fl (4) 20s 43m **28M**; dark R ○ twr. Same twr: F WR 29m **W15M**, R12M; W210°-221°, R221°-230°.

▶ ZEEGAT VAN AMELAND
Ameland ☆ W end 53°26'·92N 05°37'·52E, Fl (3) 15s 57m **30M**.

▶ ZEEGAT VAN TERSCHELLING
Otto ⚓ 53°24'·61N 05°06'·32E, VQ.
TG ⚓ 53°24'·15N 05°02'·27E, Q (9) 15s.
ZS ⚓ 53°19'·78N 04°55'·88E, Iso 4s; **Racon T**.
ZS1 ⚓ 53°19'·22N 04°57'·56E, VQ.
ZS5 ⚓ 53°18'·63N 05°01'·61E, L Fl G 8s.
ZS11-VS2 ⚓ 53°18'·67N 05°05'·96E, Q (9) 15s.

▶ WESTTERSCHELLING
Brandaris Twr ☆ 53°21'·61N 05°12'·84E, Fl 5s 54m **29M**; Y ☐ twr; partly obscured by dunes on Vlieland and Terschelling.
W hbr mole ☆, 53°21'·25N 05°13'·09E, FR 5m 5M; R post, W bands; *Horn 15s*.

▶ VLIELAND
Vlieland ☆ 53°17'·69N 05°03'·46E, Iso 4s 53m **20M**.
E mole hd ☆ 53°17'·68N 05°05'·51E, FG.

▶ EIERLANDSCHE GAT
Eierland ☆ (N tip of Texel) 53°10'·93N 04°51'·30E, Fl (2) 10s 52m **29M**; R ○ twr.

▶ OUDESCHILD
Dir lt 291°, Oc 6s; intens 291°, 53°02'·40N 04°50'·94E.
S mole head ☆ 53°02'·33N 04°51'·17E, FR 6m; *Horn (2) 30s*.

▶ DEN OEVER LOCK
LW ⚓ 52°59'·51N 04°55'·90E, L Fl 10s.
Ldg lts 131°, both Oc 10s 6m 7M; 127°-137°. Front, 52°56'·32N 05°02'·98E.
Detached bkwter N head ☆ 52°56'·76N 05°02'·29E, L Fl R 10s.

▶ APPROACHES TO ZEEGAT VAN TEXEL
NH ⚓ 53°00'·23N 04°35'·36E, VQ.
MR ⚓ 52°56'·76N 04°33'·81E, Q (9) 15s.
ZH ⚓ 52°54'·65N 04°34'·71E, VQ (6) + L Fl 10s.
TX1 ⚓ 52°48'·01N 04°15'·50E, Fl G 5s.
Vinca G ⚓ 52°45'·93N 04°12'·40E, Q (9) 15s.

▶ MOLENGAT (from the N)
MG ⚓ 53°03'·90N 04°39'·37E, Mo (A) 8s.

▶ SCHULPENGAT (from the S)
Ldg lts 026·5°, both Oc 8s **18M**; vis 024·5°-028·5°.
Front ☆, 53°00'·85N 04°44'·42E.
SG ⚓ 52°52'·90N 04°37'·90E, Mo (A) 8s; **Racon Z**.
Schilbolsnol ☆ 53°00'·50N 04°45'·68E, F WRG 27m **W15M**, R12M, G11M; W338°-002°, G002°-035°, W035°-038°, R038°-051°, W051°-068°.
Huisduinen ☆ 52°57'·13N 04°43'·29E, F WR 26m W14M, R11M; ☐ twr; vis W070°-113°, R113°-158°, W158°-208°.
Kijkduin ☆, Rear, 52°57'·33N 04°43'·58E, Fl (4) 20s 56m **30M**; brown twr; partly obscured by dunes on Texel.

▶ DEN HELDER
Ldg lts 191°, both Oc G 5s 15/24m 14M. Front, 52°57'·37N 04°47'·08E; vis 161°-221°.
Marinehaven, W bkwtrhd ☆ 52°57'·95N 04°47'·07E, QG 11m 8M; *Horn 20s*.
Ent W side, ☆ 52°57'·77N 04°47'·08E, Fl G 5s 9m 4M; 180°-067° (H24).
Grote Kaap ☆ 52°52'·85N 04°42'·88E, Oc WRG

35

NAVIGATION

10s 30m W11M, R8M, G8M; G041°-088°, W088°-094°, R094°-131°.

▶ IJMUIDEN

IJmuiden ⌕ 52°28'·44N 04°23'·78E, Mo (A) 8s; **Racon Y, 10M**.
S bkwtr hd ☆ 52°27'·82N 04°31'·94E, FG 14m 10M (in fog Fl 3s); *Horn (2) 30s*. N bkwtr hd ☆ 52°28'·05N 04°32'·55E, FR 15m 10M.

▶ AMSTERDAM

Sixhaven marina ☆ 52°22'·99N 04°53'·69E, F & FR.

▶ SCHEVENINGEN

SCH ⌕ 52°07'·75N 04°14'·11E, Iso 4s.
W mole ☆ 52°06'·23N 04°15'·16E, FG 12m 9M; G twr, W bands; *Horn (3) 30s*.

▶ NOORD HINDER TSS

Garden City ⌕ 51°29'·12N 02°17'·92E, Q (9) 15s.
Twin ⌕ 51°32'·05N 02°22'·62E, Fl (3) Y 9s.
NHR-S ⌕ 51°51'·35N 02°28'·71E, Fl Y 10s; *Bell*.
Birkenfels ⌕ 51°38'·96N 02°32'·03E, Q (9) 15s.
Track Ferry ⌕ 51°33'·78N 02°36'·33E, Fl Y 5s.
NHR-SE ⌕ 51°45'·42N 02°39'·92E, Fl G 5s.
NHR-N ⌕ 52°10'·78N 03°04'·69E, L Fl 8s;
Racon K, 10M.

▶ HOEK VAN HOLLAND APPROACHES

Noord Hinder ⌕ 52°00'·04N 02° 51'·03E, Fl (2) 10s; *Horn (2) 30s*; **Racon T, 12-15M**.
Goeree ☆ 51°55'·42N 03°40'·03E, Fl (4) 20s 32m **28M**; *Horn (4) 30s*; **Racon T, 12-15M**.
Maas Center ⌕ 52°01'12N 03°53'·44E, Iso 4s;
Racon M, 10M.
Indusbank N ⌕ 52°02'·88N 04°03'·55E, VQ.
MO ⌕ 52°00'97N 03°58'·06E, Mo (A) 8s.
MVN ⌕ 51°57'·44N 03°58'·40E, VQ.
MV ⌕ 51°57'·44N 03°58'·40E, Q (9) 15s.
Westhoofd, 51°48'·78N 03°51'·82E, Fl (3) 15s 55m **30M**; R ☐ tr.

▶ HOEK VAN HOLLAND

Maasmond ldg lts 107°, both Iso R 6s 29/43m **18M**; 099·5°-114·5°. **Front** ☆, 51°58'·55N 04°07'·53E.
Maasvlakte ☆ 51°58'·19N 04°00'·84E, Fl (5) 20s 67m **28M**, H24; 340°-267°; B 8-sided twr, Y bands.
Nieuwe Zuiderdam ☆ 51°59'·13N 04°02'·47E, FG 25m 10M; *Horn 10s*.

▶ ROTTERDAM

Maassluis, E ent ☆ 51°54'·93N 04°14'·81E, FG.
Vlaardingen, E ent ☆ 51°53'·99N 04°20'·95E, FG.
Spuihaven, W ent ☆ 51°53'·98N 04°23'·98E, FR.
Veerhaven, E ent ☆ 51°54'·40N 04°28'·74E, FG.

▶ APPROACHES TO HARINGVLIET

Buitenbank ⌕ 51°51'·14N 03°25'·69E, Iso 4s.
West Schouwen ☆ 51°42'·53N 03°41'·48E, Fl (2+1)15s 57m **30M**.
SG ⌕ 51°51'·93N 03°51'·40E, Iso 4s.

▶ STELLENDAM

N mole ☆ 51°49'·87N 04°02'·01E, FG; *Horn (2) 15s*.

▶ HELIUSHAVEN/HELLEVOETSLUIS

Heliushaven E jetty ☆ 51°49'·23N 04°07'·28E, FG 7m 3M.
Hellevoetsluis ☆ 51°49'·18N 04°07'·66E, Iso WRG 10s 16m W11M, R8M, G7M; G266°-275°, W275°-294°, R294°-316°, W316°-036°, G036°-058°, W058°-095°, R095°-140°; W twr, R top.

▶ OOSTERSCHELDE APPROACHES

Schouwenbank ⌕ 51°44'·94N 03°14'·31E, Mo (A) 8s; **Racon O, 10M**.
Middelbank ⌕ 51°40'·83N 03°18'·19E, Iso 8s.
Rabsbank ⌕ 51°38'·25N 03°09'·90E, Iso 4s.
Westpit ⌕ 51°33'·65N 03°09'·92E, Iso 8s.
SW Thornton ⌕ 51°30'·95N2 02°50'·92E, Iso 8s.

▶ OUDE ROOMPOT

Roompotsluis ldg lts 073·5°, both Oc G 5s; synch. Front, 51°37'·33N 03°40'·74E.
N bkwtr ☆ 51°37'·30N 03°40'·09E, FR 7m; *Horn (2) 30s*.
Roompot Marina, N mole head ☆ 51°35'·62N 03°43'·20E, FR.
Kaloo ⌕ 51°35'·56N 03°23'·23E, Iso 8s.
Westkapelle ☆, Common rear, 51°31'·75N 03°26'·80E, Fl 3s 49m **28M**; ☐ twr, R top.
Molenhoofd ☆ 51°31'·58N 03°26'·03E, Oc WRG 6s 10m; R306°-329°, W329°-349°, R349°-008°, G008°-034·5°, W034·5°-036·5°, G036·5°-144°, W144°-169°, R169°-198°; W mast R bands.

▶ OFFSHORE MARKS

West Hinder ☆ 51°23'·31N 02°26'·27E, Fl (4) 30s 23m 13M; *Horn Mo (U) 30s*; **Racon W**.
Oost-Dyck ⌕ 51°21'·38N 02°31'·09E, Q.
Oostdyck radar twr, 51°16'·49N 02°26'·83E; four ☆ Mo (U) 15s 15m 12M; *Horn Mo (U) 30s*; **Racon O**.

▶ SCHEUR CHANNEL

S1 ⌕ 51°23'·15N 03°00'·12E, Fl G 5s.
MOW ⊙ 51°23'·67N 03°02'·75E, Fl (5) Y 20s; *Whis*;
Racon S, 10M.

▶ WIELINGEN CHANNEL

W-Z ⌕ 51°22'·57N 03°10'·71E, Q (9) 15s.
Nieuwe Sluis ☆ 51°24'·41N 03°31'·27E, Oc WRG 10s 26m W14M, R11M, G10M; R055°-089°,

W089°-093°, G093°-105°, R105°-134°, W134°-136·5°, G136·5°-156·5°, W156·5°-236·5°, G236·5°-243°, W243°-254°, R254°-292°, W292°-055°.

▶ **VLISSINGEN**
Koopmanshaven, ☆51°26'·30N 03°34'·55E, Iso WRG 3s 15m W12M, R10M, G9M. Buitenhaven E mole ☆51°26'·41N 03°36'·36E, FG 7m 4M.

▶ **BRESKENS**
Yacht hbr. W mole ☆ 51°24'·03N 03°34'·06E, F WRG 7m; R090°-128°, W128°-157°, G157°-169·5°, W169·5°-173°, R173°-194°, G194°-296°, W296°-300°, R300°-320°, G320°-090°; in fog FY; Gy mast.

▶ **TERNEUZEN**
Marinas, W mole FG ☆51°20'·57N 03°49'·63E. Also B & W twr ☆ close SW, Oc WRG 5s 15m W9M, R7M, G6M; R090°-115°, W115°-120°, G120°-130°, W130°-245°, G245°-249°, W249°-279°, R279°-004°.

BELGIUM

▶ **ANTWERPEN**
Royerssluis, ldg lts 091°, both FR. Ent FR/G. Linkeroever marina ⚓ 51°13'·91N 04°23'·70E, F WR 9m W3M, R2M; Wshore-283°, R283°-shore.

▶ **ZEEBRUGGE**
A2 ⚓ 51°22'·42N 03°07'·05E, Iso 8s.
Ldg lts 136°, both Oc 5s 22/45m 8M.
W outer mole ☆ 51°21'·73N 03°11'·17E, Oc G 7s 31m 7M; 057°-267°; G vert strip lts; *Horn (3) 30s*.
Heist mole ☆ 51°20'·86N 03°12'·18E, Oc WR 15s 22m, **W20M, R18M**; W068°-145°, R145°-212°, W212°-296°; IPTS; *Horn (3+1) 90s*.

▶ **BLANKENBERGE**
Lt ho ☆ 51°18'·76N 03°06'·87E, Fl (2) 8s 30m **20M**.
Ldg lts 134°, both FR 5/8m 3/10M; front, R cross (X) on mast.
E pier ☆ 51°18'·91N 03°06'·56E, FR 12m 11M; 290°-245°; W ○ twr; *Bell (2) 15s*.
W pier ☆ 51°18'·89N 03°06'·43E, FG 14m 11M.

▶ **OOSTENDE**
A1 ⚓ 51°22'·37N 02°53'·34E, Iso 8s.
Ldg lts 128°, both 3 Iso 4s (vert) 22/32m 4M, 051°-201°. Front, 51°14'·13N 02°55'·55E.
Oostende lt ho ☆ 51°14'·18N 02°55'·83E, Fl (3) 10s 65m **27M**; W twr, 2 sinusoidal Bu bands.
E pier ☆ 51°14'·39N 02°55'·14E, FR 15m 12M; 333°-243°; W ○ twr; IPTS; *Horn Mo(OE) 30s*.

▶ **NIEUWPOORT**
Weststroom Bank ⚓ 51°11'·33N 02°43'·04E, Fl (4) R 20s.
Lt ho ☆ 51°09'·28N 02°43'·80E, Fl (2) R 14s 28m **16M**; R ○ twr, W bands; 2 ca E of E pier root.
E pier ☆ 51°09'·42N 02°43'·08E, FR 11m 10M; 025°-250°, 307°-347°; W ○ twr; *Horn Mo (K) 30s*.
W pier ☆ 51°09'·35N 02°43'·00E, FG 11m 9M; 025°-250°, 284°-324°; W ○ twr; IPTS from root; *Bell (2) 10s*.
Oostduinkerke ⚓ 51°09'·14N 02°39'·46E, Q.
Den Oever wreck ⚓ 51°08'·10N 02°37'·45E.
Nieuwpoort Bank ⚓ 51°10'·17N 02°36'·09E, Q (9) 15s.
Trapegeer ⚓ 51°08'·42N 02°34'·38E, Fl G 10s. E11 ⚓ 51°07'·24N 02°30'·61E, Fl G 4s.
E12 ⚓ 51°07'·90N 02°30'·59E, VQ (6) + L Fl 10s.
For Passe de Zuydcoote, see Area 14 overleaf.
Belgian/French border is between E12 and E11 buoys; see also AC 1873.

1	Delfzijl	**1**															
2	Terschelling	85	**2**														
3	Harlingen	102	19	**3**													
4	Den Oever	110	34	21	**4**												
5	Den Helder	115	39	30	11	**5**											
6	Amsterdam	159	83	81	62	51	**6**										
7	IJmuiden	146	70	68	49	38	13	**7**									
8	Scheveningen	171	95	93	74	63	38	25	**8**								
9	Rotterdam	205	129	127	108	97	72	59	34	**9**							
10	Hook of Holland	185	109	107	88	77	52	39	14	20	**10**						
11	Stellendam	201	125	123	104	93	68	55	30	36	16	**11**					
12	Roompotsluis	233	157	155	136	125	100	87	50	68	48	32	**12**				
13	Vlissingen	228	152	150	131	120	99	86	61	67	47	45	24	**13**			
14	Zeebrugge	239	163	161	142	131	106	93	68	74	54	50	28	16	**14**		
15	Blankenberge	244	168	166	147	136	111	98	73	79	59	55	33	21	5	**15**	
16	Oostende	239	163	161	142	131	110	106	81	87	67	72	40	29	13	9	**16**
17	Nieuwpoort	262	186	184	165	154	129	116	91	97	77	83	51	39	23	18	9	**17**

NAVIGATION

AREA 14, North France - *Dunkerque to Cap de la Hague*
SELECTED LIGHTS, BUOYS & WAYPOINTS | Positions are referenced to WGS84

▶ OFFSHORE MARKS
WH Zuid ⚓ 51°22'·78N 02°26'·25E, Q (6) + L Fl 15s.
Bergues N ⚓ 51°19'·92N 02°24'·50E, Q.
Oostdyck radar twr, 51°16'·49N 02°26'·83E; four ☆ Mo (U) 15s 15m 12M; *Horn Mo (U) 30s;* **Racon O**.
Bergues ⚓ 51°17'·15N 02°18'·62E, Fl G 4s.
Ruytingen N ⚓ 51°13'·10N 02°10'·28E, VQ.
Ruytingen SW ⚓ 51°04'·98N 01°46'·83E, Fl (3) G 12s; *Bell*.
Sandettié SW ⚓ 51°09'·72N 01°45'·60E, Q (9) 15s 5M.
Sandettié ⚓ 51°09'·34N 01°47'·10E, Fl 5s 12m 15M; R hull; *Horn 30s;* **Racon T, 10M**.

▶ PASSE DE ZUYDCOOTE
E12 ⚓ 51°07'·90N 02°30'·59E, VQ (6) + L Fl 10s.
E7 ⚓ 51°05'·18N 02°28'·50E, Fl (3) G 12s.

PASSE DE L'EST
E6 ⚓ 51°04'·86N 02°27'·08E, QR.
E2 ⚓ 51°04'·32N 02°22'·32E, Fl (2) R 6s.
⚓ 51°04'·28N 02°21'·71E, Q (6) + L Fl 15s.

▶ DUNKERQUE PORT EST
Jetée Est ☆ 51°03'·59N 02°21'·20E, Fl (2) R 10s 12m **16M**; R □ on W pylon, R top.
Dunkerque lt ho ☆ 51°02'·93N 02°21'·86E, Fl (2) 10s 59m **26M**.

▶ GRAVELINES
W jetty ⚓ 51°00'·94N 02°05'·48E, Fl (2) WG 6s 9m W8M, G6M; 317°-W-327-G-085°-W-244°.

▶ DUNKERQUE, WEST APPROACH
DW29 ⚓ 51°03'·85N 02°20'·21E, Fl (3) G 12s.
DW18 ⚓ 51°03'·47N 02°10'·37E, Fl (3) R 12s.
RCE ⚓ 51°02'·43N 01°53'·21E, Iso G 4s.
Dyck ⚓ 51°02'·99N 01°51'·78E, Fl 3s; **Racon B**.

▶ CALAIS
Jetée Est ☆ 50°58'·40N 01°50'·46,E Fl (2) R 6s 12m **17M**; Gy twr, R top; *Horn (2) 40s*.
Calais ☆ 50°57'·68N 01°51'·21E, Fl (4) 15s 59m **22M**; 073°-260°; W 8-sided twr, B top.

▶ CALAIS, WEST ACCESS CHAN (W-E)
CA3 ⚓ 50°56'·82N 01°41'·12E, Fl G 4s; *Whis*.
CA5 ⚓ 50°57'·64N 01°46'·13E, QG.
CA6 ⚓ 50°58'·25N 01°45'·63E, VQ R.
CA10 ⚓ 50°58'·63N 01°49'·92E, Fl (2) R 6s.
Cap Gris-Nez ☆ 50°52'·09N 01°34'·94E, Fl 5s 72m **29M**; 005°-232°; W twr, B top; *Horn 60s*.

▶ DOVER STRAIT TSS, SE Side
Vergoyer N ⚓ 50°39'·64N 01°22'·18E, VQ; **Racon C, 5-8M**.
Vergoyer E ⚓ 50°35'·74N 01°19'·65E, VQ (3) 5s.
Bassurelle ⚓ 50°32'·74N 00°57'·69E, Fl (4) R 15s 6M; *Whis;* **Racon B, 5-8m**.
Vergoyer SW ⚓ 50°26'·98N 01°00'·00E, Q (9) 10s.

▶ BOULOGNE
Boulogne Approaches ⚓ 50°45'·31N 01°31'·07E, VQ (6) + L Fl 10s 8m 6M; *Whis*.
Digue Carnot (S) ☆ 50°44'·44N 01°34'·05E, Fl (2+1) 15s 25m **19M**; W twr, G top; *Horn (2+1) 60s*.
Cap d'Alprech ☆ 50°41'·90N 01°33'·75E, Fl (3) 15s 62m **23M**; W twr, B top.

▶ LE TOUQUET/ÉTAPLES
Le Touquet ☆ 50°31'·43N 01°35'·49E, Fl (2) 10s 54m **25M**; Or twr, brown band, W&G top.
Pointe du Haut-Blanc ☆ 50°23'·89N 01°33'·62E, Fl 5s 44m **23M**; W twr, R bands, G top.

▶ ST VALÉRY-SUR-SOMME
ATSO ⚓ 50°14'·00N 01°28'·06E, Mo (A) 12s.
Training wall hd, 50°12'·25N 01°35'·85E, Q 2m 1M.
Cayeux-sur-Mer ☆ 50°11'·65N 01°30'·67E, Fl R 5s 32m **22M**; W twr, R top.

▶ LE TRÉPORT
Ault ☆ 50°06'·28N 01°27'·23E, Oc (3) WR 12s 95m W**15M**, R**11M**; 040°-W-175°-R-220°; W twr, R top.
Jetée Ouest ☆ 50°03'·87N 01°22'·13E, Fl (2) G 10s 15m **20M**; W twr, G top.

▶ DIEPPE
DI ⚓ 49°57'·05N 01°01'·25E, VQ (3) 5s; *Bell*.
Falaise du Pollet ☆ 49°55'·92N 01°05'·30E, Q 35m 11M; 105·5°-170·5°; R & W structure.
Jetée Ouest ☆ 49°56'·27N 01°04'·95E, Iso G 4s 11m 8M, W twr, G top; *Horn 30s*.
Pointe d'Ailly ☆ 49°54'·96N 00°57'·49E, Fl (3) 20s 95m **31M**; W □ twr, G top; *Horn (3) 60s*.

▶ SAINT VALÉRY-EN-CAUX
Jetée Est ☆ 49°52'·32N 00°42'·67E, Fl (2) R 6s 8m 4M; W mast.

▶ FÉCAMP
Jetée Sud ☆ 49°45'·88N 00°21'·80E, QG 14m 9M.
Cap d'Antifer ☆ 49°41'·01N 00°09'·90E, Fl 20s 128m **29M**; 021°-222°; Gy 8-sided twr, G top.

▶ **LE HAVRE**
Cap de la Hève ☆ 49°30'·74N 00°04'·15E, Fl 5s 123m **24M**; 225°-196°; W 8-sided twr, R top.
LHA Lanby 49°31'·38N 00°09'·88W, Mo (A) 12s 10m 9M; R&W; **Racon, 8-10M**.
Digue Nord ☆ 49°29'·19N 00°05'·44E, Fl R 5s 15m **21M**; W ○ twr, R top; *Horn 15s*.

▶ **CHENAL DE ROUEN/HONFLEUR**
No. 4 49°26'·97N 00°02'·60E, QR. Yachts keep N side of chan.
Ratier NW 49°26'·82N 00°02'·50E, VQ G.
No. 20 49°25'·85N 00°13'·51E, QR. Digue Ouest ☆ 49°25'·68N 00°13'·81E, QG 10m 6M.

▶ **DEAUVILLE/TROUVILLE**
Ratelets 49°25'·29N 00°01'·71E, Q (9) 15s.
E jetty 49°22'·22N 00°04'·33E. Fl (4) WR 12s 8m W7M, R4M, 131°-W-175°-R-131°; W pylon, R top.

▶ **DIVES-SUR-MER**
Dl 49°19'·18N 00°05'·84W, L Fl 10s.
No. 1 49°18'·50N 00°05'·67W.
Dir lt 159·5°, 49°17'·80N 00°05'·24W. Oc (2+1) WRG 12s 6m, W12M, 125°-G-157°-W-162°-R-194°.

▶ **OUISTREHAM/CAEN**
Ldg lts 185°, both Dir Oc (3+1) R 12s 10/30m **17M**.
Front ☆, 49°17'·09N 00°14'·80W.
Ouistreham lt ho ☆ 49°16'·85N 00°14'·80W, Oc WR 4s 37m **W17M**, R13M; 115°-R-151°-W-115°.

▶ **COURSEULLES-SUR-MER**
Courseulles 49°21'·28N 00°27'·69W, Iso 4s.
W jetty 49°20'·41N 00°27'·37W, Iso WG 4s 7m
Ver ☆ 49°20'·39N 00°31'·15W Fl (3)15s 42m **26M**.

▶ **PORT-EN-BESSIN**
W mole 49°21'·17N 00°45'·39W, Fl WG 4s 14m, W10M, G7M; G065°-114·5°, W114·5°-065°.

▶ **GRANDCAMP**
Ldg lts 146°, both Dir Q 9/12m **15M**. Front, 49°23'·42N 01°02'·92W.
Jetée Est ☆. 49°23'·52N 01°02'·98W, Oc (2) R 6s 9m 9M; *Horn Mo(N) 30s*.

▶ **CARENTAN**
C-l 49°25'·44N 01°07'·08W, Iso 4s.
Chan ent 49°21'·94N 01°09'·96W, Fl (4) G 15s.
Iles St-Marcouf ☆ 49°29'·86N 01°08'·82W, VQ (3) 5s 18m 8M; □ Gy twr, G top.

▶ **ST VAAST-LA-HOUGUE**
Le Gavendest 49°34'·36N 01°13'·89W; Q (6) + L Fl 15s; *Whis*.
Jetty 49°35'·17N 01°15'·41W, Dir Oc (2) WRG 6s 12m W10M, R/G7M; 219°-R-237°-G-310°-W-350°-R-040°; *Siren Mo(N) 30s*.

▶ **BARFLEUR**
Ldg lts 219·5°, both Oc (3) 12s 7/13m 10M; synch. Front, 49°40'·18N 01°15'·61W, W□ twr.
W jetty 49°40'·32N 01°15'·57W, Fl G 4s 8m 6M.
Pte de Barfleur ☆ 49°41'·78N 01°15'·96W, Fl (2) 10s 72m **29M**; *Horn (2) 60s*.
Les Équets 49°43'·62N 01°18'·36W, Q 8m 3M.
La Pierre Noire 49°43'·53N 01°29'·09W, Q (9) 15s 8m 4M.

▶ **CHERBOURG**
La Truite 49°40'·33N 01°35'·50W, Fl (4) R 15s.
Fort de l'Est ☆ 49°40'·28N 01°35'·93W, Iso G 4s 19m 9M.
Marina W mole 49°38'·87N 01°37'·15W, Fl (3) G 12s 7m 6M; G pylon.
Fort de l'Ouest ☆ 49°40'·45N 01°38'·87W, Fl (3) WR 15s 19m **W24M, R20M**; 122°-W-355°-R-122°; Gy twr, R top; *Horn (3) 60s*.

▶ **OMONVILLE-LA-ROGUE**
L'Étonnard 49°42'·32N 01°49'·85W.
Cap de la Hague ☆ 49°43'·31N 01° 57'·28W. Fl 5s 48m **23M**; Gy twr, W top; *Horn 30s*.

1	Dunkerque	**1**																	
2	Calais	22	**2**																
3	Boulogne	42	20	**3**															
4	Étaples	51	32	12	**4**														
5	St Valéry-sur-Somme	69	50	30	19	**5**													
6	Dieppe	96	74	54	50	35	**6**												
7	St Valéry-en-Caux	103	81	61	58	45	16	**7**											
8	Fécamp	118	96	76	70	62	29	15	**8**										
9	Le Havre	143	121	101	90	85	54	38	25	**9**									
10	Honfleur	152	130	110	100	95	63	45	34	10	**10**								
11	Deauville/Trouville	150	128	108	100	95	61	44	32	6	8	**11**							
12	Dives-sur-Mer	151	129	108	117	97	67	55	39	17	13	7	**12**						
13	Ouistreham	160	138	115	110	103	68	58	39	24	19	14	8	**13**					
14	Courseulles	162	140	118	110	103	75	55	40	28	23	21	17	11	**14**				
15	Grandcamp-Maisy	190	168	135	130	125	94	80	64	50	45	43	38	35	25	**15**			
16	Carentan	192	170	145	140	132	105	88	72	62	56	51	46	37	13	**16**			
17	St Vaast	179	157	133	130	120	95	78	63	59	53	49	45	34	16	20	**17**		
18	Barfleur	170	148	128	124	120	94	77	64	56	56	53	46	39	21	26	10	**18**	
19	Cherbourg	182	160	142	134	130	108	82	82	76	70	69	66	54	41	39	26	20	**19**

NAVIGATION

AREA 15 N Central France & Channel Is - *Cap de la Hague to St Quay*
SELECTED LIGHTS, BUOYS & WAYPOINTS | Positions are referenced to WGS84

▶ **DIELETTE**
W bkwtr Dir lt 140°, 49°33'·17N 01°51'·84W. Iso WRG 4s 12m W10M, R/G7M; G070°-135°, W135°-145°, R145°-180°; Same twr; ☆ Fl G 4s 6m 2M.

▶ **CARTERET**
Cap de Carteret ☆ 49°22'·40N 01°48'·44W, Fl (2+1) 15s 81m **26M**; Gy twr, G top.
W bkwtr ☆ 49°22'·13N 01°47'·40W, Oc R 4s 7m 7M.

▶ **PORTBAIL**
PB ⚓ 49°18'·39N 01°44'·76W.
Ldg lts 042°: Front, 49°19'·74N 01°42'·51W, Q 14m 10M. Rear, Oc 4s 20m 10M; stubby ch spire.

▶ **PASSAGE DE LA DÉROUTE**
Les Trois-Grunes ⚓ 49°21'·82N 01°55'·21W, Q (9) 15s.
Le Sénéquet ☆ 49°05'·47N 01°39'·75W, Fl (3) WR 12s 18m W13M, R10M; 083·5°-R-116·5°-W-083·5°.
Les Minquiers: NE ⚓ 49°00'·84N 01°55'·31W, VQ (3) 5s; *Bell.* SE ⚓ 48°53'·43N 02°00'·10W, Q (3) 10s; *Bell.* S ⚓ 48°53'·07N 02°10'·11W, Q (6) + L Fl 15s.

▶ **ÎLES CHAUSEY**
L'Enseigne, W twr, B top; 48°53'·73N 01°50'·27W.
Grande Île ☆ 48°52'·17N 01°49'·36W, Fl 5s 39m **23M**; Gy ☐ twr, G top; *Horn 30s.*
La Crabière Est ⚓ 48°52'·47N 01°49'·41W, Oc WRG 4s 5m, W9M, R/G 6M; W079°-291°, G291°-329°, W329°-335°, R335°-079°; Y twr.

▶ **GRANVILLE**
Pointe du Roc ☆ 48°50'·06N 01°36'·78W, Fl (4) 15s 49m **23M**.
Le Loup ⚓ 48°49'·57N 01°36'·25W, Fl (2) 6s 8m 11M.
Marina S bkwtr ☆ 48°49'·89N 01°35'·90W, Fl (2) R 6s 12m 5M; W post, R top; *Horn (2) 40s.*

▶ **CANCALE**
Pierre-de-Herpin ☆ 48°43'·77N 01°48'·92W, Oc (2) 6s 20m **17M**; *Siren Mo (N) 60s.*
Jetty hd ☆ 48°40'·08N 01°51'·14W, Oc (3) G 12s.

▶ **ST MALO, CH DE LA PETITE PORTE**
St Malo Fairway ⚓ 48°41'·38N 02°07'·28W, Iso 4s; *Whis.*
Ldg lts 128·7°, both Dir FG 20/69m **22/25M**; H24.
Front, **Les Bas Sablons** ☆ 48°38'·42N 02°01'·70W.

▶ **CHENAL DE LA GRANDE PORTE**
Ldg lts 089·1°: **Front, Le Grand Jardin** ☆ 48°40'·19N 02°04'·98W, Fl (2) R 10s 24m **15M**.
Rear, ☆ 48°40'·32N 01°58'·61W, Dir FR 40m **24M**.
Le Buron ⚓ 48°39'·32N 02°03'·66W, Fl (4) G 15s.

Môle des Noires hd ☆ 48°38'·52N 02°01'·91W, Fl R 5s 11m 13M; W twr, R top; *Horn (2) 20s.*
Écluse du Naye ldg lts 070·4°, both FR 7/23m 3/7M.
Bas-Sablons marina ☆ 48°38'·41N 02°01'·70W, Fl G 4s 7m 5M; Gy mast.

▶ **LA RANCE BARRAGE**
La Jument ⚓ Fl G 4s 6m 4M, 48°37'·44N 02°01'·76W.
Barrage lock, NW wall ☆ Fl (2) G 6s 6m 5M, 191°-291°; G pylon, 48°37'·06N 02°01'·73W.

▶ **ST CAST**
Môle ☆ 48°38'·40N 02°14'·63W, Iso WG 4s 11m, W11M, G8M; 204°-W-217°-G-233°-W-245°-G-204°.
Cap Frehel ☆ 48°41'·04N 02°19'·15W Fl (2) 10s 85m **29M**; Gy ☐ twr, G lantern; *Horn (2) 60s.*

▶ **PORT D'ERQUY**
S môle ☆ 48°38'·06N 02°28'·66W, Oc (2+1) WRG 12s 11m W11M, R/G8M; 055°-R-081°-W-094°-G-111°-W-120°-R-134°; W twr.

▶ **DAHOUET**
La Petite Muette ⚓ 48°34'·82N 02°34'·31W, Fl WRG 4s 10m W9M, R/G6M; 055°-G-114°-W-146°-R-196°.

▶ **BAIE DE SAINT BRIEUC/LE LÉGUÉ**
Grand Léjon ☆ 48°44'·90N 02°39'·87W. Fl (5) WR 20s 17m **W18M**, R14M; 015°-R-058°-W-283°-R-350°-W-015°.
Le Rohein ⚓ 48°38'·80N 02°37'·77W, VQ (9) 10s 13m, W10M, R/G7M; 072°-R-105°-W-180°-G-193°-W-237°-G-282°-W-301°-G-330°-W-072°. Le Légué ⚓ 48°34'·32N 02°41'·16W, Mo (A) 10s; *Whis.*
Pointe à l'Aigle jetty ☆ 48°32'·12N 02°43'·12W, VQ G 13m 8M; 160°-070°; W twr, G top.

▶ **BINIC**
N môle ☆ 48°36'·06N 02°48'·93W, Oc (3) 12s 12m.

▶ **SAINT QUAY-PORTRIEUX**
Herflux ⚓, 48°39'·06N 02°47'·95W. Dir ☆ 130°, Fl (2) WRG 6s 10m, W 8M, R/G 6M; G115°-125°, W125°-135°, R135°-145°.
Île Harbour ☆ 48°39'·99N 02°48'·50W, Oc (2) WRG 6s 16m, W10M, R/G 8M; 011°-R-133°-G-270°-R-306°-G-358°-W-011°.
Marina, **NE mole elbow**, 48°38'·99N 02°49'·09W, Dir lt 318·2°: Iso WRG 4s 4m **W15M**, R/G11M; W159°-179°, G179°-316°, W316°-320·5°, R320·5°-159°.
NE môle hd ☆ 48°38'·84N 02°48'·92W, Fl (3) G 12s.

CHANNEL ISLANDS

▶ THE CASQUETS AND ALDERNEY
Casquets ☆ 49°43'·32N 02°22'·62W, Fl (5) 30s 37m **24M**; H24; *Horn (2) 60s*; **Racon T, 25M**.
Quenard Pt ☆ 49°43'·75N 02°09'·86W, Fl (4) 15s 37m **23M**; 085°-027°; H24; *Horn 30s*.
Braye, ldg lts 215°, both Q 8/17m 9/12M, synch; 210°-220°. Front, 49°43'·39N 02°11'·91W.
Admiralty bkwtr ⚓ 49°43'·81N 02°11'·67W, L Fl 10s.

▶ GUERNSEY: LITTLE RUSSEL CHANNEL
Platte Fougère ☆ 49°30'·82N 02°29'·14W, Fl WR 10s 15m **16M**; W155°-085°, R085°-155°; W 8-sided twr, B band; *Horn 45s*; **Racon P**.
Roustel ⚓ 49°29'·22N 02°28'·79W, Q 8m 7M.
Platte ⚓, Fl WR 3s 6m, W7M, R5M; R024°-219°, W219°-024°; G conical twr.
Brehon ⚓ 49°28'·27N 02°29'·28W, Iso 4s 19m 9M.

▶ BIG RUSSEL
Noire Pute ⚓ 49°28'·27N 02°24'·93W, Fl (2) WR 15s 8m 6M; W220°-040°, R040°-220°.
Lower Heads ⚓ 49°25'·84N 02°28'·55W, Q (6) + L Fl 15s; *Bell*.

▶ BEAUCETTE MARINA
Petite Canupe ⚓ 49°30'·18N 02°29'·13W, Q (6) + L Fl 15s.
Ldg lts 276°, FR. Front 49°30'·19N 02°30'·21W.

▶ ST PETER PORT
Outer ldg lts 220°. **Front**, Castle bkwtr 49°27'·31N 02°31'·44W, Al WR 10s 14m **16M**; 187°-007°; *Horn 15s*. Rear, Belvedere, Oc 10s 61m 14M; 179°-269°.
White Rock pier ⚓ 49°27'·38N 02°31'·59W, Oc G 5s 11m 14M; intens 174°-354°; ○ twr; tfc sigs.
Marina app ⚓ 49°27'·36N 02°31'·67W, QG.

▶ HERM
Hbr ldg lts 078°: White drums. ⚓ F occas; 49°28'·30N 02°27'·02W.

▶ SARK
Corbée du Nez ⚓ 49°27'·08N 02°22'·17W, Fl (4) WR 15s 14m 8M; W057°-230°, R230°-057°.
Point Robert ☆ 49°26'·19N 02°20'·75W, Fl 15s 65m **20M**; 138°-353°; *Horn (2) 30s*.

▶ JERSEY (West and South coasts)
Grosnez Pt ☆ 49°15'·48N 02°14'·84W, Fl (2) WR 15s 50m **W19M, R17M**; W081°-188°, R188°-241°.
La Corbière ☆ 49°10'·85N 02°14'·92W, Iso WR 10s 36m **W18M, R16M**; Wshore-294°, R294°-328°, W328°-148°, R148°-shore; *Horn Mo (C) 60s*.

▶ WESTERN PASSAGE
Ldg lts 082°. Front, 49°10'·15N 02°05'·09W, Oc 5s 23m 14M; 034°-129°. Rear, Oc R 5s 46m 12M.
Noirmont Pt ⚓ 49°09'·91N 02°10'·08W, Fl (4) 12s 18m 13M; B twr, W band.

▶ ST HELIER
Elizabeth marina, West approach: Dir ⚓ 106°, 49°10'·76N 02°07'·12W, F WRG 4m 1M; G096°-104°, W104°-108°, R108°-119°.
Marina ent ⚓ 49°10'·69N 02°07'·21W, Oc G 4s 2M.
Red & Green Passage ldg lts 022·7°: Front, Dn ⚓ 49°10'·63N 02°06'·94W, Oc G 5s 10m 11M. Rear, Oc R 5s 18m 12M; synch.
East Rock ⚓ 49°09'·95N 02°07'·29W, QG.
Victoria pier 49°10'·57N 02°06'·88W; *Bell*; IPTS.

▶ JERSEY (South-East coast)
Demie de Pas ⚓ 49°09'·00N 02°06'·15W, Mo (D) WR 12s 11m, W14M, R10M; R130°-303°, W303°-130°; *Horn (3) 60s*; **Racon T, 10M**.
Violet ⚓ 49°07'·81N 01°57'·14W, L Fl 10s.

▶ GOREY
Ldg lts 298°. Front, ⚓ 49°11'·80N 02°01'·34W, Oc RG 5s 8m; on pierhead. Rear, Oc R 5s 24m.

▶ ST CATHERINE BAY
Verclut bkwtr ⚓ 49°13'·33N 02°00'·65W, Fl 1·5s.
La Coupe Pt, turret 49°14'·02N 02°01'·49W.

▶ JERSEY (North coast)
Sorel Point ☆ 49°15'·60N 02°09'·54W, L Fl WR 7·5s 50m **15M**; W095°-112°, R112°-173°, W173°-230°, R230°-269°, W269°-273°.

1	Cherbourg			**1**												
2	Omonville	10		**2**												
3	Braye (Alderney)	25	15	**3**												
4	St Peter Port	44	34	23	**4**											
5	Creux (Sark)	37	29	22	10	**5**										
6	St Helier	64	51	46	29	24	**6**									
7	Carteret	41	29	28	31	23	26	**7**								
8	Portbail	49	33	32	35	27	25	5	**8**							
9	Iles Chausey	69	61	58	48	43	25	33	30	**9**						
10	Granville	75	67	66	55	50	30	38	35	9	**10**					
11	Dinan	102	91	85	66	64	50	62	59	29	35	**11**				
12	St Malo	90	79	73	54	52	38	50	47	17	23	12	**12**			
13	Dahouet	88	80	72	54	52	41	60	59	37	45	41	29	**13**		
14	Le Légué/St Brieuc	96	86	76	57	56	46	69	69	41	49	45	33	8	**14**	
15	Binic	95	84	75	56	55	46	70	70	43	51	45	33	10	8	**15**
16	St Quay-Portrieux	88	80	73	56	51	46	64	64	57	47	35	11	7	4	**16**
17	Lézardrieux	88	80	76	48	38	47	48	71	53	54	61	49	33	32	30	21	**17**

NAVIGATION

AREA 16 N and S Brittany - *Paimpol to Pornichet*
SELECTED LIGHTS, BUOYS & WAYPOINTS
Positions are referenced to WGS84

▶ **OFFSHORE MARKS**
Roches Douvres ☆ 49°06'·28N 02°48'·89W, Fl 5s 60m **28M**; *Siren 60s*.
Barnouic ⚓ 49°01'·63N 02°48'·42W, VQ(3) 5s 15m 7M.

▶ **PAIMPOL**
L'Ost Pic ⚓ 48°46'·76N 02°56'·44W, Oc WR 4s 20m, W11M, R8M; W105°-116°, R116°-221°, W221°-253°, R253°-291°, W291°-329°.
La Jument ⚓ 48°47'·34N 02°57'·97W.
Ldg lts 262·2°, both QR 5/12m 7/14M. Front, Kernoa jetty, 48°47'·09N 03°02'·44W.

▶ **ÎLE DE BRÉHAT**
Kermouster Dir ⚓ 271°, 48°49'·54N 03°05'·19W, Dir Fl WRG 2s 16m, W10M, R/G 8M; G267°-270°, W270°-272°, R272°-274°; W col. (Ch du Ferlas)
Rosédo ☆ 48°51'·45N 03°00'·30W, Fl 5s 29m **20M**.
Le Paon ⚓ 48°51'·93N 02°59'·17W, F WRG 22m W11M, R/G8M; W033°-078°, G078°-181°, W181°-196°, R196°-307°, W307°-316°, R316°-348°; Y twr.
La Horaine ⚓ 48°53'·49N 02°55'·24W, Fl (3) 12s 13m 11M; Gy 8-sided twr on B hut.

▶ **LÉZARDRIEUX**
Ldg lts 224·7°. Front, **La Croix** ☆ 48°50'·22N 03°03'·24W, Dir Oc 4s 15m **19M**. Rear **Bodic** ☆, Dir Q 55m **22M**; intens 221°-229°; W ho, G gable.
Coatmer ldg lts 218·7°. Front, 48°48'·26N 03°05'·75W, F RG 16m R/G9M; R200°-250°, G250°-053°. Rear, FR 50m 9M; 197°-242°.
Les Perdrix ⚓ 48°47'·74N 03°05'·79W, Fl(2) WG 6s 5m, W6M; G165°-197°, W197°-202·5°, G202·5°-040°.

▶ **JAUDY RIVER TO TRÉGUIER**
Les Héaux de Bréhat ☆ 48°54'·50N 03°05'·18W, Oc (3) WRG 12s 48m, **W15M**, R/G11M; R227°-247°, W247°-270°, G270°-302°, W302°-227°.
Basse Crublent ⚓ 48°54'·29N 03°11'·18W, Fl (2) R 6s; *Whis*.
Grande Passe ldg lts 137°. Front, 48°51'·55N 03°07'·90W, Oc 4s 12m 11M; 042°-232°. Rear, Dir Oc R 4s 34m **15M**.
La Corne ⚓ 48°51'·34N 03°10'·63W, Fl(3) WRG 12s 14m W11M, R/G8M; W052°-059°, R059°-173°, G173°-213°, W213°-220°, R220°-052°.

▶ **PORT BLANC**
Le Voleur Dir ⚓ 150·4°. 48°50'·20N 03°18'·52W, Fl WRG 4s 17m, W14M, R/G 11M; W148°-152°.

▶ **PERROS-GUIREC**
Passe de l'Est, ldg lts 224·5°. Front, ☆ 48°47'·87N 03°26'·66W, Dir Oc(4) 12s 28m **15M**. Rear, ☆ Dir Q 79m **21M**; W twr, 1·5M from front.

Passe de l'Ouest. **Kerjean** ☆ Dir lt 143·6°, 48°47'·78N 03°23'·40W, Oc(2+1)WRG 12s 78m, **W15M**, R/G12M; G133·7°-143·2°, W143·2°-144·8°, R144·8°-154·3°.
Jetée du Linkin ⚓ 48°48'·20N 03°26'·31W, Fl (2) G 6s.

▶ **PLOUMANAC'H/LES SEPT ÎLES**
Men-Ruz 48°50'·26N 03°29'·03W, Oc WR 4s 26m W12M, R9M; W226°-242°, R242°-226°.
Île-aux-Moines ☆ 48°52'·73N 03°29'·43W, Fl (3) 15s 59m **24M**.

▶ **TRÉBEURDEN**
Ar Gouredec ⚓ 48°46'·41N 03°36'·60W, VQ (6) + L Fl 10s.
NW bkwtr ⚓ 48°46'·34N 03°35'·20W, Fl G 2·5s 8m 2M.

▶ **PRIMEL-TRÉGASTEL**
Ldg lts 152°, both FR 35/56m 6M. Front, 48°42'·45N 03°49'·20W.

▶ **BAIE DE MORLAIX**
Chenal du Tréguier ldg lts 190·5°. Front, Île Noire 48°40'·34N 03°52'·56W, Oc (2) WRG 6s 15m, W11M, R/G8M; G051°-135°, R135°-211°, W211°-051°. Rear, **La Lande** ☆ 48°38'·19N 03°53'·16W, Fl 5s 85m **23M**.
Grande Chenal ldg lts 176·4°. Front, **Île Louet** ☆ 48°40'·40N 03°53'·34W, Oc (3) WG 12s 17m **W15M**, G10M; W305°-244°, except where obsc by islands, G244°-305°. rear, **La Lande**, as above.

▶ **BLOSCON (ROSCOFF)**
Bloscon pier ⚓ 48°43'·21N 03°57'·69W, Fl WG 4s 9m W10M, G7M; W200°-210°, G210°-200°.

▶ **CANAL DE L'ÎLE DE BATZ**
Ar-Chaden ⚓ 48°43'·93N 03°58'·26W, Q(6)+L Fl WR 15s 14m, W8M, R6M; R262°-289·5°, W289·5°-293°, R293°-326°, W326°-110°.
Men-Guen-Bras ⚓ 48°43'·76N 03°58'·07W, Q WRG 14m, W9M, R/ G6M; W068°-073°, R073°-197°, W197°-257°, G257°-068°.
LW jetty hd ⚓ 48°43'·92N 03°58'·97W, Q 5m 1M.
Basse Plate ⚓ 48°44'·25N 04°02'·54W.
Lt ho ☆ 48°44'·71N 04°01'·63W, Fl(4) 25s 69m **23M**.
Same twr, auxiliary lt, FR 65m 7M; 024°-059°.

▶ **L'ABER WRAC'H**
Ile-Vierge ☆ 48°38'·33N 04°34'·06W, Fl 5s 77m **27M**; 337°-325°; Gy twr.
Outer ldg lts 100·1°: Front, 48°36'·88N 04°34'·56W, QR 20m 7M. Rear, Dir Q 55m 12M.
N bkwtr Dir ⚓ 128°; 48°35'·89N 04°33'·82W, Oc (2) WRG 6s 5m W13M, R/G11M; G125·7°-127·2°, W127·2°-128·7°, R128·7°-130·2°.

42

▶ **L'ABER BENOÎT**
Petite Fourche ⚓ 48°36'·98N 04°38'·75W.
Basse Paupian ⚓ 48°35'·31N 04°46'·28W.

▶ **CHENAUX DU FOUR & DE LA HELLE**
Le Four ☆ 48°31'·38N 04°48'·32W, Fl (5) 15s 28m **18M**; Gy ○ twr; *Horn (3+2) 60s.*
Ldg lts 158·5°. Front, **Kermorvan** ☆ 48°21'·72N 04°47'·42W, Fl 5s 20m **22M**; Horn 60s. Rear, **Pte de St Mathieu** ☆ 48°19'·79N 04°46'·27W, Fl 15s 56m **29M**.
Pte de Corsen ↙ 48°24'·89N 04°47'·63W, Dir Q WRG 33m W12M, R/G8M; R008°-012°, W012°-015°.
Grande Vinotière ⚓ 48°21'·93N 04°48'·43W, L Fl R 10s.
Les Vieux-Moines ⚓ 48°19'·33N 04°46'·63W, Fl R 4s 16m 5M; 280°-133°; R 8-sided twr.
Ldg lts 137·9°. Front, **Kermorvan** ☆, above. Rear, **Lochrist** ☆ 48°20'·55N 04°45'·82W, Dir Oc (3) 12s.

▶ **BREST AND APPROACHES**
Charles Martel ⚓ 48°18'·85N 04°42'·19W, Fl (4) R; *Whis.*
Pte du Toulinguet ☆ 48°16'·82N 04°37'·73W, Oc (3) WR 12s 49m **W15M**, R11M; Wshore-028°, R028°-090°, W090°-shore; W ☐ twr.
Pte du Petit-Minou ☆ 48°20'·19N 04°36'·87W, Fl (2) WR 6s 32m **W19M, R15M**; Rshore-252°, W252°-260°, R260°-307°, W307°-065·5°, W070·5°-shore.
Ldg lts 068°, both Dir Q 30/56m **23/22M**. Rear, **Pte du Portzic** ☆, 48°21'·49N 04°32'·06W, Oc (2) WR 12s 56m **W19M, R15M**; R219°-259°, W259°-338°, R338°-000°, W000°-065·5°, W070·5°-219°.
Moulin Blanc ⚓ 48°22'·79N 04°25'·99W, Fl (3) R 12s.

▶ **CAMARET**
N môle ↙ 48°16'·85N 04°35'·32W, Iso WG 4s 7m W12M, G9M; W135°-182°, G182°-027°.

▶ **MORGAT**
Pte de Morgat ☆ 48°13'·17N 04°29'·81W, Oc (4) WRG 12s 77m **W15M**, R11M, G10M; W shore-281°, G281°-301°, W301°-021°, R021°-043°.

▶ **DOUARNENEZ**
Île Tristan ↙ 48°06'·14N 04°20'·25W, Oc (3) WR 12s 35m; shore-W-138°-R-153°-W-shore.
↙, Dir 157°, 48°05'·40N 04°19'·80W, Fl (5) WRG 20s 16m, W5M, R/G4M; 154°-G-156°-W-158°-R-160°.

▶ **RAZ DE SEIN**
Tévennec ↙ 48°04'·28N 04°47'·73W, Q WR 28m W9M R6M; W090°-345°, R345°-090°. Same twr, Dir ↙ Fl 4s 24m 12M; intens 324°-332°.
La Vieille ☆ 48°02'·43N 04°45'·43W, Oc (2+1) WRG 12s 33m **W18M**, R13M, G14M; W290°-298°,

R298°-325°, W325°-355°, G355°-017°, W017°-035°, G035°-105°, W105°-123°, R123°-158°, W158°-205°; Gy ☐ twr; *Horn (2+1) 60s.*
La Plate ⚓ 48°02'·35N 04°45'·61W, VQ (9) 10s 19m 8M.

▶ **AUDIERNE**
Pte de Lervily ↙ 48°00'·04N 04°33'·94W, Fl (3) WR 12s 20m W14M, R11M; W211°-269°, R269°-294°, W294°-087°, R087°-121°; W twr, R top.
Kergadec Dir ↙ 006°. 48°00'·95N 04°32'·78W, Q WRG 43m W12M, R/G9M; G000°-005·3°, W005·3°-006·7°, R006·7°-017°.

▶ **POINTE DE PENMARC'H**
Eckmühl ☆ 47°47'·88N 04°22'·39W, Fl 5s 60m **23M**; Gy 8-sided twr; *Horn 60s.* Spinec ↙ 47°45'·18N 04°18'·92W, Q (6) + L Fl 15s; *Whis.*

▶ **LOCTUDY**
Pte de Langoz ↙ 47°49'·87N 04°09'·59W, Fl (4) WRG 12s 12m, **W15M**, R/G11M; W115°-257°, G257°-284°, W284°-295°, R295°-318°, W318°-328°, R328°-025°; W twr, R top.
Groyne hd ↙ 47°50'·21N 04°10'·34W, Q 3m 10M.

▶ **BENODET**
Ldg lts 345·5°. Front, ☆ 47°52'·31N 04°06'·70W, Dir Oc (2+1) G 12s 11m **17M**. Rear, Oc (2+1) 12s 48m 11M; 338°-016°.

▶ **PORT-LA-FORÊT**
Beg-Meil ↙ 47°50'·76N 03°57'·31W, Q (3) 10s.
Cap Coz mole ↙ 47°53'·48N 03°58'·28W, Fl (2) WRG 6s 5m, W7M, R/G5M; W340°-346°.

▶ **ÎLES DE GLÉNAN**
Penfret ☆ 47°43'·26N 03°57'·17W, Fl R 5s 36m **21M**; W ☐ twr, R top. Same twr, y ☆ Dir Q 34m 12M.
La Pie ⚓ 47°43'·75N 03°59'·75W, Fl (2) 6s 9m 3M.

▶ **CONCARNEAU**
Ldg lts 028·5°. Front, 47°52'·15N 03°55'·08W, Oc (3) 12s 14m 13M. Rear, ☆ Dir Q 87m **23M**.
Marina wavescreen ↙ 47°52'·20N 03°54'·72W, Fl (3) R 12s 3m 1M.

▶ **ÎLE DE GROIX**
Pen Men ☆ 47°38'·86N 03°30'·54W, Fl (4) 25s 60m **29M**; 309°-275°; W ☐ twr, B top.
Port Tudy, N môle ↙ 47°38'·70N 03°26'·74W, Iso G 4s 12m 6M; W twr, G top.

▶ **LORIENT**
Passe de l'Ouest ldg lts 057°, both Dir Q 11/22m 13/**18M**. Front, 47°42'·13N 03°21'·83W.
Passe du Sud ldg lts 008·5°, both Dir QR 16/34m **17/16M**; Front ☆, 47°43'·76N 03°21'·74W.

NAVIGATION

La Citadelle ⚓ 47°42'·59N 03°21'·94W, Oc G 4s 6m 6M; 009°-193°.
Port Louis, Jetty ☆ 47°42'·71N 03°21'·20W, Iso G 4s 7m 6M; W twr, G top.
Kernevel marina, ent between QR 1M, N end of wavebreak (47°43'·39N 03°22'·09W) and unlit ⚓.
Ste Catherine marina ☆ 47°43'·51N 03°21'·08W, QG 5m 3M.
Pen-Mané marina, bkwtr elbow ☆ 47°44'·11N 03°20'·86W, Fl (2) G 6s 4M.
No. 8 ⚓ 47°44'·55N 03°20'·98W, Fl R 2·5s.

▶ **RIVIÈRE D'ÉTEL**
W side ent ☆ 47°38'·70N 03°12'·91W, Oc (2) WRG 6s 13m W9M, R/G6M; W022°-064°, R064°-123°, W123°-330°, G330°-022°. Conspic radio mast, 47°39'·79N 03°12'·02W.

▶ **BELLE ÎLE**
Pte des Poulains ☆ 47°23'·28N 03°15'·17W, Fl 5s 34m **23M**; 023°-291°; W □ twr and dwelling.
Sauzon, Basse Gareau ⚓ 47°22'·76N 03°13'·06W. NW jetée ☆ 47°22'·51N 03°13'·10W, Fl G 4s 8m 8M.
Le Palais, N jetée ☆ 47°20'·82N 03°09'·08W, Fl (2+1) G 12s 8m 7M; W twr, G top.
Pte de Kerdonis ☆ 47°18'·59N 03°03'·61W, Fl (3) R 15s 35m **15M**. **Goulphar** ☆ 47°18'·64N 03°13'·69W, Fl (2) 10s 87m **27M**.
La Teignouse ☆ 47°27'·45N 03°02'·79W, Fl WR 4s 20m **W15M**, R11M; W033°-039°, R039°-033°.

▶ **ÎLES DE HOUAT & HOËDIC**
Port de St-Gildas N môle ☆ 47°23'·57N 02°57'·34W, Fl (2) WG 6s 8m W9M, G6M; W168°-198°, G198°-210°, W210°-240°, G240°-168°p.
Port de l'Argol bkwtr ☆ 47°20'·69N 02°52'·56W, Fl WG 4s 10m W9M, G6M; W143°-163°, G163°-183°, W183°-194°, G194°-143°; W twr, G top.

▶ **PORT HALIGUEN**
E bkwtr hd ☆ 47°29'·30N 03°05'·99W, Oc (2) WR 6s 10m, W11M, R8M; W233°-240·5°, R240·5°-299°, W299°-306°, R306°-233°; W twr, R top.

▶ **LA TRINITÉ-SUR-MER**
Ldg lts 347°. Front, 47°34'·08N 03°00'·37W, Q WRG 11m W10M, R/G7M; G321°-345°, W345°-013·5°, R013·5°-080°. **Rear** ☆, Q 21m **15M**.
Marina ☆ 47°35'·27N 03°01'·47W, Iso R 4s 8m 5M.

▶ **GOLFE DU MORBIHAN**
Pte de Port-Navalo ☆ 47°32'·87N 02°55'·11W, Oc (3) WRG 12s 32m, **W15M**, R/G11M; W155°-220°, G317°-359°, W359°-015°, R015°-105°.
359° ldg marks : Front, Grégan ⚓ 47°33'·90N 02°55'·05W, Q (6) + L Fl 15s 3m 8M. Rear, spire.

▶ **CROUESTY**
Ldg lts 058°, both Dir Q 10/27m **19M**. **Front** ☆, 47°32'·54N 02°53'·94W; R panel, W stripe.

▶ **VILAINE RIVER**
Penlan ☆ 47°30'·98N 02°30'·13W, Oc (2) WRG 6s 26m, **W15M**, R/G11M; R292·5°-025°, G025°-052°, W052°-060°, R060°-138°, G138°-180°.

▶ **PIRIAC-SUR-MER**
Grand Norven ⚓ 47°23'·55N 02°32'·90W, Q. Inner mole ☆ 47°22'·93N 02°32'·72W, Oc (2) WRG 6s 8m, W10M, R/G7M; R066°-148°, G148°-194°, W194°-201°, R201°-221°; W col; Siren 120s (occas).

▶ **LA TURBALLE**
Jetée de Garlahy ☆ 47°20'·70N 02°30'·93W, Fl (4) WR 12s 13m, W10M, R7M; R060°-315°, W315°-060°; W pylon, R top.

▶ **LE CROISIC**
Jetée du Tréhic ☆ 47°18'·49N 02°31'·43W, Iso WG 4s 12m W14M, G11M; G042°-093°, W093°-137°, G137°-345°; Gy twr, G top.

▶ **LE POULIGUEN**
Basse Martineau ⚓ 47°15'·54N 02°24'·36W. SW jetty ☆ 47°16'·39N 02°25'·40W, QR 13m 9M; 171°-081°; W col.

▶ **PORNICHET (La Baule)**
S bkwtr ☆ 47°15'·49N 02°21'·15W, Iso WRG 4s 11m, W10M, R/G7M; 303°-G-081°-W-084°-R-180°.

1	Lézardrieux	1		12	16	18	24	42	43	45	72	97	100	105	124	Pornic	12
2	Tréguier	22	2		11	12	24	39	40	41	66	87	90	95	113	St Nazaire	11
3	Perros-Guirec	28	21	3		10	13	30	30	34	55	78	80	85	106	La Baule/Pornichet	10
4	Trébeurden	40	32	17	4		9	18	22	27	48	73	75	79	100	Le Croisic	9
5	Morlaix	60	46	36	23	5		8	28	36	57	78	80	84	105	Arzal/Camoël	8
6	Roscoff	54	41	28	17	12	6		7	16	37	58	60	64	85	Crouesty	7
7	L'Aberwrac'h	84	72	60	49	48	32	7		6	26	47	48	54	74	Le Palais (Belle Ile)	6
8	Le Conquet	106	98	83	72	68	55	29	8		5	32	33	38	61	Lorient	5
9	Brest (marina)	114	107	92	83	79	67	42	18	9		4	4	12	37	Concarneau	4
10	Morgat	126	118	103	92	88	75	49	20	24	10		3	12	36	Port-la-Forêt	3
11	Douarnenez	131	123	108	97	93	80	54	25	29	11	11		2	30	Loctudy	2
12	Audierne	135	128	113	102	98	86	55	30	34	27	30	12		1	Audierne	1

AREA 17 South Biscay - *Pointe de Saint-Gildas to Hendaye*
SELECTED LIGHTS, BUOYS & WAYPOINTS

Positions are referenced to WGS84

Pte de Saint-Gildas ☆ 47°08'·02N 02°14'·76W, Q. WRG 20m, W14M, R/G10M; R264°-308°, G308°-078°, W078°-088°, R088°-174°, W174°-180°, G180°-264°.

▶ **PORNIC**

Access buoy 47°06'·45N 02°06'·64W, L Fl 10s.
Pte de Noëveillard ☆ 47°06'·62N 02°06'·92W, Oc (4) WRG 12s 22m W13M, R/G9M; G shore-051°, W051°-079°, R079°-shore; W ☐ twr, G top.

▶ **ÎLE DE NOIRMOUTIER**

Île du Pilier ☆ 47°02'·55N 02°21'·61W, Fl (3) 20s 33m **29M**; Gy twr. Same twr, auxiliary lt, QR 10m 11M, 321°-034°.
Les Boeufs 46°55'·04N 02°28'·02W, VQ (9) 10s.
L'Herbaudière, ldg lts 187·5°, both Q 5/26m 7M, Gy masts. Front, 47°01'·59N 02°17'·85W.
Basse du Martroger 47°02'·60N 02°17'·12W, Q WRG 11m W9M, R/G6M; G033°-055°, W055°-060°, R060°-095°, G095°-124°, W124°-153°, R153°-201°, W201°-240°, R240°-033°.
W jetty ☆ 47°01'·63N 02°17'·86W, Oc (2+1) WG 12s 9m W10M, G7M; W187·5°-190°, G190°-187·5°.
Noirmoutier-en-L'Île jetty ☆ 46°59'·27N 02°13'·14W, Oc (2) R 6s 6m 6M; W col, R top.

▶ **ÎLE D'YEU**

Petite Foule (main lt) ☆ 46°43'·05N 02°22'·96W Fl 5s 56m **24M**; W ☐ twr, G lantern.
Port Joinville ldg lts 219°, both QR 11/16m 6M, 169°-269°. Front, 46°43'·61N 02°20'·95W.
NW jetty ☆ 46°43'·77N 02°20'·82W, Oc (3) WG 12s 7m, W11M, G8M; G shore-150°, W150°-232°, G232°-279°, W279°-285°, G285°-shore.
Pte des Corbeaux ☆ 46°41'·42N 02°17'·11W, Fl (2+1) R 15s 25m **20M**; 083°-143° obsc by Île de Yeu.
Port de la Meule ☆ 46°41'·66N 02°20'·75W, Oc WRG 4s 9m, W9M, R/G6M; G007·5°-018°, W018°-027·5°, R027·5°-041·5°; Gy twr, R top.

▶ **ST GILLES-CROIX-DE-VIE**

Pte de Grosse Terre ☆ 46°41'·54N 01°57'·92W, Fl (4) WR 12s 25m, **W18M, R15M**; R290°-339°, W339°-125°, R125°-145°; W truncated conical twr.
Ldg lts 043·7°, both Q 7/28m **15M**; 033·5°-053·5°; W ☐ twrs, R tops. Front, 46°41'·85N 01°56'·67W.
Pilours 46°40'·98N 01°58'·10W, Q(6)+LFl 15s; *Bell*.
Jetée de la Garenne ☆ 46°41'·45N 01°57'·26W, Fl G 4s 8m 6M.

▶ **LES SABLES D'OLONNE**

Les Barges ☆ 46°29'·70N 01°50'·50W, Fl (2) R 10s 25m 13M; Gy twr.
L'Armandèche ☆ 46°29'·40N 01°48'·29W, Fl (2+1) 15s 42m **24M**; 295°-130°; W 6-sided twr.
Nouch Sud 46°28'·55N 01°47'·42W, Q(6)+LFl 15s.
Ldg lts 032·5°, both Iso 4s 12/33m **16M**, H24.
Front ☆, 46°29'·42N 01°46'·37W.
Ldg lts 320°. Front, 46°29'·44N 01°47'·51W, QG 11m 8M; W twr, G top. Rear, Q 33m 13M.
Jetée St Nicolas ☆ 46°29'·23N 01°47'·52W, QR 16m 8M; 143°-094°; W twr, R top.

▶ **BOURGENAY**

Ldg lts 040°, both QG 9/19m 7M. Front, 46°26'·37N 01°40'·61W; 020°-060°.
Landfall 46°25'·28N 01°41'·91W, L Fl 10s.
Ent ☆ 46°26'·43N 01°40'·51W, Fl R 4s 8m 9M.

▶ **ÎLE DE RÉ**

Les Baleineaux ☆ 46°15'·81N 01°35'·22W, Oc (2) 6s 23m 11M; pink twr, R top.
Les Baleines ☆ 46°14'·64N 01°33'·69W, Fl (4) 15s 53m **27M**; Gy 8-sided twr, R lantern.
Chanchardon ☆ 46°09'·73N 01°28'·44W, Fl WR 4s 15m W11M, R8M; R118°-290°, W290°-118°.
Chauveau ☆ 46°08'·03N 01°16'·42W, Oc (3) WR 12s 27m **W15M**, R11M; W057°-094°, R094°-104°, W104°-342°, R342°-057°; W ○ twr, R top.
Pte de Sablanceaux ☆ 46°09'·76N 01°15'·17W, VQ (3) 5s 10m 5M; landing stage.

▶ **ARS-EN-RÉ**

Outer ldg lts 265·8°, both Iso 4s 5/13m 11/**15M**; synch. Front, 46°14'·05N 01°28'·61W.
Le Fier d'Ars, inner ldg lts 232·5°; both Q 5/13m 9/11M. Front, 46°12'·76N 01°30'·60W.

▶ **ST MARTIN DE RÉ**

Rocha 46°14'·74N 01°20'·64W, Q.
Lt ho, ☆ 46°12'·44N 01°21'·89W, Oc (2) WR 6s 18m W10M, R7M; W shore-245°, R245°-281°, W281°-shore; W twr, R top.
W mole ☆ 46°12'·49N 01°21'·89W, Iso G 4s 10m 6M.

▶ **LA ROCHELLE**

Ldg lts 059°, both Dir Q 15/25m 13/14M; by day Fl 4s. Front, 46°09'·35N 01°09'·16W.
Pte des Minimes ☆ 46°08'·33N 01°10'·68W, Fl (3) WG 12s 8m, W8M, G5M; W059°-213°, G313°-059°.

NAVIGATION

Tour Richelieu 46°08'·89N 01°10'·36W, Fl R 4s 10m 9M; R twr.
Marina 46°08'·33N 01°10'·68W, Fl(2)G 6s 9m 7M.

▶ LA CHARENTE
Ldg lts 115°, both Dir QR 8/21m **19/20M**; W☐ twr, R top. Front, ☆ 45°57'·96N 01°04'·37W.
Île d'Aix ☆ 46°00'·60N 01°10'·67W, Fl WR 5s 24m **W24M, R20M**; R103°-118°, W118°-103°.

▶ ÎLE D'OLÉRON
Chassiron ☆ 46°02'·77N 01°24'·67W, Fl 10s **28M**.
Rocher d'Antioche 46°03'·92N 01°24'·67W, Q.

▶ ST DENIS
Dir lt 205°, 46°01'·61N 01°21'·96W; Iso WRG 4s 14m; G190°-204°, W204°-206°, R206°-220°.
E jetty 46°02'·10N 01°22'·07W, Fl(2)WG 6s 6m, W9M, G6M; G205°-277°, W277°-292°, G292°-165°.

▶ GIRONDE, PASSE DE L'OUEST
Pte de la Coubre ☆ 45°41'·78N 01°13'·99W, Fl(2) 10s 64m **28M**; W twr, R top. Also, FRG 42m, R12M, G10M; R030°-043°, G043°-060°, R060°-110°.
BXA 45°37'·53N 01°28'·69W Iso 4s 8m 7M; Whis; **Racon B, 120-150s**.
Ldg lts 081·5° (not valid E of Nos 4 & 5 buoys).
Front ☆, Dir Iso 4s 21m **20M**; intens 080·5°-082·5°. Same structure, Q(2) 5s 10m 3M.
Rear, La Palmyre ☆, 45°39'·71N 01°07'·22W, Dir Q 57m **27M**. Same twr, Dir FR 57m **17M**.
Cordouan ☆ 45°35'·16N 01°10'·39W, Oc(2+1) WRG 12s 60m, **W22M, R/G18M**.

▶ PASSE SUD (or DE GRAVE)
Ldg lts 063°. **St Nicolas Front** ☆, 45°33'·72N 01°05'·03W, Dir QG 22m **16M**.
Rear, Pte de Grave ☆, Oc WRG 4s 26m, **W19M, R/G15M**; W033°-233·5°, R233·5°-303°, W303°-312°, G312°-330°, W330°-025°.

▶ ROYAN
NE jetty 45°37'·23N 01°01'·49W, Fl(3)G 12s 2m 5M.

▶ PORT-MÉDOC
Entrance (approx) 45°33'·45N 01°03'·37W.

▶ PAUILLAC
Pauillac, NE elbow 45°11'·96N 00°44'·61W, Fl G 4s 7m 5M.
Ent E side 45°11'·86N 00°44'·60W, QG 7m 4M.

▶ BORDEAUX
Lock to Bassins Nos 1/2, 44°51'·74N 00°32'·94W.

▶ ARCACHON, PASSE NORD
Cap Ferret ☆ 44°38'·76N 01°14'·95W, Fl R 5s 53m **27M**; W○ twr, R top. Same twr, Oc(3) 12s 46m 14M; 045°-135°.
ATT-ARC 44°34'·61N 01°18'·74W, L Fl 10s 8m 5M.
1N 44°34'·58N 01°17'·83W.
11 44°37'·29N 01°14'·18W.
15 44°39'·79N 01°12'·11W.
Marina 44°39'·77N 01°09'·15W, QG 6m 6M.

▶ CAPBRETON
Digue Nord 43°39'·38N 01°27'·01W, Fl(2) R 6s 13m 12M; W○ twr, R top; *Horn 30s*.
Estacade Sud 43°39'·25N 01°26'·89W, Fl(2) G 6s 9m 12M.

▶ ANGLET/L'ADOUR
BA 43°32'·55N 01°32'·79W, L Fl 10s.
Outer S bkwtr 43°31'·60N 01°31'·68W, Q(9) 15s.
Anglet marina 43°31'·57N 01°30'·51W, Fl G 2s.

▶ ST JEAN DE LUZ
Inner ldg lts 150·7°, both Dir QG 18/27m **16M**. Front, E jetty ☆, 43°23'·25N 01°40'·15W.

▶ HENDAYE
Cabo Higuer ☆ 43°23'·51N 01°47'·53W, Fl(2) 10s 63m **23M**; 072°-340°; twr, W lantern (in Spain).
W trng wall 43°22'·82N 01°47'·36W, Fl(3) G 9s.

1	Port Joinville	**1**														
2	St Gilles-C-de-Vie	18	**2**													
3	Sables d'Olonne	31	16	**3**												
4	Bourgenay	40	25	9	**4**											
5	St Martin (I de Ré)	55	44	27	20	**5**										
6	La Rochelle	66	51	36	29	12	**6**									
7	Rochefort	84	75	61	54	36	26	**7**								
8	R La Seudre	89	71	58	52	33	24	30	**8**							
9	Port St Denis	59	48	33	30	21	13	26	22	**9**						
10	Port Bloc/Royan	97	85	71	60	56	52	68	27	42	**10**					
11	Bordeaux	152	140	126	115	111	107	123	82	97	55	**11**				
12	Cap Ferret	138	130	113	110	102	98	114	75	88	68	123	**12**			
13	Capbreton	192	186	169	166	165	156	172	131	145	124	179	58	**13**		
14	Anglet/Bayonne	200	195	181	178	177	168	184	143	157	132	187	70	12	**14**	
15	Santander	212	210	204	204	206	202	218	184	192	180	235	133	106	103	**15**
16	Cabo Finisterre	377	395	393	394	406	407	423	399	397	401	456	376	370	373	274	**16**

AREA 18 N & NW Spain - *Fuenterrabia to Bayona*
SELECTED LIGHTS, BUOYS & WAYPOINTS

Positions are referenced to WGS84

▶ **FUENTERRABIA**
Marina ent, Fl (4) G 11s and Fl (4) R 11s.

▶ **PASAJES**
Fairway ⚓ 43°21'·07N 01°56'·20W, Mo (A) 6s.
Senocozulúa Dir☆,155·75°;43°19'·90N 01°55'·61W, Oc (2) WRG 12s 50m; W154·5°-157°; *Racon M*.

▶ **SAN SEBASTIÁN**
La Concha ldg lts 158°. Front 43°18'·89N 01°59'·47W, QR 10m 7M. Rear, Oc R 4s 16m 7M.
Igueldo ☆ 43°19'·35N 02°00'·64W, Fl (2+1) 15s.

▶ **GUETARIA**
I. de San Antón ☆ 43°18'·62N 02°12'·09W, Fl (4) 15s.
N mole ☆ 43°18'·26N 02°11'·91W, Fl (3) G 9s 11m 5M.

▶ **ZUMAYA**
Lt ho ☆ 43°18'·14N 02°15'·07W, Oc (1+3) 12s 39m.
Marina ent, ☆ Fl (3) R 9s 6m 1M and Fl (2+1) G 10s.

▶ **LEQUEITIO**
Pta Amandarri ☆ 43°21'·99N 02°29'·94W, Fl G 4s.
Cabo de Santa Catalina ☆ 43°22'·67N 02°30'·69W, Fl (1+3) 20s 44m **17M**; *Horn Mo (L) 20s*.

▶ **ELANCHOVE**
Digue N, Fl G 3s 8m 4M.
Cabo Machichaco ☆ 43°27'·36N 02°45'·22W, Fl 7s 120m **24M**; *Siren Mo (M) 60s*.

▶ **BILBAO**
Punta Galea ☆ 43°22'·30N 03°02'·14W, Fl (3) 8s 82m **19M**; 011°-227°; *Siren Mo (G) 30s*.
W bkwtr hd ☆ 43°22'·67N 03°05'·04W, Fl G 5s 21m 10M; ***Racon X, 20M***.
Getxo marina ☆ 43°20'·23N 03°01'·02W, QR 3m.
Las Arenas ☆ 43°19'·83N 03°00'·97W, Oc G 4s 1m 1M and Oc R 4s 2m 1M.

▶ **CASTRO URDIALES**
Castillo de Santa Ana ☆ 43°23'·06N 03°12'·89W, Fl (4) 24s 47m **20M**; W twr; *Siren Mo (C) 60s*.
N bkwtr ☆ 43°22'·86N 03°12'·54W, Fl G 3s 12m 6M.

▶ **LAREDO and RIA DE SANTOÑA**
N bkwtr ☆ 43°24'·89'N 03°25'·20W, Fl (4) R 11s.
Santoña ldg lts 283·5°. Front, 43°26'·33N 03°27'·62W, Fl 2s 5m 8M. Rear, Oc (2) 5s 12m 11M.
C. Ajo ☆ 43°30'·70N 03°35'·72W, Oc (3) 16s 69m **17M**.

▶ **SANTANDER**
C. Mayor ☆ 43°29'·37N 03°47'·51W, Fl (2) 10s 89m

21M; W ○ twr; *Horn Mo (M) 40s*.
I de Mouro ☆ 43°28'·39N 03°45'·36W, Fl (3) 21s.
Marina del Cantabrico, ldg lts 235·6°. Front, 43°25'·75N 03°48'·83W, Iso 2s 9m 2M. Rear, Oc 5s 10m 2M. Marina ent QR and QG.
Pta del Torco de Afuera ☆ 43°26'·51N 04°02'·61W, Fl (1+2) 24s 33m **22M**; W twr.

▶ **RIBADESELLA**
Somos ☆ 43°28'·36N 05°04'·98W, Fl (2+1) 12s.
Pta del Caballo ☆ 43°28'·08N 05°03'·98W, Fl (2) R 6s 10m 5M; 278·4°-212·9°; ○ twr.
C. Lastres ☆ 43°32'·03N 05°18'·07W, Fl 12s 116m **23M**. W ○ twr.

▶ **GIJÓN**
Piedra Sacramento ☆ 43°32'·90N 05°40'·21W, QG; 8-sided twr.
Marina. N bkwtr ☆ 43°32'·85N 05°40'·08W, Fl (2) R 6s 7m 3M.
Cabo de Torres ☆ 43°34'·29N 05°41'·97W, Fl (2) 10s 80m **18M**.
C. Peñas ☆ 43°39'·31N 05°50'·90W, Fl (3) 15s 115m **35M**; Gy 8-sided twr; *Siren Mo (P) 60s*.

▶ **CUDILLERO**
Pta Rebollera ☆ 43°33'·96N 06°08'·68W, Oc (4) 16s 42m **16M**; *Siren Mo (D) 30s*.
Ent, N bkwtr ☆ Fl (3) G 9s 3m 2M.
Cabo Vidio ☆ 43°35'·60N 06°14'·79W, Fl 5s 99m **25M**; *Siren Mo (V) 60s*.
Cabo Busto ☆ 43°34'·13N 06°28'·23W, Fl (4) 20s.

▶ **LUARCA**
Pta Focicón ☆ 43°33'·03N 06°31'·85W, Oc (3) 15s 63m 14M; W □ twr; *Siren Mo (L) 30s*.
Ldg lts 170°, Front 43°32'·83N 06°32'·02W, Fl 5s 18m 2M. Rear Oc 4s 25m 2M.

▶ **RÍA DE RIBADEO**
Pta de la Cruz ☆ 43°33'·40N 07°01'·75W, Fl (4) R 11s 16m 7M.
Isla Pancha ☆ 43°33'·39N 07°02'·53W, Fl (3+1) 20s 26m **21M**; *Siren Mo (R) 30s*.
1st ldg lts 140°. Front, 43°32'·83N 07°01'·53W, Iso R 18m 5M. Rear, Oc R 4s 24m 5M.
2nd ldg lts 205°. Front, 43°32'·49N 07°02'·24W, VQ R 8m 3M; R ◊, W twr. Rear, Oc R 2s 18m 3M.
Marina ent, Fl G 5s 9m 3M; Fl R 5s 9m 1M.

NAVIGATION

▶ RÍA DE VIVERO
Pta de Faro ☆ 43°42'·74N 07°35'·03W, Fl R 5s 18m 7M.
Pta Socastro ☆ 43°43'·08N 07°36'·42W, Fl G 5s 18m.
Marina ent ☆ 43°40'·22N 07°35'·62W, Fl (3) G 9s 1M.

Pta de la Estaca de Bares ☆ 43°47'·21N 07°41'·14W, Fl (2) 7·5s 99m **25M**; *Siren Mo (B) 60s*.
Cabo Ortegal ☆ 43°46'·22N 07°52'·30W, Oc 8s 122m **18M**; W ○ twr, R band.

▶ RÍA DE CEDEIRA
Piedras de Media Mar ☆ 43°39'·37N 08°04'·80W, Fl (2) 5s 12m 4M; W ○ twr.
Bkwtr ☆ 43°39'·30N 08°04'·20W, Fl (2) R 7s 10m 4M.
Cabo Prior ☆ 43°34'·05N 08°18'·87W, Fl (1+2) 15s 105m **22M**; 055·5°-310°; 6-sided twr.

▶ RÍA DE FERROL
Cabo Prioriño Chico ☆ 43°27'·52N 08°20'·40W, Fl 5s 34m **23M**; 225°-129·5°; W 8-sided twr.

▶ RÍA DE BETANZOS
Sada marina N pier ☆ 43°21'·76N 08°14'·54W, Fl (4) G 11s 11m 5M; G twr. S bkwtr, Fl (4) R 11s 11m 3M.

▶ LA CORUÑA
Torre de Hércules ☆ 43°23'·15N 08°24'·39W, Fl (4) 20s 104m **23M**; *Siren Mo (L) 30s*.
Ldg lts 108·5°. Front, 43°23'·00N 08°21'·28W, Oc WR 4s 54m, W105·5°-114·5°; **Racon M, 18M**; 020°-196°. Rear, Fl 4s 79m 8M; 357·5°-177·5°.
Ldg lts 182°. Front, 43°20'·59N 08°22'·25W, Iso WRG 2s 27m, W180°-184°; **Racon X, 11-21M**. Rear, Oc R 4s 52m 3M.
Dique d'Abrigo ☆ 43°21'·90N 08°22'·48W, Fl G 3s.

▶ RÍA DE CORME Y LAGE
Pta Lage ☆ 43°13'·88N 09°00'·83W, Fl (5) 20s 64m.
Corme, mole ☆ 43°15'·70N 08°57'·89W, Fl (2) R 5s.
Lage, N mole ☆ 43°13'·34N 08°59'·96W, Fl G 3s.
C. Villano ☆ 43°09'·60N 09°12'·70W, Fl (2) 15s 102m **28M**; *Siren Mo (V) 60s*; **Racon M, 35M**.

▶ RÍA DE CAMARIÑAS
Ldg lts 081°. Front, 43°07'·37N 09°11'·56W, Fl 5s 13m 9M. Rear, Iso 4s 25m 11M; 043·8°-102·1°.

Camariñas bkwtr ☆ 43°07'·45N 09°10'·70W, Fl R 5s.
Cabo Toriñan ☆ 43°03'·17N 09°18'·01W, Fl (2+1) 15s 63m **24M**; **Racon T, 35M (1.7M SE of ☆)**.
Cabo Finisterre ☆ 42°52'·93N 09°16'·29W, Fl 5s 141m **23M**; *Racon O, 35M*.

▶ RÍA DE MUROS
Pta Queixal ☆ 42°44'·36N 09°04'·75W, Fl (2+1) 12s.
Muros ☆ 42°46'·64N 09°03'·31W, Fl (4) R 13s 8m 4M.
Portosin bkwtr ☆ 42°45'·94N 08°56'·93W, Fl (3) G 9s 7m 3M.
Pta Cabeiro ☆ 42°44'·37N 08°59'·44W, Oc WR 3s.

▶ RÍA DE AROUSA
Isla Sálvora ☆ 42°27'·82N 09°00'·80W, Fl (3+1) 20s 38m **21M**. Same twr, Fl (3) 20s, 126°-160°.
Sta Eugenia ☆ 42°33'·58N 08°59'·24W, Fl (2) R 7s 7m.
Isla Rúa ☆ 42°32'·95N 08°56'·38W, Fl (2+1) WR 21s 24m 13M; R121·5°-211·5°, W211·5°-121·5°; *Racon K, 211°-121°, 10-20M*.
Puebla del Caramiñal E bkwtr ☆ 42°36'·28N 08°55'·87W, Oc G 2s 8m 4M; W ○ twr G band.
Villagarcia, N mole ☆ 42°36'·11N 08°46'·33W, Iso 2s 2m 10M.
Pedras Negras marina, bkwtr ☆ 42°29'·85N 08°51'·51W, Fl (4) WR 11s 5m, W305°-315°.

▶ RÍA DE PONTEVEDRA
I. Ons ☆ 42°22'·94N 08°56'·17W, Fl (4) 24s 125m **25M**.
Sangenjo marina, ☆ 42°23'·76N 08°48'·11W, Q R.
Combarro S jetty ☆ 42°25'·60N 08°42'·20W, Oc (2) R 6s 3M.
Aguete marina, mole ☆ 42°22'·62N 08°44'·12W; Fl (2) G 7s 1M.

▶ RÍA DE VIGO
Cabo del Home, ldg lts 129°. Front 42°15'·15N 08°52'·37W, Fl 3s 36m 9M. Rear, Oc 6s 53m 11M.
Cabo Estay ldg lts 069·3°. **Front** ☆ 42°11'·12N 08°48'·89W, Iso 2s 16m **18M**; *Horn Mo (V) 60s*; *Racon B, 22M*. **Rear**, Oc 4s 48m **18M**.
Marina, 42°14'·63N 08°43'·32W, QG/QR, 10m 5M.

▶ BAYONA
Las Serralleiras ☆ 42°09'·23N 08°53'·35W, Q (9) 15s.
Ldg lts 084°. Front, 42°08'·24N 08°50'·09W, Fl 6s 7m 10M. Rear, Oc 4s 17m 9M.
C. Silleiro ☆ 42°06'·27N 08°53'·80W, Fl (2+1) 15s 83m **24M**.

1	Bilbao (ent)	1						
2	Santander	36	2					
3	Gijón	116	90	3				
4	Cabo Peñas	126	96	10	4			
5	Ría de Ribadeo	179	149	63	53	5		
6	Cabo Ortegal	214	184	98	88	40	6	
7	La Coruña	252	222	136	126	78	38	7
8	Cabo Villano	284	254	168	158	110	70	43	8
9	Bayona	355	325	239	229	181	141	114	71	9

AREA 19 Portugal - *Viana do Castelo to Vila Real de Santo Antonio*
SELECTED LIGHTS, BUOYS & WAYPOINTS | Positions are referenced to WGS84

Montedor ☆ 41°45'·09N 08°52'·49W, Fl (2) 9·5s 102m **22M**; R ☐ twr; *Horn Mo (S) 25s.*

▶ VIANA DO CASTELO
Ldg lts 012.5°. **Front** ☆ 41°41'·33N 08°50'·35W, Iso R 4s 14m **23M**; 241°-151°. **Rear** ☆, Oc R 6s 32m **23M**.
Outer mole ☆ 41°40'·45N 08°50'·66W, Fl R 3s 9M; W col, R bands; *Horn 30s.*

▶ PÓVOA DE VARZIM
Molhe N ☆ 41°22'·29N 08°46'·23W, Fl R 3s 14m 12M; *Siren 40s.*

▶ LEIXÕES
Leça ☆ 41°12'·08N 08°42'·74W, Fl (3) 14s 56m **28M**.
Outer bkwtr ☆ 41°10'·37N 08°42'·49W, Fl WR 5s 23m W12M, R9M; R001°-180°, W180°-001°; *Horn 20s.*
Marina ☆ 41°11'·08N 08°42'·27W, L Fl (2) R 12s 4m 2M.

▶ AVEIRO
Lt ho ☆ 40°38'·57N 08°44'·88W, Fl (4) 13s 65m **23M**. Same R/W twr, Fl G 4s 53m 9M, is rear 085·4° ldg lt. Front ldg lt, Fl G 3s 16m 9M, on S mole hd.
Ldg lts 065·6°, both R ○ cols. 40°38'·82N 08°44'·99W, Oc R 3s 7m 9M. Rear, Oc R 6s 8M.
Molhe Central ☆ 40°38'·64N 08°44'·95W, L Fl G 5s 8m 3M.

▶ FIGUEIRA DA FOZ
Cabo Mondego ☆ 40°11'·46N 08°54'·35W, Fl 5s 96m **28M**; *Horn 30s*; 3M NNW of Figueira da Foz.

Ldg lts 081·5°. Front, 40°08'·83N 08°51'·23W, Iso R 5s 8m 8M; Rear, Oc R 6s 12m 8M.
Molhe S ☆ 40°08'·59N 08°52'·41W, Fl G 6s 13m 7M.
Penedo da Saudade ☆ 39°45'·84N 09°01'·89W, Fl (2) 15s 54m **30M**; ☐ twr, and house

▶ NAZARÉ
Pontal da Nazaré ☆ 39°36'·25N 09°05'·18W, Oc 3s 49m 14M; 282°-192°; *Siren 35s.*
Molhe S ☆ 39°35'·34N 09°04'·76W, L Fl G 5s 14m 8M.

▶ ILHA DA BERLENGA
Ilha da Berlenga ☆ 39°24'·90N 09°30'·63W, Fl 10s 120m **27M**; *Horn 28s*; (5·7M NW of C. Carvoeiro).

▶ PENICHE
Cabo Carvoeiro ☆ 39°21'·61N 09°24'·51W, Fl (3) R 15s 56m **15M**; *Horn 35s.*
Molhe W ☆ 39°20'·85N 09°22'·56W, Fl R 3s 13m 9M; *Siren 120s.*

C. da Roca ☆ 38°46'·88N 09°29'·90W, Fl (4) 18s 164m **26M**; Aero R lt (523m) 5M E at Pena.
Cabo Raso ☆ 38°42'·56N 09°29'·15W, Fl (3) 9s 22m **15M**; 324°-189°; R twr; *Horn Mo (I) 60s.*

▶ CASCAIS
Ldg lts 284·7°. Front, **Forte de Santa Marta** 38°41'·42N 09°25'·27W, Oc WR 6s 24m **W18M**, R14M; R233°-334°, W334°-098°; W ☐ twr, Bu bands; *Horn 10s.* Rear, **Guia**, Iso WR 2s **W19M**, **R16M**; W326°-092°, R278°-292°; W twr.
Molhe Norte ☆ Fl (2) G 4s 8m 3M.

▶ LISBOA
Ldg lts 047·1°, front & middle lts visible 039·5°-054·5°, H24. Front, **Gibalta** 38°41'·94N 09°15'·97W, Oc R 3s 30m **21M**; twr & cupola. Middle, **Esteiro**, 762m from front, Oc R 6s 81m **21M**; W ☐ twr, R bands; *Racon Q, 15M.* Rear, **Mama** ☆ 38°43'·65N 09°13'·63W, Iso 6s 153m **21M**; 045·5°-048·5°.
No. 1 ⚓ 38°39'·55N 09°18'·78W, Fl G 2s.
Forte Bugio ☆ 38°39'·62N 09°17'·93W, Fl G 5s 27m 9M; ○ twr on fortress; *Horn Mo (B) 30s.*
No. 5 ⚓ 38°40'·43N 07°17'·66W, Fl G 4s.
No. 7 ⚓ 38°40'·64N 09°16'·90W, Fl G 5s.
No. 9 ⚓ 38°40'·63N 09°14'·49W, Fl G 6s.
Ponte 25 de Abril. The N (38°41'·63N 09°10'·68W) and S pillars are lit Fl (3) G 9s and Fl (3) R 9s.

Cabo Espichel ☆ 38°24'·94N 09°13'·05W, Fl 4s 167m **26M**; W 6-sided twr; *Horn 31s.*

▶ SESIMBRA
Ldg lts 003·5°, both L Fl R 5s 9/21m 7/6M. Front, 38°26'·56N 09°06'·16W. Rear 34m from front.

▶ SETÚBAL
Ldg lts 039·7°, both Iso Y 6s 12/60m **22M** (by day 5/6M). Front, fish dock 38°31'·15N 08°53'·95W.
No. 1 ⚓ 38°26'·98N 08°58'·18W, Fl G 3s 5M.
No. 2 ⚓ 38°27'·21N 08°58'·45W, Fl (2) R 10s 13m 9M; R ☐ on R column, W cupola; *Racon B, 15M.*
Forte de Outão ☆ 38°29'·31N 08°56'·06W, Oc R 6s 33m 12M.
Pinheiro da Cruz ☆ 38°15'·46N 08°46'·34W, Fl 3s.

▶ SINES
Cabo de Sines ☆ 37°57'·56N 08°52'·83W, Fl (2) 15s 55m **26M**.
W mole ☆ 37°56'·46N 08°53'·33W, Fl 3s 20m 12M.

NAVIGATION

⚓ 37°56'·12N 08°53'·25W, Fl R 3s 6M; 285m S of W mole hd.
Marina bkwtr ☆ 37°57'·04N 08°52'·04W, Fl G 4s 4M.
Cabo Sardão ☆ 37°35'·94N 08°49'·02W, Fl (3) 15s 67m **23M**.

▶ CAPE ST VINCENT/SAGRES

Cabo de São Vicente ☆ 37°01'·37N 08°59'·82W, Fl 5s 84m **32M**; W twr and bldg; *Horn Mo (I) 30s*.
Ponta de Sagres ☆ 36°59'·64N 08°56'·97W, Iso R 2s 52m 11M.
Baleeira mole ☆ 37°00'·67N 08°55'·50W, Fl WR 4s 12m, W14M, R11M; W254°-355°, R355°-254°; W ☐ twr.

▶ LAGOS

Pta da Piedade ☆ 37°04'·81N 08°40'·20W, Fl 7s 50m **20M**.
E mole ⚓ 37°05'·93N 08°39'·98W, Fl (2) G 6s 5M.
Alvor ent 37°07'·0N 08°37'·0W, Fl R/G 4s; W twrs, R/G bands.

▶ PORTIMÃO

Ponta do Altar ☆ 37°06'·34N 08°31'·17W, L Fl 5s 31m **16M**; 290°-170°; W twr and bldg.
Ldg lts 020·9°. Front 37°07'·35N 08°31'·32W, Oc R 5s 18m 8M. Rear, 87m from front, Oc R 7s 32m 8M.
E mole ⚓ 37°06'·50N 08°31'·59W, Fl G 5s 9m 7M.
W mole ⚓ 37°06'·52N 08°31'·77W, Fl R 5s 9m 7M.
No. 2 ⚓ 37°06'·96N 08°31'·54W, Fl R 4s.
Marina, S ent ☆ 37°07'·18N 08°31'·50W, Fl R 5s 3M.
N ent ☆ 37°07'·23N 08°31'·50W, Fl G 6s 3M.

Pta de Alfanzina ☆ 37°05'·22N 08°26'·59W, Fl (2) 15s 62m **29M**.
Armacão de Pera ⚓ 37°05'·92N 08°21'·21W, Oc R 5s 24m 6M.

▶ ALBUFEIRA

Ponta da Baleeira ⚓ 37°04'·84N 08°15'·88W, Oc 6s 30m 11M.
N bkwtr ☆, Fl (2) G 5s 9m 4M, approx 37°04'·90N 08°15'·52W.
S bkwtr ☆, Fl (2) R 5s 9m 4M. Olhos de Água ☆ 37°05'·47N 08°11'·40W, L Fl 5s 29m 7M.

▶ VILAMOURA

Vilamoura ☆ 37°04'·50N 08°07'·42W, Fl 5s 17m **19M**.
Marina, W mole ☆ 37°04'·19N 08°07'·49W, Fl R 4s 13m 5M.
E mole ☆ 37°04'·22N 08°07'·42W, Fl G 4s 13m 5M.

▶ FARO, OLHÃO and TAVIRA

E mole ☆ 36°57'·79N 07°52'·14W, Fl G 4s 9m 6M.
W mole ☆ 37°57'·84N 08°52'·26W, Fl R 4s 9m 6M; appr on 352°.
Access ldg lts 020·9°. Front, Barra Nova 37°58'·22N 07°52'·00W, Oc 4s 8m 6M. Rear, **C. de Santa Maria** ☆ 36°58'·48N 07°51'·88W, Fl (4) 17s 49m **25M**; W ○ twr.
No. 6 ⚓ 36°58'·49N 07°52'·12W, Fl R 6s. No. 20 ⚓ Fl R 6s, faces the commercial quay, 37°00'·13N 07°55'·11W, approx 2M before **Faro** proper. At No. 6 ⚓ the Canal de Olhão forks NE/1.6M to: No. 8 ⚓ 36°59'·90N 07°51'·07W, Fl R 3s; thence N & E to **Olhão**.

Tavira ldg lts 325·9°. Front, Fl R 3s 6m 4M. Rear, Iso R 6s 9m 5M.
W mole ☆ 37°06'·79N 07°37'·10W, Fl R 2·5s 7m 7M.

▶ VILA REAL DE SANTO ANTONIO

Lt ho ☆ 37°11'·23N 07°25'·00W, Fl 6·5s 51m **26M**; W twr, B bands.
R. Guadiano, Bar buoys ⚓ 37°08'·90N 07°23'·44W, Q (3) G 6s.
⚓ 37°09'·14N 07°23'·82W, Fl R 4s.
W trng wall ☆ 37°09'·75N 07°24'·03W, Fl R 5s 4M.
E trng wall ☆ 37°09'·93N 07°23'·63W, Fl G 3s 4M.
Marina, QR at S corner; QR/QG ent; QR at N corner.

See also Area 20 Distance Table

		1	2	3	4	5	6	7	8	9	10	11	12
1	Longships	**1**											
2	Ushant (Créac'h)	100	**2**										
3	La Coruña	418	338	**3**									
4	Cabo Villano	439	365	43	**4**								
5	Bayona	510	436	114	71	**5**							
6	Viana do Castelo	537	468	141	98	32	**6**						
7	Leixões (Pôrto)	565	491	169	126	63	33	**7**					
8	Nazaré	659	585	263	220	156	127	97	**8**				
9	Cabo Carvoeiro	670	596	274	231	171	143	114	22	**9**			
10	Cabo Raso	710	636	314	271	211	183	154	62	40	**10**		
11	Lisboa (bridge)	686	652	330	287	227	199	170	78	56	16	**11**	
12	Cabo Espichel	692	658	336	293	233	205	176	84	62	22	23	**12**

AREA 20 SW Spain & Gibraltar - *Ayamonte to Europa Point*
SELECTED LIGHTS, BUOYS & WAYPOINTS

Positions are referenced to WGS84

▶ AYAMONTE
Bar buoy ⚓ 37°08'·90N 07°23'·44W, Q (3) G 6s.
E trng wall ☆ 37°09'·93N 07°23'·63W, Fl G 3s 4M.
Vila Real de Santo Antònio ☆ 37°11'·23N 07°25'·00W, Fl 6·5s 51m **26M**; W◯ twr, B bands.

▶ ISLA CANELA and ISLA CRISTINA
No. 1 Appr ⚓ 37°10'·90N 07°19'·60W, L Fl 10s (tbc).
Ldg lts 313°. Front Q 7m 5M. Rear Fl 4s 12m 5M.
Both marinas' ent, QR and QG.

▶ RIO DE LAS PIEDRAS
No 1 Bar ⚓ 37°11'·69N 07°02'·63W, L Fl 10s.
Lateral lt buoys mark the shifting chan.
El Rompido ☆ 37°13'·12N 07°07'·69W, Fl (2) 10s 41m **24M**; W twr, B bands.

▶ RIA DE HUELVA
⚓ 37°09'·56N 06°57'·18W, VQ (6) + L Fl 10s.
Punta Umbria, bkwtr hd ☆ VQ (6) + L Fl 10s 8m 5M, 37°09'·75N 06°56'·92W, .
Marina ☆ 37°10'·76N 06°57'·36W, Fl(2) G 10s 6m 3M.
Ría de Huelva Dique ☆ 37°06'·47N 06°49'·93W, Fl (3+1) WR 20s 29m, W12M, R9M; W165°-100°, R100°-125°; **Racon K, 12M**.
⚓ 37°05'·54N 06°49'·11W, Q (9) 15s.
Dir ☆ 339·2°, WRG 59m 8M. 37°08'·57N 06°50'·66W. Fl G 337·5°-338°, FG 338°-338·6°, OcG 338·6°-339·1°, FW 339·1°-339·3°, OcR 339·3°-339·8°, FR 339·8°-340·4°, Fl R 340·4°-340·9°; W twr.
No. 1 ⚓ 37°06'·26N 06°49'·46W, Fl G 5s.
No. 3 ⚓ 37°06'·87N 06°49'·77W, Fl (2) G 10s.
No. 5 ⚓ 37°07'·38N 06°50'·03W, Fl (3) G 15s.
No. 7 ⚓ 37°07'·77N 06°50'·29W, Fl (4) G 20s.

▶ MAZAGÓN
Picacho lt ho ☆ 37°08'·10N 06°49'·56W, Fl (2+4) 30s 52m **25M**.
S Dique ☆ 37°07'·91N 06°50'·03W, QG 5m 2M.
Off Torre del Oro (ruins) ⚓ 37°04'·22N 06°43'·67W, Fl (2) 10s.
La Higuera ☆ 37°00'·47N 06°34'·16W, Fl (3) 20s 45m **20M**.

▶ CHIPIONA
Bajo Salmedina ☆ 36°44'·27N 06°28'·64W, Q (9) 15s 9m 5M.
Pta de Chipiona ☆ 36°44'·26N 06°26'·53W, Fl 10s **25M**.
Marina, No. 2 ⚓ 36°45'·14N 06°25'·59W, Fl (2) R 7s.

N bkwtr ☆ 36°44'·96N 06°25'·70W, Fl(2) G 10s 6m 5M.

▶ RÍO GUADALQUIVIR
No. 1 ⚓ 36°45'·74N 06°27'·03W, L Fl 10s; **Racon M, 10M**.
Ldg lts 068·9°. Front 36°47'·84N 06°20'·24W, Q 28m 10M. Rear, Iso 4s 60m 10M.
No. 3 ⚓ 36°46'·16N 06°25'·36W, Fl G 5s.
Selected buoys as far as Bonanza:
No. 6 ⚓ 36°46'·50N 06°24'·81W, Fl (2) R 6s.
No. 7 ⚓ 36°46'·61N 06°24'·02W, Fl (3) G 10s.
No. 11 ⚓ 36°46'·96N 06°22'·90W, Fl G 5s.
No. 12 ⚓ 36°47'·05N 06°22'·94W, Fl R 5s.
No. 14 ⚓ 36°47'·21N 06°22'·39W, Fl (2) R 6s.
No.13 ⚓ 36°47'·12N 06°22'·36W, Fl (2) G 6s.
No.17 ⚓ 36°47'·46N 06°21'·23W, Fl (4) G 12s.
No. 20 ⚓ 36°47'·81N 06°20'·71W, Fl (4) G 12s.
Up-stream the river is marked by lt bcns, lt buoys and a few ldg lights.

▶ SEVILLA
No. 52, RGR structure. 36°47'·81N 06°20'·71W, Fl (2+1) R 21s 9m 5M.
Gelves marina, ent Fl R 5s (37°20'·51N 06°01'·31W) and Fl G 3s.
Lock, 37°19'·95N 05°59'·65W, into Canal de Alfonso XIII.

▶ ROTA (Bay of Cadiz)
Rota Aero ☆ 36°38'·13N 06°20'·84W, Alt Fl WG 9s 79m **17M**; R/W chequered water twr, conspic.
Rota ☆ 36°36'·96N 06°21'·44W, Oc 4s 33m 13M; W ◯ lt ho, R band.
Marina, S pier ☆ 36°36'·96N 06°21'·44W, Fl (3) R 10s 8m 9M.

▶ PUERTO SHERRY and PUERTO DE SANTA MARIA
Puerto Sherry marina, S bkwtr ☆ 36°34'·64N 06°15'·25W, Oc R 4s 4M. N bkwtr ☆ Oc G 5s 3M.
Santa María ldg lts 040°. Front, 36°35'·77N 06°13'·36W, QG 16m 4M. Rear, 253m from front, Iso G 4s 20m 4M.
W trng wall head ☆ 36°34'·34N 06°14'·96W, Fl R 5s 10m 3M.

▶ CÁDIZ CITY and PUERTO AMERICA
⚓ 36°33'·99N 06°19'·80W, L Fl 10s.
San Felipe mole 36°32'·56N 06°16'·77W, Fl G 3s 10m 5M; G twr.

51

NAVIGATION

Puerto America marina, NE bkwtr, Fl (4) G 16s 1M.
International Free Zone hbr: No. 1 ⚓ 36°30'·66N 06°15'·45W, Fl (3) G 9s. **Puerto Elcano** marina ent 36°30'·07N 06°15'·45W.

Castillo de San Sebastián ☆ 36°31'·70N 06°18'·97W, Fl (2) 10s 38m **25M**; *Horn Mo (N) 20s.*

▶ SANCTI PETRI

Punta del Arrecife ⚓ 36°23'·66N 06°12'·99W, Q (9) 15s 7m 3M.
Sancti Petri castle ☆ 36°22'·75N 06°13'·33W, Fl 3s 18m 9M; twr.
Outer ldg lts 050°. Front, Fl 5s 12m 6M; rear, Oc (2) 6s 16m 6M.
Inner ldg lts 346·5°. Front, Fl 5s 11m 6M; rear, Oc (2) 6s 21m 6M.
'Gateway' bcns, Fl G (36°23'·10N 06°12'·65W) and Fl R 5s 7m 2M.

Cabo Roche ☆ 36°17'·75N 06°08'·59W, Fl (4) 24s 44m **20M**.
Cabo Trafalgar ☆ 36°10'·95N 06°02'·12W, Fl (2+1) 15s 50m **22M**.

▶ BARBATE

Barbate lt ho ☆ 36°11'·21N 05°55'·43W, Fl (2) WR 7s 22m, W10M, R7M; W281°-015°, R015°-095°;.
SW mole ☆ 36°10'·78N 05°55'·56W, Fl R 4s 11m 5M.
Marina ent, Fl (2) G 2M and Fl R 3s 2M.
Torre de Gracia ☆ 36°05'·38N 05°48'·69W, Oc (2) 5s 74m 13M.

▶ TARIFA

Tarifa ☆ 36°00'·06N 05°36'·60W, Fl (3) WR 10s 40m **W26M, R18M**; W113°-089°, R089°-113°; W twr; *Siren Mo (O) 60s*; **Racon C, 20M**.
Outer SE mole ☆ 36°00'·38N 05°36'·24W, Fl G 5s 11m 5M; vis 249°-045°; G twr with statue.

▶ ALGECIRAS

Pta Carnero ☆ 36°04'·61N 05°25'·57W, Fl (4) WR 20s 42m, **W16M**, R13M; W018°-325°, R325°-018°; *Siren Mo (K) 30s*.

⚓ 36°06'·73N 05°24'·76W, Q (3) 10s.
Marina, outer S jetty ☆ 36°07'·10N 05°26'·13W, Q (3) R 9s 7m 3M.

▶ LA LÍNEA

⚓ 36°09'·53N 05°22'·03W, Fl (3) G 6s.
Dique de Abrigo ☆ 36°09'·51N 05°22'·05W, Fl (2) G 6s 8m 4M.

▶ GIBRALTAR

Aero ☆ 36°08'·57N 05°20'·60W, Mo (GB) R 10s 405m **30M**.
Europa Pt ☆ 36°06'·58N 05°20'·69W, Iso 10s 49m **19M**; 197°-042° and 067°-125°; W ○ twr, R band.
Same structure, Oc R 10s 49m **15M**; 042°-067°; also FR 44m **15M**; 042°-067°; *Horn 20s.*
'A' Head ☆ 36°08'·03N 05°21'·85W, Fl 2s 18m **15M**; *Horn 10s.*
Queensway marina ☆ 36°08'·04N 05°21'·42W, 2 FR, 2 FG (vert).
'E' head ☆ 36°08'·90N 05°21'·95W, FR 28m 5M.

MOROCCO (West to east)

Cap Spartel ☆ 35°47'·46N 05°55'·44W, Fl (4) 20s 95m **30M**; Y □ twr; *Dia (4) 90s.*

▶ TANGIER

Navaids in Tangier are reported unreliable.
Monte Dirección (Le Charf) ☆ 35°46'·08N 05°47'·28W, Oc (3) WRG 12s 88m **W16M**, R12M, G11M; G140°-174·5°, W174·5°-200°, R200°-225°.

Pta Malabata ☆ 35°49'·08N 05°44'·86W, Fl 5s 77m **22M**. W □ twr.
Pte Cires ☆ 35°54'·52N 05°28'·96W, Fl (3) 10s 44m **18M**; 060°-330°.

▶ CEUTA

Pta Almina ☆ 35°53'·91N 05°16'·86W, Fl (2) 10s 148m 22M.
Digue de Poniente ☆ 35°53'·75N 05°18'·68W, Fl G 5s 13m 10M; *Siren 15s*; **Racon O, 12M**.
Marina ent ☆ Fl (4) R 11s 1M and ☆ Fl (4) G 11s.

		1											
1	Nazaré	1											
2	Cabo Carvoeiro	22	2										
3	Cabo Raso	62	40	3									
4	Lisboa (bridge)	78	56	16	4								
5	Cabo Espichel	84	62	22	23	5							
6	Sines	118	96	54	57	34	6						
7	Cabo São Vicente	169	147	104	108	85	57	7					
8	Lagos	189	167	124	128	105	77	20	8				
9	Vilamoura	212	190	147	151	128	100	43	27	9			
10	Cádiz	303	281	238	242	219	191	134	120	95	10		
11	Cabo Trafalgar	320	298	255	259	236	208	151	139	115	28	11	
12	Tarifa	344	322	279	283	260	232	175	163	139	52	24	12
13	Gibraltar	360	338	295	299	276	248	191	179	155	68	40	16	13

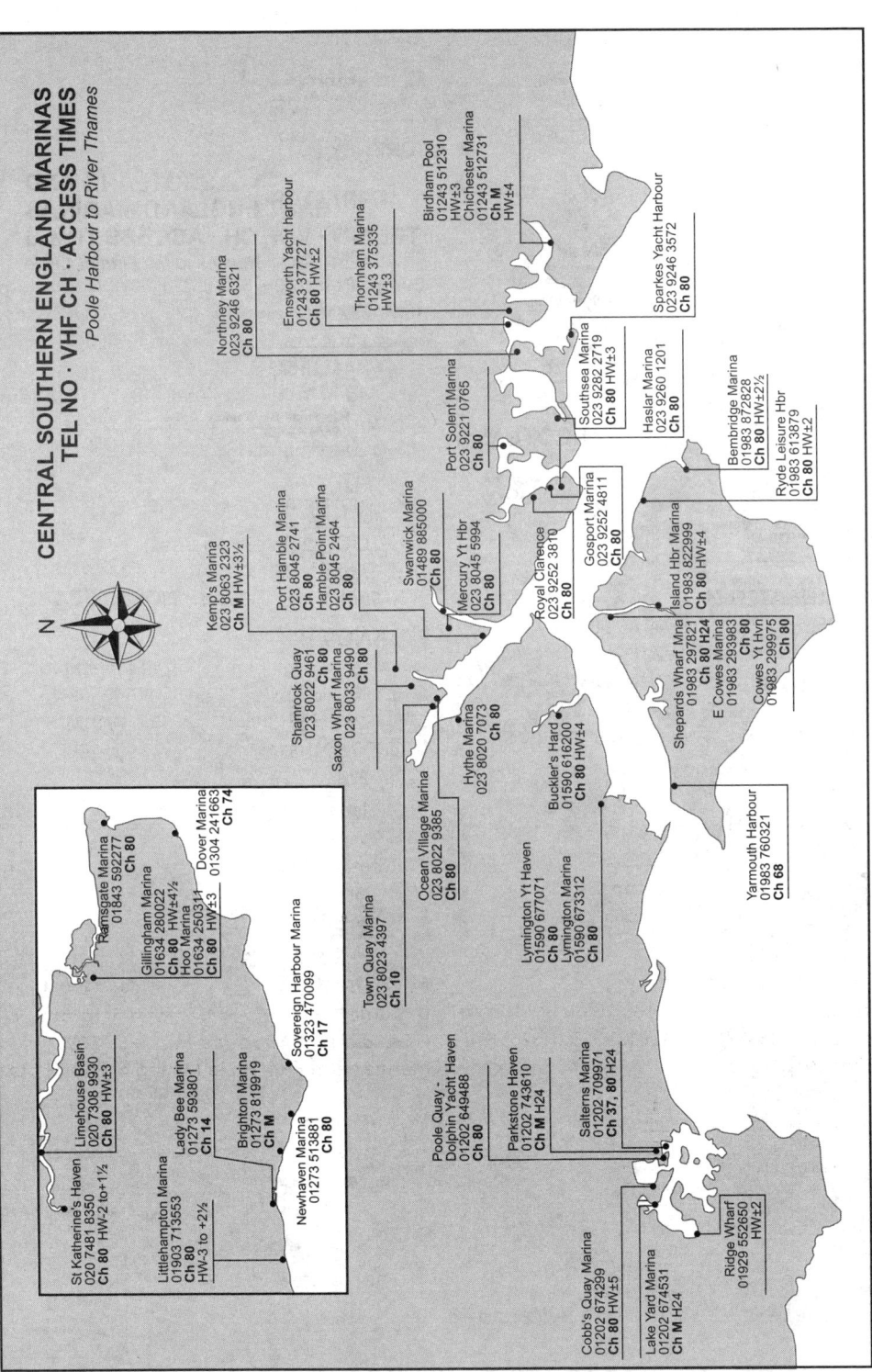

NAVIGATION

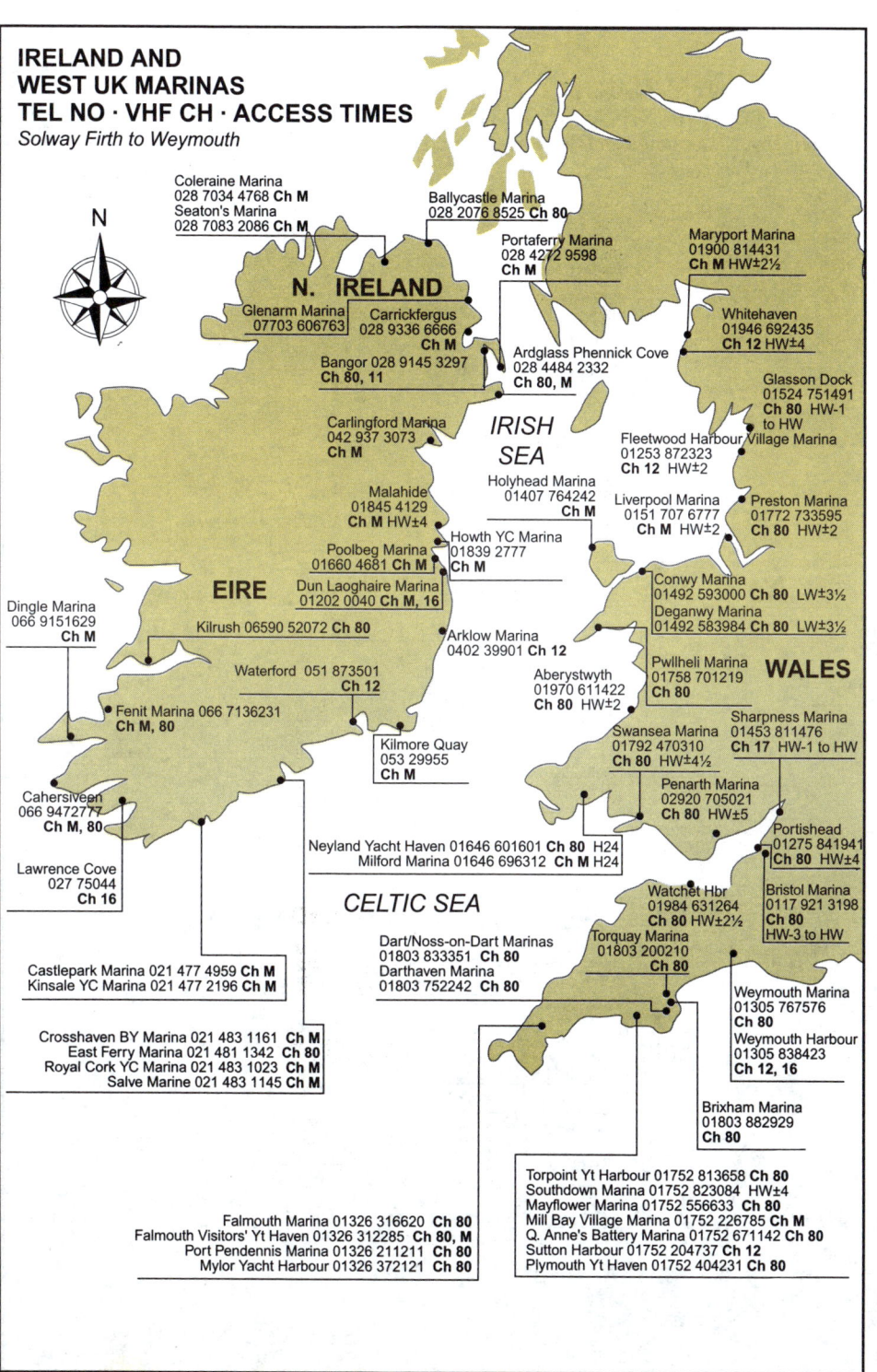

NAVIGATION

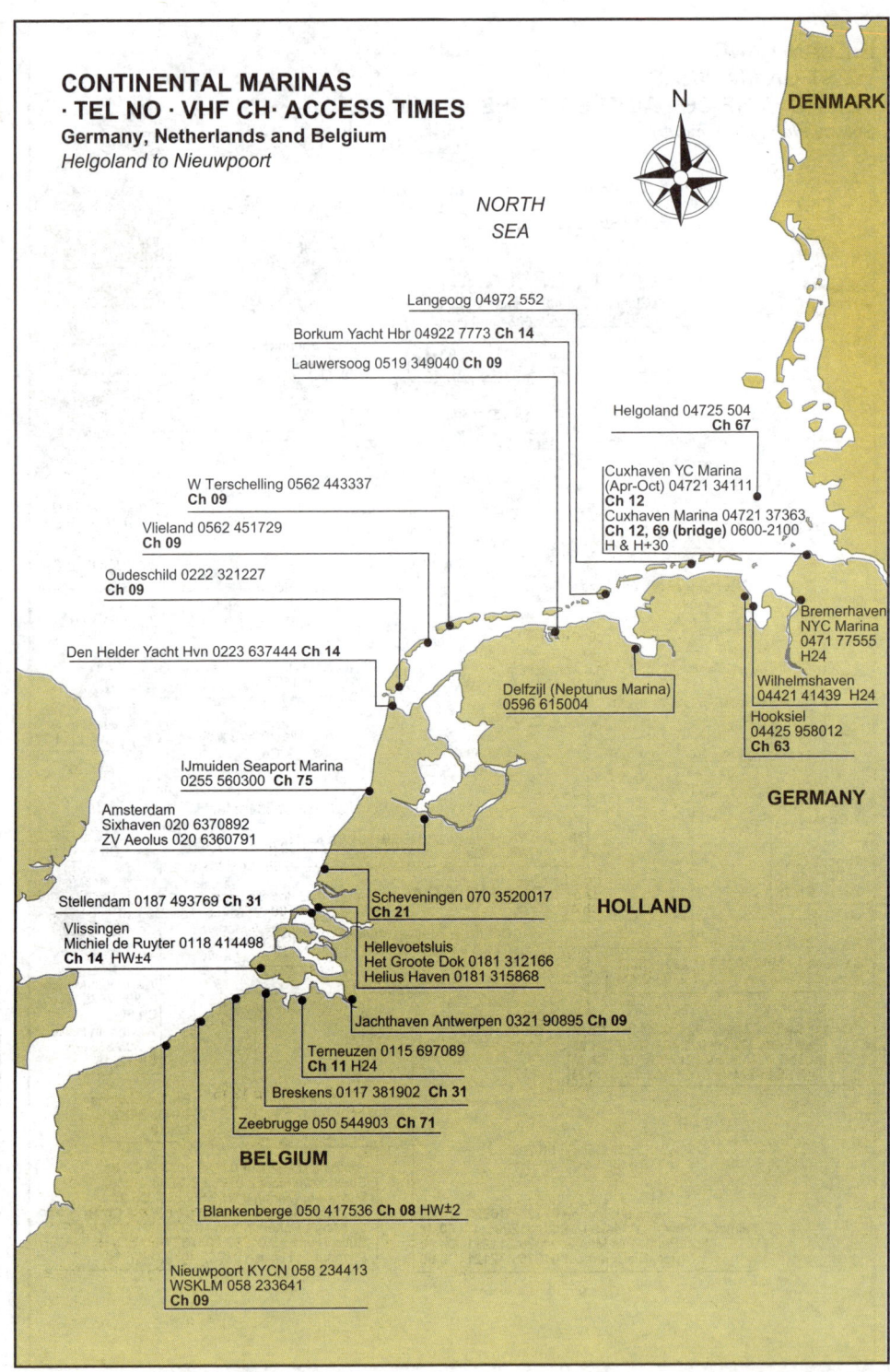

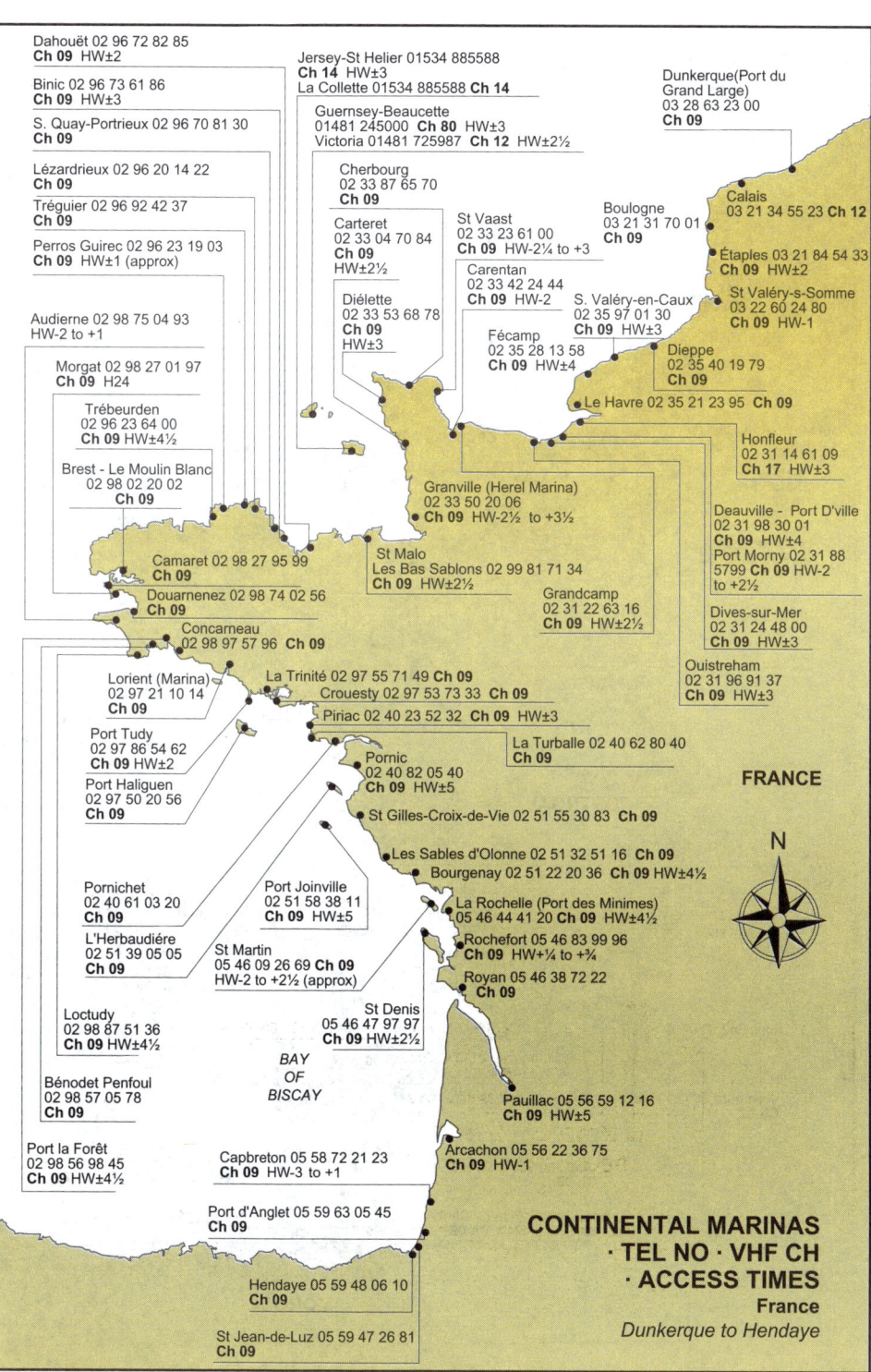

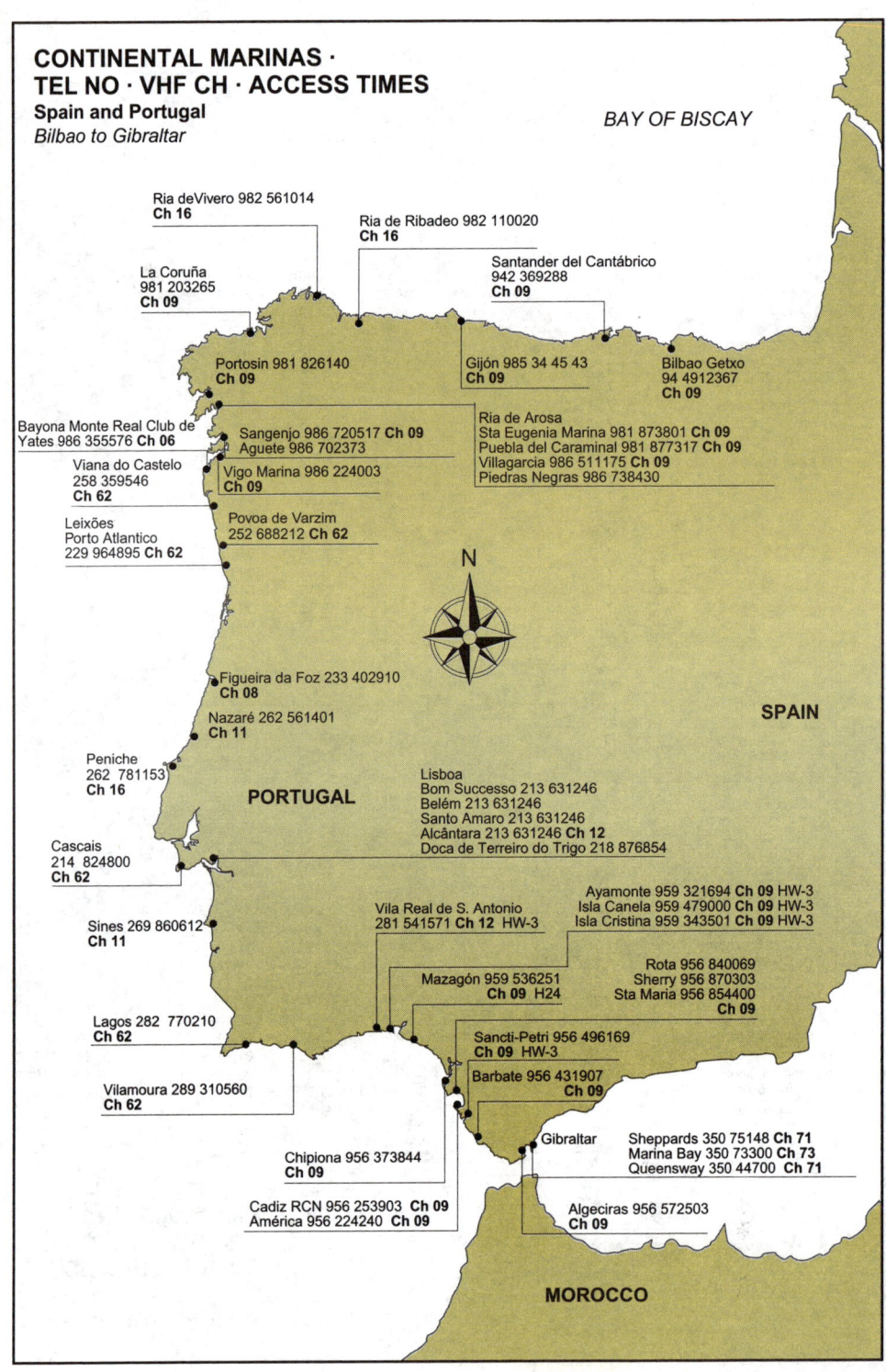

50°N 00°E/W. Times are UT - for DST add 1 hour in non-shaded areas

2005 Sunrise and Sunset Time

The times are based on LAT 50°00′N LONG 0°00′W - add 4 min for every degree West and subtract 4 min for every degree East

	Rise h m	Set h m	Rise h m	Set h m	Rise h m	Set h m	Rise h m	Set h m	Rise h m	Set h m	Rise h m	Set h m
	JANUARY		**FEBRUARY**		**MARCH**		**APRIL**		**MAY**		**JUNE**	
1	07 59	16 09	07 33	16 54	06 43	17 42	05 37	18 32	04 36	19 19	03 56	20 00
2	07 58	16 10	07 32	16 56	06 41	17 44	05 35	18 33	04 35	19 20	03 55	20 01
3	07 58	16 11	07 31	16 58	06 39	17 45	05 32	18 35	04 33	19 22	03 54	20 02
4	07 58	16 12	07 29	16 59	06 37	17 47	05 30	18 37	04 31	19 23	03 54	20 03
5	07 58	16 13	07 27	17 01	06 35	17 49	05 28	18 38	04 29	19 25	03 53	20 04
6	07 58	16 15	07 26	17 03	06 33	17 50	05 26	18 40	04 28	19 26	03 53	20 05
7	07 57	16 16	07 24	17 05	06 31	17 52	05 24	18 41	04 26	19 28	03 52	20 06
8	07 57	16 17	07 23	17 06	06 29	17 54	05 22	18 43	04 25	19 29	03 52	20 07
9	07 56	16 18	07 21	17 08	06 27	17 55	05 20	18 44	04 23	19 31	03 51	20 07
10	07 56	16 20	07 19	17 10	06 25	17 57	05 18	18 46	04 21	19 32	03 51	20 08
11	07 55	16 21	07 18	17 12	06 22	17 59	05 15	18 48	04 20	19 34	03 51	20 09
12	07 55	16 22	07 16	17 13	06 20	18 00	05 13	18 49	04 18	19 35	03 51	20 09
13	07 54	16 24	07 14	17 15	06 18	18 02	05 11	18 51	04 17	19 37	03 50	20 10
14	07 53	16 25	07 12	17 17	06 16	18 03	05 09	18 52	04 15	19 38	03 50	20 10
15	07 53	16 27	07 11	17 18	06 14	18 05	05 07	18 54	04 14	19 39	03 50	20 11
16	07 52	16 28	07 09	17 20	06 12	18 07	05 05	18 55	04 13	19 41	03 50	20 11
17	07 51	16 30	07 07	17 22	06 09	18 08	05 03	18 57	04 11	19 42	03 50	20 12
18	07 50	16 31	07 05	17 24	06 07	18 10	05 01	18 59	04 10	19 44	03 50	20 12
19	07 49	16 33	07 03	17 25	06 05	18 11	04 59	19 00	04 09	19 45	03 50	20 12
20	07 48	16 34	07 01	17 27	06 03	18 13	04 57	19 02	04 08	19 46	03 50	20 13
21	07 47	16 36	06 59	17 29	06 01	18 15	04 55	19 03	04 06	19 48	03 51	20 13
22	07 46	16 38	06 57	17 30	05 58	18 16	04 53	19 05	04 05	19 49	03 51	20 13
23	07 45	16 39	06 55	17 32	05 56	18 18	04 51	19 06	04 04	19 50	03 51	20 13
24	07 44	16 41	06 53	17 34	05 54	18 19	04 49	19 08	04 03	19 51	03 51	20 13
25	07 43	16 43	06 51	17 35	05 52	18 21	04 47	19 09	04 02	19 53	03 52	20 13
26	07 42	16 44	06 49	17 37	05 50	18 22	04 45	19 11	04 01	19 54	03 52	20 13
27	07 40	16 46	06 47	17 39	05 48	18 24	04 44	19 13	04 00	19 55	03 53	20 13
28	07 39	16 48	06 45	17 41	05 45	18 26	04 42	19 14	03 59	19 56	03 53	20 13
29	07 38	16 49			05 43	18 27	04 40	19 16	03 58	19 57	03 54	20 13
30	07 36	16 51			05 41	18 29	04 38	19 17	03 57	19 58	03 54	20 13
31	07 35	16 53			05 39	18 30			03 57	19 59		

	JULY		**AUGUST**		**SEPTEMBER**		**OCTOBER**		**NOVEMBER**		**DECEMBER**	
1	03 55	20 12	04 29	19 42	05 15	18 44	06 00	17 38	06 50	16 37	07 37	16 01
2	03 56	20 12	04 31	19 41	05 16	18 42	06 01	17 36	06 51	16 35	07 38	16 01
3	03 56	20 12	04 32	19 39	05 18	18 40	06 03	17 34	06 53	16 33	07 39	16 00
4	03 57	20 11	04 33	19 38	05 19	18 38	06 05	17 32	06 55	16 32	07 41	16 00
5	03 58	20 11	04 35	19 36	05 21	18 35	06 06	17 30	06 56	16 30	07 42	15 59
6	03 59	20 10	04 36	19 34	05 22	18 33	06 08	17 28	06 58	16 29	07 43	15 59
7	03 59	20 10	04 38	19 33	05 24	18 31	06 09	17 25	07 00	16 27	07 44	15 59
8	04 00	20 09	04 39	19 31	05 25	18 29	06 11	17 23	07 01	16 26	07 45	15 58
9	04 01	20 09	04 41	19 29	05 27	18 27	06 12	17 21	07 03	16 24	07 46	15 58
10	04 02	20 08	04 42	19 27	05 28	18 25	06 14	17 19	07 05	16 23	07 47	15 58
11	04 03	20 07	04 44	19 26	05 30	18 22	06 16	17 17	07 06	16 21	07 48	15 58
12	04 04	20 06	04 45	19 24	05 31	18 20	06 17	17 15	07 08	16 20	07 49	15 58
13	04 05	20 06	04 47	19 22	05 33	18 18	06 19	17 13	07 10	16 18	07 50	15 58
14	04 06	20 05	04 48	19 20	05 34	18 16	06 20	17 11	07 11	16 17	07 51	15 58
15	04 07	20 04	04 50	19 18	05 36	18 14	06 22	17 09	07 13	16 16	07 52	15 58
16	04 09	20 03	04 51	19 16	05 37	18 11	06 23	17 07	07 14	16 15	07 53	15 59
17	04 10	20 02	04 53	19 14	05 39	18 09	06 25	17 05	07 16	16 13	07 54	15 59
18	04 11	20 01	04 54	19 13	05 40	18 07	06 27	17 03	07 18	16 12	07 54	15 59
19	04 12	20 00	04 56	19 11	05 42	18 05	06 28	17 01	07 19	16 11	07 55	15 59
20	04 13	19 59	04 57	19 09	05 43	18 03	06 30	16 59	07 21	16 10	07 55	16 00
21	04 15	19 57	04 59	19 07	05 45	18 00	06 32	16 57	07 22	16 09	07 56	16 00
22	04 16	19 56	05 00	19 05	05 46	17 58	06 33	16 55	07 24	16 08	07 56	16 01
23	04 17	19 55	05 01	19 03	05 48	17 56	06 35	16 53	07 25	16 07	07 57	16 01
24	04 18	19 54	05 03	19 01	05 49	17 54	06 36	16 51	07 27	16 06	07 57	16 02
25	04 20	19 52	05 04	18 59	05 51	17 51	06 38	16 49	07 28	16 05	07 58	16 03
26	04 21	19 51	05 06	18 56	05 52	17 49	06 40	16 47	07 30	16 04	07 58	16 03
27	04 22	19 50	05 07	18 54	05 54	17 47	06 41	16 46	07 31	16 04	07 58	16 04
28	04 24	19 48	05 09	18 52	05 55	17 45	06 43	16 44	07 33	16 03	07 58	16 05
29	04 25	19 47	05 10	18 50	05 57	17 43	06 45	16 42	07 34	16 02	07 58	16 06
30	04 26	19 45	05 12	18 48	05 58	17 41	06 46	16 40	07 35	16 02	07 59	16 07
31	04 28	19 44	05 13	18 46			06 48	16 39			07 59	16 08

NAVIGATION

50°N 00°E/W. Times are UT - for DST add 1 hour in non-shaded areas
2005 Moonrise and Moonset Time

The times are based on **LAT 50°00'N   LONG 0°00'W** - add 4 min for every degree West and subtract 4 min for every degree East

	JANUARY Rise h m	JANUARY Set h m	FEBRUARY Rise h m	FEBRUARY Set h m	MARCH Rise h m	MARCH Set h m	APRIL Rise h m	APRIL Set h m	MAY Rise h m	MAY Set h m	JUNE Rise h m	JUNE Set h m
1	22 13	11 09	** **	10 08	** **	08 31	01 58	08 53	02 16	10 39	01 35	13 58
2	23 25	11 22	01 00	10 26	00 10	08 52	02 57	10 03	02 40	12 06	01 48	15 16
3	** **	11 34	02 23	10 49	01 33	09 21	03 41	11 25	02 58	13 30	02 02	16 33
4	00 39	11 48	03 47	11 23	02 53	10 02	04 12	12 53	03 13	14 51	02 18	17 51
5	01 56	12 04	05 08	12 12	04 05	11 01	04 34	14 21	03 27	16 10	02 38	19 08
6	03 19	12 24	06 16	13 21	05 00	12 18	04 51	15 46	03 40	17 29	03 04	20 20
7	04 46	12 53	07 07	14 47	05 40	13 46	05 06	17 08	03 55	18 48	03 38	21 24
8	06 13	13 34	07 43	16 19	06 08	15 17	05 20	18 29	04 12	20 07	04 24	22 16
9	07 32	14 35	08 08	17 52	06 29	16 46	05 34	19 50	04 34	21 24	05 20	22 55
10	08 33	15 54	08 27	19 20	06 46	18 12	05 50	21 10	05 03	22 34	06 26	23 24
11	09 17	17 26	08 42	20 43	07 01	19 35	06 09	22 29	05 41	23 34	07 36	23 45
12	09 46	18 58	08 57	22 04	07 15	20 56	06 33	23 43	06 31	** **	08 47	** **
13	10 08	20 26	09 11	23 22	07 30	22 16	07 05	** **	07 31	00 21	09 58	00 02
14	10 24	21 49	09 26	** **	07 47	23 35	07 48	00 49	08 39	00 56	11 08	00 16
15	10 39	23 08	09 44	00 39	08 08	** **	08 42	01 43	09 50	01 22	12 18	00 28
16	10 52	** **	10 07	01 54	08 35	00 50	09 46	02 25	11 01	01 41	13 30	00 40
17	11 06	00 25	10 37	03 06	09 11	02 00	10 55	02 56	12 13	01 57	14 46	00 53
18	11 22	01 40	11 17	04 12	09 58	03 01	12 07	03 19	13 24	02 10	16 06	01 07
19	11 42	02 54	12 07	05 07	10 55	03 49	13 19	03 36	14 37	02 22	17 31	01 25
20	12 06	04 07	13 08	05 51	12 02	04 26	14 32	03 51	15 52	02 35	18 58	01 50
21	12 39	05 16	14 17	06 24	13 12	04 53	15 44	04 04	17 11	02 48	20 20	02 26
22	13 22	06 18	15 28	06 49	14 25	05 14	16 59	04 16	18 35	03 04	21 26	03 19
23	14 16	07 10	16 41	07 08	15 38	05 31	18 16	04 29	20 02	03 25	22 14	04 32
24	15 20	07 50	17 53	07 23	16 50	05 44	19 37	04 43	21 28	03 55	22 46	06 00
25	16 29	08 20	19 05	07 37	18 04	05 57	21 02	05 01	22 42	04 38	23 09	07 32
26	17 41	08 43	20 18	07 49	19 19	06 09	22 28	05 25	23 38	05 39	23 27	09 01
27	18 53	09 01	21 32	08 01	20 36	06 22	23 48	05 58	** **	06 57	23 42	10 26
28	20 04	09 16	22 49	08 15	21 57	06 38	** **	06 47	00 18	08 24	23 55	11 47
29	21 15	09 29			23 21	06 57	00 54	07 53	00 45	09 53	** **	13 06
30	22 27	09 41			** **	07 23	01 42	09 13	01 05	11 18	00 09	14 23
31	23 42	09 54			00 43	08 00			01 21	12 40		

	JULY Rise h m	JULY Set h m	AUGUST Rise h m	AUGUST Set h m	SEPTEMBER Rise h m	SEPTEMBER Set h m	OCTOBER Rise h m	OCTOBER Set h m	NOVEMBER Rise h m	NOVEMBER Set h m	DECEMBER Rise h m	DECEMBER Set h m
1	00 24	15 41	00 17	18 09	02 14	18 21	03 34	17 11	06 06	16 08	07 47	15 23
2	00 43	16 57	01 06	18 55	03 26	18 38	04 44	17 23	07 25	16 26	09 07	16 08
3	01 06	18 10	02 07	19 30	04 37	18 51	05 55	17 34	08 48	16 51	10 15	17 11
4	01 38	19 16	03 14	19 55	05 47	19 03	07 08	17 47	10 09	17 27	11 07	18 31
5	02 19	20 12	04 25	20 14	06 57	19 14	08 24	18 02	11 24	18 17	11 43	19 59
6	03 13	20 54	05 37	20 30	08 07	19 26	09 43	18 22	12 25	19 25	12 08	21 27
7	04 16	21 26	06 47	20 43	09 20	19 39	11 04	18 49	13 09	20 46	12 27	22 53
8	05 25	21 50	07 56	20 54	10 35	19 55	12 22	19 28	13 40	22 13	12 42	** **
9	06 36	22 08	09 05	21 06	11 54	20 17	13 32	20 23	14 03	23 40	12 56	00 15
10	07 46	22 22	10 16	21 18	13 15	20 47	14 28	21 34	14 21	** **	13 10	01 36
11	08 56	22 35	11 29	21 32	14 32	21 30	15 08	22 59	14 35	01 04	13 25	02 56
12	10 05	22 47	12 46	21 50	15 39	22 32	15 36	** **	14 49	02 27	13 42	04 17
13	11 15	22 58	14 07	22 14	16 31	23 51	15 57	00 28	15 03	03 49	14 05	05 38
14	12 27	23 11	15 29	22 50	17 07	** **	16 14	01 56	15 19	05 12	14 35	06 57
15	13 43	23 27	16 46	23 42	17 33	01 21	16 29	03 23	15 38	06 35	15 15	08 10
16	15 04	23 48	17 50	** **	17 53	02 54	16 43	04 48	16 04	07 58	16 09	09 11
17	16 29	** **	18 36	00 53	18 09	04 25	16 58	06 13	16 38	09 16	17 13	09 58
18	17 52	00 17	19 09	02 21	18 24	05 53	17 15	07 38	17 23	10 26	18 23	10 32
19	19 06	01 01	19 32	03 55	18 38	07 19	17 37	09 02	18 21	11 21	19 35	10 57
20	20 03	02 04	19 50	05 29	18 54	08 44	18 06	10 24	19 28	12 03	20 46	11 15
21	20 43	03 26	20 06	06 59	19 13	10 08	18 44	11 38	20 39	12 33	21 56	11 30
22	21 10	04 59	20 20	08 26	19 38	11 30	19 35	12 41	21 51	12 54	23 05	11 42
23	21 31	06 33	20 35	09 49	20 10	12 47	20 36	13 30	23 02	13 11	** **	11 54
24	21 47	08 03	20 51	11 11	20 52	13 56	21 45	14 06	** **	13 25	00 13	12 05
25	22 01	09 29	21 12	12 32	21 47	14 57	22 56	14 31	00 11	13 37	01 24	12 17
26	22 15	10 51	21 38	13 50	22 51	15 34	** **	14 51	01 21	13 48	02 37	12 32
27	22 30	12 11	22 14	15 03	** **	16 05	00 08	15 06	02 31	14 00	03 55	12 51
28	22 48	13 30	23 00	16 05	00 01	16 28	01 19	15 19	03 44	14 13	05 18	13 17
29	23 09	14 47	23 58	16 55	01 12	16 45	02 29	15 30	05 02	14 29	06 40	13 55
30	23 38	16 02	** **	17 33	02 24	16 59	03 39	15 42	06 23	14 51	07 56	14 51
31	** **	17 11	01 04	18 01			04 51	15 54			08 56	16 05

55°N 00°E/W. Times are UT - for DST add 1 hour in non-shaded areas

2005 Sunrise and Sunset Time

The times are based on **LAT 55°00′N   LONG 0°** - add 4 min for every degree West and subtract 4 min for every degree East

	Rise h m	Set h m	Rise h m	Set h m	Rise h m	Set h m	Rise h m	Set h m	Rise h m	Set h m	Rise h m	Set h m
	JANUARY		FEBRUARY		MARCH		APRIL		MAY		JUNE	
1	08 25	15 43	07 51	16 37	06 50	17 36	05 32	18 37	04 20	19 36	03 29	20 28
2	08 25	15 44	07 49	16 39	06 47	17 38	05 29	18 39	04 18	19 37	03 28	20 29
3	08 24	15 45	07 47	16 41	06 45	17 40	05 27	18 41	04 16	19 39	03 27	20 30
4	08 24	15 46	07 45	16 44	06 43	17 42	05 24	18 43	04 14	19 41	03 26	20 31
5	08 23	15 48	07 43	16 46	06 40	17 44	05 22	18 45	04 11	19 43	03 25	20 33
6	08 23	15 49	07 41	16 48	06 38	17 46	05 19	18 47	04 09	19 45	03 24	20 34
7	08 22	15 51	07 39	16 50	06 35	17 48	05 17	18 49	04 07	19 47	03 24	20 35
8	08 22	15 52	07 37	16 52	06 33	17 50	05 14	18 51	04 05	19 49	03 23	20 36
9	08 21	15 54	07 35	16 54	06 30	17 52	05 12	18 53	04 03	19 51	03 22	20 37
10	08 20	15 55	07 33	16 56	06 28	17 54	05 09	18 55	04 01	19 53	03 22	20 37
11	08 19	15 57	07 31	16 58	06 25	17 56	05 07	18 57	04 00	19 54	03 21	20 38
12	08 19	15 59	07 29	17 00	06 23	17 58	05 04	18 59	03 58	19 56	03 21	20 39
13	08 18	16 00	07 27	17 03	06 20	18 00	05 02	19 01	03 56	19 58	03 21	20 40
14	08 17	16 02	07 25	17 05	06 18	18 02	04 59	19 02	03 54	20 00	03 21	20 40
15	08 16	16 04	07 22	17 07	06 15	18 04	04 57	19 04	03 52	20 02	03 20	20 41
16	08 15	16 06	07 20	17 09	06 12	18 06	04 54	19 06	03 51	20 03	03 20	20 41
17	08 13	16 07	07 18	17 11	06 10	18 08	04 52	19 08	03 49	20 05	03 20	20 42
18	08 12	16 09	07 16	17 13	06 07	18 10	04 50	19 10	03 47	20 07	03 20	20 42
19	08 11	16 11	07 13	17 15	06 05	18 12	04 47	19 12	03 46	20 08	03 20	20 43
20	08 10	16 13	07 11	17 17	06 02	18 14	04 45	19 14	03 44	20 10	03 20	20 43
21	08 08	16 15	07 09	17 19	06 00	18 16	04 42	19 16	03 42	20 12	03 20	20 43
22	08 07	16 17	07 07	17 21	05 57	18 18	04 40	19 18	03 41	20 13	03 21	20 43
23	08 06	16 19	07 04	17 23	05 55	18 20	04 38	19 20	03 39	20 15	03 21	20 43
24	08 04	16 21	07 02	17 25	05 52	18 22	04 36	19 22	03 38	20 17	03 21	20 43
25	08 02	16 23	06 59	17 28	05 50	18 23	04 33	19 24	03 37	20 18	03 22	20 43
26	08 01	16 25	06 57	17 30	05 47	18 25	04 31	19 26	03 35	20 20	03 22	20 43
27	07 59	16 27	06 55	17 32	05 44	18 27	04 29	19 28	03 34	20 21	03 23	20 43
28	07 58	16 29	06 52	17 34	05 42	18 29	04 26	19 30	03 33	20 22	03 23	20 43
29	07 56	16 31			05 39	18 31	04 24	19 32	03 32	20 24	03 24	20 42
30	07 54	16 33			05 37	18 33	04 22	19 34	03 31	20 25	03 25	20 42
31	07 52	16 35			05 34	18 35			03 30	20 27		

	JULY		AUGUST		SEPTEMBER		OCTOBER		NOVEMBER		DECEMBER	
1	03 26	20 42	04 09	20 03	05 06	18 52	06 02	17 36	07 04	16 23	08 01	15 37
2	03 26	20 41	04 11	20 01	05 08	18 50	06 04	17 33	07 06	16 21	08 03	15 36
3	03 27	20 41	04 12	19 59	05 10	18 47	06 06	17 31	07 08	16 19	08 04	15 35
4	03 28	20 40	04 14	19 57	05 12	18 45	06 08	17 28	07 10	16 16	08 06	15 35
5	03 29	20 39	04 16	19 55	05 14	18 42	06 10	17 26	07 12	16 15	08 07	15 34
6	03 30	20 39	04 18	19 53	05 16	18 40	06 12	17 23	07 14	16 13	08 09	15 33
7	03 31	20 38	04 20	19 51	05 17	18 37	06 14	17 21	07 16	16 11	08 10	15 33
8	03 32	20 37	04 21	19 48	05 19	18 35	06 16	17 18	07 18	16 09	08 11	15 32
9	03 33	20 36	04 23	19 46	05 21	18 32	06 18	17 16	07 20	16 07	08 12	15 32
10	03 35	20 35	04 25	19 44	05 23	18 30	06 20	17 13	07 22	16 05	08 14	15 32
11	03 36	20 34	04 27	19 42	05 25	18 27	06 22	17 11	07 24	16 03	08 15	15 32
12	03 37	20 33	04 29	19 40	05 27	18 24	06 24	17 08	07 26	16 02	08 16	15 31
13	03 38	20 32	04 31	19 38	05 29	18 22	06 26	17 06	07 28	16 00	08 17	15 31
14	03 40	20 31	04 33	19 35	05 30	18 19	06 28	17 03	07 30	15 58	08 18	15 31
15	03 41	20 30	04 34	19 33	05 32	18 17	06 30	17 01	07 32	15 57	08 19	15 31
16	03 43	20 29	04 36	19 31	05 34	18 14	06 31	16 59	07 34	15 55	08 20	15 32
17	03 44	20 27	04 38	19 29	05 36	18 12	06 33	16 56	07 36	15 53	08 21	15 32
18	03 46	20 26	04 40	19 26	05 38	18 09	06 35	16 54	07 38	15 52	08 21	15 32
19	03 47	20 24	04 42	19 24	05 40	18 07	06 37	16 52	07 40	15 50	08 22	15 32
20	03 49	20 23	04 44	19 22	05 42	18 04	06 39	16 49	07 42	15 49	08 23	15 33
21	03 50	20 22	04 46	19 19	05 44	18 01	06 41	16 47	07 44	15 48	08 23	15 33
22	03 52	20 20	04 48	19 17	05 45	17 59	06 43	16 45	07 46	15 46	08 24	15 34
23	03 53	20 18	04 49	19 14	05 47	17 56	06 45	16 42	07 47	15 45	08 24	15 34
24	03 55	20 17	04 51	19 12	05 49	17 54	06 47	16 40	07 49	15 44	08 24	15 35
25	03 57	20 15	04 53	19 10	05 51	17 51	06 50	16 38	07 51	15 43	08 25	15 36
26	03 58	20 14	04 55	19 07	05 53	17 49	06 52	16 36	07 53	15 41	08 25	15 36
27	04 00	20 12	04 57	19 05	05 55	17 46	06 54	16 33	07 54	15 40	08 25	15 37
28	04 02	20 10	04 59	19 02	05 57	17 43	06 56	16 31	07 56	15 39	08 25	15 38
29	04 03	20 08	05 01	19 00	05 59	17 41	06 58	16 29	07 58	15 38	08 25	15 39
30	04 05	20 06	05 02	18 57	06 00	17 38	07 00	16 27	07 59	15 38	08 25	15 40
31	04 07	20 05	05 04	18 55			07 02	16 25			08 25	15 41

NAVIGATION

55°N 00°E/W. Times are UT - for DST add 1 hour in non-shaded areas
2005 Moonrise and Moonset Time

The times are based on LAT 55°00'N LONG 0° - add 4 min for every degree West and subtract 4 min for every degree East

	Rise h m	Set h m	Rise h m	Set h m	Rise h m	Set h m	Rise h m	Set h m	Rise h m	Set h m	Rise h m	Set h m
	JANUARY		FEBRUARY		MARCH		APRIL		MAY		JUNE	
1	22 06	11 18	** **	09 55	** **	08 13	02 41	08 09	02 44	10 12	01 36	14 00
2	23 24	11 25	01 18	10 06	00 34	08 27	03 39	09 21	03 00	11 48	01 43	15 25
3	** **	11 32	02 49	10 22	02 05	08 47	04 15	10 52	03 11	13 19	01 51	16 49
4	00 45	11 39	04 22	10 47	03 34	09 21	04 37	12 29	03 19	14 48	02 00	18 14
5	02 09	11 49	05 50	11 30	04 48	10 18	04 52	14 05	03 27	16 14	02 13	19 39
6	03 40	12 02	06 59	12 39	05 40	11 39	05 02	15 38	03 34	17 40	02 31	20 58
7	05 16	12 22	07 43	14 12	06 11	13 16	05 10	17 08	03 42	19 06	02 59	22 06
8	06 52	12 55	08 09	15 54	06 31	14 56	05 17	18 36	03 52	20 33	03 41	22 57
9	08 15	13 52	08 26	17 36	06 44	16 34	05 25	20 04	04 07	21 57	04 40	23 31
10	09 13	15 16	08 37	19 12	06 53	18 08	05 34	21 31	04 28	23 14	05 51	23 53
11	09 47	16 56	08 46	20 43	07 01	19 38	05 46	22 58	05 01	** **	07 08	** **
12	10 08	18 38	08 54	22 10	07 09	21 06	06 02	** **	05 48	00 16	08 26	00 08
13	10 22	20 15	09 02	23 35	07 17	22 33	06 28	00 20	06 52	01 01	09 43	00 18
14	10 31	21 45	09 11	** **	07 27	** **	07 06	01 31	08 06	01 30	11 00	00 26
15	10 40	23 11	09 22	01 00	07 41	00 00	08 00	02 26	09 24	01 49	12 16	00 33
16	10 47	** **	09 38	02 23	08 01	01 23	09 08	03 03	10 43	02 01	13 35	00 39
17	10 55	00 34	10 01	03 42	08 31	02 40	10 25	03 27	12 01	02 11	14 57	00 46
18	11 05	01 56	10 36	04 52	09 15	03 43	11 44	03 43	13 19	02 18	16 25	00 54
19	11 17	03 17	11 26	05 49	10 15	04 30	13 04	03 54	14 38	02 24	17 59	01 05
20	11 35	04 37	12 31	06 29	11 27	05 01	14 22	04 02	15 59	02 31	19 35	01 21
21	12 02	05 53	13 45	06 56	12 45	05 22	15 42	04 09	17 26	02 38	21 03	01 49
22	12 41	06 59	15 04	07 14	14 05	05 35	17 03	04 16	18 58	02 47	22 08	02 36
23	13 36	07 50	16 24	07 27	15 25	05 45	18 27	04 22	20 34	03 01	22 48	03 51
24	14 44	08 26	17 43	07 36	16 44	05 53	19 56	04 30	22 08	03 21	23 12	05 26
25	16 00	08 50	19 01	07 43	18 04	06 00	21 29	04 41	23 26	03 57	23 26	07 08
26	17 19	09 06	20 20	07 50	19 25	06 06	23 04	04 56	** **	04 55	23 37	08 46
27	18 38	09 18	21 41	07 56	20 50	06 13	** **	05 22	00 18	06 18	23 45	10 19
28	19 55	09 26	23 05	08 04	22 19	06 22	00 31	06 04	00 49	07 55	23 52	11 47
29	21 13	09 34			23 51	06 34	01 37	07 10	01 07	09 32	** **	13 13
30	22 31	09 40			** **	06 51	02 19	08 37	01 20	11 06	00 00	14 37
31	23 52	09 47			01 22	07 20			01 29	12 35		

	JULY		AUGUST		SEPTEMBER		OCTOBER		NOVEMBER		DECEMBER	
1	00 09	16 02	** **	18 52	01 46	18 44	03 25	17 17	06 20	15 53	08 22	14 47
2	00 20	17 26	00 24	19 35	03 05	18 53	04 41	17 23	07 47	16 04	09 49	15 25
3	00 36	18 46	01 28	20 03	04 23	19 01	05 58	17 29	09 17	16 20	10 59	16 28
4	01 01	19 58	02 42	20 22	05 39	19 07	07 17	17 35	10 48	16 47	11 45	17 54
5	01 38	20 54	04 00	20 34	06 55	19 12	08 40	17 44	12 08	17 33	12 12	19 31
6	02 31	21 32	05 18	20 43	08 12	19 18	10 07	17 56	13 08	18 42	12 29	21 08
7	03 38	21 58	06 35	20 50	09 31	19 25	11 36	18 15	13 45	20 11	12 40	22 42
8	04 54	22 14	07 51	20 56	10 54	19 35	13 03	18 46	14 08	21 47	12 49	** **
9	06 12	22 26	09 06	21 02	12 21	19 48	14 17	19 38	14 22	23 23	12 56	00 12
10	07 30	22 34	10 23	21 09	13 50	20 10	15 09	20 54	14 32	** **	13 03	01 40
11	08 46	22 41	11 43	21 17	15 15	20 47	15 41	22 26	14 40	00 56	13 12	03 07
12	10 02	22 47	13 07	21 27	16 23	21 48	16 01	** **	14 47	02 26	13 22	04 35
13	11 18	22 53	14 37	21 44	17 09	23 13	16 14	00 05	14 55	03 55	13 37	06 05
14	12 36	23 00	16 07	22 11	17 37	** **	16 23	01 42	15 04	05 25	13 59	07 32
15	13 59	23 10	17 30	22 58	17 54	00 52	16 31	03 17	15 15	06 56	14 34	08 51
16	15 28	23 23	18 32	** **	18 06	02 35	16 38	04 50	15 33	08 27	15 26	09 54
17	17 01	23 44	19 11	00 11	18 15	04 14	16 46	06 22	15 59	09 54	16 34	10 37
18	18 33	** **	19 34	01 48	18 23	05 50	16 57	07 54	16 41	11 08	17 51	11 05
19	19 50	00 20	19 49	03 32	18 30	07 24	17 10	09 27	17 39	12 04	19 11	11 23
20	20 42	01 20	19 59	05 15	18 39	08 56	17 31	10 57	18 52	12 40	20 29	11 34
21	21 13	02 48	20 08	06 53	18 51	10 28	18 03	12 19	20 10	13 03	21 45	11 43
22	21 31	04 31	20 15	08 27	19 07	11 59	18 51	13 25	21 30	13 18	23 00	11 49
23	21 43	06 14	20 23	09 58	19 32	13 25	19 56	14 11	22 47	13 28	** **	11 55
24	21 52	07 53	20 33	11 28	20 09	14 43	21 11	14 40	** **	13 35	00 15	12 01
25	22 00	09 26	20 46	12 56	21 04	15 35	22 30	14 59	00 03	13 41	01 31	12 07
26	22 08	10 55	21 05	14 23	22 13	16 13	23 49	15 11	01 18	13 47	02 52	12 16
27	22 16	12 22	21 34	15 42	23 30	16 37	** **	15 20	02 35	13 53	04 17	12 27
28	22 27	13 49	22 17	16 48	** **	16 52	01 06	15 27	03 55	14 00	05 48	12 45
29	22 41	15 14	23 16	17 37	00 49	17 03	02 23	15 33	05 19	14 10	07 19	13 15
30	23 03	16 37	** **	18 09	02 07	17 11	03 39	15 39	06 49	14 24	08 40	14 06
31	23 36	17 51	00 28	18 30			04 58	15 45			09 38	15 25

SPEED, TIME AND DISTANCE (NAUTICAL MILES)

Chapter 1

Time in minutes	Speed in knots										
	1	2	3	4	5	6	7	8	9	10	15	20
1	0.0	0.0	0.1	0.1	0.1	0.1	0.1	0.1	0.2	0.2	0.3	0.3
2	0.0	0.1	0.1	0.1	0.2	0.2	0.2	0.3	0.3	0.3	0.5	0.7
3	0.1	0.1	0.2	0.2	0.3	0.3	0.4	0.4	0.5	0.5	0.8	1.0
4	0.1	0.1	0.2	0.3	0.3	0.4	0.5	0.5	0.6	0.7	1.0	1.3
5	0.1	0.2	0.3	0.3	0.4	0.5	0.6	0.7	0.8	0.8	1.3	1.7
6	0.1	0.2	0.3	0.4	0.5	0.6	0.7	0.8	0.9	1.0	1.5	2.0
7	0.1	0.2	0.4	0.5	0.6	0.7	0.8	0.9	1.1	1.2	1.8	2.3
8	0.1	0.3	0.4	0.5	0.7	0.8	0.9	1.1	1.2	1.3	2.0	2.7
9	0.2	0.3	0.5	0.6	0.8	0.9	1.1	1.2	1.4	1.5	2.3	3.0
10	0.2	0.3	0.5	0.7	0.8	1.0	1.2	1.3	1.5	1.7	2.5	3.3
11	0.2	0.4	0.6	0.7	0.9	1.1	1.3	1.5	1.7	1.8	2.8	3.7
12	0.2	0.4	0.6	0.8	1.0	1.2	1.4	1.6	1.8	2.0	3.0	4.0
13	0.2	0.4	0.7	0.9	1.1	1.3	1.5	1.7	2.0	2.2	3.3	4.3
14	0.2	0.5	0.7	0.9	1.2	1.4	1.6	1.9	2.1	2.3	3.5	4.7
15	0.3	0.5	0.8	1.0	1.3	1.5	1.8	2.0	2.3	2.5	3.8	5.0
16	0.3	0.5	0.8	1.1	1.3	1.6	1.9	2.1	2.4	2.7	4.0	5.3
17	0.3	0.6	0.9	1.1	1.4	1.7	2.0	2.3	2.6	2.8	4.3	5.7
18	0.3	0.6	0.9	1.2	1.5	1.8	2.1	2.4	2.7	3.0	4.5	6.0
19	0.3	0.6	1.0	1.3	1.6	1.9	2.2	2.5	2.9	3.2	4.8	6.3
20	0.3	0.7	1.0	1.3	1.7	2.0	2.3	2.7	3.0	3.3	5.0	6.7
21	0.4	0.7	1.1	1.4	1.8	2.1	2.5	2.8	3.2	3.5	5.3	7.0
22	0.4	0.7	1.1	1.5	1.8	2.2	2.6	2.9	3.3	3.7	5.5	7.3
23	0.4	0.8	1.2	1.5	1.9	2.3	2.7	3.1	3.5	3.8	5.8	7.7
24	0.4	0.8	1.2	1.6	2.0	2.4	2.8	3.2	3.6	4.0	6.0	8.0
25	0.4	0.8	1.3	1.7	2.1	2.5	2.9	3.3	3.8	4.2	6.3	8.3
30	0.5	1.0	1.5	2.0	2.5	3.0	3.5	4.0	4.5	5.0	7.5	10.0
35	0.6	1.2	1.8	2.3	2.9	3.5	4.1	4.7	5.3	5.8	8.8	11.7
40	0.7	1.3	2.0	2.7	3.3	4.0	4.7	5.3	6.0	6.7	10.0	13.3
45	0.8	1.5	2.3	3.0	3.8	4.5	5.3	6.0	6.8	7.5	11.3	15.0
50	0.8	1.7	2.5	3.3	4.2	5.0	5.8	6.7	7.5	8.3	12.5	16.7

NAVIGATION

DISTANCE (NAUTICAL MILES) OFF RISING/DIPPING LIGHTS

Height of light in metres	Height of eye in feet												
		2	3	4	5	6	7	8	9	10	20	30	40	50
	2	4·6	4·9	5·2	5·5	5·7	6·0	6·2	6·4	6·6	8·1	9·2	10·2	11·0
	3	5·2	5·6	5·9	6·2	6·4	6·6	6·8	7·0	7·2	8·7	9·9	10·8	11·7
	4	5·8	6·1	6·4	6·7	6·9	7·2	7·4	7·6	7·8	9·3	10·4	11·4	12·2
	5	6·3	6·6	6·9	7·2	7·4	7·7	7·9	8·1	8·3	9·8	10·9	11·9	12·7
	6	6·7	7·1	7·4	7·6	7·9	8·1	8·3	8·5	8·7	10·2	11·3	12·3	13·2
	7	7·1	7·5	7·8	8·0	8·3	8·5	8·7	8·9	9·1	10·6	11·8	12·7	13·6
	8	7·5	7·8	8·2	8·4	8·7	8·9	9·1	9·3	9·5	11·0	12·1	13·1	14·0
	9	7·8	8·2	8·5	8·8	9·0	9·2	9·5	9·7	9·8	11·3	12·5	13·5	14·3
	10	8·2	8·5	8·8	9·1	9·4	9·6	9·8	10·0	10·2	11·7	12·8	13·8	14·6
	11	8·5	8·9	9·2	9·4	9·7	9·9	10·1	10·3	10·5	12·0	13·1	14·1	15·0
	12	8·8	9·2	9·5	9·7	10·0	10·2	10·4	10·6	10·8	12·3	13·4	14·4	15·3
	13	9·1	9·5	9·8	10·0	10·3	10·5	10·7	10·9	11·1	12·6	13·7	14·7	15·6
	14	9·4	9·7	10·0	10·3	10·6	10·8	11·0	11·2	11·4	12·9	14·0	15·0	15·8
	15	9·6	10·0	10·3	10·6	10·8	11·1	11·3	11·5	11·6	13·1	14·3	15·3	16·1
	16	9·9	10·3	10·6	10·8	11·1	11·3	11·5	11·7	11·9	13·4	14·6	15·5	16·4
	17	10·2	10·5	10·8	11·1	11·3	11·6	11·8	12·0	12·2	13·7	14·8	15·8	16·6
	18	10·4	10·8	11·1	11·4	11·6	11·8	12·0	12·2	12·4	13·9	15·1	16·0	16·9
	19	10·7	11·0	11·3	11·6	11·8	12·1	12·3	12·5	12·7	14·2	15·3	16·3	17·1
	20	10·9	11·3	11·6	11·8	12·1	12·3	12·5	12·7	12·9	14·4	15·5	16·5	17·3
	25	12·0	12·3	12·6	12·9	13·2	13·4	13·6	13·8	14·0	15·5	16·6	17·6	18·4
	30	13·0	13·3	13·6	13·9	14·1	14·4	14·6	14·8	15·0	16·5	17·6	18·6	19·4
	40	14·7	15·1	15·4	15·7	15·9	16·1	16·3	16·5	16·7	18·2	19·4	20·3	21·2
	50	16·3	16·6	16·9	17·2	17·4	17·7	17·9	18·1	18·3	19·8	20·9	21·9	22·7
	60	17·7	18·0	18·3	18·6	18·8	19·1	19·3	19·5	19·7	21·2	22·3	23·3	24·1

Conversion Table

Sq inches to sq millimetres *multiply by* **645.20**	**Sq millimetres to sq inches** *multiply by* **0.0016**
Inches to millimetres *multiply by* **25.40**	**Millimetres to inches** *multiply by* **0.0394**
Sq feet to square metres *multiply by* **0.093**	**Sq metres to sq feet** *multiply by* **10.7640**
Inches to centimetres *multiply by* **2.54**	**Centimetres to inches** *multiply by* **0.3937**
Feet to metres *multiply by* **0.305**	**Metres to feet** *multiply by* **3.2810**
Nautical miles to kilometres *multiply by* **1.852**	**Kilometres to nautical miles** *multiply by* **0.5400**
Statute miles to kilometres *multiply by* **1.609**	**Kilometres to statute miles** *multiply by* **0.6214**
Statute miles to nautical miles *multiply by* **0.8684**	**Nautical miles to statute miles** *multiply by* **1.1515**
HP to metric HP *multiply by* **1.014**	**Metric HP to HP** *multiply by* **0.9862**
Pounds per sq inch to kg per sq centimetre *multiply by* **0.0703**	**Kg per sq centimetre to pounds per sq inch** *multiply by* **14.2200**
HP to kilowatts *multiply by* **0.746**	**Kilowatts to HP** *multiply by* **1.341**
Cu inches to cu centimetres *multiply by* **16.39**	**Cu centimetres to cu inches** *multiply by* **0.0610**
Imperial gallons to litres *multiply by* **4.540**	**Litres to imperial gallons** *multiply by* **0.2200**
Pints to litres *multiply by* **0.5680**	**Litres to pints** *multiply by* **1.7600**
Pounds to kilogrammes *multiply by* **0.4536**	**Kilogrammes to pounds** *multiply by* **2.2050**

WEATHER

CHAPTER 2 - WEATHER

CONTENTS

Beaufort scale & Met terminology	67
Map of UK shipping forecast areas	68
Shipping forecast record	69
Weather sources in the UK	
BBC Radio 4 broadcasts	70
BBC local radio station broadcasts	71
Navtex	73
Telephone recordings	75
Fax messages	76
Mobile phones	77
Other sources	78
Broadcasts by HM Coastguard	78
Weather sources abroad	
Channel Islands	81
Ireland	82
Denmark	83
Germany	84
Netherlands	85
Belgium	86
France	86
North and North West Spain	89
Portugal	91
South West Spain	91
Gibraltar	92
Five language weather glossary	92

Beaufort scale

Force	Wind speed (knots)	(km/h)	(m/sec)	Description	State of sea	Probable wave ht(m)
0	0–1	0–2	0–0.5	Calm	Like a mirror	0
1	1–3	2–6	0.5–1.5	Light airs	Ripples like scales are formed	0
2	4–6	7–11	2–3	Light breeze	Small wavelets, still short but more pronounced, not breaking	0.1
3	7–10	13–19	4–5	Gentle breeze	Large wavelets, crests begin to break; a few white horses	0.4
4	11–16	20–30	6–8	Moderate breeze	Small waves growing longer; fairly frequent white horses	1
5	17–21	31–39	8–11	Fresh breeze	Moderate waves, taking more pronounced form; many white horses, perhaps some spray	2
6	22–27	41–50	11–14	Strong breeze	Large waves forming; white foam crests more extensive; probably some spray	3
7	28–33	52–61	14–17	Near gale	Sea heaps up; white foam from breaking waves begins to blow in streaks	4
8	34–40	63–74	17–21	Gale	Moderately high waves of greater length; edge of crests break into spindrift; foam blown in well-marked streaks	5.5

Terms used in weather bulletins

a. Speed of movement of pressure systems

Slowly: Moving at less than 15 knots
Steadily: Moving at 15 to 25 knots
Rather quickly: Moving at 25 to 35 knots
Rapidly: Moving at 35 to 45 knots
Very rapidly: Moving at more than 45 knots

b. Visibility

Good: More than 5 miles
Moderate: 2 – 5 miles
Poor: 1000 metres – 2 miles
Fog: Less than 1000 metres

c. Barometric pressure changes (tendency)

Rising or falling slowly: Pressure change of 0.1 to 1.5 millibars in the preceding 3 hours.

Rising or falling: Pressure change of 1.6 to 3.5 millibars in the preceding 3 hours.

Rising or falling quickly: Pressure change of 3.6 to 6 millibars in the preceding 3 hours.

Rising or falling very rapidly: Pressure change of more than 6 millibars in the preceding 3 hours.

Now rising (or falling): Pressure has been falling (rising) or steady in the preceding 3 hours, but at the time of observation was definitely rising (falling).

d. Gale warnings

A '**Gale**' warning means that winds of at least force 8 (34-40 knots) or gusts reaching 43-51 knots are expected somewhere within the area, but not necessarily over the whole area. '**Severe Gale**' means winds of at least force 9 (41-47 knots) or gusts reaching 52-60 knots. '**Storm**' means winds of force 10 (48-55 knots) or gusts of 61-68 knots. '**Violent Storm**' means winds of force 11 (56-63 kn) or gusts of 69 kn or more; and '**Hurricane Force**' means winds of force 12 (64 knots or more).

Gale warnings remain in force until amended or cancelled ('gales now ceased'). If a gale persists for more than 24 hours the warning is re-issued.

e. Timing of gale warnings

Imminent Within 6 hrs of time of issue
Soon Within 6 – 12 hrs of time of issue
Later More than 12 hrs from time of issue

f. Strong wind warnings

Issued, if possible 6 hrs in advance, when winds F6 or more are expected up to 5M offshore; valid for 12 hrs.

g. Wind

Wind direction: Indicates the direction from which the wind is blowing.

Winds becoming cyclonic: Indicates that there will be considerable changes in wind direction across the path of a depression within the forecast area.

Veering: The changing of the wind in a clockwise direction, i.e. SW to W.

Backing: The changing of the wind in an anti-clockwise direction, i.e. W to SW.

WEATHER

MAP OF UK SHIPPING FORECAST AREAS

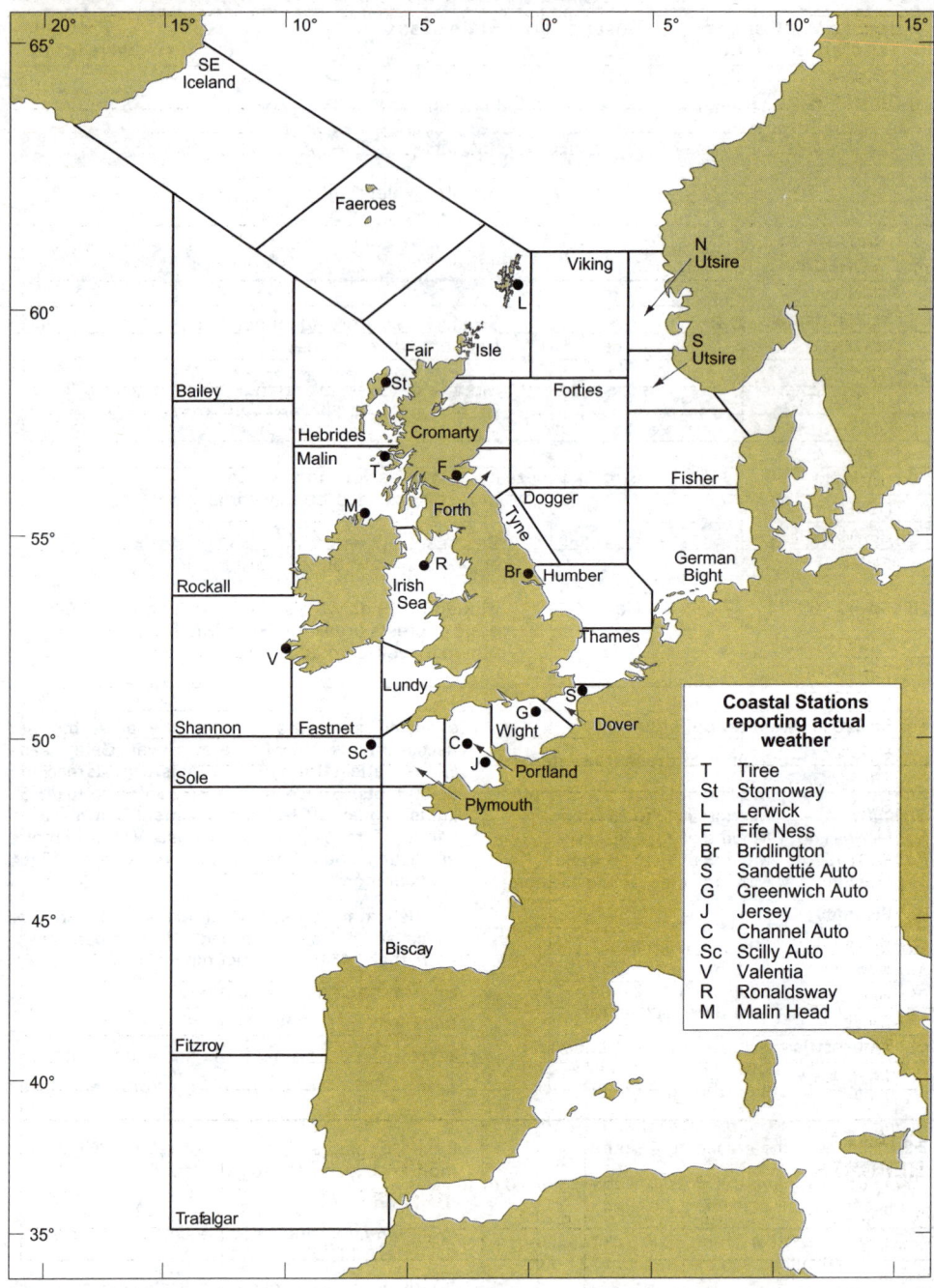

SHIPPING FORECAST RECORD   Time/Day/Date ....

GENERAL SYNOPSIS   at .... UT/BST

System position	Present position at	Movement	Forecast	

Gales	SEA AREA FORECAST	Wind (At first)	Wind (Later)	Weather	Visibility
	VIKING				
	NORTH UTSIRE				
	SOUTH UTSIRE				
	FORTIES				
	CROMARTY				
	FORTH				
	TYNE				
	DOGGER				
	FISHER				
	GERMAN BIGHT				
	HUMBER				
	THAMES				
	DOVER				
	WIGHT				
	PORTLAND				
	PLYMOUTH				
	BISCAY				
	FITZROY				
	TRAFALGAR				
	SOLE				
	LUNDY				
	FASTNET				
	IRISH SEA				
	SHANNON				
	ROCKALL				
	MALIN				
	HEBRIDES				
	BAILEY				
	FAIR ISLE				
	FAEROES				
	S E ICELAND				

COASTAL REPORTS at .... BST UTC	Wind Direction	Wind Force	Weather	Visibility	Pressure	Change	COASTAL REPORTS	Wind Direction	Wind Force	Weather	Visibility	Pressure	Change
Tiree (T)							Greenwich Lt V (G)						
Stornoway (St)							Jersey (J)						
Lerwick (L)							Channel auto (C)						
Fife Ness (F)							Scilly auto (Sc)						
Bridlington (Br)							Valentia (V)						
Sandettie auto (S)							Ronaldsway (R)						

Chapter 2

WEATHER

WEATHER SOURCES IN THE UK

RADIO BROADCASTING

1. **Shipping forecasts** are broadcast by BBC Radio 4 at the following local times:

0048[1]		LW, MW, FM
0536[1]		LW, MW, FM
1201		LW only
1754		LW, FM (Sat/Sun)

[1] Followed by the forecast for Inshore waters and weather reports from coastal stations.

The **bands/frequencies** used are:

LW	198 kHz
MW	
Newcastle:	603 kHz
Crystal Palace, Lisnagarvey and Londonderry:	720 kHz
Redruth:	756 kHz
Enniskillen & Plymouth:	774 kHz;
Aberdeen (Redmoss):	1449 kHz
Carlisle:	1485 kHz
FM	92·4-105 MHz

Contents of the shipping forecast
The forecast contains:
a. summary of gale warnings in force. (Gale warnings are also broadcast at the earliest break in Radio 4 programmes after receipt, and after the next news bulletin).
b. general synopsis for the next 24 hours with changes expected during that period; and
c. forecast for each sea area for the next 24 hours, giving wind direction and force, weather and visibility. Sea area **Trafalgar** is included only in the 0048 forecast.

2. **Weather reports from coastal stations** follow the 0048 and 0535 shipping forecasts, but not those at 1201 and 1754.

The reporting stations are: Tiree, Stornoway, Lerwick, Fife Ness, Bridlington, Sandettie*, Greenwich Lt V*, Jersey, Channel Lt V*, Scilly*, Valentia, Ronaldsway, Malin Head. * Automatic station.

They are shown on the shipping forecast map and a block is provided for their contents. These reports include wind direction and Beaufort force, present weather, visibility, and sea-level pressure and tendency (if available).

Shipping forecasts cover large sea areas and cannot readily include the detailed variations that may occur inshore. If coasting, the Inshore waters forecast (see next column) may be more helpful.

3. **Inshore waters forecast, BBC Radio 4**
The inshore waters forecast (up to 12M offshore around the UK and N Ireland) is broadcast after the 0048 and 0535 forecasts at approx 0053 and 0539 respectively. It is valid until 2359 on the day of issue and includes a general synopsis, forecasts of wind direction and force, visibility and weather.

It covers 9 stretches of inshore waters defined by places and headlands: clockwise from Duncansby Head via Berwick-upon-Tweed, Whitby, North Foreland, St Catherine's Pt, Land's End, Colwyn Bay, Mull of Kintyre (inc L. Foyle to Carlingford Lough), Cape Wrath, Orkney and Shetland.

4. After the 0048 inshore waters forecast, reports are broadcast of **actual weather** at: Boulmer, *Bridlington*, Sheerness, St Catherine's Point*, *Scilly**, Milford Haven, Aberporth, Valley, Liverpool (Crosby), *Ronaldsway*, Larne, Machrihanish*, Greenock, *Stornoway*, *Lerwick*, Wick*, Aberdeen and Leuchars. * Automatic station.

Stations in italics also feature in the 0048 and 0535 shipping forecasts.

Strong Wind Warnings are issued by the Met Office to HM Coastguard, the BBC and local radio stations. Such warnings are issued whenever winds of Force 6 or more are expected over coastal waters up to 5M offshore. Whenever possible they are issued 6 hrs before the onset of strong winds and cover a period 12 hrs ahead.

5. **BBC general (land) forecasts**
Land area forecasts may include an outlook period up to 48 hours beyond the shipping forecast, more details of frontal systems and weather along the coasts. The most comprehensive land area forecasts are broadcast by BBC Radio 4 at the times of most News bulletins.

Wind strength in land area forecasts
Wind, as described in land area forecasts, equates to the following Beaufort wind forces:

Calm:	0	Fresh:	5
Light:	1–3	Strong:	6–7
Moderate:	4	Gale:	8

Visibility in land area forecasts
Visibility, as described in land forecasts, equates to the following distances:

Mist:	Between 2000m and 1000m
Fog:	Less than 1000m
Dense fog:	Less than 50m.

6. **The UK Met Office** is at: FitzRoy Road, Exeter, Devon EX1 3PB. Tel 0845 300 0300 ;Fax 0845 300 1300. Enquiries@metoffice.com   www.met-office.gov.uk

FORECASTS FROM LOCAL RADIO STATIONS

Many local radio stations broadcast local weather reports and forecasts. This information varies from present conditions to Small Craft Warnings when Force 6 or more winds are expected. Some local and regional BBC radio stations are listed below, but note that broadcast times (LT) tend to be a little approximate and the information is subject to change.

STATIONS +TIMES   **FREQUENCIES**

BBC RADIO CORNWALL   630, 657 kHz, 95.2, 96.0, 103.9 MHz
Shipping   *Coastal Conditions*
Mon - Fri 0645   Mon - Fri 0725, 0825, 1225
Sat 0645   Sat 0725, 0825, 1310
Sun 0845 (*Tides and Shipping*)   Sun 0825
TideTimes   *Inshore waters*
Mon - Fri 0745   Mon - Fri 0610, 0715, 0815, 1030, 1225, 1725
Sat 0745   Sat 0610, 0715, 0815, 0930, 1130, 1310
Sun 0845 (*Tides and Shipping*)   Sun 0705, 0815, 0915, 1305

BBC RADIO DEVON   801, 855, 990, 1458 kHz, 94.8, 95.8, 96.0, 103.4, 104.3 MHz
Shipping Forecast
Mon - Fri 0533, 0633, 0833, 1733
Sat 0645, 0735, 0845
Sun 0633, 0733

BBC RADIO SOLENT   1359, 999 kHz, 96.1, 103.8 MHz
Weather, Shipping Forecast and Tide times
Mon-Fri Approx 0535
Shipping Forecast, Local sea conditions and Tide times
Mon - Fri 0645
Sat 0645, 0745
Sun 0645, 0745
Inshore Waters
Daily from 0630-1830 on every half hour
Shipping Movements
Mon - Fri 0533, 0645, 0845
Sat 0645
Sun 0645
'Solent Sea-Dog'
Mon - Sat 0650
Gunfacts
Tipnor Coastal Gunnery Range & Lulworth Range
Mon - Fri 0535, 0645
Sat - Sun 0745

BBC RADIO KENT   96.7, 97.6, 104.2 MHz
Inshore Forecast, Tide times
Mon - Fri 0633, 0733, 0833, 1230, 1630, 1730, 1830
Inshore Forecast, Tide times
Sat 0733, 0833, 1305
Sun 0633, 0733, 0833, 0933, 1305

BBC RADIO ESSEX   765 kHz, 95.3, 103.5 MHz
Inshore Forecast, Tide times
Mon - Fri 0744, 0844, 1744, 1844
Sat 0744, 0844, 1206, 1306
Sun 0744, 0844

Chapter 2

WEATHER

BBC RADIO SUFFOLK   95.5, 103.9 MHz
Inshore Forecast, Tide Times
Mon - Fri 0700, 0800, 1300, 1700, 1800
Sat - Sun 0600, 0700, 1300

BBC RADIO HUMBERSIDE   95.9 MHz, 1485 kHz
Coastal Forecast
Mon - Fri 0633, 0733, 0833, 1230, 1633, 1833
Sat 0833; Sun 0915

BBC RADIO YORK   95.5 MHz, 1260 kHz (E Coast), 103.7 MHz 666 kHz
(Central), 104.3 MHz (Dales)
Inshore Forecast (Whitby to The Wash)
Mon - Fri 0635, 0735, 0835, 1800
Sat - Sun approx 0630, 0730

BBC RADIO CLEVELAND   95.0 & 95.8 MHz
Inshore Forecast (Hartlepool to Flamborough Hd)
Mon - Fri 0645, 0745, 0845, 1645, 1745, 1845
Sat - Sun 0745, 0845, 0945, 1230* (*Sun only)

BBC RADIO NEWCASTLE   1458 kHz, 95.4, 96.0, 103.7, 104.4 MHz
Inshore Forecast (Berwick to Flamborough Hd) Tide Times
Mon - Fri 0555, 0655, 0755, 0855, 1155, 1255, 1655, 1755
Sat - Sun 0754, 0854, 0954, 1154* (* Sun only)

BBC RADIO SCOTLAND   810 kHz, 92.7 - 94.3 MHz
Daily Weather Forecasts for Scotland
Mon - Fri 0658, 0758, 1258, 2158
Sat - Sun 0758, 1258
Outdoor conditions
Sat - Sun 0658, 1858

BBC RADIO CUMBRIA   95.6, 96.1 MHz
Coastal Forecast
Mon - Fri 0632, 0732, 0832, 1732, 1832
Sat - Sun 0730, 0830

BBC RADIO LANCASHIRE   855, 1557 kHz, 95.5, 103.9, 104.5 MHz
Inshore Waters Forecast
Mon - Fri 0750, 0850
Long Range Weather Forecast
Sun 0805, 1230

BBC RADIO MERSEYSIDE   1485 kHz, 95.8 MHz
Inshore Waters Forecast
Mon - Fri 0700, 0800, 1200, 1300, 1715, 1745
Sat - Sun 0800, 0900, 1200, 1300, 1800

BBC RADIO WALES   657, 882, 1125 kHz, 92.4-94.6, 96.8, 103.5-105 MHz
General Forecast, in English
Mon - Fri 0606, 0658, 0903, 1003, 1150, 1359, 1629*, 1729* (*also includes a weekly outlook)
Sat 0859, 1259, 1759
Sun 0859, 1759

NAVTEX

Navtex uses a dedicated aerial, receiver and integral printer or LCD screen. The user programmes the receiver for the required station(s) and message categories. It automatically prints or displays MSI, ie weather, navigational and safety data.

All messages are transmitted in English on a single frequency of 518 kHz, with excellent coverage of Europe. Interference between stations is avoided by time sharing and by limiting the range of transmitters to about 300M. See the diagram below. Navtex information applies only to the geographic area for which each station is responsible.

A second frequency, *490 kHz (in italics throughout this section)*, is used abroad for transmissions in the national language; in the UK it is used for inshore waters forecasts. *490 kHz* stations use different identification letters to 518 kHz stations.

Weather information accounts for about 75% of all messages and Navtex is particularly valuable when out of range of other sources, or if there is a language problem.

Messages

Each message is prefixed by a four-character group. The first character is the code letter of the transmitting station (eg **E** for Niton). The second character is the message category, see above. The third and fourth are message serial numbers, running from 01 to 99 and then re-starting at 01. The serial number 00 denotes urgent messages which are always printed. Messages which are corrupt or have already been printed are rejected. Weather messages, and certain other message types, are dated and timed. All Navtex messages end with NNNN.

Note: Navareas and Metareas have the same boundaries; in this chapter they are referred to as Metareas. See also the Shipping forecast areas and boundaries for Inshore waters forecasts.

Message categories

A*	Navigational warnings
B*	Meteorological warnings
C	Ice reports
D*	SAR info and Piracy attack warnings
E	Weather forecasts
F	Pilot service
H	Loran-C
J	Satellite navigation
K	Other electronic Navaids
L	Subfacts and Gunfacts for the UK
V	Amplifying navigation warnings initially sent under A; plus weekly oil and gas rig moves
W – Y	Special service – trial allocation
Z	No messages on hand at scheduled time

G, I and **M – U** are not at present allocated

* These categories cannot be rejected by the receiver.

Navtex stations/areas – UK & W Europe

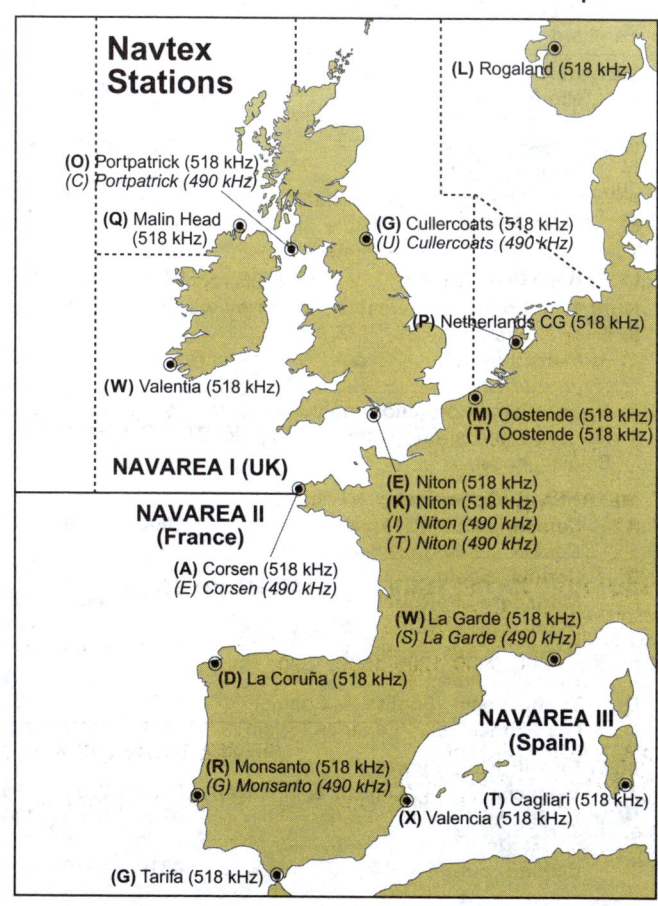

WEATHER

UK 518 kHz stations

The times (UT) of weather messages are in bold; the times of an extended outlook (a further 2 or 3 days beyond the shipping forecast period) are in italics. The Sea Areas covered follow the sequence on page 70.

G –	Cullercoats	*0100*	0500	**0900**	1300	1700	**2100**
	Fair Isle clockwise to Thames, excluding N & S Utsire, Fisher and German Bight.						
O –	Portpatrick	*0220*	**0620**	1020	1420	**1820**	*2220*
	Lundy clockwise to SE Iceland.						
E –	Niton	*0040*	0440	**0840**	1240	1640	**2040**
	Thames clockwise to Fastnet, excluding Trafalgar.						

UK 490 kHz stations

These provide forecasts for the Inshore waters (12M offshore) of the UK, including Shetland, plus a national 3 day outlook for inshore waters. Times are UT.

U –	*Cullercoats* Cape Wrath to North Foreland	0720		1920
C –	*Portpatrick* St David's Head to Cape Wrath	0820		2020
I –	*Niton* The Wash to Colwyn Bay	0520		1720

Navtex coverage abroad

Selected Navtex stations in Metareas I to III, with their identity codes and transmission times, are listed below. Times of weather messages are shown in **bold**. Gale warnings are usually transmitted 4 hourly.

METAREA I (Co-ordinator – UK)		Transmission times (UT)				
K –	Niton (Note 1)	0140	0540	**0940**	1340	1740	2140
T –	Niton (Note 2)	*0310*	**0710**	*1110*	*1510*	**1910**	*2310*
W –	Valentia, Eire	0340	**0740**	1140	1540	**1940**	2340
Q –	Malin Head, Eire	0240	**0640**	1040	1440	**1840**	2240
P –	Netherlands CG, Den Helder	**0230**	0630	1030	**1430**	1830	2230
M –	Oostende, Belgium (Note 3)	0200	0600	1000	1400	1800	2200
T –	Oostende, Belgium (Note 4)	0310	**0710**	1110	1510	**1910**	2310
L –	Rogaland, Norway	**0150**	0550	**0950**	1350	1750	2150

Note 1 In English, no weather; only Nav warnings for the French coast from Cap Gris Nez to Île de Bréhat.
2 In French, weather info (and Nav warnings) for sea areas Humber to Ouessant (Plymouth).
3 No weather information, only Nav warnings for NavArea Juliett.
4 Forecasts and strong wind warnings for Thames and Dover, plus Nav info for the Belgian coast.

METAREA II (Co-ordinator – France)						
A –	*Corsen*, Le Stiff, France	0000	0400	0800	**1200**	1600	2000
E –	*Corsen*, Le Stiff, France (In French)	*0040*	0440	**0840**	*1240*	1640	*2040*
D –	*Coruña*, Spain	0030	0430	**0830**	1230	1630	2030
R –	*Monsanto*, Portugal	0250	**0650**	1050	**1450**	1850	2250
G –	*Monsanto*, Portugal (In Portuguese)	*0100*	**0500**	*0900*	*1300*	**1700**	*2100*
F –	*Horta*, Açores, Portugal	0050	**0450**	**0850**	1250	1650	2050
J –	*Horta*, Açores, (In Portuguese)	*0130*	*0530*	*0930*	*1330*	*1730*	*2130*
G –	*Tarifa*, Spain (English & Spanish)	0100	**0500**	**0900**	1300	1700	2100
I –	*Las Palmas*, Islas Canarias, Spain	0120	0520	**0920**	1320	1720	2120

METAREA III (Co-ordinator – Spain)						
X –	*Valencia*, Spain (English & Spanish)	0350	**0750**	1150	1550	**1950**	2350
W –	*La Garde*, (Toulon), France	0340	**0740**	**1140**	1540	1940	**2340**
S –	*La Garde*, (Toulon), France (In French)	*0300*	**0700**	*1100*	*1500*	**1900**	*2300*
T –	*Cagliari*, Sardinia, Italy	0310	**0710**	1110	1510	**1910**	2310

WEATHER BY TELEPHONE

Marinecall offers 3 types of recorded forecasts as shown below.

5-day forecasts for Inshore waters

For any of 16 UK inshore areas, call **09066 526 + the Area number** shown on the map below. For a National inshore waters forecast for 3 to 5 days dial the suffix 234. 09066 calls cost 60p/min from a landline. Calls from mobiles may be subject to network charges.

Forecasts cover the waters out to 12M offshore for up to 5 days and include: General situation, strong wind or gale warnings in force, wind, weather, visibility, sea state, max air temp and mean sea temp.

The initial 2 day forecast is followed by a forecast for days 3 & 4 and outlook for day 5. Forecasts are updated at 0700 and 1900 daily. Area 250 (Channel Islands) is additionally updated at 1300.

The local inshore forecast for Shetland is only available from Shetland CG on ☎ 01595 692976.

Current weather

Current weather, updated hourly, gives summaries for next 6 hours at over 200 locations around the UK. Dial 09066 526 + the relevant area number shown below – then press 2 and select a location from the menu.

Forecasts for Offshore planning

For 2 to 5-day planning forecasts for offshore areas, updated 0800 daily, call **09066 526** + the number shown on the map), ie: **251** English Channel; **252** Southern North Sea; **253** Irish Sea; **254** Biscay; **255** NW Scotland; **256** Northern North Sea.

Contacting Marinecall

For further information contact: Marinecall Customer Services, iTouch (UK) Ltd, Avalon House, 57-63 Scrutton House, London EC2A 4PF. ☎ 0871 200 3985; 📠 0870 600 4229.
www.marinecall.co.uk
marinecall@itouch.co.uk

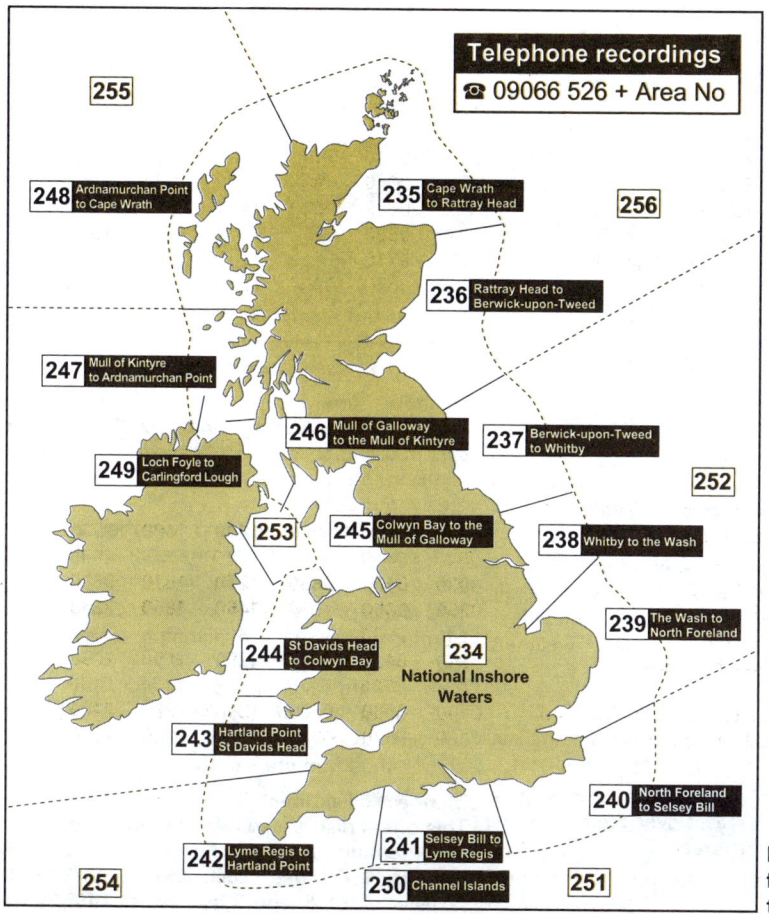

Inshore & offshore forecast areas by telephone

WEATHER

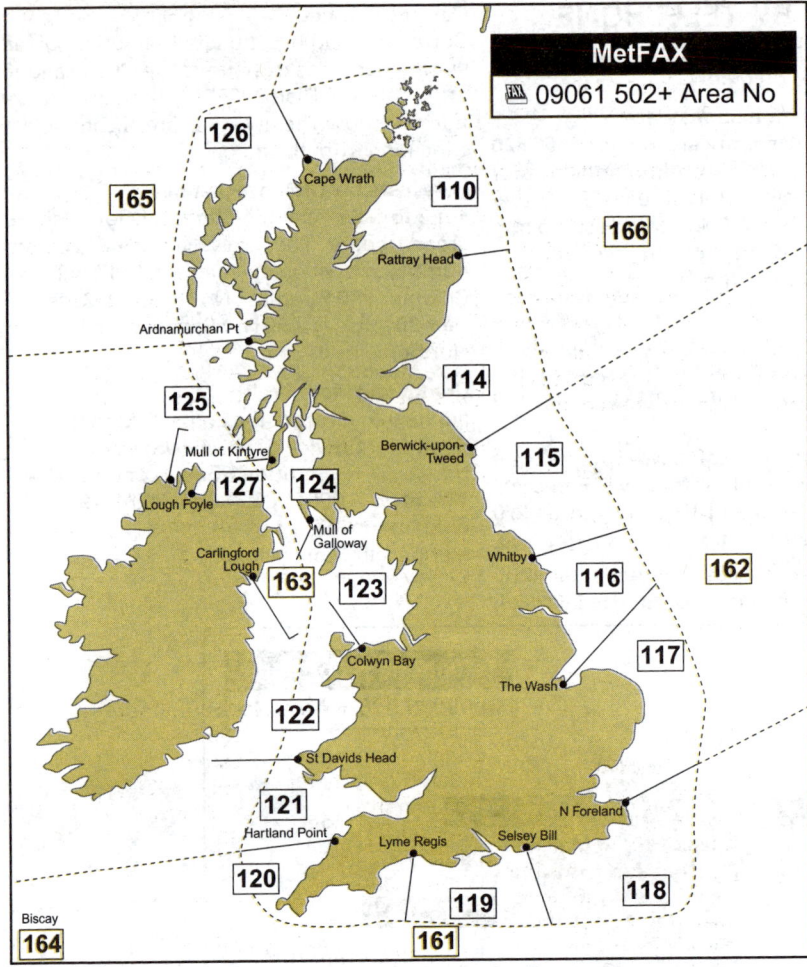

Inshore and Offshore forecast areas and codes by Fax

WEATHER BY FAX
Inshore waters forecasts

These forecasts for up to 48 hrs, plus 2 synoptic charts, are obtained by dialling 09061 502 + the Area No shown above. For a National inshore 3-5 day forecast the suffix is 109.

The forecasts include the general situation; gale and strong wind warnings in force; max air temp; sea temp; wind speed/direction; probability and strength of gusts; weather; visibility; sea state; surf; tidal data.

Two levels of service are available:
Standard, at £1/min, which gives a 48 hrs forecast and synoptic chart for today and tomorrow.
Premium at £1.50/min includes the above, plus a tabulated hourly forecast over the next 6 hrs for 4 key places in the Area.
The Fax numbers above are for the Premium service.

Offshore forecasts

For 2 – 5 day forecasts and 48/72/96/120 hour synoptic charts for the offshore Areas shown on the map above dial 09061 502 + Number of the area required.
The forecasts include wind, weather, visibility and sea states, but are briefer than those in 6.9.1. Day 5 is covered by an Outlook.

Two levels of service are available: Standard, at £1/min, which gives a planning forecast and four synoptic charts for days 2-5.
Premium at £1.50/min includes the above, plus four diagrams of significant wave height contours in the Area. The Fax numbers above are for the Premium service.

Marinecall FaxDirect

This offers discounted rates to regular users of the Premium services. For example over 6 months, 1 Fax/week costs £68.15 inc VAT; 3 faxes/week £188; and 7 faxes/week £405.38.

WEATHER BY MOBILE 'PHONE
Short Message Service (SMS, or texting)
'Marinecall Mobile' using SMS provides:
The current weather, plus the forecast for 6 hrs later, at any one of 170 coastal locations (see below), all updated hourly.

To obtain this info, type **Nautical** plus the name of the required location; then send it to 83141; the data will be received by return. Or type **Nautical Sub**, plus the required location, send it to 83141 and the info will be supplied daily by 0900. The charge is 25p per message; **Nautical Sub**(scribers) are billed at £1.50 for 6 messages.

Reports/forecasts contain: Place, date, time; max temp °C; mean wind direction and speed (kt); vis in km; % risk of precipitation. For example:

Exmouth: 1/4/05.
10am: 11c, WD 250d, WS 12kt, VIS 17.59km, RAIN 10%.
4pm: 12c, WD 290d, WS 14kt, VIS 13.50km, RAIN 12%.

The message ends with a Marinecall Tel No; press 'Dial' to get, for 60p/minute, the 2-5 day recorded forecast described under 'Weather by Telephone'.

Area 1
Anvil Point
Brixham
Dart marina
Darthaven
Exmouth
Falmouth
Fowey
Helford River
Lizard Point
Longships
Lyme Regis
Mayflower marina
Newton Ferrers
Penzance
Plymouth Yacht Haven
Portland Bill
Queen Anne's Battery
Salcombe
Start Point
Sutton Harbour
Torquay
Weymouth

Area 2
Bembridge Harbour
Birdham Pool
Buckler's Hard
Chichester
Christchurch
Cobbs Quay (Poole)
Cowes Yacht Haven
East Cowes
Emsworth
Gosport
Hamble Point
Haslar
Hythe
Island Hbr, R. Medina
Lymington marina
Lymington Yacht Haven
Mercury Yacht harbour
Swanwick marina
Needles Fairway
Northney marina
Ocean Village
Poole Town Quay
Port Hamble
Port Solent
Ryde
Salterns
Shamrock Quay
Southsea
Sparkes Yacht harbour
St Catherines Point
Town Quay (So'ton)
Wootton Creek
Yarmouth, IoW

Area 3
Beachy Head
Brighton
Dover
Dungeness
Littlehampton
Newhaven
North Foreland
Ramsgate
Rye
Selsey Bill
Shoreham
Sovereign Harbour

E England
Aldeburgh
Allington
Bradwell
Brightlingsea
Burnham Yacht H'bour
Chatham
Cuxton
Essex marina
Fox's marina
Gillingham
Great Yarmouth
Hoo
Ipswich
Landguard Point
Lowestoft
Medway Bridge marina
Orford Ness
Port Medway marina
Queenborough
Shotley Point
Southend-on-sea
Southwold
Suffolk Yacht harbour
Tidemill Yacht harbour
Titchmarsh
Tollesbury
Whitstable
Woolverstone

Area 5
No reports are given for Orkney, Shetland and W of Duncansby Head
Aberdeen
Amble
Berwick
Blyth
Boston
Bridlington
Burntisland
Cromer
Duncansby Head
Dundee
Eyemouth
Flamborough Head
Granton
Grimsby
Hartlepool
Holy Island
Hull
Inverness
King's Lynn
Lossiemouth
Montrose
Peterhead
Port Edgar
Rattray Head
Royal Quays marina
Spurn Head
St Abbs Head
St Peter's marina
Stonehaven
Sunderland
Wells-next-the-Sea
Whitby
Whitehills

Area 6
Ardfern
Corpach
Craobh
Dunstaffnage
Iona
Oban
Tobermory

Area 7
Ardrossan
Burrow Head
Campbeltown
East Loch Tarbert
Kip
Kirkcudbright
Lamlash
Largs
Mull of Kintyre
Portpatrick
Rhu
Troon

Area 8
Abersoch
Aberystwyth
Bardsey Island
Beaumaris
Caernarfon
Conwy
Glasson Dock
Holyhead
Liverpool
Maryport
Milford Dock (Haven)
Neyland (Milford Hav'n)
Port Dinorwic
Preston
Pwllheli
South Bishop (Lt ho)
Swansea
Whitehaven
Wyre Dock

Area 9
Bristol Floating Hbr
Padstow
Penarth (Cardiff)
Portishead

WEATHER

OTHER SOURCES

Internet
Meteorological information available on the Internet includes 2 and 3 to 5 day inshore forecasts, shipping forecasts, gale warnings; coastal reports charts and satellite images.
Visit the Meteorological Office site at:
   www.met-office.gov.uk
Or call their Helpline ☎ 0845 300 0300 or e-mail:
   sales@meto.gov.uk

Press forecasts
The better papers include a synoptic chart which can help to interpret the shipping forecast. However, the interval between the time of issue and the time at which they are available next day may limit their value to yachtsmen.

Television forecasts
Some TV forecasts show a synoptic chart which, with the satellite pictures, can be a useful guide to the weather situation.
In the UK Ceefax (BBC) gives the weather index on page 400, inshore waters forecasts on page 409 and 5 day forecasts on page 405. Teletext (ITN) has a weather index on page 151, shipping forecasts on page 157 and inshore waters forecasts on page 158

UK Weather Centres and Met Offices
London	020 7696 0573/020 7405 4356
Norwich	01603 763898
Newcastle	0191 232 3808
Aberdeen Airport	01224 210575
Kirkwall Airport, Orkney	01856 873802
Sella Ness, Shetland	01806 242069
Glasgow	0141 248 7272
Manchester	0161 4771017
Cardiff	029 2022 5746
Bristol	0117 927 6265

Forecasters direct
A Met Office forecaster in the UK can be called H24 on ☎ + 44 (0) 8700 767 888 for a detailed briefing on, for example, the synoptic situation, specific weather windows or the longer term outlook, plus answers to any questions. Pay a flat rate of £17·00 by credit card.

To call a forecaster in Gibraltar for weather in the Mediterranean or Canary Islands dial ☎ + 44 (0) 8700 767 818. Pay by credit card at a flat rate of £15·00; no time limit is specified, but 5-10 mins is average. For a Fax forecast, £3 by credit card, dial 📠 + 44 (0)8700 767 818.

BROADCASTS BY HM COASTGUARD

COASTGUARD BROADCASTS OF SHIPPING AND INSHORE WATERS FORECASTS

Coastguard	Shipping forecast areas	Local Inshore forecast areas	Broadcast times UT					
SOUTH COAST								
Falmouth	Plymouth, Lundy, Fastnet, Sole	8 & 9	0140	0540	*0940*	1340	1740	*2140*
Brixham	Plymouth, Portland	8	0050	0450	*0850*	1250	1650	*2050*
Portland	Plymouth, Portland, Wight	7 & 8	0220	0620	*1020*	1420	1820	*2220*
Solent	Portland, Wight	6 & 7	0040	0440	*0840*	1240	1640	*2040*
Dover	Thames, Dover, Wight	5, 6 & 7	0105	0505	*0905*	1305	1707	*2105*
EAST COAST								
Thames	Thames, Dover	5	0010	0410	*0810*	1210	1610	*2010*
Yarmouth	Humber, Thames	5	0040	0440	*0840*	1240	1640	*2040*
Humber	Humber, Tyne, Dogger, German Bight	3 & 4	0340	0740	*1140*	1540	*1940*	2340
Forth	Forth, Tyne, Dogger, Forties	2	0205	0605	*1005*	1405	1805	*2205*
Aberdeen	Fair I, Cromarty, Forth, Forties	1 & 2	0320	*0720*	1120	1520	*1920*	2320
Shetland	Faeroes, Fair I, Viking	1 & 16	0105	0505	*0905*	1305	1705	*2105*
WEST COAST								
Stornoway	Fair I, Faeroes, Bailey, Hebrides, Malin, Rockall	15	0110	0510	*0910*	1310	1710	*2110*
Clyde	Bailey, Hebrides, Rockall, Malin	13, 14 & 15	0020	0420	*0820*	1220	1620	*2020*
Belfast	Irish Sea, Malin	12	0305	*0705*	1105	1505	*1905*	2305
Liverpool	Irish Sea, Malin	11	0210	0610	*1010*	1410	1810	*2210*
Holyhead	Irish Sea	10	0235	*0635*	1035	1435	*1835*	2235
Milford Haven	Lundy, Irish Sea, Fastnet	9 & 10	0335	*0735*	1135	1535	*1935*	2335
Swansea	Lundy, Irish Sea, Fastnet	9	0005	0405	*0805*	1205	1605	*2005*

Shipping & Inshore waters forecasts

CG Centres broadcast these forecasts for their adjacent sea areas, at the times above in italics.

Inshore waters forecasts are broadcast every 4 hours as given above. The boundaries of the 16 areas used by the CG for these forecasts are shown on the map overleaf.

VHF working channels 10, 23, 73, 84 and 86 are used for all such broadcasts, after an announcement on VHF Ch 16. The positions of remote transmitters used for these broadcasts, plus their VHF channels, are listed below. Thus a relevant channel can be pre-selected and/or verified with the prior announcement on Ch 16.

FALMOUTH MRCC
Trevose Head	86	50°33'N 05°02'W
St Mary's	23	49°56'N 06°18'W
Lizard	86	49°58'N 05°12'W
Falmouth	23	50°09'N 05°06'W

Brixham MRSC
Fowey	86	50°20'N 04°38'W
Rame Head	10	50°19'N 04°13'W
Salcombe	84	50°15'N 03°45'W
East Prawle	73	50°13'N 03°42'W
Dartmouth	23	50°21'N 03°35'W
Berry Head	86	50°24'N 03°29'W
Teignmouth	10	50°34'N 03°32'W
Beer Head	84	50°41'N 03°05'W

Portland MRSC
Beer Head	86	50°41'N 03°05'W
Bincleaves (Weymouth)	73	50°36'N 02°27'W
Grove Pt (Portland Bill)	10	50°33'N 02°25'W
Hengistbury Head	73	50°43'N 01°46'W

Solent MRSC
Needles	86	50°39'N 01°35'W
Boniface (Ventnor, IoW)	23	50°36'N 01°12'W
Newhaven	86	50°47'N 00°03'E

DOVER MRCC
Fairlight (Hastings)	23	50°52'N 00°39'E
Langdon Battery (Dover)	86	51°08'N 01°21'E
North Foreland	86	51°23'N 01°27'E

Thames MRSC
Shoeburyness	23	51°31'N 00°47'E
Bradwell (R Blackwater)	86	51°44'N 00°53'E
Walton-on-the-Naze	73	51°51'N 01°17'E
Bawdsey (R Deben)	84	52°00'N 01°25'E

YARMOUTH MRCC
Lowestoft	86	52°29'N 01°46'E
Yarmouth	84	52°36'N 01°43'E
Trimingham (Cromer)	23	52°54'N 01°21'E
Langham (Blakeney)	86	52°57'N 00°58'E
Guy's Head (Wisbech)	84	52°48'N 00°13'E
Skegness	23	53°09'N 00°21'E

Humber MRSC
Easington (Spurn Hd)	84	53°39'N 00°06'E
Flamborough Head	23	54°07'N 00°05'E
Whitby	84	54°29'N 00°36'W
Hartlepool	23	54°42'N 01°10'W
Cullercoats (Blyth)	84	55°04'N 01°28'W
Newton	23	55°31'N 01°37'W

Forth MRSC
St Abbs/Cross Law	86	55°54'N 02°12'W
Craigkelly (Burntisland)	86	56°04'N 03°14'W
Fife Ness	23	56°17'N 02°35'W
Tay Law (Dundee)	86	56°28'N 02°59'W
Inverbervie	23	56°51'N 02°16'W

ABERDEEN MRCC
Greg Ness (Aberdeen)	86	57°08'N 02°03'W
Peterhead	86	57°31'N 01°46'W
Windyheads Hill	23	57°39'N 02°14'W
Banff	23	57°38'N 02°31'W
Foyers (Loch Ness)	86	57°14'N 04°31'W
Rosemarkie (Cromarty)	86	57°38'N 04°05'W
Thrumster (Wick)	84	58°24'N 03°07'W
Noss Head (Wick)	84	58°29'N 03°03'W
Dunnet Head (Thurso)	84	58°40'N 03°22'W
Ben Tongue	23	58°30'N 04°24'W
Durness (Loch Eriboll)	23	58°34'N 04°44'W

Shetland MRSC
Wideford Hill (Kirkwall)	23	58°59'N 03°01'W
Fitful Head (Sumburgh)	10	59°54'N 01°23'W
Shetland MRSC	84	60°10'N 01°08'W
Collafirth (Sullom Voe)	73	60°32'N 01°23'W
Saxa Vord (Unst)	23	60°42'N 00°51'W

Stornoway MRSC
Butt of Lewis	10	58°28'N 06°14'W
Portnaguran (Stornoway)	84	58°15'N 06°10'W
Forsneval (W Lewis)	73	58°13'N 07°00'W
Melvaig (L. Ewe)	67	57°50'N 05°47'W
Rodel (S Harris)	10	57°45'N 06°57'W
Clettreval (N Uist)	73	57°37'N 07°26'W
Skriag (Portree, Skye)	67	57°23'N 06°15'W
Drumfearn (SE Skye)	84	57°12'N 05°48'W
Barra	10	57°01'N 07°30'W
Arisaig (S of Mallaig)	73	56°55'N 06°50'W

CLYDE MRCC
Glengorm (N Mull)	23	56°38'N 06°08'W
Tiree	73	56°31'N 06°57'W
Torosay (E Mull)	10	56°27'N 05°43'W
Clyde MRCC	23	55°58'N 04°48'W
South Knapdale (L Fyne)	23	55°55'N 05°28'W
Kilchiaran (W Islay)	84	55°46'N 06°27'W
Lawhill (Ardrossan)	86	55°42'N 04°50'W
Ru Stafnish (Kintyre)	10	55°22'N 05°32'W

Belfast MRSC
Navar (Lower L. Erne)	73	54°28'N 07°54'W
Limvady (L. Foyle)	84	55°06'N 06°53'W
West Torr (Fair Head)	73	55°12'N 06°06'W
Black Mountain (Belfast)	86	54°35'N 06°01'W
Orlock Point (Bangor)	84	54°40'N 05°35'W
Slievemartin (Rostrevor)	73	54°06'N 06°10'W

Liverpool MRSC
Caldbeck (Carlisle)	10	54°46'N 03°07'W
Snaefell (Isle of Man)	86	54°16'N 04°28'W
Langthwaite (Lancaster)	73	54°02'N 02°46'W
Moel-y-Parc (Anglesey)	23	53°13'N 04°28'W

WEATHER

Holyhead MRSC
Great Ormes Head	84	53°20′N	03°51′W
Holyhead MRSC	10	53°19′N	04°38′W
Mynydd Rhiw	73	52°50′N	04°38′W

Milford Haven MRSC
Blaenplwyf (Aberystwyth)	84	52°22′N	04°06′W
Dinas Hd (Fishguard)	86	52°00′N	04°54′W
St Ann's Head	84	51°40′N	05°11′W
Tenby (Monkstone)	86	51°42′N	04°41′W

SWANSEA MRCC
Mumbles	84	51°34′N	03°59′W
St. Hillary (Barry)	86	51°27′N	03°25′W
Severn Bridges	84	51°36′N	02°38′W
Combe Martin	86	51°12′N	04°03′W
Hartland Point	84	51°01′N	04°31′W

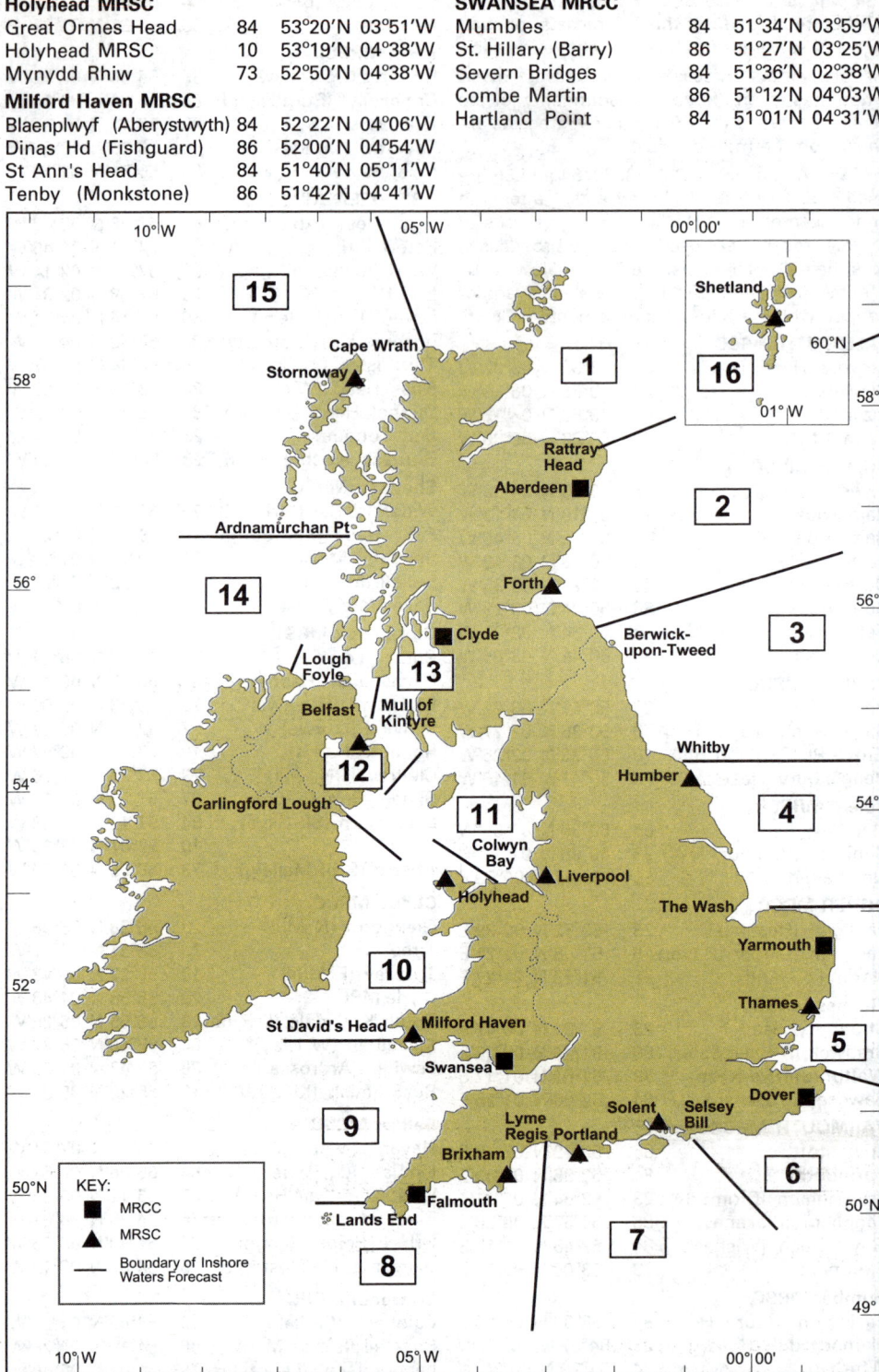

Inshore waters forecasts: Area boundaries used by the Coastguard

CHANNEL ISLANDS

Jersey Meteorological Department
Call ☎ 0900 665 0022 for the Channel Islands recorded shipping forecast. For Guernsey only, this service is available on ☎ 069 69 88 00. It is chargeable; more detailed information on request ☎ +44 (0) 1534 745550. The forecast includes a general situation, 24hr forecast for wind, weather, visibility, sea state, swell, sea temperature, plus 2 & 4 day outlooks and St Helier tide times/heights. The area is between 50°N, 03°W and the French coast from Cap de la Hague to Ile de Brehat.

Weather information by radio
Jersey Radio   1659 kHz and Ch 25 82
Storm warnings on receipt and at 0307, 0907, 1507 and 2107 UT. Near-gale warnings, synopsis, 24h forecast and outlook for next 24 hrs (Channel Islands south of 50°N and east of 03°W), plus reports from stations are broadcast at 0645[1], 0745[1], 0845[1] LT & 1245, 1845 and 2245 UT. [1] 1 hr earlier when DST in force. At St Helier mean wind speed/direction/gusts is broadcast Ch 18.

BBC Radio Jersey   1026 kHz and 88·8 MHz
Storm warnings on receipt. Wind info for local waters: Mon-Fri 0725, 0825, 1325, 1725 LT; Sat/Sun 0825. Shipping forecast for local waters: Mon-Fri @ H+00 (0600-1900, after the news) and 0625 & 1825 LT; Sat/Sun @ H+00 (0700-1300, after the news) and 0725 LT.

BBC Radio Guernsey 93·2 MHz, 1116 kHz
Weather bulletins for the waters around Guernsey, Herm and Sark are broadcast Mon-Fri at 0630, 0730 and 0830 LT; Sat/Sun at 0730 and 0830 LT. They contain forecast, synopsis, coastal forecast, storm warnings and wind strength. In the summer coastal reports are included from: Jersey, Guernsey, Alderney, Cap de la Hague, Cherbourg, Dinard, Portland and Chan Lt V.

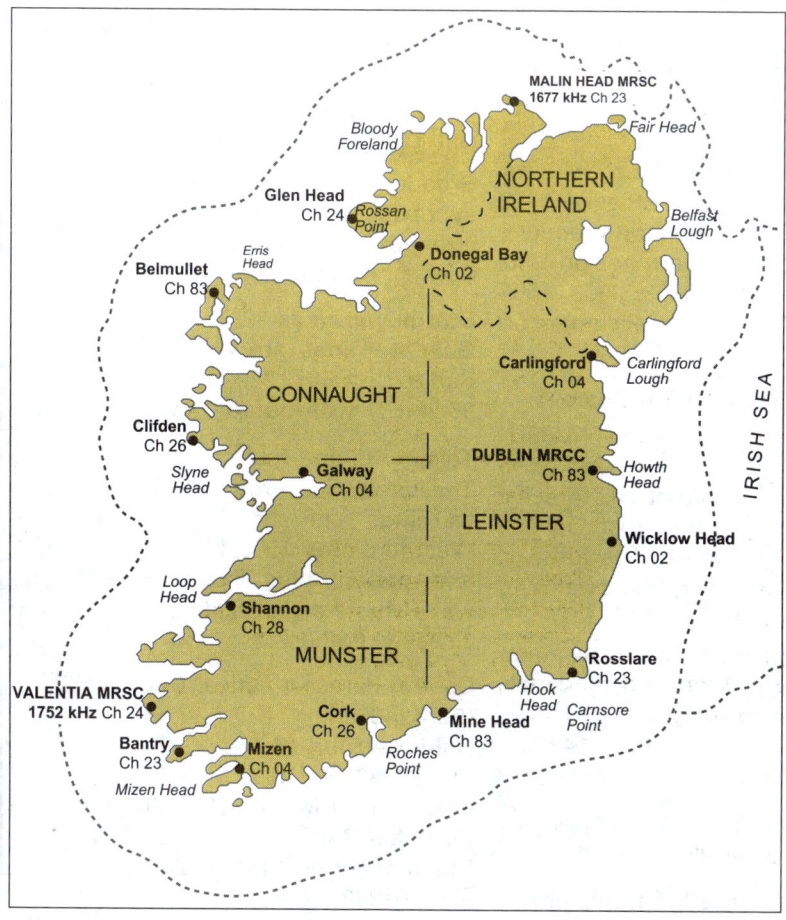

Provinces, headlands, sea areas and coastal stations referred to in weather broadcasts are shown here. Forecasts for coastal waters cover areas within 30M of the shore.

WEATHER

IRELAND

Irish Coast Radio Stations

Weather bulletins for the Irish Sea and up to 30M off the Irish coast are broadcast on VHF at 0103, 0403, 0703, 1003, 1303, 1603, 1903 & 2203UT after an announcement on Ch 16. Broadcasts are given 1 hour earlier when DST is in force. Bulletins include gale warnings, synopsis and a 24-hour forecast. Stations and VHF Ch, anti-clockwise from Malin Head, are:

MALIN HEAD	23	Mizen	04
Glen Head	24	Bantry	23
Donegal Bay	02	Cork	26
Belmullet	83	Mine Head	83
Clifden	26	Rosslare	23
Galway	04	Wicklow Head	02
Shannon	28	DUBLIN	83
VALENTIA	24	Carlingford	04

Gale warnings are broadcast on these VHF channels on receipt and at 0033, 0633, 1233 and 1833UT, after an announcement on Ch 16.

Valentia Radio broadcasts forecasts for sea areas Shannon and Fastnet on 1752 kHz at 0833 & 2033 UT, and on request. It also broadcasts gale warnings on 1752 kHz on receipt and at 0303, 0903, 1503 and 2103 (UT) after an announcement on 2182 kHz.

Radio Telefís Éireann (RTE) Radio 1

RTE Radio 1 on 567, 729kHz and FM (88·2-95·2MHz) broadcasts at 0602, 1255, 1655 and 2355LT daily a situation, forecast and coastal reports for Irish coastal waters and the Irish Sea. The forecast includes: wind, weather, vis, swell and outlook for a further 24 hrs.

Coastal reports contain wind, weather, vis, plus pressure (hPa) and tendency, which is described as:

Steady	=	0 - 0·4 hPa
Rising/falling slowly	=	0·5 -1·9
Rising/falling	=	2·0 -3·4
Rising/falling rapidly	=	3·5 -5·9
Rising/falling very rapidly	=	> 6·0

Main transmitters and FM freq's are:

East Coast Radio: Kippure 89·1 MHz. At: Every H+06 (0700-1800 LT) after the news bulletin. Broadcasts a general forecast, storm warnings and wind strength from Dublin Bay to Arklow Head.

South East Radio: Mount Leinster 89·6 MHz.
At: 0712 LT (Mon-Fri) and every H+30 (0700-1800 LT) H24 after commercial break. Broadcasts a detailed general forecast and synopsis for coastal waters, including storm warnings if adverse weather is forecast.

WLR FM: Faha Ring 95·1 & Carrickferrish 97·5 MHz.
At every H+03 and 1315 1815 LT broadcasts a general forecast, gale warnings, wind strength for area from Youghal to Kilmore Quay. Tidal information included from Jun-Sep.

Radio Kerry: Main transmitters: Mullaghanish 90·0 MHz, Three Rock 88·5, Kippure 89·1, Mount Leinster 89·6, Maghera 88·8, Truskmore 88·2, Holywell Hill 89·2 and Clermont Cairn 95·2.

Broadcasts include a general forecast, synopsis, gale warnings and wind strength for the coastal area from Cork to Shannon.

Storm warnings

Gale warnings are broadcast by: RTE Radio 1 on 567, 729 kHz and FM (88·2-95·2MHz) with hourly news bulletins.

Telephone and Fax

The latest Sea area forecast and gale warnings can be obtained through Weatherdial ☎ 1550 123 855. The same information, plus isobaric, swell and wave charts are available by Fax on ☎ 1570 131 838 (H24).

Central Forecast Office, Dublin (H24)
(01) 424655
Dublin Airport Met
(01) 379900 ext 4531
Cork Airport Met (0900–2000)
(021) 965974
Shannon Airport Met (H24)
(061) 61333.

DENMARK

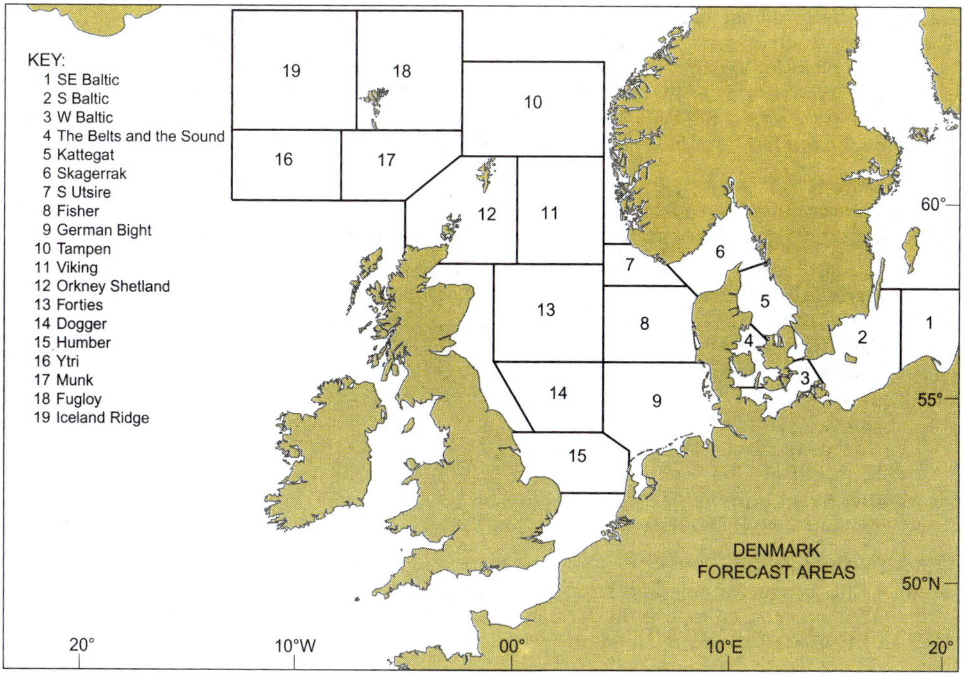

KEY:
1 SE Baltic
2 S Baltic
3 W Baltic
4 The Belts and the Sound
5 Kattegat
6 Skagerrak
7 S Utsire
8 Fisher
9 German Bight
10 Tampen
11 Viking
12 Orkney Shetland
13 Forties
14 Dogger
15 Humber
16 Ytri
17 Munk
18 Fugloy
19 Iceland Ridge
DENMARK
FORECAST AREAS
60°
55°
50°N
20°
10°W
00°
10°E
20°

8°
9°
10°E
11°
Hirtshals
Ch 66
Skagen
Ch 04
1758 kHz
Hanstholm
Ch 01
57°
Bovbjerg
Ch 02
56°
Blåvand
Ch 23
1734 kHz
55°N

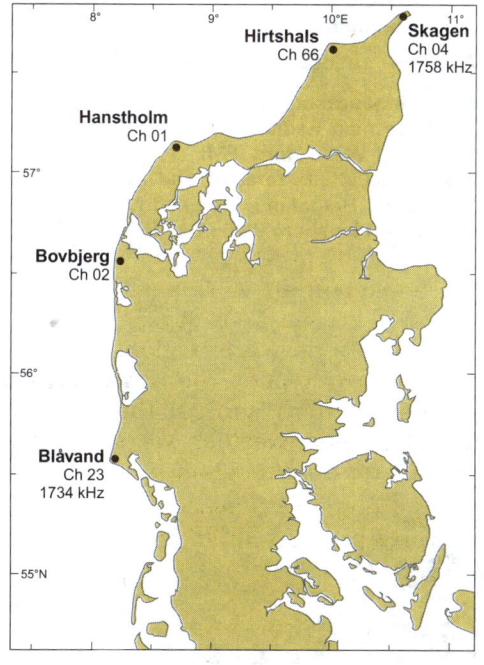

Lyngby Radio broadcasts gale warnings, synopsis and forecasts in Danish/English, on receipt or on request, from the following remote CRS, all using callsign *Lyngby Radio*:

Skagen	Ch 04, 1758 kHz	Areas 5 & 6.
Hirtshals	Ch 66	Areas 5, 6 & 8.
Hanstholm	Ch 01	Areas 6 & 8.
Bovbjerg	Ch 02	Areas 6, 8 & 9.
Blåvand	Ch 23, 1734 kHz	Areas 8 & 9.

National Radio – Danmarks Radio

Programme 1 (**Kalundborg** 243 and 1062 kHz) broadcasts in Danish every hour after the news strong wind warnings for Danish Areas 2-5, Limfjorden and, only 1 May to 31 Oct, Area 9.

Programme 3 (Stations/freqs below) broadcasts at 0445, 0745, 1045, 1645 and 2145 UT the synoptic situation and outlook for all Danish areas. Plus a 5 day outlook for Areas 2-9 & 13-15; and a 7 day outlook for Jutland, The Islands and Bornholm, followed by reports from coastal stations.

North Jutland	96·6 MHz
Limfjord (Thisted)	99·2 MHz
West Jutland	92·9 MHz
SW Jutland	92·3 MHz
South Jutland	97·2 MHz

WEATHER

GERMANY

Deutsche Wetterdienst (DWD)
The German weather service provides weather info through a databank which is updated twice daily; more often for weather reports and text forecasts. German Weather Service, Frankfurter Str 135, 63067 Offenbach. ☎ + 49 (0) 69 8062-0 📠 + 49 (0) 69 8062 4484 www.dwd.de seeschifffahrt@dwd.de. SEEWIS (Marine weather information system) allows data to be accessed by telephone/modem and fed into an onboard computer.

Traffic Centres
Traffic Centres broadcast local storm warnings, weather messages, visibility and ice reports (when appropriate) in German. (E) = in **English** and German.

Traffic Centre	VHF Ch	Every
German Bight Traffic (E)	80	H+00
Ems Traffic	15, 18, 20, 21	H+50
Jade Traffic	20, 63	H+10
Bremerhaven Weser	02, 04, 05, 07, 21, 22, 82	H+20
Bremen Weser Traffic	19, 78, 81	H+30
Hunte Traffic	63	H+30
Cuxhaven Elbe Traffic (E)	71 (outer Elbe)	H+35
Brunsbüttel Elbe Traffic (E)	68 (lower Elbe)	H+05
Kiel Kanal II (E-bound)	02	H+15 & H+45
KielKanal III (W-bound)	03	H+20 & H+50

CRS – Seefunk (DPO7)
Seefunk CRS broadcast gale and strong wind warnings, synopsis, 12hr forecast, outlook for a further 12hr and coastal reports, in German, for areas B10-B12 and N9-N11 at 0745ⓐ, **0945**, 1245, **1645** and **1945**ⓐ UT. ⓐonly in summer.

Hamburg (Control centre)	Ch 83	**Elber-Weser**	Ch 24
Borkum	Ch 28	**Nordfriesland**	Ch 26
Bremen	Ch 25		

A 4-5 day outlook for the North and Baltic Seas is broadcast at the times above in bold.

Radio broadcasting
North German Radio (NDR)
a. **NDR 1 Welle Nord (FM)**
A synopsis, 12hrs forecast and 24hrs outlook are broadcast in German at 0730 UT (1 May – 30 Sep) for Helgoland, Elbe and North Frisian coast by: **Helgoland** 88·9 MHz; **Hamburg** 89·5 & 90·3 MHz; **Flensburg** 89·6 MHz; **Heide** 90·5 MHz; **Sylt** 90·9 MHz; **Kiel** 91·3 MHz.

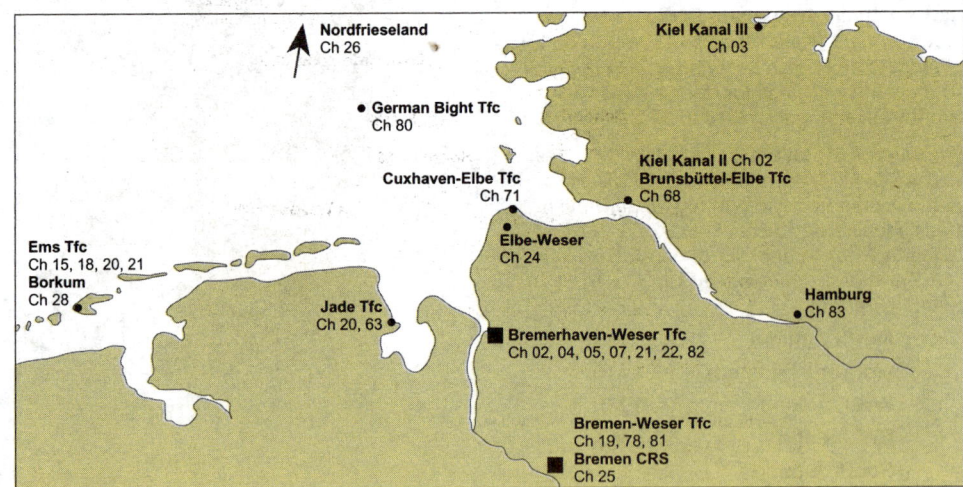

b. NDR 4 Hamburg (MW)
A synopsis, 12hrs forecast and outlook for a further 12hrs are broadcast in German at 0005, 0830 and 2200 UT on 702 (Flensburg) & 972 (Hamburg) kHz for areas B10-B14 and N9-N12; plus North Sea station reports.

Radio Bremen (MW and FM)
A 12hrs wind forecast for Areas B11 and N10 is broadcast in German on receipt by: **Bremerhaven** 936 kHz; 89·3, 92·1, 95·4 & 100·8 MHz; and **Bremen** 88·3, 93·8, 96·7 & 101·2 MHz.

Telephone forecasts
For forecast and outlook (1 April – 30 Sep) call 0190 1160 (only within Germany) plus two digits for the following areas:
- 45 North Frisian Islands and Helgoland
- 47 Weser Estuary and Jade Bay
- 53 For inland pleasure craft
- 55 Netherlands, IJsselmeer, Schelde, Maas
- 46 R Elbe to Hamburg
- 48 E Frisian Islands and Ems Estuary
- 54 Denmark

For year-round weather synopsis, forecast and outlook, call 0190 1169 plus two digits as follows:
- 20 General information
- 22 German Bight and SW North Sea
- 59 Current wind strength for North Sea coasts
- 21 North Sea and Baltic
- 31 Reports for North Sea and Baltic

For the latest wind and storm warnings for individual areas of the North Sea coasts, call +49 40 3196 628 (H24). If no warning is in force, a wind forecast for the German Bight is given.

NETHERLANDS
Netherlands Coastguard
a. VHF weather broadcasts
Forecasts for Dutch coastal waters up to 30M offshore (including IJsselmeer) are transmitted in **English** and Dutch at 0805, 1305, 1905, 2305 LT on the VHF channels shown below, without prior announcement on Ch 16. Gale warnings are broadcast on receipt and at 0333, 0733, 1133, 1533, 1933 and 2333 UT.

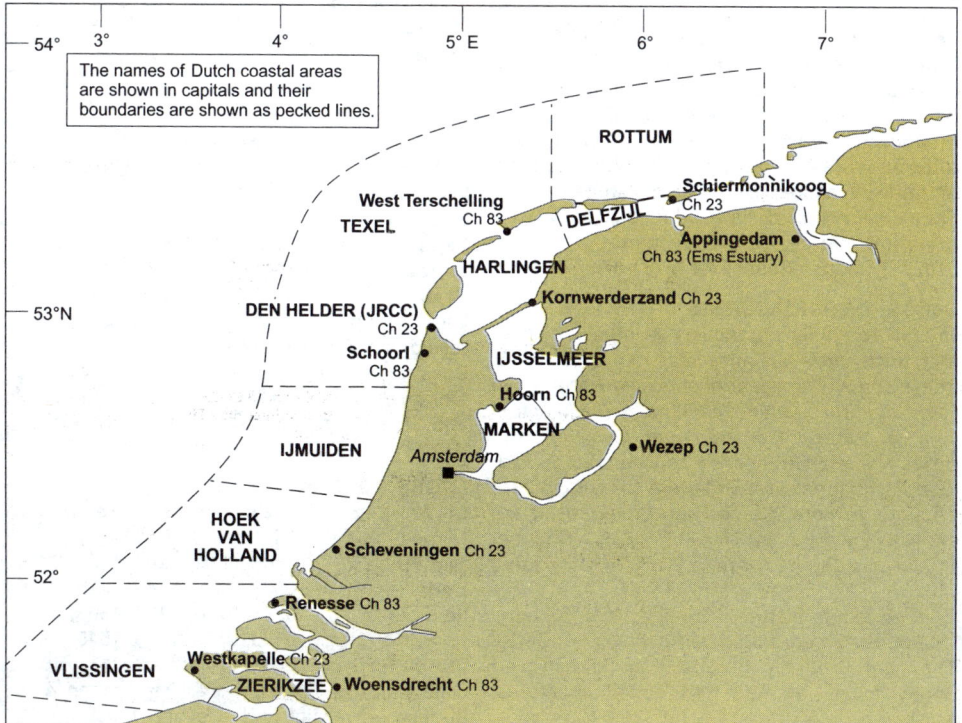

WEATHER

Westkapelle	Ch 23	Hoorn	Ch 83	Woensdrecht	Ch 83
Wezep	Ch 23	Renesse	Ch 83	Kornwerderzand	Ch 23
Scheveningen	Ch 23	West Terschelling	Ch 83	Schoorl	Ch 83
Schiermonnikoog	Ch 23	Den Helder	Ch 23	Appingedam	Ch 83

b. MF weather broadcasts
A forecast for sea areas Dover, Thames, Humber, German Bight, Dogger, Fisher, Forties and Viking is broadcast in **English** at 0940 & 2140 UT on 3673 kHz.

Gale warnings for these sea areas are broadcast in **English** on receipt and at 0333, 0733, 1133, 1533, 1933 and 2333 UT.

Radio Noord-Holland (FM)
Coastal forecasts, gale warnings and wind strength are broadcast in Dutch, Mon-Fri at 0730, 0838, 1005,1230 and 1705LT; Sat/Sun 1005, by:
Wieringermeer 93.9 MHz and **Haarlem** 97.6 MHz. In summer additional info is broadcast for leisure craft and beach areas.

BELGIUM

Coast Radio Stations

Oostende Radio broadcasts strong wind warnings and a forecast valid for sea areas Thames and Dover in **English** and Dutch on VHF Ch 27 and 2761 kHz at 0820 and 1720 UT. Strong wind warnings are also broadcast on receipt and at the end of the next two silent periods.

Antwerpen Radio broadcasts on VHF Ch 24 in **English** and Dutch for the Schelde estuary: Gale warnings on receipt, at the end of the next two silent periods and every odd H+05. Also strong wind warnings (F6+) on receipt and at every H+03 and H+48.

FRANCE

The French Met Office (Météo-France) issues a free annual booklet 'Le Guide Marine' which summarises the various means by which weather forecasts and warnings are broadcast or otherwise disseminated. It can often be obtained from marina offices, on the internet (www.meteo.fr) or from Météo-France, Direction de la Production, Service de prévision marine, 42 ave Gaspard-Coriolis, 31057 Toulouse-Cedex; tel 05.61.07.80.80.

CROSS VHF BROADCASTS
CROSS routinely broadcasts Weather bulletins in French, after an announcement on Ch 16. These contain: a repeat of any Gale warnings in force, general situation, a 24 hrs forecast (actual weather, wind, sea state and visibility) and further weather trends for coastal waters. VHF working channels, coastal areas covered to 20M offshore, remote stations and times (local) are shown below. In the English Channel broadcasts can be given in English, on request Ch 16.
Gale warnings feature in Special Met Bulletins (*Bulletins Météorologique Spéciaux* or BMS). They are routinely broadcast in French and **English** by all stations at H+03 and at other times as shown below.

CROSS GRIS-NEZ
Ch 79 Belgian border to Baie de la Somme
Dunkerque   0720, 1603, 1920
St Frieux   0710, 1545, 1910
Ailly   0703, 1533, 1903

CROSS JOBOURG
Ch 80 Baie de la Somme to Cap de la Hague
Antifer   0803, 1633, 2003
Port-en-Bessin   0745, 1615, 1945
Jobourg   0733, 1603, 1933
Cap de la Hague to Pte de Penmarc'h
Jobourg   0715, 1545, 1915
Granville   0703, 1533, 1903
Gale warnings for areas 13-14 in **English** on receipt, on request and at H+20 and H+50. Coastal BMS in French on receipt and at H+03. 'Jobourg Traffic' (VTS) broadcasts traffic info and BMS in French and **English** on Ch 80 at H+20 and H+50.

CROSS CORSEN
Ch 79 Cap de la Hague to Pte de Penmarc'h (Times in **bold** = 1 May to 30 Sep only).
Cap Fréhel   0545, 0803, **1203**, 1633, 2003
Bodic   0533, 0745, **1145**, 1615, 1945
Ile de Batz   0515, 0733, **1133**, 1603, 1933
Le Stiff   0503, 0715, **1115**, 1545, 1915
Pte du Raz   0445, 0703, **1103**, 1533, 1903
Gale warnings for areas 14-16 in French & **English** on receipt and at every H+03.

CROSS ÉTEL
Ch 80 Pte de Penmarc'h to l'Anse de l'Aiguillon (46° 15'N 01°10'W)

Penmarc'h	0703, 1533, 1903
Ile de Groix	0715, 1545, 1915
Belle Ile	0733, 1603, 1933
St Nazaire	0745, 1615, 1945
Ile d'Yeu	0803, 1633, 2003
Les Sables d'Olonne	0815, 1645, 2015

Gale warnings for areas 16-17 in French & **English** on receipt and at every H+03.

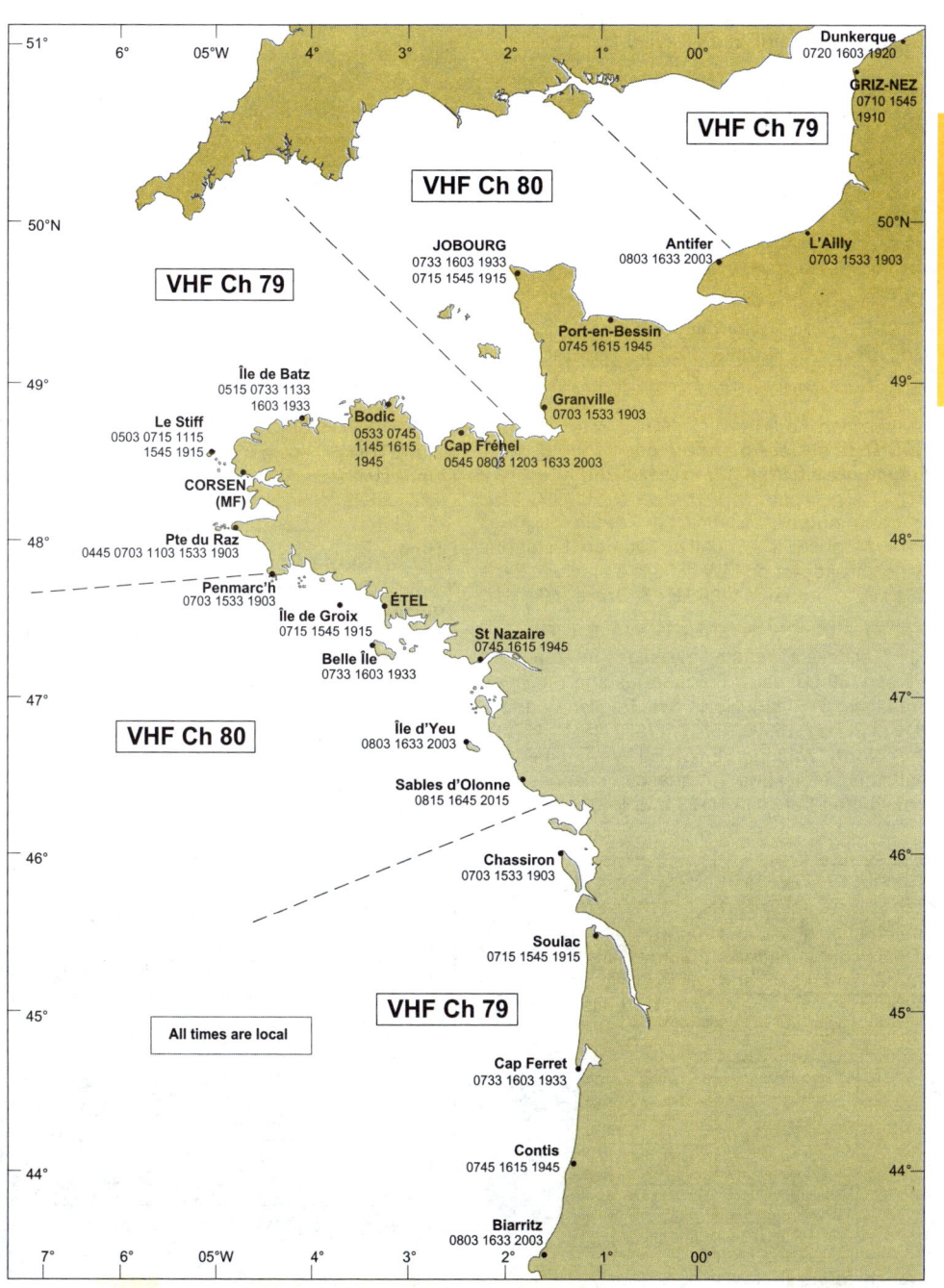

WEATHER

Ch 79 L'Anse de l'Aiguillon to Spanish border

Chassiron	0703, 1533, 1903
Soulac	0715, 1545, 1915
Cap Ferret	0733, 1603, 1933
Contis	0745, 1615, 1945
Biarritz	0803, 1633, 2003

Gale warnings for areas 17-19 in French & English on receipt and at every H+03.

CROSS MF BROADCASTS

CROSS **Gris Nez** and **Corsen** broadcast routine weather bulletins and gale warnings on 1650 kHz and 2677kHz in French at the times below. A prior announcement on 2182 kHz states the working frequency to be used. Gale warnings are broadcast on receipt, at every H+03 and at the times below.

CROSS	Routine bulletins	Areas
Gris Nez	0833, 2033 LT	10-13
Corsen	0815, 2015 LT	13-29

RADIO BROADCASTING

France Inter (LW)   162 kHz (1852m)
For all areas: storm warnings, synopsis, 24hr fcst and outlook, broadcast in French for Areas 1 to 24 at 2003 LT daily. Additional stations which broadcast on MW at 0640 LT include **Paris** 864 kHz, **Bordeaux** 1206 kHz & **Brest** 1404 kHz.

RADIO FRANCE INTERNATIONALE (RFI)

RFI broadcasts weather messages in French on HF at 1130 UT daily. Frequencies and reception areas are: 6175 kHz North Sea, English Channel, Bay of Biscay; 15300, 15515, 17570 and 21645 kHz the North Atlantic, E of 50°W. Engineering bulletins indicating frequency changes are transmitted between H+53 and H+00.

Radio Bleue (MW)

Essentially a music programme, but with forecasts in French at 0655 LT covering:
English Channel & North Sea:
Paris	864 kHz
Lille	1377 kHz

English Channel & E Atlantic:
Rennes	711 kHz
Brest	1404 kHz

Bay of Biscay & E Atlantic:
Bordeaux	1206 kHz
Bayonne	1494 kHz

LOCAL RADIO (FM)

Radio France Cherbourg   100·7 MHz
Coastal forecast, storm warnings, visibility, wind strength, tidal information, small craft warnings, in French, for the Cherbourg peninsula, broadcast 0829 LT by:

St Vaast-la-Hougue	85·0 MHz
Cherbourg	100·7 MHz
Cap de la Hague	99·8 MHz

Carteret 99·9 MHz

RECORDED FORECASTS BY TELEPHONE

a. MÉTÉO (Weather). The BQR (*Bulletin Quotidien des Renseignements*) is a very informative daily bulletin displayed in Hr Mr offices and YC's. Météo is the ☎ of a local Met Office.

Auto gives the ☎ for recorded inshore and Coastal forecasts; dial 08 36 68 08 dd (dd is the Département No, shown under each port). To select the inshore (*rivage*) or Coastal (*Côte*; out to 20M offshore) bulletin, say "STOP" as your choice is spoken. Inshore bulletins contain 5 day forecasts, local tides, signals, sea temperature, surf conditions, etc. strong wind/ gale warnings, general synopsis, 24hrs forecast and outlook.

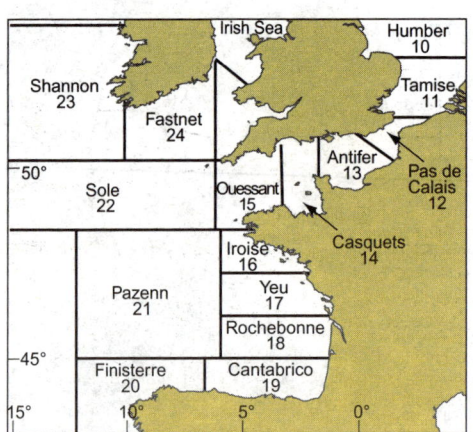

French forecast areas

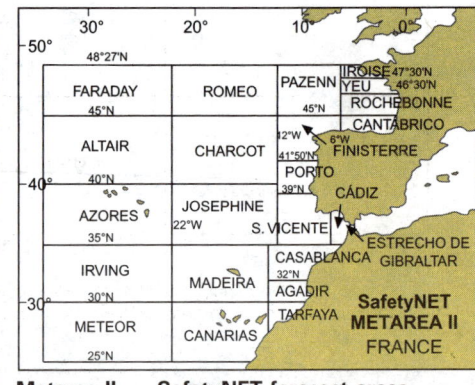

Metarea II – SafetyNET forecast areas

b. For Offshore bulletins (*zones du large*) for Channel and North Sea, Atlantic or Mediterranean, dial ☎ 08 36 68 08 08. To select desired offshore area say "STOP" as it is named.

Offshore bulletins contain strong wind/gale warnings, the general synopsis and forecast, and the 5 day outlook.

NORTH AND NORTH WEST SPAIN

Coast Radio Stations

Weather warnings and 48hr coastal forecasts are broadcast in Spanish on the VHF channels shown at 0840, 1240 & 2010 (UT) by:

Pasajes	Ch 27
Bilbao	Ch 26
Santander	Ch 24
Cabo Peñas	Ch 26
Navia	Ch 60
Cabo Ortegal	Ch 02
La Coruña	Ch 26
Finisterre	Ch 22
Vigo	Ch 65
La Guardia	Ch 21

Gale warnings, synopsis and 24/48hr forecasts for Atlantic areas are broadcast on MF at 0703 1303 1903 (UT) by:

Machichaco	1707	kHz
Cabo Peñas	1677	kHz
La Coruña	1698	kHz
Finisterre	1764	kHz

Recorded telephone forecasts

For weather recordings in Spanish, call:
☎ 906 365 372: Cantábrico and Galicia coasts.
☎ 906 365 374: High Seas bulletins.
This service is only available within Spain or for Autolink-equipped vessels.

Coastguard MRCC/MRSC

Gale warnings and coastal forecasts are broadcast in Spanish and English on receipt and as listed overleaf:

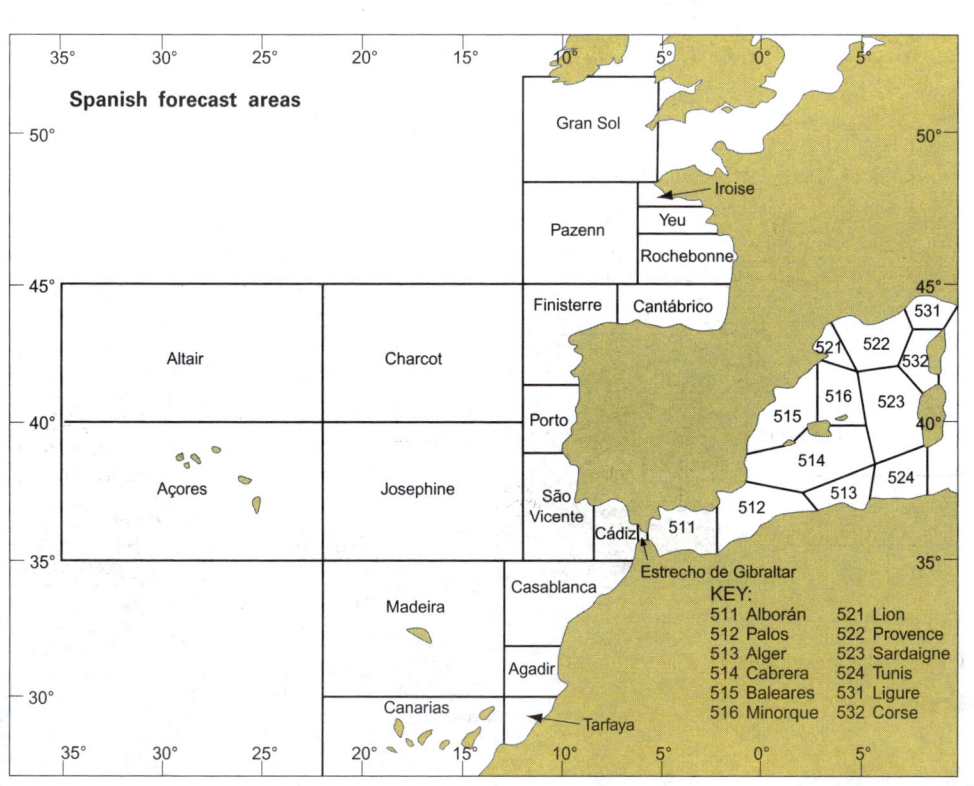

Spanish forecast areas

KEY:
511 Alborán
512 Palos
513 Alger
514 Cabrera
515 Baleares
516 Minorque
521 Lion
522 Provence
523 Sardaigne
524 Tunis
531 Ligure
532 Corse

WEATHER

Bilbao MRCC*	Ch 10	4 hrly from 0033
Santander MRSC	Ch 74	4 hrly from 0245
Gijón MRCC	Ch 10	2 hrly from 0215 to 2215
Coruña MRSC	Ch 10	4 hrly from 0005
Finisterre MRCC	Ch 11	4 hrly from 0233
Vigo MRSC	Ch 10	4 hrly from 0015

*Bilbao also broadcasts High Seas gale warnings and forecasts 4 hourly from 0233.

Radio Nacional de España (MW)
Broadcasts storm warnings, synopsis and 12hr or 18hr forecasts for Cantábrico and Galicia at 1100, 1400, 1800 & 2200 LT in Spanish. Stations/frequencies are:

San Sebastián	774 kHz
Bilbao	639 kHz
Santander	855 kHz
Oviedo	729 kHz
La Coruña	639 kHz

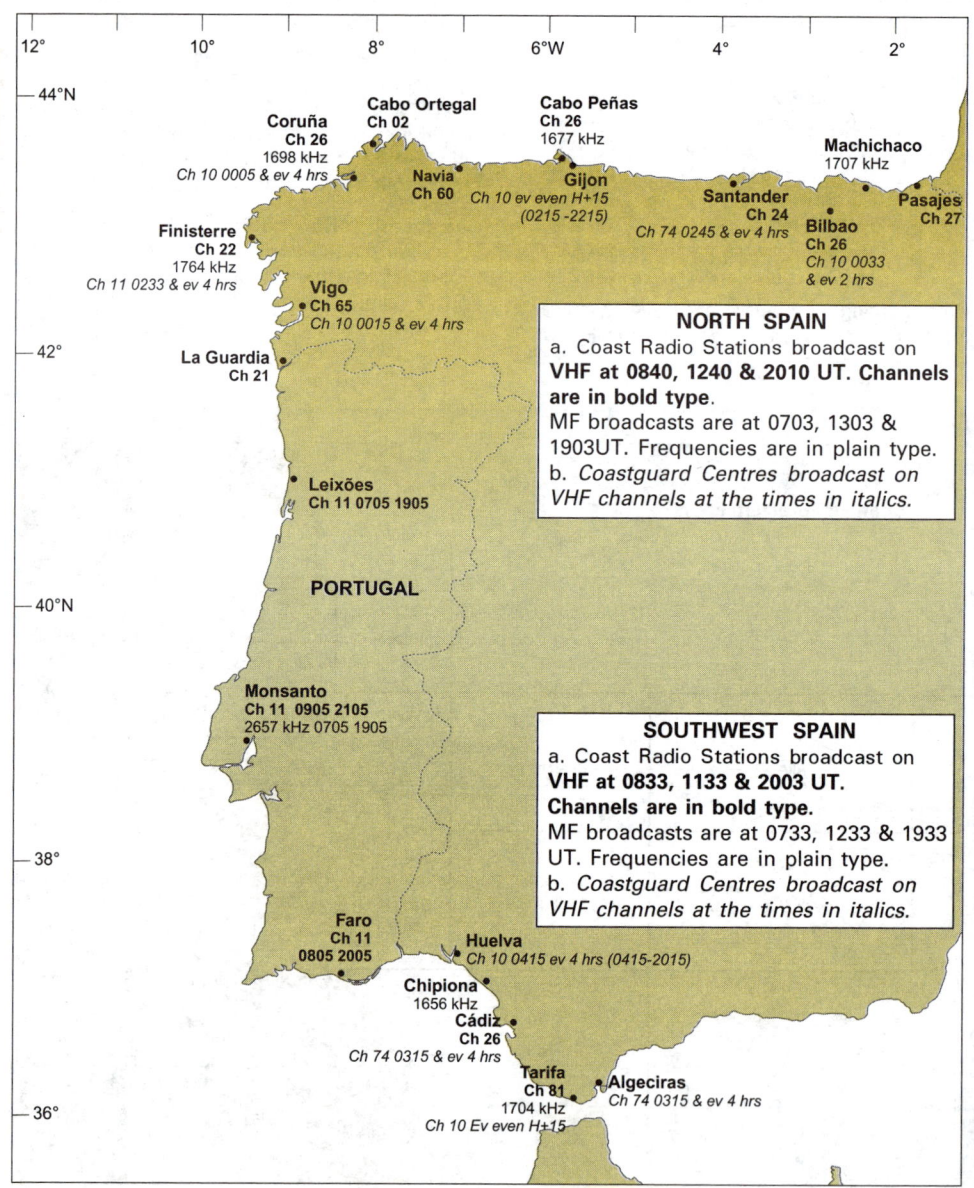

PORTUGAL

Radionaval weather broadcasts
The three stations broadcast bulletins at the times (UT), VHF channels and MF frequencies listed below.

Leixões (Porto)　　Ch 11　　　　　　0705, 1905　　Storm, gale and poor visibility warnings. Synopsis and 24hr forecast for Portuguese coastal waters within 20M, covering area Rio Minho to Cabo de São Vicente. In Portuguese, repeated in **English**.

Monsanto (Lisbon)　　Ch 11, 2657 kHz　　0905, 2105　　Storm, gale and poor visibility warnings. Synopsis and 24hr forecast for Areas 4, 6 and 16-19. In Portuguese, repeated in **English**.

Faro　　　　　　　Ch 11　　　　　　0805, 2005　　Storm, gale and poor visibility warnings. Synopsis and 24hr fcst for Portuguese coastal waters within 20M, covering area Cabo Carvoeiro to Rio Guadiana. In Portuguese, repeated in **English**.

Radiofusão Portuguesa
Broadcasts weather bulletins for the coastal waters of Portugal in Portuguese at 1100 UT. Transmitters and frequencies are:

Porto	720 kHz	Viseu	666 kHz
Montemor (Coimbra)	630 kHz	Lisboa 1	666 kHz
Miranda do Douro	630 kHz	Elvas	720 kHz
Faro	720 kHz, 97·6 MHz		

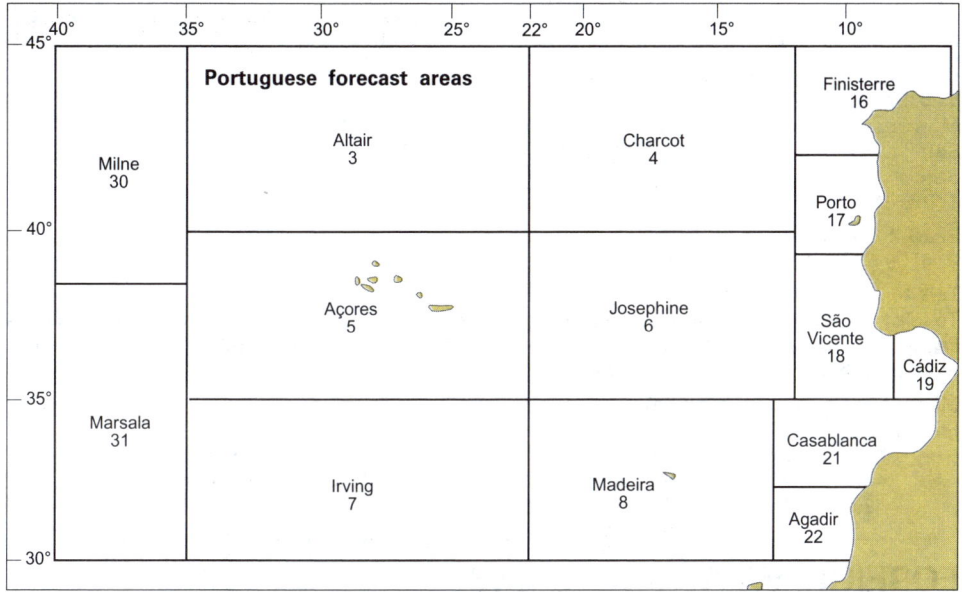

SOUTH WEST SPAIN

Coast Radio Stations
The following CRS broadcast gale warnings, synopsis and 48hr forecasts for Atlantic and Mediterranean areas, in Spanish, at the times (UT) and on the VHF or MF frequencies shown below:

Chipiona	1656 kHz	0733 1233 1933
Cadiz	Ch 26	0833 1133 2003
Tarifa	Ch 81	0833 1133 2003
	1704 kHz	0733 1233 1933
Malaga	Ch 26	0833 1133 2003
Cabo Gata	Ch 27	0833 1133 2003

Coastguard MRCC/MRSC
Broadcast in Spanish and **English** weather bulletins at the times (UT) and VHF channels listed below:

Huelva MRSC	Ch 10	4 hourly (0415-2015)
Cadiz MRSC	Ch 74	0315, 0515, 0715, 1115, 1515, 1915, 2315

WEATHER

Tarifa MRCC   Ch 10, 67   Every even H+15. Actual wind and visibility at Tarifa, followed by a forecast for Strait of Gibraltar, Cádiz Bay and Alborán, in **English** and Spanish. Fog (visibility) warnings are broadcast every even H+15, and more frequently when visibility falls below 2M.

Algeciras MRSC   Ch 74   0315, 0515, 0715, 1115, 1515, 1915, 2315

Recorded telephone forecasts
Call ☎ 906 365 373 for a coastal waters bulletin for the Atlantic coast of Andalucia. ☎ 906 365 374 for High Seas bulletins. Bulletins are in Spanish. The service is only available within Spain and to Autolink-equipped vessels.

GIBRALTAR

Radio Gibraltar (Gibraltar Broadcasting Corporation)
Broadcasts in English: General synopsis, wind force and direction, visibility and sea state, radius 5M from Gibraltar. Frequencies are 1458 kHz, 91·3 MHz, 92·6 MHz and 100·5 MHz. Times (UT):

Mon-Fri: 0530, 0630, 0730, 1030, 1230
Sat: 0530, 0630, 0730, 1030
Sun: 0630, 0730, 1030

British Forces Broadcasting Service (BFBS)   Gibraltar
Gale warnings for the Gibraltar area are broadcast on receipt by BFBS 1 and 2. All broadcasts are in English and comprise: Shipping forecast, wind, weather, visbility, sea state, swell, HW & LW times for waters within 5M of Gibraltar.

BFBS 1 frequencies and times (Local):
93·5, 97·8* MHz FM.
Mon-Fri: 0745   0845   1005   1605
Sat: 0845   0945   1202
Sun: 0845   0945   1202   1602
* This frequency is reported to have greater range.

BFBS 2 frequencies and time:
89·4, 99·5 MHz FM. Mon-Fri: 1200 **UK Local time**

Talk to a forecaster
To talk to a forecaster in Gibraltar about localised weather in the Mediterranean or Canary Islands call ☎ + 44 (0) 8700 767 818. Calls are paid by credit card at a flat rate of £15·00; there is no specified time limit, but 5-10 minutes is average.

Mediterranean forecasts by Fax
From the UK dial ℻ 09060 100 + area numbers:
   435   Gibraltar to Malaga   436   Malaga to Cartagena
   437   Cartagena to Valencia   438   Valencia to Barcelona
   439   Balearic Islands

FOREIGN WEATHER TERMS

English	German	French	Spanish	Dutch
Air mass	Luftmasse	Masse d'air	Massa de aire	Luchtmassa
Anticyclone	Antizyklonisch	Anticyclone	Anticiclón	Hogedrukgebied
Area	Gebiet	Zone	Zona	Gebied
Backing wind	Rückdrehender Wind	Vent reculant	Rolar el viento	Krimpende wind
Barometer	Barometer	Baromètre	Barómetro	Barometer
Breeze	Brise	Brise	Brisa	Bries
Calm	Flaute	Calme	Calma	Kalmte
Centre	Zentrum	Centre	Centro	Centum
Clouds	Wolken	Nuages	Nube	Wolken
Cold	Kalt	Froid	Frio	Koud
Cold front	Kaltfront	Front froid	Frente frio	Kou front
Cyclonic	Zyklonisch	Cyclonique	Ciclonica	Cycloonachtig
Decrease	Abnahme	Affaiblissement	Disminución	Afnemen
Deep	Tief	Profond	Profundo	Diep
Deepening	Vertiefend	Approfondissant	Ahondamiento	Verdiepend
Depression	Sturmtief	Dépression	Depresión	Depressie

English	German	French	Spanish	Dutch
Direction	Richtung	Direction	Direción	Richting
Dispersing	Auflösend	Se dispersant	Disipación	Oplossend
Disturbance	Störung	Perturbation	Perturbación	Verstoving
Drizzle	Niesel	Bruine	Lioviena	Motregen
East	Ost	Est	Este	Oosten
Extending	Ausdehnung	S'étendant	Extension	Uitstrekkend Exten-
sive	Ausgedehnt	Etendu	General	Uitgebreid
Falling	Fallend	Descendant	Bajando	Dalen
Filling	Auffüllend	Secomblant	Relleno	Vullend
Fog	Nebel	Brouillard	Niebla	Nevel
Fog bank	Nebelbank	Ligne de brouillard	Banco de niebla	Mist bank
Forecast	Vorhersage	Prévision	Previsión	Vooruitzicht
Frequent	Häufig	Fréquent	Frecuenta	Veelvuldig
Fresh	Frisch	Frais	Fresco	Fris
Front	Front	Front	Frente	Front
Gale	Sturm	Coup de vent	Temporal	Storm
Gale warning	Sturmwarnung	Avis de coup de vent	Aviso de temporal	Stormwaarschuwing
Good	Gut	Bon	Bueno	Goed
Gradient	Druckunterschied	Gradient	Gradiente	Gradiatie
Gust, squall	Bö	Rafalle	Ráfaga	Windvlaag
Hail	Hagel	Grêle	Granizo	Hagel
Haze	Diesig	Brume	Calina	Nevel
Heavy	Schwer	Abondant	Abunante	Zwaar
High	Hoch	Anticyclone	Alta presión	Hoog
Increasing	Zunehmend	Augmentant	Aumentar	Toenemend
Isobar	Isobar	Isobare	Isobara	Isobar
Isolated	Vereinzelt	Isolé	Aislado	Verspreid
Lightning	Blitze	Eclair de foudre	Relampago	Bliksem
Local	Örtlich	Locale	Local	Plaatselijk
Low	Tief	Dépression	Baja presión	Laag
Mist	Dunst	Brume légere	Nablina	Mist
Moderate	Mäßig	Modéré	Moderado	Matig
Moderating	Abnehmend	Se modérant	Medianente	Matigend
Moving	Bewegend	Se déplacant	Movimiento	Bewegend
North	Nord	Nord	Septentrional	Noorden
Occluded	Okklusion	Couvert	Okklusie	Bewolkt
Poor	Schlecht	Mauvais	Mal	Slecht
Precipitation	Niederschlag	Précipitation	Precipitación	Neerslag
Pressure	Druck	Pression	Presión	Druk
Rain	Regen	Pluie	Iluvia	Regen
Ridge	Hochdruckbrücke	Crête	Cresta	Rug
Rising	Ansteigend	Montant	Subiendo	Stijgen
Rough	Rauh	Agitée	Bravo o alborotado	Ruw
Sea	See	Mer	Mar	Zee
Seaway	Seegang	Haute mer	Alta mar	Zee
Scattered	Vereinzelt	Sporadiques	Difuso	Verspreid
Shower	Schauer	Averse	Aguacero	Bui
Slight	Leicht	Un peu	Leicht	Licht
Slow	Langsam	Lent	Lent	Langzaam
Snow	Schnee	Neige	Nieve	Sneeuw
South	Süd	Sud	Sur	Zuiden
Storm	Sturm	Tempête	Temporal	Storm
Sun	Sonne	Soleil	Sol	Zon
Swell	Schwell	Houle	Mar de fondo	Deining
Thunder	Donner	Tonnerre	Tormenta	Donder
Thunderstorm	Gewitter	Orage	Tronada	Onweer
Trough	Trog, Tiefausläufer	Creux	Seno	Trog
Variable	Umlaufend	Variable	Variable	Veranderlijk
Veering	Rechtdrehend	Virement de vent	Dextrogiro	Ruimende wind
Warm front	Warmfront	Front chaud	Frente calido	Warm front
Weather	Wetter	Temps	Tiempo	Weer
Wind	Wind	Vent	Viento	Wind
Weather report	Wetterbericht	Météo	Previsión	Weer bericht meteorologica

Chapter 2

COMMUNICATIONS

CHAPTER 3 - COMMUNICATIONS

CONTENTS

Radio operation 95
Radio data 97
Port Radio Stations 99
   England - South coast 99
   England - East coast 100
   Scotland 101
   England - West coast & Wales 102
   Ireland 102
   Denmark 103
   Germany 103
   Netherlands 104
   Belgium 105
   North France 106
   Channel Islands 106
   West France 106
   Spain 107
   Portugal 107
   Gibraltar 107
VTS Charts 108
   Thames & Medway 108
   Humber Estuary 109
   Netherlands - Scheldemond & Westerschelde 110
   Netherlands - Approaches to Nieuwe Waterweg 111
VHF & MF Coast Radio Stations 112
   Channel Islands 112
   Republic of Ireland 112
   Denmark 113
   Germany 113
   North Spain 113
   Portugal 114
   South West Spain 114
Sound signals and shapes 115

RADIO OPERATION

Avoiding interference

Before transmitting, first listen on the VHF channel. If occupied, wait for a break before transmitting, or choose another channel. If you cause interference you must comply immediately with any request from a Coastguard or Coast Radio Station to stop transmitting. The request will state how long to desist.

Control of communications

Ship-to-Shore: Except in the case of distress, urgency or safety, communications between ship and shore-based stations are controlled by the latter.

Intership: The ship *called* controls communication. If you call another ship, then it has control. If you are called by a ship, you assume control. If a shore-based station breaks in, both ships must comply with instructions given. A shore-based station has better aerials and equipment and so its transmission and reception ranges are greater.

Radio confidentiality

Inevitably you will overhear private conversations on VHF. It is illegal to reproduce them, pass them on or use them for any purpose.

Voice technique

There are two considerations when speaking:

What to say – i.e. voice procedure
How to say it – i.e. voice technique

Clear R/T speech is vital. If a message cannot be understood by the receiving operator it is useless.

Anyone can become a good operator by following a few rules: The voice should be pitched at a higher level than for normal conversation. Avoid dropping the voice pitch at the end of a word or phrase. Hold the microphone a few inches in front of the mouth and speak directly into it at a normal level. Speak clearly so that there can be no confusion. Emphasise words with weak syllables; 'Tower', if badly pronounced, could sound like 'tar'. People with strong accents must try to use as understandable a pronunciation as possible.

Messages which have to be written down at the receiving station should be spoken slowly. This gives time for it to be written down by the receiving operator. Remember, the average reading speed is 250 words a minute, whilst average writing speed is only 20. If the transmitting operator himself writes it down all should be well.

Difficult words may be spelled phonetically. Operators precede this with 'I spell'. If the word is pronounceable include it before and after it has been spelt. For example, if an operator sends the message 'I will moor alongside the yacht *Coila*' he would transmit: 'I will moor alongside the yacht *Coila* – I spell – Charlie Oscar India Lima Alfa – *Coila*'. When asked for your international callsign – say it is MGLA4 – transmit: 'My callsign is Mike Golf Lima Alfa Four.'

The phonetic alphabet

The syllables to emphasise are underlined

Letter	Morse	Phonetic	Spoken as
A	•–	Alfa	<u>AL</u>-fah
B	–•••	Bravo	<u>BRAH</u>-voh
C	–•–•	Charlie	<u>CHAR</u>-lee
D	–••	Delta	<u>DELL</u>-tah
E	•	Echo	<u>ECK</u>-oh
F	••–•	Foxtrot	<u>FOKS</u>-trot
G	––•	Golf	<u>GOLF</u>
H	••••	Hotel	hoh-<u>TELL</u>
I	••	India	<u>IN</u>-dee-ah
J	•–––	Juliett	<u>JEW</u>-lee-ett
K	–•–	Kilo	<u>KEY</u>-loh
L	•–••	Lima	<u>LEE</u>-mah
M	––	Mike	<u>MIKE</u>
N	–•	November	no-<u>VEM</u>-ber
O	–––	Oscar	<u>OSS</u>-car
P	•––•	Papa	pa-<u>PAH</u>
Q	––•–	Quebec	keh-<u>BECK</u>
R	•–•	Romeo	<u>ROW</u>-me-oh
S	•••	Sierra	see-<u>AIR</u>-rah
T	–	Tango	<u>TANG</u>-go
U	••–	Uniform	<u>YOU</u>-nee-form or <u>OO</u>-nee-form
V	•••–	Victor	<u>VIK</u>-tah
W	•––	Whiskey	<u>WISS</u>-key
X	–••–	X-Ray	<u>ECKS</u>-ray
Y	–•––	Yankee	<u>YANG</u>-key
Z	––••	Zulu	<u>ZOO</u>-loo

Phonetic numerals

When numerals are transmitted, the following pronunciations make them easier to understand.

No	Morse	Spoken as	No	Morse	Spoken as
1	•––––	WUN	6	–••••	SIX
2	••–––	TOO	7	––•••	SEV-EN
3	•••––	TREE	8	–––••	AIT
4	••••–	FOW-ER	9	––––•	NIN-ER
5	•••••	FIFE	0	–––––	ZERO

Chapter 3

COMMUNICATIONS

Numerals are transmitted digit by digit except that multiples of thousands may be spoken as follows:

Numeral	Spoken as
44	FOW-ER FOW-ER
90	NIN-ER ZERO
136	WUN TREE SIX
500	FIFE ZERO ZERO
1478	WUN FOW-ER SEV-EN AIT
7000	SEV-EN THOU-SAND

Punctuation

Punctuation marks should be used only where their omission would cause confusion.

Mark	Word	Spoken as
.	Decimal	DAY-SEE-MAL
,	Comma	COMMA
.	Stop	STOP

Procedure words or 'prowords'

These are used to shorten transmissions

All after: Used after proword *'say again'* to request repetition of a portion of a message

All before: Used after proword *'say again'* to request repetition of a portion of message

Correct: Reply to repetition of message that was preceded by prowords *'read back for check'* when it has been correctly repeated. Often said twice

Correction: Spoken during the transmission of a message means an error has been made in this transmission. Cancel the last word or group of words. The correct word or group follows

In figures: Following numeral or group of numerals to be written as figures

In letters: Following numeral or group of numerals to be written as figures as spoken

I say again: I am repeating transmission or portion indicated

I spell: I shall spell the next word or group of letters phonetically

Out: This is the end of working to you

Over: Invitation to reply

Read back: If receiving station is doubtful about accuracy of whole or part of message it may repeat it back to the sending station, preceding the repetition with prowords *'I read back'*

Say again: Repeat your message or portion referred to ie *'Say again all after'*, *'Say again address'*, etc

Station calling: Used when a station is uncertain of the calling station's identification

This is: This transmission is from the station whose callsign or name immediately follows

Wait: If a called station is unable to accept traffic immediately, it will reply 'WAIT.......MINUTES'. If probable delay exceeds 10 minutes the reason will be given

Word after or Word before: Used after the proword *'say again'* to request repetition

Wrong: Reply to repetition of message preceded by prowords *'read back'* when it has been incorrectly repeated

Calls, calling and callsigns

Shore-based stations normally identify themselves by using their geographical name followed by the words Coastguard or Radio, eg Solent Coastguard, Dublin Radio etc. Vessels usually identify themselves by the name on their licence but the International callsign assigned to the ship may be used in certain cases. If two yachts bear the same name or where some confusion may result, you should give your International callsign when starting communications, and thereafter use your ship's name as callsign.

'All ships' broadcast

Information to be received or used by all who intercept it, eg gale warnings, navigational warnings, weather forecasts etc, is generally broadcast by Coastguard Radio and addressed 'All stations'. No reply is needed.

Establishing communication with a shore-based station

The initial call is usually made on a working channel. Channel 16 should not be used except for distress, urgency or very briefly to establish a working channel.

- Switch to one of the station's working channels, pausing to check no-one is transmitting
- Are you close enough to try low power *(1 watt)* first? Possible at ranges up to 10 miles. Otherwise use high power *(25 watts)* with more battery drain.
- The callsign of calling station up to three times only, and prowords 'This is'
- Indication of number of R/T calls you have to make
- Proword 'Over'

Small faults can drastically reduce your transmitting range. Possibly the aerial for the channel chosen has been optimised for areas east of the station and you are to the west. If approaching the station wait 15 minutes and call again. If the range is opening, either try again in hope, or try another station within range.

Every time you call at high power, you are decreasing battery state and the range your VHF will achieve. Continued calling also clutters up the channel and denies access to other users.

RADIO DATA

SHORT, MEDIUM and LONG RANGE RADIO COMMUNICATIONS

A suitable radio receiver on board will provide weather forecasts and time signals at scheduled times on a number of frequencies in various wavebands. With a maritime receiver you are not limited to the familiar BBC and commercial broadcasts. HM Coastguard transmit navigation warnings, storm warnings and weather messages for shipping in their respective sea areas.

Short range radiotelephony (RT) transmits and receives on VHF channels in the marine VHF (Very High Frequency) band. The equipment and procedures are simple, but range is normally limited to about 20 miles from ship to shore, rather less from ship to ship. Interconnection with national telephone systems is possible on certain VHF/RT channels when a yacht is within range of a Coast Radio Station, although there are now no such stations on the mainland of the UK, France or the Netherlands. Mobile telephones are now by far the most common form of ship to shore communication.

Medium range two-way communication operate in the marine MF (medium frequency) RT band, the 2MHz 'trawler band'. Single sideband techniques are employed on these medium frequencies and SSB equipment is essential. The effective range depends on the power of the transmitter on board and the sensitivity of the associated receiver; in general this might be up to 200 miles from certain (but not all) Coast Radio Stations.

Each channel in the VHF/RT band and each frequency in the MF/RT band has its specific purpose and may not be used at random for general conversation. Calling on the wrong channel merely wastes time and causes annoyance to other users.

THE MARINE VHF BAND

VHF is used by most vessels, Coast Radio Stations, Coastguard centres and other rescue services. Its range is slightly better than the line of sight between the transmitting and receiving aerials. It pays to fit a good aerial, as high as possible.

In the Marine VHF/RT band the individual frequencies are separated from their neighbours by exactly 25kHz 'elbow-room' to eliminate mutual interference. For convenience each working frequency is given a channel number; the numbers do not run consecutively because the channels were originally spaced 50kHz apart. But it has since become possible to fit another channel in between each original one and so make fuller use of the waveband. Marine VHF frequencies are in the band 156·00–174·00 MHz. Channels 29 to 59 are allocated to other purposes. Thus 55 channels are available, plus some with special purposes (see below).

Of the 55 channels available in the Marine VHF/RT band, small craft are unlikely to need more than a selected dozen, some of which may vary with the area in which a boat operates.

The simplest and earliest VHF/RT transmitter-receivers operated only in the 'simplex' mode, ie transmit and receive on the same channel, so that only one person can talk at a time. The channel numbers are 06 (mandatory), 08 to 17, 67 to 74 and 77.

All other channels are for 'duplex' working, ie transmit and receive on different frequencies, so that conversation is normal.

For full duplex operation a more elaborate and expensive transmitter-receiver with either twin aerials or a special filter is needed, but it can interconnect with the shore telephone system so as to converse with subscribers who have no knowledge of radio procedures.

More common among yachtsmens' VHF/RTs, however, are the semi-duplex operating sets which, although involving simplex procedures, allow you to communicate with stations operating duplex systems and to link with shore telephones via Coast Radio Stations.

VHF Channel Grouping

Channels are grouped for three main purposes, but some can be used for more than one purpose. They are listed below in their preferred order of usage:

(1) *Public correspondence* (ie used to access the shore telephone system via Coast Radio Stations): Ch 26, 27, 25, 24, 23, 28, 04, 01, 03, 02, 07, 05, 84, 87, 86, 83, 85, 88, 61, 64, 65, 62, 66, 63, 60, 82, 78, 81. All channels are duplex.

(2) *Inter-ship:* Ch 06, 08, 10, 13, 09, 72, 73, 67, 69, 77, 15, 17. These are all simplex channels. It is as well to know them, so that if another vessel calls you, you can swiftly nominate a working channel from within this group.

COMMUNICATIONS

(3) Port Operations:
Simplex: Ch 12, 14, 11, 13, 09, 68, 71, 74, 69, 73, 17, 15.
Duplex: Ch 20, 22, 18, 19, 21, 05, 07, 02, 03, 01, 04, 78, 82, 79, 81, 80, 60, 63, 66, 62, 65, 64, 61, 84.

Special purposes. The following channels have one specific purpose only:

Ch 0 (156·00 MHz): SAR ops, not available to yachts.

Ch's 10 (156·500 MHz), **23** (161·750 MHz), **73** (156·675 MHz), **84** (161·825 MHz) and **86** (161·925 MHz): for MSI broadcasts by HMCG.

Ch 13 (156·650 MHz): Intership safety of navigation (sometimes referred to as bridge-to-bridge); a possible channel for calling a merchant ship if no contact on Ch 16.

Ch 16 (156·80 MHz): Distress, Safety and calling. *See Chapter 4 for Distress and Safety.* Ch 16 will be monitored by ships, CG centres (and, in some areas, any remaining Coast Radio Stations) for Distress and Safety until at least 2005, in parallel with DSC Ch 70. Yachts should monitor Ch 16. After an initial call, the stations concerned **must** switch to a working channel, except for Safety matters.

Ch 67 (156·375 MHz): the Small Craft Safety channel in the UK, accessed via Ch 16.

Ch 70 (156·525 MHz): exclusively for digital selective calling for Distress and Safety purposes.

Ch 80 (157·025 MHz): the primary working channel between yachts and UK marinas.

Ch M (157·85 MHz): the secondary working channel between yachts and UK marinas; previously known as Ch 37.

Ch M2 (161·425 MHz): for race control, with Ch M as stand-by. YCs may apply to use Ch M2.

MEDIUM RANGE MF/RT

The limited line-of-sight range of VHF/RT makes a longer-range system desirable for small craft which need to maintain contact with shore stations when offshore or in a coastal area to which VHF cover does not extend.

Single sideband MF/RT provides such contact all around the waters of the UK and Western Europe. A receiver alone gives the ability to hear weather bulletins, storm and navigation warnings for local sea areas broadcast from Coast Radio Stations in the 1.6 to 4.0MHz maritime band, ie on frequencies between 1605 and 4200 kHz. Not all radio stations are equipped to deal with this traffic but there are sufficient stations adequately spaced around the coast to cover all UK coastal waters.

Unlike VHF and HF, MF transmissions tend to follow the curvature of the earth, which makes them suitable for direction-finding equipment. For this reason, and because of their good range, the marine Distress radiotelephone frequency is in the MF band (2182 kHz).

TRAFFIC LISTS

Coast stations wishing to contact a vessel at sea will first attempt to do so by a direct call on Channel 16 which will be heard if a loudspeaker watch is kept and the vessel is within range. Failing this, the vessel's name will be added to the Traffic List broadcast at (usually) two hour intervals at the times and on the frequencies (channels) shown elsewhere in Coast Radio Stations section, pages 112 - 114. Unless you monitor that frequency at the appropriate time you may never know that there is incoming traffic awaiting attention. When such a call is received, the response is to call the station concerned on the working channel.

SILENCE PERIODS

Although there is no official silence period for VHF, it is generally advised that no transmission be made during the silence periods which are enforced for the 2182kHz distress frequency. The periods are the three minutes immediately after the whole and half hours, ie H to H+03 and H+30 to H+33.

LONG RANGE HF RADIO

HF radiotelephones use frequencies in the 4, 8, 12, 16 and 22 MHz bands (short wave) that are chosen to suit propagation conditions. HF is more expensive than MF and requires more power, but can provide worldwide coverage. A good installation and skilled operating techniques are essential for satisfactory results.

HF waves travel upwards and bounce off the ionosphere back to earth. Reception is better at night when the ionosphere is denser. The directional properties of HF transmissions are poor, so there is no HF Distress frequency.

PORT RADIO STATIONS

The following listings are derived from ALRS (Admiralty List of Radio Signals). They are therefore biassed towards 'Big Ships'. However if read in conjunction with Marina R/T details which appear in Chapter 1, pages 53 - 58, the most complete picture will emerge. (It is hoped to combine the two listings in a later edition).

Annotations: **Ch 16** is almost universally guarded; it is therefore omitted. *Call on a working channel if essential. In many larger ports it is sensible to monitor the primary port channel (in bold) before changing to a marina channel.* Times are local, unless marked **UT**. **H24** = continuous watch. **HJ** = day only. **HO** = Office hours. **HX** = no specific hours.

ENGLAND – SOUTH COAST

ST MARY'S HARBOUR, Isles of Scilly: Ch 14, 69 (Pilots). Summer 0800-1700 daily.
NEWLYN HARBOUR:
Hbr office: Ch 09 **12**
Mon-Fri: 0800-1700, Sat: 0800-1200
PENZANCE HBR RADIO:
Hbr office: Ch 09 **12** Mon-Fri: 0830-1730 and on all tides HW −2 to +1.
FALMOUTH HBR RADIO:
Ch 12 14 (Mon-Fri 0800-1700). Harbour Launch *Killigrew*: **Ch 12**
Truro Hbr office: Call *Carrick One* **Ch 12**
MEVAGISSEY:
Hbr office: Ch 14
Summer: 0900-2100, Winter: 0900-1700
CHARLESTOWN:
Hbr office: Ch 14 HW −2 to +1, only when a vessel is expected.
PAR PORT RADIO:
Hbr office: Ch 12 HO. Pilots HW ±2.
FOWEY HBR RADIO:
(0900-1700) **Hbr Patrol: Ch 12** (0900-2000). Water Taxi: **Ch** 06.
LOOE: Ch 16 Occas.
PLYMOUTH:
Movement Control: *Long Room Port Control*
Ch 14 H24.
Sutton Hbr Lock: Ch 12 H24.
Cattewater Hbr: Ch 14 (Mon-Fri 0900-1700).
SALCOMBE:
Salcombe Hbr or launch: Ch 14 May to mid-Sep: 7/7, 0600-2200; otherwise: M-F 0900-1600
Salcombe Hbr Taxi **Ch 12**. Fuel barge: **Ch 06**
Egremont (ICC Floating HQ): **Ch M**
DARTMOUTH:
Dart Nav Ch 11 M-F: 0900-1700 ±1, Sat: 0900-1200.
Fuel barge: **Ch 06**. Water taxi: **Ch 08**.
TORBAY HARBOURS:
Call *Brixham Port* or *Torquay Port* **Ch 14** May-Sep: 0800-1800; Oct-Apr: Mon-Fri: 0900-1700.
TEIGNMOUTH HBR RADIO:
Ch 12 Mon-Fri 0830-1700; Sat 0900-1200 and when vessel due.
EXETER:
Port of Exeter Ch 12 Mon-Fri: 0730-1730 and when vessel expected. **Exmouth Dock Ch 14**.
Retreat Boatyard: Ch M HW±2
LYME REGIS HARBOUR RADIO:
Ch 14. Summer: 0800-2000, Winter: 1000-1500.
Access HW±2½.
BRIDPORT RADIO:
Ch 11
PORTLAND HARBOUR RADIO:
Ch 74 (H24)
WEYMOUTH HARBOUR RADIO:
Hbr Office & Town Bridge: Ch 12 Mon-Fri: 0800-2000 (summer & when vessel is due).
Marina Ch 80. **Fuel: Ch 60**
POOLE:
Harbour Control & Bridge Ch 80 (H24)
Poole Bay Fuels: Ch M Mon-Fri: 0900-1730, weekends in season 0830-1800
YARMOUTH (IoW):
Hbr office & Yar Bridge: Ch 68 H24. Water taxi: **Ch 15**
NEWPORT (IoW):
Hr Mr: 69 0800-1600
COWES:
Hbr Office & Chain Ferry Ch 69
Mon-Fri: 0800-1700 and by arrangement
Water Taxi: Ch 77
RYDE:
Hbr office: Ch 80
Summer 0900-2000 Winter HX. Access HW±2
BEMBRIDGE:
Harbour launch **Ch M**
SOUTHAMPTON:
Monitor Port operations Ch 12 14
VTS Broadcasts Ch 12 Every H 0600-2200,
1 Jun-30 Sep
HAMBLE:
Hbr Radio: Ch 68 Apr-Sep daily: 0600-2200, Oct-Mar 0700-1830
Water Taxi: Call *Blue Star Boats* **Ch 77** 06
PORTSMOUTH:
Monitor Ch 11. Call *QHM* **Ch 11** if essential
PORTSMOUTH COMMERCIAL HARBOUR:
Call *Portsmouth Hbr Radio* **Ch 11** 14 **(H24)**
LANGSTONE:
Hbr office: Ch 12. Summer: daily 0830-1700; Winter: Mon-Fri 0830-1700; Sat-Sun 0830-1300
CHICHESTER:
Hbr office: Ch 14. 1 Apr - 30 Sep: M-Fri: 0900-1300, 1400-1700. Sat: 0900-1300. 1 Oct - 31 March: 0900-1300, 1400-1700
Water taxi **Ch 08** 0900-1800, mobile 07970 378350
LITTLEHAMPTON:
Hbr office & Bridge: Ch 71 HX

99

COMMUNICATIONS

Arun Yacht Club: Ch M Access HW±3
SHOREHAM:
Shoreham Hbr Radio: **Ch 14** (H24) and lock
BRIGHTON:
Call *Brighton Control*: **Ch M 80**. Inner hbr only, access 0800-1800 via lock
NEWHAVEN:
Newhaven Radio **Ch 12**; ditto Swing bridge
EASTBOURNE:
Sovereign Hbr, inc Lock/berthing: **Ch 17**
RYE:
Hbr radio: **Ch 14** 0900-1700 or when ship due
FOLKESTONE:
Call **Port Control: Ch 15** for clearance to enter
DOVER:
Call **Port Control Ch 74** for clearance to enter
Diesel fuel & Water Taxi: via marina **Ch 80**
DOVER STRAIT:
Channel Navigation Information Service
CNIS: Dover Coastguard **Ch 11** 67 80
Ch 11 bcsts Info H+40 plus extra bcst when visibility <2M; ditto Gris Nez Traffic **Ch 79** at H+10, plus additional bcst every H+25 when visibility <2M
RAMSGATE:
Port Control **Ch 14**

ENGLAND – EAST COAST

MEDWAY:
Monitor **Medway Radio Ch 74**
Kingsferry Bridge (W Swale): Ch 10 H24
WHITSTABLE
Hbr Radio: **Ch 09** 12, Mon-Fri: 0830-1700 and –3HW+1
PORT OF LONDON:
Port Control London: Ch 12 (from seaward approaches to Sea Reach No 4 buoy)
Port Control London: Ch 68
Sea Reach No 4 Lt buoy to Crayford Ness
Woolwich Radio: Ch 14, 22
Above Crayford Ness
Thames Barrier: Ch 14
All VHF-equipped vessels intending to navigate in the Thames Barrier Control Zone must report to Woolwich Radio on Ch 14
RIVER THAMES:
Patrol Launches: Call *Thames Patrol* **Ch 06 12 14 16 68**
King George V Dock Lock: Call *KG Control* **Ch 13**
West India Dock Lock: Ch 13
Greenwich Yacht Club: Ch M
Thames Lock (Brentford): Ch 74
Summer 0800-1800 Winter 0800-1630
Cadogan Pier: Ch 14 0900-1700
RIVER ROACH:
Havengore Bridge: Ch 72 HJ, Access HW±2
RIVER BLACKWATER:
River Bailiff: Ch 16 0900-1700

Heybridge Lock: Ch 80 –2HW+1
RIVER COLNE, BRIGHTLINGSEA:
Hbr Radio: **Ch 68** 0800-2000
RIVERS STOUR AND ORWELL:
HARWICH VTS: Ch 71 09 11 20 H24
SUNK VTS Ch 14 H24
Harwich International Port **Ch 13**
Ipswich Port Radio: Ch 68 H24
RIVER DEBEN:
Hbr office: **Ch 08**
SOUTHWOLD:
Port Radio: **Ch 09 12**;
LOWESTOFT:
Hbr Control: **Ch 11 14**
Royal Norfolk & Suffolk YC: **Ch 80** Access HW±4
Mutford Lock and Road Bridge: **Ch 09 14**
GREAT YARMOUTH:
Port Control/VTS: **Ch 09 11 12** H24
Haven Bridge: **Ch 12**
WELLS-NEXT-THE-SEA:
Wells Hbr Radio: **Ch 12**
HJ and HW–3 when vessel expected
WISBECH:
Ch 09 HW–3 when vessel expected
Sutton Bridge: **Ch 09**
KING'S LYNN:
Call *KLCB* **Ch 14** 11
Mon-Fri: 0800-1730 and –4HW+1
BOSTON:
Dock: **Ch 11 12**
Grand Sluice: **Ch 74** only when lock operates
Denver Sluice: **Ch 73** when vessel expected
RIVER HUMBER:
VTS Area 1: **Ch 14** (from sea to Clee Ness Lt F)
VTS Area 2: **Ch 12** (up-river to Garleston on R Trent and Goole on R Ouse). MSI broadcasts on Ch 12 & 14 every 2hrs from 0103
Grimsby Docks: **Ch 74**; 18 79 H24
South Ferriby sluice: **Ch 74 80**
Mon-Fri: 0930-1700; Sat, Sun & Holidays: 1030-1700. Access HW±3
RIVER TRENT TO NEAR NEWARK
Burton-upon-Stather, Flixborough, Grove, Keadby, Gunness, Gainsborough: All **Ch 17**.
Locks at Keadby, West Stockwith, Torksey and Cromwell: All **Ch 74**
RIVER OUSE TO NABURN
Blacktoft Jetty: **Ch 14**
Goole Docks: **Ch 14** H24
Goole Railway Bridge: **Ch 09**
Howdendyke: **Ch 09**
Boothferry bridge: **Ch 09**
Selby lock: **Ch 74** HJ
Selby railway and Toll bridges: **Ch 09** contact 10 mins in advance
Naburn Lock: **Ch 74**
BRIDLINGTON:
Hbr office: **Ch 12** HX. Access HW±3
SCARBOROUGH:
Scarborough Lt Ho **Ch 12** H24. Access HW±3

WHITBY:
HM & Bridge: **Ch 11**, 12 H24. Access HW±2
TEES and HARTLEPOOL:
Tees Port control: **Ch** 08, 11, 12, **14, 22**
R. Tees Barrage: **Ch M** H24
SEAHAM:
Hbr office: **Ch 12** Mon-Fri: 0800-1800
Access HW −2½ to +1½
SUNDERLAND:
Hbr Radio: **Ch 14** (H24)
TYNE, PORT OF:
Tyne Hbr Radio: **Ch** 11 **12** 14, inc Info service
Harbour Launch: **Ch** 06 08 11 12 14
BLYTH:
Port control: **Ch** 11 **12**
WARKWORTH HARBOUR (Amble):
Hbr office: **Ch 14** (Mon-Fri 0900-1700)
BERWICK-UPON-TWEED:
Hbr office: **Ch 12** Mon-Fri 0800-1700

SCOTLAND
EYEMOUTH:
Ch 12 office hours
FORTH PORTS:
Call *Forth Navigation* **Ch 71**; 12, **20** on request
Leith: **Ch 12**
Granton, Royal Forth YC: Call *Boswell* **Ch M**
Access HW±4
Grangemouth Docks: **Ch 14**
Methil Docks: **Ch 14** Access −3HW+1
Anstruther: **Ch 11** Access HW±2
PERTH:
Perth Harbour **Ch 09**
DUNDEE:
Dundee Harbour Radio **Ch 12**
Royal Tay YC: **Ch M**
ARBROATH:
Arbroath Port Control **Ch 11**
MONTROSE:
Montrose Port Control **Ch 12**
STONEHAVEN:
Stonehaven **Ch 11**
ABERDEEN:
Aberdeen Port Control **Ch** 06 11 **12** 13
PETERHEAD:
Peterhead Hbrs **Ch 14** for cl'nce to enter/exit
FRASERBURGH: Ch 12 H24
MACDUFF: Ch 12 H24
BANFF: Ch 14 HX, access HW±4
WHITEHILLS: *Whitehills Hbr Radio* **Ch 14**
BUCKIE: Ch 12 (Ch 16 is H24)
LOSSIEMOUTH:
Ch 12 0700-1700 & 1hr before vessel is due
HOPEMAN and BURGHEAD:
Burghead Radio **Ch 14** HX or when vessel due
INVERNESS:
Inverness Hbr Office: **Ch 12**
M-Fri: 0900-1700 and when vessel expected
Clachnaharry Sea Lock **Ch 74** HW±4 in HO

CROMARTY FIRTH, inc Invergordon: Ch 11
HELMSDALE: Ch 13
WICK: Ch 14 HX
SCRABSTER:
Port: **Ch 12** H24. Call on entry and exit.
ORKNEY HARBOURS NAVIGATION SERVICE:
Orkney Harbour Radio **Ch** 09 **11** 12
Kirkwall: **Ch 12**
M-Fri: 0800-1700 and when vessel expected
Stromness Harbour: Ch 12 M-Fri: 0900-1700
Pierowall (Westray Pier): Ch 14 when vessel is expected
FAIR ISLE:
Call *Shetland Coastguard* **Ch 16**
SHETLAND
Lerwick Hbr: **Ch** 11 **12**
Scalloway Hbr Radio: **Ch** 09 **12**
Mon-Fri: 0600-1800, Sat: 0600-1230
Sullom Voe VTS: Ch 14 for traffic info, weather and radar assistance on request
Balta Sound Harbour: Ch 16 HO
OUTER HEBRIDES
STORNOWAY: Hbr office **Ch 12** H24
Loch Maddy, N Uist: Ch 12 HX
St Kilda: Call *Kilda Radio* **Ch 16** HJ
MAINLAND
Kinlochbervie: Ch 14 HX
Lochinver: Ch 09 HX
ULLAPOOL: Ch 14 12 H24 fishing season, otherwise HO
Gairloch Harbour: Ch 16 0900-1400; 1900-2300
ISLE OF SKYE
Uig: **Ch 08** HX. Portree Harbour: **Ch 12** HX
Skye Bridge Crossing: **Ch 12**
KYLE OF LOCH ALSH: Ch 11
Mallaig: **Ch 09** HO
Tiree, Gott Bay Pier, : **Ch 31** HX
Isle of Coll, Arinagour Pier: **Ch 31**
Loch Sunart, Salen Jetty: **Ch 16**
ISLAND OF MULL
Tobermory: Ch 12 HJ
Craignure Pier: Ch 31 HX
Corpach/Caledonian Canal: Ch 16 74
Summer: 0700-2200; Spring/Autumn: 0830-1650; Winter: 0930-1530
OBAN:
Port **Ch 12** 0900-1700. Oban Bay, monitor **16**
CRINAN CANAL: Ch 74
May-Sep: 0800-1200, 1230-1600, 1620-1800;
Oct: Mon-Sat: 0800-1200, 1230-1600; Nov-Apr: Mon-Fri: 0900-1530
Tarbert, Loch Fyne: **Ch 14**
CAMPBELTOWN: Ch 12 13
Mon-Fri: 0900-1700
ROTHESAY, Bute: Ch 12
May-Sep: 0600-2100; Oct-Apr: 0600-1900
ARDROSSAN:
Hbr office: **Ch** 12 14

COMMUNICATIONS

CLYDEPORT:
Clydeport Estuary Radio: Ch 12 H24
QHM Faslane: Ch 73 13
Greenock Control: Ch 73
IRVINE: Ch 12
Port & Bridge: Ch 12 HX, Mon-Fri: 0800-1600
TROON: Ch 14
Seacat, daily Arr: 0930, 2030; Dep 1015, 2100
AYR: Ch 14 H24
GIRVAN: Ch 12 Mon-Fri: 0900-1700
STRANRAER: Ch 14 (H24) Monitor for ferries
KIRKCUDBRIGHT: Ch 12 0800-1700
Access HW±3

ENGLAND W COAST & WALES

Silloth Docks: Ch 12 Access –2½HW+1
WORKINGTON:
Hbr Radio: Ch 11 14 Access –2½HW+2
WHITEHAVEN:
Ch 12 Access HW±3
ISLE OF MAN
Douglas Port Control and Info: Ch 12 H24.
Note: if unable to contact other IoM hbrs below, call Douglas
Castletown: Ch 12 0830-1700
Port St Mary: Ch 12 HJ and when vessel due
Peel: Ch 12 HJ and when vessel expected
Ramsey: Ch 12 HO and when vessel due
MAINLAND
Barrow Port Control: Ch 12
Heysham Port: Ch 14 74
GLASSON DOCK Ch 69
Access –1½HW through lock
FLEETWOOD:
Fleetwood Dock Radio: Ch 12 0900-1700
Access HW±2 through lock
LIVERPOOL:
Call *Mersey Radio* Ch 12 for port operations
Information broadcasts: Ch 09 at 3h and 2h before HW. Radar assistance Ch 18
Brunswick Dock: Ch M for Liverpool marina
Canning Dock: Ch M 0900-1700. Access –2HW through lock to Albert Dock
CONWY:
Ch 12 14 Apr-Sep: 0900-1800; Oct-Mar: Mon-Fri: 0900-1800. Access –3HW+2
MENAI STRAIT
Beaumaris & Menai Bridge: Ch 69
Mon-Fri: 0800-1700
Caernarfon: Call *Caernarfon Hbr* Ch 14
Mon-Fri: 0900-1700 Sat: 0900-1200
HOLYHEAD
Port Control: Ch 14 H24
PWLLHELI
Hbr office Ch 08 0900-1715. Access –2HW+1¾
PORTHMADOG
Call *Portmadog Hbr* Ch 12 14 0900-1700, and when vessel expected. Access HW±1½

BARMOUTH
Ch 12 May-Sept: 0900-2200; Oct-April: 0900-1700 weekdays only
ABERDOVEY: Ch 12 0900-1700 Access HW±3
ABERYSTWYTH: Ch 14 Access HW±3
ABERAERON: Ch 14 Served by **NEW QUAY** Harbourmaster. 0900-1700. Access HW±3
FISHGUARD: Hbr office: Ch 14
MILFORD HAVEN
Port Control & Patrol launch: Ch 12, monitor continuously whilst under way
Milford Docks: Call *Pierhead* Ch 14 09 12 Locking approx HW±3; freeflow HW –2 to HW
Tenby: Ch 80 Access HW±2½
Saundersfoot: Ch 11 Summer: 0800-2100, Winter: Mon-Fri: 0800-1800. Access HW±2
SWANSEA BAY
Docks Radio: Ch 14 H24
Tawe Lock for marina: Ch 18
River Neath: Ch 77 H24 **Port Talbot:** Ch 12 H24
BARRY: *Barry Radio* Ch 11 Access –4HW+3
CARDIFF
Cardiff Radio Ch 14. Barrage control: Ch 18
NEWPORT:
Port: Ch 09 69 71 Access HW±4
SHARPNESS
Call *Sharpness Radio* Ch 13 for locking in
Canal operations: Ch 74 Access –5HW+1
BRISTOL
Avonmouth Sig Stn *Bristol VTS*: Ch 12 09 11 for reporting and VTS info on request
City Docks Radio: Ch 11 14 Access –3HW+1
Bristol Floating Hbr: Ch 73 Mon-Thu 0800-1700; Fri 0800-1630; other times 0800-sunset. Access –3HW+1 through lock
Prince Street Bridge and Netham Lock: Ch 73
BURNHAM-ON-SEA/BRIDGWATER
Hbr office: Ch 08 Access –3HW when vessel is expected
ILFRACOMBE:
Hbr office: Ch 12 Apr-Oct: 0815-1700, when manned; Nov-Mar: HX. Access HW±2
APPLEDORE-BIDEFORD:
Call Port/PV *'Two Rivers'* Ch 12 Access –2HW
BUDE:
Hbr office: Ch 12 When vessel expected
PADSTOW:
Ch 12 M-Fri: 0800-1700 and HW±2
ST IVES: Ch 14 HX

IRELAND

SHANNON ESTUARY: Ch 12 13
Galway: Ch 12 Access –2½HW+1
Rossaveel: Ch 12 14 Office Hours
CORK:
Port Ops: Ch 12 14
Kinsale: Ch 14. HO and when vessel expected
Bantry: Ch 06 11 12 14 H24

Castletown Bearhaven: **Ch 14**
Dingle **Ch 11 M**
Limerick: **Ch 12 13**
Office hours & when vessel expected
Fenit: **Ch 14 M** HX
ROSSLARE EUROPORT:
Hbr office: **Ch** 06 **12** 14 H24
Waterford & New Ross: **Ch 12 14** HJ &
when vessel expected
Youghal: **Ch 14** Access HW±3
ARKLOW:
Port: **Ch 14**
WICKLOW:
Port: **Ch 14** 12
DUN LAOGHAIRE:
Hbr office: **Ch 14**
DUBLIN:
Port Radio: **Ch 12** 13
Lifting Bridge: Call Eastlink **Ch 12 13**
HOWTH:
Hr Mr: **Ch 13** Mon-Fri: 0700-2300
Sat/Sun: HX
STRANGFORD HARBOUR:
Ch 12 14 M
Ardglass Harbour: **Ch 14** 12
Mon-Fri 0900-1700
Killyleagh: **Ch 12** HX
Kilkeel: **Ch 12** 14 Mon-Fri: 0900-2000
Warrenpoint: **Ch 12** H24
Greenore: **Ch 16** HJ
Dundalk: **Ch 14** Mon-Fri: 0900-1700
Drogheda: **Ch 11** Mon-Fri: 0800-1700. HX
BELFAST:
VTS: **Ch 12**
Portavogie: **Ch 12 14** Mon-Fri 0900-1700
LARNE:
Port Control: **Ch 14**
Cloghan Point: **Ch 10**
COLERAINE:
Ch 12 Mon-Fri 0900-1700
Portrush: **Ch 12** Mon-Fri 0900-1700; Sat-Sun
0900-1700, Jun-Sep only
LONDONDERRY:
Hbr radio: **Ch 14** 12
SLIGO:
Hr Mr: **Ch 12** 14
0900-1700 and when vessel expected
Killybegs: **Ch 14** when vessel expected
Burton Port: **Ch 14** 06 12

DENMARK
Skagen: **Ch 12 13** H24
Hirtshals Havn: **Ch 12** 13 HX
Torup Strand: **Ch 12 13** HX
Hanstholm Havn: **Ch 12** 13 HX
THYBORØN: Ch 12 13 HX.
Thisted (Limfjorden): **Ch 12** 13 HX.

Torsminde: **Ch 12** 13 0300-1300, 1400-2400.
Hvide Sande: **Ch 12** 13 HX.
Esbjerg Hbr Control: **Ch 12** 13 14 H24.
Rømø Havn: **Ch 10 12** 13 HX.

GERMANY
HELGOLAND:
Port: **Ch 67**
May-Aug: Mon-Thu: 0700-1200, 1300-2000.
Fri-Sat: 0700-2000. Sun: 0700-1200.
Sep-Apr: Mon-Thu: 0700-1200, 1300-1600.
Fri: 0700-1200.
List Port: Ch 11 0800-1200 1600-1800
Hornum: 67; M-Th 0700-1600, Fri 0700-1230.
Wyk Port: Ch 11
Pellworm Port: Ch 11 0700-1700
Husum Port: Ch 11. Access −4HW+2.
Information bcsts: Ch 11 every H+00.
Eider Lock: Ch 14
Büsum Port: Ch 11
**INNER DEUTSCHE BUCHT
(GERMAN BIGHT):**
VTS: Eastern part: **Ch 80**
VTS: Western part: **Ch 79**
BRUNSBÜTTEL ELBE PORT: Ch 12
NORD-OSTSEE KANAL (KIEL CANAL):
VTS Canal 1 **Ch 13**
VTS Canal 2 **Ch 02**
VTS Canal 3 **Ch 03**
VTS Canal 4 **Ch 12**
Brieholz: **Ch 73**
Ostermoor: **Ch 73**
Friedrichskoog: **Ch 10** Access HW±2
RIVER ELBE:
Cuxhaven Elbe Port: Ch 12 HX
Cuxhaven Lock: Ch 69
VTS: Ch 71
Brunsbüttel Elbe Traffic: Ch 68
Oste Bridge (flood barrage): Ch 69
Apr-Sep the bridge is opened on request
Ch 69. Oct-Mar request through Ch 03 or 16
Belum Radar or Ch 21 Cuxhaven Radar
Oste Bridge Geversdorf: Ch 69; The bridge
opens on request for small craft Apr-Sep:
0730-1930 and every H+00 and H+30
Oberndorf Bridge: Ch 69 Oct-Mar H24,
Apr-Sep 1930-0730. The bridge is opened on
request by telephone 04772 86 10 11.
Stör Lock: Ch 09 Bridge opens on request.
Glückstadt Lock: Ch 11 0700-1600 & thru HW.
Stadersand Elbe Port: Ch 12
Este Lock: Ch 10
Este Bridge: Ch 10 Opened on request
HAMBURG:
VTS: **Ch 74** 13 14
Port Traffic: **Ch 74** 13 14
Elbe Port: **Ch 12**
Rethe Bridge: **Ch 13**

COMMUNICATIONS

Kattwyk Bridge: Ch 13
Harburg Lock: Ch 13
Tiefstack Lock: Ch 11
DIE WESER AND DIE HUNTE:
Bremerhaven Weser Tfc: Ch 02 04 05 07 21 22 82
Bremen Weser Traffic: Ch 19 78 81
Hunte Traffic:
VTS: Ch 63
Info in German: Ch 02 04 05 07 21 22 82 every H+20 by Bremerhaven Weser Traffic
Info in German: Ch 19 78 81 H+30 by Bremen Weser Traffic
Info in German: Ch 63 H+30 by Hunte Traffic
BREMERHAVEN:
Port: Ch 12
Fischereihafen Lock: Ch 69 70
Bremerhaven Nord Lock: 69 70
Bremerhaven Weser:
Port: Ch 14
Brake Lock: Ch 10
Elsfleth-Ohrt Railway Bridge: Ch 73 – 2h before sunrise to 2h after sunset
Hunte Lock: Ch 73
Hunte lifting bridge: Ch 73 – 2h before sunrise to 2h after sunset
Oldenburg:
Railway Bridge: Ch 73
H24 except Sun and public holidays 0030-0630
Lock: Ch 20 Mon-Sat: 0500-2100 Sun: 0900-1200
Cäcilien Bridge: Ch 73
Oslebshausen Lock: Ch 12
BREMEN:
Port: Ch 03
Lock: Ch 20 Mon-Sat: 0600-2200, Sun: Oct-Apr 0800-1100 May-Sep: 0800-1400 1730-1930
DIE JADE:
VTS: Ch 63 20
Info bcsts (in German): Ch 20 63 every H+10
WILHEMSHAVEN:
Port: Ch 11. Lock: Ch 13
Bridges: Ch 11
VAREL Lock: Ch 13 HW±2
Wangerooge: Ch 17 0700-1700
Harlesiel: lock Ch 17 0700-2100
Bensersiel: Ch 17 Oct-Mar Mon-Fri: 0700-1230 1330-1700, Apr-Sep Mon-Fri: 0700-1900 Sat & Sun: 0700-1100 1300-1700
Langeoog: Ch 17 0700-1700
Norderney: Ch 17 Mon: 0700-1200 1230-1730, Tues: 0900-1200 1230-1900, Wed-Sun: 0700-1200 1230-1900
Norddeich: Ch 17
Mon: 0730-1900, Tue-Fri: 0700-1300 1330-1900, Sat & Sun: 0800-1200 1230-1730
BORKUM:
Port: Ch 14 All year Mon-Fri: 0700-2200, Sep-Apr Sat & Sun: 0700-1700, May-Aug Sat: 0800-1200 1500-2100 Sun: 0700-1100 1400-2000
DIE EMS VTS: Call Ems Traffic Ch 15 18 20 21
Ems Traffic broadcasts every H+50 on Ch 15 18 20 and 21 in German. All vessels must keep a continuous watch on the appropriate channel
Emden Locks: Ch 13
Oldersum Lock: Ch 13 May-Sep Mon-Fri 0700-2000 Sat & Sun 0800-2000, Oct-Apr Mon-Thu 0700-1530 Fri 0700-1400
Leer Bridge: Ch 15
Leer Lock: Ch 13 16
Weener Bridge: Ch 15
Weener Lock: Ch 13 1 Apr- 31 Oct only: Mon-Thu 0700-1600 Fri: 0700-sunset Sat & Sun: sunrise-sunset
Papenburg Lock: Ch 13

NETHERLANDS

VTS DELFZIJL/EEMSHAVEN
Delfzijl Radar: Ch 03
Eemshaven Radar: Ch 01
Port Control: Ch 66
Intership: Ch 10
DELFZIJL:
Hbr office: Ch 14 Radar assistance given when visibility falls below 2000m
Info broadcasts: Ch 66 Every even H+10
Locks: Ch 11 Mon-Sat: H24, Sun & holidays on request
Weiwerder Bridge: Ch 11
Heemskes and Handelshaven Bridges: Ch 14 Mon-Sat: 0600-1400
Farmsumerhaven: Ch 14
EEMSHAVEN:
Hbr office: Ch 14. Radar: Ch 01 19
LAUWERSOOG:
Havendienst, Ch 09. Mon 0000-1700; Tue-Wed 0800-1700; Thur-Sat 0700-1500.
Terschelling: Call Brandaris VTS Ch 02
All vessels must keep a listening watch Ch 02
Harlingen: Ch 11 Mon 0000-Sat 2200
DEN HELDER: VTS Tfc Centre Ch 12
Port Control: Ch 14
Moormanbrug Bridge: Ch 18
Koopvaarders Lock: Ch 22
IJSSELMEER
Den Oever Lock: Ch 20
Kornwerderzand: locks Ch 18
AMSTERDAM:
Port Control: Ch 04 68
Port Information: Ch 14
Beverwijk: Ch 71
Wilhelminasluis: Ch 20
Westerkeersluis: Ch 22
Haarlem: Ch 18
Oranjesluisen: Ch 18
Enkhuizen or Krabbersgat: Ch 22
Lock operates weekdays 0300-2300, Sun and

holidays 0800-2000
IJMUIDEN:
Traffic Centre: Ch 07 West of IJmuiden lt buoy
Port Control: Ch 61 From IJmuiden Lt buoy to the North Sea Locks
NORDZEE KANAAL:
VTS: Ch 68
From Ijmuiden Lt By to the IJmuiden Sluices
Noordzee sluizen: Call Sluis IJmuiden **Ch 22**
Noordzee kanaal: Ch 03 From IJmuiden Sluices to km 11·2
Zijkanaal C Sluice: Call Sluis IJmuiden **Ch 18**
SCHEVENINGEN:
Traffic Centre: Ch 21
Port: Ch 14
MAAS APPROACH: Ch 01. Oude Maas: Ch 62
HOEK VAN HOLLAND ROADS:
VTS: To cross the mouth of the Maas, Call *Maas Entrance* **Ch 03**; report vessel's name, position and course. Follow a track close W of a line joining buoys MV, MVN and Indusbank N. Whilst crossing, maintain continuous listening watch and a very sharp lookout.
NIEUWE WATERWEG:
HCC Central Traffic Control **Ch 11 14 19** See VTS Chart No 4. Report to and keep a continuous listening watch on the appropriate Tfc Centre
Bridges and locks in the Rotterdam area:
Botlekbrug: Ch 18
Koninginnebrug: Ch 18
Spijkenisserbrug: Ch 18
Brienenoordbrug: Ch 20
Sluis Weurt: Ch 18
Prins Bernhardsluis: Ch 18
Sluis S. Andries: Ch 20
Maassluis (Buitenhaven ent): Ch 80
Mandersluis: Ch 20
DORDRECHT:
Tfc Control: Dordrecht **Ch 79,** Heerjansdam **Ch 04**
Port: Ch 74
General nautical information: Ch 71
Bruggen Dordrecht: Ch 19
Alblasserdamse brug: Ch 22
Papendrechtse brug: Ch 19
Merwedesluis en Verkeersbrug: Ch 18
Algera sluis en Stuw: Ch 22
Julianasluis: Ch 18
Grote Sluis Vianen: Ch 22
Andel Wilhelminasluis: Ch 22
Dordrecht Railway and Rd Bridge: Ch 71
Broombrug/Wijnhavn: Ch 74
OOSTERSCHELDE:
Call Roompotsluis **Ch 18** Lock operating hours: Mon and Thu, 0000-2200; Tue and Sun, 0600-0000; Wed H24; Fri and Sat: 0600-2200.
Roompot Harbour: Ch 31
Ouddorp Coastguard: Ch 25
Wemeldinge Bridge and Locks: Ch 68

Zeelandbrug Bridge: Ch 18
Krammer Locks: Ch 22
Kreekraksluizen: Ch 20 Vessels should report to the locks as follows: S bound, after Tholen Hr; N bound, after Bath bridge
HARINGVLIET-SLUIZEN: Ch 20 Operating times Mon-Fri 0000-2200; 1 Nov - 1 April Sat 0800-2200 Sun 0800-1000, 1600-1800; 1 April - 1 Nov Sat & Sun 0800-2000
WESTERSCHELDE:
VTS: See VTS Chart No 3. Reporting, in English or Dutch, is compulsory for all In- and Outbound vessels, but not yachts. All vessels, including those at anchor, must keep a continuous listening watch on the VHF channel for the appropriate Traffic Area. The boundaries of each Traffic Area are marked by buoys. In emergency call the relevant Traffic Centre: Ch 67.
STEENBANK TRAFFIC AREA:
VTS Tfc Centre: Ch 64
VLISSINGEN TRAFFIC AREA:
VTS Tfc Centre: Ch 14. Info: Ch 14 every H+50
TERNEUZEN TRAFFIC AREA:
VTS Tfc Centre: Ch 03. Info: Ch 11 every H+00
GENT/TERNEUZEN TRAFFIC AREA:
VTS Tfc Centre: Ch 11
HANSWEERT TRAFFIC AREA:
VTS Tfc Centre: Ch 65
VLISSINGEN:
Call Flushing Port Control **Ch 09**
Locks & Bridge: Ch 18
TERNEUZEN:
Hr office: Ch 11
Locks: Ch 69
Westsluis and Middensluis: Ch 06
Oostsluis: Ch 18
Gent: Ch 05 11
Hansweert Locks: Ch 22

BELGIUM
ANTWERPEN TRAFFIC AREA:
VTS: Tfc Centre: Ch 12. Info: Ch 12 every H+30
ANTWERPEN:
Calling and safety: Ch 74
VTS Centre: Ch 18
Bridges: Ch 62
Boudewijnsluis & Van Cauwelaertsluis: Ch 08 71
Royerssluis Ch 74
Kattendijksluis: Ch 22
Kallosluis: Ch 08 74
Zandvlietsluis and Berendrechtsluis: Ch 06 79
Winthamsluis: Ch 68
ZEEBRUGGE TRAFFIC AREA:
VTS Tfc Centre: Ch 69. Info: Ch 69 every H+10
ZEEBRUGGE:
Port Control: Ch 71 H24. Locks: Ch 68
WANDELAAR TRAFFIC AREA:

COMMUNICATIONS

VTS Tfc Centre: Ch 65
OOSTENDE:
Port Control: **Ch 09** H24. Lock: **Ch 14**
NIEUWPOORT:
Hbr office: **Ch 09** H24

NORTH FRANCE

DUNKERQUE PORT
Port: **Ch 73** H24
CALAIS:
Port: Call Calais Port Traffic **Ch 12** H24
Ecluse Carnot: **Ch 12** HX
BOULOGNE:
Call Control Tower, Boulogne Port **Ch 12**
Le Touquet: **Ch 09**; 77 Access HW–2 to +1
Étaples-Sur-Mer: **Ch 09** Access HW±2
LE TREPORT: Ch 12 72 Access HW±3
DIEPPE:
Port: **Ch 12** HO
ST VALÉRY-EN-CAUX: lock **Ch 09** Day: HW±2¼, Night: HW±½ (Bridge opens H & H+30 during these periods)
FÉCAMP: Ch 10 **12** Access HW–3 to +1
Antifer Port: **Ch 22** H24.
LE HAVRE:
Port Operations: **Ch 67 69**
Control Tower: **Ch 12** 20
Tancarville Port: **Ch 16** H24. Lock: **Ch 18** HX
LA SEINE:
VTS: **Ch 73, 15** (Estuary), **68** (River)
Radar **Ch 13 73 82**
HONFLEUR: Port: **Ch 17 73** HX
Locks and Bridges: **Ch 17** H24
Port Jérome: Call PR **Ch 73** H24
ROUEN:
Port: **Ch 73** 68 H24
ROUEN TO PARIS – LOCKS:
Poses-Amfreville: **Ch 18**
Notre-Dame-de-la-Garenne: **Ch 22**
Mericourt: **Ch 18**
Andrésy: **Ch 22**
Bougival: **Ch 22**
Chatou: **Ch 18**
Suresnes: **Ch 22**
Paris-Arsenal: **Ch 09**
DEAUVILLE-TROUVILLE: **Ch 09** 0800-1730.
OUISTREHAM-CAEN: Ouistreham: **Ch 74.**
Lock: **Ch 12** Access HW–2 to +3. **Canal:** Monitor **Ch 68** H24. **Port de Caen Ch 74.**
Courseulles-sur-Mer: **Ch 09** HW±3
Port-en-Bessin Lock & Bridge: **Ch 18** HW±2
CHERBOURG:
Call Vigie du Homet **Ch 12** H24. Marina **Ch 09.**
Lock: **Ch 06** Access HW±¾.
GRANVILLE:
Hbr office: **Ch 12** HW±1½
ST MALO:
Hbr office: **Ch 12** H24. Marinas **Ch 09.**
Rance barrage lock: **Ch 13.** Chatelier lock **Ch 14**

DAHOUËT: Marina: **Ch 09**
LE LÉGUÉ – SAINT BRIEUC:
Call Légué Port **Ch 12** Approx HW–2 to +1½.
Paimpol Port/lock Ch 09 HW±2.
Pontrieux Lock: Ch 12 Access HW–2 to +1.
ROSCOFF-BLOSCON:
Port: **Ch 12**
0830-1200, 1330-1800

CHANNEL ISLANDS

BRAYE, Aldemey Radio:
Port: **Ch 12** 74
Apr & Sep daily: 0800-1700. May-Aug: 0800-2000 daily. Oct-Mar: Mon-Fri: 0800-1700. Outside these hours, call St Peter Port Radio.
GUERNSEY:
St Peter Port: **Ch 12** H24. Access HW±3
St Sampson: **Ch 12** H24 via St Peter Port Port Control.
JERSEY:
St Helier: **Ch 14** H24. Access HW±3
(Note: Do not use Ch M in St Helier)
Gorey: **Ch 74** HW±3.

WEST FRANCE

LE CONQUET:
Port: **Ch 08** Season 0830-1200 1330-1800;
BREST:
Port de Commerce: **Ch 12.** Naval Port: **Ch 74**
CAMARET: **Ch 09** Season 0730-2200; out of season: 0830-1200 1330-1730
DOUARNENEZ:
Hbr office: **Ch 12** 0800-1200 1330-1730
SAINT GUÉNOLÉ: Ch 12 HJ
LE GUILVINEC:
Port: **Ch 12** HX
LOCTUDY:
Hbr office: **Ch 12** Mon-Fri: 0630-1200 1400-1900; Sat: 0800-1200
CONCARNEAU: Port **Ch 12**
LORIENT:
Hbr office: Call Vigie Port Louis **Ch 12**
SAINT-NAZAIRE:
PORT: Ch 06 12 14 67 69
Loire VTS: Saint–Nazaire Port Control **Ch 12**
DONGES: Port: **Ch 12** 69 H24
Nantes: **Ch 12** 06 14 67 69
LES SABLES D'OLONNE:
Lock: **Ch 12** HM Mon-Fri: 0800-1800
LA ROCHELLE
Port: **Ch 12** H24
ROCHEFORT:
Hbr office: **Ch 12** 0800-1200, 1400-1800LT
Tonnay-Charente: **Ch 12** HX
LA GIRONDE:
VTS: **Ch 12** Compulsory from BXA Lt buoy to Bordeaux, except for leisure craft which should monitor. **Radar: Ch 12**. Height of water between Le Verdon and Bordeaux is broad-

cast automatically **Ch 17** every 5 mins.
PAUILLAC:
Hbr office: **Ch 12** 0800-1200, 1400-1800.
BLAYE:
Port: **Ch 12** 0800-1200, 1400-1800.
Ambès: **Ch 12** H24
BORDEAUX:
Hbr office: **Ch 12** H24
BAYONNE: Ch 12 H24

N & NW SPAIN
BILBAO:
Bilbao Traffic: **Ch 10**
Signal Station: **Ch 12 13** HX
SANTANDER:
Port: **Ch 14**
PUERTO DE SAN CIPRIÁN: Ch 14
FERROL: Ch 14 (H24) 10 11 12 13
LA CORUÑA:
Port: **Ch 12 13** HX
CORCUBIÓN: Ch 14 when vessel is expected
FINISTERRE TRAFFIC:
VTS: **Ch 11** 74 H24
VILLAGARCIA DE AROUSA:
Port: **Ch 12** H24
VIGO:
VTS: Call Vigo Traffic **Ch 10** H24
Port: Call Vigo Prácticos **Ch 14** HX

PORTUGAL (Marinas Ch 62)
VIANA DO CASTELO:
Ch 11 Mon-Fri 0900-1200, 1400-1700.
PÓVOA DE VARZIM:
Ch 11 Mon-Fri 0900-1200, 1400-1700.
VILA DO CONDE: Ch 11 Mon-Fri 0900-1200, 1400-1700.
LEIXÕES: Ch 12 11 13 19 60
Marina: **Ch 62**
Radar Station: **Ch 12**, H24.
DOURO: Ch 11 Mon-Fri 0900-1200, 1400-1700.
AVEIRO: Ch 11 Mon-Fri 0900-1200, 1400-1700.
FIGUEIRA DA FOZ: Ch 11 Mon-Fri 0900-1200, 1400-1700.
NAZARÉ: Ch 11 Mon-Fri 0900-1200, 1400-1700.
PENICHE: Ch 11
LISBOA: Call *Lisboa Port Control* **Ch 74**
Doca de Alcântara: **Ch 12** 05
SESIMBRA: Ch 11
Mon-Fri 0900-1200, 1400-1700.
SETÚBAL: Ch 11 H24
SINES: Ch 12 14
LAGOS: Ch 11 Mon-Fri 0900-1200, 1400-1700.
PORTIMÃO: Ch 11 H24.
VILAMOURA: Ch 62 H24
FARO: Ch 11
OLHÃO: Ch 11
VILA REAL DE SANTO ANTÓNIO: Ch 11
Mon-Fri 0900-1200, 1400-1700.

SW SPAIN
EL ROMPIDO: Marina: **Ch 09** HX
PUNTA UMBRÍA: Club: **Ch 09** HX
RÍO GUADALQUIVIR:
Call Sevilla **Ch 12**
CÁDIZ:
Call Cádiz Trafico **Ch 74** H24
Rota: Ch 09

STRAIT OF GIBRALTAR
TARIFA:
VTS: Call Tarifa Traffic **Ch 10**
Information (on request): Ch 67
Urgent messages will be bcst at any time on Ch 10 and Ch 16. Routine messages will be bcst every even H+15 on Ch 10
ALGECIRAS:
Port: Call Algeciras Prácticos **Ch 09 12** HX

GIBRALTAR
GIBRALTAR BAY Ch 12 Yachts to monitor this working channel whilst under way.
Commercial Port: Ch 06 13 14
Queen's Harbour Master: Ch 08 Mon-Thu: 0800-1630; Fri: 0800-1600.
Marinas: Queensway Quay and Sheppards Ch 71. Marina Bay Ch 73.

NOTES

COMMUNICATIONS

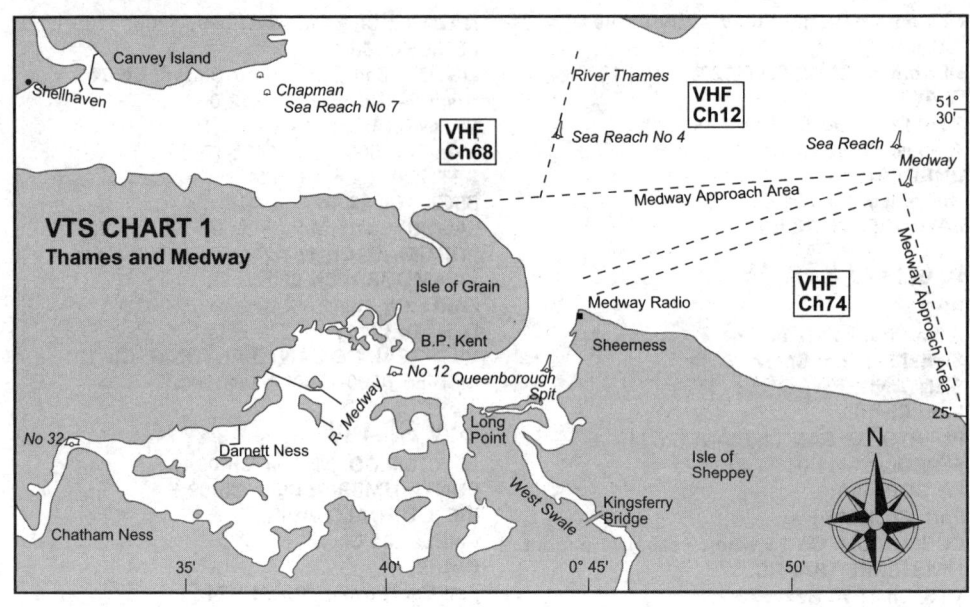
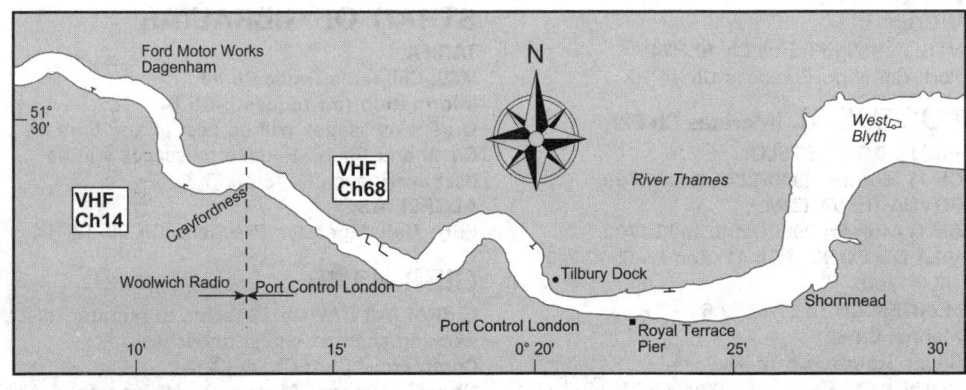
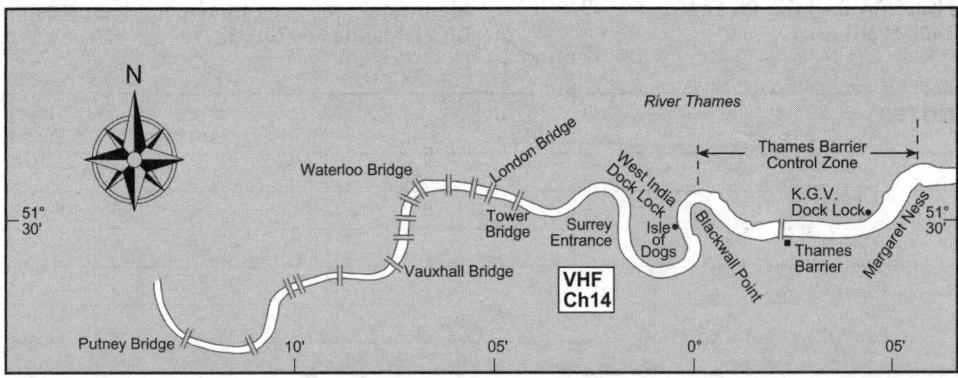

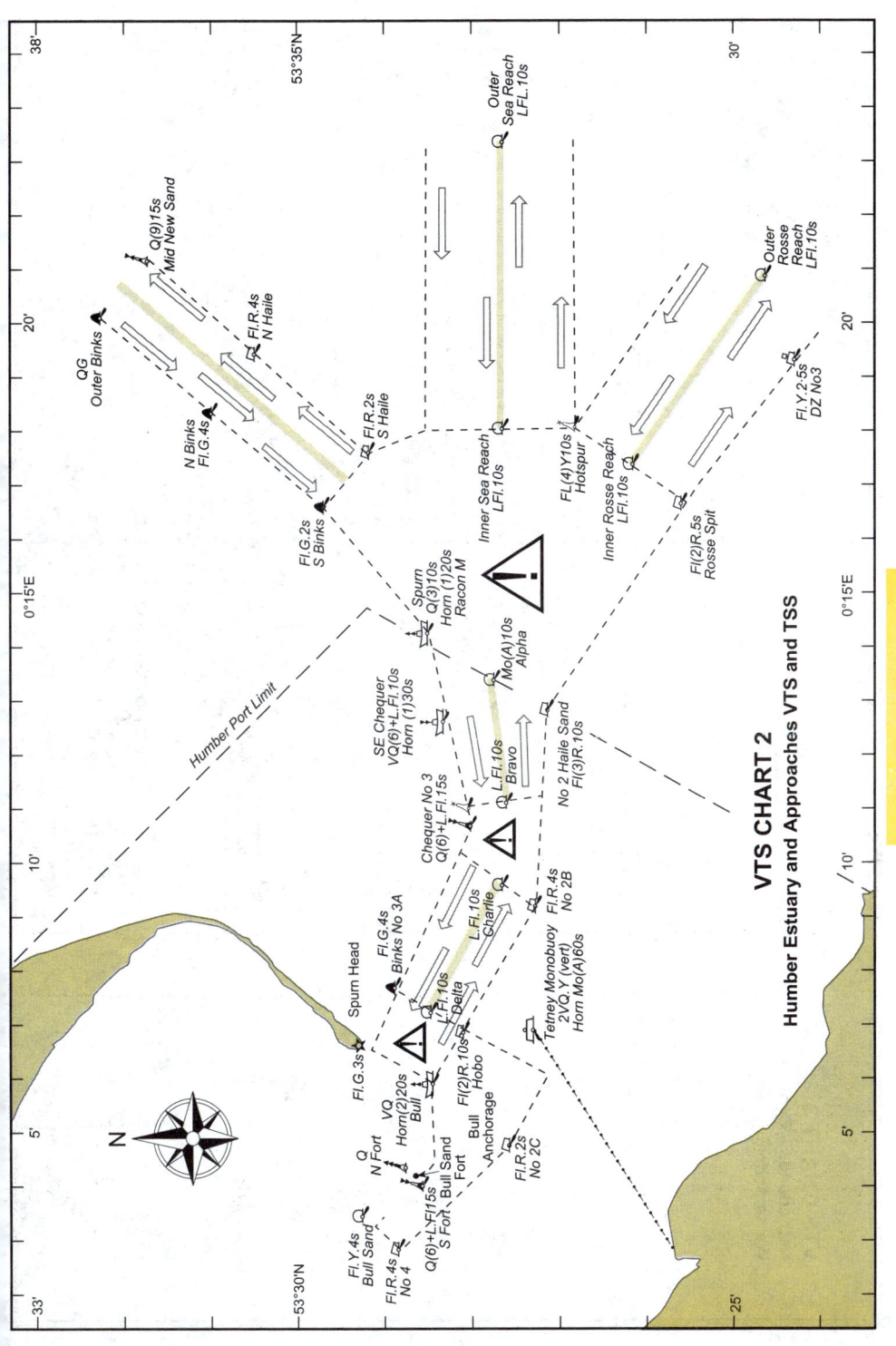

COMMUNICATIONS

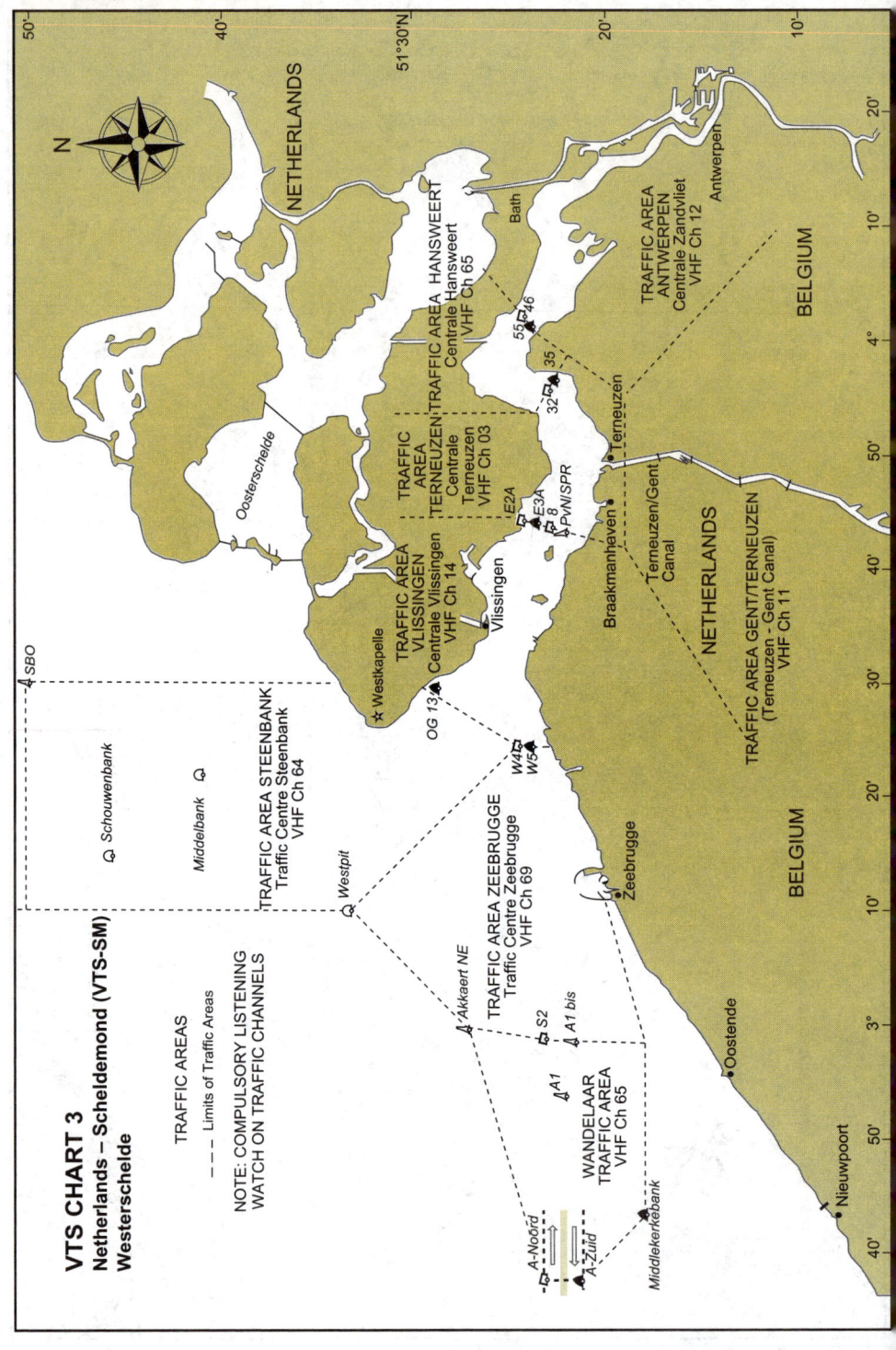

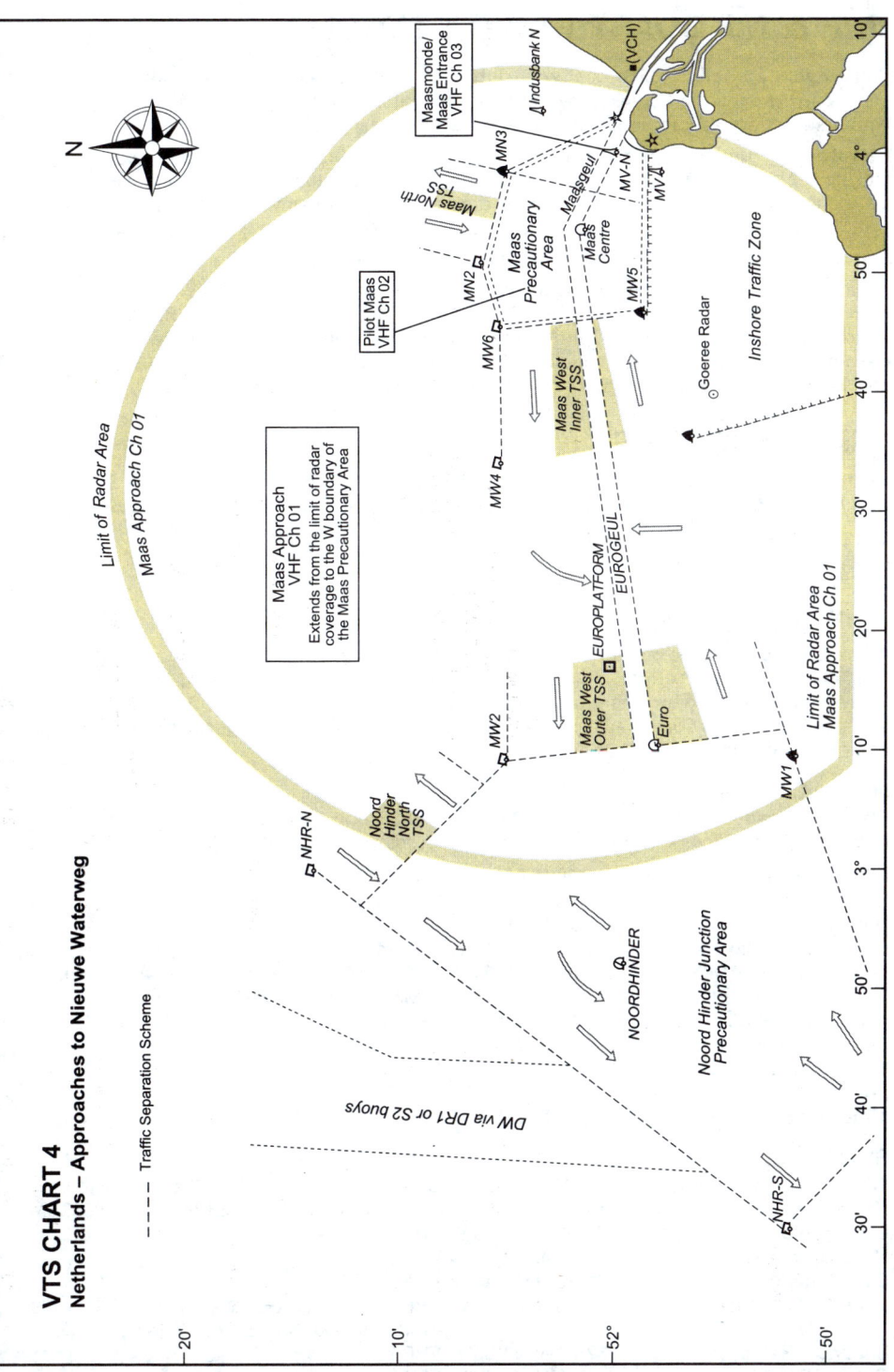

COMMUNICATIONS

VHF & MF COAST RADIO STATIONS

Coast Radio Stations* (CRS) deal with public correspondence (and a few other things). They enable a yachtsman to be linked by radio into the public telephone system in order to converse with a subscriber ashore, ie he can make or receive a Link call.

However the immensely popular and convenient mobile 'phone has to a great extent rendered Link calls obsolescent. Thus there are no longer any CRS in the UK, France and Netherlands. In Germany a limited service is provided by a commercial company (see below).

CRS still operate in the Channel Islands, Republic of Ireland, Denmark, Belgium, Spain and Portugal, as listed below. But they too may gradually be withdrawn from service.

*Readers of such arcane documents as the Admiralty List of Radio Signals will be aware that the term 'Coast Radio Station' is now used to embrace, not only the original CRS, but also Coastguard Centres, both in the UK and abroad. This is ambiguous and therefore confusing. As a general rule the CG does **not** handle Link calls, except in those countries (eg Ireland, Denmark and Belgium) where the functions of CG and CRS have always been co-located.

CHANNEL ISLANDS

ST PETER PORT RADIO 49°27'·00N 02°32'00W ☎ 01481 720672 ≋ 01534 714177
Link calls on **Ch 62** only. Ch 20 is used for navigation, pilotage and ships' business

JERSEY RADIO 49°10'·85N 02°14'30W ☎ 01534 741121 ≋ 01534 499089
Link calls on **Ch 25** only

REPUBLIC OF IRELAND

A Coast Radio service is provided by the Dept of the Marine, Leeson Lane, Dublin 2, Eire. ☎ +353 (0)1 662 0922; ext 670 for enquiries. Broadcasts are made on a working channel/frequency following a prior announcement on Ch 16 and 2182 kHz. Ch 67 is used for Safety messages only. VHF calls to an Irish Coast Radio Station should be made on a working channel. Only use Ch 16 in case of difficulty or in emergency.

NW and SE Ireland

Stations broadcast at 0033, 0433, 0833, 1233, 1633 and 2033 UT on VHF Channels listed. Navigational warnings and Traffic Lists are broadcast at every odd H+03 (except 0303 0703).

Clifden Radio	53°30'N 09°56'W	VHF 26
Belmullet Radio	54°16'N 10°03'W	VHF 83
Donegal Bay	54°22'N 08°31'W	VHF 02
Glen Head Radio	54°44'N 08°43'W	VHF 24
MALIN HEAD RADIO	55°22'N 07°21'W	VHF 23 MF 1677 kHz, ☎ +353 (0) 77 70103
		MMSI 002500100 DSC: 2187·5 kHz
Carlingford Radio	54°05'N 06°19'W	VHF 04
DUBLIN RADIO	53°23'N 06°04'W	VHF 83
Wicklow Head Radio	52°58'N 06°00'W	VHF 02
Rosslare Radio	52°15'N 06°20'W	VHF 23
Mine Head Radio	52°00'N 07°35'W	VHF 83

SW Ireland

Stations broadcast at 0233, 0633, 1033, 1433, 1833 and 2233 UT on VHF Channels listed. Navigational warnings and Traffic Lists are broadcast at every odd H+33 (not 0133 0533).

Cork Radio	51°51'N 08°29'W	VHF 26
Mizen Radio	51°34'N 09°33'W	VHF 04
Bantry Radio	51°38'N 10°00'W	VHF 23
VALENTIA RADIO	51°56'N 10°21'W	VHF 24 MF 1752 kHz, ☎ + 353 (0) 66947 6109
		MMSI 002500200, DSC: 2187·5 kHz
Shannon Radio	52°31'N 09°36'W	VHF 28
Galway Bay Radio	53°18'N 09°07'W	VHF 04

DENMARK

All VHF/MF Coast Radio Stations are remotely controlled from Lyngby Radio (55°50N 11°25'E) (MMSI 002191000). Call on working frequencies to help keep Ch 16 clear. The callsign for all stations is Lyngby Radio. Traffic lists are broadcast on all VHF channels every odd H+05. All MF stations, except Skagen, keep watch H24 on 2182 kHz. The stations listed below monitor Ch 16 H24 and Ch 70 DSC. Blåvand, Skagen and Lyngby also monitor MF 2187·5 kHz DSC. MF DSC Public correspondence facilities are available from Blåvand and Skagen on 1624·5 and 2177 kHz.

VHF AND MF

Lyngby	55°50'N 11°25'E	VHF Ch **07**, 85	MF 1704, 2170·5 kHz
Blåvand	55°33'N 08°07'E	VHF Ch 23	MF 1734, 1767, 2593
Bovbjerg	56°32'N 08°10'E	VHF Ch 02	MF 1734, 1767, 2593
Hanstholm	57°07'N 08°39'E	VHF Ch 01	
Hirtshals	57°31'N 09°57'E	VHF Ch 66	
Skagen	57°44'N 10°35'E	VHF Ch 04	MF 1758

GERMANY

Coast Radio Stations: DPO7 – Seefunk (Hamburg) *(MMSI 002113100)*

Hamburg	53°33'N 09°58'E VHF Ch 27, 83	DSC Ch 70 & 16
Borkum	53°35'N 06°40'E VHF Ch 28	DSC Ch 70 & 16
Bremen	53°05'N 08°48'E VHF Ch 25	DSC Ch 70 & 16
Elbe Weser	53°50'N 08°39'E VHF Ch 01, 24	DSC Ch 70 & 16
Nordfriesland	54°31'N 08°41'E VHF Ch 26	DSC Ch 70 & 16
Traffic Lists:	0745, 0945, 1245, 1645, 1945 and every H & H+30 on request Ch 16	

NORTH & NORTHWEST SPAIN

Call on the working channel as listed below, using the callsign of the remotely controlled station; Ch 16 is not continuously guarded. Stations are remotely controlled by Bilbao and Coruna Communications Centres.

Traffic lists are broadcast only on MF, every odd H+33, 0333-2333, except 2133. All times UT.

Pasajes	43°17'N 01°55'W *VHF 27*
Machichaco Radio	43°27'N 02°45'W *No VHF* *MF: Transmits 1707, 2182 kHz (H24);* *receives on 2132, 2045, 2048, 2182 (H24).* Traffic lists: *1707 kHz;* every odd H+33 Navigation warnings: *1707 kHz* Urgent warnings on receipt, after next silence period and at 0703 1903 in English and Spanish
BILBAO	43°22'N 03°02'W *VHF 26.* Controls Pasajes to Navia
Santander	43°25'N 03°36'W *VHF 24*
Cabo Peñas	43°26'N 05°35'W *VHF 23, MF 1677 kHz* Navigation warnings: 1677 kHz. Urgent warnings on receipt, after next silence period and at 0703 1903 in English and Spanish
Navia	43°25'N 06°50'W *VHF 60*
Cabo Ortegal	43°35'N 07°47'W *VHF 02* Navigation warnings: *VHF 02* at 0840 and 2010
CORUÑA	43°22'N 08°27'W *VHF 26, MF 1698 kHz* Navigation warnings: *VHF 26* at 0840 and 2010; *1698 kHz* at 0703, 1903
Finisterre	42°54'N 09°16'W *VHF 22, MF 1764 kHz* Navigation warnings: *VHF 22* at 0840 and 2010; *1764 kHz* at 0703, 1903
Vigo	42°10'N 08°41'W *VHF 65.* Nav warnings: *VHF 20* at 0840 and 2010
La Guardia	41°53'N 08°52'W *VHF 21.* Nav warnings: *VHF 82* at 0840 and 2010

COMMUNICATIONS

PORTUGAL

Stations are remotely controlled from Lisboa. All monitor Ch 16 H24

Arga Radio	41°48'N 08°41'W	*VHF 25 28*
Arestal Radio	40°46'N 08°21'W	*VHF 24 26*
Montejunto Radio	39°10'N 09°03'W	*VHF 25 26*
LISBOA RADIO	38°33'N 09°11'W	*VHF 23 26. MF: Transmits on 2182, 2578, 2640, 2691, 2781, 3607, 2778, 2693 kHz. Receives on 2182 (kHz) (H24)*

Traffic lists: 2693 kHz every even H+05, after announcement on 2182 kHz

Atalaia Radio	38°10'N 08°38'W	*VHF 24 25*
Picos Radio	37°50'N 08°35'W	*VHF 23 28*
Estoi Radio	37°10'N 07°50'W	*VHF 24 28*

SOUTH WEST SPAIN

Stations are remotely controlled from Malaga. Initially call Ch 16 H24 using station callsign

Chipiona Radio   36°41'N 06°25'W   *No VHF. MF: Transmits 1656, 2182 kHz (H24); receives on 2081 2182*

Traffic lists: 1656 kHz every odd H+33 (except 0133 & 2133).
Navigation warnings: 1656 kHz. Urgent warnings on receipt, and at 0733 1933, *in Spanish*

Cádiz Radio   36°21'N 06°17'W   *VHF 83*

Navigation warnings: Ch 26 on receipt, after next silence period, and at 0833, 2003, *in Spanish*

Tarifa Radio   36°03'N 05°33'W   *VHF 81; MF 1704 kHz: Transmits kHz 1704, 2182, (H24). Receives 2129, 2182 (H24), 2045, 2048, 2610, 3290 (Autolink)*

Traffic lists: *1704 kHz.* Navigation warnings: *VHF 81* at 0833 and 2003. *1704 kHz* on receipt, at 0733 1933, *in Spanish*

NOTES

SOUND SIGNALS
MANOEUVRING AND WARNING SIGNALS (Rule 34)

Short blast ● = about 1 second. Long blast ▬ = about 5 seconds

●	I am altering course to **Starboard**
● ●	I am altering course to **Port**
● ● ●	My engines are going **Astern**
● ● ● ● ●	I do not understand your intentions/actions

In a narrow channel

▬ ▬ ●	I intend to overtake you on your **Starboard** side
▬ ▬ ● ●	I intend to overtake you on your **Port** side
▬ ● ▬ ●	In response to the above two signals - **Agreed**

Nearing a bend in the channel or an area where other vessels may be hidden by obstructions

▬	Warns of a vessel's presence
▬	Acknowledgement by any approaching vessel

VESSELS IN RESTRICTED VISIBILITY (Rule 35)

▬	Power vessel underway (every 2 mins)
▬ ▬	Power vessel underway but stopped (every 2 mins)
▬ ● ●	Vessels not under command, restricted in their ability to manoeuvre, constrained by draught, sailing, fishing or towing - (every 2 mins)
▬ ● ● ●	Last vessel in tow (immediately after tug signal)
🔔 5 seconds	At ⚓ (bell, every minute)
🔔 5 seconds + 🔔 5 seconds	At anchor over 100m (bell forward, gong aft, every minute)
● ▬ ●	At ⚓, as well as above, to warn an approaching vessel

Yachts under 12m are not obliged to sound the fog signals listed above, but if they do not, they *must* make some efficient noise every two minutes

SHAPES

 ▽	Sailing vessel under sail *and* power. **Rule 25**	 ◆	Towing vessel - length of tow over 200m. **Rule 24**
●	Vessel at anchor. **Rule 30**	 ●◆●	Vessel restricted in her ability to manoeuvre. **Rule 27**
 ▽▲	Vessel fishing or trawling. **Rule 26**	 ●●	Vessel not under command. **Rule 27**
 ▽▲ + ▲	Vessel fishing with outlying gear over 150m long.	▮	Vessel constrained by her draught **Rule 28**

SAFETY

CHAPTER 4 - SAFETY

CONTENTS

Think about Safety 117

How to make a distress call 118

MAYDAY relay 118

Helicopter rescue 119

Medical help 119

First aid 120
    Essential information 120
    General medical information 121
    First Aid Kit 123

Coastguard services in the UK and abroad 124

Emergency VHF Direction Finding in the UK 132

UK & France VHF Direction Finding map 133

Emergency VHF Direction Finding in France 134

Diagrams of Military exercise areas 135

GMDSS 139
    Introduction 139
    Objective 139
    Maritime Safety Information 139
    Functions 139
    Distress alerting 139
    Communications 140
    Digital selective calling 140
    Inmarsat 140
    Cospas/Sarsat 140
    Sea areas 140

THINK ABOUT SAFETY – then do something to enhance it
The Yachtsman's Handbook, published by Nautical Data, 01243 389352, offers more comprehensive coverage of this subject.

Safety at sea is no mere abstract concept. It is very real and may save the lives of yourself and your crew, as well as your boat. It may also avoid having to call upon the safety services. There are three main requirements, all of which are in your power to implement:

KNOWLEDGE. This means knowledge of the weather (above all else) and of the sea; of the Collision Regulations; of your boat and its systems; of the waters in which you are navigating; and not least of yourself, your strengths and weaknesses. Knowledge requires training, whether it be in navigation, meteorology, boat handling, engines or electrics – and lastly survival techniques, when all else has failed and you have abandoned ship for the liferaft. We should all tackle GMDSS which will acquire increasing relevance to yachtsmen as VHF Channel 16 becomes less widely monitored in the near future.

EXPERIENCE. Nobody ever became experienced overnight. It is a long and sometimes painful process of finding out for yourself, learning and decision-making. At every stage be aware of your limitations and arrange, as far as possible, to stay within them. Read everything you can on the subject. Learn from other people's mistakes. Knowledge and experience make for sound judgement.

Recently a yacht was lost (and very nearly her crew) whilst trying to enter a harbour in an onshore gale. The skipper had been told not to attempt entry, but he was tired and desperate to find shelter. He knew conditions were marginal, to say the least, but he still persisted in his attempt. It's called "Get-home-itis" and in all its forms is a potential killer. He and his crew owe their lives to the RNLI. Do not do the same; stay at sea, however daunting the prospect – or better still avoid getting into that predicament. There are no medals for staying in harbour, but there is life.

EQUIPMENT. Shun fancy toys. Go for proven gear, whether it be the correct size of anchor, a stable dinghy (scene of so many tragic accidents), a trysail and storm jib for those sailing out of range of a safe haven, replacements for worn-out rigging, a properly maintained engine or a decent VHF radio – and don't forget that GMDSS is now affordable and training courses are widely available.

DEFINITIONS OF DISTRESS, URGENCY AND SAFETY
Yachts should keep watch on VHF Channel 16 at all times when at sea. Otherwise a distress call from another nearby craft may be missed; likewise broadcasts of navigation and weather warnings. Apart from distress, urgency and safety calls, only transmit on Channel 16 when calling/answering the Coastguard, Coast Radio Stations or other ships before transferring asap to a working channel.

The distress call 'MAYDAY' requests immediate assistance for a ship or person in grave and imminent danger. This includes a man overboard, if he is not immediately recovered. Yachts hearing a MAYDAY must give what assistance they can, provided it does not endanger their own yacht or crew.

The urgency prefix 'PAN-PAN' is used when the safety of a ship or person is at risk, or medical advice is urgently required (see PAN-PAN MEDICO overleaf).

The safety prefix 'SECURITE' is used by coast stations before navigation or weather warnings. Or ships at sea might use it to report hazards, eg a buoy adrift.

SAFETY

HOW TO MAKE A DISTRESS CALL

1. Switch on the VHF Radio
2. Select Channel 16
3. Select **HIGH POWER (25W)**
4. Switch off DUAL WATCH
5. Holding down the button on microphone or handset, say slowly and clearly:
6. **MAYDAY, MAYDAY, MAYDAY**
7. This is.............................(Say your boat's name 3 times)
8. **MAYDAY**...........(Say the boat's name once only)
9. My position is....................

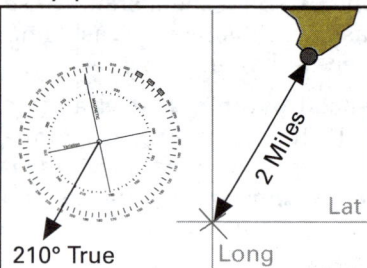

Give your position either as:

Lat and Long (from the GPS); or as

Bearing and distance from a known landmark or feature:

For example 'My position is 2 miles SSW of Portland Bill'

Say if you are not sure of position– do not guess!

10. **Tell them what is wrong:** For example, the boat is sinking; how many people (including you) on board; if you have fired flares; if you are abandoning ship, etc. If there is time, repeat your position
11. **I require immediate assistance. Over -**This means: please reply
12. Release the microphone button and listen
13. Only if you can't hear clearly, adjust the *VOLUME* and/or *SQUELCH*

If there is no reply, check the radio switches and repeat the message

MAYDAY RELAY

1. **If you hear a MAYDAY CALL, write it down**
2. If practicable, give assistance
3. If the MAYDAY is not answered, pass it on like this:
4. Select VHF Channel 16
5. Select HIGH POWER (25W)
6. Switch off DUAL WATCH
7. Then, holding down the button on microphone or handset, say slowly and clearly:
   MAYDAY RELAY, MAYDAY RELAY, MAYDAY RELAY
8. **This is**......................(say your boat's name 3 times)
9. **State the MAYDAY message, exactly as you wrote it down**
10. **Over -**This means: please reply
11. Release the button and listen

HELICOPTER RESCUE

1. **COMMUNICATE ON (CH 16) VHF**
2. Use flares or smoke when helicopter is seen or heard
3. Pilot may ask you to drop sails and motor an **EXACT COURSE**
4. You may be asked to stream tender astern with casualty in
5. Brief crew early (too noisy when helicopter is close)
6. **HELM MUST KEEP ON COURSE** and not be distracted
7. Weighted line lowered
8. Let it touch boat or water first (to earth any static charge)
9. Take in slack line only
10. **PULL IN AS DIRECTED**
11. **DO NOT SECURE IT TO THE BOAT**
12. **DO AS YOU ARE TOLD**

Note: The text and sketch relate to a Hi-line transfer, one of several techniques which may be used

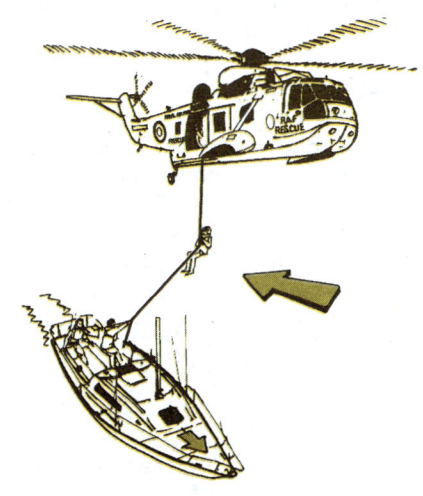

MEDICAL HELP

1. CH 16, High power, Dual watch off
2. **PAN PAN** .... (repeat 3 times)
3. **ALL STATIONS** .... (repeat 3 times)
4. **This is** .... (repeat 3 times)
5. Over
   Next message should contain:
   Yacht's name, callsign, nationality
   Yacht's position and nearest harbour
   Patient's details, symptoms and advice wanted
   The medication you have on board

SAFETY

MEDICAL ADVICE BY RADIO

European countries covered by this Almanac will give free medical advice on request. Messages are usually sent via Coastguard or Coast Radio Stations of the country concerned.

Medical Advice Link Calls (UK) Medical Advice can be obtained by contacting the nearest Co-ordination Centre on VHF 16, VHF DSC, or MF DSC, requesting Medical Advice. In a particularly urgent situation, broadcast an urgency alert using the pro-words 'PAN PAN'.

Priority is given to Medical Advice requests. A Medilink Service Doctor will be connected by telephone - VHF(usually duplex Ch's 23,84,86) or MF link to the vessel. As this call is being placed the CG will request relevant additional information. The Doctor will advise of suitable action and this call may be monitored by the CG. for operational reasons. If evacuation is necessary, then the CG is bound to act upon it. A Medilink Service call (free of charge) will always precede a request for medical evacuation.

REPUBLIC OF IRELAND Call nearest Coast Radio Station by name. Procedures are similar to UK.
DENMARK Call 'Radiomedical Lyngby': English, Danish, Norwegian, Swedish, French or German are spoken.
GERMANY Call nearest Coast Radio Station using 'Funkarzt. . . (name of station)'. English or German are spoken.
NETHERLANDS Call 'Netherlands Coastguard, Radio medical advice'. English and Dutch are spoken. Expect transfer to working Ch 23 or 83 for duty doctor.
BELGIUM Call 'Radiomedical Ostend': English, French, Dutch or German are spoken.
FRANCE Call nearest CROSS, eg 'Radiomedical CROSS Jobourg' with PAN-PAN prefix. French, English or International Code of Signals. SAMU (Urgent Medical Aid Service) in Toulouse may be contacted by the CROSS to advise on treatment and/or possible evacuation. CROSS Etel specialises in providing medical advice.
SPAIN Call 'Medrad ... (any Coast Radio Station)': Spanish.
PORTUGAL Call 'Radiomedical Lisboa': English, French, Portuguese are spoken.

FIRST AID
ESSENTIAL INFORMATION:

First ensure your own safety and that of the vessel.

GETTING HELP
Recognising signs of serious injury is not usually difficult, but it is always better to ask advice if not sure. This is available by making a **PAN-PAN** call by R/T or VHF radio, which will normally be processed by a Coast Radio Station and/or the Coastguard. You will be connected to a local doctor or hospital for advice and, if assistance is required, it will be co-ordinated by the Coastguard (see LH column).

FIRST STEPS
A - AIRWAY - NOT BREATHING: Know how to achieve and maintain an airway in all unconscious patients, by:
(1) Clearing any seaweed, excess saliva, vomit, false teeth, etc from mouth and nose.
(2) Lifting the chin to prevent choking by tongue and soft palate falling back.

B - BREATHING - Sealing mouth with own mouth and pinching nose, then blow slowly and gently until the casualty's chest rises. Ten inflations should improve colour, then continue after 2-4 seconds another 10 ventilations, then re-assess. You can use mouth to nose ventilation if the casualty's mouth cannot be opened enough to breath into. The best position for maintaining spontaneous breathing after restarting is in the semi-prone or coma position. The casualty is rolled carefully on his side keeping head and neck in line.

C - CIRCULATION - HEART NOT BEATING: You can revive an unconscious or possibly near dead patient by external cardiac massage, if there is no pulse. The best place to find a pulse is in the neck beside the Trachea (Windpipe).

The patient must be lying on a firm surface. First ventilate 1 - 2 breaths. Then apply cardiac massage by pressure over the lower third of the sternum (breastbone). The heel of one hand should be placed two fingers width above the lower extremity of the sternum, and the heel of the other hand placed on top, with the fingers interlocked, keeping the elbows straight. Press down firmly on the sternum using just enough force to depress it (4.5cm), then release keeping hands in place. Continue by pressing firmly over the sternum with both hands, one on top of the other, with intermittent mouth to mouth respiration. The rate should be 80 compresses per minute, and the ratio of breaths to pressure should be 2:15. This should be continued until either colour improves, breathing starts or a pulse becomes palpable in the neck. Then place the patient in the recovery position.

BLEEDING: Know how to deal with severe haemorrhage.

EXTERNAL BLEEDING:- 1: Remove any loose foreign bodies from wounds. 2: Press a folded handkerchief or soft pad directly on to wound, adding more padding if this becomes soaked. 3: If possible raise bleeding part. 4: If pressure is used to control bleeding check colour and temperature of parts distal to pressure pad to ensure adequate blood supply, releasing pressure frequently.

INTERNAL BLEEDING: Apparent when blood appears from the mouth or rectum, or suspected when a person collapses with pallor, sweating and a fast pulse.

All that can be done is to place the victim in the semi-prone position and prevent heat loss by covering with a blanket or sleeping bag. Supervision is necessary. *ADVICE SHOULD BE SOUGHT AS SOON AS POSSIBLE BY RADIO* (Make VHF **PAN-PAN** call).

LIVES CAN BE SAVED in all cases of injury by attending to the **A**IRWAY, **B**REATHING, **C**IRCULATION AND CONSCIOUS LEVEL of injured crew and doing this in an organised method. Using a check list prevents less important factors taking precedent. Always keep checking on anyone who has had an injury or been in the water.

GENERAL MEDICAL INFO

ARREST - of heart's action can be caused by near drowning, by blood loss and by illness such as heart attack. It is not hard to recognise as the victim is obviously near death and a pulse cannot be found.

Refer to resuscitation above and perform external cardiac massage with patient on a firm surface such as deck or cabin sole, and with mouth to mouth resuscitation in a ratio of roughly 2 breaths to 15 chest pressings. Start with 2 breaths of expired air.

BREATHING - In conscious patients, problems can be caused by pain from injured ribs or chest infection. Help is given by pain killing tablets and/or antibiotics. Crew members with asthma will usually have their own medication and should be kept propped up. Keep checking. In an unconscious patient the airway must be cleared, the jaw tipped up and mouth to mouth breathing started if necessary, or if the patient is able to breath by himself he must be placed in the semi-prone position and carefully watched in case the airway gets blocked by his tongue or by vomit or saliva.

CIRCULATION: Problems of central (the heart/pump) and peripheral (blood vessels/distribution) should be tackled as follows:
(1) Central: Failure of the Heart's Action - dealt with by External Cardiac Massage (see above)
(2) Peripheral: Attempt to stop haemorrhage by method described above (see Bleeding)

BROKEN BONES - principles are immobilisation and observation of circulation to the part beyond the probable fracture.

Skull: suspect fracture in severe blows to the head, especially if the patient is unconscious.

Priorities are (a) airway clearance and maintenance and cardiac massage if required (b) pressure if scalp bleeding is severe (c) monitoring of conscious or unconscious state (d) remember the possibility of neck injuries, keep neck and shoulders in line.

Spine: possible in falls from a height. Priority is always airway clearance and maintenance. *DO NOT USE EXCESSIVE CHIN TILT*, but if possible try to roll or lift patient from danger with head and back in a straight line – for example on a board large enough to stretch from head to buttocks with a rolled towel around the neck to minimise movement. The head should be held steady at all times in line with body in horizontal and vertical planes. *THIS IS ESSENTIAL TO PROTECT THE SPINAL CORD.*

Ribs: are often fractured in crush injuries and falls and do not take precedent over skull or spine injuries. If they appear to be the only injury then pain relief is essential to allow free movement of the chest for efficient breathing. Consider internal bleeding if patient becomes pale, clammy and collapsed. Possible internal damage if he becomes breathless.

Upper Limbs: can be splinted to the trunk whether the fracture is closed or if bone is protruding. The bone should be immobilised at the joint above and below the fracture and padding should be inserted below any bandage or strapping. This should not be too tight and the part of the limb beyond should be checked regularly for changes in colour and temperature and for swelling which can restrict the blood flow. If this happens the bindings must be loosened. If the bone is protruding, cut clothing away and if possible cover with sterile gauze. Pain killers and, in the case of open fracture, antibiotics should be given as soon as possible.

Lower Limbs: immobilise at point above and below fracture if possible. Check circulation in limb. Give pain relief or antibiotic cover for open fractures. The other limb, or an oar, is a suitable splint. Strapping should be added and distal circulation monitored.

BURNS - best treatment is immediate immersion of affected part in clean, cold sea water for at least 10 minutes. Severe burns will swell a lot

SAFETY

so any tight clothing or jewellery should be cut open or removed. The swelling around the burn is fluid from the body, which is then lost from the circulation so the victim can be shocked and dehydrated and fluid replacement is essential. Burned tissue is easily infected and should not be handled, removed or blisters pricked. If clothing is stuck it should be left. Sunburn is a form of burn and can result in severe dehydration and shock.

BRUISES - can cause a lot of pain under a finger or toenail. These can be treated safely by flaming the end of a piece of wire (such as a paper clip) and burning through the nail, just enough to release the blood.

COLD INJURY - hypothermia should be suspected after any accidental immersion. Treat, whether apparent or not, by gradual re-warming. Shelter, dry clothes, gentle warmth from another person or handwarm heat source in a sleeping bag will help. *RESUSCITATION MAY BE REQUIRED.* Continual observation is essential.

CHOKING - can be relieved by a sharp blow to the back preferably in the head down position. Alternatively grasp the victim from behind and pull clasped hands into the upper abdomen.

COLLAPSE - can complicate injuries involving loss of blood, pain and loss of fluid. If the patient is unconscious then airway clearance, resuscitation and treatment of blood loss, followed by maintenance in the semi-prone position is paramount. Heat loss must be prevented but no active heating should be used. If the patient is conscious, loosen tight clothes and elevate the lower limbs. Fluids should be given (if conscious) frequently in small amounts.

CUTS - if deep, remove any foreign body and treat bleeding with compression. Clean and dry cut. Bring the edges together using Steristrips (or adhesive tape) to hold them closed, starting in mid-cut and working to ends. Reinforce middle strips to prevent bursting.

DROWNING - Try all the resuscitation techniques in the introduction, according to need.

A - Airway: clearance and maintenance
B - Breathing: by mouth to mouth or mouth to nose
C - Circulation: External Cardiac Massage may be required.

If successful, monitor level of consciousness and check airway. Maintain semi-prone position and keep under observation.

Hypothermia: usually complicates cold water immersion. Remove wet clothes and put patient in a dry sleeping bag with either a handwarm hot water bottle or a warm dry person. Look after patient out of wind, chill and rain and warm the cabin if possible. It can help to raise lower limbs and wrap towel round abdomen. Remember to watch for deterioration during warming.

DIARRHOEA - should be treated by oral fluids only; no solid food for 24/48 hours.

EYE INJURIES - Foreign body(ies) -
(a) Try to flush out with plenty of clean water.
(b) Try pulling upper lid over lower then releasing to remove foreign body from under upper lid.
(c) Raise upper, then lower lid, asking casualty to look all around. The upper lid can be turned back on itself over a matchstick. The speck can usually be seen and removed with a Q-tip or clean handkerchief.

If the foreign body cannot be removed it may have penetrated the eye and no further attempts should be made to remove it. The eye should be covered and both eyes rested. If pain persists after the speck is removed there may be a concealed abrasion and the eyes should be rested and Chloromycetin eye drops or a solution of 1 teaspoonful salt to 1 pint of boiled cooled water inserted.

Lost contact lenses can sometimes be lodged under upper lid in upper outer part of eye. It is possible to see them by turning back the lid and massaging them back into position through the lid.

FISH HOOKS - can penetrate the skin and may have to be pushed right through until the barb can be cut off with pliers and the hook withdrawn.

HEART ATTACK - though often hard to be sure, the following treatment should at least do no harm. If the patient is conscious, make them comfortable in the half-sitting position and give the strongest available pain killers. If the patient becomes semi-conscious place them in the recovery position, and observe carefully for maintenance of clear airway, and commence resuscitation should it be necessary.

HYPOTHERMIA - nearly always complicates cold water immersion and should be considered even when not apparent. If conscious the victim may be confused and appear drunk, seeming lethargic and remote from what is going on. Shivering fits may or may not occur and poor colour, vomiting or faintness can develop. The treatment is mentioned under Cold Injury above and consists of gradual rewarming by removal from wet and cold, replacement of wet clothing and if conscious rewarming in a warm sleeping bag. Priority must be given to attention to airway and the semi-prone position if the victim is unconscious.

INTERNAL INJURIES - may occur in any of the accidents which cause broken bones and bleeding and should be suspected when the patient seems unduly distressed, collapsed or blood appears from the body openings. The abdomen may appear rigid.

The priorities are airway clearance and maintenance and the adoption of the semi-prone position with careful observation to ensure prompt treatment of respiratory or cardiac arrest. The victim should be covered to prevent heat loss.

JOINTS - can be strained and sprained on decks and winches. The treatment is rest and time, but supporting crepe bandages can be comforting.

SEASICKNESS - is best avoided by starting treatment such as Stugeron or your favourite at least 12 hours before sailing. All these drugs may cause drowsiness. Alcohol must be avoided and hangovers predispose to seasickness.

ALL SEASICK CREW ON DECK SHOULD WEAR A HARNESS and should not be allowed to vomit over the side. Oral rehydration with very small amounts of rehydration fluids should be started, and fresh air and the ability to see the horizon can help. The danger of cold should not be ignored. Stemetil anti-sickness suppositories can be useful.

SWALLOWING - Accidentally swallowed objects can usually be left to nature. Dangerous objects such as watch batteries and open safety pins should be treated as emergencies.

STINGS - from jellyfish are treated by oral antihistamines.

TOOTHACHE - caused by abscess and accompanied by swelling can be treated with antibiotics and painkillers. You can buy (OTC) dental kits.

VOMITING - Attempts should be made at rehydration using small amounts of fluid, preferably oral rehydration packs.

The information in the above list should give a casualty the best possibility of recovering until help arrives.

FIRST AID KIT

Items marked Rx require a prescription from a General Practitioner, who will have his/her own preferences and opinion on the need for a prescription. The following are mainly for guidance:

ANALGESICS - for pain relief
Paracetamol (Panadol) tabs 500mg. Dose; 2 tabs 4-6 hours for medium to moderate pain. Dihydrocodeine tabs (Rx). Dose: 1 tab 4-6 hourly for moderate to severe pain. Cause constipation with long term use. Can be used at night for cough or in the treatment of diarrhoea. Pharmacists will discuss other (OTC) painkillers which are used for moderate pain.

ANTACIDS - for heartburn and indigestion. Gaviscon tabs. Dose; 2 tabs chewed and swallowed 3/4 times daily.

ANTIBIOTICS - for infections
Amoxycillin capsules 250mg (Rx). Dose: 2 caps three times daily. Check for allergy, otherwise safe. Erythromycin tablets 250mg (Rx) For infection if allergic to Penicillin. Dose: 1 tab four times daily.

DIARRHOEALS - Imodium capsules after each loose stool. Up to 6 per day in conjunction with oral rehydration and avoiding solid food.

ANTIEMETICS - for seasickness. Prevention - Stugeron or other proprietary preparation. Stemetil suppositories (Rx) along with oral rehydration in severe cases.

ANTIHISTAMINES - for stings, bites and hay fever. Newer Antihistamine - Loratadine, 1 tablet daily is less likely to cause drowsiness.
Piriton tablets 4mg - cause drowsiness

ANTISEPTICS - Savlon, TCP, Dettol etc.

DRESSINGS - Melolin Sterile Squares 10cm x 10cm. Put shiny side to wound, can be cut up and secured with Elastoplast or Micropore Tape. Crepe bandages - assorted widths for dressings, sprains or for securing splints. Steristrips for wound closure.

EYE DROPS - for sticky, gritty or red eyes. Chloromycetin drops (Rx).

ORAL REHYDRATION - for vomiting and diarrhoea. Rehidrat or Diarolyte Powders in sachets with instructions. Start with small amounts then give freely to replace lost fluid in vomiting, diarrhoea, burns and sunburn.

SAFETY

HM Coastguard MRCCs and MRSCs

All Centres have operational A1 DSC VHF CH 70. All A2 DSC stations are operational, as indicated by 2187·5 kHz. WZ (Coastal) Navigation Warnings, Gale Warnings and Inshore Forecasts are as follows:
Stations broadcasting Gun and Subfacts are indicated by*.
Radio and telephone communications with CG Co-ordination Centres are recorded for the purpose of public safety and the prevention/detection of crime.

FALMOUTH COASTGUARD (MRCC)
50°09'N 05°03'W.
DSC MMSI 002320014 (2187·5 kHz)
E-mail   falmouthcoastguard@mcga.gov.uk
☎ 01326 317575l; 🕾 01326 318342.
Area from Marsland Mouth to Dodman Point.
On VHF Ch 16*, MF 2226 kHz   MSI Broadcast Schedules at: 0140 0540 0940 1340 1740 and 2140 UTC.

BRIXHAM COASTGUARD (MRSC)
50°24'N 03°31'W. DSC MMSI 002320013
E-mail   brixhamcoastguard@mcga.gov.uk
☎ 01803 882704; 🕾 01803 882780.
Area from Dodman Point to Topsham.
On VHF Ch 16*   MSI Broadcast Schedules at: 0050 0450 0850 1250 1650 2050 UTC.

PORTLAND COASTGUARD (MRSC)
50°36'N 02°27'W. DSC MMSI 002320012
E-mail   portlandcoastguard@mcga.gov.uk
☎ 01305 760439; 🕾 01305 760452.
Area from Topsham to Chewton Bunney.
On VHF Ch 16   MSI Broadcast Schedules at: 0220 0620 1020 1420 1820 and 2220 UTC.

SOLENT COASTGUARD (MRSC)
50°48'N 01°12'W. DSC MMSI 002320011
E-mail   solentcoastguard@mcga.gov.uk
☎ 02392 552100; 🕾 02392 551763.
Area from Chewton Bunney to Beachy Head.
Call Ch 67 (H24) for safety traffic.
On VHF Ch 16, MF 1641 kHz   MSI Broadcast Schedules at: 0040 0440 0840 1240 1640 and 2040 UTC.

DOVER COASTGUARD (MRCC)
50°08'N 01°20'E. DSC MMSI 002320010
E-mail   dovercoastguard@mcga.gov.uk
☎ 01304 210008; 🕾 01304 202137.
Area from Beachy Head to Reculver Towers.
On VHF Ch 16, MSI Broadcast Schedules at: 0105 0505 0905 1305 1705 and 2105 UTC.
Operates Channel Navigation Information Service (CNIS) which broadcasts nav and tfc info on Ch 11 every H+40 (and H+55 in bad vis).

LONDON COASTGUARD
51°30'N 00°05'E.
E-mail   londoncoastguard@mcga.gov.uk
☎ 0208 312 7380; 🕾 0208 312 7679.
Area River Thames from Shell Haven Pt (North Bank) and Egypt (South Bank) to Teddington.
NOTE: Does not broadcast MSI. Call on VHF Ch 16 *London Coastguard.*

THAMES COASTGUARD (MRSC)
51°51'N 01°17'E. DSC MMSI 002320009

E-mail   thamescoastguard@mcga.gov.uk
☎ 01255 675518; 🕾 01255 675249.
Area from Reculver Towers to Southwold.
On VHF Ch 16   MSI Broadcast Schedules at: 0010 0410 0810 1210 1610 and 2010 UTC.

YARMOUTH COASTGUARD (MRCC)
52°37'N 01°43'E. DSC MMSI 002320008
E-mail   yarmouthcoastguard@mcga.gov.uk
☎ 01493 851338; 🕾 01493 852307.
Area from Southwold to Haile Sand Fort.
On VHF Ch 16, MF 1869 kHz MSI Broadcast Schedules at: 0040 0440 0840 1240 1640 and 2040 UTC.

HUMBER COASTGUARD (MRSC)
54°06'N 00°11'W.
DSC MMSI 002320007 (2187·5 kHz)
E-mail   humbercoastguard@mcga.gov.uk
☎ 01262 672317; 🕾 01262 606915.
Area from Haile Sand Fort to the Scottish border.
On VHF Ch 16, MF 2226 kHz   MSI Broadcast SchedulesN at: 0340 0740 1140 1540 1940 and 2340 UTC.

FORTH COASTGUARD (MRSC)
56°17'N 02°35'W. DSC MMSI 002320005
E-mail   forthcoastguard@mcga.gov.uk
☎ 01333 450666; 🕾 01333 450725.
Area from English border to Doonies Point.
On VHF Ch 16   MSI Broadcast Schedules at: 0205 0605 1005 1405 1805 and 2205 UTC.

ABERDEEN COASTGUARD (MRCC)
57°08'N 02°05'W.
DSC MMSI 002320004 (2187·5 kHz)
E-mail   aberdeencoastguard@mcga.gov.uk
☎ 01224 592334; 🕾 01224 575920.
Area from Doonies Pt to Cape Wrath, incl Pentland Firth.On VHF Ch 16, On MF 2226 kHz   MSI Broadcast Schedules at: 0320 0720 1120 1520 1920 and 2320 UTC.

SHETLAND COASTGUARD (MRSC)
60°09'N 01°08'W.
DSC MMSI 002320001(2187·5 kHz)
E-mail   shetlandcoastguard@mcga.gov.uk
☎ 01595 692976; 🕾 01595 694810.
Area from Covers Shetland, Orkney and Fair Isle. On VHF Ch 16, MF 1770 kHz   MSI Broadcast Schedules at: 0105 0505 0905 1305 1705 2105 UTC.

STORNOWAY COASTGUARD (MRSC)
58°12'N 06°22'W.
DSC MMSI 002320024 (2187·5 kHz)
E-mail   stornowaycoastguard@mcga.gov.uk
☎ 01851 702013; 🕾 01851 704387.
Area from Cape Wrath to Ardnamurchan Pt. Mainland, Barra to Butt of Lewis, Western Is and St Kilda.On VHF Ch 16, MF 1743 kHz MSI Broadcast Schedules at: 0110 0510 0910 1310 1710 2110 UTC.

CLYDE COASTGUARD (MRCC)
55°58'N 04°48'W.
DSC MMSI 002320022 (2187·5 kHz)
E-mail   clydecoastguard@mcga.gov.uk
☎ 01475 729988;   01475 786955.
Area from Ardnamurchan Point to Mull of Galloway. On VHF Ch 16*, MF 1883 kHz   MSI Broadcast Schedules at: 0020 0420 0820 1220 1620 2020 UTC.

BELFAST COASTGUARD (MRSC)
54°40'N 05°40'W.
DSC MMSI 002320021
E-mail   belfastcoastguard@mcga.gov.uk
☎ 02891 463933;   02891 465886.
Area covers Northern Ireland.
On VHF Ch 16*   MSI Broadcast Schedules at: 0305 0705 1105 1505 1905 and 2305 UTC.

LIVERPOOL COASTGUARD (MRSC)
53°30'N 03°03'W.
DSC MMSI 002320019
E-mail   liverpoolcoastguard@mcga.gov.uk
☎ 0151 9313341;   0151 9313347
Area from Mull of Galloway to Queensferry.
On VHF Ch 16   MSI Broadcast Schedules at: 0210 0610 1010 1410 1810 and 2210 UTC.

HOLYHEAD COASTGUARD (MRSC)
53°19'N 04°38'W.
DSC MMSI 002320018 (2187·5 kHz)
E-mail   holyheadcoastguard@mcga.g.v.uk
☎ 01407 762051;   01407 764373
Area from Queensferry to Friog
On VHF Ch 16, MF 1880 kHz,   MSI Broadcast Schedules at: 0235 0635 1035 1435 1835 and 2235 UTC.

MILFORD HAVEN COASTGUARD (MRSC)
51°41'N 05°10'W.
DSC MMSI 002320017 (2187·5 kHz)
E-mail   milfordcoastguard@mcga.gov.uk
☎ 01646 690909;   01646 692176.
Area from Friog to River Towy.
On VHF Ch 16, MF 1767 kHz   MSI Broadcast Schedules at: 0335 0735 1135 1535 1935 and 2335 UTC.

SWANSEA COASTGUARD (MRCC)
51°34'N 03°58'W.
DSC MMSI 002320016
E-mail   swanseacoastguard@mcga.gov.uk
☎ 01792 366534;   01792 369005.
Area from River Towy to Marsland Mouth.
On VHF Ch 16   MSI Broadcast Schedules at: 0005 0405 0805 1205 1605 and 2005 UTC.

CHANNEL ISLANDS
ST PETER PORT RADIO (CRS)
49°27'·00N 02°32'00W.
DSC MMSI 002320064
☎ 01481 720672;   01534 714177
Area covers the Channel Islands Northern area; Alderney Radio keeps watch Ch 16 HJ.
On VHF Ch 20, MF 1764 kHz   MSI Broadcast Schedules at: 0133 0533 0933 1333 1733 and 2133 UTC.

JERSEY RADIO   (CRS)
49°10'·85N 02°14'30W.
DSC MMSI 002320060
☎ 01534 741121.   01534 499089
Area covers the Channel Is Southern area.
On VHF Ch 25 82, MF 1658 kHz   MSI Broadcast Schedules at: 0645 0433 0745 0845 1245 1633 1845 2033 2245 UTC.

IRISH COASTGUARD

The Irish Coastguard is part of the Department of Marine, Leeson Lane, Dublin 2. ☎ (01) 6620922;   (01) 662 0795.

The Coastguard co-ordinates all SAR operations around the coast of Ireland through Dublin MRCC, Malin Head MRSC and Valentia MRSC. It liaises with UK and France during any rescue operation within 100M of the Irish coast.

The MRCC/MRSCs are co-located with the Coast Radio Stations of the same name and manned by the same staff. All stations maintain H24 listening watch on VHF Ch 16. If ashore dial 999 and ask for Marine Rescue in an emergency.

Details of the MRCC/MRSCs are as follows:

DUBLIN (MRCC)
53°20'N 06°15W.
DSC MMSI 002500300 (+2187·5 kHz).
☎ +353 1 662 0922/3;   +353 1 662 0795.
Covers Carlingford Lough to Youghal.

VALENTIA (MRSC)
51°56'N 10°21'W.
DSC MMSI 002500200 (+2187·5 kHz).
☎ +353 669 476 109;   +353 669 476 289.
Covers Youghal to Slyne Head.

MALIN HEAD (MRSC)
55°22'N 07°20W.
DSC MMSI 002500100 (+2187·5 kHz).
☎ +353 77 70103;   +353 77 70221.
Covers Slyne Head to Lough Foyle.

SAFETY

SAR RESOURCES

The Irish Coastguard provides some 50 units around the coast and is on call 24 hours a day. Some of these units have a specialist cliff climbing capability.

A helicopter, based at Shannon, can respond within 15 to 45 minutes and operate to a radius of 200M. It is equipped with infrared search equipment and can uplift 14 survivors. In addition helicopters (based at Finner Camp in Donegal and at Baldonnel, Dublin) can operate to 150 miles by day and 70 miles at night.

Other military and civilian aircraft and vessels, together with the Garda and lighthouse service, can be called upon.

The RNLI maintains four stations around the coast and some 26 lifeboats. Additionally, six individually community-run inshore rescue boats are available.

COAST AND CLIFF RESCUE SERVICES

This comprises about 50 stations manned by volunteers, who are trained in first aid and equipped with inflatables, breeches buoys, cliff ladders etc. Their ☎ numbers (the Leader's residence) are given, where appropriate, under each port.

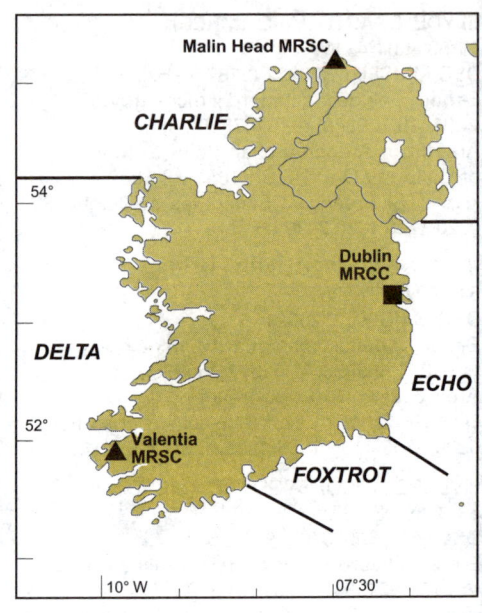

Irish Coastguard centres

DANISH COASTGUARD

The Danish Coastguard is controlled remotely from Lyngby through Blavand and Skagen CRS.

Lyngby is an operational Coast DSC station working via Blavand and Skagen on VHF Ch 70 MMSI 002191000.

There are at least 12 lifeboats stationed at the major harbours along this west facing coast.

MSI Navigational Warnings are broadcast on VHF from Lyngby at 0133 0533 0933 1333 1733 2133 on channels shown.

MF broadcasts are transmitted on 1758KHz from Skajen and 1734KHz from Blavand.

Firing Practice areas exist at:

Tranum and Blokhus ☎ 98235088 or call *Tranum* on VHF Ch 16.

Nymindegab ☎ 75289355 or call *Nymindegab* on VHF Ch 16.

Oksbøl ☎ 76541213 or call *Oksbøl* on VHF Ch 16; (Lyngby Radio broadcasts firing warnings at 0705 1705).

Rømø E ☎ 74755219 or call *Fly Rømø* on VHF Ch 16; Rømø W ☎ 74541340.

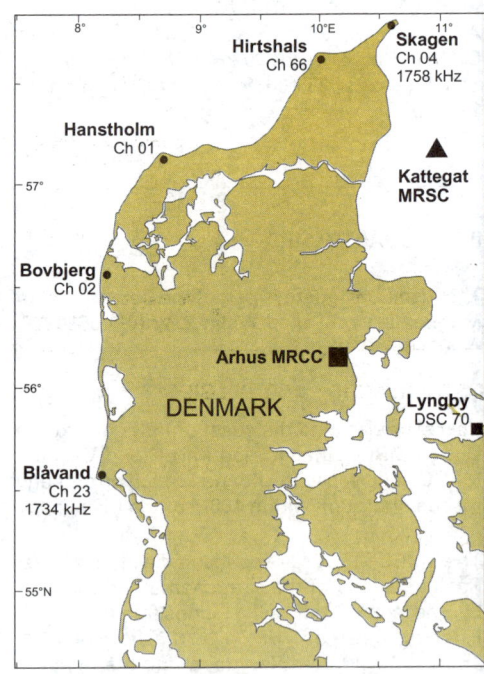

Danish Coastguard centres

GERMANY

SAFETY SERVICES

Maritime Rescue Co-ordination Centre Bremen MRCC (☎ 0421 536870; 📠 0421 5368714; MMSI 002111240) callsign *Bremen Rescue Radio*, coordinates SAR operations in the Search & Rescue Region (SRR) which abuts the UK SRR at about 55°12'N 03°30'E. A 24 hrs watch is kept on VHF Ch 16 and DSC Ch 70 via remote stations at Norddeich, Elbe Weser, Bremen, Helgoland, Hamburg, Eiderstedt and Nordfriesland.

DGzRS, the German Sea Rescue Service *(Deutsch Gesellschaft zur Rettung Schiffbrüchiger)*, is also based at Bremen (☎ 0421 537 0777; 📠 0421 537 0714). It monitors Ch 16 H24. Offshore lifeboats are based at Borkum, Norderney, Langeoog, Wilhelmshaven, Bremerhaven, Cuxhaven, Helgoland, Amrum and List. There are also many inshore lifeboats. The German Navy provides ships and SAR helicopters.

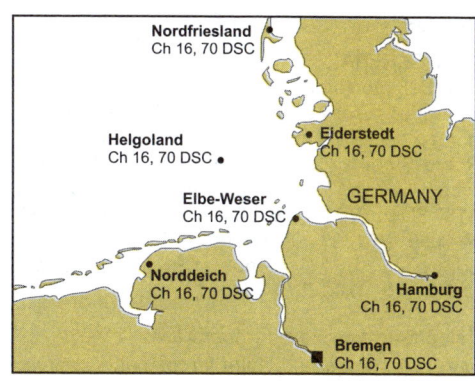

German Coastguard Radio Stations

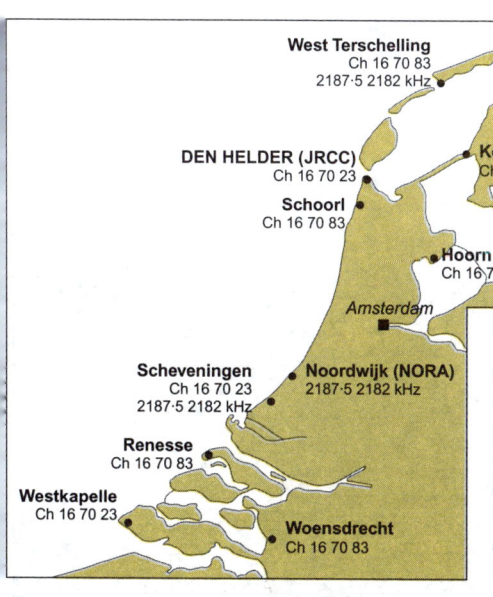

Netherlands Coastguard Radio Stations

NETHERLANDS AND BELGIUM

Netherlands

The Netherlands Coastguard (JRCC Den Helder) coordinates SAR operations using callsign *Den Helder Rescue*. A JRCC is a Joint Rescue Coordination Centre (marine and aeronautical).

The JRCC keeps a listening watch H24 on Ch 16 (until 1 Feb 2005), DSC Ch 70, and MF DSC 2187·5kHz (but not on 2182kHz); MMSI 002442000. Working channels are VHF 67 & 73. There are 24 lifeboat stations along the coast and 10 inshore lifeboat stations. Helicopters, fixed wing aircraft and ships of the RNLN can also be used.

Medical advice: initial call on Ch 16, DSC Ch 70 (MMSI 002442000) or 2187·5 kHz (MMSI 002442000). Working chans are VHF 23 & 83 or MF 2824 kHz transmit, 2520 kHz listen.

JRCC Operations (Joint Rescue Coordination Centre - marine and aeronautical) can be contacted H24 through the following:

For emergency:
☎ + 31 (0) 900 0111; 📠 + 31 (0) 223 658358.

Operational telephone number:
☎ + 31 (0) 223 542300.

or HO for Admin/info
☎+ 31 (0) 255 546546; 📠+31 223 658300.

Inmarsat 'C': 424477710

Navigational warnings
Navigational warnings (*Nautische Warnnachricht*) for the North Sea coast are contained in IJmuiden Navtex (P) transmissions. Dangers to navigation should be reported to Seewarn Cuxhaven.

SAFETY

Belgium

SAR GENERAL

The Belgian Pilotage Service coordinates SAR operations from Oostende MRCC. The MRCC is connected by telephone to the Oostende Coast Radio Station (OST) which maintains listening watch H24 on Ch 16, 2182kHz and DSC Ch 70 and 2187·5kHz. MMSI 002050480. ☎ 059 706565; 📠 059 701339. Antwerpen CRS, remotely controlled by Oostende CRS, has MMSI 002050485. DSC Ch 70.

Telephone and Fax numbers are:

MRCC Oostende ☎ +32(0) 59 701000;
📠 +32(0) 59 703605.

MRSC Nieuwpoort ☎ +32(0) 58 230000;
📠 +32(0) 58 231575.

MRSC Zeebrugge ☎ +32(0) 50 550801;
📠 +32(0) 50 547400.

RCC Brussels (Point of contact for Cospas/Sarsat):
☎ +32(0) 2 226 8856 (Mon-Fri 0600-1500 UT).

Offshore and inshore lifeboats are based at Nieuwpoort, Oostende and Zeebrugge.

The Belgian Air Force provides helicopters from Koksijde near the French border. The Belgian Navy also cooperates in SAR operations.

Navigational warnings are broadcast by Oostende Radio on receipt and at scheduled times on 2761 kHz and VHF Ch 27. Also by Oostende Navtex (M) at: 0200, 0600, 1000, 1400, 1800, 2200 UT for the SW part of the North Sea.

FRANCE – CROSS

Four Centres Régionaux Opérationnels de Surveillance et de Sauvetage (CROSS) cover the Channel and Atlantic coasts; see below. CROSS is an MRCC. CROSS provides a permanent, H24, all weather operational presence along the French coast and liaises with foreign CGs. CROSS' main functions include:

(1) Co-ordinating Search and Rescue.
(2) Navigational surveillance.
(3) Broadcasting navigational warnings.
(4) Broadcasting weather information.
(5) Anti-pollution control.
(6) Marine and fishery surveillance.

CROSS and sous-Cross centres

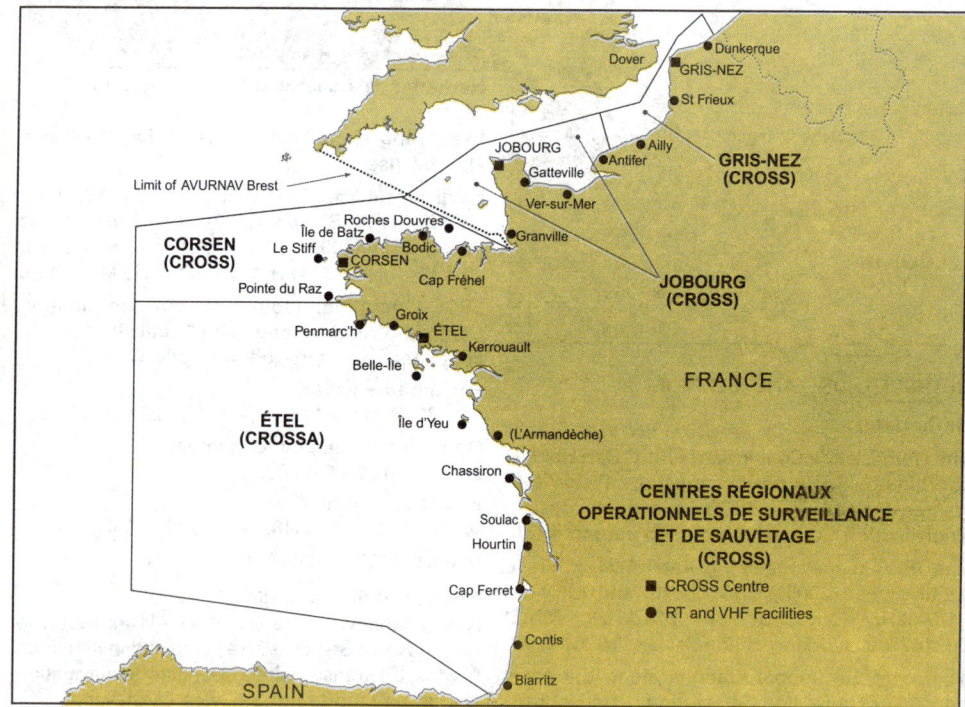

All centres keep watch on VHF Ch 16 as well as Ch 70 (DSC), and broadcast gale warnings along with weather forecasts and local navigational warnings.

CROSSA Étel specialises in providing medical advice and responds to alerts from Cospas/Sarsat satellites.

CROSS can be contacted by R/T, by ☎, through Coast Radio Stations, via the National Gendarmerie or Affaires Maritimes, or via a Semaphore station. Call *Semaphore* stations on Ch 16 (working Ch 10) or by ☎ as listed later in this section.

In addition to their safety and SAR functions, CROSS stations using, for example, the callsign *Corsen Traffic* monitor Traffic Separation Schemes in the Dover Strait, off Casquets and off Ouessant. They also broadcast navigational warnings and weather forecasts. See Chapter 2 for times and VHF channels.

CROSS stations
All stations co-ordinate SAR on VHF Ch 15 67 68 73. DSC Ch 70. All stations have Emergency ☎ 1616.

CROSS Gris-Nez
50°52'N 01°35'E   MMSI 002275100
☎ 03 21 87 21 87; 📠 03 21 87 78 55
Belgian Border to Cap d'Antifer
DSC Ch 70 MF 2187·5 kHz

Navigation Warnings
On VHF Ch 79: From: Dunkerque, Gris-Nez, Saint-Frieux and L'Ailly every H+10
On MF 1650 kHz: Gris-Nez at 0833 2033 UT

CROSS Jobourg
49°41'N 01°54'W   MMSI 002275200
☎ 02 33 52 72 13; 📠 02 33 52 71 72
Cap de la Hague to Mont St Michel

Navigation Warnings
On VHF Ch 80: From: Antifer, Ver-sur-Mer, Gatteville, Jobourg, Granville and Roche Douvres every H+20/H+50.
On MF 1650 kHz: Gris-Nez at 0915 2115 LT

CROSS Corsen
48°24'N 04°47'W   MMSI 002275300
☎ 02 98 89 31 31; 📠 02 98 89 65 75
Mont St Michel to Pointe de Penmarc'h

Navigation Warnings
On MF 2677 kHz: From CROSS Corsen at 0735 1935 LT

CROSS Étel
47°39'N 03°12'W   MMSI 002275000
☎ 02 97 55 35 35; 📠 02 97 55 49 34
Pointe de Penmarc'h to the Spanish Border

Navigation Warnings
On VHF Ch 80: From: Penmarc'h 0703 1533 1903 LT, Ile de Groix at 0715 1545 1915 LT. Belle-Ile at 0733 1603 1933 LT, Saint-Nazaire at 0745 1615 1945 LT, Ile d'Yeu at 0803 1633 2003 LT, and Les Sable d'Olonne at 0815 1645 2015 LT.

On VHF Ch 79 From: Chassiron at 1903 LT, Soulac at 1915 LT, Cap Ferrat at 1933 LT, Contis at 1945 LT and Biarritz at 2003 LT.

Semaphore (Signal) stations

* Dunkerque	03·28·66·86·18	
Boulogne	03·21·31·32·10	
Ault	03·22·60·47·33	
Dieppe	02·35·84·23·82	
* Fécamp	02·35·28·00·91	
* La Hève	02·35·46·07·81	
* Le Havre	02·35·21·74·39	
Villerville	02·31·88·11·13	
* Port-en-Bessin	02·31·21·81·51	
St-Vaast	02·33·54·44·50	
* Barfleur	02·33·54·04·37	
Lévy	02·33·54·31·17	
* Le Homet	02·33·92·60·08	
La Hague	02·33·52·71·07	
Carteret	02·33·53·85·08	
Barneville Le Roc	02·33·50·05·85	
St-Cast	02·96·41·85·30	
* St Quay-Portrieux	02·96·70·42·18	
Bréhat	02·96·20·00·12	
* Ploumanac'h	02·96·91·46·51	
Batz	02·98·61·76·06	
* Brignogan	02·98·83·50·84	
* Ouessant Stiff	02·98·48·81·50	
* St-Mathieu	02·98·89·01·59	
* Portzic (Ch 08)	02·98·22·21·47	
Toulinguet	02·98·27·90·02	
Cap-de-la-Chèvre	02·98·27·09·55	
* Pointe-du-Raz	02·98·70·66·57	
* Penmarc'h	02·98·58·61·00	
Beg Meil	02·98·94·98·92	
* Port-Louis	02·97·82·52·10	
Étel Mât Fenoux	02·97·55·35·35	
Beg Melen (Groix)	02·97·86·80·13	
Talut (Belle-Île)	02·97·31·85·07	
St-Julien	02·97·50·09·35	
Piriac-sur-Mer	02·40·23·59·87	
* Chemoulin	02·40·91·99·00	
St-Sauveur (Yeu)	02·51·58·31·01	
Les Baleines (Ré)	05·46·29·42·06	
Chassiron (Oléron)	05·46·47·85·43	
* Pointe-de-Grave	05·56·09·60·03	
Cap Ferret	05·56·60·60·03	
Messanges	05·58·48·94·10	
* Socoa	05·59·47·18·54	

* H24. Remainder sunrise to sunset.

SAFETY

EMERGENCY VHF DF SERVICE
A yacht in emergency can call CROSS on VHF Ch 16, 11 or 67 to obtain a bearing. This will be passed as the true bearing of the yacht *from* the DF station. The Semaphore stations listed above are also equipped with VHF DF. They keep watch on Ch 16 and other continuously scanned frequencies, which include Ch 1-29, 36, 39, 48, 50, 52, 55, 56 and 60-88.

MEDICAL
The Service d'Aide Médicale Urgente (SAMU) can be contacted via CROSS. CROSS Étel specialises in providing medical advice. It can be contacted via:

Lille – 03·20·54·22·22
Le Havre – 02·35·47·15·15
Caen – 02·31·44·88·88
Saint Brieuc – 02·96·94·28·95
Brest – 02·98·46·11·33
Vannes – 02·97·54·22·11
Nantes – 02·40·08·37·77
La Rochelle – 05·46·27·32·15
Bordeaux – 05·56·96·70·70
Bayonne – 05·59·63·33·33

Semaphore stations
These stations keep a visual, radar and radio watch (VHF Ch 16) around the coast. They show visual gale warning signals, will repeat forecasts and offer local weather reports. They relay emergency calls to CROSS and are equipped with VHF DF; see above.

Lifeboats
The lifeboat service Société National de Sauvetage en Mer (SNSM) comes under CROSS, but ashore it is best to contact local lifeboat stations direct. A hefty charge may be levied if a SNSM lifeboat attends a vessel not in distress.

Navigation warnings
Long-range warnings are broadcast by Inmarsat SafetyNet for Navarea II, which includes the west coast of France. The north coast lies in Navarea I.

Avurnavs (AVis URgents aux NAVigateurs) are regional Coastal and Local warnings issued by two regional authorities:

(1) **Brest** – for the west coast of France and the western Channel to Mont St Michel; and

(2) **Cherbourg** – for the eastern Channel from Mont St Michel to the Belgian frontier.

Avurnavs are broadcast by Niton and Brest on Navtex, and on MF by Jobourg and CROSS Gris Nez; urgent ones on receipt and after next silence period, and at scheduled times. Warnings are prefixed by '*Sécurité Avurnav*', followed by the name of the station.

Local warnings for coastal waters are broadcast in French and **English** by CROSS as follows:

CROSS	VHF Ch	Times (local)
Dunkerque	79	H+10
CROSS Gris Nez	79	H+10
	1650 kHz	0833 2033 LT
Saint Frieux	79	H+10
L'Ailly	79	H+10
CROSS Jobourg	80	H+20 & H+50
	1650 kHz	0915 2115 LT
Granville	80	H+20
Roche Douvre	80	H+20 & H+50
CROSS Corsen	79	H+10 & H+40
	2677 kHz	0735 1935 LT
Bodic	79	H+10 & H+40
Ile de Batz	79	H+10 & H+40
Le Stiff	79	H+10 & H+40
Pointe du Raz	79	H+10 & H+40
CROSS Étel	80	On receipt

SPAIN AND PORTUGAL
Spain and Portugal – MRCC/MRSC
MRCCs and MRSCs are primarily responsible for handling Distress, Safety and Urgency communications. Madrid MRCC coordinates SAR on the N and NW coasts of Spain through six MRCC/MRSCs. All stations monitor VHF Ch 16 and 2182 kHz H24 and VHF DSC Ch 70 (H24).

In Portugal, the Portuguese Navy coordinates SAR in two regions, Lisboa and Santa Maria (Azores).

In SW Spain and the Gibraltar Strait MRCC Tarifa coordinates SAR.

Digital Selective Calling (DSC) is operational as shown below. MRCC/MRSCs also broadcast weather as shown in Chapter 2. MRCC/MRSCs do not handle commercial link calls.

Search and Rescue operations and the prevention of pollution in Spain are undertaken by the National Society for Maritime Rescue and Safety (Salvamento y Seguridad – SASEMA).

A shipping forecast is broadcast, in Spanish, every two hours from Salvamento Marítimao's regional centres and copies of this can usually be obtained from most yacht clubs.

NORTH AND NORTH-WEST SPAIN

Bilbao MRCC MMSI 002240996	43°21'N 03°02'W ☎ 94 483 9286; 📠 94 483 9161	Ch 10: Nav warnings every 4 hours from 0233 UT. DSC Ch 70, 2187·5 kHz
Santander MRSC MMSI 002241009	43°28'N 03°43'W ☎ 942 213 030; 📠 942 213 638	Ch 11: Nav warnings every 4 hours from 0045 UT. DSC Ch 70 2187·5 kHz
Gijón MRCC MMSI 002240997	43°37'N 05°42'W ☎ 985 326 050; 📠 985 320 908	Ch 10 Nav warnings every H+15 DSC Ch 70, 2187·5 kHz
Coruña MRSC MMSI 002241022	43°22'N 08°23'W ☎ 981 209 548; 📠 981 209 518 Call: *Coruña Traffic*	Ch 13, 16, 67 Ch 13: Nav warnings every 4 hours from 0205 UT. DSC Ch 70, 2187·5 kHz
Finisterre MRCC MMSI 002240993	42°42'N 08°59'W ☎ 981 767 320; 📠 981 767 740 Call: *Finisterre Traffic*	Ch 11, 16 2182 kHz Ch 11: Nav warnings every 4 hours from 0033 UT. DSC Ch 70, 2187·5 kHz
Vigo MRSC MMSI 002240998	42°10'N 08°41'W ☎ 986 297 403; 📠 986 290 455	Ch 11, 16 2182 kHz DSC Ch 70, 2187·5 kHz Ch 10: Nav warnings every 4 hours from 0215 UT

PORTUGAL

Lisboa MRCC 38°41'N 09°19'W
Ch 23 25 26 27 28 MF 2182 2578 2693 kHz.
MMSI 002630100
☎ 351 21 419 0098
📠 351 21 419 9900
DSC Ch 70; 2187·5 kHz
VHF Services controlled from Lisboa:

Arga	Ch 25 28 83
Arestal	Ch 24 26 85
Montejunto	Ch 23 27 87
Atalaia	Ch 24 26 85
Picos	Ch 23 27 85
Estoi	Ch 24 28 86

Spanish & Portuguese Coastguard Radio Stations

SOUTH WEST SPAIN

Tarifa MRCC MMSI 002240994	36°01'N 05°35'W ☎ 956 681 452; 📠 956 680 606	Ch 16 10 74, 2182 kHz (all H24); Call: *Tarifa Traffic* Ch 10 74: Nav warnings every even H+15 and on receipt DSC Ch 70, 2187·5 kHz (H24)
Algeciras MRSC MMSI 002241001	36°08'N 05°26'W ☎ 956 585 404; 📠 956 585 402	Ch 15 16 74 DSC Ch 70 Nav warnings on request

SAFETY

UK EMERGENCY VHF DIRECTION FINDING SERVICE

Remotely controlled H24 by a Coastguard Maritime Rescue Co-ordination Centre (MRCC) or Maritime Rescue Sub-Centre (MRSC), this equipment is for emergency use only. It is not a free navigational service and should only be used 'one stage down' from real distress. It is in all yachtsmen's interests not to abuse the service.

After contact on Ch 16, invariably Ch 67 is used for the DF procedure; this may be a count from 1-10. Note that the bearing obtained is from the station to the vessel.

VHF-DF stations are marked on charts by a dot and magenta circle, suffixed 'RG'.

STATION	CONTROLLED BY	POSITION	
Barra	MRSC Stornoway	57°00'·81N	07°30'·42W
Bawdsey	MRSC Thames	51°59'·60N	01°25'·00E
Berry Head	MRSC Brixham	50°23'·97N	03°29'·05W
Boniface	MRSC Solent	50°36'·21N	01°12'·03W
Compass Head	MRSC Shetland	59°52'·05N	01°16'·30W
Crosslaw	MRSC Forth	55°54'·48N	02°12'·31W
Cullercoats	MRSC Humber	55°04'·00N	01°28'·00W
Dunnet Head	MRCC Aberdeen	58°40'·31N	03°22'·52W
Easington	MRSC Humber	53°39'·13N	00°05'·90E
East Prawle	MRSC Brixham	50°13'·10N	03°42'·50W
Fairlight	MRCC Dover	50°52'·19N	00°38'·74E
Fife Ness	MRSC Forth	56°16'·70N	02°35'·30W
Flamborough	MRSC Humber	54°07'·08N	00°05'·21W
Great Ormes Head	MRSC Holyhead	53°19'·96N	03°51'·25W
Grove Point	MRSC Portland	50°32'·93N	02°25'·20W
Hartland Pt	MRCC Swansea	51°01'·22N	04°31'·40W
Hartlepool	MRSC Humber	54°41'·79N	01°10'·57W
Hengistbury Head	MRSC Portland	50°42'·95N	01°45'·64W
Inverbervie	MRSC Forth	56°51'·10N	02°15'·65W
Kilchiaran	MRCC Clyde	55°45'·90N	06°27'·19W
Lands End	MRCC Falmouth	50°08'·13N	05°38'·19W
Landgon Battery	MRCC Dover	51°07'·97N	01°20'·59E
Law Hill	MRCC Clyde	55°41'·76N	04°50'·46W
Lizard	MRCC Falmouth	49°57'·60N	05°12'·06W
Lowestoft	MRCC Yarmouth	52°28'·60N	01°42'·20E
Newhaven	MRSC Solent	50°46'·93N	00°03'·01E
Newton	MRSC Humber	55°31'·01N	01°37'·10W
North Foreland	MRCC Dover	51°22'·53N	01°26'·72E
Noss Head	MRCC Aberdeen	58°28'·80N	03°03'·00W
Rame Head	MRSC Brixham	50°19'·03N	04°13'·20W
Rhiw	MRSC Holyhead	52°50'·00N	04°37'·82W
Rodel	MRSC Stornoway	57°44'·90N	06°57'·41W
St Ann's Head	MRSC Milford Haven	51°40'·97N	05°10'·52W
St Mary's, Isles of Scilly	MRCC Falmouth	49°55'·73N	06°18'·25W
Sandwick	MRSC Stornoway	58°12'·65N	06°21'·27W
Selsey	MRSC Solent	50°43'·80N	00°48'·22W
Shoeburyness	MRSC Thames	51°31'·38N	00°46'·50E
Skegness	MRCC Yarmouth	53°09'·00N	00°21'·00E
Snaefell	MRSC Liverpool	54°15'·84N	04°27'·66W
Tiree	MRSC Clyde	56°30'·62N	06°57'·68W
Trevose Head	MRCC Falmouth	50°32'·91N	05°01'·99W
Trimingham	MRCC Yarmouth	52°54'·57N	01°20'·60E
Tynemouth	MRSC Humber	55°01'·07N	01°24'·99W
Walney Island	MRSC Liverpool	54°06'·61N	03°16'·00W
Whitby	MRSC Humber	54°29'·40N	00°36'·30W
Wideford Hill	MRSC Shetland	58°59'·29N	03°01'·40W
Windyhead	MRCC Aberdeen	57°38'·90N	02°14'·50W

CHANNEL ISLANDS

Guernsey	Ship transmits on Ch 16 (Distress only)	49°26'·27N	02°35'·77W
Jersey	or Ch 67 (Guernsey) or Ch 82 (Jersey)	49°10'·85N	02°14'·30W

IRELAND

Orlock Head	MRSC Belfast	54°40'·41N	05°34'·97W
West Torr	MRSC Belfast	55°11'·70N	06°05'·20W

SAFETY

FRENCH EMERGENCY VHF DIRECTION FINDING SERVICE

This service is for EMERGENCY USE ONLY. Each VHF direction-finding station is remotely controlled either by a Centre Régional Opérationnel de Surveillance et du Sauvetage (CROSS), Signal Station or Naval Lookout Station. See associated diagram. CROSS Stations guard Ch 16 or 11; (if a maritime rescue operation is already underway on Ch 11, then Ch 67 is used). Signal Stations and Lookout Stations keep a priority watch on Ch 16. Seven additional frequencies are retained in memory (scanner sweeping) from amongst the following channels:

1-29	:	156.050 MHz-157.450 MHz	52	:	155.625 MHz
36	:	162.400 MHz	55	:	155.775 MHz
39	:	162.550 MHz	56	:	155.825 MHz
48	:	121.500 MHz	60-88	:	156.025 MHz-157.425 MHz
50	:	155.525 MHz			

Ship transmits on Ch 16 (distress only) or Ch 11 in order that the station can determine its bearing. Ship's bearing from the station is transmitted on Ch 16 (distress only) or Ch 11

STATION	HOURS	CONTROLLED BY	POSITION	
Ault	HJ	Sig Stn	50°06'·50N	01°27'·50E
Barfleur	H24	Sig Stn	49°41'·90N	01°15'·90W
Batz	HJ	Sig Stn	48°44'·80N	04°00'·60W
Beg-Meil	HJ	Sig Stn	47°51'·30N	03°58'·40W
Beg Melen	HJ	Sig Stn	47°39'·20N	03°30'·10W
Boulogne	HJ	Sig Stn	50°44'·00N	01°36'·00E
Bréhat	HJ	Sig Stn	48°51'·30N	03°00'·10W
Brignogan	H24	Sig Stn	48°40'·60N	04°19'·70W
Cap de La Chèvre	HJ	Sig Stn	48°10'·20N	04°33'·00W
Cap Ferret	HJ	Sig Stn	44°37'·50N	01°15'·00W
Carteret	HJ	Sig Stn	49°22'·40N	01°48'·30W
Chassiron	HJ	Sig Stn	46°02'·80N	01°24'·50W
Chemoulin	H24	Sig Stn	47°14'·10N	02°17'·80W
Créach (Ouessant)	H24	CROSS Corsen	48°27'·60N	05°07'·80W
Créach (Ouessant)	HJ	Sig Stn	48°27'·60N	05°07'·70W
Dieppe	HJ	Sig Stn	49°56'·00N	01°05'·20W
Dunkerque	H24	Sig Stn	51°03'·40N	02°20'·40E
Étel	H24	CROSS Étel	47°39'·80N	03°12'·00W
Fécamp	H24	Sig Stn	49°46'·10N	00°22'·20E
Gris-Nez	H24	CROSS Gris Nez	50°52'·20N	01°35'·01E
Grouin (Cancale)	HJ	Sig Stn	48°42'·60N	01°50'·60W
Homet	H24	Lookout Stn	49°39'·50N	01°37'·90W
Jobourg	H24	CROSS Jobourg	49°41'·50N	01°54'·50W
La Coubre	H24	Sig Stn	45°41'·90N	01°13'·40W
La Hague	HJ	Sig Stn	49°43'·60N	01°56'·30W
La Hève	H24	Sig Stn	49°30'·60N	00°04'·20E
Le Roc	HJ	Sig Stn	48°50'·10N	01°36'·90W
Le Talut	HJ	Sig Stn	47°17'·70N	03°13'·00W
Les Baleines	HJ	Sig Stn	46°14'·60N	01°33'·70W
Levy	HJ	Sig Stn	49°41'·70N	01°28'·20W
Messanges	HJ	Sig Stn	43°48'·80N	01°23'·90W
Penmarc'h	H24	Sig Stn	47°47'·90N	04°22'·40W
Piriac	HJ	Sig Stn	47°22'·50N	02°33'·40W
Ploumanach	H24	Sig Stn	48°49'·50N	03°28'·20W
Pointe de Grave	HJ	Sig Stn	45°34'·30N	01°03'·90W
Pointe du Raz	H24	Sig Stn	48°02'·30N	04°43·80W
Port-en-Bessin	H24	Sig Stn	49°21'·10N	00°46'·30W
Port-Louis	H24	Lookout Stn	47°42'·60N	03°21'·80W
Roches-Douvres	H24	CROSS Jobourg	49°06'·39N	02°48'·80W
Saint-Cast	HJ	Sig Stn	48°38'·60N	02°14'·70W
Saint-Julien	HJ	Sig Stn	47°29'·70N	03°07'·50W
Saint-Mathieu	H24	Lookout Stn	48°19'·80N	04°46'·20W
Saint-Quay-Portrieux	H24	Sig Stn	48°39'·30N	02°49'·50W
Saint-Sauveur	HJ	Sig Stn	46°41'·70N	02°18'·80W
Saint-Vaast	HJ	Sig Stn	49°34'·50N	01°16'·50W
Sangatte	H24	Sig Stn	50°57'·10N	01°46'·39E
Socoa	H24	Sig Stn	43°23'·30N	01°41'·10W
Taillefer	HJ	Sig Stn	47°21'·80N	03°09'·00W
Toulinguet (Camaret)	HJ	Sig Stn	48°16'·80N	04°37'·50W
Villerville	HJ	Sig Stn	49°23'·20N	00°06'·50E

MILITARY EXERCISE AREAS

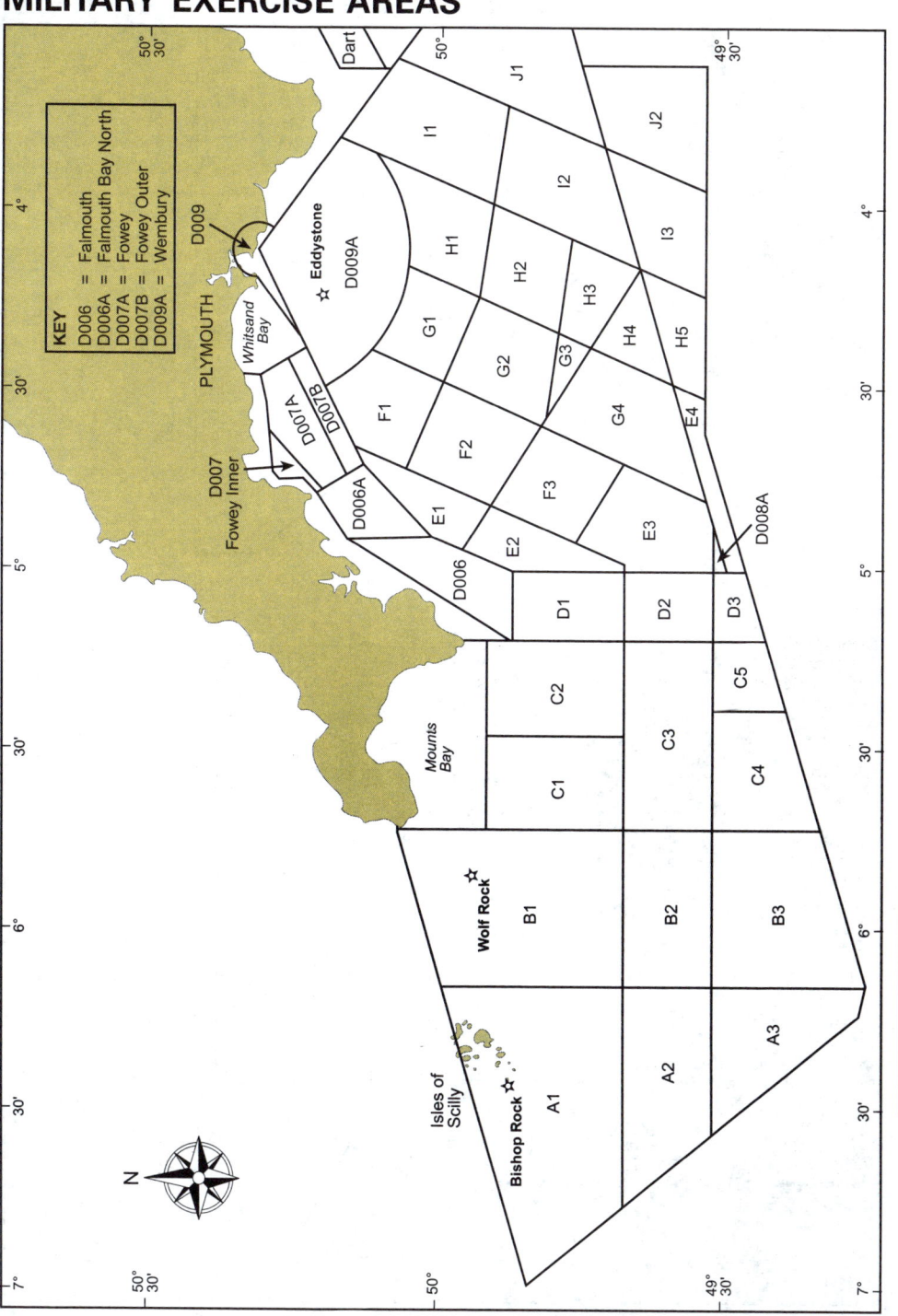

SAFETY

MILITARY EXERCISE AREAS

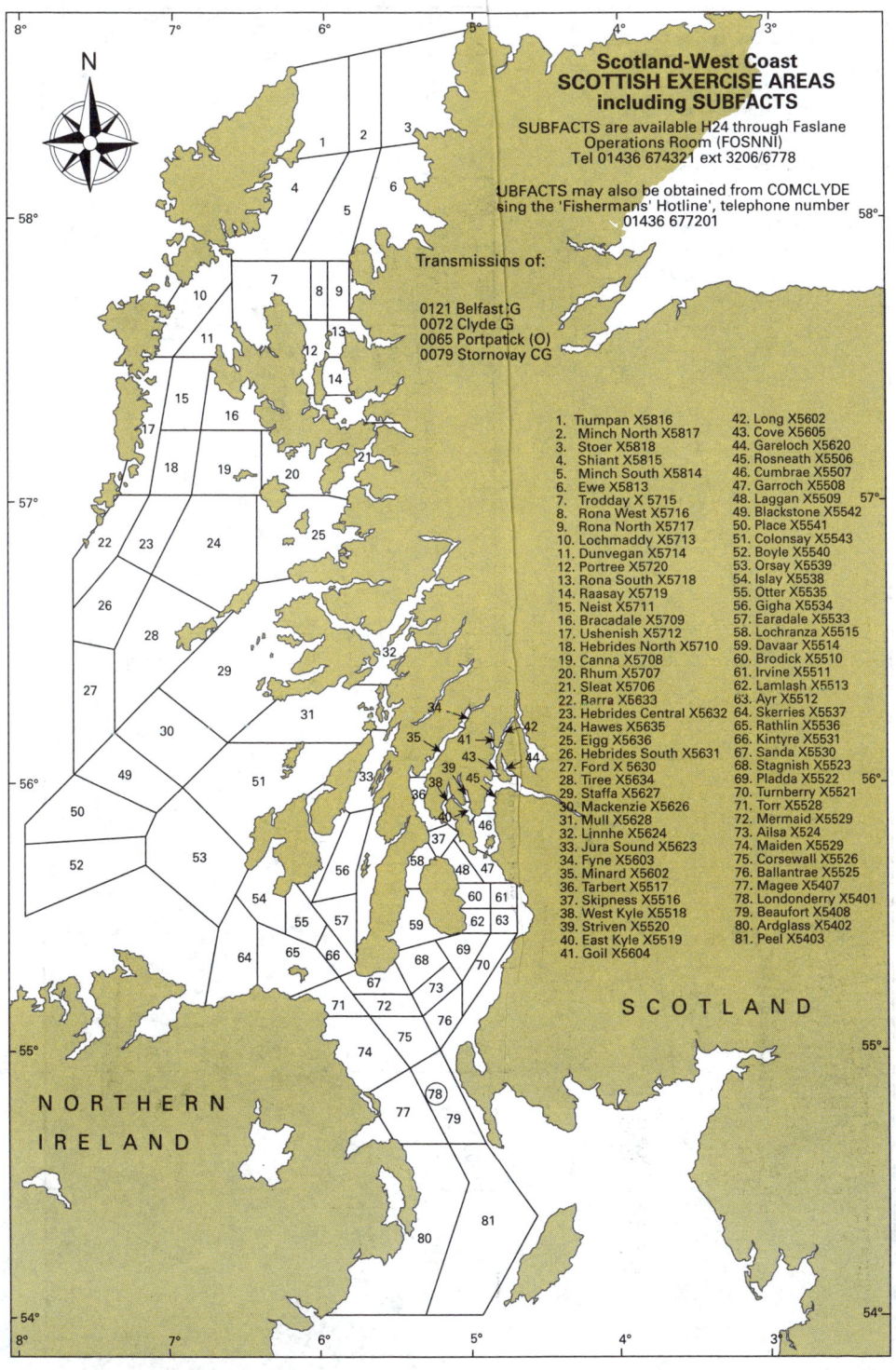

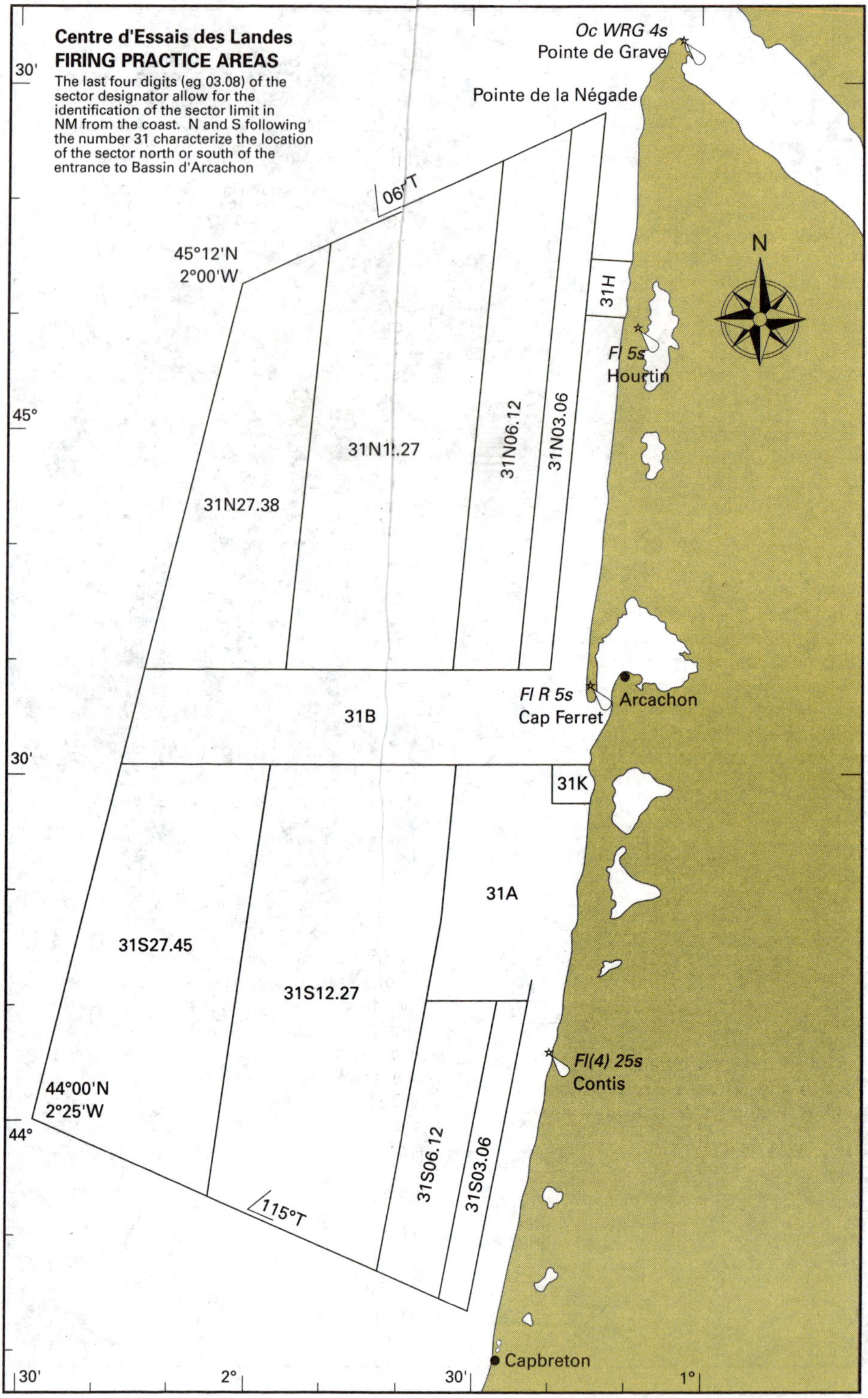

Centre d'Essais des Landes
FIRING PRACTICE AREAS
The last four digits (eg 03.08) of the sector designator allow for the identification of the sector limit in NM from the coast. N and S following the number 31 characterize the location of the sector north or south of the entrance to Bassin d'Arcachon
Oc WRG 4s
Pointe de Grave
Pointe de la Négade
06°T
45°12'N
2°00'W
31H
Fl 5s
Hourtin
N
31N27.38
31N12.27
31N06.12
31N03.06
31B
Fl R 5s
Cap Ferret
Arcachon
31K
31A
31S27.45
31S12.27
31S06.12
31S03.06
Fl(4) 25s
Contis
44°00'N
2°25'W
115°T
Capbreton
30'
45°
30'
44°
30'
2°
30'
1°

GMDSS

INTRODUCTION

The Global Maritime Distress and Safety System (GMDSS) is a third generation maritime distress and safety communications system adopted by the International Maritime Organisation (IMO).

Before the advent of GMDSS, maritime distress and safety relied heavily on ships and Coast Radio Stations keeping continuous watch on the three main international distress frequencies: 500 kHz (Morse) and R/T on 2182 kHz and VHF Ch 16. When out of range of Coast Radio Stations, only ships in the vicinity of a distress incident could render assistance.

GMDSS was introduced in Feb 1992 and became operational in most respects on 1 Feb 1999. The speed with which the various elements of GMDSS are put in place varies from sea area to sea area according to national policies.

On 31 Jan 2005 the Coastguard will cease its dedicated headset Watch on Ch 16. But this does not dispense with Ch 16, which is still needed to talk to a distressed vessel after the GMDSS DSC electronic alert. It is also still required to maintain communications with other ships assisting in the distress situation. From 31 January 2005 HM Coastguard will keep a loudspeaker watch on Ch 16.

Recommended reading:

ALRS, Vol 5 (UK Hydrographic Office).

GMDSS for small craft (Clemmetsen/Fernhurst).

VHF DSC Handbook (Fletcher/Reed's Publications).

OBJECTIVE

The objective of GMDSS is to alert SAR authorities ashore and ships in the vicinity to a distress incident by means of a combination of satellite and terrestrial communication, and navigation systems. As a result a coordinated SAR operation can be mounted rapidly and reliably anywhere in the world. GMDSS also provides urgency and safety communications, and promulgates Maritime Safety Information (MSI).

MARITIME SAFETY INFORMATION (MSI)

MSI refers to the vital meteorological, navigational and SAR messages which, traditionally, have been broadcast to vessels at sea by CRSs in Morse and by RT on VHF and MF. MSI is prepared/coordinated by the nations which control the 16 Navareas/Metareas used for Nav and Met warnings. The UK controls Navarea 1, which covers the Atlantic between 48°N and 71°N, out to 40°W. Navareas and Metreas have the same boundaries.

GMDSS broadcasts MSI in English by two independent but complementary means, Navex and SafetyNet:

Navex on MF (518kHz) covers coastal/offshore waters out to about 300 miles from transmitters.

SafetyNet uses Inmarsat satellites to cover beyond MF range. Enhanced Group Calling (EGC is a part of SafetyNet which enables MSI to be sent selectively by Inmarsat-C satellites to groups of users in any of the four oceans.

FUNCTIONS

Regardless of the sea areas in which they operate, vessels complying with GMDSS must be able to perform certain functions:

- transmit ship-to-shore distress alerts by two independent means;
- transmit ship-to-ship distress alerts;
- transmit and receive safety information, e.g. navigation and weather warnings;
- transmit signals for locating incidents;
- receive shore-to-ship distress alerts;
- receive ship-to-ship distress alerts;
- transmit and receive communications for SAR co-ordination.

GMDSS regulations apply to all ships over 300 tons engaged in international voyages, but they affect all seagoing craft. Although not obligatory for yachts, some features of GMDSS are of interest and, as equipment becomes more affordable, yachtsmen may decide to fit GMDSS voluntarily. This will become an increasing necessity as the present system for sending/receiving distress calls is run down.

DISTRESS ALERTING

GMDSS requires participating ships to be able to send distress alerts by two out of three independent means. These are:

1. Digital Selective Calling (DSC) using VHF Ch 70, MF 2187.5 kHz, or HF distress and alerting frequencies in the 4, 6, 8, 12 and 16 MHz bands.

SAFETY

2. EPIRBs (406 MHz via Cospas/Sarsat satellites; 121.5 MHz aeronautical civil distress; and 243MHz UHF aeronautical military distress; float-free or manually operated); or the Inmarsat system in the 1.6 GHz band. All types transmit distress messages which include the position and identification of the vessel in distress.

3. Inmarsat, via ship terminals.

COMMUNICATIONS

GMDSS uses both terrestrial and satellite based communications. Terrestrial communications, ie VHF, MF and HF, are employed in Digital Selective Calling (see below). Satellite communications come in the form of INMARSAT and Cospas/Sarsat.

DIGITAL SELECTIVE CALLING (DSC)

DSC is a fundamental part of GMDSS. It is so called because information is sent by a burst of digital code; selective because it is addressed to another DSC radio-telephone.

Under GMDSS, every vessel and relevant shore stations have a 9-digit identification number, known as an MMSI (Maritime Mobile Service Identity) that is used for identification in all DSC messages.

DSC is used to transmit distress alerts from ships, and to receive distress acknowledgments from ships or shore stations. DSC can also be used for relay purposes and for Urgency, Safety and Routine calling and answering.

In practice, a DSC distress call sent on VHF works broadly as follows:

Yachtsman presses the distress button; the set automatically switches to Ch 70 and transmits a coded distress message before reverting to Ch 16.

Any ship will reply directly by voice on Ch 16. But a CRS would send a distress acknowledgment on Ch 70 (automatically turning off the distress transmission), before replying on Ch 16. If a distress acknowledgment is not received from a CRS, the call will automatically be repeated about every 4 mins.

INMARSAT

Inmarsat (International Maritime Satellite System), via four geostationary satellites, provides near-global communications except in the polar regions above about 70°N and 70°S.

1.6 GHz satellite EPIRBs, operating through Inmarsat, can also be used for alerting, in addition to 406 MHz EPIRBs which use Cospas/Sarsat.

COSPAS/SARSAT

The US/Russian Cospas/Sarsat satellites complement the various other Satcom systems. They not only detect an emergency signal transmitted by an EPIRB, but also locate it with a high degree of accuracy.

There are four Cospas/Sarsat satellites operating in low polar orbits. In addition to these, there are four GEOSAR geostationary earth orbit satellites capable of receiving alerts from 406 MHz beacons.

Note that satellite tracking of 121.5MHz EPIRBS will cease in 2009.

SEA AREAS

For the purposes of GMDSS, the world's sea areas are divided into four categories in each of which ships must carry certain types of radio equipment.

The categories of areas are:

A1 an area within RT coverage of at least one VHF Coast Radio Station or Coastguard Centre in which continuous alerting via DSC is available. Range: roughly 40 miles from the CRS/CG.

A2 an area, excluding sea area A1, within RT coverage of at least one MF CRS/CG in which continuous DSC alerting is available. Range: roughly 100-150 miles from the CRS/CG.

A3 an area, excluding sea areas A1 and A2, within coverage of an Inmarsat satellite between 70°N and 70°S in which continuous alerting is available.

A4 an area outside sea areas A1, A2 and A3; ie in practice the polar regions.

The UK has declared its coastal waters to be an A1 area, but intends to continue guarding VHF Channel 16 until 01 Feb 2005. VHF DSC is fully operational at all UK Coastguard Radio Stations. France declared the English Channel to be an A1 area.

As most UK yachtsmen will operate in an A1 area, a VHF radio and a Navtex receiver will initially meet GMDSS requirements. As suitable VHF DSC sets become available (and affordable) it will make sense to re-equip with DSC equipment.

CHAPTER 5 - TIDES

CONTENTS

Dover Ranges and times of HW 142
Brest tidal coefficients 143
Tidal Calculations 144
Special instructions: Bournemouth to Selsey Bill 148
Tidal curves Bournemouth to Selsey Bill
Secondary ports: time & height differences 152
Tidal gates 171
Tidal stream charts 180
English Channel & S Brittany, Portland, Isle of Wight, Channel Islands,
North Sea, Scotland, West UK and Ireland,

Tidal curves & predictions

Southern England 218
Falmouth, Plymouth, Dartmouth, Portland, Poole, Southampton,
Portsmouth, Shoreham, Dover

Eastern England 254
Sheerness, London Bridge, Burnham-on-Crouch, Walton-on-the-Naze,
Lowestoft, Immingham, River Tyne

Scotland 282
Leith, Aberdeen, Wick, Lerwick, Stornoway, Ullapool, Oban, Greenock

Western England and Wales 314
Liverpool, Holyhead, Milford Haven, Avonmouth

Ireland 330
Dublin, Belfast, Galway, Cobh

Denmark 346
Esbjerg

Germany 350
Helgoland, Cuxhaven, Wilhelmshaven

Netherlands 362
Hoek van Holland, Vlissingen

Northern France 370
Dunkerque, Dieppe, Le Havre, Cherbourg, St Malo

Channel Islands 390
St Peter Port, St Helier

Western France 398
Brest, Pointe de Grave

Portugal & Gibraltar 406
Lisboa, Gibraltar

TIDES

DOVER RANGES & TIMES OF HW 2005

Day	HW	Range	HW		Day	HW	Range	HW		Day	HW	Range	HW		Day	HW	Range	HW		Day	HW	Range	HW
January					15	0200	5.5	1421		28	0147	5.0	1416		8	0047	5.0	1301		21	0055	5.5	1312
1	0158	4.6	1414		16	0236	4.7	1500		29	0251	4.6	1519		9	0112	5.0	1326		22	0133	4.9	1351
2	0235	4.2	1454		17	0317	3.8	1550		30	0404	4.2	1625		10	0136	4.9	1353		23	0215	4.2	1435
3	0320	3.9	1544		18	0413	2.9	1658		31	0521	3.8	1736		11	0204	4.7	1426		24	0305	3.3	1533
4	0415	3.3	1647		19	0530	2.4	1820							12	0240	4.4	1507		25	0408	2.6	1644
5	0523	3.5	1806		20	0659	2.4	1948		**June**					13	0325	3.9	1558		26	0520	2.6	1802
6	0635	4.1	1918		21	0835	2.9	2057		1	0636	4.1	1850		14	0426	3.3	1710		27	0639	2.6	1928
7	0742	4.8	2020		22	0927	3.7	2140		2	0743	4.3	1955		15	0605	3.0	1849		28	0752	3.2	2027
8	0843	5.5	2117		23	1000	4.4	2213		3	0838	4.6	2050		16	0743	3.4	2013		29	0841	3.8	2105
9	0939	6.0	2211		24	1029	4.9	2243		4	0925	4.8	2138		17	0852	4.1	2120		30	0916	4.5	2136
10	1035	6.2	2303		25	1059	5.3	2312		5	1006	5.0	2222		18	0949	4.9	2217		31	0947	4.9	2206
11	1128	6.4	2352		26	1128	5.5	2341		6	1046	5.1	2303		19	1039	5.6	2307					
12	1219	6.3			27	1156	5.6			7	1124	5.1	2342		20	1124	6.1	2352		**November**			
13	0040	5.9	1308		28	0011	5.7	1225		8	1202	5.0			21	1207	6.3			1	1017	5.2	2236
14	0127	5.4	1357		29	0042	5.7	1256		9	0019	4.9	1240		22	0034	6.5	1249		2	1048	5.4	2306
15	0214	4.6	1445		30	0116	5.5	1332		10	0056	4.7	1316		23	0114	6.3	1329		3	1121	5.5	2337
16	0302	5.1	1535		31	0154	5.0	1415		11	0131	4.4	1352		24	0153	6.0	1411		4	1154	5.5	
17	0351	4.5	1628							12	0208	4.2	1427		25	0234	5.4	1453		5	0012	5.3	1232
18	0445	4.2	1728		**April**					13	0248	3.8	1507		26	0320	4.5	1539		6	0052	5.0	1314
19	0547	3.5	1836		1	0241	4.2	1508		14	0336	3.6	1555		27	0412	3.6	1634		7	0138	4.5	1406
20	0659	3.2	1947		2	0345	3.3	1632		15	0434	3.1	1652		28	0517	2.9	1743		8	0237	3.8	1520
21	0812	3.4	2051		3	0538	2.9	1828		16	0538	3.3	1754		29	0635	2.6	1912		9	0400	3.4	1702
22	0915	3.7	2143		4	0721	3.3	1954		17	0640	3.5	1855		30	0804	2.8	2050		10	0531	3.4	1827
23	1006	4.2	2227		5	0839	4.1	2059		18	0735	3.9	1950		31	0912	3.5	2146		11	0650	3.8	1938
24	1046	4.5	2305		6	0936	5.0	2149		19	0824	4.3	2040							12	0755	4.4	2036
25	1121	4.8	2339		7	1022	5.7	2232		20	0911	4.8	2129		**September**					13	0849	5.1	2124
26	1153	4.8			8	1101	6.1	2311		21	0959	5.2	2218		1	0957	4.2	2225		14	0935	5.5	2205
27	0010	5.0	1224		9	1136	6.3	2348		22	1047	5.5	2309		2	1034	4.6	2255		15	1017	5.7	2243
28	0040	5.1	1253		10	1209	6.2			23	1137	5.6			3	1105	5.0	2322		16	1057	5.8	2319
29	0107	5.1	1318		11	0024	6.1	1243		24	0000	5.7	1227		4	1135	5.1	2349		17	1136	5.7	2357
30	0135	5.0	1346		12	0059	5.7	1317		25	0054	5.6	1319		5	1202	5.2			18	1214	5.5	
31	0207	4.9	1421		13	0132	5.2	1352		26	0149	5.5	1411		6	0015	5.2	1228		19	0035	5.1	1252
					14	0206	4.6	1430		27	0246	5.2	1504		7	0039	5.2	1253		20	0114	4.7	1331
February					15	0245	3.8	1516		28	0345	4.9	1559		8	0102	5.2	1320		21	0155	4.2	1414
1	0245	4.6	1503		16	0341	3.0	1621		29	0445	4.3	1657		9	0131	5.1	1352		22	0239	3.6	1505
2	0331	4.2	1554		17	0458	2.4	1738		30	0548	4.2	1800		10	0207	4.6	1432		23	0331	3.1	1607
3	0429	3.9	1703		18	0618	2.4	1857							11	0252	3.9	1522		24	0432	2.8	1714
4	0549	3.3	1843		19	0739	2.9	2006		**July**					12	0352	3.0	1645		25	0539	2.9	1823
5	0722	3.5	2009		20	0836	3.6	2053		1	0654	4.0	1909		13	0600	2.6	1851		26	0644	3.0	1922
6	0840	4.1	2116		21	0915	4.3	2129		2	0757	4.0	2015		14	0736	3.2	2013		27	0739	3.5	2010
7	0945	4.8	2213		22	0949	4.8	2202		3	0853	4.0	2113		15	0844	4.1	2117		28	0823	4.0	2050
8	1041	5.5	2303		23	1021	5.3	2235		4	0943	4.3	2205		16	0938	5.1	2209		29	0901	4.5	2126
9	1131	6.0	2347		24	1054	5.5	2308		5	1028	4.5	2249		17	1024	5.8	2254		30	0939	4.9	2203
10	1215	6.2			25	1126	5.7	2342		6	1109	4.7	2329		18	1106	6.3	2333					
11	0029	6.4	1256		26	1200	5.8			7	1147	4.8			19	1145	6.5			**December**			
12	0111	6.3	1335		27	0018	5.7	1238		8	0006	4.8	1224		20	0009	6.6	1224		1	1017	5.2	2240
13	0151	5.9	1414		28	0058	5.4	132		9	0041	4.8	1258		21	0045	6.3	1302		2	1057	5.5	2320
14	0231	5.4	1455		29	0144	4.9	1411		10	0113	4.7	1329		22	0122	5.8	1340		3	1139	5.4	
15	0313	4.6	1540		30	0241	4.2	1516		11	0143	4.5	1358		23	0201	5.2	1420		4	0003	5.3	1225
16	0359	3.8	1634							12	0212	4.4	1428		24	0244	4.3	1504		5	0050	5.2	1315
17	0456	3.3	1742		**May**					13	0244	4.3	1505		25	0336	3.3	1601		6	0142	4.8	1412
18	0609	2.7	1902		1	0402	3.6	1640		14	0324	3.9	1551		26	0441	2.8	1713		7	0241	4.4	1521
19	0737	2.7	2024		2	0539	3.3	180		15	0416	3.5	1648		27	0559	2.3	1841		8	0346	4.1	1637
20	0901	3.2	2126		3	0707	3.7	1929		16	0523	3.5	1757		28	0731	2.6	2028		9	0455	4.2	1752
21	0954	3.9	2210		4	0818	4.3	2032		17	0644	3.5	1910		29	0843	3.4	2119		10	0607	4.1	1900
22	1031	4.4	2245		5	0912	5.0	2122		18	0754	3.9	2016		30	0928	4.1	2153		11	0715	4.2	2000
23	1101	4.8	2316		6	0956	5.4	2206		19	0855	4.4	2118							12	0815	4.5	2053
24	1130	5.1	2345		7	1034	5.7	2246		20	0952	5.0	2215		**October**					13	0908	4.7	2140
25	1159	5.2			8	1110	5.8	2324		21	1044	5.4	2309		1	1001	4.7	2220		14	0956	5.0	2223
26	0013	5.4	1226		9	1144	5.7			22	1134	5.7			2	1031	5.0	2246		15	1040	5.1	2303
27	0040	5.5	1252		10	0000	5.6	1220		23	0001	6.0	1222		3	1058	5.3	2313		16	1122	5.1	2343
28	0108	5.5	1320		11	0036	5.3	1256		24	0050	6.2	1308		4	1126	5.4	2340		17	1201	5.0	
					12	0111	4.9	1332		25	0137	6.0	1354		5	1153	5.4			18	0021	4.9	1239
March					13	0146	4.4	1410		26	0224	5.8	1440		6	0005	5.4	1221		19	0100	4.7	1316
1	0140	5.4	1353		14	0225	3.9	1452		27	0311	5.3	1527		7	0033	5.3	1251		20	0136	4.4	1354
2	0216	5.0	1434		15	0317	3.3	1546		28	0401	4.7	1617		8	0106	5.1	1327		21	0212	4.1	1432
3	0300	4.4	1523		16	0424	2.8	1651		29	0456	3.8	1714		9	0145	4.6	1409		22	0248	3.8	1514
4	0356	3.5	1630		17	0534	2.5	1759		30	0600	3.5	1821		10	0234	3.7	1507		23	0329	3.4	1604
5	0526	3.0	1834		18	0642	3.0	1903		31	0714	3.2	1942		11	0347	3.0	1704		24	0420	3.1	1707
6	0722	3.2	2006		19	0739	3.5	1956							12	0554	2.8	1846		25	0523	3.3	1814
7	0844	3.9	2113		20	0825	4.1	2039		**August**					13	0719	3.4	2002		26	0629	3.7	1918
8	0947	4.8	2207		21	0905	4.7	2118		1	0827	3.4	2058		14	0825	4.4	2102		27	0728	3.5	2006
9	1038	5.7	2252		22	0943	5.1	2157		2	0927	3.7	2156		15	0917	5.2	2150		28	0821	4.1	2054
10	1122	6.2	2333		23	1021	5.5	2238		3	1014	4.2	2240		16	1001	5.9	2231		29	0910	4.6	2140
11	1200	6.4			24	1101	5.7	2319		4	1054	4.7	2316		17	1042	6.2	2308		30	0959	5.1	2227
12	0011	6.5	1235		25	1143	5.7			5	1130	4.8	2343		18	1121	6.3	2343		31	1047	5.4	2314
13	0048	6.3	1309		26	0004	5.6	1229		6	1203	4.9			19	1158	6.2						
14	0125	6.0	1344		27	0052	5.4	1320		7	0019	5.0	1234		20	0018	6.0	1235					

142

BREST TIDAL COEFFICIENTS 2005

Date	Jan am	Jan pm	Feb am	Feb pm	Mar am	Mar pm	Apr am	Apr pm	May am	May pm	June am	June pm	July am	July pm	Aug am	Aug pm	Sept am	Sept pm	Oct am	Oct pm	Nov am	Nov pm	Dec am	Dec pm
1	59	56	60	56	78	73	55	48	47	45	57		53	52	43	46	58	63	69	74	83	86	82	85
2	53	51	52	48	68	62	42	39	47		59	62	52	54	50	54	68	73	78	82	88	90	87	87
3	48	46	45	43	55	49	39		50	55	65	68	55	58	58	62	76	80	85	88	90	89	87	87
4	45	44	43			43	39	43	50	61	67	70	73	60	62	66	69	82	84	90	91	88	86	85	83
5	45		45	50	38		58	67	73	78	74	76	64	68	72	74	86	86	91	90	83	78	80	76
6	47	50	56	64	40	46	75	83	83	87	76	77	68	69	76	77	86	86	88	85	74	68	72	68
7	54	60	72	80	54	63	89	95	89	91	76	76	70	71	78	79	84	82	82	77	62	57	64	61
8	65	71	88	94	73	82	100	103	91	91	75	73	71	71	78	77	79	75	73	66	51	47	58	56
9	77	83	100	104	90	97	104	104	90	88	71	69	70	70	76	74	71	65	60	53	45	45	55	55
10	88	93	107	108	103	107	103	100	85	81	66	64	69	67	72	68	60	54	47	41	47		57	
11	96	99	108	105	109	110	96	91	77	73	61	58	65	63	65	61	48	42	37	36	52	57	59	62
12	100	100	102	97	109	107	86	79	68	63	55	51	61	58	57	52	37	35	39		64	70	65	67
13	99	97	91	83	103	97	73	65	58	52	48	46	55	52	48	44	36		46	54	76	81	70	73
14	93	88	76	68	91	84	58	51	47	42	43	41	50	47	41	39	41	49	63	71	85	88	75	76
15	83	77	60	51	76	68	44	37	38	34	41	41	45	44	40		58	68	80	87	91	92	78	78
16	71	64	44	37	60	51	31	26	32	32	42		44		43	49	77	86	94	99	92	91	78	78
17	57	51	31	28	43	35	26	31	33		44	47	45	47	56	64	94	101	103	105	90	87	77	75
18	46	42	28		29	24	29		36	40	51	55	51	55	73	81	106	109	105	104	83	80	73	71
19	39		31	35	23		35	41	45	51	60	64	61	67	89	96	111	111	102	98	75	70	68	65
20	39	40	41	47	25	30	48	55	56	62	69	74	73	79	102	106	109	106	93	87	65	59	62	59
21	42	45	53	58	37	44	61	67	68	73	79	83	85	90	109	110	100	94	81	74	54	49	56	52
22	49	53	64	69	51	57	74	79	78	82	86	89	95	98	109	106	87	79	66	59	44	39	49	46
23	57	61	74	78	64	70	84	88	86	89	91	92	100	101	102	96	70	61	51	44	35	33	42	40
24	65	68	81	84	76	80	91	93	91	92	92	92	101	99	89	82	52	44	37	31	31	32	38	38
25	71	73	87	88	85	89	95	95	92	91	90	88	96	92	73	65	36	29	26	25	34		38	
26	75	77	89	89	92	94	95	93	89	86	85	81	86	80	56	48	24	23	26		37	42	40	42
27	78	79	89	87	95	95	90	86	83	79	77	73	73	67	40	34	26		30	35	46	51	46	50
28	79	78	85	82	94	93	81	76	74	69	68	64	59	53	29		31	38	41	48	56	62	55	60
29	77	76			90	86	69	63	65	61	60	57	47	43	28	31	44	51	54	60	67	71	65	71
30	74	71			81	76	57	51	58	56	54		40		35	41	58	64	65	71	76	79	75	80
31	68	64			69	63			55	56			39	40	46	52			75	80			84	88

These tidal coefficients indicate at a glance the magnitude of the tide on any particular day by assigning a non-dimensional coefficient to the twice-daily range of tide. The coefficient is based on a scale of 45 for mean neap (morte eau) and 95 for mean spring (vive eau) ranges at Brest. The coefficient is 70 for an average tide. A very small neap tide may have a coefficient of only 20, whilst a very big spring tide might be as high as 120. The ratio of the coefficients of different tides equals the ratio of their ranges; the range, for example, of the largest spring tide (120) is six times that of the smallest neap tide (20). The table above is for Brest, but holds good elsewhere along the Channel and Atlantic coasts of France.

French translations of common tidal terms are as follows:

HW	Pleine mer (PM)	MHWS	Pleine mer moyenne de VE
LW	Basse mer (BM)	MHWN	Pleine mer moyenne de ME
Springs	Vive eau (VE)	MLWN	Basse mer moyenne de ME
Neaps	Morte eau (ME)	MLWS	Basse mer moyenne de VE

TIDES

TIDAL CALCULATIONS

Find the height at a given time (STANDARD PORT)

1. On Standard Curve diagram, plot heights of H.W. and L.W. occuring either side of required time and join by sloping line.
2. Enter H.W. Time and sufficient others to bracket required time.
3. From required time, proceed vertically to curves, using heights plotted in (1) to help interpolation between Spring and Neaps. Do NOT extrapolate.
4. Proceed horizontally to sloping line, thence vertically to Height scale.
5. Read off height.

EXAMPLE:
Find the height of tide at ULLAPOOL at 1900 on 6th January

From tables	JANUARY	
ULLAPOOL	**6** 0420	4.6
	1033	1.6
	1641	4.6
	F 2308	1.2

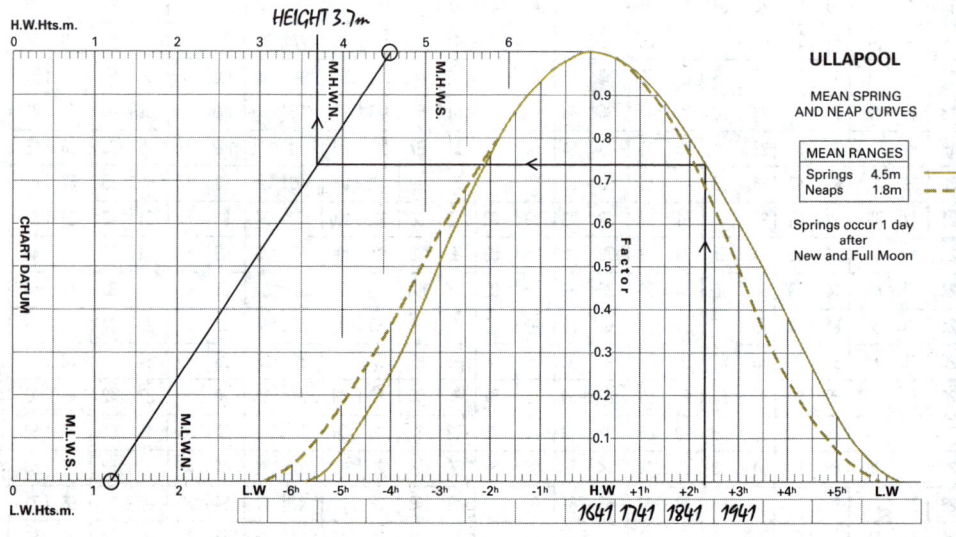

Find the time for a given height (STANDARD PORT)

1. On Standard Curve diagram, plot heights of H.W. and L.W. occurring either side of required event and join by sloping line.
2. Enter H.W. time and those for half-tidal cycle covering required event.
3. From required height, proceed vertically to sloping line, thence horizontally to curves, using heights plotted in (1) to assist interpolation between Spring and Neaps. Do NOT extrapolate.
4. Proceed vertically to Time scale.
5. Read off time.

EXAMPLE:
Find the time at which the afternoon tide at ULLAPOOL falls to 3.7m on 6 January

From tables	JANUARY	
ULLAPOOL	**6** 0420	4.6
	1033	1.6
	1641	4.6
	F 2308	1.2

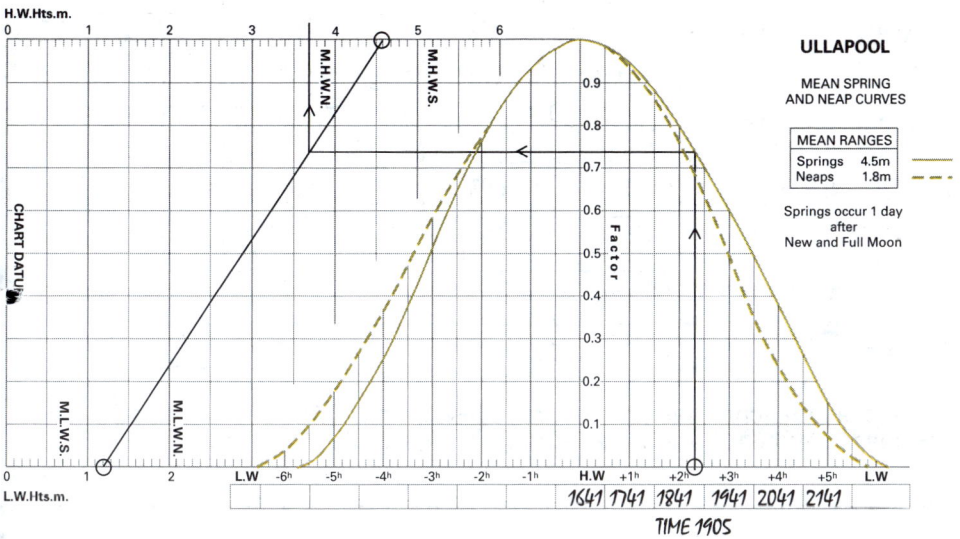

Find the time and height of H.W. and L.W. at a Secondary Port

EXAMPLE:
Find the time and height of the afternoon H.W. and L.W. at ST MARY's (Isles of Scilly) on 14th July (BST)
Note: *The data used in this example do not refer to the year of these tables.*

from tables	JULY	
PLYMOUTH (DEVONPORT)	**14** 0309	1.0
	0927	5.3
	1532	1.1
	SA 2149	5.0

From tables										
Location	Lat	Long	High Water		Low Water		MHWS	MHWN	MLWN	MLWS
DEVONPORT *Standard port*	50°22'N	4°11'W	0000 and 1200	0600 and 1800	0000 and 1200	0600 and 1800	5.5	4.4	2.2	0.8
St. Mary's, *Scilly*	49°55'N	6°19'W	−0035	−0100	−0040	−0025	+0.2	−0.1	−0.2	−0.1

145

TIDES

TIDAL PREDICTION FORM (NP 204)

STANDARD PORT _Devonport_   TIME/HEIGHT REQUIRED _pm_
SECONDARY PORT _St Mary's_   DATE _14 July_   TIME ZONE _B.S.T_

	TIME		HEIGHT		
STANDARD PORT	HW	LW	HW	LW	RANGE
	¹ 2149	² 1532	³ 5.0	⁴ 1.1	⁵ 3.9
Seasonal change	Standard Ports −		⁶ 0.0	⁶ 0.0	
DIFFERENCES	⁷ −0044	⁸ −0032	⁹ 0.1	¹⁰ −0.1	
Seasonal change *	Secondary Ports +		¹¹ 0.0	¹¹ 0.0	
SECONDARY PORT	¹² 2105	¹³ 1500	¹⁴ 5.1	¹⁵ 1.0	
Duration	¹⁶ 0605		LW 1500 UT = 1600 BST		
			HW 2105 UT = 2205 BST		

* The seasonal changes are generally less than ± 0.1m and for most purposes can be ignored. See Admiraly Tide Tables Vol 1. for details

---

INTERMEDIATE TIMES/HEIGHTS (SECONDARY PORT)

These are the same as the appropriate calculations for a Standard Port except that the Standard Curve diagram for the Standard Port must be entered with H.W. and L.W. heights and times for the Secondary Port obtained on Form N.P. 204. When interpolating between the Spring and Neap curves the Range at the Standard Port must be used.

EXAMPLES:

Find the height of the tide at PADSTOW at 1100 on 28th February. Find the time at which the morning tide at PADSTOW falls to 4.9m on 28th February.

Notes:
The data in these examples do not refer to the year of these tables.

From tables	FEBRUARY	
MILFORD HAVEN	**28** 0315	1.1
	0922	6.6
	1538	1.3
	TU 2145	6.3

From tables Location	Lat	Long	High Water		Low Water		MHWS	MHWN	MLWN	MLWS
MILFORD HAVEN Standard port	51°42'N	5°03'W	0100 and 1300	0700 and 1900	0100 and 1300	0700 and 1900	7.0	5.2	2.5	0.7
River Camel										
Padstow	50°33'N	4°56'W	−0055	−0050	−0040	−0050	+0.3	+0.4	+0.1	+0.1
Wadebridge	50°31'N	4°50'W	−0052	−0052	+0235	+0245	−3.8	−3.8	−2.5	−0.4

TIDAL PREDICTION FORM (NP 204)

STANDARD PORT *Milford Haven*   TIME/HEIGHT REQUIRED *1100 : 4.9*

SECONDARY PORT *Padstow*   DATE *28 Feb* TIME ZONE *UT*

	TIME		HEIGHT		
STANDARD PORT	HW	LW	HW	LW	RANGE
	¹ 0922	² 1538	³ 6.6	⁴ 1.3	⁵ 5.3
Seasonal change	Standard Ports +		⁶ 0.0	⁶ 0.0	
DIFFERENCES	⁷* −0052	⁸ −	⁹ +0.3	¹⁰ +0.1	
Seasonal change *	Secondary Ports −		¹¹ 0.0	¹¹ 0.0	
SECONDARY PORT	¹² 0830	¹³ −	¹⁴ 6.9	¹⁵ 1.4	
Duration	¹⁶ −				

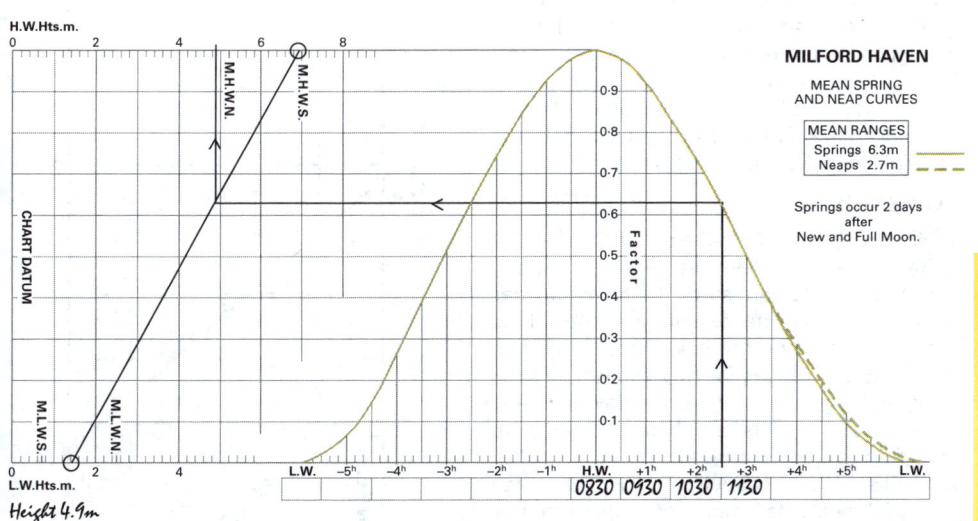

MILFORD HAVEN
MEAN SPRING AND NEAP CURVES

MEAN RANGES
Springs 6.3m
Neaps 2.7m

Springs occur 2 days after New and Full Moon.

Height 4.9m

TIDES

SPECIAL INSTRUCTIONS FOR PLACES BETWEEN BOURNEMOUTH AND SELSEY BILL

- Owing to the rapid change of tidal characteristics and distortion of the tidal curve in this area, curves are shown for individual ports. It is a characteristic of the tide here that Low Water is more sharply defined than High Water and these curves have therefore been drawn with their times relative to that of Low Water.
- Apart from differences caused by referring the times to Low Water the procedure for obtaining intermediate heights at places whose curves are shown is identical to that used for normal Secondary Ports.
- The **height** differences for ports between Bournemouth and Yarmouth always refer to the higher High Water, i.e. that which is shown as reaching a factor of 1.0 on the curves. Note that the **time** differences, which are not required for this calculation, also refer to the higher High Water.
- The tide at ports between Bournemouth and Christchurch shows considerable change of shape and duration between Springs and Neaps and it is not practical to define the tide with only two curves. A third curve has therefore been drawn for the range at Portsmouth at which the two High Waters are equal at the port concerned – this range being marked on the body of the graph. Interpolation here should be between this "critical" curve and either the Spring or Neap curve as appropriate.

Note that while the critical curve extends throughout the tidal cycle the Spring and Neap curves stop at the higher High Water. Thus for a range at Portsmouth of 3.5m the factor for 7 hours after LW at Bournemouth should be referred to the following Low Water, whereas had the range at Portsmouth been 2.5, it should be referred to the preceding Low Water.

NOTES

1. NEWPORT. Owing to the constriction of the River Medina, Newport requires slightly different treatment since the harbour dries out at 1.4m. The calculation should be performed using the Low Water Time and Height Differences for Cowes and the High Water Height Differences for Newport. Any calculated heights which fall below 1.4m should be treated as 1.4m.
2. CHRISTCHURCH (Tuckton). Low Waters do not fall below 0.7m except under very low river flow conditions.

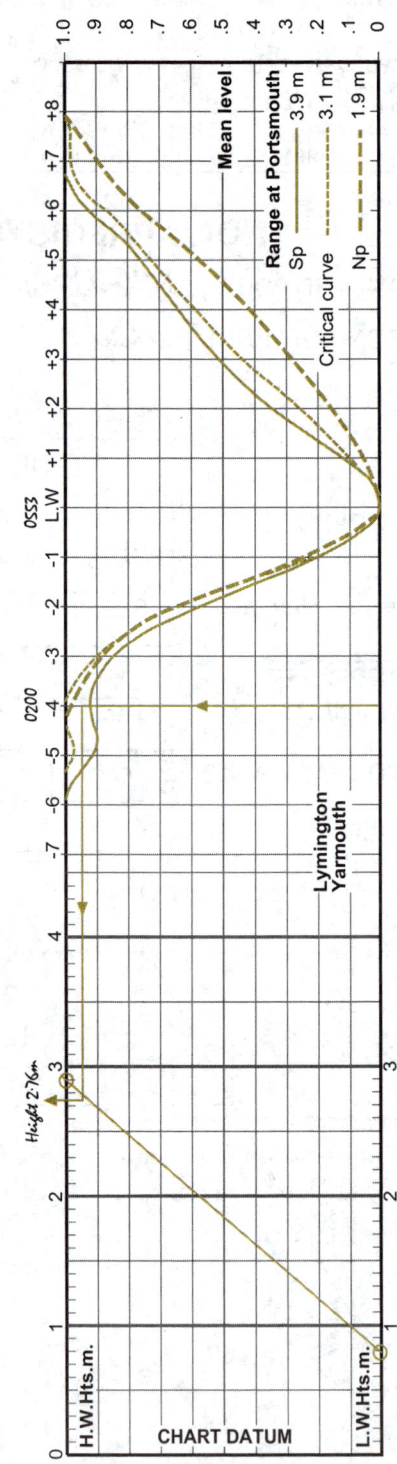

To find the Height of tide at a given time at any Secondary Port between Bournemouth and Selsey Bill

1. Complete top section of N.P. 204 (as below). Omit H.W. time column (Boxes 1, 7, 12)
2. On Standard Curve diagram (previous page), plot Secondary Port H.W. and L.W. heights and join by sloping line.
3. From the time required, using Secondary Port L.W. time, proceed vertically to curve, interpolating as necessary using Range at Portsmouth. Do NOT extrapolate.
4. Proceed horizontally to sloping line, thence vertically to Height Scale.
5. Read off height.

EXAMPLE:
Find the height of tide at LYMINGTON at 0200 UT on 18th November

From tables	NOVEMBER	
PORTSMOUTH	**18** 0110	4.6
	0613	1.1
	1318	4.6
	SA 1833	1.0

From tables Location	Lat	Long	High Water		Low Water		MHWS	MHWN	MLWN	MLWS
			0000	0600	0500	1100				
PORTSMOUTH *Standard port*	50°48′N	1°07′W	and	and	and	and	4.7	3.8	1.9	0.8
			1200	1800	1700	2300				
Lymington	50°46′N	1°32′W	−0110	+0005	−0020	−0020	−1.7	−1.2	−0.5	−0.1

STANDARD PORT __Portsmouth__ TIME/HEIGHT REQUIRED __0200__

SECONDARY PORT __Lymington__ DATE __18 Nov__ TIME ZONE __UT__

	TIME		HEIGHT		
STANDARD PORT	HW	LW	HW	LW	RANGE
	1 —	2 0613	3 4.6	4 1.1	5 3.5
Seasonal change	Standard Ports −		6 0.0	6 0.0	
DIFFERENCES	7* —	8 −0020	9 −1.7	10 −0.2	
Seasonal change *	Secondary Ports +		11 0.0	11 0.0	
SECONDARY PORT	12 —	13 0553	14 2.9	15 0.9	
Duration	16 —				

* The Seasonal changes are generally less than ± 0.1m and for most purposes can be ignored. See Admiralty Tide Tables Vol 1 for full details.

TIDAL CURVES - BOURNEMOUTH TO FRESHWATER

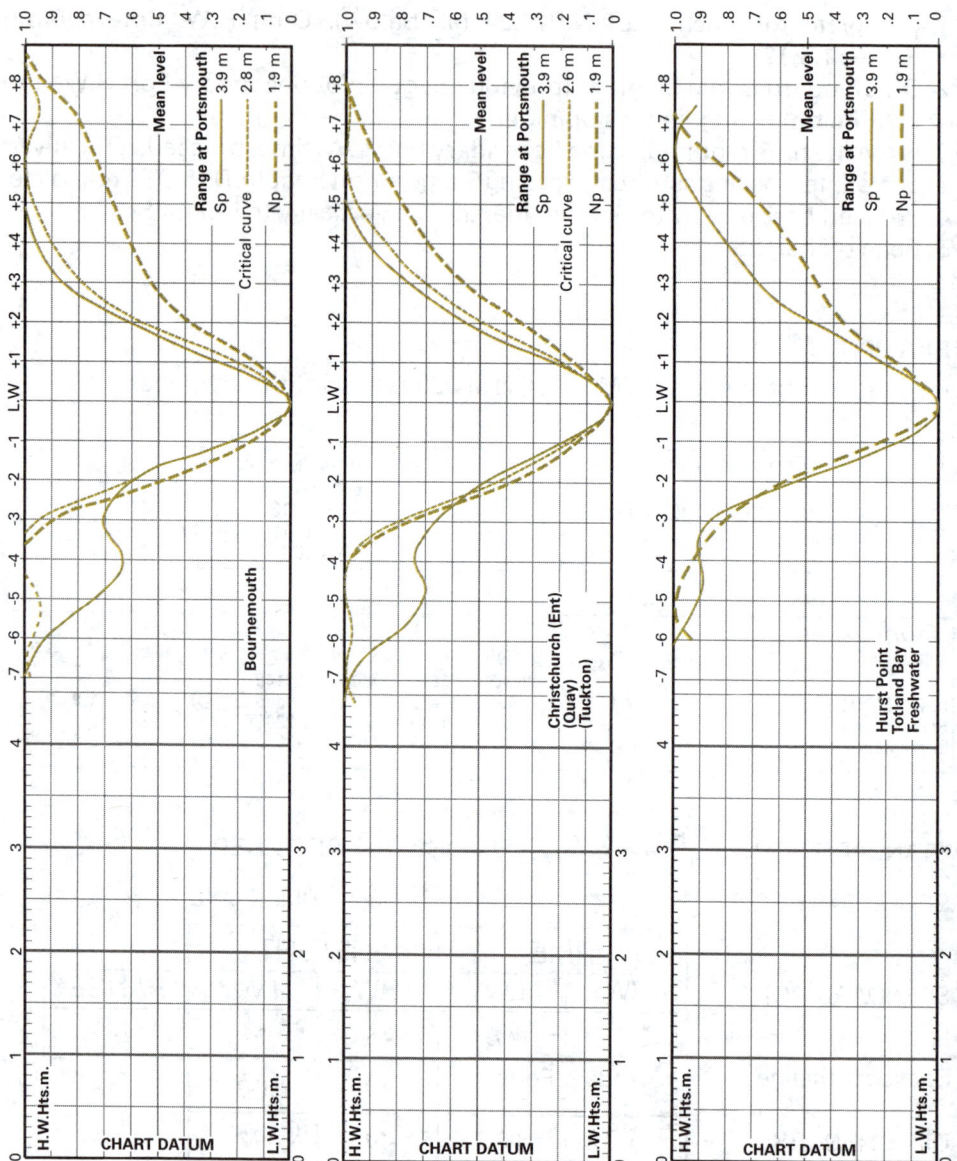

Note: The curves for Lymington and Yarmouth are on page 148, together with a worked example.

TIDAL CURVES - BUCKLERS HARD TO SELSEY BILL

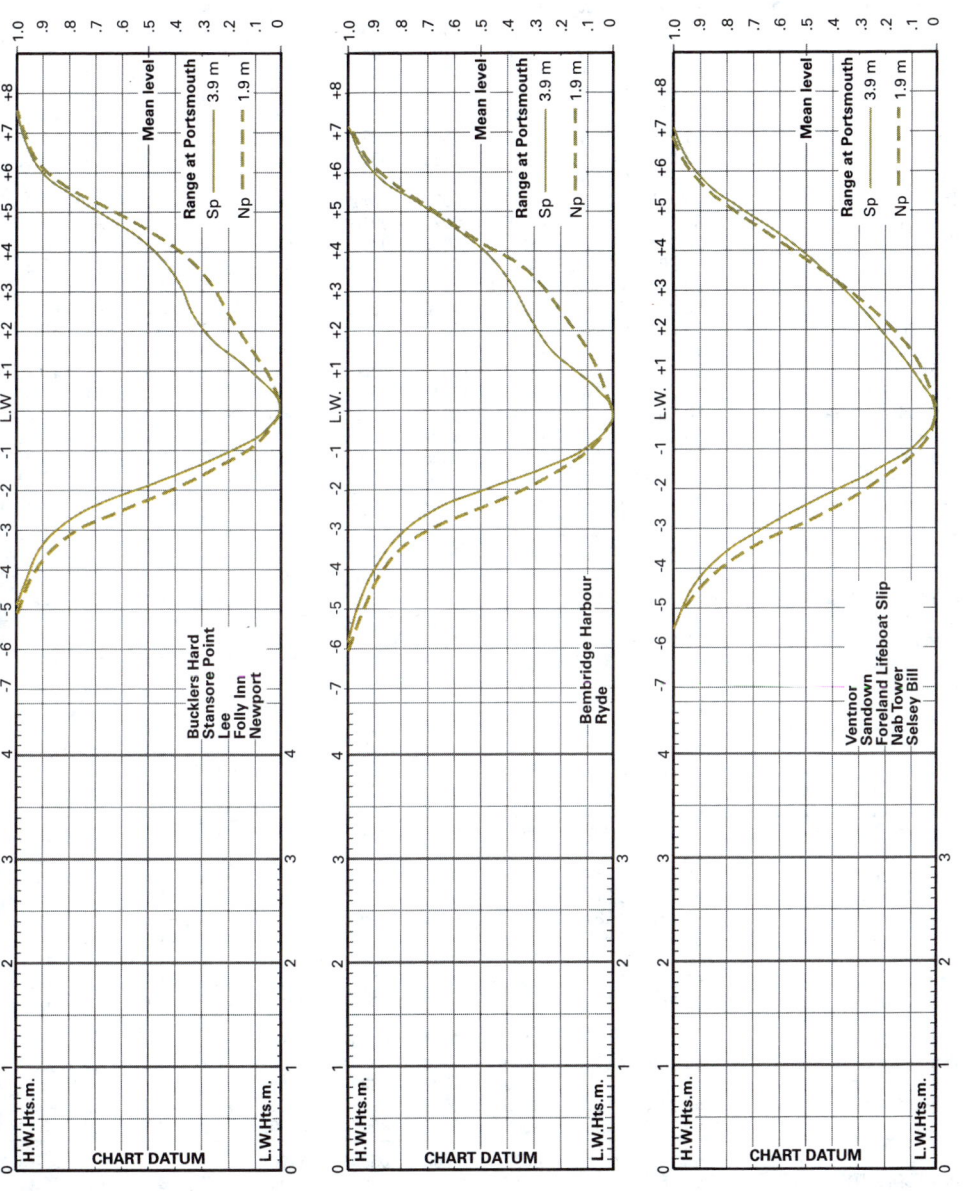

TIDES

SECONDARY PORTS: TIME & HEIGHT DIFFERENCES
SOUTH COAST OF ENGLAND *Time Zone UT*

Location	Lat	Long	High Water 0000	0600	Low Water 0000	0600	MHWS	MHWN	MLWN	MLWS
PLYMOUTH (DEVONPORT)	50 22N	4 11W	and	and	and	and	5.5	4.4	2.2	0.8
Standard port			1200	1800	1200	1800				
Isles of Scilly, St. Mary's	49 55N	6 19W	–0035	–0100	–0040	–0025	+0.2	–0.1	–0.2	–0.1
Penzance & Newlyn	50 06N	5 33W	–0040	–0110	–0035	–0025	+0.1	0.0	–0.2	0.0
Porthleven	50 05N	5 19W	–0045	–0105	–0030	–0025	0.0	–0.1	0.0	0.0
Lizard Point	49 57N	5 12W	–0045	–0100	–0030	–0030	–0.2	–0.2	–0.3	–0.2
Coverack	50 01N	5 05W	–0030	–0050	–0020	–0015	–0.2	–0.2	–0.3	–0.2
Helford River Entrance	50 05N	5 05W	–0030	–0035	–0015	–0010	–0.2	–0.2	–0.3	–0.2
FALMOUTH	50 09N	5 03W	standard port (no secondaries)							
Truro	50 16N	5 03W	–0020	–0025	dries	dries	–2.0	–2.0	dries	dries
Mevagissey	50 16N	4 47W	–0015	–0020	–0010	–0005	–0.1	–0.1	–0.2	–0.1
Par	50 21N	4 42W	–0010	–0015	–0010	–0005	–0.4	–0.4	–0.4	–0.2
Fowey	50 20N	4 38W	–0010	–0015	–0010	–0005	–0.1	–0.1	–0.2	–0.2
Lostwithiel	50 24N	4 40W	+0005	–0010	dries	dries	–4.1	–4.1	dries	dries
Looe	50 21N	4 27W	–0010	–0010	–0005	–0005	–0.1	–0.2	–0.2	–0.2
Whitsand Bay	50 20N	4 15W	0000	0000	0000	0000	0.0	+0.1	–0.1	+0.2
River Tamar										
Saltash	50 24N	4 12W	0000	+0010	0000	–0005	+0.1	+0.1	+0.1	+0.1
Cargreen	50 26N	4 12W	0000	+0010	+0020	+0020	0.0	0.0	–0.1	0.0
Cotehele Quay	50 29N	4 13W	0000	+0020	+0045	+0045	–0.9	–0.9	–0.8	–0.4
Lopwell, R Tavy	50 28N	4 09W	no data	no data	dries	dries	–2.6	–2.7	dries	dries
Jupiter Point	50 23N	4 14W	+0010	+0005	0000	–0005	0.0	0.0	+0.1	0.0
St. Germans	50 23N	4 18W	0000	0000	+0020	+0020	–0.3	–0.1	0.0	+0.2
Turnchapel	50 22N	4 07W	0000	0000	+0010	–0015	0.0	+0.1	+0.2	+0.1
Bovisand Pier	50 20N	4 08W	0000	–0020	0000	–0010	–0.2	–0.1	0.0	+0.1
River Yealm Entrance	50 18N	4 04W	+0006	+0006	+0002	+0002	–0.1	–0.1	–0.1	–0.1
			0100	0600	0100	0600				
PLYMOUTH (DEVONPORT)	50 22N	4 11W	and	and	and	and	5.5	4.4	2.2	0.8
Standard port			1300	1800	1300	1800				
Salcombe	50 13N	3 47W	0000	+0010	+0005	–0005	–0.2	–0.3	–0.1	–0.1
Start Point	50 13N	3 39W	+0015	+0015	+0005	+0010	–0.1	–0.2	+0.1	+0.2
River Dart										
DARTMOUTH	50 21N	3 34W	standard port (no secondaries)							
Greenway Quay	50 23N	3 35W	+0030	+0045	+0025	+0005	–0.6	–0.6	–0.2	–0.2
Totnes	50 26N	3 41W	+0030	+0040	+0115	+0030	–2.0	–2.1	dries	dries
Torquay	50 28N	3 31W	+0025	+0045	+0010	0000	–0.6	–0.7	–0.2	–0.1
Teignmouth Approaches	50 33N	3 29W	+0020	+0050	+0025	0000	–0.9	–0.8	–0.2	–0.1
Teignmouth New Quay	50 33N	3 30W	+0025	+0055	+0040	+0005	–0.8	–0.8	–0.2	+0.1
Exmouth Approaches	50 36N	3 23W	+0030	+0050	+0015	+0005	–0.9	–1.0	–0.5	–0.3
River Exe										
Exmouth Dock	50 37N	3 25W	+0035	+0055	+0050	+0020	–1.5	–1.6	–0.9	–0.6
Starcross	50 38N	3 27W	+0040	+0110	+0055	+0025	–1.4	–1.5	–0.8	–0.1
Topsham	50 41N	3 28W	+0045	+0105	no data	no data	–1.5	–1.6	no data	
Lyme Regis	50 43N	2 56W	+0040	+0100	+0005	–0005	–1.2	–1.3	–0.5	–0.2
Bridport West Bay	50 42N	2 45W	+0025	+0040	0000	0000	–1.4	–1.4	–0.6	–0.2
Chesil Beach	50 37N	2 33W	+0040	+0055	–0005	+0010	–1.6	–1.5	–0.5	0.0
Chesil Cove	50 34N	2 28W	+0035	+0050	–0010	+0005	–1.5	–1.6	–0.5	–0.2
			0100	0700	0100	0700				
PORTLAND			50 34N	2 26W	and	and	and	and	2.1	1.4	0.8	0.1
Standard port			1300	1900	1300	1900				
Lulworth Cove	50 37N	2 15W	+0005	+0015	–0005	0000	+0.1	+0.1	+0.2	+0.1
Mupe Bay	50 37N	2 13W	+0005	+0015	–0005	0000	+0.1	+0.1	+0.2	+0.1
			0000	0600	0500	1100				
PORTSMOUTH	50 48N	1 07W	and	and	and	and	4.7	3.8	1.9	0.8
standard port			1200	1800	1700	2300				
Swanage	50 37N	1 57W	–0250	+0105	–0105	–0105	–2.7	–2.2	–0.7	–0.3
Poole Harbour Entrance	50 41N	1 57W	–0230	+0115	–0045	–0020	–2.5	–2.1	–0.6	–0.2
POOLE, TOWN QUAY	50 43N	1 59W	standard port							
Pottery Pier	50 42N	1 59W	–0150	+0200	–0010	0000	–2.7	–2.1	–0.6	0.0
Wareham *River Frome*	50 41N	2 06W	–0140	+0205	+0110	+0035	–2.5	–2.1	–0.7	+0.1
Cleavel Point	50 40N	2 00W	–0220	+0130	–0025	–0015	–2.6	–2.3	–0.7	–0.3
Bournemouth	50 43N	1 52W	–0240	+0055	–0050	–0030	–2.7	–2.2	–0.8	–0.3
Christchurch *Entrance*	50 43N	1 45W	–0230	+0030	–0035	–0035	–2.9	–2.4	–1.2	–0.2
Christchurch *Quay*	50 44N	1 46W	–0210	+0100	+0105	+0055	–2.9	–2.4	–1.0	0.0
Christchurch *Tuckton*	50 44N	1 47W	–0205	+0110	+0110	+0105	–3.0	–2.5	–1.0	+0.1

Location	Lat	Long	High Water		Low Water		MHWS	MHWN	MLWN	MLWS
Hurst Point	50 42N	1 33W	−0115	−0005	−0030	−0025	−2.0	−1.5	−0.5	−0.1
Lymington	50 46N	1 32W	−0110	+0005	−0020	−0020	−1.7	−1.2	−0.5	−0.1
Bucklers Hard	50 48N	1 25W	−0040	−0010	+0010	−0010	−1.0	−0.8	−0.2	−0.3
Stansore Point	50 47N	1 21W	−0050	−0010	−0005	−0010	−0.8	−0.5	−0.3	−0.1
Isle of Wight										
Yarmouth	50 42N	1 30W	−0105	+0005	−0025	−0030	−1.7	−1.2	−0.3	0.0
Totland Bay	50 41N	1 33W	−0130	−0045	−0035	−0045	−2.2	−1.7	−0.4	−0.1
Freshwater	50 40N	1 31W	−0210	+0025	−0040	−0020	−2.1	−1.5	−0.4	0.0
Ventnor	50 36N	1 12W	−0025	−0030	−0025	−0030	−0.8	−0.6	−0.2	+0.2
Sandown	50 39N	1 09W	0000	+0005	+0010	+0025	−0.6	−0.5	−0.2	0.0
Foreland *Lifeboat Slip*	50 41N	1 04W	−0005	0000	+0005	+0010	+0.1	+0.1	0.0	+0.1
Bembridge Harbour	50 42N	1 06W	+0020	0000	+0100	+0020	−1.5	−1.4	−1.3	−1.0
Ryde	50 44N	1 07W	−0010	+0010	−0005	−0010	−0.2	−0.1	0.0	+0.1
Medina River										
Cowes	50 46N	1 18W	−0015	+0015	0000	−0020	−0.5	−0.3	−0.1	0.0
Folly Inn	50 44N	1 17W	−0015	+0015	0000	−0020	−0.6	−0.4	−0.1	+0.2
Newport	50 42N	1 17W	no data	no data	no data	no data	−0.6	−0.4	+0.1	+0.8
			0400	1100	0000	0600				
SOUTHAMPTON	50 54N	1 24W	and	and	and	and	4.5	3.7	1.8	0.5
standard port			1600	2300	1200	1800				
Calshot Castle	50 49N	1 18W	0000	+0025	0000	0000	0.0	0.0	+0.2	+0.3
Redbridge	50 55N	1 28W	−0020	+0005	0000	−0005	−0.1	−0.1	−0.1	−0.1
River Hamble										
Warsash	50 51N	1 18W	+0020	+0010	+0010	0000	0.0	+0.1	+0.1	+0.3
Bursledon	50 53N	1 18W	+0020	+0020	+0010	+0010	+0.1	+0.1	+0.2	+0.2
			0500	1000	0000	0600				
PORTSMOUTH	50 48N	1 07W	and	and	and	and	4.7	3.8	1.9	0.8
standard port			1700	2200	1200	1800				
Lee-on-the-Solent	50 48N	1 12W	−0005	+0005	−0015	−0010	−0.2	−0.1	+0.1	+0.2
Chichester Harbour										
Entrance	50 47N	0 56W	−0010	+0005	+0015	+0020	+0.2	+0.2	0.0	+0.1
Northney	50 50N	0 58W	+0010	+0015	+0015	+0025	+0.2	0.0	−0.2	−0.3
Bosham	50 50N	0 52W	0000	+0010	no data	no data	+0.2	+0.1	no data	
Itchenor	50 48N	0 52W	−0005	+0005	+0005	+0025	+0.1	0.0	−0.2	−0.2
Dell Quay	50 49N	0 49W	+0005	+0015	no data	no data	+0.2	+0.1	no data	
Selsey Bill	50 43N	0 47W	+0010	−0010	+0035	+0020	+0.5	+0.2	−0.2	−0.2
Nab Tower	50 40N	0 57W	+0015	0000	+0015	+0015	−0.2	0.0	+0.2	0.0
			0500	1000	0000	0600				
SHOREHAM	50 50N	0 15W	and	and	and	and	6.3	4.8	1.9	0.6
standard port			1700	2200	1200	1800				
Pagham	50 46N	0 43W	+0015	0000	−0015	−0025	−0.7	−0.5	−0.1	−0.1
Bognor Regis	50 47N	0 40W	+0010	−0005	−0005	−0020	−0.6	−0.5	−0.2	−0.1
River Arun										
Littlehampton *Entrance*	50 48N	0 32W	+0010	0000	−0005	−0010	−0.4	−0.4	−0.2	−0.2
Littlehampton *UMA wharf*	50 48N	0 33W	+0015	+0005	0000	+0045	−0.7	−0.7	−0.3	+0.2
Arundel	50 51N	0 33W	no data	+0120	no data	no data	−3.1	−2.8	no data	
Worthing	50 48N	0 22W	+0010	0000	−0005	−0010	−0.1	−0.2	0.0	0.0
Brighton	50 49N	0 08W	0000	−0005	0000	0000	+0.3	+0.2	+0.1	0.0
Newhaven	50 47N	0 04E	−0015	−0010	0000	0000	+0.2	+0.1	−0.1	−0.2
Eastbourne	50 46N	0 17E	−0010	−0005	+0015	+0020	+1.1	+0.6	+0.2	+0.1
			0000	0600	0100	0700				
DOVER	51 07N	1 19E	and	and	and	and	6.8	5.3	2.1	0.8
standard port			1200	1800	1300	1900				
Hastings	50 51N	0 35E	0000	−0010	−0030	−0030	+0.8	+0.5	+0.1	−0.1
Rye *Approaches*	50 55N	0 47E	+0005	−0010	no data	no data	+1.0	+0.7	no data	
Rye *Harbour*	50 56N	0 46E	+0005	−0010	dries	dries	−1.4	−1.7	dries	
Dungeness	50 54N	0 58E	−0010	−0015	−0020	−0010	+1.0	+0.6	+0.4	+0.1
Folkestone	51 05N	1 12E	−0020	−0005	−0010	−0010	+0.4	+0.4	0.0	−0.1
Deal	51 13N	1 25E	+0010	+0020	+0010	+0005	−0.6	−0.3	0.0	0.0
Richborough	51 18N	1 21E	+0015	+0015	+0030	+0030	−3.4	−2.6	−1.7	−0.7
Ramsgate	51 20N	1 25E	+0030	+0030	+0017	+0007	−1.6	−1.3	−0.7	−0.2

EAST COAST ENGLAND *Time Zone UT*

Location	Lat	Long	High Water		Low Water		MHWS	MHWN	MLWN	MLWS
			0200	0800	0200	0700				
SHEERNESS	51 27N	0 45E	and	and	and	and	5.8	4.7	1.5	0.6
standard port			1400	2000	1400	1900				
Margate	51 23N	1 23E	−0050	−0040	−0020	−0050	−0.9	−0.9	−0.1	0.0
Herne Bay	51 23N	1 07E	−0025	−0015	0000	−0025	−0.5	−0.5	−0.1	−0.1
Whitstable	51 22N	1 02E	−0008	−0011	+0005	0000	−0.3	−0.3	0.0	−0.1

TIDES

Location	Lat	Long	High Water		Low Water		MHWS	MHWN	MLWN	MLWS
River Swale										
Grovehurst Jetty	51 22N	0 46E	−0007	0000	0000	+0016	0.0	0.0	0.0	−0.1
Faversham	51 19N	0 54E	no data	no data	no data	no data	−0.2	−0.2	no data	
River Medway										
Bee Ness	51 25N	0 39E	+0002	+0002	0000	+0005	+0.2	+0.1	0.0	0.0
Bartlett Creek	51 23N	0 38E	+0016	+0008	no data	no data	+0.1	0.0	no data	
Darnett Ness	51 24N	0 36E	+0004	+0004	0000	+0010	+0.2	+0.1	0.0	−0.1
Chatham *Lock approaches*	51 24N	0 33E	+0010	+0012	+0012	+0018	+0.3	+0.1	−0.1	−0.2
Upnor	51 25N	0 32E	+0015	+0015	+0015	+0025	+0.2	+0.2	−0.1	−0.1
Rochester *Strood Pier*	51 24N	0 30E	+0018	+0018	+0018	+0028	+0.2	+0.2	−0.2	−0.3
Wouldham	51 21N	0 27E	+0030	+0025	+0035	+0120	−0.2	−0.3	−1.0	−0.3
New Hythe	51 19N	0 28E	+0035	+0035	+0220	+0240	−1.6	−1.7	−1.2	−0.3
Allington Lock	51 17N	0 30E	+0050	+0035	no data	no data	−2.1	−2.2	−1.3	−0.4
River Thames										
Southend–on–Sea	51 31N	0 43E	−0005	0000	0000	+0005	0.0	0.0	−0.1	−0.1
Coryton	51 30N	0 31E	+0005	+0010	+0010	+0015	+0.4	+0.3	+0.1	−0.1
			0300	0900	0400	1100				
LONDON BRIDGE	51 30N	0 05W	and	and	and	and	7.1	5.9	1.3	0.5
standard port			1500	2100	1600	2300				
Albert Bridge	51 29N	0 10W	+0025	+0020	+0105	+0110	−0.9	−0.8	−0.7	−0.4
Hammersmith Bridge	51 29N	0 14W	+0040	+0035	+0205	+0155	−1.4	−1.3	−1.0	−0.5
Kew Bridge	51 29N	0 17W	+0055	+0050	+0255	+0235	−1.8	−1.8	−1.2	−0.5
Richmond Lock	51 28N	0 19W	+0105	+0055	+0325	+0305	−2.2	−2.2	−1.3	−0.5
			0200	0700	0100	0700				
SHEERNESS	51 27N	0 45E	and	and	and	and	5.8	4.7	1.5	0.6
standard port			1400	1900	1300	1900				
Thames Estuary *Shivering Sand*	51 30N	1 05E	−0025	−0019	−0008	−0026	−0.6	−0.6	−0.1	−0.1
			0000	0600	0500	1100				
WALTON–ON–THE–NAZE	51 51N	1 17E	and	and	and	and	4.2	3.4	1.1	0.4
standard port			1200	1800	1700	2300				
Whitaker Beacon	51 40N	1 06E	+0022	+0024	+0033	+0027	+0.6	+0.5	+0.2	+0.1
Holliwell Point	51 38N	0 56E	+0034	+0037	+0100	+0037	+1.1	+0.9	+0.3	+0.1
River Roach *Rochford*	51 35N	0 43E	+0050	+0040	dries	dries	−0.8	−1.1	dries	
River Crouch										
BURNHAM–ON–CROUCH	51 37N	0 48E	standard port - see full predictions page 263							
North Fambridge	51 38N	0 41E	+0115	+0050	+0130	+0100	+1.1	+0.8	0.0	−0.1
Hullbridge	51 38N	0 38E	+0115	+0050	+0135	+0105	+1.1	+0.8	0.0	−0.1
Battlesbridge	51 37N	0 34E	+0120	+0110	dries	dries	−1.8	−2.0	dries	
River Blackwater										
Bradwell Waterside	51 45N	0 53E	+0035	+0023	+0047	+0004	+1.0	+0.8	+0.2	0.0
Osea Island	51 43N	0 46E	+0057	+0045	+0050	+0007	+1.1	+0.9	+0.1	0.0
Maldon	51 44N	0 42E	+0107	+0055	no data	no data	−1.3	−1.1	no data	
West Mersea	51 47N	0 54E	+0035	+0015	+0055	+0010	+0.9	+0.4	+0.1	+0.1
River Colne										
Brightlingsea	51 48N	1 00E	+0025	+0021	+0046	+0004	+0.8	+0.4	+0.1	0.0
Colchester	51 53N	0 56E	+0035	+0025	dries	dries	0.0	−0.3	dries	
Clacton–on–Sea	51 47N	1 09E	+0012	+0010	+0025	+0008	+0.3	+0.1	+0.1	+0.1
Bramble Creek	51 53N	1 14E	+0010	−0007	−0005	+0010	+0.3	+0.3	+0.3	+0.3
Sunk Head	51 46N	1 30E	0000	+0002	−0002	+0002	−0.3	−0.3	−0.1	−0.1
Harwich	51 57N	1 17E	+0007	+0002	−0010	−0012	−0.2	0.0	0.0	0.0
Wrabness	51 57N	1 10E	+0017	+0015	−0010	−0012	−0.1	0.0	0.0	0.0
Mistley	51 57N	1 05E	+0032	+0027	−0010	−0012	0.0	0.0	−0.1	−0.1
Pin Mill	52 00N	1 17E	+0012	+0015	−0008	−0012	−0.1	0.0	0.0	0.0
Ipswich	52 03N	1 10E	+0022	+0027	0000	−0012	0.0	0.0	−0.1	−0.1
			0100	0700	0100	0700				
WALTON–ON–THE–NAZE	51 51N	1 17E	and	and	and	and	4.2	3.4	1.1	0.4
standard port			1300	1900	1300	1900				
Felixstowe Pier	51 57N	1 21E	−0005	−0007	−0018	−0020	−0.5	−0.4	0.0	0.0
River Deben										
Woodbridge Haven	51 59N	1 24E	0000	−0005	−0020	−0025	−0.5	−0.5	−0.1	+0.1
Woodbridge	52 05N	1 19E	+0045	+0025	+0025	−0020	−0.2	−0.3	−0.2	0.0
Bawdsey	52 00N	1 26E	−0016	−0020	−0030	−0032	−0.8	−0.6	−0.1	−0.1
Orford Haven										
Bar	52 02N	1 28E	−0026	−0030	−0036	−0038	−1.0	−0.8	−0.1	0.0
Orford Quay	52 05N	1 32E	+0040	+0040	+0055	+0055	−1.4	−1.1	0.0	+0.2
Slaughden Quay	52 08N	1 36E	+0105	+0105	+0125	+0125	−1.3	−0.8	−0.1	+0.2
Iken Cliffs	52 09N	1 31E	+0130	+0130	+0155	+0155	−1.3	−1.0	0.0	+0.2

Location	Lat	Long	High Water		Low Water		MHWS	MHWN	MLWN	MLWS
			0300	0900	0200	0800				
LOWESTOFT	52 28N	1 45E	and	and	and	and	2.4	2.1	1.0	0.5
standard port			1500	2100	1400	2000				
Orford Ness	52 05N	1 35E	+0135	+0135	+0135	+0125	+0.4	+0.6	−0.1	0.0
Aldeburgh	52 09N	1 36E	+0130	+0130	+0115	+0120	+0.3	+0.2	−0.1	−0.2
Minsmere Sluice	52 14N	1 38E	+0110	+0110	+0110	+0110	0.0	−0.1	−0.2	−0.2
Southwold	52 19N	1 40E	+0105	+0105	+0055	+0055	0.0	0.0	−0.1	0.0
Great Yarmouth										
Gorleston–on–Sea	52 34N	1 44E	−0035	−0035	−0030	−0030	0.0	0.0	0.0	0.0
Britannia Pier	52 36N	1 45E	−0105	−0100	−0040	−0055	+0.1	+0.1	0.0	0.0
Caister–on–Sea	52 39N	1 44E	−0120	−0120	−0100	−0100	0.0	−0.1	0.0	0.0
Winterton–on–Sea	52 43N	1 42E	−0225	−0215	−0135	−0135	+0.8	+0.5	+0.2	+0.1
			0100	0700	0100	0700				
IMMINGHAM	53 38N	0 11E	and	and	and	and	7.3	5.8	2.6	0.9
standard port			1300	1900	1300	1900				
Cromer	52 56N	1 18E	+0050	+0030	+0050	+0130	−2.1	−1.7	−0.5	−0.1
Blakeney Bar	52 59N	0 59E	+0035	+0025	+0030	+0040	−1.6	−1.3	no data	
Blakeney	52 57N	1 01E	+0115	+0055	no data	no data	−3.9	−3.8	no data	
Wells Bar	52 59N	0 49E	+0020	+0020	+0020	+0020	−1.3	−1.0	no data	
Wells	52 57N	0 51E	+0035	+0045	+0340	+0310	−3.8	−3.8	not below CD	
Burnham Overy Staithe	52 58N	0 48E	+0045	+0055	no data	no data	−5.0	−4.9	no data	
The Wash										
Hunstanton	52 56N	0 29E	+0010	+0020	+0105	+0025	+0.1	−0.2	−0.1	0.0
West Stones	52 50N	0 21E	+0025	+0025	+0115	+0040	−0.3	−0.4	−0.3	+0.2
King's Lynn	52 45N	0 24E	+0030	+0030	+0305	+0140	−0.5	−0.8	−0.8	+0.1
Wisbech Cut	52 48N	0 13E	+0020	+0025	+0200	+0030	−0.3	−0.7	−0.4	no data
Lawyer's Creek	52 53N	0 05E	+0010	+0020	no data	no data	−0.3	−0.6	no data	
Tabs Head	52 56N	0 05E	0000	+0005	+0125	+0020	+0.2	−0.2	−0.2	−0.2
Boston	52 58N	0 01W	0000	+0010	+0140	+0050	−0.5	−1.0	−0.9	−0.5
Skegness	53 09N	0 21E	+0010	+0015	+0030	+0020	−0.4	−0.5	−0.1	0.0
Inner Dowsing Light Tower	53 20N	0 34E	0000	0000	+0010	+0010	−0.9	−0.7	−0.1	+0.3
River Humber										
Bull Sand Fort	53 34N	0 04E	−0020	−0030	−0035	−0015	−0.4	−0.3	+0.1	+0.2
Grimsby	53 35N	0 04W	−0012	−0012	−0015	−0015	−0.2	−0.1	0.0	+0.2
Hull King George Dock	53 44N	0 16W	+0010	+0010	+0021	+0017	+0.3	+0.2	−0.1	−0.2
Hull Albert Dock	53 44N	0 21W	+0019	+0019	+0033	+0027	+0.3	+0.1	−0.1	−0.2
Humber Bridge	53 43N	0 27W	+0027	+0022	+0049	+0039	−0.1	−0.4	−0.7	−0.6
River Trent										
Burton Stather	53 39N	0 42W	+0105	+0045	+0335	+0305	−2.1	−2.3	−2.3	dries
Flixborough Wharf	53 37N	0 42W	+0120	+0100	+0400	+0340	−2.3	−2.6	dries	
Keadby	53 36N	0 44W	+0135	+0120	+0425	+0410	−2.5	−2.8	dries	
Owston Ferry	53 29N	0 46W	+0155	+0145	dries	dries	−3.5	−3.9	dries	
River Ouse										
Blacktoft	53 42N	0 43W	+0100	+0055	+0325	+0255	−1.6	−1.8	−2.2	−1.1
Goole	53 42N	0 52W	+0130	+0115	+0355	+0350	−1.6	−2.1	−1.9	−0.6
			0200	0800	0100	0800				
R. TYNE, N. SHIELDS	55 01N	1 26W	and	and	and	and	5.0	3.9	1.8	0.7
standard port			1400	2000	1300	2000				
Bridlington	54 05N	0 11W	+0119	+0109	+0109	+0104	+1.1	+0.8	+0.5	+0.4
Filey Bay	54 13N	0 16W	+0101	+0101	+0101	+0048	+0.8	+1.0	+0.6	+0.3
Scarborough	54 17N	0 23W	+0059	+0059	+0044	+0044	+0.7	+0.7	+0.5	+0.2
Whitby	54 29N	0 37W	+0034	+0049	+0034	+0019	+0.6	+0.4	+0.1	+0.1
Middlesborough	54 35N	1 13W	+0019	+0021	+0014	+0011	+0.6	+0.6	+0.3	+0.1
Hartlepool	54 41N	1 11W	+0015	+0015	+0008	+0008	+0.4	+0.3	0.0	+0.1
Seaham	54 50N	1 19W	+0004	+0004	−0001	−0001	+0.2	+0.2	+0.2	0.0
Sunderland	54 55N	1 21W	+0002	−0002	−0002	−0002	+0.2	+0.3	+0.2	+0.1
Newcastle–upon–Tyne	54 58N	1 36W	+0003	+0003	+0008	+0008	+0.3	+0.2	+0.1	+0.1
Blyth	55 07N	1 29W	+0005	−0007	−0001	+0009	0.0	0.0	−0.1	+0.1
Coquet Island	55 20N	1 32W	−0010	−0010	−0020	−0020	+0.1	+0.1	0.0	+0.1
Amble	55 20N	1 34W	−0013	−0013	−0016	−0020	0.0	0.0	+0.1	+0.1
North Sunderland	55 34N	1 38W	−0048	−0044	−0058	−0102	−0.2	−0.2	−0.2	0.0
Holy Island	55 40N	1 47W	−0043	−0039	−0105	−0110	−0.2	−0.2	−0.3	−0.1
Berwick	55 47N	2 00W	−0053	−0053	−0109	−0109	−0.3	−0.1	−0.5	−0.1
SCOTLAND Time Zone UT			0300	0900	0300	0900				
LEITH	55 59N	3 11W	and	and	and	and	5.6	4.4	2.0	0.8
standard port			1500	2100	1500	2100				
Eyemouth	55 52N	2 05W	−0003	+0008	+0011	+0005	−0.5	−0.4	−0.1	0.0
Dunbar	56 00N	2 31W	−0003	+0003	+0003	−0003	−0.3	−0.3	0.0	+0.1
Fidra	56 04N	2 47W	−0001	0000	−0002	+0001	−0.2	−0.2	0.0	0.0

TIDES

Location	Lat	Long	High Water		Low Water		MHWS	MHWN	MLWN	MLWS
Cockenzie	55 58N	2 57W	–0007	–0015	–0013	–0005	–0.2	0.0	no data	
Granton	55 59N	3 13W	0000	0000	0000	0000	0.0	0.0	0.0	0.0
Grangemouth	56 02N	3 41W	+0025	+0010	–0052	–0015	–0.1	–0.2	–0.3	–0.3
Kincardine	56 04N	3 43W	+0015	+0030	–0030	–0030	0.0	–0.2	–0.5	–0.3
Alloa	56 07N	3 48W	+0040	+0040	+0025	+0025	–0.2	–0.5	no data	–0.7
Stirling	56 07N	3 56W	+0100	+0100	no data		–2.9	–3.1	–2.3	–0.7
Firth of Forth										
Burntisland	56 03N	3 14W	+0013	+0004	–0002	+0007	+0.1	0.0	+0.1	+0.2
Kirkcaldy	56 09N	3 09W	+0005	0000	–0004	–0001	–0.3	–0.3	–0.2	–0.2
Methil	56 11N	3 00W	–0005	–0001	–0001	–0001	–0.1	–0.1	–0.1	–0.1
Anstruther Easter	56 13N	2 42W	–0018	–0012	–0006	–0008	–0.3	–0.2	0.0	0.0
			0000	0600	0100	0700				
ABERDEEN	57 09N	2 05W	and	and	and	and	**4.3**	**3.4**	**1.6**	**0.6**
standard port			1200	1800	1300	1900				
River Tay										
Bar	56 27N	2 38W	+0100	+0100	+0050	+0110	+0.9	+0.8	+0.3	+0.1
Dundee	56 27N	2 58W	+0140	+0120	+0055	+0145	+1.1	+0.9	+0.3	+0.1
Newburgh	56 21N	3 14W	+0215	+0200	+0250	+0335	–0.2	–0.4	–1.1	–0.5
Perth	56 24N	3 27W	+0220	+0225	+0510	+0530	–0.9	–1.4	–1.2	–0.3
Arbroath	56 33N	2 35W	+0056	+0037	+0034	+0055	+0.7	+0.7	+0.2	+0.1
Montrose	56 42N	2 27W	+0055	+0055	+0030	+0040	+0.5	+0.4	+0.2	0.0
Stonehaven	56 58N	2 12W	+0013	+0008	+0013	+0009	+0.2	+0.2	+0.1	0.0
Peterhead	57 30N	1 46W	–0035	–0045	–0035	–0040	–0.5	–0.3	–0.1	–0.1
Fraserburgh	57 41N	2 00W	–0105	–0115	–0120	–0110	–0.6	–0.5	–0.2	0.0
			0200	0900	0400	0900				
ABERDEEN	57 09N	2 05W	and	and	and	and	**4.3**	**3.4**	**1.6**	**0.6**
standard port			1400	2100	1600	2100				
Banff	57 40N	2 31W	–0100	–0150	–0150	–0050	–0.4	–0.2	–0.1	+0.2
Whitehills	57 41N	2 35W	–0122	–0137	–0117	–0127	–0.4	–0.3	+0.1	+0.1
Buckie	57 40N	2 58W	–0130	–0145	–0125	–0140	–0.2	–0.2	0.0	+0.1
Lossiemouth	57 43N	3 18W	–0125	–0200	–0130	–0130	–0.2	–0.2	0.0	0.0
Burghead	57 42N	3 29W	–0120	–0150	–0135	–0120	–0.2	–0.2	0.0	0.0
Nairn	57 36N	3 52W	–0120	–0150	–0135	–0130	0.0	–0.1	0.0	+0.1
McDermott Base	57 36N	3 59W	–0110	–0140	–0120	–0115	–0.1	–0.1	+0.1	+0.3
			0300	1000	0000	0700				
ABERDEEN	57 09N	2 05W	and	and	and	and	**4.3**	**3.4**	**1.6**	**0.6**
standard port			1500	2200	1200	1900				
Inverness Firth										
Fortrose	57 35N	4 08W	–0125	–0125	–0125	–0125	0.0	0.0	no data	
Inverness	57 30N	4 15W	–0050	–0150	–0200	–0150	+0.5	+0.3	+0.2	+0.1
Cromarty Firth										
Cromarty	57 42N	4 03W	–0120	–0155	–0155	–0120	0.0	0.0	+0.1	+0.2
Invergordon	57 41N	4 10W	–0105	–0200	–0200	–0110	+0.1	+0.1	+0.1	+0.1
Dingwall	57 36N	4 25W	–0045	–0145	no data	no data	+0.1	+0.2	no data	
			0300	0800	0200	0800				
ABERDEEN	57 09N	2 05W	and	and	and	and	**4.3**	**3.4**	**1.6**	**0.6**
standard port			1500	2000	1400	2000				
Dornoch Firth										
Portmahomack	57 50N	3 50W	–0120	–0210	–0140	–0110	–0.2	–0.1	+0.1	+0.1
Meikle Ferry	57 51N	4 08W	–0100	–0140	–0120	–0055	+0.1	0.0	–0.1	0.0
Golspie	57 58N	3 59W	–0130	–0215	–0155	–0130	–0.3	–0.3	–0.1	0.0
			0000	0700	0200	0700				
WICK	58 26N	3 05W	and	and	and	and	**3.5**	**2.8**	**1.4**	**0.7**
standard port			1200	1900	1400	1900				
Helmsdale	58 07N	3 39W	+0025	+0015	+0035	+0030	+0.4	+0.3	+0.1	0.0
Duncansby Head	58 39N	3 02W	–0115	–0115	–0110	–0110	–0.4	–0.4	no data	
Orkney Islands										
Muckle Skerry	58 41N	2 55W	–0025	–0025	–0020	–0020	–0.9	–0.8	–0.4	–0.3
Burray Ness	58 51N	2 52W	+0005	+0005	+0015	+0015	–0.2	–0.3	–0.1	–0.1
Deer Sound	58 58N	2 50W	–0040	–0040	–0035	–0035	–0.3	–0.3	–0.1	–0.1
Kirkwall	58 59N	2 58W	–0042	–0042	–0041	–0041	–0.5	–0.4	–0.1	–0.1
Loth	59 12N	2 42W	–0052	–0052	–0058	–0058	–0.1	0.0	+0.3	+0.4
Kettletoft Pier	59 14N	2 36W	–0025	–0025	–0015	–0015	0.0	0.0	+0.2	+0.2
Rapness	59 15N	2 52W	–0205	–0205	–0205	–0205	+0.1	0.0	+0.2	0.0
Pierowall	59 19N	2 58W	–0150	–0150	–0145	–0145	+0.2	0.0	0.0	–0.1

Location	Lat	Long	High Water		Low Water		MHWS	MHWN	MLWN	MLWS
Tingwall	59 05N	3 02W	−0200	−0125	−0145	−0125	−0.4	−0.4	−0.1	−0.1
Stromness	58 58N	3 18W	−0225	−0135	−0205	−0205	+0.1	−0.1	0.0	0.0
St. Mary's	58 54N	2 55W	−0140	−0140	−0140	−0140	−0.2	−0.2	0.0	−0.1
Widewall Bay	58 49N	3 01W	−0155	−0155	−0150	−0150	+0.1	−0.1	−0.1	−0.3
Bur Wick	58 44N	2 58W	−0100	−0100	−0150	−0150	−0.1	−0.1	+0.2	+0.1
			0000	0600	0100	0800				
LERWICK	60 09N	1 08W	and	and	and	and	2.1	1.7	0.9	0.5
standard port			1200	1800	1300	2000				
Fair Isle	59 32N	1 36W	−0006	−0015	−0031	−0037	+0.1	0.0	+0.1	+0.1
Shetland Islands										
Sumburgh *Grutness Voe*	59 53N	1 17W	+0006	+0008	+0004	−0002	−0.3	−0.3	−0.2	−0.1
Dury Voe	60 21N	1 10W	−0015	−0015	−0010	−0010	0.0	−0.1	0.0	−0.2
Out Skerries	60 25N	0 45W	−0025	−0025	−0010	−0010	+0.1	0.0	0.0	−0.1
Toft Pier	60 28N	1 12W	−0105	−0100	−0125	−0115	+0.2	+0.1	−0.1	−0.1
Burra Voe *Yell Sound*	60 30N	1 03W	−0025	−0025	−0025	−0025	+0.2	+0.1	0.0	−0.1
Mid Yell	60 36N	1 03W	−0030	−0020	−0035	−0025	+0.3	+0.2	+0.2	+0.1
Balta Sound	60 45N	0 50W	−0055	−0055	−0045	−0045	+0.2	+0.1	0.0	−0.1
Burra Firth	60 48N	0 52W	−0110	−0110	−0115	−0115	+0.4	+0.2	0.0	0.0
Bluemull Sound	60 42N	1 00W	−0135	−0135	−0155	−0155	+0.5	+0.2	+0.1	0.0
Sullom Voe	60 27N	1 18W	−0135	−0125	−0135	−0120	0.0	0.0	−0.2	−0.2
Hillswick	60 29N	1 29W	−0220	−0220	−0200	−0200	−0.1	−0.1	−0.1	−0.1
Scalloway	60 08N	1 16W	−0150	−0150	−0150	−0150	−0.5	−0.4	−0.3	0.0
Bay of Quendale	59 54N	1 20W	−0025	−0025	−0030	−0030	−0.4	−0.3	0.0	+0.1
Foula	60 07N	2 03W	−0140	−0130	−0140	−0120	−0.1	−0.1	0.0	0.0
			0200	0700	0100	0700				
WICK	58 26N	3 05W	and	and	and	and	3.5	2.8	1.4	0.7
Standard port			1400	1900	1300	1900				
Stroma	58 40N	3 08W	−0115	−0115	−0110	−0110	−0.4	−0.5	−0.1	−0.2
Gills Bay	58 38N	3 10W	−0150	−0150	−0202	−0202	+0.7	+0.7	+0.6	+0.3
Scrabster	58 37N	3 33W	−0255	−0225	−0240	−0230	+1.5	+1.2	+0.8	+0.3
Sule Skerry	59 05N	4 24W	−0320	−0255	−0315	−0250	+0.4	+0.3	+0.2	+0.1
Loch Eriboll Portnancon	58 30N	4 42W	−0340	−0255	−0315	−0255	+1.6	+1.3	+0.8	+0.4
Kyle of Durness	58 36N	4 47W	−0350	−0350	−0315	−0315	+1.1	+0.7	+0.4	−0.1
Rona	59 08N	5 49W	−0410	−0345	−0330	−0340	−0.1	−0.2	−0.2	−0.1
			0100	0700	0300	0900				
STORNOWAY	58 12N	6 23W	and	and	and	and	4.8	3.7	2.0	0.7
standard port			1300	1900	1500	2100				
Outer Hebrides										
Loch Shell	58 00N	6 25W	−0013	0000	0000	−0017	0.0	−0.1	−0.1	0.0
E. Loch Tarbert	57 54N	6 48W	−0025	−0010	−0010	−0020	+0.2	0.0	+0.1	+0.1
Loch Maddy	57 36N	7 06W	−0044	−0014	−0016	−0030	0.0	−0.1	−0.1	0.0
Loch Carnan	57 22N	7 16W	−0050	−0010	−0020	−0040	−0.3	−0.5	−0.1	−0.1
Loch Skiport	57 20N	7 16W	−0100	−0025	−0024	−0024	−0.2	−0.4	−0.3	−0.2
Loch Boisdale	57 09N	7 16W	−0055	−0030	−0020	−0040	−0.7	−0.7	−0.3	−0.2
Barra *North Bay*	57 00N	7 24W	−0103	−0031	−0034	−0048	−0.6	−0.5	−0.2	−0.1
Castle Bay	56 57N	7 29W	−0115	−0040	−0045	−0100	−0.5	−0.6	−0.3	−0.1
Barra Head	56 47N	7 38W	−0115	−0040	−0045	−0055	−0.8	−0.7	−0.2	+0.1
Shillay	57 31N	7 41W	−0103	−0043	−0047	−0107	−0.6	−0.7	−0.7	−0.3
Balivanich	57 29N	7 23W	−0103	−0017	−0031	−0045	−0.7	−0.6	−0.5	−0.2
Scolpaig	57 39N	7 29W	−0033	−0033	−0040	−0040	−1.0	−0.9	−0.5	0.0
Leverburgh	57 46N	7 01W	−0025	−0025	−0015	−0025	−0.2	−0.2	−0.1	−0.1
W. Loch Tarbert	57 55N	6 55W	−0015	−0015	−0046	−0046	−1.1	−0.9	−0.5	0.0
Little Bernera	58 16N	6 52W	−0021	−0011	−0017	−0027	−0.5	−0.6	−0.4	−0.2
Carloway	58 17N	6 47W	−0040	+0020	−0035	−0015	−0.6	−0.5	−0.4	−0.1
St Kilda *Village Bay*	57 48N	8 34W	−0040	−0040	−0045	−0045	−1.4	−1.2	−0.8	−0.3
Flannan Isles	58 16N	7 36W	−0026	−0016	−0016	−0026	−0.9	−0.7	−0.6	−0.2
Rockall	57 36N	13 41W	−0055	−0055	−0105	−0105	−1.8	−1.5	−0.9	−0.2
			0000	0600	0300	0900				
ULLAPOOL	57 54N	5 10W	and	and	and	and	5.2	3.9	2.1	0.7
standard port			1200	1800	1500	2100				
Loch Bervie	58 27N	5 03W	+0030	+0010	+0010	+0020	−0.3	−0.3	−0.2	0.0
Loch Laxford	58 24N	5 05W	+0015	+0015	+0005	+0005	−0.3	−0.4	−0.2	0.0
Eddrachillis Bay										
Badcall Bay	58 19N	5 08W	+0005	+0005	+0005	+0005	−0.7	−0.5	−0.5	+0.2
Loch Nedd	58 14N	5 10W	0000	0000	0000	0000	−0.3	−0.2	−0.2	0.0
Loch Inver	58 09N	5 18W	−0005	−0005	−0005	−0005	−0.2	0.0	0.0	+0.1

TIDES

Location	Lat	Long	High Water		Low Water		MHWS	MHWN	MLWN	MLWS
Summer Isles Tanera Mor	58 01N	5 24W	−0005	−0005	−0010	−0010	−0.1	+0.1	0.0	+0.1
Loch Ewe Mellon Charles	57 51N	5 38W	−0010	−0010	−0010	−0010	−0.1	−0.1	−0.1	0.0
Loch Gairloch Gairloch	57 43N	5 41W	−0020	−0020	−0010	−0010	0.0	+0.1	−0.3	−0.1
Loch Torridon Shieldaig	57 31N	5 39W	−0020	−0020	−0015	−0015	+0.4	+0.3	+0.1	0.0
Inner Sound Applecross	57 26N	5 49W	−0010	−0015	−0010	−0010	0.0	0.0	0.0	+0.1
Loch Carron Plockton	57 20N	5 39W	+0005	−0025	−0005	−0010	+0.5	+0.5	+0.5	+0.2
Rona Loch a' Bhraige	57 35N	5 58W	−0020	0000	−0010	0000	−0.1	−0.1	−0.1	−0.2
Skye										
Broadford Bay	57 15N	5 54W	−0015	−0015	−0010	−0015	+0.2	+0.1	+0.1	0.0
Portree	57 24N	6 11W	−0025	−0025	−0025	−0025	+0.1	−0.2	−0.2	0.0
Loch Snizort (Uig Bay)	57 35N	6 22W	−0045	−0020	−0005	−0025	+0.1	−0.4	−0.2	0.0
Loch Dunvegan	57 27N	6 38W	−0105	−0030	−0020	−0040	0.0	−0.1	0.0	0.0
Loch Harport	57 20N	6 25W	−0115	−0035	−0020	−0100	−0.1	−0.1	0.0	+0.1
Soay Camus nan Gall	57 09N	6 13W	−0055	−0025	−0025	−0045	−0.4	−0.2	no data	
Loch Alsh										
Kyle of Lochalsh	57 17N	5 43W	−0040	−0020	−0005	−0025	+0.1	0.0	0.0	−0.1
Dornie Bridge	57 17N	5 31W	−0040	−0010	−0005	−0020	+0.1	−0.1	0.0	0.0
Kyle Rhea Glenelg Bay	57 13N	5 38W	−0105	−0035	−0035	−0055	−0.4	−0.4	−0.9	−0.1
Loch Hourn	57 06N	5 34W	−0125	−0050	−0040	−0110	−0.2	−0.1	−0.1	+0.1
			0000	0600	0100	0700				
OBAN	56 25N	5 29W	and	and	and	and	4.0	2.9	1.8	0.7
standard port			1200	1800	1300	1900				
Loch Nevis										
Inverie Bay	57 02N	5 41W	+0030	+0020	+0035	+0020	+1.0	+0.9	+0.2	0.0
Mallaig	57 00N	5 50W	+0017	+0017	+0017	+0017	+1.0	+0.7	+0.3	+0.1
Eigg Bay of Laig	56 55N	6 10W	+0015	+0030	+0040	+0005	+0.7	+0.6	−0.2	−0.2
Loch Moidart	56 47N	5 53W	+0015	+0015	+0040	+0020	+0.8	+0.6	−0.2	−0.2
Coll Loch Eatharna	56 37N	6 31W	+0025	+0010	+0015	+0025	+0.4	+0.3	no data	
Tiree Gott Bay	56 31N	6 48W	0000	+0010	+0005	+0010	0.0	+0.1	0.0	0.0
			0100	0700	0100	0800				
OBAN	56 25N	5 29W	and	and	and	and	4.0	2.9	1.8	0.7
standard port			1300	1900	1300	2000				
Mull										
Carsaig Bay	56 19N	5 59W	−0015	−0005	−0030	+0020	+0.1	+0.2	0.0	−0.1
Iona	56 19N	6 23W	−0010	−0005	−0020	+0015	0.0	+0.1	−0.3	−0.2
Bunessan	56 19N	6 14W	−0015	−0015	−0010	−0015	+0.3	+0.1	−0.1	−0.1
Ulva Sound	56 29N	6 08W	−0010	−0015	0000	−0005	+0.4	+0.3	0.0	−0.1
Loch Sunart Salen	56 42N	5 47W	−0015	+0015	+0010	+0005	+0.6	+0.5	−0.1	−0.1
Sound of Mull										
Tobermory	56 37N	6 04W	+0025	+0010	+0015	+0025	+0.4	+0.4	0.0	0.0
Salen	56 31N	5 57W	+0045	+0015	+0020	+0030	+0.2	+0.2	−0.1	0.0
Loch Aline	56 32N	5 46W	+0012	+0012	no data	no data	+0.5	+0.3	no data	
Craignure	56 28N	5 42W	+0030	+0005	+0010	+0015	0.0	+0.1	−0.1	−0.1
Loch Linnhe										
Corran	56 43N	5 14W	+0007	+0007	+0004	+0004	+0.4	+0.4	−0.1	0.0
Corpach	56 50N	5 07W	0000	+0020	+0040	0000	0.0	0.0	−0.2	−0.2
Loch Eil Head	56 51N	5 20W	+0025	+0045	+0105	+0025	no data		no data	
Loch Leven Head	56 43N	5 00W	+0045	+0045	+0045	+0045	no data		no data	
Loch Linnhe Port Appin	56 33N	5 25W	−0005	−0005	−0030	0000	+0.2	+0.2	+0.1	+0.1
Loch Creran										
Barcaldine Pier	56 32N	5 19W	+0010	+0020	+0040	+0015	+0.1	+0.1	0.0	+0.1
Loch Creran Head	56 33N	5 16W	+0015	+0025	+0120	+0020	−0.3	−0.3	−0.4	−0.3
Loch Etive										
Dunstaffnage Bay	56 27N	5 26W	+0005	0000	0000	+0005	+0.1	+0.1	+0.1	+0.1
Connel	56 27N	5 24W	+0020	+0005	+0010	+0015	−0.3	−0.2	−0.1	+0.1
Bonawe	56 27N	5 13W	+0150	+0205	+0240	+0210	−2.0	−1.7	−1.3	−0.5
Seil Sound	56 18N	5 35W	−0035	−0015	−0040	−0015	−1.3	−0.9	−0.7	−0.3
Colonsay Scalasaig	56 04N	6 10W	−0020	−0005	−0015	+0005	−0.1	−0.2	−0.2	−0.2
Jura Glengarrisdale Bay	56 06N	5 47W	−0020	0000	−0010	0000	−0.4	−0.2	−0.2	−0.2
Islay										
Rubha A'Mhail	55 56N	6 07W	−0020	0000	+0005	−0015	−0.3	−0.1	−0.3	−0.1
Ardnave Point	55 52N	6 20W	−0035	+0010	0000	−0025	−0.4	−0.2	−0.3	−0.1
Orsay	55 41N	6 31W	−0110	−0110	−0040	−0040	−1.4	−0.6	−0.5	−0.2
Bruichladdich	55 48N	6 22W	−0105	−0035	−0110	−0110	−1.8	−1.3	−0.4	+0.1
Port Ellen	55 38N	6 11W	−0530	−0050	−0045	−0530	−3.1	−2.1	−1.3	−0.4
Port Askaig	55 51N	6 06W	−0110	−0030	−0020	−0020	−1.9	−1.4	−0.8	−0.3
Sound of Jura										
Craighouse	55 50N	5 57W	−0230	−0250	−0150	−0230	−3.0	−2.4	−1.3	−0.6

Location	Lat	Long	High Water		Low Water		MHWS	MHWN	MLWN	MLWS
Loch Melfort	56 15N	5 29W	−0055	−0025	−0040	−0035	−1.2	−0.8	−0.5	−0.1
Loch Beag	56 09N	5 36W	−0110	−0045	−0035	−0045	−1.6	−1.2	−0.8	−0.4
Carsaig Bay	56 02N	5 38W	−0105	−0040	−0050	−0050	−2.1	−1.6	−1.0	−0.4
Sound of Gigha	55 41N	5 44W	−0450	−0210	−0130	−0410	−2.5	−1.6	−1.0	−0.1
Machrihanish	55 25N	5 45W	−0520	−0350	−0340	−0540	Mean range 0.5 metres			
			0000	0600	0000	0600				
GREENOCK	55 57N	4 46W	and	and	and	and	3.4	2.8	1.0	0.3
standard port			1200	1800	1200	1800				
Firth of Clyde										
Southend, Kintyre	55 19N	5 38W	−0030	−0010	+0005	+0035	−1.3	−1.2	−0.5	−0.2
Campbeltown	55 25N	5 36W	−0025	−0005	−0015	+0005	−0.5	−0.3	+0.1	+0.2
Carradale	55 36N	5 28W	−0015	−0005	−0005	+0005	−0.3	−0.2	+0.1	+0.1
Loch Ranza	55 43N	5 18W	−0015	−0005	−0010	−0005	−0.4	−0.3	−0.1	0.0
Loch Fyne										
East Loch Tarbert	55 52N	5 24W	−0005	−0005	0000	−0005	+0.2	+0.1	0.0	0.0
Inveraray	56 14N	5 04W	+0011	+0011	+0034	+0034	−0.1	+0.1	−0.5	−0.2
Kyles of Bute										
Rubha a'Bhodaich	55 55N	5 09W	−0020	−0010	−0007	−0007	−0.2	−0.1	+0.2	+0.2
Tighnabruich	55 55N	5 13W	+0007	−0010	−0002	−0015	0.0	+0.2	+0.4	+0.5
Firth of Clyde – continued										
Millport	55 45N	4 56W	−0005	−0025	−0025	−0005	0.0	−0.1	0.0	+0.1
Rothesay Bay	55 51N	5 03W	−0020	−0015	−0010	−0002	+0.2	+0.2	+0.2	+0.2
Wemyss Bay	55 53N	4 53W	−0005	−0005	−0005	−0005	0.0	0.0	+0.1	+0.1
Loch Long										
Coulport	56 03N	4 53W	−0011	−0011	−0008	−0008	0.0	0.0	0.0	0.0
Lochgoilhead	56 10N	4 54W	+0015	0000	−0005	−0005	−0.2	−0.3	−0.3	−0.3
Arrochar	56 12N	4 45W	−0005	−0005	−0005	−0005	0.0	0.0	−0.1	−0.1
Gareloch										
Rosneath	56 01N	4 47W	−0005	−0005	−0005	−0005	0.0	−0.1	0.0	0.0
Faslane	56 04N	4 49W	−0010	−0010	−0010	−0010	0.0	0.0	−0.1	−0.2
Garelochhead	56 05N	4 50W	0000	0000	0000	0000	0.0	0.0	0.0	−0.1
River Clyde										
Helensburgh	56 00N	4 44W	0000	0000	0000	0000	0.0	0.0	0.0	0.0
Port Glasgow	55 56N	4 41W	+0010	+0005	+0010	+0020	+0.2	+0.1	0.0	0.0
Bowling	55 56N	4 29W	+0020	+0010	+0030	+0055	+0.6	+0.5	+0.3	+0.1
Clydebank *Rothesay Dock*	55 54N	4 24W	+0025	+0015	+0035	+0100	+1.0	+0.8	+0.5	+0.4
Glasgow	55 51N	4 16W	+0025	+0015	+0035	+0105	+1.3	+1.2	+0.6	+0.4
Firth of Clyde – continued										
Brodick Bay	55 35N	5 08W	0000	0000	+0005	+0005	−0.2	−0.2	0.0	0.0
Lamlash	55 32N	5 07W	−0016	−0036	−0024	−0004	−0.2	−0.2	no data	
Ardrossan	55 38N	4 49W	−0020	−0010	−0010	−0010	−0.2	−0.2	+0.1	+0.1
Irvine	55 36N	4 41W	−0020	−0020	−0030	−0010	−0.3	−0.3	−0.1	0.0
Troon	55 33N	4 41W	−0025	−0025	−0020	−0020	−0.2	−0.2	0.0	0.0
Ayr	55 28N	4 39W	−0025	−0025	−0030	−0015	−0.4	−0.3	+0.1	+0.1
Girvan	55 15N	4 52W	−0025	−0040	−0035	−0010	−0.3	−0.3	−0.1	0.0
Loch Ryan Stranraer	54 55N	5 03W	−0030	−0025	−0010	−0010	−0.2	−0.1	0.0	+0.1

WEST COAST ENGLAND *Time Zone UT*

Location	Lat	Long	High Water		Low Water		MHWS	MHWN	MLWN	MLWS
			0000	0600	0200	0800				
LIVERPOOL	53 24N	3 01W	and	and	and	and	9.3	7.4	2.9	0.9
standard port			1200	1800	1400	2000				
Portpatrick	54 50N	5 07W	+0018	+0026	0000	−0035	−5.5	−4.4	−2.0	−0.6
Luce Bay										
Drummore	54 41N	4 53W	+0030	+0040	+0015	+0020	−3.4	−2.5	−0.9	−0.3
Port William	54 46N	4 35W	+0030	+0030	+0025	0000	−2.9	−2.2	−0.8	no data
Wigtown Bay										
Isle of Whithorn	54 42N	4 22W	+0020	+0025	+0025	+0005	−2.4	−2.0	−0.8	−0.2
Garlieston	54 47N	4 22W	+0025	+0035	+0030	+0005	−2.3	−1.7	−0.5	no data
Solway Firth										
Kirkcudbright Bay	54 48N	4 04W	+0015	+0015	+0010	0000	−1.8	−1.5	−0.5	−0.1
Hestan Islet	54 50N	3 48W	+0025	+0025	+0020	+0025	−1.0	−1.1	−0.5	0.0
Southerness Point	54 52N	3 36W	+0030	+0030	+0030	+0010	−0.7	−0.7	no data	
Annan Waterfoot	54 58N	3 16W	+0050	+0105	+0220	+0310	−2.2	−2.6	−2.7	
Torduff Point	54 58N	3 09W	+0105	+0140	+0520	+0410	−4.1	−4.9		
Redkirk	54 59N	3 06W	+0110	+0215	+0715	+0445	−5.5	−6.2		
Silloth	54 52N	3 24W	+0030	+0040	+0045	+0055	−0.1	−0.3	−0.6	−0.1
Maryport	54 43N	3 30W	+0017	+0032	+0020	+0005	−0.7	−0.8	−0.4	0.0
Workington	54 39N	3 34W	+0020	+0020	+0020	+0010	−1.2	−1.1	−0.3	0.0
Whitehaven	54 33N	3 36W	+0005	+0015	+0010	+0005	−1.3	−1.1	−0.5	+0.1
Tarn Point	54 17N	3 25W	+0005	+0005	+0010	0000	−1.0	−1.0	−0.4	0.0
Duddon Bar	54 09N	3 20W	+0003	+0003	+0008	+0002	−0.8	−0.8	−0.3	0.0

TIDES

Location	Lat	Long	High Water		Low Water		MHWS	MHWN	MLWN	MLWS
			0000 and 1200	0600 and 1800	0200 and 1400	0700 and 1900				
LIVERPOOL standard port	53 24N	3 01W					9.3	7.4	2.9	0.9
Barrow-in-Furness	54 06N	3 12W	+0015	+0015	+0015	+0015	0.0	−0.3	+0.1	+0.2
Ulverston	54 11N	3 04W	+0020	+0040	no data	no data	0.0	−0.1	no data	
Arnside	54 12N	2 51W	+0100	+0135	no data	no data	+0.5	+0.2	no data	
Morecambe	54 04N	2 52W	+0005	+0010	+0030	+0015	+0.2	0.0	0.0	+0.2
Heysham	54 02N	2 55W	+0005	+0005	+0015	0000	+0.1	0.0	0.0	+0.2
River Lune Glasson Dock	54 00N	2 51W	+0020	+0030	+0220	+0240	−2.7	−3.0	no data	
Lancaster	54 03N	2 49W	+0110	+0030	dries	dries	−5.0	−4.9	dries	
River Wyre										
Wyre Lighthouse	53 57N	3 02W	−0010	−0010	+0005	0000	−0.1	−0.1	no data	
Fleetwood	53 56N	3 00W	−0008	−0008	−0003	−0003	−0.1	−0.1	+0.1	+0.3
Blackpool	53 49N	3 04W	−0015	−0005	−0005	−0015	−0.4	−0.4	−0.1	+0.1
River Ribble Preston	53 46N	2 45W	+0010	+0010	+0335	+0310	−4.0	−4.1	−2.8	−0.8
Liverpool Bay										
Southport	53 39N	3 01W	−0020	−0010	no data	no data	−0.3	−0.3	no data	
Formby	53 32N	3 07W	−0015	−0010	−0020	−0020	−0.3	−0.1	0.0	+0.1
River Mersey										
Gladstone Dock	53 27N	3 01W	−0003	−0003	−0003	−0003	−0.1	−0.1	0.0	−0.1
Eastham	53 19N	2 57W	+0010	+0010	+0009	+0009	+0.3	+0.1	−0.1	−0.3
Hale Head	53 19N	2 48W	+0030	+0025	no data	no data	−2.4	−2.5	no data	
Widnes	53 21N	2 44W	+0040	+0045	+0400	+0345	−4.2	−4.4	−2.5	−0.3
Fiddler's Ferry	53 22N	2 39W	+0100	+0115	+0540	+0450	−5.9	−6.3	−2.4	−0.4
River Dee										
Hilbre Island	53 23N	3 13W	−0015	−0012	−0010	−0015	−0.3	−0.2	+0.2	+0.4
Mostyn Docks	53 19N	3 16W	−0020	−0015	−0020	−0020	−0.8	−0.7	no data	
Connah's Quay	53 13N	3 03W	0000	+0015	+0355	+0340	−4.6	−4.4	dries	
Chester	53 12N	2 54W	+0105	+0105	+0500	+0500	−5.3	−5.4	dries	
Isle of Man										
Peel	54 14N	4 42W	+0005	+0005	−0015	−0025	−4.1	−3.1	−1.4	−0.5
Ramsey	54 19N	4 22W	+0005	+0015	−0005	−0015	−1.9	−1.5	−0.6	0.0
Douglas	54 09N	4 28W	+0005	+0015	−0015	−0025	−2.4	−2.0	−0.5	−0.1
Port St. Mary	54 04N	4 44W	+0005	+0015	−0010	−0030	−3.4	−2.6	−1.3	−0.4
Calf Sound	54 04N	4 48W	+0005	+0005	−0015	−0025	−3.2	−2.6	−0.9	−0.3
Port Erin	54 05N	4 46W	−0005	+0015	−0010	−0050	−4.1	−3.2	−1.3	−0.5

WALES Time Zone UT

Location	Lat	Long	High Water		Low Water		MHWS	MHWN	MLWN	MLWS
Colwyn Bay	53 18N	3 43W	−0020	−0020	no data	no data	−1.5	−1.3	no data	
Llandudno	53 20N	3 50W	−0020	−0020	−0035	−0040	−1.7	−1.4	−0.7	−0.3
			0000 and 1200	0600 and 1800	0500 and 1700	1100 and 2300				
HOLYHEAD standard port	53 19N	4 37W					5.6	4.4	2.0	0.7
Conwy	53 17N	3 50W	+0025	+0035	+0120	+0105	+2.3	+1.8	+0.6	+0.4
Menai Strait										
Beaumaris	53 16N	4 05W	+0025	+0010	+0055	+0035	+2.0	+1.6	+0.5	+0.1
Menai Bridge	53 13N	4 09W	+0030	+0010	+0100	+0035	+1.7	+1.4	+0.3	0.0
Port Dinorwic	53 11N	4 13W	−0015	−0025	+0030	0000	0.0	0.0	0.0	+0.1
Caernarfon	53 09N	4 16W	−0030	−0030	+0015	−0005	−0.4	−0.4	−0.1	−0.1
Fort Belan	53 07N	4 20W	−0040	−0015	−0025	−0005	−1.0	−0.9	−0.2	−0.1
Trwyn Dinmor	53 19N	4 03W	+0025	+0015	+0050	+0035	+1.9	+1.5	+0.5	+0.2
Moelfre	53 20N	4 14W	+0025	+0020	+0050	+0035	+1.9	+1.4	+0.5	+0.2
Amlwch	53 25N	4 20W	+0020	+0010	+0035	+0025	+1.6	+1.3	+0.5	+0.2
Cemaes Bay	53 25N	4 27W	+0020	+0025	+0040	+0035	+1.0	+0.7	+0.3	+0.1
Trearddur Bay	53 16N	4 37W	−0045	−0025	−0015	−0015	−0.4	−0.4	0.0	+0.1
Porth Trecastell	53 12N	4 30W	−0045	−0025	−0005	−0015	−0.6	−0.6	0.0	0.0
Llanddwyn Island	53 08N	4 25W	−0115	−0055	−0030	−0020	−0.7	−0.5	−0.1	0.0
Trefor	53 00N	4 25W	−0115	−0100	−0030	−0020	−0.8	−0.9	−0.2	−0.1
Porth Dinllaen	52 57N	4 34W	−0120	−0105	−0035	−0025	−1.0	−1.0	−0.2	−0.2
Porth Ysgaden	52 54N	4 39W	−0125	−0110	−0040	−0035	−1.1	−1.0	−0.1	−0.1
Bardsey Island	52 46N	4 47W	−0220	−0240	−0145	−0140	−1.2	−1.2	−0.5	−0.1
			0100 and 1300	0800 and 2000	0100 and 1300	0700 and 1900				
MILFORD HAVEN standard port	51 42N	5 03W					7.0	5.2	2.5	0.7
Cardigan Bay										
Aberdaron	52 48N	4 43W	+0210	+0200	+0240	+0310	−2.4	−1.9	−0.6	−0.2
St. Tudwal's Roads	52 49N	4 29W	+0155	+0145	+0240	+0310	−2.2	−1.7	−0.7	−0.2
Pwllheli	52 53N	4 24W	+0210	+0150	+0245	+0320	−2.0	−1.8	−0.6	−0.2
Criccieth	52 55N	4 14W	+0210	+0155	+0255	+0320	−2.0	−1.8	−0.7	−0.3
Porthmadog	52 55N	4 08W	+0235	+0210	no data	no data	−1.9	−1.8	no data	
Barmouth	52 43N	4 03W	+0215	+0205	+0310	+0320	−2.0	−1.7	−0.7	0.0

EXAMPLE:
Find the time at which the afternoon tide at ULLAPOOL falls to 3.7m on 6 January

From tables	JANUARY	
ULLAPOOL	**6** 0420	4.6
	1033	1.6
	1641	4.6
	F 2308	1.2

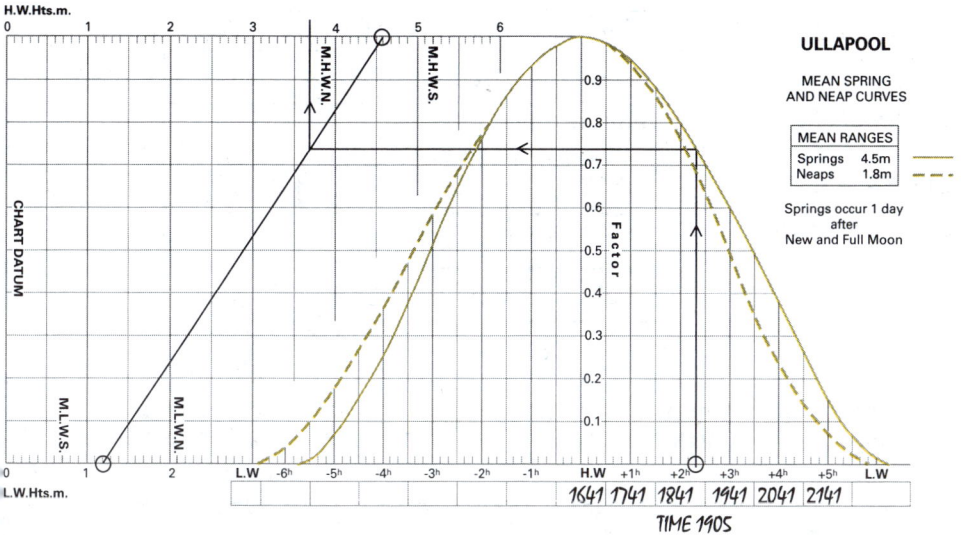

Find the time and height of H.W. and L.W. at a Secondary Port

EXAMPLE:
Find the time and height of the afternoon H.W. and L.W. at ST MARY's (Isles of Scilly) on 14th July (BST)
Note: *The data used in this example do not refer to the year of these tables.*

from tables	JULY	
PLYMOUTH (DEVONPORT)	**14** 0309	1.0
	0927	5.3
	1532	1.1
	SA 2149	5.0

From tables										
Location	Lat	Long	High Water		Low Water		MHWS	MHWN	MLWN	MLWS
DEVONPORT *Standard port*	50°22′N	4°11′W	0000 and 1200	0600 and 1800	0000 and 1200	0600 and 1800	5.5	4.4	2.2	0.8
St. Mary's, *Scilly*	49° 55′N	6°19′W	−0035	−0100	−0040	−0025	+0.2	−0.1	−0.2	−0.1

TIDES

TIDAL PREDICTION FORM (NP 204)

STANDARD PORT __Devonport__   TIME/HEIGHT REQUIRED __pm__
SECONDARY PORT __St Mary's__   DATE __14 July__   TIME ZONE __B.S.T__

	TIME		HEIGHT		
STANDARD PORT	HW	LW	HW	LW	RANGE
	¹ 2149	² 1532	³ 5.0	⁴ 1.1	⁵ 3.9
Seasonal change	Standard Ports −		⁶ 0.0	⁶ 0.0	
DIFFERENCES	⁷* −0044	⁸ −0032	⁹ 0.1	¹⁰ −0.1	
Seasonal change *	Secondary Ports +		¹¹ 0.0	¹¹ 0.0	
SECONDARY PORT	¹² 2105	¹³ 1500	¹⁴ 5.1	¹⁵ 1.0	
Duration	¹⁶ 0605		LW 1500 UT = 1600 BST		
			HW 2105 UT = 2205 BST		

* The seasonal changes are generally less than ± 0.1m and for most purposes can be ignored. See Admiraly Tide Tables Vol 1. for details

INTERMEDIATE TIMES/HEIGHTS (SECONDARY PORT)

These are the same as the appropriate calculations for a Standard Port except that the Standard Curve diagram for the Standard Port must be entered with H.W. and L.W. heights and times for the Secondary Port obtained on Form N.P. 204. When interpolating between the Spring and Neap curves the Range at the Standard Port must be used.

EXAMPLES:

Find the height of the tide at PADSTOW at 1100 on 28th February. Find the time at which the morning tide at PADSTOW falls to 4.9m on 28th February.

Notes:
The data in these examples do not refer to the year of these tables.

From tables	FEBRUARY	
MILFORD HAVEN	**28** 0315	1.1
	0922	6.6
	1538	1.3
	TU 2145	6.3

146

From tables Location	Lat	Long	High Water		Low Water		MHWS	MHWN	MLWN	MLWS
MILFORD HAVEN Standard port	51°42'N	5°03'W	0100 and 1300	0700 and 1900	0100 and 1300	0700 and 1900	7.0	5.2	2.5	0.7
River Camel Padstow	50°33'N	4°56'W	−0055	−0050	−0040	−0050	+0.3	+0.4	+0.1	+0.1
Wadebridge	50°31'N	4°50'W	−0052	−0052	+0235	+0245	−3.8	−3.8	−2.5	−0.4

TIDAL PREDICTION FORM (NP 204)

STANDARD PORT Milford Haven   TIME/HEIGHT REQUIRED 1100 : 4.9

SECONDARY PORT Padstow   DATE 28 Feb   TIME ZONE UT

	TIME		HEIGHT		
STANDARD PORT	HW	LW	HW	LW	RANGE
	1 0922	2 1538	3 6.6	4 1.3	5 5.3
Seasonal change	Standard Ports +		6 0.0	6 0.0	
DIFFERENCES	7* −0052	8 −	9 +0.3	10 +0.1	
Seasonal change *	Secondary Ports −		11 0.0	11 0.0	
SECONDARY PORT	12 0830	13 −	14 6.9	15 1.4	
Duration	16 −				

MILFORD HAVEN
MEAN SPRING AND NEAP CURVES

MEAN RANGES
Springs 6.3m
Neaps 2.7m

Springs occur 2 days after New and Full Moon.

Height 4.9m

TIDES

SPECIAL INSTRUCTIONS FOR PLACES BETWEEN BOURNEMOUTH AND SELSEY BILL

- Owing to the rapid change of tidal characteristics and distortion of the tidal curve in this area, curves are shown for individual ports. It is a characteristic of the tide here that Low Water is more sharply defined than High Water and these curves have therefore been drawn with their times relative to that of Low Water.
- Apart from differences caused by referring the times to Low Water the procedure for obtaining intermediate heights at places whose curves are shown is identical to that used for normal Secondary Ports.
- The **height** differences for ports between Bournemouth and Yarmouth always refer to the higher High Water, i.e. that which is shown as reaching a factor of 1.0 on the curves. Note that the **time** differences, which are not required for this calculation, also refer to the higher High Water.
- The tide at ports between Bournemouth and Christchurch shows considerable change of shape and duration between Springs and Neaps and it is not practical to define the tide with only two curves. A third curve has therefore been drawn for the range at Portsmouth at which the two High Waters are equal at the port concerned – this range being marked on the body of the graph. Interpolation here should be between this "critical" curve and either the Spring or Neap curve as appropriate.

Note that while the critical curve extends throughout the tidal cycle the Spring and Neap curves stop at the higher High Water. Thus for a range at Portsmouth of 3.5m the factor for 7 hours after LW at Bournemouth should be referred to the following Low Water, whereas had the range at Portsmouth been 2.5, it should be referred to the preceding Low Water.

NOTES

1. NEWPORT. Owing to the constriction of the River Medina, Newport requires slightly different treatment since the harbour dries out at 1.4m. The calculation should be performed using the Low Water Time and Height Differences for Cowes and the High Water Height Differences for Newport. Any calculated heights which fall below 1.4m should be treated as 1.4m.
2. CHRISTCHURCH (Tuckton). Low Waters do not fall below 0.7m except under very low river flow conditions.

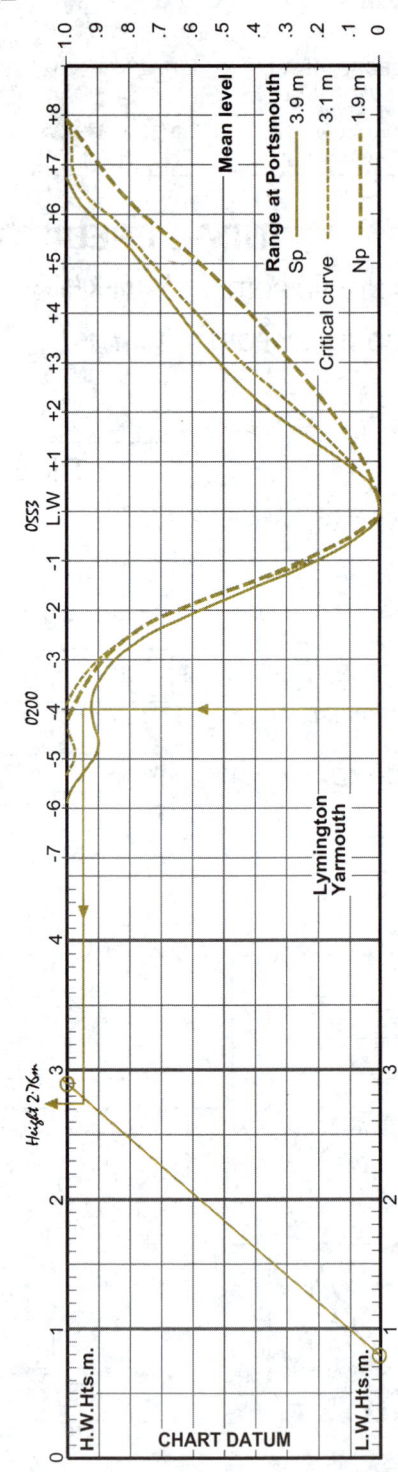

To find the Height of tide at a given time at any Secondary Port between Bournemouth and Selsey Bill

1. Complete top section of N.P. 204 (as below). Omit H.W. time column (Boxes 1,7,12)
2. On Standard Curve diagram (previous page), plot Secondary Port H.W. and L.W. heights and join by sloping line.
3. From the time required, using Secondary Port L.W. time, proceed vertically to curve, interpolating as necessary using Range at Portsmouth. Do NOT extrapolate.
4. Proceed horizontally to sloping line, thence vertically to Height Scale.
5. Read off height.

EXAMPLE:
Find the height of tide at LYMINGTON at 0200 UT on 18th November

From tables PORTSMOUTH	NOVEMBER 18 SA	0110 0613 1318 1833	4.6 1.1 4.6 1.0

From tables Location	Lat	Long	High Water 0000 and 1200	High Water 0600 and 1800	Low Water 0500 and 1700	Low Water 1100 and 2300	MHWS	MHWN	MLWN	MLWS
PORTSMOUTH Standard port	50°48'N	1°07'W					4.7	3.8	1.9	0.8
Lymington	50°46'N	1°32'W	−0110	+0005	−0020	−0020	−1.7	−1.2	−0.5	−0.1

STANDARD PORT ..... *Portsmouth* ..... TIME/HEIGHT REQUIRED 0200

SECONDARY PORT ..... *Lymington* ..... DATE *18 Nov* ..... TIME ZONE ..... UT

	TIME	TIME	HEIGHT	HEIGHT	
STANDARD PORT	HW	LW	HW	LW	RANGE
	1 −	2 0613	3 4.6	4 1.1	5 3.5
Seasonal change	Standard Ports −	Standard Ports −	6 0.0	6 0.0	
DIFFERENCES	7* −	8 −0020	9 −1.7	10 −0.2	
Seasonal change *	Secondary Ports +	Secondary Ports +	11 0.0	11 0.0	
SECONDARY PORT	12 −	13 0553	14 2.9	15 0.9	
Duration	16	−			

* The Seasonal changes are generally less than ± 0.1m and for most purposes can be ignored. See Admiralty Tide Tables Vol 1 for full details.

TIDES

TIDAL CURVES - BOURNEMOUTH TO FRESHWATER

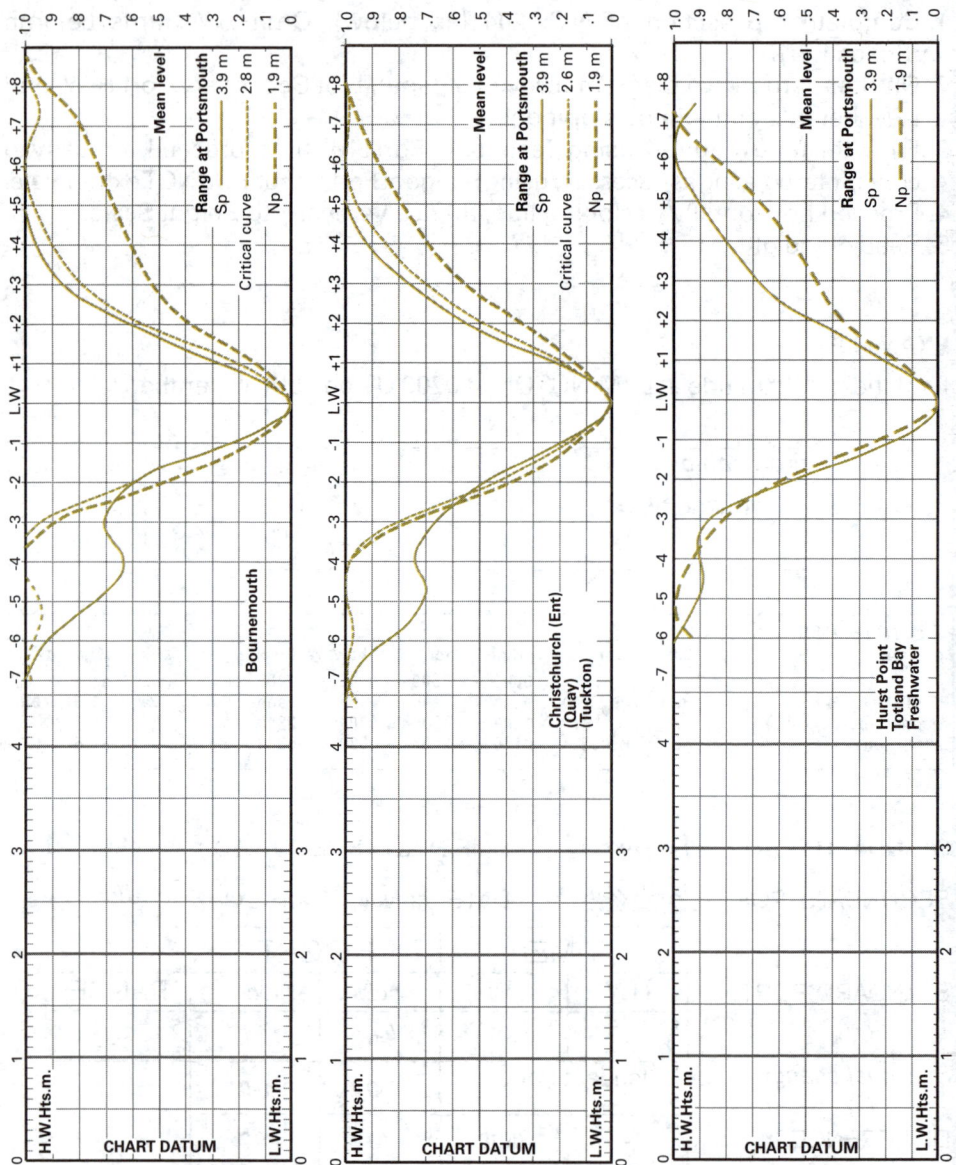

Note: The curves for Lymington and Yarmouth are on page 148, together with a worked example.

TIDAL CURVES - BUCKLERS HARD TO SELSEY BILL

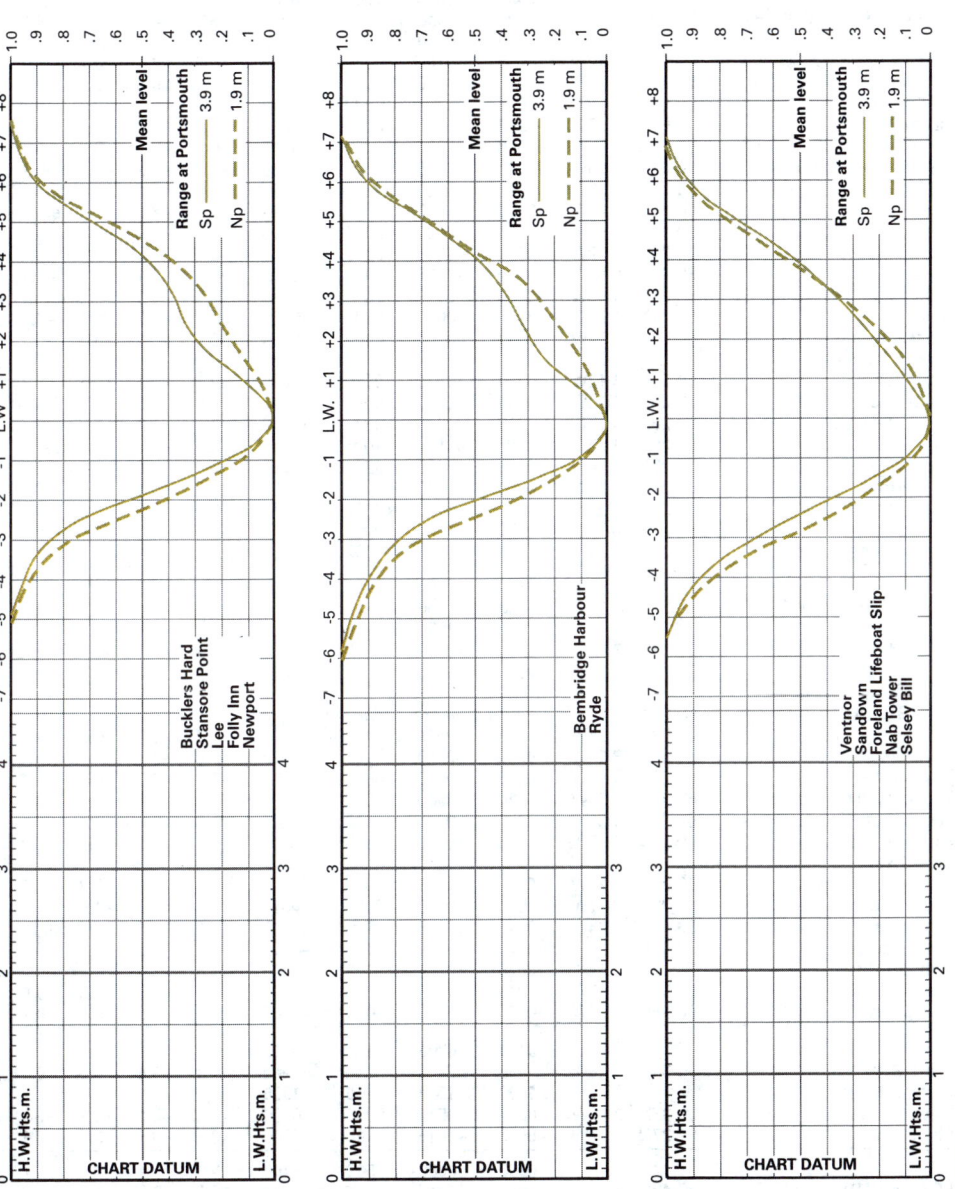

TIDES

SECONDARY PORTS: TIME & HEIGHT DIFFERENCES
SOUTH COAST OF ENGLAND *Time Zone UT*

Location	Lat	Long	High Water		Low Water		MHWS	MHWN	MLWN	MLWS
			0000	0600	0000	0600				
PLYMOUTH (DEVONPORT)	50 22N	4 11W	and	and	and	and	5.5	4.4	2.2	0.8
Standard port			1200	1800	1200	1800				
Isles of Scilly, St. Mary's	49 55N	6 19W	−0035	−0100	−0040	−0025	+0.2	−0.1	−0.2	−0.1
Penzance & Newlyn	50 06N	5 33W	−0040	−0110	−0035	−0025	+0.1	0.0	−0.2	0.0
Porthleven	50 05N	5 19W	−0045	−0105	−0030	−0025	0.0	−0.1	−0.2	0.0
Lizard Point	49 57N	5 12W	−0045	−0100	−0030	−0030	−0.2	−0.2	−0.3	−0.2
Coverack	50 01N	5 05W	−0030	−0050	−0020	−0015	−0.2	−0.2	−0.3	−0.2
Helford River Entrance	50 05N	5 05W	−0030	−0035	−0015	−0010	−0.2	−0.2	−0.3	−0.2
FALMOUTH	50 09N	5 03W	standard port (no secondaries)							
Truro	50 16N	5 03W	−0020	−0025	dries	dries	−2.0	−2.0	dries	
Mevagissey	50 16N	4 47W	−0015	−0020	−0010	−0005	−0.1	−0.1	−0.2	−0.1
Par	50 21N	4 42W	−0010	−0015	−0010	−0005	−0.4	−0.4	−0.4	−0.2
Fowey	50 20N	4 38W	−0010	−0015	−0010	−0005	−0.1	−0.1	−0.2	−0.2
Lostwithiel	50 24N	4 40W	+0005	−0010	dries	dries	−4.1	−4.1	dries	
Looe	50 21N	4 27W	−0010	−0010	−0005	−0005	−0.1	−0.2	−0.2	−0.2
Whitsand Bay	50 20N	4 15W	0000	0000	0000	0000	0.0	+0.1	−0.1	+0.2
River Tamar										
Saltash	50 24N	4 12W	0000	+0010	0000	−0005	+0.1	+0.1	+0.1	+0.1
Cargreen	50 26N	4 12W	0000	+0010	+0020	+0020	0.0	0.0	−0.1	0.0
Cotehele Quay	50 29N	4 13W	0000	+0020	+0045	+0045	−0.9	−0.9	−0.8	−0.4
Lopwell, R Tavy	50 28N	4 09W	no data	no data	dries	dries	−2.6	−2.7	dries	
Jupiter Point	50 23N	4 14W	+0010	+0005	0000	−0005	0.0	0.0	+0.1	0.0
St. Germans	50 23N	4 18W	0000	0000	+0020	+0020	−0.3	−0.1	0.0	+0.2
Turnchapel	50 22N	4 07W	0000	0000	+0010	−0015	0.0	+0.1	+0.2	+0.1
Bovisand Pier	50 20N	4 08W	0000	−0020	0000	−0010	−0.2	−0.1	0.0	+0.1
River Yealm Entrance	50 18N	4 04W	+0006	+0006	+0002	+0002	−0.1	−0.1	−0.1	−0.1
			0100	0600	0100	0600				
PLYMOUTH (DEVONPORT)	50 22N	4 11W	and	and	and	and	5.5	4.4	2.2	0.8
Standard port			1300	1800	1300	1800				
Salcombe	50 13N	3 47W	0000	+0010	+0005	−0005	−0.2	−0.3	−0.1	−0.1
Start Point	50 13N	3 39W	+0015	+0015	+0005	+0010	−0.1	−0.2	+0.1	+0.2
River Dart										
DARTMOUTH	50 21N	3 34W	standard port (no secondaries)							
Greenway Quay	50 23N	3 35W	+0030	+0045	+0025	+0005	−0.6	−0.6	−0.2	−0.2
Totnes	50 26N	3 41W	+0030	+0040	+0115	+0030	−2.0	−2.1	dries	
Torquay	50 28N	3 31W	+0025	+0045	+0010	0000	−0.6	−0.7	−0.2	−0.1
Teignmouth Approaches	50 33N	3 29W	+0020	+0050	+0025	0000	−0.9	−0.8	−0.2	−0.1
Teignmouth New Quay	50 33N	3 30W	+0025	+0055	+0040	+0005	−0.8	−0.8	−0.2	+0.1
Exmouth Approaches	50 36N	3 23W	+0030	+0050	+0015	+0005	−0.9	−1.0	−0.5	−0.3
River Exe										
Exmouth Dock	50 37N	3 25W	+0035	+0055	+0050	+0020	−1.5	−1.6	−0.9	−0.6
Starcross	50 38N	3 27W	+0040	+0110	+0055	+0025	−1.4	−1.5	−0.8	−0.1
Topsham	50 41N	3 28W	+0045	+0105	no data	no data	−1.5	−1.6	no data	
Lyme Regis	50 43N	2 56W	+0040	+0100	+0005	−0005	−1.2	−1.3	−0.5	−0.2
Bridport West Bay	50 42N	2 45W	+0025	+0040	0000	0000	−1.4	−1.4	−0.6	−0.2
Chesil Beach	50 37N	2 33W	+0040	+0055	−0005	+0010	−1.6	−1.5	−0.5	0.0
Chesil Cove	50 34N	2 28W	+0035	+0050	−0010	+0005	−1.5	−1.6	−0.5	−0.2
			0100	0700	0100	0700				
PORTLAND			and	and	and	and	2.1	1.4	0.8	0.1
Standard port	50 34N	2 26W	1300	1900	1300	1900				
Lulworth Cove	50 37N	2 15W	+0005	+0015	−0005	0000	+0.1	+0.1	+0.2	+0.1
Mupe Bay	50 37N	2 13W	+0005	+0015	−0005	0000	+0.1	+0.1	+0.2	+0.1
			0000	0600	0500	1100				
PORTSMOUTH	50 48N	1 07W	and	and	and	and	4.7	3.8	1.9	0.8
standard port			1200	1800	1700	2300				
Swanage	50 37N	1 57W	−0250	+0105	−0105	−0105	−2.7	−2.2	−0.7	−0.3
Poole Harbour Entrance	50 41N	1 57W	−0230	+0115	−0045	−0020	−2.5	−2.1	−0.6	−0.2
POOLE, TOWN QUAY	50 43N	1 59W	standard port							
Pottery Pier	50 42N	1 59W	−0150	+0200	−0010	0000	−2.7	−2.1	−0.6	0.0
Wareham *River Frome*	50 41N	2 06W	−0140	+0205	+0110	+0035	−2.5	−2.1	−0.7	+0.1
Cleavel Point	50 40N	2 00W	−0220	+0130	−0025	−0015	−2.6	−2.3	−0.7	−0.3
Bournemouth	50 43N	1 52W	−0240	+0055	−0050	−0030	−2.7	−2.2	−0.8	−0.3
Christchurch *Entrance*	50 43N	1 45W	−0230	+0030	−0035	−0035	−2.9	−2.4	−1.2	−0.2
Christchurch *Quay*	50 44N	1 46W	−0210	+0100	+0105	+0055	−2.9	−2.4	−1.0	0.0
Christchurch *Tuckton*	50 44N	1 47W	−0205	+0110	+0110	+0105	−3.0	−2.5	−1.0	+0.1

Location	Lat	Long	High Water		Low Water		MHWS	MHWN	MLWN	MLWS
Hurst Point	50 42N	1 33W	−0115	−0005	−0030	−0025	−2.0	−1.5	−0.5	−0.1
Lymington	50 46N	1 32W	−0110	+0005	−0020	−0020	−1.7	−1.2	−0.5	−0.1
Bucklers Hard	50 48N	1 25W	−0040	−0010	+0010	−0010	−1.0	−0.8	−0.2	−0.3
Stansore Point	50 47N	1 21W	−0050	−0010	−0005	−0010	−0.8	−0.5	−0.3	−0.1
Isle of Wight										
Yarmouth	50 42N	1 30W	−0105	+0005	−0025	−0030	−1.7	−1.2	−0.3	0.0
Totland Bay	50 41N	1 33W	−0130	−0045	−0035	−0045	−2.2	−1.7	−0.4	−0.1
Freshwater	50 40N	1 31W	−0210	+0025	−0040	−0020	−2.1	−1.5	−0.4	0.0
Ventnor	50 36N	1 12W	−0025	−0030	−0025	−0030	−0.8	−0.6	−0.2	+0.2
Sandown	50 39N	1 09W	0000	+0005	+0010	+0025	−0.6	−0.5	−0.2	0.0
Foreland *Lifeboat Slip*	50 41N	1 04W	−0005	0000	+0005	+0010	+0.1	+0.1	0.0	+0.1
Bembridge Harbour	50 42N	1 06W	+0020	0000	+0100	+0020	−1.5	−1.4	−1.3	−1.0
Ryde	50 44N	1 07W	−0010	+0010	−0005	−0010	−0.2	−0.1	0.0	+0.1
Medina River										
Cowes	50 46N	1 18W	−0015	+0015	0000	−0020	−0.5	−0.3	−0.1	0.0
Folly Inn	50 44N	1 17W	−0015	+0015	0000	−0020	−0.6	−0.4	−0.1	+0.2
Newport	50 42N	1 17W	no data	no data	no data	no data	−0.6	−0.4	+0.1	+0.8
SOUTHAMPTON	50 54N	1 24W	0400 and 1600	1100 and 2300	0000 and 1200	0600 and 1800	4.5	3.7	1.8	0.5
standard port										
Calshot Castle	50 49N	1 18W	0000	+0025	0000	0000	0.0	0.0	+0.2	+0.3
Redbridge	50 55N	1 28W	−0020	+0005	0000	−0005	−0.1	−0.1	−0.1	−0.1
River Hamble										
Warsash	50 51N	1 18W	+0020	+0010	+0010	0000	0.0	+0.1	+0.1	+0.3
Bursledon	50 53N	1 18W	+0020	+0020	+0010	+0010	+0.1	+0.1	+0.2	+0.2
PORTSMOUTH	50 48N	1 07W	0500 and 1700	1000 and 2200	0000 and 1200	0600 and 1800	4.7	3.8	1.9	0.8
standard port										
Lee-on-the-Solent	50 48N	1 12W	−0005	+0005	−0015	−0010	−0.2	−0.1	+0.1	+0.2
Chichester Harbour										
Entrance	50 47N	0 56W	−0010	+0005	+0015	+0020	+0.2	+0.2	0.0	+0.1
Northney	50 50N	0 58W	+0010	+0015	+0015	+0025	+0.2	0.0	−0.2	−0.3
Bosham	50 50N	0 52W	0000	+0010	no data	no data	+0.2	+0.1	no data	
Itchenor	50 48N	0 52W	−0005	+0005	+0005	+0025	+0.1	0.0	−0.2	−0.2
Dell Quay	50 49N	0 49W	+0005	+0015	no data	no data	+0.2	+0.1	no data	
Selsey Bill	50 43N	0 47W	+0010	−0010	+0035	+0020	+0.5	+0.2	−0.2	−0.2
Nab Tower	50 40N	0 57W	+0015	0000	+0015	+0015	−0.2	0.0	+0.2	0.0
SHOREHAM	50 50N	0 15W	0500 and 1700	1000 and 2200	0000 and 1200	0600 and 1800	6.3	4.8	1.9	0.6
standard port										
Pagham	50 46N	0 43W	+0015	0000	−0015	−0025	−0.7	−0.5	−0.1	−0.1
Bognor Regis	50 47N	0 40W	+0010	−0005	−0005	−0020	−0.6	−0.5	−0.2	−0.1
River Arun										
Littlehampton *Entrance*	50 48N	0 32W	+0010	0000	−0005	−0010	−0.4	−0.4	−0.2	−0.2
Littlehampton *UMA wharf*	50 48N	0 33W	+0015	+0005	0000	+0045	−0.7	−0.7	−0.3	+0.2
Arundel	50 51N	0 33W	no data	+0120	no data	no data	−3.1	−2.8	no data	
Worthing	50 48N	0 22W	+0010	0000	−0005	−0010	−0.1	−0.2	0.0	0.0
Brighton	50 49N	0 08W	0000	−0005	0000	0000	+0.3	+0.2	+0.1	0.0
Newhaven	50 47N	0 04E	−0015	−0010	0000	0000	+0.2	+0.1	−0.1	−0.2
Eastbourne	50 46N	0 17E	−0010	−0005	+0015	+0020	+1.1	+0.6	+0.2	+0.1
DOVER	51 07N	1 19E	0000 and 1200	0600 and 1800	0100 and 1300	0700 and 1900	6.8	5.3	2.1	0.8
standard port										
Hastings	50 51N	0 35E	0000	−0010	−0030	−0030	+0.8	+0.5	+0.1	−0.1
Rye *Approaches*	50 55N	0 47E	+0005	−0010	no data	no data	+1.0	+0.7	no data	
Rye *Harbour*	50 56N	0 46E	+0005	−0010	dries	dries	−1.4	−1.7	dries	
Dungeness	50 54N	0 58E	−0010	−0015	−0020	−0010	+1.0	+0.6	+0.4	+0.1
Folkestone	51 05N	1 12E	−0020	−0005	−0010	−0010	+0.4	+0.4	0.0	−0.1
Deal	51 13N	1 25E	+0010	+0020	+0010	+0005	−0.6	−0.3	0.0	0.0
Richborough	51 18N	1 21E	+0015	+0015	+0030	+0030	−3.4	−2.6	−1.7	−0.7
Ramsgate	51 20N	1 25E	+0030	+0030	+0017	+0007	−1.6	−1.3	−0.7	−0.2

EAST COAST ENGLAND *Time Zone UT*

Location	Lat	Long	High Water		Low Water		MHWS	MHWN	MLWN	MLWS
SHEERNESS	51 27N	0 45E	0200 and 1400	0800 and 2000	0200 and 1400	0700 and 1900	5.8	4.7	1.5	0.6
standard port										
Margate	51 23N	1 23E	−0050	−0040	−0020	−0050	−0.9	−0.9	−0.1	0.0
Herne Bay	51 23N	1 07E	−0025	−0015	0000	−0025	−0.5	−0.5	−0.1	−0.1
Whitstable	51 22N	1 02E	−0008	−0011	+0005	0000	−0.3	−0.3	0.0	−0.1

TIDES

Location	Lat	Long	High Water		Low Water		MHWS	MHWN	MLWN	MLWS
River Swale										
Grovehurst Jetty	51 22N	0 46E	−0007	0000	0000	+0016	0.0	0.0	0.0	−0.1
Faversham	51 19N	0 54E	no data	no data	no data	no data	−0.2	−0.2	no data	
River Medway										
Bee Ness	51 25N	0 39E	+0002	+0002	0000	+0005	+0.2	+0.1	0.0	0.0
Bartlett Creek	51 23N	0 38E	+0016	+0008	no data	no data	+0.1	0.0	no data	
Darnett Ness	51 24N	0 36E	+0004	+0004	0000	+0010	+0.2	+0.1	0.0	−0.1
Chatham *Lock approaches*	51 24N	0 33E	+0010	+0012	+0012	+0018	+0.3	+0.1	−0.1	−0.2
Upnor	51 25N	0 32E	+0015	+0015	+0015	+0025	+0.2	+0.2	−0.1	−0.1
Rochester *Strood Pier*	51 24N	0 30E	+0018	+0018	+0018	+0028	+0.2	+0.2	−0.2	−0.3
Wouldham	51 21N	0 27E	+0030	+0025	+0035	+0120	−0.2	−0.3	−1.0	−0.3
New Hythe	51 19N	0 28E	+0035	+0035	+0220	+0240	−1.6	−1.7	−1.2	−0.3
Allington Lock	51 17N	0 30E	+0050	+0035	no data	no data	−2.1	−2.2	−1.3	−0.4
River Thames										
Southend-on-Sea	51 31N	0 43E	−0005	0000	0000	+0005	0.0	0.0	−0.1	−0.1
Coryton	51 30N	0 31E	+0005	+0010	+0010	+0015	+0.4	+0.3	+0.1	−0.1
			0300	0900	0400	1100				
LONDON BRIDGE	51 30N	0 05W	and	and	and	and	7.1	5.9	1.3	0.5
standard port			1500	2100	1600	2300				
Albert Bridge	51 29N	0 10W	+0025	+0020	+0105	+0110	−0.9	−0.8	−0.7	−0.4
Hammersmith Bridge	51 29N	0 14W	+0040	+0035	+0205	+0155	−1.4	−1.3	−1.0	−0.5
Kew Bridge	51 29N	0 17W	+0055	+0050	+0255	+0235	−1.8	−1.8	−1.2	−0.5
Richmond Lock	51 28N	0 19W	+0105	+0055	+0325	+0305	−2.2	−2.2	−1.3	−0.5
			0200	0700	0100	0700				
SHEERNESS	51 27N	0 45E	and	and	and	and	5.8	4.7	1.5	0.6
standard port			1400	1900	1300	1900				
Thames Estuary *Shivering Sand*	51 30N	1 05E	−0025	−0019	−0008	−0026	−0.6	−0.6	−0.1	−0.1
			0000	0600	0500	1100				
WALTON-ON-THE-NAZE	51 51N	1 17E	and	and	and	and	4.2	3.4	1.1	0.4
standard port			1200	1800	1700	2300				
Whitaker Beacon	51 40N	1 06E	+0022	+0024	+0033	+0027	+0.6	+0.5	+0.2	+0.1
Holliwell Point	51 38N	0 56E	+0034	+0037	+0100	+0037	+1.1	+0.9	+0.3	+0.1
River Roach *Rochford*	51 35N	0 43E	+0050	+0040	dries	dries	−0.8	−1.1	dries	
River Crouch										
BURNHAM-ON-CROUCH	51 37N	0 48E	standard port - see full predictions page 263							
North Fambridge	51 38N	0 41E	+0115	+0050	+0130	+0100	+1.1	+0.8	0.0	−0.1
Hullbridge	51 38N	0 38E	+0115	+0050	+0135	+0105	+1.1	+0.8	0.0	−0.1
Battlesbridge	51 37N	0 34E	+0120	+0110	dries	dries	−1.8	−2.0	dries	
River Blackwater										
Bradwell Waterside	51 45N	0 53E	+0035	+0023	+0047	+0004	+1.0	+0.8	+0.2	0.0
Osea Island	51 43N	0 46E	+0057	+0045	+0050	+0007	+1.1	+0.9	+0.1	0.0
Maldon	51 44N	0 42E	+0107	+0055	no data	no data	−1.3	−1.1	no data	
West Mersea	51 47N	0 54E	+0035	+0015	+0055	+0010	+0.9	+0.4	+0.1	+0.1
River Colne										
Brightlingsea	51 48N	1 00E	+0025	+0021	+0046	+0004	+0.8	+0.4	+0.1	0.0
Colchester	51 53N	0 56E	+0035	+0025	dries	dries	0.0	−0.3	dries	
Clacton-on-Sea	51 47N	1 09E	+0012	+0010	+0025	+0008	+0.3	+0.1	+0.1	+0.1
Bramble Creek	51 53N	1 14E	+0010	−0007	−0005	+0010	+0.3	+0.3	+0.3	+0.3
Sunk Head	51 46N	1 30E	0000	+0002	−0002	+0002	−0.3	−0.3	−0.1	−0.1
Harwich	51 57N	1 17E	+0007	+0002	−0010	−0012	−0.2	0.0	0.0	0.0
Wrabness	51 57N	1 10E	+0017	+0015	−0010	−0012	−0.1	0.0	0.0	0.0
Mistley	51 57N	1 05E	+0032	+0027	−0010	−0012	0.0	0.0	−0.1	−0.1
Pin Mill	52 00N	1 17E	+0012	+0015	−0008	−0012	−0.1	0.0	0.0	0.0
Ipswich	52 03N	1 10E	+0022	+0027	0000	−0012	0.0	0.0	−0.1	−0.1
			0100	0700	0100	0700				
WALTON-ON-THE-NAZE	51 51N	1 17E	and	and	and	and	4.2	3.4	1.1	0.4
standard port			1300	1900	1300	1900				
Felixstowe Pier	51 57N	1 21E	−0005	−0007	−0018	−0020	−0.5	−0.4	0.0	0.0
River Deben										
Woodbridge Haven	51 59N	1 24E	0000	−0005	−0020	−0025	−0.5	−0.5	−0.1	+0.1
Woodbridge	52 05N	1 19E	+0045	+0025	+0025	−0020	−0.2	−0.3	−0.2	0.0
Bawdsey	52 00N	1 26E	−0016	−0020	−0030	−0032	−0.8	−0.6	−0.1	−0.1
Orford Haven										
Bar	52 02N	1 28E	−0026	−0030	−0036	−0038	−1.0	−0.8	−0.1	0.0
Orford Quay	52 05N	1 32E	+0040	+0040	+0055	+0055	−1.4	−1.1	0.0	+0.2
Slaughden Quay	52 08N	1 36E	+0105	+0105	+0125	+0125	−1.3	−0.8	−0.1	+0.2
Iken Cliffs	52 09N	1 31E	+0130	+0130	+0155	+0155	−1.3	−1.0	0.0	+0.2

Location	Lat	Long	High Water		Low Water		MHWS	MHWN	MLWN	MLWS
			0300	0900	0200	0800				
LOWESTOFT	52 28N	1 45E	and	and	and	and	2.4	2.1	1.0	0.5
standard port			1500	2100	1400	2000				
Orford Ness	52 05N	1 35E	+0135	+0135	+0135	+0125	+0.4	+0.6	−0.1	0.0
Aldeburgh	52 09N	1 36E	+0130	+0130	+0115	+0120	+0.3	+0.2	−0.1	−0.2
Minsmere Sluice	52 14N	1 38E	+0110	+0110	+0110	+0110	0.0	−0.1	−0.2	−0.2
Southwold	52 19N	1 40E	+0105	+0105	+0055	+0055	0.0	0.0	−0.1	0.0
Great Yarmouth										
Gorleston-on-Sea	52 34N	1 44E	−0035	−0035	−0030	−0030	0.0	0.0	0.0	0.0
Britannia Pier	52 36N	1 45E	−0105	−0100	−0040	−0055	+0.1	+0.1	0.0	0.0
Caister-on-Sea	52 39N	1 44E	−0120	−0120	−0100	−0100	0.0	−0.1	0.0	0.0
Winterton-on-Sea	52 43N	1 42E	−0225	−0215	−0135	−0135	+0.8	+0.5	+0.2	+0.1
			0100	0700	0100	0700				
IMMINGHAM	53 38N	0 11E	and	and	and	and	7.3	5.8	2.6	0.9
standard port			1300	1900	1300	1900				
Cromer	52 56N	1 18E	+0050	+0030	+0050	+0130	−2.1	−1.7	−0.5	−0.1
Blakeney Bar	52 59N	0 59E	+0035	+0025	+0030	+0040	−1.6	−1.3	*no data*	
Blakeney	52 57N	1 01E	+0115	+0055	*no data*	*no data*	−3.9	−3.8	*no data*	
Wells Bar	52 59N	0 49E	+0020	+0020	+0020	+0020	−1.3	−1.0	*no data*	
Wells	52 57N	0 51E	+0035	+0045	+0340	+0310	−3.8	−3.8	*not below CD*	
Burnham *Overy Staithe*	52 58N	0 48E	+0045	+0055	*no data*	*no data*	−5.0	−4.9	*no data*	
The Wash										
Hunstanton	52 56N	0 29E	+0010	+0020	+0105	+0025	+0.1	−0.2	−0.1	0.0
West Stones	52 50N	0 21E	+0025	+0025	+0115	+0040	−0.3	−0.4	−0.3	+0.2
King's Lynn	52 45N	0 24E	+0030	+0030	+0305	+0140	−0.5	−0.8	−0.8	+0.1
Wisbech Cut	52 48N	0 13E	+0020	+0025	+0200	+0030	−0.3	−0.7	−0.4	*no data*
Lawyer's Creek	52 53N	0 05E	+0010	+0020	*no data*	*no data*	−0.3	−0.6	*no data*	
Tabs Head	52 56N	0 05E	0000	+0005	+0125	+0020	+0.2	−0.2	−0.2	−0.2
Boston	52 58N	0 01W	0000	+0010	+0140	+0050	−0.5	−1.0	−0.9	−0.5
Skegness	53 09N	0 21E	+0010	+0015	+0030	+0020	−0.4	−0.5	−0.1	0.0
Inner Dowsing Light Tower	53 20N	0 34E	0000	0000	+0010	+0010	−0.9	−0.7	−0.1	+0.3
River Humber										
Bull Sand Fort	53 34N	0 04E	−0020	−0030	−0035	−0015	−0.4	−0.3	+0.1	+0.2
Grimsby	53 35N	0 04W	−0012	−0012	−0015	−0015	−0.2	−0.1	0.0	+0.2
Hull *King George Dock*	53 44N	0 16W	+0010	+0010	+0021	+0017	+0.3	+0.2	−0.1	−0.2
Hull *Albert Dock*	53 44N	0 21W	+0019	+0019	+0033	+0027	+0.3	+0.1	−0.1	−0.2
Humber Bridge	53 43N	0 27W	+0027	+0022	+0049	+0039	−0.1	−0.4	−0.7	−0.6
River Trent										
Burton Stather	53 39N	0 42W	+0105	+0045	+0335	+0305	−2.1	−2.3	−2.3	*dries*
Flixborough Wharf	53 37N	0 42W	+0120	+0100	+0400	+0340	−2.3	−2.6	*dries*	
Keadby	53 36N	0 44W	+0135	+0120	+0425	+0410	−2.5	−2.8	*dries*	
Owston Ferry	53 29N	0 46W	+0155	+0145	*dries*	*dries*	−3.5	−3.9	*dries*	
River Ouse										
Blacktoft	53 42N	0 43W	+0100	+0055	+0325	+0255	−1.6	−1.8	−2.2	−1.1
Goole	53 42N	0 52W	+0130	+0115	+0355	+0350	−1.6	−2.1	−1.9	−0.6
			0200	0800	0100	0800				
R. TYNE, N. SHIELDS	55 01N	1 26W	and	and	and	and	5.0	3.9	1.8	0.7
standard port			1400	2000	1300	2000				
Bridlington	54 05N	0 11W	+0119	+0109	+0109	+0104	+1.1	+0.8	+0.5	+0.4
Filey Bay	54 13N	0 16W	+0101	+0101	+0101	+0048	+0.8	+1.0	+0.6	+0.2
Scarborough	54 17N	0 23W	+0059	+0059	+0044	+0044	+0.7	+0.7	+0.5	+0.2
Whitby	54 29N	0 37W	+0034	+0049	+0034	+0019	+0.6	+0.4	+0.1	+0.1
Middlesbrough	54 35N	1 13W	+0019	+0021	+0014	+0011	+0.6	+0.6	+0.3	+0.1
Hartlepool	54 41N	1 11W	+0015	+0015	+0008	+0008	+0.4	+0.3	0.0	+0.1
Seaham	54 50N	1 19W	+0004	+0004	−0001	−0001	+0.2	+0.2	+0.2	0.0
Sunderland	54 55N	1 21W	+0002	−0002	−0002	−0002	+0.2	+0.3	+0.2	+0.1
Newcastle-upon-Tyne	54 58N	1 36W	+0003	+0003	+0008	+0008	+0.3	+0.2	+0.1	+0.1
Blyth	55 07N	1 29W	+0005	−0007	−0001	+0009	0.0	0.0	−0.1	+0.1
Coquet Island	55 20N	1 32W	−0010	−0010	−0020	−0020	+0.1	+0.1	0.0	+0.1
Amble	55 20N	1 34W	−0013	−0013	−0016	−0020	0.0	0.0	+0.1	+0.1
North Sunderland	55 34N	1 38W	−0048	−0044	−0058	−0102	−0.2	−0.2	−0.2	0.0
Holy Island	55 40N	1 47W	−0043	−0039	−0105	−0110	−0.2	−0.2	−0.3	−0.1
Berwick	55 47N	2 00W	−0053	−0053	−0109	−0109	−0.3	−0.1	−0.5	−0.1
SCOTLAND *Time Zone UT*			0300	0900	0300	0900				
LEITH	55 59N	3 11W	and	and	and	and	5.6	4.4	2.0	0.8
standard port			1500	2100	1500	2100				
Eyemouth	55 52N	2 05W	−0003	+0008	+0011	+0005	−0.5	−0.4	−0.1	0.0
Dunbar	56 00N	2 31W	−0003	+0003	+0003	−0003	−0.3	−0.3	0.0	+0.1
Fidra	56 04N	2 47W	−0001	0000	−0002	+0001	−0.2	−0.2	0.0	0.0

TIDES

Location	Lat	Long	High Water		Low Water		MHWS	MHWN	MLWN	MLWS
Cockenzie	55 58N	2 57W	−0007	−0015	−0013	−0005	−0.2	0.0	no data	
Granton	55 59N	3 13W	0000	0000	0000	0000	0.0	0.0	0.0	0.0
Grangemouth	56 02N	3 41W	+0025	+0010	−0052	−0015	−0.1	−0.2	−0.3	−0.3
Kincardine	56 04N	3 43W	+0015	+0030	−0030	−0030	0.0	−0.2	−0.5	−0.3
Alloa	56 07N	3 48W	+0040	+0040	+0025	+0025	−0.2	−0.5	no data	−0.7
Stirling	56 07N	3 56W	+0100	+0100	no data		−2.9	−3.1	−2.3	−0.7
Firth of Forth										
Burntisland	56 03N	3 14W	+0013	+0004	−0002	+0007	+0.1	0.0	+0.1	+0.2
Kirkcaldy	56 09N	3 09W	+0005	0000	−0004	−0001	−0.3	−0.3	−0.2	−0.2
Methil	56 11N	3 00W	−0005	−0001	−0001	−0001	−0.1	−0.1	−0.1	−0.1
Anstruther Easter	56 13N	2 42W	−0018	−0012	−0006	−0008	−0.3	−0.2	0.0	0.0
ABERDEEN standard port	57 09N	2 05W	0000 and 1200	0600 and 1800	0100 and 1300	0700 and 1900	4.3	3.4	1.6	0.6
River Tay										
Bar	56 27N	2 38W	+0100	+0100	+0050	+0110	+0.9	+0.8	+0.3	+0.1
Dundee	56 27N	2 58W	+0140	+0120	+0055	+0145	+1.1	+0.9	+0.3	+0.1
Newburgh	56 21N	3 14W	+0215	+0200	+0250	+0335	−0.2	−0.4	−1.1	−0.5
Perth	56 24N	3 27W	+0220	+0225	+0510	+0530	−0.9	−1.4	−1.2	−0.3
Arbroath	56 33N	2 35W	+0056	+0037	+0034	+0055	+0.7	+0.7	+0.2	+0.1
Montrose	56 42N	2 27W	+0055	+0055	+0030	+0040	+0.5	+0.4	+0.2	0.0
Stonehaven	56 58N	2 12W	+0013	+0008	+0013	+0009	+0.2	+0.2	+0.1	0.0
Peterhead	57 30N	1 46W	−0035	−0045	−0035	−0040	−0.5	−0.3	−0.1	−0.1
Fraserburgh	57 41N	2 00W	−0105	−0115	−0120	−0110	−0.6	−0.5	−0.2	0.0
ABERDEEN standard port	57 09N	2 05W	0200 and 1400	0900 and 2100	0400 and 1600	0900 and 2100	4.3	3.4	1.6	0.6
Banff	57 40N	2 31W	−0100	−0150	−0150	−0050	−0.4	−0.2	−0.1	+0.2
Whitehills	57 41N	2 35W	−0122	−0137	−0117	−0127	−0.4	−0.3	+0.1	+0.1
Buckie	57 40N	2 58W	−0130	−0145	−0125	−0140	−0.2	−0.2	0.0	+0.1
Lossiemouth	57 43N	3 18W	−0125	−0200	−0130	−0130	−0.2	−0.2	0.0	0.0
Burghead	57 42N	3 29W	−0120	−0150	−0135	−0120	−0.2	−0.2	0.0	0.0
Nairn	57 36N	3 52W	−0120	−0150	−0135	−0130	0.0	−0.1	0.0	+0.1
McDermott Base	57 36N	3 59W	−0110	−0140	−0120	−0115	−0.1	−0.1	+0.1	+0.3
ABERDEEN standard port	57 09N	2 05W	0300 and 1500	1000 and 2200	0000 and 1200	0700 and 1900	4.3	3.4	1.6	0.6
Inverness Firth										
Fortrose	57 35N	4 08W	−0125	−0125	−0125	−0125	0.0	0.0	no data	
Inverness	57 30N	4 15W	−0050	−0150	−0200	−0150	+0.5	+0.3	+0.2	+0.1
Cromarty Firth										
Cromarty	57 42N	4 03W	−0120	−0155	−0155	−0120	0.0	0.0	+0.1	+0.2
Invergordon	57 41N	4 10W	−0105	−0200	−0200	−0110	+0.1	+0.1	+0.1	+0.1
Dingwall	57 36N	4 25W	−0045	−0145	no data	no data	+0.1	+0.2	no data	
ABERDEEN standard port	57 09N	2 05W	0300 and 1500	0800 and 2000	0200 and 1400	0800 and 2000	4.3	3.4	1.6	0.6
Dornoch Firth										
Portmahomack	57 50N	3 50W	−0120	−0210	−0140	−0110	−0.2	−0.1	+0.1	+0.1
Meikle Ferry	57 51N	4 08W	−0100	−0140	−0120	−0055	+0.1	0.0	−0.1	0.0
Golspie	57 58N	3 59W	−0130	−0215	−0155	−0130	−0.3	−0.3	−0.1	0.0
WICK standard port	58 26N	3 05W	0000 and 1200	0700 and 1900	0200 and 1400	0700 and 1900	3.5	2.8	1.4	0.7
Helmsdale	58 07N	3 39W	+0025	+0015	+0035	+0030	+0.4	+0.3	+0.1	0.0
Duncansby Head	58 39N	3 02W	−0115	−0115	−0110	−0110	−0.4	−0.4	no data	
Orkney Islands										
Muckle Skerry	58 41N	2 55W	−0025	−0025	−0020	−0020	−0.9	−0.8	−0.4	−0.3
Burray Ness	58 51N	2 52W	+0005	+0005	+0015	+0015	−0.2	−0.3	−0.1	−0.1
Deer Sound	58 58N	2 50W	−0040	−0040	−0035	−0035	−0.3	−0.3	−0.1	−0.1
Kirkwall	58 59N	2 58W	−0042	−0042	−0041	−0041	−0.5	−0.4	−0.1	−0.1
Loth	59 12N	2 42W	−0052	−0052	−0058	−0058	−0.1	0.0	+0.3	+0.4
Kettletoft Pier	59 14N	2 36W	−0025	−0025	−0015	−0015	0.0	0.0	+0.2	+0.2
Rapness	59 15N	2 52W	−0205	−0205	−0205	−0205	+0.1	0.0	+0.2	0.0
Pierowall	59 19N	2 58W	−0150	−0150	−0145	−0145	+0.2	0.0	0.0	−0.1

Location	Lat	Long	High Water		Low Water		MHWS	MHWN	MLWN	MLWS
Tingwall	59 05N	3 02W	−0200	−0125	−0145	−0125	−0.4	−0.4	−0.1	−0.1
Stromness	58 58N	3 18W	−0225	−0135	−0205	−0205	+0.1	−0.1	0.0	0.0
St. Mary's	58 54N	2 55W	−0140	−0140	−0140	−0140	−0.2	−0.2	0.0	−0.1
Widewall Bay	58 49N	3 01W	−0155	−0155	−0150	−0150	+0.1	−0.1	−0.1	−0.3
Bur Wick	58 44N	2 58W	−0100	−0100	−0150	−0150	−0.1	−0.1	+0.2	+0.1
			0000	0600	0100	0800				
LERWICK	60 09N	1 08W	and	and	and	and	2.1	1.7	0.9	0.5
standard port			1200	1800	1300	2000				
Fair Isle	59 32N	1 36W	−0006	−0015	−0031	−0037	+0.1	0.0	+0.1	+0.1
Shetland Islands										
Sumburgh *Grutness Voe*	59 53N	1 17W	+0006	+0008	+0004	−0002	−0.3	−0.3	−0.2	−0.1
Dury Voe	60 21N	1 10W	−0015	−0015	−0010	−0010	0.0	−0.1	0.0	−0.2
Out Skerries	60 25N	0 45W	−0025	−0025	−0010	−0010	+0.1	0.0	0.0	−0.1
Toft Pier	60 28N	1 12W	−0105	−0100	−0125	−0115	+0.2	+0.1	−0.1	−0.1
Burra Voe *Yell Sound*	60 30N	1 03W	−0025	−0025	−0025	−0025	+0.2	+0.1	0.0	−0.1
Mid Yell	60 36N	1 03W	−0030	−0020	−0035	−0025	+0.3	+0.2	+0.2	+0.1
Balta Sound	60 45N	0 50W	−0055	−0055	−0045	−0045	+0.2	+0.1	0.0	−0.1
Burra Firth	60 48N	0 52W	−0110	−0110	−0115	−0115	+0.4	+0.2	0.0	0.0
Bluemull Sound	60 42N	1 00W	−0135	−0135	−0155	−0155	+0.5	+0.2	+0.1	0.0
Sullom Voe	60 27N	1 18W	−0135	−0125	−0135	−0120	0.0	0.0	−0.2	−0.2
Hillswick	60 29N	1 29W	−0220	−0220	−0200	−0200	−0.1	−0.1	−0.1	−0.1
Scalloway	60 08N	1 16W	−0150	−0150	−0150	−0150	−0.5	−0.4	−0.3	0.0
Bay of Quendale	59 54N	1 20W	−0025	−0025	−0030	−0030	−0.4	−0.3	0.0	+0.1
Foula	60 07N	2 03W	−0140	−0130	−0140	−0120	−0.1	−0.1	0.0	0.0
			0200	0700	0100	0700				
WICK	58 26N	3 05W	and	and	and	and	3.5	2.8	1.4	0.7
Standard port			1400	1900	1300	1900				
Stroma	58 40N	3 08W	−0115	−0115	−0110	−0110	−0.4	−0.5	−0.1	−0.2
Gills Bay	58 38N	3 10W	−0150	−0150	−0202	−0202	+0.7	+0.7	+0.6	+0.3
Scrabster	58 37N	3 33W	−0255	−0225	−0240	−0230	+1.5	+1.2	+0.8	+0.3
Sule Skerry	59 05N	4 24W	−0320	−0255	−0315	−0250	+0.4	+0.3	+0.2	+0.1
Loch Eriboll Portnancon	58 30N	4 42W	−0340	−0255	−0315	−0255	+1.6	+1.3	+0.8	+0.4
Kyle of Durness	58 36N	4 47W	−0350	−0350	−0315	−0315	+1.1	+0.7	+0.4	−0.1
Rona	59 08N	5 49W	−0410	−0345	−0330	−0340	−0.1	−0.2	−0.2	−0.1
			0100	0700	0300	0900				
STORNOWAY	58 12N	6 23W	and	and	and	and	4.8	3.7	2.0	0.7
standard port			1300	1900	1500	2100				
Outer Hebrides										
Loch Shell	58 00N	6 25W	−0013	0000	0000	−0017	0.0	−0.1	−0.1	0.0
E. Loch Tarbert	57 54N	6 48W	−0025	−0010	−0010	−0020	+0.2	0.0	+0.1	+0.1
Loch Maddy	57 36N	7 06W	−0044	−0014	−0016	−0030	0.0	−0.1	−0.1	0.0
Loch Carnan	57 22N	7 16W	−0050	−0010	−0020	−0040	−0.3	−0.5	−0.1	−0.1
Loch Skiport	57 20N	7 16W	−0100	−0025	−0024	−0024	−0.2	−0.4	−0.3	−0.2
Loch Boisdale	57 09N	7 16W	−0055	−0030	−0020	−0040	−0.7	−0.7	−0.3	−0.2
Barra *North Bay*	57 00N	7 24W	−0103	−0031	−0034	−0048	−0.6	−0.5	−0.2	−0.1
Castle Bay	56 57N	7 29W	−0115	−0040	−0045	−0100	−0.5	−0.6	−0.3	−0.1
Barra Head	56 47N	7 38W	−0115	−0040	−0045	−0055	−0.8	−0.7	−0.2	+0.1
Shillay	57 31N	7 41W	−0103	−0043	−0047	−0107	−0.6	−0.7	−0.7	−0.3
Balivanich	57 29N	7 23W	−0103	−0017	−0031	−0045	−0.7	−0.6	−0.5	−0.2
Scolpaig	57 39N	7 29W	−0033	−0033	−0040	−0040	−1.0	−0.9	−0.5	0.0
Leverburgh	57 46N	7 01W	−0025	−0025	−0015	−0025	−0.2	−0.2	−0.1	−0.1
W. Loch Tarbert	57 55N	6 55W	−0015	−0015	−0046	−0046	−1.1	−0.9	−0.5	0.0
Little Bernera	58 16N	6 52W	−0021	−0011	−0017	−0027	−0.5	−0.6	−0.4	−0.2
Carloway	58 17N	6 47W	−0040	+0020	−0035	−0015	−0.6	−0.5	−0.4	−0.1
St Kilda Village Bay	57 48N	8 34W	−0040	−0040	−0045	−0045	−1.4	−1.2	−0.8	−0.3
Flannan Isles	58 16N	7 36W	−0026	−0016	−0016	−0026	−0.9	−0.7	−0.6	−0.2
Rockall	57 36N	13 41W	−0055	−0055	−0105	−0105	−1.8	−1.5	−0.9	−0.2
			0000	0600	0300	0900				
ULLAPOOL	57 54N	5 10W	and	and	and	and	5.2	3.9	2.1	0.7
standard port			1200	1800	1500	2100				
Loch Bervie	58 27N	5 03W	+0030	+0010	+0010	+0020	−0.3	−0.3	−0.2	0.0
Loch Laxford	58 24N	5 05W	+0015	+0015	+0005	+0005	−0.3	−0.4	−0.2	0.0
Eddrachillis Bay										
Badcall Bay	58 19N	5 08W	+0005	+0005	+0005	+0005	−0.7	−0.5	−0.5	+0.2
Loch Nedd	58 14N	5 10W	0000	0000	0000	0000	−0.3	−0.2	−0.2	0.0
Loch Inver	58 09N	5 18W	−0005	−0005	−0005	−0005	−0.2	0.0	0.0	+0.1

TIDES

Location	Lat	Long	High Water		Low Water		MHWS	MHWN	MLWN	MLWS
Summer Isles Tanera Mor	58 01N	5 24W	−0005	−0005	−0010	−0010	−0.1	+0.1	0.0	+0.1
Loch Ewe Mellon Charles	57 51N	5 38W	−0010	−0010	−0010	−0010	−0.1	−0.1	−0.1	0.0
Loch Gairloch Gairloch	57 43N	5 41W	−0020	−0020	−0010	−0010	0.0	+0.1	−0.3	−0.1
Loch Torridon Shieldaig	57 31N	5 39W	−0020	−0020	−0015	−0015	+0.4	+0.3	+0.1	0.0
Inner Sound Applecross	57 26N	5 49W	−0010	−0015	−0010	−0010	0.0	0.0	0.0	+0.1
Loch Carron Plockton	57 20N	5 39W	+0005	−0025	−0005	−0010	+0.5	+0.5	+0.5	+0.2
Rona Loch a' Bhraige	57 35N	5 58W	−0020	0000	−0010	0000	−0.1	−0.1	−0.1	−0.2
Skye										
Broadford Bay	57 15N	5 54W	−0015	−0015	−0010	−0015	+0.2	+0.1	+0.1	0.0
Portree	57 24N	6 11W	−0025	−0025	−0025	−0025	+0.1	−0.2	−0.2	0.0
Loch Snizort (Uig Bay)	57 35N	6 22W	−0045	−0025	−0005	−0025	+0.1	−0.4	−0.2	0.0
Loch Dunvegan	57 27N	6 38W	−0105	−0030	−0020	−0040	0.0	−0.1	0.0	0.0
Loch Harport	57 20N	6 25W	−0115	−0035	−0020	−0100	−0.1	−0.1	0.0	+0.1
Soay Camus nan Gall	57 09N	6 13W	−0055	−0025	−0025	−0045	−0.4	−0.2	no data	
Loch Alsh										
Kyle of Lochalsh	57 17N	5 43W	−0040	−0020	−0005	−0025	+0.1	0.0	0.0	−0.1
Dornie Bridge	57 17N	5 31W	−0040	−0010	−0005	−0020	+0.1	−0.1	0.0	0.0
Kyle Rhea Glenelg Bay	57 13N	5 38W	−0105	−0035	−0035	−0055	−0.4	−0.4	−0.9	−0.1
Loch Hourn	57 06N	5 34W	−0125	−0050	−0040	−0110	−0.2	−0.1	−0.1	+0.1
			0000 and 1200	0600 and 1800	0100 and 1300	0700 and 1900				
OBAN *standard port*	56 25N	5 29W					4.0	2.9	1.8	0.7
Loch Nevis										
Inverie Bay	57 02N	5 41W	+0030	+0020	+0035	+0020	+1.0	+0.9	+0.2	0.0
Mallaig	57 00N	5 50W	+0017	+0017	+0017	+0017	+1.0	+0.7	+0.3	+0.1
Eigg Bay of Laig	56 55N	6 10W	+0015	+0030	+0040	+0005	+0.7	+0.6	−0.2	−0.2
Loch Moidart	56 47N	5 53W	+0015	+0015	+0040	+0020	+0.8	+0.6	−0.2	−0.2
Coll Loch Eatharna	56 37N	6 31W	+0025	+0010	+0015	+0025	+0.4	+0.3	no data	
Tiree Gott Bay	56 31N	6 48W	0000	+0010	+0005	+0010	0.0	+0.1	0.0	0.0
			0100 and 1300	0700 and 1900	0100 and 1300	0800 and 2000				
OBAN *standard port*	56 25N	5 29W					4.0	2.9	1.8	0.7
Mull										
Carsaig Bay	56 19N	5 59W	−0015	−0005	−0030	+0020	+0.1	+0.2	0.0	−0.1
Iona	56 19N	6 23W	−0010	−0005	−0020	+0015	0.0	+0.1	−0.3	−0.2
Bunessan	56 19N	6 14W	−0015	−0015	−0010	−0015	+0.3	+0.1	0.0	−0.1
Ulva Sound	56 29N	6 08W	−0010	−0015	0000	−0005	+0.4	+0.3	0.0	−0.1
Loch Sunart Salen	56 42N	5 47W	−0015	+0015	+0010	+0005	+0.6	+0.5	−0.1	−0.1
Sound of Mull										
Tobermory	56 37N	6 04W	+0025	+0010	+0015	+0025	+0.4	+0.4	0.0	0.0
Salen	56 31N	5 57W	+0045	+0015	+0020	+0030	+0.2	+0.2	−0.1	0.0
Loch Aline	56 32N	5 46W	+0012	+0012	no data	no data	+0.5	+0.3	no data	
Craignure	56 28N	5 42W	+0030	+0005	+0010	+0015	0.0	+0.1	−0.1	−0.1
Loch Linnhe										
Corran	56 43N	5 14W	+0007	+0007	+0004	+0004	+0.4	+0.4	−0.1	0.0
Corpach	56 50N	5 07W	0000	+0020	+0040	0000	0.0	0.0	−0.2	−0.2
Loch Eil Head	56 51N	5 20W	+0025	+0045	+0105	+0025	no data		no data	
Loch Leven Head	56 43N	5 00W	+0045	+0045	+0045	+0045	no data		no data	
Loch Linnhe Port Appin	56 33N	5 25W	−0005	−0005	−0030	0000	+0.2	+0.2	+0.1	+0.1
Loch Creran										
Barcaldine Pier	56 32N	5 19W	+0010	+0020	+0040	+0015	+0.1	+0.1	0.0	+0.1
Loch Creran Head	56 33N	5 16W	+0015	+0025	+0120	+0020	−0.3	−0.3	−0.4	−0.3
Loch Etive										
Dunstaffnage Bay	56 27N	5 26W	+0005	0000	0000	+0005	+0.1	+0.1	+0.1	+0.1
Connel	56 27N	5 24W	+0020	+0005	+0010	+0015	−0.3	−0.2	−0.1	+0.1
Bonawe	56 27N	5 13W	+0150	+0205	+0240	+0210	−2.0	−1.7	−1.3	−0.5
Seil Sound	56 18N	5 35W	−0035	−0015	−0040	−0015	−1.3	−0.9	−0.7	−0.3
Colonsay Scalasaig	56 04N	6 10W	−0020	−0005	−0015	+0005	−0.1	−0.2	−0.2	−0.2
Jura Glengarrisdale Bay	56 06N	5 47W	−0020	0000	−0010	0000	−0.4	−0.2	0.0	−0.2
Islay										
Rubha A'Mhail	55 56N	6 07W	−0020	0000	+0005	−0015	−0.3	−0.1	−0.3	−0.1
Ardnave Point	55 52N	6 20W	−0035	+0010	0000	−0025	−0.4	−0.2	−0.3	−0.1
Orsay	55 41N	6 31W	−0110	−0110	−0040	−0040	−1.4	−0.6	−0.5	−0.2
Bruichladdich	55 48N	6 22W	−0105	−0035	−0110	−0110	−1.8	−1.3	−0.4	+0.1
Port Ellen	55 38N	6 11W	−0530	−0050	−0045	−0530	−3.1	−2.1	−1.3	−0.4
Port Askaig	55 51N	6 06W	−0110	−0030	−0020	−0020	−1.9	−1.4	−0.8	−0.3
Sound of Jura										
Craighouse	55 50N	5 57W	−0230	−0250	−0150	−0230	−3.0	−2.4	−1.3	−0.6

Location	Lat	Long	High Water		Low Water		MHWS	MHWN	MLWN	MLWS
Loch Melfort	56 15N	5 29W	−0055	−0025	−0040	−0035	−1.2	−0.8	−0.5	−0.1
Loch Beag	56 09N	5 36W	−0110	−0045	−0035	−0045	−1.6	−1.2	−0.8	−0.4
Carsaig Bay	56 02N	5 38W	−0105	−0040	−0050	−0050	−2.1	−1.6	−1.0	−0.4
Sound of Gigha	55 41N	5 44W	−0450	−0210	−0130	−0410	−2.5	−1.6	−1.0	−0.1
Machrihanish	55 25N	5 45W	−0520	−0350	−0340	−0540	Mean range 0.5 metres			
			0000	0600	0000	0600				
GREENOCK	55 57N	4 46W	and	and	and	and	**3.4**	**2.8**	**1.0**	**0.3**
standard port			1200	1800	1200	1800				
Firth of Clyde										
Southend, Kintyre	55 19N	5 38W	−0030	−0010	+0005	+0035	−1.3	−1.2	−0.5	−0.2
Campbeltown	55 25N	5 36W	−0025	−0005	−0015	+0005	−0.5	−0.3	+0.1	+0.2
Carradale	55 36N	5 28W	−0015	−0005	−0005	+0005	−0.3	−0.2	+0.1	+0.1
Loch Ranza	55 43N	5 18W	−0015	−0005	−0010	−0005	−0.4	−0.3	−0.1	0.0
Loch Fyne										
East Loch Tarbert	55 52N	5 24W	−0005	−0005	0000	−0005	+0.2	+0.1	0.0	0.0
Inveraray	56 14N	5 04W	+0011	+0011	+0034	+0034	−0.1	+0.1	−0.5	−0.2
Kyles of Bute										
Rubha a'Bhodaich	55 55N	5 09W	−0020	−0010	−0007	−0007	−0.2	−0.1	+0.2	+0.2
Tighnabruich	55 55N	5 13W	+0007	−0010	−0002	−0015	0.0	+0.2	+0.4	+0.5
Firth of Clyde – continued										
Millport	55 45N	4 56W	−0005	−0025	−0025	−0005	0.0	−0.1	0.0	+0.1
Rothesay Bay	55 51N	5 03W	−0020	−0015	−0010	−0002	+0.2	+0.2	+0.2	+0.2
Wemyss Bay	55 53N	4 53W	−0005	−0005	−0005	−0005	0.0	0.0	+0.1	+0.1
Loch Long										
Coulport	56 03N	4 53W	−0011	−0011	−0008	−0008	0.0	0.0	0.0	0.0
Lochgoilhead	56 10N	4 54W	+0015	0000	−0005	−0005	−0.2	−0.3	−0.3	−0.3
Arrochar	56 12N	4 45W	−0005	−0005	−0005	−0005	0.0	0.0	−0.1	−0.1
Gareloch										
Rosneath	56 01N	4 47W	−0005	−0005	−0005	−0005	0.0	−0.1	0.0	0.0
Faslane	56 04N	4 49W	−0010	−0010	−0010	−0010	0.0	0.0	−0.1	−0.2
Garelochhead	56 05N	4 50W	0000	0000	0000	0000	0.0	0.0	0.0	−0.1
River Clyde										
Helensburgh	56 00N	4 44W	0000	0000	0000	0000	0.0	0.0	0.0	0.0
Port Glasgow	55 56N	4 41W	+0010	+0005	+0010	+0020	+0.2	+0.1	0.0	0.0
Bowling	55 56N	4 29W	+0020	+0010	+0030	+0055	+0.6	+0.5	+0.3	+0.1
Clydebank *Rothesay Dock*	55 54N	4 24W	+0025	+0015	+0035	+0100	+1.0	+0.8	+0.5	+0.4
Glasgow	55 51N	4 16W	+0025	+0015	+0035	+0105	+1.3	+1.2	+0.6	+0.4
Firth of Clyde – continued										
Brodick Bay	55 35N	5 08W	0000	0000	+0005	+0005	−0.2	−0.2	0.0	0.0
Lamlash	55 32N	5 07W	−0016	−0036	−0024	−0004	−0.2	−0.2	no data	
Ardrossan	55 38N	4 49W	−0020	−0010	−0010	−0010	−0.2	−0.2	+0.1	+0.1
Irvine	55 36N	4 41W	−0020	−0020	−0030	−0010	−0.3	−0.3	−0.1	0.0
Troon	55 33N	4 41W	−0025	−0025	−0020	−0020	−0.2	−0.2	0.0	0.0
Ayr	55 28N	4 39W	−0025	−0025	−0030	−0015	−0.4	−0.3	+0.1	+0.1
Girvan	55 15N	4 52W	−0025	−0040	−0035	−0010	−0.3	−0.3	−0.1	0.0
Loch Ryan *Stranraer*	54 55N	5 03W	−0030	−0025	−0010	−0010	−0.2	−0.1	0.0	+0.1

WEST COAST ENGLAND *Time Zone UT*

Location	Lat	Long	High Water		Low Water		MHWS	MHWN	MLWN	MLWS
			0000	0600	0200	0800				
LIVERPOOL	53 24N	3 01W	and	and	and	and	**9.3**	**7.4**	**2.9**	**0.9**
standard port			1200	1800	1400	2000				
Portpatrick	54 50N	5 07W	+0018	+0026	0000	−0035	−5.5	−4.4	−2.0	−0.6
Luce Bay										
Drummore	54 41N	4 53W	+0030	+0040	+0015	+0020	−3.4	−2.5	−0.9	−0.3
Port William	54 46N	4 35W	+0030	+0030	+0025	0000	−2.9	−2.2	−0.8	no data
Wigtown Bay										
Isle of Whithorn	54 42N	4 22W	+0020	+0025	+0025	+0005	−2.4	−2.0	−0.8	−0.2
Garlieston	54 47N	4 22W	+0025	+0035	+0030	+0005	−2.3	−1.7	−0.5	no data
Solway Firth										
Kirkcudbright Bay	54 48N	4 04W	+0015	+0015	+0010	0000	−1.8	−1.5	−0.5	−0.1
Hestan Islet	54 50N	3 48W	+0025	+0025	+0020	+0025	−1.0	−1.1	−0.5	0.0
Southerness Point	54 52N	3 36W	+0030	+0030	+0030	+0010	−0.7	−0.7	no data	
Annan Waterfoot	54 58N	3 16W	+0050	+0105	+0220	+0310	−2.2	−2.6	−2.7	
Torduff Point	54 58N	3 09W	+0105	+0140	+0520	+0410	−4.1	−4.9		
Redkirk	54 59N	3 06W	+0110	+0215	+0715	+0445	−5.5	−6.2		
Silloth	54 52N	3 24W	+0030	+0040	+0045	+0055	−0.1	−0.3	−0.6	−0.1
Maryport	54 43N	3 30W	+0017	+0032	+0020	+0005	−0.7	−0.8	−0.4	0.0
Workington	54 39N	3 34W	+0020	+0020	+0020	+0010	−1.2	−1.1	−0.3	0.0
Whitehaven	54 33N	3 36W	+0005	+0015	+0010	+0005	−1.3	−1.1	−0.5	+0.1
Tarn Point	54 17N	3 25W	+0005	+0005	+0010	0000	−1.0	−1.0	−0.4	0.0
Duddon Bar	54 09N	3 20W	+0003	+0003	+0008	+0002	−0.8	−0.8	−0.3	0.0

TIDES

Location	Lat	Long	High Water		Low Water		MHWS	MHWN	MLWN	MLWS
			0000 and 1200	0600 and 1800	0200 and 1400	0700 and 1900				
LIVERPOOL standard port	53 24N	3 01W					9.3	7.4	2.9	0.9
Barrow-in-Furness	54 06N	3 12W	+0015	+0015	+0015	+0015	0.0	−0.3	+0.1	+0.2
Ulverston	54 11N	3 04W	+0020	+0040	no data	no data	0.0	−0.1	no data	
Arnside	54 12N	2 51W	+0100	+0135	no data	no data	+0.5	+0.2	no data	
Morecambe	54 04N	2 52W	+0005	+0010	+0030	+0015	+0.2	0.0	0.0	+0.2
Heysham	54 02N	2 55W	+0005	+0005	+0015	0000	+0.1	0.0	0.0	+0.2
River Lune Glasson Dock	54 00N	2 51W	+0020	+0030	+0220	+0240	−2.7	−3.0	no data	
Lancaster	54 03N	2 49W	+0110	+0030	dries	dries	−5.0	−4.9	dries	
River Wyre										
Wyre Lighthouse	53 57N	3 02W	−0010	−0010	+0005	0000	−0.1	−0.1	no data	
Fleetwood	53 56N	3 00W	−0008	−0008	−0003	−0003	−0.1	−0.1	+0.1	+0.3
Blackpool	53 49N	3 04W	−0015	−0005	−0005	−0015	−0.4	−0.4	−0.1	+0.1
River Ribble Preston	53 46N	2 45W	+0010	+0010	+0335	+0310	−4.0	−4.1	−2.8	−0.8
Liverpool Bay										
Southport	53 39N	3 01W	−0020	−0010	no data	no data	−0.3	−0.3	no data	
Formby	53 32N	3 07W	−0015	−0010	−0020	−0020	−0.3	−0.1	0.0	+0.1
River Mersey										
Gladstone Dock	53 27N	3 01W	−0003	−0003	−0003	−0003	−0.1	−0.1	0.0	−0.1
Eastham	53 19N	2 57W	+0010	+0010	+0009	+0009	+0.3	+0.1	−0.1	−0.3
Hale Head	53 19N	2 48W	+0030	+0025	no data	no data	−2.4	−2.5	no data	
Widnes	53 21N	2 44W	+0040	+0045	+0400	+0345	−4.2	−4.4	−2.5	−0.3
Fiddler's Ferry	53 22N	2 39W	+0100	+0115	+0540	+0450	−5.9	−6.3	−2.4	−0.4
River Dee										
Hilbre Island	53 23N	3 13W	−0015	−0012	−0010	−0015	−0.3	−0.2	+0.2	+0.4
Mostyn Docks	53 19N	3 16W	−0020	−0015	−0020	−0020	−0.8	−0.7	no data	
Connah's Quay	53 13N	3 03W	0000	+0015	+0355	+0340	−4.6	−4.4	dries	
Chester	53 12N	2 54W	+0105	+0105	+0500	+0500	−5.3	−5.4	dries	
Isle of Man										
Peel	54 14N	4 42W	+0005	+0005	−0015	−0025	−4.1	−3.1	−1.4	−0.5
Ramsey	54 19N	4 22W	+0005	+0015	−0005	−0015	−1.9	−1.5	−0.6	0.0
Douglas	54 09N	4 28W	+0005	+0015	−0015	−0025	−2.4	−2.0	−0.5	−0.1
Port St. Mary	54 04N	4 44W	+0005	+0015	−0010	−0030	−3.4	−2.6	−1.3	−0.4
Calf Sound	54 04N	4 48W	+0005	+0015	−0015	−0025	−3.2	−2.6	−0.9	−0.3
Port Erin	54 05N	4 46W	−0005	+0015	−0010	−0050	−4.1	−3.2	−1.3	−0.5

WALES *Time Zone UT*

Location	Lat	Long	High Water		Low Water		MHWS	MHWN	MLWN	MLWS
Colwyn Bay	53 18N	3 43W	−0020	−0020	no data	no data	−1.5	−1.3	no data	
Llandudno	53 20N	3 50W	−0020	−0020	−0035	−0040	−1.7	−1.4	−0.7	−0.3
			0000 and 1200	0600 and 1800	0500 and 1700	1100 and 2300				
HOLYHEAD standard port	53 19N	4 37W					5.6	4.4	2.0	0.7
Conwy	53 17N	3 50W	+0025	+0035	+0120	+0105	+2.3	+1.8	+0.6	+0.4
Menai Strait										
Beaumaris	53 16N	4 05W	+0025	+0010	+0055	+0035	+2.0	+1.6	+0.5	+0.1
Menai Bridge	53 13N	4 09W	+0030	+0010	+0100	+0035	+1.7	+1.4	+0.3	0.0
Port Dinorwic	53 11N	4 13W	−0015	−0025	+0030	0000	0.0	0.0	0.0	+0.1
Caernarfon	53 09N	4 16W	−0030	−0030	+0015	−0005	−0.4	−0.4	−0.1	−0.1
Fort Belan	53 07N	4 20W	−0040	−0015	−0025	−0005	−1.0	−0.9	−0.2	−0.1
Trwyn Dinmor	53 19N	4 03W	+0025	+0015	+0050	+0035	+1.9	+1.5	+0.5	+0.2
Moelfre	53 20N	4 14W	+0025	+0020	+0050	+0035	+1.9	+1.4	+0.5	+0.2
Amlwch	53 25N	4 20W	+0020	+0010	+0035	+0025	+1.6	+1.3	+0.5	+0.2
Cemaes Bay	53 25N	4 27W	+0020	+0025	+0040	+0035	+1.0	+0.7	+0.3	+0.1
Trearddur Bay	53 16N	4 37W	−0045	−0025	−0015	−0015	−0.4	−0.4	0.0	+0.1
Porth Trecastell	53 12N	4 30W	−0045	−0025	−0005	−0015	−0.6	−0.6	0.0	0.0
Llanddwyn Island	53 08N	4 25W	−0115	−0055	−0030	−0020	−0.7	−0.5	−0.1	0.0
Trefor	53 00N	4 25W	−0115	−0100	−0030	−0020	−0.8	−0.9	−0.2	−0.1
Porth Dinllaen	52 57N	4 34W	−0120	−0105	−0035	−0025	−1.0	−1.0	−0.2	−0.2
Porth Ysgaden	52 54N	4 39W	−0125	−0110	−0040	−0035	−1.1	−1.0	−0.1	−0.1
Bardsey Island	52 46N	4 47W	−0220	−0240	−0145	−0140	−1.2	−1.2	−0.5	−0.1
			0100 and 1300	0800 and 2000	0100 and 1300	0700 and 1900				
MILFORD HAVEN standard port	51 42N	5 03W					7.0	5.2	2.5	0.7
Cardigan Bay										
Aberdaron	52 48N	4 43W	+0210	+0200	+0240	+0310	−2.4	−1.9	−0.6	−0.2
St. Tudwal's Roads	52 49N	4 29W	+0155	+0145	+0240	+0310	−2.2	−1.9	−0.7	−0.2
Pwllheli	52 53N	4 24W	+0210	+0150	+0245	+0320	−2.0	−1.8	−0.6	−0.2
Criccieth	52 55N	4 14W	+0210	+0155	+0255	+0320	−2.0	−1.8	−0.7	−0.3
Porthmadog	52 55N	4 08W	+0235	+0210	no data	no data	−1.9	−1.8	no data	
Barmouth	52 43N	4 03W	+0215	+0205	+0310	+0320	−2.0	−1.7	−0.7	0.0

Location	Lat	Long	High Water		Low Water		MHWS	MHWN	MLWN	MLWS
Aberdovey	52 32N	4 03W	+0215	+0200	+0230	+0305	−2.0	−1.7	−0.5	0.0
Aberystwyth	52 24N	4 05W	+0145	+0130	+0210	+0245	−2.0	−1.7	−0.7	0.0
New Quay	52 13N	4 21W	+0150	+0125	+0155	+0230	−2.1	−1.8	−0.6	−0.1
Aberporth	52 08N	4 33W	+0135	+0120	+0150	+0220	−2.1	−1.8	−0.6	−0.1
Port Cardigan	52 07N	4 42W	+0140	+0120	+0220	+0130	−2.3	−1.8	−0.5	0.0
Cardigan *Town*	52 05N	4 40W	+0220	+0150	no data	no data	−2.2	−1.6	no data	
Fishguard	52 00N	4 58W	+0115	+0100	+0110	+0135	−2.2	−1.8	−0.5	+0.1
Porthgain	51 57N	5 11W	+0055	+0045	+0045	+0100	−2.5	−1.8	−0.6	0.0
Ramsey Sound	51 53N	5 19W	+0030	+0030	+0030	+0030	−1.9	−1.3	−0.3	0.0
Solva	51 52N	5 12W	+0015	+0010	+0035	+0015	−1.5	−1.0	−0.2	0.0
Little Haven	51 46N	5 06W	+0010	+0010	+0025	+0015	−1.1	−0.8	−0.2	0.0
Martin's Haven	51 44N	5 15W	+0010	+0010	+0015	+0015	−0.8	−0.5	+0.1	+0.1
Skomer Island	51 44N	5 17W	−0005	−0005	+0005	+0005	−0.4	−0.1	0.0	0.0
Dale Roads	51 42N	5 09W	−0005	−0005	−0008	−0008	0.0	0.0	0.0	−0.1
Cleddau River										
Neyland	51 42N	4 57W	+0002	+0010	0000	0000	0.0	0.0	0.0	0.0
Black Tar	51 45N	4 54W	+0010	+0020	+0005	0000	+0.1	+0.1	0.0	−0.1
Haverfordwest	51 48N	4 58W	+0010	+0025	dries	dries	−4.8	−4.9	dries	
Stackpole Quay	51 37N	4 54W	−0005	+0025	−0010	−0010	+0.9	+0.7	+0.2	+0.3
Tenby	51 40N	4 42W	−0015	−0010	−0015	−0020	+1.4	+1.1	+0.5	+0.2
Towy River										
Ferryside	51 46N	4 22W	0000	−0010	+0220	0000	−0.3	−0.7	−1.7	−0.6
Carmarthen	51 51N	4 18W	+0010	0000	dries	dries	−4.4	−4.8	dries	
Burry Inlet										
Burry Port	51 41N	4 15W	+0003	+0003	+0007	+0007	+1.6	+1.4	+0.5	+0.4
Llanelli	51 40N	4 10W	−0003	−0003	+0150	+0020	+0.8	+0.6	no data	
Mumbles	51 34N	3 58W	+0005	+0010	−0020	−0015	+2.3	+1.7	+0.6	+0.2
River Neath Entrance	51 37N	3 51W	+0002	+0011	dries	dries	+2.7	+2.2	dries	
Port Talbot	51 35N	3 49W	+0003	+0005	−0010	−0003	+2.6	+2.2	+1.0	+0.5
Porthcawl	51 28N	3 42W	+0005	+0010	−0010	−0005	+2.9	+2.3	+0.8	+0.3
			0600	1100	0300	0800				
BRISTOL, AVONMOUTH	51 30N	2 44W	and	and	and	and	**13.2**	**9.8**	**3.8**	**1.0**
standard port			1800	2300	1500	2000				
Barry	51 23N	3 16W	−0030	−0015	−0125	−0030	−1.8	−1.3	+0.2	0.0
Flat Holm	51 23N	3 07W	−0015	−0015	−0045	−0045	−1.3	−1.1	−0.2	+0.2
Steep Holm	51 20N	3 06W	−0020	−0020	−0050	−0050	−1.6	−1.2	−0.2	−0.2
Cardiff	51 27N	3 09W	−0015	−0015	−0100	−0030	−1.0	−0.6	+0.1	0.0
Newport	51 33N	2 59W	−0020	−0010	0000	−0020	−1.1	−1.0	−0.6	−0.7
River Wye Chepstow	51 39N	2 40W	+0020	+0020	no data	no data	no data		no data	
			0000	0600	0000	0700				
BRISTOL, AVONMOUTH	51 30N	2 44W	and	and	and	and	**13.2**	**9.8**	**3.8**	**1.0**
standard port			1200	1800	1200	1900				

WEST COAST ENGLAND Time Zone UT

Location	Lat	Long	High Water		Low Water		MHWS	MHWN	MLWN	MLWS
River Severn										
Sudbrook	51 35N	2 43W	+0010	+0010	+0025	+0015	+0.2	+0.1	−0.1	+0.1
Beachley *Aust*	51 36N	2 38W	+0010	+0015	+0040	+0025	−0.2	−0.2	−0.5	−0.3
Inward Rocks	51 39N	2 37W	+0020	+0020	+0105	+0045	−1.0	−1.1	−1.4	−0.6
Narlwood Rocks	51 39N	2 36W	+0025	+0025	+0120	+0100	−1.9	−2.0	−2.3	−0.8
White House	51 40N	2 33W	+0025	+0025	+0145	+0120	−3.0	−3.1	−3.6	−1.0
Berkeley	51 42N	2 30W	+0030	+0045	+0245	+0220	−3.8	−3.9	−3.4	−0.5
Sharpness Dock	51 43N	2 29W	+0035	+0050	+0305	+0245	−3.9	−4.2	−3.3	−0.4
Wellhouse Rock	51 44N	2 29W	+0040	+0055	+0320	+0305	−4.1	−4.4	−3.1	−0.2
Epney	51 42N	2 24W	+0130	no data	no data	no data	−9.4	no data	no data	
Minsterworth	51 50N	2 23W	+0140	no data	no data	no data	−10.1	no data	no data	
Llanthony	51 51N	2 21W	+0215	no data	no data	no data	−10.7	no data	no data	
			0200	0800	0300	0800				
BRISTOL, AVONMOUTH	51 30N	2 44W	and	and	and	and	**13.2**	**9.8**	**3.8**	**1.0**
standard port			1400	2000	1500	2000				
River Avon										
Shirehampton	51 29N	2 41W	0000	0000	+0035	+0010	−0.7	−0.7	−0.8	0.0
Sea Mills	51 29N	2 39W	+0005	+0005	+0105	+0030	−1.4	−1.5	−1.7	−0.1
Cumberland Basin *Entrance*	51 27N	2 37W	+0010	+0010	dries	dries	−2.9	−3.0	dries	
Portishead	51 30N	2 45W	−0002	0000	no data	no data	−0.1	−0.1	no data	
Clevedon	51 27N	2 52W	−0010	−0020	−0025	−0015	−0.4	−0.2	+0.2	0.0
St Thomas Head	51 24N	2 56W	0000	0000	−0030	−0030	−0.4	−0.2	+0.1	+0.1
English & Welsh Grounds	51 28N	2 59W	−0008	−0008	−0030	−0030	−0.5	−0.8	−0.3	0.0
Weston–super–Mare	51 21N	2 59W	−0020	−0030	−0130	−0030	−1.2	−1.0	−0.8	−0.2
River Parrett										
Burnham-on-Sea	51 14N	3 00W	−0020	−0025	−0030	0000	−2.3	−1.9	−1.4	−1.1
Bridgwater	51 08N	3 00W	−0015	−0030	+0305	+0455	−8.6	−8.1	dries	

TIDES

Location	Lat	Long	High Water		Low Water		MHWS	MHWN	MLWN	MLWS
Hinkley Point	51 13N	3 08W	−0020	−0025	−0100	−0040	−1.7	−1.4	−0.2	−0.2
Watchet	51 11N	3 20W	−0035	−0050	−0145	−0040	−1.9	−1.5	+0.1	+0.1
Minehead	51 13N	3 28W	−0037	−0052	−0155	−0045	−2.6	−1.9	−0.2	0.0
Porlock Bay	51 13N	3 38W	−0045	−0055	−0205	−0050	−3.0	−2.2	−0.1	−0.1
Lynmouth	51 14N	3 49W	−0055	−0115	no data	no data	−3.6	−2.7	no data	
			0100	0700	0100	0700				
MILFORD HAVEN	51 42N	5 03W	and	and	and	and	7.0	5.2	2.5	0.7
standard port			1300	1900	1300	1900				
Ilfracombe	51 13N	4 07W	−0016	−0016	−0041	−0031	+2.3	+1.8	+0.6	+0.3
Rivers Taw & Torridge										
Appledore	51 03N	4 12W	−0020	−0025	+0015	−0045	+0.5	0.0	−0.9	−0.5
Yelland Marsh	51 04N	4 10W	−0010	−0015	+0100	−0015	+0.1	−0.4	−1.2	−0.6
Fremington	51 05N	4 07W	−0010	−0015	+0030	−0030	−1.1	−1.8	−2.2	−0.5
Barnstaple	51 05N	4 04W	0000	−0015	−0155	−0245	−2.9	−3.8	−2.2	−0.4
Bideford	51 01N	4 12W	−0020	−0025	0000	0000	−1.1	−1.6	−2.5	−0.7
Clovelly	51 00N	4 24W	−0030	−0030	−0020	−0040	+1.3	+1.1	+0.2	+0.2
Lundy	51 10N	4 40W	−0025	−0025	−0020	−0035	+1.0	+0.7	+0.2	0.0
Bude	50 50N	4 33W	−0040	−0040	−0035	−0045	+0.7	+0.6	no data	
Boscastle	50 41N	4 42W	−0045	−0010	−0110	−0100	+0.3	+0.4	+0.2	+0.2
Port Isaac	50 35N	4 50W	−0100	−0100	−0100	−0100	+0.5	+0.6	0.0	+0.2
River Camel										
Padstow	50 33N	4 56W	−0055	−0050	−0040	−0050	+0.3	+0.4	+0.1	+0.1
Wadebridge	50 31N	4 50W	−0052	−0052	+0235	+0245	−3.8	−3.8	−2.5	−0.4
Newquay	50 25N	5 05W	−0100	−0110	−0105	−0050	0.0	+0.1	0.0	−0.1
Perranporth	50 21N	5 09W	−0100	−0110	−0110	−0050	−0.1	0.0	0.0	+0.1
St. Ives	50 13N	5 28W	−0050	−0115	−0105	−0040	−0.4	−0.3	−0.1	−0.1
Cape Cornwall	50 08N	5 42 W	−0130	−0145	−0120	−0120	−1.0	−0.9	−0.5	−0.1
Sennen Cove	50 04N	5 42W	−0130	−0145	−0125	−0125	−0.9	−0.4	no data	

IRELAND *Time Zone UT*

Location	Lat	Long	High Water		Low Water		MHWS	MHWN	MLWN	MLWS
			0000	0700	0000	0500				
DUBLIN, NORTH WALL	53 21N	6 13W	and	and	and	and	4.1	3.4	1.5	0.7
standard port			1200	1900	1200	1700				
Courtown	52 39N	6 13W	−0328	−0242	−0158	−0138	−2.8	−2.4	−0.5	0.0
Arklow	52 47N	6 08W	−0315	−0201	−0140	−0134	−2.7	−2.2	−0.6	−0.1
Wicklow	52 59N	6 02W	−0019	−0019	−0024	−0026	−1.4	−1.1	−0.4	0.0
Greystones	53 09N	6 04W	−0008	−0008	−0008	−0008	−0.5	−0.4	no data	
Dun Laoghaire	53 18N	6 08W	−0006	−0001	−0002	−0003	0.0	0.0	0.0	+0.1
Dublin Bar	53 21N	6 09W	−0006	−0001	−0002	−0003	0.0	0.0	0.0	+0.1
Howth	53 23N	6 04W	−0007	−0005	+0001	+0005	0.0	−0.1	−0.2	−0.2
Malahide	53 27N	6 09W	+0002	+0003	+0009	+0009	+0.1	−0.2	−0.4	−0.2
Balbriggan	53 37N	6 11W	−0021	−0015	+0010	+0002	+0.3	+0.2	no data	
River Boyne Bar	53 43N	6 14W	−0005	0000	+0020	+0030	+0.4	+0.3	−0.1	−0.2
Dunany Point	53 52N	6 14W	−0028	−0018	−0008	−0006	+0.7	+0.9	no data	
Dundalk Soldiers Point	54 00N	6 21W	−0010	−0010	0000	+0045	+1.0	+0.8	+0.1	−0.1

NORTHERN IRELAND *Time Zone UT*

Location	Lat	Long	High Water		Low Water		MHWS	MHWN	MLWN	MLWS
Carlingford Lough										
Cranfield Point	54 01N	6 03W	−0027	−0011	+0005	−0010	+0.7	+0.9	+0.3	+0.2
Warrenpoint	54 06N	6 15W	−0020	−0010	+0025	+0035	+1.0	+0.7	+0.2	+0.0
Newry *Victoria Lock*	54 09N	6 19W	+0005	+0015	+0045	dries	+1.2	+0.9	+0.1	dries
			0100	0700	0000	0600				
BELFAST	54 36N	5 55W	and	and	and	and	3.5	3.0	1.1	0.4
standard port			1300	1900	1200	1800				
Kilkeel	54 03N	5 59W	+0040	+0030	+0010	+0010	+1.2	+1.1	+0.4	+0.4
Newcastle	54 12N	5 53W	+0025	+0035	+0020	+0040	+1.6	+1.1	+0.4	+0.1
Killough Harbour	54 15N	5 38W	0000	+0020	no data	no data	+1.8	+1.6	no data	
Ardglass	54 16N	5 36W	+0010	+0015	+0005	+0010	+1.7	+1.2	+0.6	+0.3
Strangford Lough										
Killard Point	54 19N	5 31W	+0011	+0021	+0005	+0025	+1.0	+0.8	+0.1	+0.1
Strangford	54 22N	5 33W	+0147	+0157	+0148	+0208	+0.1	+0.1	−0.2	0.0
Quoile Barrier	54 22N	5 41W	+0150	+0200	+0150	+0300	+0.2	+0.2	−0.3	−0.1
Killyleagh	54 24N	5 39W	+0157	+0207	+0211	+0231	+0.3	+0.3	no data	
South Rock	54 24N	5 25W	+0023	+0023	+0025	+0025	+1.0	+0.8	+0.1	+0.1
Portavogie	54 28N	5 26W	+0010	+0020	+0010	+0020	+1.2	+0.9	+0.3	+0.2
Donaghadee	54 38N	5 32W	+0020	+0020	+0023	+0023	+0.5	+0.4	0.0	+0.1
Carrickfergus	54 43N	5 48W	+0005	+0005	+0005	+0005	−0.3	−0.3	−0.2	−0.1
Larne	54 51N	5 47W	+0005	0000	+0010	−0005	−0.7	−0.5	−0.3	0.0
Red Bay	55 04N	6 03W	+0022	−0010	+0007	−0017	−1.9	−1.5	−0.8	−0.2
Cushendun	55 08N	6 02W	+0010	−0030	0000	−0025	−1.7	−1.5	−0.6	−0.2
Portrush	55 12N	6 40W	−0433	−0433	−0433	−0433	−1.6	−1.6	−0.3	0.0
Coleraine	55 08N	6 40W	−0403	−0403	−0403	−0403	−1.3	−1.2	−0.2	0.0

Location	Lat	Long	High Water		Low Water		MHWS	MHWN	MLWN	MLWS
			0200 and 1400	0900 and 2100	0200 and 1400	0800 and 2000				
GALWAY standard port	53 16N	9 03W					5.1	3.9	2.0	0.6
Londonderry	55 00N	7 19W	+0254	+0319	+0322	+0321	–2.4	–1.8	–0.8	–0.1
IRELAND *Time Zone UT*										
Inishtrahull	55 26N	7 14W	+0100	+0100	+0115	+0200	–1.8	–1.4	–0.4	–0.2
Portmore	55 22N	7 20W	+0120	+0120	+0135	+0135	–1.3	–1.1	–0.4	–0.1
Trawbreaga Bay	55 19N	7 23W	+0115	+0059	+0109	+0125	–1.1	–0.8	no data	
Lough Swilly										
Rathmullan	55 05N	7 31W	+0125	+0050	+0126	+0118	–0.8	–0.7	–0.1	–0.1
Fanad Head	55 16N	7 38W	+0115	+0040	+0125	+0120	–1.1	–0.9	–0.5	–0.1
Mulroy Bay										
Bar	55 15N	7 46W	+0108	+0052	+0102	+0118	–1.2	–1.0	no data	
Fanny's Bay	55 12N	7 49W	+0145	+0129	+0151	+0207	–2.2	–1.7	no data	
Seamount Bay	55 11N	7 44W	+0210	+0154	+0226	+0242	–3.1	–2.3	no data	
Cranford Bay	55 09N	7 42W	+0329	+0313	+0351	+0407	–3.7	–2.8	no data	
Sheephaven										
Downies Bay	55 11N	7 50W	+0057	+0043	+0053	+0107	–1.1	–0.9	no data	
Inishbofin Bay	55 10N	8 10W	+0040	+0026	+0032	+0046	–1.2	–0.9	no data	
			0600 and 1800	1100 and 2300	0000 and 1200	0700 and 1900				
GALWAY standard port	53 16N	9 03W					5.1	3.9	2.0	0.6
Gweedore Harbour	55 04N	8 19W	+0048	+0100	+0055	+0107	–1.3	–1.0	–0.5	–0.1
Burtonport	54 59N	8 26W	+0042	+0055	+0115	+0055	–1.2	–1.0	–0.6	–0.1
Loughros More Bay	54 47N	8 30W	+0042	+0054	+0046	+0058	–1.1	–0.9	no data	
Donegal Bay										
Killybegs	54 38N	8 26W	+0040	+0050	+0055	+0035	–1.0	–0.9	–0.5	0.0
Donegal Hbr *Salt Hill Quay*	54 38N	8 13W	+0038	+0050	+0052	+0104	–1.2	–0.9	no data	
Mullaghmore	54 28N	8 27W	+0036	+0048	+0047	+0059	–1.4	–1.0	–0.4	–0.2
Sligo Harbour *Oyster Island*	54 18N	8 34W	+0043	+0055	+0042	+0054	–1.0	–0.9	–0.5	–0.1
Ballysadare Bay *Culleenamore*	54 16N	8 36W	+0059	+0111	+0111	+0123	–1.2	–0.9	no data	
Killala Bay *Inishcrone*	54 13N	9 06W	+0035	+0055	+0030	+0050	–1.3	–1.2	–0.7	–0.2
Broadhaven	54 16N	9 53W	+0040	+0050	+0040	+0050	–1.4	–1.1	–0.4	–0.1
Blacksod Bay										
Blacksod Quay	54 06N	10 03W	+0025	+0035	+0040	+0040	–1.2	–1.0	–0.6	–0.2
Bull's Mouth	54 02N	9 55W	+0101	+0057	+0109	+0105	–1.5	–1.0	–0.6	–0.1
Clare Island	53 48N	9 57W	+0019	+0013	+0029	+0023	–1.0	–0.7	–0.4	–0.1
Westport Bay										
Inishraher	53 48N	9 38W	+0030	+0012	+0058	+0026	–0.6	–0.5	–0.3	–0.1
Killary Harbour	53 38N	9 53W	+0021	+0015	+0035	+0029	–1.0	–0.8	–0.4	–0.1
Inishbofin Bofin Harbour	53 37N	10 13W	+0013	+0009	+0021	+0017	–1.0	–0.8	–0.4	–0.1
Clifden Bay	53 29N	10 04W	+0005	+0005	+0016	+0016	–0.7	–0.5	no data	
Slyne Head	53 24N	10 14W	–0002	–0002	+0010	+0010	–0.7	–0.5	no data	
Roundstone Bay	53 23N	9 55W	+0003	+0003	+0008	+0008	–0.7	–0.5	–0.3	–0.1
Kilkieran Cove	53 20N	9 44W	+0005	+0005	+0016	+0016	–0.3	–0.2	–0.1	0.0
Aran Islands Killeany Bay	53 07N	9 39W	–0008	–0008	+0003	+0003	–0.4	–0.3	–0.2	–0.1
Liscannor	52 56N	9 23W	–0003	–0007	+0006	+0002	–0.4	–0.3	no data	
Seafield Point	52 48N	9 30W	–0006	–0014	+0004	–0004	–0.5	–0.4	no data	
Kilrush	52 38N	9 30W	–0006	+0027	+0057	–0016	–0.1	–0.2	–0.3	–0.1
Limerick Dock	52 40N	8 38W	+0135	+0141	+0141	+0219	+1.0	+0.7	–0.8	–0.2
			0500 and 1700	1100 and 2300	0500 and 1700	1100 and 2300				
COBH standard port	51 51N	8 18 W					4.1	3.2	1.3	0.4
Tralee Bay *Fenit Pier*	52 16N	9 52W	–0057	–0017	–0029	–0109	+0.5	+0.2	+0.3	+0.1
Smerwick Harbour	52 12N	10 24W	–0107	–0027	–0041	–0121	–0.3	–0.4	no data	
Dingle Harbour	52 07N	10 15W	–0111	–0041	–0049	–0119	–0.1	0.0	+0.3	+0.4
Castlemaine Hbr										
Cromane Point	52 09N	9 54W	–0026	–0006	–0017	–0037	+0.4	+0.2	+0.4	+0.2
Valentia Harbour										
Knights Town	51 56N	10 18W	–0118	–0038	–0056	–0136	–0.6	–0.4	–0.1	0.0
Ballinskelligs Bay										
Castle	51 49N	10 16W	–0119	–0039	–0054	–0134	–0.5	–0.5	–0.1	0.0
Kenmare River										
West Cove	51 46N	10 03W	–0113	–0033	–0049	–0129	–0.6	–0.5	–0.1	0.0
Dunkerron Harbour	51 52N	9 38W	–0117	–0027	–0050	–0140	–0.2	–0.3	+0.1	0.0
Coulagh Bay										
Ballycrovane Hbr	51 43N	9 57W	–0116	–0036	–0053	–0133	–0.6	–0.5	–0.1	0.0

TIDES

Location	Lat	Long	High Water		Low Water		MHWS	MHWN	MLWN	MLWS
Black Ball Harbour	51 36N	10 02W	−0115	−0035	−0047	−0127	−0.7	−0.6	−0.1	+0.1
Bantry Bay										
Castletown Bearhaven	51 39N	9 54W	−0048	−0012	−0025	−0101	−0.9	−0.6	−0.1	0.0
Bantry	51 41N	9 28W	−0045	−0025	−0040	−0105	−0.9	−0.8	−0.2	0.0
Dunmanus Bay										
Dunbeacon Harbour	51 37N	9 33W	−0057	−0025	−0032	−0104	−0.8	−0.7	−0.3	−0.1
Dunmanus Harbour	51 32N	9 40W	−0107	−0031	−0044	−0120	−0.7	−0.6	−0.2	0.0
Crookhaven	51 28N	9 43W	−0057	−0033	−0048	−0112	−0.8	−0.6	−0.4	−0.1
Schull	51 31N	9 32W	−0040	−0015	−0015	−0110	−0.9	−0.6	−0.2	0.0
Baltimore	51 29N	9 23W	−0025	−0005	−0010	−0050	−0.6	−0.3	+0.1	+0.2
Castletownshend	51 32N	9 10W	−0020	−0030	−0020	−0050	−0.4	−0.2	+0.1	+0.3
Clonakilty Bay	51 35N	8 50W	−0033	−0011	−0019	−0041	−0.3	−0.2	*no data*	
Courtmacsherry	51 38N	8 42W	−0029	−0007	+0005	−0017	−0.4	−0.3	−0.2	−0.1
Kinsale	51 42N	8 31W	−0019	−0005	−0009	−0023	−0.2	0.0	+0.1	+0.2
Roberts Cove	51 45N	8 19W	−0005	−0005	−0005	−0005	−0.1	0.0	0.0	+0.1
Cork Harbour										
Ringaskiddy	51 50N	8 19W	+0005	+0020	+0007	+0013	+0.1	+0.1	+0.1	+0.1
Marino Point	51 53N	8 20W	0000	+0010	0000	+0010	+0.1	+0.1	0.0	0.0
Cork City	51 54N	8 27W	+0005	+0010	+0020	+0010	+0.4	+0.4	+0.3	+0.2
Ballycotton	51 50N	8 01W	−0011	+0001	+0003	−0009	0.0	0.0	−0.1	0.0
Youghal	51 57N	7 51W	0000	+0010	+0010	0000	−0.2	−0.1	−0.1	−0.1
Dungarvan Harbour	52 05N	7 34W	+0004	+0012	+0007	−0001	0.0	+0.1	−0.2	0.0
Waterford Harbour										
Dunmore East	52 09N	6 59W	+0008	+0003	0000	0000	+0.1	0.0	+0.1	+0.2
Cheekpoint	52 16N	7 00W	+0022	+0020	+0020	+0020	+0.3	+0.2	+0.2	+0.1
Kilmokea Point	52 17N	7 00W	+0026	+0022	+0020	+0020	+0.2	+0.1	+0.1	+0.1
Waterford	52 16N	7 07W	+0057	+0057	+0046	+0046	+0.4	+0.3	−0.1	+0.1
New Ross	52 24N	6 57W	+0100	+0030	+0055	+0130	+0.3	+0.4	+0.3	+0.4
Baginbun Head	52 10N	6 50W	+0003	+0003	−0008	−0008	−0.2	−0.1	+0.2	+0.2
Great Saltee	52 07N	6 38W	+0019	+0009	−0004	+0006	−0.3	−0.4	*no data*	
Carnsore Point	52 10N	6 22W	+0029	+0019	−0002	+0008	−1.1	−1.0	*no data*	
Rosslare Harbour	52 15N	6 21W	+0045	+0035	+0015	−0005	−2.2	−1.8	−0.5	−0.1
Wexford Harbour	52 20N	6 27W	+0126	+0126	+0118	+0108	−2.1	−1.7	−0.3	+0.1

DENMARK *Time Zone −0100*

Location	Lat	Long	High Water		Low Water		MHWS	MHWN	MLWN	MLWS
			0300	0700	0100	0800				
ESBJERG	55 28N	8 27E	and	and	and	and	1.9	1.5	0.5	0.1
Standard port			1500	1900	1300	2000				
Hirtshals	57 36N	9 58E	+0055	+0320	+0340	+0100	−1.6	−1.3	−0.4	−0.1
Hanstholm	57 08N	8 36E	+0100	+0340	+0340	+0130	−1.6	−1.2	−0.4	−0.1
Thyborøn	56 42N	8 13E	+0120	+0230	+0410	+0210	−1.5	−1.2	−0.4	−0.1
Torsminde	56 22N	8 07E	+0045	+0050	+0040	+0010	−1.3	−1.0	−0.4	−0.1
Hvide Sande	56 00N	8 07E	0000	+0010	−0015	−0025	−1.1	−0.8	−0.3	−0.1
Blavandshuk	55 33N	8 05E	−0120	−0110	−0050	−0100	−0.1	−0.1	−0.2	−0.1
Gradyb Bar	55 26N	8 15E	−0130	−0115	*no data*	*no data*	−0.4	−0.3	−0.2	−0.1
Rømø Havn	55 05N	8 34E	−0040	−0005	0000	−0020	0.0	+0.1	−0.2	−0.2
Hojer	54 58N	8 40E	−0020	+0015	*no data*	*no data*	+0.5	+0.6	−0.1	−0.1

GERMANY *Time Zone −0100*

Location	Lat	Long	High Water		Low Water		MHWS	MHWN	MLWN	MLWS
			0100	0600	0100	0800				
HELGOLAND	54 11N	7 53E	and	and	and	and	2.7	2.4	0.4	0.0
Standard port			1300	1800	1300	2000				
Lister Tief, List	55 01N	8 27E	+0252	+0240	+0201	+0210	−0.8	−0.6	−0.2	0.0
Hörnum	54 45N	8 18E	+0223	+0218	+0131	+0137	−0.5	−0.4	−0.2	0.0
Amrum–Hafen	54 38N	8 23E	+0138	+0137	+0128	+0134	+0.1	+0.2	−0.1	0.0
Dagebüll	54 44N	8 41E	+0226	+0217	+0211	+0225	+0.5	+0.5	+0.1	0.0
Suderoogsand	54 25N	8 30E	+0116	+0102	+0038	+0122	+0.5	+0.4	+0.1	0.0
Hever, Husum	54 28N	9 01E	+0205	+0152	+0118	+0200	+1.2	+1.1	+0.1	0.0
Suederhoeft	54 16N	8 42E	+0103	+0056	+0051	+0112	+0.7	+0.6	−0.1	0.0
Eidersperrwerk	54 16N	8 51E	+0120	+0115	+0130	+0155	+0.7	+0.6	−0.1	0.0
Linnenplate	54 13N	8 40E	+0047	+0046	+0034	+0046	+0.7	+0.6	0.0	−0.1
Büsum	54 07N	8 52E	+0054	+0049	−0001	+0027	+0.9	+0.8	+0.1	+0.1
			0200	0800	0200	0900				
CUXHAVEN	53 52N	8 43E	and	and	and	and	3.3	2.9	0.4	0.1
Standard port			1400	2000	1400	2100				
River Elbe										
Großer Vogelsand	54 00N	8 29E	−0044	−0046	−0101	−0103	0.0	0.0	+0.1	0.0
Scharhörn	53 58N	8 28E	−0045	−0047	−0101	−0103	+0.1	+0.1	+0.1	0.0
Otterndorf	53 50N	8 52E	+0025	+0025	+0022	+0022	−0.1	−0.1	0.0	0.0
Brunsbüttel	53 53N	9 08E	+0057	+0105	+0121	+0112	−0.2	−0.2	−0.1	0.0

Location	Lat	Long	High Water		Low Water		MHWS	MHWN	MLWN	MLWS
Glückstadt	53 47N	9 25E	+0205	+0214	+0220	+0213	−0.3	−0.2	−0.2	0.0
Stadersand	53 38N	9 32E	+0241	+0245	+0300	+0254	−0.1	0.0	−0.2	0.0
Schulau	53 34N	9 42E	+0304	+0315	+0337	+0321	+0.1	+0.2	−0.3	−0.1
Seemannshoeft	53 32N	9 53E	+0324	+0332	+0403	+0347	+0.2	+0.3	−0.4	−0.2
Hamburg	53 33N	9 58E	+0338	+0346	+0422	+0406	+0.3	+0.4	−0.4	−0.3
Harburg	53 28N	10 00E	+0344	+0350	+0430	+0416	+0.4	+0.4	−0.4	−0.3
			0200	0800	0200	0900				
WILHELMSHAVEN	53 31N	8 09E	and	and	and	and	4.3	3.8	0.6	0.0
Standard port			1400	2000	1400	2100				
River Weser										
Alter Weser Lt Hse	53 32N	8 08E	−0055	−0048	−0015	−0029	−1.1	−0.9	−0.2	−0.1
Bremerhaven	53 33N	8 34E	+0029	+0046	+0033	+0038	−0.2	−0.1	−0.2	0.0
Nordenham	53 28N	8 29E	+0051	+0109	+0055	+0058	−0.2	−0.1	−0.4	−0.2
Brake	53 19N	8 29E	+0120	+0119	+0143	+0155	−0.3	−0.2	−0.4	−0.2
Elsfleth	53 16N	8 29E	+0137	+0137	+0206	+0216	−0.2	−0.1	−0.3	0.0
Vegesack	53 10N	8 37E	+0208	+0204	+0250	+0254	−0.2	−0.2	−0.5	−0.2
Bremen	53 07N	8 43E	+0216	+0211	+0311	+0314	−0.1	−0.1	−0.6	−0.3
River Jade										
Wangerooge East	53 46N	7 59E	−0058	−0053	−0024	−0034	−0.9	−0.9	−0.1	0.0
Wangerooge West	53 47N	7 52E	−0101	−0058	−0035	−0045	−1.1	−1.0	−0.2	0.0
Schillig	53 42N	8 03E	−0031	−0025	−0006	−0014	−0.7	−0.6	0.0	0.0
Hooksiel	53 39N	8 05E	−0023	−0022	−0008	−0012	−0.5	−0.4	0.0	0.0
			0200	0700	0200	0800				
HELGOLAND	54 11N	7 53E	and	and	and	and	2.7	2.4	0.4	0.0
Standard port			1400	1900	1400	2000				
East Frisian Islands and coast										
Spiekeroog	53 45N	7 41E	+0003	−0003	−0031	−0012	+0.4	+0.3	0.0	0.0
Neuharlingersiel	53 42N	7 42E	+0014	+0008	−0024	−0013	+0.5	+0.4	0.0	−0.1
Langeoog	53 43N	7 30E	+0003	−0001	−0034	−0018	+0.4	+0.2	0.0	0.0
Norderney (Riffgat)	53 42N	7 09E	−0024	−0030	−0056	−0045	+0.1	0.0	0.0	0.0
Norddeich Hafen	53 37N	7 10E	−0018	−0017	−0029	−0012	+0.1	+0.1	0.0	−0.1
Juist	53 40N	7 00E	−0026	−0032	−0019	−0008	+0.2	+0.1	0.0	0.0
River Ems										
Memmert	53 38N	6 54E	−0032	−0038	−0114	−0103	+0.1	+0.1	0.0	0.0
Borkum (Fischerbalje)	53 33N	6 45E	−0048	−0052	−0124	−0105	0.0	0.0	0.0	0.0
Emshorn	53 30N	6 50E	−0037	−0041	−0108	−0047	+0.1	+0.1	0.0	0.0
Knock	53 20N	7 02E	+0018	+0005	−0028	+0004	+0.6	+0.6	0.0	0.0
Emden	53 20N	7 11E	+0041	+0028	−0011	+0022	+0.8	+0.8	0.0	0.0

NETHERLANDS *Time Zone −0100*

Location	Lat	Long	High Water		Low Water		MHWS	MHWN	MLWN	MLWS
			0200	0700	0200	0800				
HELGOLAND	54 11N	7 53E	and	and	and	and	2.7	2.4	0.4	0.0
Standard port			1400	1900	1400	2000				
Nieuwe Statenzijl	53 14N	7 13E	+0101	+0045	+0026	+0026	+1.0	+0.8	+0.9	+0.6
Delfzijl	53 20N	6 56E	+0020	−0005	−0040	0000	+0.8	+0.8	+0.2	+0.2
Eemshaven	53 26N	6 52E	−0025	−0045	−0115	−0045	+0.5	+0.4	+0.3	+0.3
Schiermonnikoog	53 28N	6 12E	−0120	−0130	−0240	−0220	+0.1	+0.1	+0.3	+0.3
Waddenzee										
Lauwersoog	53 25N	6 12E	−0130	−0145	−0235	−0220	+0.1	+0.1	+0.2	+0.2
Nes	53 26N	5 47E	−0135	−0150	−0245	−0225	+0.1	0.0	+0.2	+0.2
West Terschelling	53 22N	5 13E	−0220	−0250	−0335	−0310	−0.4	−0.4	+0.1	+0.2
Vlieland−Haven	53 18N	5 06E	−0250	−0320	−0355	−0330	−0.4	−0.4	+0.1	+0.2
Harlingen	53 10N	5 25E	−0155	−0245	−0210	−0130	−0.5	−0.5	−0.1	+0.2
Kornwerderzand	53 04N	5 20E	−0210	−0315	−0300	−0215	−0.5	−0.5	−0.1	+0.2
Den Oever	52 56N	5 02E	−0245	−0410	−0400	−0305	−0.8	−0.7	0.0	+0.2
Oudeschild	53 02N	4 51E	−0310	−0420	−0445	−0400	−1.0	−0.8	0.0	+0.2
Den Helder	52 58N	4 45E	−0410	−0520	−0520	−0430	−1.0	−0.8	0.0	+0.2
Noordwinning (Platform K13−A)	53 13N	3 13E	−0420	−0430	−0520	−0530	−1.1	−1.1	+0.1	+0.1
			0300	0900	0400	1000				
VLISSINGEN	51 27N	3 36E	and	and	and	and	4.7	3.8	0.8	0.2
Standard port			1500	2100	1600	2200				
Ijmuiden	52 28N	4 35E	+0145	+0140	+0305	+0325	−2.6	−2.1	−0.5	0.0
Scheveningen	52 06N	4 16E	+0105	+0100	+0220	+0245	−2.6	−2.1	−0.6	0.0
Europlatform	52 00N	3 17E	+0005	−0005	−0030	−0055	−2.6	−2.1	−0.5	0.0

TIDES

Location	Lat	Long	High Water		Low Water		MHWS	MHWN	MLWN	MLWS
Nieuwe Waterweg										
HOEK VAN HOLLAND			*standard port*							
Maassluis	51 55N	4 15E	+0155	+0115	+0100	+0310	−2.7	−2.1	−0.6	0.0
Nieuwe Maas, Vlaardingen	51 54N	4 21E	+0150	+0120	+0130	+0330	−2.6	−2.1	−0.6	0.0
Lek										
Krimpen Aan de Lek	51 53N	4 38E	+0225	+0200	+0325	+0445	−3.1	−2.5	−0.7	0.0
Schoonhoven	51 57N	4 51E	+0415	+0315	+0435	+0545	−3.1	−2.3	−0.4	+0.2
Oude Maas										
Spijkenisse	51 52N	4 20E	+0145	+0120	+0145	+0310	−2.9	−2.3	−0.6	0.0
Goidschalxoord	51 50N	4 27E	+0200	+0140	+0240	+0410	−3.3	−2.7	−0.7	0.0
Merwede										
Dordrecht	51 49N	4 39E	+0220	+0210	+0420	+0510	−3.7	−3.0	−0.7	−0.1
Werkendam	51 49N	4 53E	+0425	+0410	+0550	+0650	−4.0	−3.2	−0.5	+0.1
Moerdijk	51 42N	4 36E	+0525	+0450	+0520	+0605	−4.2	−3.3	−0.6	+0.1
Haringvlietsluizen	51 50N	4 02E	+0015	+0015	+0015	−0020	−1.7	−1.6	−0.4	+0.1
Brouwershavensche Gat	51 45N	3 49E	0000	+0010	0000	−0030	−1.5	−1.3	−0.3	+0.1
Ooster Schelde										
Roompot Buiten	51 37N	3 40E	−0015	+0005	+0005	−0020	−1.1	−0.9	−0.2	+0.1
Stavenisse	51 36N	4 01E	+0150	+0120	+0055	+0115	−1.2	−0.8	−0.4	+0.1
Bergse Diepsluis (West)	51 30N	4 12E	+0145	+0125	+0105	+0115	−0.6	−0.3	−0.2	+0.1
Zijpe, Philipsdam (West)	51 40N	4 11E	+0215	+0125	+0100	+0110	−1.1	−0.7	−0.4	0.0
Walcheren, Westkapelle	51 31N	3 27E	−0025	−0015	−0010	−0025	−0.5	−0.5	−0.1	+0.1
Westerschelde										
Terneuzen	51 20N	3 50E	+0020	+0020	+0020	+0030	+0.4	+0.4	0.0	+0.1
Hansweert	51 27N	4 00E	+0100	+0050	+0040	+0100	+0.6	+0.7	0.0	+0.1
Bath	51 24N	4 13E	+0125	+0115	+0115	+0140	+1.0	+1.0	0.0	+0.1

BELGIUM *Time Zone −0100*

Location	Lat	Long	High Water		Low Water		MHWS	MHWN	MLWN	MLWS
Antwerpen	51 21N	4 14E	+0128	+0116	+0121	+0144	+1.2	+1.0	+0.1	+0.1
Zeebrugge	51 21N	3 12E	−0035	−0015	−0020	−0035	+0.2	+0.2	+0.4	+0.2
Blankenberge	51 19N	3 07E	−0040	−0040	−0040	−0040	−0.3	0.0	+0.3	+0.2
Oostende	51 14N	2 56E	−0055	−0040	−0030	−0045	+0.5	+0.5	+0.4	+0.2
Nieuwpoort	51 09N	2 43E	−0110	−0050	−0035	−0045	+0.7	+0.6	+0.5	+0.2

FRANCE *Time Zone −0100*

Location	Lat	Long	High Water		Low Water		MHWS	MHWN	MLWN	MLWS
			0200	0800	0200	0900				
DUNKERQUE	51 03N	2 22E	and	and	and	and	6.0	5.0	1.5	0.6
Standard port			1400	2000	1400	2100				
Gravelines	51 01N	2 06E	−0005	−0015	−0005	+0005	+0.3	+0.1	−0.1	−0.1
Sandettie Bank	51 09N	1 47E	−0015	−0025	−0020	−0005	+0.1	−0.1	−0.1	−0.1
Calais	51 58N	1 51E	−0020	−0030	−0015	−0005	+1.2	+0.9	+0.6	+0.3
Wissant	50 53N	1 40E	−0035	−0050	−0030	−0010	+1.9	+1.5	+0.8	+0.4
			0100	0600	0100	0700				
DIEPPE	49 56N	1 05E	and	and	and	and	9.3	7.4	2.5	0.8
Standard port			1300	1800	1300	1900				
Boulogne	50 44N	1 35E	+0014	+0027	+0035	+0033	−0.4	−0.2	+0.1	+0.3
Le Touquet, Étaples	50 31N	1 35E	+0007	+0017	+0032	+0032	+0.2	+0.3	+0.4	+0.4
Berck	50 24N	1 34E	+0007	+0017	+0028	+0028	+0.5	+0.5	+0.4	+0.4
La Somme										
Le Hourdel	50 13N	1 34E	+0020	+0020	no data	no data	+0.8	+0.6	no data	
St Valéry	50 11N	1 37E	+0035	+0035	no data	no data	+0.9	+0.7	no data	
Cayeux	50 11N	1 29E	0000	+0005	+0015	+0010	+0.4	+0.5	+0.5	+0.5
Le Tréport	50 04N	1 22E	+0005	0000	+0007	+0007	+0.1	+0.1	0.0	+0.1
St. Valéry–en–Caux	49 52N	0 42E	−0005	−0005	−0015	−0020	−0.5	−0.4	−0.1	−0.1
Fécamp	49 46N	0 22E	−0015	−0010	−0030	−0040	−1.0	−0.6	+0.3	+0.4
Etretat	49 42N	0 12E	−0020	−0020	−0045	−0050	−1.2	−0.8	+0.3	+0.4
			0000	0500	0000	0700				
LE HAVRE	49 29N	0 07E	and	and	and	and	7.9	6.6	2.8	1.2
Standard port			1200	1700	1200	1900				
Antifer (Le Havre)	49 39N	0 09E	+0025	+0015	+0005	−0007	+0.1	0.0	0.0	0.0
La Seine										
Honfleur	49 25N	0 14E	−0135	−0135	+0015	+0040	+0.1	+0.1	+0.1	+0.3
Tancarville	49 28N	0 28E	−0105	−0100	+0105	+0140	−0.1	−0.1	0.0	+1.0
Quilleboeuf	49 28N	0 32E	−0045	−0050	+0120	+0200	0.0	0.0	+0.2	+1.4
Vatteville	49 29N	0 40E	+0005	−0020	+0225	+0250	0.0	−0.1	+0.8	+2.3
Caudebec	49 32N	0 44E	+0020	−0015	+0230	+0300	−0.3	−0.2	+0.9	+2.4
Heurteauville	49 27N	0 49E	+0110	+0025	+0310	+0330	−0.5	−0.2	+1.1	+2.7

Location	Lat	Long	High Water		Low Water		MHWS	MHWN	MLWN	MLWS
Duclair	49 29N	0 53E	+0225	+0150	+0355	+0410	−0.4	−0.3	+1.4	+3.3
Rouen	49 27N	1 06E	+0440	+0415	+0525	+0525	−0.2	−0.1	+1.6	+3.6
Trouville	49 22N	0 05E	−0100	−0010	0000	+0005	+0.4	+0.3	+0.3	+0.1
Dives	49 18N	0 05W	−0100	−0010	0000	0000	+0.3	+0.2	+0.2	+0.1
Ouistreham	49 17N	0 15W	−0045	−0010	−0005	0000	−0.3	−0.3	−0.2	−0.3
Courseulles-sur-Mer	49 20N	0 27W	−0045	−0015	−0020	−0025	−0.5	−0.5	−0.1	−0.1
Arromanches	49 21N	0 37W	−0055	−0025	−0027	−0035	−0.6	−0.6	−0.2	−0.2
Port-en-Bessin	49 21N	0 45W	−0055	−0030	−0030	−0035	−0.7	−0.7	−0.2	−0.1
Alpha–Baie de Seine	49 49N	0 20W	+0030	+0020	−0005	−0020	−1.0	−0.9	−0.4	−0.2
			0300	1000	0400	1000				
CHERBOURG	49 39N	1 38W	and	and	and	and	6.4	5.0	2.5	1.1
Standard port			1500	2200	1600	2200				
Rade de la Capelle	49 25N	1 05W	+0115	+0050	+0130	+0117	+0.8	+0.9	+0.1	+0.1
Îles Saint Marcouf	49 30N	1 08W	+0118	+0052	+0125	+0110	+0.6	+0.7	+0.1	+0.1
St. Vaast-la-Hougue	49 34N	1 16W	+0120	+0050	+0120	+0115	+0.3	+0.5	0.0	−0.1
Barfleur	49 40N	1 15W	+0110	+0055	+0052	+0052	+0.1	+0.3	0.0	0.0
Omonville	49 42N	1 50W	−0010	−0010	−0015	−0015	−0.1	−0.1	0.0	0.0
Goury	49 43N	1 57W	−0100	−0040	−0105	−0120	+1.7	+1.6	+1.0	+0.3

CHANNEL ISLANDS Time Zone UT

Location	Lat	Long	High Water		Low Water		MHWS	MHWN	MLWN	MLWS
			0300	0900	0200	0900				
ST. HELIER	49 11N	2 07W	and	and	and	and	11.0	8.1	4.0	1.4
Standard port			1500	2100	1400	2100				
Alderney, Braye	49 43N	2 12W	+0050	+0040	+0025	+0105	−4.8	−3.4	−1.5	−0.5
Sark, Maseline Pier	49 26N	2 21W	+0005	+0015	+0005	+0010	−2.1	−1.5	−0.6	−0.3
Guernsey, St PETER PORT	49 27N	2 31W	standard port (no secondaries)							
Jersey										
St. Catherine Bay	49 13N	2 01W	0000	+0010	+0010	+0010	0.0	−0.1	0.0	+0.1
Bouley Bay	49 14N	2 05W	+0002	+0002	+0004	+0004	−0.3	−0.3	−0.1	−0.1
Les Ecrehou	49 17N	1 56W	+0005	+0009	+0011	+0009	−0.2	+0.1	−0.2	0.0
Les Minquiers	48 57N	2 08W	−0014	−0018	−0001	−0008	+0.5	+0.6	+0.1	+0.1

FRANCE Time Zone −0100

Location	Lat	Long	High Water		Low Water		MHWS	MHWN	MLWN	MLWS
			0100	0800	0300	0800				
ST. MALO	48 38N	2 02W	and	and	and	and	12.2	9.3	4.2	1.5
Standard port			1300	2000	1500	2000				
Îles Chausey	48 52N	1 49W	+0005	+0005	+0015	+0015	+0.8	+0.7	+0.6	+0.4
Diélette	49 33N	1 52W	+0045	+0035	+0020	+0035	−2.5	−1.9	−0.7	−0.3
Carteret	49 22N	1 47W	+0030	+0020	+0015	+0030	−1.6	−1.2	−0.5	−0.2
Portbail	49 18N	1 45W	+0030	+0025	+0025	+0030	−0.8	−0.6	−0.2	−0.1
St. Germain sur Ay	49 14N	1 36W	+0025	+0025	+0035	+0035	−0.7	−0.5	0.0	+0.1
Le Sénéquet	49 05N	1 40W	+0015	+0015	+0023	+0023	−0.3	−0.3	+0.1	+0.1
Regnéville sur Mer	49 01N	1 33W	+0010	+0010	+0030	+0020	+0.4	+0.3	+0.2	0.0
Granville	48 50N	1 36W	+0005	+0005	+0020	+0010	+0.7	+0.5	+0.3	+0.1
Cancale	48 40N	1 51W	−0002	−0002	+0010	+0010	+0.8	+0.6	+0.3	+0.1
Île des Hebihens	48 37N	2 11W	−0002	−0002	−0005	−0005	−0.2	−0.2	−0.1	−0.1
St. Cast	48 38N	2 15W	−0002	−0002	−0005	−0005	−0.2	−0.2	−0.1	−0.1
Erquy	48 38N	2 28W	−0010	−0005	−0023	−0017	−0.6	−0.5	0.0	0.0
Dahouët	48 35N	2 34W	−0010	−0010	−0025	−0020	−0.9	−0.7	−0.2	−0.2
Le Légué (Buoy)	48 34N	2 41W	−0010	−0005	−0020	−0015	−0.8	−0.5	−0.2	−0.1
Binic	48 36N	2 49W	−0008	−0008	−0030	−0015	−0.8	−0.7	−0.2	−0.2
St Quay-Portrieux	48 38N	2 49W	−0010	−0005	−0025	−0020	−0.9	−0.7	−0.2	−0.1
Paimpol	48 47N	3 02W	−0010	−0005	−0035	−0025	−1.4	−1.0	−0.4	−0.2
Île de Bréhat	48 51N	3 00W	−0015	−0010	−0045	−0035	−1.9	−1.4	−0.6	−0.3
Les Héaux de Bréhat	48 55N	3 05W	−0020	−0015	−0055	−0035	−2.4	−1.7	−0.7	−0.3
Lézardrieux	48 47N	3 06W	−0020	−0015	−0055	−0045	−1.7	−1.3	−0.5	−0.2
Port-Béni	48 51N	3 10W	−0025	−0025	−0105	−0050	−2.4	−1.7	−0.6	−0.2
Tréguier	48 47N	3 13W	−0020	−0020	−0100	−0045	−2.3	−1.6	−0.6	−0.2
Perros-Guirec	48 49N	3 28W	−0040	−0045	−0120	−0105	−2.9	−2.0	−0.8	−0.3
Ploumanac'h	48 50N	3 29W	−0035	−0040	−0120	−0100	−2.9	−2.0	−0.7	−0.2
			0000	0600	0000	0600				
BREST	48 23N	4 30W	and	and	and	and	6.9	5.4	2.6	1.0
Standard port			1200	1800	1200	1800				
Trébeurden	48 46N	3 35W	+0100	+0110	+0120	+0100	+2.3	+1.9	+0.9	+0.4
Locquirec	48 42N	3 38W	+0058	+0108	+0120	+0100	+2.2	+1.8	+0.8	+0.3
Anse de Primel	48 43N	3 50W	+0100	+0110	+0120	+0100	+2.1	+1.7	+0.8	+0.3

TIDES

Location	Lat	Long	High Water		Low Water		MHWS	MHWN	MLWN	MLWS
Chateau du Taureau (Morlaix)	48 41N	3 53W	+0055	+0105	+0115	+0055	+2.0	+1.7	+0.8	+0.3
Roscoff	48 43N	3 58W	+0055	+0105	+0115	+0055	+1.9	+1.6	+0.8	+0.3
Ile de Batz	48 44N	4 00W	+0045	+0100	+0105	+0055	+2.0	+1.6	+0.9	+0.4
Brignogan	48 40N	4 19W	+0040	+0045	+0058	+0038	+1.5	+1.2	+0.6	+0.2
L'Aber Vrac'h, Ile Cézon	48 36N	4 34W	+0030	+0030	+0040	+0035	+0.8	+0.7	+0.2	0.0
Aber Benoit	48 35N	4 37W	+0022	+0025	+0035	+0020	+0.9	+0.7	+0.3	+0.1
Portsall	48 34N	4 43W	+0015	+0020	+0025	+0015	+0.6	+0.5	+0.1	0.0
L'Aber Ildut	48 28N	4 45W	+0010	+0010	+0023	+0010	+0.4	+0.3	0.0	0.0
Ouessant, Baie de Lampaul	48 27N	5 06W	+0005	+0005	−0005	+0003	0.0	−0.1	−0.1	0.0
Molene	48 24N	4 58W	+0012	+0012	+0017	+0017	+0.4	+0.3	+0.2	+0.1
Le Conquet	48 22N	4 47W	−0005	0000	+0007	+0007	−0.1	−0.1	−0.1	0.0
Le Trez Hir	48 21N	4 42W	−0010	−0005	−0008	−0008	−0.3	−0.3	−0.1	0.0
Camaret	48 17N	4 35W	−0010	−0010	−0013	−0013	−0.3	−0.3	−0.1	0.0
Morgat	48 13N	4 30W	−0008	−0008	−0020	−0010	−0.4	−0.4	−0.2	0.0
Douarnenez	48 06N	4 19W	−0010	−0015	−0018	−0008	−0.5	−0.5	−0.3	−0.1
Ile de Sein	48 02N	4 51W	−0005	−0005	−0010	−0005	−0.7	−0.6	−0.2	−0.1
Audierne	48 01N	4 33W	−0035	−0030	−0035	−0030	−1.7	−1.3	−0.6	−0.2
Le Guilvinec	47 48N	4 17W	−0010	−0025	−0025	−0015	−1.8	−1.4	−0.6	−0.1
Lesconil	47 48N	4 13W	−0008	−0028	−0028	−0018	−1.9	−1.4	−0.6	−0.1
Pont l'Abbe River, Loctudy	47 50N	4 10W	−0010	−0030	−0030	−0020	−2.0	−1.6	−0.7	−0.3
Odet River										
Bénodet	47 53N	4 07W	0000	−0020	−0023	−0013	−1.8	−1.4	−0.6	−0.2
Corniguel	47 58N	4 06W	+0015	+0010	−0015	−0010	−2.0	−1.6	−1.0	−0.7
Concarneau	47 52N	3 55W	−0010	−0030	−0030	−0020	−1.9	−1.5	−0.7	−0.2
Iles de Glenan, Ile de Penfret	47 44N	3 57W	−0005	−0030	−0028	−0018	−1.9	−1.5	−0.7	−0.2
Port Louis	47 42N	3 21W	+0004	−0021	−0022	−0012	−1.8	−1.4	−0.6	−0.1
Lorient	47 45N	3 21W	+0003	−0022	−0020	−0010	−1.8	−1.4	−0.6	−0.2
Hennebont	47 48N	3 17W	+0015	−0017	+0005	+0003	−1.9	−1.5	−0.8	−0.2
Ile de Groix, Port Tudy	47 39N	3 27W	0000	−0025	−0025	−0015	−1.8	−1.4	−0.6	−0.1
Port d'Etel	47 39N	3 12W	+0020	−0010	+0030	+0010	−2.0	−1.3	−0.4	+0.5
Port–Haliguen	47 29N	3 06W	+0015	−0020	−0015	−0010	−1.7	−1.3	−0.6	−0.3
Port Maria	47 29N	3 08W	+0010	−0025	−0025	−0015	−1.6	−1.3	−0.6	−0.1
Belle–Ile, Le Palais	47 21N	3 09W	+0007	−0028	−0025	−0020	−1.8	−1.4	−0.7	−0.3
Crac'h River, La Trinité	47 35N	3 01W	+0020	−0020	−0015	−0005	−1.5	−1.1	−0.5	−0.2
Golfe du Morbihan										
Port–Navalo	47 33N	2 55W	+0030	−0005	−0010	−0005	−2.0	−1.5	−0.8	−0.3
Auray	47 40N	2 59W	+0055	0000	+0020	+0005	−2.0	−1.4	−0.8	−0.2
Arradon	47 37N	2 50W	+0155	+0145	+0145	+0130	−3.7	−2.7	−1.6	−0.5
Vannes	47 39N	2 46W	+0220	+0200	+0200	+0125	−3.6	−2.7	−1.6	−0.5
St Armel (Le Passage)	47 36N	2 43W	+0205	+0200	+0210	+0140	−3.5	−2.5	−1.5	−0.5
Le Logeo	47 33N	2 51W	+0155	+0140	+0145	+0125	−3.7	−2.7	−1.6	−0.5
Port du Crouesty	47 32N	2 54W	+0013	−0022	−0017	−0012	−1.6	−1.2	−0.6	−0.3
Ile de Houat	47 24N	2 57W	+0010	−0025	−0020	−0015	−1.7	−1.3	−0.6	−0.2
Ile de Hoedic	47 20N	2 52W	+0010	−0035	−0027	−0022	−1.8	−1.4	−0.7	−0.3
Pénerf	47 31N	2 37W	+0020	−0025	−0015	−0015	−1.5	−1.1	−0.6	−0.3
Tréhiguier	47 30N	2 27W	+0035	−0020	−0005	−0010	−1.4	−1.0	−0.5	−0.3
Le Croisic	47 18N	2 31W	+0015	−0040	−0020	−0015	−1.5	−1.1	−0.6	−0.3
Le Pouliguen	47 17N	2 25W	+0020	−0025	−0020	−0025	−1.5	−1.1	−0.6	−0.3
Le Grand–Charpentier	47 13N	2 19W	+0015	−0045	−0025	−0020	−1.5	−1.1	−0.6	−0.3
Pornichet	47 16N	2 21W	+0020	−0045	−0022	−0022	−1.4	−1.0	−0.5	−0.2
La Loire										
St. Nazaire	47 16N	2 12W	+0030	−0040	−0010	−0010	−1.1	−0.8	−0.4	−0.2
Donges	47 18N	2 05W	+0035	−0035	+0005	+0005	−1.0	−0.7	−0.5	−0.4
Cordemais	47 17N	1 54W	+0055	−0005	+0105	+0030	−0.7	−0.5	−0.7	−0.4
Le Pellerin	47 12N	1 46W	+0110	+0010	+0145	+0100	−0.7	−0.5	−0.9	−0.4
Nantes (Chantenay)	47 12N	1 35W	+0135	+0055	+0215	+0125	−0.6	−0.3	−0.8	−0.1
BREST	48 23N	4 30W	0500 and 1700	1100 and 2300	0500 and 1700	1100 and 2300	6.9	5.4	2.6	1.0
Standard port										
Pointe de Saint–Gildas	47 08N	2 15W	−0045	+0025	−0020	−0020	−1.3	−1.0	−0.5	−0.2
Pornic	47 06N	2 07W	−0050	+0030	−0010	−0010	−1.1	−0.8	−0.4	−0.2
Ile de Noirmoutier, L'Herbaudière	47 02N	2 18W	−0047	+0023	−0020	−0020	−1.4	−1.0	−0.5	−0.2
Fromentine	46 54N	2 10W	−0050	+0020	−0020	+0010	−1.6	−1.2	−0.7	0.0
Ile de Yeu, Port Joinville	46 44N	2 21W	−0040	+0015	−0030	−0035	−1.9	−1.4	−0.7	−0.3
St. Gilles–Croix-de-Vie	46 41N	1 56W	−0030	+0015	−0032	−0032	−1.8	−1.3	−0.6	−0.3
Les Sables d'Olonne	46 30N	1 48W	−0030	+0015	−0035	−0035	−1.7	−1.3	−0.6	−0.3

Location	Lat	Long	High Water		Low Water		MHWS	MHWN	MLWN	MLWS
			0000 and 1200	0600 and 1800	0500 and 1700	1200 and 2400				
POINTE DE GRAVE	45 34N	1 04W					5.4	4.4	2.1	1.0
Standard port										
Ile de Ré, St Martin	46 12N	1 22W	+0015	−0030	−0025	−0020	+0.6	+0.5	+0.3	−0.1
La Pallice	46 10N	1 13W	+0015	−0030	−0025	−0020	+0.6	+0.5	+0.3	−0.1
La Rochelle	46 09N	1 09W	+0015	−0030	−0025	−0020	+0.6	+0.5	+0.3	−0.1
Ile d'Aix	46 01N	1 10W	+0015	−0040	−0030	−0025	+0.7	+0.5	+0.3	−0.1
La Charente, Rochefort	45 57N	0 58W	+0035	−0010	+0030	+0125	+1.1	+0.9	+0.1	−0.2
Le Chapus	45 51N	1 11W	+0015	−0040	−0025	−0015	+0.6	+0.6	+0.4	+0.2
La Cayenne	45 47N	1 08W	+0030	−0015	−0010	−0005	+0.2	+0.2	+0.3	0.0
Pointe de Gatseau	45 48N	1 14W	+0005	−0005	−0015	−0025	−0.1	−0.1	+0.2	+0.2
Cordouan	45 35N	1 10W	−0010	−0010	−0015	−0025	−0.5	−0.4	−0.1	−0.3
La Gironde										
Royan	45 37N	1 01W	0000	−0005	−0005	−0005	−0.3	−0.2	0.0	0.0
Richard	45 27N	0 56W	+0018	+0018	+0028	+0033	−0.1	−0.1	−0.4	−0.5
Lamena	45 20N	0 48W	+0035	+0045	+0100	+0125	+0.2	+0.1	−0.5	−0.3
Pauillac	45 12N	0 45W	+0100	+0100	+0135	+0205	+0.1	0.0	−1.0	−0.5
La Reuille	45 03N	0 36W	+0135	+0145	+0230	+0305	−0.2	−0.3	−1.3	−0.7
La Garonne										
Le Marquis	45 00N	0 33W	+0145	+0150	+0247	+0322	−0.3	−0.4	−1.5	−0.9
Bordeaux	44 52N	0 33W	+0200	+0225	+0330	+0405	−0.1	−0.2	−1.7	−1.0
La Dordogne, Libourne	44 55N	0 15W	+0250	+0305	+0525	+0540	−0.7	−0.9	−2.0	−0.4
Bassin d' Arcachon										
Cap Ferret	44 37N	1 15W	−0015	+0005	−0005	+0015	−1.4	−1.2	−0.8	−0.5
Arcachon (Eyrac)	44 40N	1 10W	+0010	+0025	0000	+0020	−1.1	−1.0	−0.8	−0.6
L'Adour, Boucau	43 31N	1 31W	−0030	−0035	−0025	−0040	−1.2	−1.1	−0.4	−0.3
St Jean de Luz, Socoa	43 23N	1 40W	−0040	−0045	−0030	−0045	−1.1	−1.1	−0.6	−0.4

SPAIN *Time Zone −0100*

Location	Lat	Long	High Water		Low Water		MHWS	MHWN	MLWN	MLWS
Pasajes	43 20N	1 56W	−0050	−0030	−0015	−0045	−1.2	−1.3	−0.5	−0.5
San Sebastian	43 19N	1 59W	−0110	−0030	−0020	−0040	−1.2	−1.2	−0.5	−0.4
Guetaria	43 18N	2 12W	−0110	−0030	−0020	−0040	−1.0	−1.0	−0.5	−0.4
Lequeitio	43 22N	2 30W	−0115	−0035	−0025	−0045	−1.2	−1.2	−0.5	−0.4
Bermeo	43 25N	2 43W	−0055	−0015	−0005	−0025	−0.8	−0.7	−0.5	−0.4
Abra de Bilbao	43 21N	3 02W	−0125	−0045	−0035	−0055	−1.2	−1.2	−0.5	−0.4
Portugalete (Bilbao)	43 20N	3 02W	−0100	−0020	−0010	−0030	−0.7	−1.2	−0.2	−0.6
Castro Urdiales	43 23N	3 13W	−0040	−0120	−0020	−0110	−1.4	−1.5	−0.6	−0.6
Ria de Santona	43 26N	3 28W	−0005	−0045	+0015	−0035	−0.7	−1.2	−0.3	−0.7
Santander	43 28N	3 47W	−0020	−0100	0000	−0050	−0.7	−1.2	−0.3	−0.7
Ria de Suances	43 27N	4 03W	0000	−0030	+0020	−0020	−1.5	−1.5	−0.6	−0.6
San Vicente de la Barquera	43 23N	4 24W	−0020	−0100	0000	−0050	−1.5	−1.5	−0.6	−0.6
Ria de Tina Mayor	43 24N	4 31W	−0020	−0100	0000	−0050	−1.4	−1.5	−0.6	−0.6
Ribadesella	43 28N	5 04W	+0005	−0020	+0020	−0020	−1.4	−1.3	−0.6	−0.4
Gijon	43 34N	5 42W	−0005	−0030	+0010	−0030	−1.0	−1.4	−0.4	−0.7
Luanco	43 37N	5 47W	−0010	−0035	+0005	−0035	−1.4	−1.3	−0.6	−0.4
Aviles	43 35N	5 56W	−0100	−0040	−0015	−0050	−1.2	−1.6	−0.5	−0.7
San Esteban de Pravia	43 34N	6 05W	−0005	−0030	+0010	−0030	−1.4	−1.3	−0.6	−0.4
Luarca	43 33N	6 32W	+0010	−0015	+0025	−0015	−1.2	−1.1	−0.5	−0.3
Ribadeo	43 33N	7 02W	+0010	−0015	+0025	−0015	−1.3	−1.5	−0.7	−0.8
Burela	43 39N	7 21W	+0010	−0015	+0025	−0015	−1.5	−1.5	−0.7	−0.6
Ria de Vivero	43 43N	7 36W	+0010	−0015	+0025	−0015	−1.4	−1.3	−0.6	−0.4
Santa Marta de Ortigueira	43 41N	7 51W	−0020	0000	+0020	−0010	−1.3	−1.2	−0.6	−0.4
El Ferrol del Caudillo	43 28N	8 16W	−0045	−0100	−0010	−0105	−1.6	−1.4	−0.7	−0.4
La Coruna	43 22N	8 24W	−0110	−0050	−0030	−0100	−1.6	−1.6	−0.6	−0.5
Ria de Corme	43 16N	8 58W	−0025	−0005	+0015	−0015	−1.7	−1.6	−0.6	−0.5
Ria de Camarinas	43 08N	9 11W	−0115	−0055	0000	−0105	−1.6	−1.6	−0.6	−0.5

			0500 and 1700	1000 and 2200	0300 and 1500	0800 and 2000				
LISBOA	38 42N	9 07W					3.8	3.0	1.5	0.6
Standard port										
Corcubion	42 57N	9 12W	+0055	+0110	+0120	+0135	−0.5	−0.4	−0.3	−0.1
Muros	42 46N	9 03W	+0050	+0105	+0115	+0130	−0.3	−0.3	−0.2	−0.1
Ria de Arosa, Villagarcia	42 37N	8 47W	+0040	+0100	+0110	+0120	−0.3	−0.2	−0.2	−0.1
Ria de Pontevedra, Marin	42 24N	8 42W	+0050	+0110	+0120	+0130	−0.5	−0.4	−0.3	−0.1
Vigo	42 15N	8 43W	+0040	+0100	+0105	+0125	−0.4	−0.3	−0.2	−0.1
Bayona	42 07N	8 51W	+0035	+0050	+0100	+0115	−0.3	−0.3	−0.2	−0.1
La Guardia	41 54N	8 53W	+0040	+0055	+0105	+0120	−0.5	−0.4	−0.3	−0.2

TIDES

Location	Lat	Long	High Water		Low Water		MHWS	MHWN	MLWN	MLWS
			0400 and 1600	0900 and 2100	0400 and 1600	0900 and 2100				
LISBOA *Standard port*	38 42N	9 07W					3.8	3.0	1.5	0.6
PORTUGAL *Time Zone UT*										
Viana do Castelo	41 41N	8 50W	–0020	0000	+0010	+0015	–0.4	–0.4	–0.1	0.0
Esposende	41 32N	8 47W	–0020	0000	+0010	+0015	–0.6	–0.5	–0.2	–0.1
Povoa de Varzim	41 22N	8 46W	–0020	0000	+0010	+0015	–0.3	–0.3	–0.1	–0.1
Porto de Leixoes	41 11N	8 42W	–0025	–0010	0000	+0010	–0.4	–0.4	–0.1	0.0
Rio Douro										
Entrance	41 09N	8 40W	–0010	+0005	+0015	+0025	–0.6	–0.5	–0.2	–0.1
Oporto (Porto)	41 08N	8 37W	+0002	+0002	+0040	+0040	–0.5	–0.4	–0.2	0.0
Porto de Aveiro	40 39N	8 45W	+0005	+0010	+0010	+0015	–0.6	–0.4	–0.1	0.0
Figueira da Foz	40 09N	8 51W	–0015	0000	+0010	+0020	–0.4	–0.4	–0.1	0.0
Nazare (Pederneira)	39 35N	9 04W	–0030	–0015	–0005	+0005	–0.5	–0.4	–0.1	0.0
Peniche	39 21N	9 22W	–0035	–0015	–0005	0000	–0.4	–0.4	–0.1	0.0
Ericeira	38 58N	9 25W	–0040	–0025	–0010	–0010	–0.4	–0.3	–0.1	0.0
River Tagus (Rio Tejo)										
Cascais	38 42N	9 25W	–0040	–0025	–0015	–0010	–0.3	–0.3	0.0	+0.1
Paco de Arcos	38 41N	9 18W	–0020	–0030	–0005	–0005	–0.4	–0.4	–0.2	–0.1
Pedroucos	38 42N	9 13W	–0010	–0015	0000	0000	–0.2	–0.1	–0.1	–0.1
Alfeite	38 40N	9 09W	+0005	0000	0000	+0005	0.0	0.0	–0.1	–0.1
Alcochete	38 45N	8 58W	+0010	+0010	+0010	+0010	+0.5	+0.4	+0.1	0.0
Vila Franca de Xira	38 57N	8 59W	+0045	+0040	+0100	+0140	+0.3	+0.2	–0.2	+0.3
Sesimbra	38 26N	9 07W	–0045	–0030	–0020	–0010	–0.4	–0.4	–0.1	0.0
Setubal	38 30N	8 54W	–0020	–0015	–0005	+0005	–0.4	–0.4	–0.1	–0.1
Porto de Sines	37 57N	8 53W	–0050	–0030	–0020	–0010	–0.4	–0.4	–0.1	0.0
Milfontes	37 43N	8 47W	–0040	–0030	no data	no data	–0.1	–0.1	0.0	+0.1
Arrifana	37 17N	8 52W	–0030	–0020	no data	no data	–0.1	0.0	–0.1	+0.1
Enseada de Belixe	37 01N	8 58W	–0050	–0030	–0020	–0015	+0.3	+0.2	+0.2	+0.2
Lagos	37 06N	8 40W	–0100	–0040	–0030	–0025	–0.4	–0.4	–0.1	0.0
Portimao	37 07N	8 32W	–0100	–0040	–0030	–0025	–0.5	–0.4	–0.1	+0.1
Ponta do Altar	37 06N	8 31W	–0100	–0040	–0030	–0025	–0.3	–0.3	–0.1	0.0
Enseada de Albufeira	37 05N	8 15W	–0035	+0015	–0005	0000	–0.2	–0.2	0.0	+0.1
Porto de Faro-Olhao	36 59N	7 52W	–0050	–0030	–0015	+0005	–0.4	–0.4	–0.1	0.0
Rio Guadiana										
Vila Real de Santo António	37 12N	7 25W	–0050	–0015	–0010	0000	–0.4	–0.4	–0.1	+0.1
			0500 and 1700	1000 and 2200	0500 and 1700	1100 and 2300				
LISBOA *Standard port*	38 42N	9 07W					3.8	3.0	1.5	0.6
SPAIN *Time Zone –0100*										
Ayamonte	37 13N	7 25W	+0005	+0015	+0025	+0045	–0.7	–0.6	–0.1	–0.2
Ria de Huelva										
Bar	37 08N	6 52W	0000	+0015	+0035	+0030	–0.1	–0.6	–0.1	–0.4
Huelva, Muelle de Fabrica	37 15N	6 58W	+0010	+0025	+0045	+0040	–0.3	–0.3	–0.3	–0.1
Rio Guadalquivir										
Bar	36 45N	6 26W	–0005	+0005	+0020	+0030	–0.6	–0.5	–0.2	–0.2
Bonanza	36 48N	6 20W	+0025	+0040	+0100	+0120	–0.8	–0.6	–0.4	–0.1
Corta de los Jerónimos	37 08N	6 06W	+0210	+0230	+0255	+0345	–1.2	–0.9	–0.5	–0.1
Sevilla	37 23N	6 00W	+0400	+0430	+0510	+0545	–1.7	–1.2	–0.6	–0.1
Rota	36 37N	6 21W	–0010	+0010	+0025	+0015	–0.7	–0.6	–0.3	–0.1
Puerto de Santa Maria	36 36N	6 13W	+0006	+0006	+0027	+0027	–0.6	–0.4	–0.4	–0.1
Cadiz										
Puerto Cadiz	36 32N	6 17W	0000	+0020	+0040	+0025	–0.5	–0.5	–0.3	0.0
La Carraca	36 30N	6 11W	+0020	+0050	+0100	+0040	–0.5	–0.4	–0.1	0.0
Cabo Trafalgar	36 11N	6 02W	–0003	–0003	+0026	+0026	–1.4	–1.1	–0.6	–0.1
Barbate	36 11N	5 56W	+0016	+0016	+0045	+0045	–1.9	–1.5	–0.5	+0.1
Punta Camarinal	36 05N	5 48W	–0007	–0007	+0013	+0013	–1.7	–1.4	–0.7	–0.2
GIBRALTAR *Time Zone –0100*										
			0000 and 1200	0700 and 1900	0100 and 1300	0600 and 1800				
GIBRALTAR *Standard port*	36 08N	5 21W					1.0	0.7	0.3	0.1
Tarifa	36 00N	5 36W	–0038	–0038	–0042	–0042	+0.4	+0.3	+0.3	+0.2
Punta Carnero	36 04N	5 26W	–0010	–0010	0000	0000	0.0	+0.1	+0.1	+0.1
Algeciras	36 07N	5 27W	–0010	–0010	–0010	–0010	+0.1	+0.2	+0.1	+0.1

TIDAL GATES - SOUTHERN ENGLAND

A guide to the time of tide turn at tidal gates, the approximate maximum strength of the tidal flow (spring rates shown - neaps are approximately 60% of these), and the position and timing of races, counter tides, etc.

LAND'S END (AC 1148)

Tidal streams set hard north/south round Land's End, and east/west around Gwennap and Pendeen. But the inshore currents run counter to the tidal streams. By staying close inshore, this tidal gate favours a N-bound passage. With careful timing nearly 9½hrs of fair tide can be carried, from HWD–3 to HWD+5. The chartlets, referenced to HW Dover, depict both tidal streams and inshore currents.

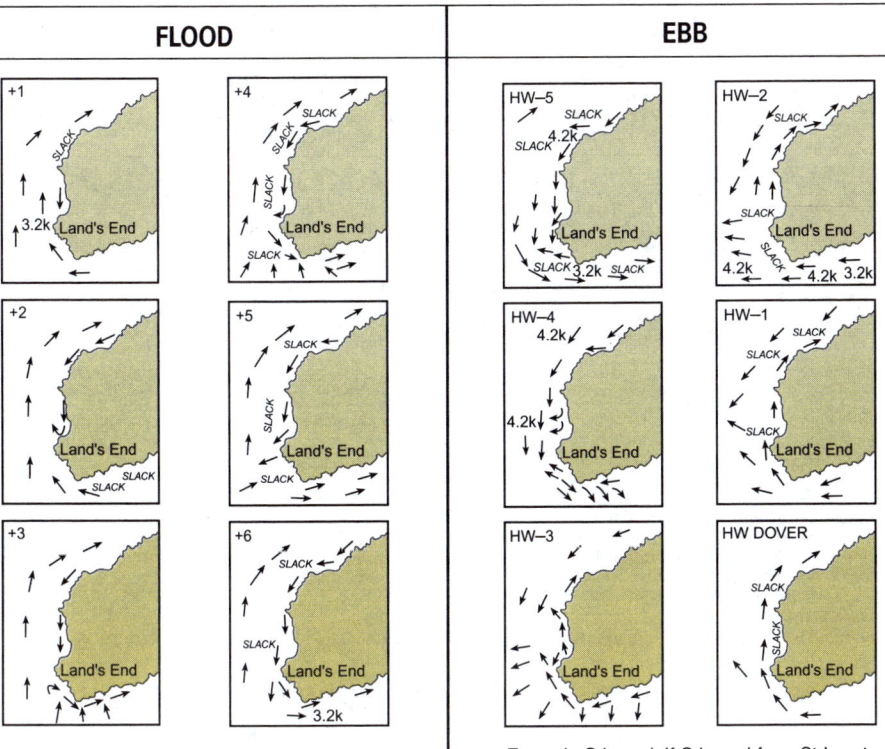

Example N-bound: At HWD+1 the N-going flood starts off Gwennap and does not turn NE along the N Cornish coast until HWD+3. But as early as HWD–3 an inshore current is beginning to set north. Utilise this by arriving off Runnel Stone at HWD–2 and then keeping within ¼M of the shore. If abeam the Brisons at HWD, the tide and current should serve for the next 6 or 7 hours to make good St Ives, or even Newquay and Padstow.

Example S-bound: If S-bound from St Ives to Newlyn, aim to reach the Runnel Stone by HWD+5, ie with 2hrs of E-going tide in hand for the remaining 9M to Newlyn. To achieve this 20M passage, leave St Ives 5 hours earlier, ie at HWD. Buck a foul tide for the first 3 hours, then use the S-going inshore current, keeping as close inshore as is prudent, only moving seaward to clear the Wra and the Brisons. This timing would also suit a passage from S Wales or the Bristol Channel, going inshore of Longships if conditions allow.

From Ireland, ie Cork or further W, the inshore passage would not benefit. But aim to be off the Runnel Stone at HWD+5 if bound for Newlyn; or at HWD+3 if bound for Helford/Falmouth, with the W-going stream slackening and 5hrs of fair tide to cover the remaining 20M past the Lizard.

With acknowledgements to the Royal Cruising Club Pilotage Foundation for their kind permission to use the tidal stream chartlets and text written by Hugh Davies, as first published in Yachting Monthly *magazine.*

TIDES

TIDAL GATES - SOUTHERN ENGLAND

A guide to the time of tide turn at tidal gates, the approximate maximum strength of the tidal flow (spring rates shown - neaps are approximately 60% of these), and the position and timing of races, counter tides, etc.

FLOOD   EBB

THE LIZARD (AC 777, 2345)

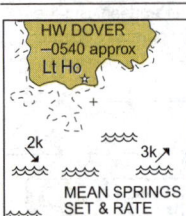

HW DOVER
−0540 approx
Lt Ho
2k
3k
MEAN SPRINGS SET & RATE

Drying rocks lie approx 5 cables S of the Lizard Lt ho and extend westwards. 49°57′N is about as far N as yachts may safely pass inshore of the Race, which extends 2-3M to seaward of these rocks. Race conditions may also exist SE of the Lizard with short, heavy seas in westerlies. If passing S of the Race, route via 49°55′N 05°13′W to clear the worst of the Race.

Inshore the E-going Channel flood, 2kn max @ springs, begins at HW Dover +0145; and outside the Race at approx HWD +0300.	Inshore the W-going Channel ebb, 3kn max @ springs, begins at HW Dover −0345; and outside the Race at HWD −0240.

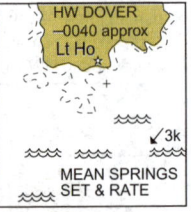

HW DOVER
−0040 approx
Lt Ho
3k
MEAN SPRINGS SET & RATE

START POINT (AC 1634)

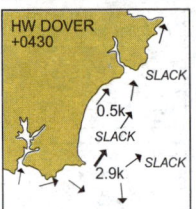

HW DOVER
+0430
SLACK
0.5k
SLACK
2.9k
SLACK

Start Pt, and to a lesser extent Prawle Pt (3.3M WSW), can be slow to round when W-bound with a fair tide against a W'ly wind raising a bad sea. Drying rocks extend 3 cables SSE of the lt ho and a Race may extend up to 1.7M ESE and 1.0M S of the lt ho. It is safe to pass between the Race and the rocks, but in bad weather wiser to go outside the Race. The Skerries Bank (least depth 2.1m) lies 8 cables NE of Start Pt. On both the flood and the ebb back eddies form between Start Pt and Hallsands, 1M NW.

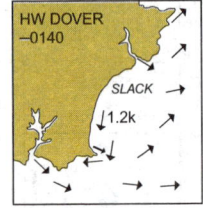

HW DOVER
−0140
SLACK
1.2k

The NE-going Channel flood, 3.1kn max @ springs, begins at HW Dover +0430.	The SW-going Channel ebb, 2.2kn max @ springs, begins at HW Dover −0140, but an hour earlier it is possible to round Start Pt close inshore using the back eddy.

PORTLAND (AC 2255)

A dangerous Race forms between 200 metres and 2 miles south of Portland Bill. The Race shifts westward on the W-going stream and eastward on the E-going stream. In the latter case it is not advisable to pass between the Race and the Shambles Bank. Study carefully the hourly tidal stream chartlets on pp.184-185 or in NP 257. The Race may be avoided either by passing to seaward of it, ie 3-5M south of the Bill and east of the Shambles; or by using the inshore passage – if conditions suit.

Seaward of the Race.

E-bound: The Channel flood sets east from HW Dover +6 to HWD −1.	W-bound: The ebb sets west from HW Dover to HWD +5½.

The inshore passage, (a narrow stretch of relatively smooth water between the Bill and the Race), should be started, in either direction, from a position 2M north of the Bill, keeping close inshore to the Portland peninsula. It should not be used at night (due to pot floats), nor in winds >F4/5, nor at springs especially with wind against tide.

If E-bound via the inshore passage, slackish water or a fair stream occurs around the Bill from HW Portland −3 to +1. The passage across Lyme Bay should be specifically timed to meet this critical window.	W-bound, similar conditions occur from HW Portland +4 to −6. The W-bound timing is easy if you have started from Weymouth, Portland harbour or Lulworth Cove.

ST ALBAN'S HEAD (AC 2610)

A sometimes vicious Race forms over St Alban's Ledge, a rocky dorsal ridge (least depth 8.5m) which extends approx 4M SW from St Alban's Head. Three yellow naval target buoys (DZ A, B and C) straddle the middle and outer sections, but are only occasionally used. In settled weather and at neaps the Race may be barely perceptible in which case it can be crossed with impunity. Avoid it either by keeping to seaward via 50°31′.40N 02°07′.80W; or by using the narrow inshore passage at the foot of St Alban's Head.

Based on a position 1M S of St Alban's Head, the tidal stream windows are:

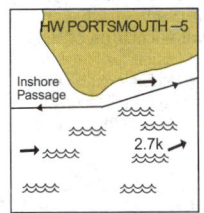

HW PORTSMOUTH −5
Inshore Passage
2.7k

ESE-going stream starts at HW Portsmouth +0530. Spring rates are the same, max 4kn. Along the W side of St Alban's Head the stream runs almost continuously SE due to a back eddy.	WNW-going stream starts at HW Portsmouth. Overfalls extend 2.5M further SW than on the E-going stream and are more dangerous to small craft. Slack water lasts barely half an hour.

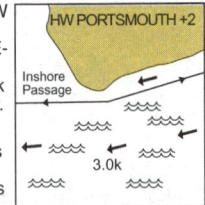

HW PORTSMOUTH +2
Inshore Passage
3.0k

The inshore passage lies as close to the foot of St Alban's Head as feels comfortable. It may be hard to see the width of clear water in the inshore passage until committed to it, but except in onshore gales when it is better to stay offshore, the passage will be swiftly made with only a few, if any, overfalls. The NCI station on the Head (☎ 01929 439220) may advise on conditions.

TIDAL GATES - SOUTHERN ENGLAND

A guide to the time of tide turn at tidal gates, the approximate maximum strength of the tidal flow (spring rates shown - neaps are approximately 60% of these), and the position and timing of races, counter tides, etc.

FLOOD	EBB

THE NEEDLES CHANNEL (AC 2035)

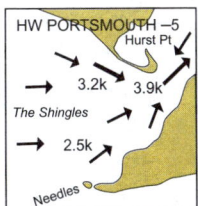 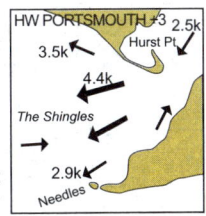

The Needles Channel lies between the SW Shingles PHM buoy and the Bridge WCM buoy. Once through this narrow section the channel widens with the Island shore to starboard and the long, drying 1.2m, Shingles bank to port. Abeam Hurst Castle the channel again narrows (assisted by The Trap, a shoal spit south of Hurst Castle) before opening out into the west Solent.

Study carefully the hourly tidal stream chartlets for the Isle of Wight on pp.186-191 and the values shown on AC 2035 at tidal diamonds B, C, D and E.

The ENE-going flood runs from HW Portsmouth +5 until HW P $-1\frac{1}{2}$, at springs reaching 3.1kn at The Bridge and 3.9kn at Hurst.	The WSW-going ebb runs from HW P -1 until HW P $+4\frac{1}{2}$, reaching 4.4kn at Hurst and 3.4kn at The Bridge, both spring rates. The ebb sets strongly WSW across the Shingles which with adequate rise is routinely crossed by racing yachts; but cruisers should stay clear even in calm conditions when any swell causes the sea to break heavily.

Prevailing W/SW winds, even if only F4, against the ebb raise dangerous breaking seas in the Needles Channel and at The Bridge, a shallow ridge extending 9 cables west from the Needles light. Worst conditions are often found just after LW slack. In such conditions it is safer to go via the North Channel to Hurst. In W/SW gales avoid the Needles altogether by sheltering at Poole or going east-about via Nab Tower.

ON PASSAGE UP CHANNEL

The following 3 tidal gates (The Looe, Beachy Head and Dungeness) are components in the tidal conveyor belt which, if stepped onto at the outset, can enable a fastish yacht to carry a fair tide for 88M from Selsey Bill to Dover. Go through the Looe at slackish water, HW Portsmouth $+4\frac{1}{2}$ (HW Dover +5). Based on a mean SOG of 7 knots, Beachy Head will be passed at HW D -1, Dungeness at HW D $+3$ and Dover at HW $+5\frac{1}{2}$, only bucking the first of the ebb in the last hour. A faster boat could make Ramsgate. The down-Channel passage is less rewarding and many yachts will pause at Brighton.

THE LOOE (AC 2045, 1652)

This channel is little shorter than the detour south of the Owers, but is much used by yachts on passage from/to points east of the Solent. Although adequately lit, it is best not attempted at night due to many lobster floats; nor in onshore gales as searoom is limited by extensive shoals on which the sea breaks.

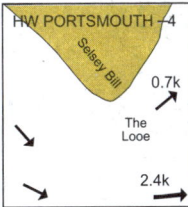

The E-going flood runs from HW Portsmouth $+4\frac{1}{2}$ (HW Dover +5) until HW P $-1\frac{1}{2}$ (HW D -1), at springs reaching 2.4kn near the Boulder and Street light buoys which mark its narrow western end; they may be hard to see in other than good visibility. Max neap rate is 1.2kn.	The W-going ebb runs from HW P $-1\frac{1}{2}$ (HW D -1) until HW P $+4\frac{1}{2}$ (HW D +5), at springs reaching 2.6kn near Boulder and Street. Max neap rate is 1.3kn.

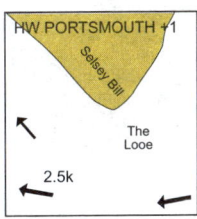

At the wider eastern end of the channel (near E Borough Head buoy) rates are greatly reduced.

BEACHY HEAD (AC 1652, 536)

Stay at least 5 cables to seaward of the towering chalk cliffs to avoid isolated boulders and rocky, part-drying ridges such as Head Ledge. The lt ho stands on a drying rock ledge. Close inshore many fishing floats are a trap for the unwary. In bad weather stay 2M offshore to avoid overfalls caused by a ridge of uneven ground which extends 1M SSE from Beachy Head.

2M south of Beachy Head the E-going flood starts at HW Dover +0530, max spring rate 2.6kn.	The W-going ebb starts at HW Dover +0030, max spring rate 2.0kn.

Between 5M and 7M east of Beachy Head avoid breakers and eddies caused by the Horse of Willingdon, Royal Sovereign and other shoals.

DUNGENESS (AC 536, 1892)

Tidal stream atlases: Dungeness is on the east and west edges respectively of NP 250 (English Channel) and NP 233 (Dover Strait). The nearest tidal stream diamond (2.2M SE of Dungeness) is 'H' on AC 536 and 'B' on AC 1892; their positions and values are the same.

The NE-going flood starts at HW Dover -0100, max spring rate 1.9kn.	The SW-going ebb starts at HW Dover $+0430$, max spring rate 2.1kn.

TIDES

TIDAL GATES - NORTH EAST SCOTLAND

A guide to the time of tide turn at tidal gates, and in straits and estuaries, showing the approximate strength of the tidal flow (spring rates shown - neaps are approximately 60% of these), and the position and timing of races, counter tides etc.

FLOOD	EBB

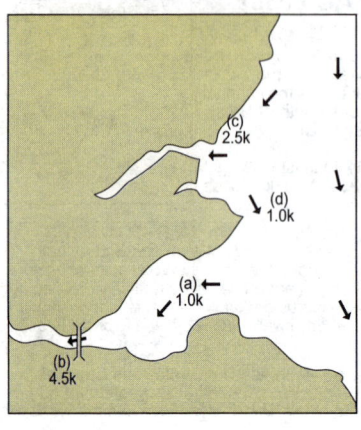

FIRTHS of FORTH (AC 175) & TAY (AC 1481)

Tidal streams are quite weak in the outer part of the Firth, increasing as the narrows at islands and the bridges are approached. Apart from the stream of the Tay, which attains 5 knots in most places, the coastwise tidal streams between Fife Ness and Arbroath are weak.

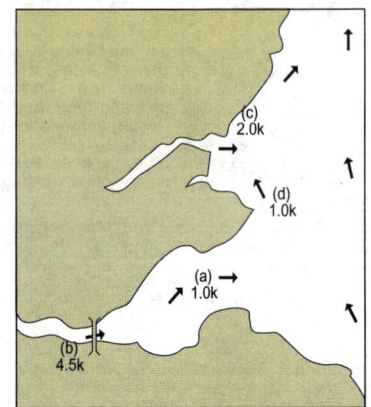

(a) Dover –0225 to Dover +0330   (a) Dover +0330 to Dover –0225
(b) Dover –0200 to Dover +0400   (b) Dover +0400 to Dover –0200
(c) Dover –0210 to Dover +0420   (c) Dover +0420 to Dover –0210
(d) Dover –0110 to Dover +0520   (d) Dover +0520 to Dover –0110

PASSAGES FROM FORTH & TAY

Northbound. Leave before HW (Dover +0400) to be at N Carr at Dover +0600. Bound from Forth to Tay aim to arrive at Abertay By at LW slack (Dover –0200).

Southbound. Leave before LW (Dover -0200) to be at Bass Rk at HW Dover. Similar timings if bound from Tay to Forth, leave late in ebb to pick up early flood off St Andrews to N Carr and into Forth.

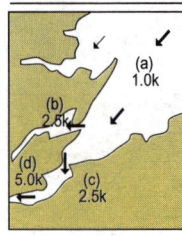

INVERNESS & CROMARTY FIRTHS (AC 1077)

Tidal streams in the Inverness Firth and approaches are not strong, except in the Cromarty Firth Narrows, the Fort George Narrows and the Kessock Road, including off the entrance to the Caledonian Canal.

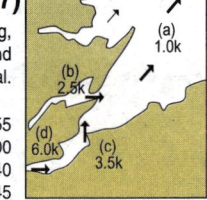

(a) Dover –0555 to Dover +0030   (a) Dover +0030 to Dover –0555
(b) Dover –0400 to Dover +0115   (b) Dover +0115 to Dover –0400
(c) Dover –0400 to Dover –0220   (c) Dover +0115 to Dover –0440
(d) Dover –0430 to Dover +0100   (d) Dover –0130 to Dover +0545

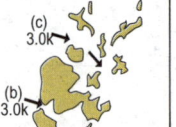

PENTLAND FIRTH & ORKNEYS (AC 1954)

The tide flows strongly around and through the Orkney Islands. The Pentland Firth is a dangerous area for all craft, tidal flows reach 12 knots between Duncansby Head and S Ronaldsay. W of Dunnet Hd & Hoy is less violent. There is little tide within Scapa Flow.

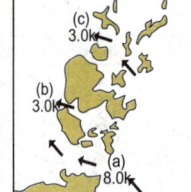

(a) Dover –0500 to Dover +0100   (a) Dover +0115 to Dover –0535
(b) Dover +0500 to Dover –0110   (b) Dover –0110 to Dover +0050
(c) Dover –0530 to Dover +0040   (c) Dover +0040 to Dover –0530

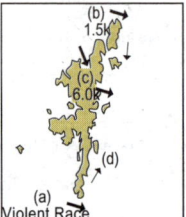

SHETLAND ISLANDS (AC 219)

The tidal flow around the Shetland Islands rotates as the cycle progresses. When the flood begins, at –0400 HW Dover, the tidal flow is to the E, at HW Dover it is S, at Dover +0300 it is W, and at –0600 Dover it is N.

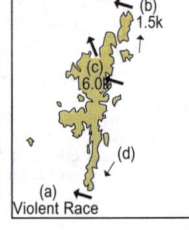

(a) Dover –0410 to Dover +0020   (a) Dover +0050 to Dover –0410
(b) Dover –0400 to Dover +0030   (b) Dover +0130 to Dover –0500
(c) Dover –0530 to Dover +0100   (c) Dover +0100 to Dover –0530
(d) Dover –0400 to Dover –0200   (d) Dover +0200 to Dover +0500

TIDAL GATES - NORTH WEST SCOTLAND

A guide to the time of tide turn at tidal gates, the approximate maximum strength of the tidal flow (spring rates shown - neaps are approximately 60% of these), and the position and timing of races, counter tides, etc.

FLOOD	EBB

SOUND OF HARRIS (AC 2642)

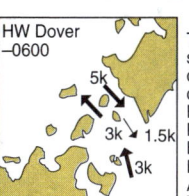

HW Dover
−0600

The behaviour of tidal streams in the Sd of Harris varies from day to night, springs to neaps, and winter to summer. The following data applies to daylight, in summer at spring tides in the Cope Channel. Further information can be sought in the Admiralty West of Scotland Pilot.
HW Dover - HW D +0200: SE stream.
HW D +0300 - HW D +0600: Incoming stream from both ends.
HW D −0600 - HW D −0500: NW stream.
HW D −0500 - HW Dover: Outgoing stream from both ends.
At neaps in summer the stream will run SE for most of the day.
Tide rates shown are the maxima likely to be encountered at any time.

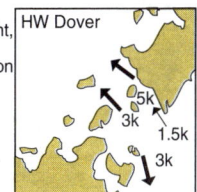

HW Dover

THE LITTLE MINCH (AC 1795)

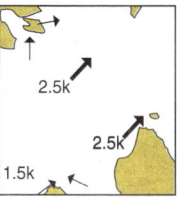

The N going stream on both shores begins at HW Dover +0430 (HW Ullapool -0345), with the strongest flow from mid channel to the Skye coast. There is a W going counter tide E of Vaternish Point.

The S going stream on both shores begins at HW Dover −0130 (HW Ullapool +0240), with the strongest flow from mid channel to the Skye coast. The E going stream in Sound of Scalpay runs at up to 2k. The E going flood and W going ebb in Sound of Scalpay run at up to 2k.

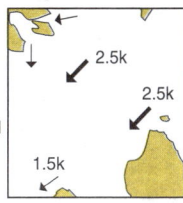

KYLE OF LOCHALSH & KYLERHEA (AC 2540)
NOTE: THESE STREAMS ARE SUBJECT TO VARIATION

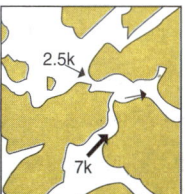

N going stream in Kyle Rhea begins HW Dover +0140 (HW Ullapool +0555) and runs for 6 hours. The E going stream in Kyle Akin begins (Sp) HW Dover +0350 (HW Ullapool −0415). (Nps) HW Dover −0415 (HW Ullapool).

S going stream in Kyle Rhea begins HW Dover -0415 (HW Ullapool) and runs for 6 hours. The W going stream in Kyle Akin begins (Sp) HW Dover −0015 (HW Ullapool +0400). (Nps) HW Dover +0140 (HW Ullapool +0555).

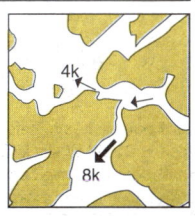

SOUND OF MULL - WEST (AC 2171)

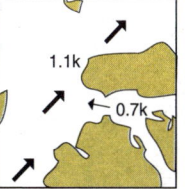

The N going stream off Ardnamurchan begins at HW Dover +0130 (HW Oban −0525). The E going stream in the Sound of Mull begins at HW Dover +0555 (HW Oban −0100).

The S going stream off Ardnamurchan begins at HW Dover −0430 (HW Oban +0100). The W going stream in the Sound of Mull begins at HW Dover −0130 (HW Oban +0400).

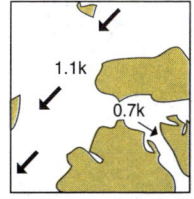

SOUND OF MULL - EAST (AC 2171)

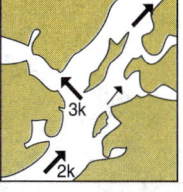

The N going stream in the Firth of Lorne begins at HW Dover −0100 (HW Oban +0430). The W going stream in the Sound of Mull begins at HW Dover +0105 (HW Oban −0550). The ingoing tides at Lochs Feochan, Etive and Creran begin at HW Dover +0300, −0100 & +0030.

The S going stream in the Firth of Lorne begins at HW Dover +0500 (HW Oban −0155). The E going stream in the Sound of Mull begins at HW Dover +0555 (HW Oban −0025). The outgoing tides at Lochs Feochan, Etive and Creran begin at HW Dover −0500, −0520 & −0505.

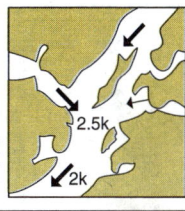

SOUND OF LUING & DORUS MOR (AC 2343)

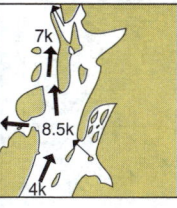

The N or W going stream begins as follows:
Dorus Mor: HW Dover −0200 (HW Oban +0330). Springs: 8 knots.
Corryvreckan: HW D −0120 (HW O +0410). Sp: 8.5 knots.
Cuan Sound: HW D −0110 (HW O +0420). Sp: 6 knots.
Sound of Jura: HW D −0130 (HW O +0400). Sp: 4 knots.
Sound of Luing: HW D −0100 (HW O +0430). Sp: 7 knots.
The S or E going stream begins as follows:
Dorus Mor: HW Dover +0440 (HW Oban −0215). Springs: 8 knots.
Corryvreckan: HW D +0445 (HW O −0210). Sp: 8.5 knots.
Cuan Sound: HW D +0455 (HW O −0200). Sp: 6 knots.
Sound of Jura: HW D +0450 (HW O −0205). Sp: 4 knots.
Sound of Luing: HW D +0500 (HW O −0155). Sp: 7 knots.

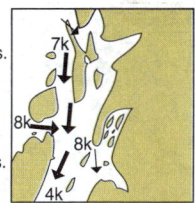

TIDES

TIDAL GATES - SOUTH WEST SCOTLAND

A guide to the time of tide turn at tidal gates, the approximate maximum strength of the tidal flow (spring rates shown - neaps are approximately 60% of these), and the position and timing of races, counter tides, etc.

FLOOD	EBB

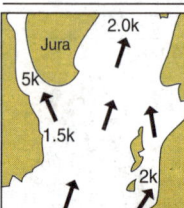

SOUNDS OF ISLAY AND GIGHA (AC 2168)

Main flood begins +0015 HW Dover (HW Oban +0545). Streams turn approx 1 hr earlier in Gigha Sd & at Kintyre & Jura shores. S going stream for 9hrs close inshore between Gigha and Machrihanish starting HW Dover (HW Oban −0530).

Main ebb begins HW Dover −0545 (HW Oban −0015). Streams turn 1 hr earlier in Gigha Sd, Kintyre & Jura shores. Overfalls off McArthur's Hd.

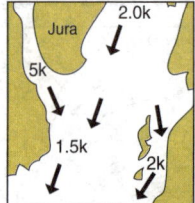

NORTH CHANNEL - NORTH (AC 2798)

Main flood begins HW Dover −0600 (HW Greenock +0505). Races off Mull of Kintyre, Altacarry Hd & Fair Hd. Counter tides in bays of Antrim coast. W-going streams in Rathlin Sd, counter tide from Sanda Sd to Machrihanish last 1h30 - 2 hrs.

Main ebb begins HW Dover (HW Greenock −0120). Races off Mull of Kintyre & Altacarry Hd. Counter tides in bays of Antrim coast, counter tide from Macrihanish to Sanda Sd last 1h30 - 2 hrs.

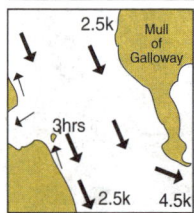

NORTH CHANNEL - SOUTH (AC 2198)

Irish coast - flood begins HW Dover +0610 (HW Belfast −0600). Scottish coast - HW Dover +0430 (HW Greenock +0310). Races off Copeland Is. & Mull of Galloway. Counter tide off Donaghadee and Island Magee last 3 hrs of flood.

Irish coast - ebb begins HW Dover −0015 (HW Belfast). Scottish coast - HW Dover −0130 (HW Greenock −0250). Races off Copeland Is. & Mull of Galloway. Flood begins 2 hrs early close inshore N of Mull of Galloway.

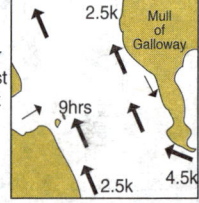

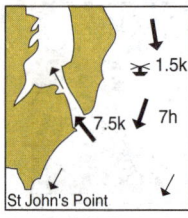

APPROACHES TO STRANGFORD LOUGH (AC 2156)

The tide cycle is approx 3 hours later than in the N Channel

Flood runs for 6 hours from HW Dover −0345 (HW Belfast −0330), with a maximum rate of 7.5 knots at Rue Point. The strong flow flattens the sea in onshore winds and entrance can be made in strong winds.

Ebb runs for 6 hours from HW Dover +0215 (HW Belfast +0230), max rate 7.5k, E of Angus Rk. If entering against ebb use West Channel with care. Smoothest water near Bar Pladdy Buoy when leaving.

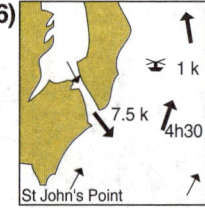

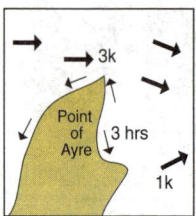

ISLE OF MAN - NORTH (AC 2094)

E going stream at Point of Ayre begins HW Dover −0545 (HW Liverpool −0600). Counter tide inside banks E of Point. In Ramsey Bay the S Going tide runs for 3h from +0530 Dover (+0515 Liverpool).

W going stream at Point of Ayre begins HW Dover +0015 (HW Liverpool). Counter tide inside banks W of Point. In Ramsey Bay the N going tide runs for 9h from −0330 Dover (−0345 Liverpool).

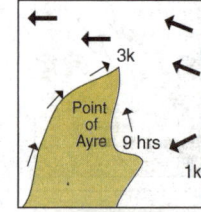

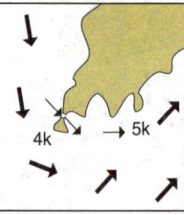

ISLE OF MAN - SOUTH (AC 2094)

E going stream begins −0600 Dover (Liverpool +0610). Overfalls and race E of Chicken Rock. Calf Sound: The E going stream begins earlier, at approximately Dover +0400 (Liverpool +0345).

W going stream begins +0015 Dover (HW Liverpool). Overfalls and race N of Chicken Rock. Calf Sound: The W going stream begins earlier, at approximately −0130 Dover (−0145 Liverpool). Note: all times may vary due to weather conditions.

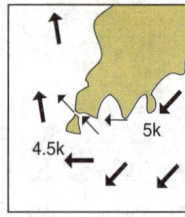

TIDAL GATES - IRISH SEA

A guide to the time of tide turn at tidal gates, the approximate strength of the tidal flow (spring rates shown — neaps are approximately 60% of these), and the position and timing of races, counter tides, etc.

FLOOD	EBB

DUBLIN BAY (AC 1415)

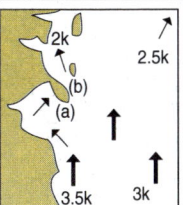

Tide between Rosbeg bank and Howth Hd (a) runs NE from HW Dublin +0300 for 9h30. In Howth Sd (b) the stream is NW going from +0430 to –0130. New flood and ebb tides begin close to the S shore and N of Baily up to 1h before HW Dublin.

The tide between Rosbeg bank and Howth Hd (a) runs SW from HW Dublin for 3h. In Howth Sd (b) the stream is SE going from –0130 to +0430. Strengths of streams increase S of Dublin Bay, and decrease N of it.

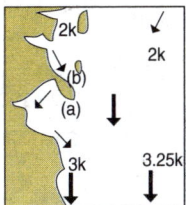

N W ANGLESEY (AC 1977)

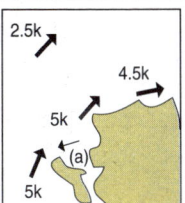

Flood tide close to the coast runs at over 5k springs, and at about 2.5k 7 miles offshore. The brief period of slack water offshore is 1h before HW Dover (1h15 before HW L'pool). Slack water lasts longer in Holyhead Bay.

Ebb tide close to the coast runs at over 5k springs, and at about 2.5k 7 miles offshore. Slack water is 5h after HW Dover (4h45 after HW L'pool). There is no significant counter tide in Holyhead Bay, but the ebb starts first there, giving about 9h W-going tide N of the harbour (a).

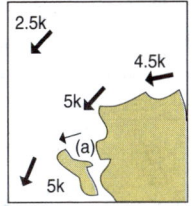

BARDSEY SOUND (AC 1971)

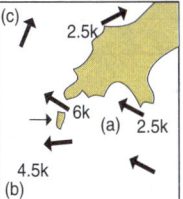

The tide turns to the NW or NE (flood) as follows:
at (a): HW Dover +0300;
at (b): HW D +0500;
at (c): –0545 HW D.
These times are approximate. There is a strong eddy down tide of Bardsey Island and overfalls throughout the area.

The tide turns to the SW or SE (ebb) as follows:
at (a): HW Dover –0300;
at (b): HW D –0100 ;
at (c): at HW D –0030.
These times are approximate. There is a strong eddy down tide of Bardsey Island and overfalls throughout the area.

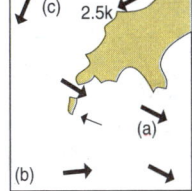

S W WALES (AC 1478)

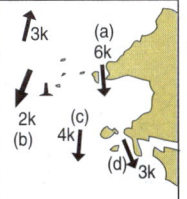

The tide turns to the S or SE (Bristol Channel flood) as follows:
at (a): HW Dover –0200;
at (b) & (c): HW D –0100 ;
at (d): –0300 HW D

The tide turns to the N or NW (Bristol Channel ebb) as follows:
at (a): HW Dover +0400;
at (b) & (c): HW D +0500 ;
at (d): +0300 HW D

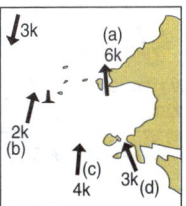

CARNSORE POINT (AC 2049)

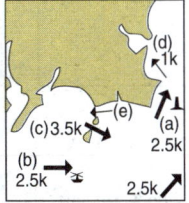

The tide turns to the NE or N (Irish Sea flood) as follows:
at (a): HW Dover +0500; at (b): HW D +0520; at (c): HW D +0600;
at (d): –0600 HW D. NE going streams are shorter in duration and weaker than SE going - careful passage planning is essential.

The tide turns to the SW or S as follows:
at (a): –0200 HW D ; at (b): HW D –0020; at (c): –0015 HW D; at (d): –0300 HW Dover. Leaving Rosslare at –0300 HW D a yacht can carry a fair tide for about 8h until HW D +0515 off Hook Head.

NOTE: The tide turns on St Patrick's Bridge (e) up to 2 hours earlier than in Saltee Sound

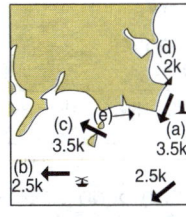

CORK COAST (AC 2049)

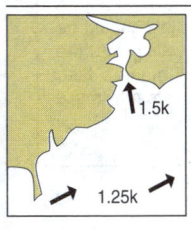

The tide, which flows coastwise, turns to the NE at HW Dover +0045. There is an eddy 5 miles ESE of Old Head of Kinsale at HW Dover +0400. The ingoing Cork Harbour tide begins at HW Dover +0055.

The tide turns SW at HW Dover +0500. The outgoing Cork Harbour tide begins at HW Dover –0540.

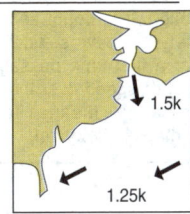

TIDES

MENAI STRAIT (AC 1464) - TIDAL GATES

FLOOD

(T) : turning → : < 2k ➡ : 2-4k ⫸ : 4k +

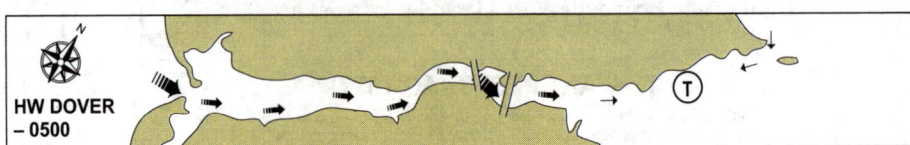

HW DOVER −0600

LOCAL LW: Caernarfon: HW Dover −0555. Port Dinorwic: −0620. Menai: −0540. Beaumaris: −0605.

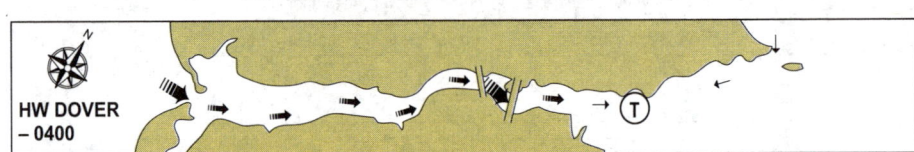

HW DOVER −0500

HW DOVER −0400

HW DOVER −0300

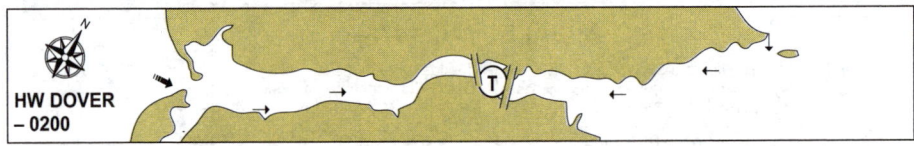

HW DOVER −0200

SLACK WATER IN THE SWELLIES: HW Dover −0200 to −0230.

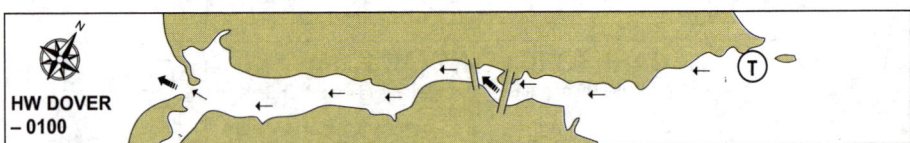

HW DOVER −0100

LOCAL HW: Belan: HW Dover −0115. Caernarfon: −0105. Port Dinorwic: −0050.

THE SWELLIES

WESTBOUND: Leave or pass Beaumaris in time to arrive at the Swellies by HW Dover −0230 to −0200. If in doubt about passage speed, leave early; the adverse tide will check your progress. For a first time passage this is useful, as the yacht's speed over the ground is reduced. Late arrival will mean a faster passage, but with perhaps less control.

EASTBOUND: Leave or pass Port Dinorwic in time to arrive at Menai Bridge by HW Dover −0230 to −0200. Progress towards the Swellies should be closely monitored, as you are travelling with the last of the flood. Early arrival will mean a fast, perhaps dangerous passage, being late may make it impossible.

MENAI STRAIT (AC 1464) - TIDAL GATES contd

EBB

(T) : turning → : < 2k ⇒ : 2-4k ⇛ : 4k +

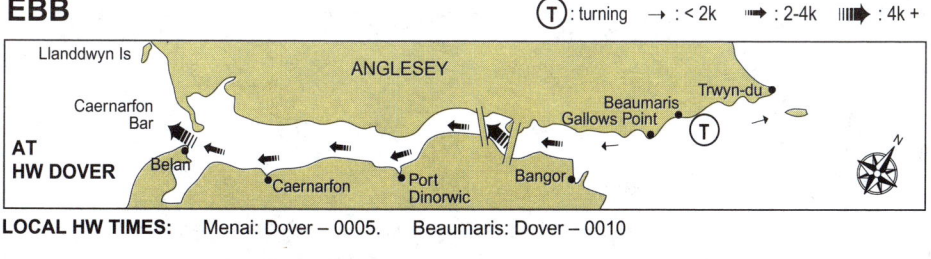

AT HW DOVER

LOCAL HW TIMES: Menai: Dover – 0005. Beaumaris: Dover – 0010

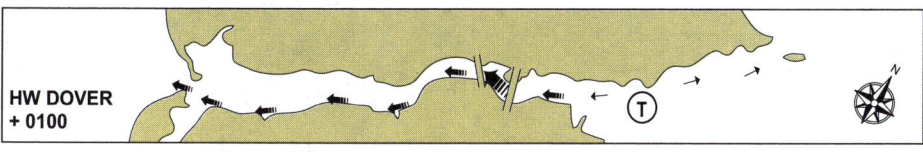

HW DOVER + 0100

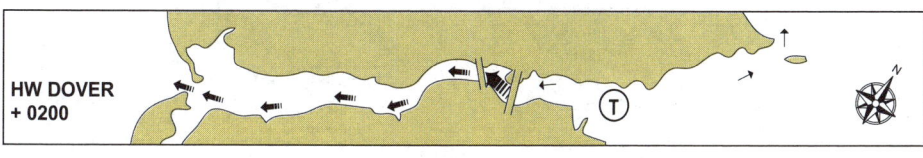

HW DOVER + 0200

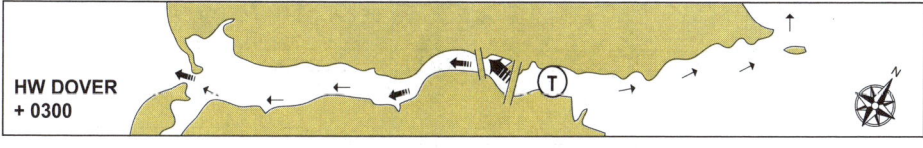

HW DOVER + 0300

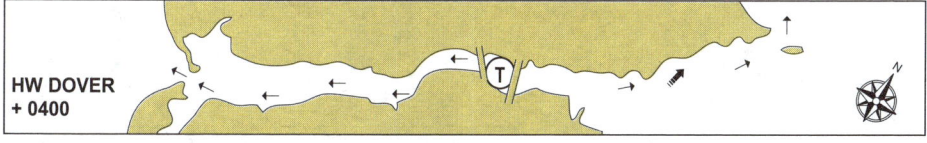

HW DOVER + 0400

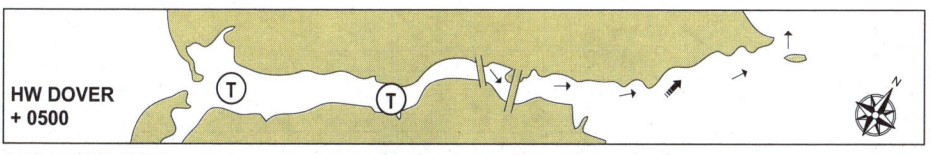

HW DOVER + 0500

LOCAL LW TIMES: Belan: Dover + 0520.

CAERNARFON BAR

CAERNARFON BAR is without question highly dangerous in certain conditions. Buoys are located to suit changing channel; positions obtainable from Caernarfon Port Radio - VHF Ch 16; 06, 12: 2h–HW, or when vessel expected. Beware cross track tides near high water. Bar impassable during or after fresh or strong onshore weather. Keep strictly in channel.

OUTWARD BOUND: Do not leave Belan Narrows after half tide, better as soon as possible after the ebb commences, which gives maximum depth and duration of fair tide if bound S & W.

INWARD BOUND: Locating the bar buoys may be difficult; head for Llanddwyn I. until they are located. Only cross after half tide (HW Dover –0400), which inevitably limits onward passage to max of 3 hours.

TIDES

ENGLISH CHANNEL AND SOUTH BRITTANY

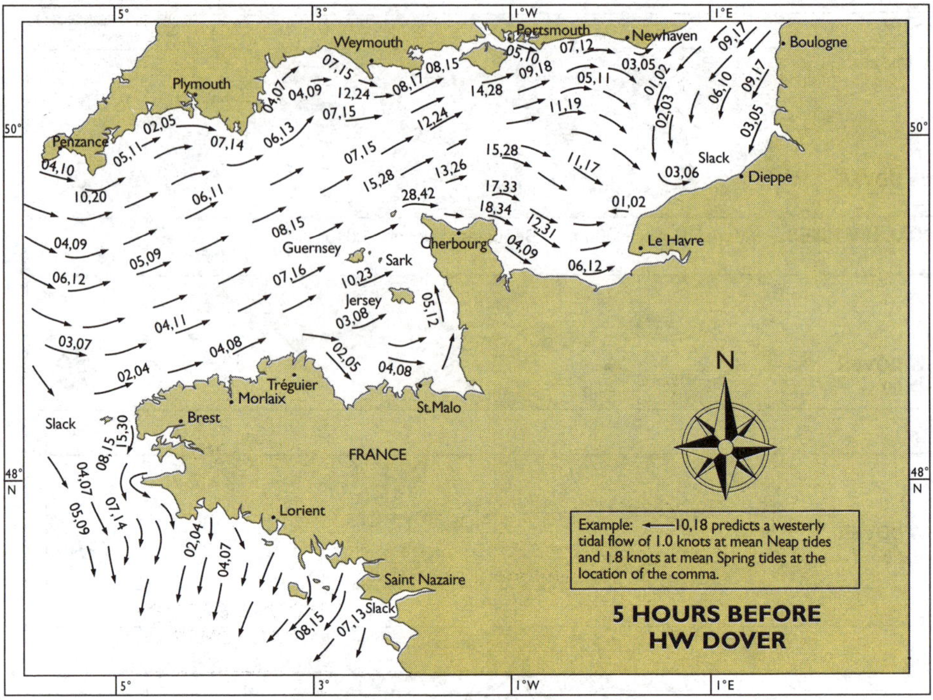

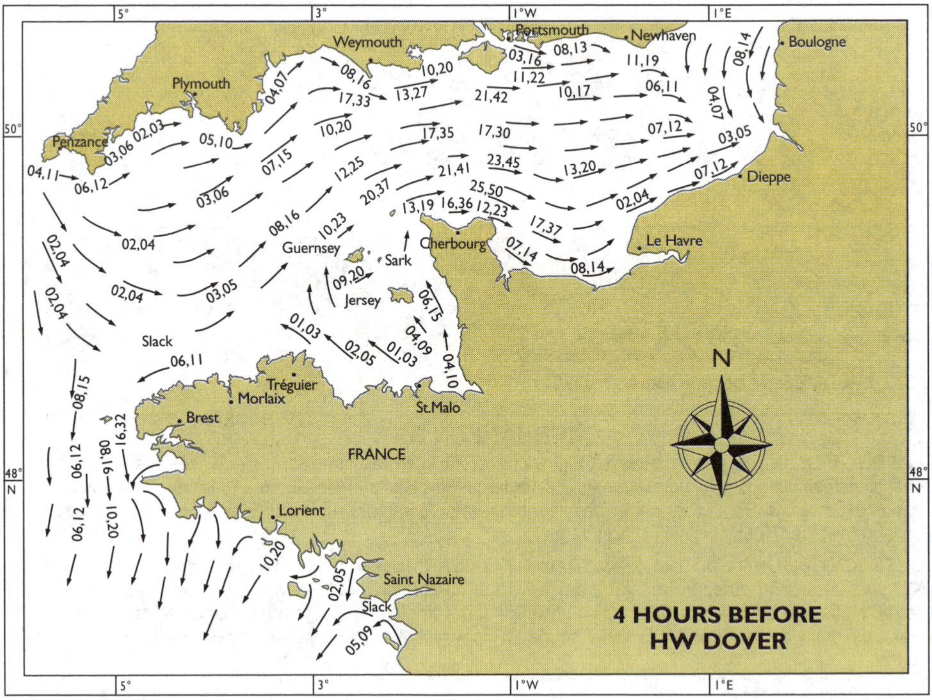

5 HOURS BEFORE HW DOVER

Example: ←—— 10,18 predicts a westerly tidal flow of 1.0 knots at mean Neap tides and 1.8 knots at mean Spring tides at the location of the comma.

4 HOURS BEFORE HW DOVER

ENGLISH CHANNEL AND SOUTH BRITTANY

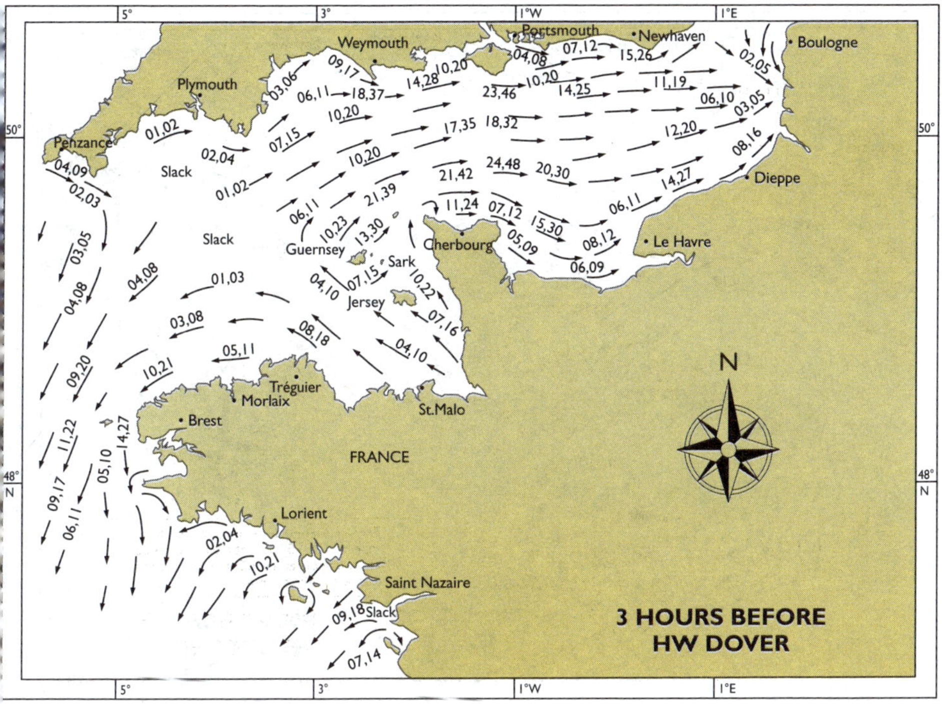

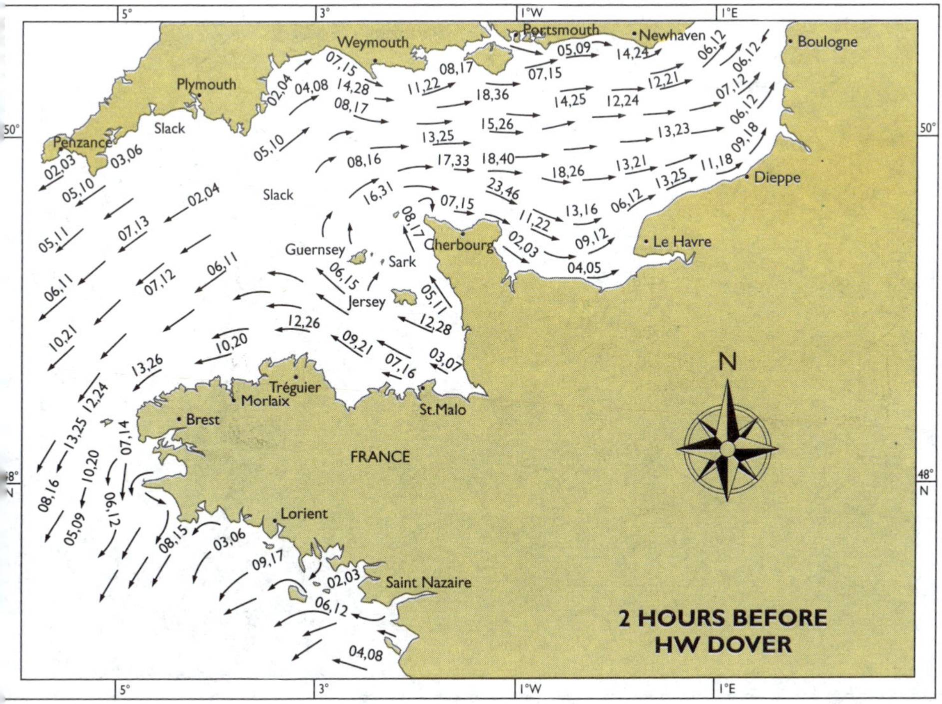

TIDES

ENGLISH CHANNEL AND SOUTH BRITTANY

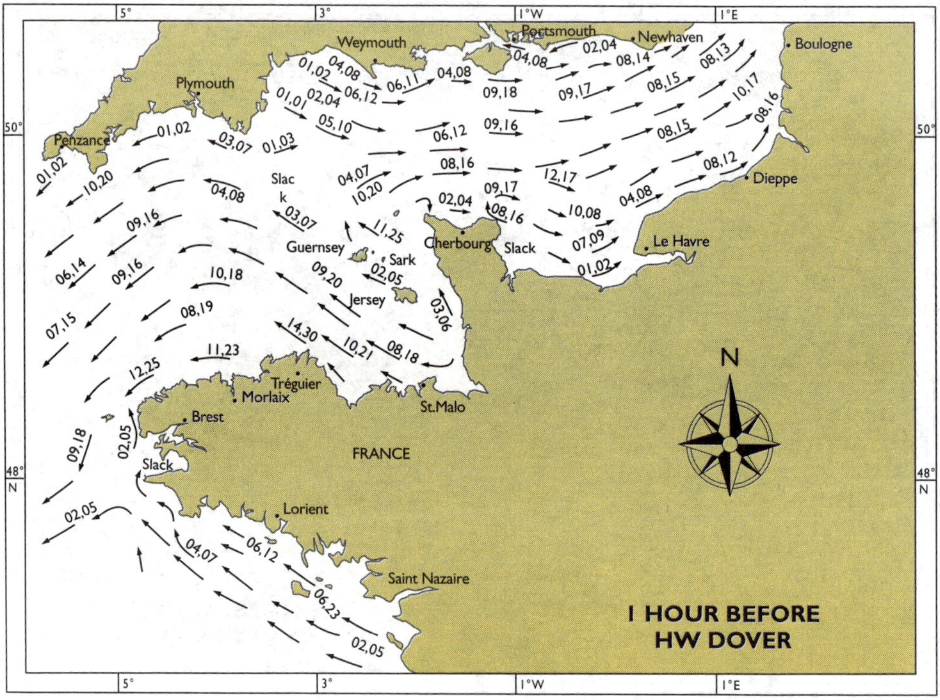

1 HOUR BEFORE HW DOVER

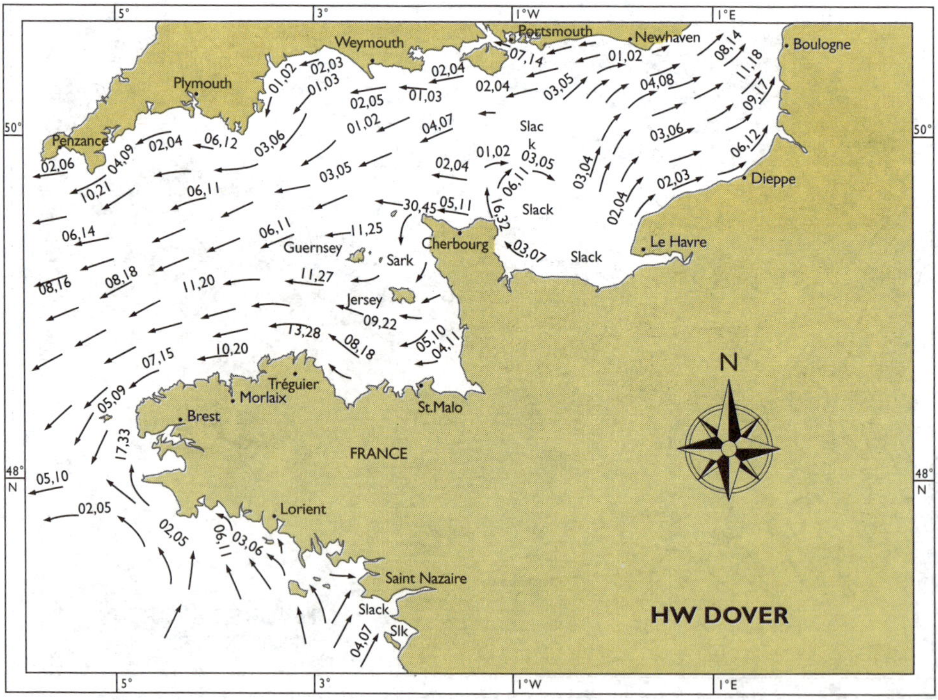

HW DOVER

ENGLISH CHANNEL AND SOUTH BRITTANY

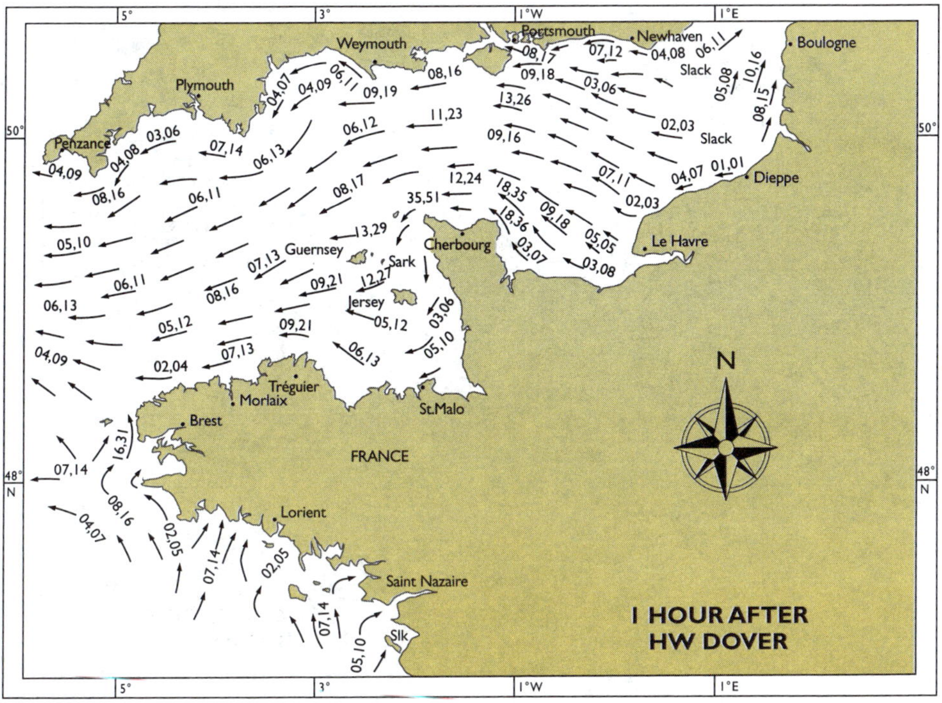

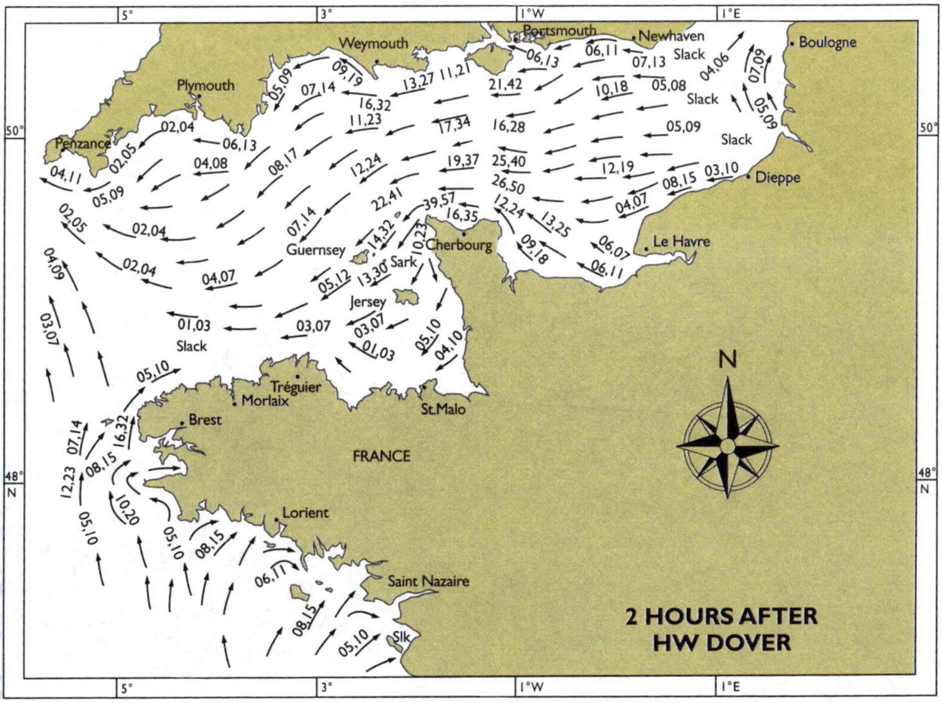

TIDES

ENGLISH CHANNEL AND SOUTH BRITTANY

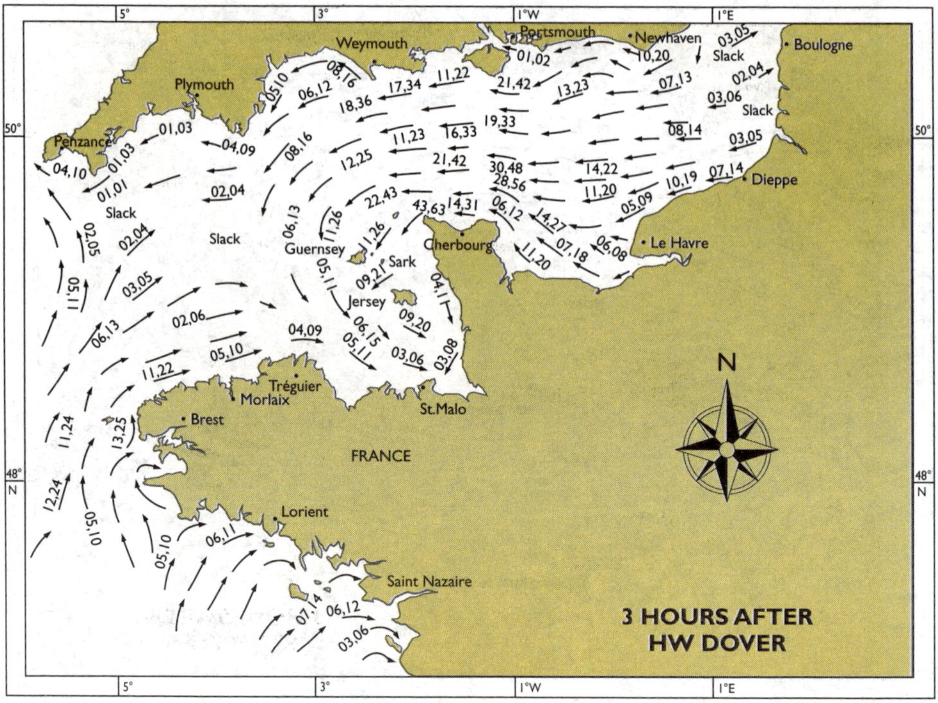

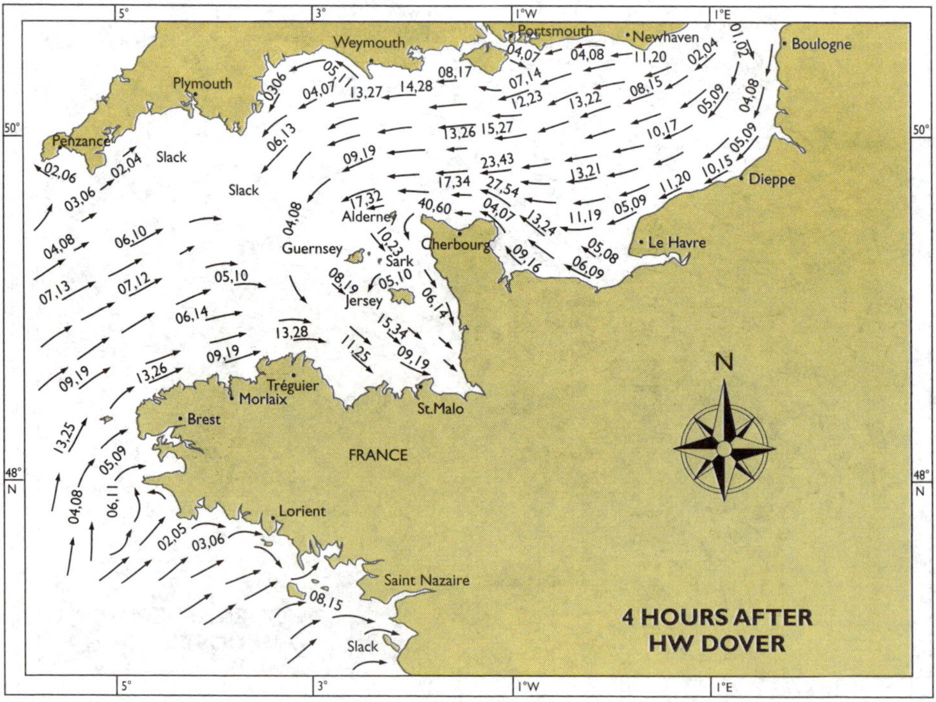

3 HOURS AFTER HW DOVER

4 HOURS AFTER HW DOVER

ENGLISH CHANNEL AND SOUTH BRITTANY

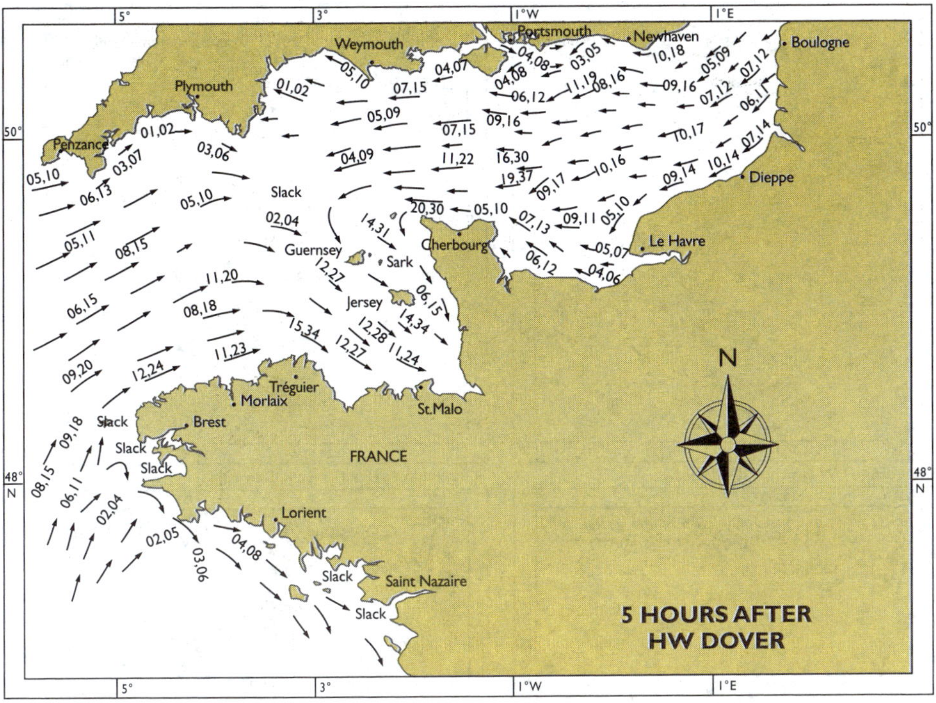

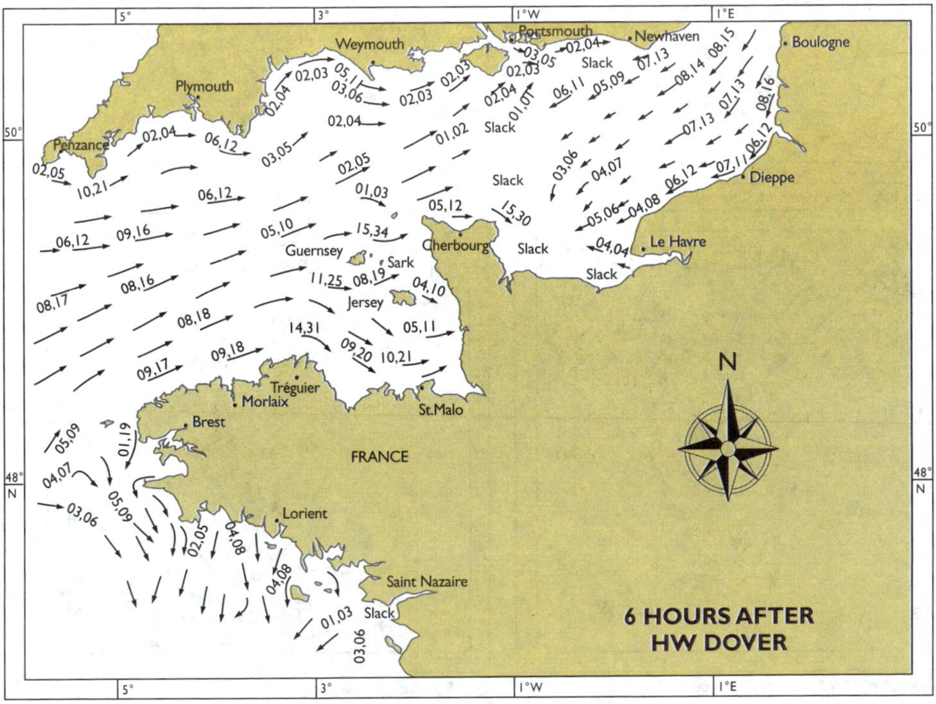

TIDES

PORTLAND

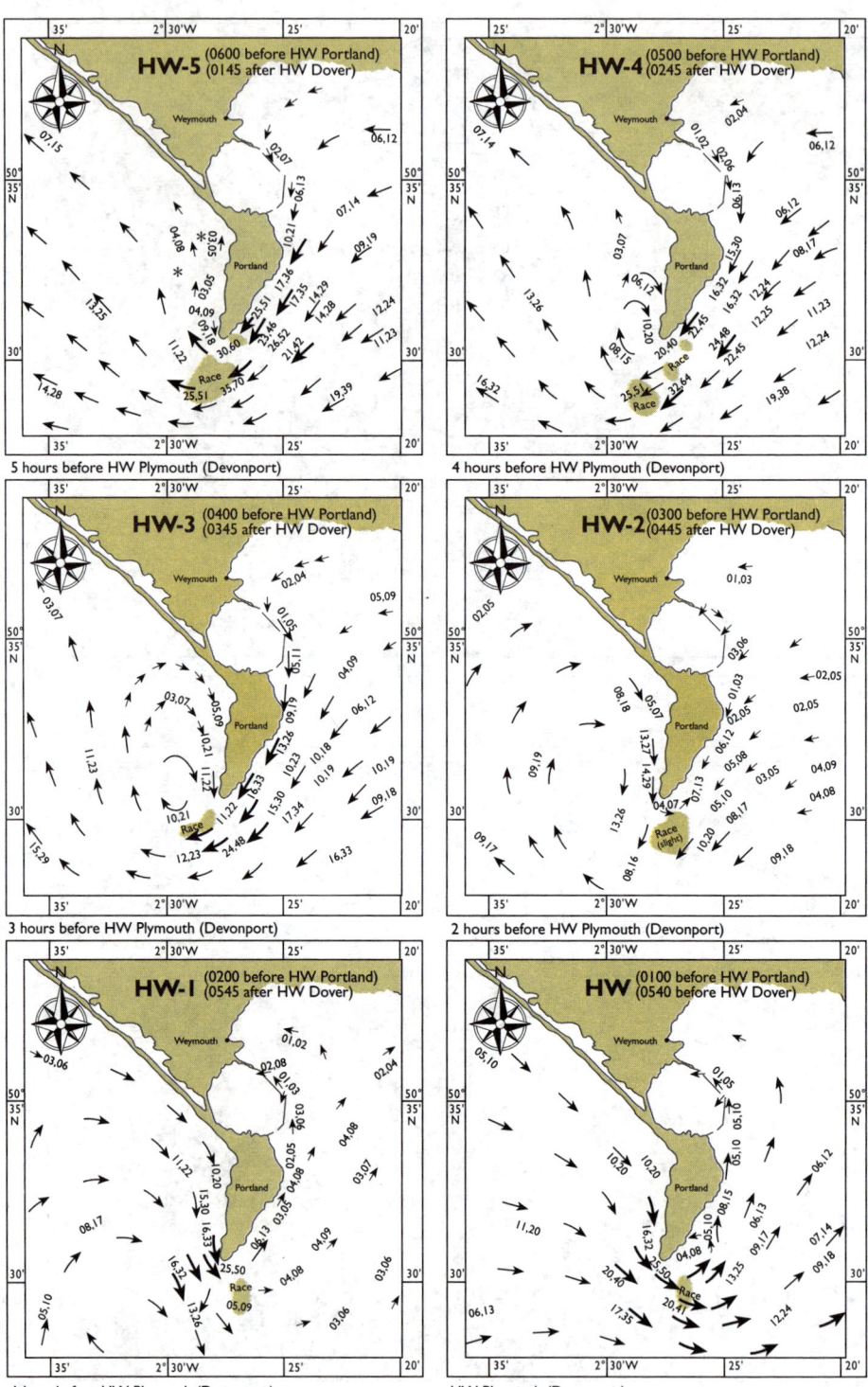

PORTLAND

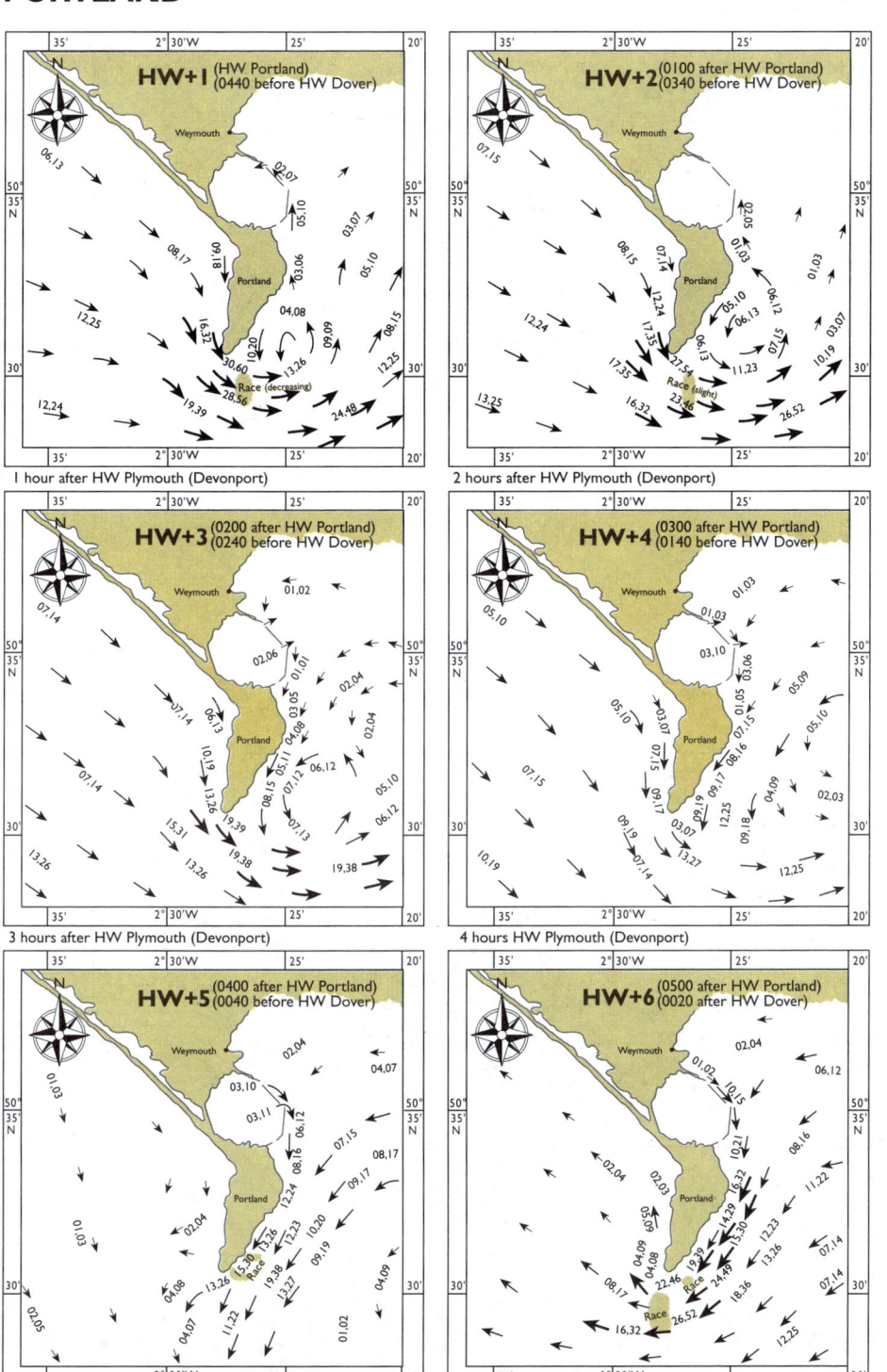

TIDES

ISLE OF WIGHT

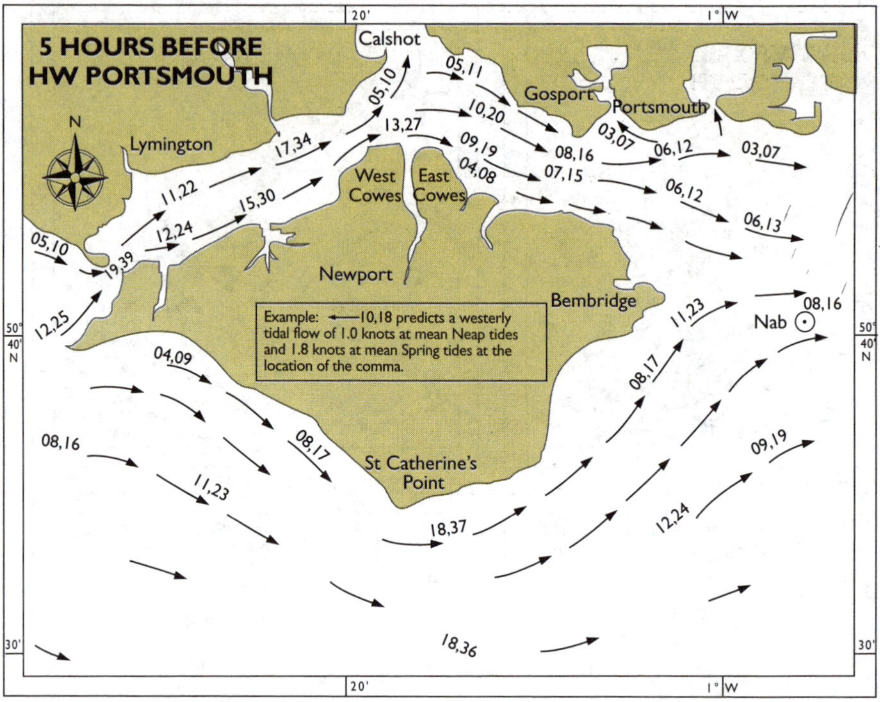

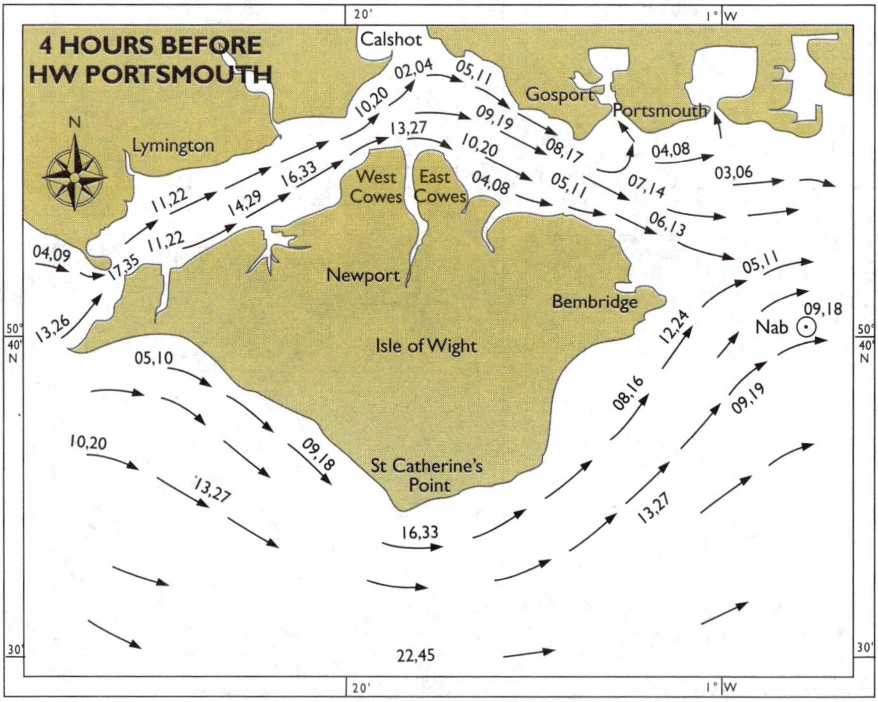

5 HOURS BEFORE HW PORTSMOUTH

Example: ←10,18 predicts a westerly tidal flow of 1.0 knots at mean Neap tides and 1.8 knots at mean Spring tides at the location of the comma.

4 HOURS BEFORE HW PORTSMOUTH

ISLE OF WIGHT

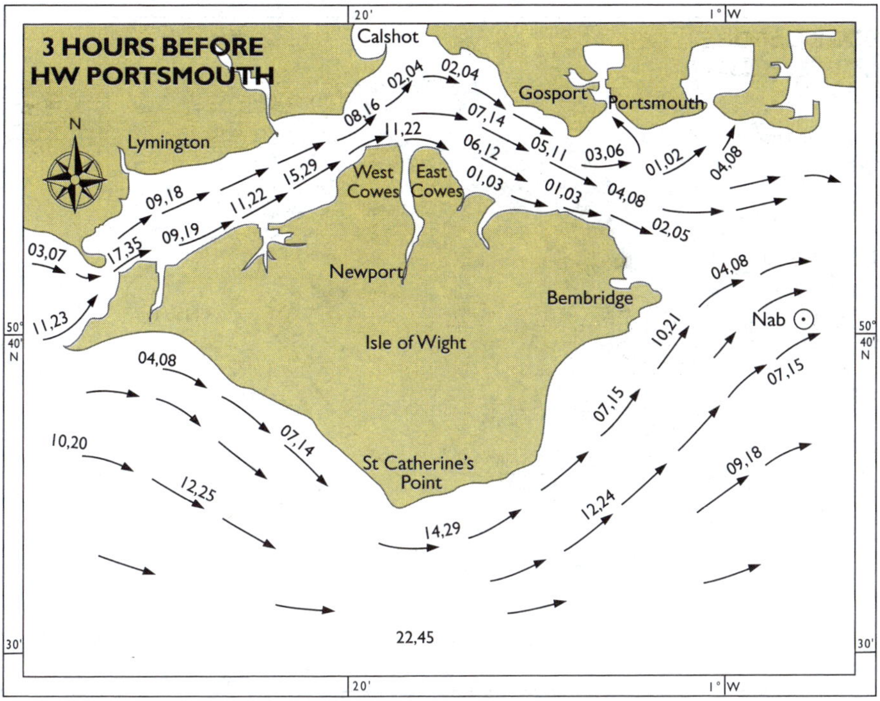

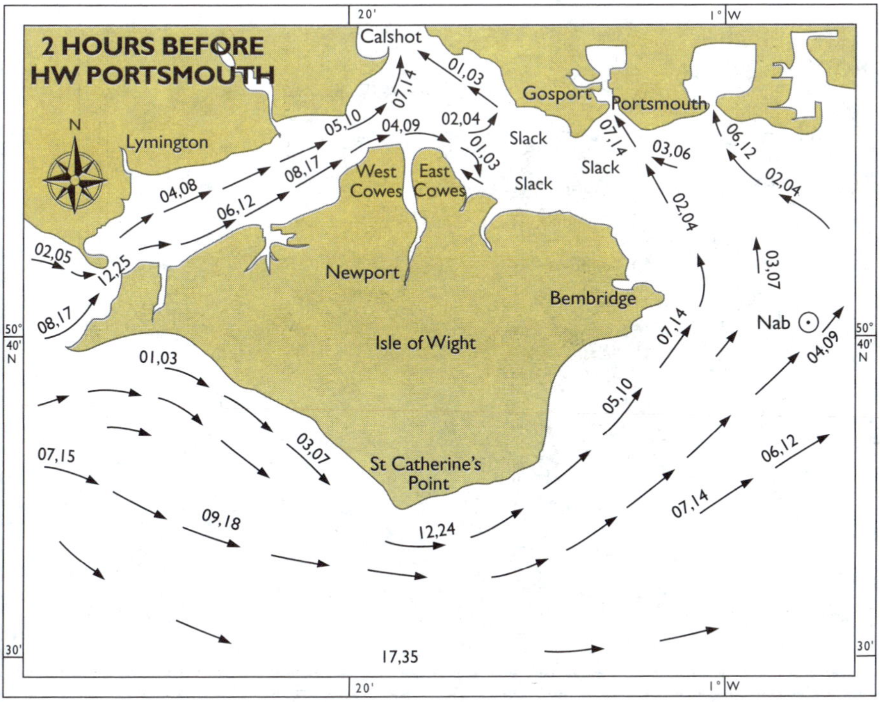

TIDES

ISLE OF WIGHT

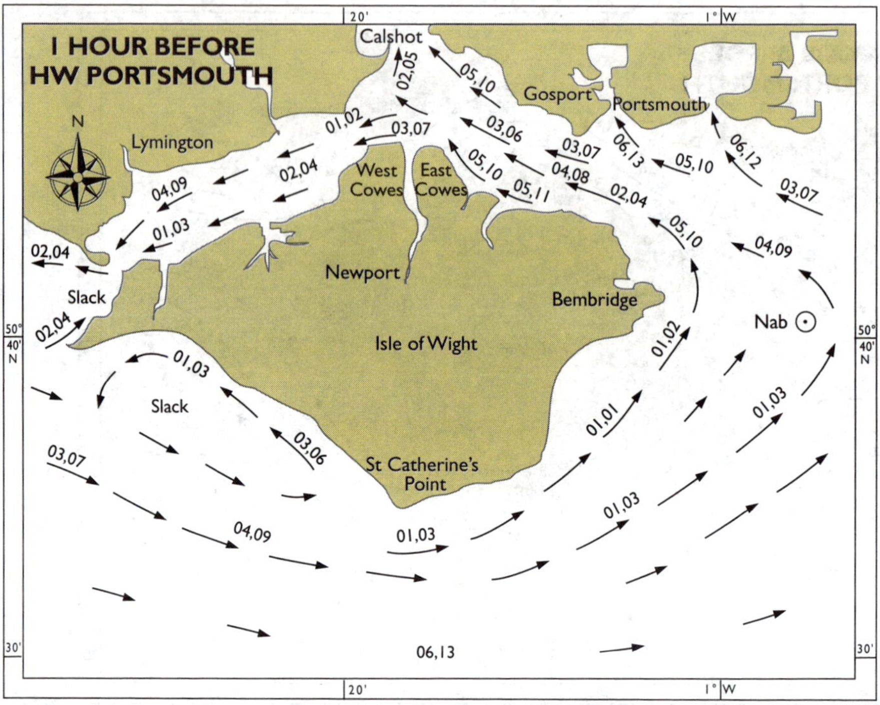

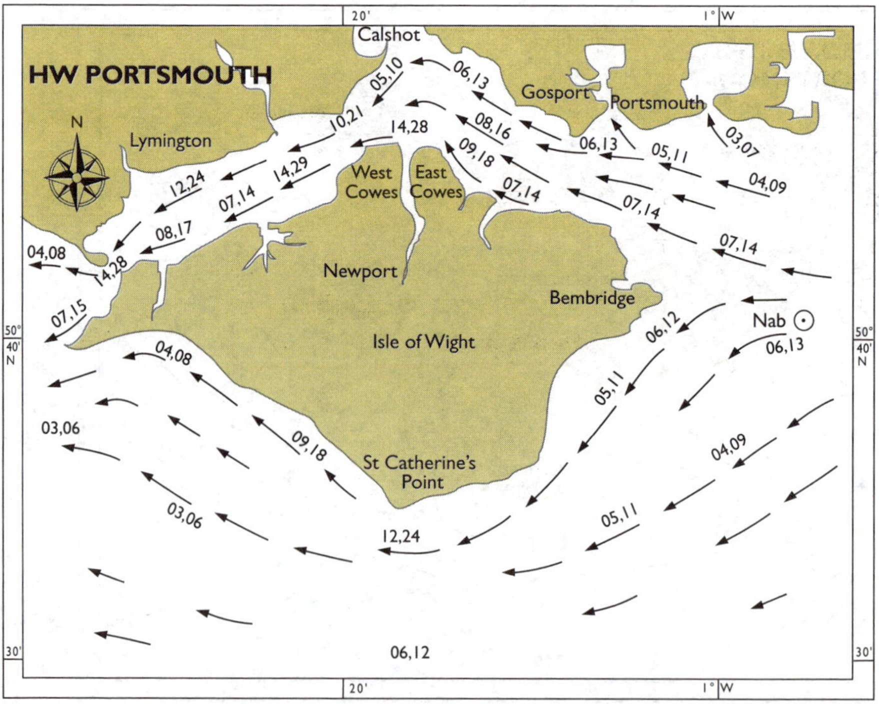

1 HOUR BEFORE HW PORTSMOUTH

HW PORTSMOUTH

ISLE OF WIGHT

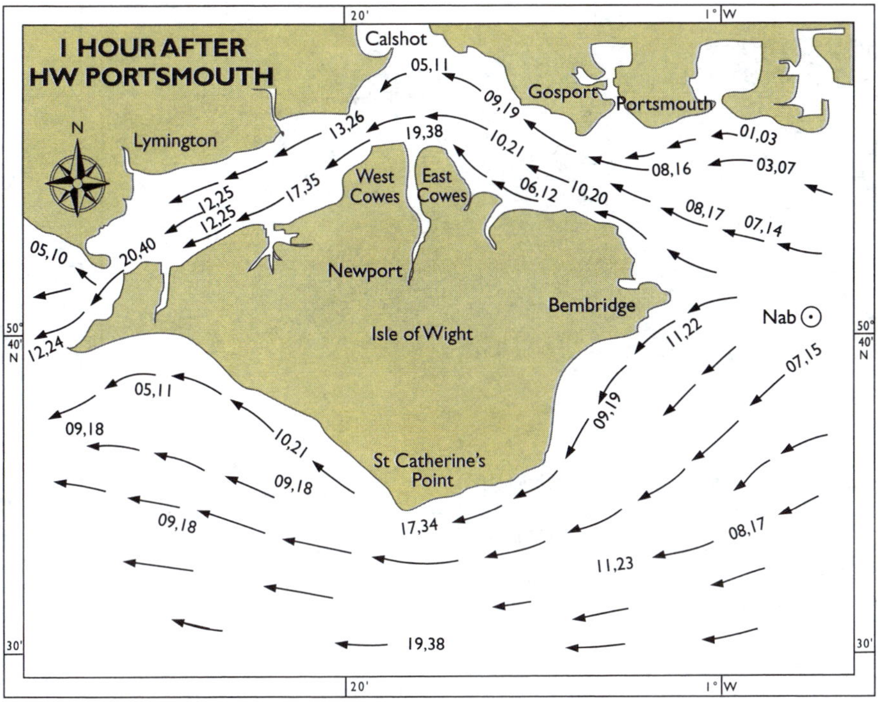

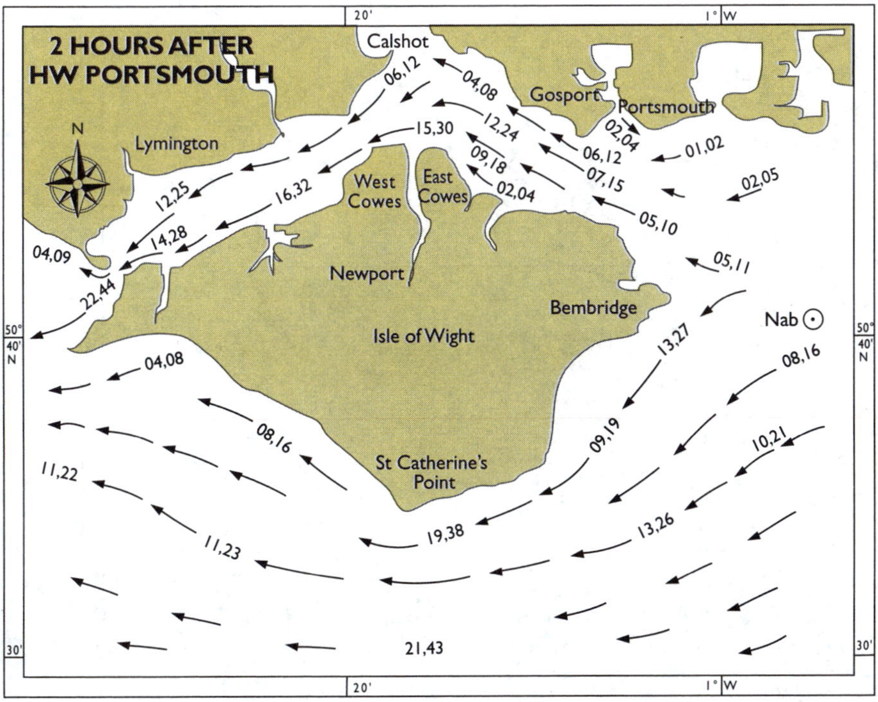

TIDES

ISLE OF WIGHT

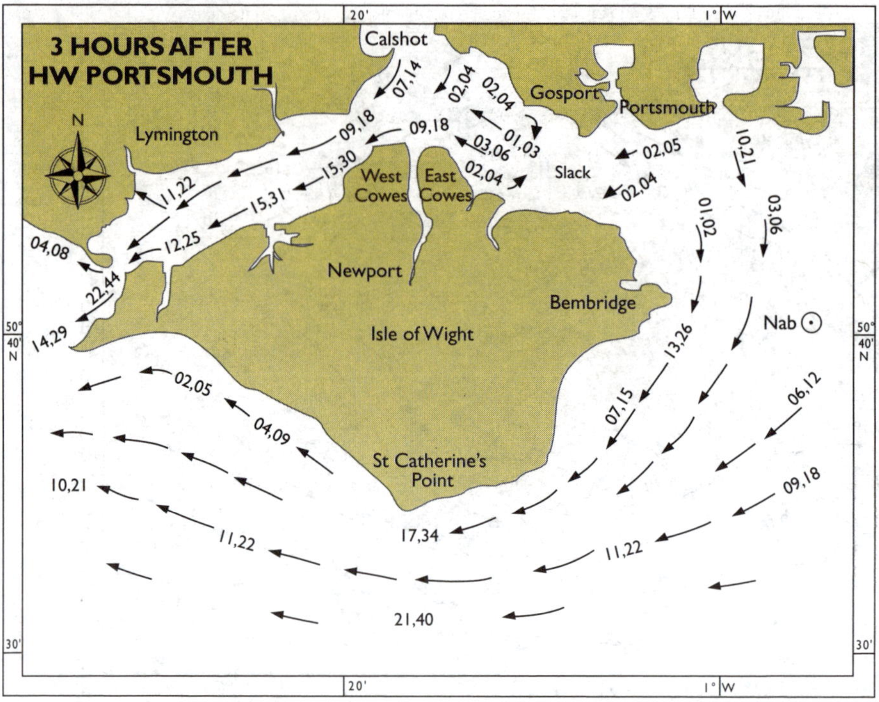

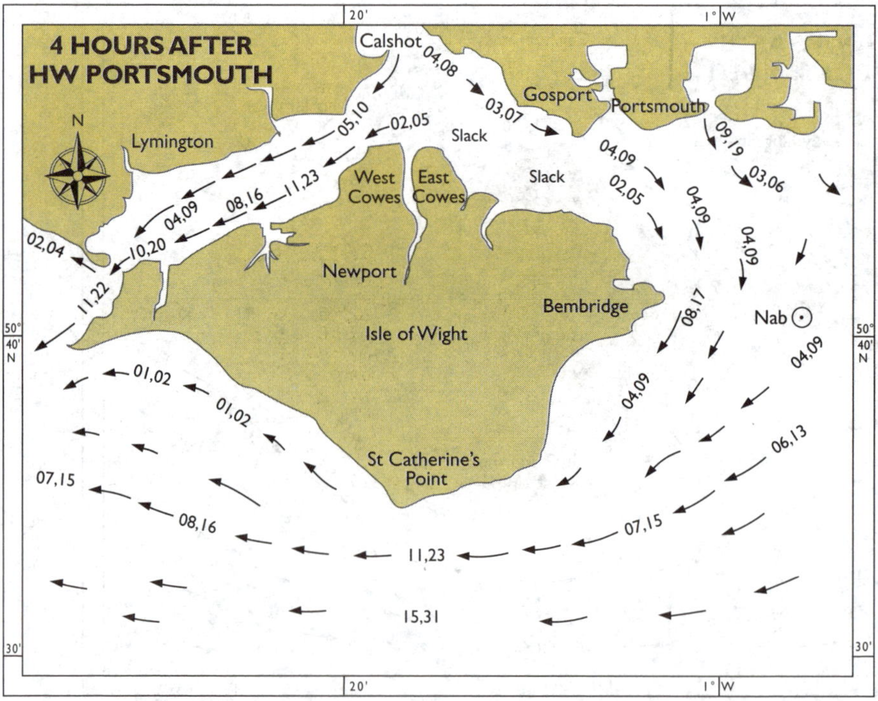

ISLE OF WIGHT

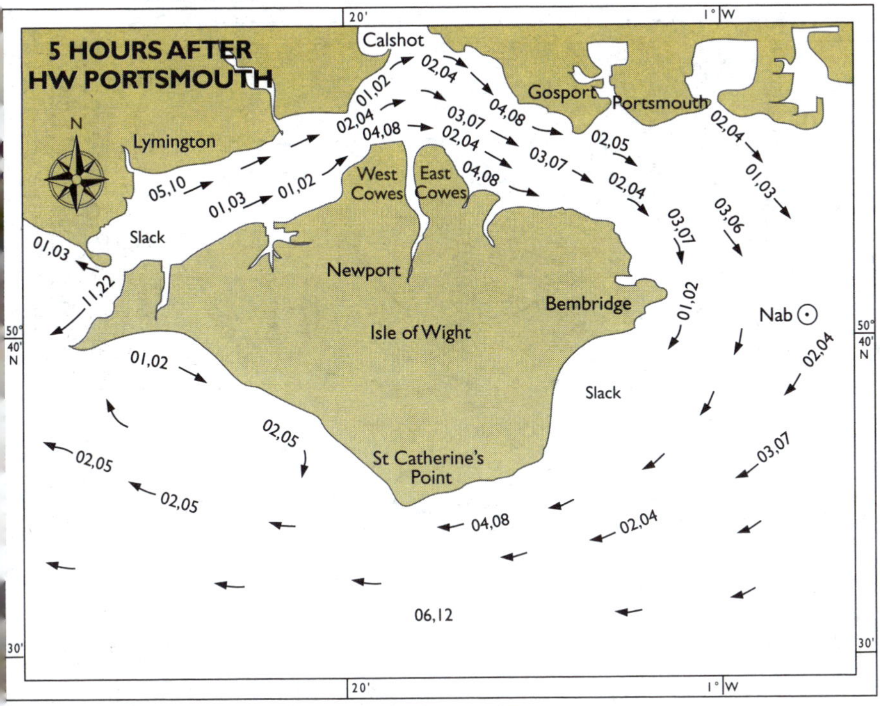

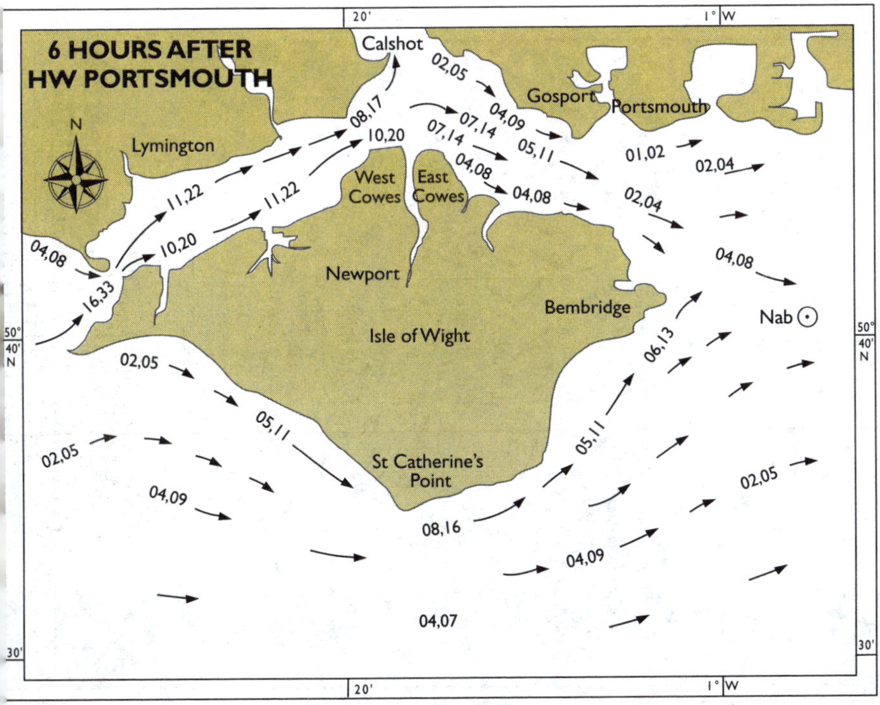

5 HOURS AFTER HW PORTSMOUTH

6 HOURS AFTER HW PORTSMOUTH

TIDES

CHANNEL ISLANDS

Example: ←—10,18 predicts a westerly tidal flow of 1.0 knots at mean Neap tides and 1.8 knots at mean Spring tides at the location of the comma.

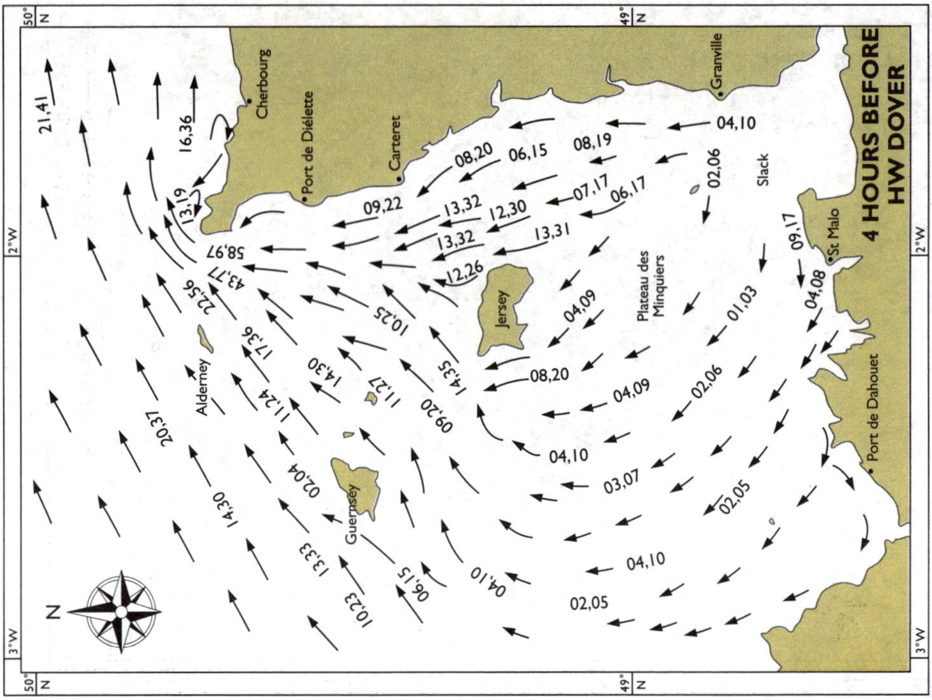

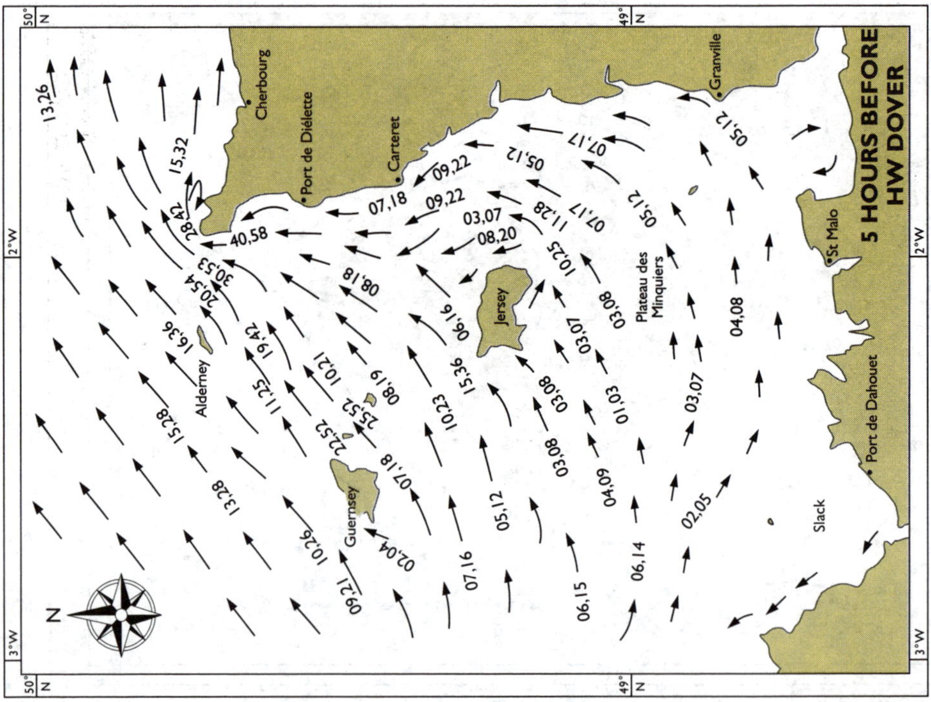

4 HOURS BEFORE HW DOVER

5 HOURS BEFORE HW DOVER

CHANNEL ISLANDS

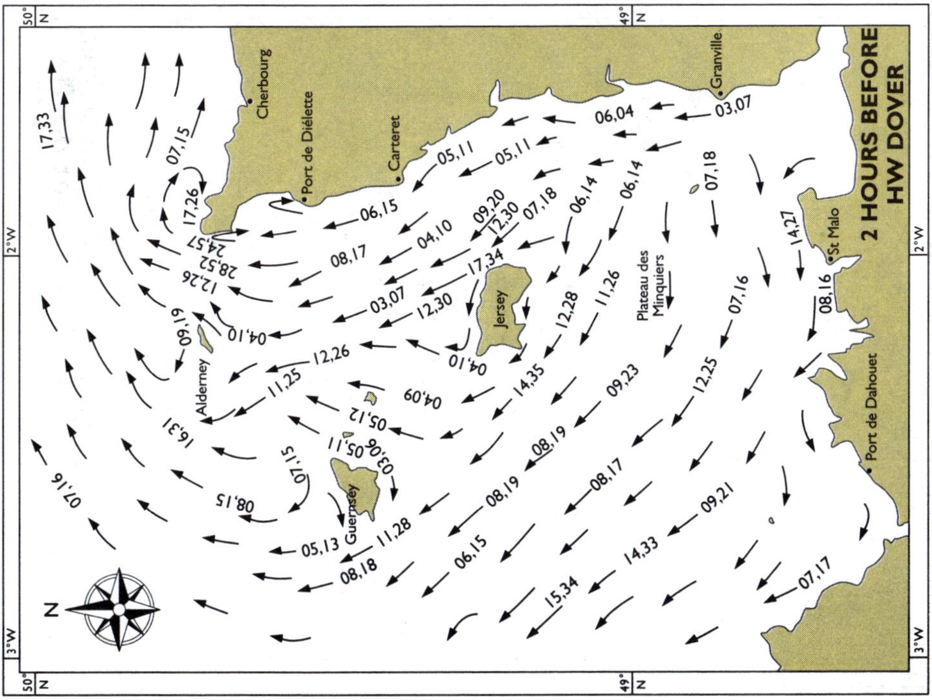

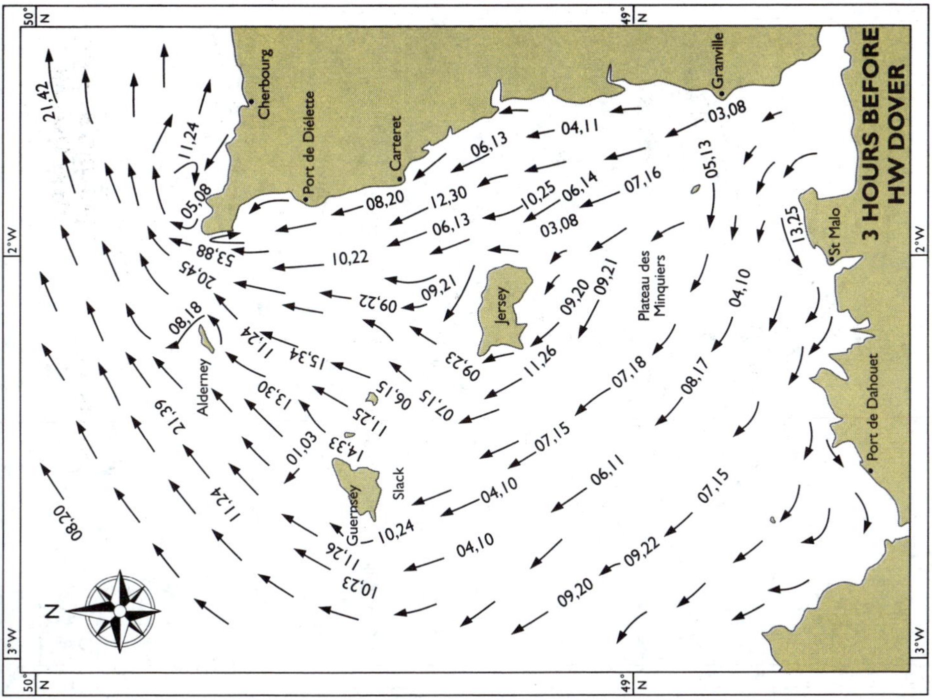

TIDES

CHANNEL ISLANDS

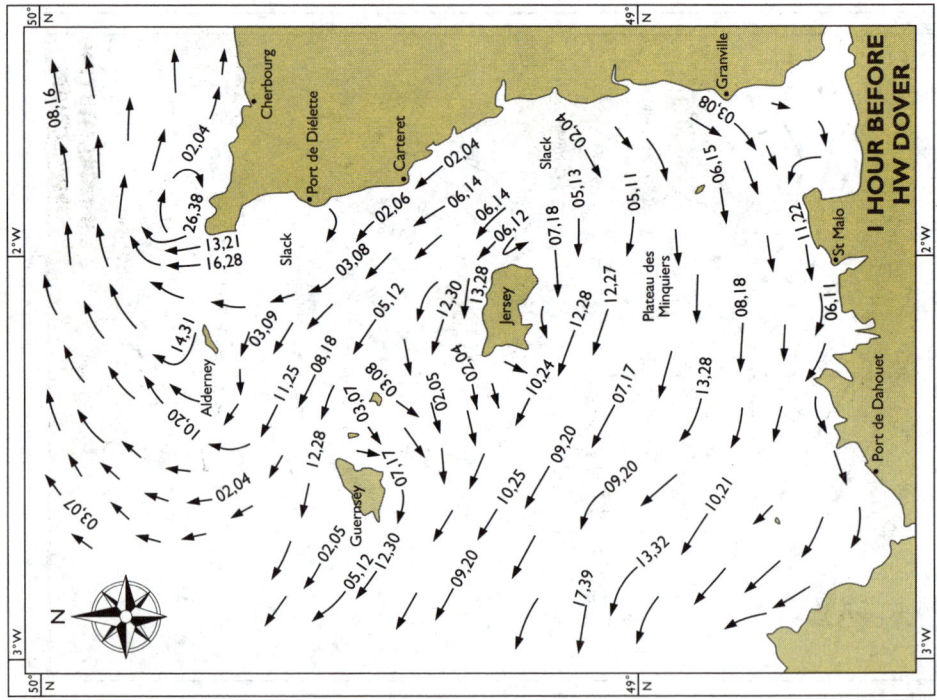

CHANNEL ISLANDS

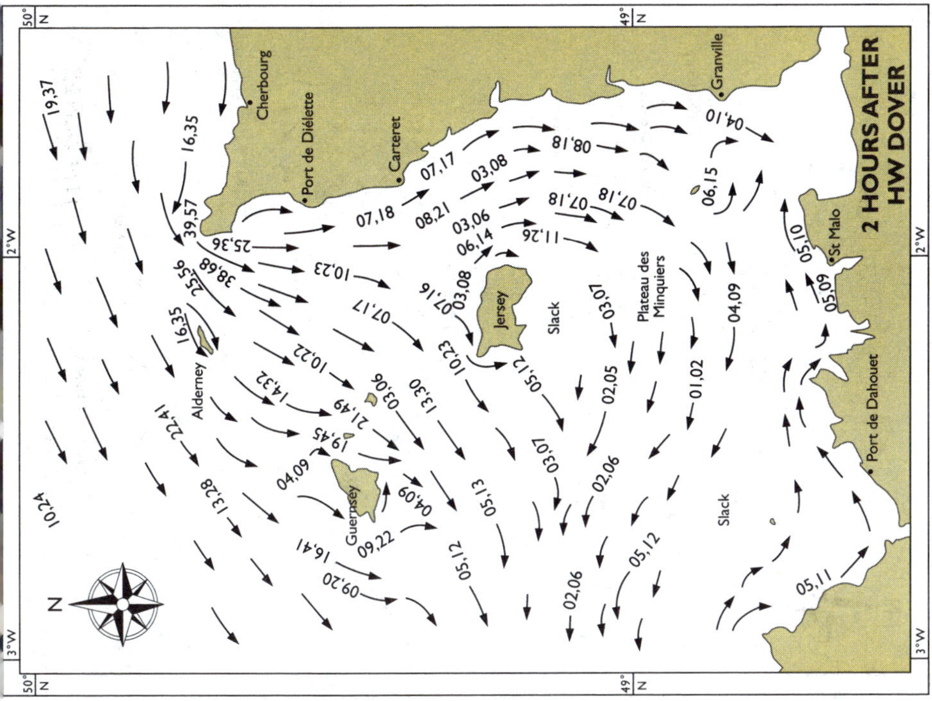

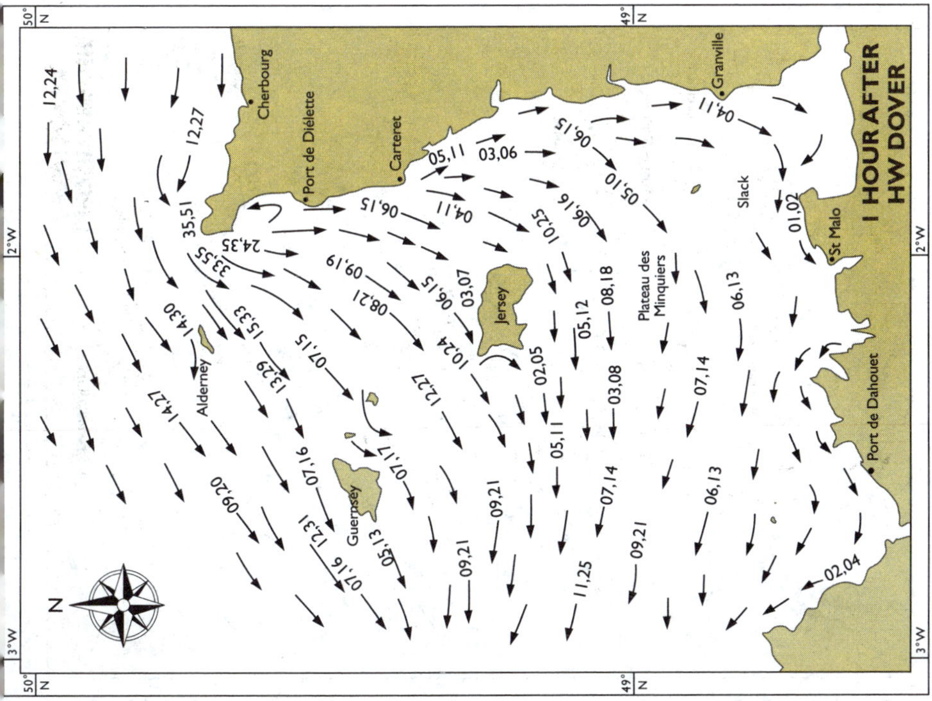

TIDES

CHANNEL ISLANDS

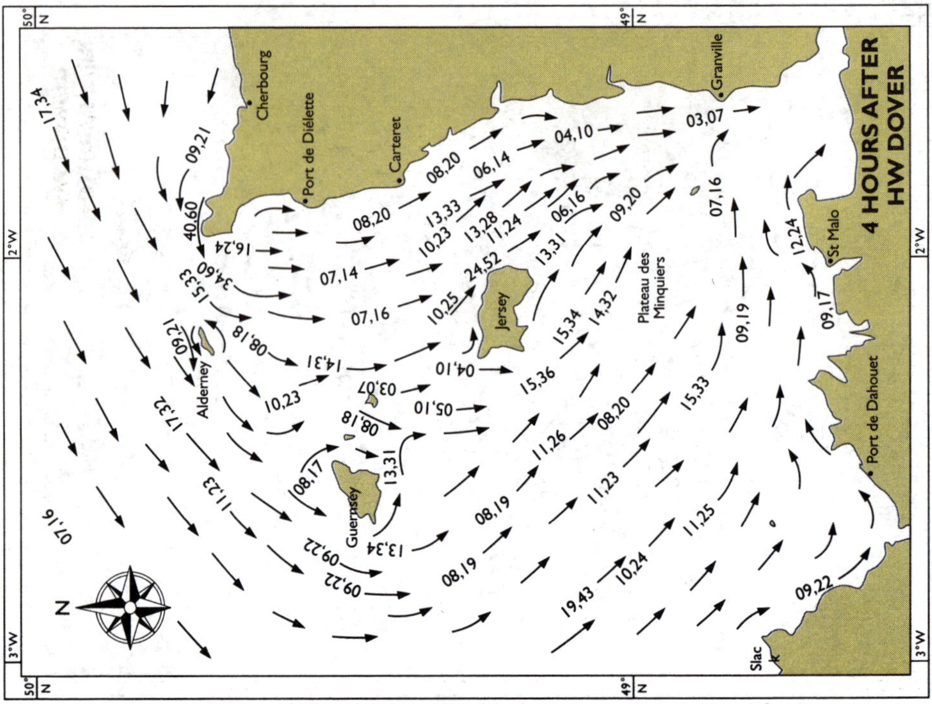

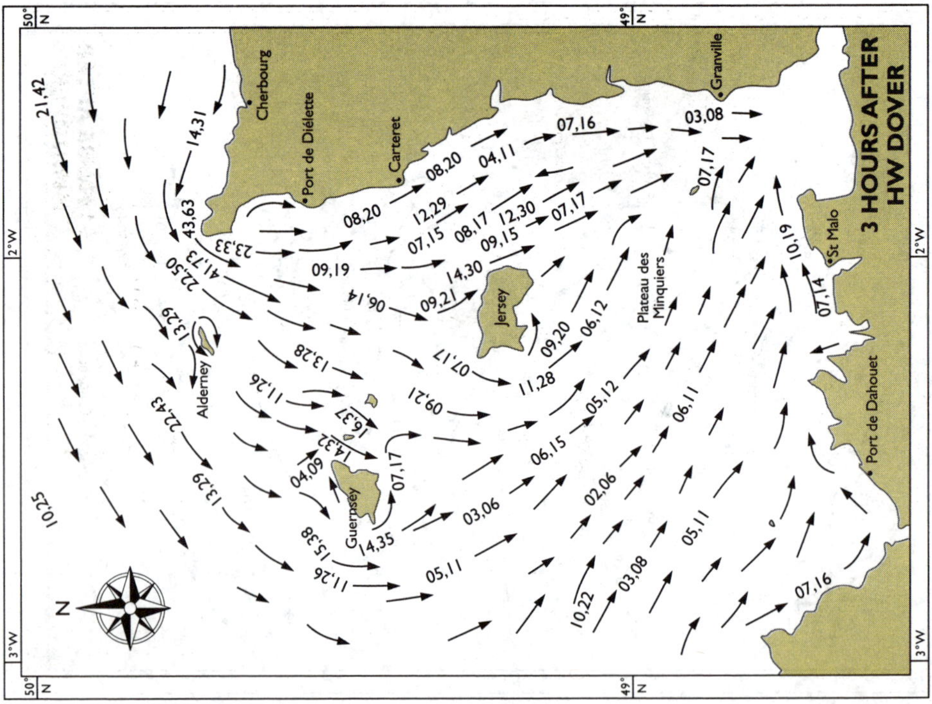

CHANNEL ISLANDS

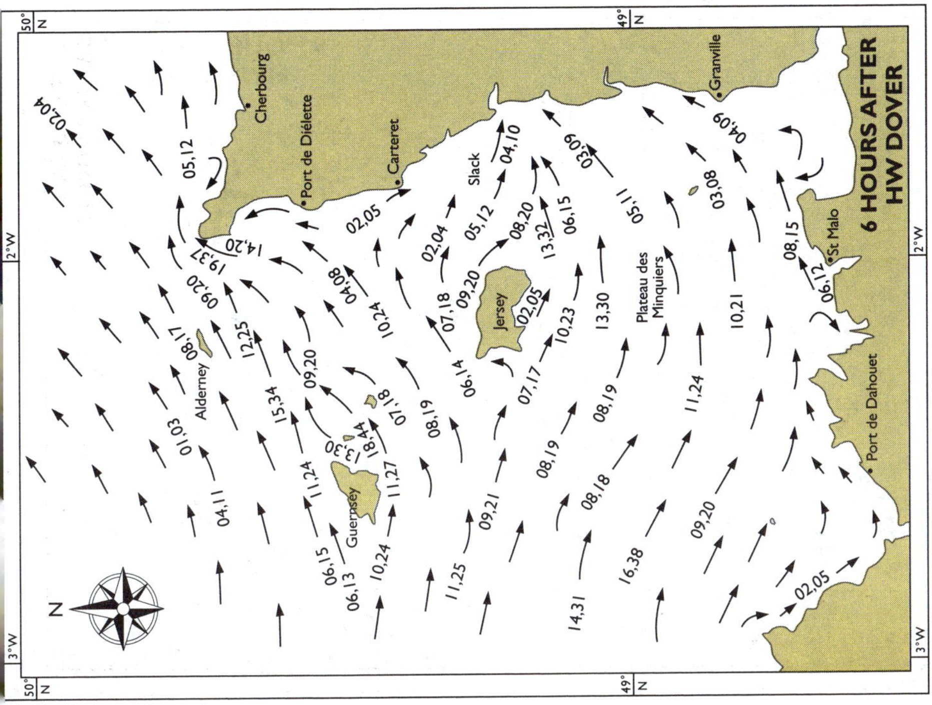

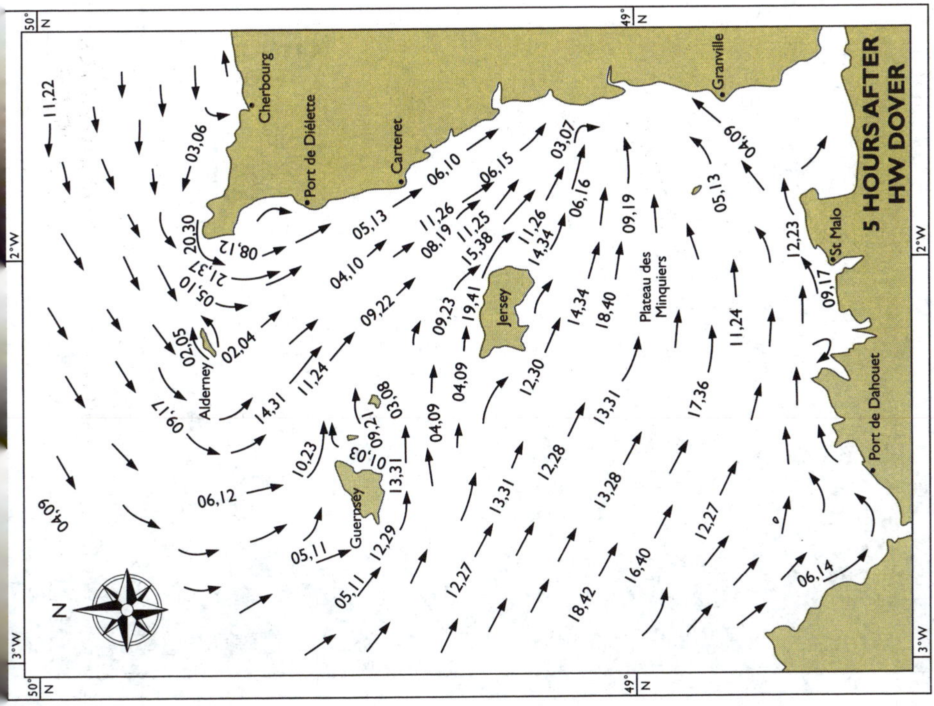

TIDES
NORTH SEA

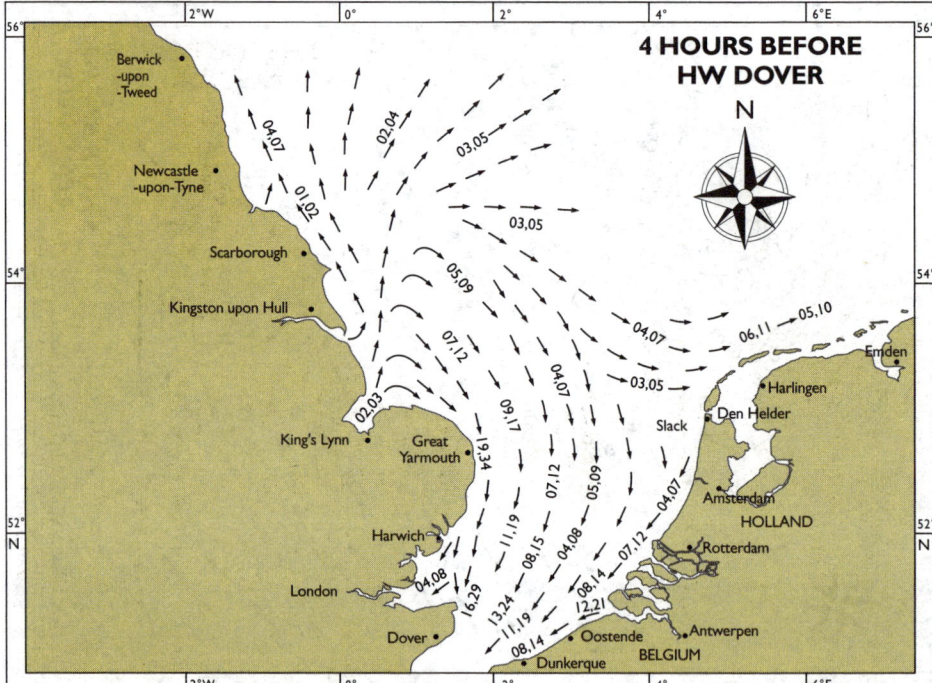

NORTH SEA

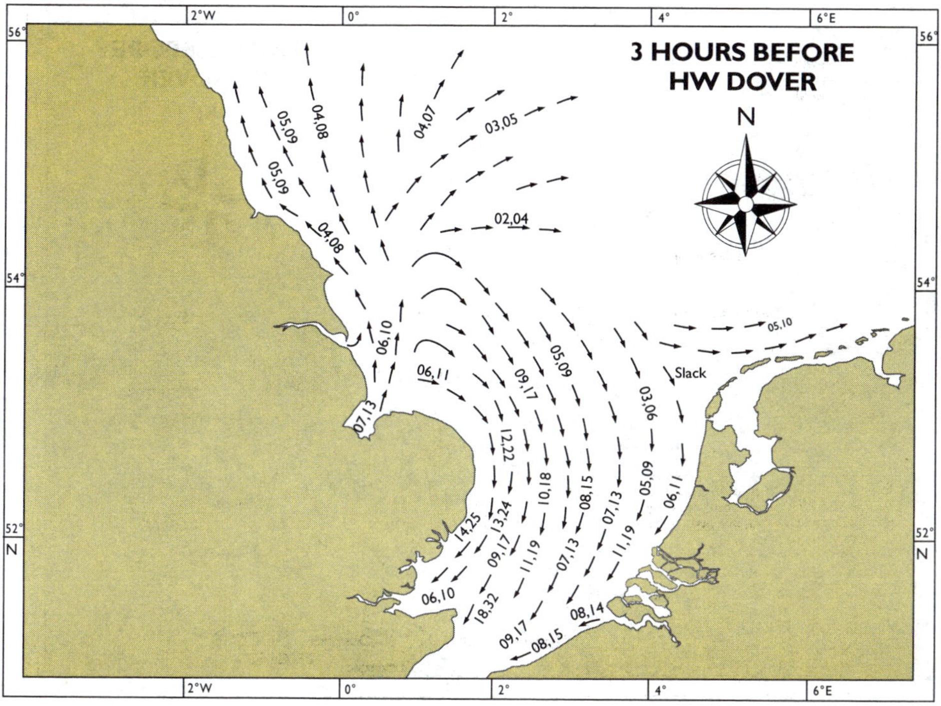

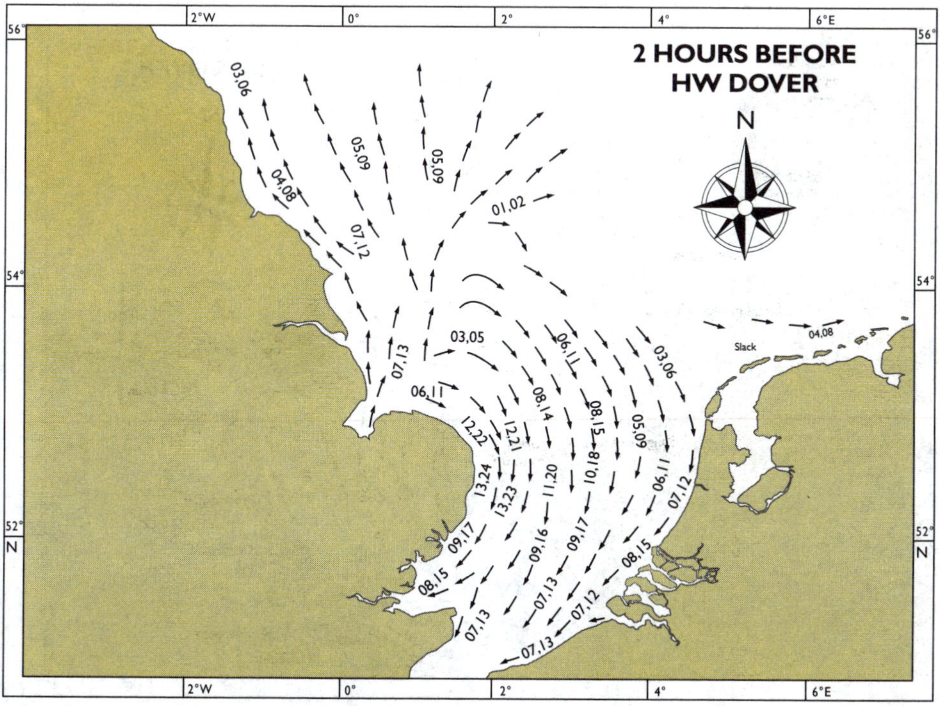

TIDES

NORTH SEA

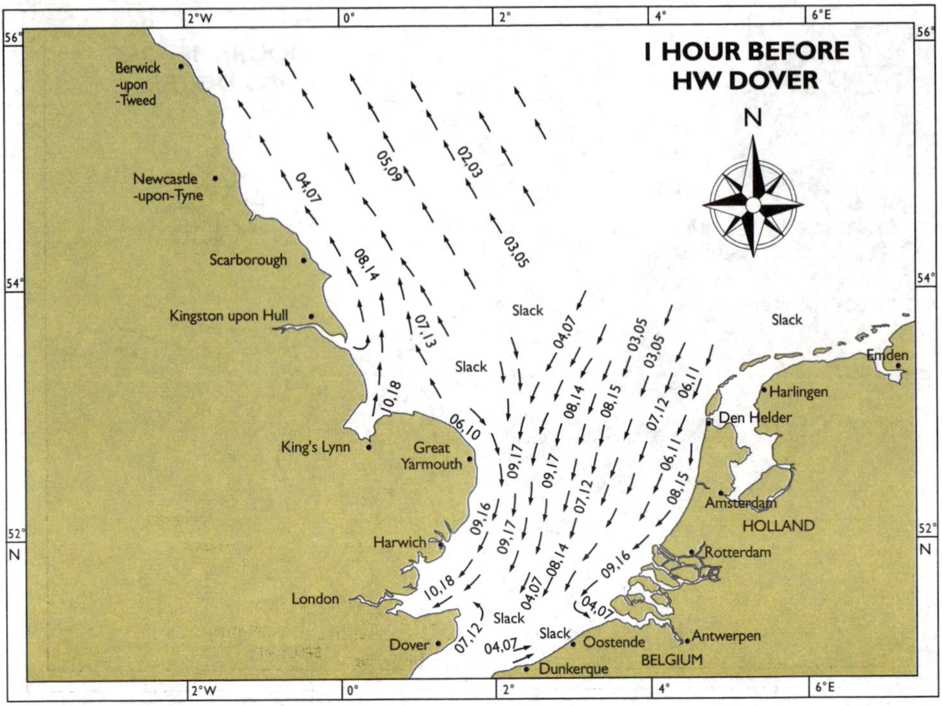

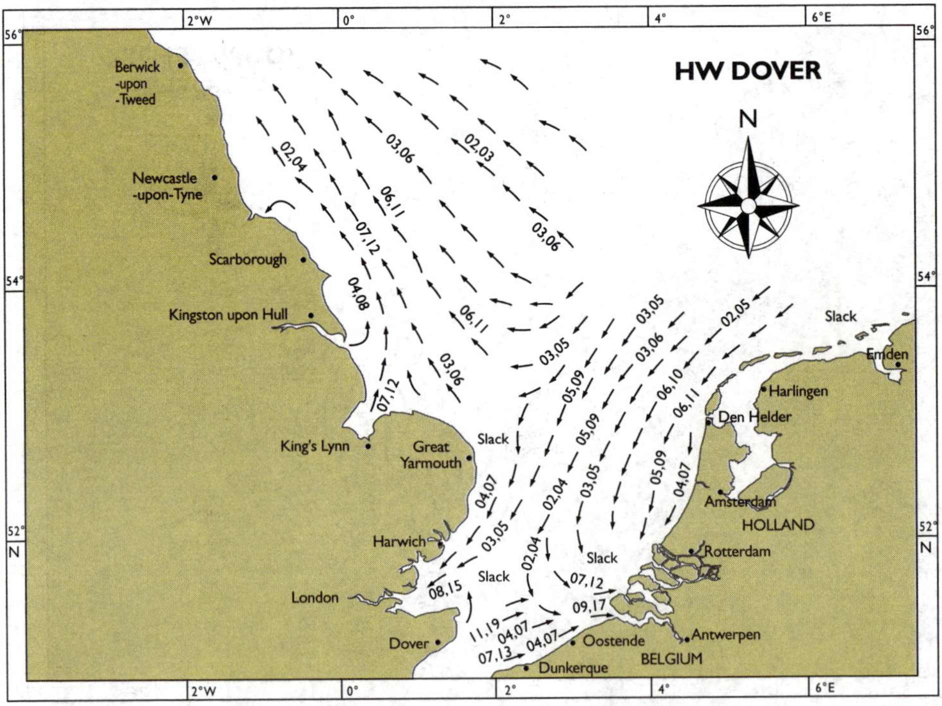

NORTH SEA

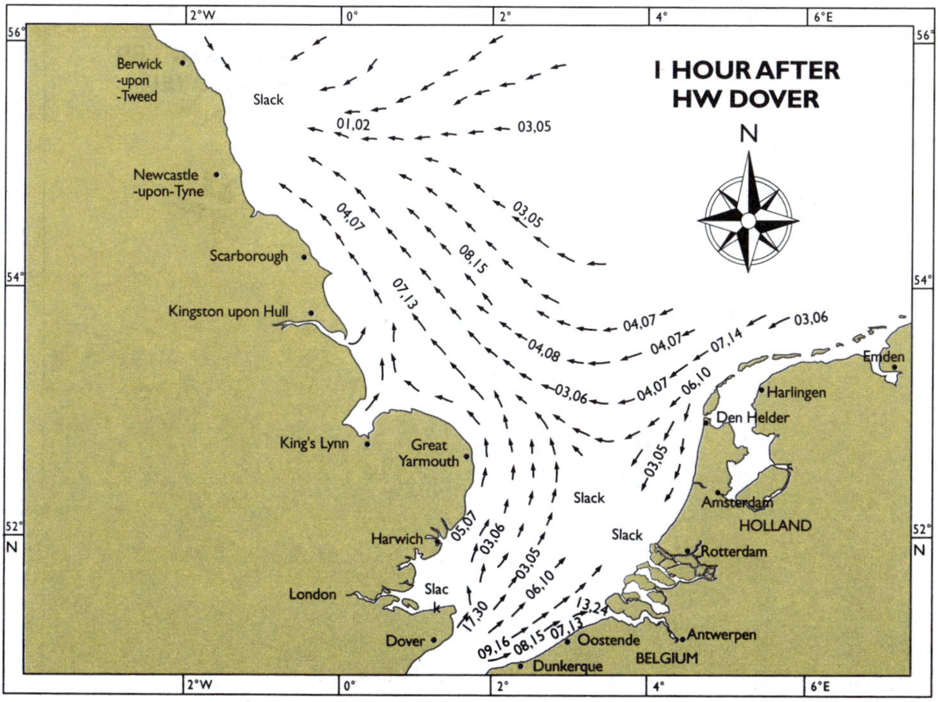

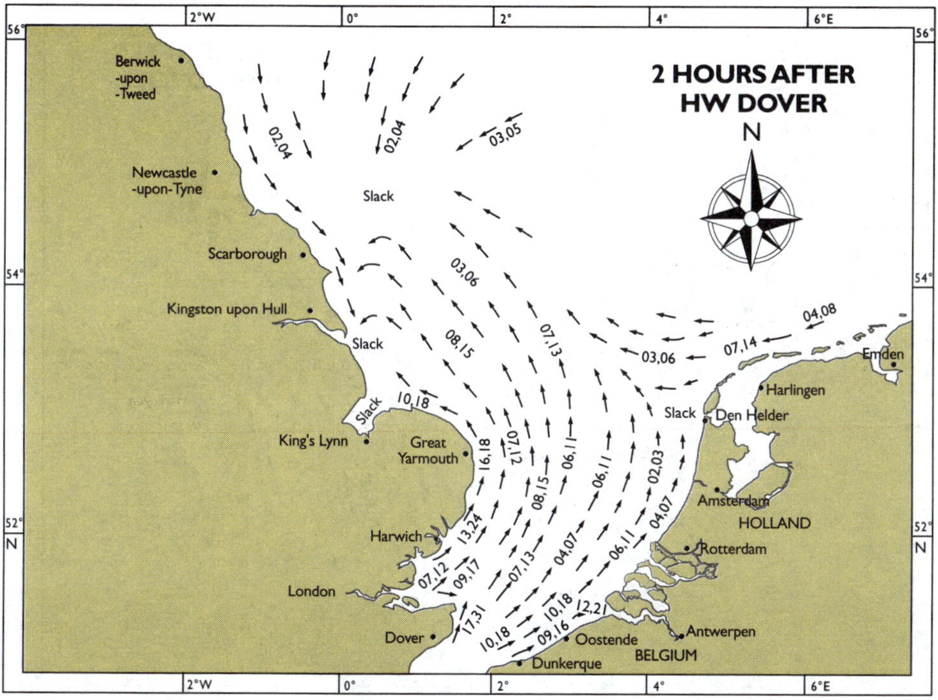

203

TIDES

NORTH SEA

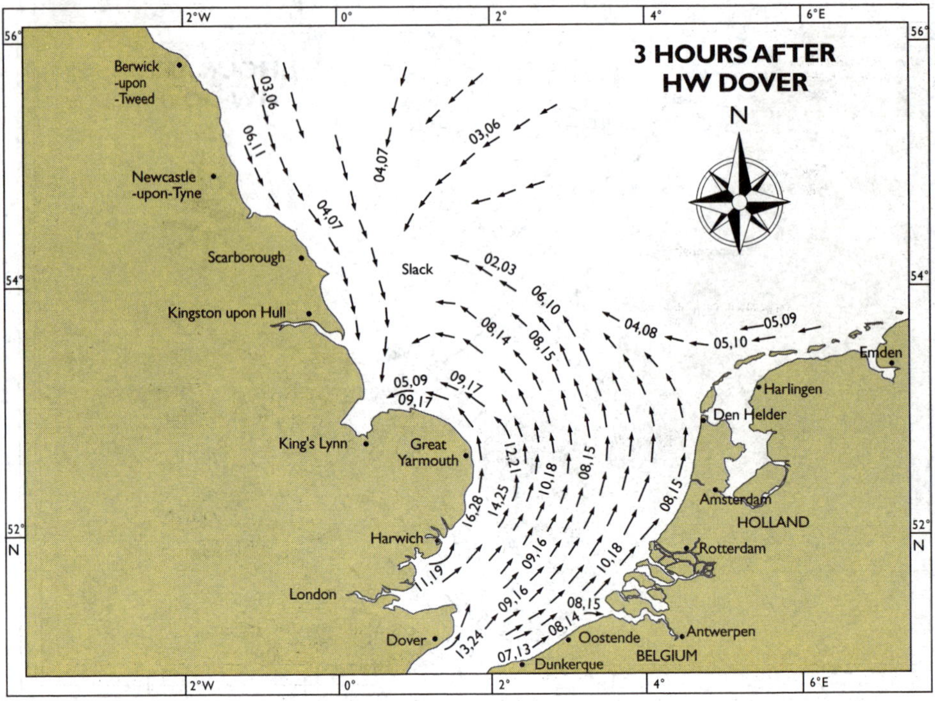

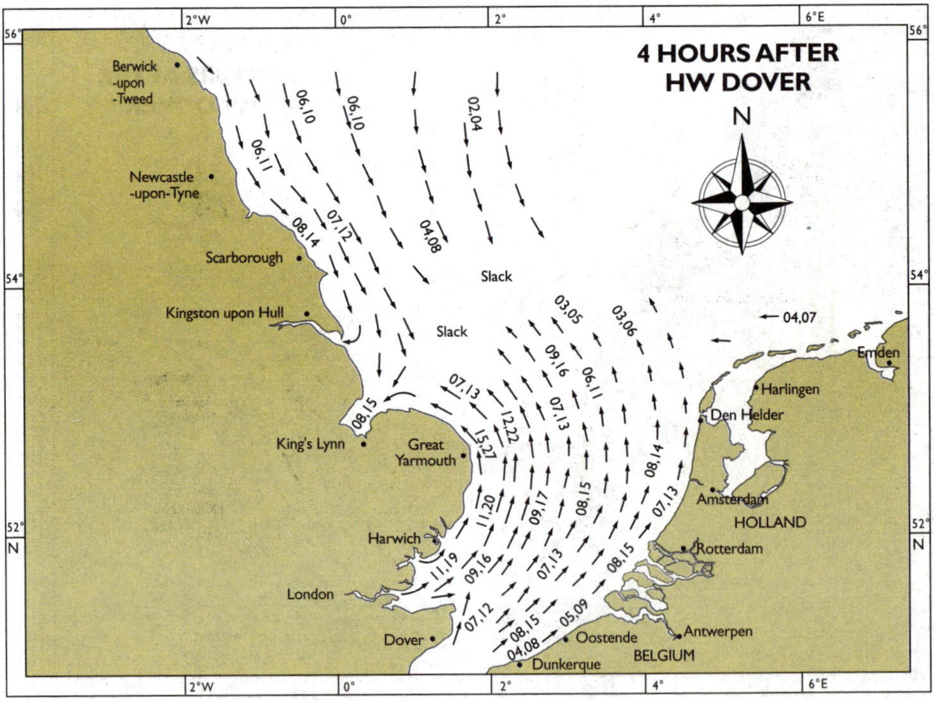

NORTH SEA

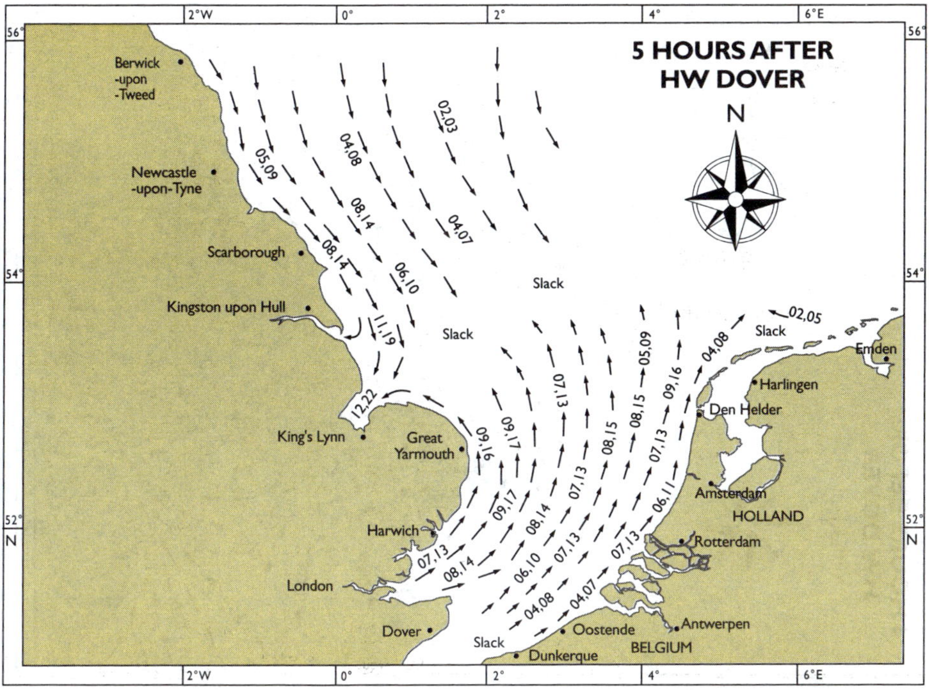

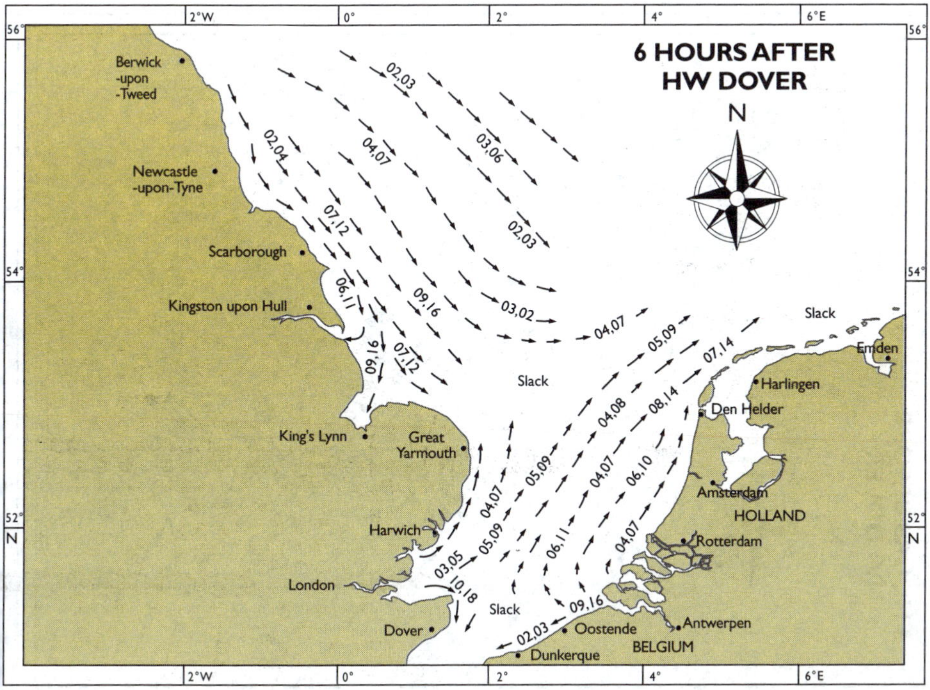

TIDES

SCOTLAND

Example: ←—10,18 predicts a westerly tidal flow of 1.0 knots at mean Neap tides and 1.8 knots at mean Spring tides at the location of the comma.

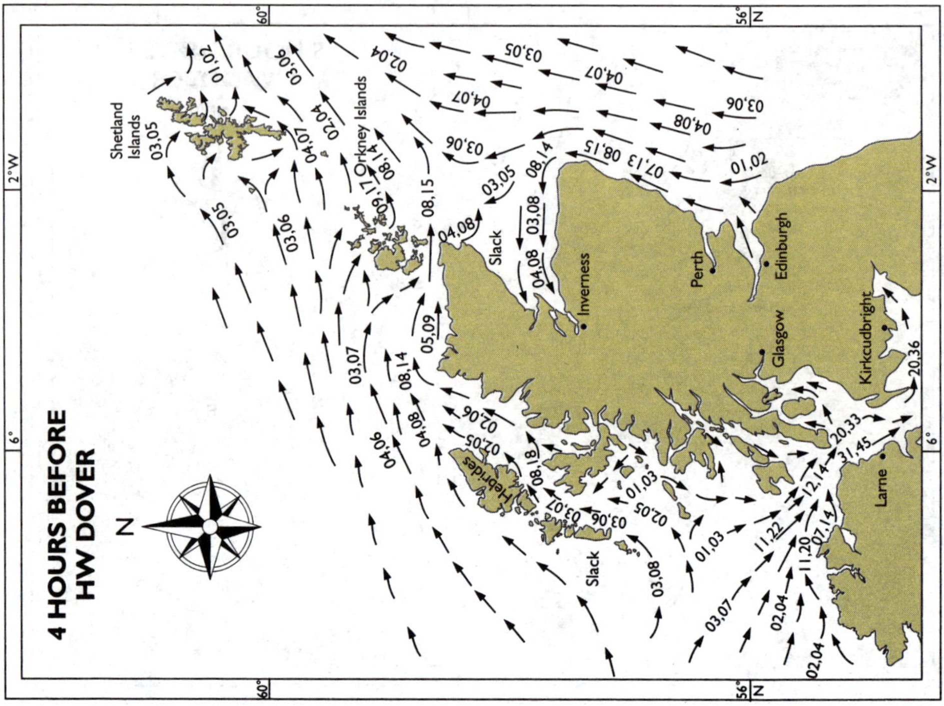

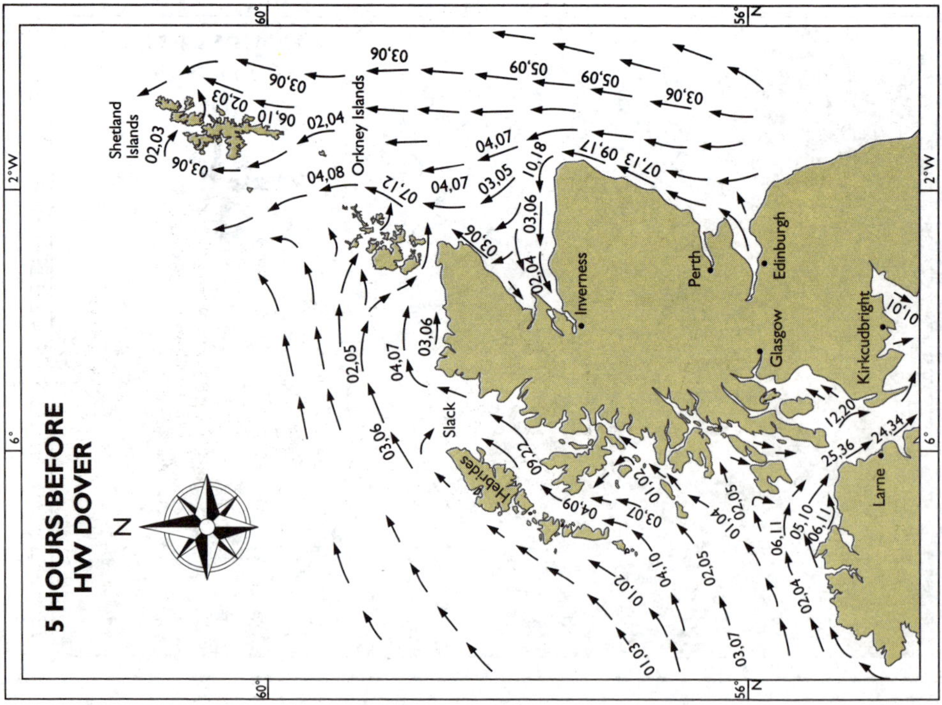

4 HOURS BEFORE HW DOVER

5 HOURS BEFORE HW DOVER

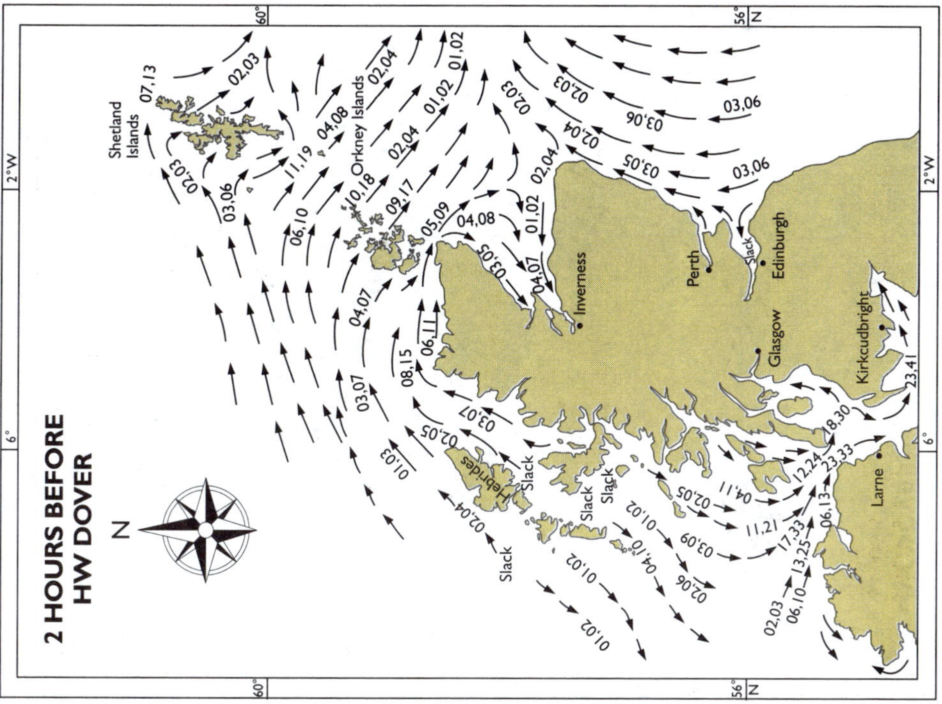

SCOTLAND

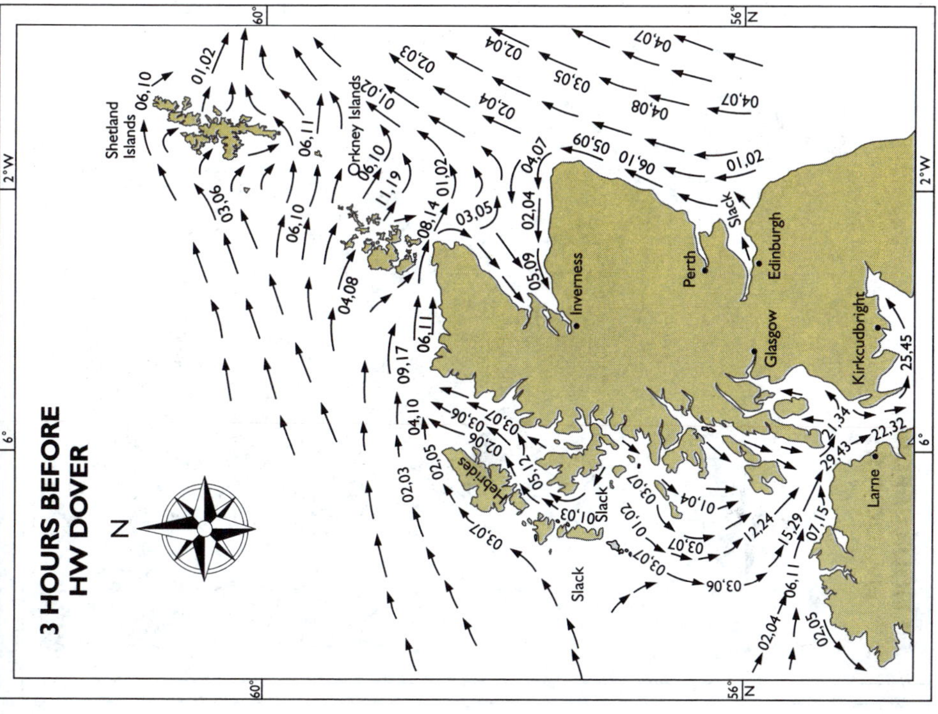

TIDES

SCOTLAND

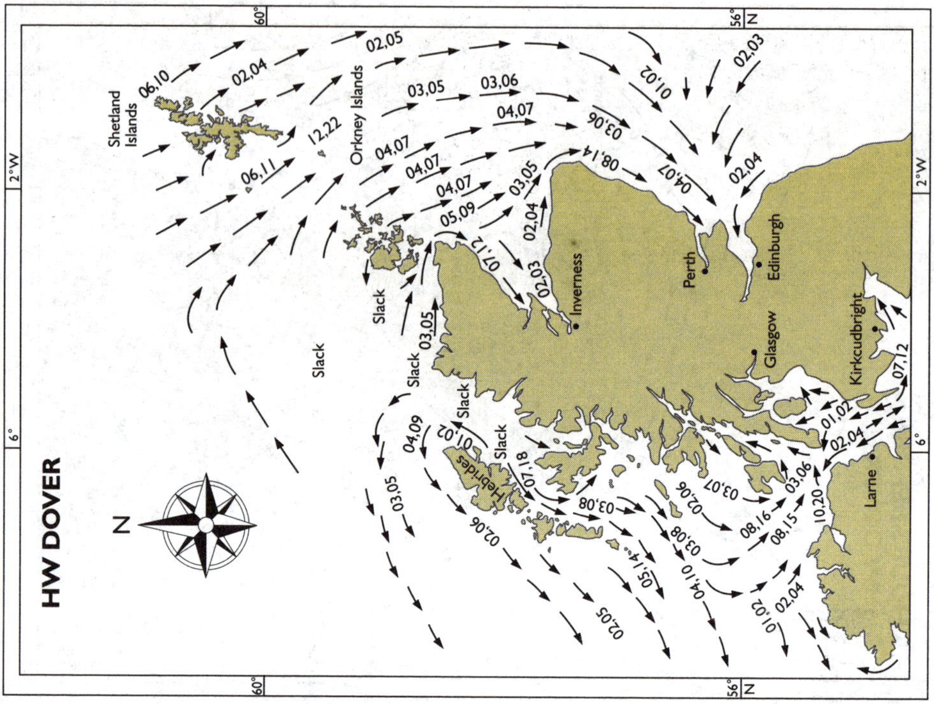

HW DOVER

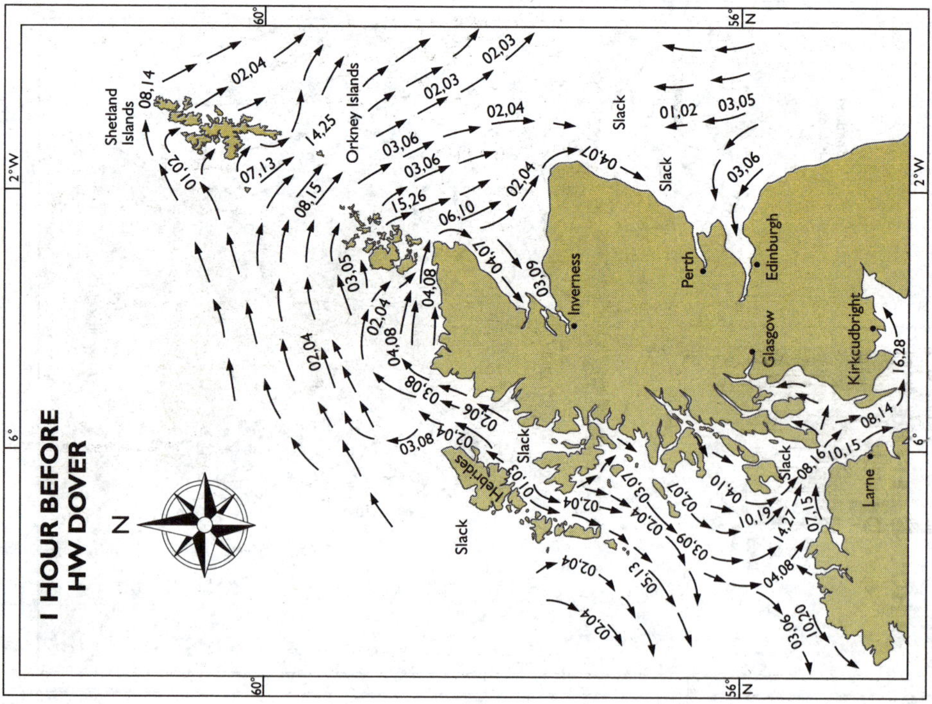

1 HOUR BEFORE HW DOVER

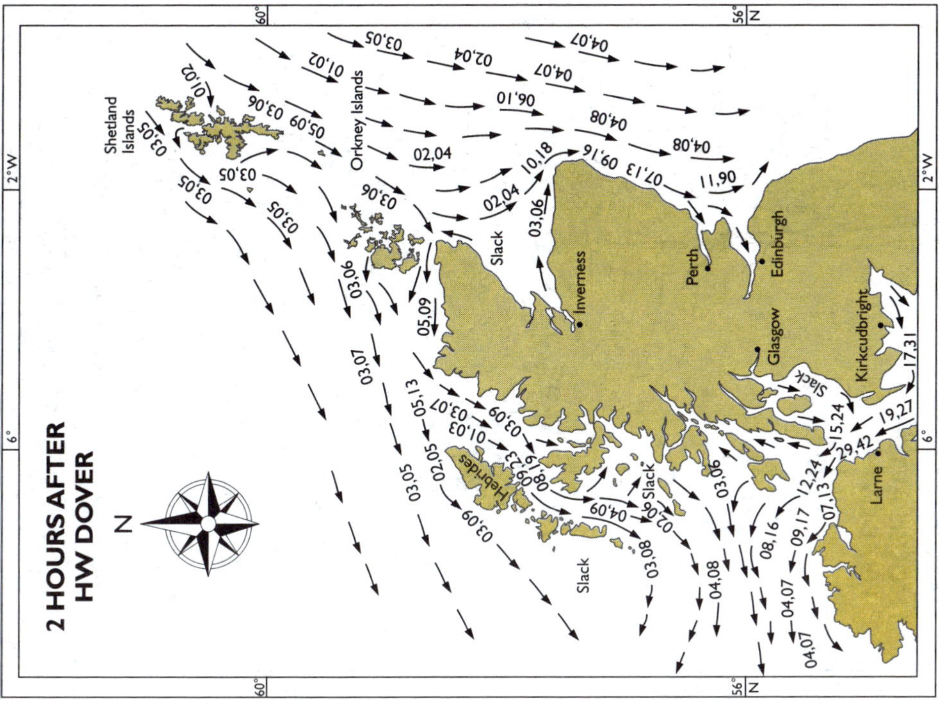

SCOTLAND

2 HOURS AFTER HW DOVER

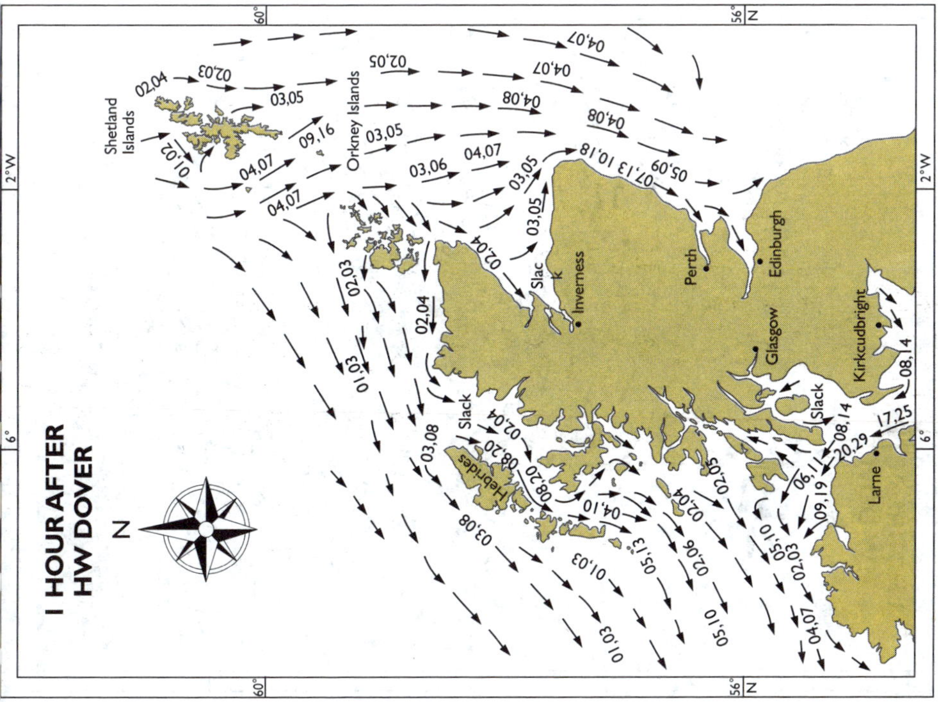

1 HOUR AFTER HW DOVER

TIDES

SCOTLAND

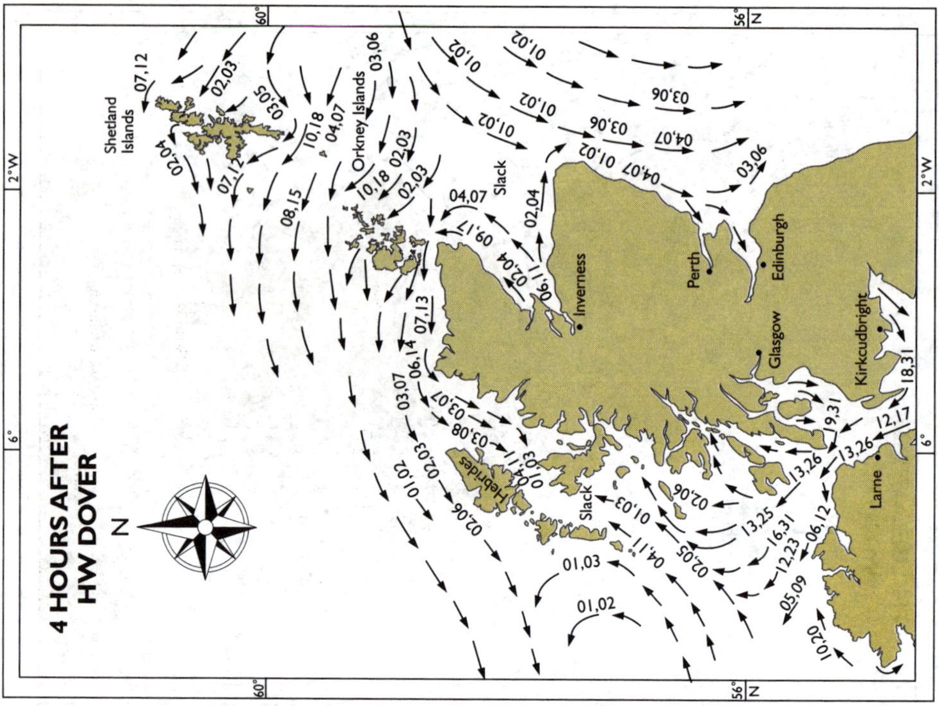

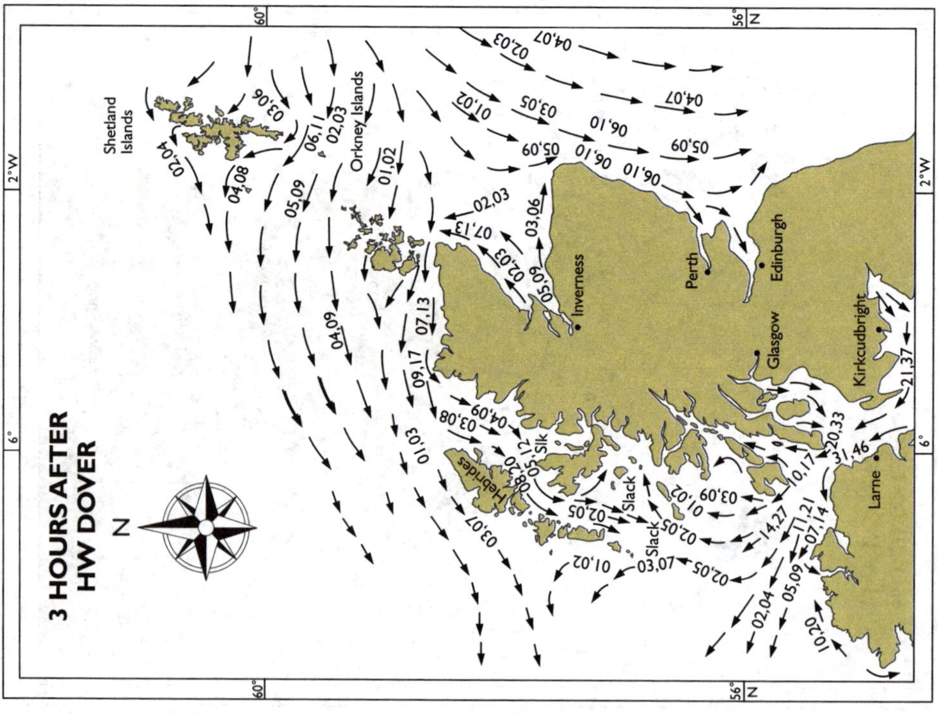

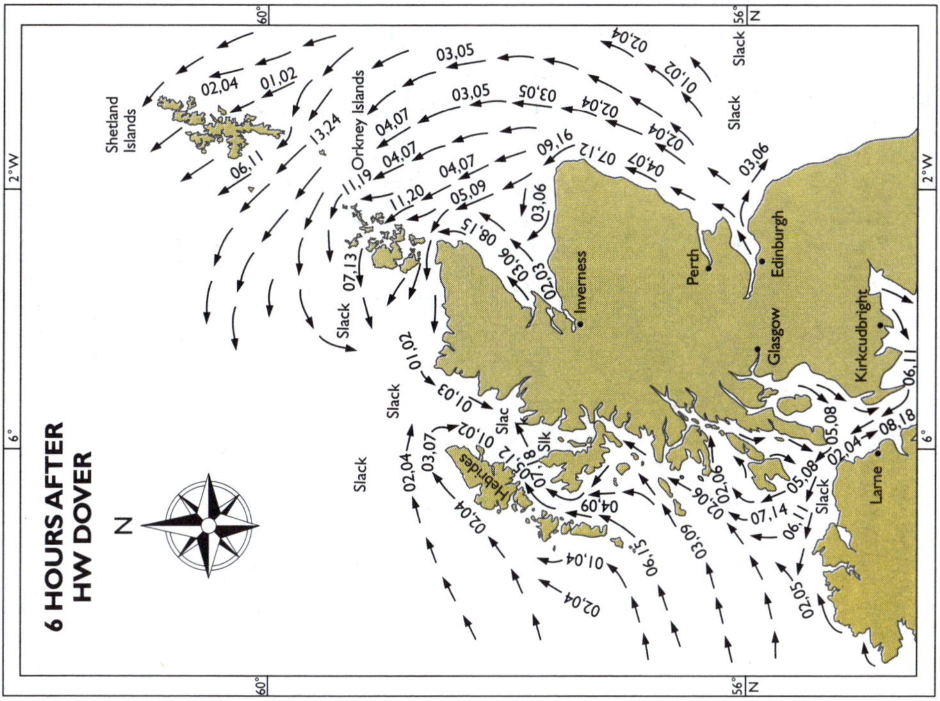

SCOTLAND

6 HOURS AFTER HW DOVER

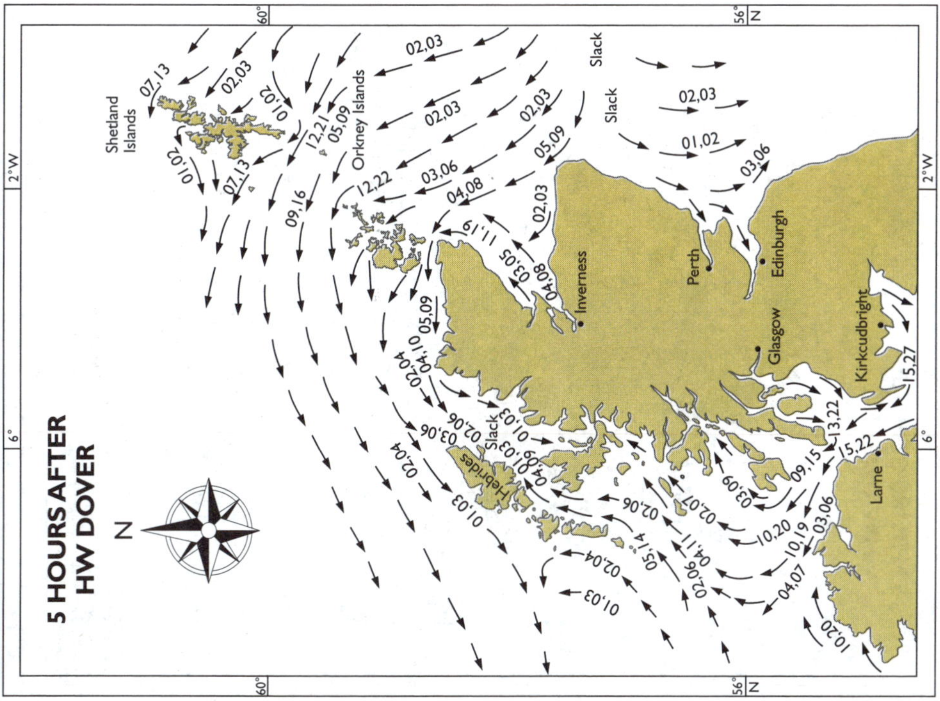

5 HOURS AFTER HW DOVER

Chapter 5

TIDES

WEST UK AND IRELAND

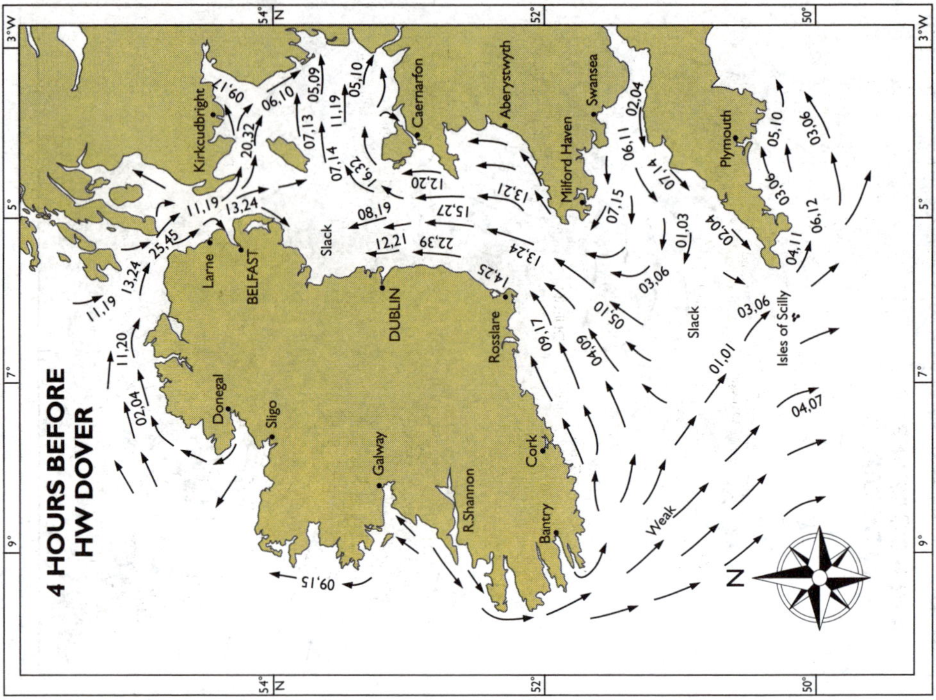

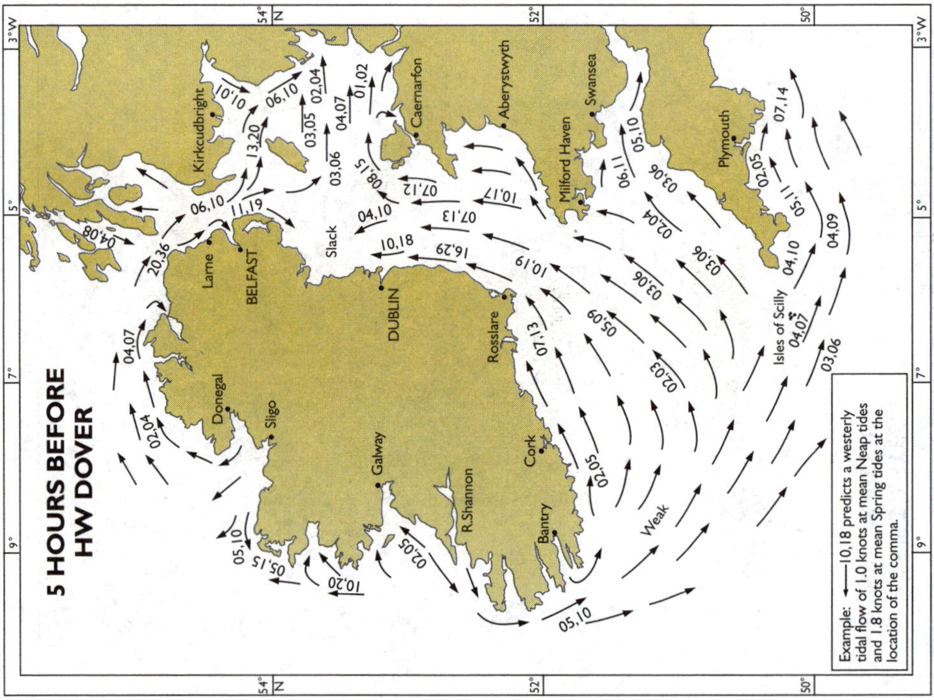

WEST UK AND IRELAND

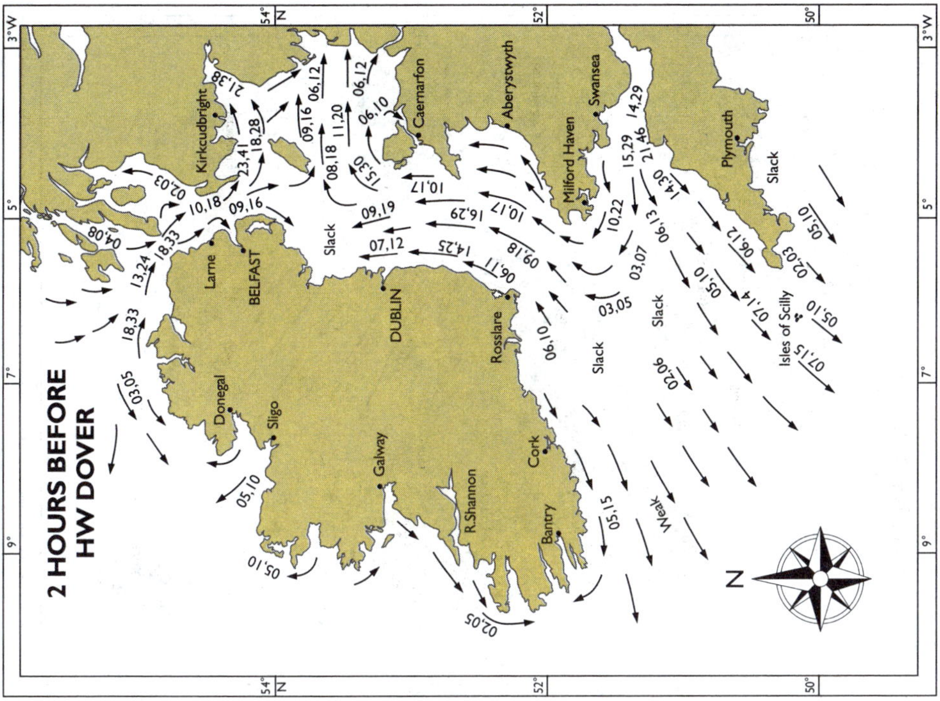

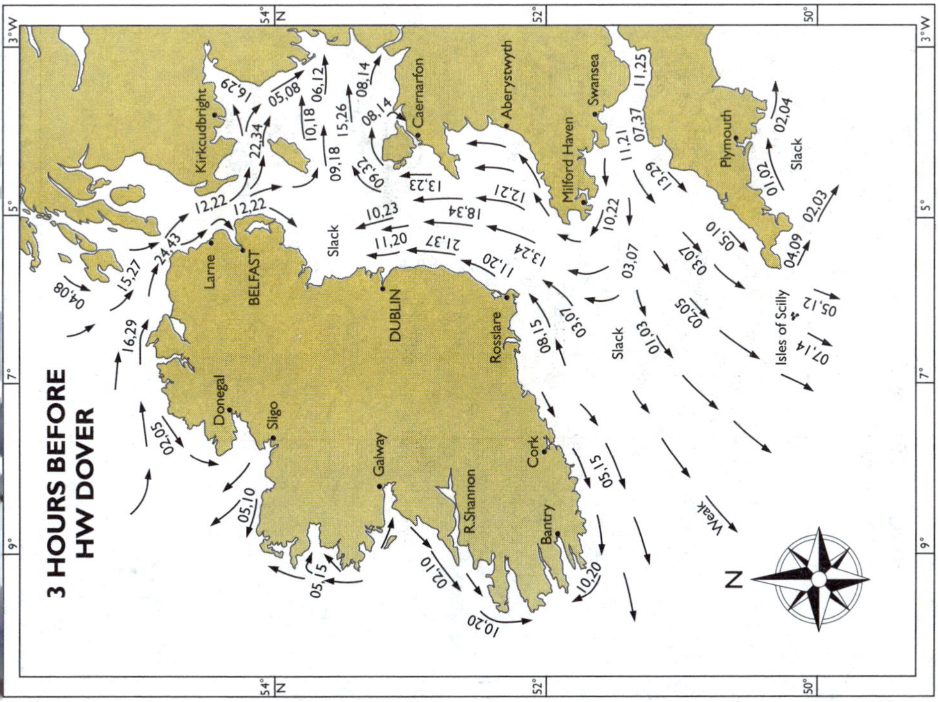

TIDES
WEST UK AND IRELAND

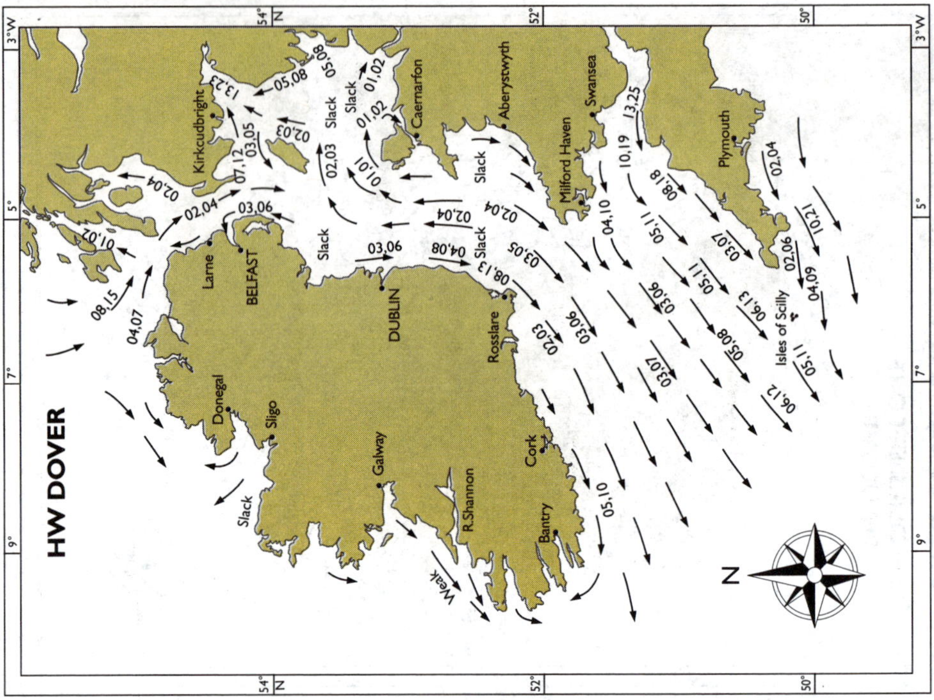

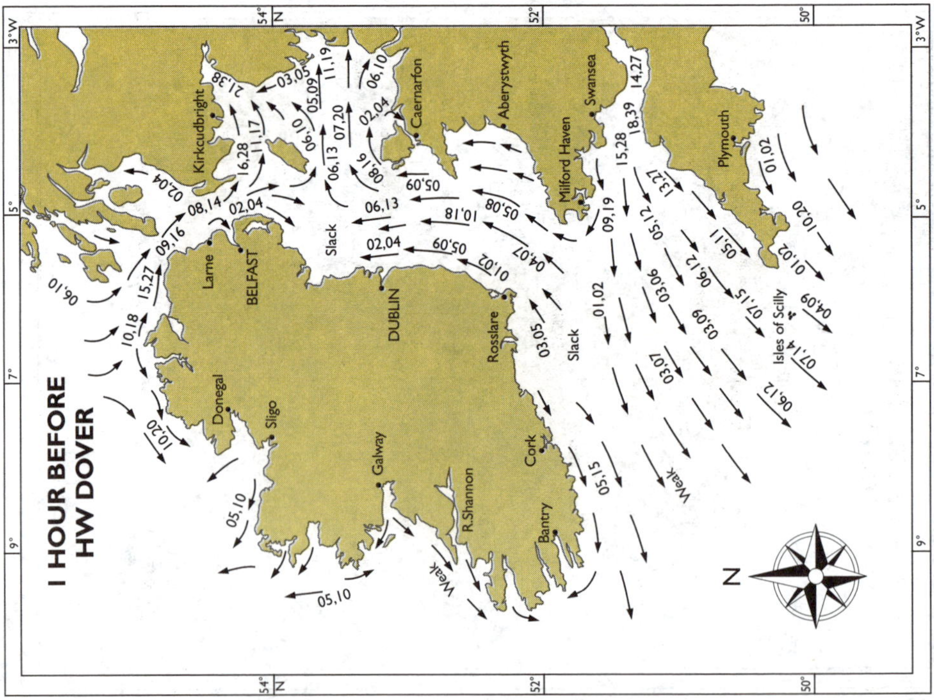

WEST UK AND IRELAND

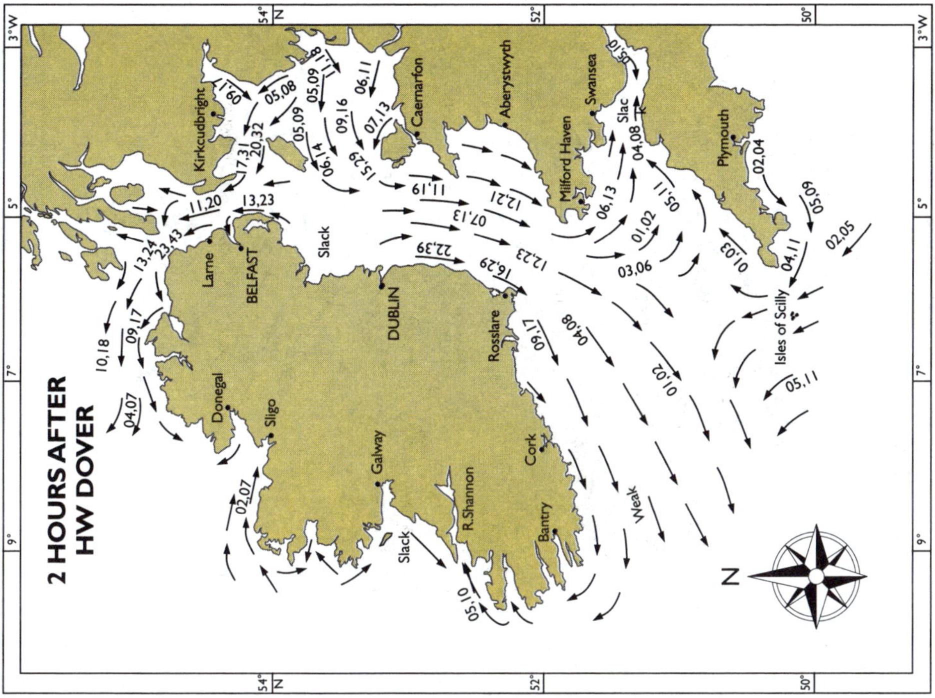

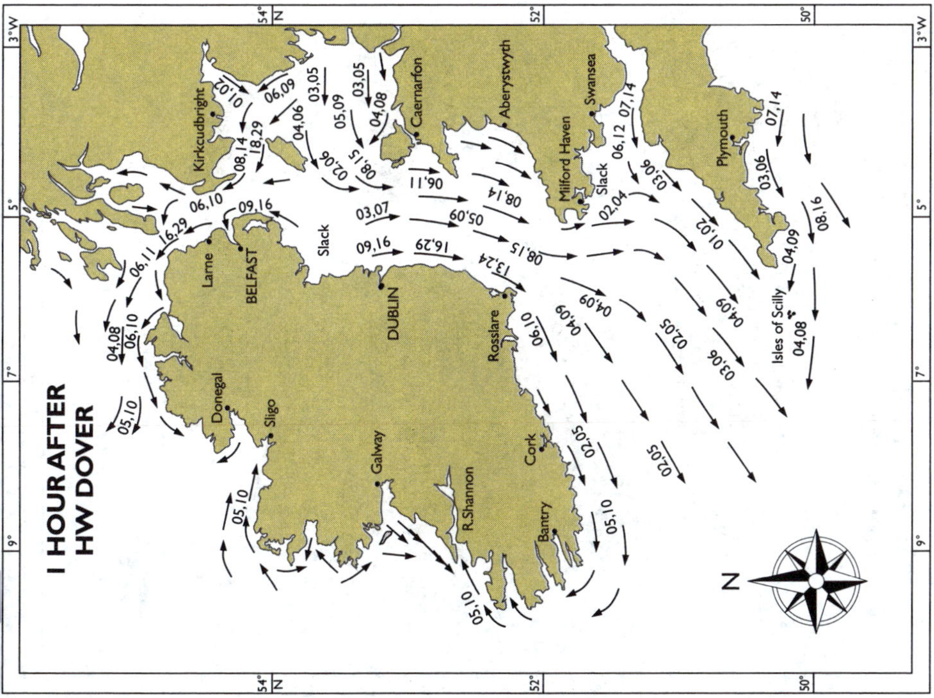

TIDES

WEST UK AND IRELAND

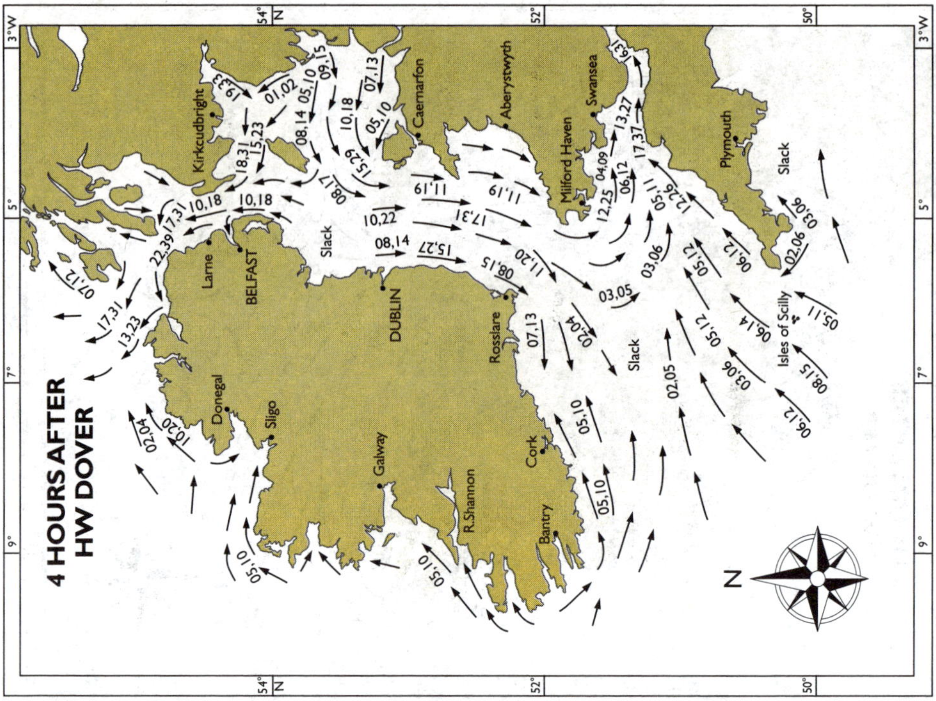

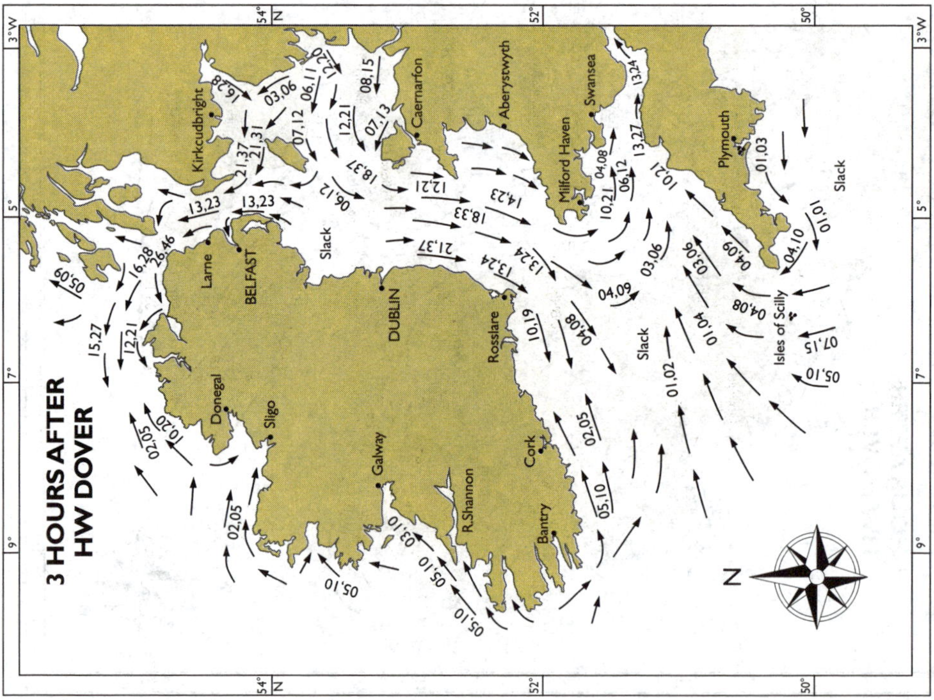

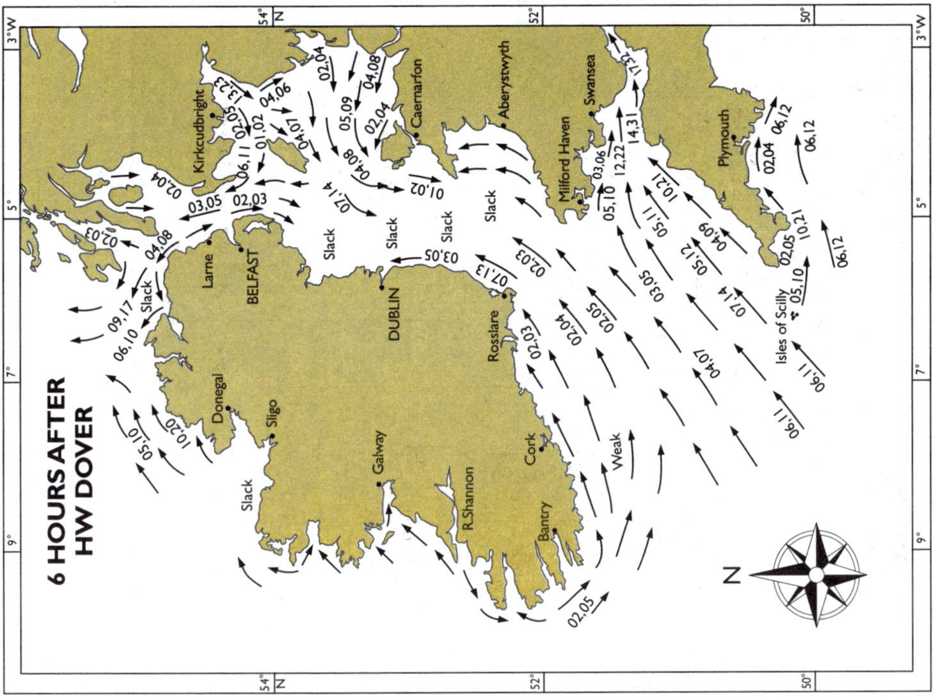

WEST UK AND IRELAND

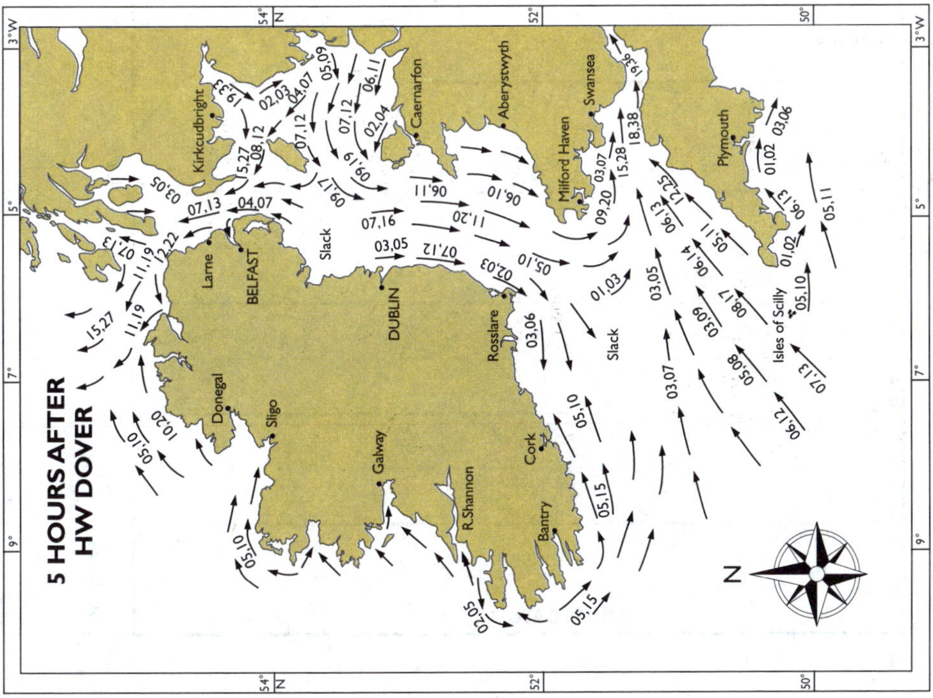

TIDES

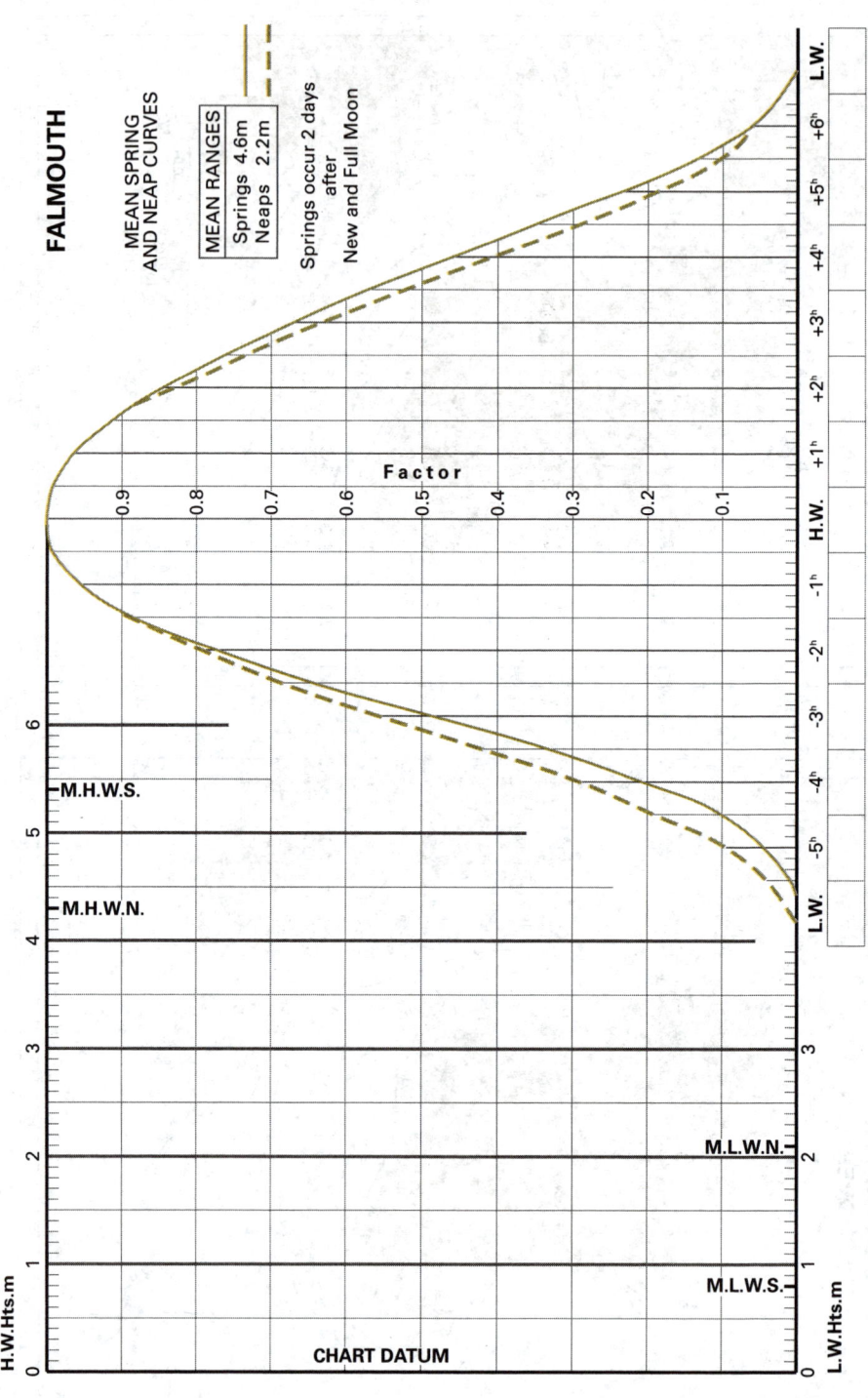

ENGLAND – FALMOUTH

TIME ZONE (UT) For Summer Time add ONE hour in **non-shaded areas**

LAT 50°09′N LONG 5°03′W

TIMES AND HEIGHTS OF HIGH AND LOW WATERS

YEAR 2005

JANUARY

Time	m	Time	m
1 SA	0224 1.6 / 0820 4.8 / 1450 1.6 / 2046 4.5	**16** SU	0337 1.2 / 0933 5.1 / 1604 1.2 / 2201 4.7
2 SU	0259 1.7 / 0859 4.7 / 1528 1.7 / 2127 4.4	**17** M	0418 1.5 / 1015 4.8 / 1646 1.5 / ◑ 2245 4.5
3 M	0340 1.8 / 0942 4.6 / 1614 1.8 / ◐ 2216 4.3	**18** TU	0503 1.7 / 1104 4.5 / 1735 1.8 / 2342 4.3
4 TU	0432 1.9 / 1035 4.5 / 1715 1.9 / 2316 4.3	**19** W	0600 2.0 / 1208 4.3 / 1837 2.1
5 W	0543 2.0 / 1140 4.5 / 1832 1.9	**20** TH	0049 4.2 / 0713 2.2 / 1320 4.2 / 1951 2.1
6 TH	0023 4.4 / 0706 2.0 / 1252 4.5 / 1946 1.8	**21** F	0155 4.3 / 0834 2.1 / 1426 4.3 / 2105 1.9
7 F	0136 4.5 / 0820 1.8 / 1405 4.6 / 2053 1.6	**22** SA	0254 4.5 / 0942 1.9 / 1522 4.4 / 2203 1.8
8 SA	0244 4.7 / 0927 1.5 / 1514 4.8 / 2157 1.4	**23** SU	0344 4.7 / 1034 1.6 / 1609 4.6 / 2250 1.5
9 SU	0347 5.0 / 1029 1.3 / 1616 5.0 / 2256 1.2	**24** M	0427 4.9 / 1117 1.5 / 1656 4.8 / 2330 1.5
10 M	0442 5.3 / 1126 1.0 / 1711 5.3 / ● 2350 1.0	**25** TU	0505 5.1 / 1156 1.3 / 1727 4.9 / ○
11 TU	0533 5.5 / 1220 0.7 / 1805 5.3	**26** W	0007 1.3 / 0543 5.1 / 1232 1.2 / 1806 4.9
12 W	0042 0.8 / 0626 5.6 / 1310 0.6 / 1859 5.3	**27** TH	0041 1.3 / 0621 5.2 / 1304 1.2 / 1844 4.9
13 TH	0130 0.7 / 0717 5.6 / 1358 0.6 / 1949 5.2	**28** F	0113 1.2 / 0659 5.1 / 1335 1.2 / 1920 4.8
14 F	0215 0.8 / 0805 5.6 / 1442 0.7 / 2036 5.1	**29** SA	0142 1.3 / 0732 5.1 / 1403 1.2 / 1952 4.8
15 SA	0257 0.9 / 0851 5.4 / 1524 0.9 / 2120 4.9	**30** SU	0210 1.3 / 0803 5.0 / 1432 1.3 / 2022 4.7
		31 M	0239 1.4 / 0833 4.9 / 1502 1.4 / 2053 4.6

FEBRUARY

Time	m	Time	m
1 TU	0313 1.5 / 0906 4.8 / 1537 1.5 / 2131 4.5	**16** W	0417 1.6 / 0959 4.5 / 1639 1.8 / ◑ 2219 4.3
2 W	0353 1.6 / 0951 4.6 / 1623 1.7 / ◐ 2225 4.4	**17** TH	0501 2.0 / 1046 4.1 / 1730 2.2 / 2322 4.1
3 TH	0448 1.9 / 1055 4.4 / 1728 1.9 / 2339 4.3	**18** F	0609 2.3 / 1217 3.9 / 1846 2.4
4 F	0613 2.0 / 1216 4.3 / 1904 2.0	**19** SA	0108 4.0 / 0745 2.4 / 1356 3.9 / 2027 2.3
5 SA	0103 4.3 / 0753 1.9 / 1346 4.4 / 2034 1.8	**20** SU	0225 4.2 / 0925 2.1 / 1501 4.2 / 2145 2.0
6 SU	0226 4.6 / 0915 1.6 / 1506 4.6 / 2147 1.5	**21** M	0321 4.5 / 1019 1.7 / 1552 4.5 / 2234 1.6
7 M	0335 4.9 / 1022 1.3 / 1610 4.9 / 2249 1.2	**22** TU	0407 4.8 / 1101 1.4 / 1634 4.7 / 2314 1.4
8 TU	0433 5.3 / 1119 0.8 / 1704 5.1 / ● 2342 0.8	**23** W	0447 5.0 / 1139 1.2 / 1711 4.9 / 2351 1.2
9 W	0523 5.5 / 1211 0.5 / 1755 5.3	**24** TH	0525 5.1 / 1214 1.0 / 1749 5.0 / ○
10 TH	0031 0.6 / 0614 5.7 / 1258 0.3 / 1844 5.4	**25** F	0025 1.0 / 0603 5.2 / 1246 0.9 / 1826 5.0
11 F	0116 0.4 / 0701 5.7 / 1342 0.3 / 1929 5.3	**26** SA	0055 1.0 / 0639 5.2 / 1315 0.9 / 1859 5.0
12 SA	0158 0.4 / 0746 5.6 / 1422 0.4 / 2010 5.3	**27** SU	0124 0.9 / 0712 5.2 / 1343 0.9 / 1928 5.0
13 SU	0235 0.6 / 0825 5.4 / 1458 0.6 / 2046 5.1	**28** M	0151 1.0 / 0740 5.1 / 1410 1.0 / 1955 4.9
14 M	0309 0.9 / 0859 5.2 / 1530 1.0 / 2114 4.8		
15 TU	0342 1.3 / 0928 4.8 / 1602 1.5 / 2142 4.6		

MARCH

Time	m	Time	m
1 TU	0218 1.1 / 0808 5.0 / 1438 1.1 / 2023 4.8	**16** W	0307 1.3 / 0843 4.7 / 1523 1.5 / 2052 4.6
2 W	0250 1.2 / 0839 4.8 / 1510 1.4 / 2058 4.6	**17** TH	0337 1.6 / 0912 4.4 / 1553 1.8 / ◑ 2128 4.4
3 TH	0327 1.5 / 0924 4.5 / 1551 1.6 / ◐ 2151 4.4	**18** F	0414 2.0 / 0954 4.0 / 1637 2.2 / 2221 4.1
4 F	0419 1.8 / 1029 4.3 / 1652 2.0 / 2309 4.2	**19** SA	0521 2.4 / 1106 3.8 / 1759 2.5 / 2357 3.9
5 SA	0546 2.1 / 1159 4.1 / 1843 2.2	**20** SU	0659 2.5 / 1329 3.8 / 1941 2.4
6 SU	0047 4.2 / 0746 2.0 / 1345 4.2 / 2029 1.9	**21** M	0155 4.1 / 0858 2.1 / 1437 4.1 / 2115 2.0
7 M	0220 4.5 / 0912 1.5 / 1506 4.5 / 2142 1.5	**22** TU	0253 4.4 / 0950 1.7 / 1526 4.4 / 2204 1.6
8 TU	0327 4.9 / 1015 1.1 / 1603 4.9 / 2238 1.0	**23** W	0340 4.7 / 1031 1.4 / 1608 4.7 / 2244 1.4
9 W	0420 5.3 / 1107 0.6 / 1652 5.2 / ● 2328 0.7	**24** TH	0421 5.0 / 1108 1.1 / 1646 4.9 / 2321 1.1
10 TH	0507 5.5 / 1154 0.3 / 1737 5.3 / ●	**25** F	0500 5.1 / 1143 0.9 / 1722 5.0 / ○ 2356 0.9
11 F	0013 0.4 / 0553 5.6 / 1238 0.2 / 1821 5.4	**26** SA	0536 5.2 / 1217 0.8 / 1758 5.1
12 SA	0055 0.3 / 0637 5.6 / 1318 0.2 / 1901 5.4	**27** SU	0029 0.8 / 0613 5.2 / 1249 0.7 / 1831 5.1
13 SU	0133 0.3 / 0717 5.5 / 1355 0.3 / 1935 5.3	**28** M	0100 0.7 / 0646 5.2 / 1319 0.7 / 1902 5.1
14 M	0208 0.5 / 0751 5.3 / 1427 0.7 / 2004 5.1	**29** TU	0130 0.8 / 0718 5.1 / 1348 0.9 / 1930 5.1
15 TU	0238 0.9 / 0819 5.0 / 1455 1.1 / 2027 4.9	**30** W	0200 0.9 / 0750 5.0 / 1418 1.1 / 2002 4.9
		31 TH	0233 1.2 / 0827 4.8 / 1452 1.4 / 2042 4.7

APRIL

Time	m	Time	m
1 F	0314 1.5 / 0914 4.5 / 1536 1.7 / 2138 4.5	**16** SA	0339 2.0 / 0925 4.0 / 1556 2.2 / 2146 4.2
2 SA	0410 1.8 / 1022 4.2 / 1643 2.1 / ◐ 2256 4.2	**17** SU	0444 2.3 / 1031 3.8 / 1722 2.5 / 2303 4.0
3 SU	0547 2.1 / 1201 4.0 / 1844 2.2	**18** M	0619 2.4 / 1244 3.8 / 1856 2.4
4 M	0043 4.3 / 0745 1.9 / 1347 4.2 / 2022 1.8	**19** TU	0106 4.1 / 0752 2.1 / 1358 4.1 / 2018 2.1
5 TU	0212 4.6 / 0900 1.5 / 1456 4.6 / 2126 1.4	**20** W	0213 4.4 / 0856 1.7 / 1448 4.4 / 2114 1.7
6 W	0312 5.0 / 0956 1.0 / 1548 4.9 / 2219 1.0	**21** TH	0301 4.6 / 0943 1.4 / 1532 4.6 / 2200 1.4
7 TH	0401 5.3 / 1045 0.6 / 1632 5.2 / 2305 0.6	**22** F	0345 4.9 / 1025 1.1 / 1612 4.9 / 2242 1.1
8 F	0445 5.5 / 1130 0.4 / 1712 5.3 / ● 2348 0.4	**23** SA	0426 5.0 / 1105 0.9 / 1650 5.0 / 2321 0.9
9 SA	0527 5.5 / 1211 0.3 / 1751 5.4	**24** SU	0506 5.1 / 1143 0.8 / 1726 5.1 / ○ 2359 0.8
10 SU	0028 0.4 / 0607 5.5 / 1250 0.4 / 1827 5.3	**25** M	0544 5.2 / 1220 0.7 / 1802 5.2
11 M	0105 0.5 / 0644 5.3 / 1324 0.6 / 1858 5.2	**26** TU	0036 0.7 / 0623 5.2 / 1256 0.8 / 1838 5.2
12 TU	0138 0.7 / 0715 5.1 / 1355 0.9 / 1922 5.1	**27** W	0112 0.8 / 0701 5.1 / 1331 0.9 / 1914 5.2
13 W	0208 1.0 / 0740 4.9 / 1422 1.2 / 1947 4.9	**28** TH	0149 0.9 / 0740 5.0 / 1407 1.1 / 1953 5.0
14 TH	0236 1.3 / 0807 4.6 / 1448 1.5 / 2016 4.7	**29** F	0229 1.4 / 0825 4.7 / 1448 1.4 / 2038 4.7
15 F	0304 1.6 / 0839 4.3 / 1515 1.9 / 2054 4.4	**30** SA	0316 1.5 / 0919 4.4 / 1538 1.7 / 2135 4.6

Chart Datum: 2·91 metres below Ordnance Datum (Newlyn)

》》 **FREE** monthly updates from 《《
www.reedsalmanac.co.uk

Chapter 5

219

TIDES

TIME ZONE (UT)
For Summer Time add ONE hour in **non-shaded areas**

ENGLAND – FALMOUTH
LAT 50°09′N   LONG 5°03′W
TIMES AND HEIGHTS OF HIGH AND LOW WATERS

YEAR 2005

	MAY			JUNE			JULY			AUGUST	
	Time m	Time m		Time m	Time m		Time m	Time m		Time m	Time m
1 SU ☽	0419 1.7 1027 4.2 1651 2.0 2252 4.4	**16** M	0417 2.1 1010 4.0 1645 2.3 2228 4.2	**1** W	0004 4.6 0648 1.5 1253 4.4 1917 1.7	**16** TH	0550 1.9 1147 4.2 1819 2.0 2358 4.4	**1** F	0029 4.5 0705 1.6 1308 4.4 1934 1.8	**16** SA	0548 1.8 1149 4.3 1825 1.9	**1** M	0203 4.1 0841 2.0 1433 4.4 2121 1.9	**16** TU	0103 4.2 0759 1.9 1353 4.5 2041 1.7
2 M	0551 1.9 1204 4.2 1834 2.0	**17** TU	0535 2.2 1134 3.9 1808 2.3 2351 4.2	**2** TH	0113 4.6 0754 1.5 1352 4.6 2020 1.5	**17** F	0655 1.8 1249 4.3 1924 1.8	**2** SA	0133 4.4 0810 1.7 1406 4.5 2039 1.7	**17** SU	0008 4.4 0705 1.8 1300 4.3 1943 1.8	**2** TU	0303 4.3 0948 1.8 1526 4.6 2218 1.7	**17** W	0233 4.5 0915 1.6 1506 4.8 2151 1.4
3 TU	0032 4.4 0725 1.7 1328 4.3 1957 1.7	**18** W	0650 2.0 1258 4.1 1919 2.1	**3** F	0212 4.7 0852 1.3 1444 4.7 2116 1.4	**18** SA	0755 1.6 1348 4.4 2023 1.6	**3** SU	0231 4.5 0911 1.6 1459 4.6 2139 1.6	**18** M	0125 4.4 0818 1.7 1411 4.5 2053 1.6	**3** W	0354 4.5 1039 1.6 1610 4.8 2305 1.5	**18** TH	0342 4.8 1020 1.3 1604 5.2 2250 0.9
4 W	0148 4.7 0833 1.4 1429 4.6 2058 1.4	**19** TH	0111 4.3 0753 1.7 1355 4.3 2018 1.8	**4** SA	0304 4.8 0944 1.2 1531 4.9 2207 1.2	**19** SU	0208 4.6 0853 1.5 1445 4.6 2121 1.5	**4** M	0324 4.5 1005 1.5 1547 4.8 2231 1.5	**19** TU	0241 4.6 0925 1.5 1516 4.8 2158 1.4	**4** TH	0437 4.6 1122 1.4 1649 5.0 2346 1.3	**19** F	0438 5.0 1116 0.9 1655 5.5 ○ 2344 0.6
5 TH	0245 4.9 0928 1.1 1519 4.9 2150 1.1	**20** F	0209 4.5 0847 1.5 1444 4.5 2110 1.5	**5** SU	0352 4.9 1032 1.1 1614 5.0 2253 1.1	**20** M	0309 4.7 0949 1.3 1540 4.9 2217 1.3	**5** TU	0411 4.6 1053 1.5 1629 4.9 2317 1.4	**20** W	0349 4.8 1028 1.3 1615 5.1 2259 1.1	**5** F ●	0514 4.8 1201 1.3 1726 5.1	**20** SA	0528 5.3 1206 0.6 1744 5.7
6 F	0335 5.1 1017 0.8 1603 5.1 2237 0.8	**21** SA	0259 4.7 0937 1.3 1530 4.8 2159 1.3	**6** M ●	0434 4.9 1115 1.1 1652 5.1 2335 1.1	**21** TU	0405 4.9 1044 1.2 1632 5.1 2311 1.0	**6** W ●	0452 4.7 1135 1.4 1706 5.0 2358 1.3	**21** TH	0447 5.0 1126 1.0 1708 5.3 ○ 2355 0.8	**6** SA	0023 1.2 0552 4.8 1236 1.2 1803 5.1	**21** SU	0033 0.3 0618 5.4 1254 0.4 1833 5.7
7 SA	0420 5.2 1101 0.7 1643 5.2 2320 0.7	**22** SU	0348 4.9 1024 1.1 1614 5.0 2246 1.1	**7** TU	0511 4.9 1154 1.1 1725 5.1	**22** W	0459 5.0 1137 1.0 1720 5.2 ○	**7** TH	0529 4.8 1214 1.3 1741 5.0	**22** F	0542 5.1 1220 0.8 1759 5.5	**7** SU	0057 1.1 0630 4.8 1307 1.2 1840 5.1	**22** M	0119 0.2 0706 5.4 1337 0.4 1919 5.7
8 SU ●	0500 5.3 1143 0.6 1720 5.2	**23** M	0434 5.0 1110 0.9 1656 5.1 ○ 2332 0.9	**8** W	0014 1.1 0547 4.9 1230 1.2 1757 5.1	**23** TH	0003 0.9 0552 5.1 1228 0.9 1809 5.4	**8** F	0037 1.3 0607 4.8 1250 1.3 1818 5.0	**23** SA	0048 0.5 0636 5.2 1310 0.6 1851 5.6	**8** M	0126 1.2 0707 4.8 1335 1.2 1915 5.0	**23** TU	0200 0.3 0749 5.4 1416 0.5 2001 5.5
9 M	0000 0.7 0537 5.2 1221 0.7 1753 5.2	**24** TU	0518 5.1 1155 0.9 1737 5.2	**9** TH	0050 1.2 0622 4.8 1303 1.3 1829 5.0	**24** F	0055 0.7 0645 5.1 1318 0.9 1901 5.4	**9** SA	0112 1.3 0645 4.7 1323 1.4 1854 5.0	**24** SU	0137 0.4 0728 5.3 1357 0.6 1940 5.6	**9** TU	0153 1.2 0740 4.8 1401 1.3 1947 5.0	**24** W	0238 0.5 0828 5.2 1452 0.8 2038 5.3
10 TU	0037 0.8 0613 5.1 1254 0.9 1823 5.2	**25** W	0016 0.8 0603 5.1 1239 0.9 1821 5.3	**10** F	0123 1.3 0655 4.7 1335 1.5 1904 4.9	**25** SA	0145 0.7 0738 5.1 1406 0.9 1951 5.4	**10** SU	0144 1.4 0724 4.6 1354 1.5 1931 4.9	**25** M	0222 0.4 0816 5.2 1440 0.7 2027 5.5	**10** W	0218 1.3 0810 4.7 1426 1.4 2015 4.9	**25** TH	0313 0.9 0902 5.0 1526 1.1 2110 4.9
11 W	0111 1.0 0643 4.9 1325 1.1 1849 5.1	**26** TH	0101 0.8 0650 5.1 1322 1.0 1905 5.3	**11** SA	0156 1.5 0732 4.5 1407 1.7 1940 4.8	**26** SU	0234 0.8 0830 5.0 1453 1.0 2040 5.3	**11** M	0215 1.4 0802 4.6 1424 1.6 2008 4.8	**26** TU	0305 0.6 0900 5.1 1520 0.9 2110 5.3	**11** TH	0244 1.4 0839 4.6 1454 1.5 2043 4.7	**26** F ☽	0346 1.3 0932 4.7 1601 1.5 2141 4.6
12 TH	0141 1.2 0712 4.8 1354 1.4 1919 4.9	**27** F	0146 0.9 0738 5.0 1407 1.1 1952 5.2	**12** SU	0229 1.5 0813 4.4 1441 1.7 2022 4.7	**27** M	0322 0.9 0921 4.9 1540 1.2 2131 5.1	**12** TU	0245 1.5 0839 4.5 1454 1.6 2043 4.7	**27** W	0345 0.9 0942 4.9 1600 1.2 2151 5.0	**12** F	0314 1.5 0912 4.5 1528 1.6 2121 4.6	**27** SA	0421 1.7 1006 4.4 1644 1.8 2221 4.2
13 F	0211 1.3 0744 4.6 1423 1.6 1953 4.8	**28** SA	0233 1.0 0830 4.8 1454 1.3 2041 5.0	**13** M	0305 1.6 0858 4.3 1518 1.9 2106 4.5	**28** TU	0410 1.0 1013 4.7 1629 1.4 ☽ 2224 4.9	**13** W	0317 1.5 0917 4.4 1527 1.7 2121 4.6	**28** TH	0425 1.5 1024 4.6 1642 1.5 ☽ 2235 4.6	**13** SA	0352 1.8 0957 4.4 1615 1.8 ☽ 2216 4.4	**28** SU	0509 2.2 1101 4.1 1749 2.3 2350 3.9
14 SA	0242 1.6 0821 4.3 1454 1.9 2033 4.5	**29** SU	0324 1.2 0925 4.6 1546 1.5 2137 4.8	**14** TU	0349 1.7 0946 4.2 1605 2.0 2155 4.4	**29** W	0503 1.4 1109 4.6 1724 1.5 2325 4.7	**14** TH	0354 1.7 0956 4.3 1609 1.8 ☽ 2204 4.5	**29** F	0510 1.8 1114 4.4 1733 1.8 2334 4.3	**14** SU	0447 1.9 1103 4.2 1729 2.1 2333 4.2	**29** M	0624 2.4 1255 4.0 1933 2.4
15 SU	0320 1.9 0908 4.1 1536 2.1 2124 4.3	**30** M	0423 1.5 1029 4.5 1649 1.7 ☽ 2245 4.7	**15** W	0444 1.9 1042 4.1 1708 2.1 ☽ 2254 4.4	**30** TH	0601 1.5 1209 4.4 1827 1.7	**15** F	0441 1.9 1046 4.3 1706 1.9 2300 4.4	**30** SA	0605 2.1 1219 4.2 1841 2.1	**15** M	0620 2.1 1225 4.3 1918 2.0	**30** TU	0142 3.9 0823 2.4 1411 4.3 2112 2.1
		31 TU	0534 1.5 1145 4.4 1804 1.8						**31** SU	0050 4.1 0718 2.1 1330 4.2 2004 2.1			**31** W	0246 4.1 0935 2.0 1507 4.5 2204 1.7

Chart Datum: 2·91 metres below Ordnance Datum (Newlyn)

》 FREE monthly updates from 《
www.reedsalmanac.co.uk

TIME ZONE (UT)
For Summer Time add ONE hour in **non-shaded areas**

ENGLAND – FALMOUTH
LAT 50°09′N   LONG 5°03′W
TIMES AND HEIGHTS OF HIGH AND LOW WATERS

YEAR 2005

SEPTEMBER		OCTOBER		NOVEMBER		DECEMBER	
Time m	Time m	Time m	Time m	Time m	Time m	Time m	Time m
1 0337 4.4 1022 1.6 TH 1552 4.8 2247 1.5	**16** 0335 4.9 1009 1.2 F 1551 5.3 2236 0.8	**1** 0352 4.8 1031 1.5 SA 1603 5.0 2251 1.2	**16** 0403 5.3 1036 0.8 SU 1617 5.6 2300 0.5	**1** 0432 5.1 1102 1.2 TU 1645 5.2 2320 1.0	**16** 0459 5.4 1137 0.9 W 1715 5.4 ○ 2356 0.9	**1** 0439 5.1 1110 1.2 TH 1658 5.1 ● 2330 1.1	**16** 0513 5.2 1159 1.2 F 1733 5.0
2 0418 4.7 1103 1.4 F 1630 5.0 2325 1.2	**17** 0424 5.2 1059 0.8 SA 1639 5.6 2325 0.4	**2** 0429 5.0 1106 1.2 SU 1640 5.2 2325 1.0	**17** 0445 5.4 1121 0.6 M 1700 5.7 ○ 2343 0.5	**2** 0507 5.2 1138 1.1 W 1721 5.3 ● 2355 1.0	**17** 0534 5.4 1217 0.9 TH 1753 5.2	**2** 0518 5.3 1153 1.1 F 1741 5.2	**17** 0014 1.3 0548 5.2 SA 1238 1.3 1809 4.9
3 0455 4.9 1139 1.2 SA 1707 5.2 ●	**18** 0509 5.4 1146 0.5 SU 1723 5.7 ○	**3** 0504 5.1 1139 1.1 M 1715 5.3 ● 2356 0.9	**18** 0525 5.5 1203 0.5 TU 1741 5.6	**3** 0542 5.3 1214 1.0 TH 1758 5.0	**18** 0034 1.0 0608 5.3 F 1254 1.1 1827 5.1	**3** 0012 1.1 0600 5.3 SA 1237 1.0 1825 5.2	**18** 0050 1.4 0622 5.2 SU 1314 1.4 1843 4.8
4 0000 1.1 0530 5.0 SU 1213 1.1 1742 5.2	**19** 0010 0.3 0553 5.5 M 1230 0.4 1807 5.8	**4** 0537 5.2 1211 1.0 TU 1750 5.3	**19** 0024 0.5 0604 5.5 W 1243 0.6 1820 5.5	**4** 0030 1.0 0617 5.3 F 1248 1.0 1834 5.2	**19** 0107 1.2 0639 5.2 SA 1328 1.3 1858 4.9	**4** 0055 1.2 0643 5.3 SU 1321 1.1 1910 5.1	**19** 0124 1.5 0655 5.1 M 1348 1.5 1919 4.7
5 0031 1.0 0606 5.0 M 1242 1.0 1818 5.2	**20** 0053 0.2 0636 5.5 TU 1311 0.4 1850 5.7	**5** 0026 0.9 0610 5.2 W 1240 1.0 1823 5.2	**20** 0101 0.7 0639 5.4 TH 1318 0.8 1854 5.3	**5** 0103 1.1 0651 5.2 SA 1323 1.2 1912 5.0	**20** 0139 1.5 0709 5.1 SU 1400 1.5 1928 4.7	**5** 0138 1.3 0728 5.3 M 1406 1.2 1959 4.9	**20** 0156 1.6 0732 5.0 TU 1421 1.6 1957 4.6
6 0059 1.0 0640 5.0 TU 1309 1.1 1850 5.2	**21** 0132 0.4 0715 5.4 W 1347 0.6 1928 5.5	**6** 0055 1.0 0641 5.2 TH 1308 1.0 1852 5.2	**21** 0134 1.0 0709 5.3 F 1351 1.1 1924 5.0	**6** 0138 1.3 0729 5.1 SU 1401 1.4 1954 4.8	**21** 0209 1.7 0741 4.9 M 1434 1.8 2004 4.5	**6** 0223 1.4 0817 5.2 TU 1455 1.4 2051 4.8	**21** 0229 1.7 0812 4.8 W 1455 1.7 2039 4.4
7 0124 1.0 0711 5.0 W 1333 1.1 1919 5.1	**22** 0206 0.7 0749 5.3 TH 1421 0.9 2000 5.2	**7** 0122 1.1 0710 5.1 F 1336 1.2 1922 5.0	**22** 0204 1.3 0734 5.1 SA 1422 1.5 1950 4.7	**7** 0216 1.5 0813 5.0 M 1446 1.5 2046 4.6	**22** 0242 2.0 0822 4.7 TU 1511 2.0 2050 4.3	**7** 0312 1.5 0908 5.0 W 1548 1.5 2147 4.6	**22** 0302 1.9 0855 4.7 TH 1531 1.9 2124 4.3
8 0149 1.1 0738 4.9 TH 1358 1.2 1945 5.0	**23** 0238 1.1 0816 5.0 F 1452 1.3 2027 4.8	**8** 0150 1.2 0740 5.0 SA 1407 1.4 1957 4.8	**23** 0233 1.7 0803 4.8 SU 1453 1.8 2021 4.4	**8** 0303 1.8 0908 4.8 TU 1543 1.9 2147 4.4	**23** 0322 2.2 0911 4.5 W 1601 2.3 ◐ 2147 4.1	**8** 0408 1.7 1008 4.9 TH 1650 1.6 ◐ 2254 4.5	**23** 0340 2.0 0940 4.5 F 1615 2.0 ◐ 2214 4.2
9 0214 1.3 0804 4.8 F 1426 1.4 2013 4.8	**24** 0307 1.5 0840 4.7 SA 1524 1.7 2054 4.5	**9** 0222 1.5 0819 4.8 SU 1444 1.6 2043 4.6	**24** 0303 2.0 0840 4.6 M 1531 2.2 2105 4.1	**9** 0407 2.1 1015 4.6 W 1705 2.0 ◐ 2311 4.3	**24** 0419 2.4 1012 4.3 TH 1710 2.4 2304 4.0	**9** 0516 1.9 1117 4.7 F 1804 1.7	**24** 0430 2.2 1031 4.4 SA 1713 2.1 2313 4.2
10 0243 1.5 0837 4.6 SA 1500 1.5 2052 4.6	**25** 0338 1.9 0913 4.5 SU 1602 2.1 ◐ 2133 4.1	**10** 0301 1.8 0911 4.6 M 1534 1.9 ◐ 2146 4.3	**25** 0344 2.4 0931 4.3 TU 1630 2.5 ◐ 2209 3.9	**10** 0546 2.2 1145 4.5 TH 1845 1.9	**25** 0539 2.5 1130 4.3 F 1828 2.3	**10** 0007 4.5 0633 1.9 SA 1231 4.7 1915 1.7	**25** 0537 2.2 1133 4.4 SU 1821 2.1
11 0319 1.7 0925 4.4 SU 1545 1.9 ◐ 2152 4.3	**26** 0421 2.4 1004 4.2 M 1706 2.5 2239 3.8	**11** 0359 2.2 1022 4.4 TU 1701 2.3 2312 4.1	**26** 0500 2.7 1045 4.1 W 1804 2.6	**11** 0047 4.4 0719 2.0 F 1311 4.7 1958 1.6	**26** 0032 4.1 0656 2.4 SA 1250 4.4 1934 2.0	**11** 0114 4.6 0744 1.8 SU 1337 4.8 2019 1.5	**26** 0018 4.2 0651 2.1 M 1239 4.4 1927 2.0
12 0412 2.1 1035 4.3 M 1700 2.2 2316 4.1	**27** 0540 2.7 1149 4.0 TU 1857 2.6	**12** 0557 2.4 1158 4.3 W 1908 2.1	**27** 0030 3.9 0642 2.6 TH 1254 4.2 1951 2.3	**12** 0156 4.6 0826 1.6 SA 1414 5.0 2055 1.3	**27** 0135 4.3 0759 2.1 SU 1350 4.6 2028 1.8	**12** 0213 4.7 0846 1.6 M 1435 4.9 2115 1.5	**27** 0122 4.4 0757 2.0 TU 1346 4.5 2028 1.8
13 0556 2.3 1207 4.2 TU 1911 2.2	**28** 0118 3.8 0756 2.6 W 1344 4.2 2049 2.2	**13** 0109 4.2 0748 2.1 TH 1338 4.6 2026 1.6	**28** 0144 4.1 0813 2.3 F 1358 4.4 2046 1.9	**13** 0249 4.9 0920 1.4 SU 1506 5.2 2146 1.1	**28** 0225 4.6 0852 1.8 M 1442 4.7 2116 1.6	**13** 0306 4.9 0942 1.5 TU 1527 5.0 2206 1.4	**28** 0224 4.6 0858 1.8 W 1448 4.6 2125 1.6
14 0103 4.2 0755 2.1 W 1347 4.5 2038 1.7	**29** 0223 4.1 0908 2.1 TH 1440 4.5 2136 1.8	**14** 0225 4.6 0855 1.6 F 1442 5.0 2124 1.2	**29** 0233 4.4 0904 1.9 SA 1445 4.7 2128 1.6	**14** 0337 5.2 1009 1.1 M 1553 5.3 2233 0.9	**29** 0312 4.9 0940 1.5 TU 1529 4.9 2202 1.4	**14** 0354 5.0 1032 1.3 W 1614 5.0 2253 1.3	**29** 0321 4.8 0955 1.5 TH 1547 4.8 2220 1.4
15 0235 4.5 0910 1.6 TH 1458 4.9 2142 1.3	**30** 0312 4.5 0952 1.7 F 1524 4.8 2215 1.5	**15** 0317 5.0 0948 1.2 SA 1532 5.4 2214 0.8	**30** 0315 4.7 0946 1.5 SU 1527 4.9 2206 1.4	**15** 0419 5.3 1055 1.0 TU 1637 5.4 2316 0.8	**30** 0357 5.0 1026 1.4 W 1614 5.0 2246 1.2	**15** 0436 5.2 1117 1.2 TH 1656 5.0 2335 1.2	**30** 0414 5.1 1050 1.3 F 1640 5.0 2312 1.2
			31 0355 5.0 1025 1.4 M 1607 5.1 2244 1.2				**31** 0502 5.2 1141 1.1 SA 1728 5.1 ●

Chart Datum: 2·91 metres below Ordnance Datum (Newlyn)

》 **FREE** monthly updates from 《
www.reedsalmanac.co.uk

Chapter 5

221

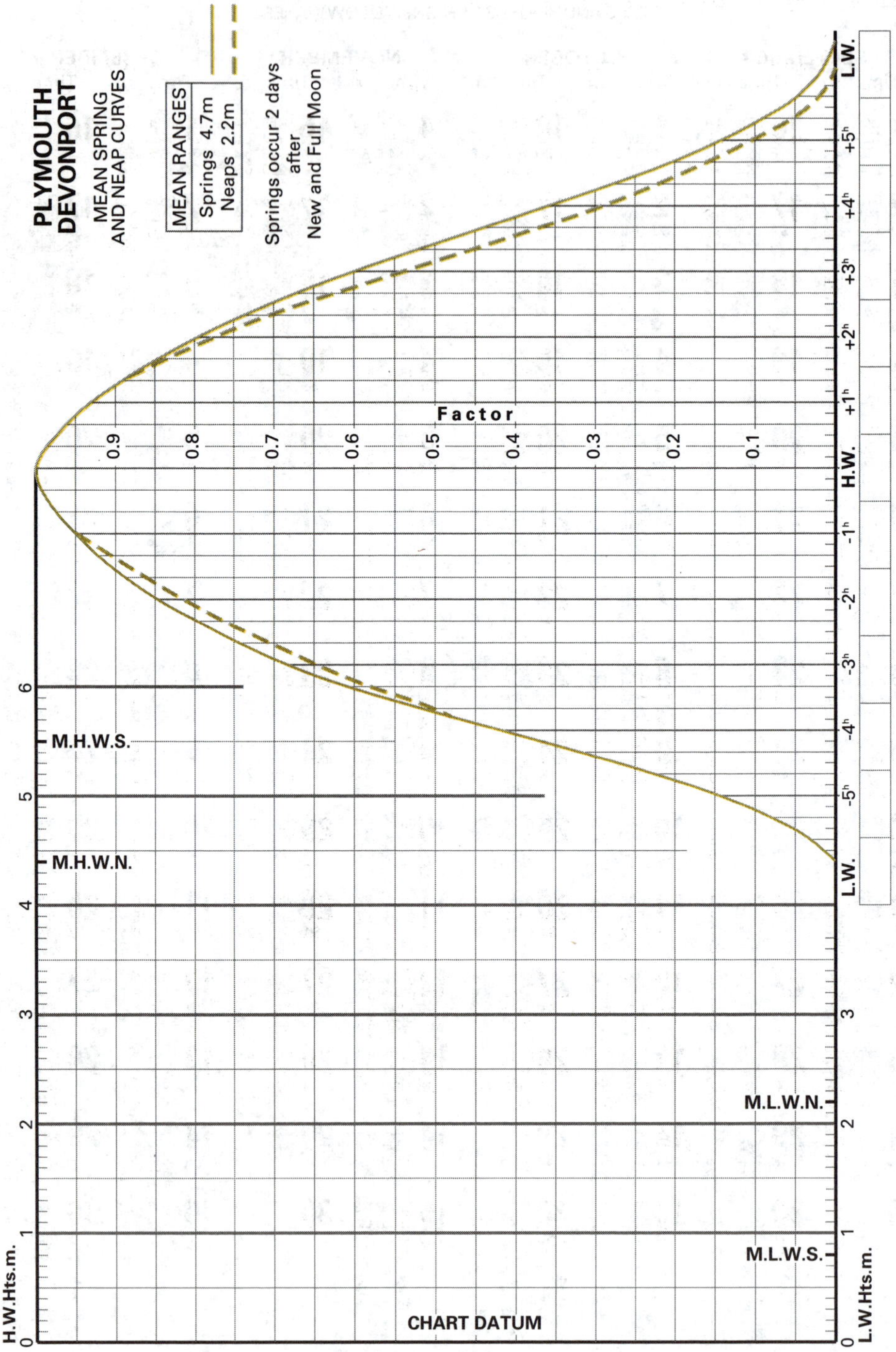
PLYMOUTH
DEVONPORT
MEAN SPRING
AND NEAP CURVES
MEAN RANGES
Springs 4.7m
Neaps 2.2m
Springs occur 2 days
after
New and Full Moon
Factor
0.9
0.8
0.7
0.6
0.5
0.4
0.3
0.2
0.1
L.W.
-5h
-4h
-3h
-2h
-1h
H.W.
+1h
+2h
+3h
+4h
+5h
L.W.
H.W.Hts.m.
M.H.W.S.
M.H.W.N.
CHART DATUM
M.L.W.N.
M.L.W.S.
L.W.Hts.m.

TIME ZONE (UT)
For Summer Time add ONE hour in **non-shaded areas**

ENGLAND – PLYMOUTH
LAT 50°22′N   LONG 4°11′W
TIMES AND HEIGHTS OF HIGH AND LOW WATERS

YEAR 2005

JANUARY		FEBRUARY		MARCH		APRIL	
Time m	Time m	Time m	Time m	Time m	Time m	Time m	Time m
1 0234 1.7 / 0850 4.9 / SA 1500 1.7 / 2115 4.6	**16** 0347 1.2 / 1001 5.2 / SU 1614 1.2 / 2229 4.8	**1** 0323 1.5 / 0935 4.9 / TU 1547 1.6 / 2159 4.6	**16** 0427 1.7 / 1027 4.6 / W 1649 1.9 / ◐ 2246 4.4	**1** 0228 1.1 / 0839 5.1 / TU 1448 1.1 / 2053 4.9	**16** 0317 1.3 / 0913 4.8 / W 1533 1.5 / 2121 4.7	**1** 0324 1.5 / 0943 4.6 / F 1546 1.8 / 2206 4.6	**16** 0349 2.1 / 0953 4.1 / SA 1606 2.3 / ◐ 2214 4.3
2 0309 1.7 / 0928 4.8 / SU 1538 1.8 / 2155 4.5	**17** 0428 1.5 / 1042 4.9 / M 1656 1.6 / ◐ 2312 4.6	**2** 0403 1.7 / 1019 4.7 / W 1633 1.8 / ◐ 2252 4.5	**17** 0511 2.1 / 1113 4.2 / TH 1740 2.3 / 2347 4.2	**2** 0300 1.2 / 0909 4.9 / W 1520 1.4 / 2127 4.7	**17** 0347 1.5 / 0941 4.5 / TH 1603 1.9 / ◐ 2156 4.5	**2** 0420 1.9 / 1049 4.3 / SA 1653 2.2 / ◐ 2322 4.3	**17** 0454 2.4 / 1058 3.7 / SU 1732 2.6 / 2329 4.1
3 0350 1.9 / 1010 4.7 / M 1624 1.9 / ◐ 2243 4.4	**18** 0513 1.8 / 1130 4.6 / TU 1745 1.9	**3** 0458 2.0 / 1121 4.5 / TH 1738 2.0	**18** 0619 2.4 / 1243 4.0 / F 1856 2.5	**3** 0337 1.5 / 0952 4.6 / TH 1601 1.7 / ◐ 2219 4.5	**18** 0424 2.1 / 1022 4.1 / F 1647 2.3 / 2248 4.2	**3** 0557 2.2 / 1227 4.1 / SU 1854 2.3	**18** 0629 2.5 / 1311 3.9 / M 1906 2.5
4 0442 2.0 / 1102 4.6 / TU 1725 2.0 / 2342 4.4	**19** 0007 4.4 / 0610 2.1 / W 1234 4.4 / 1847 2.2	**4** 0004 4.4 / 0623 2.1 / F 1242 4.4 / 1914 2.1	**19** 0136 4.1 / 0755 2.5 / SA 1425 4.0 / 2037 2.4	**4** 0429 1.9 / 1056 4.4 / F 1702 2.1 / 2335 4.3	**19** 0531 2.5 / 1132 3.9 / SA 1809 2.6	**4** 0110 4.4 / 0755 2.0 / M 1416 4.3 / 2032 1.9	**19** 0134 4.2 / 0802 2.2 / TU 1427 4.2 / 2028 2.2
5 0553 2.1 / 1205 4.6 / W 1842 2.0	**20** 0116 4.3 / 0723 2.3 / TH 1348 4.3 / 2001 2.2	**5** 0131 4.4 / 0803 2.0 / SA 1414 4.5 / 2044 1.9	**20** 0255 4.3 / 0935 2.2 / SU 1532 4.3 / 2155 2.1	**5** 0556 2.2 / 1225 4.2 / SA 1853 2.3	**20** 0023 4.0 / 0709 2.6 / SU 1357 3.9 / 1951 2.5	**5** 0241 4.7 / 0910 1.5 / TU 1527 4.7 / 2136 1.4	**20** 0242 4.5 / 0906 1.8 / W 1519 4.5 / 2124 1.8
6 0050 4.5 / 0716 2.1 / TH 1319 4.6 / 1956 1.9	**21** 0224 4.4 / 0844 2.2 / F 1456 4.4 / 2115 2.1	**6** 0256 4.7 / 0925 1.7 / SU 1537 4.7 / 2157 1.6	**21** 0353 4.6 / 1029 1.8 / M 1624 4.6 / 2244 1.7	**6** 0114 4.3 / 0756 2.1 / SU 1413 4.3 / 2039 2.0	**21** 0224 4.2 / 0908 2.2 / M 1507 4.2 / 2125 2.1	**6** 0343 5.1 / 1006 1.0 / W 1620 5.0 / 2229 1.0	**21** 0332 4.7 / 0953 1.4 / TH 1604 4.7 / 2210 1.4
7 0204 4.6 / 0830 1.9 / F 1434 4.7 / 2103 1.7	**22** 0325 4.6 / 0952 2.0 / SA 1554 4.5 / 2213 1.9	**7** 0407 5.0 / 1032 1.3 / M 1643 5.0 / 2259 1.2	**22** 0440 4.9 / 1111 1.4 / TU 1707 4.8 / 2324 1.4	**7** 0250 4.6 / 0922 1.6 / M 1537 4.6 / 2152 1.5	**22** 0324 4.5 / 1000 1.8 / TU 1558 4.5 / 2214 1.7	**7** 0434 5.4 / 1055 0.6 / TH 1705 5.3 / 2315 0.6	**22** 0417 5.0 / 1035 1.1 / F 1645 5.0 / 2252 1.1
8 0315 4.8 / 0937 1.6 / SA 1546 4.9 / 2207 1.4	**23** 0416 4.8 / 1044 1.7 / SU 1642 4.7 / 2300 1.6	**8** 0506 5.4 / 1129 0.8 / TU 1738 5.2 / ● 2352 0.8	**23** 0521 5.1 / 1149 1.2 / W 1746 5.0	**8** 0359 5.0 / 1025 1.1 / TU 1636 5.0 / 2248 1.0	**23** 0412 4.8 / 1041 1.4 / W 1641 4.8 / 2254 1.4	**8** 0519 5.6 / 1140 0.4 / F 1747 5.4 / ● 2358 0.4	**23** 0459 5.1 / 1115 0.9 / SA 1724 5.1 / 2331 0.9
9 0419 5.1 / 1039 1.3 / SU 1649 5.1 / 2306 1.2	**24** 0500 5.0 / 1127 1.5 / M 1724 4.9 / 2340 1.5	**9** 0558 5.4 / 1221 0.5 / W 1829 5.4	**24** 0001 1.2 / 0600 5.2 / TH 1224 1.0 / ◯ 1823 5.1	**9** 0453 5.4 / 1117 0.6 / W 1726 5.3 / 2338 0.7	**24** 0454 5.1 / 1118 1.1 / TH 1720 5.0 / 2331 1.1	**9** 0602 5.6 / 1221 0.3 / SA 1825 5.5	**24** 0540 5.2 / 1153 0.8 / SU 1801 5.2 / ◯
10 0516 5.4 / 1136 1.0 / M 1746 5.3 / ●	**25** 0539 5.2 / 1206 1.3 / TU 1802 5.0 / ◯	**10** 0041 0.6 / 0647 5.8 / TH 1308 0.3 / 1917 5.5	**25** 0035 1.0 / 0637 5.3 / F 1256 0.9 / 1859 5.1	**10** 0541 5.6 / 1204 0.3 / TH 1812 5.4 / ●	**25** 0534 5.2 / 1153 0.9 / F 1757 5.1	**10** 0038 0.4 / 0641 5.6 / SU 1300 0.4 / 1900 5.4	**25** 0009 0.8 / 0618 5.3 / M 1230 0.7 / 1836 5.3
11 0000 1.0 / 0608 5.6 / TU 1230 0.7 / 1839 5.4	**26** 0017 1.3 / 0617 5.2 / W 1242 1.2 / 1840 5.0	**11** 0126 0.4 / 0733 5.8 / F 1352 0.3 / 2001 5.4	**26** 0105 1.0 / 0712 5.3 / SA 1325 0.9 / 1931 5.1	**11** 0023 0.4 / 0627 5.7 / F 1248 0.2 / 1854 5.5	**26** 0006 0.9 / 0611 5.3 / SA 1227 0.8 / 1832 5.2	**11** 0115 0.5 / 0717 5.4 / M 1334 0.8 / 1930 5.3	**26** 0046 0.7 / 0656 5.3 / TU 1306 0.8 / 1911 5.3
12 0052 0.8 / 0659 5.7 / W 1320 5.7 / 1931 5.4	**27** 0051 1.3 / 0654 5.3 / TH 1314 1.2 / 1917 5.0	**12** 0208 0.4 / 0817 5.7 / SA 1432 0.4 / 2041 5.4	**27** 0134 0.9 / 0744 5.3 / SU 1353 0.9 / 2000 5.1	**12** 0105 0.3 / 0710 5.7 / SA 1328 0.3 / 1933 5.5	**27** 0039 0.8 / 0646 5.3 / SU 1259 0.7 / 1904 5.2	**12** 0148 0.7 / 0747 5.2 / TU 1405 0.9 / 1954 5.2	**27** 0122 0.7 / 0733 5.2 / W 1341 0.9 / 1946 5.3
13 0140 0.7 / 0749 5.7 / TH 1408 0.6 / 2020 5.3	**28** 0123 1.2 / 0731 5.2 / F 1345 1.2 / 1952 4.9	**13** 0245 0.6 / 0855 5.5 / SU 1508 0.6 / 2115 5.2	**28** 0201 1.0 / 0812 5.2 / M 1420 1.0 / 2026 5.0	**13** 0143 0.3 / 0749 5.6 / SU 1405 0.4 / 2007 5.4	**28** 0110 0.7 / 0719 5.2 / M 1329 0.7 / 1934 5.2	**13** 0218 1.0 / 0812 4.9 / W 1432 1.2 / 2018 5.0	**28** 0159 0.9 / 0812 5.1 / TH 1417 1.1 / 2024 5.1
14 0225 0.7 / 0836 5.7 / F 1452 0.7 / 2106 5.2	**29** 0152 1.3 / 0804 5.2 / SA 1413 1.2 / 2023 4.9	**14** 0319 0.9 / 0928 5.3 / M 1540 1.0 / 2143 4.9		**14** 0218 0.5 / 0822 5.4 / M 1437 0.7 / 2035 5.2	**29** 0140 0.8 / 0750 5.2 / TU 1358 0.9 / 2002 5.2	**14** 0246 1.3 / 0838 4.7 / TH 1458 1.6 / 2046 4.8	**29** 0239 1.2 / 0855 4.9 / F 1458 1.4 / 2108 4.9
15 0307 0.9 / 0920 5.5 / SA 1534 0.9 / 2148 5.0	**30** 0220 1.3 / 0834 5.1 / SU 1442 1.3 / 2052 4.8	**15** 0352 1.3 / 0956 4.9 / TU 1612 1.5 / 2210 4.7		**15** 0248 0.9 / 0849 5.1 / TU 1505 1.1 / 2057 5.0	**30** 0210 0.9 / 0821 5.1 / W 1428 1.1 / 2033 5.0	**15** 0314 1.7 / 0909 4.4 / F 1525 2.0 / 2123 4.5	**30** 0326 1.5 / 0947 4.7 / SA 1548 1.8 / 2203 4.7
	31 0249 1.4 / 0903 5.0 / M 1512 1.4 / 2122 4.7				**31** 0243 1.2 / 0857 4.9 / TH 1502 1.4 / 2112 4.8		

Chart Datum: 3·22 metres below Ordnance Datum (Newlyn)

》 **FREE** monthly updates from 《
www.reedsalmanac.co.uk

Chapter 5

TIDES

TIME ZONE (UT)
For Summer Time add ONE hour in **non-shaded areas**

ENGLAND – PLYMOUTH
LAT 50°22'N   LONG 4°11'W
TIMES AND HEIGHTS OF HIGH AND LOW WATERS

YEAR 2005

	MAY			JUNE			JULY			AUGUST	
	Time m	Time m		Time m	Time m		Time m	Time m		Time m	Time m
1 SU	0429 1.8 / 1054 4.3 / 1701 2.1 / ☽2318 4.5	**16** M	0427 2.2 / 1037 4.1 / 1655 2.4 / ☾2255 4.3	**1** W	0030 4.7 / 0658 1.6 / 1320 4.5 / 1927 1.8	**16** TH	0600 2.0 / 1212 4.3 / 1829 2.1	**1** F	0056 4.6 / 0715 1.7 / 1336 4.5 / 1944 1.9	**16** SA	0558 1.9 / 1214 4.4 / 1835 2.0	**1** M	0232 4.2 / 0851 2.1 / 1503 4.5 / 2131 2.0	**16** TU	0131 4.3 / 0809 2.0 / 1422 4.6 / 2051 1.8
2 M	0601 2.0 / 1230 4.3 / 1844 2.1	**17** TU	0545 2.3 / 1159 4.0 / 1818 2.4	**2** TH	0141 4.7 / 0804 1.5 / 1421 4.7 / 2030 1.6	**17** F	0024 4.5 / 0705 1.9 / 1316 4.4 / 1934 1.9	**2** SA	0201 4.5 / 0820 1.8 / 1435 4.6 / 2049 1.8	**17** SU	0034 4.5 / 0715 1.9 / 1327 4.4 / 1953 1.9	**2** TU	0334 4.4 / 0958 1.9 / 1558 4.7 / 2228 1.8	**17** W	0303 4.6 / 0925 1.7 / 1537 4.9 / 2201 1.4
3 TU	0059 4.5 / 0735 1.8 / 1356 4.4 / 2007 1.8	**18** W	0017 4.3 / 0700 2.1 / 1325 4.2 / 1929 2.2	**3** F	0241 4.8 / 0902 1.3 / 1515 4.8 / 2126 1.4	**18** SA	0132 4.6 / 0805 1.7 / 1417 4.5 / 2033 1.7	**3** SU	0301 4.6 / 0921 1.7 / 1530 4.7 / 2149 1.7	**18** M	0153 4.5 / 0828 1.8 / 1440 4.6 / 2103 1.7	**3** W	0426 4.6 / 1049 1.7 / 1643 4.9 / 2315 1.5	**18** TH	0414 4.9 / 1030 1.3 / 1637 5.3 / 2300 0.9
4 W	0217 4.8 / 0843 1.4 / 1459 4.7 / 2108 1.4	**19** TH	0139 4.4 / 0803 1.8 / 1424 4.4 / 2028 1.9	**4** SA	0335 4.9 / 0954 1.2 / 1603 5.0 / 2217 1.2	**19** SU	0237 4.7 / 0903 1.5 / 1516 4.7 / 2131 1.5	**4** M	0356 4.6 / 1015 1.6 / 1619 4.9 / 2241 1.5	**19** TU	0311 4.7 / 0935 1.5 / 1548 4.9 / 2208 1.4	**4** TH	0510 4.7 / 1132 1.4 / 1723 5.1 / 2356 1.3	**19** F	0511 5.1 / 1126 0.9 / 1729 5.6 / ○2354 0.6
5 TH	0316 5.0 / 0938 1.1 / 1551 5.0 / 2200 1.1	**20** F	0238 4.6 / 0857 1.5 / 1515 4.6 / 2120 1.6	**5** SU	0424 5.0 / 1042 1.1 / 1647 5.1 / 2303 1.1	**20** M	0340 4.8 / 0959 1.3 / 1612 5.0 / 2227 1.3	**5** TU	0444 4.7 / 1103 1.5 / 1702 5.0 / 2327 1.4	**20** W	0421 4.9 / 1038 1.3 / 1648 5.2 / 2309 1.1	**5** F	0549 4.9 / 1211 1.3 / 1801 5.2 / ●	**20** SA	0603 5.4 / 1216 0.6 / 1818 5.8
6 F	0407 5.2 / 1027 0.8 / 1636 5.2 / 2247 0.8	**21** SA	0330 4.8 / 0947 1.3 / 1602 4.9 / 2209 1.3	**6** M	0507 5.0 / 1125 1.1 / 1726 5.2 / ●2345 1.1	**21** TU	0438 5.0 / 1054 1.2 / 1705 5.2 / 2321 1.0	**6** W	0526 4.8 / 1145 1.4 / 1740 5.1 / ●	**21** TH	0521 5.1 / 1136 1.0 / 1742 5.4 / ○	**6** SA	0033 1.2 / 0626 4.9 / 1246 1.2 / 1837 5.2	**21** SU	0043 0.5 / 0651 5.5 / 1304 0.4 / 1906 5.8
7 SA	0453 5.3 / 1111 0.7 / 1717 5.3 / 2330 0.7	**22** SU	0420 5.0 / 1034 1.1 / 1647 5.1 / 2256 1.1	**7** TU	0546 5.0 / 1204 1.1 / 1800 5.2	**22** W	0533 5.1 / 1147 1.1 / 1755 5.3 / ○	**7** TH	0008 1.3 / 0604 4.9 / 1224 1.3 / 1815 5.1	**22** F	0005 0.8 / 0616 5.2 / 1230 0.8 / 1833 5.6	**7** SU	0107 1.1 / 0703 4.9 / 1317 1.2 / 1913 5.2	**22** M	0129 0.2 / 0738 5.5 / 1347 0.3 / 1951 5.8
8 SU	0534 5.4 / 1153 0.6 / 1755 5.3 / ●	**23** M	0507 5.1 / 1120 0.9 / 1730 5.2 / ○2342 0.9	**8** W	0024 1.1 / 0621 5.0 / 1240 1.2 / 1831 5.2	**23** TH	0013 0.9 / 0626 5.2 / 1238 0.9 / 1843 5.5	**8** F	0047 1.3 / 0641 4.9 / 1300 1.3 / 1851 5.1	**23** SA	0058 0.5 / 0709 5.3 / 1320 0.6 / 1924 5.7	**8** M	0136 1.2 / 0739 4.9 / 1345 1.2 / 1947 5.1	**23** TU	0210 0.3 / 0820 5.5 / 1426 0.5 / 2032 5.6
9 M	0010 0.7 / 0612 5.3 / 1231 0.7 / 1827 5.3	**24** TU	0553 5.2 / 1205 0.9 / 1812 5.3	**9** TH	0100 1.2 / 0655 4.9 / 1313 1.3 / 1902 5.1	**24** F	0105 0.7 / 0718 5.2 / 1328 0.9 / 1933 5.5	**9** SA	0122 1.3 / 0718 4.8 / 1333 1.4 / 1927 5.1	**24** SU	0147 0.4 / 0800 5.4 / 1407 0.6 / 2012 5.7	**9** TU	0203 1.2 / 0812 4.9 / 1411 1.3 / 2018 5.1	**24** W	0248 0.5 / 0858 5.3 / 1502 0.8 / 2108 5.4
10 TU	0047 0.8 / 0646 5.2 / 1304 0.9 / 1856 5.3	**25** W	0026 0.8 / 0637 5.2 / 1249 0.9 / 1854 5.4	**10** F	0133 1.3 / 0728 4.8 / 1345 1.5 / 1936 5.0	**25** SA	0155 0.7 / 0810 5.2 / 1416 0.9 / 2022 5.5	**10** SU	0154 1.4 / 0756 4.7 / 1404 1.5 / 2003 5.0	**25** M	0232 0.4 / 0846 5.3 / 1450 0.7 / 2057 5.6	**10** W	0228 1.3 / 0841 4.8 / 1436 1.4 / 2045 5.0	**25** TH	0323 0.9 / 0931 5.1 / 1536 1.1 / 2139 5.0
11 W	0121 1.0 / 0716 5.0 / 1335 1.1 / 1922 5.2	**26** TH	0111 0.8 / 0723 5.2 / 1332 1.0 / 1937 5.4	**11** SA	0206 1.5 / 0804 4.6 / 1417 1.6 / 2012 4.9	**26** SU	0244 0.9 / 0900 5.1 / 1503 1.0 / 2110 5.4	**11** M	0225 1.4 / 0833 4.7 / 1434 1.5 / 2039 4.9	**26** TU	0315 0.6 / 0929 5.2 / 1530 0.9 / 2139 5.4	**11** TH	0254 1.4 / 0909 4.7 / 1504 1.5 / 2113 4.8	**26** F	0356 1.3 / 1000 4.8 / 1611 1.5 / ☽2209 4.8
12 TH	0151 1.2 / 0744 4.9 / 1404 1.4 / 1951 5.0	**27** F	0156 0.9 / 0810 5.1 / 1417 1.1 / 2023 5.3	**12** SU	0239 1.6 / 0844 4.5 / 1451 1.8 / 2052 4.8	**27** M	0332 0.9 / 0949 4.9 / 1550 1.2 / 2159 5.2	**12** TU	0255 1.5 / 0909 4.6 / 1504 1.7 / 2113 4.8	**27** W	0355 0.9 / 1010 4.9 / 1610 1.2 / 2219 5.1	**12** F	0324 1.5 / 0941 4.6 / 1538 1.7 / 2149 4.7	**27** SA	0431 1.7 / 1033 4.6 / 1654 1.9 / 2248 4.3
13 F	0221 1.5 / 0815 4.7 / 1433 1.7 / 2024 4.9	**28** SA	0243 1.0 / 0900 5.0 / 1504 1.3 / 2111 5.1	**13** M	0315 1.8 / 0927 4.4 / 1528 2.0 / 2135 4.6	**28** TU	0420 1.1 / 1040 4.8 / 1639 1.4 / ☽2251 5.0	**13** W	0327 1.6 / 0945 4.6 / 1537 1.7 / 2149 4.7	**28** TH	0435 1.3 / 1051 4.7 / 1652 1.5 / ☽2302 4.7	**13** SA	0402 1.7 / 1025 4.4 / 1625 1.9 / ☽2243 4.5	**28** SU	0519 2.3 / 1127 4.3 / 1759 2.4
14 SA	0252 1.7 / 0851 4.4 / 1504 2.0 / 2103 4.6	**29** SU	0334 1.3 / 0953 4.8 / 1556 1.6 / 2205 4.9	**14** TU	0359 1.9 / 1014 4.3 / 1615 2.1 / 2223 4.5	**29** W	0513 1.4 / 1135 4.7 / 1734 1.6 / 2350 4.8	**14** TH	0404 1.7 / 1024 4.4 / 1619 1.8 / ☾2231 4.6	**29** F	0520 1.7 / 1140 4.4 / 1743 1.9 / 2359 4.4	**14** SU	0457 2.0 / 1129 4.3 / 1739 2.2 / 2358 4.3	**29** M	0016 4.0 / 0634 2.7 / 1322 4.0 / 1943 2.5
15 SU	0330 2.0 / 0937 4.2 / 1546 2.2 / 2152 4.4	**30** M	0433 1.5 / 1056 4.6 / 1659 1.8 / ☽2312 4.8	**15** W	0454 2.1 / 1109 4.2 / 1718 2.2 / ☽2320 4.5	**30** TH	0611 1.6 / 1235 4.5 / 1837 1.8	**15** F	0451 1.9 / 1109 4.4 / 1718 2.0 / 2326 4.5	**30** SA	0615 2.0 / 1246 4.2 / 1851 2.2	**15** M	0630 2.2 / 1252 4.4 / 1928 2.1	**30** TU	0210 4.0 / 0833 2.4 / 1440 4.3 / 2122 2.2
		31 TU	0544 1.7 / 1210 4.5 / 1814 1.9						**31** SU	0117 4.2 / 0728 2.2 / 1358 4.3 / 2014 2.2			**31** W	0317 4.2 / 0945 2.2 / 1538 4.6 / 2214 1.8

Chart Datum: 3·22 metres below Ordnance Datum (Newlyn)

》》 **FREE** monthly updates from 《《
www.reedsalmanac.co.uk

ENGLAND – PLYMOUTH

TIME ZONE (UT)
For Summer Time add ONE hour in **non-shaded areas**

LAT 50°22'N   LONG 4°11'W

YEAR 2005

TIMES AND HEIGHTS OF HIGH AND LOW WATERS

SEPTEMBER				OCTOBER				NOVEMBER				DECEMBER			
Time	m	Time	m	Time	m	Time	m	Time	m	Time	m	Time	m	Time	m
1 0409 4.5 1032 1.7 TH 1624 4.9 2257 1.5		**16** 0407 5.0 1019 1.2 F 1623 5.4 2246 0.8		**1** 0424 4.9 1041 1.5 SA 1636 5.1 2301 1.2		**16** 0436 5.4 1046 0.8 SU 1650 5.7 2310 0.5		**1** 0505 5.2 1112 1.2 TU 1719 5.3 2330 1.0		**16** 0533 5.5 1147 0.9 W 1750 5.5 ○		**1** 0512 5.2 1120 1.2 TH 1732 5.2 ● 2340 1.1		**16** 0548 5.3 1209 1.5 F 1808 5.1	
2 0451 4.8 1113 1.4 F 1703 5.1 2335 1.2		**17** 0457 5.3 1109 0.8 SA 1712 5.7 2335 0.4		**2** 0502 5.1 1116 1.2 SU 1713 5.3 2335 1.0		**17** 0519 5.5 1131 0.6 M 1734 5.8 ○ 2353 0.5		**2** 0541 5.3 1148 1.1 W 1756 5.4 ●		**17** 0006 0.9 0609 5.5 TH 1227 0.9 1827 5.4		**2** 0553 5.4 1203 1.1 F 1815 5.3		**17** 0024 1.3 0622 5.3 SA 1248 1.3 1843 5.0	
3 0529 5.0 1149 1.2 SA 1741 5.3 ●		**18** 0543 5.5 1156 0.5 SU 1758 5.8 ○		**3** 0538 5.2 1149 1.1 M 1750 5.4 ●		**18** 0600 5.6 1213 0.5 TU 1815 5.7		**3** 0005 1.0 0616 5.4 TH 1224 1.0 1832 5.3		**18** 0044 1.0 0642 5.4 F 1304 1.1 1900 5.2		**3** 0022 1.1 0634 5.4 SA 1247 1.0 1858 5.3		**18** 0100 1.4 0655 5.3 SU 1324 1.4 1916 4.9	
4 0010 1.1 0605 5.1 SU 1223 1.1 1816 5.3		**19** 0020 0.3 0627 5.6 M 1240 0.4 1841 5.9		**4** 0006 0.9 0612 5.3 TU 1221 1.0 1824 5.4		**19** 0034 0.5 0638 5.6 W 1253 0.6 1853 5.6		**4** 0040 1.0 0650 5.4 F 1258 1.0 1907 5.3		**19** 0117 1.2 0712 5.3 SA 1338 1.3 1930 5.0		**4** 0105 1.2 0716 5.4 SU 1331 1.1 1942 5.2		**19** 0134 1.5 0728 5.2 M 1358 1.5 1951 4.8	
5 0041 1.0 0640 5.1 M 1252 1.0 1851 5.3		**20** 0103 0.2 0709 5.6 TU 1321 0.4 1923 5.8		**5** 0036 0.9 0644 5.3 W 1250 1.0 1856 5.4		**20** 0111 0.7 0712 5.5 TH 1328 0.8 1927 5.4		**5** 0113 1.1 0724 5.3 SA 1333 1.2 1944 5.1		**20** 0149 1.5 0741 5.2 SU 1410 1.6 2000 4.8		**5** 0148 1.3 0800 5.4 M 1416 1.2 2030 5.0		**20** 0206 1.7 0804 5.1 TU 1431 1.7 2028 4.7	
6 0109 1.0 0713 5.1 TU 1319 1.1 1923 5.3		**21** 0142 0.4 0747 5.5 W 1357 0.6 2000 5.6		**6** 0105 1.0 0714 5.3 TH 1318 1.0 1925 5.3		**21** 0144 1.0 0741 5.4 F 1401 1.1 1956 5.1		**6** 0148 1.3 0801 5.2 SU 1411 1.4 2025 4.9		**21** 0219 1.8 0813 5.0 M 1444 1.9 2035 4.6		**6** 0233 1.4 0847 5.3 TU 1505 1.4 2120 4.9		**21** 0239 1.8 0843 4.9 W 1505 1.8 2109 4.5	
7 0134 1.0 0743 5.1 W 1343 1.1 1951 5.2		**22** 0216 0.7 0820 5.4 TH 1431 0.9 2031 5.3		**7** 0132 1.1 0742 5.2 F 1346 1.2 1954 5.1		**22** 0214 1.3 0806 5.2 SA 1432 1.5 2021 4.8		**7** 0226 1.6 0844 5.1 M 1456 1.6 2115 4.7		**22** 0252 2.1 0852 4.8 TU 1521 2.1 2119 4.4		**7** 0322 1.6 0937 5.1 W 1558 1.6 2215 4.7		**22** 0312 2.0 0924 4.8 TH 1541 2.0 2152 4.4	
8 0159 1.1 0810 5.0 TH 1408 1.2 2016 5.1		**23** 0248 1.1 0846 5.1 F 1502 1.3 2057 4.9		**8** 0200 1.3 0812 5.1 SA 1417 1.4 2028 4.9		**23** 0243 1.7 0834 5.0 SU 1503 1.9 2051 4.5		**8** 0313 1.9 0937 4.9 TU 1553 2.0 2215 4.5		**23** 0332 2.3 0940 4.6 W 1611 2.4 ● 2215 4.2		**8** 0418 1.8 1035 5.0 TH 1700 1.7 ● 2320 4.6		**23** 0350 2.1 1008 4.6 F 1625 2.1 ● 2241 4.3	
9 0224 1.3 0835 4.9 F 1436 1.4 2044 4.9		**24** 0317 1.5 0910 4.8 SA 1534 1.8 2123 4.6		**9** 0232 1.5 0849 4.9 SU 1454 1.7 2113 4.7		**24** 0313 2.1 0910 4.7 M 1541 2.3 2134 4.2		**9** 0417 2.2 1042 4.7 W 1715 2.1 ● 2337 4.4		**24** 0429 2.5 1039 4.4 TH 1720 2.5 2330 4.1		**9** 0526 2.0 1143 4.8 F 1814 1.8		**24** 0440 2.3 1058 4.5 SA 1723 2.2 2339 4.3	
10 0253 1.5 0907 4.7 SA 1510 1.6 2121 4.7		**25** 0348 2.0 0942 4.6 SU 1612 2.2 ● 2201 4.2		**10** 0311 1.9 0940 4.7 M 1544 2.0 ● 2214 4.4		**25** 0354 2.5 0959 4.4 TU 1640 2.6 ● 2236 4.0		**10** 0556 2.3 1210 4.6 TH 1855 2.0		**25** 0549 2.6 1155 4.4 F 1838 2.4		**10** 0033 4.6 0643 2.0 SA 1258 4.8 1925 1.8		**25** 0547 2.3 1158 4.5 SU 1831 2.2	
11 0329 1.8 0953 4.6 SU 1555 2.0 ● 2220 4.4		**26** 0431 2.5 1031 4.3 M 1716 2.6 2306 3.9		**11** 0409 2.3 1049 4.5 TU 1711 2.4 2338 4.2		**26** 0510 2.8 1112 4.2 W 1814 2.7		**11** 0114 4.5 0729 2.1 F 1339 4.8 2008 1.7		**26** 0059 4.2 0706 2.5 SA 1317 4.5 1944 2.1		**11** 0142 4.7 0754 1.9 SU 1405 4.9 2029 1.6		**26** 0044 4.3 0701 2.2 M 1306 4.5 1937 2.1	
12 0422 2.2 1102 4.4 M 1710 2.3 2342 4.2		**27** 0550 2.8 1214 4.1 TU 1907 2.7		**12** 0607 2.5 1224 4.4 W 1918 2.2		**27** 0057 4.0 0652 2.7 TH 1321 4.3 2001 2.4		**12** 0225 4.7 0835 1.7 SA 1443 5.1 2105 1.3		**27** 0203 4.4 0809 2.2 SU 1419 4.7 2038 1.9		**12** 0242 4.8 0856 1.7 M 1505 5.0 2125 1.5		**27** 0150 4.5 0807 2.0 TU 1414 4.6 2038 1.9	
13 0606 2.4 1233 4.3 TU 1921 2.3		**28** 0146 3.9 0806 2.7 W 1412 4.3 2059 2.3		**13** 0137 4.3 0758 2.2 TH 1406 4.7 2036 1.7		**28** 0212 4.2 0823 2.0 F 1427 4.5 2056 2.0		**13** 0320 5.0 0930 1.4 SU 1537 5.3 2156 1.1		**28** 0255 4.7 0902 1.9 M 1512 4.8 2126 1.6		**13** 0337 5.0 0952 1.4 TU 1559 5.1 2216 1.4		**28** 0254 4.7 0908 1.7 W 1519 4.7 2135 1.7	
14 0131 4.3 0805 2.2 W 1416 4.6 2048 1.8		**29** 0253 4.3 0918 2.2 TH 1510 4.6 2146 1.9		**14** 0255 4.6 0905 1.7 F 1512 5.1 2134 1.2		**29** 0303 4.5 0914 1.7 SA 1516 4.8 2138 1.7		**14** 0409 5.3 1019 1.1 M 1625 5.4 2243 0.9		**29** 0343 4.9 0950 1.6 TU 1601 5.0 2212 1.5		**14** 0426 5.1 1042 1.3 W 1647 5.1 2303 1.3		**29** 0353 4.9 1005 1.4 TH 1619 4.9 2230 1.4	
15 0305 4.6 0920 1.7 TH 1529 5.0 2152 1.3		**30** 0343 4.6 1002 1.8 F 1556 4.9 2225 1.5		**15** 0349 5.1 0958 1.2 SA 1604 5.5 2224 0.8		**30** 0347 4.7 0956 1.6 SU 1559 5.1 2216 1.4		**15** 0452 5.4 1105 0.9 TU 1710 5.5 2326 0.8		**30** 0429 5.1 1036 1.4 W 1647 5.1 2256 1.2		**15** 0509 5.3 1127 1.3 TH 1730 5.1 ○ 2345 1.2		**30** 0447 5.1 1100 1.3 F 1713 5.1 2322 1.1	
						31 0427 5.1 1035 1.4 M 1640 5.2 2254 1.2								**31** 0536 5.3 1151 1.1 SA 1803 5.2	

Chart Datum: 3·22 metres below Ordnance Datum (Newlyn)

》》 **FREE** monthly updates from 《《
www.reedsalmanac.co.uk

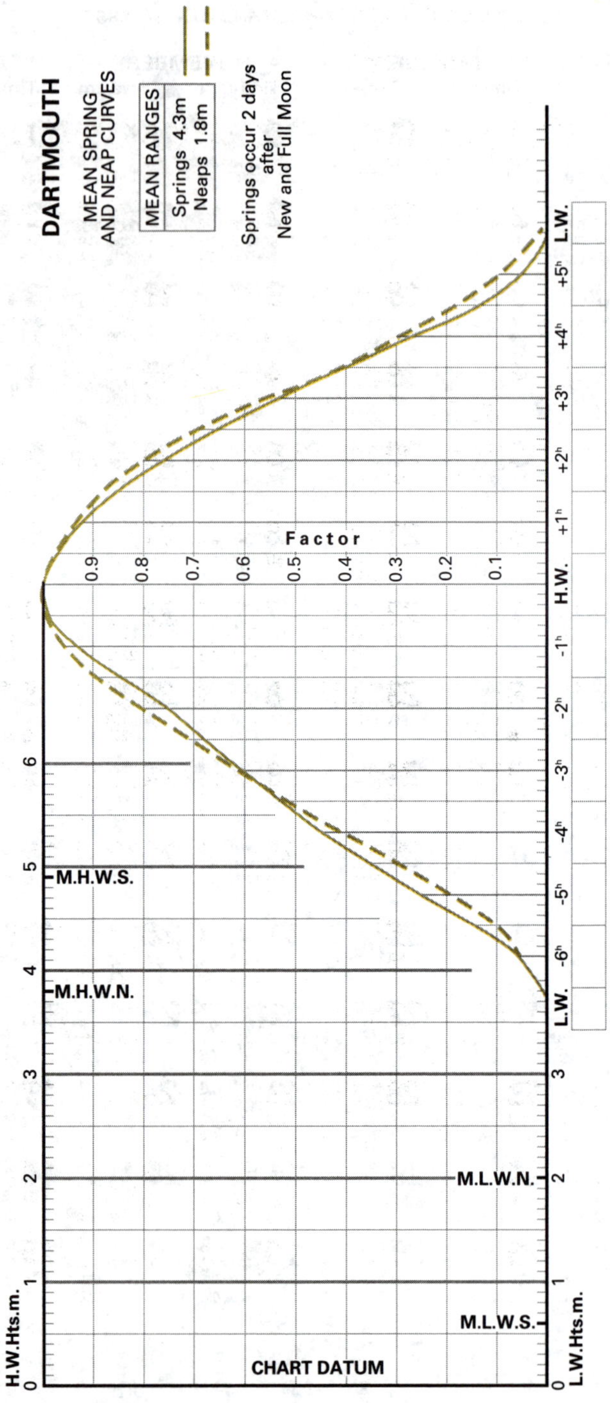

DARTMOUTH
MEAN SPRING AND NEAP CURVES
MEAN RANGES
Springs 4.3m
Neaps 1.8m
Springs occur 2 days after New and Full Moon
Factor
0.9
0.8
0.7
0.6
0.5
0.4
0.3
0.2
0.1
L.W.
-6h
-5h
-4h
-3h
-2h
-1h
H.W.
+1h
+2h
+3h
+4h
+5h
L.W.
H.W.Hts.m.
0
1
2
3
4
5
6
M.H.W.S.
M.H.W.N.
M.L.W.N.
M.L.W.S.
CHART DATUM
L.W.Hts.m.

TIME ZONE (UT)
For Summer Time add ONE hour in **non-shaded areas**

ENGLAND - DARTMOUTH

LAT 50°21'N   LONG 3°34'W

TIMES AND HEIGHTS OF HIGH AND LOW WATERS

YEAR 2005

JANUARY				FEBRUARY				MARCH				APRIL			
Time	m	Time	m	Time	m	Time	m	Time	m	Time	m	Time	m	Time	m
1 0232 1.5 0911 4.3 SA 1458 1.5 2135 4.0		**16** 0344 1.0 1020 4.6 SU 1611 1.0 2248 4.2		**1** 0321 1.3 0955 4.3 TU 1544 1.4 2218 4.0		**16** 0424 1.5 1046 4.0 W 1645 1.7 ○ 2304 3.8		**1** 0227 0.9 0900 4.5 TU 1446 0.9 2114 4.3		**16** 0315 1.1 0934 4.2 W 1530 1.3 2141 4.1		**1** 0322 1.3 1003 4.0 F 1543 1.6 2225 4.0		**16** 0346 1.9 1012 3.5 SA 1603 2.1 ○ 2233 3.7	
2 0307 1.6 0948 4.2 SU 1535 1.6 2214 3.9		**17** 0425 1.3 1100 4.3 M 1652 1.4 ○ 2330 4.0		**2** 0400 1.5 1038 4.1 W 1629 1.6 ○ 2310 3.9		**17** 0507 1.9 1131 3.6 TH 1735 2.1		**2** 0258 1.0 0930 4.3 W 1518 1.2 2147 4.1		**17** 0344 1.5 1001 3.9 TH 1600 1.7 ○ 2215 3.9		**2** 0417 1.7 1107 3.7 SA 1649 2.0 2339 3.7		**17** 0450 2.2 1116 3.3 SU 1727 2.4 2346 3.5	
3 0347 1.7 1029 4.1 M 1621 1.7 ○ 2301 3.8		**18** 0509 1.6 1147 4.0 TU 1740 1.7		**3** 0454 1.8 1138 3.9 TH 1733 1.8		**18** 0003 3.6 0614 2.2 F 1258 3.4 1852 2.3		**3** 0334 1.3 1011 4.0 TH 1558 1.5 ○ 2238 3.9		**18** 0421 1.9 1041 3.5 F 1643 2.1 2306 3.6		**3** 0552 2.0 1243 3.5 SU 1850 2.1		**18** 0624 2.3 1326 3.3 M 1902 2.3	
4 0438 1.8 1120 4.0 TU 1721 1.8 2359 3.8		**19** 0023 3.8 0605 1.9 W 1249 3.8 1843 2.0		**4** 0020 3.8 0618 1.9 F 1257 3.8 1910 1.9		**19** 0152 3.5 0751 2.3 SA 1443 3.4 2034 2.2		**4** 0426 1.7 1114 3.8 F 1658 1.9 2352 3.7		**19** 0526 2.3 1149 3.3 SA 1804 2.4		**4** 0125 3.8 0751 1.8 M 1434 3.7 2029 1.7		**19** 0150 3.6 0758 2.0 TU 1445 3.6 2024 2.0	
5 0548 1.9 1221 4.0 W 1838 1.8		**20** 0132 3.7 0719 2.1 TH 1405 3.7 1957 2.0		**5** 0147 3.8 0759 1.8 SA 1431 3.9 2041 1.7		**20** 0314 3.7 0933 2.0 SU 1552 3.7 2153 1.9		**5** 0551 2.0 1241 3.6 SA 1849 2.1		**20** 0039 3.4 0705 2.4 SU 1414 3.3 1947 2.3		**5** 0259 4.1 0907 1.3 TU 1547 4.1 2134 1.2		**20** 0300 3.9 0903 1.6 W 1539 3.9 2121 1.6	
6 0105 3.9 0712 1.9 TH 1335 4.0 1952 1.7		**21** 0242 3.8 0841 2.0 F 1515 3.8 2112 1.9		**6** 0315 4.1 0922 1.5 SU 1557 4.1 2155 1.4		**21** 0414 4.0 1027 1.6 M 1646 4.0 2243 1.5		**6** 0129 3.7 0752 1.9 SU 1430 3.7 2036 1.8		**21** 0242 3.6 0905 2.0 M 1526 3.6 2122 1.9		**6** 0403 4.5 1004 0.8 W 1642 4.4 2227 0.8		**21** 0352 4.1 0951 1.2 TH 1625 4.1 2208 1.2	
7 0221 4.0 0827 1.7 F 1452 4.1 2100 1.5		**22** 0345 4.0 0950 1.8 SA 1615 3.9 2211 1.7		**7** 0428 4.4 1031 1.1 M 1705 4.4 2258 1.0		**22** 0502 4.2 1110 1.2 TU 1730 4.2 2323 1.2		**7** 0309 4.0 0919 1.4 M 1557 4.0 2150 1.3		**22** 0344 3.9 0958 1.6 TU 1619 3.9 2212 1.5		**7** 0456 4.8 1054 0.4 TH 1728 4.7 2314 0.4		**22** 0439 4.4 1034 0.9 F 1708 4.4 2251 0.9	
8 0335 4.2 0935 1.4 SA 1607 4.3 2205 1.2		**23** 0438 4.2 1043 1.5 SU 1704 4.1 2259 1.4		**8** 0529 4.8 1128 0.6 TU 1802 4.7 ● 2351 0.6		**23** 0545 4.5 1148 1.0 W 1811 4.4		**8** 0420 4.5 1023 0.9 TU 1658 4.4 2247 0.8		**23** 0433 4.2 1040 1.2 W 1703 4.2 2253 1.2		**8** 0543 5.0 1139 0.2 F 1812 4.8 ● 2357 0.2		**23** 0522 4.5 1114 0.7 SA 1748 4.5 2330 0.7	
9 0441 4.5 1038 1.1 SU 1712 4.5 2305 1.0		**24** 0523 4.4 1126 1.3 M 1748 4.3 2339 1.3		**9** 0623 5.0 1220 0.3 W 1854 4.8		**24** 0000 1.0 0625 4.6 TH 1223 0.8 ○ 1848 4.5		**9** 0516 4.8 1116 0.4 W 1750 4.7 2337 0.5		**24** 0517 4.5 1117 0.9 TH 1744 4.5 2330 0.9		**9** 0627 5.0 1220 0.1 SA 1850 4.9 ○		**24** 0604 4.6 1152 0.6 SU 1826 4.6 ○	
10 0540 4.8 1135 0.8 M 1811 4.7 ● 2359 0.8		**25** 0603 4.6 1205 1.1 TU 1827 4.4 ○		**10** 0041 0.4 0711 5.2 TH 1308 0.1 1940 4.9		**25** 0035 0.8 0701 4.7 F 1256 0.7 1923 4.5		**10** 0605 5.0 1203 0.1 TH 1837 4.8 ●		**25** 0558 4.6 1152 0.7 F 1822 4.5 ○		**10** 0038 0.2 0705 5.0 SU 1300 0.2 1924 4.8		**25** 0008 0.6 0643 4.7 M 1230 0.5 1900 4.7	
11 0633 5.0 1230 0.5 TU 1903 4.8		**26** 0016 1.1 0642 4.6 W 1242 1.0 1904 4.4		**11** 0126 0.2 0756 5.2 F 1351 0.1 2023 4.8		**26** 0105 0.8 0736 4.5 SA 1325 0.7 1954 4.5		**11** 0022 0.2 0652 5.1 F 1248 0.0 1918 4.9		**26** 0005 0.7 0636 4.6 SA 1226 0.6 1856 4.6		**11** 0115 0.3 0740 4.8 M 1333 0.4 1953 4.7		**26** 0046 0.5 0720 4.7 TU 1306 0.5 1935 4.7	
12 0052 0.6 0723 5.1 W 1320 0.4 1954 4.8		**27** 0051 1.1 0718 4.7 TH 1314 1.0 1940 4.4		**12** 0207 0.2 0839 5.1 SA 1430 0.2 2102 4.8		**27** 0133 0.7 0807 4.7 SU 1352 0.7 2022 4.5		**12** 0105 0.1 0734 5.1 SA 1328 0.1 1956 4.9		**27** 0039 0.6 0710 4.7 SU 1259 0.5 1928 4.6		**12** 0147 0.5 0809 4.7 TU 1404 0.7 2016 4.6		**27** 0122 0.6 0756 4.6 W 1340 0.7 2008 4.7	
13 0139 0.5 0811 5.1 TH 1407 0.4 2042 4.7		**28** 0123 1.0 0754 4.6 F 1344 1.0 2014 4.3		**13** 0243 0.9 0916 4.9 SU 1506 0.7 2135 4.6		**28** 0200 0.8 0834 4.6 M 1419 0.8 2048 4.4		**13** 0142 0.2 0811 5.0 SU 1404 0.1 2029 4.8		**28** 0110 0.5 0742 4.7 M 1329 0.5 1957 4.6		**13** 0217 0.8 0834 4.4 W 1430 1.0 2040 4.4		**28** 0158 0.7 0834 4.5 TH 1416 0.9 2046 4.5	
14 0224 0.6 0857 5.1 F 1450 0.5 2127 4.6		**29** 0151 1.1 0826 4.6 SA 1412 1.0 2045 4.3		**14** 0317 1.4 0948 4.7 M 1537 1.0 2203 4.3					**14** 0217 0.3 0844 4.7 M 1435 0.5 2056 4.6		**28** 0139 0.6 0812 4.6 TU 1357 0.7 2024 4.6		**14** 0244 1.1 0859 4.1 TH 1456 1.4 2107 4.3		**29** 0237 0.9 0916 4.2 F 1456 1.2 2129 4.3	
15 0305 0.7 0940 4.9 SA 1531 0.7 2207 4.4		**30** 0219 1.1 0855 4.5 SU 1440 1.1 2113 4.2		**15** 0349 1.7 1015 4.3 TU 1609 1.3 2229 4.1					**15** 0246 0.7 0910 4.5 TU 1503 0.9 2118 4.4		**29** 0209 0.7 0843 4.5 W 1427 0.9 2054 4.5		**15** 0312 1.5 0930 3.8 F 1523 1.8 2143 3.9		**30** 0324 1.1 1006 4.0 SA 1545 1.6 2222 4.1	
		31 0247 1.2 0924 4.4 M 1510 1.2 2142 4.1								**30** 0241 1.0 0918 4.3 TH 1500 1.2 2133 4.3					
										31 0315 1.2 1000 4.0 TH 1538 1.6 2222 4.0					

Chart Datum: 2·62 metres below Ordnance Datum (Newlyn)

》》 **FREE** monthly updates from 《《
www.reedsalmanac.co.uk

TIDES

TIME ZONE (UT) — For Summer Time add ONE hour in **non-shaded areas**

ENGLAND - DARTMOUTH
LAT 50°21'N   LONG 3°34'W
TIMES AND HEIGHTS OF HIGH AND LOW WATERS

YEAR 2005

	MAY			JUNE			JULY			AUGUST	
	Time m	Time m		Time m	Time m		Time m	Time m		Time m	Time m
1 SU	0426 1.6 1112 3.7 1657 1.9 ☽ 2335 3.9	**16** M	0424 2.0 1055 3.5 1651 2.2 ☾ 2313 3.7	**1** W	0045 4.1 0654 1.4 1336 3.9 1923 1.6	**16** TH	0555 1.8 1228 3.7 1824 1.9	**1** F	0111 4.0 0711 1.5 1352 3.9 1940 1.7	**16** SA	0553 1.7 1230 3.8 1831 1.8	**1** M	0250 3.6 0848 1.9 1522 3.9 2129 1.8	**16** TU	0147 3.7 0805 1.8 1440 4.0 2048 1.6
2 M	0556 1.8 1245 3.7 1840 1.9	**17** TU	0540 2.1 1215 3.4 1813 2.2	**2** TH	0157 4.1 0800 1.3 1439 4.1 2027 1.4	**17** F	0040 3.9 0701 1.7 1332 3.8 1930 1.7	**2** SA	0218 3.9 0816 1.6 1453 4.0 2046 1.6	**17** SU	0049 3.9 0711 1.7 1343 3.8 1949 1.7	**2** TU	0354 3.8 0956 1.7 1619 4.1 2226 1.6	**17** W	0322 4.0 0922 1.5 1557 4.3 2159 1.2
3 TU	0114 3.9 0731 1.6 1413 3.8 2003 1.6	**18** W	0033 3.7 0656 1.9 1341 3.6 1925 2.0	**3** F	0259 4.2 0859 1.1 1535 4.2 2123 1.2	**18** SA	0148 4.0 0801 1.5 1435 3.9 2030 1.5	**3** SU	0320 4.0 0918 1.5 1550 4.1 2147 1.5	**18** M	0210 3.9 0824 1.6 1458 4.0 2100 1.5	**3** W	0448 4.0 1048 1.5 1705 4.3 2314 1.3	**18** TH	0435 4.3 1029 1.1 1659 4.5 2259 0.7
4 W	0235 4.2 0840 1.2 1518 4.1 2105 1.2	**19** TH	0155 3.8 0759 1.6 1442 3.8 2024 1.7	**4** SA	0355 4.3 0952 1.0 1624 4.4 2215 0.5	**19** SU	0255 4.1 0900 1.3 1536 4.1 2129 1.3	**4** M	0417 4.0 1013 1.4 1641 4.3 2240 1.3	**19** TU	0330 4.1 0933 1.3 1609 4.3 2206 1.0	**4** TH	0533 4.1 1131 1.2 1747 4.5 2355 1.1	**19** F	0534 4.5 1125 0.7 1753 5.0 ○ 2353 0.4
5 TH	0336 4.4 0936 0.9 1612 4.4 2158 0.9	**20** F	0256 4.0 0854 1.3 1535 4.0 2117 1.4	**5** SU	0446 4.4 1041 0.9 1710 4.5 2302 0.9	**20** M	0400 4.2 0957 1.1 1633 4.4 2225 1.1	**5** TU	0506 4.1 1102 1.3 1725 4.4 2326 1.2	**20** W	0443 4.3 1037 1.1 1711 4.6 2308 0.9	**5** F	0614 4.3 1210 1.1 1826 4.6 ●	**20** SA	0628 4.8 1215 0.3 1843 5.2
6 F	0428 4.6 1025 0.6 1658 4.6 2246 0.6	**21** SA	0350 4.2 0945 1.1 1623 4.3 2207 1.1	**6** M	0530 4.4 1124 0.9 1750 4.6 ● 2344 0.9	**21** TU	0500 4.4 1053 1.0 1728 4.6 2320 0.8	**6** W	0550 4.2 1144 1.2 1804 4.5 ○	**21** TH	0545 4.5 1135 0.8 1806 4.8 ○	**6** SA	0033 1.0 0651 4.3 1246 1.0 1901 4.6	**21** SU	0043 0.1 0715 4.9 1304 0.2 1930 5.2
7 SA	0516 4.7 1110 0.5 1741 4.7 2329 0.5	**22** SU	0442 4.4 1033 0.9 1710 4.5 2255 0.9	**7** TU	0611 4.4 1203 0.9 1825 4.6	**22** W	0557 4.5 1146 0.8 1820 4.7 ○	**7** TH	0007 1.1 0629 4.3 1223 1.1 1840 4.5	**22** F	0004 0.6 0641 4.6 1230 0.6 1857 5.0	**7** SU	0107 0.9 0727 4.3 1317 1.0 1937 4.6	**22** M	0129 0.0 0801 4.9 1346 0.2 2013 5.2
8 SU	0558 4.8 1152 0.4 1820 4.7 ●	**23** M	0530 4.5 1119 0.7 1754 4.6 ○ 2341 0.7	**8** W	0023 0.9 0646 4.4 1240 1.0 1855 4.6	**23** TH	0012 0.7 0651 4.6 1238 0.7 1907 4.9	**8** F	0047 1.1 0705 4.3 1300 1.1 1915 4.5	**23** SA	0058 0.3 0733 4.7 1320 0.4 1947 5.1	**8** M	0135 1.0 0802 4.3 1344 1.0 2009 4.5	**23** TU	0209 0.1 0842 4.9 1425 0.3 2053 5.0
9 M	0009 0.5 0637 4.7 1231 0.5 1852 4.7	**24** TU	0618 4.6 1204 0.7 1837 4.7	**9** TH	0100 1.0 0719 4.3 1313 1.1 1926 4.5	**24** F	0105 0.5 0741 4.6 1328 0.7 1956 4.9	**9** SA	0122 1.1 0741 4.2 1332 1.2 1950 4.5	**24** SU	0146 0.2 0822 4.8 1406 0.4 2034 5.1	**9** TU	0202 1.0 0834 4.3 1410 1.1 2040 4.5	**24** W	0246 0.3 0919 4.7 1500 0.6 2129 4.8
10 TU	0047 0.6 0710 4.6 1304 0.7 1920 4.7	**25** W	0025 0.6 0701 4.6 1249 0.7 1918 4.8	**10** F	0132 1.1 0751 4.2 1344 1.3 1959 4.4	**25** SA	0154 0.5 0832 4.6 1415 0.7 2044 4.9	**10** SU	0153 1.2 0818 4.1 1403 1.3 2025 4.4	**25** M	0230 0.2 0907 4.7 1448 0.5 2118 5.0	**10** W	0227 1.1 0902 4.2 1434 1.2 2106 4.4	**25** TH	0321 0.7 0951 4.5 1533 0.9 2159 4.4
11 W	0121 0.8 0739 4.4 1334 0.9 1945 4.6	**26** TH	0111 0.6 0746 4.6 1331 0.8 2000 4.8	**11** SA	0205 1.3 0826 4.0 1416 1.4 2034 4.3	**26** SU	0242 0.6 0921 4.5 1501 0.8 2131 4.8	**11** M	0224 1.2 0854 4.0 1432 1.4 2100 4.3	**26** TU	0313 0.4 0949 4.6 1527 0.7 2159 4.8	**11** TH	0252 1.2 0930 4.2 1502 1.3 2134 4.2	**26** F	0353 1.1 1019 4.3 1608 1.4 ☽ 2228 4.1
12 TH	0150 1.0 0807 4.3 1403 1.2 2013 4.4	**27** F	0155 0.7 0832 4.5 1416 0.9 2045 4.7	**12** SU	0237 1.4 0905 3.9 1449 1.6 2113 4.2	**27** M	0329 0.7 1008 4.4 1547 1.0 2218 4.6	**12** TU	0253 1.3 0930 4.0 1502 1.5 2134 4.2	**27** W	0352 0.7 1029 4.4 1607 1.0 2238 4.5	**12** F	0322 1.3 1001 4.1 1535 1.5 2208 4.1	**27** SA	0427 1.6 1051 3.9 1650 1.9 2306 3.7
13 F	0220 1.3 0837 4.1 1431 1.4 2046 4.3	**28** SA	0241 0.8 0921 4.3 1502 1.1 2132 4.5	**13** M	0313 1.6 0947 3.8 1526 1.8 2155 4.0	**28** TU	0417 1.0 1058 4.2 1635 1.3 ☽ 2309 4.4	**13** W	0325 1.4 1004 3.9 1534 1.6 2208 4.0	**28** TH	0431 1.1 1109 4.1 1648 1.3 ☽ 2320 4.1	**13** SA	0359 1.4 1039 3.9 1622 1.7 ☽ 2301 3.9	**28** SU	0515 2.2 1144 3.6 1754 2.2
14 SA	0250 1.5 0912 3.8 1502 1.7 2124 4.0	**29** SU	0331 1.1 1012 4.1 1553 1.4 2224 4.3	**14** TU	0356 1.7 1033 3.7 1612 1.9 2242 3.9	**29** W	0509 1.2 1152 4.1 1729 1.4	**14** TH	0401 1.5 1043 3.8 1616 1.7 2249 4.0	**29** F	0516 1.5 1157 3.9 1738 1.7	**14** SU	0453 1.7 1146 3.7 1734 2.0	**29** M	0032 3.4 0630 2.3 1338 3.5 1939 2.3
15 SU	0327 1.8 0957 3.6 1543 2.0 2211 3.8	**30** M	0429 1.3 1114 4.0 1655 1.6 ☽ 2330 4.2	**15** W	0450 1.8 1127 3.6 1714 2.0 ☽ 2337 3.9	**30** TH	0006 4.2 0606 1.4 1250 3.9 1833 1.6	**15** F	0447 1.6 1131 3.8 1712 1.8 2343 3.9	**30** SA	0015 3.8 0610 1.8 1301 3.7 1847 2.0	**15** M	0014 3.7 0626 1.8 1307 3.8 1924 1.9	**30** TU	0227 3.4 0830 2.3 1458 3.7 2119 2.0
		31 TU	0539 1.4 1226 3.9 1809 1.7						**31** SU	0133 3.6 0724 2.0 1415 3.7 2010 2.0			**31** W	0337 3.6 0943 1.9 1558 4.0 2212 1.6

Chart Datum: 2·62 metres below Ordnance Datum (Newlyn)

》》 **FREE** monthly updates from 《《
www.reedsalmanac.co.uk

ENGLAND - DARTMOUTH

YEAR 2005

LAT 50°21'N   LONG 3°34'W

TIMES AND HEIGHTS OF HIGH AND LOW WATERS

TIME ZONE (UT)
For Summer Time add ONE hour in non-shaded areas

SEPTEMBER

Day	Time	m	Time	m	Day	Time	m
1 TH	0430 / 1031 / 1646 / 2256	3.9 / 1.5 / 4.3 / 1.3			16 F	0428 / 1017 / 1645 / 2245	4.4 / 1.0 / 4.8 / 0.6
2 F	0514 / 1112 / 1726 / 2334	4.2 / 1.2 / 4.5 / 1.0			17 SA	0520 / 1108 / 1735 / 2334	4.7 / 0.6 / 5.1 / 0.2
3 SA ●	0553 / 1148 / 1805	4.4 / 1.0 / 4.7			18 SU ○	0607 / 1155 / 1823	4.9 / 0.3 / 5.2
4 SU	0009 / 0630 / 1222 / 1841	0.9 / 4.5 / 0.9 / 4.7			19 M	0019 / 0652 / 1240 / 1905	0.1 / 5.0 / 0.2 / 5.3
5 M	0041 / 0704 / 1252 / 1915	0.8 / 4.5 / 0.8 / 4.7			20 TU	0103 / 0733 / 1321 / 1946	0.0 / 5.0 / 0.2 / 5.2
6 TU	0109 / 0737 / 1319 / 1946	0.8 / 4.5 / 0.9 / 4.7			21 W	0141 / 0809 / 1356 / 2022	0.2 / 4.9 / 0.4 / 5.0
7 W	0133 / 0806 / 1342 / 2013	0.8 / 4.5 / 0.9 / 4.6			22 TH	0215 / 0842 / 1429 / 2052	0.5 / 4.8 / 0.7 / 4.7
8 TH	0158 / 0832 / 1407 / 2038	0.9 / 4.4 / 1.0 / 4.5			23 F	0246 / 0907 / 1500 / 2118	0.9 / 4.5 / 1.1 / 4.3
9 F	0223 / 0856 / 1434 / 2105	1.1 / 4.3 / 1.2 / 4.3			24 SA	0315 / 0931 / 1531 / 2143	1.3 / 4.2 / 1.6 / 4.0
10 SA	0251 / 0928 / 1508 / 2141	1.3 / 4.1 / 1.4 / 4.1			25 SU ◐	0345 / 1002 / 1609 / 2220	1.8 / 4.0 / 2.1 / 3.6
11 SU ◐	0327 / 1012 / 1552 / 2239	1.6 / 3.9 / 1.8 / 3.8			26 M	0427 / 1049 / 1712 / 2324	2.3 / 3.7 / 2.4 / 3.3
12 M	0419 / 1120 / 1706 / 2359	2.0 / 3.8 / 2.1 / 3.6			27 TU	0545 / 1230 / 1903	2.6 / 3.5 / 2.5
13 TU	0601 / 1248 / 1917	2.2 / 3.7 / 2.1			28 W	0203 / 0802 / 1429 / 2056	3.3 / 2.5 / 3.7 / 2.1
14 W	0147 / 0801 / 1434 / 2045	3.7 / 2.0 / 4.0 / 1.6			29 TH	0312 / 0915 / 1529 / 2144	3.6 / 2.0 / 4.0 / 1.7
15 TH	0324 / 0917 / 1549 / 2150	4.0 / 1.5 / 4.4 / 1.1			30 F	0403 / 1000 / 1617 / 2223	4.0 / 1.6 / 4.3 / 1.3

OCTOBER

Day	Time	m	Day	Time	m
1 SA	0446 / 1040 / 1658 / 2300	4.3 / 1.3 / 4.5 / 1.0	16 SU	0458 / 1045 / 1713 / 2309	4.8 / 0.6 / 5.1 / 0.3
2 SU	0525 / 1115 / 1736 / 2334	4.5 / 1.0 / 4.7 / 0.8	17 M	0543 / 1130 / 1758 / 2352	4.9 / 0.4 / 5.2 / 0.3
3 M ●	0602 / 1148 / 1815	4.6 / 0.9 / 4.8	18 TU	0625 / 1212 / 1840	5.0 / 0.3 / 5.1
4 TU	0005 / 0637 / 1220 / 1849	0.7 / 4.7 / 0.8 / 4.8	19 W	0034 / 0702 / 1253 / 1917	0.3 / 5.0 / 0.4 / 4.9
5 W	0036 / 0708 / 1250 / 1920	0.7 / 4.7 / 0.8 / 4.7	20 TH	0111 / 0736 / 1328 / 1950	0.5 / 4.9 / 0.6 / 4.8
6 TH	0105 / 0738 / 1318 / 1948	0.8 / 4.7 / 0.8 / 4.7	21 F	0143 / 0804 / 1400 / 2018	0.8 / 4.7 / 0.9 / 4.5
7 F	0131 / 0805 / 1345 / 2016	0.9 / 4.6 / 1.0 / 4.5	22 SA	0213 / 0828 / 1430 / 2043	1.1 / 4.6 / 1.3 / 4.2
8 SA	0159 / 0834 / 1416 / 2050	1.1 / 4.5 / 1.2 / 4.3	23 SU	0241 / 0855 / 1501 / 2112	1.5 / 4.3 / 1.7 / 3.9
9 SU	0230 / 0910 / 1452 / 2134	1.3 / 4.2 / 1.5 / 4.1	24 M	0311 / 0931 / 1538 / 2154	1.9 / 4.1 / 2.1 / 3.6
10 M	0309 / 1000 / 1541 / 2233	1.7 / 4.1 / 1.8 / 3.8	25 TU ◐	0351 / 1018 / 1636 / 2254	2.3 / 3.8 / 2.4 / 3.4
11 TU	0406 / 1107 / 1707 / 2355	2.1 / 3.9 / 2.2 / 3.6	26 W	0506 / 1130 / 1809	2.6 / 3.6 / 2.5
12 W	0602 / 1240 / 1914	2.3 / 3.8 / 2.0	27 TH	0112 / 0648 / 1337 / 1957	3.4 / 2.5 / 3.7 / 2.2
13 TH	0153 / 0754 / 1423 / 2033	3.7 / 2.0 / 4.1 / 1.5	28 F	0229 / 0819 / 1445 / 2053	3.8 / 2.2 / 3.9 / 1.8
14 F	0314 / 0902 / 1531 / 2132	4.1 / 1.5 / 4.5 / 1.0	29 SA	0322 / 0911 / 1536 / 2136	4.1 / 1.8 / 4.2 / 1.5
15 SA	0410 / 0956 / 1625 / 2222	4.5 / 1.0 / 4.9 / 0.6	30 SU	0408 / 0954 / 1620 / 2214	4.2 / 1.4 / 4.5 / 1.2
			31 M	0449 / 1034 / 1702 / 2253	4.5 / 1.2 / 4.6 / 1.0

NOVEMBER

Day	Time	m	Day	Time	m
1 TU	0528 / 1111 / 1743 / 2329	4.6 / 1.0 / 4.7 / 0.8	16 W ○	0557 / 1146 / 1815	4.9 / 0.7 / 4.9
2 W ●	0605 / 1147 / 1821	4.7 / 0.9 / 4.8	17 TH	0005 / 0634 / 1226 / 1852	0.7 / 4.9 / 0.7 / 4.8
3 TH	0004 / 0641 / 1223 / 1856	0.8 / 4.8 / 0.8 / 4.7	18 F	0044 / 0706 / 1304 / 1924	0.8 / 4.8 / 0.9 / 4.6
4 F	0040 / 0714 / 1258 / 1931	0.8 / 4.8 / 0.8 / 4.7	19 SA	0117 / 0736 / 1337 / 1953	1.0 / 4.7 / 1.1 / 4.4
5 SA	0113 / 0747 / 1332 / 2007	0.9 / 4.7 / 1.0 / 4.5	20 SU	0148 / 0804 / 1409 / 2022	1.3 / 4.6 / 1.4 / 4.2
6 SU	0147 / 0823 / 1410 / 2047	1.1 / 4.6 / 1.2 / 4.3	21 M	0218 / 0835 / 1442 / 2056	1.5 / 4.4 / 1.7 / 4.0
7 M	0225 / 0905 / 1454 / 2135	1.4 / 4.5 / 1.4 / 4.1	22 TU	0250 / 0913 / 1519 / 2139	1.9 / 4.2 / 2.0 / 3.8
8 TU	0311 / 0957 / 1550 / 2234	1.7 / 4.3 / 1.7 / 3.9	23 W ◐	0329 / 1000 / 1608 / 2234	2.1 / 4.0 / 2.2 / 3.6
9 W	0414 / 1100 / 1711 / ◐2354	2.0 / 4.1 / 1.9 / 3.8	24 TH	0426 / 1057 / 1716 / 2347	2.3 / 3.8 / 2.3 / 3.5
10 TH	0551 / 1226 / 1851	2.1 / 4.0 / 1.9	25 F	0544 / 1211 / 1834	2.4 / 3.8 / 2.2
11 F	0129 / 0725 / 1355 / 2004	3.9 / 1.9 / 4.2 / 1.5	26 SA	0114 / 0702 / 1333 / 1940	3.6 / 2.2 / 3.9 / 1.9
12 SA	0243 / 0832 / 1501 / 2102	4.1 / 1.5 / 4.5 / 1.1	27 SU	0220 / 0805 / 1437 / 2035	3.8 / 2.0 / 4.1 / 1.7
13 SU	0340 / 0928 / 1557 / 2154	4.4 / 1.2 / 4.7 / 0.9	28 M	0314 / 0859 / 1531 / 2123	3.9 / 1.7 / 4.2 / 1.4
14 M	0430 / 1017 / 1647 / 2242	4.7 / 0.9 / 4.8 / 0.7	29 TU	0403 / 0948 / 1622 / 2210	4.1 / 1.4 / 4.4 / 1.1
15 TU	0515 / 1104 / 1733 / 2325	4.8 / 0.7 / 4.9 / 0.6	30 W	0451 / 1035 / 1710 / 2255	4.3 / 1.2 / 4.5 / 1.0

DECEMBER

Day	Time	m	Day	Time	m
1 TH	0535 / 1119 / 1756 / 2339	4.6 / 1.0 / 4.6 / 0.9	16 F	0613 / 1208 / 1833	4.7 / 1.0 / 4.5
2 F	0618 / 1202 / 1840	4.8 / 0.9 / 4.7	17 SA	0023 / 0647 / 1248 / 1907	1.1 / 4.7 / 1.1 / 4.4
3 SA	0021 / 0658 / 1247 / 1922	0.9 / 4.8 / 0.8 / 4.7	18 SU	0100 / 0719 / 1324 / 1939	1.1 / 4.7 / 1.2 / 4.3
4 SU	0105 / 0739 / 1330 / 2005	1.0 / 4.8 / 0.9 / 4.6	19 M	0133 / 0751 / 1357 / 2013	1.3 / 4.6 / 1.4 / 4.2
5 M	0147 / 0822 / 1415 / 2051	1.1 / 4.8 / 1.0 / 4.4	20 TU	0205 / 0826 / 1429 / 2050	1.5 / 4.5 / 1.5 / 4.1
6 TU	0231 / 0908 / 1503 / 2140	1.2 / 4.7 / 1.2 / 4.3	21 W ◐	0237 / 0904 / 1503 / 2130	1.6 / 4.4 / 1.6 / 3.9
7 W	0320 / 0957 / 1555 / 2234	1.4 / 4.5 / 1.4 / 4.1	22 TH	0310 / 0944 / 1538 / 2211	1.8 / 4.2 / 1.8 / 3.8
8 TH	0415 / 1053 / 1656 / ◐2337	1.6 / 4.4 / 1.5 / 4.0	23 F ◐	0347 / 1027 / 1622 / 2259	1.9 / 4.0 / 1.9 / 3.7
9 F	0522 / 1200 / 1809	1.8 / 4.2 / 1.6	24 SA	0436 / 1116 / 1719 / 2356	2.1 / 3.9 / 2.0 / 3.7
10 SA	0048 / 0639 / 1313 / 1921	4.0 / 1.8 / 4.2 / 1.6	25 SU	0542 / 1214 / 1827	2.1 / 3.9 / 2.0
11 SU	0158 / 0750 / 1422 / 2025	4.1 / 1.7 / 4.2 / 1.4	26 M	0059 / 0657 / 1321 / 1933	3.7 / 2.1 / 3.9 / 1.9
12 M	0300 / 0853 / 1524 / 2122	4.2 / 1.5 / 4.4 / 1.3	27 TU	0207 / 0803 / 1431 / 2035	3.9 / 1.9 / 4.0 / 1.7
13 TU	0357 / 0950 / 1620 / 2214	4.4 / 1.2 / 4.5 / 1.2	28 W	0313 / 0905 / 1539 / 2133	4.1 / 1.7 / 4.1 / 1.5
14 W	0448 / 1041 / 1710 / 2302	4.5 / 1.1 / 4.6 / 1.1	29 TH	0414 / 1003 / 1641 / 2229	4.3 / 1.4 / 4.3 / 1.3
15 TH	0532 / 1126 / 1754 / ○2344	4.7 / 1.0 / 4.5 / 1.0	30 F	0510 / 1059 / 1736 / 2321	4.5 / 1.1 / 4.5 / 1.1
			31 SA	0600 / 1150 / 1828	4.7 / 0.9 / 4.6

Chart Datum: 2·62 metres below Ordnance Datum (Newlyn)

》》 **FREE** monthly updates from 《《
www.reedsalmanac.com

Chapter 5

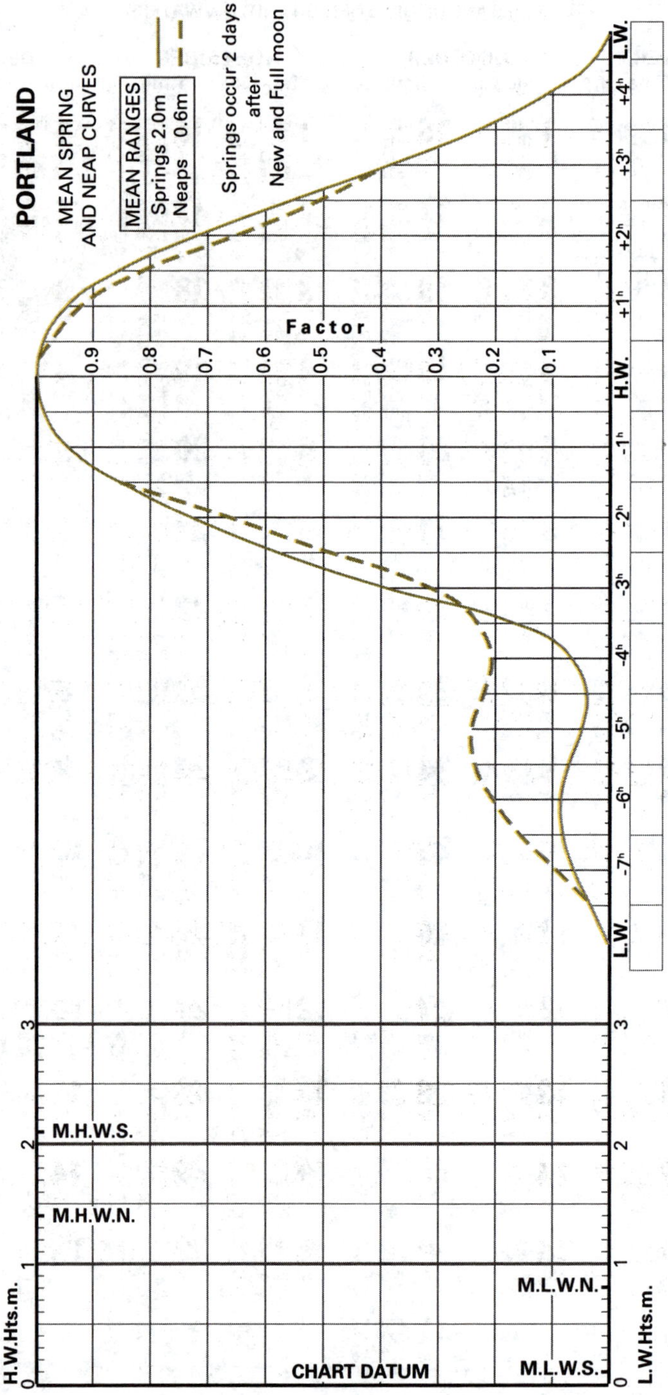
PORTLAND
MEAN SPRING
AND NEAP CURVES
MEAN RANGES
Springs 2.0m
Neaps 0.6m
Springs occur 2 days
after
New and Full moon
Factor
0.9
0.8
0.7
0.6
0.5
0.4
0.3
0.2
0.1
L.W.
+4h
+3h
+2h
+1h
H.W.
-1h
-2h
-3h
-4h
-5h
-6h
-7h
L.W.
H.W.Hts.m.
M.H.W.S.
M.H.W.N.
CHART DATUM
M.L.W.N.
M.L.W.S.
L.W.Hts.m.
0
1
2
3

TIME ZONE (UT)
For Summer Time add ONE hour in **non-shaded areas**
YEAR 2005

ENGLAND – PORTLAND
LAT 50°34′N   LONG 2°26′W
TIMES AND HEIGHTS OF HIGH AND LOW WATERS

Note - Double LWs occur at Portland. The predictions are for the first LW. The second LW occurs from 3 to 4 Hrs later and may, at Springs, on occasions be lower than the first.

JANUARY				FEBRUARY				MARCH				APRIL			
Time	m	Time	m	Time	m	Time	m	Time	m	Time	m	Time	m	Time	m
1 0222 0.5 0925 1.7 SA 1447 0.5 2156 1.5		**16** 0328 0.4 1047 1.9 SU 1606 0.4 2311 1.6		**1** 0313 0.4 1020 1.6 TU 1538 0.3 2244 1.5		**16** 0406 0.5 1111 1.5 W 1638 0.6 2331 1.4		**1** 0225 0.2 0935 1.8 TU 1442 0.2 2149 1.7		**16** 0259 0.3 1004 1.6 W 1517 0.4 2213 1.6		**1** 0311 0.4 1024 1.5 F 1531 0.5 2241 1.5		**16** 0321 0.6 1029 1.2 SA 1515 0.7 ◐ 2233 1.4	
2 0253 0.6 0957 1.6 SU 1523 0.5 2233 1.4		**17** 0411 0.5 1124 1.7 M 1654 0.5 ◐ 2350 1.5		**2** 0350 0.5 1057 1.5 W 1624 0.4 ◐ 2331 1.4		**17** 0447 0.7 1150 1.3 TH 1724 0.7		**2** 0252 0.2 1002 1.6 W 1511 0.3 2218 1.6		**17** 0324 0.5 1029 1.4 TH 1532 0.5 ◐ 2240 1.4		**2** 0404 0.6 1119 1.4 SA 1640 0.7 ◐ 2349 1.4		**17** 0414 0.8 1134 1.1 SU 1609 0.9 2345 1.3	
3 0331 0.6 1037 1.6 M 1610 0.5 ◐ 2322 1.4		**18** 0459 0.7 1204 1.5 TU 1746 0.6		**3** 0444 0.6 1150 1.4 TH 1730 0.5		**18** 0021 1.3 0610 0.8 F 1252 1.2 1852 0.8		**3** 0324 0.4 1035 1.5 TH 1549 0.4 ◐ 2257 1.5		**18** 0350 0.6 1102 1.2 F 1553 0.7 2321 1.3		**3** 0552 0.7 1250 1.3 SU 1849 0.8		**18** 0705 0.8 1334 1.1 M 1916 0.9	
4 0425 0.7 1129 1.5 TU 1714 0.6		**19** 0038 1.4 0600 0.8 W 1255 1.4 1846 0.7		**4** 0040 1.4 0606 0.7 F 1309 1.4 1859 0.6		**19** 0140 1.3 0817 0.8 SA 1440 1.2 2028 0.8		**4** 0410 0.5 1124 1.4 F 1647 0.6		**19** 0445 0.8 1204 1.1 SA 1651 0.8		**4** 0141 1.4 0802 0.7 M 1503 1.4 2029 0.7		**19** 0138 1.3 0828 0.7 TU 1534 1.3 2031 0.8	
5 0029 1.4 0540 0.7 W 1240 1.5 1828 0.6		**20** 0143 1.4 0716 0.8 TH 1405 1.4 1952 0.7		**5** 0219 1.4 0751 0.7 SA 1455 1.4 2033 0.6		**20** 0329 1.4 0936 0.7 SU 1624 1.3 2134 0.7		**5** 0001 1.4 0537 0.7 SA 1245 1.3 1842 0.7		**20** 0038 1.3 0757 0.8 SU 1408 1.1 1957 0.8		**5** 0330 1.6 0916 0.5 TU 1625 1.6 2132 0.5		**20** 0316 1.5 0914 0.5 W 1624 1.5 2121 0.6	
6 0153 1.4 0703 0.7 TH 1406 1.5 1941 0.5		**21** 0304 1.4 0839 0.8 F 1530 1.3 2057 0.7		**6** 0355 1.6 0923 0.6 SU 1633 1.5 2149 0.5		**21** 0439 1.6 1020 0.6 M 1721 1.4 2223 0.5		**6** 0145 1.4 0756 0.7 SU 1450 1.3 2035 0.7		**21** 0235 1.3 0916 0.7 M 1614 1.3 2108 0.7		**6** 0439 1.8 1007 0.3 W 1721 1.8 2221 0.3		**21** 0419 1.6 0952 0.4 TH 1708 1.7 2204 0.4	
7 0314 1.6 0818 0.7 F 1530 1.6 2049 0.5		**22** 0409 1.5 0944 0.7 SA 1636 1.4 2152 0.6		**7** 0508 1.8 1029 0.4 M 1746 1.7 2248 0.3		**22** 0531 1.7 1059 0.4 TU 1809 1.6 2306 0.4		**7** 0342 1.5 0928 0.6 M 1637 1.5 2147 0.5		**22** 0409 1.5 0955 0.5 TU 1703 1.5 2156 0.5		**7** 0534 2.0 1050 0.1 TH 1809 2.0 2304 0.2		**22** 0511 1.8 1029 0.2 F 1750 1.8 2244 0.3	
8 0421 1.7 0926 0.6 SA 1642 1.7 2152 0.4		**23** 0501 1.7 1033 0.6 SU 1729 1.5 2241 0.5		**8** 0609 2.0 1122 0.3 TU 1845 1.9 ● 2339 0.2		**23** 0617 1.9 1137 0.3 W 1852 1.8 2347 0.2		**8** 0500 1.8 1025 0.3 TU 1742 1.8 2240 0.3		**23** 0503 1.7 1031 0.4 W 1746 1.7 2239 0.4		**8** 0623 2.2 1131 0.0 F 1851 2.1 ○ 2345 0.1		**23** 0557 2.0 1105 0.1 SA 1830 2.0 2322 0.2	
9 0520 1.9 1027 0.5 SU 1747 1.8 2249 0.3		**24** 0547 1.8 1116 0.5 M 1818 1.6 2325 0.4		**9** 0703 2.2 1210 0.1 W 1935 2.1		**24** 0659 2.0 1214 0.2 TH 1931 1.9 ○		**9** 0558 2.1 1112 0.1 W 1833 2.0 2326 0.1		**24** 0550 1.9 1107 0.2 TH 1827 1.8 2319 0.2		**9** 0706 2.3 1210 -0.1 SA 1930 2.2		**24** 0641 2.0 1141 0.0 SU 1908 2.1 ○ 2358 0.1	
10 0616 2.1 1122 0.3 M 1846 1.9 ○ 2343 0.3		**25** 0630 1.9 1157 0.4 TU 1902 1.7 ○		**10** 0025 0.1 0750 2.4 TH 1255 0.0 2019 2.1		**25** 0025 0.2 0737 2.1 F 1249 0.1 2006 1.9		**10** 0648 2.3 1155 0.0 TH 1918 2.1 ●		**25** 0634 2.0 1143 0.1 F 1905 1.9 ○ 2356 0.1		**10** 0023 0.0 0744 2.3 SU 1248 -0.1 2004 2.2		**25** 0721 2.1 1217 0.0 M 1943 2.1	
11 0709 2.2 1214 0.2 TU 1940 2.0		**26** 0006 0.4 0710 2.0 W 1236 0.3 1942 1.8		**11** 0108 0.0 0833 2.4 F 1337 -0.1 2058 2.1		**26** 0100 0.1 0812 2.1 SA 1319 0.1 2037 1.9		**11** 0008 0.0 0731 2.4 F 1236 -0.1 1958 2.2		**26** 0713 2.1 1217 0.0 SA 1941 2.0		**11** 0100 0.0 0818 2.2 M 1322 0.0 2033 2.1		**26** 0034 0.1 0756 2.1 TU 1253 0.1 2015 2.1	
12 0032 0.2 0758 2.3 W 1304 0.1 2029 2.1		**27** 0045 0.3 0749 2.0 TH 1311 0.3 2019 1.8		**12** 0148 0.0 0911 2.3 SA 1417 0.0 2133 2.0		**27** 0131 0.1 0843 2.0 SU 1348 0.1 2104 1.8		**12** 0048 -0.1 0811 2.3 SA 1315 -0.2 2033 2.2		**27** 0031 0.0 0749 2.1 SU 1249 0.1 2012 2.0		**12** 0133 0.1 0846 2.0 TU 1353 0.1 2056 1.9		**27** 0110 0.1 0830 2.0 W 1329 0.1 2045 2.0	
13 0119 0.2 0845 2.3 TH 1351 0.2 2114 2.0		**28** 0120 0.3 0824 2.0 F 1342 0.2 2051 1.8		**13** 0225 0.1 0945 2.1 SU 1454 0.1 2203 1.9				**13** 0125 -0.1 0846 2.2 SU 1351 -0.1 2104 2.1		**28** 0104 0.0 0821 2.1 M 1321 0.0 2040 2.0		**13** 0204 0.2 0909 1.8 W 1420 0.3 2116 1.8		**28** 0146 0.2 0903 1.9 TH 1406 0.3 2117 1.9	
14 0204 0.2 0929 2.2 F 1436 0.2 2156 1.9		**29** 0150 0.3 0856 1.9 SA 1408 0.2 2120 1.7		**14** 0300 0.2 1015 1.9 M 1530 0.2 2230 1.7				**14** 0200 0.0 0916 2.1 M 1424 0.0 2130 1.9		**28** 0135 0.1 0850 2.0 TU 1351 0.1 2104 1.9		**14** 0231 0.4 0932 1.6 TH 1438 0.4 2136 1.6		**29** 0226 0.3 0940 1.7 F 1447 0.4 2154 1.7	
15 0246 0.3 1009 2.1 SA 1521 0.3 2234 1.8		**30** 0217 0.3 0924 1.8 SU 1434 0.3 2145 1.6		**15** 0333 0.3 1042 1.7 TU 1604 0.4 2257 1.5				**15** 0231 0.1 0941 1.9 TU 1453 0.2 2151 1.7		**30** 0204 0.1 0916 1.8 W 1421 0.2 2129 1.8		**15** 0254 0.5 0957 1.4 F 1451 0.6 2159 1.5		**30** 0314 0.5 1026 1.5 SA 1539 0.6 2244 1.6	
		31 0243 0.3 0951 1.7 M 1503 0.3 2211 1.5								**31** 0234 0.2 0946 1.7 TH 1452 0.3 2159 1.6					

Chart Datum: 0·93 metres below Ordnance Datum (Newlyn)

》》 **FREE** monthly updates from 《《
www.reedsalmanac.co.uk

TIDES

TIME ZONE (UT)
For Summer Time add ONE hour in **non-shaded areas**

YEAR 2005

ENGLAND – PORTLAND
LAT 50°34'N   LONG 2°26'W
TIMES AND HEIGHTS OF HIGH AND LOW WATERS

Note - Double LWs occur at Portland. The predictions are for the first LW. The second LW occurs from 3 to 4 Hrs later and may, at Springs, on occasions be lower than the first.

MAY		JUNE		JULY		AUGUST	
Time m	Time m	Time m	Time m	Time m	Time m	Time m	Time m
1 0421 0.6 / 1131 1.4 / SU 1657 0.7 / ☽ 2358 1.5	**16** 0358 0.7 / 1115 1.2 / M 1602 0.8 / ☽ 2307 1.4	**1** 0117 1.6 / 0657 0.5 / W 1409 1.6 / 1922 0.7	**16** 0536 0.6 / 1309 1.3 / TH 1812 0.8	**1** 0137 1.6 / 0711 0.5 / F 1423 1.5 / 1937 0.7	**16** 0539 0.5 / 1304 1.4 / SA 1817 0.7	**1** 0317 1.3 / 0850 0.7 / M 1600 1.5 / 2136 0.8	**16** 0204 1.3 / 0759 0.7 / TU 1522 1.5 / 2054 0.7
2 0559 0.7 / 1310 1.4 / M 1839 0.8	**17** 0535 0.7 / 1248 1.2 / TU 1805 0.9	**2** 0227 1.7 / 0804 0.5 / TH 1513 1.7 / 2027 0.6	**17** 0103 1.4 / 0650 0.6 / F 1424 1.4 / 1927 0.7	**2** 0244 1.5 / 0816 0.6 / SA 1528 1.6 / 2045 0.7	**17** 0109 1.4 / 0654 0.6 / SU 1431 1.4 / 1938 0.7	**2** 0433 1.4 / 0950 0.7 / TU 1658 1.6 / 2225 0.7	**17** 0400 1.5 / 0926 0.6 / W 1642 1.8 / 2204 0.5
3 0140 1.5 / 0740 0.6 / TU 1446 1.5 / 2005 0.7	**18** 0040 1.4 / 0718 0.7 / W 1422 1.3 / 1938 0.8	**3** 0330 1.7 / 0859 0.4 / F 1609 1.7 / 2121 0.6	**18** 0225 1.5 / 0755 0.5 / SA 1529 1.5 / 2029 0.6	**3** 0350 1.5 / 0915 0.6 / SU 1627 1.6 / 2144 0.7	**18** 0244 1.4 / 0813 0.5 / M 1549 1.6 / 2056 0.6	**3** 0530 1.5 / 1037 0.6 / W 1747 1.8 / 2306 0.6	**18** 0519 1.7 / 1027 0.4 / TH 1746 2.0 / 2258 0.3
4 0304 1.7 / 0847 0.4 / W 1554 1.7 / 2105 0.6	**19** 0215 1.4 / 0816 0.6 / TH 1528 1.5 / 2035 0.7	**4** 0427 1.7 / 0948 0.4 / SA 1700 1.8 / 2208 0.5	**19** 0337 1.6 / 0853 0.4 / SU 1626 1.7 / 2124 0.5	**4** 0450 1.5 / 1007 0.5 / M 1718 1.7 / 2235 0.6	**19** 0410 1.6 / 0927 0.5 / TU 1655 1.8 / 2203 0.5	**4** 0619 1.6 / 1119 0.5 / TH 1830 1.9 / 2346 0.4	**19** 0620 1.9 / 1119 0.2 / F 1841 2.2 / ○ 2346 0.1
5 0408 1.8 / 0937 0.3 / TH 1648 1.8 / 2154 0.4	**20** 0326 1.6 / 0901 0.4 / F 1620 1.6 / 2121 0.5	**5** 0519 1.8 / 1032 0.3 / SU 1746 1.9 / 2252 0.4	**20** 0440 1.7 / 0947 0.3 / M 1719 1.9 / 2216 0.4	**5** 0543 1.6 / 1054 0.5 / TU 1804 1.8 / 2320 0.5	**20** 0522 1.7 / 1030 0.3 / W 1755 2.0 / 2302 0.4	**5** 0701 1.7 / 1200 0.4 / F 1909 2.0 / ●	**20** 0712 2.1 / 1205 0.1 / SA 1930 2.3
6 0502 1.9 / 1021 0.2 / F 1735 2.0 / 2237 0.3	**21** 0425 1.7 / 0943 0.3 / SA 1707 1.8 / 2204 0.4	**6** 0607 1.8 / 1114 0.3 / M 1828 2.0 / ● 2335 0.4	**21** 0538 1.8 / 1040 0.3 / TU 1810 2.0 / 2307 0.3	**6** 0630 1.7 / 1137 0.4 / W 1845 1.9 / ●	**21** 0626 1.9 / 1126 0.3 / TH 1851 2.1 / ○ 2355 0.2	**6** 0024 0.3 / 0739 1.8 / SA 1239 0.3 / 1945 2.0	**21** 0031 0.0 / 0758 2.2 / SU 1249 0.0 / 2014 2.5
7 0552 2.0 / 1102 0.1 / SA 1819 2.1 / 2318 0.2	**22** 0518 1.8 / 1024 0.2 / SU 1753 2.0 / 2246 0.3	**7** 0649 1.8 / 1155 0.3 / TU 1905 2.0	**22** 0634 1.9 / 1131 0.2 / W 1900 2.1 / ○ 2358 0.3	**7** 0002 0.4 / 0712 1.7 / TH 1219 0.4 / 1922 1.9	**22** 0723 2.0 / 1217 0.2 / F 1943 2.3	**7** 0102 0.3 / 0812 1.8 / SU 1316 0.3 / 2018 2.0	**22** 0115 -0.1 / 0838 2.2 / M 1331 0.0 / 2054 2.4
8 0636 2.1 / 1142 0.1 / SU 1858 2.1 / ● 2357 0.2	**23** 0607 1.9 / 1106 0.2 / M 1836 2.1 / ○ 2328 0.2	**8** 0015 0.4 / 0726 1.8 / W 1234 0.3 / 1937 2.0	**23** 0727 2.0 / 1222 0.2 / TH 1949 2.2	**8** 0043 0.4 / 0750 1.7 / F 1258 0.4 / 1956 1.9	**23** 0044 0.1 / 0813 2.1 / SA 1305 0.1 / 2031 2.3	**8** 0135 0.2 / 0843 1.8 / M 1348 0.2 / 2048 2.0	**23** 0156 -0.1 / 0915 2.2 / TU 1410 0.0 / 2130 2.3
9 0716 2.1 / 1219 0.1 / M 1933 2.1	**24** 0653 2.0 / 1148 0.1 / TU 1917 2.1	**9** 0055 0.4 / 0759 1.7 / TH 1311 0.4 / 2006 1.9	**24** 0047 0.2 / 0817 2.0 / F 1311 0.2 / 2036 2.2	**9** 0121 0.4 / 0824 1.7 / SA 1335 0.4 / 2028 1.9	**24** 0131 0.1 / 0859 2.1 / SU 1350 0.1 / 2114 2.3	**9** 0203 0.2 / 0911 1.8 / TU 1414 0.3 / 2116 1.9	**24** 0235 0.0 / 0948 2.0 / W 1447 0.2 / 2202 2.0
10 0034 0.2 / 0749 2.0 / TU 1255 0.2 / 2002 2.0	**25** 0010 0.2 / 0736 2.0 / W 1232 0.2 / 1957 2.1	**10** 0132 0.4 / 0829 1.7 / F 1344 0.5 / 2034 1.8	**25** 0137 0.2 / 0905 2.0 / SA 1400 0.3 / 2123 2.1	**10** 0156 0.3 / 0856 1.7 / SU 1407 0.4 / 2059 1.8	**25** 0217 0.1 / 0940 2.1 / M 1433 0.2 / 2155 2.2	**10** 0226 0.3 / 0936 1.7 / W 1437 0.4 / 2140 1.7	**25** 0312 0.2 / 1018 1.8 / TH 1523 0.3 / 2232 1.8
11 0111 0.2 / 0818 1.8 / W 1328 0.3 / 2026 1.9	**26** 0053 0.2 / 0819 2.0 / TH 1316 0.2 / 2037 2.1	**11** 0206 0.4 / 0900 1.6 / SA 1413 0.5 / 2102 1.7	**26** 0227 0.3 / 0953 1.9 / SU 1448 0.3 / 2209 2.0	**11** 0224 0.4 / 0927 1.6 / M 1433 0.5 / 2128 1.7	**26** 0301 0.1 / 1019 1.9 / TU 1515 0.3 / 2233 2.0	**11** 0249 0.3 / 0959 1.6 / TH 1500 0.4 / 2204 1.6	**26** 0348 0.4 / 1046 1.6 / F 1600 0.5 / ☽ 2300 1.5
12 0144 0.3 / 0844 1.7 / TH 1356 0.4 / 2048 1.8	**27** 0138 0.2 / 0901 1.9 / F 1401 0.3 / 2118 2.0	**12** 0235 0.5 / 0933 1.5 / SU 1438 0.6 / 2131 1.6	**27** 0317 0.3 / 1039 1.8 / M 1536 0.4 / 2255 1.9	**12** 0248 0.4 / 0957 1.5 / TU 1457 0.5 / 2156 1.6	**27** 0344 0.2 / 1056 1.8 / W 1557 0.4 / 2310 1.8	**12** 0316 0.3 / 1026 1.5 / F 1529 0.5 / 2233 1.5	**27** 0425 0.6 / 1119 1.5 / SA 1645 0.7 / 2335 1.3
13 0214 0.5 / 0910 1.5 / F 1417 0.5 / 2112 1.7	**28** 0227 0.3 / 0947 1.8 / SA 1450 0.5 / 2204 1.9	**13** 0303 0.5 / 1010 1.4 / M 1507 0.7 / 2203 1.5	**28** 0410 0.4 / 1128 1.7 / TU 1628 0.5 / ☽ 2344 1.8	**13** 0315 0.4 / 1028 1.5 / W 1526 0.5 / 2226 1.5	**28** 0429 0.4 / 1134 1.6 / TH 1642 0.5 / ☽ 2348 1.6	**13** 0352 0.4 / 1104 1.4 / SA 1612 0.6 / ☽ 2314 1.4	**28** 0511 0.8 / 1205 1.2 / SU 1802 0.9
14 0240 0.7 / 0939 1.4 / SA 1436 0.6 / 2136 1.6	**29** 0321 0.4 / 1040 1.7 / SU 1546 0.6 / 2258 1.7	**14** 0338 0.6 / 1054 1.3 / TU 1549 0.7 / 2245 1.5	**29** 0506 0.5 / 1220 1.6 / W 1724 0.6	**14** 0349 0.4 / 1104 1.4 / TH 1606 0.6 / ☽ 2304 1.5	**29** 0518 0.5 / 1217 1.5 / F 1735 0.7	**14** 0445 0.5 / 1202 1.3 / SU 1724 0.7	**29** 0032 1.2 / 0638 0.9 / M 1329 1.3 / 2020 0.9
15 0310 0.6 / 1016 1.3 / SU 1505 0.7 / 2210 1.5	**30** 0424 0.5 / 1143 1.6 / M 1651 0.7 / ○	**15** 0428 0.6 / 1154 1.3 / W 1651 0.8 / ☽ 2344 1.4	**30** 0036 1.7 / 0606 0.6 / TH 1318 1.5 / 1827 0.7	**15** 0436 0.5 / 1154 1.4 / F 1702 0.6 / ☽ 2356 1.4	**30** 0032 1.4 / 0615 0.6 / SA 1316 1.4 / 1845 0.8	**15** 0020 1.3 / 0610 0.7 / M 1332 1.3 / 1911 0.8	**30** 0315 1.2 / 0831 0.9 / TU 1544 1.4 / 2133 0.8
	31 0003 1.7 / 0538 0.5 / TU 1257 1.5 / 1806 0.7				**31** 0138 1.3 / 0728 0.7 / SU 1443 1.4 / 2018 0.8		**31** 0431 1.3 / 0932 0.7 / W 1641 1.6 / 2210 0.7

Chart Datum: 0·93 metres below Ordnance Datum (Newlyn)

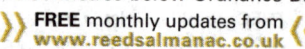
FREE monthly updates from www.reedsalmanac.co.uk

TIME ZONE (UT) For Summer Time add ONE hour in non-shaded areas YEAR 2005	ENGLAND – PORTLAND LAT 50°34′N LONG 2°26′W TIMES AND HEIGHTS OF HIGH AND LOW WATERS	Note - Double LWs occur at Portland. The predictions are for the first LW. The second LW occurs from 3 to 4 Hrs later and may, at Springs, on occasions be lower than the first.

SEPTEMBER

Time	m	Time	m
1 0519 TH 1015 1726 2244	1.5 0.6 1.8 0.5	**16** 0512 F 1016 1729 2244	1.8 0.4 2.1 0.2
2 0600 F 1054 1807 2320	1.7 0.5 1.9 0.4	**17** 0604 SA 1102 1820 2328	2.0 0.2 2.3 0.1
3 0639 SA 1134 1846 ● 2357	1.8 0.3 2.0 0.2	**18** 0650 SU 1145 1906 ○	2.2 0.1 2.4
4 0715 SU 1212 1922	1.9 0.2 2.1	**19** 0009 M 0732 1227 1948	-0.1 2.3 0.0 2.5
5 0032 M 0748 1248 1956	0.2 2.0 0.2 2.1	**20** 0050 TU 0810 1306 2026	-0.1 2.3 0.0 2.4
6 0105 TU 0819 1320 2026	0.1 2.0 0.2 2.0	**21** 0128 W 0843 1342 2059	-0.1 2.2 0.1 2.2
7 0133 W 0845 1347 2053	0.1 1.9 0.2 1.9	**22** 0203 TH 0913 1417 2128	0.1 2.1 0.2 2.0
8 0157 TH 0908 1410 2117	0.2 1.8 0.3 1.8	**23** 0235 F 0937 1449 2152	0.3 1.9 0.4 1.7
9 0220 F 0929 1433 2140	0.3 1.7 0.4 1.7	**24** 0303 SA 0959 1520 2216	0.5 1.7 0.6 1.5
10 0245 SA 0955 1459 2209	0.4 1.6 0.5 1.5	**25** 0323 SU 1025 1556 ◐ 2246	0.7 1.5 0.8 1.3
11 0314 SU 1029 1537 ◐ 2249	0.5 1.5 0.6 1.4	**26** 0337 M 1104 1728 2345	0.8 1.4 0.9 1.1
12 0400 M 1125 1656	0.6 1.4 0.8	**27** 0420 TU 1219 2020	1.0 1.3 0.9
13 0000 TU 0552 1301 1921	1.3 0.8 1.4 0.8	**28** 0337 W 0758 1514 2110	1.2 1.0 1.4 0.8
14 0207 W 0807 1510 2058	1.3 0.8 1.6 0.7	**29** 0420 TH 0902 1609 2139	1.4 0.8 1.6 0.6
15 0406 TH 0923 1630 2156	1.5 0.6 1.8 0.5	**30** 0454 F 0944 1650 2211	1.5 0.7 1.8 0.5

OCTOBER

Time	m	Time	m
1 0529 SA 1023 1731 2246	1.7 0.5 1.9 0.3	**16** 0537 SU 1039 1751 2301	2.1 0.3 2.2 0.1
2 0605 SU 1102 1811 2322	1.9 0.4 2.0 0.2	**17** 0620 M 1121 1837 ○ 2342	2.2 0.2 2.3 0.0
3 0641 M 1139 1849 ● 2356	2.0 0.2 2.1 0.1	**18** 0701 TU 1200 1918	2.2 0.1 2.3
4 0716 TU 1214 1925	2.1 0.2 2.1	**19** 0020 W 0737 1238 1955	0.0 2.3 0.1 2.2
5 0028 W 0747 1246 1958	0.1 2.1 0.2 2.1	**20** 0057 TH 0810 1314 2027	0.1 2.2 0.2 2.1
6 0058 TH 0815 1315 2026	0.2 2.1 0.2 2.0	**21** 0130 F 0836 1348 2053	0.2 2.1 0.3 1.9
7 0126 F 0839 1342 2052	0.2 2.0 0.3 1.9	**22** 0159 SA 0858 1420 2116	0.4 1.9 0.5 1.6
8 0152 SA 0903 1409 2119	0.3 1.9 0.4 1.7	**23** 0222 SU 0917 1450 2140	0.6 1.7 0.7 1.4
9 0219 SU 0931 1441 2152	0.4 1.7 0.5 1.6	**24** 0235 M 0939 1523 2210	0.7 1.6 0.8 1.3
10 0250 M 1008 1528 ◐ 2241	0.6 1.6 0.7 1.4	**25** 0248 TU 1011 1651 2311	0.9 1.5 0.9 1.2
11 0341 TU 1109 1718	0.8 1.5 0.8	**26** 0319 W 1119 1900	1.0 1.4 0.9
12 0005 W 0607 1256 1928	1.3 0.9 1.5 0.8	**27** 0303 TH 0703 1318 2012	1.2 1.0 1.4 0.8
13 0232 TH 0801 1457 2043	1.4 0.8 1.6 0.6	**28** 0341 F 0818 1504 2053	1.4 0.9 1.5 0.6
14 0356 F 0906 1607 2135	1.6 0.7 1.9 0.4	**29** 0413 SA 0906 1559 2130	1.6 0.7 1.7 0.5
15 0450 SA 0955 1702 2219	1.9 0.5 2.1 0.2	**30** 0447 SU 0947 1645 2206	1.8 0.6 1.9 0.4
		31 0524 M 1026 1730 2241	1.9 0.4 2.0 0.3

NOVEMBER

Time	m	Time	m
1 0603 TU 1102 1812 ● 2316	2.1 0.3 2.0 0.2	**16** 0629 W 1134 1849 ○ 2351	2.2 0.3 2.1 0.2
2 0640 W 1137 1852 ● 2350	2.1 0.3 2.0 0.2	**17** 0707 TH 1213 1927	2.2 0.3 2.0
3 0715 TH 1211 1929	2.2 0.3 2.1	**18** 0028 F 0739 1252 1959	0.3 2.1 0.4 1.9
4 0024 F 0747 1246 2002	0.2 2.1 0.3 2.0	**19** 0103 SA 0806 1328 2027	0.4 2.1 0.4 1.8
5 0058 SA 0817 1320 2034	0.3 2.0 0.4 1.9	**20** 0134 SU 0829 1403 2053	0.5 1.9 0.5 1.6
6 0133 SU 0847 1357 2109	0.4 1.8 0.5 1.7	**21** 0200 M 0853 1436 2121	0.6 1.8 0.6 1.5
7 0210 M 0921 1443 2151	0.5 1.8 0.6 1.6	**22** 0220 TU 0918 1510 2156	0.7 1.7 0.7 1.3
8 0255 TU 1006 1549 2250	0.7 1.6 0.7 1.5	**23** 0242 W 0949 1601 ◐ 2249	0.8 1.6 0.8 1.3
9 0407 W 1112 1725 ●	0.9 1.6 0.8	**24** 0325 TH 1040 1741	0.9 1.5 0.9
10 0022 TH 0555 1254 1901	1.4 0.9 1.6 0.7	**25** 0016 F 0527 1207 1900	1.2 1.0 1.4 0.8
11 0211 F 0730 1428 2010	1.5 0.9 1.7 0.6	**26** 0158 SA 0717 1344 1955	1.3 0.9 1.5 0.7
12 0323 SA 0836 1534 2103	1.7 0.8 1.8 0.4	**27** 0307 SU 0817 1459 2039	1.5 0.9 1.6 0.5
13 0416 SU 0927 1630 2149	1.9 0.7 2.0 0.3	**28** 0357 M 0904 1558 2118	1.7 0.7 1.7 0.4
14 0504 M 1012 1720 2232	2.0 0.5 2.1 0.2	**29** 0442 TU 0945 1650 2157	1.8 0.6 1.8 0.3
15 0548 TU 1054 1806 2312	2.1 0.4 2.1 0.2	**30** 0525 W 1024 1738 2237	2.0 0.5 1.9 0.3

DECEMBER

Time	m	Time	m
1 0608 TH 1104 1824 ● 2319	2.1 0.4 2.0 0.3	**16** 0642 F 1158 1908	2.0 0.5 1.8
2 0649 F 1145 1908	2.2 0.4 2.0	**17** 0010 SA 0717 1239 1944	0.4 2.1 0.4 1.8
3 0001 SA 0728 1228 1950	0.3 2.2 0.4 2.0	**18** 0049 SU 0748 1318 2016	0.4 2.0 0.4 1.7
4 0044 SU 0807 1312 2032	0.3 2.1 0.4 1.9	**19** 0124 M 0815 1355 2046	0.5 2.0 0.5 1.6
5 0129 M 0847 1359 2115	0.4 2.0 0.4 1.8	**20** 0156 TU 0846 1429 2117	0.5 1.9 0.5 1.6
6 0215 TU 0930 1452 2203	0.5 1.9 0.5 1.7	**21** 0223 W 0916 1457 2151	0.6 1.8 0.6 1.5
7 0307 W 1019 1552 2300	0.6 1.8 0.6 1.6	**22** 0247 TH 0947 1525 2229	0.7 1.7 0.7 1.4
8 0407 TH 1119 1702 ◐	0.7 1.7 0.6	**23** 0318 F 1022 1604 2318	0.7 1.6 0.6 1.5
9 0008 F 0519 1230 1815	1.6 0.8 1.6 0.6	**24** 0406 SA 1112 1702	0.8 1.5 0.6
10 0124 SA 0637 1344 1923	1.6 0.8 1.6 0.6	**25** 0026 SU 0520 1222 1814	1.3 0.8 1.4 0.6
11 0235 SU 0750 1453 2022	1.6 0.7 1.7 0.5	**26** 0146 M 0648 1347 1923	1.4 0.8 1.4 0.6
12 0336 TU 0851 1554 2115	1.7 0.7 1.7 0.5	**27** 0259 TU 0800 1505 2022	1.5 0.7 1.5 0.5
13 0430 W 0944 1649 2203	1.8 0.6 1.8 0.4	**28** 0359 W 0859 1612 2117	1.7 0.6 1.6 0.5
14 0518 TH 1031 1740 2248	1.9 0.6 1.7 0.4	**29** 0453 TH 0952 1711 2210	1.8 0.6 1.7 0.4
15 0602 F 1116 1826 ○ 2330	2.0 0.5 1.8 0.4	**30** 0543 SA 1044 1806 ○ 2302	2.0 0.5 1.8 0.4
		31 0633 SU 1133 1859 ● 2353	2.1 0.4 1.9 0.3

Chart Datum: 0·93 metres below Ordnance Datum (Newlyn)

》》 **FREE** monthly updates from 《《
www.reedsalmanac.co.uk

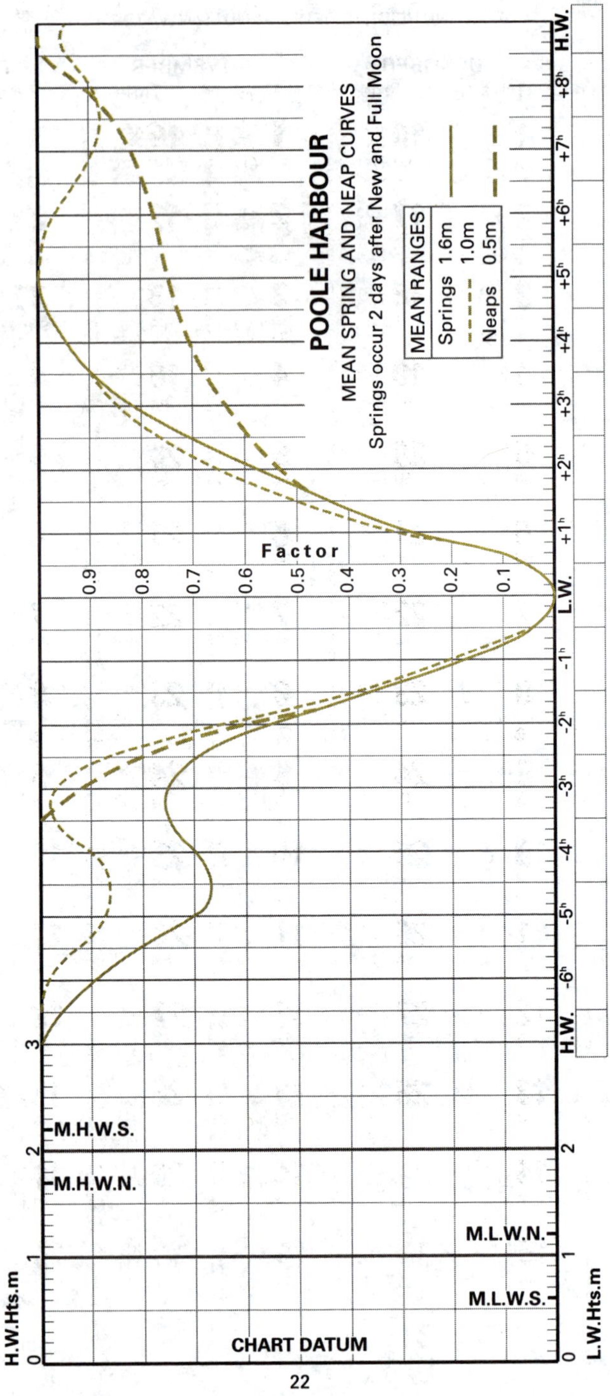
POOLE HARBOUR
MEAN SPRING AND NEAP CURVES
Springs occur 2 days after New and Full Moon
MEAN RANGES
Springs 1.6m
1.0m
Neaps 0.5m
Factor
0.9
0.8
0.7
0.6
0.5
0.4
0.3
0.2
0.1
H.W.
-6h
-5h
-4h
-3h
-2h
-1h
L.W.
+1h
+2h
+3h
+4h
+5h
+6h
+7h
+8h
H.W.
H.W.Hts.m
L.W.Hts.m
M.H.W.S.
M.H.W.N.
M.L.W.N.
M.L.W.S.
CHART DATUM
0
1
2
3
22

TIME ZONE (UT) For Summer Time add ONE hour in **non-shaded areas** YEAR **2005**	ENGLAND – POOLE HARBOUR LAT 50°42′N LONG 1°59′W TIMES AND HEIGHTS OF HIGH AND LOW WATERS	Note - HW times are not shown because they cannot be predicted with reasonable accuracy. Approximate times can be gained using LW times and the Tidal Curves at the start of this section.

JANUARY / FEBRUARY / MARCH / APRIL

JANUARY Time m	Time m	FEBRUARY Time m	Time m	MARCH Time m	Time m	APRIL Time m	Time m
1 0728 2.0 / 1.0 SA 1948 1.9 / 0.9	**16** 0841 2.1 / 0.8 SU 2103 2.0 / 0.8	**1** 0821 2.0 / 0.9 TU 2042 1.9 / 0.9	**16** 0931 1.9 / 1.0 W 2152 1.7 / 1.2	**1** 0714 2.1 / 0.7 TU 1933 2.0 / 0.7	**16** 0802 2.0 / 0.8 W 2020 1.9 / 1.0	**1** 0821 1.9 / 0.9 F 2054 1.8 / 1.1	**16** 0856 1.7 / 1.2 SA 2142 1.6 / 1.4
2 0809 1.9 / 1.1 SU 2030 1.8 / 1.0	**17** 0932 2.0 / 1.0 M 2152 1.9 / 0.9	**2** 0910 1.9 / 1.0 W 2136 1.8 / 1.0	**17** 1034 1.8 / 1.2 TH 2304 1.6 / 1.3	**2** 0752 2.0 / 0.8 W 2014 1.9 / 0.9	**17** 0840 1.9 / 1.0 TH 2105 1.8 / 1.2	**2** 0930 1.8 / 1.1 SA 2221 1.7 / 1.2	**17** 1025 1.6 / 1.3 SU 2326 1.6 / 1.4
3 0858 1.9 / 1.2 M 2121 1.8 / 1.0	**18** 1029 1.9 / 1.1 TU 2248 1.8 / 1.1	**3** 1013 1.9 / 1.2 TH 2246 1.7 / 1.2	**18** 1202 1.6 / 1.3 F 1.5	**3** 0838 1.9 / 0.9 TH 2106 1.8 / 1.0	**18** 0935 1.7 / 1.2 F 2219 1.6 / 1.4	**3** 1117 1.6 / 1.2 SU 1.7	**18** 1206 1.5 / 1.3 M 1.6
4 0956 1.9 / 1.2 TU 2221 1.8 / 1.1	**19** 1135 1.8 / 1.2 W 2356 1.6 / 1.2	**4** 1137 1.8 / 1.2 F 1.7	**19** 0036 1.4 / 1.6 SA 1324 1.3 / 1.6	**4** 0941 1.8 / 1.1 F 2222 1.7 / 1.2	**19** 1115 1.5 / 1.4 SA 1.5	**4** 0010 1.2 / 1.7 M 1257 1.0 / 1.8	**19** 0050 1.3 / 1.6 TU 1314 1.2 / 1.8
5 1103 1.9 / 1.2 W 2329 1.8 / 1.1	**20** 1247 1.8 / 1.2 TH 1.6	**5** 0014 1.2 / 1.7 SA 1309 1.2 / 1.7 / 1.1 / 1.8	**20** 0152 1.3 / 1.7 SU 1423 1.2 / 1.1 / 1.8	**5** 1119 1.7 / 1.2 SA 1.7	**20** 0007 1.4 / 1.7 SU 1253 1.3 / 1.6	**5** 0133 1.0 / 1.8 TU 1403 0.9 / 2.0	**20** 0145 1.2 / 1.7 W 1401 1.0 / 1.9
6 1215 1.9 / 1.2 TH 1.8	**21** 0108 1.2 / 1.8 F 1350 1.2 / 1.7	**6** 0140 1.1 / 1.8 SU 1422 0.9 / 2.0	**21** 0246 1.1 / 1.8 M 1508 1.0 / 1.9	**6** 0011 1.3 / 1.7 SU 1307 1.1 / 1.8	**21** 0131 1.3 / 1.7 M 1356 1.2 / 1.8	**6** 0231 0.8 / 2.1 W 1455 0.7 / 2.1	**21** 0227 1.0 / 1.8 TH 1441 0.8 / 2.0
7 0040 1.0 / 2.0 F 1324 1.0 / 1.9	**22** 0209 1.2 / 1.9 SA 1442 1.0 / 1.8	**7** 0247 0.9 / 2.1 M 1521 0.7 / 2.1	**22** 0328 1.0 / 1.9 TU 1547 0.8 / 2.0	**7** 0142 1.1 / 1.8 M 1419 0.9 / 2.0	**22** 0224 1.2 / 1.8 TU 1440 1.0 / 2.0	**7** 0318 0.7 / 2.1 TH 1539 0.5 / 2.3	**22** 0303 0.8 / 1.9 F 1517 0.7 / 2.0
8 0148 1.0 / 2.1 SA 1426 0.9 / 1.9	**23** 0300 1.1 / 1.9 SU 1527 0.9 / 1.9	**8** 0343 0.8 / 2.2 TU 1613 0.6 / 2.2	**23** 0405 0.8 / 2.0 W 1624 0.7 / 2.0	**8** 0245 0.9 / 2.0 TU 1513 0.7 / 2.1	**23** 0304 0.9 / 1.9 W 1519 0.8 / 2.0	**8** 0401 0.5 / 2.2 F 1621 0.4 / 2.3	**23** 0338 0.7 / 2.0 SA 1553 0.7 / 2.1
9 0248 0.9 / 2.2 SU 1523 0.7 / 2.1	**24** 0343 1.0 / 2.0 M 1607 0.9 / 2.0	**9** 0433 0.6 / 2.3 W 1701 0.4 / 2.2	**24** 0441 0.8 / 2.0 TH 1659 0.7 / 2.1	**9** 0336 0.7 / 2.1 W 1601 0.5 / 2.3	**24** 0340 0.8 / 1.9 TH 1555 0.7 / 2.0	**9** 0441 0.4 / 2.2 SA 1700 0.4 / 2.3	**24** 0412 0.6 / 2.0 SU 1628 0.6 / 2.1
10 0344 0.8 / 2.3 M 1617 0.6 / 2.3	**25** 0422 0.9 / 2.0 TU 1644 0.8 / 2.0	**10** 0520 2.3 / 0.6 TH 1746 2.3 / 0.4	**25** 0514 0.7 / 2.0 F 1732 0.6	**10** 0422 0.6 / 2.2 TH 1645 0.4 / 2.3	**25** 0414 0.7 / 2.0 F 1630 0.6 / 2.1	**10** 0519 2.3 / 0.4 SU 1736 2.2 / 0.4	**25** 0446 0.6 / 2.1 M 1703 0.6
11 0437 0.7 / 2.3 TU 1708 0.6	**26** 0459 0.8 / 2.0 W 1720 0.7	**11** 0604 2.3 / 0.5 F 1829 2.3 / 0.4	**26** 0544 2.1 / 0.7 SA 1801 2.0 / 0.6	**11** 0504 0.4 / 2.3 F 1726 0.4	**26** 0446 0.6 / 2.0 SA 1702 0.6	**11** 0554 2.3 / 0.5 M 1809 2.2 / 0.6	**26** 0521 2.2 / 0.6 TU 1739 2.1 / 0.6
12 0528 2.3 / 2.3 W 1757 0.5	**27** 0533 2.0 / 0.8 TH 1753 2.0 / 0.7	**12** 0647 2.1 / 0.5 SA 1909 2.2 / 0.6	**27** 0612 2.1 / 2.0 SU 1829 2.0 / 0.6	**12** 0544 2.3 / 0.4 SA 1805 2.3 / 0.4	**27** 0516 2.1 / 0.6 SU 1733 2.1 / 0.6	**12** 0627 2.2 / 0.6 TU 1841 2.1 / 0.7	**27** 0559 2.2 / 0.6 W 1819 2.1 / 0.7
13 0617 2.3 / 2.3 TH 1845 0.5	**28** 0605 2.0 / 0.8 F 1823 2.0 / 0.7	**13** 0727 2.3 / 0.6 SU 1946 2.1 / 0.6	**28** 0642 2.1 / 0.7 M 1859 2.0 / 0.7	**13** 0622 2.3 / 0.4 SU 1840 2.2 / 0.4	**28** 0547 2.1 / 0.6 M 1803 2.1 / 0.6	**13** 0657 2.1 / 0.7 W 1913 2.0 / 0.8	**28** 0640 2.1 / 0.6 TH 1902 2.1 / 0.8
14 0705 2.3 / 0.7 F 1931 0.6 / 2.1	**29** 0635 2.0 / 0.8 SA 1852 2.0 / 0.7	**14** 0805 2.1 / 0.7 M 2023 2.0 / 0.8		**14** 0656 2.3 / 0.6 M 1913 2.1 / 0.6	**29** 0618 2.1 / 0.6 TU 1836 2.1 / 0.7	**14** 0729 2.1 / 0.8 TH 1948 1.9 / 1.0	**29** 0726 2.0 / 0.7 F 1953 2.0 / 0.9
15 0753 2.2 / 0.7 SA 2017 0.7	**30** 0706 2.0 / 0.8 SU 1924 2.0 / 0.7	**15** 0845 0.9 / 2.0 TU 2103 1.9 / 0.9		**15** 0729 2.1 / 0.7 TU 1945 2.0 / 0.8	**30** 0653 2.1 / 0.6 W 1913 2.0 / 0.7	**15** 0806 1.0 / 2.0 F 2033 1.8 / 1.2	**30** 0822 1.9 / 0.9 SA 2058 1.9 / 1.0
	31 0740 2.0 / 0.9 M 2000 1.9 / 0.8				**31** 0732 2.0 / 0.7 TH 1956 2.0 / 0.9		

Chart Datum: 1·40 metres below Ordnance Datum (Newlyn)

》》 **FREE** monthly updates 《《
www.reedsalmanac.co.uk

TIDES

TIME ZONE (UT)
For Summer Time add ONE hour in **non-shaded areas**

YEAR 2005

ENGLAND – POOLE HARBOUR
LAT 50°42′N   LONG 1°59′W
TIMES AND HEIGHTS OF HIGH AND LOW WATERS

Note - HW times are not shown because they cannot be predicted with reasonable accuracy. Approximate times can be gained using LW times and the Tidal Curves at the start of this section.

	MAY			JUNE			JULY			AUGUST	
	Time m	Time m		Time m	Time m		Time m	Time m		Time m	Time m
1 SU	0936 1.8 / 1.0 / 1.8 / 2221 1.2	**16** M 0936 1.6 / 1.2 / 1.7 / 2225 1.4	**1** W	1149 1.8 / 0.9 / 2.0	**16** TH 1049 1.7 / 1.1 / 1.8 / 2330 1.2	**1** F	1208 1.8 / 1.0 / 1.9	**16** SA 1052 1.8 / 1.1 / 1.8 / 2336 1.2	**1** M	0124 1.2 / 1.7 / 1.8 / 1348 1.8	**16** TU 0034 1.3 / 1.8 / 1310 1.2 / 1.8
2 M	1106 1.7 / 1.0 / 2350 1.1	**17** TU 1058 1.6 / 1.3 / 1.7 / 2346 1.3	**2** TH	0026 1.0 / 1254 1.8 / 2.0	**17** F 1152 1.7 / 1.1 / 1.9	**2** SA	0048 1.0 / 1.8 / 1312 1.0 / 1.9	**17** SU 1204 1.8 / 1.1 / 1.9	**2** TU	0224 1.2 / 1.8 / 1444 1.1 / 1.9	**17** W 0154 1.0 / 1.9 / 1420 1.0 / 2.0
3 TU	1230 1.8 / 1.0 / 1.9	**18** W 1210 1.6 / 1.2 / 1.8	**3** F	0127 0.9 / 1.9 / 1350 0.8 / 2.0	**18** SA 0032 1.1 / 1.8 / 1252 1.0 / 1.9	**3** SU	0149 1.0 / 1.8 / 1409 1.0 / 1.9	**18** M 0050 1.0 / 1.8 / 1318 1.0 / 1.9	**3** W	0312 0.9 / 1.9 / 1530 0.9 / 1.9	**18** TH 0254 0.8 / 2.1 / 1517 0.8 / 2.1
4 W	0105 1.0 / 1.9 / 1334 0.8 / 2.0	**19** TH 0048 1.2 / 1.6 / 1305 1.0 / 1.9	**4** SA	0219 0.8 / 1.9 / 1438 0.8 / 2.1	**19** SU 0128 1.0 / 1.9 / 1347 0.9 / 2.0	**4** M	0242 0.9 / 1.9 / 1500 1.0 / 2.0	**19** TU 0159 0.9 / 1.9 / 1423 0.9 / 2.0	**4** TH	0353 0.8 / 1.9 / 1611 0.8 / 2.0	**19** F 0346 0.6 / 2.2 / 1608 0.7 / 2.2
5 TH	0203 0.8 / 1.9 / 1426 0.7 / 2.1	**20** F 0136 1.0 / 1.8 / 1350 0.9 / 2.0	**5** SU	0306 0.8 / 2.0 / 1523 0.8 / 2.1	**20** M 0220 0.9 / 2.0 / 1439 0.8 / 2.1	**5** TU	0328 0.9 / 1.9 / 1545 0.9 / 2.0	**20** W 0258 0.8 / 2.0 / 1521 0.8 / 2.1	**5** F	0432 0.8 / 1.9 / 1648 0.8 / 2.0	**20** SA 0435 0.4 / 2.3 / 1655 0.6 / 2.3
6 F	0251 0.7 / 1.9 / 1510 0.6 / 2.2	**21** SA 0217 0.9 / 1.9 / 1432 0.8 / 2.0	**6** M	0349 0.7 / 2.0 / 1605 0.8 / 2.1	**21** TU 0310 0.7 / 2.0 / 1531 0.8 / 2.1	**6** W	0411 0.8 / 1.9 / 1626 0.9 / 2.0	**21** TH 0353 0.7 / 2.1 / 1615 0.7 / 2.2	**6** SA	0508 0.7 / 1.9 / 1724 0.8 / 2.0	**21** SU 0521 0.4 / 2.3 / 1741 0.5
7 SA	0334 0.6 / 2.1 / 1552 0.6 / 2.2	**22** SU 0257 0.8 / 2.0 / 1512 0.7 / 2.1	**7** TU	0429 0.7 / 2.0 / 1644 0.8 / 2.1	**22** W 0401 0.7 / 2.1 / 1622 0.7 / 2.2	**7** TH	0450 0.7 / 2.0 / 1705 0.9 / 2.0	**22** F 0445 0.5 / 2.3 / 1707 0.6 / 2.3	**7** SU	0541 0.7 / 2.0 / 1756 0.8 / 2.0	**22** M 0604 0.4 / 2.4 / 1824 0.5 / 2.3
8 SU	0415 0.6 / 2.1 / 1631 0.6 / 2.2	**23** M 0337 0.7 / 2.1 / 1554 0.7 / 2.1	**8** W	0507 0.7 / 2.0 / 1721 0.8	**23** TH 0451 0.6 / 2.2 / 1714 0.7	**8** F	0527 0.8 / 2.0 / 1742 0.9	**23** SA 0535 0.4 / 2.3 / 1756 0.6 / 2.3	**8** M	0612 0.7 / 2.0 / 1826 0.8 / 2.0	**23** TU 0646 0.4 / 2.3 / 1905 0.6
9 M	0453 0.6 / 2.1 / 1708 0.6	**24** TU 0418 0.6 / 2.1 / 1637 0.7 / 2.2	**9** TH	0543 0.7 / 2.1 / 1757 0.8	**24** F 0542 0.6 / 2.2 / 1805 0.7 / 2.2	**9** SA	0602 0.8 / 2.0 / 1817 0.9	**24** SU 0623 0.4 / 2.3 / 1844 0.6	**9** TU	0640 0.7 / 2.0 / 1854 0.8	**24** W 0726 0.6 / 2.2 / 1946 0.7
10 TU	0528 0.6 / 2.1 / 1742 0.7	**25** W 0502 0.6 / 2.1 / 1722 0.6 / 2.2	**10** F	0617 0.8 / 2.0 / 1833 0.9	**25** SA 0633 0.6 / 2.2 / 1856 0.7	**10** SU	0634 0.8 / 2.0 / 1850 0.9	**25** M 0710 0.6 / 2.3 / 1931 0.6	**10** W	0708 0.8 / 2.0 / 1925 0.8	**25** TH 0804 0.7 / 2.1 / 2026 0.8
11 W	0602 0.7 / 2.1 / 1816 0.8	**26** TH 0547 0.6 / 2.2 / 1809 0.7	**11** SA	0651 0.9 / 2.0 / 1909 1.0	**26** SU 0724 0.6 / 2.2 / 1948 0.7	**11** M	0706 0.8 / 1.9 / 1923 0.9	**26** TU 0755 0.6 / 2.2 / 2017 0.7	**11** TH	0739 0.8 / 2.0 / 2001 0.9	**26** F 0845 0.9 / 1.9 / 2111 1.0
12 TH	0634 0.8 / 2.0 / 1850 0.9	**27** F 0636 0.6 / 2.1 / 1900 0.7	**12** SU	0727 1.0 / 1.9 / 1948 1.1	**27** M 0816 0.6 / 2.1 / 2042 0.8	**12** TU	0738 0.9 / 1.9 / 1958 1.0	**27** W 0840 0.7 / 2.1 / 2105 0.8	**12** F	0817 0.9 / 1.9 / 2044 1.0	**27** SA 0934 1.1 / 1.8 / 2211 1.1
13 F	0707 0.9 / 2.0 / 1926 1.0	**28** SA 0728 0.7 / 2.1 / 1955 0.8	**13** M	0806 1.0 / 1.8 / 2032 1.2	**28** TU 0910 0.7 / 2.0 / 2138 0.9	**13** W	0814 0.9 / 1.9 / 2039 1.0	**28** TH 0927 0.9 / 2.0 / 2157 0.9	**13** SA	0905 1.0 / 1.9 / 2140 1.1	**28** SU 1043 1.3 / 1.6 / 2335 1.3
14 SA	0744 1.0 / 1.9 / 2010 1.2	**29** SU 0826 0.8 / 2.0 / 2056 0.9	**14** TU	0852 1.1 / 1.8 / 2125 1.2	**29** W 1006 0.9 / 2.0 / 2238 1.0	**14** TH	0857 1.0 / 1.8 / 2127 1.1	**29** F 1020 1.1 / 1.8 / 2258 1.1	**14** SU	1009 1.2 / 1.8 / 2257 1.2	**29** M 1214 1.6 / 1.6
15 SU	0831 1.1 / 1.8 / 2107 1.3	**30** M 0930 0.9 / 1.9 / 2204 0.9	**15** W	0947 1.1 / 1.7 / 2225 1.2	**30** TH 1105 0.9 / 1.9 / 2342 1.0	**15** F	0949 1.0 / 1.8 / 2226 1.2	**30** SA 1124 1.2 / 1.7 / 1.8	**15** M	1137 1.3 / 1.7 / 1.8	**30** TU 0104 1.3 / 1.7 / 1334 1.3 / 1.7
		31 TU 1039 0.9 / 1.8 / 2316 1.0						**31** SU 0010 1.2 / 1.6 / 1239 1.2 / 1.8			**31** W 0208 1.2 / 1.8 / 1430 1.2 / 1.8

Chart Datum: 1·40 metres below Ordnance Datum (Newlyn)

》》 FREE monthly updates from 《《
www.reedsalmanac.co.uk

ENGLAND – POOLE HARBOUR

LAT 50°42'N   LONG 1°59'W

TIMES AND HEIGHTS OF HIGH AND LOW WATERS

TIME ZONE (UT)
For Summer Time add ONE hour in **non-shaded areas**

YEAR 2005

Note - HW times are not shown because they cannot be predicted with reasonable accuracy. Approximate times can be gained using LW times and the Tidal Curves at the start of this section.

	SEPTEMBER			OCTOBER			NOVEMBER			DECEMBER	
	Time m	Time m		Time m	Time m		Time m	Time m		Time m	Time m
1 TH	0254 1.0 / 1.9 / 1513 1.0 / 1.9	**16** F 0245 0.8 / 2.1 / 1506 0.8 / 2.1	**1** SA	0303 0.9 / 2.0 / 1521 0.9	**16** SU 0309 0.6 / 2.3 / 1529 0.6 / 2.3	**1** TU	0334 0.8 / 2.1 / 1552 0.8 / 2.1	**16** W 0405 0.7 / 2.3 / 1628 0.6 / 2.2 ○	**1** TH	0333 0.8 / 2.2 / 1557 0.7 / 2.1 ●	**16** F 0425 0.8 / 2.1 / 1651 0.8 / 2.1
2 F	0332 0.8 / 2.0 / 1550 0.9 / 2.0	**17** SA 0332 0.6 / 2.3 / 1552 0.6 / 2.3	**2** SU	0338 0.7 / 2.1 / 1555 0.8 / 2.0	**17** M 0351 0.5 / 2.4 / 1611 0.6 ○ / 2.3	**2** W	0407 0.7 / 2.1 / 1624 0.7 ● / 2.1	**17** TH 0444 0.7 / 2.3 / 1706 0.7	**2** F	0414 0.8 / 2.2 / 1638 0.7 / 2.2	**17** SA 0504 0.8 / 2.1 / 1729 0.8
3 SA	0408 0.7 / 2.1 / 1625 0.8 ● / 2.0	**18** SU 0416 0.4 / 2.4 / 1636 0.5 ○ / 2.3	**3** M	0411 0.7 / 2.1 / 1627 0.7 ● / 2.1	**18** TU 0432 0.4 / 2.4 / 1651 0.5 / 2.3	**3** TH	0440 0.7 / 2.2 / 1658 0.7	**18** F 0521 0.7 / 2.2 / 1743 0.7	**3** SA	0456 0.8 / 2.2 / 1722 0.7	**18** SU 0542 0.9 / 2.1 / 1804 0.8
4 SU	0443 0.7 / 2.1 / 1659 0.7 / 2.0	**19** M 0459 0.4 / 2.4 / 1718 0.4	**4** TU	0443 0.7 / 2.1 / 1658 0.7 / 2.1	**19** W 0510 0.5 / 2.3 / 1730 0.6	**4** F	0514 0.7 / 2.2 / 1733 0.7	**19** SA 0557 0.8 / 2.1 / 1818 0.8	**4** SU	0541 0.8 / 2.2 / 1808 0.7	**19** M 0618 0.9 / 2.1 / 1840 0.9
5 M	0516 0.6 / 2.1 / 1730 0.7	**20** TU 0538 0.4 / 2.3 / 1757 0.4	**5** W	0513 0.6 / 2.1 / 1726 0.7	**20** TH 0546 0.6 / 2.3 / 1805 0.6	**5** SA	0551 0.8 / 2.2 / 1812 0.7	**20** SU 0634 0.9 / 2.1 / 1854 0.9	**5** M	0630 0.8 / 2.2 / 1858 0.7	**20** TU 0655 1.0 / 2.0 / 1915 0.9
6 TU	0544 0.6 / 2.0 / 1757 0.7	**21** W 0616 0.4 / 2.3 / 1835 0.6	**6** TH	0541 0.7 / 2.1 / 1755 0.7	**21** F 0621 0.7 / 2.2 / 1840 0.8	**6** SU	0632 0.9 / 2.1 / 1856 0.8	**21** M 0712 1.1 / 1.9 / 1933 1.0	**6** TU	0722 0.8 / 2.1 / 1952 0.8	**21** W 0732 1.1 / 1.9 / 1951 1.0
7 W	0611 0.7 / 2.0 / 1824 0.7	**22** TH 0652 0.6 / 2.2 / 1911 0.7	**7** F	0610 0.7 / 2.1 / 1828 0.8	**22** SA 0656 0.9 / 2.0 / 1915 0.9	**7** M	0721 1.0 / 2.0 / 1949 0.9	**22** TU 0757 1.3 / 1.8 / 2019 1.2	**7** W	0821 0.9 / 2.0 / 2051 0.9	**22** TH 0813 1.2 / 1.8 / 2032 1.1
8 TH	0638 0.7 / 2.0 / 1854 0.8	**23** F 0727 0.8 / 2.1 / 1947 0.8	**8** SA	0644 0.8 / 2.1 / 1905 0.8	**23** SU 0733 1.0 / 1.9 / 1955 1.1	**8** TU	0822 1.2 / 1.9 / 2057 1.1	**23** W 0853 1.4 / 1.8 / 2118 1.3 ◐	**8** TH	0926 1.0 / 1.9 / 2156 0.9 ◐	**23** F 0900 1.3 / 1.7 / 2120 1.2
9 F	0708 0.8 / 2.0 / 1928 0.9	**24** SA 0804 1.0 / 1.9 / 2028 1.0	**9** SU	0725 1.0 / 2.0 / 1951 1.0	**24** M 0821 1.3 / 1.8 / 2047 1.3	**9** W	0942 1.2 / 1.8 / 2222 1.2 ◐	**24** TH 1008 1.4 / 1.8 / 2234 1.3	**9** F	1036 1.1 / 1.9 / 2305 1.0	**24** SA 0957 1.3 / 1.7 / 2217 1.2
10 SA	0745 0.9 / 1.9 / 2010 1.0	**25** SU 0852 1.2 / 1.8 / 2124 1.3 ◐	**10** M	0818 1.2 / 1.9 / 2054 1.2	**25** TU 0932 1.4 / 1.7 / 2211 1.4 ◐	**10** TH	1110 1.2 / 1.9 / 2347 1.1	**25** F 1127 1.4 / 1.8 / 2347 1.3	**10** SA	1147 1.1 / 2.0 / (no pm)	**25** SU 1102 1.3 / 1.8 / 2321 1.2
11 SU	0832 1.1 / 1.9 / 2107 1.2 ◐	**26** M 1007 1.4 / 1.6 / 2258 1.4	**11** TU	0941 1.3 / 1.8 / 2235 1.3	**26** W 1111 1.5 / 1.6 / 2348 1.4	**11** F	1227 1.1 / 1.9	**26** SA 1231 1.3 / 1.8 / (1.7)	**11** SU	0013 1.0 / 1252 1.0 / 2.0 / 1.9	**26** M 1209 1.3 / 1.7
12 M	0943 1.2 / 1.7 / 2238 1.3	**27** TU 1150 1.5 / 1.6	**12** W	1131 1.3 / 1.7	**27** TH 1233 1.4 / 1.6	**12** SA	0058 0.9 / 2.1 / 1328 0.9 / 2.0	**27** SU 0046 1.2 / 1.8 / 1319 1.2 / 1.8	**12** M	0115 0.9 / 2.0 / 1350 0.9 / 2.0	**27** TU 0027 1.2 / 1.9 / 1310 1.2 / 1.8
13 TU	1134 1.6 / 1.4 / 1.7	**28** W 0037 1.4 / 1313 1.4 / 1.7 / 1.7	**13** TH	0020 1.2 / 1.9 / 1257 1.2 / 1.9	**28** F 0058 1.3 / 1.8 / 1328 1.3 / 1.8	**13** SU	0153 0.8 / 2.2 / 1418 0.8 / 2.1	**28** M 0133 1.1 / 2.0 / 1401 1.0 / 1.9	**13** TU	0210 0.8 / 2.1 / 1440 0.9 / 2.0	**28** W 0127 1.1 / 2.0 / 1403 1.0 / 1.9
14 W	0033 1.2 / 1.8 / 1310 1.2 / 1.9	**29** TH 0143 1.2 / 1.9 / 1407 1.2 / 1.8	**14** F	0131 1.0 / 2.0 / 1357 0.9 / 1.9	**29** SA 0145 1.1 / 1.9 / 1409 1.1 / 1.9	**14** M	0240 0.7 / 2.3 / 1504 0.7 / 2.2	**29** TU 0215 1.0 / 2.1 / 1439 0.9 / 2.0	**14** W	0259 0.8 / 2.1 / 1527 0.8 / 2.1	**29** TH 0220 1.0 / 2.1 / 1452 0.9 / 2.0
15 TH	0150 1.0 / 2.0 / 1415 1.0 / 2.0	**30** F 0226 1.0 / 2.0 / 1446 1.0 / 1.9	**15** SA	0224 0.8 / 2.2 / 1445 0.8 / 2.1	**30** SU 0224 0.9 / 2.0 / 1445 0.9 / 2.0	**15** TU	0324 0.7 / 2.3 / 1547 0.7 / 2.2	**30** W 0254 0.9 / 2.1 / 1517 0.8 / 2.1	**15** TH	0343 0.8 / 2.2 / 1610 0.8 / 2.1 ○	**30** F 0310 0.9 / 2.1 / 1541 0.8 / 2.1
					31 M 0300 0.8 / 2.1 / 1519 0.8 / 2.0						**31** SA 0400 0.8 / 2.2 / 1629 0.7 ● / 2.2

Chart Datum: 1·40 metres below Ordnance Datum (Newlyn)

》 FREE monthly updates from **《**
www.reedsalmanac.co.uk

TIDES

SOUTHAMPTON
MEAN SPRING AND NEAP CURVES
Springs occur 2 days after New and Full Moon

MEAN RANGES
Springs 4.0m
Neaps 1.9m

238

ENGLAND – SOUTHAMPTON

LAT 50°54′N   LONG 1°24′W

TIMES AND HEIGHTS OF HIGH AND LOW WATERS

TIME ZONE (UT) For Summer Time add ONE hour in **non-shaded areas**

YEAR 2005

Note - Double HWs occur at Southampton. The predictions are for the first HW.

	JANUARY			FEBRUARY			MARCH			APRIL	
	Time m	Time m		Time m	Time m		Time m	Time m		Time m	Time m
1 SA	0150 4.2 / 0734 1.5 / 1402 4.1 / 1950 1.4	**16** SU 0250 4.4 / 0844 1.1 / 1506 4.2 / 2104 1.1	**1** TU	0237 4.1 / 0823 1.3 / 1450 4.0 / 2041 1.3	**16** W 0338 3.9 / 0930 1.6 / 1600 3.7 / ◐ 2150 1.7	**1** TU	0128 4.3 / 0718 0.9 / 1341 4.3 / 1933 0.9	**16** W 0213 4.2 / 0805 1.1 / 1432 4.0 / 2018 1.4	**1** F	0225 4.1 / 0822 1.3 / 1455 3.9 / 2048 1.6	**16** SA 0259 3.6 / 0852 1.8 / 1545 3.5 / ◐ 2129 2.2
2 SU	0231 4.1 / 0814 1.6 / 1443 4.0 / 2032 1.5	**17** M 0341 4.2 / 0933 1.4 / 1558 4.0 / ◐ 2153 1.4	**2** W	0321 4.0 / 0911 1.5 / 1540 3.9 / ◐ 2134 1.6	**17** TH 0432 3.7 / 1031 1.9 / 1707 3.5 / 2303 2.1	**2** W	0204 4.2 / 0753 1.1 / 1420 4.1 / 2011 1.2	**17** TH 0251 3.9 / 0841 1.5 / 1516 3.7 / ◐ 2059 1.8	**2** SA	0324 3.9 / 0927 1.6 / 1610 3.7 / ◐ 2210 1.9	**17** SU 0403 3.4 / 1010 2.1 / 1713 3.5 / 2319 2.3
3 M	0317 4.0 / 0902 1.7 / 1531 3.9 / ◐ 2123 1.6	**18** TU 0435 4.0 / 1029 1.6 / 1656 3.8 / 2252 1.7	**3** TH	0418 3.9 / 1013 1.7 / 1646 3.8 / 2245 1.8	**18** F 0548 3.5 / 1200 2.1 / 1846 3.4	**3** TH	0245 4.1 / 0838 1.3 / 1507 3.9 / ◐ 2100 1.5	**18** F 0337 3.6 / 0932 1.9 / 1618 3.5 / 2207 2.2	**3** SU	0450 3.7 / 1107 1.8 / 1753 3.7	**18** M 0539 3.4 / 1156 2.1 / 1851 3.6
4 TU	0411 3.9 / 1001 1.8 / 1630 3.8 / 2226 1.7	**19** W 0537 3.8 / 1135 1.8 / 1806 3.6	**4** F	0532 3.9 / 1136 1.8 / 1811 3.7	**19** SA 0041 2.2 / 0723 3.6 / 1328 2.0 / 2014 3.6	**4** F	0340 3.9 / 0938 1.6 / 1615 3.7 / 2213 1.8	**19** SA 0448 3.4 / 1104 2.2 / 1802 3.4	**4** M	0002 1.9 / 0634 3.7 / 1249 1.6 / 1928 3.9	**19** TU 0049 2.2 / 0710 3.5 / 1310 1.9 / 1954 3.8
5 W	0514 3.9 / 1109 1.8 / 1738 3.8 / 2338 1.7	**20** TH 0001 1.8 / 0646 3.8 / 1247 1.8 / 1923 3.7	**5** SA	0015 1.8 / 0655 3.9 / 1306 1.6 / 1938 3.9	**20** SU 0200 2.0 / 0834 3.7 / 1430 1.7 / 2111 3.8	**5** SA	0458 3.7 / 1110 1.8 / 1751 3.6	**20** SU 0008 2.3 / 0639 3.4 / 1254 2.1 / 1946 3.5	**5** TU	0130 1.6 / 0755 3.9 / 1401 1.2 / 2033 4.2	**20** W 0145 1.8 / 0808 3.7 / 1400 1.5 / 2037 4.0
6 TH	0622 4.0 / 1221 1.7 / 1851 3.9	**21** F 0112 1.9 / 0754 3.9 / 1352 1.7 / 2031 3.8	**6** SU	0140 1.6 / 0812 4.1 / 1422 1.3 / 2050 4.1	**21** M 0252 1.7 / 0922 4.0 / 1515 1.4 / 2151 4.1	**6** SU	0001 1.9 / 0638 3.7 / 1258 1.7 / 1932 3.8	**21** M 0137 2.1 / 0804 3.6 / 1400 1.8 / 2043 3.8	**6** W	0232 1.2 / 0853 4.2 / 1456 0.8 / 2122 4.5	**21** TH 0227 1.5 / 0850 3.9 / 1442 1.2 / 2112 4.2
7 F	0049 1.6 / 0727 4.2 / 1329 1.5 / 1958 4.1	**22** SA 0214 1.8 / 0851 4.1 / 1446 1.5 / 2123 3.9	**7** M	0249 1.3 / 0916 4.3 / 1524 1.0 / 2149 4.4	**22** TU 0334 1.4 / 1000 4.1 / 1554 1.1 / 2225 4.2	**7** M	0137 1.7 / 0805 4.0 / 1417 1.3 / 2046 4.1	**22** TU 0229 1.8 / 0855 3.8 / 1446 1.4 / 2122 4.0	**7** TH	0322 0.8 / 0940 4.4 / 1543 0.5 / 2205 4.6	**22** F 0305 1.1 / 0925 4.1 / 1521 0.9 / 2144 4.3
8 SA	0155 1.4 / 0828 4.3 / 1432 1.2 / 2059 4.3	**23** SU 0304 1.6 / 0937 4.1 / 1531 1.3 / 2205 4.1	**8** TU	0347 1.0 / 1009 4.6 / 1618 0.6 / ● 2240 4.6	**23** W 0412 1.1 / 1033 4.3 / 1630 0.8 / 2255 4.3	**8** TU	0246 1.3 / 0908 4.2 / 1516 0.9 / 2140 4.4	**23** W 0308 1.4 / 0932 4.0 / 1524 1.1 / 2154 4.2	**8** F	0406 0.5 / 1022 4.6 / ● 2245 4.7 / 1625 0.3	**23** SA 0342 0.8 / 0959 4.3 / 1558 0.7 / 2217 4.5
9 SU	0255 1.2 / 0924 4.5 / 1529 0.9 / 2154 4.5	**24** M 0348 1.4 / 1016 4.2 / 1612 1.1 / 2242 4.2	**9** W	0439 0.7 / 1058 4.7 / 1707 0.5 / 2326 4.7	**24** TH 0447 0.9 / 1103 4.3 / 1705 0.5 / ○ 2323 4.4	**9** W	0340 0.9 / 0959 4.5 / 1606 0.5 / 2227 4.6	**24** TH 0344 1.1 / 1004 4.2 / 1600 0.8 / 2223 4.3	**9** SA	0447 0.5 / 1100 4.6 / 1705 0.2 / 2322 4.7	**24** SU 0417 0.6 / 1033 4.4 / 1634 0.6 / ○ 2251 4.5
10 M	0351 1.0 / 1016 4.6 / 1623 0.7 / ● 2246 4.6	**25** TU 0428 1.2 / 1051 4.3 / 1649 0.9 / ○ 2315 4.3	**10** TH	0527 0.4 / 1143 4.8 / 1752 0.4	**25** F 0520 0.8 / 1133 4.4 / 1737 0.6 / 2353 4.4	**10** TH	0428 0.5 / 1043 4.6 / ● 2309 4.8 / 1651 0.2	**25** F 0418 0.8 / 1034 4.3 / 1635 0.6 / ○ 2252 4.4	**10** SU	0525 0.2 / 1137 4.6 / 1741 0.2 / 2357 4.6	**25** M 0453 0.5 / 1108 4.5 / 1710 0.5 / 2326 4.6
11 TU	0444 0.8 / 1106 4.7 / 1714 0.5 / 2336 4.7	**26** W 0505 1.1 / 1124 4.3 / 1725 0.8 / 2346 4.3	**11** F	0011 4.8 / 0611 0.3 / 1227 4.7 / 1833 0.1	**26** SA 0551 0.7 / 1203 4.4 / 1806 0.6	**11** F	0511 0.3 / 1124 4.7 / 1732 0.0 / 2348 4.8	**26** F 0451 0.6 / 1104 4.4 / 1708 0.5 / 2322 4.5	**11** M	0600 0.3 / 1213 4.5 / 1815 0.4	**26** TU 0528 0.5 / 1145 4.5 / 1745 0.6
12 W	0535 0.7 / 1155 4.6 / 1803 0.4	**27** TH 0540 1.0 / 1156 4.3 / 1758 0.8	**12** SA	0053 4.7 / 0653 0.4 / 1308 4.7 / 1912 0.3	**27** SU 0023 4.4 / 0619 0.8 / 1235 4.4 / 1833 0.6	**12** SA	0551 0.2 / 1203 4.7 / 1810 0.1	**27** SA 0523 0.5 / 1135 4.5 / 1739 0.5 / 2354 4.5	**12** TU	0031 4.5 / 0632 0.5 / 1249 4.4 / 1845 0.7	**27** W 0004 4.6 / 0604 0.5 / 1226 4.5 / 1822 0.7
13 TH	0025 4.7 / 0623 0.7 / 1243 4.7 / 1849 0.4	**28** F 0018 4.3 / 0612 1.0 / 1229 4.3 / 1827 0.8	**13** SU	0134 4.6 / 0731 0.6 / 1348 4.5 / 1949 0.5	**28** M 0055 4.5 / 0647 0.7 / 1307 4.4 / 1901 0.7	**13** SU	0025 4.7 / 0628 0.2 / 1241 4.6 / 1845 0.2	**28** SU 0553 0.5 / 1208 4.5 / 1808 0.5	**13** W	0105 4.3 / 0702 0.7 / 1325 4.2 / 1914 1.1	**28** TH 0044 4.5 / 0643 0.7 / 1309 4.4 / 1903 1.0
14 F	0114 4.6 / 0711 0.7 / 1331 4.6 / 1934 0.6	**29** SA 0051 4.3 / 0641 1.1 / 1302 4.3 / 1856 0.9	**14** M	0214 4.6 / 0809 0.8 / 1429 4.3 / 2024 0.9		**14** M	0103 4.6 / 0702 0.4 / 1318 4.5 / 1916 0.5	**28** M 0027 4.6 / 0624 0.6 / 1243 4.5 / 1839 0.7	**14** TH	0139 4.1 / 0731 1.1 / 1402 4.0 / 1946 1.5	**29** F 0128 4.3 / 0727 1.1 / 1358 4.2 / 1951 1.3
15 SA	0202 4.5 / 0757 0.9 / 1418 4.4 / 2019 0.8	**30** SU 0124 4.3 / 0711 1.1 / 1335 4.2 / 1926 1.0	**15** TU	0255 4.2 / 0847 1.2 / 1511 4.0 / 2102 1.3		**15** TU	0138 4.4 / 0734 0.7 / 1354 4.2 / 1946 0.9	**30** W 0102 4.4 / 0657 0.7 / 1320 4.3 / 1913 0.9	**15** F	0215 3.9 / 0806 1.5 / 1446 3.7 / 2026 1.9	**30** SA 0220 4.0 / 0821 1.3 / 1459 4.0 / 2054 1.6
		31 M 0159 4.2 / 0744 1.2 / 1410 4.1 / 2000 1.1						**31** TH 0140 4.3 / 0735 1.0 / 1402 4.2 / 1954 1.2			

Chart Datum: 2·74 metres below Ordnance Datum (Newlyn)

》》 **FREE** monthly updates from 《《
www.reedsalmanac.co.uk

TIDES

TIME ZONE (UT)
For Summer Time add ONE hour in **non-shaded areas**

YEAR 2005

ENGLAND – SOUTHAMPTON
LAT 50°54'N   LONG 1°24'W
TIMES AND HEIGHTS OF HIGH AND LOW WATERS

Note - Double HWs occur at Southampton. The predictions are for the first HW.

Day	MAY Time m		MAY Time m		JUNE Time m		JUNE Time m		JULY Time m		JULY Time m		AUGUST Time m		AUGUST Time m	
1	0326	3.9	**16** 0332	3.6	**1** 0554	3.9	**16** 0456	3.6	**1** 0619	3.8	**16** 0500	3.7	**1** 0128	1.8	**16** 0029	1.8
	0932	1.5	0928	1.9	1151	1.4	1052	1.7	1211	1.5	1055	1.7	0809	3.7	0704	3.8
	SU 1619	3.8	M 1626	3.6	W 1837	4.1	TH 1740	3.8	F 1857	4.0	SA 1743	3.9	M 1354	1.9	TU 1306	1.8
	◐ 2219	1.8	◐ 2221	2.2			2336	1.8			2341	1.8	2033	3.9	1941	4.0
2	0452	3.7	**17** 0443	3.5	**2** 0031	1.4	**17** 0601	3.7	**2** 0051	1.5	**17** 0612	3.7	**2** 0230	1.6	**17** 0152	1.6
	1102	1.6	1048	1.9	0700	4.0	1157	1.7	0724	3.8	1209	1.7	0909	3.9	0822	4.0
	M 1751	3.9	TU 1741	3.7	TH 1254	1.3	F 1840	3.9	SA 1313	1.5	SU 1852	4.0	TU 1451	1.7	W 1421	1.5
	2352	1.7	2342	2.1	1935	4.2			1955	4.0			2125	4.0	2049	4.2
3	0622	3.8	**18** 0600	3.5	**3** 0130	1.3	**18** 0037	1.7	**3** 0150	1.5	**18** 0053	1.6	**3** 0319	1.4	**18** 0257	1.2
	1226	1.5	1203	1.8	0758	4.0	0704	3.8	0824	3.9	0725	3.9	0956	4.0	0924	4.3
	TU 1909	4.0	W 1848	3.8	F 1349	1.2	SA 1258	1.5	SU 1410	1.5	M 1322	1.6	W 1538	1.5	TH 1523	1.2
					2026	4.3	1936	4.1	2048	4.1	1958	4.1	2207	4.1	2144	4.5
4	0106	1.5	**19** 0045	1.8	**4** 0221	1.1	**19** 0133	1.4	**4** 0243	1.3	**19** 0201	1.4	**4** 0401	1.2	**19** 0353	0.8
	0733	4.0	0706	3.7	0848	4.1	0801	4.0	0917	4.0	0832	4.0	1034	4.1	1016	4.5
	W 1332	1.2	TH 1302	1.6	SA 1439	1.1	SU 1354	1.3	M 1502	1.4	TU 1427	1.4	TH 1620	1.3	F 1617	0.8
	2008	4.3	1940	4.0	2111	4.3	2027	4.3	2135	4.1	2058	4.3	2242	4.2	○ 2233	4.7
5	0205	1.2	**20** 0135	1.5	**5** 0307	1.0	**20** 0226	1.2	**5** 0330	1.2	**20** 0303	1.1	**5** 0439	1.0	**20** 0443	0.4
	0829	4.2	0758	3.9	0933	4.2	0853	4.1	1003	4.0	0931	4.3	1108	4.2	1103	4.7
	TH 1425	0.9	F 1351	1.3	SU 1524	1.0	M 1447	1.2	TU 1548	1.3	W 1527	1.2	F 1658	1.1	SA 1706	0.5
	2056	4.4	2024	4.2	2152	4.3	2116	4.4	2216	4.2	2153	4.5	● 2315	4.3	2319	4.8
6	0254	0.9	**21** 0219	1.2	**6** 0350	0.9	**21** 0317	0.9	**6** 0413	1.1	**21** 0359	0.8	**6** 0515	0.9	**21** 0530	0.2
	0915	4.3	0842	4.1	1015	4.2	0943	4.3	1044	4.1	1024	4.4	1139	4.3	1148	4.8
	F 1512	0.7	SA 1436	1.1	M 1607	1.0	TU 1538	1.0	W 1632	1.3	TH 1623	0.9	SA 1734	1.0	SU 1752	0.4
	2139	4.5		2104	4.3	● 2231	4.3	2204	4.5	● 2254	4.2	○ 2244	4.6	2346	4.3		
7	0338	0.7	**22** 0302	1.0	**7** 0431	0.8	**22** 0407	0.8	**7** 0453	1.0	**22** 0452	0.6	**7** 0549	0.8	**22** 0003	4.8
	0957	4.4	0923	4.2	1054	4.2	1032	4.4	1121	4.2	1115	4.6	1209	4.3		0613	0.1
	SA 1554	0.6	SU 1519	0.9	TU 1647	1.0	W 1629	0.9	TH 1712	1.2	F 1715	0.7	SU 1806	1.0	M 1232	4.8
	2217	4.5	2144	4.5	2307	4.3	○ 2252	4.6	2330	4.2	2333	4.7			1834	0.4
8	0418	0.5	**23** 0343	0.8	**8** 0509	0.8	**23** 0457	0.6	**8** 0531	1.0	**23** 0542	0.4	**8** 0017	4.3	**23** 0046	4.4
	1036	4.4	1004	4.4	1132	4.2	1122	4.5	1156	4.2	1204	4.7	0619	0.8	0653	0.2
	SU 1634	0.5	M 1602	0.8	W 1725	1.1	TH 1720	0.8	F 1750	1.2	SA 1805	0.6	M 1240	4.3	TU 1314	4.7
	● 2254	4.5	○ 2224	4.6	2343	4.2	2341	4.6					1835	1.0	1915	0.5
9	0457	0.5	**24** 0426	0.6	**9** 0545	0.9	**24** 0547	0.5	**9** 0005	4.2	**24** 0021	4.7	**9** 0049	4.2	**24** 0128	4.6
	1113	4.4	1046	4.5	1209	4.2	1212	4.5	0605	1.0	0629	0.3	0646	0.9	0732	0.4
	M 1712	0.6	TU 1645	0.7	TH 1802	1.2	F 1810	0.8	SA 1232	4.2	SU 1253	4.7	TU 1311	4.2	W 1356	4.6
	2329	4.4	2305	4.6					1824	1.2	1852	0.6	1903	1.1	1953	0.8
10	0532	0.6	**25** 0508	0.6	**10** 0019	4.2	**25** 0031	4.6	**10** 0040	4.2	**25** 0109	4.6	**10** 0121	4.2	**25** 0210	4.4
	1149	4.3	1130	4.5	0618	1.0	0636	0.6	0638	1.0	0715	0.4	0713	1.0	0809	0.8
	TU 1747	0.8	W 1728	0.7	F 1247	4.1	SA 1304	4.5	SU 1306	4.2	M 1341	4.6	W 1344	4.2	TH 1437	4.3
			2349	4.6	1837	1.3	1901	0.9	1857	1.3	1938	0.7	1931	1.2	2032	1.1
11	0003	4.4	**26** 0552	0.6	**11** 0057	4.1	**26** 0123	4.5	**11** 0115	4.1	**26** 0156	4.5	**11** 0153	4.1	**26** 0253	4.1
	0604	0.7	1216	4.5	0651	1.1	0726	0.7	0709	1.1	0759	0.6	0743	1.2	0847	1.2
	W 1225	4.2	TH 1813	0.8	SA 1326	4.1	SU 1358	4.4	M 1342	4.1	TU 1428	4.5	TH 1418	4.1	F 1522	4.1
	1819	1.0			1912	1.5	1953	1.0	1929	1.4	2024	0.9	2004	1.4	◐ 2115	1.5
12	0038	4.2	**27** 0035	4.5	**12** 0135	4.0	**27** 0216	4.3	**12** 0151	4.0	**27** 0243	4.3	**12** 0229	4.0	**27** 0342	3.8
	0636	0.9	0638	0.7	0726	1.3	0818	0.8	0741	1.2	0843	0.8	0818	1.4	0933	1.7
	TH 1303	4.1	F 1306	4.4	SU 1407	4.0	M 1454	4.3	TU 1419	4.1	W 1517	4.3	F 1457	4.0	SA 1615	3.8
	1851	1.3	1902	1.0	1950	1.7	2048	1.2	2004	1.5	2110	1.1	2045	1.5	2212	1.9
13	0114	4.1	**28** 0126	4.3	**13** 0216	3.9	**28** 0312	4.2	**13** 0228	3.9	**28** 0333	4.1	**13** 0312	3.9	**28** 0448	3.6
	0707	1.2	0728	0.9	0805	1.5	0911	1.1	0816	1.3	0929	1.1	0903	1.6	1040	2.1
	F 1342	4.0	SA 1402	4.3	M 1452	3.9	TU 1552	4.2	W 1459	4.0	TH 1608	4.1	SA 1546	3.9	SU 1729	3.6
	1925	1.6	1956	1.2	2035	1.8	◐ 2145	1.3	2043	1.6	◐ 2201	1.4	◐ 2139	1.8	2337	2.1
14	0152	3.9	**29** 0223	4.2	**14** 0302	3.8	**29** 0411	4.0	**14** 0310	3.9	**29** 0428	3.9	**14** 0411	3.8	**29** 0626	3.5
	0742	1.4	0824	1.1	0851	1.7	1008	1.2	0859	1.5	1021	1.5	1005	1.8	1220	2.2
	SA 1426	3.9	SU 1504	4.1	TU 1542	3.8	W 1652	4.1	TH 1544	3.9	F 1706	3.9	SU 1653	3.8	M 1906	3.6
	2007	1.8	2059	1.5	2129	1.9	2245	1.4	2131	1.7	2301	1.7	2255	1.9		
15	0236	3.7	**30** 0327	4.0	**15** 0355	3.7	**30** 0514	3.9	**15** 0359	3.8	**30** 0533	3.8	**15** 0532	3.7	**30** 0112	2.1
	0827	1.7	0929	1.3	0947	1.7	1108	1.4	0951	1.6	1126	1.8	1132	2.0	0759	3.6
	SU 1520	3.7	M 1615	4.0	W 1639	3.8	TH 1755	4.1	F 1639	3.9	SA 1814	3.8	M 1818	3.8	TU 1346	2.1
	2103	2.1	◐ 2211	1.6	◐ 2231	1.9	2348	1.5	2231	1.8					2020	3.8
			31 0440	3.9					**31** 0014	1.8					**31** 0218	1.8
			1041	1.4					0652	3.6					0858	4.0
			TU 1729	4.0					SU 1242	1.9					W 1442	1.9
			2324	1.6					1928	3.8					2111	4.0

Chart Datum: 2·74 metres below Ordnance Datum (Newlyn)

》》 **FREE** monthly updates from 《《
www.reedsalmanac.co.uk

TIME ZONE (UT)
For Summer Time add ONE hour in **non-shaded areas**

YEAR 2005

ENGLAND – SOUTHAMPTON
LAT 50°54′N   LONG 1°24′W

Note – Double HWs occur at Southampton. The predictions are for the first HW.

TIMES AND HEIGHTS OF HIGH AND LOW WATERS

SEPTEMBER		OCTOBER		NOVEMBER		DECEMBER	
Time m	Time m	Time m	Time m	Time m	Time m	Time m	Time m
1 0303 1.5 / 0940 4.1 / TH 1524 1.6 / 2149 4.2	**16** 0247 1.1 / 0912 4.4 / F 1513 1.1 / 2131 4.6	**1** 0309 1.3 / 0941 4.3 / SA 1530 1.3 / 2150 4.3	**16** 0314 0.7 / 0937 4.8 / SU 1539 0.7 / 2154 4.7	**1** 0340 0.9 / 1001 4.5 / TU 1600 0.9 / 2216 4.5	**16** 0410 0.7 / 1031 4.7 / W 1635 0.7 / ○ 2251 4.6	**1** 0343 1.0 / 1006 4.6 / TH 1607 0.9 / ● 2228 4.5	**16** 0429 1.1 / 1052 4.4 / F 1654 0.9 / 2316 4.3
2 0341 1.2 / 1014 4.2 / F 1600 1.3 / 2222 4.3	**17** 0338 0.7 / 1000 4.7 / SA 1602 0.7 / 2216 4.7	**2** 0344 1.0 / 1010 4.4 / SU 1604 1.0 / 2219 4.4	**17** 0358 0.4 / 1018 4.9 / M 1622 0.5 / ○ 2234 4.8	**2** 0415 0.8 / 1033 4.6 / W 1635 0.8 / ● 2250 4.5	**17** 0450 0.7 / 1109 4.6 / TH 1714 0.7 / 2330 4.5	**2** 0424 0.9 / 1046 4.7 / F 1648 0.8 / 2310 4.6	**17** 0510 1.1 / 1130 4.4 / SA 1733 0.9 / 2355 4.3
3 0417 1.0 / 1044 4.3 / SA 1635 1.1 / ● 2251 4.3	**18** 0425 0.3 / 1043 4.8 / SU 1647 0.4 / ○ 2258 4.8	**3** 0418 0.8 / 1037 4.5 / M 1636 0.9 / ● 2248 4.4	**18** 0440 0.3 / 1057 4.9 / TU 1702 0.4 / 2313 4.7	**3** 0450 0.8 / 1107 4.6 / TH 1709 0.8 / 2325 4.6	**18** 0528 0.9 / 1146 4.5 / F 1750 0.9	**3** 0506 0.9 / 1128 4.7 / SA 1730 0.8 / 2353 4.6	**18** 0548 1.2 / 1207 4.3 / SU 1808 1.0
4 0451 0.8 / 1111 4.4 / SU 1709 0.9 / 2319 4.4	**19** 0508 0.2 / 1124 4.9 / M 1730 0.3 / 2339 4.8	**4** 0451 0.7 / 1105 4.5 / TU 1708 0.8 / 2317 4.5	**19** 0519 0.4 / 1135 4.8 / W 1740 0.5 / 2351 4.7	**4** 0524 0.9 / 1143 4.6 / F 1744 0.8	**19** 0008 4.4 / 0604 1.1 / SA 1224 4.4 / 1824 1.0	**4** 0549 1.0 / 1212 4.6 / SU 1815 0.9	**19** 0033 4.3 / 0624 1.3 / M 1245 4.3 / 1842 1.1
5 0524 0.7 / M 1740 0.8 / 2348 4.4	**20** 0548 0.1 / 1204 4.9 / TU 1809 0.3	**5** 0521 0.7 / 1135 4.5 / W 1737 0.8 / 2349 4.5	**20** 0555 0.6 / 1212 4.7 / TH 1816 0.7	**5** 0003 4.5 / 0559 1.0 / SA 1222 4.5 / 1821 1.0	**20** 0048 4.3 / 0639 1.3 / SU 1301 4.2 / 1858 1.3	**5** 0040 4.5 / 0635 1.1 / M 1259 4.5 / 1901 1.0	**20** 0112 4.2 / 0700 1.4 / TU 1322 4.2 / 1916 1.3
6 0553 0.7 / 1208 4.4 / TU 1808 0.9	**21** 0018 4.8 / 0625 0.3 / W 1243 4.7 / 1846 0.5	**6** 0550 0.8 / 1207 4.5 / TH 1806 0.8	**21** 0029 4.5 / 0629 0.8 / F 1249 4.5 / 1849 0.9	**6** 0045 4.4 / 0638 1.2 / SU 1304 4.4 / 1903 1.2	**21** 0129 4.1 / 0715 1.6 / M 1341 4.1 / 1934 1.5	**6** 0131 4.4 / 0725 1.3 / TU 1352 4.3 / 1954 1.2	**21** 0151 4.1 / 0737 1.6 / W 1402 4.0 / 1952 1.4
7 0018 4.4 / 0619 0.8 / W 1238 4.4 / 1833 0.9	**22** 0058 4.6 / 0700 0.6 / TH 1321 4.5 / 1920 0.8	**7** 0022 4.5 / 0618 0.9 / F 1241 4.5 / 1836 1.0	**22** 0108 4.3 / 0702 1.2 / SA 1325 4.3 / 1921 1.3	**7** 0131 4.3 / 0724 1.4 / M 1353 4.2 / 1953 1.4	**22** 0213 4.0 / 0757 1.9 / TU 1426 3.9 / 2017 1.7	**7** 0229 4.3 / 0823 1.5 / W 1451 4.2 / 2054 1.3	**22** 0233 4.0 / 0817 1.8 / TH 1444 3.9 / 2032 1.6
8 0049 4.3 / 0644 0.9 / TH 1310 4.3 / 1900 1.1	**23** 0136 4.4 / 0734 1.0 / F 1359 4.3 / 1954 1.2	**8** 0058 4.4 / 0650 1.1 / SA 1318 4.4 / 1911 1.2	**23** 0149 4.1 / 0736 1.6 / SU 1405 4.0 / 1958 1.6	**8** 0228 4.1 / 0822 1.7 / TU 1454 4.0 / 2058 1.7	**23** 0306 3.9 / 0851 2.1 / W 1520 3.7 / ◐ 2114 2.0	**8** 0333 4.2 / 0929 1.6 / TH 1557 4.1 / ◐ 2201 1.4	**23** 0319 3.9 / 0905 1.9 / F 1532 3.8 / ◐ 2122 1.8
9 0122 4.3 / 0713 1.1 / F 1343 4.3 / 1932 1.2	**24** 0217 4.1 / 0808 1.4 / SA 1439 4.0 / 2032 1.6	**9** 0138 4.2 / 0729 1.4 / SU 1400 4.2 / 1955 1.5	**24** 0235 3.9 / 0819 2.0 / M 1452 3.8 / 2046 2.0	**9** 0342 4.0 / 0940 1.9 / W 1614 3.9 / ◐ 2223 1.8	**24** 0409 3.8 / 1004 2.3 / TH 1627 3.6 / 2230 2.1	**9** 0444 4.1 / 1041 1.6 / F 1709 4.0 / 2311 1.5	**24** 0412 3.9 / 1002 2.0 / SA 1628 3.7 / 2223 1.9
10 0157 4.2 / 0747 1.3 / SA 1421 4.1 / 2012 1.5	**25** 0304 3.8 / 0850 1.9 / SU 1528 3.7 / ◐ 2124 2.0	**10** 0227 4.0 / 0819 1.7 / M 1455 4.0 / ◐ 2056 1.8	**25** 0337 3.7 / 0924 2.3 / TU 1558 3.6 / 2204 2.2	**10** 0510 4.0 / 1112 1.9 / TH 1742 3.9 / 2350 1.7	**25** 0521 3.8 / 1124 2.2 / F 1742 3.6 / 2345 2.0	**10** 0554 4.1 / 1151 1.6 / SA 1819 4.0	**25** 0512 3.8 / 1108 2.0 / SU 1734 3.7 / 2332 1.9
11 0240 4.0 / 0832 1.6 / SU 1511 4.0 / ◐ 2107 1.8	**26** 0409 3.6 / 0959 2.3 / M 1643 3.5 / 2255 2.3	**11** 0337 3.8 / 0934 2.0 / TU 1616 3.8 / 2229 2.0	**26** 0505 3.6 / 1109 2.4 / W 1732 3.6 / 2345 2.2	**11** 0631 4.1 / 1230 1.7 / F 1857 4.1	**26** 0629 3.9 / 1228 2.0 / SA 1850 3.8	**11** 0018 1.4 / 0658 4.2 / SU 1255 1.5 / 1923 4.1	**26** 0616 3.9 / 1215 1.9 / M 1842 3.7
12 0342 3.8 / 0937 2.0 / M 1623 3.8 / 2231 2.0	**27** 0554 3.5 / 1156 2.4 / TU 1832 3.5	**12** 0516 3.8 / 1124 2.1 / W 1758 3.8	**27** 0638 3.7 / 1236 2.3 / TH 1859 3.7	**12** 0058 1.4 / 0734 4.3 / SA 1332 1.4 / 1956 4.3	**27** 0046 1.8 / 0724 4.0 / SU 1320 1.8 / 1944 3.9	**12** 0118 1.3 / 0755 4.3 / M 1352 1.3 / 2019 4.2	**27** 0038 1.8 / 0716 4.0 / TU 1315 1.7 / 1944 3.9
13 0514 3.7 / 1120 2.1 / TU 1803 3.7	**28** 0042 2.2 / 0733 3.7 / W 1325 2.2 / 1953 3.7	**13** 0014 1.8 / 0652 4.0 / TH 1256 1.8 / 1922 4.0	**28** 0056 2.0 / 0739 3.9 / F 1331 2.0 / 1955 3.9	**13** 0155 1.1 / 0826 4.5 / SU 1424 1.1 / 2046 4.4	**28** 0136 1.6 / 0809 4.2 / M 1404 1.5 / 2029 4.1	**13** 0212 1.2 / 0845 4.4 / TU 1443 1.1 / 2109 4.3	**28** 0137 1.6 / 0811 4.2 / W 1410 1.5 / 2038 4.1
14 0022 1.9 / 0658 3.8 / W 1305 1.9 / 1934 4.0	**29** 0148 1.9 / 0830 4.0 / TH 1416 1.9 / 2042 4.0	**14** 0139 1.4 / 0801 4.3 / F 1400 1.4 / 2022 4.3	**29** 0146 1.7 / 0823 4.1 / SA 1413 1.7 / 2037 4.1	**14** 0243 0.9 / 0911 4.7 / M 1510 0.9 / 2130 4.5	**29** 0220 1.4 / 0849 4.4 / TU 1446 1.3 / 2109 4.3	**14** 0301 1.1 / 0931 4.5 / W 1530 1.0 / 2155 4.3	**29** 0230 1.4 / 0900 4.4 / TH 1500 1.2 / 2128 4.3
15 0146 1.6 / 0816 4.1 / TH 1417 1.5 / 2040 4.3	**30** 0232 1.6 / 0909 4.2 / F 1455 1.6 / 2119 4.1	**15** 0226 1.0 / 0853 4.6 / SA 1452 1.0 / 2111 4.6	**30** 0226 1.4 / 0858 4.3 / SU 1450 1.4 / 2111 4.2	**15** 0328 0.7 / 0952 4.7 / TU 1554 0.7 / 2211 4.6	**30** 0302 1.2 / 0928 4.5 / W 1527 1.1 / 2149 4.4	**15** 0346 1.1 / 1013 4.5 / TH 1614 1.0 / ○ 2237 4.3	**30** 0320 1.2 / 0947 4.5 / F 1549 1.0 / 2214 4.4
			31 0304 1.1 / 0930 4.4 / M 1526 1.1 / 2144 4.4				**31** 0408 1.0 / 1033 4.6 / SA 1637 0.8 / ● 2301 4.6

Chart Datum: 2·74 metres below Ordnance Datum (Newlyn)

》》 **FREE** monthly updates from 《《
www.reedsalmanac.co.uk

241

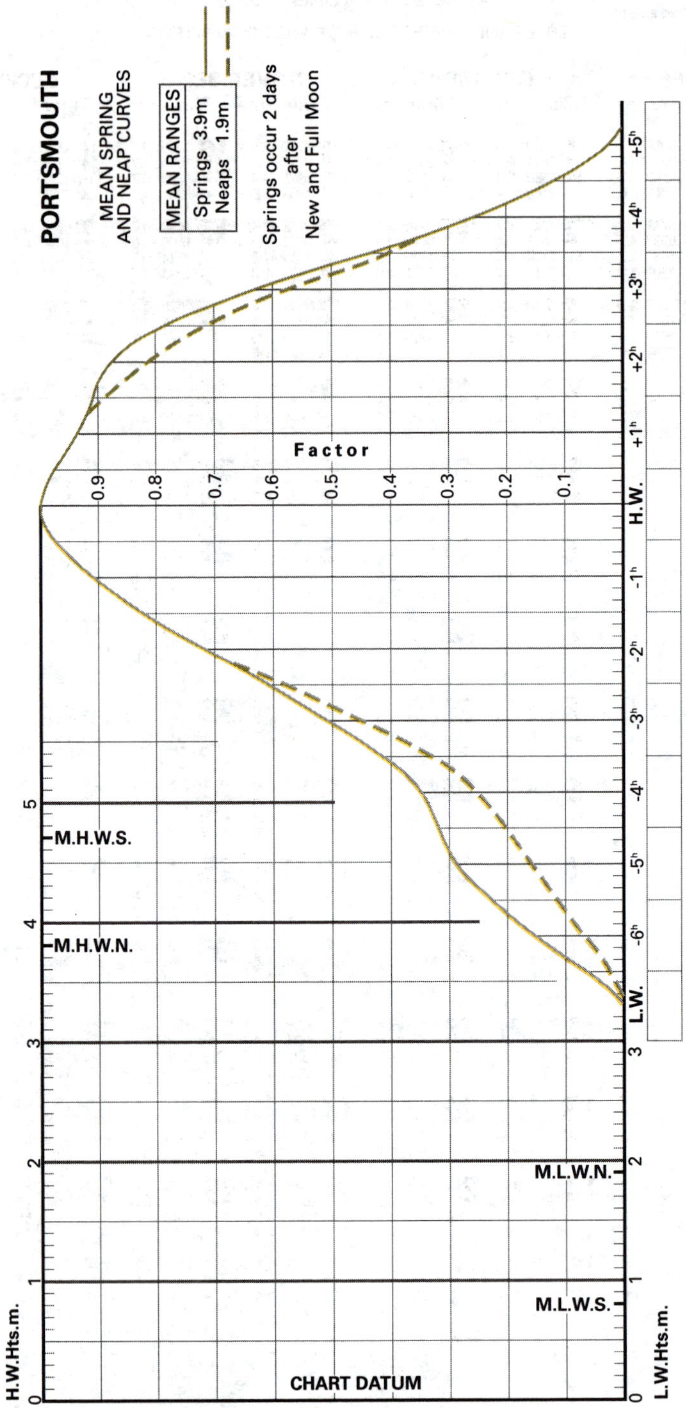
PORTSMOUTH
MEAN SPRING
AND NEAP CURVES
MEAN RANGES
Springs 3.9m
Neaps 1.9m
Springs occur 2 days
after
New and Full Moon
Factor
0.9
0.8
0.7
0.6
0.5
0.4
0.3
0.2
0.1
L.W.
-6h
-5h
-4h
-3h
-2h
-1h
H.W.
+1h
+2h
+3h
+4h
+5h
H.W.Hts.m.
0
1
2
3
4
5
M.H.W.S.
M.H.W.N.
CHART DATUM
L.W.Hts.m.
M.L.W.S.
M.L.W.N.

TIME ZONE (UT) For Summer Time add ONE hour in **non-shaded areas**	ENGLAND – PORTSMOUTH LAT 50°48′N LONG 1°07′W TIMES AND HEIGHTS OF HIGH AND LOW WATERS		YEAR 2005

JANUARY

Time m	Time m
1 0224 4.3 / 0743 1.6 / SA 1427 4.1 / 2003 1.4	**16** 0332 4.6 / 0856 1.2 / SU 1543 4.3 / 2118 1.1
2 0305 4.2 / 0824 1.7 / SU 1508 4.1 / 2045 1.5	**17** 0419 4.4 / 0947 1.5 / M 1632 4.1 / ◐ 2207 1.4
3 0350 4.2 / 0913 1.8 / M 1556 4.0 / ◐ 2136 1.6	**18** 0509 4.2 / 1044 1.7 / TU 1725 3.9 / 2303 1.7
4 0443 4.1 / 1011 1.9 / TU 1652 3.9 / 2236 1.7	**19** 0606 4.0 / 1150 1.9 / W 1831 3.7
5 0544 4.1 / 1118 1.9 / W 1800 3.9 / 2344 1.7	**20** 0011 1.9 / 0712 3.9 / TH 1302 1.9 / 1949 3.7
6 0653 4.2 / 1230 1.8 / TH 1917 4.0	**21** 0123 1.9 / 0819 4.0 / F 1405 1.8 / 2058 3.8
7 0055 1.6 / 0759 4.3 / F 1339 1.6 / 2028 4.2	**22** 0224 1.8 / 0916 4.1 / SA 1457 1.6 / 2152 4.0
8 0203 1.5 / 0859 4.5 / SA 1441 1.3 / 2132 4.4	**23** 0315 1.7 / 1002 4.2 / SU 1542 1.4 / 2235 4.2
9 0303 1.3 / 0955 4.7 / SU 1538 1.0 / 2229 4.6	**24** 0358 1.5 / 1041 4.3 / M 1622 1.3 / 2312 4.3
10 0359 1.1 / 1047 4.8 / M 1632 0.8 / ● 2324 4.8	**25** 0437 1.3 / 1117 4.4 / TU 1659 1.1 / ○ 2346 4.4
11 0452 1.0 / 1138 4.8 / TU 1723 0.7	**26** 0514 1.2 / 1151 4.4 / W 1735 1.0
12 0016 4.8 / 0543 0.9 / W 1229 4.8 / 1812 0.6	**27** 0020 4.4 / 0548 1.2 / TH 1226 4.4 / 1808 1.0
13 0107 4.9 / 0632 0.9 / TH 1319 4.8 / 1900 0.6	**28** 0054 4.4 / 0620 1.2 / F 1300 4.4 / 1838 1.0
14 0157 4.8 / 0720 0.9 / F 1408 4.6 / 1946 0.7	**29** 0127 4.4 / 0650 1.2 / SA 1333 4.3 / 1907 1.0
15 0245 4.7 / 0808 1.0 / SA 1456 4.5 / 2032 0.9	**30** 0200 4.4 / 0721 1.2 / SU 1407 4.3 / 1939 1.0
	31 0234 4.4 / 0755 1.3 / M 1442 4.2 / 2015 1.1

FEBRUARY

Time m	Time m
1 0312 4.3 / 0836 1.4 / TU 1523 4.1 / 2057 1.3	**16** 0412 4.1 / 0946 1.6 / W 1633 3.8 / ◐ 2207 1.8
2 0355 4.2 / 0925 1.6 / W 1612 4.0 / 2151 1.6	**17** 0459 3.9 / 1049 1.9 / TH 1732 3.6 / 2319 2.1
3 0451 4.1 / 1028 1.8 / TH 1718 3.9 / 2301 1.8	**18** 0607 3.7 / 1217 2.1 / F 1904 3.5
4 0605 4.0 / 1152 1.8 / F 1844 3.8	**19** 0051 2.2 / 0741 3.7 / SA 1339 2.0 / 2039 3.7
5 0029 1.8 / 0729 4.0 / SA 1324 1.7 / 2012 4.0	**20** 0207 2.0 / 0856 3.8 / SU 1438 1.7 / 2137 4.0
6 0155 1.7 / 0843 4.2 / SU 1437 1.4 / 2124 4.3	**21** 0301 1.7 / 0946 4.0 / M 1523 1.5 / 2219 4.2
7 0302 1.4 / 0945 4.5 / M 1536 1.0 / 2224 4.5	**22** 0343 1.5 / 1026 4.2 / TU 1602 1.2 / 2255 4.3
8 0358 1.1 / 1039 4.7 / TU 1628 0.7 / ● 2317 4.7	**23** 0420 1.2 / 1101 4.3 / W 1639 1.0 / 2328 4.4
9 0448 0.8 / 1130 4.8 / W 1716 0.5	**24** 0456 1.1 / 1135 4.3 / TH 1714 0.9 / ○ 2359 4.5
10 0006 4.9 / 0535 0.7 / TH 1219 4.8 / 1801 0.4	**25** 0529 0.9 / 1207 4.4 / F 1747 0.9
11 0052 4.9 / 0619 0.6 / F 1305 4.8 / 1844 0.4	**26** 0030 4.5 / 0559 0.9 / SA 1240 4.4 / 1816 0.8
12 0136 4.9 / 0702 0.6 / SA 1348 4.7 / 1924 0.5	**27** 0102 4.5 / 0627 0.9 / SU 1313 4.4 / 1844 0.8
13 0217 4.8 / 0742 0.8 / SU 1429 4.5 / 2001 0.8	**28** 0133 4.5 / 0657 0.9 / M 1346 4.4 / 1914 0.9
14 0255 4.6 / 0820 1.0 / M 1509 4.3 / 2038 1.1	
15 0333 4.4 / 0900 1.3 / TU 1549 4.1 / 2118 1.4	

MARCH

Time m	Time m
1 0205 4.5 / 0729 1.0 / TU 1420 4.4 / 1948 1.0	**16** 0249 4.4 / 0817 1.2 / W 1512 4.1 / 2035 1.5
2 0240 4.4 / 0807 1.1 / W 1459 4.2 / 2029 1.3	**17** 0324 4.1 / 0855 1.6 / TH 1555 3.9 / ◐ 2120 1.9
3 0321 4.2 / 0853 1.4 / TH 1548 4.0 / ◐ 2121 1.6	**18** 0408 3.8 / 0950 1.9 / F 1651 3.6 / 2234 2.2
4 0415 4.0 / 0956 1.7 / F 1656 3.8 / 2237 1.9	**19** 0511 3.5 / 1130 2.2 / SA 1820 3.5
5 0533 3.8 / 1134 1.9 / SA 1830 3.8	**20** 0022 2.3 / 0654 3.5 / SU 1308 2.1 / 2013 3.7
6 0026 2.0 / 0710 3.8 / SU 1322 1.7 / 2008 3.9	**21** 0146 2.1 / 0831 3.7 / M 1411 1.8 / 2111 4.0
7 0157 1.7 / 0835 4.1 / M 1434 1.3 / 2120 4.3	**22** 0239 1.8 / 0922 3.9 / TU 1455 1.5 / 2152 4.2
8 0300 1.3 / 0937 4.4 / TU 1528 1.0 / 2215 4.6	**23** 0319 1.6 / 1001 4.1 / W 1534 1.2 / 2226 4.3
9 0351 1.0 / 1029 4.6 / W 1616 0.6 / 2303 4.8	**24** 0355 1.1 / 1035 4.2 / TH 1610 0.9 / 2258 4.4
10 0437 0.7 / 1116 4.7 / TH 1700 0.4 / ● 2347 4.9	**25** 0429 0.9 / 1108 4.3 / F 1645 0.8 / ○ 2329 4.5
11 0519 0.5 / 1201 4.7 / F 1741 0.4	**26** 0501 0.8 / 1142 4.4 / SA 1717 0.8
12 0028 4.9 / 0559 0.4 / SA 1243 4.8 / 1820 0.4	**27** 0001 4.5 / 0531 0.7 / SU 1216 4.5 / 1748 0.7
13 0107 4.9 / 0637 0.5 / SU 1322 4.6 / 1855 0.5	**28** 0033 4.6 / 0602 0.7 / M 1250 4.5 / 1818 0.7
14 0143 4.8 / 0711 0.7 / M 1400 4.6 / 1928 0.8	**29** 0106 4.6 / 0633 0.7 / TU 1326 4.5 / 1851 0.8
15 0217 4.6 / 0744 0.9 / TU 1436 4.4 / 2000 1.1	**30** 0140 4.5 / 0708 0.8 / W 1403 4.4 / 1928 1.0
	31 0217 4.3 / 0747 1.0 / TH 1446 4.3 / 2011 1.3

APRIL

Time m	Time m
1 0300 4.2 / 0836 1.4 / F 1540 4.0 / 2109 1.7	**16** 0331 3.8 / 0911 1.9 / SA 1621 3.7 / ◐ 2157 2.2
2 0358 3.9 / 0945 1.7 / SA 1652 3.8 / ◐ 2236 1.9	**17** 0430 3.6 / 1040 2.1 / SU 1739 3.6 / 2341 2.3
3 0520 3.7 / 1132 1.8 / SU 1830 3.8	**18** 0556 3.4 / 1221 2.1 / M 1919 3.7
4 0025 1.9 / 0701 3.8 / M 1312 1.8 / 2001 4.0	**19** 0105 2.1 / 0736 3.6 / TU 1329 1.8 / 2024 3.9
5 0148 1.6 / 0824 4.0 / TU 1418 1.3 / 2105 4.4	**20** 0200 1.8 / 0836 3.8 / W 1416 1.5 / 2107 4.1
6 0246 1.2 / 0922 4.3 / W 1510 0.9 / 2156 4.6	**21** 0242 1.5 / 0918 4.0 / TH 1456 1.2 / 2144 4.3
7 0333 0.9 / 1011 4.5 / TH 1554 0.6 / 2241 4.8	**22** 0318 1.2 / 0956 4.1 / F 1532 1.0 / 2219 4.4
8 0416 0.6 / 1056 4.7 / F 1636 0.5 / ● 2322 4.9	**23** 0353 1.0 / 1033 4.3 / SA 1608 0.9 / 2254 4.5
9 0456 0.5 / 1138 4.7 / SA 1715 0.5	**24** 0427 0.8 / 1111 4.4 / SU 1643 0.8 / ○ 2329 4.6
10 0001 4.9 / 0534 0.5 / SU 1218 4.7 / 1751 0.5	**25** 0501 0.7 / 1150 4.5 / M 1718 0.7
11 0037 4.8 / 0609 0.6 / M 1255 4.7 / 1824 0.7	**26** 0006 4.7 / 0536 0.7 / TU 1230 4.6 / 1754 0.8
12 0110 4.7 / 0642 0.7 / TU 1331 4.5 / 1856 0.9	**27** 0043 4.7 / 0614 0.7 / W 1310 4.6 / 1834 0.9
13 0142 4.5 / 0712 0.9 / W 1406 4.4 / 1928 1.2	**28** 0122 4.6 / 0655 0.8 / TH 1354 4.5 / 1917 1.1
14 0214 4.3 / 0744 1.2 / TH 1443 4.2 / 2003 1.5	**29** 0205 4.4 / 0741 1.0 / F 1443 4.3 / 2008 1.3
15 0248 4.1 / 0821 1.6 / F 1526 3.9 / 2048 1.9	**30** 0254 4.2 / 0837 1.2 / SA 1543 4.1 / 2113 1.6

Chart Datum: 2·73 metres below Ordnance Datum (Newlyn)

》》 **FREE** monthly updates from 《《
www.reedsalmanac.co.uk

TIDES

TIME ZONE (UT)
For Summer Time add ONE hour in **non-shaded areas**

ENGLAND – PORTSMOUTH
LAT 50°48′N LONG 1°07′W
TIMES AND HEIGHTS OF HIGH AND LOW WATERS

YEAR 2005

	MAY			JUNE			JULY			AUGUST	
	Time m	Time m		Time m	Time m		Time m	Time m		Time m	Time m
1 SU	0357 4.0 0951 1.5 1656 4.0 ◐ 2236 1.8	**16** M	0358 3.7 0951 1.9 1658 3.8 ● 2240 2.2	**1** W	0618 4.0 1204 1.4 1905 4.3	**16** TH	0518 3.8 1104 1.7 1809 4.0 2345 1.9	**1** F	0645 3.9 1223 1.5 1924 4.2	**16** SA	0528 3.9 1107 1.7 1811 4.0 2351 1.8	**1** M	0139 1.8 0837 3.8 1403 1.9 2057 4.0	**16** TU	0049 1.8 0742 3.9 1325 1.9 2011 4.1
2 M	0516 3.8 1121 1.6 1823 4.0	**17** TU	0505 3.6 1113 2.0 1809 3.8	**2** TH	0041 1.5 0726 4.0 1309 1.3 2004 4.4	**17** F	0623 3.8 1207 1.7 1910 4.1	**2** SA	0103 1.5 0752 3.9 1327 1.6 2023 4.2	**17** SU	0642 3.9 1219 1.7 1922 4.1	**2** TU	0239 1.6 0938 4.0 1459 1.7 2150 4.1	**17** W	0209 1.5 0858 4.2 1435 1.6 2117 4.4
3 TU	0005 1.7 0646 3.9 1245 1.5 1939 4.2	**18** W	0001 2.1 0620 3.6 1225 1.8 1916 3.9	**3** F	0142 1.3 0826 4.1 1405 1.2 2057 4.4	**18** SA	0047 1.7 0729 3.9 1307 1.6 2006 4.2	**3** SU	0204 1.5 0854 4.0 1424 1.5 2118 4.2	**18** M	0105 1.6 0759 4.0 1333 1.6 2029 4.2	**3** W	0327 1.4 1025 4.2 1545 1.5 2232 4.2	**18** TH	0309 1.1 0959 4.5 1532 1.2 2212 4.6
4 W	0120 1.5 0800 4.1 1349 1.2 2039 4.4	**19** TH	0103 1.9 0729 3.7 1320 1.6 2009 4.1	**4** SA	0234 1.2 0919 4.2 1453 1.1 2145 4.5	**19** SU	0143 1.5 0830 4.1 1402 1.4 2059 4.4	**4** M	0257 1.4 0949 4.1 1515 1.5 2205 4.3	**19** TU	0214 1.4 0907 4.2 1438 1.4 2129 4.4	**4** TH	0408 1.2 1105 4.3 1626 1.4 2308 4.3	**19** F	0401 0.8 1052 4.7 1623 0.9 ○ 2303 4.7
5 TH	0218 1.2 0857 4.3 1441 1.0 2129 4.6	**20** F	0151 1.6 0824 3.9 1405 1.4 2055 4.3	**5** SU	0321 1.1 1008 4.3 1538 1.1 2228 4.5	**20** M	0235 1.3 0926 4.3 1454 1.2 2149 4.5	**5** TU	0343 1.3 1037 4.2 1600 1.4 2247 4.3	**20** W	0313 1.1 1007 4.4 1536 1.2 2223 4.6	**5** F	0447 1.1 1140 4.4 1703 1.2 ● 2341 4.3	**20** SA	0450 0.5 1141 4.9 1710 0.7 2351 4.8
6 F	0306 1.0 0946 4.4 1525 0.8 2214 4.7	**21** SA	0232 1.3 0911 4.1 1447 1.2 2137 4.4	**6** M	0404 1.0 1052 4.4 1620 1.1 ● 2307 4.5	**21** TU	0325 1.0 1020 4.4 1546 1.1 2238 4.6	**6** W	0426 1.2 1118 4.3 1641 1.3 ● 2324 4.4	**21** TH	0408 0.9 1102 4.6 1630 1.0 ○ 2315 4.7	**6** SA	0523 1.0 1213 4.4 1739 1.1	**21** SU	0536 0.4 1227 5.0 1756 0.6
7 SA	0349 0.8 1031 4.5 1607 0.7 2255 4.7	**22** SU	0312 1.1 0956 4.3 1527 1.0 2219 4.5	**7** TU	0444 1.0 1133 4.4 1659 1.1 2343 4.5	**22** W	0416 0.9 1112 4.6 1637 1.0 ○ 2327 4.7	**7** TH	0505 1.1 1156 4.4 1720 1.3 2358 4.4	**22** F	0500 0.7 1155 4.8 1722 0.8	**7** SU	0014 4.3 0556 0.9 1245 4.4 1811 1.1	**22** M	0037 4.8 0619 0.4 1312 5.0 1839 0.6
8 SU	0430 0.7 1114 4.6 1646 0.7 ● 2333 4.7	**23** M	0352 0.9 1042 4.5 1609 0.9 ○ 2301 4.6	**8** W	0522 1.0 1211 4.4 1736 1.2	**23** TH	0506 0.7 1203 4.7 1729 0.9	**8** F	0542 1.1 1231 4.4 1757 1.3	**23** SA	0006 4.7 0550 0.5 1246 4.9 1811 0.7	**8** M	0047 4.3 0627 0.9 1317 4.4 1841 1.1	**23** TU	0123 4.8 0701 0.5 1355 4.9 1920 0.7
9 M	0508 0.7 1153 4.6 1723 0.8	**24** TU	0433 0.8 1127 4.6 1652 0.9 2343 4.7	**9** TH	0017 4.5 0558 1.0 1247 4.4 1812 1.2	**24** F	0016 4.7 0557 0.7 1255 4.7 1820 0.9	**9** SA	0032 4.3 0617 1.1 1306 4.4 1832 1.3	**24** SU	0056 4.7 0638 0.5 1335 4.9 1859 0.7	**9** TU	0120 4.3 0655 1.0 1349 4.4 1909 1.2	**24** W	0205 4.7 0741 0.7 1435 4.7 2001 0.9
10 TU	0008 4.7 0543 0.8 1231 4.5 1757 0.9	**25** W	0517 0.7 1213 4.6 1737 0.9	**10** F	0051 4.4 0632 1.1 1324 4.3 1848 1.4	**25** SA	0106 4.7 0648 0.7 1347 4.7 1911 0.9	**10** SU	0108 4.3 0649 1.1 1342 4.3 1905 1.3	**25** M	0145 4.7 0725 0.5 1423 4.8 1946 0.8	**10** W	0152 4.3 0723 1.1 1420 4.3 1940 1.2	**25** TH	0247 4.5 0819 1.0 1514 4.5 2041 1.2
11 W	0041 4.6 0617 0.9 1307 4.5 1831 1.1	**26** TH	0027 4.7 0602 0.7 1301 4.7 1824 0.9	**11** SA	0126 4.3 0706 1.3 1402 4.2 1924 1.5	**26** SU	0157 4.6 0739 0.7 1440 4.6 2003 1.0	**11** M	0143 4.2 0721 1.2 1418 4.3 1938 1.4	**26** TU	0233 4.6 0810 0.7 1509 4.7 2032 0.9	**11** TH	0225 4.2 0754 1.2 1453 4.3 2016 1.4	**26** F	0329 4.2 0900 1.3 1553 4.2 ◑ 2126 1.5
12 TH	0113 4.5 0649 1.1 1343 4.4 1905 1.3	**27** F	0113 4.6 0651 0.8 1351 4.6 1915 1.0	**12** SU	0203 4.1 0742 1.4 1443 4.2 2003 1.7	**27** M	0250 4.5 0831 0.8 1534 4.6 2057 1.1	**12** TU	0219 4.1 0753 1.3 1455 4.2 2013 1.5	**27** W	0320 4.4 0855 0.9 1554 4.4 2120 1.2	**12** F	0302 4.1 0832 1.4 1530 4.2 2059 1.5	**27** SA	0415 3.9 0949 1.7 1639 4.0 2226 1.9
13 F	0147 4.3 0722 1.3 1421 4.2 1941 1.6	**28** SA	0201 4.5 0743 1.0 1445 4.5 2010 1.2	**13** M	0243 4.0 0821 1.5 1527 4.1 2047 1.8	**28** TU	0345 4.3 0925 1.0 1628 4.5 ◑ 2153 1.3	**13** W	0257 4.1 0829 1.4 1533 4.2 2054 1.6	**28** TH	0407 4.2 0942 1.2 1640 4.3 ◑ 2212 1.4	**13** SA	0347 4.0 0920 1.7 1618 4.1 ◑ 2155 1.7	**28** SU	0514 3.7 1058 2.1 1742 3.7 2350 2.1
14 SA	0223 4.1 0759 1.5 1504 4.0 2025 1.8	**29** SU	0255 4.3 0841 1.1 1545 4.4 2111 1.4	**14** TU	0328 3.9 0907 1.7 1616 4.0 2140 2.0	**29** W	0441 4.2 1021 1.2 1724 4.3 2253 1.4	**14** TH	0338 4.0 0912 1.5 1616 4.1 ◑ 2142 1.7	**29** F	0458 4.0 1035 1.5 1732 4.1 2313 1.7	**14** SU	0447 3.9 1024 1.9 1723 4.0 2312 1.9	**29** M	0649 3.6 1224 2.1 1923 3.7
15 SU	0305 3.9 0846 1.7 1555 3.9 2122 2.1	**30** M	0356 4.3 0945 1.3 1650 4.3 ◑ 2219 1.5	**15** W	0419 3.8 1002 1.7 1710 4.0 ◐ 2240 1.9	**30** TH	0540 4.1 1120 1.4 1823 4.2	**15** F	0427 3.9 1004 1.6 1707 4.0 ◐ 2240 1.9	**30** SA	0559 3.8 1139 1.8 1836 3.9	**15** M	0609 3.8 1152 2.0 1848 3.9	**30** TU	0119 2.0 0827 3.8 1349 2.1 2044 3.8
		31 TU	0505 4.0 1054 1.4 1759 4.2 2331 1.5							**31** SU	0025 1.8 0718 3.7 1254 1.9 1950 3.9			**31** W	0231 1.8 0925 4.0 1445 1.8 2136 4.1

Chart Datum: 2·73 metres below Ordnance Datum (Newlyn)

》》 **FREE** monthly updates from 《《
www.reedsalmanac.co.uk

ENGLAND – PORTSMOUTH

LAT 50°48′N   LONG 1°07′W

TIME ZONE (UT) For Summer Time add ONE hour in **non-shaded areas**

YEAR 2005

TIMES AND HEIGHTS OF HIGH AND LOW WATERS

SEPTEMBER

Day	Time m	Day	Time m
1 TH	0309 1.5 / 1009 4.2 / 1528 1.6 / 2215 4.2	**16** F	0300 1.1 / 0946 4.6 / 1521 1.1 / 2159 4.6
2 F	0347 1.2 / 1045 4.4 / 1605 1.3 / 2249 4.3	**17** SA	0347 0.7 / 1034 4.8 / 1607 0.8 / 2246 4.8
3 SA	0423 1.0 / 1117 4.5 / 1640 1.1 / 2320 4.4	**18** SU	0431 0.5 / 1119 5.0 / 1651 0.6 / ○ 2330 4.9
4 SU	0458 0.9 / 1147 4.5 / 1714 1.0 / 2350 4.4	**19** M	0514 0.4 / 1202 5.0 / 1733 0.5
5 M	0531 0.8 / 1216 4.5 / 1745 1.0	**20** TU	0014 4.9 / 0553 0.4 / 1243 5.0 / 1812 0.5
6 TU	0021 4.4 / 0559 0.8 / 1247 4.5 / 1812 1.0	**21** W	0056 4.8 / 0631 0.5 / 1322 4.9 / 1850 0.7
7 W	0053 4.4 / 0626 0.9 / 1316 4.5 / 1839 1.0	**22** TH	0135 4.7 / 0707 0.8 / 1358 4.7 / 1926 0.9
8 TH	0124 4.4 / 0653 1.0 / 1346 4.5 / 1909 1.1	**23** F	0214 4.5 / 0742 1.1 / 1433 4.5 / 2002 1.2
9 F	0157 4.4 / 0723 1.1 / 1418 4.4 / 1943 1.3	**24** SA	0253 4.3 / 0819 1.5 / 1510 4.2 / 2043 1.6
10 SA	0233 4.2 / 0800 1.4 / 1455 4.2 / 2025 1.5	**25** SU	0337 4.0 / 0907 1.9 / 1553 3.9 / ◐ 2139 2.0
11 SU	0318 4.1 / 0847 1.7 / 1543 4.0 / ◐ 2122 1.8	**26** M	0436 3.7 / 1022 2.3 / 1655 3.6 / 2313 2.2
12 M	0422 3.8 / 0958 2.0 / 1653 3.9 / 2253 2.0	**27** TU	0616 3.6 / 1206 2.4 / 1850 3.6
13 TU	0554 3.7 / 1149 2.2 / 1829 3.8	**28** W	0052 2.2 / 0805 3.8 / 1328 2.2 / 2023 3.8
14 W	0048 1.9 / 0737 3.9 / 1325 1.9 / 2002 4.1	**29** TH	0158 1.9 / 0900 4.1 / 1422 1.9 / 2112 4.0
15 TH	0205 1.5 / 0851 4.3 / 1430 1.5 / 2107 4.4	**30** F	0241 1.6 / 0939 4.3 / 1501 1.6 / 2148 4.2

OCTOBER

Day	Time m	Day	Time m
1 SA	0318 1.3 / 1013 4.4 / 1536 1.3 / 2220 4.3	**16** SU	0324 0.8 / 1010 4.9 / 1544 0.8 / 2224 4.8
2 SU	0353 1.0 / 1043 4.5 / 1610 1.1 / 2250 4.4	**17** M	0406 0.6 / 1053 5.0 / 1626 0.7 / ○ 2307 4.9
3 M	0426 0.9 / 1113 4.6 / 1642 1.0 / ● 2321 4.5	**18** TU	0447 0.5 / 1134 5.0 / 1706 0.6 / 2349 4.9
4 TU	0458 0.9 / 1143 4.6 / 1713 0.9 / 2353 4.5	**19** W	0525 0.6 / 1213 4.9 / 1745 0.7
5 W	0528 0.9 / 1213 4.6 / 1741 0.9	**20** TH	0029 4.8 / 0601 0.8 / 1250 4.8 / 1820 0.8
6 TH	0025 4.6 / 0556 0.9 / 1245 4.6 / 1810 1.0	**21** F	0108 4.7 / 0636 1.0 / 1324 4.7 / 1855 1.1
7 F	0100 4.6 / 0625 1.0 / 1317 4.5 / 1843 1.1	**22** SA	0145 4.5 / 0711 1.3 / 1358 4.4 / 1930 1.3
8 SA	0135 4.5 / 0659 1.2 / 1352 4.4 / 1920 1.2	**23** SU	0224 4.3 / 0748 1.6 / 1434 4.2 / 2010 1.7
9 SU	0215 4.3 / 0740 1.5 / 1432 4.3 / 2006 1.5	**24** M	0308 4.0 / 0836 2.0 / 1517 3.9 / 2102 2.0
10 M	0305 4.1 / 0833 1.8 / 1525 4.0 / ◐ 2109 1.8	**25** TU	0405 3.8 / 0947 2.3 / 1616 3.7 / ◐ 2226 2.2
11 TU	0416 3.9 / 0956 2.1 / 1641 3.8 / 2250 2.0	**26** W	0528 3.7 / 1126 2.4 / 1743 3.6
12 W	0550 3.8 / 1146 2.1 / 1819 3.8	**27** TH	0003 2.2 / 0712 3.8 / 1248 2.2 / 1930 3.7
13 TH	0035 1.8 / 0727 4.1 / 1312 1.8 / 1948 4.1	**28** F	0113 2.0 / 0813 4.0 / 1343 2.0 / 2026 3.9
14 F	0146 1.5 / 0833 4.4 / 1412 1.4 / 2049 4.4	**29** SA	0200 1.7 / 0854 4.2 / 1424 1.7 / 2105 4.1
15 SA	0239 1.1 / 0924 4.7 / 1500 1.1 / 2139 4.6	**30** SU	0239 1.4 / 0929 4.4 / 1500 1.4 / 2140 4.3
		31 M	0315 1.2 / 1002 4.5 / 1534 1.2 / 2214 4.4

NOVEMBER

Day	Time m	Day	Time m
1 TU	0349 1.1 / 1035 4.6 / 1607 1.1 / 2249 4.5	**16** W	0420 0.9 / 1107 4.9 / 1643 0.8 / ○ 2328 4.7
2 W	0422 1.0 / 1109 4.6 / 1639 1.0 / ● 2326 4.6	**17** TH	0459 0.9 / 1146 4.8 / 1721 0.9
3 TH	0455 1.0 / 1143 4.7 / 1713 0.9	**18** F	0008 4.7 / 0536 1.0 / 1222 4.7 / 1758 1.0
4 F	0003 4.7 / 0529 1.0 / 1220 4.7 / 1748 0.9	**19** SA	0046 4.6 / 0612 1.2 / 1257 4.6 / 1833 1.2
5 SA	0042 4.7 / 0606 1.1 / 1257 4.6 / 1827 1.0	**20** SU	0123 4.5 / 0649 1.4 / 1331 4.4 / 1909 1.4
6 SU	0123 4.6 / 0647 1.3 / 1337 4.5 / 1911 1.2	**21** M	0202 4.3 / 0727 1.7 / 1408 4.2 / 1948 1.6
7 M	0210 4.4 / 0736 1.5 / 1423 4.3 / 2004 1.4	**22** TU	0246 4.1 / 0812 2.0 / 1450 4.0 / 2034 1.8
8 TU	0306 4.2 / 0837 1.8 / 1522 4.1 / 2112 1.7	**23** W	0336 4.0 / 0908 2.2 / 1541 3.8 / ◐ 2133 2.0
9 W	0417 4.1 / 0957 1.9 / 1635 4.0 / ◐ 2237 1.8	**24** TH	0438 3.9 / 1023 2.3 / 1644 3.7 / 2249 2.1
10 TH	0541 4.1 / 1125 1.9 / 1802 4.0	**25** F	0549 3.9 / 1142 2.3 / 1758 3.7
11 F	0002 1.7 / 0701 4.2 / 1242 1.7 / 1921 4.1	**26** SA	0002 2.0 / 0657 4.0 / 1246 2.1 / 1909 3.8
12 SA	0113 1.4 / 0804 4.5 / 1343 1.4 / 2022 4.3	**27** SU	0101 1.9 / 0751 4.2 / 1334 1.9 / 2006 3.9
13 SU	0208 1.2 / 0856 4.7 / 1433 1.2 / 2114 4.5	**28** M	0148 1.7 / 0837 4.3 / 1416 1.6 / 2054 4.1
14 M	0255 1.0 / 0943 4.8 / 1519 1.0 / 2201 4.7	**29** TU	0230 1.5 / 0919 4.5 / 1454 1.4 / 2138 4.3
15 TU	0339 0.9 / 1027 4.9 / 1602 0.9 / 2246 4.7	**30** W	0309 1.3 / 0959 4.6 / 1532 1.2 / 2221 4.5

DECEMBER

Day	Time m	Day	Time m
1 TH	0348 1.2 / 1039 4.7 / 1612 1.0 / ● 2304 4.6	**16** F	0440 1.2 / 1125 4.6 / 1706 1.1 / 2353 4.5
2 F	0429 1.1 / 1120 4.7 / 1653 0.9 / 2347 4.7	**17** SA	0519 1.2 / 1201 4.6 / 1744 1.1
3 SA	0511 1.1 / 1201 4.7 / 1737 0.9	**18** SU	0031 4.5 / 0557 1.3 / 1237 4.5 / 1819 1.2
4 SU	0032 4.7 / 0556 1.1 / 1245 4.7 / 1823 0.9	**19** M	0108 4.5 / 0633 1.4 / 1312 4.4 / 1855 1.3
5 M	0120 4.7 / 0645 1.2 / 1331 4.6 / 1913 1.0	**20** TU	0145 4.4 / 0710 1.6 / 1348 4.2 / 1930 1.4
6 TU	0211 4.6 / 0737 1.5 / 1422 4.4 / 2007 1.2	**21** W	0224 4.3 / 0747 1.7 / 1427 4.1 / 2006 1.5
7 W	0307 4.5 / 0836 1.5 / 1519 4.3 / 2106 1.3	**22** TH	0306 4.2 / 0828 1.8 / 1508 4.0 / 2047 1.7
8 TH	0410 4.4 / 0941 1.6 / 1623 4.1 / ◐ 2211 1.4	**23** F	0352 4.1 / 0915 2.0 / 1555 3.8 / ◐ 2135 1.8
9 F	0517 4.3 / 1051 1.7 / 1732 4.0 / 2320 1.5	**24** SA	0443 4.0 / 1012 2.1 / 1648 3.8 / 2232 1.9
10 SA	0625 4.3 / 1202 1.6 / 1844 4.1	**25** SU	0542 3.8 / 1117 2.1 / 1752 3.8 / 2336 1.9
11 SU	0028 1.5 / 0728 4.4 / 1307 1.5 / 1949 4.2	**26** M	0644 4.0 / 1224 2.0 / 1902 3.8
12 M	0130 1.4 / 0825 4.5 / 1405 1.3 / 2048 4.3	**27** TU	0042 1.8 / 0745 4.2 / 1325 1.8 / 2008 4.0
13 TU	0225 1.3 / 0916 4.6 / 1455 1.2 / 2141 4.5	**28** W	0142 1.7 / 0839 4.3 / 1418 1.6 / 2106 4.2
14 W	0314 1.2 / 1003 4.6 / 1542 1.2 / 2230 4.5	**29** TH	0235 1.5 / 0930 4.5 / 1507 1.3 / 2159 4.4
15 TH	0358 1.2 / 1046 4.6 / 1625 1.1 / ○ 2313 4.5	**30** F	0325 1.3 / 1017 4.6 / 1556 1.1 / 2249 4.6
		31 SA	0415 1.2 / 1104 4.7 / 1644 0.9 / ● 2338 4.7

Chart Datum: 2·73 metres below Ordnance Datum (Newlyn)

》》 **FREE** monthly updates from 《《
www.reedsalmanac.co.uk

TIDES

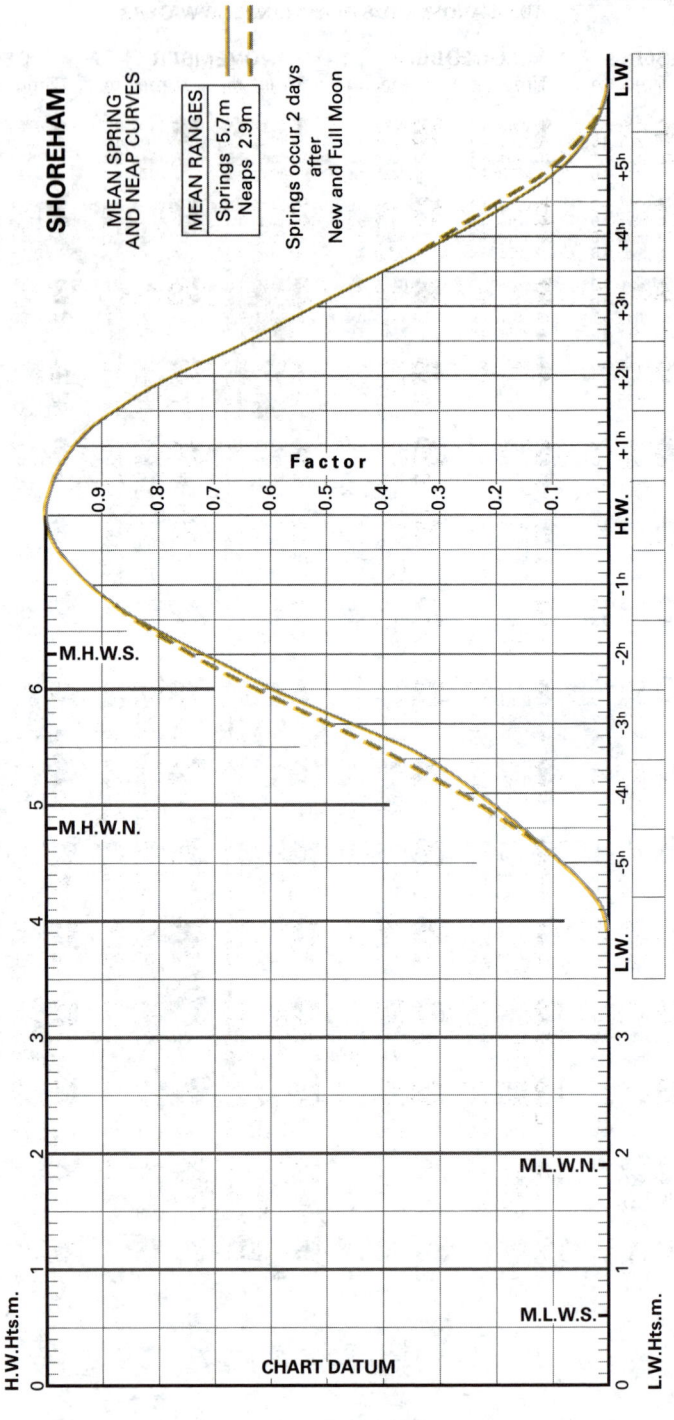

ENGLAND - SHOREHAM
LAT 50°50'N   LONG 0°15'W
TIMES AND HEIGHTS OF HIGH AND LOW WATERS

TIME ZONE (UT) For Summer Time add ONE hour in **non-shaded areas**

YEAR 2005

JANUARY		FEBRUARY		MARCH		APRIL	
Time m	Time m	Time m	Time m	Time m	Time m	Time m	Time m
1 0211 5.6 0824 1.5 SA 1420 5.4 2043 1.5	**16** 0323 6.1 0934 1.2 SU 1540 5.7 2157 1.1	**1** 0258 5.7 0910 1.4 TU 1513 5.5 2130 1.4	**16** 0407 5.4 1020 1.7 W 1632 5.0 ◐ 2241 1.8	**1** 0153 6.0 0802 0.9 TU 1407 5.9 2019 1.0	**16** 0243 5.7 0853 1.2 W 1503 5.4 2110 1.4	**1** 0250 5.5 0912 1.4 F 1520 5.3 2142 1.7	**16** 0322 4.8 0948 1.9 SA 1618 4.6 ◐ 2223 2.2
2 0249 5.5 0904 1.7 SU 1501 5.3 2124 1.6	**17** 0409 5.7 1025 1.4 M 1629 5.3 ◐ 2248 1.4	**2** 0342 5.5 1000 1.6 W 1604 5.2 ◐ 2223 1.6	**17** 0500 4.9 1117 2.0 TH 1736 4.6 2349 2.2	**2** 0228 5.9 0840 1.1 W 1446 5.7 2100 1.2	**17** 0316 5.3 0931 1.6 TH 1547 5.0 ◐ 2154 1.9	**2** 0348 5.0 1021 1.7 SA 1638 4.8 ◐ 2306 2.0	**17** 0437 4.4 1058 2.2 SU 1737 4.5 2348 2.4
3 0333 5.3 0952 1.8 M 1550 5.1 ◐ 2213 1.7	**18** 0459 5.4 1122 1.7 TU 1725 5.0 2346 1.8	**3** 0439 5.2 1104 1.8 TH 1710 5.0 2334 1.9	**18** 0609 4.6 1251 2.2 F 1855 4.4	**3** 0310 5.6 0927 1.4 TH 1534 5.3 ◐ 2153 1.6	**18** 0402 4.8 1023 2.0 F 1652 4.5 2256 2.3	**3** 0524 4.7 1200 1.9 SU 1828 4.7	**18** 0606 4.3 1238 2.2 M 1857 4.6
4 0427 5.2 1050 1.8 TU 1650 5.0 2313 1.8	**19** 0557 5.1 1229 1.9 W 1829 4.8	**4** 0557 5.0 1228 1.9 F 1843 4.9	**19** 0135 2.3 0730 4.6 SA 1418 2.1 2031 4.6	**4** 0404 5.2 1031 1.7 F 1640 4.9 2308 2.0	**19** 0521 4.4 1140 2.3 SA 1815 4.3	**4** 0056 2.0 0710 4.8 M 1340 1.7 2002 5.1	**19** 0135 2.2 0726 4.5 TU 1401 2.0 2011 4.9
5 0533 5.2 1157 1.8 W 1804 5.0	**20** 0057 2.0 0702 5.0 TH 1340 1.9 1944 4.8	**5** 0106 1.9 0727 5.1 SA 1355 1.7 2010 5.1	**20** 0247 2.1 0855 4.8 SU 1515 1.8 2135 5.0	**5** 0526 4.8 1204 2.0 SA 1829 4.7	**20** 0048 2.5 0648 4.3 SU 1344 2.2 1952 4.5	**5** 0218 1.6 0831 5.2 TU 1446 1.2 2107 5.6	**20** 0232 1.9 0831 4.9 W 1450 1.6 2101 5.3
6 0023 1.8 0647 5.2 TH 1309 1.7 1920 5.1	**21** 0208 2.0 0814 5.0 F 1442 1.8 2056 4.9	**6** 0230 1.7 0842 5.4 SU 1506 1.3 2121 5.5	**21** 0339 1.7 0948 5.2 M 1600 1.4 2218 5.4	**6** 0056 2.1 0715 4.8 SU 1348 1.8 2007 5.0	**21** 0221 2.2 0825 4.6 M 1447 1.9 2107 4.9	**6** 0314 1.1 0929 5.7 W 1537 0.8 2158 6.1	**21** 0314 1.5 0916 5.2 TH 1530 1.3 2140 5.6
7 0136 1.7 0754 5.5 F 1415 1.5 2027 5.4	**22** 0307 1.8 0916 5.2 SA 1535 1.6 2150 5.2	**7** 0335 1.3 0945 5.8 M 1604 0.9 2221 5.9	**22** 0420 1.4 1028 5.5 TU 1638 1.2 2254 5.7	**7** 0227 1.7 0839 5.2 M 1500 1.3 2120 5.5	**22** 0313 1.8 0922 5.0 TU 1532 1.5 2149 5.4	**7** 0401 0.7 1017 6.1 TH 1622 0.5 2242 6.4	**22** 0351 1.2 0953 5.6 F 1607 1.0 2215 5.9
8 0242 1.5 0855 5.8 SA 1516 1.2 2127 5.7	**23** 0356 1.6 1003 5.4 SU 1619 1.4 2234 5.5	**8** 0429 0.9 1040 6.1 TU 1655 0.6 ● 2315 6.3	**23** 0456 1.2 1102 5.7 W 1714 1.0 2327 5.9	**8** 0329 1.3 0942 5.7 TU 1555 0.9 2215 6.0	**23** 0353 1.4 1001 5.4 W 1609 1.2 2224 5.7	**8** 0444 0.5 1101 6.3 F 1704 0.4 ● 2324 6.6	**23** 0427 0.9 1029 5.9 SA 1643 0.9 2249 6.1
9 0341 1.2 0951 6.0 SU 1611 0.9 2224 6.0	**24** 0438 1.4 1043 5.6 M 1659 1.2 2312 5.7	**9** 0519 0.7 1131 6.4 W 1744 0.4 ○ 2357 0.9	**24** 0530 1.0 1133 5.9 TH 1748 0.9 ○ 2357 0.9	**9** 0419 0.8 1033 6.1 W 1642 0.6 2303 6.4	**24** 0428 1.1 1034 5.7 TH 1644 1.0 2256 5.9	**9** 0525 0.4 1142 6.4 SA 1744 0.4	**24** 0502 0.8 1105 6.0 SU 1718 0.8 ○ 2323 6.2
10 0435 1.0 1044 6.2 M 1703 0.7 ○ 2319 6.2	**25** 0516 1.3 1119 5.7 TU 1735 1.1 ○ 2347 5.8	**10** 0004 6.5 0606 0.5 TH 1220 6.6 1830 0.3	**25** 0603 0.9 1202 6.0 F 1821 0.8	**10** 0505 0.5 1120 6.4 TH 1727 0.3 ● 2347 6.6	**25** 0502 0.9 1105 5.9 F 1718 0.8 ○ 2326 6.1	**10** 0002 6.6 0603 0.4 SU 1221 6.4 1821 0.5	**25** 0537 0.7 1141 6.1 M 1753 0.7 2358 6.3
11 0527 0.8 1136 6.4 TU 1754 0.6	**26** 0551 1.2 1152 5.8 W 1810 1.0	**11** 0050 6.7 0651 0.5 F 1305 6.5 1915 0.3	**26** 0024 6.1 0634 0.9 SA 1232 6.0 1851 0.8	**11** 0548 0.4 1204 6.5 F 1809 0.2	**26** 0535 0.7 1135 6.0 SA 1751 0.8 2355 6.2	**11** 0038 6.5 0640 0.5 M 1256 6.3 1856 0.6	**26** 0613 0.6 1218 6.2 TU 1830 0.7
12 0011 6.4 0617 0.7 W 1228 6.4 1844 0.5	**27** 0019 5.9 0625 1.1 TH 1223 5.9 1844 1.0	**12** 0132 6.6 0735 0.6 SA 1347 6.4 1957 0.4	**27** 0052 6.1 0703 0.9 SU 1302 6.0 1918 0.8	**12** 0028 6.7 0630 0.3 SA 1245 6.5 1849 0.3	**27** 0607 0.7 1207 6.1 SU 1822 0.7	**12** 0110 6.2 0714 0.7 TU 1329 6.0 1930 0.8	**27** 0035 6.2 0650 0.6 W 1257 6.1 1909 0.8
13 0102 6.5 0706 0.7 TH 1318 6.4 1933 0.5	**28** 0049 5.9 0657 1.1 F 1253 5.9 1915 1.0	**13** 0212 6.5 0817 0.7 SU 1426 6.2 2037 0.7	**28** 0121 6.1 0731 0.9 M 1333 6.0 1946 0.8	**13** 0107 6.6 0709 0.4 SU 1323 6.4 1923 0.5	**28** 0025 6.2 0637 0.7 M 1239 6.2 1851 0.7	**13** 0139 6.0 0746 0.8 W 1400 5.8 2003 1.1	**28** 0113 6.1 0731 0.8 TH 1338 6.0 1952 1.0
14 0151 6.4 0756 0.8 F 1406 6.2 2021 0.6	**29** 0117 5.9 0728 1.1 SA 1324 5.8 1944 1.0	**14** 0249 6.2 0857 1.0 M 1503 5.8 2115 1.0		**14** 0141 6.4 0745 0.5 TU 1357 6.1 1923 0.7	**29** 0056 6.2 0708 0.7 TU 1312 6.1 1923 0.7	**14** 0207 5.6 0820 1.1 TH 1433 5.4 2039 1.5	**29** 0156 5.8 0818 1.0 F 1426 5.7 2043 1.3
15 0237 6.3 0845 0.9 SA 1453 6.0 2109 0.8	**30** 0147 5.9 0757 1.1 SU 1357 5.8 2013 1.1	**15** 0326 5.8 0936 1.3 TU 1544 5.4 2154 1.4		**15** 0213 6.1 0819 0.8 TU 1429 5.8 2035 1.0	**30** 0130 6.1 0742 0.8 W 1348 6.0 2000 0.9	**15** 0239 5.3 0859 1.5 F 1515 5.0 2122 1.9	**30** 0246 5.5 0914 1.3 SA 1527 5.3 2147 1.6
	31 0220 5.8 0830 1.2 M 1432 5.7 2048 1.2				**31** 0207 5.9 0822 1.0 TH 1429 5.7 2044 1.2		

Chart Datum: 3·27 metres below Ordnance Datum (Newlyn)

》 **FREE** monthly updates from 《
www.reedsalmanac.co.uk

Chapter 5

TIDES

TIME ZONE (UT)
For Summer Time add ONE
hour in **non-shaded areas**

ENGLAND – SHOREHAM
LAT 50°50'N LONG 0°15'W

YEAR 2005

TIMES AND HEIGHTS OF HIGH AND LOW WATERS

MAY		JUNE		JULY		AUGUST	
Time m	Time m	Time m	Time m	Time m	Time m	Time m	Time m
1 0354 5.1 / 1025 1.6 / SU 1648 5.0 / ◐ 2310 1.8	**16** 0400 4.6 / 1024 2.0 / M 1656 4.7 / ◐ 2304 2.2	**1** 0013 1.5 / 0624 5.1 / W 1245 1.4 / 1903 5.4	**16** 0526 4.7 / 1142 1.8 / TH 1805 5.0	**1** 0040 1.5 / 0646 5.1 / F 1307 1.5 / 1918 5.3	**16** 0524 4.9 / 1144 1.8 / SA 1804 5.1	**1** 0217 1.8 / 0833 4.8 / M 1444 1.9 / 2057 5.0	**16** 0119 1.8 / 0740 4.9 / TU 1358 1.9 / 2012 5.2
2 0525 4.8 / 1155 1.7 / M 1819 5.0	**17** 0519 4.5 / 1135 2.0 / TU 1804 4.7	**2** 0120 1.4 / 0733 5.2 / TH 1346 1.3 / 2005 5.6	**17** 0022 1.8 / 0632 4.8 / F 1246 1.8 / 1905 5.1	**2** 0142 1.5 / 0754 5.1 / SA 1407 1.5 / 2022 5.3	**17** 0030 1.8 / 0642 4.9 / SU 1258 1.8 / 1918 5.2	**2** 0315 1.6 / 0936 5.1 / TU 1538 1.7 / 2152 5.3	**17** 0238 1.5 / 0854 5.3 / W 1509 1.5 / 2118 5.6
3 0042 1.8 / 0655 4.9 / TU 1319 1.5 / 1940 5.3	**18** 0021 2.1 / 0630 4.5 / W 1251 1.9 / 1907 4.9	**3** 0217 1.2 / 0832 5.4 / F 1439 1.2 / 2059 5.7	**18** 0124 1.7 / 0733 5.0 / SA 1346 1.6 / 2001 5.4	**3** 0239 1.4 / 0856 5.2 / SU 1503 1.5 / 2118 5.4	**18** 0142 1.6 / 0757 5.1 / M 1411 1.7 / 2025 5.4	**3** 0402 1.4 / 1023 5.4 / W 1623 1.5 / 2236 5.5	**18** 0339 1.1 / 0955 5.8 / TH 1605 1.1 / 2215 6.0
4 0155 1.4 / 0808 5.3 / W 1421 1.2 / 2041 5.7	**19** 0131 1.9 / 0731 4.8 / TH 1353 1.7 / 2002 5.2	**4** 0307 1.1 / 0924 5.6 / SA 1528 1.1 / 2146 5.8	**19** 0220 1.4 / 0829 5.3 / SU 1442 1.4 / 2054 5.6	**4** 0331 1.3 / 0949 5.3 / M 1553 1.4 / 2206 5.5	**19** 0248 1.4 / 0901 5.4 / TU 1516 1.4 / 2125 5.7	**4** 0444 1.2 / 1104 5.6 / TH 1703 1.3 / 2313 5.7	**19** 0430 0.7 / 1049 6.2 / F 1654 0.8 / ○ 2306 6.3
5 0250 1.1 / 0904 5.6 / TH 1511 0.9 / 2131 6.0	**20** 0223 1.6 / 0824 5.1 / F 1441 1.4 / 2049 5.5	**5** 0353 1.0 / 1011 5.7 / SU 1612 1.0 / 2229 5.9	**20** 0312 1.2 / 0922 5.6 / M 1534 1.2 / 2144 5.9	**5** 0417 1.2 / 1036 5.5 / TU 1638 1.3 / 2249 5.6	**20** 0346 1.1 / 1001 5.8 / W 1612 1.1 / 2221 6.0	**5** 0521 1.1 / 1139 5.8 / F 1739 1.2 / ● 2346 5.7	**20** 0518 0.5 / 1139 6.5 / SA 1742 0.5 / 2355 6.5
6 0336 0.8 / 0952 5.9 / F 1555 0.7 / 2215 6.2	**21** 0307 1.3 / 0910 5.4 / SA 1524 1.2 / 2132 5.8	**6** 0435 0.9 / 1053 5.8 / M 1655 1.0 / ● 2308 5.9	**21** 0402 0.9 / 1013 5.8 / TU 1625 1.0 / 2233 6.1	**6** 0459 1.1 / 1117 5.6 / W 1719 1.2 / ● 2327 5.7	**21** 0440 0.8 / 1056 6.1 / TH 1705 0.9 / ○ 2314 6.2	**6** 0556 1.0 / 1213 5.9 / SA 1814 1.1	**21** 0604 0.3 / 1225 6.7 / SU 1828 0.4
7 0419 0.6 / 1036 6.1 / SA 1637 0.6 / 2256 6.3	**22** 0348 1.0 / 0953 5.7 / SU 1605 1.0 / 2213 6.0	**7** 0516 0.9 / 1133 5.8 / TU 1734 1.0 / 2344 5.8	**22** 0451 0.8 / 1104 6.0 / W 1715 0.9 / ○ 2322 6.2	**7** 0539 1.1 / 1155 5.7 / TH 1757 1.2	**22** 0531 0.6 / 1150 6.3 / F 1756 0.7	**7** 0017 5.8 / 0630 1.0 / SU 1243 5.9 / 1846 1.1	**22** 0041 6.6 / 0649 0.3 / M 1310 6.7 / 1912 0.4
8 0459 0.6 / 1117 6.1 / SU 1717 0.7 / ● 2334 6.3	**23** 0428 0.8 / 1036 5.9 / M 1647 0.9 / ○ 2254 6.2	**8** 0554 0.9 / 1210 5.8 / W 1812 1.1	**23** 0541 0.6 / 1156 6.1 / TH 1805 0.8	**8** 0002 5.7 / 0615 1.1 / F 1231 5.8 / 1833 1.2	**23** 0006 6.3 / 0620 0.5 / SA 1241 6.5 / 1845 0.6	**8** 0046 5.8 / 0703 1.0 / M 1310 5.9 / 1918 1.1	**23** 0125 6.5 / 0733 0.4 / TU 1351 6.6 / 1956 0.6
9 0538 0.6 / 1156 6.1 / M 1755 0.7	**24** 0510 0.7 / 1119 6.1 / TU 1730 0.8 / 2336 6.2	**9** 0019 5.8 / 0630 1.0 / TH 1247 5.8 / 1848 1.2	**24** 0012 6.2 / 0631 0.6 / F 1248 6.2 / 1855 0.8	**9** 0036 5.6 / 0650 1.1 / SA 1305 5.7 / 1908 1.2	**24** 0057 6.4 / 0710 0.4 / SU 1330 6.5 / 1934 0.6	**9** 0114 5.7 / 0732 1.0 / TU 1336 5.9 / 1947 1.2	**24** 0206 6.3 / 0815 0.6 / W 1429 6.4 / 2037 0.8
10 0009 6.1 / 0614 0.7 / TU 1231 6.0 / 1831 0.9	**25** 0554 0.6 / 1203 6.1 / W 1815 0.8	**10** 0052 5.6 / 0706 1.1 / F 1322 5.7 / 1923 1.3	**25** 0104 6.2 / 0722 0.6 / SA 1340 6.2 / 1947 0.8	**10** 0108 5.6 / 0725 1.1 / SU 1337 5.7 / 1942 1.3	**25** 0145 6.3 / 0758 0.5 / M 1416 6.5 / 2023 0.7	**10** 0143 5.7 / 0759 1.1 / W 1405 5.8 / 2016 1.2	**25** 0245 6.0 / 0855 0.9 / TH 1507 6.0 / 2118 1.1
11 0041 6.0 / 0649 0.8 / W 1305 5.9 / 1905 1.0	**26** 0020 6.2 / 0639 0.6 / TH 1250 6.1 / 1901 0.8	**11** 0125 5.5 / 0742 1.2 / SA 1358 5.5 / 2001 1.4	**26** 0155 6.1 / 0814 0.7 / SU 1432 6.1 / 2040 0.9	**11** 0139 5.5 / 0759 1.2 / M 1407 5.6 / 2017 1.4	**26** 0231 6.2 / 0846 0.6 / TU 1500 6.3 / 2111 0.8	**11** 0215 5.6 / 0829 1.2 / TH 1438 5.7 / 2050 1.3	**26** 0325 5.6 / 0936 1.3 / F 1548 5.6 / ◑ 2202 1.5
12 0112 5.8 / 0722 1.0 / TH 1339 5.7 / 1940 1.2	**27** 0106 6.1 / 0727 0.7 / F 1339 6.0 / 1951 1.0	**12** 0200 5.3 / 0820 1.4 / SU 1434 5.4 / 2042 1.6	**27** 0248 5.9 / 0908 0.8 / M 1524 6.0 / 2136 1.1	**12** 0212 5.4 / 0833 1.3 / TU 1439 5.5 / 2053 1.5	**27** 0317 5.9 / 0933 0.8 / W 1545 6.0 / 2200 1.1	**12** 0252 5.5 / 0906 1.2 / F 1518 5.5 / 2133 1.5	**27** 0413 5.1 / 1023 1.8 / SA 1638 5.1 / 2258 2.0
13 0142 5.5 / 0758 1.2 / F 1414 5.4 / 2017 1.5	**28** 0156 5.9 / 0819 0.8 / SA 1433 5.8 / 2046 1.2	**13** 0238 5.1 / 0902 1.5 / M 1515 5.2 / 2128 1.8	**28** 0343 5.7 / 1004 1.0 / TU 1618 5.8 / ◑ 2235 1.2	**13** 0248 5.3 / 0909 1.4 / W 1516 5.4 / 2134 1.6	**28** 0404 5.6 / 1022 1.2 / TH 1631 5.6 / ◑ 2253 1.4	**13** 0337 5.2 / 0954 1.6 / SA 1607 5.2 / ◑ 2230 1.8	**28** 0515 4.7 / 1128 2.2 / SU 1744 4.7
14 0216 5.2 / 0837 1.5 / SA 1455 5.2 / 2102 1.8	**29** 0252 5.6 / 0916 0.9 / SU 1534 5.6 / 2148 1.4	**14** 0323 4.9 / 0949 1.6 / TU 1604 5.1 / 2220 1.9	**29** 0440 5.4 / 1102 1.2 / W 1714 5.6 / 2336 1.4	**14** 0330 5.2 / 0950 1.5 / TH 1601 5.3 / 2220 1.7	**29** 0455 5.2 / 1116 1.5 / F 1724 5.3 / 2354 1.7	**14** 0435 4.9 / 1058 1.9 / SU 1715 5.0 / 2348 1.9	**29** 0027 2.2 / 0632 4.5 / M 1313 2.5 / 1907 4.6
15 0259 4.9 / 0925 1.7 / SU 1548 4.9 / 2156 2.0	**30** 0357 5.3 / 1022 1.3 / M 1641 5.4 / ◑ 2259 1.5	**15** 0419 4.8 / 1043 1.7 / W 1702 5.0 / ◐ 2320 1.9	**30** 0541 5.2 / 1203 1.4 / TH 1814 5.4	**15** 0421 5.0 / 1041 1.7 / F 1656 5.1 / 2321 1.8	**30** 0556 4.8 / 1223 1.9 / SA 1827 5.0	**15** 0604 4.8 / 1225 2.0 / M 1850 4.9	**30** 0157 2.1 / 0818 4.6 / TU 1428 2.2 / 2044 4.8
	31 0509 5.1 / 1134 1.4 / TU 1753 5.4				**31** 0107 1.9 / 0710 4.7 / SU 1338 2.0 / 1943 4.9		**31** 0258 1.8 / 0923 5.1 / W 1522 1.8 / 2139 5.2

Chart Datum: 3·27 metres below Ordnance Datum (Newlyn)

》》 **FREE** monthly updates from 《《
www.reedsalmanac.co.uk

TIME ZONE (UT)
For Summer Time add ONE hour in **non-shaded areas**

ENGLAND – SHOREHAM
LAT 50°50′N   LONG 0°15′W
TIMES AND HEIGHTS OF HIGH AND LOW WATERS

YEAR 2005

SEPTEMBER				OCTOBER				NOVEMBER				DECEMBER			
Time	m	Time	m	Time	m	Time	m	Time	m	Time	m	Time	m	Time	m
1 0344 1.5 1007 5.5 TH 1604 1.5 2220 5.5		**16** 0328 1.0 0947 6.0 F 1553 1.0 2205 6.1		**1** 0354 1.3 1011 5.8 SA 1612 1.2 2223 5.8		**16** 0354 0.7 1012 6.5 SU 1616 0.6 2232 6.4		**1** 0427 1.1 1031 6.1 TU 1645 1.0 2247 6.0		**16** 0453 0.8 1108 6.4 W 1715 0.7 ○ 2331 6.3		**1** 0430 1.2 1033 6.1 TH 1652 1.0 ● 2257 6.1		**16** 0517 1.1 1126 6.0 F 1739 1.0 2354 6.0	
2 0423 1.2 1043 5.8 F 1641 1.3 2254 5.7		**17** 0415 0.6 1035 6.4 SA 1638 0.6 2252 6.5		**2** 0428 1.1 1042 6.0 SU 1645 1.1 2252 5.9		**17** 0436 0.5 1055 6.7 M 1658 0.5 ○ 2314 6.6		**2** 0500 1.0 1103 6.2 W 1719 0.9 ● 2321 6.1		**17** 0533 0.8 1146 6.3 TH 1755 0.8		**2** 0510 1.1 1113 6.2 F 1733 0.9 2339 6.2		**17** 0557 1.2 1203 5.9 SA 1817 1.0	
3 0458 1.0 1116 5.9 SA 1715 1.1 ● 2324 5.9		**18** 0459 0.4 1119 6.7 SU 1722 0.4 ○ 2337 6.6		**3** 0501 0.9 1111 6.1 M 1718 1.0 ● 2320 6.0		**18** 0517 0.5 1135 6.7 TU 1739 0.5 2355 6.5		**3** 0534 1.0 1136 6.2 TH 1753 0.9 2356 6.2		**18** 0010 6.2 0611 1.0 F 1222 6.2 1832 0.9		**3** 0552 1.0 1155 6.2 SA 1816 0.9		**18** 0031 5.9 0633 1.2 SU 1239 5.8 1853 1.1	
4 0531 0.9 1146 6.0 SU 1748 1.0 2351 5.9		**19** 0542 0.3 1202 6.8 M 1804 0.4		**4** 0533 0.9 1138 6.2 TU 1750 0.9 2349 6.1		**19** 0557 0.5 1213 6.6 W 1818 0.6		**4** 0607 1.0 1211 6.2 F 1828 0.9		**19** 0047 6.1 0648 1.1 SA 1256 5.9 1908 1.1		**4** 0023 6.2 0635 1.0 SU 1239 6.2 1901 0.9		**19** 0108 5.8 0710 1.3 M 1313 5.7 1929 1.2	
5 0604 0.9 1213 6.1 M 1820 1.0		**20** 0019 6.6 0623 0.3 TU 1243 6.8 1845 0.4		**5** 0604 0.9 1205 6.2 W 1819 0.9		**20** 0033 6.4 0634 0.7 TH 1249 6.4 1854 0.8		**5** 0032 6.1 0644 1.0 SA 1248 6.1 1906 1.0		**20** 0123 5.9 0725 1.4 SU 1330 5.7 1944 1.3		**5** 0110 6.1 0722 1.1 M 1326 6.0 1950 1.0		**20** 0145 5.7 0746 1.5 TU 1348 5.5 2007 1.4	
6 0018 6.0 0634 0.9 TU 1238 6.1 1849 1.0		**21** 0100 6.5 0703 0.5 W 1320 6.6 1924 0.6		**6** 0019 6.1 0631 0.9 TH 1235 6.2 1847 0.9		**21** 0109 6.2 0710 0.9 F 1322 6.1 1930 1.1		**6** 0111 6.0 0725 1.2 SU 1328 5.9 1950 1.2		**21** 0201 5.6 0803 1.6 M 1406 5.4 2024 1.6		**6** 0200 5.9 0814 1.3 TU 1418 5.8 2043 1.2		**21** 0220 5.5 0825 1.6 W 1424 5.3 2046 1.6	
7 0046 6.0 0701 0.9 W 1305 6.0 1915 1.0		**22** 0137 6.3 0741 0.7 TH 1355 6.3 2001 0.9		**7** 0050 6.1 0700 1.0 F 1307 6.1 1919 1.0		**22** 0144 5.9 0746 1.2 SA 1354 5.8 2005 1.3		**7** 0156 5.8 0813 1.5 M 1415 5.6 2042 1.5		**22** 0244 5.3 0847 1.9 TU 1450 5.0 2111 1.9		**7** 0256 5.8 0912 1.4 W 1518 5.5 2143 1.4		**22** 0258 5.4 0909 1.8 TH 1504 5.1 2130 1.7	
8 0115 6.0 0726 1.0 TH 1333 6.0 1943 1.1		**23** 0212 6.0 0817 1.1 F 1428 5.9 2037 1.2		**8** 0123 6.0 0735 1.2 SA 1341 5.9 1957 1.2		**23** 0221 5.6 0824 1.6 SU 1429 5.3 2045 1.7		**8** 0251 5.4 0913 1.7 TU 1517 5.2 2148 1.7		**23** 0335 5.0 0940 2.1 W 1548 4.7 ○ 2207 2.1		**8** 0401 5.6 1020 1.5 TH 1627 5.3 ○ 2251 1.5		**23** 0340 5.2 0957 2.0 F 1552 4.9 ○ 2219 1.9	
9 0146 5.9 0757 1.1 F 1406 5.9 2017 1.2		**24** 0249 5.6 0854 1.5 SA 1505 5.4 2117 1.7		**9** 0201 5.7 0817 1.4 SU 1421 5.6 2044 1.5		**24** 0306 5.2 0909 2.0 M 1516 4.9 2136 2.1		**9** 0408 5.1 1029 2.0 W 1645 5.0 ○ 2311 1.9		**24** 0439 4.9 1045 2.3 TH 1701 4.6 2315 2.2		**9** 0511 5.5 1130 1.6 F 1740 5.2		**24** 0432 5.0 1053 2.1 SA 1653 4.8 2315 2.0	
10 0221 5.7 0835 1.4 SA 1444 5.6 2100 1.5		**25** 0335 5.1 0939 1.9 SU 1554 4.9 ○ 2209 2.1		**10** 0248 5.3 0911 1.8 M 1514 5.1 ○ 2148 1.9		**25** 0408 4.8 1009 2.4 TU 1630 4.5 ○ 2244 2.4		**10** 0540 5.1 1159 2.0 TH 1816 5.0		**25** 0545 4.8 1159 2.3 F 1811 4.6		**10** 0001 1.5 0621 5.5 SA 1240 1.6 1852 5.3		**25** 0536 5.0 1154 2.1 SU 1804 4.8	
11 0304 5.3 0923 1.7 SU 1532 5.2 ○ 2159 1.8		**26** 0439 4.7 1042 2.3 M 1707 4.5 2328 2.4		**11** 0358 4.9 1028 2.1 TU 1642 4.8 2318 2.1		**26** 0523 4.6 1135 2.5 W 1752 4.4		**11** 0038 1.7 0701 5.6 F 1318 1.7 1931 5.3		**26** 0029 2.2 0648 5.0 SA 1312 2.1 1913 4.8		**11** 0108 1.5 0727 5.6 SU 1343 1.4 1957 5.4		**26** 0018 2.0 0641 5.0 M 1259 2.0 1910 4.9	
12 0404 4.9 1033 2.1 M 1645 4.8 2325 2.1		**27** 0559 4.4 1238 2.6 TU 1833 4.4		**12** 0552 4.8 1213 2.2 W 1835 4.8		**27** 0027 2.4 0643 4.7 TH 1320 2.4 1916 4.6		**12** 0147 1.4 0806 5.7 SA 1418 1.4 2031 5.7		**27** 0135 2.0 0745 5.2 SU 1407 1.8 2007 5.1		**12** 0208 1.4 0826 5.6 M 1438 1.3 2054 5.6		**27** 0123 2.0 0740 5.2 TU 1400 1.8 2009 5.1	
13 0552 4.7 1214 2.2 TU 1841 4.8		**28** 0128 2.3 0747 4.6 W 1404 2.3 2020 4.7		**13** 0104 1.9 0726 5.1 TH 1345 1.8 1957 5.2		**28** 0147 2.1 0800 5.1 F 1417 2.0 2023 5.0		**13** 0241 1.1 0859 6.1 SU 1507 1.1 2122 6.0		**28** 0226 1.7 0832 5.5 M 1451 1.5 2053 5.4		**13** 0301 1.3 0917 5.7 TU 1528 1.1 2145 5.7		**28** 0224 1.8 0834 5.4 W 1455 1.5 2103 5.4	
14 0112 2.0 0735 4.9 W 1356 1.9 2007 5.1		**29** 0231 1.7 0855 5.1 TH 1457 1.9 2114 5.1		**14** 0216 1.5 0835 5.6 F 1445 1.3 2058 5.7		**29** 0236 1.5 0849 5.4 SA 1459 1.6 2105 5.3		**14** 0328 0.8 0945 6.3 M 1552 0.8 2208 6.2		**29** 0310 1.5 0914 5.8 TU 1532 1.3 2135 5.7		**14** 0350 1.2 1004 5.8 W 1615 1.0 2231 5.9		**29** 0317 1.5 0924 5.8 TH 1545 1.2 2153 5.7	
15 0233 1.5 0850 5.5 TH 1502 1.4 2113 5.7		**30** 0317 1.3 0937 5.5 F 1537 1.5 2151 5.5		**15** 0309 0.9 0927 6.1 SA 1533 0.9 2147 6.2		**30** 0316 1.2 0926 5.7 SU 1536 1.3 2140 5.6		**15** 0411 1.1 1028 6.4 TU 1634 0.7 2251 6.3		**30** 0350 1.2 0954 6.0 W 1612 1.1 2216 5.9		**15** 0435 1.1 1046 5.8 TH 1658 1.0 ○ 2314 5.9		**30** 0407 1.1 1012 6.0 F 1633 1.0 2242 6.0	
						31 0352 1.2 0959 5.9 M 1611 1.1 2213 5.9								**31** 0454 1.1 1059 6.2 SA 1720 0.8 ● 2331 6.2	

Chart Datum: 3·27 metres below Ordnance Datum (Newlyn)

》》 **FREE** monthly updates from 《《
www.reedsalmanac.co.uk

TIDES

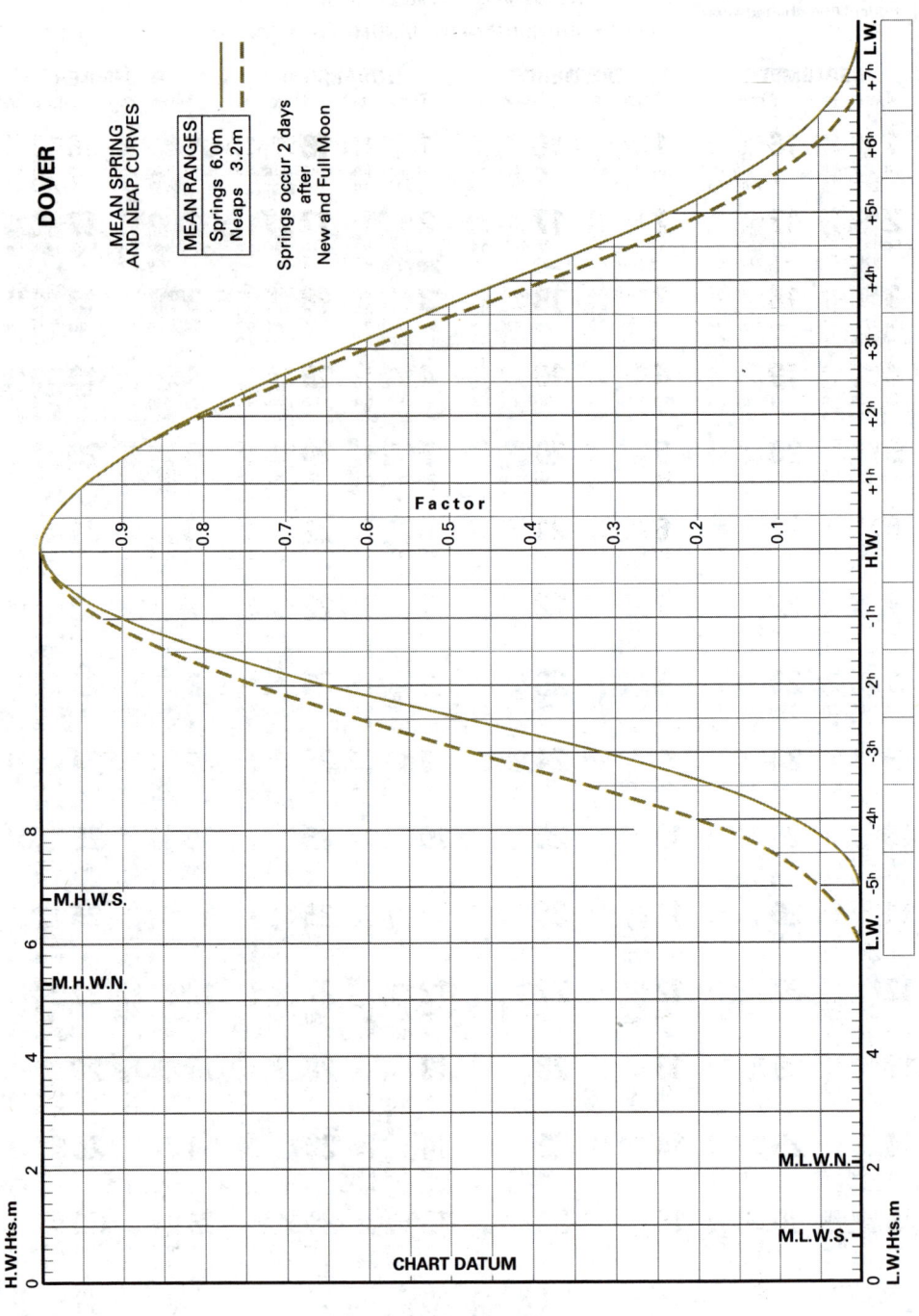

ENGLAND – DOVER

LAT 51°07'N   LONG 1°19'E

TIMES AND HEIGHTS OF HIGH AND LOW WATERS

TIME ZONE (UT) For Summer Time add ONE hour in **non-shaded areas**

YEAR 2005

JANUARY		FEBRUARY		MARCH		APRIL	
Time m	Time m	Time m	Time m	Time m	Time m	Time m	Time m
1 0158 6.1 / 0917 1.6 / SA 1414 5.8 / 2128 1.8	**16** 0302 6.5 / 1037 1.0 / SU 1535 6.0 / 2248 1.4	**1** 0245 6.3 / 1008 1.4 / TU 1503 6.0 / 2220 1.7	**16** 0359 5.9 / 1113 1.7 / W 1634 5.4 / ☾ 2323 2.0	**1** 0140 6.6 / 0907 1.1 / TU 1353 6.4 / 2117 1.2	**16** 0236 6.3 / 0952 1.3 / W 1500 5.9 / 2156 1.6	**1** 0241 6.1 / 1002 1.7 / F 1508 5.8 / 2227 1.8	**16** 0341 5.3 / 1018 2.2 / SA 1621 5.2 / ☾ 2247 2.4
2 0235 6.0 / 0957 1.7 / SU 1454 5.7 / 2209 1.9	**17** 0351 6.2 / 1120 1.3 / M 1628 5.7 / ☾ 2332 1.7	**2** 0331 6.1 / 1051 1.7 / W 1554 5.8 / ☾ 2308 1.9	**17** 0456 5.5 / 1203 2.2 / TH 1742 5.1	**2** 0216 6.5 / 0940 1.3 / W 1434 6.2 / 2153 1.5	**17** 0317 5.9 / 1019 1.8 / TH 1550 5.5 / ☾ 2230 2.0	**2** 0345 5.6 / 1101 2.1 / SA 1632 5.3 / ☾ 2340 2.2	**17** 0458 5.0 / 1122 2.6 / SU 1738 5.0
3 0320 5.9 / 1041 1.8 / M 1544 5.6 / ☾ 2255 2.0	**18** 0445 5.9 / 1207 1.7 / TU 1728 5.4	**3** 0429 5.8 / 1147 1.9 / TH 1703 5.4	**18** 0027 2.4 / 0609 5.1 / F 1316 2.4 / 1902 5.0	**3** 0300 6.2 / 1021 1.6 / TH 1523 5.9 / ☾ 2240 1.8	**18** 0413 5.4 / 1059 2.3 / F 1658 5.1 / 2324 2.4	**3** 0538 5.2 / 1235 2.3 / SU 1828 5.2	**18** 0025 2.6 / 0618 4.9 / M 1319 2.6 / 1857 5.1
4 0415 5.8 / 1133 1.9 / TU 1647 5.5 / 2353 2.1	**19** 0024 2.0 / 0547 5.6 / W 1303 2.0 / 1836 5.3	**4** 0015 2.2 / 0549 5.6 / F 1306 2.1 / 1843 5.3	**19** 0153 2.5 / 0737 5.1 / SA 1433 2.4 / 2024 5.2	**4** 0356 5.8 / 1115 2.0 / F 1630 5.4 / SA 1820 4.9	**19** 0530 5.0 / 1221 2.6 / SA 1820 4.9	**4** 0124 2.2 / 0721 5.3 / M 1416 2.1 / 1954 5.5	**19** 0157 2.4 / 0739 5.1 / TU 1434 2.3 / 2006 5.4
5 0523 5.7 / 1238 1.9 / W 1806 5.5	**20** 0127 2.2 / 0659 5.4 / TH 1406 2.1 / 1947 5.3	**5** 0147 2.2 / 0722 5.6 / SA 1434 2.0 / 2009 5.5	**20** 0311 2.3 / 0901 5.3 / SU 1543 2.1 / 2126 5.5	**5** 0526 5.3 / 1239 2.3 / SA 1834 5.1	**20** 0112 2.6 / 0659 4.9 / SU 1400 2.6 / 1948 5.0	**5** 0254 1.8 / 0839 5.7 / TU 1537 1.7 / 2059 5.9	**20** 0300 2.0 / 0836 5.4 / W 1530 1.9 / 2053 5.7
6 0107 2.2 / 0635 5.7 / TH 1351 1.9 / 1918 5.6	**21** 0236 2.2 / 0812 5.5 / F 1512 2.1 / 2051 5.5	**6** 0311 1.9 / 0840 5.8 / SU 1551 1.7 / 2116 5.9	**21** 0415 1.9 / 0954 5.6 / M 1641 1.8 / 2210 5.9	**6** 0128 2.3 / 0722 5.3 / SU 1422 2.1 / 2006 5.4	**21** 0239 2.4 / 0835 5.1 / M 1513 2.3 / 2057 5.4	**6** 0410 1.3 / 0936 6.1 / W 1644 1.2 / 2149 6.4	**21** 0352 1.6 / 0915 5.8 / TH 1618 1.6 / 2129 6.0
7 0225 2.2 / 0742 5.9 / F 1501 1.7 / 2020 5.8	**22** 0344 2.1 / 0915 5.6 / SA 1613 1.9 / 2143 5.7	**7** 0424 1.5 / 0945 6.1 / M 1702 1.3 / 2213 6.2	**22** 0506 1.6 / 1031 5.9 / TU 1727 1.6 / 2245 6.1	**7** 0300 2.0 / 0844 5.7 / M 1545 1.8 / 2113 5.8	**22** 0344 2.0 / 0927 5.5 / TU 1612 1.9 / 2140 5.8	**7** 0513 0.9 / 1022 6.4 / TH 1738 0.9 / 2232 6.7	**22** 0438 1.3 / 0949 6.0 / F 1701 1.4 / 2202 6.3
8 0334 1.8 / 0843 6.1 / SA 1606 1.4 / 2117 6.1	**23** 0440 1.8 / 1006 5.8 / SU 1703 1.7 / 2227 6.0	**8** 0531 1.1 / 1041 6.5 / TU 1806 1.0 / ● 2303 6.6	**23** 0547 1.4 / 1101 6.1 / W 1806 1.4 / 2316 6.3	**8** 0419 1.5 / 0947 6.1 / TU 1659 1.3 / 2207 6.3	**23** 0436 1.6 / 1000 5.8 / W 1700 1.6 / 2213 6.1	**8** 0604 0.6 / 1101 6.6 / F 1823 0.7 / ● 2311 6.9	**23** 0521 1.1 / 1021 6.3 / SA 1741 1.2 / 2235 6.5
9 0437 1.6 / 0939 6.4 / SU 1708 1.2 / 2211 6.4	**24** 0526 1.6 / 1046 6.0 / M 1744 1.6 / 2305 6.2	**9** 0632 0.8 / 1131 6.7 / W 1902 0.8 / 2347 6.8	**24** 0624 1.2 / 1130 6.2 / TH 1841 1.3 / ○ 2345 6.4	**9** 0528 1.0 / 1038 6.5 / W 1759 0.9 / 2252 6.7	**24** 0519 1.3 / 1029 6.1 / TH 1740 1.3 / 2243 6.3	**9** 0648 0.4 / 1136 6.7 / SA 1901 0.6 / 2348 6.9	**24** 0602 1.0 / 1054 6.4 / SU 1819 1.1 / ○ 2308 6.6
10 0536 1.2 / 1035 6.6 / M 1807 1.0 / ● 2303 6.6	**25** 0605 1.4 / 1121 6.1 / TU 1821 1.4 / 2339 6.3	**10** 0726 0.5 / 1215 6.7 / TH 1950 0.6	**25** 0700 1.1 / 1159 6.3 / F 1914 1.2	**10** 0624 0.6 / 1122 6.7 / TH 1848 0.6 / ● 2333 6.9	**25** 0557 1.1 / 1059 6.3 / F 1815 1.2 / ○ 2312 6.5	**10** 0726 0.5 / 1209 6.7 / SU 1935 0.7	**25** 0641 0.9 / 1126 6.5 / M 1856 1.0 / 2342 6.7
11 0632 0.9 / 1128 6.7 / TU 1903 0.9 / 2352 6.7	**26** 0641 1.3 / 1153 6.1 / W 1856 1.4	**11** 0029 7.0 / 0812 0.4 / F 1256 6.8 / 2030 0.6	**26** 0013 6.5 / 0734 1.0 / SA 1226 6.3 / 1945 1.1	**11** 0712 0.4 / 1200 6.8 / F 1930 0.5	**26** 0634 1.0 / 1128 6.4 / SA 1849 1.1 / 2341 6.6	**11** 0024 6.9 / 0757 0.6 / M 1243 6.6 / 2004 0.8	**26** 0718 0.8 / 1200 6.6 / TU 1931 0.9
12 0728 0.8 / 1219 6.7 / W 1956 0.9	**27** 0010 6.4 / 0716 1.3 / TH 1224 6.2 / 1929 1.4	**12** 0111 7.0 / 0854 0.4 / SA 1335 6.6 / 2106 0.7	**27** 0040 6.6 / 0807 1.0 / SU 1252 6.4 / 2016 1.1	**12** 0011 7.0 / 0753 0.3 / SA 1235 6.8 / 2005 0.5	**27** 0709 0.9 / 1156 6.5 / SU 1921 1.0	**12** 0059 6.7 / 0825 0.8 / TU 1317 6.5 / 2030 1.0	**27** 0018 6.7 / 0752 0.9 / W 1238 6.6 / 2007 1.0
13 0040 6.8 / 0820 0.7 / TH 1308 6.6 / 2044 0.9	**28** 0040 6.4 / 0751 1.2 / F 1253 6.2 / 2003 1.3	**13** 0151 6.9 / 0930 0.6 / SU 1414 6.4 / 2139 0.9	**28** 0108 6.6 / 0837 1.1 / M 1320 6.5 / 2046 1.1	**13** 0048 7.0 / 0828 0.4 / SU 1309 6.7 / 2036 0.7	**28** 0011 6.7 / 0742 0.9 / M 1225 6.6 / 1953 1.0	**13** 0132 6.5 / 0848 1.1 / W 1352 6.3 / 2054 1.3	**28** 0058 6.6 / 0828 1.1 / TH 1320 6.5 / 2046 1.1
14 0127 6.7 / 0909 0.7 / F 1357 6.5 / 2127 1.0	**29** 0107 6.4 / 0826 1.2 / SA 1318 6.2 / 2037 1.3	**14** 0231 6.7 / 1004 0.8 / M 1455 6.2 / 2210 1.2		**14** 0125 6.9 / 0859 0.6 / M 1344 6.6 / 2104 0.9	**29** 0042 6.7 / 0813 0.9 / TU 1256 6.6 / 2024 1.0	**14** 0206 6.2 / 0910 1.5 / TH 1430 6.0 / 2120 1.6	**29** 0144 6.4 / 0909 1.3 / F 1411 6.2 / 2132 1.5
15 0214 6.7 / 0954 0.8 / SA 1445 6.3 / 2208 1.2	**30** 0135 6.4 / 0900 1.2 / SU 1346 6.2 / 2109 1.4	**15** 0313 6.3 / 1037 1.3 / TU 1540 5.8 / 2242 1.6		**15** 0200 6.7 / 0925 0.9 / TU 1421 6.3 / 2130 1.3	**30** 0116 6.7 / 0844 1.0 / W 1332 6.5 / 2057 1.2	**15** 0245 5.8 / 0938 1.9 / F 1516 5.6 / 2156 2.0	**30** 0241 6.1 / 0958 1.7 / SA 1516 5.8 / 2230 1.8
	31 0207 6.4 / 0933 1.3 / M 1421 6.2 / 2142 1.5				**31** 0154 6.5 / 0919 1.3 / TH 1415 6.2 / 2137 1.5		

Chart Datum: 3·67 metres below Ordnance Datum (Newlyn)

》》 **FREE** monthly updates from 《《
www.reedsalmanac.co.uk

TIDES

ENGLAND – DOVER
LAT 51°07′N LONG 1°19′E
TIMES AND HEIGHTS OF HIGH AND LOW WATERS

TIME ZONE (UT) For Summer Time add ONE hour in **non-shaded areas**

YEAR 2005

MAY				JUNE				JULY				AUGUST			
Time	m	Time	m	Time	m	Time	m	Time	m	Time	m	Time	m	Time	m
1 0402 5.6 / 1104 2.0 / SU 1640 5.5 / ☾ 2349 2.0		**16** 0424 5.1 / 1051 2.4 / M 1651 5.2 / ☽ 2338 2.3		**1** 0057 1.5 / 0636 5.6 / W 1328 1.8 / 1850 5.8		**16** 0002 2.0 / 0538 5.3 / TH 1227 2.2 / 1754 5.5		**1** 0120 1.5 / 0654 5.5 / F 1344 1.8 / 1909 5.7		**16** 0004 1.9 / 0523 5.4 / SA 1229 2.2 / 1757 5.6		**1** 0245 2.1 / 0827 5.4 / M 1519 2.1 / 2058 5.5		**16** 0204 2.2 / 0743 5.4 / TU 1443 2.1 / 2013 5.7	
2 0539 5.4 / 1236 2.1 / M 1809 5.4		**17** 0534 5.0 / 1216 2.5 / TU 1759 5.2		**2** 0203 1.4 / 0743 5.7 / TH 1430 1.6 / 1955 5.9		**17** 0108 1.9 / 0640 5.4 / F 1337 2.1 / 1855 5.6		**2** 0220 1.7 / 0757 5.6 / SA 1447 1.8 / 2015 5.8		**17** 0116 2.0 / 0644 5.4 / SU 1350 2.1 / 1910 5.7		**2** 0355 2.0 / 0927 5.6 / TU 1624 1.9 / 2156 5.7		**17** 0324 1.9 / 0852 5.8 / W 1557 1.7 / 2120 6.0	
3 0118 1.9 / 0707 5.5 / TU 1400 1.9 / 1929 5.6		**18** 0103 2.2 / 0642 5.1 / W 1338 2.3 / 1903 5.4		**3** 0307 1.3 / 0838 5.9 / F 1531 1.5 / 2050 6.1		**18** 0211 1.8 / 0735 5.6 / SA 1441 1.9 / 1950 5.8		**3** 0324 1.7 / 0853 5.7 / SU 1550 1.8 / 2113 5.8		**18** 0232 1.9 / 0754 5.6 / M 1506 1.9 / 2016 5.9		**3** 0454 1.8 / 1014 5.9 / W 1717 1.6 / 2240 5.9		**18** 0433 1.5 / 0949 6.2 / TH 1702 1.3 / 2217 6.4	
4 0236 1.6 / 0818 5.8 / W 1511 1.6 / 2032 6.0		**19** 0208 2.0 / 0739 5.4 / TH 1438 2.0 / 1956 5.6		**4** 0408 1.2 / 0925 6.0 / SA 1628 1.4 / 2138 6.2		**19** 0310 1.6 / 0824 5.8 / SU 1539 1.7 / 2040 6.1		**4** 0425 1.6 / 0943 5.8 / M 1647 1.6 / 2205 6.0		**19** 0340 1.6 / 0855 5.9 / TU 1611 1.6 / 2118 6.1		**4** 0540 1.6 / 1054 6.2 / TH 1800 1.4 / 2316 6.1		**19** 0537 1.2 / 1039 6.6 / F 1804 0.9 / ○ 2307 6.6	
5 0345 1.2 / 0912 6.1 / TH 1612 1.3 / 2122 6.3		**20** 0302 1.7 / 0825 5.7 / F 1531 1.8 / 2039 5.9		**5** 0502 1.2 / 1006 6.1 / SU 1717 1.3 / 2222 6.3		**20** 0407 1.4 / 0911 6.1 / M 1635 1.4 / 2129 6:3		**5** 0516 1.6 / 1028 6.0 / TU 1734 1.5 / 2249 6.1		**20** 0443 1.4 / 0952 6.2 / W 1712 1.3 / 2215 6.4		**5** 0619 1.5 / 1130 6.3 / F 1837 1.3 / ● 2348 6.1		**20** 0635 0.9 / 1124 6.9 / SA 1900 0.6 / 2352 6.8	
6 0445 0.9 / 0956 6.3 / F 1705 1.1 / 2206 6.5		**21** 0353 1.4 / 0905 6.0 / SA 1619 1.5 / 2118 6.2		**6** 0547 1.2 / 1046 6.2 / M 1759 1.2 / ● 2303 6.3		**21** 0502 1.2 / 0959 6.3 / TU 1728 1.2 / 2218 6.5		**6** 0558 1.5 / 1109 6.2 / W 1815 1.4 / ● 2329 6.1		**21** 0544 1.2 / 1042 6.4 / TH 1810 1.0 / ○ 2309 6.5		**6** 0652 1.5 / 1203 6.4 / SA 1910 1.3		**21** 0726 0.7 / 1207 7.0 / SU 1949 0.6	
7 0536 0.8 / 1034 6.4 / SA 1751 0.9 / 2246 6.6		**22** 0442 1.2 / 0943 6.2 / SU 1706 1.3 / 2157 6.4		**7** 0624 1.2 / 1124 6.3 / TU 1836 1.2 / 2342 6.3		**22** 0555 1.1 / 1047 6.4 / W 1818 1.0 / ○ 2309 6.6		**7** 0634 1.5 / 1147 6.3 / TH 1852 1.4		**22** 0642 1.0 / 1134 6.7 / F 1907 0.8		**7** 0019 6.2 / 0723 1.4 / SU 1234 6.4 / 1942 1.2		**22** 0034 6.8 / 0809 0.6 / M 1249 7.1 / 2032 0.4	
8 0619 0.7 / 1110 6.5 / SU 1830 0.9 / 2324 6.7		**23** 0530 1.0 / 1021 6.4 / M 1751 1.1 / ○ 2238 6.6		**8** 0657 1.3 / 1202 6.3 / W 1910 1.3		**23** 0647 1.0 / 1137 6.6 / TH 1909 0.9		**8** 0006 6.1 / 0707 1.5 / F 1224 6.3 / 1925 1.4		**23** 0001 6.6 / 0737 0.9 / SA 1222 6.8 / 2001 0.6		**8** 0047 6.1 / 0754 1.4 / M 1301 6.4 / 2015 1.2		**23** 0114 6.8 / 0846 0.7 / TU 1329 7.0 / 2110 0.5	
9 0655 0.8 / 1144 6.5 / M 1904 0.9		**24** 0615 0.9 / 1101 6.5 / TU 1834 1.0 / 2319 6.7		**9** 0019 6.2 / 0725 1.4 / TH 1240 6.3 / 1940 1.3		**24** 0000 6.6 / 0738 1.0 / F 1227 6.6 / 2001 0.9		**9** 0041 6.1 / 0739 1.5 / SA 1258 6.3 / 1959 1.4		**24** 0050 6.7 / 0827 0.8 / SU 1308 6.9 / 2050 0.5		**9** 0112 6.1 / 0825 1.4 / TU 1326 6.4 / 2047 1.2		**24** 0153 6.6 / 0920 0.8 / W 1411 6.9 / 2144 0.7	
10 0000 6.6 / 0725 1.0 / TU 1220 6.5 / 1934 1.0		**25** 0658 0.9 / 1143 6.6 / W 1916 1.0		**10** 0056 6.1 / 0753 1.5 / F 1316 6.2 / 2011 1.4		**25** 0054 6.5 / 0829 1.0 / SA 1319 6.6 / 2054 0.9		**10** 0113 6.0 / 0811 1.5 / SU 1329 6.2 / 2034 1.4		**25** 0137 6.6 / 0911 0.8 / M 1354 6.8 / 2135 0.6		**10** 0136 6.1 / 0856 1.4 / W 1353 6.3 / 2118 1.3		**25** 0234 6.4 / 0952 1.1 / TH 1453 6.6 / 2218 1.2	
11 0036 6.5 / 0752 1.1 / W 1256 6.4 / 2001 1.2		**26** 0004 6.6 / 0740 1.0 / TH 1229 6.6 / 1959 1.0		**11** 0131 5.9 / 0824 1.6 / SA 1352 6.1 / 2046 1.6		**26** 0149 6.4 / 0920 1.1 / SU 1411 6.5 / 2146 0.9		**11** 0143 5.9 / 0845 1.6 / M 1358 6.1 / 2109 1.4		**26** 0224 6.5 / 0950 0.9 / TU 1440 6.7 / 2216 0.7		**11** 0204 6.1 / 0927 1.3 / TH 1426 6.3 / 2150 1.5		**26** 0320 6.0 / 1026 1.5 / F 1539 6.1 / ◐ 2255 1.6	
12 0111 6.3 / 0815 1.4 / TH 1332 6.2 / 2027 1.4		**27** 0052 6.5 / 0824 1.1 / F 1320 6.5 / 2047 1.1		**12** 0208 5.8 / 0859 1.7 / SU 1427 5.9 / 2124 1.7		**27** 0246 6.2 / 1009 1.2 / M 1504 6.4 / 2237 1.1		**12** 0212 5.8 / 0920 1.6 / TU 1428 6.1 / 2146 1.5		**27** 0311 6.2 / 1029 1.1 / W 1527 6.5 / 2257 1.0		**12** 0240 6.0 / 1001 1.4 / F 1507 6.1 / 2227 1.7		**27** 0412 5.6 / 1106 2.0 / SA 1634 5.7 / 2343 2.1	
13 0146 6.0 / 0840 1.6 / F 1410 6.0 / 2058 1.6		**28** 0147 6.3 / 0912 1.3 / SA 1416 6.3 / 2140 1.3		**13** 0248 5.6 / 0939 1.9 / M 1507 5.7 / 2209 1.8		**28** 0345 6.0 / 1057 1.4 / TU 1559 6.2 / ◐ 2329 1.2		**13** 0244 5.8 / 0957 1.7 / W 1505 6.0 / 2225 1.6		**28** 0401 5.8 / 1109 1.4 / TH 1617 6.2 / ◐ 2341 1.4		**13** 0325 5.8 / 1042 1.7 / SA 1558 5.8 / ◐ 2315 2.0		**28** 0517 5.3 / 1205 2.3 / SU 1743 5.3	
14 0225 5.7 / 0913 1.8 / SA 1452 5.7 / 2137 1.9		**29** 0251 6.0 / 1007 1.5 / SU 1519 6.1 / 2241 1.5		**14** 0336 5.4 / 1025 2.0 / TU 1555 5.6 / 2300 1.9		**29** 0445 5.7 / 1148 1.6 / W 1657 6.0		**14** 0324 5.7 / 1037 1.9 / TH 1551 5.8 / ◐ 2309 1.8		**29** 0456 5.6 / 1156 1.8 / F 1714 5.8		**14** 0426 5.5 / 1139 2.2 / SU 1710 5.5		**29** 0054 2.5 / 0635 5.1 / M 1332 2.6 / 1912 5.1	
15 0317 5.4 / 0955 2.1 / SU 1546 5.4 / 2227 2.1		**30** 0404 5.8 / 1111 1.7 / M 1625 5.9 / ☾ 2348 1.6		**15** 0434 5.3 / 1119 2.2 / W 1652 5.5 / ☽		**30** 0022 1.4 / 0548 5.7 / TH 1244 1.7 / 1800 5.8		**15** 0416 5.5 / 1125 2.0 / F 1648 5.7		**30** 0032 1.8 / 0600 5.4 / SA 1256 2.1 / 1821 5.5		**15** 0025 2.2 / 0605 5.2 / M 1308 2.4 / 1849 5.4		**30** 0216 2.5 / 0804 5.2 / TU 1457 2.4 / 2050 5.3	
		31 0521 5.6 / 1220 1.8 / TU 1736 5.8								**31** 0136 2.1 / 0714 5.3 / SU 1406 2.2 / 1942 5.4				**31** 0334 2.3 / 0912 5.6 / W 1608 2.0 / 2146 5.6	

Chart Datum: 3·67 metres below Ordnance Datum (Newlyn)

)) **FREE** monthly updates from ((
www.reedsalmanac.co.uk

TIME ZONE (UT)
For Summer Time add ONE hour in **non-shaded areas**

ENGLAND – DOVER
LAT 51°07′N   LONG 1°19′E
TIMES AND HEIGHTS OF HIGH AND LOW WATERS

YEAR 2005

SEPTEMBER Time m	Time m	OCTOBER Time m	Time m	NOVEMBER Time m	Time m	DECEMBER Time m	Time m
1 0436 1.9 / 0957 6.0 / TH 1701 1.6 / 2225 5.9	**16** 0425 1.5 / 0938 6.3 / F 1654 1.2 / 2209 6.5	**1** 0452 1.7 / 1001 6.2 / SA 1709 1.4 / 2220 6.2	**16** 0502 1.1 / 1001 6.8 / SU 1730 0.7 / 2231 6.7	**1** 0523 1.4 / 1017 6.5 / TU 1740 1.2 / 2236 6.4	**16** 0602 1.0 / 1057 6.8 / W 1828 0.9 / ○ 2319 6.6	**1** 0530 1.4 / 1017 6.5 / TH 1751 1.2 / ● 2240 6.5	**16** 0618 1.3 / 1122 6.4 / F 1839 1.3 / 2343 6.4
2 0523 1.7 / 1034 6.2 / F 1742 1.4 / 2255 6.1	**17** 0525 1.1 / 1024 6.7 / SA 1751 0.8 / 2254 6.8	**2** 0529 1.5 / 1031 6.4 / SU 1743 1.2 / 2246 6.3	**17** 0550 0.9 / 1042 7.0 / M 1816 0.6 / ○ 2308 6.8	**2** 0558 1.3 / 1048 6.6 / W 1817 1.1 / ● 2306 6.5	**17** 0640 1.0 / 1136 6.7 / TH 1903 1.0 / 2357 6.6	**2** 0611 1.2 / 1057 6.6 / F 1832 1.1 / 2320 6.6	**17** 0655 1.3 / 1201 6.3 / SA 1912 1.4
3 0600 1.5 / 1105 6.4 / SA 1816 1.3 / ● 2322 6.3	**18** 0617 0.8 / 1106 7.0 / SU 1842 0.5 / ○ 2333 6.9	**3** 0600 1.3 / 1058 6.5 / M 1815 1.1 / ● 2313 6.4	**18** 0631 0.8 / 1121 7.1 / TU 1857 0.6 / 2343 6.9	**3** 0633 1.2 / 1121 6.7 / TH 1853 1.1 / 2337 6.6	**18** 0714 1.1 / 1214 6.6 / F 1933 1.2	**3** 0652 1.2 / 1139 6.6 / SA 1913 1.2	**18** 0021 6.4 / 0729 1.4 / SU 1239 6.2 / 1942 1.5
4 0631 1.4 / 1135 6.5 / SU 1847 1.2 / 2349 6.3	**19** 0702 0.7 / 1145 7.2 / M 1926 0.4	**4** 0630 1.3 / 1126 6.6 / TU 1848 1.1 / 2340 6.5	**19** 0708 0.8 / 1158 7.0 / W 1933 0.7	**4** 0708 1.2 / 1154 6.7 / F 1927 1.2	**19** 0035 6.5 / 0746 1.3 / SA 1252 6.4 / 2001 1.5	**4** 0003 6.6 / 0734 1.2 / SU 1225 6.5 / 1954 1.3	**19** 0100 6.4 / 0802 1.5 / M 1316 6.1 / 2012 1.7
5 0700 1.3 / 1202 6.5 / M 1918 1.1	**20** 0009 6.9 / 0740 0.6 / TU 1224 7.2 / 2004 0.4	**5** 0700 1.2 / 1153 6.6 / W 1920 1.1	**20** 0018 6.8 / 0741 0.9 / TH 1235 6.9 / 2003 0.9	**5** 0012 6.6 / 0743 1.3 / SA 1232 6.6 / 2001 1.3	**20** 0114 6.4 / 0816 1.5 / SU 1331 6.1 / 2027 1.7	**5** 0050 6.6 / 0818 1.2 / M 1315 6.4 / 2039 1.4	**20** 0136 6.2 / 0835 1.6 / TU 1354 5.9 / 2044 1.8
6 0015 6.3 / 0728 1.3 / TU 1228 6.5 / 1949 1.1	**21** 0045 6.8 / 0814 0.7 / W 1302 7.1 / 2037 0.6	**6** 0005 6.5 / 0731 1.2 / TH 1221 6.6 / 1950 1.1	**21** 0055 6.6 / 0812 1.1 / F 1312 6.7 / 2031 1.3	**6** 0052 6.5 / 0820 1.4 / SU 1314 6.4 / 2039 1.5	**21** 0155 6.2 / 0847 1.7 / M 1414 5.8 / 2058 2.0	**6** 0142 6.4 / 0908 1.4 / TU 1412 6.1 / 2130 1.6	**21** 0212 6.1 / 0911 1.7 / W 1432 5.7 / 2121 1.9
7 0039 6.3 / 0758 1.3 / W 1253 6.5 / 2019 1.2	**22** 0122 6.7 / 0845 0.9 / TH 1340 6.8 / 2108 1.0	**7** 0033 6.6 / 0802 1.3 / F 1251 6.6 / 2020 1.3	**22** 0133 6.4 / 0840 1.4 / SA 1351 6.3 / 2056 1.6	**7** 0138 6.3 / 0903 1.6 / M 1406 6.1 / 2125 1.8	**22** 0239 5.9 / 0924 2.0 / TU 1505 5.5 / 2138 2.3	**7** 0241 6.2 / 1004 1.5 / W 1521 5.9 / 2228 1.8	**22** 0248 5.9 / 0951 1.8 / TH 1514 5.5 / 2203 2.1
8 0102 6.4 / 0828 1.3 / TH 1320 6.5 / 2047 1.3	**23** 0201 6.4 / 0914 1.2 / F 1420 6.5 / 2136 1.4	**8** 0106 6.5 / 0834 1.4 / SA 1327 6.5 / 2053 1.5	**23** 0215 6.1 / 0908 1.7 / SU 1435 5.9 / 2124 2.0	**8** 0237 5.9 / 0955 1.9 / TU 1520 5.7 / 2222 2.1	**23** 0331 5.6 / 1011 2.2 / W 1607 5.2 / ◑ 2229 2.5	**8** 0346 6.0 / 1107 1.7 / TH 1637 5.7 / ◑ 2333 1.9	**23** 0329 5.7 / 1036 2.0 / F 1604 5.3 / ◑ 2250 2.2
9 0131 6.4 / 0857 1.4 / F 1352 6.5 / 2118 1.5	**24** 0244 6.1 / 0943 1.6 / SA 1504 6.0 / 2206 1.9	**9** 0145 6.3 / 0910 1.6 / SU 1409 6.2 / 2133 1.8	**24** 0305 5.7 / 0943 2.1 / M 1533 5.4 / 2202 2.4	**9** 0400 5.6 / 1106 2.1 / W 1702 5.5 / ◑ 2346 2.3	**24** 0432 5.4 / 1116 2.4 / TH 1714 5.1 / 2342 2.5	**9** 0455 5.9 / 1213 1.7 / F 1752 5.7	**24** 0420 5.5 / 1129 2.1 / SA 1707 5.2 / 2347 2.4
10 0207 6.3 / 0931 1.6 / SA 1432 6.2 / 2154 1.7	**25** 0336 5.6 / 1017 2.1 / SU 1601 5.5 / ◑ 2244 2.4	**10** 0234 5.9 / 0956 2.0 / M 1507 5.7 / ◑ 2224 2.2	**25** 0408 5.4 / 1033 2.5 / TU 1644 5.1 / 2302 2.8	**10** 0531 5.5 / 1236 2.1 / TH 1827 5.5	**25** 0539 5.3 / 1237 2.4 / F 1823 5.1	**10** 0041 1.9 / 0607 5.9 / SA 1320 1.7 / 1900 5.7	**25** 0523 5.4 / 1233 2.1 / SU 1814 5.2
11 0252 5.9 / 1015 2.0 / SU 1522 5.8 / ◑ 2242 2.1	**26** 0441 5.3 / 1110 2.5 / M 1713 5.1	**11** 0347 5.4 / 1100 2.5 / TU 1704 5.3 / 2344 2.5	**26** 0520 5.1 / 1211 2.7 / W 1802 5.0	**11** 0119 2.2 / 0650 5.7 / F 1357 1.8 / 1938 5.8	**26** 0111 2.6 / 0644 5.4 / SA 1346 2.2 / 1922 5.3	**11** 0148 1.9 / 0715 5.9 / SU 1424 1.5 / 2000 5.8	**26** 0058 2.4 / 0629 5.5 / M 1341 2.0 / 1914 5.4
12 0352 5.4 / 1110 2.5 / M 1645 5.3 / 2354 2.4	**27** 0005 2.8 / 0559 5.0 / TU 1259 2.7 / 1841 5.0	**12** 0554 5.2 / 1244 2.6 / W 1846 5.4	**27** 0103 2.8 / 0639 5.1 / TH 1346 2.5 / 1928 5.2	**12** 0233 1.9 / 0755 6.0 / SA 1506 1.4 / 2036 6.1	**27** 0218 2.3 / 0739 5.6 / SU 1442 1.9 / 2010 5.6	**12** 0251 1.7 / 0815 6.1 / M 1529 1.4 / 2053 6.0	**27** 0212 2.3 / 0728 5.6 / TU 1445 1.9 / 2006 5.6
13 0600 5.1 / 1246 2.5 / TU 1851 5.3	**28** 0149 2.8 / 0731 5.2 / W 1432 2.5 / 2028 5.2	**13** 0141 2.4 / 0719 5.5 / TH 1421 2.0 / 2002 5.7	**28** 0223 2.5 / 0752 5.5 / F 1451 2.1 / 2027 5.5	**13** 0335 1.5 / 0849 6.4 / SU 1607 1.1 / 2124 6.3	**28** 0312 2.1 / 0823 5.8 / M 1533 1.7 / 2050 5.9	**13** 0353 1.6 / 0908 6.2 / TU 1629 1.3 / 2140 6.1	**28** 0316 2.0 / 0821 5.9 / W 1544 1.7 / 2054 5.9
14 0150 2.4 / 0736 5.4 / W 1431 2.2 / 2013 5.6	**29** 0308 2.4 / 0843 5.6 / TH 1541 2.1 / 2119 5.6	**14** 0303 1.9 / 0825 6.0 / F 1534 1.5 / 2102 6.2	**29** 0321 2.2 / 0841 5.8 / SA 1540 1.8 / 2105 5.8	**14** 0430 1.3 / 0935 6.6 / M 1701 0.9 / 2205 6.5	**29** 0401 1.8 / 0901 6.1 / TU 1621 1.4 / 2126 6.1	**14** 0449 1.4 / 0956 6.3 / W 1720 1.3 / 2223 6.3	**29** 0414 1.7 / 0910 6.1 / TH 1640 1.4 / 2140 6.1
15 0316 2.0 / 0844 5.8 / TH 1548 1.7 / 2117 6.1	**30** 0407 2.0 / 0928 5.9 / F 1630 1.7 / 2153 5.9	**15** 0407 1.5 / 0917 6.5 / SA 1636 1.1 / 2150 6.5	**30** 0407 2.0 / 0917 6.1 / SU 1623 1.5 / 2136 6.1	**15** 0519 1.1 / 1017 6.7 / TU 1748 0.9 / 2243 6.6	**30** 0446 1.6 / 0939 6.3 / W 1707 1.3 / 2203 6.3	**15** 0536 1.3 / 1040 6.4 / TH 1803 1.3 / ○ 2303 6.4	**30** 0506 1.4 / 0959 6.3 / F 1731 1.2 / 2227 6.4
			31 0446 1.6 / 0947 6.3 / M 1702 1.3 / 2206 6.3				**31** 0555 1.2 / 1047 6.5 / SA 1820 1.1 / ● 2314 6.6

Chart Datum: 3·67 metres below Ordnance Datum (Newlyn)

》 **FREE** monthly updates from 《
www.reedsalmanac.co.uk

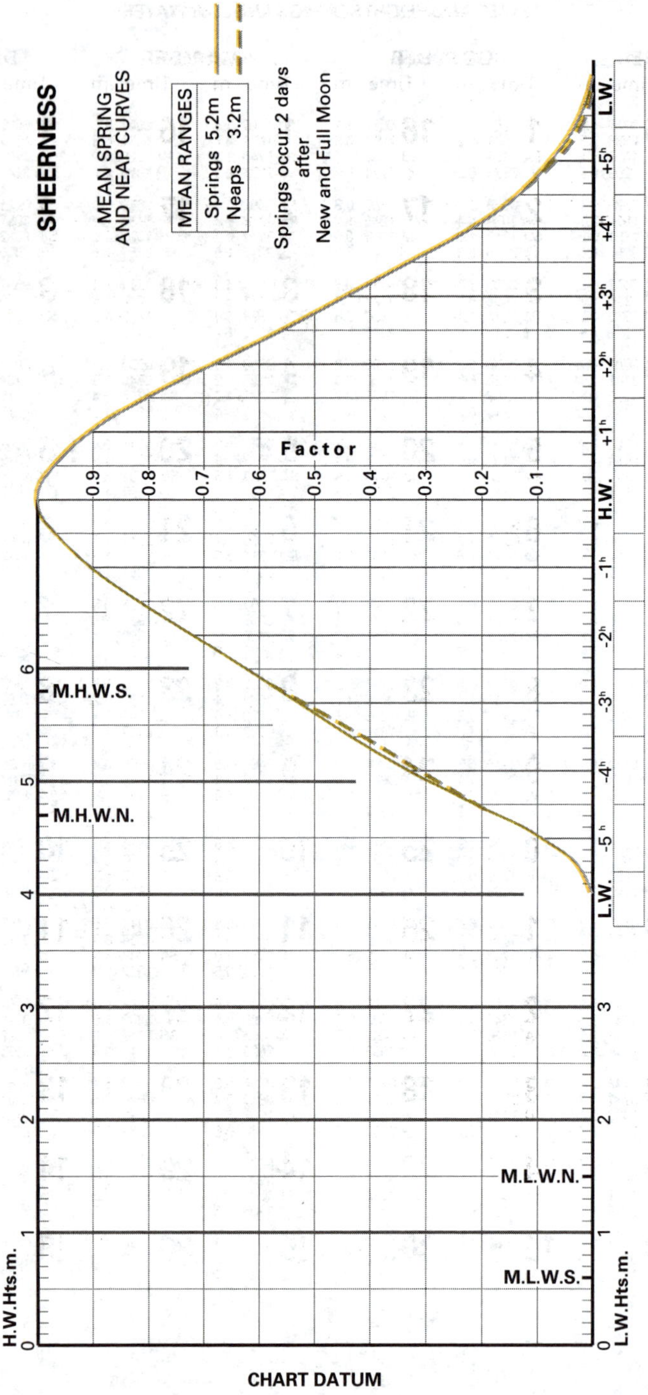
SHEERNESS
MEAN SPRING AND NEAP CURVES
MEAN RANGES
Springs 5.2m
Neaps 3.2m
Springs occur 2 days after New and Full Moon
Factor
0.9
0.8
0.7
0.6
0.5
0.4
0.3
0.2
0.1
L.W.
-5h
-4h
-3h
-2h
-1h
H.W.
+1h
+2h
+3h
+4h
+5h
L.W.
M.H.W.S.
M.H.W.N.
M.L.W.N.
M.L.W.S.
H.W.Hts.m.
L.W.Hts.m.
0
1
2
3
4
5
6
CHART DATUM

TIME ZONE (UT)
For Summer Time add ONE hour in **non-shaded areas**

ENGLAND – SHEERNESS
LAT 51°27'N   LONG 0°45'E
TIMES AND HEIGHTS OF HIGH AND LOW WATERS

YEAR 2005

JANUARY		FEBRUARY		MARCH		APRIL	
Time m	Time m	Time m	Time m	Time m	Time m	Time m	Time m
1 0327 5.2 0946 1.0 SA 1602 5.1 2145 1.3	**16** 0429 5.5 1102 0.6 SU 1709 5.4 2255 1.2	**1** 0418 5.2 1029 0.9 TU 1655 5.1 2229 1.2	**16** 0521 5.1 1127 1.1 W 1759 4.8 ● 2339 1.4	**1** 0318 5.5 0936 0.7 TU 1547 5.4 2130 0.9	**16** 0403 5.5 1009 0.9 W 1628 5.1 2217 1.1	**1** 0419 5.3 1015 1.1 F 1646 5.0 2237 1.1	**16** 0458 4.7 1044 1.6 SA 1711 4.5 ● 2315 1.5
2 0405 5.1 1024 1.0 SU 1643 5.0 2224 1.4	**17** 0516 5.3 1144 0.8 M 1759 5.1 ● 2341 1.3	**2** 0459 5.1 1102 1.0 W 1742 4.9 ● 2314 1.3	**17** 0615 4.8 1216 1.4 TH 1856 4.5	**2** 0353 5.4 0958 0.8 W 1624 5.2 2200 1.0	**17** 0442 5.1 1038 1.2 TH 1706 4.8 ● 2255 1.3	**2** 0517 5.0 1114 1.4 SA 1749 4.7 ● 2351 1.3	**17** 0600 4.4 1148 1.9 SU 1819 4.2
3 0447 5.0 1104 1.1 M 1730 4.9 ● 2309 1.5	**18** 0608 5.1 1231 1.0 TU 1855 4.9	**3** 0551 5.0 1152 1.2 TH 1842 4.8	**18** 0045 1.6 0727 4.5 F 1336 1.7 2010 4.4	**3** 0433 5.3 1028 1.0 TH 1708 5.0 ● 2244 1.2	**18** 0530 4.7 1122 1.5 F 1756 4.5 2352 1.6	**3** 0636 4.8 1249 1.6 SU 1915 4.5	**18** 0041 1.6 0724 4.3 M 1332 2.0 1954 4.2
4 0536 4.9 1151 1.2 TU 1825 4.9	**19** 0036 1.5 0708 4.9 W 1330 1.3 1956 4.7	**4** 0017 1.5 0702 4.8 F 1310 1.3 1958 4.7	**19** 0220 1.7 0856 4.4 SA 1505 1.7 2133 4.4	**4** 0525 5.0 1119 1.2 F 1807 4.7 2349 1.4	**19** 0639 4.4 1235 1.9 SA 1912 4.2	**4** 0147 1.4 0813 4.8 M 1436 1.6 2049 4.6	**19** 0233 1.5 0851 4.4 TU 1500 1.8 2114 4.5
5 0004 1.6 0635 4.8 W 1251 1.2 1929 4.8	**20** 0146 1.6 0818 4.7 TH 1437 1.4 2103 4.7	**5** 0151 1.5 0829 4.8 SA 1457 1.4 2118 4.5	**20** 0346 1.5 1016 4.6 SU 1615 1.6 2239 4.7	**5** 0639 4.8 1245 1.5 SA 1929 4.5	**20** 0135 1.7 0815 4.2 SU 1428 1.9 2050 4.2	**5** 0326 1.1 0941 5.1 TU 1555 1.3 2205 5.0	**20** 0340 1.2 0955 4.8 W 1558 1.5 2211 4.8
6 0114 1.6 0747 4.9 TH 1407 1.2 2040 4.9	**21** 0300 1.5 0931 4.7 F 1542 1.4 2208 4.8	**6** 0330 1.4 0952 5.0 SU 1617 1.2 2231 5.0	**21** 0453 1.2 1113 4.9 M 1709 1.4 2329 5.0	**6** 0135 1.5 0815 4.7 SU 1444 1.5 2101 4.6	**21** 0318 1.5 0945 4.5 M 1546 1.7 2205 4.6	**6** 0443 0.7 1047 5.5 W 1658 1.0 2303 5.3	**21** 0431 1.0 1043 5.1 TH 1644 1.2 2256 5.1
7 0234 1.6 0902 5.0 F 1525 1.1 2147 5.1	**22** 0409 1.4 1036 4.9 SA 1638 1.4 2303 5.0	**7** 0450 1.1 1104 5.3 M 1724 1.0 2332 5.3	**22** 0543 1.0 1156 5.2 TU 1751 1.2	**7** 0326 1.3 0947 5.0 M 1608 1.3 2220 4.9	**22** 0425 1.2 1043 4.9 TU 1642 1.4 2257 4.9	**7** 0541 0.4 1139 5.7 TH 1748 0.8 2350 5.6	**22** 0515 0.8 1124 5.4 F 1724 1.1 2336 5.4
8 0350 1.3 1010 5.2 SA 1633 1.0 2247 5.3	**23** 0508 1.2 1129 5.0 SU 1726 1.3 2349 5.1	**8** 0601 0.7 1204 5.7 TU 1821 0.8	**23** 0009 5.2 0623 0.8 W 1233 5.4 1825 1.1	**8** 0451 0.9 1059 5.4 TU 1716 1.0 2322 5.3	**23** 0515 1.0 1126 5.2 W 1725 1.2 2338 5.2	**8** 0628 0.3 1223 5.9 F 1831 0.7	**23** 0555 0.7 1201 5.5 SA 1802 0.9
9 0458 1.1 1112 5.5 SU 1733 0.9 2343 5.5	**24** 0557 1.0 1213 5.2 M 1806 1.2	**9** 0026 5.5 0659 0.4 W 1257 5.9 1911 0.7	**24** 0044 5.3 0658 0.7 TH 1306 5.4 ● 1857 1.0	**9** 0557 0.5 1156 5.7 W 1810 0.8	**24** 0555 0.8 1203 5.4 TH 1801 1.0	**9** 0031 5.7 0707 0.2 SA 1303 6.0 1909 0.6	**24** 0012 5.5 0632 0.6 SU 1237 5.7 ○ 1840 0.8
10 0601 0.8 1209 5.7 M 1828 0.8 ●	**25** 0028 5.2 0638 0.9 TU 1252 5.4 ○ 1840 1.1	**10** 0114 5.7 0750 0.2 TH 1345 6.0 1956 0.6	**25** 0116 5.4 0731 0.6 F 1337 5.5 ○ 1930 0.8	**10** 0012 5.6 0649 0.3 TH 1244 5.9 ● 1855 0.7	**25** 0014 5.4 0630 0.7 F 1237 5.5 ○ 1833 0.9	**10** 0110 5.8 0743 0.3 SU 1340 5.9 1945 0.5	**25** 0048 5.6 0710 0.6 M 1313 5.7 1918 0.7
11 0035 5.6 0701 0.7 TU 1303 5.8 1919 0.7	**26** 0103 5.3 0715 0.8 W 1326 5.4 1913 1.0	**11** 0158 5.8 0836 0.1 F 1430 6.0 2037 0.6	**26** 0147 5.5 0806 0.5 SA 1409 5.6 2004 0.8	**11** 0056 5.8 0733 0.1 F 1327 6.0 1936 0.5	**26** 0047 5.5 0705 0.6 SA 1309 5.6 1907 0.8	**11** 0147 5.9 0815 0.4 M 1414 5.8 2021 0.5	**26** 0124 5.7 0747 0.6 TU 1348 5.7 1956 0.7
12 0124 5.7 0756 0.4 W 1355 5.9 2007 0.7	**27** 0136 5.4 0749 0.7 TH 1359 5.4 1946 0.9	**12** 0239 5.8 0917 0.1 SA 1512 5.9 2114 0.7	**27** 0217 5.6 0839 0.5 SU 1441 5.6 2036 0.8	**12** 0136 5.9 0813 0.1 SA 1407 6.0 2013 0.5	**27** 0119 5.6 0740 0.6 SU 1341 5.7 1942 0.7	**12** 0223 5.8 0844 0.6 TU 1447 5.6 2053 0.7	**27** 0202 5.7 0822 0.6 W 1425 5.6 2033 0.7
13 0212 5.7 0847 0.3 TH 1444 5.9 2052 0.8	**28** 0207 5.4 0824 0.7 F 1432 5.4 2021 0.9	**13** 0319 5.5 0954 0.3 SU 1553 5.6 2148 0.8		**13** 0214 5.9 0849 0.3 SU 1445 5.9 2048 0.6	**28** 0150 5.7 0814 0.5 M 1414 5.7 2015 0.7	**13** 0258 5.6 0910 0.8 W 1519 5.4 2121 0.8	**28** 0242 5.5 0855 0.8 TH 1503 5.5 2110 0.8
14 0258 5.6 0935 0.3 F 1533 5.8 2134 0.9	**29** 0239 5.4 0859 0.6 SA 1505 5.4 2055 0.9	**14** 0358 5.4 1025 0.5 M 1633 5.4 2220 1.0		**14** 0251 5.9 0920 0.3 M 1520 5.7 2119 0.6	**29** 0223 5.7 0845 0.6 TU 1447 5.6 2045 0.8	**14** 0334 5.4 0934 1.0 TH 1550 5.1 2148 1.1	**29** 0326 5.6 0932 1.0 F 1546 5.3 2154 0.9
15 0343 5.6 1020 0.4 SA 1620 5.6 2215 1.0	**30** 0310 5.4 0932 0.7 SU 1539 5.4 2126 1.0	**15** 0438 5.4 1054 0.8 TU 1713 5.1 2254 1.2		**15** 0327 5.7 0946 0.6 TU 1554 5.4 2147 0.9	**30** 0257 5.6 0912 0.7 W 1522 5.5 2113 0.8	**15** 0412 5.1 1002 1.3 F 1625 4.8 2223 1.2	**30** 0417 5.3 1018 1.3 SA 1638 5.0 2251 1.0
	31 0343 5.3 1002 0.8 M 1615 5.2 2156 1.1				**31** 0335 5.5 0937 0.9 TH 1600 5.3 2148 0.9		

Chart Datum: 2·90 metres below Ordnance Datum (Newlyn)

FREE monthly updates from www.reedsalmanac.co.uk

Chapter 5

TIDES

TIME ZONE (UT)
For Summer Time add ONE hour in **non-shaded areas**

ENGLAND – SHEERNESS
LAT 51°27′N   LONG 0°45′E
TIMES AND HEIGHTS OF HIGH AND LOW WATERS

YEAR 2005

	MAY			JUNE			JULY			AUGUST	
	Time m	Time m		Time m	Time m		Time m	Time m		Time m	Time m
1 SU ◐	0521 5.1 1123 1.5 1745 4.7	**16** M	0529 4.6 1113 1.8 1740 4.5 ◐ 2358 1.4	**1** W	0132 0.8 0742 5.2 1343 1.4 2000 5.0	**16** TH	0023 1.2 0649 4.7 1239 1.7 1905 4.7	**1** F	0156 0.9 0811 5.1 1404 1.4 2027 5.1	**16** SA	0023 1.2 0658 4.8 1242 1.6 1914 4.8	**1** M	0317 1.5 0943 4.8 1550 1.4 2216 4.9	**16** TU	0225 1.5 0846 4.7 1503 1.5 2123 4.9
2 M	0013 1.1 0640 4.9 1250 1.6 1907 4.7	**17** TU	0635 4.5 1226 1.9 1855 4.4	**2** TH	0240 0.7 0850 5.3 1449 1.3 2106 5.1	**17** F	0128 1.2 0753 4.8 1348 1.6 2013 4.8	**2** SA	0257 1.0 0914 5.1 1509 1.3 2132 5.1	**17** SU	0133 1.3 0807 4.8 1401 1.6 2030 4.8	**2** TU	0422 1.4 1046 5.0 1658 1.2 2316 5.1	**17** W	0350 1.3 1003 5.0 1625 1.2 2239 5.3
3 TU	0150 1.1 0805 5.0 1416 1.5 2030 4.8	**18** W	0124 1.4 0747 4.5 1350 1.8 2011 4.5	**3** F	0343 0.7 0951 5.3 1549 1.2 2204 5.3	**18** SA	0236 1.1 0857 5.0 1456 1.5 2117 5.0	**3** SU	0356 1.1 1013 5.1 1612 1.2 2232 5.1	**18** M	0256 1.3 0917 5.0 1524 1.5 2143 5.0	**3** W	0516 1.4 1137 5.1 1752 1.0	**18** TH	0459 1.1 1108 5.3 1736 0.8 2341 5.6
4 W	0311 0.8 0921 5.3 1527 1.3 2139 5.1	**19** TH	0239 1.2 0854 4.8 1458 1.6 2114 4.8	**4** SA	0437 0.7 1044 5.4 1643 1.1 2255 5.3	**19** SU	0339 1.0 0956 5.2 1559 1.3 2215 5.2	**4** M	0448 1.1 1106 5.2 1709 1.1 2326 5.2	**19** TU	0408 1.1 1022 5.2 1635 1.2 2249 5.3	**4** TH	0004 5.2 0559 1.3 1219 5.3 1835 0.9	**19** F ○	0558 0.9 1203 5.6 1837 0.5
5 TH	0419 0.6 1023 5.5 1628 1.1 2236 5.3	**20** F	0337 1.0 0950 5.0 1552 1.4 2207 5.1	**5** SU	0522 0.8 1130 5.4 1731 1.0 2341 5.4	**20** M	0437 0.9 1050 5.3 1657 1.1 2309 5.4	**5** TU	0533 1.1 1152 5.3 1800 1.0	**20** W	0511 1.0 1122 5.4 1741 0.9 2349 5.6	**5** F ●	0044 5.3 0635 1.2 1256 5.3 1912 0.8	**20** SA	0035 5.9 0649 0.6 1252 5.8 1928 0.2
6 F	0514 0.5 1114 5.6 1718 0.9 2323 5.5	**21** SA	0427 0.9 1039 5.3 1641 1.2 2254 5.3	**6** M ●	0601 0.8 1211 5.5 1815 0.8	**21** TU	0530 0.9 1140 5.5 1752 1.0	**6** W ●	0013 5.3 0613 1.1 1234 5.3 1845 0.9	**21** TH ○	0608 0.9 1215 5.5 1842 0.7	**6** SA	0120 5.4 0708 1.1 1329 5.4 1946 0.8	**21** SU	0124 6.1 0736 0.7 1336 5.9 2015 0.1
7 SA	0557 0.5 1157 5.7 1800 0.8	**22** SU	0514 0.8 1124 5.5 1727 1.0 2338 5.5	**7** TU	0024 5.5 0636 0.9 1249 5.5 1857 0.8	**22** W ○	0001 5.6 0621 0.8 1229 5.6 1846 0.8	**7** TH	0056 5.3 0650 1.1 1311 5.3 1925 0.8	**22** F	0044 5.8 0700 0.8 1306 5.7 1938 0.4	**7** SU	0152 5.4 0740 1.0 1400 5.5 2018 0.7	**22** M	0208 6.1 0818 0.6 1418 6.0 2058 0.1
8 SU ●	0004 5.6 0634 0.5 1236 5.7 1840 0.7	**23** M ○	0559 0.7 1206 5.6 1813 0.9	**8** W	0105 5.5 0710 0.9 1324 5.4 1937 0.7	**23** TH	0051 5.7 0710 0.8 1315 5.6 1940 0.6	**8** F	0134 5.3 0724 1.1 1345 5.3 2002 0.8	**23** SA	0136 5.9 0750 0.7 1353 5.7 2030 0.2	**8** M	0223 5.5 0813 1.0 1430 5.5 2051 0.7	**23** TU	0251 6.1 0858 0.7 1458 6.0 2137 0.2
9 M	0044 5.7 0708 0.5 1312 5.7 1919 0.6	**24** TU	0021 5.6 0642 0.7 1247 5.7 1858 0.8	**9** TH	0144 5.4 0744 1.0 1357 5.4 2014 0.8	**24** F	0142 5.8 0757 0.7 1402 5.6 2032 0.5	**9** SA	0210 5.3 0758 1.1 1417 5.3 2036 0.8	**24** SU	0225 6.0 0836 0.7 1439 5.8 2118 0.1	**9** TU	0255 5.5 0846 1.0 1500 5.4 2123 0.7	**24** W	0332 5.9 0934 0.8 1538 5.9 2211 0.4
10 TU	0122 5.7 0740 0.6 1346 5.6 1956 0.6	**25** W	0104 5.7 0724 0.7 1328 5.7 1944 0.7	**10** F	0221 5.4 0815 1.1 1430 5.3 2047 0.9	**25** SA	0232 5.9 0845 0.8 1449 5.6 2124 0.4	**10** SU	0244 5.3 0831 1.1 1450 5.3 2110 0.8	**25** M	0313 6.0 0920 0.8 1523 5.8 2203 0.2	**10** W	0327 5.4 0918 1.1 1531 5.4 2152 0.8	**25** TH	0413 5.6 1007 1.0 1618 5.6 2241 0.8
11 W	0159 5.6 0811 0.8 1418 5.5 2030 0.7	**26** TH	0148 5.8 0806 0.7 1410 5.6 2030 0.6	**11** SA	0258 5.2 0846 1.2 1503 5.2 2120 1.0	**26** SU	0324 5.8 0931 0.9 1538 5.5 2215 0.4	**11** M	0318 5.3 0905 1.1 1523 5.2 2143 0.8	**26** TU	0359 5.9 1001 0.9 1607 5.7 2245 0.3	**11** TH	0400 5.3 0946 1.2 1602 5.2 2219 1.0	**26** F ◐	0454 5.3 1042 1.1 1702 5.3 2313 1.1
12 TH	0236 5.5 0839 1.0 1449 5.3 2101 0.9	**27** F	0235 5.7 0848 0.8 1454 5.5 2118 0.6	**12** SU	0336 5.1 0920 1.3 1539 5.1 2155 1.0	**27** M	0416 5.7 1019 1.0 1629 5.4 2307 0.5	**12** TU	0354 5.2 0940 1.2 1557 5.2 2218 0.9	**27** W	0446 5.6 1040 1.0 1653 5.6 2325 0.6	**12** F	0435 5.2 1015 1.3 1639 5.2 2247 1.1	**27** SA	0538 5.0 1124 1.4 1754 5.0 2357 1.4
13 F	0313 5.3 0906 1.2 1521 5.1 2130 1.0	**28** SA	0325 5.6 0933 0.9 1542 5.3 2210 0.7	**13** M	0416 5.0 0959 1.4 1620 4.9 2237 1.1	**28** TU	0511 5.5 1108 1.1 1722 5.3 ◐	**13** W	0431 5.1 1016 1.3 1634 5.0 2254 1.0	**28** TH	0534 5.4 1122 1.3 1742 5.3	**13** SA	0517 5.0 1052 1.4 1726 5.0 ◐ 2327 1.3	**28** SU	0634 4.7 1225 1.7 1904 4.7
14 SA	0352 5.0 0937 1.3 1557 4.9 2204 1.2	**29** SU	0421 5.4 1024 1.2 1637 5.1 2309 0.9	**14** TU	0501 5.0 1044 1.5 1707 4.8 2326 1.2	**29** W ◐	0000 0.6 0607 5.4 1201 1.3 1820 5.2	**14** TH ◐	0512 5.0 1055 1.4 1716 5.0 2333 1.1	**29** F	0007 0.9 0626 5.1 1212 1.3 1838 5.1	**14** SU	0611 4.8 1148 1.6 1829 4.8	**29** M	0110 1.8 0746 4.5 1400 1.7 2034 4.5
15 SU	0436 4.8 1018 1.6 1641 4.7 2252 1.3	**30** M ◐	0523 5.3 1123 1.3 1740 5.0	**15** W ◐	0551 4.9 1137 1.6 1802 4.7	**30** TH	0056 0.7 0708 5.2 1300 1.3 1922 5.1	**15** F	0600 4.9 1137 1.6 1802 4.7	**30** SA	0059 1.1 0725 4.9 1315 1.7 1946 4.9	**15** M	0035 1.5 0722 4.7 1315 1.7 1954 4.7	**30** TU	0244 1.7 0912 4.5 1533 1.5 2159 4.7
		31 TU	0019 0.8 0631 5.2 1233 1.4 1850 5.0						**31** SU	0206 1.4 0833 4.8 1433 1.5 2103 4.8			**31** W	0401 1.7 1023 4.8 1644 1.2 2259 5.0

Chart Datum: 2·90 metres below Ordnance Datum (Newlyn)

》》 **FREE** monthly updates from 《《
www.reedsalmanac.co.uk

ENGLAND – SHEERNESS

TIME ZONE (UT)
For Summer Time add ONE hour in **non-shaded areas**

LAT 51°27′N   LONG 0°45′E

TIMES AND HEIGHTS OF HIGH AND LOW WATERS

YEAR 2005

SEPTEMBER

Time	m	Time	m
1 0458 1115 TH 1735 2345	1.5 5.1 1.0 5.3	**16** 0446 1053 F 1728 2329	1.1 5.3 0.7 5.8
2 0541 1157 F 1815	1.3 5.3 0.9	**17** 0542 1145 SA 1823	0.9 5.6 0.4
3 0022 0616 SA 1232 ● 1848	5.4 1.2 5.4 0.8	**18** 0019 0630 SU 1230 ○ 1909	6.0 0.8 5.9 0.2
4 0055 0647 SU 1304 1920	5.5 1.1 5.5 0.7	**19** 0103 0712 M 1311 1950	6.1 0.7 6.0 0.1
5 0126 0718 M 1334 1952	5.6 1.0 5.6 0.6	**20** 0144 0752 TU 1351 2028	6.1 0.6 6.1 0.2
6 0155 0750 TU 1403 2024	5.6 0.9 5.6 0.6	**21** 0223 0829 W 1429 2102	6.0 0.7 6.0 0.4
7 0226 0822 W 1432 2055	5.6 0.9 5.6 0.7	**22** 0300 0904 TH 1507 2132	5.8 0.8 5.9 0.7
8 0256 0852 TH 1502 2122	5.6 1.0 5.6 0.8	**23** 0336 0935 F 1546 2157	5.6 1.0 5.6 1.0
9 0328 0917 F 1534 2144	5.4 1.1 5.4 1.0	**24** 0412 1006 SA 1627 2225	5.3 1.2 5.3 1.3
10 0402 0943 SA 1612 2208	5.3 1.2 5.3 1.2	**25** 0451 1043 SU 1716 ◐ 2306	4.9 1.4 4.9 1.7
11 0443 1020 SU 1659 ◐ 2252	5.1 1.3 5.1 1.4	**26** 0541 1139 M 1824	4.6 1.7 4.5
12 0536 1119 M 1805	4.8 1.5 4.8	**27** 0015 0655 TU 1325 1958	2.0 4.3 1.8 4.4
13 0008 0650 TU 1258 1936	1.7 4.6 1.7 4.7	**28** 0208 0831 W 1507 2128	2.1 4.3 1.6 4.6
14 0209 0824 W 1456 2113	1.7 4.6 1.5 4.9	**29** 0330 0949 TH 1613 2229	1.9 4.7 1.3 5.0
15 0337 0948 TH 1620 2230	1.5 4.9 1.1 5.4	**30** 0427 1042 F 1702 2313	1.6 5.0 1.0 5.3

OCTOBER

Time	m	Time	m
1 0510 1123 SA 1741 2350	1.3 5.3 0.9 5.5	**16** 0517 1120 SU 1759 2355	1.0 5.7 0.4 5.9
2 0546 1159 SU 1816	1.2 5.5 0.8	**17** 0603 1203 M 1841	0.8 5.9 0.4
3 0022 0618 M 1231 ● 1848	5.6 1.0 5.6 0.7	**18** 0037 0643 TU 1244 1919	6.0 0.7 6.0 0.4
4 0053 0650 TU 1302 1920	5.6 0.9 5.7 0.7	**19** 0116 0723 W 1323 1953	6.0 0.7 6.0 0.5
5 0124 0723 W 1333 1953	5.7 0.9 5.7 0.7	**20** 0153 0800 TH 1401 2025	5.9 0.7 6.0 0.6
6 0155 0756 TH 1404 2024	5.7 0.9 5.7 0.8	**21** 0228 0836 F 1440 2054	5.7 0.8 5.8 0.9
7 0227 0827 F 1437 2052	5.6 1.0 5.6 0.9	**22** 0302 0908 SA 1519 2119	5.5 1.0 5.5 1.2
8 0300 0855 SA 1513 2117	5.5 1.1 5.5 1.1	**23** 0335 0938 SU 1559 2147	5.2 1.2 5.2 1.5
9 0336 0926 SU 1555 2149	5.3 1.2 5.3 1.3	**24** 0411 1011 M 1647 2227	4.9 1.4 4.8 1.8
10 0419 1010 M 1648 ◐ 2242	5.1 1.3 5.1 1.5	**25** 0457 1101 TU 1748 ◐ 2326	4.6 1.6 4.5 2.0
11 0515 1117 TU 1759	4.8 1.5 4.8	**26** 0604 1227 W 1909	4.4 1.8 4.4
12 0006 0633 W 1306 1931	1.8 4.6 1.5 4.8	**27** 0105 0735 TH 1420 2033	2.2 4.3 1.6 4.5
13 0156 0808 TH 1450 2102	1.8 4.7 1.3 5.1	**28** 0240 0855 F 1525 2139	2.0 4.5 1.4 4.8
14 0318 0928 F 1607 2213	1.5 4.9 0.9 5.5	**29** 0340 0953 SA 1616 2227	1.7 4.9 1.1 5.1
15 0423 1030 SA 1709 2309	1.2 5.4 0.6 5.8	**30** 0427 1039 SU 1658 2307	1.4 5.2 0.9 5.4
		31 0506 1118 M 1736 2343	1.2 5.4 0.8 5.5

NOVEMBER

Time	m	Time	m
1 0543 1154 TU 1812	1.1 5.5 0.8	**16** 0010 0614 W 1219 ○ 1844	5.7 0.8 5.8 0.7
2 0018 0619 W 1230 ● 1847	5.6 1.0 5.6 0.8	**17** 0049 0655 TH 1300 1919	5.7 0.7 5.8 0.8
3 0053 0656 TH 1305 1922	5.7 0.9 5.7 0.8	**18** 0126 0736 F 1340 1951	5.7 0.7 5.7 0.9
4 0127 0733 F 1341 1957	5.7 0.9 5.7 0.8	**19** 0201 0814 SA 1420 2022	5.6 0.8 5.6 1.1
5 0202 0810 SA 1420 2030	5.6 1.0 5.7 1.0	**20** 0235 0848 SU 1500 2050	5.4 1.0 5.4 1.3
6 0239 0847 SU 1502 2105	5.5 1.0 5.6 1.1	**21** 0308 0918 M 1540 2120	5.2 1.1 5.1 1.5
7 0320 0928 M 1550 2148	5.3 1.1 5.4 1.3	**22** 0343 0951 TU 1624 2158	5.0 1.3 4.9 1.7
8 0408 1020 TU 1649 2246	5.1 1.2 5.2 1.5	**23** 0426 1035 W 1716 ◐ 2248	4.8 1.4 4.6 1.9
9 0508 1132 W 1800 ◐	4.9 1.3 5.0	**24** 0521 1135 TH 1815 2354	4.6 1.5 4.5 2.0
10 0004 0623 TH 1307 1921	1.7 4.7 1.2 5.0	**25** 0631 1256 F 1923	4.4 1.6 4.5
11 0132 0746 F 1430 2040	1.7 4.8 1.0 5.2	**26** 0116 0745 SA 1416 2030	2.0 4.5 1.4 4.7
12 0246 0859 SA 1540 2146	1.5 5.1 0.8 5.4	**27** 0232 0850 SU 1516 2128	1.8 4.7 1.3 4.8
13 0349 1000 SU 1639 2241	1.3 5.3 0.7 5.6	**28** 0330 0945 M 1606 2218	1.6 5.0 1.1 5.2
14 0443 1051 M 1728 2328	1.1 5.6 0.6 5.7	**29** 0420 1034 TU 1652 2303	1.4 5.2 1.0 5.2
15 0531 1136 TU 1809	0.9 5.7 0.6	**30** 0505 1118 W 1735 2345	0.9 5.4 0.9 5.5

DECEMBER

Time	m	Time	m
1 0550 1201 TH 1817	1.1 5.5 0.9	**16** 0029 0638 F 1247 1852	5.5 0.8 5.5 1.0
2 0025 0633 F 1243 1857	5.6 0.9 5.6 0.9	**17** 0108 0721 SA 1329 1926	5.4 0.8 5.5 1.1
3 0106 0718 SA 1326 1938	5.6 0.9 5.7 0.9	**18** 0144 0800 SU 1409 1959	5.4 0.8 5.4 1.1
4 0146 0803 SU 1411 2020	5.6 0.8 5.7 0.9	**19** 0218 0836 M 1447 2030	5.3 0.9 5.3 1.2
5 0229 0850 M 1459 2103	5.5 0.8 5.7 1.0	**20** 0251 0907 TU 1524 2101	5.2 1.0 5.2 1.3
6 0314 0940 TU 1551 2151	5.4 0.8 5.5 1.2	**21** 0325 0939 W 1602 2137	5.1 1.1 5.0 1.4
7 0405 1035 W 1648 2245	5.2 0.8 5.4 1.3	**22** 0403 1015 TH 1643 2217	5.0 1.1 4.9 1.5
8 0502 1137 TH 1751 ◐ 2347	5.1 0.9 5.2 1.5	**23** 0445 1058 F 1728 ◐ 2305	4.8 1.2 4.7 1.7
9 0606 1246 F 1859	5.0 0.9 5.1	**24** 0533 1149 SA 1820	4.7 1.3 4.6
10 0055 0715 SA 1355 2007	1.5 4.9 0.9 5.2	**25** 0000 0631 SU 1249 1920	1.8 4.6 1.4 4.6
11 0204 0823 SU 1501 2112	1.5 4.9 0.9 5.2	**26** 0107 0739 M 1400 2025	1.8 4.6 1.4 4.7
12 0308 0926 M 1601 2210	1.3 5.1 0.9 5.4	**27** 0222 0848 TU 1511 2128	1.7 4.7 1.3 4.9
13 0408 1023 TU 1653 2301	1.2 5.3 0.9 5.4	**28** 0332 0951 W 1611 2225	1.5 5.0 1.2 5.1
14 0502 1115 W 1737 2347	1.1 5.4 1.0 5.4	**29** 0432 1047 TH 1705 2317	1.3 5.2 1.0 5.3
15 0552 1202 TH 1816 ○	0.9 5.5 0.9	**30** 0527 1140 F 1755	1.1 5.4 0.9
		31 0006 0619 SA 1230 ● 1842	5.5 0.9 5.6 0.9

Chart Datum: 2·90 metres below Ordnance Datum (Newlyn)

》》 **FREE** monthly updates from 《《
www.reedsalmanac.co.uk

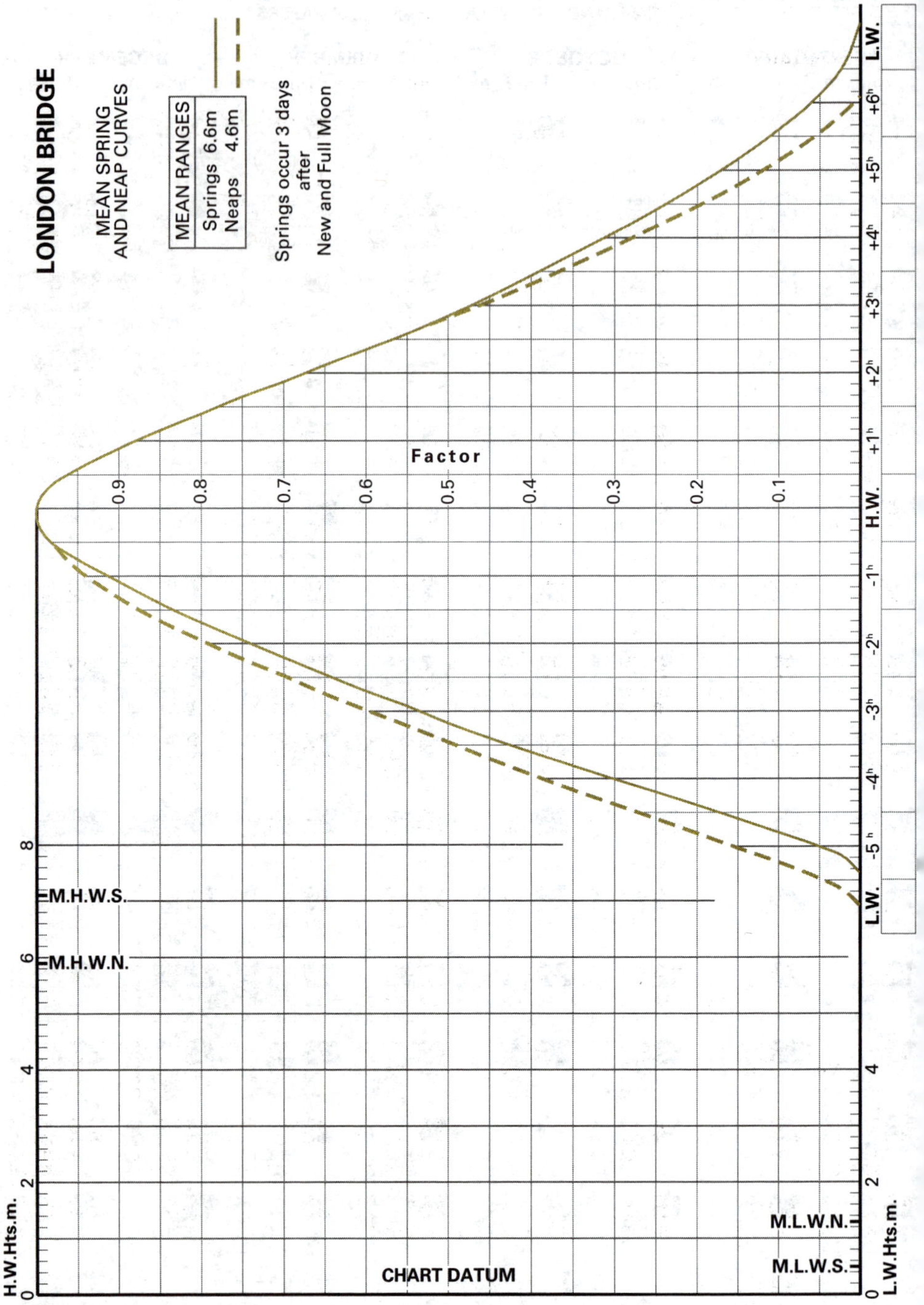
LONDON BRIDGE
MEAN SPRING AND NEAP CURVES
MEAN RANGES
Springs 6.6m
Neaps 4.6m
Springs occur 3 days after New and Full Moon
Factor
0.9
0.8
0.7
0.6
0.5
0.4
0.3
0.2
0.1
L.W.
-5 h
-4h
-3h
-2h
-1h
H.W.
+1h
+2h
+3h
+4h
+5h
+6h
L.W.
M.H.W.S.
M.H.W.N.
M.L.W.N.
M.L.W.S.
CHART DATUM
H.W.Hts.m.
L.W.Hts.m.
0
2
4
6
8

TIME ZONE (UT)
For Summer Time add ONE hour in **non-shaded areas**

ENGLAND – LONDON BRIDGE
LAT 51°30'N   LONG 0°05'W
TIMES AND HEIGHTS OF HIGH AND LOW WATERS

YEAR 2005

JANUARY

Time m	Time m
1 0441 6.4 / 1113 1.0 / SA 1723 6.4 / 2313 1.1	**16** 0549 6.7 / 1233 0.5 / SU 1830 6.7
2 0520 6.3 / 1149 1.0 / SU 1805 6.4 / 2354 1.2	**17** 0030 1.1 / 0634 6.5 / M 1309 0.8 / ◐ 1919 6.4
3 0603 6.2 / 1231 1.1 / M 1852 6.2 / ◑	**18** 0111 1.2 / 0724 6.3 / TU 1349 1.0 / 2011 6.1
4 0039 1.3 / 0654 6.1 / TU 1321 1.2 / 1946 6.1	**19** 0157 1.4 / 0822 6.1 / W 1438 1.3 / 2109 5.8
5 0134 1.5 / 0755 5.9 / W 1424 1.3 / 2049 5.9	**20** 0253 1.6 / 0929 5.9 / TH 1536 1.5 / 2210 5.7
6 0243 1.7 / 0906 5.9 / TH 1540 1.4 / 2159 6.0	**21** 0357 1.7 / 1038 5.8 / F 1644 1.6 / 2313 5.8
7 0406 1.6 / 1019 6.0 / F 1701 1.3 / 2307 6.2	**22** 0511 1.6 / 1142 6.0 / SA 1755 1.5
8 0525 1.4 / 1129 6.3 / SA 1812 1.1	**23** 0011 6.0 / 0631 1.4 / SU 1240 6.2 / 1853 1.4
9 0008 6.5 / 0638 1.1 / SU 1231 6.7 / 1912 0.9	**24** 0102 6.2 / 0728 1.1 / M 1328 6.4 / 1941 1.2
10 0103 6.7 / 0744 0.9 / M 1328 6.9 / ● 2008 0.8	**25** 0145 6.4 / 0815 0.9 / TU 1410 6.5 / ○ 2024 1.2
11 0154 6.9 / 0844 0.6 / TU 1422 7.1 / 2101 0.7	**26** 0221 6.5 / 0857 0.9 / W 1446 6.6 / 2059 1.0
12 0243 6.9 / 0939 0.4 / W 1514 7.2 / 2149 0.7	**27** 0253 6.4 / 0935 0.9 / TH 1519 6.5 / 2128 1.3
13 0331 6.9 / 1030 0.3 / TH 1605 7.2 / 2234 0.8	**28** 0323 6.4 / 1008 1.0 / F 1551 6.5 / 2154 1.2
14 0418 6.9 / 1115 0.3 / F 1654 7.1 / 2315 0.8	**29** 0352 6.4 / 1034 1.0 / SA 1625 6.6 / 2225 1.2
15 0504 6.8 / 1156 0.4 / SA 1742 7.0 / 2353 0.9	**30** 0423 6.5 / 1100 1.0 / SU 1700 6.6 / 2258 1.1
	31 0458 6.5 / 1128 0.9 / M 1739 6.6 / 2333 1.0

FEBRUARY

Time m	Time m
1 0538 6.5 / 1201 0.9 / TU 1821 6.4	**16** 0029 1.0 / 0632 6.5 / W 1256 1.0 / ◐ 1905 6.1
2 0011 1.1 / 0624 6.4 / W 1241 1.0 / ◑ 1910 6.2	**17** 0106 1.3 / 0719 6.1 / TH 1338 1.4 / 1951 5.7
3 0056 1.3 / 0719 6.1 / TH 1331 1.3 / 2007 5.9	**18** 0158 1.6 / 0823 5.6 / F 1438 1.8 / 2057 5.3
4 0154 1.5 / 0826 5.9 / F 1442 1.6 / 2115 5.7	**19** 0306 1.8 / 0958 5.4 / SA 1548 2.0 / 2232 5.3
5 0315 1.8 / 0943 5.8 / SA 1619 1.7 / 2234 5.7	**20** 0419 1.8 / 1119 5.6 / SU 1709 1.9 / 2344 5.6
6 0455 1.7 / 1107 5.9 / SU 1755 1.5 / 2349 6.0	**21** 0604 1.5 / 1219 6.0 / M 1831 1.5
7 0637 1.3 / 1221 6.4 / M 1905 1.1	**22** 0039 6.1 / 0710 1.1 / TU 1308 6.4 / 1923 1.2
8 0051 6.4 / 0745 0.8 / TU 1322 6.8 / ● 2002 0.8	**23** 0124 6.4 / 0756 0.8 / W 1349 6.6 / 2007 1.1
9 0144 6.8 / 0841 0.4 / W 1414 7.1 / 2052 0.6	**24** 0202 6.5 / 0839 0.7 / TH 1425 6.7 / ○ 2045 1.1
10 0231 7.0 / 0931 0.1 / TH 1503 7.3 / 2139 0.5	**25** 0235 6.5 / 0918 0.8 / F 1457 6.7 / 2118 1.2
11 0316 7.1 / 1017 0.0 / F 1549 7.3 / 2221 0.5	**26** 0305 6.5 / 0953 0.9 / SA 1529 6.6 / 2145 1.2
12 0358 7.1 / 1058 0.0 / SA 1632 7.3 / 2259 0.6	**27** 0332 6.5 / 1021 0.9 / SU 1601 6.6 / 2213 1.1
13 0438 7.1 / 1132 0.2 / SU 1713 7.1 / 2331 0.7	**28** 0402 6.6 / 1043 0.9 / M 1635 6.7 / 2241 1.0
14 0516 7.0 / 1200 0.5 / M 1752 6.8	
15 0000 0.8 / 0553 6.8 / TU 1226 0.7 / 1828 6.5	

MARCH

Time m	Time m
1 0437 6.7 / 1106 0.9 / TU 1712 6.6 / 2312 0.9	**16** 0519 6.9 / 1143 0.8 / W 1743 6.5 / 2351 0.9
2 0517 6.7 / 1134 0.9 / W 1753 6.5 / 2346 0.9	**17** 0558 6.5 / 1208 1.1 / TH 1817 6.2 / ◑
3 0602 6.5 / 1210 1.0 / TH 1838 6.2 / ◐	**18** 0022 1.1 / 0642 6.0 / F 1245 1.4 / 1859 5.7
4 0027 1.1 / 0654 6.2 / F 1257 1.3 / 1931 5.8	**19** 0112 1.5 / 0738 5.5 / SA 1346 1.9 / 1954 5.3
5 0121 1.5 / 0759 5.8 / SA 1403 1.7 / 2039 5.4	**20** 0229 1.8 / 0908 5.2 / SU 1506 2.1 / 2138 5.1
6 0241 1.8 / 0921 5.5 / SU 1551 2.0 / 2210 5.4	**21** 0346 1.8 / 1050 5.4 / M 1628 2.0 / 2312 5.5
7 0502 1.8 / 1102 5.7 / M 1750 1.7 / 2338 5.8	**22** 0518 1.5 / 1152 5.9 / TU 1801 1.6
8 0640 1.1 / 1217 6.3 / TU 1856 1.1	**23** 0010 6.0 / 0641 1.0 / W 1240 6.7 / 1857 1.3
9 0040 6.3 / 0736 0.5 / W 1313 6.9 / 1948 0.7	**24** 0056 6.3 / 0728 0.7 / TH 1320 6.7 / 1940 1.1
10 0130 6.8 / 0826 0.1 / TH 1401 7.3 / ● 2035 0.4	**25** 0134 6.5 / 0810 0.6 / F 1356 6.8 / ○ 2019 1.0
11 0213 7.1 / 0911 -0.1 / F 1445 7.4 / 2118 0.3	**26** 0208 6.6 / 0850 0.7 / SA 1429 6.7 / 2055 1.1
12 0254 7.2 / 0953 -0.1 / SA 1526 7.4 / 2159 0.3	**27** 0238 6.5 / 0927 0.8 / SU 1502 6.7 / 2128 1.1
13 0332 7.2 / 1030 0.0 / SU 1604 7.2 / 2234 0.4	**28** 0308 6.6 / 0958 0.9 / M 1535 6.7 / 2158 1.0
14 0409 7.2 / 1100 0.3 / M 1639 7.0 / 2304 0.6	**29** 0341 6.7 / 1022 0.9 / TU 1611 6.7 / 2227 0.9
15 0444 7.1 / 1123 0.6 / TU 1711 6.8 / 2328 0.7	**30** 0419 6.8 / 1046 0.9 / W 1648 6.6 / 2256 0.8
	31 0501 6.7 / 1115 0.9 / TH 1729 6.4 / 2330 0.9

APRIL

Time m	Time m
1 0547 6.5 / 1152 1.1 / F 1814 6.1	**16** 0617 6.0 / 1208 1.4 / SA 1826 5.8 / ◑
2 0012 1.1 / 0642 6.1 / SA 1242 1.5 / ◐ 1907 5.7	**17** 0039 1.4 / 0710 5.6 / SU 1304 1.8 / 1918 5.4
3 0109 1.5 / 0750 5.7 / SU 1351 1.9 / 2021 5.3	**18** 0156 1.7 / 0822 5.3 / M 1423 2.1 / 2034 5.2
4 0242 1.8 / 0923 5.5 / M 1553 2.1 / 2202 5.4	**19** 0313 1.7 / 1004 5.4 / TU 1543 2.0 / 2225 5.4
5 0515 1.5 / 1058 5.9 / TU 1734 1.6 / 2321 5.9	**20** 0430 1.5 / 1110 5.8 / W 1703 1.8 / 2329 5.8
6 0623 0.8 / 1203 6.5 / W 1834 1.0	**21** 0551 1.1 / 1201 6.3 / TH 1811 1.4
7 0019 6.5 / 0713 0.2 / TH 1255 7.1 / 1923 0.5	**22** 0017 6.2 / 0646 0.8 / F 1243 6.6 / 1900 1.1
8 0106 6.9 / 0759 -0.1 / F 1339 7.3 / ● 2008 0.3	**23** 0057 6.4 / 0732 0.7 / SA 1321 6.8 / 1943 1.0
9 0148 7.2 / 0842 -0.1 / SA 1420 7.4 / 2052 0.2	**24** 0134 6.6 / 0814 0.6 / SU 1358 6.8 / ○ 2024 0.9
10 0228 7.2 / 0921 0.0 / SU 1459 7.3 / 2132 0.3	**25** 0209 6.7 / 0853 0.6 / M 1434 6.8 / 2104 0.9
11 0306 7.2 / 0957 0.3 / M 1534 7.0 / 2208 0.4	**26** 0245 6.8 / 0929 0.7 / TU 1511 6.8 / 2141 0.8
12 0342 7.1 / 1026 0.5 / TU 1605 6.8 / 2238 0.6	**27** 0324 6.8 / 1001 0.8 / W 1550 6.7 / 2216 0.8
13 0417 6.9 / 1049 0.8 / W 1635 6.6 / 2300 0.7	**28** 0407 6.8 / 1032 0.9 / TH 1631 6.6 / 2251 0.8
14 0454 6.7 / 1107 1.0 / TH 1707 6.5 / 2322 0.8	**29** 0453 6.6 / 1107 1.0 / F 1714 6.3 / 2330 0.9
15 0533 6.4 / 1132 1.1 / F 1743 6.2 / 2352 1.1	**30** 0544 6.4 / 1149 1.2 / SA 1802 6.0

Chart Datum: 2·90 metres below Ordnance Datum (Newlyn)

》》 **FREE** monthly updates from 《《
www.reedsalmanac.co.uk

TIDES

TIME ZONE (UT)
For Summer Time add ONE hour in **non-shaded areas**

ENGLAND – LONDON BRIDGE
LAT 51°30′N   LONG 0°05′W
TIMES AND HEIGHTS OF HIGH AND LOW WATERS

YEAR 2005

	MAY			JUNE			JULY			AUGUST		
	Time m	Time m		Time m	Time m		Time m	Time m		Time m	Time m
1 SU	0018 1.1 0644 6.1 1243 1.5 ☾ 1901 5.7	**16** M	0020 1.2 0646 5.8 1234 1.6 ☽ 1849 5.7	**1** W	0252 1.0 0903 6.3 1505 1.5 2118 6.1	**16** TH	0146 1.2 0806 5.8 1400 1.7 2016 5.7	**1** F	0310 0.9 0930 6.3 1523 1.4 2142 6.3	**16** SA	0154 1.2 0823 5.9 1419 1.6 2034 5.8	**1** M	0414 1.6 1051 5.8 1644 1.6 2320 5.9	**16** TU	0343 1.7 1003 5.6 1622 1.7 2233 5.8
2 M	0125 1.4 0758 5.8 1357 1.8 2023 5.5	**17** TU	0122 1.4 0744 5.6 1337 1.8 1952 5.4	**2** TH	0407 0.8 1006 6.5 1618 1.3 2219 6.3	**17** F	0252 1.3 0910 5.8 1510 1.7 2126 5.7	**2** SA	0412 1.0 1027 6.3 1629 1.4 2242 6.2	**17** SU	0306 1.3 0929 5.8 1535 1.7 2146 5.8	**2** TU	0533 1.5 1153 6.0 1819 1.4	**17** W	0519 1.5 1123 5.9 1803 1.4 2356 6.2
3 TU	0307 1.5 0924 5.9 1539 1.8 2146 5.7	**18** W	0234 1.5 0855 5.5 1451 1.9 2113 5.4	**3** F	0509 0.7 1103 6.7 1722 1.1 2316 6.6	**18** SA	0400 1.2 1017 6.0 1621 1.6 2234 5.9	**3** SU	0515 1.1 1123 6.3 1738 1.3 2342 6.3	**18** M	0425 1.3 1039 6.0 1651 1.5 2300 6.0	**3** W	0022 6.2 0638 1.3 1248 6.3 1920 1.0	**18** TH	0636 1.1 1228 6.4 1920 0.8
4 W	0448 1.1 1037 6.3 1702 1.4 2253 6.2	**19** TH	0343 1.4 1009 5.8 1604 1.8 2229 5.7	**4** SA	0602 0.5 1155 6.8 1818 0.8	**19** SU	0509 1.1 1118 6.3 1729 1.3 2335 6.2	**4** M	0612 1.0 1217 6.4 1840 1.1	**19** TU	0539 1.1 1144 6.3 1807 1.2	**4** TH	0115 6.5 0730 1.1 1335 6.5 2008 0.8	**19** F	0059 6.7 0735 0.8 1322 6.8 ○ 2016 0.3
5 TH	0551 0.6 1136 6.7 1802 0.9 2349 6.6	**20** F	0453 1.2 1110 6.1 1713 1.5 2327 6.0	**5** SU	0008 6.7 0649 0.5 1244 6.9 1908 0.7	**20** M	0611 0.9 1212 6.6 1832 1.1	**5** TU	0038 6.4 0702 1.0 1307 6.5 1934 0.9	**20** W	0008 6.4 0644 0.9 1243 6.6 1919 0.9	**5** F	0200 6.6 0815 1.0 1415 6.6 ● 2052 0.7	**20** SA	0152 7.2 0827 0.5 1410 7.1 2108 0.0
6 F	0641 0.2 1227 7.1 1852 0.5	**21** SA	0556 0.9 1200 6.5 1813 1.2	**6** M	0057 6.8 0733 0.5 1328 6.8 ● 1956 0.6	**21** TU	0030 6.6 0705 0.7 1302 6.8 1930 0.8	**6** W	0129 6.5 0749 1.0 1352 6.5 ● 2023 0.8	**21** TH	0108 6.8 0743 0.7 1335 6.8 ○ 2022 0.6	**6** SA	0239 6.7 0856 1.1 1450 6.6 2131 0.7	**21** SU	0240 7.4 0916 0.4 1454 7.2 2155 -0.2
7 SA	0037 6.9 0725 0.1 1312 7.2 1938 0.3	**22** SU	0015 6.4 0649 0.7 1245 6.7 1905 1.0	**7** TU	0143 6.8 0815 0.7 1409 6.7 2040 0.6	**22** W	0122 6.8 0757 0.6 1350 6.9 ○ 2026 0.6	**7** TH	0215 6.6 0832 1.0 1431 6.5 2107 0.8	**22** F	0202 7.1 0838 0.6 1425 7.0 2118 0.3	**7** SU	0313 6.6 0931 1.2 1520 6.5 2206 0.8	**22** M	0326 7.5 1000 0.4 1537 7.3 2237 -0.1
8 SU	0122 7.1 0807 0.1 1353 7.1 ● 2023 0.3	**23** M	0100 6.6 0736 0.6 1328 6.9 ○ 1954 0.8	**8** W	0227 6.7 0854 0.9 1445 6.5 2122 0.7	**23** TH	0212 7.0 0847 0.6 1437 6.9 2121 0.5	**8** F	0256 6.5 0911 1.1 1505 6.4 2147 0.8	**23** SA	0254 7.2 0929 0.6 1513 7.0 2210 0.1	**8** M	0343 6.5 0958 1.3 1548 6.4 2234 0.9	**23** TU	0410 7.4 1041 0.4 1618 7.3 2313 0.0
9 M	0203 7.1 0847 0.3 1432 7.0 2105 0.4	**24** TU	0142 6.8 0821 0.6 1409 6.9 2041 0.7	**9** TH	0307 6.6 0929 1.0 1518 6.4 2158 0.8	**24** F	0303 7.1 0936 0.7 1525 6.8 2213 0.4	**9** SA	0332 6.5 0944 1.2 1536 6.4 2220 0.9	**24** SU	0344 7.3 1017 0.6 1600 7.0 2256 0.0	**9** TU	0413 6.5 1020 1.3 1616 6.4 2254 1.0	**24** W	0452 7.2 1117 0.6 1658 7.2 2344 0.3
10 TU	0243 6.9 0923 0.6 1506 6.7 2142 0.6	**25** W	0226 6.9 0904 0.7 1452 6.9 2127 0.7	**10** F	0345 6.4 0958 1.2 1549 6.3 2228 0.9	**25** SA	0355 7.0 1023 0.8 1614 6.8 2303 0.4	**10** SU	0405 6.4 1009 1.3 1607 6.4 2247 0.9	**25** M	0433 7.2 1100 0.6 1645 7.0 2338 0.1	**10** W	0445 6.5 1048 1.2 1646 6.5 2314 0.9	**25** TH	0532 6.9 1149 0.7 1737 7.0
11 W	0321 6.8 0955 0.8 1537 6.6 2215 0.7	**26** TH	0312 6.9 0945 0.7 1536 6.7 2213 0.6	**11** SA	0421 6.4 1022 1.2 1622 6.3 2255 0.9	**26** SU	0447 7.0 1109 0.8 1703 6.7 2349 0.4	**11** M	0438 6.4 1036 1.2 1639 6.4 2312 0.9	**26** TU	0521 7.1 1140 0.7 1730 7.0	**11** TH	0520 6.5 1120 1.1 1722 6.5 2341 0.9	**26** F	0010 0.6 0611 6.6 1221 1.1 ☽ 1816 6.7
12 TH	0358 6.6 1020 1.0 1607 6.5 2240 0.8	**27** F	0400 6.9 1026 0.8 1621 6.6 2258 0.7	**12** SU	0458 6.3 1051 1.2 1658 6.3 2325 1.0	**27** M	0540 6.9 1154 0.9 1753 6.6	**12** TU	0514 6.4 1108 1.2 1714 6.3 2341 0.9	**27** W	0015 0.2 0608 6.9 1218 1.0 1813 6.8	**12** F	0559 6.4 1155 1.1 1804 6.4	**27** SA	0039 0.9 0650 6.1 1257 1.5 1901 6.2
13 F	0435 6.5 1041 1.1 1641 6.4 2304 0.9	**28** SA	0452 6.8 1108 1.0 1709 6.4 2344 0.7	**13** M	0538 6.3 1127 1.3 1738 6.1	**28** TU	0035 0.6 0635 6.7 1240 1.0 ☽ 1845 6.5	**13** W	0552 6.3 1145 1.2 1753 6.3	**28** TH	0050 0.6 0656 6.6 1256 1.0 ☽ 1900 6.6	**13** SA	0015 1.0 0644 6.1 1237 1.3 SU 1853 6.2	**28** SU	0118 1.5 0737 5.7 1346 1.8 2003 5.7
14 SA	0514 6.3 1108 1.2 1718 6.2 2336 1.0	**29** SU	0547 6.5 1155 1.2 1802 6.2	**14** TU	0002 1.0 0621 6.1 1210 1.4 1822 6.0	**29** W	0122 0.6 0732 6.6 1329 1.2 1942 6.4	**14** TH	0015 0.9 0635 6.2 1227 1.3 ☽ 1836 6.1	**29** F	0127 1.0 0748 6.2 1339 1.2 1953 6.3	**14** SU	0100 1.2 0738 5.9 1331 1.6 1955 5.9	**29** M	0215 1.8 0852 5.4 1450 1.8 2137 5.4
15 SU	0558 6.0 1145 1.3 1800 6.0	**30** M	0036 0.9 0647 6.3 1248 1.4 ☽ 1902 6.0	**15** W	0049 1.1 0710 5.9 1300 1.5 ☽ 1913 5.8	**30** TH	0213 0.7 0831 6.4 1423 1.3 2041 6.3	**15** F	0058 1.0 0724 6.0 1317 1.4 1930 6.0	**30** SA	0211 1.4 0845 6.0 1430 1.4 2057 6.0	**15** M	0206 1.5 0844 5.6 1451 1.8 2108 5.7	**30** TU	0327 2.0 1019 5.5 1604 1.8 2300 5.6
		31 TU	0138 1.0 0755 6.2 1352 1.5 2011 6.0					**31** SU	0307 1.4 0947 5.8 1531 1.6 2209 5.8			**31** W	0457 1.9 1129 5.7 1804 1.5

Chart Datum: 2·90 metres below Ordnance Datum (Newlyn)
)) **FREE** monthly updates from ((
www.reedsalmanac.co.uk

ENGLAND – LONDON BRIDGE

YEAR 2005

LAT 51°30'N   LONG 0°05'W

TIMES AND HEIGHTS OF HIGH AND LOW WATERS

TIME ZONE (UT)
For Summer Time add ONE hour in **non-shaded areas**

SEPTEMBER

Time	m		Time	m
1 0003	6.1	**16**	0626	1.2
0620	1.5		1213	6.4
TH 1225	6.2	F	1908	0.6
1901	1.0			
2 0054	6.5	**17**	0047	6.9
0711	1.1		0719	0.7
F 1311	6.5	SA	1304	6.9
1946	0.7		1959	0.1
3 0137	6.8	**18**	0135	7.3
0755	1.0		0808	0.4
SA 1351	6.7	SU	1348	7.2
● 2028	0.6	○	2045	-0.2
4 0214	6.8	**19**	0219	7.5
0835	1.0		0853	0.3
SU 1425	6.6	M	1429	7.4
2107	0.6		2129	-0.2
5 0246	6.7	**20**	0301	7.5
0911	1.1		0936	0.3
M 1455	6.5	TU	1509	7.4
2142	0.8		2208	0.0
6 0315	6.6	**21**	0341	7.4
0939	1.2		1015	0.4
TU 1521	6.4	W	1548	7.3
2211	1.0		2241	0.2
7 0344	6.6	**22**	0418	7.1
1002	1.3		1050	0.6
W 1547	6.5	TH	1626	7.2
2229	1.1		2308	0.5
8 0414	6.6	**23**	0453	6.8
1026	1.2		1119	0.7
TH 1618	6.6	F	1703	7.0
2246	1.0		2330	0.8
9 0448	6.6	**24**	0525	6.5
1055	1.1		1146	1.0
F 1655	6.6	SA	1742	6.6
2310	0.9		2353	1.1
10 0526	6.4	**25**	0559	6.1
1127	1.1		1218	1.2
SA 1737	6.5	SU	1826	6.1
2342	1.0	◐		
11 0609	6.2	**26**	0027	1.5
1205	1.2		0638	5.7
SU 1827	6.2	M	1307	1.6
◐			1922	5.6
12 0024	1.3	**27**	0125	2.0
0700	5.8		0735	5.3
M 1257	1.6	TU	1418	1.9
1928	5.8		2104	5.2
13 0125	1.7	**28**	0247	2.3
0806	5.5		0944	5.2
TU 1417	1.9	W	1534	1.9
2043	5.5		2233	5.5
14 0309	2.0	**29**	0418	2.1
0933	5.4		1058	5.6
W 1614	1.9	TH	1729	1.5
2222	5.6		2334	6.0
15 0512	1.8	**30**	0552	1.7
1108	5.8		1154	6.1
TH 1807	1.3	F	1829	1.0
2349	6.2			

OCTOBER

Time	m		Time	m
1 0024	6.5	**16**	0026	7.0
0643	1.2		0654	0.6
SA 1240	6.5	SU	1237	7.0
1913	0.7		1931	0.0
2 0106	6.8	**17**	0112	7.4
0726	1.0		0741	0.3
SU 1319	6.6	M	1321	7.3
1954	0.6	○	2015	-0.1
3 0141	6.8	**18**	0154	7.5
0804	1.0		0826	0.2
M 1353	6.6	TU	1402	7.4
● 2033	0.7		2056	0.0
4 0213	6.8	**19**	0233	7.4
0839	1.1		0908	0.3
TU 1423	6.6	W	1442	7.3
2109	0.8		2134	0.2
5 0243	6.7	**20**	0311	7.2
0910	1.2		0948	0.5
W 1451	6.5	TH	1521	7.2
2138	1.0		2207	0.5
6 0313	6.6	**21**	0345	6.9
0939	1.2		1023	0.7
TH 1521	6.6	F	1559	7.0
2200	1.1		2233	0.8
7 0345	6.6	**22**	0417	6.7
1007	1.1		1052	0.9
F 1556	6.6	SA	1638	6.7
2220	1.0		2254	1.0
8 0420	6.6	**23**	0448	6.4
1036	1.1		1118	1.0
SA 1636	6.7	SU	1710	6.4
2247	1.0		2317	1.3
9 0459	6.5	**24**	0522	6.2
1109	1.1		1149	1.3
SU 1721	6.5	M	1802	6.0
2323	1.1		2350	1.6
10 0543	6.2	**25**	0602	5.8
1149	1.2		1237	1.5
M 1813	1.6	TU	1855	5.6
◐		◐		
11 0008	1.4	**26**	0039	1.9
0634	5.8		0654	5.4
TU 1244	1.6	W	1346	1.8
1916	5.6		2010	5.3
12 0110	1.9	**27**	0158	2.3
0742	5.4		0827	5.2
W 1415	1.8	TH	1500	1.8
2038	5.5		2147	5.4
13 0258	2.2	**28**	0324	2.2
0921	5.4		1012	5.4
TH 1625	1.6	F	1617	1.6
2219	5.8		2252	5.8
14 0455	1.8	**29**	0448	1.9
1048	5.9		1111	5.8
F 1748	1.0	SA	1735	1.2
2332	6.4		2343	6.1
15 0602	1.2	**30**	0555	1.5
1148	6.5		1159	6.2
SA 1843	0.4	SU	1828	0.9
		31	0025	6.5
			0641	1.2
		M	1240	6.5
			1911	0.8

NOVEMBER

Time	m		Time	m
1 0103	6.7	**16**	0127	7.2
0722	1.1		0757	0.4
TU 1316	6.6	W	1338	7.2
1952	0.8	○	2023	0.4
2 0138	6.8	**17**	0207	7.1
0801	1.1		0841	0.5
W 1350	6.6	TH	1420	7.1
● 2030	0.8		2102	0.6
3 0212	6.8	**18**	0245	6.9
0834	1.0		0923	0.7
TH 1424	6.7	F	1501	6.9
2104	0.9		2137	0.9
4 0247	6.8	**19**	0319	6.7
0916	1.0		1000	0.8
F 1501	6.7	SA	1542	6.7
2135	1.0		2206	1.0
5 0323	6.7	**20**	0350	6.5
0952	1.0		1032	1.0
SA 1542	6.8	SU	1621	6.5
2204	1.0		2228	1.2
6 0401	6.6	**21**	0421	6.4
1028	1.0		1100	1.1
SU 1627	6.7	M	1701	6.3
2231	1.1		2253	1.3
7 0443	6.4	**22**	0457	6.2
1107	1.1		1131	1.2
M 1716	6.5	TU	1742	6.1
2318	1.2		2325	1.5
8 0528	6.2	**23**	0537	6.0
1155	1.2		1212	1.4
TU 1811	6.2	W	1829	5.9
9 0007	1.5	**24**	0009	1.7
0622	5.8		0624	5.7
W 1259	1.4	TH	1308	1.6
◐ 1917	5.9		1922	5.6
10 0112	1.9	**25**	0105	2.0
0736	5.6		0724	5.5
TH 1428	1.4	F	1413	1.6
2038	5.8		2027	5.5
11 0247	2.0	**26**	0217	2.1
0907	5.7		0847	5.4
F 1605	1.3	SA	1519	1.6
2158	6.1		2140	5.6
12 0421	1.6	**27**	0333	2.0
1018	6.1		1006	5.6
SA 1715	0.8	SU	1626	1.4
2302	6.5		2244	5.9
13 0528	1.2	**28**	0443	1.6
1116	6.6		1105	5.9
SU 1810	0.5	M	1728	1.2
2356	6.9		2336	6.3
14 0622	0.8	**29**	0544	1.3
1207	6.9		1154	6.2
M 1858	0.3	TU	1823	1.0
15 0044	7.2	**30**	0022	6.6
0711	0.5		0637	1.0
TU 1254	7.1	W	1239	6.5
1942	0.3		1910	0.9

DECEMBER

Time	m		Time	m
1 0105	6.8	**16**	0147	6.7
0725	1.0		0820	0.8
TH 1321	6.7	F	1406	6.7
● 1955	0.8		2036	1.0
2 0146	6.9	**17**	0227	6.6
0812	0.9		0905	0.8
F 1403	6.8	SA	1450	6.6
2037	0.8		2115	1.1
3 0227	6.9	**18**	0302	6.5
0859	0.8		0946	0.9
SA 1448	6.9	SU	1531	6.5
2118	0.9		2148	1.3
4 0308	6.8	**19**	0333	6.4
0946	0.8		1022	1.0
SU 1534	6.9	M	1608	6.4
2158	1.0		2212	1.4
5 0351	6.7	**20**	0405	6.3
1033	0.8		1051	1.1
M 1624	6.8	TU	1644	6.3
2240	1.1		2236	1.4
6 0437	6.5	**21**	0439	6.3
1121	0.9		1117	1.2
TU 1716	6.6	W	1721	6.3
2324	1.2		2306	1.3
7 0525	6.3	**22**	0516	6.2
1211	1.0		1148	1.2
W 1812	6.4	TH	1800	6.2
			2343	1.4
8 0013	1.4	**23**	0557	6.1
0620	6.1		1227	1.3
TH 1308	1.0	F	1844	6.0
◐ 1913	6.3	◐		
9 0110	1.5	**24**	0027	1.5
0727	6.0		0644	5.9
F 1413	1.1	SA	1316	1.4
2020	6.2		1933	5.9
10 0218	1.6	**25**	0120	1.7
0838	6.1		0740	5.7
SA 1524	1.1	SU	1416	1.5
2126	6.3		2031	5.8
11 0333	1.6	**26**	0226	1.8
0943	6.2		0849	5.6
SU 1631	1.0	M	1523	1.5
2228	6.4		2137	5.8
12 0444	1.4	**27**	0341	1.8
1043	6.3		1001	5.7
M 1730	0.9	TU	1632	1.4
2324	6.6		2244	6.0
13 0547	1.1	**28**	0453	1.6
1138	6.4		1107	5.9
TU 1823	0.8	W	1738	1.2
			2344	6.3
14 0015	6.7	**29**	0558	1.3
0642	0.9		1206	6.4
W 1231	6.7	TH	1836	1.0
1910	0.8			
15 0103	6.7	**30**	0037	6.6
0732	0.8		0657	1.0
TH 1320	6.8	F	1259	6.7
○ 1955	0.9		1929	0.9
		31	0126	6.8
			0755	0.8
		SA	1349	6.9
		●	2020	0.8

Chart Datum: 2·90 metres below Ordnance Datum (Newlyn)

》》 **FREE** monthly updates from 《《
www.reedsalmanac.co.uk

Chapter 5

TIDES

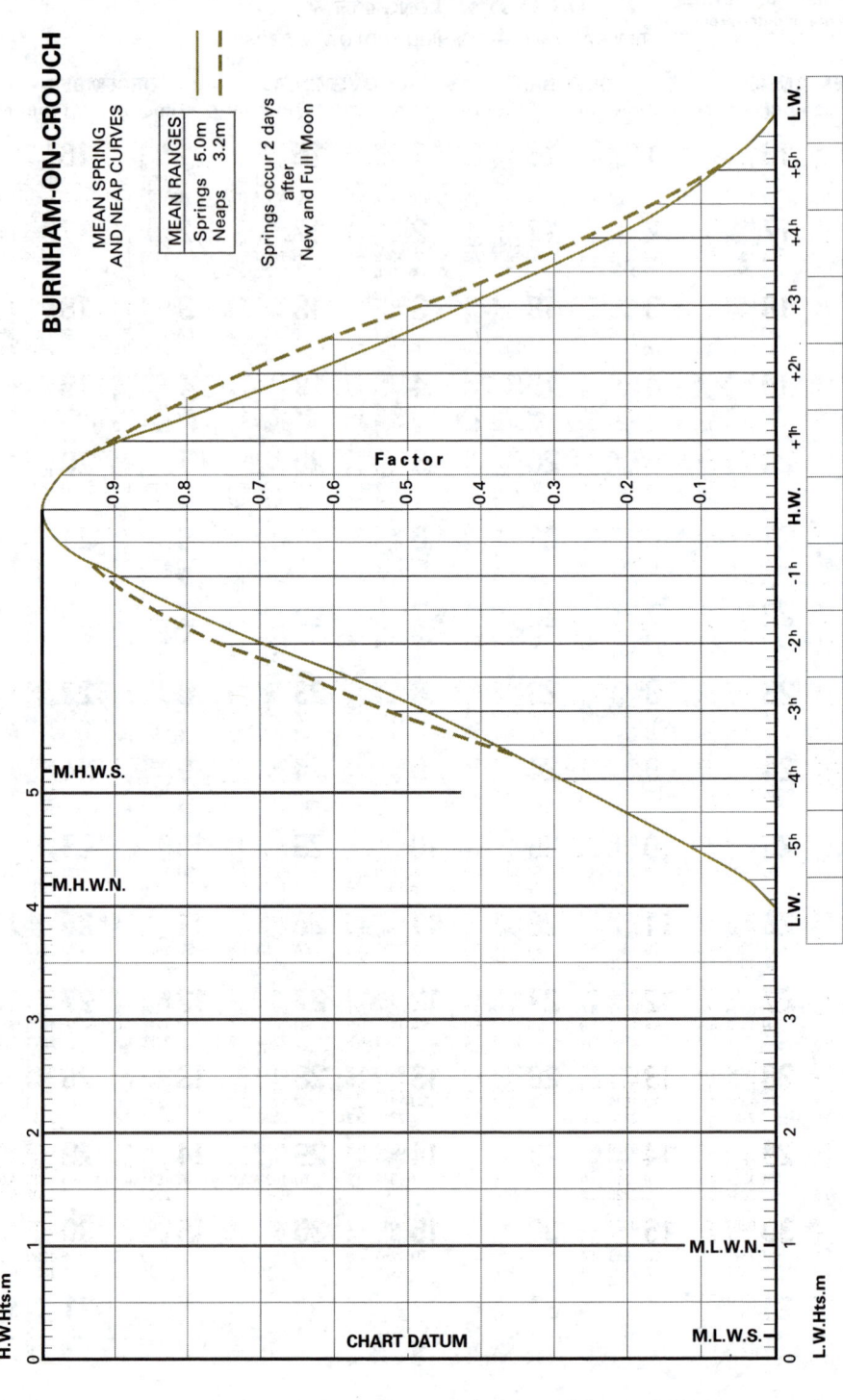

TIME ZONE (UT)	ENGLAND – BURNHAM-ON-CROUCH	YEAR 2005
For Summer Time add ONE hour in **non-shaded areas**	LAT 51°37′N LONG 0°48′E TIMES AND HEIGHTS OF HIGH AND LOW WATERS	

JANUARY

Time	m	Time	m
1 0318 0956 SA 1549 2151	4.7 0.5 4.6 0.9	**16** 0417 1059 SU 1654 2253	5.0 0.2 4.8 0.9
2 0357 1035 SU 1630 2233	4.6 0.5 4.6 1.0	**17** 0502 1146 M 1742 ☽ 2343	4.8 0.4 4.6 1.0
3 0440 1120 M 1720 ☽ 2321	4.5 0.7 4.5 1.1	**18** 0553 1244 TU 1836	4.6 0.7 4.3
4 0532 1216 TU 1816	4.3 0.8 4.3	**19** 0048 0653 W 1348 1942	1.1 4.3 0.9 4.1
5 0023 0633 W 1323 1922	1.1 4.1 0.8 4.3	**20** 0202 0804 TH 1458 2049	1.2 4.2 1.0 4.1
6 0137 0744 TH 1436 2032	1.1 4.3 0.8 4.3	**21** 0321 0917 F 1602 2154	1.1 4.3 1.0 4.2
7 0252 0854 F 1547 2138	1.1 4.5 0.7 4.6	**22** 0432 1021 SA 1658 2249	0.9 4.5 1.0 4.5
8 0404 1000 SA 1651 2238	0.9 4.7 0.5 4.7	**23** 0531 1117 SU 1746 2339	0.8 4.6 0.9 4.6
9 0512 1101 SU 1750 2334	0.7 5.0 0.5 4.8	**24** 0621 1205 M 1827	0.7 4.7 0.9
10 0616 1200 M 1841 ●	0.4 5.1 0.4	**25** 0021 0700 TU 1246 ○ 1901	4.7 0.5 4.7 0.8
11 0028 0709 TU 1257 1926	5.0 0.3 5.3 0.4	**26** 0059 0733 W 1321 1930	4.8 0.4 4.8 0.8
12 0118 0759 W 1348 2008	5.1 0.2 5.3 0.5	**27** 0131 0803 TH 1352 1958	4.8 0.4 4.8 0.8
13 0205 0846 TH 1435 2049	5.1 0.2 5.3 0.5	**28** 0204 0832 F 1420 2027	4.8 0.4 4.8 0.8
14 0250 0930 F 1522 2129	5.2 0.2 5.3 0.7	**29** 0229 0901 SA 1451 2057	4.8 0.4 4.8 0.7
15 0334 1014 SA 1608 2209	5.1 0.1 5.1 0.8	**30** 0259 0931 SU 1525 2129	4.8 0.3 4.8 0.7
		31 0332 1004 M 1603 2204	4.8 0.4 4.8 0.7

FEBRUARY

Time	m	Time	m
1 0410 1039 TU 1645 2244	4.7 0.4 4.6 0.8	**16** 0507 1142 W 1739 ☽ 2348	4.7 0.8 4.2 1.0
2 0453 1123 W 1735 ☽ 2333	4.6 0.5 4.3 1.0	**17** 0558 1239 TH 1831	4.3 1.0 4.0
3 0547 1223 TH 1834	4.5 0.8 4.2	**18** 0059 0712 F 1355 1956	1.1 4.0 1.2 3.8
4 0043 0657 F 1346 1950	1.1 4.2 0.9 4.1	**19** 0235 0846 SA 1520 2122	1.2 4.0 1.3 4.0
5 0211 0822 SA 1519 2110	1.1 4.2 0.9 4.2	**20** 0408 1004 SU 1633 2226	1.0 4.2 1.1 4.2
6 0346 0945 SU 1638 2223	1.0 4.5 0.8 4.5	**21** 0513 1101 M 1727 2318	0.8 4.5 1.1 4.6
7 0510 1056 M 1741 2325	0.7 4.8 0.7 4.7	**22** 0602 1147 TU 1810	0.5 4.7 0.9
8 0616 1157 TU 1832 ●	0.3 5.1 0.5	**23** 0000 0640 W 1227 1842	4.7 0.4 4.8 0.8
9 0020 0705 W 1251 1914	4.8 0.1 5.3 0.4	**24** 0039 0711 TH 1302 ○ 1911	4.8 0.4 4.8 0.8
10 0108 0750 TH 1338 1953	5.2 0.0 5.5 0.4	**25** 0111 0740 F 1332 1937	4.8 0.3 4.8 0.7
11 0153 0832 F 1421 2031	5.2 -0.1 5.5 0.4	**26** 0140 0808 SA 1359 2006	4.8 0.3 5.0 0.7
12 0233 0911 SA 1502 2108	5.3 -0.1 5.4 0.4	**27** 0209 0837 SU 1429 2037	4.8 0.3 5.0 0.5
13 0311 0948 SU 1541 2144	5.3 0.0 5.2 0.5	**28** 0237 0906 M 1501 2108	5.0 0.2 5.0 0.4
14 0349 1023 M 1619 2220	5.2 0.2 5.0 0.7		
15 0426 1100 TU 1656 2300	5.0 0.4 4.6 0.8		

MARCH

Time	m	Time	m
1 0309 0935 TU 1537 2141	5.0 0.3 5.0 0.4	**16** 0353 1019 W 1614 2225	5.0 0.5 4.6 0.7
2 0345 1008 W 1616 2218	5.0 0.4 4.7 0.5	**17** 0430 1055 TH 1650 ☽ 2308	4.7 0.8 4.3 0.9
3 0426 1047 TH 1701 ☽ 2305	4.8 0.5 4.5 0.8	**18** 0517 1145 F 1733	4.3 1.1 4.0
4 0517 1143 F 1757	4.5 0.9 4.1	**19** 0012 0621 SA 1303 1842	1.1 4.0 1.3 3.7
5 0011 0626 SA 1314 1915	1.0 4.2 1.1 3.8	**20** 0149 0808 SU 1439 2041	1.2 3.8 1.5 3.8
6 0151 0808 SU 1506 2055	1.1 4.1 1.1 4.0	**21** 0336 0939 M 1603 2155	1.0 4.1 1.2 4.1
7 0351 0947 M 1632 2216	0.9 4.3 0.9 4.3	**22** 0443 1035 TU 1659 2247	0.7 4.5 1.0 4.5
8 0510 1056 TU 1730 2315	0.5 4.8 0.7 4.7	**23** 0530 1119 W 1741 2329	0.5 4.7 0.9 4.7
9 0608 1150 W 1818 ●	0.2 5.2 0.5	**24** 0610 1157 TH 1816	0.4 4.8 0.8
10 0006 0652 TH 1239 ● 1857	5.0 0.0 5.3 0.4	**25** 0008 0640 F 1232 ○ 1844	4.8 0.3 5.0 0.7
11 0052 0732 F 1322 1933	5.2 -0.1 5.5 0.3	**26** 0042 0710 SA 1304 1913	4.8 0.3 5.0 0.7
12 0133 0810 SA 1401 2010	5.3 -0.1 5.5 0.3	**27** 0113 0740 SU 1334 1944	4.8 0.3 5.0 0.6
13 0210 0845 SU 1437 2045	5.3 -0.1 5.3 0.4	**28** 0145 0812 M 1406 2016	5.0 0.2 5.0 0.4
14 0245 0917 M 1511 2119	5.2 0.1 5.1 0.4	**29** 0216 0842 TU 1439 2050	5.1 0.2 5.0 0.3
15 0319 0947 TU 1543 2151	5.1 0.2 4.8 0.5	**30** 0251 0913 W 1515 2125	5.1 0.3 5.0 0.3
		31 0328 0947 TH 1554 2204	5.0 0.4 4.7 0.4

APRIL

Time	m	Time	m
1 0412 1029 F 1638 2253	4.8 0.7 4.3 0.7	**16** 0449 1106 SA 1659 2342	4.3 1.2 4.1 1.0
2 0507 1127 SA 1735 ☽	4.5 1.0 4.0	**17** 0547 1220 SU 1802	4.0 1.5 3.8
3 0004 0623 SU 1305 1857	0.9 4.1 1.3 3.8	**18** 0110 0720 M 1353 1941	1.1 3.8 1.5 3.8
4 0201 0812 M 1459 2043	1.0 4.1 1.2 4.0	**19** 0247 0855 TU 1519 2106	1.0 4.0 1.3 4.1
5 0350 0943 TU 1616 2200	0.7 4.5 1.0 4.3	**20** 0356 0954 W 1618 2202	0.8 4.3 1.1 4.3
6 0457 1042 W 1710 2254	0.3 4.8 0.7 4.7	**21** 0445 1039 TH 1700 2246	0.5 4.7 0.9 4.6
7 0549 1132 TH 1755 2343	0.0 5.2 0.5 5.0	**22** 0526 1118 F 1737 2326	0.4 4.8 0.8 4.7
8 0632 1217 F 1835 ●	-0.1 5.3 0.4	**23** 0603 1155 SA 1813	0.3 5.0 0.7
9 0027 0709 SA 1259 1912	5.2 -0.1 5.3 0.3	**24** 0005 0638 SU 1231 ○ 1847	4.8 0.3 5.0 0.5
10 0107 0743 SU 1336 1947	5.2 0.0 5.2 0.3	**25** 0043 0714 M 1307 1923	5.0 0.3 5.0 0.3
11 0145 0815 M 1411 2022	5.2 0.1 5.1 0.3	**26** 0120 0748 TU 1344 2000	5.0 0.3 5.0 0.3
12 0219 0846 TU 1441 2056	5.2 0.3 5.0 0.3	**27** 0158 0823 W 1420 2038	5.1 0.3 5.0 0.3
13 0253 0915 W 1511 2127	5.1 0.4 4.8 0.4	**28** 0238 0859 TH 1459 2118	5.1 0.4 4.8 0.3
14 0328 0944 TH 1541 2200	4.8 0.7 4.6 0.6	**29** 0322 0938 F 1542 2202	4.8 0.5 4.6 0.4
15 0405 1019 F 1615 2242	4.6 0.9 4.3 0.8	**30** 0411 1024 SA 1630 2258	4.5 0.9 4.3 0.5

Chart Datum: 2·35 metres below Ordnance Datum (Newlyn)

》》 **FREE** monthly updates from 《《
www.reedsalmanac.co.uk

TIDES

TIME ZONE (UT)
For Summer Time add ONE hour in **non-shaded areas**

ENGLAND – BURNHAM-ON-CROUCH
LAT 51°37'N LONG 0°48'E
TIMES AND HEIGHTS OF HIGH AND LOW WATERS

YEAR 2005

	MAY			JUNE			JULY			AUGUST	
	Time m	Time m		Time m	Time m		Time m	Time m		Time m	Time m
1 SU ○	0512 4.5 1126 1.1 1731 4.1	**16** M	0520 4.1 1136 1.3 1734 4.1	**1** W	0143 0.4 0731 4.6 1356 1.1 1943 4.3	**16** TH	0047 0.8 0640 4.2 1301 1.2 1901 4.2	**1** F	0212 0.5 0758 4.5 1422 1.1 2010 4.5	**16** SA	0051 0.8 0652 4.3 1308 1.2 1913 4.3	**1** M	0335 1.1 0931 4.3 1613 1.0 2201 4.3	**16** TU	0242 1.1 0839 4.2 1520 1.1 2116 4.3
2 M	0018 0.8 0628 4.2 1258 1.3 1851 4.0	**17** TU	0029 0.9 0625 4.0 1255 1.5 1844 4.0	**2** TH	0259 0.3 0839 4.6 1508 1.0 2049 4.6	**17** F	0151 0.7 0747 4.3 1410 1.2 2006 4.2	**2** SA	0317 0.5 0901 4.5 1531 1.0 2116 4.5	**17** SU	0201 0.8 0801 4.3 1424 1.1 2023 4.3	**2** TU	0439 1.0 1034 4.5 1718 0.8 2302 4.6	**17** W	0407 1.0 0959 4.5 1646 0.9 2231 4.7
3 TU	0205 0.7 0801 4.3 1435 1.2 2017 4.1	**18** W	0145 0.9 0746 4.1 1413 1.3 2002 4.1	**3** F	0400 0.3 0940 4.7 1607 0.8 2148 4.7	**18** SA	0255 0.7 0849 4.5 1514 1.1 2106 4.5	**3** SU	0414 0.7 1001 4.6 1634 0.8 2217 4.6	**18** M	0315 0.8 0909 4.5 1539 1.1 2133 4.5	**3** W	0531 1.0 1126 4.7 1812 0.7 2353 4.7	**18** TH	0514 0.8 1102 4.7 1753 0.6 2333 5.1
4 W	0332 0.4 0917 4.6 1547 1.0 2127 4.5	**19** TH	0254 0.8 0854 4.3 1518 1.1 2103 4.2	**4** SA	0451 0.2 1032 4.8 1659 0.7 2242 4.8	**19** SU	0354 0.5 0947 4.6 1612 0.9 2203 4.6	**4** M	0505 0.7 1054 4.6 1730 0.7 2313 4.6	**19** TU	0423 0.7 1014 4.6 1651 0.9 2237 4.7	**4** TH	0616 0.9 1213 4.8 1852 0.5	**19** F ○	0609 0.5 1157 5.1 1844 0.2
5 TH	0433 0.2 1015 5.0 1641 0.7 2223 4.7	**20** F	0350 0.5 0947 4.6 1608 1.0 2155 4.5	**5** SU	0534 0.3 1120 4.8 1747 0.5 2332 4.8	**20** M	0450 0.4 1040 4.7 1709 0.8 2257 4.8	**5** TU	0550 0.8 1144 4.7 1822 0.5 2339 5.0	**20** W	0525 0.7 1113 4.8 1757 0.5	**5** F ●	0038 4.8 0650 0.9 1253 5.0 1928 0.4	**20** SA	0027 5.3 0652 0.5 1247 5.2 1929 0.0
6 F	0523 0.1 1104 5.1 1727 0.5 2312 5.0	**21** SA	0438 0.4 1032 4.7 1653 0.8 2241 4.7	**6** M ●	0616 0.4 1206 4.8 1833 0.4	**21** TU	0543 0.4 1131 4.8 1805 0.5 2351 5.0	**6** W ●	0005 4.7 0631 0.8 1229 4.7 1904 0.5	**21** TH ○	0621 0.5 1209 5.0 1851 0.3	**6** SA	0115 4.8 0722 0.9 1328 5.0 1958 0.4	**21** SU	0116 5.5 0732 0.5 1332 5.5 2010 -0.1
7 SA	0605 0.0 1150 5.1 1812 0.4 2358 5.0	**22** SU	0524 0.3 1114 4.8 1738 0.7 2327 4.8	**7** TU	0019 4.8 0650 0.5 1248 4.8 1913 0.4	**22** W ○	0633 0.4 1222 5.0 1855 0.4	**7** TH	0051 4.7 0706 0.8 1310 4.7 1942 0.4	**22** F	0037 5.2 0706 0.5 1302 5.1 1941 0.1	**7** SU	0148 4.8 0751 0.9 1357 4.8 2025 0.4	**22** M	0201 5.6 0812 0.4 1414 5.5 2050 -0.1
8 SU ●	0642 0.1 1231 5.1 1850 0.3	**23** M	0610 0.2 1158 5.0 1823 0.5 ○	**8** W	0103 4.8 0724 0.7 1325 4.7 1951 0.4	**23** TH	0045 5.1 0718 0.4 1311 5.0 1945 0.3	**8** F	0131 4.7 0739 0.8 1344 4.7 2016 0.4	**23** SA	0129 5.3 0749 0.5 1349 5.2 2027 0.0	**8** M	0215 4.8 0818 0.8 1422 4.8 2051 0.4	**23** TU	0243 5.5 0850 0.4 1453 5.5 2127 0.0
9 M	0042 5.0 0716 0.2 1310 5.0 1928 0.3	**24** TU	0013 5.0 0650 0.3 1242 5.0 1905 0.4	**9** TH	0141 4.7 0756 0.7 1357 4.7 2027 0.4	**24** F	0136 5.2 0801 0.5 1359 5.0 2032 0.2	**9** SA	0205 4.7 0810 0.9 1415 4.7 2047 0.4	**24** SU	0217 5.5 0831 0.5 1434 5.2 2110 -0.1	**9** TU	0242 4.8 0847 0.8 1450 4.8 2119 0.4	**24** W	0324 5.3 0928 0.5 1531 5.3 2203 0.1
10 TU	0120 5.0 0746 0.3 1345 4.8 2003 0.3	**25** W	0059 5.1 0730 0.3 1325 5.0 1948 0.3	**10** F	0217 4.7 0828 0.8 1428 4.7 2100 0.4	**25** SA	0226 5.2 0844 0.6 1446 5.0 2119 0.1	**10** SU	0235 4.7 0840 0.9 1443 4.7 2116 0.4	**25** M	0303 5.5 0911 0.5 1517 5.3 2152 0.0	**10** W	0312 4.8 0919 0.8 1520 4.8 2148 0.4	**25** TH	0403 5.1 1005 0.7 1610 5.2 2238 0.3
11 W	0157 5.0 0818 0.4 1416 4.7 2038 0.3	**26** TH	0145 5.1 0811 0.4 1408 5.0 2033 0.3	**11** SA	0252 4.6 0858 0.8 1459 4.6 2132 0.5	**26** SU	0316 5.2 0927 0.6 1532 5.0 2207 0.1	**11** M	0307 4.6 0910 0.9 1515 4.7 2146 0.4	**26** TU	0349 5.3 0952 0.7 1559 5.2 2234 0.1	**11** TH	0347 4.8 0951 0.8 1553 4.8 2219 0.5	**26** F ◐	0442 4.8 1046 0.8 1651 5.0 2319 0.7
12 TH	0232 4.8 0848 0.5 1445 4.7 2110 0.4	**27** F	0232 5.1 0852 0.6 1452 4.8 2119 0.2	**12** SU	0328 4.6 0931 0.9 1535 4.6 2209 0.5	**27** M	0407 5.1 1012 0.8 1620 4.8 2259 0.1	**12** TU	0341 4.6 0943 0.9 1550 4.7 2220 0.5	**27** W	0434 5.1 1033 0.8 1642 5.1 2319 0.2	**12** F	0426 4.7 1028 0.9 1631 4.7 2258 0.7	**27** SA	0524 4.5 1133 1.0 1740 4.5
13 F	0307 4.7 0919 0.8 1517 4.6 2144 0.5	**28** SA	0321 4.8 0934 0.7 1538 4.7 2208 0.3	**13** M	0407 4.6 1009 1.0 1616 4.5 2252 0.7	**28** TU	0459 5.0 1101 0.9 1711 4.8 ◐ 2354 0.2	**13** W	0419 4.6 1021 0.9 1629 4.6 2301 0.5	**28** TH ◐	0521 4.8 1120 0.9 1729 4.8	**13** SA	0511 4.5 1114 1.1 1721 4.5 ◐ 2349 0.9	**28** SU	0012 1.0 0616 4.2 1242 1.1 1849 4.1
14 SA	0346 4.6 0952 0.9 1552 4.5 2226 0.7	**29** SU	0413 4.7 1022 0.9 1630 4.6 2306 0.4	**14** TU	0451 4.5 1056 1.2 1704 4.3 2343 0.7	**29** W	0554 5.0 1157 1.0 1805 4.7	**14** TH	0502 4.5 1104 1.1 1714 4.5 ◐ 2347 0.6	**29** F	0009 0.5 0611 4.6 1217 1.0 1823 4.6	**14** SU	0606 4.3 1218 1.2 1825 4.2	**29** M	0126 1.2 0734 4.1 1420 1.2 2023 4.1
15 SU	0428 4.3 1035 1.1 1637 4.2 2319 0.8	**30** M ◐	0513 4.7 1120 1.1 1728 4.3	**15** W	0542 4.2 1152 1.2 1759 4.2	**30** TH ◐	0103 0.4 0653 4.6 1308 1.1 1904 4.6	**15** F	0553 4.3 1159 1.2 1807 4.3	**30** SA	0112 0.7 0711 4.3 1330 1.1 1931 4.3	**15** M	0110 1.0 0716 4.1 1344 1.2 1948 4.2	**30** TU	0255 1.1 0902 4.2 1554 1.1 2145 4.2
		31 TU	0019 0.4 0618 4.6 1235 1.2 1833 4.3						**31** SU	0223 1.0 0820 4.2 1454 1.1 2047 4.2			**31** W	0413 1.3 1011 4.3 1701 0.9 2245 4.5

Chart Datum: 2·35 metres below Ordnance Datum (Newlyn)

⟫ **FREE** monthly updates from ⟪
www.reedsalmanac.co.uk

TIME ZONE (UT)
For Summer Time add ONE hour in **non-shaded areas**

ENGLAND – BURNHAM-ON-CROUCH
LAT 51°37'N   LONG 0°48'E
TIMES AND HEIGHTS OF HIGH AND LOW WATERS

YEAR 2005

SEPTEMBER		OCTOBER		NOVEMBER		DECEMBER	
Time m	Time m	Time m	Time m	Time m	Time m	Time m	Time m
1 0510 1.1 1104 4.7 TH 1752 0.7 2333 4.8	**16** 0459 0.9 1047 4.8 F 1741 0.3 2322 5.3	**1** 0524 1.0 1113 4.8 SA 1757 0.4 2342 5.0	**16** 0524 0.7 1111 5.1 SU 1806 0.0 2347 5.3	**1** 0554 0.8 1145 5.0 TU 1822 0.4	**16** 0002 5.2 0626 0.4 W 1214 5.2 ○ 1854 0.3	**1** 0601 0.8 1151 5.0 TH 1830 0.5 ●	**16** 0023 4.8 0654 0.4 F 1243 5.0 1908 0.7
2 0554 1.0 1149 5.0 F 1831 0.4	**17** 0549 0.7 1139 5.1 SA 1829 0.0	**2** 0600 0.9 1152 5.0 SU 1828 0.4	**17** 0609 0.5 1156 5.3 M 1845 0.0 ○	**2** 0010 5.0 0629 0.8 W 1220 5.0 ● 1854 0.4	**17** 0044 5.1 0706 0.4 TH 1257 5.1 1928 0.4	**2** 0017 5.0 0645 0.7 F 1237 5.1 1909 0.5	**17** 0104 4.8 0736 0.4 SA 1325 4.8 1941 0.8
3 0015 5.0 0630 0.9 SA 1227 5.0 ● 1903 0.4	**18** 0011 5.5 0633 0.5 SU 1225 5.3 ○ 1909 -0.1	**3** 0017 5.1 0630 0.9 M 1226 5.0 ● 1856 0.4	**18** 0030 5.5 0648 0.4 TU 1240 5.3 1920 0.1	**3** 0045 5.0 0704 0.7 TH 1259 5.0 1928 0.5	**18** 0122 5.0 0746 0.4 F 1337 5.1 2000 0.5	**3** 0100 5.0 0728 0.5 SA 1321 5.1 1947 0.5	**18** 0140 4.8 0815 0.4 SU 1403 4.8 2014 0.9
4 0051 5.0 0659 0.9 SU 1302 5.0 1930 0.4	**19** 0057 5.6 0710 0.4 M 1308 5.5 1946 -0.1	**4** 0048 5.0 0658 0.8 TU 1257 5.0 1924 0.4	**19** 0111 5.3 0726 0.4 W 1320 5.3 1954 0.2	**4** 0119 5.0 0741 0.5 F 1335 5.1 2001 0.5	**19** 0157 4.8 0825 0.4 SA 1416 5.0 2032 0.8	**4** 0141 5.0 0813 0.4 SU 1406 5.1 2027 0.7	**19** 0213 4.5 0852 0.5 M 1437 4.5 2043 0.9
5 0122 5.0 0726 0.9 M 1330 5.0 1956 0.4	**20** 0138 5.5 0748 0.4 TU 1348 5.5 2023 0.0	**5** 0116 5.0 0728 0.8 W 1327 5.0 1953 0.4	**20** 0148 5.2 0804 0.4 TH 1358 5.3 2027 0.3	**5** 0156 5.0 0820 0.5 SA 1414 5.1 2035 0.5	**20** 0229 4.8 0903 0.5 SU 1453 4.8 2103 0.9	**5** 0223 5.0 0858 0.3 M 1452 5.1 2107 0.8	**20** 0243 4.7 0925 0.5 TU 1512 4.6 2113 1.0
6 0148 5.0 0754 0.8 TU 1357 5.0 2022 0.4	**21** 0216 5.3 0827 0.4 W 1425 5.5 2056 0.1	**6** 0146 5.0 0800 0.7 TH 1357 5.0 2022 0.4	**21** 0223 5.1 0842 0.4 F 1435 5.2 2057 0.5	**6** 0233 5.0 0900 0.5 SU 1456 5.0 2111 0.8	**21** 0300 4.7 0939 0.7 M 1531 4.6 2134 1.0	**6** 0307 4.8 0944 0.3 TU 1542 5.0 2151 0.9	**21** 0316 4.6 0958 0.5 W 1548 4.5 2147 1.1
7 0215 5.0 0824 0.7 W 1422 5.0 2049 0.4	**22** 0253 5.2 0903 0.4 TH 1501 5.3 2129 0.3	**7** 0216 5.0 0834 0.7 F 1429 5.1 2052 0.5	**22** 0255 5.0 0918 0.5 SA 1512 5.0 2128 0.8	**7** 0313 4.7 0942 0.5 M 1542 4.8 2153 1.0	**22** 0335 4.6 1019 0.8 TU 1612 4.5 2213 1.2	**7** 0355 4.7 1036 0.4 W 1635 4.7 2241 1.1	**22** 0353 4.6 1036 0.7 TH 1627 4.3 2228 1.1
8 0243 5.0 0855 0.7 TH 1452 5.0 2117 0.4	**23** 0328 5.1 0939 0.5 F 1537 5.2 2200 0.5	**8** 0251 5.0 0908 0.7 SA 1504 5.0 2123 0.7	**23** 0327 4.7 0954 0.7 SU 1551 4.7 2201 1.0	**8** 0358 4.5 1034 0.7 TU 1637 4.5 2247 1.2	**23** 0417 4.3 1110 0.9 W 1700 4.2 ◐ 2307 1.5	**8** 0449 4.6 1136 0.5 TH 1737 4.6 ◐ 2342 1.2	**23** 0436 4.5 1121 0.8 F 1713 4.2 ◐ 2317 1.1
9 0316 5.0 0927 0.7 F 1525 5.0 2146 0.5	**24** 0402 4.8 1017 0.8 SA 1616 4.8 2236 0.9	**9** 0328 4.8 0946 0.7 SU 1546 4.8 2200 0.9	**24** 0401 4.5 1038 0.9 M 1635 4.3 2245 1.3	**9** 0454 4.2 1143 0.9 W 1747 4.3 ◐	**24** 0511 4.2 1213 1.0 TH 1802 4.0	**9** 0551 4.5 1252 0.5 F 1844 4.5	**24** 0527 4.2 1205 0.9 SA 1806 4.1
10 0353 4.8 1002 0.8 SA 1602 4.8 2221 0.7	**25** 0437 4.5 1101 1.0 SU 1702 4.5 ◐ 2324 1.2	**10** 0411 4.6 1033 0.9 M 1636 4.5 ◐ 2251 1.1	**25** 0443 4.2 1138 1.1 TU 1734 4.1 ◐ 2352 1.6	**10** 0004 1.3 0608 4.1 TH 1319 0.8 1915 4.3	**25** 0021 1.6 0619 4.1 F 1326 1.0 1920 4.0	**10** 0059 1.2 0700 4.5 SA 1411 0.5 1957 4.5	**25** 0020 1.3 0626 4.2 SU 1320 0.9 1910 4.2
11 0435 4.6 1046 1.0 SU 1649 4.6 ◐ 2310 1.0	**26** 0522 4.1 1206 1.2 M 1808 4.0	**11** 0503 4.2 1139 1.1 TU 1746 4.2	**26** 0546 4.0 1306 1.1 W 1905 3.8	**11** 0142 1.3 0735 4.2 F 1449 0.7 2037 4.6	**26** 0142 1.5 0737 4.1 SA 1434 0.9 2031 4.2	**11** 0218 1.1 0810 4.6 SU 1520 0.4 2102 4.6	**26** 0130 1.3 0734 4.2 M 1424 0.9 2017 4.2
12 0529 4.2 1146 1.2 M 1754 4.2	**27** 0039 1.6 0634 3.8 TU 1346 1.2 1955 4.0	**12** 0015 1.5 0618 4.0 W 1324 1.1 1928 4.1	**27** 0128 1.7 0726 4.0 TH 1435 1.1 2035 4.1	**12** 0303 1.2 0848 4.5 SA 1557 0.4 2140 4.8	**27** 0251 1.3 0842 4.3 SU 1531 0.8 2125 4.5	**12** 0326 1.0 0914 4.7 M 1619 0.4 2159 4.7	**27** 0239 1.2 0840 4.3 TU 1528 0.8 2120 4.5
13 0032 1.2 0639 4.0 TU 1324 1.2 1930 4.1	**28** 0216 1.6 0825 4.0 W 1523 1.1 2120 4.5	**13** 0209 1.5 0802 4.1 TH 1513 0.9 2105 4.5	**28** 0255 1.6 0847 4.2 F 1541 0.9 2136 4.5	**13** 0404 0.9 0948 4.7 SU 1651 0.2 2231 5.1	**28** 0345 1.1 0935 4.5 M 1619 0.7 2211 4.7	**13** 0425 0.8 1011 4.8 TU 1709 0.4 2249 4.8	**28** 0341 1.1 0940 4.5 W 1625 0.7 2215 4.6
14 0224 1.1 0818 4.1 W 1519 1.1 2115 4.3	**29** 0341 1.1 0939 4.3 TH 1629 0.9 2218 4.6	**14** 0336 1.1 0924 4.5 F 1625 0.4 2210 4.7	**29** 0356 1.3 0944 4.5 SA 1630 0.7 2221 4.7	**14** 0455 0.7 1040 5.0 M 1738 0.1 2318 5.1	**29** 0430 1.0 1021 4.7 TU 1704 0.6 2252 4.8	**14** 0518 0.7 1105 4.8 W 1754 0.4 2338 4.8	**29** 0441 0.9 1036 4.7 TH 1720 0.5 2306 4.8
15 0355 1.1 0946 4.3 TH 1642 0.7 2226 4.8	**30** 0439 0.7 1031 4.7 F 1717 0.4 2303 4.8	**15** 0435 0.8 1021 4.8 SA 1720 0.2 2301 5.2	**30** 0442 1.0 1028 4.7 SU 1711 0.5 2300 5.0	**15** 0542 0.5 1128 5.1 TU 1819 0.2	**30** 0515 0.8 1106 4.8 W 1748 0.5 2334 5.0	**15** 0611 0.5 1155 5.0 TH 1833 0.5 ○	**30** 0539 0.8 1129 5.0 F 1812 0.5 2356 4.8
			31 0518 0.9 1107 4.8 M 1747 0.4 2335 5.0				**31** 0633 0.5 1222 5.1 SA 1856 0.5

Chart Datum: 2·35 metres below Ordnance Datum (Newlyn)

>> **FREE** monthly updates from <<
www.reedsalmanac.co.uk

Chapter 5

265

TIDES

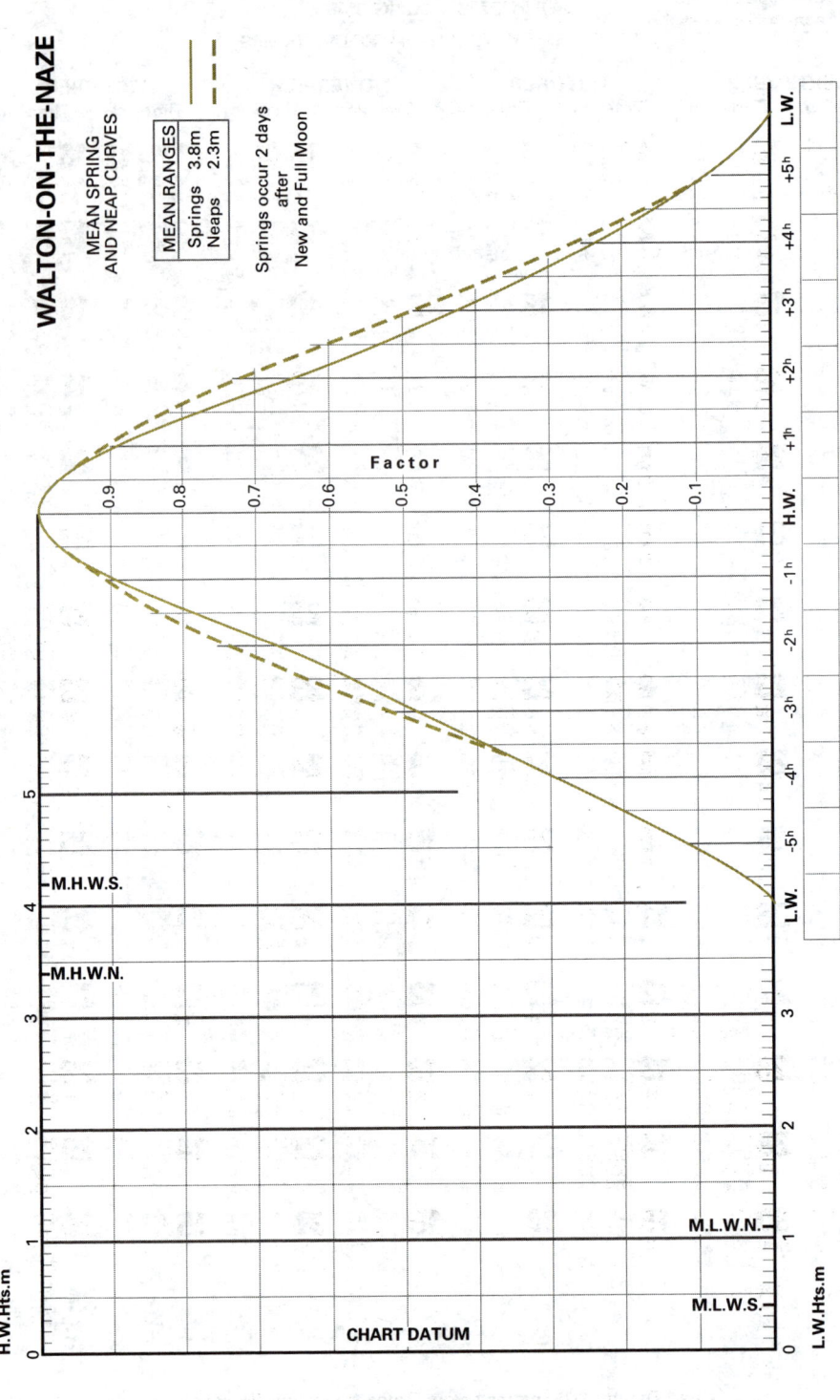

| TIME ZONE (UT) For Summer Time add ONE hour in **non-shaded areas** | ENGLAND – WALTON-ON-THE-NAZE LAT 51°51′N   LONG 1°17′E TIMES AND HEIGHTS OF HIGH AND LOW WATERS | YEAR **2005** |

JANUARY

Time m	Time m
1 0234 3.8 / 0858 0.7 / SA 1506 3.7 / 2052 1.0	**16** 0336 4.0 / 1005 0.4 / SU 1614 3.9 / 2159 1.0
2 0315 3.7 / 0940 0.7 / SU 1550 3.7 / 2137 1.1	**17** 0423 3.9 / 1056 0.6 / M 1704 3.7 / ☾ 2252 1.1
3 0400 3.6 / 1028 0.8 / M 1641 3.6 / ☽ 2229 1.2	**18** 0516 3.7 / 1151 0.8 / TU 1801 3.5 / 2354 1.2
4 0454 3.5 / 1124 0.9 / TU 1740 3.5 / 2331 1.2	**19** 0617 3.5 / 1251 1.0 / W 1904 3.3
5 0558 3.5 / 1227 0.9 / W 1845 3.5	**20** 0104 1.3 / 0725 3.4 / TH 1355 1.1 / 2009 3.3
6 0040 1.2 / 0706 3.5 / TH 1335 0.9 / 1952 3.5	**21** 0217 1.2 / 0835 3.4 / F 1455 1.1 / 2111 3.4
7 0150 1.2 / 0813 3.6 / F 1441 0.8 / 2055 3.7	**22** 0323 1.0 / 0937 3.6 / SA 1548 1.1 / 2204 3.6
8 0257 1.0 / 0916 3.8 / SA 1541 0.7 / 2153 3.8	**23** 0419 0.9 / 1030 3.7 / SU 1633 1.0 / 2251 3.7
9 0401 0.8 / 1015 4.0 / SU 1637 0.7 / 2247 3.9	**24** 0506 0.8 / 1116 3.8 / M 1713 1.0 / 2332 3.8
10 0501 0.6 / 1112 4.1 / M 1728 0.6 / ● 2339 4.0	**25** 0548 0.7 / 1156 3.8 / TU 1749 0.9 / ○
11 0558 0.5 / 1207 4.3 / TU 1816 0.6	**26** 0009 3.9 / 0624 0.6 / W 1232 3.9 / 1820 0.9
12 0029 4.1 / 0651 0.3 / W 1300 4.3 / 1901 0.7	**27** 0042 3.9 / 0656 0.6 / TH 1304 3.9 / 1850 0.9
13 0118 4.1 / 0742 0.2 / TH 1350 4.3 / 1945 0.7	**28** 0113 3.9 / 0727 0.6 / F 1334 3.9 / 1921 0.9
14 0205 4.2 / 0830 0.2 / F 1438 4.3 / 2028 0.8	**29** 0143 3.9 / 0758 0.6 / SA 1406 3.9 / 1954 0.8
15 0251 4.1 / 0917 0.3 / SA 1526 4.1 / 2112 0.9	**30** 0215 3.9 / 0831 0.5 / SU 1441 3.9 / 2028 0.8
	31 0249 3.9 / 0906 0.6 / M 1521 3.9 / 2106 0.8

FEBRUARY

Time m	Time m
1 0328 3.8 / 0944 0.6 / TU 1605 3.7 / 2149 0.9	**16** 0428 3.8 / 1051 0.9 / W 1701 3.4 / ☾ 2258 1.1
2 0413 3.5 / 1031 0.7 / W 1657 3.5 / ☽ 2242 1.1	**17** 0521 3.5 / 1146 1.1 / TH 1756 3.2
3 0509 3.6 / 1131 0.9 / TH 1759 3.4 / 2350 1.2	**18** 0005 1.2 / 0635 3.2 / F 1257 1.3 / 1917 3.1
4 0621 3.4 / 1249 1.0 / F 1912 3.3	**19** 0134 1.3 / 0806 3.2 / SA 1416 1.4 / 2040 3.2
5 0112 1.2 / 0743 3.4 / SA 1415 1.1 / 2029 3.4	**20** 0301 1.1 / 0920 3.4 / SU 1524 1.2 / 2142 3.4
6 0240 1.1 / 0902 3.6 / SU 1529 0.9 / 2139 3.6	**21** 0402 0.9 / 1015 3.6 / M 1615 1.1 / 2231 3.7
7 0359 0.8 / 1010 3.9 / M 1628 0.8 / 2238 3.8	**22** 0448 0.7 / 1059 3.8 / TU 1655 1.0 / 2312 3.8
8 0501 0.5 / 1109 4.1 / TU 1718 0.7 / ● 2331 4.0	**23** 0527 0.6 / 1138 3.9 / W 1729 0.9 / 2349 3.9
9 0554 0.3 / 1201 4.3 / W 1803 0.6	**24** 0600 0.6 / 1212 3.9 / TH 1800 0.9 / ○
10 0019 4.2 / 0642 0.2 / TH 1250 4.4 / 1845 0.6	**25** 0022 3.9 / 0631 0.5 / F 1243 3.9 / 1828 0.8
11 0105 4.2 / 0727 0.1 / F 1335 4.4 / 1926 0.6	**26** 0052 3.9 / 0701 0.5 / SA 1312 4.0 / 1859 0.8
12 0147 4.3 / 0809 0.1 / SA 1418 4.3 / 2006 0.7	**27** 0122 3.9 / 0732 0.5 / SU 1343 4.0 / 1932 0.7
13 0227 4.3 / 0849 0.2 / SU 1458 4.2 / 2045 0.7	**28** 0152 4.0 / 0803 0.4 / M 1417 4.0 / 2005 0.6
14 0306 4.2 / 0927 0.4 / M 1538 4.0 / 2124 0.8	
15 0345 4.0 / 1006 0.6 / TU 1617 3.7 / 2206 0.9	

MARCH

Time m	Time m
1 0225 4.0 / 0835 0.5 / TU 1454 4.0 / 2041 0.6	**16** 0311 4.0 / 0922 0.7 / W 1533 3.7 / 2129 0.8
2 0302 4.0 / 0911 0.6 / W 1535 3.8 / 2121 0.7	**17** 0350 3.8 / 1001 0.9 / TH 1610 3.5 / ☾ 2215 1.0
3 0345 3.9 / 0953 0.7 / TH 1622 3.6 / ☽ 2212 0.9	**18** 0438 3.5 / 1055 1.2 / F 1655 3.2 / 2321 1.2
4 0438 3.6 / 1052 1.0 / F 1720 3.3 / 2320 1.1	**19** 0545 3.2 / 1208 1.4 / SA 1807 3.0
5 0551 3.4 / 1219 1.2 / SA 1838 3.1	**20** 0052 1.3 / 0733 3.1 / SU 1338 1.5 / 2001 3.1
6 0053 1.2 / 0729 3.3 / SU 1403 1.2 / 2014 3.3	**21** 0231 1.1 / 0856 3.3 / M 1456 1.3 / 2112 3.3
7 0245 1.0 / 0904 3.5 / M 1523 1.0 / 2132 3.5	**22** 0334 0.9 / 0950 3.6 / TU 1549 1.1 / 2202 3.6
8 0359 0.7 / 1010 3.8 / TU 1618 0.8 / 2229 3.8	**23** 0418 0.7 / 1032 3.8 / W 1628 1.0 / 2242 3.8
9 0453 0.4 / 1102 4.2 / W 1703 0.7 / 2317 4.0	**24** 0455 0.6 / 1109 3.9 / TH 1701 0.9 / 2319 3.9
10 0540 0.2 / 1149 4.3 / TH 1745 0.6 / ●	**25** 0527 0.5 / 1143 4.0 / F 1731 0.8 / ○ 2352 3.9
11 0002 4.2 / 0623 0.1 / F 1233 4.4 / 1824 0.5	**26** 0559 0.5 / 1214 4.0 / SA 1802 0.8
12 0044 4.3 / 0703 0.1 / SA 1314 4.4 / 1903 0.5	**27** 0024 3.9 / 0631 0.5 / SU 1246 4.0 / 1835 0.7
13 0123 4.3 / 0741 0.1 / SU 1352 4.3 / 1941 0.5	**28** 0057 4.0 / 0705 0.4 / M 1319 4.0 / 1910 0.7
14 0200 4.3 / 0815 0.3 / M 1427 4.1 / 2017 0.5	**29** 0130 4.1 / 0738 0.2 / TU 1354 4.0 / 1946 0.5
15 0235 4.2 / 0848 0.4 / TU 1500 3.9 / 2052 0.6	**30** 0206 4.1 / 0811 0.2 / W 1431 4.0 / 2024 0.5
	31 0245 4.0 / 0848 0.6 / TH 1512 3.8 / 2106 0.6

APRIL

Time m	Time m
1 0331 3.9 / 0933 0.8 / F 1558 3.5 / 2159 0.8	**16** 0409 3.5 / 1013 1.3 / SA 1620 3.3 / ☾ 2251 1.1
2 0428 3.6 / 1035 1.1 / SA 1657 3.2 / 2313 1.0	**17** 0510 3.2 / 1128 1.5 / SU 1725 3.1
3 0547 3.3 / 1210 1.4 / SU 1821 3.1	**18** 0015 1.2 / 0643 3.1 / M 1255 1.5 / 1903 3.1
4 0103 1.1 / 0733 3.3 / M 1356 1.3 / 2003 3.2	**19** 0145 1.1 / 0814 3.3 / TU 1415 1.4 / 2025 3.3
5 0244 0.8 / 0900 3.6 / TU 1508 1.1 / 2116 3.5	**20** 0250 0.9 / 0911 3.5 / W 1510 1.2 / 2118 3.5
6 0347 0.5 / 0957 3.8 / W 1559 0.8 / 2209 3.8	**21** 0336 0.7 / 0954 3.8 / TH 1550 1.0 / 2201 3.7
7 0436 0.2 / 1045 4.2 / TH 1641 0.7 / 2255 4.0	**22** 0414 0.6 / 1031 3.9 / F 1624 0.9 / 2239 3.9
8 0518 0.1 / 1128 4.3 / F 1721 0.6 / ● 2338 4.2	**23** 0449 0.5 / 1107 4.0 / SA 1658 0.8 / 2316 3.9
9 0558 0.1 / 1209 4.3 / SA 1801 0.5	**24** 0525 0.5 / 1142 4.0 / SU 1734 0.7 / ○ 2353 4.0
10 0018 4.2 / 0634 0.2 / SU 1248 4.2 / 1839 0.5	**25** 0603 0.5 / 1218 4.0 / M 1813 0.6
11 0057 4.2 / 0709 0.3 / M 1324 4.1 / 1916 0.5	**26** 0031 4.0 / 0640 0.5 / TU 1256 4.0 / 1852 0.5
12 0133 4.2 / 0742 0.4 / TU 1356 4.0 / 1952 0.5	**27** 0111 4.1 / 0717 0.5 / W 1334 4.0 / 1933 0.5
13 0208 4.1 / 0813 0.6 / W 1427 3.9 / 2026 0.6	**28** 0153 4.1 / 0756 0.6 / TH 1415 3.9 / 2016 0.5
14 0244 3.9 / 0845 0.8 / TH 1458 3.7 / 2102 0.7	**29** 0238 4.0 / 0838 0.7 / F 1459 3.7 / 2104 0.6
15 0323 3.7 / 0922 1.0 / F 1534 3.5 / 2147 0.9	**30** 0330 3.8 / 0928 1.0 / SA 1549 3.5 / 2204 0.7

Chart Datum: 2·16 metres below Ordnance Datum (Newlyn)

》》 **FREE** monthly updates from 《《
www.reedsalmanac.co.uk

TIDES

TIME ZONE (UT)
For Summer Time add ONE hour in **non-shaded areas**

ENGLAND – WALTON-ON-THE-NAZE
LAT 51°51′N   LONG 1°17′E
TIMES AND HEIGHTS OF HIGH AND LOW WATERS

YEAR 2005

	MAY			JUNE			JULY			AUGUST	
	Time m	Time m	Time m	Time m	Time m	Time m	Time m	Time m

1 0433 3.6 / 1034 1.2 / SU 1653 3.3 / ☾ 2326 0.9
16 0441 3.3 / 1045 1.4 / M 1656 3.3 / ☽ 2337 1.0
1 0046 0.6 / 0653 3.7 / W 1258 1.2 / 1905 3.5
16 0605 3.4 / 1207 1.3 / TH 1825 3.4
1 0113 0.7 / 0719 3.6 / F 1322 1.2 / 1931 3.6
16 0616 3.5 / 1213 1.3 / SA 1836 3.5
1 0230 1.2 / 0849 3.5 / M 1506 1.1 / 2117 3.5
16 0141 1.2 / 0759 3.4 / TU 1416 1.2 / 2034 3.5

2 0553 3.4 / 1204 1.4 / M 1815 3.2
17 0549 3.2 / 1201 1.5 / TU 1809 3.2
2 0156 0.5 / 0759 3.7 / TH 1405 1.1 / 2009 3.7
17 0053 0.8 / 0709 3.5 / F 1311 1.3 / 1927 3.4
2 0213 0.7 / 0820 3.6 / SA 1426 1.1 / 2034 3.6
17 0103 0.9 / 0722 3.5 / SU 1324 1.3 / 1944 3.5
2 0330 1.1 / 0949 3.6 / TU 1607 0.9 / 2216 3.7
17 0300 1.1 / 0915 3.6 / W 1537 1.0 / 2146 3.8

3 0106 0.8 / 0722 3.5 / TU 1334 1.3 / 1938 3.3
18 0048 1.0 / 0708 3.3 / W 1314 1.4 / 1923 3.3
3 0253 0.5 / 0857 3.8 / F 1500 0.9 / 2105 3.8
18 0153 0.8 / 0809 3.6 / SA 1410 1.2 / 2025 3.6
3 0307 0.8 / 0917 3.7 / SU 1525 0.9 / 2133 3.7
18 0211 0.9 / 0828 3.6 / M 1434 1.2 / 2050 3.6
3 0419 1.1 / 1039 3.8 / W 1657 0.8 / 2305 3.8
18 0403 0.9 / 1016 3.8 / TH 1639 0.6 / 2246 4.1

4 0227 0.6 / 0835 3.7 / W 1441 1.1 / 2045 3.6
19 0152 0.9 / 0813 3.5 / TH 1414 1.2 / 2022 3.4
4 0341 0.4 / 0947 3.9 / SA 1549 0.8 / 2157 3.9
19 0248 0.7 / 0904 3.7 / SU 1505 1.0 / 2119 3.7
4 0354 0.8 / 1009 3.7 / M 1618 0.8 / 2227 3.7
19 0315 0.8 / 0930 3.7 / TU 1541 1.0 / 2152 3.8
4 0501 1.0 / 1124 3.9 / TH 1740 0.7 / 2348 3.9
19 0454 0.8 / 1109 4.1 / F 1731 0.4 / ○ 2338 4.3

5 0324 0.4 / 0931 4.0 / TH 1532 0.8 / 2139 3.8
20 0244 0.7 / 0904 3.7 / F 1501 1.1 / 2112 3.6
5 0422 0.5 / 1033 3.9 / SU 1634 0.7 / 2245 3.9
20 0340 0.6 / 0955 3.8 / M 1558 0.9 / 2211 3.9
5 0437 0.9 / 1056 3.8 / TU 1707 0.7 / 2316 3.8
20 0413 0.8 / 1027 3.9 / W 1643 0.7 / 2251 4.0
5 0538 1.0 / 1203 4.0 / F 1818 0.6 / ●
20 0540 0.7 / 1157 4.2 / SA 1819 0.2

6 0411 0.3 / 1018 4.1 / F 1615 0.7 / 2226 4.0
21 0329 0.6 / 0947 3.8 / SA 1543 0.9 / 2156 3.8
6 0501 0.6 / 1117 3.9 / M 1719 0.6 / ● 2330 3.9
21 0430 0.6 / 1044 3.9 / TU 1651 0.7 / 2303 4.0
6 0517 0.9 / 1140 3.8 / W 1752 0.7 / ●
21 0506 0.7 / 1120 4.0 / TH 1739 0.5 / ○ 2347 4.2
6 0026 3.9 / 0612 1.0 / SA 1239 4.0 / 1850 0.6
21 0027 4.4 / 0623 0.7 / SU 1243 4.5 / 1903 0.1

7 0451 0.2 / 1102 4.1 / SA 1657 0.6 / 2310 4.0
22 0412 0.5 / 1028 3.9 / SU 1625 0.8 / 2240 3.9
7 0538 0.7 / 1158 3.9 / TU 1802 0.6
22 0519 0.6 / 1133 4.0 / W 1743 0.6 / ○ 2355 4.1
7 0001 3.8 / 0555 0.9 / TH 1221 3.8 / 1833 0.6
22 0555 0.7 / 1212 4.1 / F 1832 0.3
7 0100 3.9 / 0643 1.0 / SU 1309 3.9 / 1919 0.6
22 0114 4.5 / 0705 0.6 / M 1327 4.4 / 1946 0.1

8 0529 0.3 / 1142 4.1 / SU 1737 0.5 / ● 2352 4.0
23 0455 0.5 / 1110 4.0 / M 1709 0.7 / ○ 2324 4.0
8 0013 3.9 / 0614 0.8 / W 1236 3.8 / 1843 0.6
23 0607 0.6 / 1222 4.0 / TH 1836 0.5
8 0042 3.8 / 0630 0.9 / F 1256 3.8 / 1910 0.6
23 0040 4.3 / 0641 0.7 / SA 1301 4.2 / 1921 0.2
8 0128 3.9 / 0712 0.9 / M 1336 3.9 / 1947 0.6
23 0158 4.4 / 0746 0.7 / TU 1408 4.4 / 2026 0.2

9 0605 0.4 / 1221 4.1 / M 1818 0.5
24 0537 0.5 / 1152 4.0 / TU 1754 0.6
9 0053 3.8 / 0648 0.8 / TH 1310 3.8 / 1921 0.6
24 0048 4.2 / 0654 0.7 / F 1312 4.0 / 1927 0.4
9 0118 3.8 / 0703 1.0 / SA 1328 3.8 / 1943 0.6
24 0131 4.4 / 0726 0.7 / SU 1348 4.3 / 2008 0.1
9 0157 3.9 / 0743 0.9 / TU 1405 3.9 / 2017 0.6
24 0240 4.3 / 0827 0.7 / W 1448 4.3 / 2105 0.3

10 0031 4.0 / 0638 0.5 / TU 1257 3.9 / 1856 0.5
25 0009 4.1 / 0620 0.5 / W 1236 4.0 / 1840 0.5
10 0131 3.8 / 0722 0.9 / F 1342 3.8 / 1957 0.6
25 0140 4.2 / 0740 0.7 / SA 1401 4.0 / 2018 0.3
10 0150 3.8 / 0735 1.0 / SU 1358 3.8 / 2014 0.6
25 0219 4.4 / 0809 0.7 / M 1433 4.3 / 2054 0.2
10 0228 3.9 / 0817 0.9 / W 1436 3.9 / 2049 0.6
25 0321 4.1 / 0908 0.8 / TH 1528 4.2 / 2143 0.5

11 0110 4.0 / 0712 0.6 / W 1329 3.8 / 1933 0.5
26 0057 4.1 / 0704 0.6 / TH 1321 4.0 / 1928 0.4
11 0207 3.7 / 0755 0.9 / SA 1415 3.7 / 2032 0.7
26 0232 4.2 / 0826 0.8 / SU 1449 4.0 / 2110 0.3
11 0223 3.7 / 0808 1.0 / M 1431 3.8 / 2047 0.6
26 0306 4.3 / 0853 0.8 / TU 1517 4.2 / 2139 0.3
11 0304 3.9 / 0852 0.9 / TH 1511 3.9 / 2123 0.7
26 0402 3.9 / 0951 0.9 / F 1611 4.0 / ☾ 2227 0.8

12 0146 3.9 / 0744 0.7 / TH 1400 3.8 / 2008 0.6
27 0146 4.1 / 0748 0.7 / F 1407 3.9 / 2018 0.4
12 0244 3.7 / 0831 1.0 / SU 1452 3.7 / 2112 0.7
27 0325 4.1 / 0915 0.9 / M 1539 3.9 / 2205 0.3
12 0258 3.7 / 0844 1.0 / TU 1507 3.8 / 2124 0.7
27 0354 4.1 / 0938 0.9 / W 1602 4.1 / 2227 0.4
12 0345 3.8 / 0932 0.9 / F 1551 3.8 / 2204 0.8
27 0446 3.6 / 1042 1.1 / SA 1702 3.8 / 2321 1.1

13 0223 3.8 / 0817 0.9 / F 1433 3.7 / 2045 0.7
28 0237 4.1 / 0834 0.8 / SA 1455 3.8 / 2111 0.5
13 0325 3.6 / 0912 1.0 / M 1535 3.6 / 2158 0.7
28 0420 4.0 / 1007 1.0 / TU 1632 3.9 / ☾ 2304 0.4
13 0338 3.7 / 0925 1.0 / W 1548 3.7 / 2207 0.7
28 0442 3.9 / 1028 1.0 / TH 1651 3.9 / ☾ 2318 0.7
13 0432 3.6 / 1021 1.2 / SA 1642 3.6 / ☾ 2259 1.0
28 0540 3.4 / 1149 1.3 / SU 1813 3.5

14 0303 3.7 / 0853 1.0 / SA 1510 3.6 / 2130 0.8
29 0332 3.9 / 0926 0.9 / SU 1549 3.7 / 2213 0.5
14 0411 3.5 / 1002 1.1 / TU 1625 3.5 / 2253 0.9
29 0517 3.8 / 1107 1.1 / W 1728 3.8
14 0423 3.6 / 1011 1.2 / TH 1635 3.6 / ☾ 2257 0.9
29 0535 3.6 / 1125 1.1 / F 1747 3.7
14 0530 3.4 / 1126 1.3 / SU 1749 3.4
29 0030 1.4 / 0656 3.2 / M 1320 1.3 / 1944 3.3

15 0347 3.5 / 0940 1.2 / SU 1557 3.4 / 2227 0.9
30 0434 3.8 / 1028 1.2 / M 1650 3.5 / ☾ 2327 0.6
15 0504 3.4 / 1102 1.3 / W 1722 3.4 / ☾ 2353 0.9
30 0008 0.6 / 0617 3.7 / TH 1213 1.2 / 1828 3.7
15 0516 3.5 / 1108 1.3 / F 1731 3.5 / ☾ 2357 0.9
30 0017 0.9 / 0634 3.5 / SA 1234 1.2 / 1853 3.5
15 0015 1.1 / 0639 3.3 / M 1247 1.3 / 1910 3.4
30 0153 1.5 / 0821 3.2 / TU 1448 1.2 / 2103 3.4

31 0542 3.6 / 1142 1.3 / TU 1758 3.5
31 0123 1.1 / 0741 3.4 / SU 1352 1.2 / 2007 3.4
31 0306 1.4 / 0927 3.3 / W 1551 1.0 / 2200 3.7

Chart Datum: 2·16 metres below Ordnance Datum (Newlyn)
)) **FREE** monthly updates from ((
www.reedsalmanac.co.uk

ENGLAND – WALTON-ON-THE-NAZE

TIME ZONE (UT) For Summer Time add ONE hour in **non-shaded areas**

LAT 51°51'N   LONG 1°17'E

YEAR 2005

TIMES AND HEIGHTS OF HIGH AND LOW WATERS

SEPTEMBER				OCTOBER				NOVEMBER				DECEMBER			
Time	m	Time	m	Time	m	Time	m	Time	m	Time	m	Time	m	Time	m
1 0359 1.2 1018 3.8 TH 1638 0.8 2246 3.9		**16** 0349 1.0 1002 3.9 F 1628 0.5 2235 4.2		**1** 0412 1.1 1027 3.9 SA 1643 0.6 2254 4.0		**16** 0412 0.8 1025 4.1 SU 1652 0.2 2259 4.3		**1** 0440 0.9 1057 4.0 TU 1707 0.6 2321 4.0		**16** 0512 0.6 1125 4.2 W 1742 0.5 ○ 2354 4.1		**1** 0447 0.9 1103 4.0 TH 1716 0.7 ● 2328 4.0		**16** 0542 0.6 1153 4.0 F 1757 0.8	
2 0440 1.1 1101 4.0 F 1717 0.6 2326 4.0		**17** 0436 0.8 1051 4.1 SA 1715 0.2 2322 4.4		**2** 0446 1.0 1104 4.0 SU 1714 0.6 2328 4.1		**17** 0454 0.7 1108 4.3 M 1732 0.2 ○ 2341 4.4		**2** 0515 0.9 1133 4.0 W 1742 0.6 ● 2355 4.0		**17** 0555 0.6 1207 4.1 TH 1818 0.6		**2** 0532 0.8 1147 4.1 F 1758 0.7		**17** 0014 3.9 0627 0.6 SA 1236 3.9 1832 0.9	
3 0516 1.0 1138 4.0 SA 1751 0.6 ●		**18** 0519 0.7 1136 4.3 SU 1758 0.1 ○		**3** 0516 1.0 1137 4.0 M 1744 0.6 ● 2358 4.0		**18** 0535 0.6 1150 4.3 TU 1810 0.3		**3** 0553 0.8 1209 4.0 TH 1818 0.7		**18** 0033 4.0 0638 0.6 F 1249 4.1 1853 0.7		**3** 0010 4.0 0618 0.7 SA 1232 4.1 1839 0.7		**18** 0052 3.9 0709 0.6 SU 1316 3.9 1907 1.0	
4 0001 4.0 0547 1.0 SU 1212 4.0 1820 0.6		**19** 0007 4.5 0559 0.6 M 1219 4.4 1838 0.1		**4** 0546 0.9 1207 4.0 TU 1814 0.6		**19** 0022 4.3 0616 0.6 W 1231 4.3 1846 0.4		**4** 0030 4.0 0632 0.7 F 1247 4.1 1854 0.7		**19** 0110 3.9 0719 0.6 SA 1329 4.0 1927 0.9		**4** 0053 4.0 0706 0.6 SU 1319 4.1 1921 0.8		**19** 0126 3.9 0748 0.6 M 1352 3.8 1939 1.0	
5 0033 4.0 0616 1.0 M 1241 4.0 1848 0.6		**20** 0050 4.4 0640 0.6 TU 1300 4.4 1917 0.2		**5** 0027 4.0 0618 0.9 W 1238 4.0 1845 0.6		**20** 0100 4.2 0657 0.6 TH 1311 4.3 1921 0.5		**5** 0108 4.0 0714 0.7 SA 1327 4.1 1930 0.7		**20** 0143 3.9 0800 0.7 SU 1408 3.9 2000 1.0		**5** 0137 4.0 0755 0.5 M 1407 4.1 2004 0.9		**20** 0158 3.8 0824 0.7 TU 1428 3.7 2011 1.1	
6 0100 4.0 0646 0.9 TU 1309 4.0 1916 0.6		**21** 0130 4.3 0721 0.6 W 1339 4.4 1953 0.3		**6** 0058 4.0 0653 0.8 TH 1309 4.0 1916 0.6		**21** 0137 4.1 0737 0.6 F 1349 4.2 1954 0.7		**6** 0147 4.0 0757 0.7 SU 1411 4.0 2009 0.9		**21** 0216 3.8 0839 0.8 M 1448 3.7 2034 1.1		**6** 0223 3.9 0845 0.5 TU 1459 4.0 2052 1.0		**21** 0232 3.7 0900 0.7 W 1505 3.6 2048 1.1	
7 0128 4.0 0718 0.9 W 1336 4.0 1945 0.6		**22** 0208 4.2 0800 0.7 TH 1417 4.3 2028 0.5		**7** 0130 4.0 0729 0.8 F 1343 4.1 1948 0.7		**22** 0210 4.0 0816 0.7 SA 1428 4.0 2027 0.9		**7** 0229 3.8 0843 0.7 M 1459 3.9 2055 1.1		**22** 0252 3.7 0923 0.9 TU 1531 3.6 2116 1.3		**7** 0313 3.8 0941 0.6 W 1555 3.8 2146 1.2		**22** 0311 3.7 0941 0.8 TH 1546 3.5 2132 1.2	
8 0158 4.0 0751 0.8 TH 1407 4.0 2015 0.6		**23** 0245 4.1 0839 0.7 F 1454 4.2 2102 0.7		**8** 0206 4.0 0806 0.8 SA 1420 4.0 2022 0.8		**23** 0243 3.8 0856 0.8 SU 1508 3.8 2103 1.1		**8** 0316 3.6 0939 0.8 TU 1557 3.7 2153 1.3		**23** 0336 3.5 1017 1.0 W 1621 3.4 ○ 2214 1.5		**8** 0409 3.7 1045 0.7 TH 1659 3.7 ● 2251 1.3		**23** 0356 3.6 1029 0.9 F 1634 3.4 ● 2225 1.3	
9 0232 3.9 0826 0.8 F 1441 4.0 2047 0.7		**24** 0320 3.9 0920 0.9 SA 1535 3.9 2141 1.0		**9** 0245 3.9 0847 0.8 SU 1503 3.9 2102 1.0		**24** 0319 3.6 0943 1.0 M 1555 3.5 2150 1.4		**9** 0415 3.4 1052 1.0 W 1710 3.5 ○ 2313 1.4		**24** 0432 3.4 1122 1.1 TH 1725 3.2 2329 1.6		**9** 0514 3.6 1158 0.7 F 1809 3.6		**24** 0449 3.4 1124 1.0 SA 1729 3.4 2328 1.4	
10 0311 3.9 0904 0.9 SA 1520 3.9 2125 0.8		**25** 0357 3.6 1008 1.1 SU 1623 3.6 ○ 2232 1.3		**10** 0329 3.7 0938 1.0 M 1556 3.6 ○ 2157 1.2		**25** 0403 3.4 1047 1.2 TU 1656 3.3 ● 2302 1.6		**10** 0532 3.3 1223 0.9 TH 1838 3.5		**25** 0543 3.3 1230 1.1 F 1843 3.2		**10** 0005 1.3 0624 3.6 SA 1312 0.7 1918 3.6		**25** 0551 3.4 1224 1.0 SU 1833 3.4	
11 0355 3.7 0951 1.1 SU 1609 3.7 ○ 2217 1.1		**26** 0443 3.3 1115 3.2 M 1732 3.2 2346 1.6		**11** 0424 3.4 1048 1.2 TU 1708 3.4 2323 1.5		**26** 0508 3.2 1211 1.2 W 1829 3.1		**11** 0045 1.4 0657 3.4 F 1347 0.8 1957 3.7		**26** 0045 1.5 0659 3.3 SA 1333 1.0 1951 3.4		**11** 0118 1.2 0731 3.7 SU 1416 0.6 2021 3.7		**26** 0034 1.4 0656 3.4 M 1324 1.0 1938 3.4	
12 0451 3.4 1056 1.3 M 1717 3.4 2339 1.3		**27** 0559 3.1 1249 1.2 TU 1916 3.2		**12** 0542 3.2 1228 1.2 W 1850 3.3		**27** 0032 1.7 0649 3.1 TH 1334 1.2 1955 3.3		**12** 0200 1.3 0808 3.6 SA 1451 0.6 2057 3.9		**27** 0149 1.4 0802 3.5 SU 1426 0.9 2043 3.5		**12** 0222 1.1 0832 3.8 M 1511 0.6 2115 3.8		**27** 0138 1.3 0800 3.5 TU 1423 0.9 2038 3.6	
13 0604 3.2 1228 1.3 TU 1852 3.3		**28** 0117 1.6 0745 3.2 W 1419 1.2 2038 3.4		**13** 0110 1.5 0723 3.3 TH 1409 1.0 2024 3.6		**28** 0153 1.6 0807 3.4 F 1436 1.1 2053 3.6		**13** 0257 1.0 0905 3.9 SU 1541 0.4 2146 4.1		**28** 0239 1.2 0852 3.7 M 1511 0.8 2127 3.8		**13** 0317 0.9 0927 3.9 TU 1558 0.6 2204 3.9		**28** 0236 1.2 0857 3.6 W 1517 0.8 2131 3.7	
14 0124 1.4 0739 3.3 W 1415 1.2 2033 3.5		**29** 0236 1.5 0856 3.5 TH 1521 1.0 2134 3.7		**14** 0231 1.2 0842 3.6 F 1517 0.6 2126 4.0		**29** 0250 1.3 0901 3.6 SA 1522 0.8 2137 3.8		**14** 0345 0.8 0955 4.1 M 1625 0.3 2231 4.2		**29** 0322 1.1 0937 3.8 TU 1553 0.7 2207 3.9		**14** 0407 0.7 1019 3.9 W 1640 0.7 2250 3.9		**29** 0332 1.1 0951 3.8 TH 1608 0.8 2220 3.9	
15 0249 1.2 0903 3.5 TH 1533 0.8 2142 3.9		**30** 0330 1.3 0946 3.8 F 1606 0.8 2217 3.9		**15** 0326 0.9 0937 3.9 SA 1608 0.4 2215 4.2		**30** 0333 1.1 0944 3.8 SU 1600 0.7 2214 4.0		**15** 0429 0.7 1041 4.1 TU 1704 0.4 2314 4.2		**30** 0404 1.0 1020 3.9 W 1635 0.7 2247 4.0		**15** 0456 0.7 1107 4.0 TH 1719 0.7 ○ 2334 3.9		**30** 0426 0.9 1042 3.9 F 1657 0.7 2308 3.9	
						31 0407 1.0 1021 3.9 M 1634 0.6 2248 4.0								**31** 0519 0.7 1133 4.1 SA 1744 0.7 ● 2356 4.0	

Chart Datum: 2·16 metres below Ordnance Datum (Newlyn)

》FREE monthly updates from 《
www.reedsalmanac.co.uk

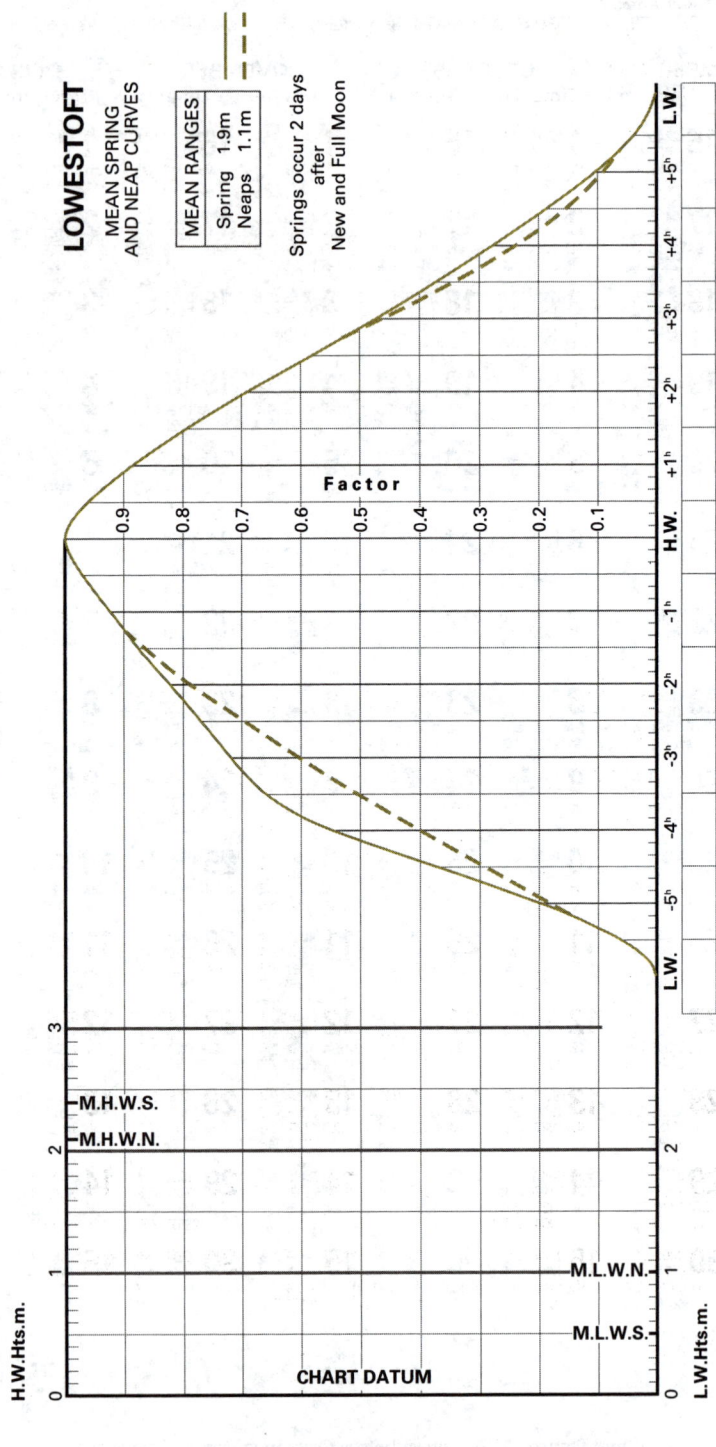

TIME ZONE (UT)
For Summer Time add ONE hour in **non-shaded areas**

ENGLAND – LOWESTOFT
LAT 52°28′N   LONG 1°45′E
TIMES AND HEIGHTS OF HIGH AND LOW WATERS

YEAR 2005

JANUARY		FEBRUARY		MARCH		APRIL	
Time m	Time m	Time m	Time m	Time m	Time m	Time m	Time m
1 0023 2.4 / 0654 0.8 / SA 1305 2.1 / 1838 1.1	**16** 0105 2.6 / 0753 0.4 / SU 1420 2.1 / 1937 1.1	**1** 0115 2.4 / 0742 0.7 / TU 1353 2.1 / 1936 1.0	**16** 0214 2.3 / 0846 0.9 / W 1520 2.0 / ○ 2040 1.1	**1** 0010 2.5 / 0632 0.6 / TU 1240 2.2 / 1827 0.8	**16** 0057 2.4 / 0713 0.8 / W 1323 2.1 / 1918 0.9	**1** 0119 2.3 / 0725 0.9 / F 1343 2.1 / 1949 0.8	**16** 0243 2.0 / 0750 1.3 / SA 1417 2.1 / ○ 2057 1.0
2 0105 2.4 / 0737 0.8 / SU 1348 2.1 / 1922 1.2	**17** 0154 2.5 / 0845 0.6 / M 1530 2.1 / ○ 2024 1.2	**2** 0157 2.4 / 0828 0.8 / W 1445 2.0 / ○ 2027 1.1	**17** 0323 2.2 / 0954 1.1 / TH 1634 2.0 / 2206 1.2	**2** 0047 2.4 / 0706 0.6 / W 1320 2.1 / 1908 0.9	**17** 0147 2.2 / 0752 1.0 / TH 1406 2.0 / ○ 2009 1.0	**2** 0226 2.2 / 0825 1.1 / SA 1446 2.0 / ○ 2109 0.9	**17** 0418 2.0 / 0854 1.4 / SU 1525 2.0 / 2250 0.9
3 0148 2.4 / 0823 0.8 / M 1439 2.0 / ○ 2012 1.2	**18** 0248 2.4 / 0944 0.7 / TU 1635 2.0 / 2125 1.2	**3** 0248 2.3 / 0927 0.8 / TH 1602 2.0 / 2132 1.2	**18** 0455 2.1 / 1124 1.2 / F 1740 2.0 / 2357 1.1	**3** 0131 2.3 / 0749 0.8 / TH 1407 2.1 / ○ 1959 1.0	**18** 0259 2.1 / 0843 1.2 / F 1506 2.0 / 2127 1.1	**3** 0409 2.1 / 1004 1.2 / SU 1606 2.0 / 2300 0.8	**18** 0532 2.0 / 1139 1.4 / M 1647 2.0 / 2352 0.9
4 0234 2.3 / 0918 0.8 / TU 1554 1.9 / 2109 1.3	**19** 0359 2.3 / 1050 0.9 / W 1734 2.1 / 2256 1.2	**4** 0402 2.2 / 1048 0.9 / F 1726 2.1 / 2310 1.1	**19** 0626 2.0 / 1235 1.2 / SA 1845 2.1	**4** 0228 2.2 / 0846 0.9 / F 1511 2.0 / 2107 1.0	**19** 0440 2.0 / 1053 1.4 / SA 1633 2.0 / 2330 1.0	**4** 0545 2.2 / 1143 1.2 / M 1724 2.1	**19** 0638 2.1 / 1232 1.3 / TU 1753 2.1
5 0328 2.3 / 1022 0.8 / W 1713 2.1 / 2220 1.3	**20** 0516 2.2 / 1153 1.0 / TH 1830 2.1	**5** 0533 2.2 / 1206 0.9 / SA 1826 2.1	**20** 0107 1.0 / 0743 2.1 / SU 1333 1.2 / 1938 2.1	**5** 0352 2.2 / 1018 1.1 / SA 1640 2.0 / 2300 1.0	**20** 0608 2.0 / 1218 1.3 / SU 1747 2.0	**5** 0015 0.6 / 0700 2.3 / TU 1250 1.1 / 1829 2.2	**20** 0040 0.8 / 0726 2.1 / W 1310 1.2 / 1846 2.1
6 0439 2.3 / 1129 0.8 / TH 1808 2.2 / 2342 1.2	**21** 0018 1.2 / 0630 2.1 / F 1251 1.0 / 1922 2.2	**6** 0033 1.0 / 0646 2.3 / SU 1309 0.9 / 1919 2.2	**21** 0159 0.9 / 0831 2.2 / M 1415 1.1 / 2017 2.2	**6** 0534 2.2 / 1154 1.1 / SU 1754 2.1	**21** 0035 0.9 / 0720 2.1 / M 1313 1.2 / 1850 2.1	**6** 0119 0.5 / 0755 2.3 / W 1344 1.0 / 1926 2.3	**21** 0123 0.7 / 0802 2.2 / TH 1342 1.1 / 1931 2.2
7 0553 2.3 / 1228 0.7 / F 1858 2.2	**22** 0124 1.2 / 0744 2.2 / SA 1341 1.1 / 2005 2.2	**7** 0140 0.8 / 0756 2.4 / M 1407 0.8 / 2010 2.3	**22** 0240 0.7 / 0907 2.2 / TU 1448 1.0 / 2049 2.3	**7** 0025 0.8 / 0655 2.2 / M 1302 1.0 / 1855 2.2	**22** 0126 0.8 / 0805 2.2 / TU 1352 1.1 / 1937 2.2	**7** 0214 0.3 / 0837 2.4 / TH 1430 0.8 / 2015 2.4	**22** 0201 0.6 / 0831 2.2 / F 1413 0.9 / 2010 2.3
8 0049 1.1 / 0654 2.4 / SA 1323 0.7 / 1943 2.3	**23** 0216 0.9 / 0839 2.2 / SU 1424 1.1 / 2040 2.3	**8** 0242 0.6 / 0857 2.4 / TU 1501 0.8 / ● 2058 2.4	**23** 0316 0.6 / 0936 2.2 / W 1517 0.9 / 2119 2.4	**8** 0133 0.6 / 0803 2.3 / TU 1400 0.9 / 1950 2.3	**23** 0207 0.7 / 0839 2.2 / W 1423 1.0 / 2014 2.3	**8** 0301 0.2 / 0914 2.4 / F 1510 0.7 / ● 2101 2.5	**23** 0238 0.5 / 0859 2.3 / SA 1448 0.8 / 2049 2.4
9 0149 0.9 / 0753 2.4 / SU 1416 0.6 / 2028 2.4	**24** 0259 0.8 / 0920 2.2 / M 1500 1.0 / 2111 2.4	**9** 0338 0.3 / 0948 2.5 / W 1549 0.7 / 2145 2.6	**24** 0350 0.6 / 1003 2.2 / TH 1545 0.8 / ○ 2152 2.5	**9** 0233 0.4 / 0853 2.4 / W 1450 0.8 / 2039 2.4	**24** 0243 0.6 / 0907 2.2 / TH 1450 0.9 / 2048 2.3	**9** 0342 0.2 / 0950 2.4 / SA 1548 0.6 / 2145 2.6	**24** 0314 0.4 / 0929 2.3 / SU 1524 0.7 / ○ 2127 2.5
10 0247 0.7 / 0853 2.5 / M 1508 0.7 / ● 2114 2.5	**25** 0337 0.7 / 0956 2.2 / TU 1531 1.0 / ○ 2141 2.4	**10** 0427 0.2 / 1035 2.5 / TH 1633 0.7 / ○ 2230 2.7	**25** 0423 0.5 / 1030 2.3 / F 1616 0.8 / 2226 2.5	**10** 0323 0.2 / 0935 2.4 / TH 1533 0.7 / ● 2124 2.6	**25** 0317 0.5 / 0933 2.3 / F 1519 0.8 / ○ 2123 2.4	**10** 0420 0.2 / 1025 2.4 / SU 1625 0.5 / 2228 2.6	**25** 0351 0.4 / 1001 2.4 / M 1602 0.6 / 2207 2.5
11 0343 0.5 / 0951 2.6 / TU 1558 0.7 / 2200 2.5	**26** 0413 0.7 / 1027 2.2 / W 1600 0.9 / 2214 2.5	**11** 0513 0.1 / 1119 2.4 / F 1713 0.7 / 2313 2.7	**26** 0456 0.5 / 1059 2.3 / SA 1648 0.7 / 2300 2.5	**11** 0408 0.1 / 1015 2.4 / F 1612 0.6 / 2208 2.7	**26** 0350 0.4 / 1000 2.4 / SA 1552 0.7 / 2158 2.5	**11** 0456 0.3 / 1101 2.3 / M 1702 0.6 / 2310 2.5	**26** 0428 0.4 / 1036 2.4 / TU 1641 0.6 / 2248 2.5
12 0437 0.3 / 1046 2.6 / W 1646 0.8 / 2246 2.6	**27** 0447 0.6 / 1056 2.2 / TH 1632 0.9 / 2249 2.5	**12** 0556 0.1 / 1202 2.3 / SA 1750 0.8 / 2356 2.5	**27** 0528 0.5 / 1131 2.3 / SU 1721 0.7 / 2335 2.5	**12** 0449 0.1 / 1054 2.3 / SA 1650 0.6 / 2251 2.7	**27** 0424 0.4 / 1030 2.4 / SU 1625 0.6 / 2233 2.5	**12** 0530 0.5 / 1136 2.3 / TU 1738 0.6 / 2352 2.4	**27** 0505 0.5 / 1113 2.4 / W 1721 0.6 / 2331 2.4
13 0528 0.2 / 1137 2.5 / TH 1731 0.8 / 2333 2.6	**28** 0521 0.6 / 1127 2.2 / F 1706 0.9 / 2325 2.5	**13** 0637 0.2 / 1245 2.2 / SU 1827 0.8	**28** 0600 0.5 / 1204 2.2 / M 1753 0.8	**13** 0527 0.2 / 1132 2.3 / SU 1725 0.6 / 2332 2.6	**28** 0458 0.5 / 1102 2.3 / M 1659 0.6 / 2309 2.5	**13** 0601 0.7 / 1209 2.2 / W 1815 0.7	**28** 0543 0.6 / 1152 2.3 / TH 1804 0.6
14 0617 0.2 / 1228 2.4 / F 1813 0.9	**29** 0556 0.6 / 1159 2.1 / SA 1740 0.9	**14** 0039 2.6 / 0717 0.4 / M 1329 2.1 / 1904 0.9		**14** 0604 0.3 / 1209 2.2 / M 1801 0.7	**29** 0530 0.5 / 1136 2.3 / TU 1734 0.7 / 2347 2.5	**14** 0036 2.2 / 0632 0.9 / TH 1244 2.2 / 1855 0.8	**29** 0020 2.4 / 0624 0.8 / F 1237 2.3 / 1854 0.6
15 0019 2.6 / 0704 0.3 / SA 1321 2.2 / 1854 1.0	**30** 0000 2.5 / 0629 0.6 / SU 1234 2.2 / 1815 0.9	**15** 0124 2.5 / 0758 0.6 / TU 1416 2.0 / 1947 1.0		**15** 0014 2.5 / 0638 0.5 / TU 1245 2.1 / 1837 0.7	**30** 0604 0.6 / 1213 2.3 / W 1810 0.7	**15** 0127 2.1 / 0706 1.1 / F 1325 2.1 / 1945 0.9	**30** 0120 2.3 / 0714 1.0 / SA 1329 2.2 / 1958 0.7
	31 0037 2.4 / 0704 0.6 / M 1311 2.1 / 1853 1.0				**31** 0028 2.4 / 0640 0.7 / TH 1254 2.2 / 1853 0.8		

Chart Datum: 1·50 metres below Ordnance Datum (Newlyn)

》》 **FREE** monthly updates from 《《
www.reedsalmanac.co.uk

Chapter 5

271

TIDES

TIME ZONE (UT)
For Summer Time add ONE hour in **non-shaded areas**

ENGLAND – LOWESTOFT
LAT 52°28′N   LONG 1°45′E

TIMES AND HEIGHTS OF HIGH AND LOW WATERS

YEAR 2005

	MAY			JUNE			JULY			AUGUST	
	Time m	Time m		Time m	Time m		Time m	Time m		Time m	Time m
1	0239 2.2 0816 1.2 SU 1431 2.1 ◐ 2125 0.7	**16** 0341 2.0 0807 1.3 M 1441 2.1 2148 0.9	**1**	0517 2.2 1034 1.2 W 1628 2.3 2327 0.5	**16** 0448 2.0 0929 1.3 TH 1554 2.2 2248 0.8	**1**	0541 2.1 1059 1.2 F 1709 2.3 2354 0.7	**16** 0439 2.0 0945 1.3 SA 1608 2.2 2256 0.8	**1**	0029 1.1 0655 2.2 M 1305 1.0 1928 2.2	**16** 0557 2.2 1206 1.1 TU 1824 2.3
2	0423 2.2 0949 1.3 M 1542 2.1 2248 0.6	**17** 0448 2.0 0916 1.4 TU 1545 2.1 2257 0.8	**2**	0616 2.2 1143 1.2 TH 1735 2.3	**17** 0541 2.1 1044 1.3 F 1701 2.2 2344 0.7	**2**	0635 2.2 1212 1.1 SA 1816 2.2	**17** 0542 2.1 1110 1.2 SU 1727 2.2	**2**	0128 1.1 0745 2.3 TU 1404 0.9 2028 2.2	**17** 0041 1.0 0653 2.2 W 1314 0.9 1934 2.4
3	0541 2.2 1117 1.2 TU 1656 2.2 2354 0.5	**18** 0545 2.0 1103 1.4 W 1655 2.1 2348 0.8	**3**	0025 0.5 0706 2.2 F 1243 1.1 1835 2.3	**18** 0628 2.1 1156 1.2 SA 1803 2.2	**3**	0050 0.8 0723 2.2 SU 1317 1.0 1921 2.2	**18** 0001 0.8 0634 2.2 M 1226 1.1 1833 2.3	**3**	0217 1.1 0826 2.3 W 1450 0.8 2112 2.2	**18** 0140 0.9 0745 2.4 TH 1416 0.6 2036 2.4
4	0645 2.3 1221 1.1 W 1802 2.2	**19** 0635 2.1 1203 1.3 TH 1755 2.1	**4**	0118 0.6 0748 2.3 SA 1336 0.9 1930 2.3	**19** 0036 0.7 0711 2.2 SU 1255 1.1 1858 2.3	**4**	0141 0.9 0805 2.3 M 1412 0.9 2022 2.2	**19** 0059 0.8 0722 2.3 TU 1327 0.9 1935 2.3	**4**	0256 1.1 0901 2.4 TH 1530 0.7 2149 2.3	**19** 0235 0.8 0833 2.5 F 1512 0.4 ○ 2126 2.5
5	0054 0.4 0734 2.3 TH 1316 1.0 1900 2.3	**20** 0033 0.7 0715 2.2 F 1249 1.1 1845 2.2	**5**	0204 0.6 0826 2.3 SU 1424 0.8 2022 2.3	**20** 0125 0.6 0752 2.3 M 1347 0.9 1950 2.3	**5**	0226 0.9 0844 2.3 TU 1500 0.8 2113 2.2	**20** 0153 0.8 0808 2.3 W 1425 0.7 2036 2.4	**5**	0329 1.0 0932 2.4 F 1606 0.6 ● 2221 2.3	**20** 0325 0.8 0920 2.6 SA 1603 0.2 2212 2.5
6	0147 0.4 0814 2.3 F 1403 0.9 1951 2.4	**21** 0117 0.6 0751 2.2 SA 1332 1.0 1932 2.3	**6**	0246 0.6 0901 2.4 M 1508 0.7 ● 2112 2.3	**21** 0213 0.6 0832 2.3 TU 1439 0.8 2042 2.4	**6**	0306 0.9 0919 2.4 W 1543 0.7 ● 2158 2.2	**21** 0246 0.8 0854 2.4 TH 1522 0.5 ○ 2133 2.5	**6**	0358 1.0 1004 2.5 SA 1639 0.6 2250 2.3	**21** 0410 0.7 1005 2.7 SU 1649 0.1 2255 2.5
7	0233 0.4 0849 2.3 SA 1445 0.7 2038 2.5	**22** 0158 0.5 0824 2.3 SU 1415 0.9 2016 2.4	**7**	0324 0.7 0937 2.4 TU 1550 0.7 2159 2.3	**22** 0300 0.6 0913 2.4 W 1530 0.6 ○ 2136 2.4	**7**	0341 1.0 0953 2.4 TH 1622 0.6 2238 2.2	**22** 0337 0.7 0940 2.5 F 1616 0.3 2226 2.5	**7**	0426 0.9 1037 2.5 SU 1711 0.5 2319 2.3	**22** 0451 0.7 1049 2.8 M 1733 0.1 2338 2.4
8	0313 0.4 0924 2.4 SU 1525 0.6 ● 2124 2.5	**23** 0240 0.5 0859 2.3 M 1459 0.7 ○ 2101 2.4	**8**	0359 0.8 1011 2.4 W 1631 0.6 2244 2.2	**23** 0348 0.6 0956 2.5 TH 1622 0.5 2230 2.5	**8**	0413 1.0 1025 2.4 F 1659 0.6 2314 2.2	**23** 0426 0.7 1025 2.6 SA 1707 0.2 2316 2.5	**8**	0455 0.9 1111 2.6 M 1743 0.6 2348 2.2	**23** 0530 0.7 1133 2.8 TU 1814 0.2
9	0350 0.5 0959 2.4 M 1605 0.6 2209 2.4	**24** 0322 0.5 0935 2.4 TU 1543 0.6 2146 2.5	**9**	0431 0.9 1044 2.4 TH 1710 0.6 2327 2.2	**24** 0436 0.7 1040 2.5 F 1715 0.4 2325 2.5	**9**	0443 1.0 1059 2.5 SA 1735 0.6 2348 2.2	**24** 0511 0.7 1111 2.7 SU 1755 0.1	**9**	0527 0.9 1146 2.5 TU 1814 0.6	**24** 0020 2.3 0608 0.8 W 1217 2.7 1854 0.4
10	0425 0.6 1034 2.4 TU 1643 0.6 2253 2.4	**25** 0404 0.5 1013 2.4 W 1629 0.6 2234 2.5	**10**	0501 1.0 1117 2.4 F 1748 0.7	**25** 0523 0.8 1127 2.5 SA 1807 0.3	**10**	0514 1.0 1134 2.5 SU 1809 0.6	**25** 0004 2.4 0553 0.8 M 1157 2.7 1841 0.2	**10**	0020 2.2 0600 0.9 W 1221 2.5 1846 0.6	**25** 0103 2.2 0646 0.9 TH 1302 2.6 1934 0.6
11	0457 0.7 1107 2.3 W 1720 0.6 2336 2.3	**26** 0447 0.6 1054 2.4 TH 1716 0.5 2326 2.4	**11**	0009 2.1 0531 1.0 SA 1153 2.4 1827 0.7	**26** 0020 2.4 0609 0.9 SU 1215 2.5 1859 0.3	**11**	0021 2.1 0547 1.0 M 1212 2.4 1844 0.6	**26** 0053 2.3 0634 0.9 TU 1242 2.7 1927 0.3	**11**	0055 2.2 0636 1.0 TH 1257 2.4 1920 0.7	**26** 0149 2.2 0729 1.1 F 1353 2.5 ◐ 2020 0.9
12	0527 0.9 1140 2.3 TH 1758 0.7	**27** 0531 0.7 1138 2.3 F 1807 0.5	**12**	0051 2.1 0607 1.0 SU 1233 2.3 1909 0.7	**27** 0117 2.3 0656 1.0 M 1303 2.5 1953 0.3	**12**	0056 2.1 0625 1.0 TU 1251 2.4 1921 0.7	**27** 0145 2.2 0715 1.0 W 1329 2.6 2015 0.4	**12**	0134 2.2 0716 1.1 F 1337 2.4 2001 0.8	**27** 0244 2.1 0822 1.1 SA 1501 2.3 2119 1.1
13	0021 2.2 0557 1.0 F 1215 2.3 1839 0.7	**28** 0022 2.4 0617 0.9 SA 1226 2.4 1902 0.5	**13**	0137 2.0 0648 1.1 M 1318 2.3 1955 0.8	**28** 0223 2.2 0744 1.1 TU 1355 2.5 ◐ 2050 0.4	**13**	0135 2.1 0705 1.1 W 1331 2.4 2002 0.7	**28** 0246 2.1 0800 1.0 TH 1421 2.5 ◐ 2109 0.6	**13**	0220 2.1 0804 1.1 SA 1425 2.3 ◐ 2052 0.9	**28** 0359 2.1 0940 1.3 SU 1636 2.2 2254 1.3
14	0112 2.1 0631 1.1 SA 1255 2.2 1927 0.8	**29** 0126 2.3 0708 1.0 SU 1318 2.3 2006 0.5	**14**	0230 2.0 0735 1.2 TU 1405 2.2 2048 0.8	**29** 0339 2.1 0837 1.1 W 1451 2.4 2151 0.5	**14**	0218 2.1 0750 1.1 TH 1414 2.3 ◐ 2049 0.8	**29** 0356 2.1 0855 1.1 F 1526 2.3 2213 0.9	**14**	0322 2.1 0904 1.2 SU 1531 2.2 2206 1.0	**29** 0509 2.1 1134 1.1 M 1805 2.1
15	0218 2.0 0713 1.2 SU 1344 2.2 2027 0.9	**30** 0244 2.2 0806 1.2 M 1415 2.3 ◐ 2116 0.5	**15**	0343 2.0 0827 1.3 W 1456 2.2 ◐ 2147 0.8	**30** 0443 2.1 0942 1.2 TH 1557 2.3 2254 0.6	**15**	0315 2.1 0841 1.2 F 1504 2.3 2146 0.8	**30** 0458 2.1 1015 1.2 SA 1648 2.2 2323 1.0	**15**	0450 2.1 1034 1.2 M 1704 2.2 2334 1.0	**30** 0014 1.3 0615 2.1 TU 1249 1.0 1926 2.2
		31 0410 2.2 0917 1.2 TU 1518 2.3 2224 0.5						**31** 0557 2.1 1150 1.1 SU 1807 2.2			**31** 0117 1.3 0715 2.2 W 1345 0.9 2016 2.3

Chart Datum: 1·50 metres below Ordnance Datum (Newlyn)

》》 **FREE** monthly updates from 《《
www.reedsalmanac.co.uk

TIME ZONE (UT)
For Summer Time add ONE hour in **non-shaded areas**

ENGLAND – LOWESTOFT
LAT 52°28′N   LONG 1°45′E
TIMES AND HEIGHTS OF HIGH AND LOW WATERS

YEAR 2005

SEPTEMBER		OCTOBER		NOVEMBER		DECEMBER	
Time m	Time m	Time m	Time m	Time m	Time m	Time m	Time m
1 0203 1.2 / 0759 2.3 / TH 1427 0.8 / 2054 2.3	**16** 0127 1.1 / 0718 2.4 / F 1402 0.5 / 2027 2.5	**1** 0207 1.2 / 0753 2.4 / SA 1427 0.7 / 2053 2.3	**16** 0155 1.0 / 0741 2.6 / SU 1429 0.4 / 2046 2.5	**1** 0227 1.0 / 0826 2.5 / TU 1452 0.6 / 2110 2.4	**16** 0258 0.8 / 0855 2.6 / W 1526 0.6 / ○ 2134 2.5	**1** 0236 0.9 / 0838 2.5 / TH 1457 0.7 / ● 2113 2.5	**16** 0331 0.7 / 0938 2.4 / F 1541 0.9 / 2151 2.5
2 0238 1.1 / 0833 2.4 / F 1504 0.7 / 2125 2.3	**17** 0219 1.0 / 0808 2.6 / SA 1455 0.3 / 2110 2.5	**2** 0235 1.1 / 0827 2.5 / SU 1500 0.6 / 2119 2.4	**17** 0239 0.9 / 0829 2.7 / M 1514 0.3 / ○ 2123 2.5	**2** 0302 0.9 / 0905 2.5 / W 1527 0.6 / ● 2141 2.5	**17** 0342 0.7 / 0943 2.6 / TH 1603 0.7 / 2211 2.5	**2** 0319 0.8 / 0923 2.5 / F 1538 0.7 / 2150 2.5	**17** 0415 0.7 / 1027 2.3 / SA 1617 1.0 / 2227 2.5
3 0307 1.1 / 0904 2.5 / SA 1537 0.6 / ● 2153 2.3	**18** 0305 0.8 / 0855 2.7 / SU 1541 0.2 / ○ 2150 2.5	**3** 0302 1.0 / 0902 2.6 / M 1532 0.6 / ● 2144 2.4	**18** 0321 0.8 / 0915 2.8 / TU 1555 0.3 / 2200 2.5	**3** 0340 0.8 / 0944 2.6 / TH 1603 0.6 / 2214 2.5	**18** 0424 0.7 / 1031 2.5 / F 1639 0.8 / 2248 2.5	**3** 0405 0.7 / 1009 2.5 / SA 1620 0.7 / 2230 2.5	**18** 0457 0.7 / 1112 2.3 / SU 1650 1.0 / 2302 2.5
4 0334 1.0 / 0935 2.5 / SU 1609 0.5 / 2218 2.3	**19** 0347 0.7 / 0940 2.8 / M 1624 0.1 / 2229 2.5	**4** 0332 0.9 / 0937 2.6 / TU 1603 0.5 / 2212 2.4	**19** 0401 0.7 / 1001 2.8 / W 1633 0.4 / 2238 2.5	**4** 0418 0.8 / 1024 2.6 / F 1639 0.7 / 2250 2.5	**19** 0505 0.7 / 1119 2.4 / SA 1712 1.0 / 2323 2.5	**4** 0452 0.7 / 1059 2.5 / SU 1704 0.8 / 2312 2.5	**19** 0538 0.7 / 1155 2.2 / M 1720 1.1 / 2337 2.5
5 0402 0.9 / 1009 2.6 / M 1640 0.5 / 2245 2.3	**20** 0426 0.7 / 1024 2.8 / TU 1704 0.2 / 2308 2.5	**5** 0405 0.8 / 1012 2.6 / W 1635 0.5 / 2243 2.4	**20** 0441 0.7 / 1046 2.7 / TH 1709 0.6 / 2315 2.5	**5** 0458 0.8 / 1107 2.5 / SA 1717 0.8 / 2328 2.5	**20** 0547 0.8 / 1207 2.3 / SU 1744 1.1 / 2358 2.4	**5** 0542 0.6 / 1152 2.4 / M 1749 1.0 / 2358 2.5	**20** 0617 0.7 / 1236 2.2 / TU 1752 1.1
6 0432 0.8 / 1043 2.6 / TU 1710 0.5 / 2315 2.3	**21** 0504 0.7 / 1108 2.8 / W 1742 0.4 / 2346 2.4	**6** 0439 0.8 / 1048 2.6 / TH 1707 0.6 / 2316 2.4	**21** 0520 0.7 / 1131 2.6 / F 1743 0.8 / 2351 2.4	**6** 0540 0.8 / 1154 2.4 / SU 1757 0.9	**21** 0631 0.8 / 1259 2.2 / M 1817 1.2	**6** 0635 0.6 / 1250 2.4 / TU 1837 1.1	**21** 0015 2.4 / 0656 0.8 / W 1318 2.1 / 1829 1.2
7 0503 0.8 / 1117 2.6 / W 1740 0.6 / 2347 2.3	**22** 0542 0.7 / 1152 2.7 / TH 1818 0.6	**7** 0513 0.8 / 1125 2.5 / F 1739 0.7 / 2352 2.4	**22** 0601 0.8 / 1219 2.4 / SA 1816 1.0	**7** 0011 2.4 / 0629 0.8 / M 1249 2.4 / 1843 1.1	**22** 0038 2.4 / 0718 0.9 / TU 1403 2.1 / 1856 1.3	**7** 0048 2.5 / 0733 0.6 / W 1355 2.3 / 1929 1.2	**22** 0057 2.4 / 0738 0.8 / TH 1404 2.0 / 1911 1.3
8 0536 0.9 / 1151 2.5 / TH 1811 0.6	**23** 0024 2.3 / 0621 0.8 / F 1238 2.5 / 1854 0.8	**8** 0549 0.9 / 1205 2.5 / SA 1814 0.8	**23** 0028 2.4 / 0644 0.9 / SU 1314 2.2 / 1851 1.2	**8** 0101 2.4 / 0728 0.8 / TU 1356 2.3 / 1939 1.2	**23** 0126 2.3 / 0816 0.9 / W 1519 2.1 / ◐ 1945 1.4	**8** 0141 2.4 / 0837 0.6 / TH 1519 2.2 / ◐ 2028 1.3	**23** 0143 2.3 / 0825 0.9 / F 1504 2.0 / ◐ 1959 1.3
9 0021 2.3 / 0609 0.9 / F 1228 2.5 / 1843 0.9	**24** 0104 2.3 / 0704 0.9 / SA 1330 2.3 / 1933 1.1	**9** 0031 2.4 / 0631 0.9 / SU 1253 2.4 / 1856 1.0	**24** 0109 2.3 / 0736 1.0 / M 1431 2.1 / 1934 1.4	**9** 0158 2.3 / 0845 0.8 / W 1533 2.2 / ◐ 2051 1.4	**24** 0220 2.3 / 0927 1.0 / TH 1626 2.1 / 2045 1.5	**9** 0238 2.4 / 0944 0.6 / F 1638 2.2 / 2137 1.3	**24** 0231 2.3 / 0918 0.9 / SA 1617 2.0 / 2054 1.4
10 0059 2.3 / 0648 1.0 / SA 1309 2.4 / 1922 1.0	**25** 0149 2.2 / 0756 1.0 / SU 1445 2.2 / ◐ 2022 1.3	**10** 0118 2.3 / 0723 1.0 / M 1353 2.3 / ◐ 1950 1.2	**25** 0201 2.2 / 0850 1.0 / TU 1600 2.1 / 2034 1.5	**10** 0303 2.3 / 1009 0.8 / TH 1702 2.3 / 2223 1.4	**25** 0320 2.2 / 1036 0.9 / F 1725 2.1 / 2210 1.5	**10** 0342 2.4 / 1049 0.6 / SA 1738 2.2 / 2252 1.3	**25** 0325 2.2 / 1019 0.9 / SU 1715 2.1 / 2201 1.4
11 0144 2.2 / 0736 1.1 / SU 1402 2.3 / ◐ 2013 1.0	**26** 0248 2.2 / 0915 1.1 / M 1623 2.1 / 2212 1.5	**11** 0216 2.2 / 0836 1.1 / TU 1521 2.2 / 2106 1.3	**26** 0306 2.2 / 1030 1.0 / W 1713 2.1 / 2307 1.6	**11** 0413 2.3 / 1118 0.6 / F 1807 2.3 / 2335 1.3	**26** 0426 2.2 / 1130 0.9 / SA 1816 2.2 / 2336 1.4	**11** 0453 2.4 / 1148 0.6 / SU 1831 2.3 / 2359 1.2	**26** 0431 2.2 / 1120 0.9 / M 1805 2.1 / 2324 1.3
12 0241 2.2 / 0839 1.1 / M 1516 2.2 / 2126 1.2	**27** 0409 2.2 / 1109 1.1 / TU 1747 2.1 / 2353 1.4	**12** 0327 2.2 / 1022 1.0 / W 1710 2.3 / 2257 1.3	**27** 0423 2.2 / 1133 0.9 / TH 1818 2.2	**12** 0522 2.4 / 1217 0.6 / SA 1900 2.4	**27** 0529 2.3 / 1215 0.8 / SU 1858 2.2	**12** 0558 2.4 / 1244 0.7 / M 1917 2.3	**27** 0539 2.2 / 1213 0.9 / TU 1850 2.2
13 0359 2.1 / 1022 1.2 / TU 1703 2.2 / 2315 1.2	**28** 0521 2.2 / 1216 1.2 / W 1901 2.2	**13** 0444 2.2 / 1140 0.8 / TH 1825 2.4	**28** 0007 1.5 / 0527 2.2 / F 1223 0.9 / 1909 2.3	**13** 0033 1.2 / 1022 2.5 / SU 1312 0.5 / 1943 2.4	**28** 0026 1.3 / 0622 2.5 / M 1257 0.8 / 1933 2.3	**13** 0059 1.1 / 0656 2.4 / TU 1335 0.7 / 1958 2.4	**28** 0030 1.2 / 0636 2.3 / W 1302 0.8 / 1931 2.3
14 0520 2.1 / 1155 0.9 / W 1827 2.3	**29** 0051 1.4 / 0624 2.2 / TH 1308 0.8 / 1949 2.3	**14** 0008 1.1 / 0552 2.3 / F 1243 0.6 / 1922 2.5	**29** 0050 1.4 / 0621 2.3 / SA 1306 0.8 / 1946 2.3	**14** 0126 1.1 / 0715 2.6 / M 1401 0.5 / 2021 2.4	**29** 0110 1.2 / 0709 2.4 / TU 1337 0.7 / 2006 2.3	**14** 0155 0.9 / 0752 2.4 / W 1421 0.8 / 2036 2.4	**29** 0124 1.1 / 0729 2.3 / TH 1349 0.8 / 2011 2.3
15 0028 1.2 / 0623 2.3 / TH 1302 0.7 / 1935 2.4	**30** 0134 1.3 / 0714 2.3 / F 1351 0.8 / 2025 2.3	**15** 0105 1.1 / 0649 2.5 / SA 1339 0.5 / 2007 2.5	**30** 0124 1.2 / 0707 2.4 / SU 1343 0.7 / 2016 2.3	**15** 0213 0.9 / 0806 2.6 / TU 1445 0.5 / 2057 2.5	**30** 0153 1.0 / 0754 2.4 / W 1417 0.7 / 2039 2.4	**15** 0245 0.8 / 0847 2.4 / TH 1503 0.8 / ○ 2114 2.5	**30** 0215 0.9 / 0821 2.2 / F 1435 0.8 / 2051 2.4
			31 0154 1.1 / 0748 2.4 / M 1418 0.7 / 2042 2.4				**31** 0306 0.8 / 0913 2.1 / SA 1522 0.8 / ● 2132 2.5

Chart Datum: 1·50 metres below Ordnance Datum (Newlyn)

》》 **FREE** monthly updates from 《《
www.reedsalmanac.co.uk

TIDES

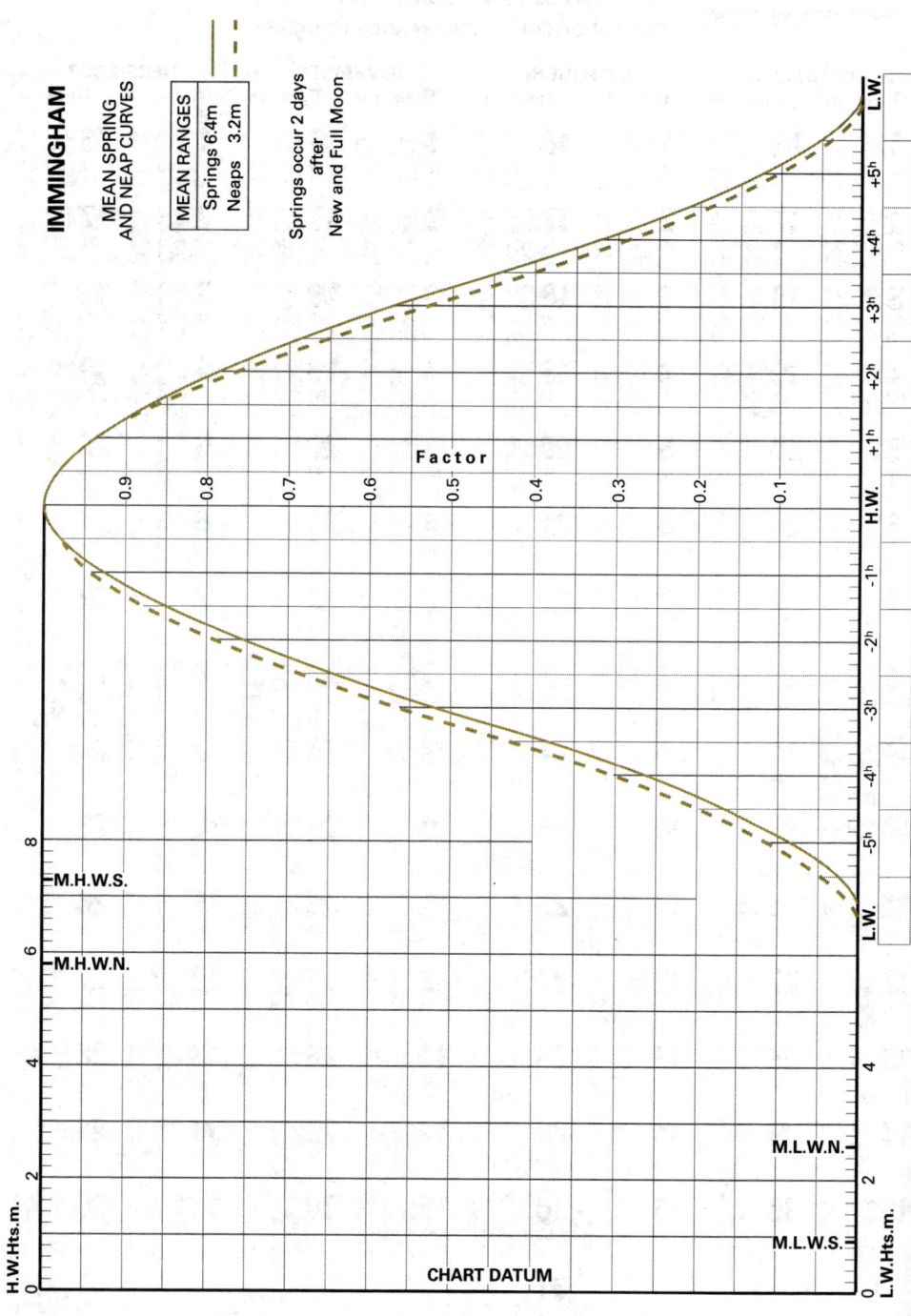

TIME ZONE (UT)
For Summer Time add ONE hour in **non-shaded areas**

ENGLAND – IMMINGHAM
LAT 53°38′N LONG 0°11′W
TIMES AND HEIGHTS OF HIGH AND LOW WATERS

YEAR 2005

JANUARY		FEBRUARY		MARCH		APRIL	
Time m	Time m	Time m	Time m	Time m	Time m	Time m	Time m
1 0312 1.8 / 0916 6.2 / SA 1509 2.2 / 2112 6.5	**16** 0419 1.2 / 1029 6.5 / SU 1619 2.0 / 2222 6.8	**1** 0356 1.7 / 1002 6.2 / TU 1600 2.1 / 2206 6.6	**16** 0452 2.1 / 1104 5.8 / W 1701 2.5 / ◐ 2326 5.9	**1** 0256 1.4 / 0852 6.6 / TU 1459 1.6 / 2059 6.9	**16** 0333 1.7 / 0929 6.3 / W 1542 1.9 / 2152 6.3	**1** 0345 2.0 / 0946 6.2 / F 1610 2.0 / 2223 6.1	**16** 0411 2.7 / 1008 5.6 / SA 1649 2.6 / ◐ 2331 5.3
2 0351 2.0 / 0958 6.1 / SU 1549 2.4 / 2153 6.4	**17** 0504 1.6 / 1120 6.1 / M 1704 2.3 / ◐ 2316 6.5	**2** 0438 2.0 / 1047 6.0 / W 1649 2.3 / ◐ 2258 6.3	**17** 0538 2.6 / 1206 5.5 / TH 1758 2.8	**2** 0325 1.6 / 0927 6.4 / W 1534 1.8 / 2140 6.7	**17** 0404 2.2 / 1002 5.9 / TH 1620 2.3 / ◐ 2240 5.7	**2** 0443 2.5 / 1046 5.8 / SA 1724 2.4 / ◐ 2352 5.6	**17** 0512 3.1 / 1139 5.3 / SU 1806 2.8
3 0436 2.1 / 1046 5.9 / M 1637 2.5 / ◐ 2243 6.2	**18** 0552 2.0 / 1214 5.8 / TU 1757 2.6	**3** 0534 2.2 / 1147 5.8 / TH 1754 2.6	**18** 0045 5.5 / 0643 3.0 / F 1325 5.4 / 1922 3.0	**3** 0402 1.9 / 1009 6.1 / TH 1619 2.1 / ◐ 2231 6.3	**18** 0447 2.7 / 1052 5.5 / F 1715 2.8	**3** 0611 2.9 / 1223 5.6 / SU 1907 2.4	**18** 0109 5.2 / 0637 3.3 / M 1320 5.4 / 1943 2.7
4 0529 2.2 / 1144 5.8 / TU 1735 2.7 / 2343 6.1	**19** 0018 6.1 / 0647 2.4 / W 1314 5.7 / 1903 2.8	**4** 0006 6.1 / 0651 2.4 / F 1311 5.7 / 1920 2.7	**19** 0212 5.4 / 0817 3.1 / SA 1441 5.5 / 2120 2.8	**4** 0456 2.3 / 1105 5.8 / F 1725 2.5 / 2343 5.8	**19** 0007 5.3 / 0550 3.2 / SA 1235 5.3 / 1836 3.0	**4** 0155 5.7 / 0755 2.8 / M 1406 5.8 / 2048 2.0	**19** 0225 5.4 / 0818 3.1 / TU 1430 5.6 / 2104 2.3
5 0631 2.2 / 1252 5.8 / W 1844 2.7	**20** 0129 5.9 / 0753 2.6 / TH 1417 5.7 / 2027 2.8	**5** 0140 5.9 / 0819 2.4 / SA 1438 5.9 / 2052 2.4	**20** 0328 5.6 / 0937 2.8 / SU 1544 5.9 / 2219 2.3	**5** 0618 2.7 / 1233 5.5 / SA 1901 2.7	**20** 0146 5.2 / 0725 3.3 / SU 1405 5.4 / 2053 2.8	**5** 0318 6.1 / 0915 2.4 / TU 1517 6.3 / 2157 1.5	**20** 0323 5.8 / 0925 2.7 / W 1523 6.0 / 2154 1.9
6 0054 6.1 / 0741 2.2 / TH 1403 5.9 / 2000 2.6	**21** 0240 5.8 / 0900 2.6 / F 1518 5.8 / 2139 2.5	**6** 0313 6.1 / 0935 2.2 / SU 1547 6.2 / 2211 1.9	**21** 0427 5.9 / 1030 2.4 / M 1634 6.3 / 2305 1.9	**6** 0140 5.7 / 0803 2.7 / SU 1420 5.7 / 2049 2.4	**21** 0304 5.5 / 0913 3.0 / M 1514 5.7 / 2153 2.3	**6** 0420 6.6 / 1014 1.8 / W 1612 6.8 / 2250 0.9	**21** 0408 6.2 / 1011 2.3 / TH 1605 6.3 / 2237 1.5
7 0211 6.3 / 0850 2.0 / F 1507 6.2 / 2114 2.3	**22** 0346 5.9 / 0957 2.5 / SA 1610 6.1 / 2234 2.2	**7** 0427 6.5 / 1039 1.9 / M 1645 6.7 / 2315 1.4	**22** 0511 6.2 / 1114 2.1 / TU 1714 6.6 / 2346 1.6	**7** 0320 6.0 / 0928 2.4 / M 1535 6.2 / 2210 1.8	**22** 0403 5.9 / 1007 2.6 / TU 1605 6.1 / 2237 1.9	**7** 0507 7.0 / 1102 1.4 / TH 1659 7.2 / 2336 0.6	**22** 0444 6.5 / 1050 1.9 / F 1642 6.6 / 2317 1.3
8 0322 6.5 / 0953 1.8 / SA 1604 6.5 / 2219 1.9	**23** 0440 6.1 / 1045 2.3 / SU 1654 6.4 / 2320 1.9	**8** 0528 6.9 / 1135 1.5 / TU 1736 7.1 / ●	**23** 0548 6.5 / 1153 1.9 / W 1749 6.8	**8** 0430 6.5 / 1032 1.8 / TU 1633 6.7 / 2309 1.1	**23** 0446 6.2 / 1050 2.2 / W 1645 6.5 / 2317 1.5	**8** 0548 7.2 / 1147 1.1 / F 1741 7.4 / ●	**23** 0517 6.7 / 1127 1.6 / SA 1718 6.9 / 2356 1.1
9 0425 6.8 / 1050 1.6 / SU 1655 6.8 / 2319 1.5	**24** 0525 6.3 / 1128 2.1 / M 1733 6.7	**9** 0011 0.9 / 0622 7.2 / W 1226 1.2 / 1822 7.4	**24** 0025 1.4 / 0620 6.6 / TH 1230 1.7 / ◯ 1822 6.9	**9** 0525 6.9 / 1123 1.5 / W 1721 7.1 / 2359 0.7	**24** 0521 6.5 / 1128 1.9 / TH 1720 6.7 / 2355 1.3	**9** 0019 0.5 / 0624 7.3 / SA 1229 0.9 / 1822 7.5	**24** 0549 6.9 / 1204 1.4 / SU 1754 7.1 / ◯
10 0524 7.0 / 1143 1.4 / M 1744 7.1 / ●	**25** 0003 1.7 / 0604 6.5 / TU 1208 1.9 / ◯ 1809 6.8	**10** 0102 0.5 / 0709 7.3 / TH 1312 1.1 / 1905 7.6	**25** 0101 1.2 / 0651 6.7 / F 1301 1.6 / 1854 7.0	**10** 0611 7.2 / 1210 1.1 / TH 1805 7.5 / ●	**25** 0552 6.7 / 1203 1.6 / F 1753 6.9 / ◯	**10** 0058 0.5 / 0657 7.2 / SU 1308 0.9 / 1901 7.5	**25** 0032 1.0 / 0622 7.0 / M 1241 1.2 / 1831 7.2
11 0015 1.1 / 0620 7.2 / TU 1234 1.3 / 1831 7.4	**26** 0043 1.5 / 0639 6.6 / W 1245 1.8 / 1844 6.9	**11** 0148 0.4 / 0753 7.4 / F 1355 1.0 / 1947 7.7	**26** 0135 1.2 / 0722 6.8 / SA 1330 1.5 / 1925 7.1	**11** 0045 0.4 / 0651 7.4 / F 1253 0.9 / 1846 7.7	**26** 0031 1.1 / 0622 6.9 / SA 1236 1.4 / 1825 7.1	**11** 0133 0.7 / 0728 7.1 / M 1343 1.0 / 1938 7.3	**26** 0108 1.0 / 0655 7.1 / TU 1318 1.1 / 1909 7.2
12 0109 0.8 / 0714 7.3 / W 1323 1.2 / 1917 7.5	**27** 0120 1.4 / 0713 6.6 / TH 1318 1.8 / 1917 6.9	**12** 0230 0.4 / 0832 7.3 / SA 1434 1.1 / 2028 7.6	**27** 0204 1.2 / 0752 6.8 / SU 1359 1.5 / 1955 7.1	**12** 0127 0.3 / 0728 7.4 / SA 1333 0.8 / 1925 7.7	**27** 0106 1.0 / 0652 7.0 / SU 1307 1.4 / 1857 7.2	**12** 0204 1.0 / 0757 6.9 / TU 1415 1.2 / 2014 7.0	**27** 0142 1.1 / 0730 7.0 / W 1356 1.1 / 1950 7.1
13 0200 0.7 / 0806 7.2 / TH 1410 1.3 / 2003 7.5	**28** 0154 1.4 / 0746 6.6 / F 1348 1.8 / 1949 6.9	**13** 0309 0.7 / 0909 6.9 / SU 1510 1.3 / 2107 7.4	**28** 0231 1.2 / 0821 6.8 / M 1428 1.5 / 2025 7.1	**13** 0204 0.4 / 0801 7.2 / SU 1410 0.9 / 2003 7.6	**28** 0137 1.0 / 0722 7.0 / M 1338 1.3 / 1930 7.2	**13** 0232 1.4 / 0824 6.7 / W 1444 1.5 / 2048 6.6	**28** 0218 1.3 / 0807 6.9 / TH 1436 1.3 / 2035 6.8
14 0248 0.7 / 0854 7.1 / F 1454 1.4 / 2047 7.4	**29** 0226 1.4 / 0818 6.6 / SA 1417 1.8 / 2019 6.9	**14** 0344 1.1 / 0944 6.6 / M 1544 1.7 / 2147 6.9		**14** 0237 0.7 / 0832 7.0 / M 1442 1.2 / 2039 7.3	**29** 0205 1.1 / 0753 6.9 / TU 1409 1.3 / 2004 7.2	**14** 0259 1.8 / 0851 6.4 / TH 1515 1.8 / 2124 6.1	**29** 0256 1.6 / 0849 6.7 / F 1522 1.5 / 2127 6.4
15 0334 0.8 / 0941 6.8 / SA 1536 1.7 / 2133 7.2	**30** 0255 1.5 / 0850 6.5 / SU 1448 1.8 / 2050 6.8	**15** 0417 1.6 / 1021 6.2 / TU 1619 2.1 / 2230 6.4		**15** 0306 1.2 / 0901 6.6 / TU 1512 1.5 / 2114 6.8	**30** 0234 1.2 / 0825 6.8 / W 1443 1.4 / 2042 7.0	**15** 0330 2.3 / 0923 6.1 / F 1554 2.2 / 2210 5.6	**30** 0343 2.1 / 0938 6.4 / SA 1621 1.9 / 2235 6.0
	31 0324 1.6 / 0924 6.4 / M 1522 1.9 / 2124 6.7				**31** 0305 1.6 / 0902 6.6 / TH 1520 1.6 / 2126 6.5		

Chart Datum: 3·90 metres below Ordnance Datum (Newlyn)

》》 **FREE** monthly updates from 《《
www.reedsalmanac.co.uk

TIDES

TIME ZONE (UT)
For Summer Time add ONE hour in **non-shaded areas**

ENGLAND – IMMINGHAM
LAT 53°38′N   LONG 0°11′W
TIMES AND HEIGHTS OF HIGH AND LOW WATERS

YEAR 2005

	MAY			JUNE			JULY			AUGUST	
	Time m	Time m		Time m	Time m		Time m	Time m		Time m	Time m
1 SU	0446 2.5 / 1045 6.0 / 1739 2.1 ☽	**16** M	0440 2.9 / 1053 5.6 / 1737 2.5	**1** W	0119 6.1 / 0704 2.4 / 1311 6.3 / 1953 1.6	**16** TH	0018 5.6 / 0604 2.8 / 1222 5.8 / 1900 2.2	**1** F	0137 6.0 / 0730 2.4 / 1338 6.2 / 2013 1.9	**16** SA	0018 5.7 / 0612 2.6 / 1226 6.0 / 1908 2.3	**1** M	0253 5.7 / 0922 2.5 / 1527 5.8 / 2143 2.5	**16** TU	0211 5.8 / 0821 2.6 / 1448 6.0 / 2110 2.4
2 M	0018 5.8 / 0609 2.7 / 1219 5.9 / 1907 2.0	**17** TU	0014 5.4 / 0549 3.1 / 1219 5.5 / 1848 2.5	**2** TH	0223 6.2 / 0811 2.3 / 1416 6.4 / 2053 1.5	**17** F	0122 5.7 / 0710 2.7 / 1325 5.9 / 2002 2.1	**2** SA	0235 6.0 / 0838 2.3 / 1442 6.2 / 2112 2.0	**17** SU	0130 5.8 / 0726 2.6 / 1342 6.0 / 2020 2.2	**2** TU	0351 6.0 / 1021 2.2 / 1629 6.0 / 2235 2.3	**17** W	0323 6.1 / 0947 2.1 / 1604 6.4 / 2217 2.0
3 TU	0147 5.9 / 0736 2.6 / 1344 6.1 / 2027 1.7	**18** W	0126 5.5 / 0706 3.0 / 1329 5.6 / 1958 2.3	**3** F	0320 6.3 / 0912 2.0 / 1514 6.5 / 2146 1.4	**18** SA	0222 5.9 / 0817 2.5 / 1426 6.1 / 2102 1.9	**3** SU	0330 6.1 / 0940 2.2 / 1544 6.2 / 2205 2.0	**18** M	0239 5.9 / 0843 2.4 / 1457 6.2 / 2128 2.0	**3** W	0440 6.3 / 1111 1.9 / 1718 6.2 / 2320 2.1	**18** TH	0422 6.6 / 1054 1.5 / 1706 6.8 / 2314 1.6
4 W	0258 6.2 / 0847 2.3 / 1450 6.4 / 2129 1.3	**19** TH	0227 5.7 / 0817 2.8 / 1426 5.9 / 2058 2.0	**4** SA	0407 6.5 / 1006 1.8 / 1607 6.7 / 2234 1.4	**19** SU	0316 6.2 / 0920 2.2 / 1523 6.4 / 2157 1.7	**4** M	0418 6.2 / 1034 1.9 / 1638 6.3 / 2252 2.0	**19** TU	0340 6.2 / 0954 2.0 / 1604 6.5 / 2228 1.8	**4** TH	0521 6.6 / 1155 1.6 / 1758 6.4 ○	**19** F	0513 7.1 / 1150 1.0 / 1800 7.2
5 TH	0355 6.6 / 0945 1.9 / 1545 6.8 / 2221 1.0	**20** F	0317 6.0 / 0916 2.4 / 1515 6.2 / 2149 1.7	**5** SU	0448 6.6 / 1054 1.6 / 1654 6.7 / 2317 1.4	**20** M	0406 6.4 / 1017 1.9 / 1617 6.7 / 2249 1.5	**5** TU	0500 6.4 / 1123 1.7 / 1727 6.4 / 2336 1.9	**20** W	0435 6.6 / 1057 1.6 / 1705 6.8 / 2324 1.5	**5** F	0002 1.9 / 0558 6.8 / 1237 1.4 ● 1833 6.5	**20** SA	0005 1.3 / 0559 7.4 / 1242 0.5 / 1848 7.4
6 F	0440 6.8 / 1035 1.5 / 1633 7.0 / 2306 0.9	**21** SA	0400 6.3 / 1005 2.1 / 1600 6.5 / 2236 1.4	**6** M ●	0525 6.7 / 1140 1.4 / 1739 6.7 / 2358 1.5	**21** TU	0452 6.7 / 1110 1.6 / 1710 6.9 / 2338 1.3	**6** W ●	0539 6.6 / 1208 1.6 / 1810 6.4	**21** TH ○	0525 6.9 / 1156 1.2 / 1803 7.0	**6** SA	0041 1.8 / 0633 6.9 / 1315 1.3 / 1906 6.6	**21** SU	0052 1.0 / 0644 7.7 / 1328 0.3 / 1932 7.5
7 SA	0519 7.0 / 1120 1.2 / 1717 7.2 / 2348 0.9	**22** SU	0439 6.6 / 1050 1.7 / 1644 6.8 / 2319 1.2	**7** TU	0600 6.7 / 1222 1.4 / 1822 6.7	**22** W	0537 6.9 / 1203 1.2 / 1803 7.0 ○	**7** TH	0017 1.9 / 0615 6.7 / 1251 1.5 / 1849 6.4	**22** F	0016 1.3 / 0612 7.2 / 1252 0.8 / 1857 7.2	**7** SU	0116 1.7 / 0707 6.9 / 1350 1.3 / 1938 6.6	**22** M	0136 0.9 / 0726 7.8 / 1411 0.2 / 2012 7.4
8 SU ●	0554 7.0 / 1203 1.1 / 1758 7.2	**23** M	0518 6.8 / 1134 1.4 / 1727 7.0 ○	**8** W	0035 1.6 / 0634 6.7 / 1302 1.4 / 1902 6.6	**23** TH	0027 1.2 / 0621 7.1 / 1255 1.0 / 1856 7.1	**8** F	0055 1.8 / 0651 6.8 / 1330 1.5 / 1926 6.4	**23** SA	0107 1.2 / 0659 7.4 / 1343 0.5 / 1948 7.3	**8** M	0146 1.7 / 0740 6.9 / 1421 1.4 / 2009 6.6	**23** TU	0217 0.9 / 0808 7.8 / 1451 0.5 / 2050 7.2
9 M	0026 1.0 / 0626 7.0 / 1243 1.1 / 1838 7.1	**24** TU	0002 1.1 / 0555 7.0 / 1218 1.2 / 1811 7.1	**9** TH	0111 1.7 / 0707 6.7 / 1339 1.5 / 1940 6.5	**24** F	0115 1.1 / 0707 7.2 / 1348 0.8 / 1949 7.1	**9** SA	0131 1.8 / 0727 6.8 / 1406 1.5 / 2001 6.4	**24** SU	0154 1.1 / 0745 7.5 / 1431 0.4 / 2036 7.2	**9** TU	0213 1.8 / 0811 6.9 / 1449 1.5 / 2040 6.6	**24** W	0255 1.1 / 0849 7.5 / 1527 0.8 / 2127 6.8
10 TU	0102 1.2 / 0658 6.9 / 1319 1.2 / 1917 6.9	**25** W	0044 1.1 / 0635 7.1 / 1303 1.1 / 1858 7.2	**10** F	0144 1.8 / 0741 6.7 / 1414 1.6 / 2017 6.3	**25** SA	0203 1.1 / 0754 7.2 / 1439 0.8 / 2044 7.0	**10** SU	0203 1.9 / 0801 6.7 / 1440 1.6 / 2035 6.4	**25** M	0238 1.2 / 0830 7.5 / 1517 0.5 / 2122 7.0	**10** W	0240 1.9 / 0841 6.8 / 1515 1.6 / 2111 6.4	**25** TH	0331 1.5 / 0931 7.1 / 1603 1.4 / 2205 6.4
11 W	0134 1.4 / 0728 6.8 / 1353 1.3 / 1954 6.7	**26** TH	0126 1.2 / 0715 7.1 / 1349 1.0 / 1946 7.2	**11** SA	0216 2.0 / 0815 6.5 / 1449 1.7 / 2054 6.1	**26** SU	0251 1.4 / 0842 7.2 / 1531 0.8 / 2140 6.8	**11** M	0233 2.0 / 0835 6.7 / 1513 1.7 / 2110 6.3	**26** TU	0321 1.3 / 0915 7.4 / 1601 0.8 / 2207 6.8	**11** TH	0310 1.9 / 0912 6.6 / 1542 1.8 / 2144 6.3	**26** F ☽	0407 1.9 / 1017 6.6 / 1638 2.0 / 2249 6.0
12 TH	0204 1.7 / 0757 6.6 / 1425 1.6 / 2030 6.4	**27** F	0209 1.4 / 0758 7.0 / 1438 1.1 / 2038 6.8	**12** SU	0249 2.2 / 0850 6.3 / 1528 1.9 / 2134 6.0	**27** M	0339 1.6 / 0933 7.0 / 1623 1.0 / 2238 6.5	**12** TU	0305 2.1 / 0908 6.6 / 1547 1.8 / 2146 6.1	**27** W	0404 1.6 / 1002 7.1 / 1644 1.2 / 2255 6.4	**12** F	0344 2.1 / 0949 6.5 / 1616 2.0 / 2225 6.0	**27** SA	0447 2.4 / 1114 6.1 / 1721 2.6 / 2348 5.6
13 F	0233 1.9 / 0828 6.4 / 1458 1.8 / 2108 6.0	**28** SA	0255 1.6 / 0845 6.8 / 1531 1.3 / 2137 6.5	**13** M	0327 2.4 / 0930 6.2 / 1612 2.1 / 2221 5.8	**28** TU	0430 1.9 / 1028 6.8 / 1718 1.2 ☽ 2338 6.3	**13** W	0340 2.2 / 0945 6.4 / 1624 1.9 / 2228 6.0	**28** TH	0447 2.0 / 1054 6.7 / 1730 1.7 ☽ 2347 6.0	**13** SA	0427 2.3 / 1036 6.2 / 1705 2.3 ☽ 2318 5.8	**28** SU	0542 2.8 / 1229 5.7 / 1825 3.0
14 SA	0306 2.3 / 0903 6.2 / 1539 2.1 / 2153 5.7	**29** SU	0346 2.0 / 0939 6.6 / 1631 1.5 / 2250 6.2	**14** TU	0410 2.6 / 1018 6.0 / 1703 2.2 / 2316 5.7	**29** W	0525 2.1 / 1130 6.6 / 1814 1.5	**14** TH	0421 2.4 / 1028 6.2 / 1707 2.1 ☽ 2317 5.8	**29** F	0537 2.3 / 1153 6.3 / 1822 2.2	**14** SU	0526 2.6 / 1139 5.9 / 1817 2.5	**29** M	0104 5.4 / 0721 3.1 / 1353 5.5 / 2010 3.1
15 SU	0346 2.6 / 0947 5.8 / 1631 2.4 / 2255 5.4	**30** M	0446 2.3 / 1044 6.4 / 1738 1.6 ☽	**15** W	0503 2.7 / 1116 5.8 / 1800 2.2	**30** TH	0037 6.1 / 0624 2.3 / 1234 6.4 / 1913 1.7	**15** F	0511 2.5 / 1120 6.0 / 1800 2.2	**30** SA	0044 5.8 / 0638 2.6 / 1301 5.9 / 1927 2.5	**15** M	0038 5.6 / 0647 2.7 / 1313 5.8 / 1947 2.6	**30** TU	0220 5.6 / 0910 2.9 / 1511 5.6 / 2126 2.9
		31 TU	0009 6.1 / 0553 2.4 / 1200 6.2 / 1847 1.6						**31** SU	0148 5.6 / 0803 2.7 / 1415 5.8 / 2040 2.6			**31** W	0326 5.9 / 1007 2.3 / 1615 6.0 / 2218 2.5

Chart Datum: 3·90 metres below Ordnance Datum (Newlyn)

FREE monthly updates from
www.reedsalmanac.co.uk

TIME ZONE (UT)
For Summer Time add ONE hour in **non-shaded areas**

ENGLAND – IMMINGHAM
LAT 53°38'N   LONG 0°11'W
TIMES AND HEIGHTS OF HIGH AND LOW WATERS

YEAR 2005

SEPTEMBER

#	Time m	#	Time m
1 TH	0418 6.3 / 1053 1.9 / 1701 6.3 / 2303 2.1	**16** F	0406 6.7 / 1044 1.3 / 1657 7.0 / 2259 1.6
2 F	0459 6.6 / 1134 1.5 / 1737 6.5 / 2343 1.7	**17** SA	0455 7.2 / 1135 0.7 / 1744 7.3 / 2346 1.2
3 SA	0535 6.9 / 1213 1.3 / 1809 6.7 ●	**18** SU	0539 7.6 / 1221 0.4 / 1826 7.5 ○
4 SU	0019 1.7 / 0608 7.0 / 1249 1.2 / 1839 6.8	**19** M	0030 0.9 / 0620 7.8 / 1304 0.3 / 1904 7.5
5 M	0053 1.6 / 0641 7.1 / 1323 1.2 / 1909 6.8	**20** TU	0112 0.8 / 0702 7.9 / 1343 0.4 / 1940 7.4
6 TU	0122 1.6 / 0712 7.1 / 1353 1.3 / 1938 6.8	**21** W	0150 0.9 / 0742 7.8 / 1419 0.7 / 2013 7.2
7 W	0148 1.6 / 0742 7.1 / 1419 1.4 / 2006 6.8	**22** TH	0226 1.1 / 0821 7.5 / 1450 1.1 / 2045 6.8
8 TH	0214 1.6 / 0811 7.0 / 1442 1.5 / 2035 6.7	**23** F	0258 1.5 / 0900 7.0 / 1519 1.7 / 2117 6.5
9 F	0243 1.7 / 0842 6.8 / 1507 1.7 / 2106 6.5	**24** SA	0330 1.9 / 0942 6.4 / 1549 2.3 / 2152 6.0
10 SA	0315 1.9 / 0919 6.6 / 1539 2.0 / 2145 6.2	**25** SU	0407 2.4 / 1037 5.9 / 1629 2.8 ◐ 2245 5.6
11 SU	0357 2.2 / 1006 6.2 / 1626 2.4 ◐ 2236 5.8	**26** M	0501 2.8 / 1201 5.4 / 1731 3.3
12 M	0457 2.6 / 1115 5.8 / 1742 2.8 / 2359 5.6	**27** TU	0022 5.4 / 0630 3.1 / 1330 5.3 / 1923 3.4
13 TU	0629 2.8 / 1313 5.6 / 1930 2.9	**28** W	0148 5.5 / 0846 2.8 / 1446 5.6 / 2101 3.1
14 W	0153 5.7 / 0818 2.6 / 1451 6.0 / 2101 2.6	**29** TH	0256 5.9 / 0940 2.3 / 1547 6.0 / 2153 2.6
15 TH	0309 6.2 / 0945 1.9 / 1602 6.5 / 2207 2.1	**30** F	0349 6.3 / 1024 1.9 / 1631 6.3 / 2236 2.2

OCTOBER

#	Time m	#	Time m
1 SA	0430 6.6 / 1102 1.5 / 1707 6.6 / 2314 1.9	**16** SU	0430 7.3 / 1109 0.7 / 1719 7.3 / 2321 1.2
2 SU	0505 6.9 / 1139 1.3 / 1737 6.8 / 2349 1.7	**17** M	0513 7.6 / 1152 0.6 / 1757 7.4 ○
3 M	0537 7.1 / 1215 1.2 / 1807 6.9 ●	**18** TU	0004 1.0 / 0555 7.7 / 1233 0.6 / 1832 7.4
4 TU	0021 1.6 / 0609 7.1 / 1249 1.2 / 1836 7.0	**19** W	0045 0.9 / 0636 7.7 / 1311 0.8 / 1906 7.3
5 W	0052 1.5 / 0641 7.2 / 1319 1.2 / 1905 7.0	**20** TH	0123 1.0 / 0716 7.5 / 1344 1.1 / 1938 7.1
6 TH	0121 1.5 / 0713 7.2 / 1347 1.3 / 1935 7.0	**21** F	0158 1.2 / 0756 7.2 / 1415 1.5 / 2009 6.9
7 F	0150 1.5 / 0745 7.1 / 1413 1.5 / 2005 6.8	**22** SA	0230 1.5 / 0835 6.8 / 1443 1.9 / 2039 6.6
8 SA	0222 1.6 / 0820 6.9 / 1442 1.7 / 2038 6.6	**23** SU	0302 1.9 / 0916 6.3 / 1513 2.4 / 2112 6.2
9 SU	0258 1.9 / 0902 6.6 / 1518 2.1 / 2119 6.3	**24** M	0340 2.3 / 1007 5.8 / 1552 2.8 / 2158 5.8
10 M	0344 2.2 / 0955 6.1 / 1610 2.6 ◐ 2214 5.9	**25** TU	0434 2.7 / 1128 5.4 / 1650 3.2 / 2328 5.5
11 TU	0452 2.5 / 1119 5.7 / 1730 3.0 / 2343 5.7	**26** W	0554 2.9 / 1254 5.3 / 1817 3.4
12 W	0630 2.6 / 1321 5.7 / 1917 3.0	**27** TH	0102 5.5 / 0745 2.8 / 1406 5.5 / 2006 3.2
13 TH	0133 5.9 / 0814 2.3 / 1443 6.1 / 2043 2.6	**28** F	0212 5.8 / 0853 2.4 / 1505 5.9 / 2111 2.8
14 F	0246 6.3 / 0928 1.7 / 1546 6.6 / 2145 2.1	**29** SA	0307 6.2 / 0940 2.0 / 1552 6.3 / 2156 2.4
15 SA	0342 6.9 / 1022 1.1 / 1636 7.0 / 2235 1.6	**30** SU	0350 6.5 / 1020 1.7 / 1629 6.6 / 2235 2.1
		31 M	0427 6.8 / 1059 1.4 / 1701 6.8 / 2311 1.8

NOVEMBER

#	Time m	#	Time m
1 TU	0501 7.0 / 1136 1.3 / 1732 7.0 / 2346 1.6	**16** W	0532 7.4 / 1202 1.1 / 1803 7.2 ○
2 W	0536 7.1 / 1212 1.2 / 1804 7.1	**17** TH	0020 1.2 / 0615 7.3 / 1240 1.2 / 1837 7.1
3 TH	0020 1.5 / 0612 7.2 / 1246 1.2 / 1836 7.1	**18** F	0100 1.3 / 0657 7.1 / 1314 1.5 / 1911 7.0
4 F	0056 1.4 / 0649 7.2 / 1319 1.4 / 1909 7.1	**19** SA	0137 1.4 / 0737 6.9 / 1346 1.7 / 1943 6.9
5 SA	0132 1.4 / 0728 7.1 / 1352 1.5 / 1944 7.0	**20** SU	0211 1.6 / 0817 6.6 / 1416 2.0 / 2015 6.7
6 SU	0211 1.5 / 0811 6.9 / 1429 1.8 / 2023 6.8	**21** M	0245 1.9 / 0858 6.2 / 1449 2.3 / 2050 6.4
7 M	0255 1.7 / 0900 6.5 / 1512 2.2 / 2108 6.5	**22** TU	0324 2.2 / 0943 5.9 / 1527 2.7 / 2132 6.1
8 TU	0349 2.0 / 1002 6.1 / 1608 2.6 / 2208 6.2	**23** W	0414 2.4 / 1042 5.6 / 1616 2.9 ◐ 2233 5.8
9 W	0500 2.2 / 1134 5.8 / 1721 2.9 ◐ 2332 6.0	**24** TH	0517 2.6 / 1154 5.5 / 1721 3.2 / 2354 5.7
10 TH	0626 2.2 / 1306 5.9 / 1852 2.9	**25** F	0627 2.6 / 1303 5.5 / 1837 3.2
11 F	0103 6.1 / 0749 1.9 / 1418 6.2 / 2009 2.6	**26** SA	0106 5.7 / 0736 2.5 / 1405 5.7 / 1952 3.0
12 SA	0213 6.5 / 0855 1.6 / 1518 6.5 / 2112 2.1	**27** SU	0206 5.9 / 0837 2.3 / 1458 6.0 / 2055 2.7
13 SU	0311 6.8 / 0950 1.3 / 1608 6.8 / 2205 1.7	**28** M	0258 6.2 / 0929 2.0 / 1543 6.3 / 2145 2.4
14 M	0402 7.1 / 1038 1.1 / 1650 7.0 / 2253 1.4	**29** TU	0343 6.5 / 1014 1.8 / 1622 6.6 / 2230 2.0
15 TU	0448 7.3 / 1121 1.0 / 1728 7.1 / 2338 1.2	**30** W	0426 6.8 / 1057 1.5 / 1700 6.8 / 2312 1.7

DECEMBER

#	Time m	#	Time m
1 TH	0508 7.0 / 1138 1.4 / 1737 7.0 ● 2355 1.5	**16** F	0002 1.5 / 0601 6.8 / 1216 1.7 / 1816 6.9
2 F	0551 7.1 / 1218 1.4 / 1814 7.1	**17** SA	0045 1.4 / 0645 6.8 / 1253 1.8 / 1852 6.9
3 SA	0038 1.3 / 0635 7.1 / 1259 1.4 / 1853 7.2	**18** SU	0125 1.5 / 0725 6.6 / 1327 1.9 / 1927 6.9
4 SU	0123 1.3 / 0722 7.1 / 1340 1.5 / 1933 7.1	**19** M	0201 1.6 / 0804 6.5 / 1359 2.1 / 2001 6.8
5 M	0209 1.3 / 0811 7.0 / 1424 1.7 / 2017 7.0	**20** TU	0236 1.7 / 0841 6.3 / 1432 2.2 / 2035 6.6
6 TU	0259 1.4 / 0905 6.6 / 1511 2.0 / 2106 6.9	**21** W	0312 1.9 / 0918 6.1 / 1506 2.3 / 2112 6.4
7 W	0355 1.5 / 1008 6.3 / 1605 2.3 / 2203 6.6	**22** TH	0351 2.1 / 0959 5.9 / 1545 2.5 / 2154 6.2
8 TH	0457 1.7 / 1121 6.0 / 1708 2.5 ◐ 2311 6.5	**23** F	0437 2.2 / 1047 5.8 / 1631 2.8 ◐ 2244 6.0
9 F	0604 1.8 / 1233 6.1 / 1817 2.6	**24** SA	0530 2.3 / 1145 5.7 / 1727 2.9 / 2345 5.9
10 SA	0025 6.4 / 0711 1.8 / 1339 6.1 / 1928 2.5	**25** SU	0629 2.4 / 1249 5.6 / 1833 3.0
11 SU	0134 6.5 / 0816 1.7 / 1439 6.2 / 2035 2.3	**26** M	0052 5.9 / 0731 2.4 / 1353 5.7 / 1943 2.9
12 M	0237 6.6 / 0914 1.6 / 1533 6.4 / 2135 2.1	**27** TU	0159 6.0 / 0837 2.3 / 1453 5.9 / 2051 2.6
13 TU	0335 6.7 / 1006 1.6 / 1620 6.6 / 2228 2.0	**28** W	0301 6.2 / 0931 2.1 / 1545 6.2 / 2151 2.3
14 W	0428 6.8 / 1052 1.6 / 1701 6.7 / 2317 1.6	**29** TH	0357 6.5 / 1023 1.9 / 1632 6.6 / 2245 1.9
15 TH	0516 6.8 / 1135 1.6 / 1740 6.9 ○	**30** F	0449 6.7 / 1112 1.6 / 1717 6.9 / 2337 1.5
		31 SA	0541 6.9 / 1159 1.5 / 1800 7.1

Chart Datum: 3·90 metres below Ordnance Datum (Newlyn)

》》 FREE monthly updates from 《《
www.reedsalmanac.co.uk

TIDES

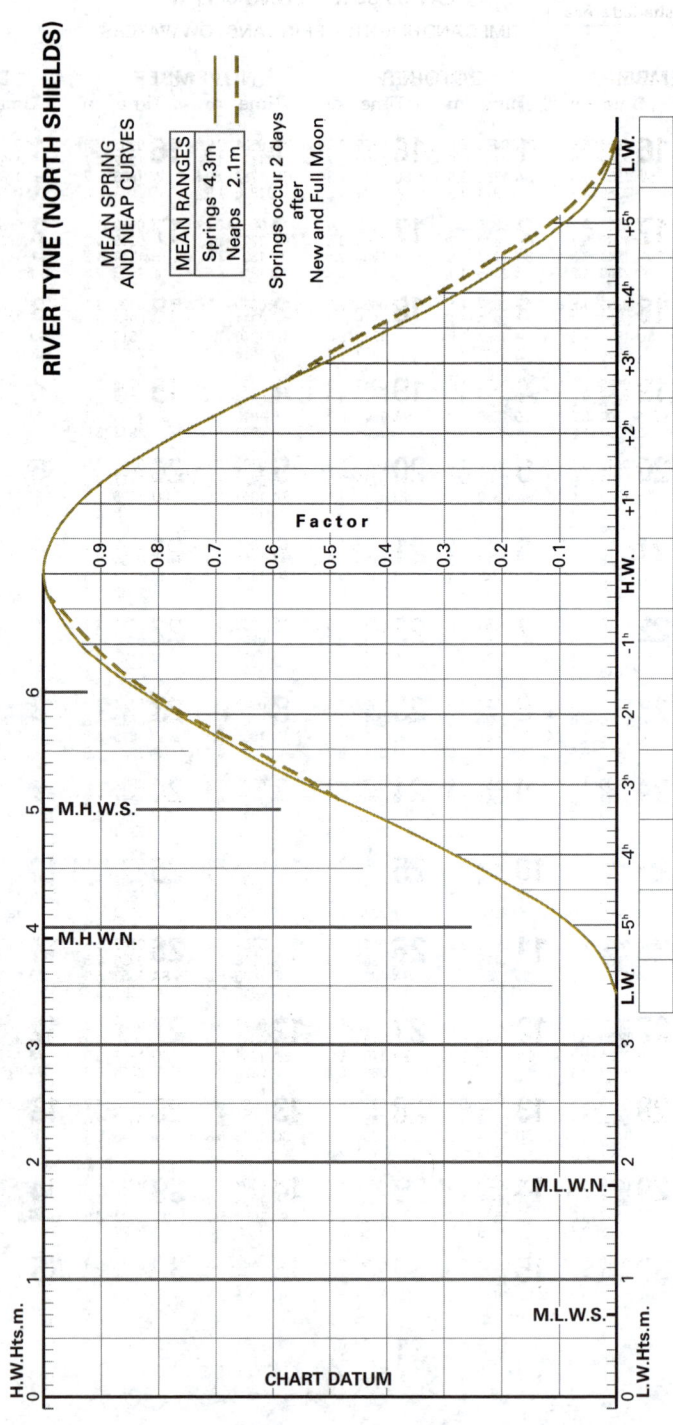

TIME ZONE (UT)
For Summer Time add ONE hour in **non-shaded areas**

ENGLAND – NORTH SHIELDS
LAT 55°01′N   LONG 1°26′W
TIMES AND HEIGHTS OF HIGH AND LOW WATERS

YEAR 2005

	JANUARY			FEBRUARY			MARCH			APRIL	
	Time m	Time m		Time m	Time m		Time m	Time m		Time m	Time m
1 SA	0045 1.3 0651 4.3 1240 1.7 1852 4.6	**16** SU 0146 0.8 0754 4.5 1349 1.6 1955 4.8	**1** TU	0133 1.2 0738 4.3 1330 1.6 1943 4.5	**16** W 0234 1.6 0850 4.0 1446 1.9 ◐ 2109 4.1	**1** TU	0024 0.9 0623 4.6 1224 1.2 1830 4.8	**16** W 0105 1.3 0712 4.3 1315 1.4 1933 4.3	**1** F	0119 1.4 0727 4.3 1341 1.5 2007 4.2	**16** SA 0149 2.1 0812 3.9 1441 1.9 ◐ 2109 3.7
2 SU	0127 1.4 0734 4.2 1322 1.9 1936 4.4	**17** M 0236 1.1 0848 4.3 1440 1.8 ◐ 2052 4.5	**2** W	0217 1.4 0828 4.2 1420 1.8 ◐ 2038 4.4	**17** TH 0331 2.0 0953 3.8 1604 2.1 2226 3.8	**2** W	0059 1.1 0702 4.4 1301 1.4 1915 4.6	**17** TH 0142 1.7 0757 4.0 1404 1.8 ◐ 2029 4.0	**2** SA	0222 1.8 0833 4.0 1502 1.7 ◐ 2134 4.0	**17** SU 0304 2.4 0925 3.7 1611 2.0 2235 3.6
3 M	0213 1.5 0823 4.1 1411 2.0 2026 4.4	**18** TU 0331 1.5 0947 4.1 1544 2.0 2158 4.3	**3** TH	0314 1.6 0929 4.1 1528 1.9 2148 4.2	**18** F 0452 2.2 1112 3.8 1745 2.1 2356 3.8	**3** TH	0140 1.3 0750 4.2 1350 1.6 ◐ 2012 4.3	**18** F 0232 2.1 0856 3.8 1516 2.0 2145 3.7	**3** SU	0358 2.0 1001 3.9 1648 1.6 2314 4.0	**18** M 0456 2.4 1055 3.7 1744 1.8 2359 3.7
4 TU	0306 1.6 0919 4.1 1512 2.1 2125 4.3	**19** W 0435 1.7 1052 4.0 1700 2.1 2310 4.1	**4** F	0428 1.7 1043 4.0 1658 2.0 2314 4.2	**19** SA 0624 2.2 1232 3.9 1906 1.9	**4** F	0237 1.7 0851 4.0 1500 1.8 2130 4.1	**19** SA 0356 2.4 1018 3.6 1703 2.1 2324 3.6	**4** M	0540 2.0 1133 4.0 1820 1.3	**19** TU 0618 2.2 1212 3.9 1845 1.6
5 W	0407 1.6 1022 4.1 1623 2.1 2232 4.3	**20** TH 0545 1.9 1158 4.0 1818 2.1	**5** SA	0554 1.7 1202 4.1 1830 1.7	**20** SU 0113 3.9 0729 2.0 1333 4.1 2000 1.6	**5** SA	0402 1.9 1014 3.9 1644 1.9 2310 4.0	**20** SU 0552 2.4 1154 3.7 1837 1.9	**5** TU	0036 4.3 0652 1.7 1245 4.3 1925 0.9	**20** W 0056 4.0 0708 1.9 1304 4.1 1929 1.3
6 TH	0514 1.6 1127 4.2 1738 1.9 2341 4.4	**21** F 0022 4.1 0650 1.9 1300 4.1 1922 1.8	**6** SU	0040 4.3 0710 1.6 1311 4.4 1943 1.4	**21** M 0206 4.2 0814 1.8 1418 4.3 2041 1.4	**6** SU	0546 1.9 1146 4.0 1827 1.6	**21** M 0048 3.8 0704 2.1 1303 4.0 1932 1.6	**6** W	0135 4.6 0746 1.3 1339 4.7 2016 0.6	**21** TH 0137 4.2 0746 1.6 1343 4.4 2006 1.0
7 F	0620 1.5 1229 4.4 1847 1.7	**22** SA 0126 4.2 0743 1.8 1351 4.3 2014 1.6	**7** M	0150 4.6 0812 1.3 1408 4.7 2042 0.9	**22** TU 0246 4.4 0851 1.6 1454 4.6 2116 1.1	**7** M	0041 4.2 0705 1.7 1301 4.3 1938 1.2	**22** TU 0141 4.1 0750 1.8 1349 4.2 2012 1.3	**7** TH	0221 4.8 0831 1.0 1423 5.0 2100 0.4	**22** F 0211 4.5 0820 1.3 1416 4.6 2041 0.8
8 SA	0049 4.6 0721 1.3 1326 4.6 1949 1.4	**23** SU 0217 4.3 0827 1.7 1434 4.5 2056 1.4	**8** TU	0247 4.9 0904 1.1 1457 5.0 ● 2135 0.5	**23** W 0319 4.5 0923 1.4 1525 4.7 2149 0.9	**8** TU	0148 4.6 0804 1.4 1357 4.7 2034 0.7	**23** W 0219 4.3 0825 1.5 1425 4.5 2047 1.0	**8** F	0302 5.0 0911 0.8 1503 5.2 ● 2140 0.3	**23** SA 0243 4.7 0853 1.1 1448 4.8 2115 0.7
9 SU	0151 4.8 0818 1.2 1417 4.8 2046 1.0	**24** M 0259 4.4 0905 1.6 1511 4.6 2134 1.2	**9** W	0337 5.1 0951 0.9 1542 5.2 2223 0.3	**24** TH 0350 4.7 0953 1.2 1554 4.9 ○ 2220 0.8	**9** W	0239 4.9 0852 1.1 1443 5.0 ● 2122 0.4	**24** TH 0251 4.5 0857 1.3 1456 4.7 2119 0.8	**9** SA	0339 5.0 0948 0.7 1541 5.3 2217 0.3	**24** SU 0314 4.8 0925 0.9 1521 5.0 ○ 2148 0.6
10 M	0248 5.0 0910 1.0 1506 5.0 ● 2140 0.7	**25** TU 0336 4.5 0939 1.5 1544 4.8 ○ 2208 1.1	**10** TH	0424 5.2 1034 0.8 1625 5.4 2308 0.2	**25** F 0419 4.7 1022 1.1 1623 5.0 2250 0.7	**10** TH	0324 5.1 0934 0.8 1525 5.3 ● 2205 0.2	**25** F 0320 4.7 0927 1.1 1525 4.9 ○ 2150 0.6	**10** SU	0414 5.0 1025 0.6 1620 5.2 2251 0.5	**25** M 0346 4.9 0959 0.8 1556 5.0 2223 0.6
11 TU	0342 5.1 1000 0.9 1553 5.2 2231 0.5	**26** W 0410 4.6 1011 1.4 1615 4.8 2241 1.0	**11** F	0508 5.2 1115 0.7 1708 5.4 2350 0.2	**26** SA 0449 4.8 1051 1.0 1652 5.0 2321 0.7	**11** F	0404 5.1 1014 0.7 1605 5.4 2246 0.1	**26** SA 0349 4.8 0956 0.9 1553 5.0 2221 0.5	**11** M	0449 4.9 1100 0.7 1659 5.1 2324 0.7	**26** TU 0420 4.9 1035 0.7 1634 5.0 2259 0.7
12 W	0434 5.2 1048 0.8 1639 5.3 2322 0.4	**27** TH 0442 4.7 1042 1.3 1646 4.9 2314 0.9	**12** SA	0550 5.0 1153 0.8 1750 5.3	**27** SU 0519 4.8 1121 1.0 1722 5.0 2352 0.7	**12** SA	0443 5.1 1051 0.6 1644 5.4 2323 0.2	**27** SU 0418 4.9 1026 0.8 1623 5.0 2252 0.5	**12** TU	0523 4.8 1135 0.8 1739 4.8 2355 1.1	**27** W 0456 4.9 1113 0.8 1717 4.9 2337 0.9
13 TH	0524 5.1 1133 0.8 1726 5.3	**28** F 0514 4.7 1113 1.3 1717 4.9 2347 0.9	**13** SU	0031 0.4 0632 4.8 1231 1.0 1833 5.1	**28** M 0550 4.7 1151 1.1 1754 4.9	**13** SU	0520 5.0 1126 0.7 1724 5.3 2358 0.5	**28** M 0448 4.9 1056 0.8 1655 5.0 2324 0.6	**13** W	0558 4.6 1210 1.0 1821 4.5	**28** TH 0537 4.8 1156 0.9 1807 4.7
14 F	0010 0.4 0614 5.0 1218 1.2 1813 5.2	**29** SA 0547 4.6 1143 1.3 1749 4.9	**14** M	0110 0.8 0714 4.5 1310 1.3 1918 4.8		**14** M	0557 4.8 1201 0.9 1804 5.0	**29** TU 0520 4.8 1129 0.9 1731 5.0 2357 0.8	**14** TH	0026 1.4 0635 4.4 1250 1.4 1906 4.2	**29** F 0020 1.2 0623 4.6 1247 1.1 1904 4.5
15 SA	0059 0.6 0704 4.8 1302 1.3 1903 5.0	**30** SU 0020 1.0 0621 4.5 1216 1.4 1822 4.8	**15** TU	0149 1.2 0758 4.3 1352 1.6 2008 4.5		**15** TU	0031 0.9 0633 4.6 1237 1.1 1846 4.7	**30** W 0556 4.6 1204 1.0 1813 4.8	**15** F	0102 1.8 0718 4.1 1337 1.6 2000 3.9	**30** SA 0114 1.5 0718 4.4 1351 1.3 2015 4.2
		31 M 0055 1.1 0657 4.4 1250 1.5 1859 4.7						**31** TH 0033 1.1 0637 4.5 1246 1.2 1902 4.5			

Chart Datum: 2·60 metres below Ordnance Datum (Newlyn)

》》 **FREE** monthly updates from 《《
www.reedsalmanac.co.uk

TIDES

TIME ZONE (UT)
For Summer Time add ONE hour in non-shaded areas

ENGLAND – NORTH SHIELDS
LAT 55°01'N   LONG 1°26'W
TIMES AND HEIGHTS OF HIGH AND LOW WATERS

YEAR 2005

	MAY			JUNE			JULY			AUGUST		
	Time m	Time m		Time m	Time m		Time m	Time m		Time m	Time m
1 SU	0224 1.8 / 0827 4.2 / 1512 1.4 / ☾ 2139 4.1	**16** M	0221 2.2 / 0841 3.9 / 1521 1.8 / ☽ 2142 3.7	**1** W	0443 1.8 / 1041 4.4 / 1727 1.1 / 2341 4.3	**16** TH	0346 2.1 / 0955 4.0 / 1634 1.5 / 2249 3.9	**1** F	0506 1.7 / 1112 4.4 / 1750 1.4	**16** SA	0346 1.9 / 0959 4.2 / 1637 1.6 / 2252 4.0	**1** M	0032 4.1 / 0700 1.7 / 1305 4.1 / 1924 1.8	**16** TU	0557 1.8 / 1210 4.2 / 1840 1.7
2 M	0353 2.0 / 0950 4.1 / 1636 1.3 / 2304 4.1	**17** TU	0344 2.3 / 0952 3.8 / 1636 1.7 / 2253 3.8	**2** TH	0549 1.6 / 1147 4.5 / 1828 1.0	**17** F	0455 2.0 / 1057 4.1 / 1734 1.4 / 2346 4.1	**2** SA	0001 4.2 / 0613 1.7 / 1217 4.3 / 1849 1.4	**17** SU	0501 1.9 / 1109 4.2 / 1746 1.5 / 2358 4.2	**2** TU	0130 4.3 / 0758 1.5 / 1402 4.2 / 2013 1.7	**17** W	0041 4.3 / 0715 1.4 / 1324 4.5 / 1944 1.4
3 TU	0519 1.9 / 1112 4.2 / 1759 1.1	**18** W	0507 2.2 / 1103 3.9 / 1742 1.6 / 2354 3.9	**3** F	0037 4.4 / 0646 1.5 / 1244 4.6 / 1920 1.0	**18** SA	0557 1.8 / 1155 4.2 / 1830 1.3	**3** SU	0057 4.3 / 0714 1.5 / 1316 4.3 / 1940 1.4	**18** M	0617 1.7 / 1221 4.3 / 1853 1.4	**3** W	0217 4.4 / 0844 1.3 / 1447 4.4 / 2053 1.6	**18** TH	0141 4.6 / 0815 1.0 / 1422 4.8 / 2038 1.2
4 W	0014 4.3 / 0625 1.6 / 1202 4.1 / 1900 0.9	**19** TH	0609 1.9 / 1202 4.1 / 1835 1.3	**4** SA	0126 4.5 / 0736 1.3 / 1334 4.6 / 2004 1.0	**19** SU	0039 4.3 / 0653 1.6 / 1251 4.4 / 1921 1.1	**4** M	0146 4.4 / 0806 1.4 / 1408 4.4 / 2025 1.4	**19** TU	0059 4.4 / 0723 1.5 / 1328 4.5 / 1953 1.3	**4** TH	0256 4.6 / 0922 1.1 / 1525 4.5 / 2128 1.5	**19** F	0231 5.0 / 0908 0.6 / 1512 5.1 / ○ 2125 0.9
5 TH	0110 4.5 / 0719 1.4 / 1313 4.7 / 1950 0.7	**20** F	0043 4.2 / 0656 1.7 / 1250 4.3 / 1919 1.1	**5** SU	0208 4.6 / 0822 1.2 / 1420 4.7 / 2044 1.0	**20** M	0127 4.5 / 0744 1.3 / 1343 4.6 / 2010 1.0	**5** TU	0230 4.5 / 0852 1.2 / 1454 4.5 / 2104 1.4	**20** W	0154 4.6 / 0823 1.1 / 1427 4.8 / 2047 1.1	**5** F	0331 4.7 / 0957 1.0 / 1559 4.6 / ● 2200 1.3	**20** SA	0316 5.2 / 0957 0.2 / 1558 5.3 / 2209 0.8
6 F	0155 4.7 / 0804 1.1 / 1358 4.9 / 2033 0.6	**21** SA	0125 4.4 / 0737 1.4 / 1332 4.5 / 2000 0.9	**6** M	0247 4.7 / 0904 1.0 / 1503 4.7 / ● 2121 1.1	**21** TU	0213 4.7 / 0834 1.1 / 1434 4.8 / 2059 0.9	**6** W	0309 4.6 / 0934 1.1 / 1536 4.5 / ● 2141 1.4	**21** TH	0244 4.9 / 0917 0.7 / 1521 5.0 / ○ 2138 0.9	**6** SA	0402 4.8 / 1030 0.9 / 1630 4.6 / 2230 1.3	**21** SU	0359 5.4 / 1042 0.1 / 1642 5.3 / 2251 0.7
7 SA	0235 4.8 / 0845 0.9 / 1439 5.0 / 2112 0.6	**22** SU	0203 4.6 / 0817 1.2 / 1412 4.7 / 2039 0.8	**7** TU	0324 4.7 / 0945 1.0 / 1544 4.7 / 2157 1.2	**22** W	0257 4.9 / 0924 0.8 / 1526 4.9 / ○ 2147 0.9	**7** TH	0345 4.7 / 1012 1.0 / 1614 4.5 / 2215 1.4	**22** F	0331 5.1 / 1009 0.4 / 1612 5.1 / 2226 0.9	**7** SU	0433 4.9 / 1101 0.8 / 1702 4.7 / 2300 1.2	**22** M	0442 5.5 / 1126 0.1 / 1725 5.2 / 2331 0.7
8 SU	0311 4.9 / 0924 0.8 / 1453 4.9 / ● 2147 0.7	**23** M	0240 4.6 / 0856 1.0 / 1453 4.9 / ○ 2119 0.7	**8** W	0400 4.7 / 1023 1.0 / 1625 4.6 / 2231 1.3	**23** TH	0342 5.0 / 1014 0.6 / 1618 5.0 / 2235 0.9	**8** F	0420 4.7 / 1048 1.0 / 1650 4.5 / 2248 1.4	**23** SA	0417 5.2 / 1059 0.2 / 1702 5.2 / 2312 0.8	**8** M	0503 4.9 / 1133 0.8 / 1733 4.6 / 2330 1.2	**23** TU	0525 5.5 / 1207 0.2 / 1808 5.0
9 M	0346 4.9 / 1002 0.8 / 1559 4.9 / 2221 0.8	**24** TU	0318 4.9 / 0937 0.8 / 1536 5.0 / 2200 0.7	**9** TH	0435 4.7 / 1101 1.0 / 1705 4.5 / 2304 1.4	**24** F	0429 5.0 / 1106 0.5 / 1711 5.0 / 2323 1.0	**9** SA	0453 4.7 / 1123 1.0 / 1726 4.5 / 2321 1.4	**24** SU	0503 5.3 / 1147 0.2 / 1750 5.1 / 2356 0.9	**9** TU	0535 4.9 / 1204 0.9 / 1806 4.6	**24** W	0010 0.9 / 0609 5.3 / 1248 0.6 / 1850 4.7
10 TU	0421 4.8 / 1039 0.8 / 1639 4.8 / 2253 1.0	**25** W	0357 4.9 / 1021 0.7 / 1622 5.0 / 2243 0.8	**10** F	0511 4.6 / 1138 1.1 / 1745 4.4 / 2338 1.5	**25** SA	0517 5.0 / 1158 0.4 / 1805 4.9	**10** SU	0527 4.7 / 1157 1.0 / 1802 4.4 / 2354 1.4	**25** M	0550 5.3 / 1234 0.3 / 1839 4.9	**10** W	0001 1.3 / 0607 4.8 / 1237 1.0 / 1839 4.5	**25** TH	0050 1.1 / 0656 5.0 / 1328 1.0 / 1935 4.5
11 W	0455 4.7 / 1115 0.9 / 1719 4.6 / 2325 1.3	**26** TH	0440 4.9 / 1107 0.7 / 1713 4.9 / 2328 1.0	**11** SA	0547 4.5 / 1216 1.2 / 1826 4.3	**26** SU	0012 1.1 / 0607 5.0 / 1251 0.5 / 1900 4.7	**11** M	0603 4.6 / 1233 1.1 / 1839 4.3	**26** TU	0039 1.0 / 0638 5.2 / 1321 0.5 / 1927 4.7	**11** TH	0034 1.4 / 0641 4.6 / 1312 1.2 / 1917 4.3	**26** F	0134 1.4 / 0747 4.6 / 1412 1.4 / ☾ 2026 4.2
12 TH	0531 4.6 / 1152 1.1 / 1801 4.4 / 2358 1.5	**27** F	0526 4.9 / 1158 0.7 / 1808 4.8	**12** SU	0015 1.6 / 0627 4.4 / 1258 1.3 / 1909 4.1	**27** M	0103 1.3 / 0700 4.8 / 1345 0.6 / 1957 4.5	**12** TU	0029 1.5 / 0640 4.5 / 1312 1.2 / 1919 4.1	**27** W	0125 1.2 / 0728 5.0 / 1408 0.8 / 2018 4.4	**12** F	0110 1.5 / 0722 4.4 / 1352 1.4 / 2002 4.0	**27** SA	0228 1.7 / 0848 4.4 / 1508 1.9 / 2128 4.0
13 F	0608 4.4 / 1231 1.3 / 1846 4.2	**28** SA	0018 1.2 / 0616 4.7 / 1254 0.8 / 1908 4.6	**13** M	0056 1.7 / 0711 4.3 / 1344 1.4 / 1957 4.0	**28** TU	0156 1.4 / 0756 4.7 / 1442 0.8 / 2056 4.4	**13** W	0108 1.6 / 0720 4.3 / 1353 1.3 / 2002 4.1	**28** TH	0213 1.5 / 0823 4.7 / 1500 1.2 / ☾ 2114 4.2	**13** SA	0156 1.7 / 0812 4.3 / 1443 1.6 / ☾ 2057 4.1	**28** SU	0343 2.0 / 1004 4.1 / 1627 2.2 / 2246 4.0
14 SA	0034 1.8 / 0650 4.2 / 1317 1.5 / 1935 4.0	**29** SU	0114 1.6 / 0713 4.6 / 1356 0.9 / 2014 4.4	**14** TU	0143 1.9 / 0800 4.2 / 1436 1.5 / 2051 3.9	**29** W	0254 1.6 / 0859 4.6 / 1542 1.0 / 2158 4.4	**14** TH	0150 1.7 / 0805 4.3 / 1439 1.4 / 2051 4.0	**29** F	0311 1.7 / 0925 4.3 / 1559 1.5 / 2216 4.0	**14** SU	0257 1.8 / 0917 4.1 / 1551 1.8 / 2207 4.0	**29** M	0523 2.0 / 1135 3.8 / 1802 2.2
15 SU	0120 2.0 / 0740 4.0 / 1413 1.7 / 2034 3.8	**30** M	0218 1.7 / 0818 4.4 / 1505 0.9 / ☾ 2125 4.3	**15** W	0240 1.9 / 0855 4.1 / 1533 1.6 / ☾ 2149 3.9	**30** TH	0358 1.7 / 1004 4.5 / 1646 1.2 / 2300 4.2	**15** F	0242 1.8 / 0857 4.2 / 1534 1.5 / 2148 4.0	**30** SA	0423 1.8 / 1037 4.2 / 1709 1.8 / 2324 4.1	**15** M	0422 2.0 / 1041 4.1 / 1717 1.8 / 2327 4.1	**30** TU	0008 4.0 / 0648 1.9 / 1256 4.0 / 1912 2.1
		31 TU	0330 1.8 / 0929 4.4 / 1618 1.1 / 2236 4.2						**31** SU	0546 1.9 / 1154 4.1 / 1823 1.9			**31** W	0113 4.2 / 0745 1.6 / 1351 4.2 / 1959 1.9

Chart Datum: 2·60 metres below Ordnance Datum (Newlyn)

》》 **FREE** monthly updates from 《《
www.reedsalmanac.co.uk

TIME ZONE (UT)
For Summer Time add ONE hour in **non-shaded areas**

ENGLAND – NORTH SHIELDS
LAT 55°01'N LONG 1°26'W
TIMES AND HEIGHTS OF HIGH AND LOW WATERS

YEAR 2005

SEPTEMBER		OCTOBER		NOVEMBER		DECEMBER	
Time m	Time m	Time m	Time m	Time m	Time m	Time m	Time m
1 0200 4.4 / 0827 1.3 / TH 1432 4.4 / 2036 1.6	**16** 0127 4.7 / 0804 0.8 / F 1411 4.9 / 2022 1.2	**1** 0207 4.6 / 0830 1.1 / SA 1434 4.6 / 2039 1.4	**16** 0152 5.1 / 0830 0.5 / SU 1433 5.1 / 2042 1.0	**1** 0232 4.9 / 0855 0.9 / TU 1457 4.9 / 2107 1.2	**16** 0254 5.2 / 0924 0.8 / W 1523 5.1 / ○ 2140 0.9	**1** 0237 4.9 / 0859 1.0 / TH 1500 4.9 / ● 2119 1.1	**16** 0327 4.8 / 0941 1.3 / F 1543 4.9 / 2210 1.1
2 0237 4.6 / 0902 1.1 / F 1505 4.6 / 2108 1.4	**17** 0214 5.1 / 0852 0.4 / SA 1456 5.2 / 2106 0.9	**2** 0238 4.6 / 0901 0.9 / SU 1503 4.8 / 2108 1.2	**17** 0233 5.4 / 0912 0.4 / M 1511 5.2 / ○ 2121 0.8	**2** 0303 5.0 / 0928 0.8 / W 1527 5.0 / ● 2139 1.1	**17** 0336 5.2 / 1000 1.0 / TH 1559 5.1 / 2220 0.9	**2** 0318 5.0 / 0939 1.0 / F 1537 5.0 / 2200 1.0	**17** 0410 4.8 / 1017 1.4 / SA 1620 4.9 / 2249 1.1
3 0309 4.8 / 0933 0.9 / SA 1535 4.7 / ● 2138 1.3	**18** 0256 5.4 / 0937 0.2 / SU 1537 5.3 / ○ 2146 0.7	**3** 0307 5.0 / 0931 0.8 / M 1531 4.9 / ● 2137 1.1	**18** 0313 5.5 / 0950 0.4 / TU 1548 5.2 / 2200 0.7	**3** 0337 5.1 / 1001 0.8 / TH 1559 5.0 / 2214 1.0	**18** 0418 5.0 / 1035 1.2 / F 1636 5.0 / 2259 1.0	**3** 0401 5.0 / 1019 1.1 / SA 1617 5.0 / 2244 0.9	**18** 0450 4.7 / 1051 1.5 / SU 1656 4.8 / 2327 1.1
4 0338 4.9 / 1003 0.8 / SU 1603 4.8 / 2206 1.1	**19** 0337 5.6 / 1018 0.1 / M 1616 5.3 / 2225 0.6	**4** 0335 5.1 / 1000 0.7 / TU 1559 4.9 / 2206 1.0	**19** 0354 5.5 / 1027 0.5 / W 1624 5.2 / 2238 0.8	**4** 0413 5.1 / 1035 0.9 / F 1633 5.0 / 2251 1.0	**19** 0501 4.8 / 1109 1.4 / SA 1713 4.8 / 2338 1.2	**4** 0449 5.0 / 1102 1.2 / SU 1700 5.0 / 2332 0.9	**19** 0530 4.6 / 1125 1.6 / M 1732 4.8
5 0406 5.0 / 1033 0.7 / M 1632 4.8 / 2234 1.1	**20** 0417 5.6 / 1058 0.2 / TU 1655 5.2 / 2303 0.7	**5** 0404 5.1 / 1030 0.7 / W 1628 5.0 / 2236 1.0	**20** 0435 5.3 / 1102 0.8 / TH 1701 5.0 / 2316 0.9	**5** 0453 5.0 / 1111 1.1 / SA 1711 4.9 / 2332 1.1	**20** 0545 4.6 / 1143 1.7 / SU 1751 4.7	**5** 0540 4.9 / 1149 1.4 / M 1747 4.9	**20** 0004 1.2 / 0609 4.4 / TU 1200 1.7 / 1810 4.6
6 0434 5.0 / 1102 0.7 / TU 1701 4.8 / 2303 1.1	**21** 0459 5.5 / 1135 0.5 / W 1733 5.0 / 2341 0.9	**6** 0435 5.1 / 1101 0.8 / TH 1658 4.9 / 2308 1.1	**21** 0517 5.0 / 1136 1.1 / F 1738 4.8 / 2355 1.2	**6** 0539 4.8 / 1152 1.4 / SU 1755 4.8	**21** 0019 1.4 / 0630 4.4 / M 1219 1.9 / 1833 4.5	**6** 0025 1.0 / 0635 4.7 / TU 1240 1.6 / 1839 4.8	**21** 0043 1.4 / 0651 4.3 / W 1237 1.9 / 1851 4.5
7 0504 5.0 / 1132 0.8 / W 1731 4.8 / 2332 1.1	**22** 0541 5.2 / 1210 0.8 / TH 1812 4.8	**7** 0508 5.0 / 1132 1.0 / F 1732 4.8 / 2342 1.2	**22** 0602 4.7 / 1209 1.5 / SA 1817 4.6	**7** 0020 1.3 / 0634 4.6 / M 1241 1.7 / 1846 4.6	**22** 0105 1.6 / 0720 4.1 / TU 1303 2.1 / 1922 4.3	**7** 0123 1.1 / 0737 4.5 / W 1338 1.8 / 1939 4.7	**22** 0125 1.5 / 0736 4.1 / TH 1319 2.0 / 1937 4.4
8 0535 4.9 / 1202 0.9 / TH 1803 4.7	**23** 0019 1.1 / 0626 4.9 / F 1247 1.3 / 1853 4.5	**8** 0547 4.8 / 1206 1.3 / SA 1811 4.7	**23** 0036 1.5 / 0650 4.4 / SU 1246 1.9 / 1901 4.3	**8** 0120 1.4 / 0740 4.4 / TU 1345 2.0 / 1951 4.4	**23** 0159 1.8 / 0816 3.9 / W 1359 2.3 / ○ 2021 4.1	**8** 0226 1.2 / 0844 4.4 / TH 1444 1.9 / ● 2045 4.6	**23** 0213 1.6 / 0826 4.0 / F 1409 2.1 / ○ 2029 4.2
9 0004 1.3 / 0609 4.8 / F 1235 1.1 / 1838 4.5	**24** 0101 1.4 / 0715 4.5 / SA 1325 1.7 / 1940 4.2	**9** 0022 1.4 / 0635 4.6 / SU 1249 1.6 / 1858 4.4	**24** 0126 1.7 / 0746 4.1 / M 1334 2.2 / 1957 4.1	**9** 0235 1.6 / 0858 4.2 / W 1508 2.1 / ○ 2108 4.3	**24** 0303 1.9 / 0922 3.8 / TH 1516 2.4 / 2130 4.0	**9** 0335 1.3 / 0954 4.3 / F 1556 2.0 / 2157 4.5	**24** 0306 1.7 / 0921 3.9 / SA 1510 2.2 / 2127 4.1
10 0040 1.4 / 0650 4.6 / SA 1313 1.6 / 1923 4.3	**25** 0153 1.8 / 0815 4.1 / SU 1417 2.1 / ○ 2040 4.0	**10** 0114 1.6 / 0736 4.3 / M 1347 1.9 / ○ 2000 4.2	**25** 0232 2.0 / 0856 3.8 / TU 1448 2.5 / ○ 2110 3.9	**10** 0400 1.5 / 1023 4.2 / TH 1640 2.1 / 2230 4.4	**25** 0415 1.9 / 1032 3.9 / F 1640 2.4 / 2242 4.1	**10** 0445 1.3 / 1101 4.3 / SA 1706 1.9 / 2306 4.6	**25** 0406 1.8 / 1021 3.9 / SU 1621 2.3 / 2230 4.1
11 0125 1.7 / 0744 4.3 / SU 1405 1.7 / ○ 2020 4.1	**26** 0306 2.0 / 0932 3.8 / M 1540 2.4 / 2201 3.8	**11** 0229 1.8 / 0858 4.1 / TU 1515 2.0 / 2122 4.1	**26** 0401 2.1 / 1022 3.7 / W 1637 2.5 / 2239 3.9	**11** 0520 1.3 / 1137 4.4 / F 1748 1.9 / 2341 4.6	**26** 0522 1.8 / 1135 4.0 / SA 1747 2.2 / 2343 4.2	**11** 0551 1.3 / 1203 4.4 / SU 1811 1.7	**26** 0509 1.8 / 1123 4.0 / M 1732 2.2 / 2333 4.2
12 0231 1.9 / 0857 4.1 / M 1523 2.0 / 2138 4.0	**27** 0453 2.1 / 1109 3.7 / TU 1734 2.5 / 2334 3.9	**12** 0410 1.8 / 1036 4.1 / W 1700 2.1 / 2255 4.1	**27** 0529 1.9 / 1143 3.9 / TH 1759 2.3 / 2354 4.1	**12** 0625 1.1 / 1236 4.5 / SA 1845 1.6	**27** 0617 1.6 / 1227 4.2 / SU 1838 2.0	**12** 0009 4.7 / 0648 1.2 / M 1257 4.5 / 1907 1.6	**27** 0609 1.7 / 1219 4.2 / TU 1835 2.0
13 0408 2.0 / 1035 4.0 / TU 1707 2.1 / 2310 4.0	**28** 0623 1.9 / 1232 3.9 / W 1847 2.2	**13** 0544 1.5 / 1201 4.3 / TH 1818 1.9	**28** 0629 1.7 / 1240 4.1 / F 1850 2.1	**13** 0039 4.8 / 0718 0.9 / SU 1325 4.8 / 1933 1.4	**28** 0033 4.4 / 0702 1.5 / M 1310 4.4 / 1921 1.7	**13** 0106 4.7 / 0739 1.2 / TU 1344 4.7 / 1958 1.4	**28** 0033 4.3 / 0703 1.5 / W 1311 4.4 / 1928 1.7
14 0553 1.7 / 1209 4.2 / W 1833 1.8	**29** 0044 4.1 / 0716 1.6 / TH 1325 4.2 / 1932 1.9	**14** 0009 4.4 / 0651 1.1 / F 1303 4.7 / 1913 1.5	**29** 0046 4.3 / 0712 1.5 / SA 1321 4.4 / 1928 1.8	**14** 0128 5.0 / 0804 0.8 / M 1407 4.9 / 2017 1.1	**29** 0117 4.6 / 0743 1.3 / TU 1348 4.6 / 2000 1.5	**14** 0157 4.8 / 0823 1.1 / W 1426 4.8 / 2045 1.2	**29** 0128 4.5 / 0753 1.4 / TH 1357 4.6 / 2018 1.4
15 0028 4.3 / 0707 1.3 / TH 1319 4.6 / 1933 1.5	**30** 0131 4.4 / 0756 1.4 / F 1403 4.4 / 2008 1.7	**15** 0106 4.8 / 0744 0.8 / SA 1351 4.9 / 2000 1.2	**30** 0126 4.6 / 0749 1.2 / SU 1355 4.6 / 2003 1.5	**15** 0212 5.1 / 0845 0.7 / TU 1446 5.0 / 2059 1.0	**30** 0157 4.7 / 0821 1.1 / W 1424 4.8 / 2039 1.3	**15** 0243 4.8 / 0904 1.3 / TH 1506 4.9 / ○ 2128 1.1	**30** 0219 4.7 / 0840 1.3 / F 1440 4.8 / 2106 1.1
			31 0200 4.8 / 0823 1.0 / M 1427 4.8 / 2035 1.3				**31** 0308 4.9 / 0926 1.1 / SA 1523 5.0 / ● 2154 0.9

Chart Datum: 2·60 metres below Ordnance Datum (Newlyn)

》》 **FREE** monthly updates from 《《
www.reedsalmanac.co.uk

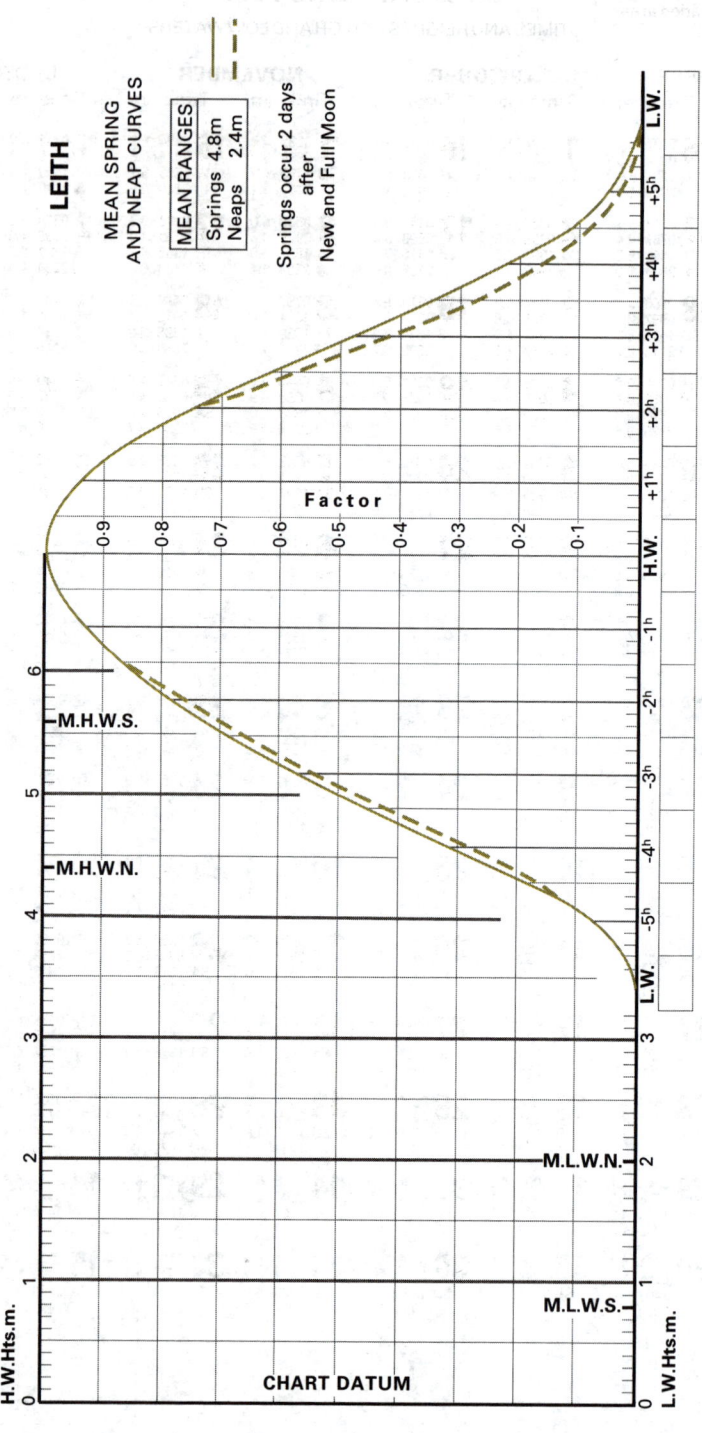

| TIME ZONE (UT) For Summer Time add ONE hour in **non-shaded areas** | SCOTLAND – LEITH LAT 55°59′N LONG 3°11′W TIMES AND HEIGHTS OF HIGH AND LOW WATERS | YEAR **2005** |

SCOTLAND – LEITH
LAT 55°59′N LONG 3°11′W
TIMES AND HEIGHTS OF HIGH AND LOW WATERS

TIME ZONE (UT) — For Summer Time add ONE hour in **non-shaded areas**

YEAR 2005

JANUARY		FEBRUARY		MARCH		APRIL	
Time m	Time m	Time m	Time m	Time m	Time m	Time m	Time m
1 0558 4.8 / 1113 1.8 / SA 1806 4.9	**16** 0034 0.9 / 0700 5.0 / SU 1230 1.6 / 1912 5.2	**1** 0000 1.3 / 0651 4.8 / TU 1149 1.7 / 1856 4.9	**16** 0049 1.7 / 0801 4.4 / W 1308 2.0 / ◐ 2025 4.5	**1** 0539 5.1 / 1048 1.2 / TU 1748 5.2 / 2321 1.1	**16** 0629 4.7 / 1138 1.5 / W 1850 4.7 / 2357 1.8	**1** 0641 4.7 / 1155 1.6 / F 1917 4.7	**16** 0005 2.2 / 0732 4.2 / SA 1301 2.1 / ◐ 2012 4.1
2 0000 1.5 / 0641 4.7 / SU 1150 2.0 / 1848 4.8	**17** 0117 1.3 / 0755 4.8 / M 1314 1.9 / ◐ 2011 4.9	**2** 0037 1.5 / 0738 4.6 / W 1237 1.9 / ◐ 1948 4.7	**17** 0141 2.1 / 0900 4.2 / TH 1436 2.3 / 2133 4.2	**2** 0619 4.9 / 1119 1.4 / W 1831 5.0 / 2354 1.4	**17** 0716 4.4 / 1221 1.9 / TH 1945 4.3 / ◐	**2** 0034 2.0 / 0739 4.5 / SA 1321 1.9 / ◐ 2034 4.4	**17** 0130 2.6 / 0839 4.1 / SU 1514 2.2 / 2121 4.0
3 0044 1.6 / 0729 4.6 / M 1237 2.1 / ◐ 1937 4.7	**18** 0205 1.7 / 0852 4.5 / TU 1416 2.1 / 2113 4.7	**3** 0130 1.7 / 0835 4.5 / TH 1347 2.1 / 2057 4.5	**18** 0323 2.4 / 1008 4.1 / F 1630 2.3 / 2252 4.1	**3** 0704 4.7 / 1204 1.6 / TH 1924 4.7 / ◐	**18** 0044 2.2 / 0812 4.2 / F 1338 2.2 / 2050 4.1	**3** 0247 2.3 / 0902 4.3 / SU 1550 1.9 / 2206 4.5	**18** 0352 2.6 / 0954 4.1 / M 1650 2.0 / 2238 4.1
4 0136 1.7 / 0823 4.5 / TU 1343 2.2 / 2036 4.6	**19** 0312 2.0 / 0953 4.4 / W 1539 2.2 / 2219 4.5	**4** 0248 1.9 / 0946 4.4 / F 1535 2.1 / 2224 4.5	**19** 0505 2.4 / 1128 4.2 / SA 1754 2.1	**4** 0046 1.8 / 0759 4.5 / F 1313 2.0 / 2036 4.5	**19** 0219 2.6 / 0921 4.0 / SA 1605 2.3 / 2207 4.0	**4** 0436 2.1 / 1032 4.4 / M 1720 1.5 / 2330 4.7	**19** 0504 2.3 / 1110 4.2 / TU 1743 1.7 / 2351 4.3
5 0238 1.8 / 0924 4.6 / W 1505 2.2 / 2145 4.6	**20** 0431 2.1 / 1058 4.4 / TH 1657 2.1 / 2328 4.5	**5** 0442 1.9 / 1101 4.5 / SA 1721 1.9 / 2345 4.7	**20** 0016 4.3 / 0611 2.2 / SU 1241 4.5 / 1852 1.8	**5** 0219 2.1 / 0915 4.3 / SA 1527 2.1 / 2210 4.4	**20** 0438 2.5 / 1042 4.1 / SU 1733 2.1 / 2344 4.1	**5** 0542 1.8 / 1147 4.8 / TU 1824 1.1	**20** 0552 2.0 / 1209 4.5 / W 1825 1.5
6 0352 1.8 / 1029 4.6 / TH 1625 2.1 / 2255 4.7	**21** 0536 2.1 / 1204 4.5 / F 1803 2.0	**6** 0603 1.7 / 1212 4.8 / SU 1835 1.5	**21** 0114 4.5 / 0656 2.0 / M 1329 4.7 / 1933 1.5	**6** 0442 2.1 / 1043 4.4 / SU 1724 1.8 / 2339 4.6	**21** 0549 2.3 / 1206 4.3 / M 1828 1.8	**6** 0034 5.1 / 0635 1.4 / W 1244 5.2 / 1915 0.7	**21** 0038 4.6 / 0629 1.7 / TH 1253 4.8 / 1900 1.2
7 0506 1.6 / 1132 4.8 / F 1734 1.8	**22** 0034 4.5 / 0625 2.0 / SA 1301 4.7 / 1857 1.7	**7** 0054 5.1 / 0705 1.5 / M 1313 5.1 / 1937 1.0	**22** 0155 4.8 / 0731 1.7 / TU 1407 5.0 / 2007 1.2	**7** 0559 1.8 / 1201 4.7 / M 1836 1.3	**22** 0047 4.4 / 0634 2.0 / TU 1259 4.6 / 1908 1.5	**7** 0123 5.4 / 0720 1.1 / TH 1329 5.5 / 1959 0.4	**22** 0115 4.9 / 0704 1.4 / F 1330 5.1 / 1933 0.9
8 0001 5.0 / 0610 1.5 / SA 1230 5.0 / 1836 1.5	**23** 0127 4.7 / 0705 1.8 / SU 1346 4.9 / 1940 1.5	**8** 0150 5.4 / 0759 1.2 / TU 1404 5.5 / ● 2032 0.6	**23** 0227 5.0 / 0804 1.5 / W 1439 5.1 / 2038 1.0	**8** 0048 5.1 / 0656 1.5 / TU 1302 5.1 / 1932 0.8	**23** 0126 4.7 / 0709 1.7 / W 1337 4.9 / 1941 1.2	**8** 0204 5.5 / 0802 0.8 / F 1410 5.7 / ● 2039 0.3	**23** 0149 5.1 / 0738 1.1 / SA 1404 5.3 / 2006 0.7
9 0102 5.2 / 0709 1.3 / SU 1324 5.3 / 1936 1.1	**24** 0209 4.9 / 0741 1.7 / M 1424 5.0 / 2017 1.3	**9** 0239 5.7 / 0846 0.9 / W 1450 5.7 / 2120 0.3	**24** 0256 5.1 / 0835 1.2 / TH 1509 5.3 / ○ 2109 0.8	**9** 0140 5.4 / 0745 1.1 / W 1350 5.5 / 2021 0.4	**24** 0158 5.0 / 0740 1.4 / TH 1409 5.1 / 2011 0.9	**9** 0242 5.6 / 0842 0.6 / SA 1451 5.8 / 2115 0.3	**24** 0223 5.3 / 0812 0.9 / SU 1438 5.5 / ○ 2039 0.6
10 0157 5.5 / 0804 1.1 / M 1413 5.5 / ● 2033 0.8	**25** 0245 5.0 / 0815 1.5 / TU 1458 5.1 / ○ 2051 1.1	**10** 0325 5.9 / 0931 0.7 / TH 1534 5.9 / 2205 0.1	**25** 0326 5.2 / 0907 1.1 / F 1539 5.4 / 2140 0.7	**10** 0225 5.7 / 0828 0.8 / TH 1432 5.7 / ● 2104 0.1	**25** 0227 5.1 / 0811 1.1 / F 1440 5.3 / ○ 2042 0.7	**10** 0320 5.5 / 0919 0.5 / SU 1532 5.7 / 2148 0.5	**25** 0257 5.4 / 0846 0.8 / M 1513 5.5 / 2113 0.6
11 0248 5.7 / 0856 1.0 / TU 1500 5.7 / 2127 0.5	**26** 0317 5.1 / 0849 1.4 / W 1529 5.2 / 2125 1.0	**11** 0410 5.8 / 1011 0.7 / F 1619 5.9 / 2247 0.2	**26** 0356 5.3 / 0938 1.0 / SA 1608 5.4 / 2211 0.7	**11** 0306 5.7 / 0908 0.6 / F 1514 5.9 / 2143 0.1	**26** 0256 5.2 / 0843 0.9 / SA 1509 5.4 / 2113 0.6	**11** 0359 5.4 / 0953 0.6 / M 1613 5.5 / 2215 0.8	**26** 0332 5.4 / 0920 0.7 / TU 1552 5.5 / 2146 0.7
12 0338 5.8 / 0944 1.0 / W 1549 5.7 / 2218 0.4	**27** 0348 5.1 / 0923 1.3 / TH 1601 5.3 / 2158 0.9	**12** 0454 5.6 / 1048 1.0 / SA 1703 5.8 / 2324 0.4	**27** 0429 5.3 / 1005 1.0 / SU 1638 5.4 / 2239 0.7	**12** 0346 5.7 / 0944 0.5 / SA 1555 5.9 / 2220 0.2	**27** 0327 5.4 / 0914 0.8 / SU 1540 5.5 / 2143 0.5	**12** 0437 5.2 / 1022 1.0 / TU 1654 5.3 / 2233 1.1	**27** 0410 5.4 / 0954 0.8 / W 1634 5.4 / 2218 1.0
13 0427 5.8 / 1030 1.0 / TH 1637 5.7 / 2306 0.4	**28** 0421 5.1 / 0956 1.3 / F 1632 5.2 / 2232 0.9	**13** 0539 5.4 / 1119 1.3 / SU 1748 5.5 / 2355 0.8		**13** 0427 5.5 / 1017 0.6 / SU 1637 5.7 / 2251 0.5	**28** 0400 5.4 / 0941 0.7 / M 1613 5.5 / 2210 0.7	**13** 0515 5.0 / 1045 1.1 / W 1736 5.0 / 2250 1.5	**28** 0451 5.2 / 1031 0.9 / TH 1721 5.1 / 2254 1.3
14 0517 5.6 / 1113 1.1 / F 1726 5.6 / 2351 0.6	**29** 0455 5.1 / 1026 1.3 / SA 1704 5.2 / 2303 1.0	**14** 0623 5.0 / 1145 1.5 / M 1835 5.2		**14** 0507 5.3 / 1043 0.9 / M 1719 5.5 / 2312 0.9	**29** 0435 5.3 / 1005 0.8 / TU 1650 5.4 / 2232 0.9	**14** 0554 4.7 / 1112 1.4 / TH 1822 4.6 / 2319 1.8	**29** 0536 5.0 / 1112 1.2 / F 1814 5.0 / 2346 1.7
15 0608 5.3 / 1152 1.4 / SA 1818 5.4	**30** 0531 5.1 / 1051 1.4 / SU 1737 5.1 / 2332 1.1	**15** 0018 1.3 / 0710 4.7 / TU 1218 1.6 / 1925 4.8		**15** 0547 5.1 / 1110 1.1 / TU 1802 5.1 / 2328 1.3	**30** 0512 5.2 / 1030 1.0 / W 1731 5.2 / 2255 1.2	**15** 0638 4.5 / 1154 1.7 / F 1913 4.3	**30** 0628 4.8 / 1224 1.4 / SA 1917 4.7
	31 0609 4.9 / 1116 1.5 / M 1814 5.0				**31** 0554 5.0 / 1105 1.3 / TH 1819 5.0 / 2332 1.5		

Chart Datum: 2·90 metres below Ordnance Datum (Newlyn)

Chapter 5

TIDES

TIME ZONE (UT)
For Summer Time add ONE hour in **non-shaded areas**

SCOTLAND – LEITH
LAT 55°59′N LONG 3°11′W

TIMES AND HEIGHTS OF HIGH AND LOW WATERS

YEAR 2005

	MAY			JUNE			JULY			AUGUST	
	Time m	Time m		Time m	Time m		Time m	Time m		Time m	Time m
1	0108 2.1 0733 4.6 SU 1400 1.6 ☽ 2034 4.6	**16** 0053 2.4 0757 4.2 M 1352 2.0 ☾ 2034 4.2	**1** 0332 1.9 0951 4.8 W 1624 1.3 2238 4.8	**16** 0232 2.2 0910 4.4 TH 1515 1.7 2144 4.4	**1** 0350 1.9 1022 4.8 F 1643 1.6 2302 4.6	**16** 0224 2.1 0913 4.5 SA 1511 1.8 2155 4.5	**1** 0544 1.9 1210 4.5 M 1810 2.0	**16** 0453 2.0 1114 4.6 TU 1735 1.9 2342 4.7
2	0249 2.2 0856 4.5 M 1544 1.5 2155 4.6	**17** 0227 2.5 0904 4.2 TU 1533 2.0 2137 4.2	**2** 0433 1.8 1054 4.9 TH 1725 1.2 2338 4.9	**17** 0344 2.1 1011 4.5 F 1621 1.6 2243 4.5	**2** 0454 1.8 1124 4.7 SA 1741 1.6	**17** 0348 2.1 1023 4.5 SU 1631 1.7 2259 4.6	**2** 0038 4.6 0646 1.7 TU 1311 4.6 1855 1.9	**17** 0608 1.6 1227 5.0 W 1838 1.6
3	0411 2.0 1016 4.6 TU 1659 1.3 2309 4.8	**18** 0358 2.3 1009 4.3 W 1640 1.8 2240 4.3	**3** 0528 1.6 1152 5.0 F 1817 1.2	**18** 0446 1.9 1109 4.6 SA 1717 1.5 2339 4.7	**3** 0001 4.7 0554 1.6 SU 1225 4.8 1829 1.6	**18** 0506 1.9 1133 4.7 M 1742 1.6	**3** 0129 4.8 0734 1.4 W 1357 4.8 1932 1.7	**18** 0046 5.1 0710 1.1 TH 1326 5.4 1931 1.2
4	0512 1.8 1124 4.9 W 1759 1.0	**19** 0455 2.1 1109 4.5 TH 1728 1.5 2337 4.6	**4** 0030 5.0 0619 1.4 SA 1243 5.1 1900 1.1	**19** 0540 1.7 1205 4.8 SU 1808 1.3	**4** 0055 4.8 0649 1.5 M 1318 4.8 1909 1.6	**19** 0002 4.8 0611 1.6 TU 1238 5.0 1843 1.4	**4** 0210 5.0 0812 1.2 TH 1434 5.0 2005 1.5	**19** 0139 5.4 0805 0.6 F 1415 5.7 ○ 2020 0.9
5	0009 5.0 0603 1.5 TH 1219 5.1 1849 0.8	**20** 0541 1.8 1200 4.7 F 1810 1.3	**5** 0116 5.1 0707 1.2 SU 1330 5.1 1937 1.1	**20** 0032 4.9 0629 1.4 M 1258 5.1 1857 1.1	**5** 0141 4.9 0737 1.3 TU 1405 4.9 1946 1.5	**20** 0100 5.0 0711 1.2 W 1336 5.3 1939 1.2	**5** 0246 5.1 0845 1.1 F 1507 5.0 ● 2038 1.4	**20** 0224 5.7 0854 0.2 SA 1501 5.9 2105 0.7
6	0058 5.2 0649 1.2 F 1306 5.3 1931 0.7	**21** 0026 4.8 0621 1.5 SA 1246 5.0 1849 1.1	**6** 0157 5.1 0752 1.0 M 1414 5.1 ● 2011 1.1	**21** 0121 5.1 0719 1.1 TU 1348 5.3 1948 1.0	**6** 0222 5.0 0820 1.2 W 1446 5.0 ● 2020 1.5	**21** 0152 5.3 0809 0.8 TH 1428 5.6 ○ 2032 1.0	**6** 0318 5.2 0916 0.9 SA 1537 5.1 2111 1.3	**21** 0308 5.9 0940 0.0 SU 1545 5.9 2148 0.6
7	0139 5.3 0733 0.9 SA 1348 5.4 2009 0.6	**22** 0109 5.1 0701 1.2 SU 1328 5.2 1928 0.9	**7** 0236 5.2 0833 1.0 TU 1456 5.1 2043 1.2	**22** 0207 5.3 0812 0.9 W 1438 5.5 ○ 2039 0.9	**7** 0300 5.1 0857 1.1 TH 1523 5.0 2054 1.4	**22** 0240 5.5 0904 0.5 F 1516 5.8 2122 0.8	**7** 0348 5.3 0947 0.8 SU 1608 5.1 2144 1.2	**22** 0352 6.0 1023 0.0 M 1629 5.8 2228 0.6
8	0218 5.4 0815 0.8 SU 1430 5.5 ● 2043 0.7	**23** 0149 5.2 0741 1.0 M 1409 5.3 ○ 2008 0.8	**8** 0314 5.1 0911 1.0 W 1537 5.1 2113 1.3	**23** 0252 5.4 0905 0.6 TH 1527 5.6 2130 0.9	**8** 0335 5.1 0931 1.0 F 1558 5.0 2128 1.4	**23** 0326 5.7 0955 0.2 SA 1604 5.8 2209 0.8	**8** 0420 5.3 1018 0.8 M 1641 5.1 2214 1.2	**23** 0437 6.0 1102 0.2 TU 1713 5.6 2304 0.8
9	0256 5.3 0854 0.7 M 1512 5.4 2114 0.8	**24** 0229 5.4 0823 0.8 TU 1452 5.5 2050 0.8	**9** 0350 5.1 0945 1.0 TH 1616 5.0 2143 1.4	**24** 0339 5.5 0959 0.5 F 1616 5.6 2220 1.0	**9** 0409 5.1 1004 1.0 SA 1633 5.0 2201 1.4	**24** 0413 5.8 1043 0.2 SU 1652 5.7 2253 0.8	**9** 0451 5.2 1049 0.9 TU 1716 5.0 2240 1.3	**24** 0523 5.8 1138 0.6 W 1759 5.3 2335 1.1
10	0334 5.3 0930 0.8 TU 1553 5.3 2140 1.1	**25** 0309 5.4 0908 0.7 W 1537 5.5 2134 0.9	**10** 0426 5.0 1017 1.1 F 1654 4.9 2214 1.6	**25** 0427 5.5 1052 0.5 SA 1708 5.5 2309 1.1	**10** 0443 5.1 1038 1.1 SU 1709 4.9 2235 1.5	**25** 0501 5.8 1128 0.3 M 1741 5.5 2334 1.0	**10** 0524 5.1 1117 1.0 W 1753 4.9 2304 1.5	**25** 0610 5.4 1207 1.1 TH 1846 4.9
11	0411 5.1 1002 1.0 W 1634 5.1 2202 1.3	**26** 0352 5.4 0956 0.7 TH 1624 5.5 2221 1.1	**11** 0504 4.9 1051 1.3 SA 1733 4.7 2249 1.7	**26** 0517 5.4 1144 0.6 SU 1801 5.4 2358 1.3	**11** 0519 5.0 1112 1.1 M 1746 4.8 2308 1.6	**26** 0550 5.6 1211 0.6 TU 1831 5.2	**11** 0559 5.0 1143 1.2 TH 1832 4.8 2331 1.6	**26** 0007 1.5 0702 5.0 F 1236 1.6 ☽ 1938 4.4
12	0448 5.0 1029 1.2 TH 1715 4.9 2227 1.6	**27** 0437 5.3 1047 0.8 F 1715 5.4 2311 1.4	**12** 0543 4.8 1129 1.5 SU 1815 4.6 2329 1.9	**27** 0611 5.3 1236 0.7 M 1858 5.1	**12** 0556 4.9 1148 1.3 TU 1827 4.7 2341 1.7	**27** 0013 1.3 0641 5.2 W 1253 0.9 1924 5.0	**12** 0639 4.9 1213 1.5 F 1916 4.7 2329 1.9	**27** 0054 1.9 0804 4.5 SA 1323 2.2 2038 4.4
13	0526 4.8 1100 1.4 F 1757 4.6 2259 1.9	**28** 0526 5.2 1143 1.0 SA 1811 5.2	**13** 0627 4.6 1214 1.6 M 1901 4.5	**28** 0047 1.5 0710 5.2 TU 1332 1.0 ☽ 1958 4.9	**13** 0636 4.8 1226 1.4 W 1910 4.6 ☽ 2020 4.7	**28** 0054 1.5 0738 4.7 TH 1336 1.4 ☽ 2008 4.5	**13** 0011 1.8 0726 4.7 SA 1259 1.7 ☽ 2008 4.5	**28** 0217 2.2 0913 4.3 SU 1458 2.3 2146 4.3
14	0608 4.6 1141 1.6 SA 1844 4.4 2345 2.1	**29** 0007 1.6 0622 5.0 SU 1246 1.1 1913 4.9	**14** 0018 2.1 0715 4.5 TU 1307 1.7 1950 4.4	**29** 0142 1.7 0815 5.0 W 1432 1.2 2059 4.7	**14** 0020 1.7 0719 4.7 TH 1310 1.6 ☾ 1958 4.5	**29** 0147 1.8 0841 4.5 F 1433 1.8 2120 4.5	**14** 0113 2.0 0829 4.5 SU 1410 2.0 2113 4.4	**29** 0415 2.2 1030 4.2 M 1650 2.3 2303 4.3
15	0658 4.4 1236 1.9 SU 1936 4.3	**30** 0111 1.7 0727 4.9 M 1358 1.2 ☽ 2022 4.8	**15** 0120 2.2 0810 4.4 W 1408 1.8 ☽ 2046 4.4	**30** 0243 1.8 0918 4.9 TH 1538 1.4 2201 4.6	**15** 0113 1.9 0810 4.6 F 1404 1.7 2053 4.5	**30** 0303 2.0 0947 4.3 SA 1553 2.0 2224 4.4	**15** 0255 2.1 0951 4.4 M 1606 2.1 2228 4.5	**30** 0544 2.1 1156 4.3 TU 1801 2.3
		31 0223 1.7 0841 4.8 TU 1516 1.3 2132 4.7					**31** 0429 2.0 1058 4.4 SU 1710 2.1 2333 4.5		**31** 0018 4.5 0642 1.7 W 1259 4.6 1845 2.1

Chart Datum: 2·90 metres below Ordnance Datum (Newlyn)

FREE monthly updates from www.reedsalmanac.co.uk

TIME ZONE (UT)
For Summer Time add ONE hour in **non-shaded areas**

SCOTLAND – LEITH
LAT 55°59'N   LONG 3°11'W
TIMES AND HEIGHTS OF HIGH AND LOW WATERS

YEAR 2005

	SEPTEMBER			OCTOBER			NOVEMBER			DECEMBER	
	Time m	Time m		Time m	Time m		Time m	Time m		Time m	Time m
1 TH	0111 4.8 0723 1.5 1341 4.8 1918 1.8	**16** F	0031 5.2 0702 0.9 1312 5.5 1914 1.2	**1** SA	0119 5.1 0725 1.2 1343 5.1 1921 1.5	**16** SU	0058 5.6 0729 0.5 1335 5.7 1932 0.9	**1** TU	0146 5.3 0745 0.9 1404 5.3 1951 1.2	**16** W	0203 5.7 0819 0.8 1431 5.6 ○ 2032 0.9	**1** TH	0152 5.3 0746 1.1 1410 5.4 ● 2003 1.1	**16** F	0237 5.3 0829 1.4 1456 5.3 2100 1.1
2 F	0151 5.0 0756 1.2 1414 5.0 1948 1.5	**17** SA	0121 5.6 0751 0.5 1357 5.8 1959 0.9	**2** SU	0151 5.3 0753 1.0 1411 5.2 1951 1.3	**17** M	0141 5.9 0810 0.4 1415 5.8 ○ 2014 0.7	**2** W	0219 5.5 0816 0.9 1437 5.4 ● 2024 1.0	**17** TH	0247 5.6 0854 1.0 1511 5.5 2113 0.9	**2** F	0233 5.4 0825 1.1 1449 5.5 2045 1.0	**17** SA	0320 5.2 0901 1.4 1535 5.3 2137 1.1
3 SA	0223 5.2 0825 1.0 1443 5.1 ● 2019 1.3	**18** SU	0204 5.9 0836 0.2 1439 5.9 ○ 2041 0.6	**3** M	0221 5.4 0822 0.8 1439 5.3 ● 2022 1.1	**18** TU	0222 6.0 0849 0.3 1454 5.8 2055 0.6	**3** TH	0254 5.5 0847 0.9 1512 5.5 2057 1.0	**18** F	0331 5.5 0924 1.2 1551 5.4 2149 1.0	**3** SA	0316 5.5 0906 1.1 1529 5.5 2131 0.9	**18** SU	0400 5.1 0931 1.5 1612 5.2 2210 1.2
4 SU	0253 5.3 0853 0.8 1511 5.2 2050 1.1	**19** M	0245 6.1 0917 0.0 1520 5.9 2121 0.5	**4** TU	0251 5.5 0850 0.7 1509 5.4 2052 1.0	**19** W	0305 5.9 0925 0.5 1534 5.7 2133 0.7	**4** F	0331 5.5 0918 1.0 1548 5.4 2130 1.0	**19** SA	0415 5.3 0949 1.4 1630 5.2 2221 1.3	**4** SU	0401 5.5 0951 1.2 1612 5.4 2220 1.0	**19** M	0439 5.0 1000 1.6 1649 5.1 2240 1.3
5 M	0322 5.4 0922 0.7 1540 5.4 2120 1.0	**20** TU	0328 6.1 0956 0.1 1601 5.8 2159 0.6	**5** W	0321 5.5 0919 0.7 1540 5.4 2120 1.0	**20** TH	0348 5.8 0957 0.8 1614 5.5 2208 0.9	**5** SA	0412 5.4 0948 1.2 1627 5.3 2206 1.2	**20** SU	0458 5.0 1013 1.7 1710 5.0 2251 1.5	**5** M	0449 5.4 1039 1.4 1659 5.3 2313 1.1	**20** TU	0518 4.9 1032 1.8 1727 5.0 2314 1.5
6 TU	0351 5.4 0952 0.7 1611 5.3 2148 1.0	**21** W	0411 6.0 1031 0.4 1643 5.5 2233 0.8	**6** TH	0353 5.5 0945 0.8 1614 5.4 2145 1.1	**21** F	0433 5.5 1020 1.2 1655 5.2 2236 1.2	**6** SU	0457 5.3 1022 1.5 1710 5.2 2250 1.3	**21** M	0542 4.8 1044 2.0 1753 4.8 2329 1.7	**6** TU	0541 5.3 1132 1.7 1750 5.2	**21** W	0559 4.7 1109 1.9 1809 4.8 2353 1.6
7 W	0422 5.4 1019 0.8 1644 5.2 2211 1.1	**22** TH	0456 5.7 1059 0.9 1726 5.3 2301 1.1	**7** F	0429 5.4 1006 1.0 1650 5.3 2209 1.2	**22** SA	0518 5.2 1036 1.6 1737 5.0 2304 1.5	**7** M	0547 5.1 1108 1.8 1800 5.0 2352 1.6	**22** TU	0629 4.6 1126 2.2 1843 4.6	**7** W	0011 1.2 0637 5.1 1231 1.9 1847 5.1	**22** TH	0642 4.6 1150 2.1 1855 4.7
8 TH	0454 5.3 1040 1.0 1720 5.1 2231 1.3	**23** F	0542 5.3 1118 1.3 1810 4.9 2329 1.5	**8** SA	0509 5.2 1028 1.3 1730 5.1 2240 1.4	**23** SU	0606 4.8 1103 2.0 1824 4.7 2345 1.9	**8** TU	0646 4.9 1225 2.2 1859 4.8	**23** W	0020 2.0 0721 4.4 1226 2.5 ◐ 1943 4.4	**8** TH	0116 1.3 0741 4.9 1337 2.1 ◐ 1955 5.0	**23** F	0040 1.8 0729 4.5 1242 2.3 ◐ 1947 4.5
9 F	0530 5.1 1059 1.2 1758 5.0 2258 1.5	**24** SA	0632 4.9 1142 1.8 1859 4.6	**9** SU	0556 5.0 1101 1.7 1816 4.9 2325 1.7	**24** M	0700 4.5 1148 2.4 1921 4.4	**9** W	0118 1.8 0756 4.7 1403 2.3 ◐ 2014 4.7	**24** TH	0130 2.1 0819 4.3 1351 2.6 2047 4.4	**9** F	0228 1.4 0851 4.8 1447 2.1 2108 4.9	**24** SA	0135 1.9 0822 4.6 1348 2.4 2044 4.5
10 SA	0611 5.0 1127 1.5 1841 4.8 2337 1.7	**25** SU	0012 1.9 0730 4.5 1228 2.3 ◐ 1958 4.4	**10** M	0651 4.8 1153 2.1 1911 4.6	**25** TU	0051 2.2 0801 4.2 1308 2.7 ◐ 2029 4.3	**10** TH	0300 1.7 0916 4.7 1531 2.2 2137 4.8	**25** F	0312 2.1 0920 4.3 1529 2.6 2150 4.4	**10** SA	0341 1.5 0959 4.8 1554 2.0 2215 5.0	**25** SU	0239 2.0 0919 4.5 1506 2.4 2145 4.5
11 SU	0702 4.7 1211 1.9 1934 4.6	**26** M	0133 2.3 0839 4.2 1400 2.7 2108 4.2	**11** TU	0044 2.0 0801 4.6 1400 2.4 2026 4.5	**26** W	0316 2.3 0910 4.1 1532 2.8 2141 4.3	**11** F	0421 1.5 1030 4.9 1637 2.0 2246 5.0	**26** SA	0423 2.0 1020 4.4 1634 2.4 2248 4.6	**11** SU	0447 1.4 1102 4.9 1655 1.8 2317 5.1	**26** M	0352 1.9 1018 4.4 1621 2.3 2246 4.5
12 M	0039 2.0 0808 4.5 1336 2.2 2042 4.4	**27** TU	0402 2.3 0956 4.1 1626 2.7 2227 4.3	**12** W	0309 2.0 0929 4.6 1600 2.3 2155 4.6	**27** TH	0438 2.1 1026 4.2 1646 2.5 2253 4.4	**12** SA	0523 1.2 1134 5.1 1731 1.7 2344 5.3	**27** SU	0512 1.8 1117 4.6 1723 2.1 2341 4.7	**12** M	0545 1.4 1158 5.0 1751 1.6	**27** TU	0457 1.8 1116 4.6 1722 2.1 2345 4.7
13 TU	0247 2.2 0936 4.4 1608 2.3 2209 4.5	**28** W	0524 2.1 1127 4.3 1735 2.4 2346 4.5	**13** TH	0447 1.7 1052 4.8 1710 2.0 2311 4.9	**28** F	0530 1.8 1137 4.5 1733 2.2 2351 4.7	**13** SU	0616 1.0 1207 5.3 1819 1.4	**28** M	0554 1.6 1207 4.8 1805 1.8	**13** TU	0013 5.2 0634 1.3 1249 5.1 1843 1.4	**28** W	0552 1.7 1212 4.8 1814 1.8
14 W	0455 1.8 1104 4.6 1729 2.0 2328 4.7	**29** TH	0616 1.8 1231 4.6 1818 2.1	**14** F	0550 1.2 1200 5.1 1803 1.6	**29** SA	0610 1.6 1224 4.7 1811 1.9	**14** M	0034 5.5 0702 0.9 1311 5.5 1905 1.1	**29** TU	0027 4.9 0632 1.4 1251 5.0 1844 1.5	**14** W	0105 5.2 0716 1.3 1334 5.2 1932 1.2	**29** TH	0040 4.9 0640 1.5 1303 5.0 1903 1.5
15 TH	0606 1.4 1217 5.1 1826 1.6	**30** F	0039 4.8 0654 1.5 1312 4.8 1851 1.8	**15** SA	0010 5.2 0643 0.8 1252 5.5 1849 1.3	**30** SU	0035 5.0 0643 1.3 1300 5.0 1845 1.6	**15** TU	0120 5.6 0742 0.9 1351 5.5 1949 1.0	**30** W	0111 5.0 0708 1.3 1332 5.2 1923 1.3	**15** TH	0152 5.3 0754 1.3 1416 5.3 ○ 2018 1.1	**30** F	0132 5.1 0728 1.3 1350 5.2 1952 1.2
						31 M	0112 5.2 0714 1.1 1332 5.2 1918 1.4							**31** SA	0220 5.4 0815 1.2 1434 5.4 ● 2043 0.9

Chart Datum: 2·90 metres below Ordnance Datum (Newlyn)

》》 **FREE** monthly updates from 《《
www.reedsalmanac.co.uk

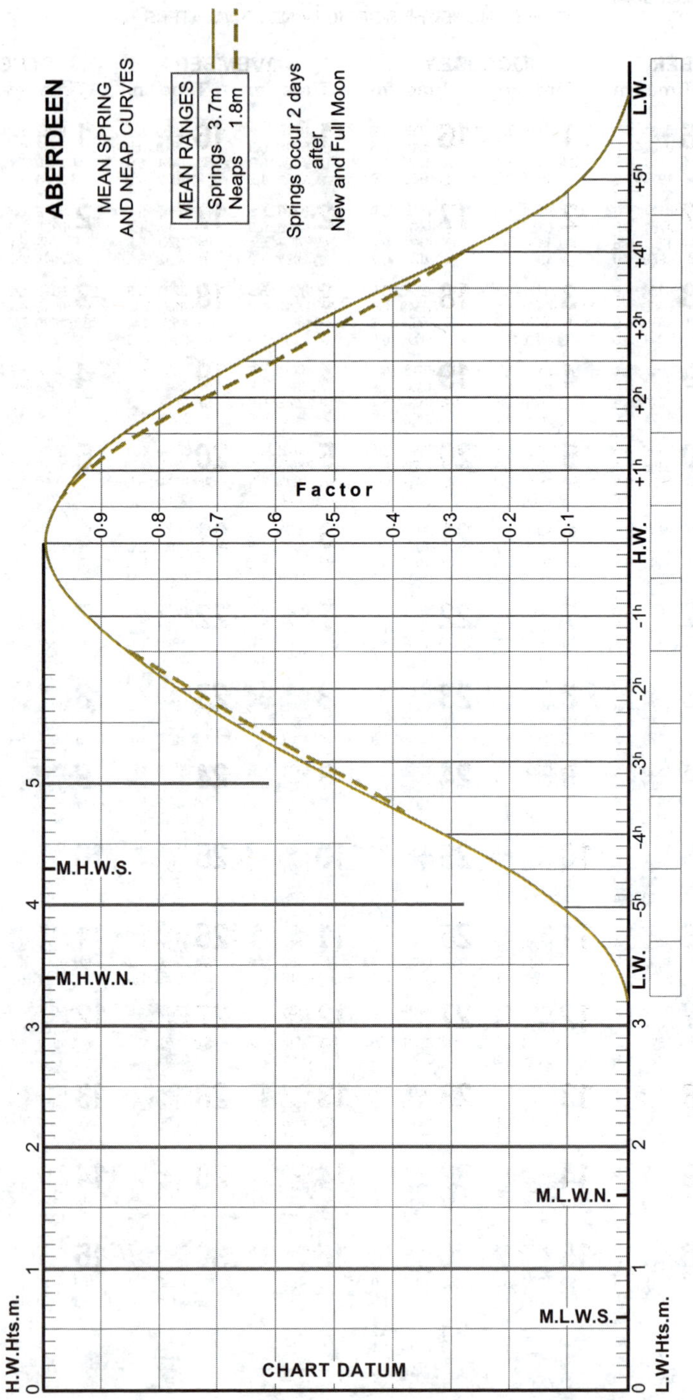
ABERDEEN
MEAN SPRING AND NEAP CURVES
MEAN RANGES
Springs 3.7m
Neaps 1.8m
Springs occur 2 days after New and Full Moon
Factor
0·9 0·8 0·7 0·6 0·5 0·4 0·3 0·2 0·1
L.W. -5h -4h -3h -2h -1h H.W. +1h +2h +3h +4h +5h L.W.
H.W.Hts.m.
0 1 2 3 4 5
M.H.W.S.
M.H.W.N.
CHART DATUM
M.L.W.S.
M.L.W.N.
L.W.Hts.m.

TIME ZONE (UT)
For Summer Time add ONE hour in **non-shaded areas**

SCOTLAND – ABERDEEN
LAT 57°09′N   LONG 2°05′W
TIMES AND HEIGHTS OF HIGH AND LOW WATERS

YEAR 2005

JANUARY				FEBRUARY				MARCH				APRIL			
Time	m	Time	m	Time	m	Time	m	Time	m	Time	m	Time	m	Time	m
1 0446 3.7 1020 1.6 SA 1645 3.9 2303 1.3		**16** 0549 3.8 1127 1.4 SU 1749 4.1		**1** 0534 3.7 1109 1.5 TU 1738 3.8 2355 1.3		**16** 0013 1.4 0644 3.4 W 1230 1.7 ☾ 1904 3.5		**1** 0418 3.9 1000 1.1 TU 1626 4.1 2233 1.0		**16** 0506 3.6 1054 1.3 W 1727 3.7 2321 1.5		**1** 0520 3.6 1119 1.3 F 1804 3.6		**16** 0608 3.3 1224 1.7 SA 1908 3.1 ☾	
2 0531 3.6 1102 1.7 SU 1729 3.8 2350 1.3		**17** 0013 1.1 0642 3.6 M 1221 1.6 ☽ 1846 3.9		**2** 0625 3.5 1202 1.6 W 1834 3.7 ☾		**17** 0112 1.8 0748 3.3 TH 1347 1.9 2023 3.3		**2** 0457 3.8 1039 1.2 W 1711 3.9 2317 1.2		**17** 0552 3.4 1145 1.6 TH 1826 3.3 ☽		**2** 0001 1.6 0627 3.4 SA 1242 1.5 ☽ 1930 3.4		**17** 0050 2.1 0721 3.1 SU 1359 1.7 2031 3.1	
3 0621 3.5 1153 1.8 M 1821 3.7 ☾		**18** 0109 1.3 0741 3.5 TU 1324 1.8 1951 3.6		**3** 0053 1.4 0727 3.5 TH 1313 1.8 1946 3.6		**18** 0233 2.0 0908 3.2 F 1532 1.9 2155 3.2		**3** 0545 3.6 1129 1.4 TH 1809 3.7 ☾		**18** 0015 1.9 0652 3.2 F 1301 1.8 1943 3.1		**3** 0137 1.8 0753 3.3 SU 1428 1.5 2107 3.4		**18** 0242 2.1 0847 3.1 M 1533 1.6 2155 3.2	
4 0044 1.4 0716 3.5 TU 1256 1.9 1921 3.6		**19** 0212 1.6 0848 3.4 W 1438 1.9 2106 3.5		**4** 0207 1.5 0839 3.5 F 1439 1.8 2111 3.6		**19** 0413 2.0 1026 3.3 SA 1650 1.7 2309 3.4		**4** 0016 1.5 0648 3.4 F 1243 1.6 1928 3.5		**19** 0140 2.1 0813 3.1 SA 1454 1.9 2121 3.1		**4** 0319 1.8 0923 3.4 M 1601 1.2 2231 3.6		**19** 0404 1.9 1003 3.3 TU 1630 1.4 2251 3.4	
5 0146 1.4 0818 3.5 W 1407 1.9 2028 3.7		**20** 0326 1.7 0956 3.6 TH 1601 1.8 2219 3.5		**5** 0329 1.6 0956 3.6 SA 1608 1.6 2234 3.7		**20** 0511 1.8 1124 3.5 SU 1739 1.5		**5** 0141 1.7 0809 3.3 SA 1424 1.7 2104 3.4		**20** 0344 2.1 0945 3.2 SU 1624 1.7 2244 3.2		**5** 0432 1.5 1036 3.7 TU 1703 0.9 2329 3.9		**20** 0450 1.7 1055 3.5 W 1711 1.1 2330 3.6	
6 0251 1.4 0923 3.6 TH 1518 1.7 2138 3.7		**21** 0435 1.7 1055 3.7 F 1705 1.7 2321 3.6		**6** 0448 1.4 1103 3.8 SU 1721 1.2 2343 4.0		**21** 0000 3.5 0553 1.6 M 1209 3.7 1818 1.2		**6** 0322 1.7 0937 3.4 SU 1606 1.4 2235 3.6		**21** 0448 1.9 1053 3.4 M 1713 1.4 2335 3.4		**6** 0524 1.2 1130 3.9 W 1752 0.6		**21** 0526 1.4 1134 3.7 TH 1745 0.9	
7 0356 1.3 1025 3.8 F 1625 1.5 2246 3.9		**22** 0526 1.7 1144 3.7 SA 1754 1.5		**7** 0549 1.3 1159 4.0 M 1818 0.9		**22** 0039 3.7 0628 1.5 TU 1244 3.9 1852 1.0		**7** 0445 1.5 1052 3.7 M 1717 1.1 2341 3.9		**22** 0530 1.6 1139 3.6 TU 1751 1.2		**7** 0014 4.1 0607 1.0 TH 1214 4.2 1835 0.4		**22** 0004 3.7 0558 1.2 F 1210 3.9 1817 0.7	
8 0458 1.2 1120 3.9 SA 1727 1.3 2346 4.1		**23** 0012 3.7 0607 1.6 SU 1226 3.8 1834 1.3		**8** 0040 4.2 0640 1.1 TU 1249 4.3 ● 1908 0.5		**23** 0112 3.8 0700 1.3 W 1316 4.0 1924 0.9		**8** 0542 1.3 1148 4.0 TU 1810 0.7		**23** 0011 3.6 0603 1.4 W 1215 3.8 1824 0.9		**8** 0054 4.2 0646 0.7 F 1255 4.4 ● 1914 0.3		**23** 0036 3.9 0629 1.0 SA 1243 4.0 1849 0.6	
9 0555 1.1 1210 4.1 SU 1822 1.0		**24** 0054 3.8 0644 1.5 M 1302 4.0 1911 1.1		**9** 0131 4.4 0726 0.9 W 1334 4.5 1956 0.3		**24** 0143 3.9 0730 1.1 TH 1344 4.1 ○ 1955 0.7		**9** 0032 4.1 0628 1.0 W 1235 4.2 1856 0.4		**24** 0043 3.8 0633 1.2 TH 1247 3.9 1854 0.8		**9** 0130 4.2 0724 0.6 SA 1334 4.4 1951 0.3		**24** 0108 4.0 0701 0.8 SU 1316 4.2 ○ 1923 0.5	
10 0042 4.3 0646 1.0 M 1258 4.3 ● 1914 0.7		**25** 0130 3.9 0717 1.4 TU 1336 4.1 ○ 1945 1.0		**10** 0217 4.4 0809 0.8 TH 1417 4.6 2040 0.2		**25** 0212 4.0 0759 1.0 F 1415 4.2 2025 0.6		**10** 0116 4.3 0709 0.8 TH 1317 4.5 ● 1938 0.2		**25** 0112 3.9 0702 1.0 F 1317 4.1 ○ 1924 0.6		**10** 0205 4.2 0800 0.6 SU 1412 4.4 2025 0.5		**25** 0140 4.1 0734 0.7 M 1352 4.3 1957 0.5	
11 0136 4.4 0735 0.9 TU 1345 4.4 2005 0.5		**26** 0204 3.9 0749 1.3 W 1407 4.1 2018 0.9		**11** 0301 4.4 0849 0.8 F 1500 4.6 2123 0.2		**26** 0241 4.0 0827 0.9 SA 1445 4.2 2056 0.6		**11** 0157 4.4 0748 0.6 F 1357 4.6 2018 0.2		**26** 0141 4.0 0731 0.9 SA 1347 4.2 1955 0.5		**11** 0240 4.1 0835 0.6 M 1451 4.3 2058 0.7		**26** 0214 4.1 0810 0.7 TU 1431 4.2 2033 0.6	
12 0228 4.4 0822 0.8 W 1431 4.5 2054 0.4		**27** 0236 3.9 0820 1.2 TH 1438 4.2 2050 0.9		**12** 0343 4.3 0929 0.9 SA 1543 4.5 2205 0.5		**27** 0312 4.0 0857 0.9 SU 1516 4.2 2126 0.7		**12** 0235 4.3 0825 0.6 SA 1437 4.6 2056 0.3		**27** 0211 4.1 0801 0.8 SU 1418 4.3 2026 0.5		**12** 0315 4.0 0911 0.8 TU 1532 4.1 2131 1.0		**27** 0250 4.1 0848 0.7 W 1513 4.1 2112 0.8	
13 0319 4.4 0908 0.8 TH 1519 4.5 2144 0.4		**28** 0308 3.9 0851 1.2 F 1509 4.2 2122 0.9		**13** 0425 4.1 1007 1.0 SU 1627 4.4 2245 0.7		**28** 0343 4.0 0927 1.0 M 1549 4.2 2158 0.8		**13** 0312 4.2 0901 0.7 SU 1516 4.5 2131 0.5		**28** 0241 4.1 0831 0.7 M 1451 4.3 2057 0.6		**13** 0350 3.8 0947 1.0 W 1614 3.8 2204 1.3		**28** 0329 4.0 0931 0.8 TH 1601 4.0 2156 1.1	
14 0409 4.1 0953 1.1 F 1607 4.4 2233 0.6		**29** 0341 3.9 0922 1.2 SA 1541 4.1 2156 0.9		**14** 0508 3.8 1048 1.2 M 1712 4.1 2327 1.1				**14** 0349 4.0 0937 0.8 M 1557 4.3 2206 0.8		**29** 0314 4.0 0903 0.8 TU 1527 4.2 2130 0.8		**14** 0427 3.7 1027 1.2 TH 1701 3.5 2242 1.6		**29** 0415 3.8 1022 1.0 F 1659 3.8 2251 1.4	
15 0458 4.1 1039 1.2 SA 1657 4.3 2322 0.8		**30** 0415 3.8 0954 1.3 SU 1615 4.1 2230 1.0		**15** 0553 3.6 1133 1.4 TU 1803 3.8				**15** 0426 3.8 1013 1.0 TU 1639 4.0 2241 1.2		**30** 0350 3.9 0939 0.9 W 1609 4.0 2208 1.2		**15** 0511 3.5 1116 1.5 F 1758 3.3 2331 1.9		**30** 0510 3.7 1128 1.1 SA 1811 3.6	
		31 0452 3.7 1029 1.4 M 1653 4.0 2308 1.1										**31** 0431 3.8 1022 1.1 TH 1659 3.8 2255 1.3					

Chart Datum: 2·25 metres below Ordnance Datum (Newlyn)

》》 **FREE** monthly updates from 《《
www.reedsalmanac.co.uk

TIDES

TIME ZONE (UT)
For Summer Time add ONE hour in **non-shaded areas**

SCOTLAND – ABERDEEN
LAT 57°09'N   LONG 2°05'W
TIMES AND HEIGHTS OF HIGH AND LOW WATERS

YEAR 2005

	MAY				JUNE				JULY				AUGUST			
	Time	m	Time	m	Time	m	Time	m	Time	m	Time	m	Time	m	Time	m
1 SU ◐	0003 0620 1251 1932	1.6 3.5 1.2 3.4	**16** M	0005 0637 1305 1937	1.9 3.3 1.5 3.1	**1** W	0222 0832 1506 2137	1.6 3.7 1.0 3.6	**16** TH	0131 0750 1414 2043	1.8 3.4 1.3 3.3	**1** F	0245 0906 1530 2158	1.5 3.6 1.2 3.5	**16** SA	0131 0756 1416 2049	1.7 3.5 1.4 3.4	**1** M	0444 1103 1708 2324	1.5 3.5 1.6 3.6	**16** TU	0337 1005 1618 2234	1.6 3.6 1.5 3.6
2 M	0133 0741 1422 2058	1.8 3.4 1.2 3.5	**17** TU	0129 0745 1420 2046	2.0 3.2 1.5 3.2	**2** TH	0328 0940 1607 2233	1.5 3.7 0.9 3.7	**17** F	0237 0851 1512 2142	1.7 3.4 1.3 3.4	**2** SA	0354 1012 1631 2253	1.5 3.6 1.3 3.6	**17** SU	0244 0906 1523 2154	1.7 3.5 1.4 3.5	**2** TU	0539 1159 1754	1.4 3.6 1.6	**17** W	0455 1118 1724 2333	1.3 3.8 1.3 3.9
3 TU	0258 0903 1540 2211	1.7 3.5 1.0 3.6	**18** W	0248 0855 1524 2150	1.9 3.3 1.4 3.3	**3** F	0426 1038 1659 2320	1.3 3.8 0.9 3.8	**18** SA	0337 0952 1607 2235	1.6 3.5 1.2 3.6	**3** SU	0456 1112 1722 2341	1.4 3.6 1.3 3.7	**18** M	0356 1019 1630 2254	1.6 3.6 1.3 3.7	**3** W	0010 0622 1244 1832	3.8 1.2 3.7 1.4	**18** TH	0554 1216 1816	0.9 4.1 1.1
4 W	0405 1011 1639 2305	1.5 3.7 0.8 3.8	**19** TH	0349 0956 1615 2239	1.7 3.4 1.2 3.5	**4** SA	0516 1128 1744	1.2 3.9 0.9	**19** SU	0432 1048 1658 2323	1.4 3.7 1.0 3.8	**4** M	0547 1204 1806	1.2 3.7 1.3	**19** TU	0502 1124 1731 2347	1.3 3.8 1.2 3.9	**4** TH	0049 0700 1321 1907	3.9 1.0 3.8 1.3	**19** F ○	0023 0644 1307 1902	4.2 0.5 4.3 0.9
5 TH	0457 1105 1728 2349	1.2 3.9 0.6 3.9	**20** F	0436 1045 1658 2320	1.5 3.6 1.0 3.7	**5** SU	0002 0601 1214 1823	3.8 1.0 3.9 0.9	**20** M	0523 1140 1747	1.2 3.9 0.9	**5** TU	0024 0632 1250 1845	3.8 1.1 3.7 1.3	**20** W	0600 1222 1825	1.0 4.0 1.0	**5** F ●	0124 0734 1354 1939	4.0 0.9 3.8 1.2	**20** SA	0109 0731 1353 1945	4.4 0.2 4.4 0.7
6 F	0542 1150 1810	1.0 4.1 0.6	**21** SA	0516 1128 1737 2358	1.3 3.8 0.8 3.8	**6** M	0040 0643 1257 1900	3.9 0.9 3.9 1.0	**21** TU	0007 0611 1231 1835	3.9 1.0 4.0 0.9	**6** W ●	0103 0712 1332 1921	3.9 1.0 3.8 1.3	**21** TH ○	0036 0653 1316 1914	4.1 0.7 4.2 0.9	**6** SA	0155 0807 1426 2009	4.1 0.8 3.9 1.1	**21** SU	0153 0816 1437 2027	4.6 0.1 4.5 0.7
7 SA	0027 0622 1232 1847	4.0 0.8 4.2 0.6	**22** SU	0554 1208 1815	1.1 3.9 0.7	**7** TU	0117 0723 1339 1936	4.0 0.9 3.9 1.1	**22** W ○	0051 0700 1321 1923	4.1 0.8 4.2 0.8	**7** TH	0139 0750 1410 1956	3.9 0.9 3.8 1.2	**22** F	0124 0743 1407 2001	4.3 0.4 4.3 0.8	**7** SU	0226 0838 1457 2039	4.1 0.7 3.9 1.1	**22** M	0236 0859 1519 2107	4.7 0.1 4.4 0.7
8 SU ●	0103 0700 1312 1923	4.1 0.7 4.2 0.6	**23** M ○	0035 0632 1250 1854	4.0 0.9 4.1 0.7	**8** W	0152 0801 1420 2011	4.0 0.8 3.8 1.2	**23** TH	0136 0749 1413 2011	4.2 0.6 4.2 0.8	**8** F	0213 0826 1447 2029	4.0 0.9 3.8 1.2	**23** SA	0210 0832 1457 2047	4.4 0.2 4.4 0.8	**8** M	0257 0909 1528 2109	4.1 0.8 3.9 1.1	**23** TU	0319 0941 1602 2147	4.6 0.3 4.2 0.8
9 M	0138 0738 1352 1957	4.1 0.7 4.1 0.8	**24** TU	0113 0713 1332 1935	4.1 0.7 4.2 0.7	**9** TH	0228 0839 1500 2045	3.9 0.9 3.7 1.3	**24** F	0221 0840 1506 2059	4.1 0.5 4.2 0.9	**9** SA	0247 0901 1522 2102	3.9 0.9 3.8 1.3	**24** SU	0256 0921 1545 2132	4.5 0.2 4.3 0.8	**9** TU	0328 0941 1600 2140	4.1 0.8 3.8 1.2	**24** W	0404 1023 1645 2228	4.5 0.4 4.0 1.0
10 TU	0212 0815 1432 2031	4.0 0.7 4.0 0.9	**25** W	0151 0756 1418 2018	4.2 0.6 4.2 0.8	**10** F	0303 0916 1541 2120	3.9 1.0 3.6 1.4	**25** SA	0309 0932 1600 2149	4.2 0.4 4.1 1.0	**10** SU	0321 0935 1558 2137	3.9 0.9 3.7 1.3	**25** M	0344 1009 1633 2217	4.5 0.3 4.1 1.0	**10** W	0401 1013 1635 2212	4.0 0.9 3.7 1.3	**25** TH	0451 1105 1730 2314	4.2 0.9 3.8 1.3
11 W	0247 0852 1513 2104	4.0 0.8 3.9 1.2	**26** TH	0233 0842 1508 2104	4.1 0.6 4.1 0.9	**11** SA	0340 0955 1623 2157	3.8 1.1 3.6 1.5	**26** SU	0400 1026 1656 2241	4.2 0.5 4.0 1.2	**11** M	0356 1011 1635 2210	3.9 1.0 3.6 1.4	**26** TU	0432 1057 1722 2303	4.4 0.5 3.9 1.1	**11** TH	0437 1048 1714 2250	3.9 1.0 3.7 1.4	**26** F ◐	0543 1152 1822	3.9 1.2 3.6
12 TH	0322 0930 1556 2138	3.8 1.0 3.7 1.4	**27** F	0317 0932 1603 2154	4.1 0.7 4.0 1.1	**12** SU	0420 1036 1707 2238	3.7 1.2 3.4 1.6	**27** M	0454 1122 1752 2336	4.1 0.6 3.8 1.3	**12** TU	0434 1049 1715 2248	3.8 1.1 3.5 1.5	**27** W	0523 1146 1813 2354	4.2 0.7 3.7 1.3	**12** F	0518 1129 1759 2336	3.8 1.2 3.5 1.6	**27** SA	0011 0644 1249 1925	1.6 3.5 1.6 3.4
13 F	0400 1010 1642 2216	3.7 1.1 3.5 1.6	**28** SA	0408 1029 1704 2251	4.0 0.8 3.8 1.3	**13** M	0505 1123 1755 2325	3.6 1.3 3.3 1.7	**28** TU ◐	0552 1220 1850	4.0 0.7 3.6	**13** W	0515 1133 1759 2341	3.7 1.3 3.5 1.6	**28** TH ◐	0618 1238 1908	3.9 1.0 3.5	**13** SA	0609 1221 1856	3.6 1.4 3.4	**28** SU	0126 0802 1407 2042	1.8 3.3 1.8 3.3
14 SA	0442 1057 1734 2303	3.5 1.3 3.3 1.8	**29** SU	0506 1133 1810 2358	3.8 0.8 3.7 1.5	**14** TU	0556 1215 1848	3.6 1.3 3.3	**29** W ◐	0035 0652 1321 1951	1.4 3.9 0.9 3.5	**14** TH	0600 1217 1849 ◐	1.3 3.4	**29** F	0053 0719 1337 2011	1.5 3.7 1.4 3.4	**14** SU	0041 0716 1331 2005	1.7 3.4 1.6 3.4	**29** M	0311 0935 1551 2202	1.8 3.3 2.0 3.4
15 SU	0535 1154 1833	3.4 1.5 3.2	**30** M ◐	0612 1244 1919	3.7 0.9 3.6	**15** W ◐	0023 0651 1314 1943	1.8 3.4 1.4 3.3	**30** TH	0139 0757 1424 2056	1.5 3.7 1.1 3.5	**15** F	0025 0654 1313 1945	1.7 3.5 1.3 3.4	**30** SA	0204 0833 1449 2121	1.7 3.5 1.6 3.5	**15** M	0206 0839 1455 2122	1.8 3.4 1.6 3.5	**30** TU	0434 1100 1655 2305	1.6 3.5 1.9 3.6
			31 TU	0110 0721 1357 2030	1.6 3.7 1.0 3.5							**31** SU	0329 0952 1608 2228	1.7 3.4 1.7 3.5				**31** W	0525 1147 1739 2351	1.3 3.7 1.7 3.8

Chart Datum: 2·25 metres below Ordnance Datum (Newlyn)

》 **FREE** monthly updates from 《《
www.reedsalmanac.co.uk

SCOTLAND – ABERDEEN

TIME ZONE (UT)
For Summer Time add ONE hour in **non-shaded areas**

LAT 57°09'N   LONG 2°05'W

TIMES AND HEIGHTS OF HIGH AND LOW WATERS

YEAR 2005

SEPTEMBER

Time	m	Time	m
1 0605 1226 TH 1814	1.2 3.7 1.5	**16** 0542 1205 F 1801	0.8 4.2 1.1
2 0028 0639 F 1259 1846	3.9 1.0 3.8 1.3	**17** 0006 0628 SA 1250 1843	4.3 0.4 4.4 0.9
3 0100 0710 SA 1329 ● 1915	4.1 0.8 3.9 1.2	**18** 0049 0711 SU 1331 ○ 1923	4.5 0.2 4.5 0.7
4 0130 0740 SU 1357 1944	4.2 0.7 3.9 1.0	**19** 0130 0752 M 1410 2001	4.7 0.1 4.5 0.6
5 0159 0809 M 1426 2012	4.2 0.7 4.0 1.0	**20** 0211 0831 TU 1448 2039	4.7 0.2 4.4 0.7
6 0228 0838 TU 1455 2040	4.3 0.7 4.0 1.0	**21** 0252 0909 W 1526 2117	4.6 0.4 4.2 0.8
7 0258 0907 W 1525 2109	4.2 0.7 4.0 1.0	**22** 0335 0946 TH 1606 2157	4.4 0.8 4.0 1.0
8 0331 0938 TH 1558 2141	4.2 0.9 3.9 1.1	**23** 0421 1024 F 1648 2240	4.1 1.2 3.8 1.3
9 0406 1010 F 1635 2217	4.0 1.0 3.8 1.3	**24** 0512 1105 SA 1736 2334	3.8 1.6 3.6 1.6
10 0449 1050 SA 1720 2304	3.9 1.3 3.6 1.5	**25** 0614 1200 SU 1839 ◐	3.5 1.9 3.4
11 0543 1143 SU 1818 ◐	3.7 1.6 3.5	**26** 0051 0732 M 1324 1958	1.8 3.2 2.2 3.3
12 0012 0658 M 1304 1936	1.7 3.5 1.8 3.4	**27** 0243 0908 TU 1524 2126	1.9 3.2 2.2 3.4
13 0150 0830 TU 1445 2102	1.8 3.4 1.9 3.5	**28** 0410 1030 W 1631 2234	1.7 3.4 2.0 3.5
14 0334 1004 W 1614 2220	1.6 3.6 1.7 3.7	**29** 0458 1120 TH 1713 2321	1.4 3.6 1.8 3.7
15 0448 1113 TH 1714 2319	1.2 3.9 1.4 4.0	**30** 0536 1157 F 1747	1.2 3.7 1.5

OCTOBER

Time	m	Time	m
1 0609 1227 SA 1817	1.0 3.9 1.3	**16** 0607 1226 SU 1820	0.5 4.3 0.9
2 0029 0639 SU 1256 1846	4.1 0.9 4.0 1.2	**17** 0026 0647 M 1304 ○ 1858	4.5 0.4 4.4 0.8
3 0059 0708 M 1324 ● 1914	4.2 0.7 4.1 1.0	**18** 0107 0725 TU 1341 1936	4.6 0.4 4.4 0.7
4 0129 0736 TU 1353 1943	4.3 0.7 4.1 1.0	**19** 0147 0802 W 1417 2014	4.6 0.5 4.4 0.7
5 0159 0806 W 1422 2012	4.3 0.7 4.1 0.9	**20** 0229 0838 TH 1454 2053	4.5 0.8 4.2 0.9
6 0231 0836 TH 1454 2044	4.3 0.8 4.0 1.0	**21** 0312 0913 F 1531 2132	4.3 1.1 4.1 1.1
7 0306 0907 F 1528 2118	4.2 0.9 4.1 1.1	**22** 0357 0948 SA 1611 2215	4.0 1.4 3.9 1.3
8 0346 0942 SA 1606 2158	4.1 1.1 3.9 1.2	**23** 0448 1027 SU 1656 2307	3.7 1.7 3.7 1.6
9 0433 1025 SU 1653 2252	3.9 1.4 3.8 1.4	**24** 0547 1117 M 1755	3.4 2.0 3.5
10 0534 1126 M 1755 ◐	3.7 1.7 3.6	**25** 0016 0657 TU 1234 ◐ 1908	1.8 3.3 2.2 3.4
11 0008 0656 TU 1256 1918	1.6 3.5 2.0 3.5	**26** 0148 0818 W 1420 2030	1.8 3.2 2.3 3.4
12 0150 0829 W 1439 2045	1.6 3.5 1.9 3.6	**27** 0318 0940 TH 1543 2144	1.7 3.3 2.1 3.5
13 0325 0956 TH 1558 2201	1.6 3.7 1.8 3.8	**28** 0415 1035 F 1632 2237	1.5 3.5 1.9 3.7
14 0432 1058 F 1654 2258	1.4 4.0 1.4 4.3	**29** 0455 1115 SA 1709 2317	1.3 3.7 1.6 3.9
15 0523 1145 SA 1739 2344	0.7 4.2 1.1 4.3	**30** 0530 1148 SU 1742 2352	1.1 3.9 1.4 4.0
31 0602 1219 M 1813	1.0 4.0 1.2		

NOVEMBER

Time	m	Time	m
1 0025 0632 TU 1250 1844	4.2 0.9 4.2 1.1	**16** 0048 0701 W 1316 ○ 1917	4.4 0.8 4.3 0.9
2 0059 0704 W 1321 ● 1916	4.3 0.8 4.2 1.0	**17** 0130 0737 TH 1352 1957	4.4 0.9 4.3 0.9
3 0133 0736 TH 1354 1950	4.3 0.8 4.3 0.9	**18** 0212 0813 F 1428 2036	4.3 1.1 4.2 1.0
4 0210 0810 F 1428 2027	4.3 0.9 4.3 1.0	**19** 0256 0848 SA 1505 2116	4.1 1.3 4.1 1.1
5 0250 0847 SA 1506 2108	4.2 1.1 4.2 1.0	**20** 0340 0924 SU 1544 2158	3.9 1.5 4.0 1.3
6 0336 0929 SU 1548 2156	4.1 1.3 4.1 1.2	**21** 0428 1002 M 1627 2245	3.7 1.7 3.8 1.4
7 0430 1019 M 1639 2256	3.9 1.5 3.9 1.3	**22** 0520 1046 TU 1718 2340	3.5 1.9 3.6 1.6
8 0537 1124 TU 1744	3.7 1.8 3.7	**23** 0617 1143 W 1819 ◐	3.4 2.1 3.5
9 0013 0654 W 1249 ◐ 1902	1.4 3.6 1.9 3.7	**24** 0046 0718 TH 1301 1924	1.7 3.3 2.2 3.4
10 0140 0816 TH 1415 2021	1.4 3.6 1.9 3.7	**25** 0159 0826 F 1421 2033	1.7 3.3 2.1 3.5
11 0300 0933 F 1527 2133	1.2 3.8 1.7 3.9	**26** 0305 0930 SA 1528 2136	1.6 3.4 2.0 3.6
12 0405 1032 SA 1624 2232	1.0 3.9 1.5 4.1	**27** 0358 1022 SU 1618 2228	1.5 3.6 1.8 3.7
13 0457 1119 SU 1713 2321	0.9 4.1 1.3 4.2	**28** 0442 1104 M 1700 2312	1.3 3.8 1.6 3.8
14 0542 1201 M 1756	0.7 4.2 1.1	**29** 0521 1142 TU 1739 2352	1.2 3.9 1.4 3.9
15 0005 0622 TU 1239 1837	4.4 0.7 4.3 0.9	**30** 0558 1218 W 1816	1.1 4.1 1.1

DECEMBER

Time	m	Time	m
1 0032 0635 TH 1254 ● 1855	4.2 1.0 4.2 1.1	**16** 0122 0720 F 1336 1947	4.1 1.2 4.2 1.0
2 0114 0714 F 1331 1936	4.3 1.0 4.3 0.9	**17** 0204 0756 SA 1412 2026	4.0 1.3 4.2 1.0
3 0157 0755 SA 1410 2020	4.3 1.0 4.3 0.9	**18** 0246 0832 SU 1449 2104	4.0 1.4 4.1 1.1
4 0244 0839 SU 1452 2108	4.3 1.1 4.3 0.9	**19** 0326 0906 M 1525 2142	3.9 1.5 4.1 1.1
5 0335 0926 M 1539 2200	4.2 1.3 4.2 0.9	**20** 0407 0941 TU 1603 2221	3.8 1.6 4.0 1.2
6 0431 1018 TU 1632 2258	4.0 1.5 4.1 1.0	**21** 0449 1019 W 1645 2304	3.6 1.8 3.8 1.3
7 0533 1117 W 1732	3.9 1.6 4.0	**22** 0534 1101 TH 1732 2352	3.5 1.9 3.7 1.5
8 0004 0638 TH 1225 ◐ 1839	1.1 3.7 1.7 4.0	**23** 0623 1151 F 1824 ◐	3.4 1.9 3.6
9 0114 0747 F 1336 1948	1.2 3.7 1.7 3.9	**24** 0046 0717 SA 1254 1922	1.6 3.4 2.0 3.5
10 0223 0856 SA 1445 2058	1.2 3.7 1.6 3.9	**25** 0147 0816 SU 1404 2024	1.6 3.4 1.9 3.5
11 0329 0958 SU 1550 2203	1.2 3.8 1.6 3.9	**26** 0247 0918 M 1512 2129	1.6 3.5 1.8 3.6
12 0428 1051 M 1647 2300	1.1 3.9 1.4 4.0	**27** 0346 1016 TU 1613 2230	1.5 3.6 1.7 3.7
13 0518 1138 TU 1738 2350	1.1 4.0 1.3 4.1	**28** 0440 1105 W 1707 2324	1.4 3.8 1.5 3.9
14 0603 1219 W 1824	1.1 4.1 1.1	**29** 0530 1150 TH 1755	1.3 4.0 1.3
15 0037 0643 TH 1259 ○ 1906	4.1 1.2 4.2 1.1	**30** 0014 0616 F 1234 1842	4.0 1.2 4.1 1.1
		31 0103 0702 SA 1316 ● 1929	4.2 1.1 4.3 0.8

Chart Datum: 2·25 metres below Ordnance Datum (Newlyn)

》 **FREE** monthly updates from 《
www.reedsalmanac.co.uk

Chapter 5

289

TIDES

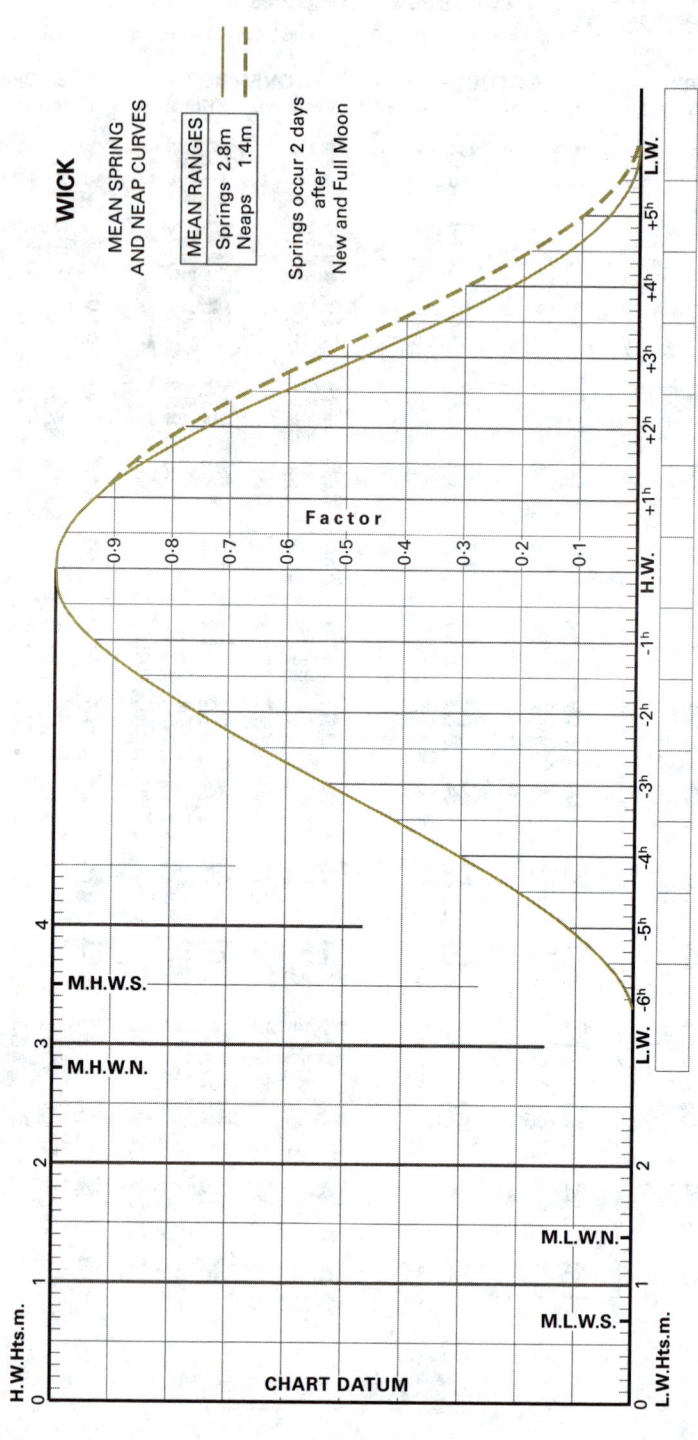

TIME ZONE (UT)
For Summer Time add ONE hour in **non-shaded areas**

SCOTLAND – WICK
LAT 58°26′N   LONG 3°05′W

YEAR 2005

TIMES AND HEIGHTS OF HIGH AND LOW WATERS

JANUARY		FEBRUARY		MARCH		APRIL	
Time m	Time m	Time m	Time m	Time m	Time m	Time m	Time m
1 0231 2.9 0758 1.4 SA 1433 3.2 2048 1.1	**16** 0341 3.1 0906 1.3 SU 1542 3.4 2206 1.0	**1** 0321 2.9 0847 1.3 TU 1527 3.1 2135 1.1	**16** 0432 2.7 1002 1.4 W 1652 2.8 ◐ 2257 1.5	**1** 0210 3.1 0744 0.9 TU 1419 3.3 2018 0.9	**16** 0257 2.9 0831 1.1 W 1517 2.9 2056 1.3	**1** 0310 2.9 0856 1.1 F 1551 2.8 2138 1.4	**16** 0350 2.6 1021 1.4 SA 1652 2.4 ◐ 2228 1.7
2 0314 2.9 0838 1.4 SU 1516 3.1 2135 1.2	**17** 0432 2.9 0958 1.4 M 1637 3.2 ◐ 2304 1.2	**2** 0410 2.8 0934 1.4 W 1621 3.0 ◐ 2236 1.2	**17** 0532 2.6 1139 1.6 TH 1805 2.6	**2** 0248 3.0 0820 1.1 W 1502 3.1 2058 1.0	**17** 0339 2.7 0920 1.3 TH 1611 2.7 ◐ 2143 1.6	**2** 0411 2.9 1028 1.2 SA 1717 2.7 ◐ 2335 1.5	**17** 0504 2.5 1204 1.4 SU 1821 2.4
3 0403 2.8 0925 1.5 M 1606 3.0 ◐ 2233 1.2	**18** 0528 2.8 1107 1.5 TU 1738 3.0	**3** 0511 2.8 1045 1.5 TH 1733 2.9	**18** 0028 1.6 0648 2.6 F 1332 1.6 1936 2.6	**3** 0333 2.9 0905 1.2 TH 1556 2.9 ◐ 2153 1.3	**18** 0436 2.6 1055 1.5 F 1727 2.5 2328 1.7	**3** 0535 2.7 1234 1.2 SU 1857 2.7	**18** 0030 1.7 0631 2.5 M 1328 1.2 1945 2.5
4 0501 2.8 1028 1.6 TU 1706 3.0 2342 1.2	**19** 0010 1.4 0629 2.8 W 1232 1.6 1846 2.9	**4** 0002 1.3 0623 2.8 F 1235 1.5 1857 2.9	**19** 0202 1.6 0809 2.7 SA 1444 1.4 2053 2.7	**4** 0432 2.8 1013 1.4 F 1713 2.8 2335 1.5	**19** 0556 2.5 1257 1.5 SA 1906 2.4	**4** 0115 1.5 0705 2.7 M 1359 0.9 2021 2.9	**19** 0151 1.6 0747 2.6 TU 1421 1.1 2040 2.6
5 0604 2.8 1153 1.6 W 1815 3.0	**20** 0122 1.4 0737 2.8 TH 1356 1.5 2001 2.8	**5** 0128 1.3 0739 2.9 SA 1406 1.3 2023 3.0	**20** 0300 1.5 0910 2.9 SU 1531 1.2 2145 2.8	**5** 0551 2.7 1228 1.4 SA 1851 2.7	**20** 0131 1.7 0727 2.6 SU 1416 1.3 2030 2.6	**5** 0225 1.3 0822 2.9 TU 1457 0.7 2120 3.1	**20** 0238 1.4 0841 2.8 W 1501 0.9 2121 2.8
6 0049 1.2 0708 2.9 TH 1311 1.5 1925 3.0	**21** 0225 1.5 0840 2.9 F 1458 1.4 2106 2.9	**6** 0241 1.2 0850 3.1 SU 1516 1.1 2135 3.2	**21** 0341 1.4 0956 3.0 M 1609 1.0 2226 3.0	**6** 0120 1.5 0718 2.8 SU 1407 1.2 2025 2.9	**21** 0237 1.6 0837 2.7 M 1504 1.1 2121 2.7	**6** 0315 1.1 0921 3.2 W 1544 0.5 2207 3.2	**21** 0313 1.2 0924 2.9 TH 1536 0.7 2156 2.9
7 0153 1.2 0811 3.0 F 1418 1.4 2035 3.2	**22** 0314 1.4 0932 3.0 SA 1546 1.3 2158 3.0	**7** 0340 1.1 0950 3.3 M 1611 0.8 2233 3.4	**22** 0416 1.3 1034 3.2 TU 1643 0.9 2301 3.1	**7** 0238 1.3 0838 3.0 M 1512 0.9 2133 3.1	**22** 0318 1.4 0926 2.9 TU 1541 0.9 2200 2.9	**7** 0355 0.9 1009 3.4 TH 1624 0.3 2249 3.3	**22** 0345 1.0 1002 3.1 F 1608 0.6 2230 3.1
8 0251 1.1 0909 3.2 SA 1518 1.1 2139 3.3	**23** 0354 1.4 1015 3.2 SU 1626 1.1 2241 3.1	**8** 0429 1.0 1043 3.5 TU 1700 0.5 ● 2325 3.5	**23** 0447 1.1 1109 3.3 W 1714 0.7 2334 3.2	**8** 0331 1.1 0939 3.2 TU 1602 0.6 2225 3.3	**23** 0351 1.2 1005 3.0 W 1614 0.8 2233 3.0	**8** 0432 0.7 1053 3.5 F 1701 0.2 ● 2328 3.4	**23** 0415 0.8 1038 3.2 SA 1639 0.5 2303 3.2
9 0344 1.0 1003 3.4 SU 1613 0.9 2236 3.5	**24** 0431 1.3 1054 3.3 M 1702 1.0 2319 3.1	**9** 0513 0.8 1130 3.7 W 1746 0.3 O	**24** 0516 1.0 1141 3.4 TH 1744 0.6 O	**9** 0416 0.9 1029 3.5 W 1646 0.3 ● 2311 3.5	**24** 0420 1.0 1039 3.2 TH 1644 0.6 2305 3.1	**9** 0508 0.6 1134 3.6 SA 1737 0.3	**24** 0447 0.7 1114 3.3 SU 1711 0.4 O 2337 3.3
10 0435 0.9 1053 3.6 M 1704 0.8 ● 2331 3.6	**25** 0504 1.2 1129 3.4 TU 1736 0.9 O 2354 3.2	**10** 0012 3.6 0554 0.8 TH 1216 3.8 1829 0.2	**25** 0005 3.2 0543 0.9 F 1213 3.4 1813 0.6	**10** 0456 0.7 1114 3.7 TH 1727 0.2 ● 2353 3.6	**25** 0448 0.9 1112 3.3 F 1714 0.5 O 2336 3.2	**10** 0004 3.4 0544 0.5 SU 1213 3.6 1810 0.4	**25** 0520 0.6 1150 3.4 M 1744 0.5
11 0523 0.9 1141 3.7 TU 1755 0.5	**26** 0535 1.2 1202 3.4 W 1808 0.8	**11** 0057 3.6 0634 0.7 F 1300 3.8 1911 0.3	**26** 0036 3.2 0611 0.8 SA 1243 3.5 1842 0.6	**11** 0533 0.6 1157 3.8 F 1806 0.2	**26** 0516 0.7 1144 3.5 SA 1743 0.5	**11** 0039 3.3 0619 0.6 M 1251 3.4 1843 0.6	**26** 0011 3.3 0555 0.6 TU 1229 3.4 1819 0.6
12 0023 3.6 0609 0.9 W 1229 3.8 1844 0.4	**27** 0027 3.2 0605 1.1 TH 1234 3.4 1839 0.8	**12** 0140 3.4 0712 0.8 SA 1342 3.7 1952 0.6	**27** 0106 3.2 0641 0.8 SU 1313 3.4 1912 0.6	**12** 0033 3.5 0609 0.6 SA 1238 3.8 1842 0.3	**27** 0007 3.3 0545 0.7 SU 1217 3.4 1812 0.5	**12** 0112 3.2 0655 0.7 TU 1328 3.3 1914 0.8	**27** 0047 3.3 0634 0.7 W 1310 3.3 1858 0.7
13 0114 3.6 0654 0.9 TH 1317 3.8 1933 0.4	**28** 0100 3.2 0634 1.1 F 1305 3.4 1910 0.8	**13** 0220 3.3 0749 1.0 SU 1424 3.6 2030 0.9	**28** 0137 3.2 0711 0.9 M 1344 3.4 1943 0.7	**13** 0110 3.4 0645 0.6 SU 1316 3.7 1917 0.5	**28** 0038 3.3 0616 0.6 M 1249 3.4 1844 0.5	**13** 0145 3.1 0730 0.8 W 1406 3.0 1944 1.1	**28** 0126 3.2 0716 0.7 TH 1356 3.1 1940 0.9
14 0203 3.4 0737 1.0 F 1404 3.7 2023 0.5	**29** 0132 3.1 0704 1.1 SA 1336 3.4 1941 0.8	**14** 0301 3.1 0826 1.0 M 1507 3.3 2109 1.0		**14** 0146 3.2 0719 0.7 M 1354 3.5 1949 0.7	**29** 0110 3.2 0649 0.7 TU 1324 3.3 1917 0.7	**14** 0219 3.0 0809 1.0 TH 1448 2.8 2017 1.3	**29** 0209 3.1 0805 0.8 F 1451 3.0 2031 1.2
15 0252 3.3 0821 1.1 SA 1452 3.6 2113 0.7	**30** 0205 3.1 0735 1.1 SU 1408 3.3 2014 0.9	**15** 0343 2.9 0906 1.2 TU 1554 3.1 2154 1.3		**15** 0220 3.1 0754 0.9 TU 1434 3.2 2021 1.0	**30** 0145 3.2 0725 0.8 W 1403 3.2 1953 0.9	**15** 0259 2.8 0858 1.2 F 1540 2.6 2100 1.5	**30** 0300 3.0 0912 1.0 SA 1559 2.8 2147 1.4
	31 0240 3.0 0809 1.2 M 1444 3.2 2051 1.0				**31** 0223 3.1 0805 0.9 TH 1450 3.0 2036 1.1		

Chart Datum: 1·71 metres below Ordnance Datum (Newlyn)

》 **FREE** monthly updates from 《
www.reedsalmanac.co.uk

TIDES

TIME ZONE (UT)
For Summer Time add ONE hour in **non-shaded areas**

SCOTLAND – WICK
LAT 58°26′N   LONG 3°05′W

TIMES AND HEIGHTS OF HIGH AND LOW WATERS

YEAR 2005

MAY

Day	Time	m	Day	Time	m
1 SU	0405 / 1053 / 1723 / ☽ 2328	2.8 / 1.0 / 2.7 / 1.5	**16** M	0418 / 1107 / 1727 / 2314	2.6 / 1.2 / 2.4 / 1.6
2 M	0526 / 1223 / 1848	2.8 / 0.9 / 2.7	**17** TU	0531 / 1219 / 1838	2.6 / 1.2 / 2.5
3 TU	0052 / 0645 / 1337 / 2000	1.4 / 2.8 / 0.8 / 2.8	**18** W	0035 / 0641 / 1321 / 1939	1.6 / 2.6 / 1.1 / 2.6
4 W	0157 / 0756 / 1433 / 2055	1.2 / 3.0 / 0.6 / 3.0	**19** TH	0137 / 0742 / 1410 / 2029	1.4 / 2.7 / 0.9 / 2.7
5 TH	0247 / 0855 / 1519 / 2141	1.0 / 3.1 / 0.5 / 3.1	**20** F	0224 / 0833 / 1451 / 2111	1.2 / 2.8 / 0.8 / 2.9
6 F	0329 / 0944 / 1558 / 2222	0.9 / 3.3 / 0.5 / 3.2	**21** SA	0304 / 0919 / 1528 / 2151	1.1 / 3.0 / 0.7 / 3.0
7 SA	0408 / 1029 / 1634 / 2300	0.7 / 3.3 / 0.5 / 3.2	**22** SU	0342 / 1002 / 1605 / 2229	0.9 / 3.1 / 0.6 / 3.2
8 SU	0445 / 1110 / 1708 / ● 2336	0.6 / 3.4 / 0.5 / 3.3	**23** M	0420 / 1045 / 1642 / 2308	0.8 / 3.3 / 0.6 / 3.3
9 M	0523 / 1150 / 1742	0.6 / 3.3 / 0.6	**24** TU	0500 / 1129 / 1722 / 2348	0.6 / 3.3 / 0.6 / 3.3
10 TU	0011 / 0600 / 1229 / 1815	3.3 / 0.6 / 3.2 / 0.8	**25** W	0542 / 1215 / 1804	0.6 / 3.3 / 0.7
11 W	0044 / 0638 / 1306 / 1847	3.2 / 0.7 / 3.1 / 1.0	**26** TH	0030 / 0628 / 1304 / 1849	3.4 / 0.5 / 3.3 / 0.8
12 TH	0118 / 0716 / 1345 / 1919	3.1 / 0.8 / 2.9 / 1.2	**27** F	0114 / 0719 / 1356 / 1939	3.3 / 0.6 / 3.2 / 1.0
13 F	0152 / 0756 / 1427 / 1954	3.0 / 1.0 / 2.7 / 1.3	**28** SA	0202 / 0817 / 1455 / 2035	2.8 / 0.6 / 3.0 / 1.2
14 SA	0231 / 0844 / 1516 / 2036	2.9 / 1.1 / 2.6 / 1.5	**29** SU	0257 / 0927 / 1600 / 2144	3.1 / 0.7 / 2.9 / 1.3
15 SU	0318 / 0948 / 1616 / 2139	2.7 / 1.2 / 2.5 / 1.6	**30** M	0400 / 1044 / 1710 / ☽ 2301	3.0 / 0.8 / 2.8 / 1.4
			31 TU	0509 / 1157 / 1819	2.9 / 0.8 / 2.7

JUNE

Day	Time	m	Day	Time	m
1 W	0013 / 0617 / 1304 / 1924	1.3 / 2.9 / 0.8 / 2.8	**16** TH	0535 / 1213 / 1831	2.7 / 1.1 / 2.6
2 TH	0119 / 0724 / 1402 / 2021	1.2 / 3.0 / 0.7 / 2.9	**17** F	0026 / 0637 / 1311 / 1929	1.4 / 2.7 / 1.0 / 2.7
3 F	0216 / 0825 / 1450 / 2111	1.1 / 3.0 / 0.7 / 3.0	**18** SA	0128 / 0738 / 1403 / 2023	1.3 / 2.8 / 0.9 / 2.8
4 SA	0304 / 0919 / 1531 / 2155	1.0 / 3.1 / 0.6 / 3.1	**19** SU	0223 / 0837 / 1451 / 2113	1.2 / 2.9 / 0.9 / 3.0
5 SU	0348 / 1008 / 1609 / 2235	0.9 / 3.1 / 0.8 / 3.1	**20** M	0312 / 0927 / 1537 / 2200	1.0 / 3.1 / 0.8 / 3.1
6 M	0429 / 1052 / 1645 / ● 2313	0.8 / 3.1 / 0.8 / 3.2	**21** TU	0400 / 1025 / 1623 / 2246	0.8 / 3.2 / 0.7 / 3.3
7 TU	0510 / 1133 / 1721 / 2349	0.8 / 3.1 / 0.9 / 3.2	**22** W	0449 / 1117 / 1710 / ○ 2332	0.7 / 3.3 / 0.7 / 3.4
8 W	0550 / 1213 / 1756	0.7 / 3.1 / 1.0	**23** TH	0538 / 1208 / 1757	0.5 / 3.4 / 0.8
9 TH	0024 / 0628 / 1251 / 1829	3.2 / 0.8 / 3.0 / 1.1	**24** F	0018 / 0628 / 1301 / 1845	3.5 / 0.4 / 3.4 / 0.8
10 F	0059 / 0706 / 1329 / 1903	3.1 / 0.8 / 2.9 / 1.2	**25** SA	0106 / 0721 / 1354 / 1934	3.5 / 0.4 / 3.3 / 0.9
11 SA	0134 / 0745 / 1409 / 1938	3.1 / 0.9 / 2.8 / 1.2	**26** SU	0156 / 0817 / 1448 / 2024	3.4 / 0.4 / 3.1 / 1.0
12 SU	0211 / 0826 / 1451 / 2015	3.0 / 0.9 / 2.7 / 1.3	**27** M	0248 / 0915 / 1544 / 2119	3.3 / 0.5 / 3.0 / 1.1
13 M	0251 / 0913 / 1538 / 2100	2.9 / 1.0 / 2.6 / 1.4	**28** TU	0343 / 1016 / 1641 / ☽ 2219	3.2 / 0.6 / 2.9 / 1.2
14 TU	0338 / 1008 / 1632 / 2158	2.8 / 1.1 / 2.5 / 1.5	**29** W	0442 / 1119 / 1739 / 2326	3.1 / 0.8 / 2.8 / 1.3
15 W	0433 / 1111 / 1731 / ☽ 2313	2.7 / 1.1 / 2.5 / 1.5	**30** TH	0543 / 1222 / 1840	3.0 / 0.9 / 2.7

JULY

Day	Time	m	Day	Time	m
1 F	0036 / 0648 / 1325 / 1942	1.3 / 2.9 / 1.0 / 2.8	**16** SA	0541 / 1213 / 1833	2.8 / 1.1 / 2.7
2 SA	0146 / 0756 / 1422 / 2040	1.3 / 2.9 / 1.1 / 2.8	**17** SU	0036 / 0652 / 1320 / 1938	1.4 / 2.8 / 1.1 / 2.8
3 SU	0247 / 0859 / 1510 / 2130	1.2 / 2.9 / 1.1 / 3.0	**18** M	0151 / 0805 / 1424 / 2041	1.3 / 2.9 / 1.1 / 2.9
4 M	0337 / 0953 / 1552 / 2215	1.0 / 2.9 / 1.1 / 3.1	**19** TU	0256 / 0914 / 1521 / 2138	1.1 / 3.0 / 1.0 / 3.1
5 TU	0422 / 1040 / 1630 / 2256	0.9 / 3.0 / 1.1 / 3.2	**20** W	0353 / 1015 / 1613 / 2230	0.9 / 3.2 / 0.9 / 3.3
6 W	0502 / 1122 / 1707 / ● 2333	0.9 / 3.0 / 1.1 / 3.2	**21** TH	0444 / 1109 / 1702 / ○ 2319	0.6 / 3.4 / 0.8 / 3.5
7 TH	0540 / 1201 / 1741	0.8 / 3.1 / 1.1	**22** F	0534 / 1201 / 1748	0.4 / 3.5 / 0.8
8 F	0009 / 0616 / 1238 / 1814	3.3 / 0.8 / 3.1 / 1.1	**23** SA	0007 / 0622 / 1252 / 1833	3.6 / 0.2 / 3.5 / 0.7
9 SA	0043 / 0651 / 1313 / 1846	3.2 / 0.7 / 3.0 / 1.1	**24** SU	0055 / 0710 / 1340 / 1916	3.7 / 0.2 / 3.4 / 0.8
10 SU	0116 / 0725 / 1347 / 1918	3.2 / 0.7 / 2.9 / 1.1	**25** M	0141 / 0758 / 1428 / 1959	3.7 / 0.3 / 3.3 / 0.9
11 M	0150 / 0759 / 1423 / 1950	3.1 / 0.7 / 2.9 / 1.1	**26** TU	0228 / 0846 / 1515 / 2043	3.6 / 0.4 / 3.1 / 1.0
12 TU	0224 / 0835 / 1500 / 2025	3.1 / 0.8 / 2.8 / 1.2	**27** W	0317 / 0936 / 1603 / 2132	3.4 / 0.7 / 2.9 / 1.1
13 W	0302 / 0915 / 1543 / 2106	3.0 / 0.9 / 2.7 / 1.3	**28** TH	0409 / 1031 / 1655 / ☽ 2234	3.2 / 0.9 / 2.8 / 1.3
14 TH	0345 / 1003 / 1632 / ● 2157	3.0 / 1.0 / 2.7 / 1.4	**29** F	0507 / 1133 / 1754 / 2355	3.0 / 1.2 / 2.7 / 1.4
15 F	0437 / 1104 / 1730 / 2310	2.9 / 1.1 / 2.6 / 1.5	**30** SA	0614 / 1245 / 1901	2.8 / 1.3 / 2.7
			31 SU	0125 / 0732 / 1359 / 2011	1.4 / 2.7 / 1.4 / 2.8

AUGUST

Day	Time	m	Day	Time	m
1 M	0239 / 0846 / 1456 / 2111	1.3 / 2.7 / 1.4 / 2.9	**16** TU	0138 / 0752 / 1413 / 2019	1.3 / 2.8 / 1.3 / 2.9
2 TU	0331 / 0944 / 1541 / 2159	1.1 / 2.8 / 1.3 / 3.1	**17** W	0252 / 0909 / 1515 / 2122	1.1 / 3.0 / 1.1 / 3.1
3 W	0413 / 1030 / 1618 / 2240	1.0 / 2.9 / 1.2 / 3.2	**18** TH	0348 / 1009 / 1605 / 2216	0.8 / 3.2 / 1.0 / 3.4
4 TH	0450 / 1109 / 1652 / 2317	0.9 / 3.0 / 1.2 / 3.3	**19** F	0436 / 1101 / 1650 / ○ 2305	0.5 / 3.4 / 0.9 / 3.6
5 F	0524 / 1145 / 1724 / ● 2351	0.8 / 3.1 / 1.1 / 3.3	**20** SA	0521 / 1148 / 1732 / 2351	0.2 / 3.6 / 0.7 / 3.8
6 SA	0557 / 1218 / 1754	0.7 / 3.1 / 1.0	**21** SU	0605 / 1233 / 1812	0.1 / 3.7 / 0.6
7 SU	0023 / 0627 / 1250 / 1823	3.3 / 0.6 / 3.1 / 1.0	**22** M	0035 / 0647 / 1316 / 1850	3.8 / 0.1 / 3.7 / 0.6
8 M	0054 / 0657 / 1321 / 1852	3.3 / 0.6 / 3.1 / 1.0	**23** TU	0119 / 0728 / 1358 / 1929	3.8 / 0.3 / 3.5 / 0.7
9 TU	0124 / 0727 / 1352 / 1921	3.3 / 0.7 / 3.0 / 1.0	**24** W	0202 / 0808 / 1439 / 2007	3.7 / 0.5 / 3.3 / 0.9
10 W	0155 / 0758 / 1424 / 1953	3.2 / 0.8 / 2.9 / 1.1	**25** TH	0246 / 0848 / 1521 / 2050	3.4 / 0.8 / 3.0 / 1.1
11 TH	0228 / 0831 / 1501 / 2028	3.1 / 0.9 / 2.8 / 1.2	**26** F	0334 / 0933 / 1609 / ☽ 2146	3.2 / 1.2 / 2.8 / 1.3
12 F	0307 / 0909 / 1544 / 2110	3.0 / 1.0 / 2.7 / 1.3	**27** SA	0431 / 1033 / 1707 / 2321	2.9 / 1.5 / 2.7 / 1.5
13 SA	0355 / 1000 / 1639 / ☽ 2210	2.9 / 1.2 / 2.7 / 1.4	**28** SU	0544 / 1202 / 1821	2.7 / 1.7 / 2.7
14 SU	0500 / 1120 / 1748 / ☽ 2359	2.7 / 1.3 / 2.7 / 1.5	**29** M	0111 / 0714 / 1341 / 1943	1.5 / 2.7 / 1.5 / 2.7
15 M	0623 / 1253 / 1904	2.7 / 1.4 / 2.8	**30** TU	0228 / 0837 / 1444 / 2049	1.4 / 2.9 / 1.3 / 2.9
			31 W	0317 / 0931 / 1526 / 2138	1.2 / 2.8 / 1.4 / 3.1

Chart Datum: 1·71 metres below Ordnance Datum (Newlyn)

》》 **FREE** monthly updates from 《《
www.reedsalmanac.co.uk

SCOTLAND – WICK

TIME ZONE (UT)
For Summer Time add ONE hour in **non-shaded areas**

LAT 58°26'N LONG 3°05'W

TIMES AND HEIGHTS OF HIGH AND LOW WATERS

YEAR 2005

	SEPTEMBER			OCTOBER			NOVEMBER			DECEMBER	
	Time m	Time m		Time m	Time m		Time m	Time m		Time m	Time m
1 TH	0355 1.0 1013 3.0 1601 1.3 2218 3.3	**16** F	0335 0.6 0958 3.3 1550 1.0 2200 3.5	**1** SA	0358 0.9 1018 3.1 1603 1.2 2222 3.3	**16** SU	0357 0.4 1021 3.5 1606 0.8 2223 3.7	**1** TU	0421 0.8 1045 3.4 1629 1.0 2254 3.5	**16** W	0447 0.7 1113 3.5 1702 0.8 ○ 2328 3.6	**1** TH	0423 0.9 1048 3.5 1642 1.0 ● 2309 3.5	**16** F	0505 1.1 1132 3.5 1735 0.9 2358 3.3
2 F	0428 0.8 1048 3.1 1631 1.1 2253 3.3	**17** SA	0420 0.4 1044 3.5 1630 0.8 2246 3.7	**2** SU	0428 0.7 1049 3.2 1631 1.0 2255 3.4	**17** M	0435 0.4 1101 3.6 1643 0.7 ○ 2306 3.8	**2** W	0452 0.7 1117 3.4 1701 0.9 ● 2330 3.5	**17** TH	0522 0.8 1150 3.5 1743 0.8	**2** F	0501 0.9 1127 3.5 1722 0.9 2353 3.5	**17** SA	0542 1.2 1209 3.5 1815 0.9
3 SA	0459 0.7 1121 3.1 1700 1.0 ● 2326 3.4	**18** SU	0501 0.2 1127 3.6 1708 0.7 ○ 2330 3.9	**3** M	0456 0.6 1119 3.3 1659 0.9 ● 2326 3.5	**18** TU	0512 0.4 1139 3.6 1721 0.7 2348 3.8	**3** TH	0523 0.7 1150 3.5 1735 0.8	**18** F	0009 3.5 0557 1.0 1226 3.5 1823 0.9	**3** SA	0541 0.9 1207 3.6 1806 0.8	**18** SU	0038 3.2 0616 1.3 1246 3.4 1854 1.0
4 SU	0529 0.6 1151 3.2 1728 0.9 2357 3.4	**19** M	0540 0.2 1208 3.6 1746 0.6	**4** TU	0524 0.6 1149 3.3 1728 0.8 2357 3.5	**19** W	0548 0.5 1216 3.5 1759 0.7	**4** F	0007 3.5 0556 0.8 1225 3.5 1812 0.9	**19** SA	0050 3.3 0632 1.2 1302 3.4 1903 1.0	**4** SU	0039 3.5 0623 1.0 1250 3.5 1853 0.8	**19** M	0117 3.1 0650 1.3 1321 3.4 1932 1.0
5 M	0558 0.6 1221 3.2 1756 0.9	**20** TU	0012 3.9 0618 0.2 1247 3.5 1823 0.6	**5** W	0553 0.6 1218 3.4 1757 0.8	**20** TH	0028 3.7 0623 0.7 1252 3.5 1837 0.8	**5** SA	0047 3.4 0632 1.0 1302 3.4 1852 0.9	**20** SU	0131 3.2 0706 1.4 1339 3.3 1946 1.1	**5** M	0129 3.4 0709 1.2 1335 3.5 1946 0.8	**20** TU	0155 3.0 0723 1.4 1357 3.3 2011 1.1
6 TU	0026 3.4 0625 0.6 1250 3.2 1824 0.9	**21** W	0053 3.8 0655 0.4 1324 3.4 1900 0.7	**6** TH	0029 3.5 0622 0.7 1250 3.3 1829 0.9	**21** F	0109 3.5 0656 1.0 1327 3.3 1915 1.0	**6** SU	0131 3.3 0713 1.1 1343 3.3 1939 1.0	**21** M	0214 3.0 0740 1.5 1418 3.1 2033 1.3	**6** TU	0223 3.3 0800 1.3 1426 3.4 2048 0.9	**21** W	0235 2.9 0758 1.5 1436 3.2 2052 1.2
7 W	0056 3.4 0654 0.6 1320 3.2 1853 0.9	**22** TH	0134 3.6 0730 0.7 1401 3.2 1937 0.9	**7** F	0103 3.4 0653 0.8 1322 3.3 1903 0.9	**22** SA	0150 3.2 0729 1.2 1404 3.2 1958 1.2	**7** M	0222 3.1 0800 1.4 1431 3.2 2039 1.1	**22** TU	0303 2.8 0821 1.7 1505 3.0 2133 1.4	**7** W	0324 3.1 0859 1.4 1523 3.3 2200 1.0	**22** TH	0319 2.8 0836 1.6 1518 3.0 2141 1.3
8 TH	0126 3.4 0723 0.8 1351 3.1 1924 1.0	**23** F	0215 3.4 0804 1.0 1439 3.1 2018 1.1	**8** SA	0140 3.3 0727 1.0 1359 3.2 1941 1.1	**23** SU	0235 3.0 0803 1.5 1445 3.0 2051 1.4	**8** TU	0324 3.0 0903 1.6 1531 3.1 2210 1.2	**23** W	0402 2.7 0915 1.8 1603 2.9 ○ 2247 1.4	**8** TH	0430 3.0 1011 1.5 1629 3.2 ○ 2314 1.0	**23** F	0408 2.7 0923 1.6 1609 2.9 ○ 2240 1.3
9 F	0159 3.2 0755 0.9 1426 3.0 1959 1.1	**24** SA	0301 3.1 0840 1.4 1523 2.9 2111 1.4	**9** SU	0224 3.1 0807 1.2 1443 3.1 2029 1.2	**24** M	0330 2.8 0846 1.7 1539 2.9 2216 1.5	**9** W	0444 2.9 1041 1.7 1647 3.0 ○ 2344 1.2	**24** TH	0509 2.6 1041 1.8 1713 2.8	**9** F	0538 2.9 1127 1.6 1737 3.2	**24** SA	0504 2.7 1028 1.7 1708 2.9 2345 1.4
10 SA	0239 3.1 0831 1.1 1508 2.9 2041 1.3	**25** SU	0358 2.8 0929 1.6 1621 2.8 ○ 2251 1.5	**10** M	0321 2.9 0901 1.5 1540 2.9 ○ 2147 1.4	**25** TU	0442 2.6 1011 1.9 1653 2.8 ○ 2353 1.5	**10** TH	0607 2.9 1210 1.6 1807 3.0	**25** F	0000 1.4 0618 2.6 1209 1.8 1822 2.8	**10** SA	0024 1.0 0644 3.0 1238 1.5 1844 3.2	**25** SU	0605 2.7 1151 1.7 1812 2.9
11 SU	0329 2.9 0919 1.3 1602 2.8 ○ 2141 1.4	**26** M	0515 2.6 1114 1.8 1739 2.7	**11** TU	0440 2.8 1037 1.7 1659 2.8 2359 1.3	**26** W	0608 2.6 1209 1.9 1816 2.7	**11** F	0100 1.0 0722 3.0 1320 1.5 1918 3.2	**26** SA	0103 1.3 0721 2.7 1316 1.7 1923 2.9	**11** SU	0127 1.0 0746 3.1 1341 1.4 1949 3.2	**26** M	0047 1.3 0705 2.8 1305 1.7 1915 2.9
12 M	0440 2.8 1048 1.5 1716 2.8 2355 1.5	**27** TU	0046 1.5 0651 2.5 1314 1.8 1907 2.7	**12** W	0619 2.8 1237 1.6 1828 2.9	**27** TH	0113 1.4 0728 2.6 1333 1.8 1929 2.8	**12** SA	0201 0.8 0822 3.1 1415 1.3 2020 3.3	**27** SU	0154 1.2 0812 2.9 1407 1.5 2015 3.0	**12** M	0222 1.0 0841 3.1 1437 1.3 2049 3.2	**27** TU	0144 1.3 0802 2.9 1406 1.5 2017 3.0
13 TU	0616 2.7 1245 1.5 1843 2.8	**28** W	0202 1.4 0815 2.7 1420 1.7 2018 2.9	**13** TH	0125 1.1 0746 2.9 1351 1.5 1945 3.1	**28** F	0207 1.3 0824 2.8 1421 1.6 2024 3.0	**13** SU	0250 0.7 0911 3.3 1501 1.1 2113 3.5	**28** M	0235 1.0 0855 3.0 1449 1.4 2102 3.2	**13** TU	0308 1.1 0929 3.2 1526 1.1 2143 3.3	**28** W	0234 1.2 0853 3.1 1458 1.4 2114 3.1
14 W	0137 1.3 0752 2.9 1408 1.4 2004 3.0	**29** TH	0249 1.2 0906 2.8 1501 1.5 2108 3.0	**14** F	0227 0.8 0849 3.1 1444 1.2 2047 3.3	**29** SA	0246 1.1 0905 2.9 1457 1.4 2107 3.1	**14** M	0332 0.7 0955 3.4 1542 1.0 2201 3.6	**29** TU	0313 0.9 0933 3.2 1527 1.2 2144 3.3	**14** W	0349 1.1 1013 3.3 1611 1.0 2231 3.3	**29** TH	0320 1.2 0941 3.2 1546 1.2 2206 3.3
15 TH	0245 1.0 0904 3.1 1505 1.2 2108 3.2	**30** F	0326 1.0 0944 3.0 1534 1.3 2147 3.2	**15** SA	0315 0.6 0938 3.4 1527 1.0 2138 3.5	**30** SU	0320 0.9 0940 3.1 1529 1.2 2144 3.3	**15** TU	0410 0.7 1035 3.5 1622 0.9 2245 3.6	**30** W	0348 0.9 1011 3.3 1604 1.1 2226 3.4	**15** TH	0428 1.1 1054 3.4 1654 1.0 ○ 2316 3.3	**30** F	0405 1.1 1026 3.4 1632 1.0 2256 3.4
						31 M	0351 0.8 1013 3.2 1559 1.1 2220 3.4							**31** SA	0449 1.0 1110 3.5 1718 0.8 ● 2345 3.5

Chart Datum: 1·71 metres below Ordnance Datum (Newlyn)

》》 **FREE** monthly updates from 《《
www.reedsalmanac.co.uk

TIDES

LERWICK
MEAN SPRING AND NEAP CURVES

MEAN RANGES
Springs 1.6m
Neaps 0.8m

Springs occur 1 day after New and Full Moon

TIME ZONE (UT)
For Summer Time add ONE hour in **non-shaded areas**

SCOTLAND – LERWICK
LAT 60°09′N   LONG 1°08′W
TIMES AND HEIGHTS OF HIGH AND LOW WATERS

YEAR 2005

	JANUARY			FEBRUARY			MARCH			APRIL	
	Time m	Time m		Time m	Time m		Time m	Time m		Time m	Time m
1	0213 1.8 0750 1.0 SA 1412 2.0 2039 0.8	**16** 0316 1.9 0853 0.9 SU 1518 2.1 2142 0.7	**1**	0301 1.8 0843 0.9 TU 1508 1.9 2129 0.8	**16** 0402 1.7 1000 0.9 W 1623 1.7 ☾ 2244 1.0	**1**	0145 1.9 0737 0.6 TU 1356 2.0 2011 0.6	**16** 0230 1.8 0827 0.7 W 1453 1.8 2048 0.9	**1**	0240 1.8 0900 0.7 F 1532 1.7 2133 0.9	**16** 0319 1.6 1017 0.9 SA 1617 1.4 ☾ 2228 1.1
2	0256 1.7 0831 1.0 SU 1456 1.9 2125 0.8	**17** 0405 1.8 0946 1.0 M 1611 1.9 ☾ 2243 0.8	**2**	0351 1.7 0935 1.0 W 1604 1.8 ☾ 2227 0.8	**17** 0500 1.6 1141 1.0 TH 1742 1.6	**2**	0222 1.8 0818 0.7 W 1439 1.9 2055 0.7	**17** 0310 1.7 0920 0.9 TH 1543 1.6 ☾ 2136 1.0	**2**	0343 1.7 1020 0.8 SA 1656 1.6 ☾ 2310 1.0	**17** 0422 1.5 1148 0.9 SU 1810 1.4
3	0344 1.7 0921 1.1 M 1547 1.9 ☾ 2218 0.8	**18** 0500 1.7 1056 1.0 TU 1714 1.8 2358 0.9	**3**	0450 1.7 1047 1.0 TH 1715 1.8 2345 0.9	**18** 0024 1.1 0628 1.6 F 1321 1.0 1925 1.6	**3**	0308 1.8 0909 0.8 TH 1537 1.8 ☾ 2151 0.9	**18** 0400 1.6 1055 1.0 F 1653 1.5 2326 1.1	**3**	0506 1.6 1216 0.7 SU 1844 1.6	**18** 0017 1.1 0609 1.5 M 1303 0.8 1933 1.5
4	0439 1.7 1023 1.1 TU 1647 1.9 2323 0.9	**19** 0606 1.7 1227 1.0 W 1831 1.7	**4**	0602 1.7 1229 1.0 F 1842 1.8	**19** 0148 1.1 0749 1.7 SA 1429 0.9 2039 1.6	**4**	0408 1.7 1022 0.9 F 1655 1.7 2316 1.0	**19** 0515 1.5 1244 0.9 SA 1903 1.4	**4**	0055 1.0 0647 1.6 M 1337 0.6 2004 1.7	**19** 0132 1.0 0734 1.5 TU 1359 0.7 2020 1.5
5	0541 1.7 1146 1.1 W 1756 1.9	**20** 0110 1.0 0714 1.7 TH 1344 1.0 1945 1.7	**5**	0110 0.9 0721 1.8 SA 1352 0.9 2006 1.8	**20** 0245 1.0 0847 1.8 SU 1517 0.8 2127 1.7	**5**	0526 1.6 1217 0.9 SA 1836 1.6	**20** 0115 1.1 0715 1.6 SU 1359 0.9 2018 1.5	**5**	0202 0.8 0803 1.8 TU 1435 0.4 2059 1.8	**20** 0220 0.9 0822 1.6 W 1439 0.6 2057 1.7
6	0032 0.8 0648 1.8 TH 1305 1.0 1910 1.9	**21** 0210 1.0 0815 1.8 F 1443 0.9 2048 1.8	**6**	0220 0.9 0829 1.9 SU 1456 0.7 2115 2.0	**21** 0327 1.0 0932 1.9 M 1555 0.7 2205 1.8	**6**	0102 1.0 0701 1.7 SU 1347 0.8 2009 1.7	**21** 0220 1.0 0818 1.7 M 1448 0.7 2102 1.6	**6**	0253 0.7 0859 1.9 W 1521 0.3 2145 1.9	**21** 0255 0.8 0902 1.7 TH 1513 0.5 2130 1.8
7	0135 0.8 0751 1.9 F 1407 0.9 2017 2.0	**22** 0258 1.0 0906 1.9 SA 1530 0.9 2139 1.8	**7**	0319 0.8 0927 2.1 M 1550 0.5 2213 2.1	**22** 0402 0.9 1010 2.0 TU 1627 0.6 2240 1.9	**7**	0216 0.9 0819 1.8 M 1450 0.6 2114 1.9	**22** 0302 0.9 0904 1.8 TU 1524 0.6 2137 1.7	**7**	0335 0.5 0946 2.1 TH 1602 0.2 2226 2.0	**22** 0327 0.6 0937 1.9 F 1546 0.4 2203 1.9
8	0232 0.8 0846 2.0 SA 1503 0.8 2117 2.1	**23** 0340 1.0 0950 2.0 SU 1611 0.8 2221 1.9	**8**	0409 0.7 1018 2.2 TU 1639 0.3 ● 2305 2.2	**23** 0432 0.8 1045 2.0 W 1657 0.5 2313 1.9	**8**	0311 0.7 0917 2.0 TU 1540 0.4 2205 2.0	**23** 0335 0.8 0941 1.9 W 1555 0.5 2210 1.8	**8**	0413 0.4 1029 2.1 F 1640 0.1 ● 2303 2.0	**23** 0359 0.5 1012 2.0 SA 1619 0.3 2235 1.9
9	0325 0.7 0937 2.2 SU 1555 0.6 2215 2.2	**24** 0417 0.9 1029 2.1 M 1646 0.7 2259 1.9	**9**	0454 0.6 1107 2.3 W 1724 0.2 2352 2.2	**24** 0501 0.7 1117 2.1 TH 1726 0.4 ○ 2343 2.0	**9**	0356 0.6 1006 2.1 W 1624 0.2 ● 2250 2.1	**24** 0404 0.7 1015 1.9 TH 1624 0.4 2241 1.9	**9**	0451 0.3 1109 2.2 SA 1717 0.2 2338 2.0	**24** 0433 0.4 1047 2.0 SU 1653 0.3 ○ 2308 2.0
10	0416 0.7 1027 2.3 M 1646 0.5 ● 2311 2.2	**25** 0450 0.8 1105 2.1 TU 1720 0.6 ○ 2334 2.0	**10**	0536 0.5 1152 2.4 TH 1807 0.1	**25** 0529 0.6 1147 2.1 F 1756 0.4	**10**	0436 0.5 1051 2.3 TH 1705 0.1 ● 2331 2.1	**25** 0432 0.6 1047 2.0 F 1654 0.3 ○ 2311 1.9	**10**	0528 0.3 1148 2.2 SU 1753 0.3	**25** 0508 0.4 1124 2.1 M 1729 0.3 2342 2.0
11	0504 0.7 1116 2.3 TU 1735 0.3	**26** 0521 0.8 1138 2.1 W 1752 0.6	**11**	0036 2.2 0616 0.4 F 1236 2.4 1849 0.2		**11**	0514 0.4 1133 2.3 F 1744 0.1	**26** 0502 0.5 1118 2.0 SA 1725 0.3 2341 1.9	**11**	0011 2.0 0605 0.3 M 1226 2.1 1827 0.4	**26** 0545 0.4 1202 2.1 TU 1806 0.4
12	0004 2.3 0551 0.7 W 1205 2.4 1823 0.3	**27** 0007 2.0 0551 0.8 TH 1210 2.2 1823 0.5	**12**	0117 2.1 0656 0.5 SA 1319 2.3 1931 0.3	**27** 0042 2.0 0629 0.6 SU 1248 2.1 1859 0.4	**12**	0009 2.1 0552 0.3 SA 1213 2.3 1821 0.2	**27** 0533 0.4 1150 2.1 SU 1757 0.3	**12**	0044 2.0 0643 0.4 TU 1304 2.0 1901 0.6	**27** 0017 2.0 0625 0.4 W 1245 2.0 1846 0.5
13	0055 2.2 0636 0.8 TH 1253 2.4 1911 0.3	**28** 0040 2.0 0622 0.8 F 1240 2.1 1855 0.5	**13**	0157 2.0 0736 0.6 SU 1401 2.2 2012 0.5	**28** 0112 1.9 0702 0.6 M 1320 2.1 1933 0.5	**13**	0046 2.0 0630 0.4 SU 1252 2.2 1859 0.3	**28** 0011 2.0 0606 0.4 M 1223 2.1 1830 0.3	**13**	0117 1.9 0721 0.6 W 1343 1.8 1934 0.7	**28** 0054 2.0 0709 0.4 TH 1333 1.9 1930 0.6
14	0143 2.1 0721 0.9 F 1341 2.3 1959 0.4	**29** 0111 2.0 0653 0.8 SA 1312 2.1 1929 0.5	**14**	0236 1.9 0817 0.7 M 1443 2.0 2055 0.7		**14**	0120 2.0 0708 0.5 M 1331 2.1 1936 0.5	**29** 0042 2.0 0641 0.4 TU 1258 2.0 1906 0.4	**14**	0151 1.8 0803 0.7 TH 1426 1.7 2007 0.9	**29** 0137 1.9 0800 0.5 F 1431 1.8 2022 0.8
15	0229 2.0 0806 0.9 SA 1429 2.2 2049 0.5	**30** 0144 1.9 0726 0.8 SU 1346 2.1 2005 0.6	**15**	0317 1.8 0901 0.8 TU 1529 1.9 2141 0.9		**15**	0154 1.9 0746 0.6 TU 1410 1.9 2011 0.7	**30** 0115 1.9 0719 0.5 W 1338 2.0 1946 0.6	**15**	0230 1.8 0856 0.8 F 1515 1.5 2050 1.0	**30** 0229 1.8 0903 0.6 SA 1540 1.6 2129 0.9
		31 0220 1.8 0802 0.8 M 1423 2.0 2044 0.7						**31** 0153 1.9 0804 0.6 TH 1427 1.8 2032 0.7			

Chart Datum: 1·22 metres below Ordnance Datum (Local)

》 **FREE** monthly updates from 《
www.reedsalmanac.co.uk

TIDES

TIME ZONE (UT)
For Summer Time add ONE hour in **non-shaded areas**

SCOTLAND – LERWICK
LAT 60°09'N   LONG 1°08'W
TIMES AND HEIGHTS OF HIGH AND LOW WATERS

YEAR 2005

MAY

	Time	m		Time	m
1	0337	1.7	**16**	0346	1.6
	1028	0.6		1051	0.8
SU	1700	0.6	M	1652	1.3
☾	2304	1.0	☽	2310	1.0
2	0457	1.6	**17**	0452	1.5
	1202	0.6		1157	0.7
M	1831	1.6	TU	1820	1.4
3	0032	0.9	**18**	0024	1.0
	0627	1.7		0617	1.5
TU	1314	0.5	W	1256	0.7
	1939	1.7		1922	1.5
4	0136	0.8	**19**	0122	0.9
	0737	1.8		0725	1.6
W	1410	0.4	TH	1344	0.6
	2031	1.7		2006	1.6
5	0227	0.7	**20**	0208	0.8
	0833	1.9		0813	1.7
TH	1456	0.3	F	1426	0.5
	2116	1.8		2045	1.7
6	0310	0.5	**21**	0247	0.7
	0921	2.0		0855	1.8
F	1537	0.3	SA	1506	0.4
	2156	1.9		2122	1.8
7	0350	0.4	**22**	0326	0.6
	1005	2.0		0937	1.9
SA	1614	0.3	SU	1545	0.4
	2233	1.9		2200	1.9
8	0428	0.4	**23**	0405	0.5
	1046	2.0		1020	2.0
SU	1650	0.4	M	1625	0.4
●	2307	2.0	○	2239	2.0
9	0507	0.4	**24**	0446	0.4
	1126	2.0		1104	2.0
M	1725	0.4	TU	1706	0.4
	2341	2.0		2318	2.1
10	0545	0.4	**25**	0530	0.3
	1204	1.9		1151	2.0
TU	1800	0.6	W	1749	0.5
				2359	2.1
11	0014	2.0	**26**	0616	0.3
	0624	0.4		1241	2.0
W	1244	1.8	TH	1835	0.6
	1833	0.7			
12	0049	1.9	**27**	0043	2.0
	0704	0.5		0705	0.3
TH	1324	1.7	F	1337	1.9
	1906	0.8		1924	0.7
13	0124	1.8	**28**	0133	2.0
	0747	0.6		0800	0.4
F	1406	1.6	SA	1436	1.8
	1942	0.9		2018	0.8
14	0204	1.7	**29**	0230	1.9
	0837	0.7		0903	0.4
SA	1454	1.5	SU	1538	1.7
	2027	1.0		2121	0.9
15	0251	1.7	**30**	0333	1.8
	0939	0.7		1016	0.5
SU	1547	1.5	M	1645	1.6
	2135	1.0	☽	2235	0.9

JUNE

	Time	m		Time	m
1	0557	1.7	**16**	0506	1.6
	1242	0.5		1153	0.7
W	1901	1.6	TH	1804	1.5
2	0101	0.8	**17**	0019	0.9
	0705	1.8		0613	1.6
TH	1341	0.5	F	1250	0.7
	1956	1.7		1906	1.6
3	0158	0.7	**18**	0118	0.8
	0805	1.8		0719	1.7
F	1429	0.5	SA	1341	0.6
	2043	1.8		1958	1.7
4	0246	0.6	**19**	0209	0.8
	0857	1.8		0816	1.8
SA	1511	0.5	SU	1429	0.5
	2126	1.8		2045	1.8
5	0330	0.5	**20**	0257	0.6
	0944	1.9		0909	1.9
SU	1550	0.5	M	1517	0.5
	2206	1.9		2131	1.9
6	0411	0.5	**21**	0344	0.5
	1029	1.9		1000	2.0
M	1627	0.6	TU	1604	0.5
●	2243	1.9		2217	2.0
7	0452	0.5	**22**	0432	0.4
	1110	1.9		1052	2.0
TU	1704	0.6	W	1652	0.5
	2320	2.0	○	2303	2.1
8	0532	0.5	**23**	0521	0.3
	1151	1.8		1146	2.1
W	1740	0.7	TH	1739	0.5
	2355	2.0		2350	2.1
9	0612	0.5	**24**	0610	0.2
	1230	1.8		1240	2.0
TH	1815	0.8	F	1827	0.6
10	0030	1.9	**25**	0039	2.1
	0651	0.5		0701	0.2
F	1309	1.7	SA	1334	2.0
	1849	0.8		1915	0.6
11	0107	1.9	**26**	0130	2.1
	0731	0.6		0753	0.2
SA	1348	1.7	SU	1427	1.9
	1926	0.9		2005	0.7
12	0145	1.9	**27**	0223	2.0
	0814	0.6		0847	0.3
SU	1430	1.6	M	1520	1.8
	2006	0.9		2057	0.7
13	0227	1.7	**28**	0318	2.0
	0901	0.6		0947	0.4
M	1515	1.5	TU	1615	1.7
	2053	0.9	☽	2156	0.8
14	0315	1.7	**29**	0416	1.9
	0954	0.7		1053	0.5
TU	1605	1.5	W	1714	1.6
	2151	1.0	☽	2305	0.8
15	0407	1.6	**30**	0521	1.8
	1053	0.7		1204	0.6
W	1701	1.5	TH	1816	1.6
☾	2305	1.0			

JULY

	Time	m		Time	m
1	0023	0.8	**16**	0520	1.7
	0631	1.7		1153	0.8
F	1308	0.7	SA	1808	1.6
	1917	1.6			
2	0131	0.8	**17**	0028	0.9
	0738	1.7		0632	1.7
SA	1404	0.7	SU	1302	0.8
	2012	1.7		1915	1.7
3	0229	0.7	**18**	0138	0.8
	0838	1.7		0747	1.7
SU	1451	0.7	M	1403	0.7
	2102	1.8		2016	1.8
4	0319	0.7	**19**	0237	0.7
	0932	1.8		0852	1.8
M	1534	0.8	TU	1459	0.7
	2147	1.9		2110	1.9
5	0403	0.6	**20**	0332	0.5
	1019	1.8		0951	2.0
TU	1614	0.8	W	1553	0.6
	2228	1.9		2202	2.1
6	0444	0.6	**21**	0423	0.4
	1101	1.8		1047	2.1
W	1651	0.8	TH	1642	0.6
●	2306	2.0	○	2252	2.2
7	0523	0.5	**22**	0513	0.2
	1140	1.9		1140	2.1
TH	1727	0.8	F	1729	0.5
	2342	2.0		2341	2.2
8	0559	0.5	**23**	0600	0.1
	1217	1.8		1230	2.1
F	1801	0.8	SA	1814	0.5
9	0017	2.0	**24**	0029	2.3
	0634	0.5		0647	0.1
SA	1252	1.8	SU	1318	2.1
	1833	0.9		1857	0.5
10	0051	2.0	**25**	0117	2.3
	0709	0.5		0733	0.2
SU	1326	1.9	M	1404	2.0
	1905	0.8		1941	0.6
11	0124	1.9	**26**	0204	2.2
	0745	0.5		0820	0.3
M	1401	1.7	TU	1450	1.9
	1940	0.7		2027	0.6
12	0201	1.9	**27**	0253	2.1
	0822	0.6		0910	0.5
TU	1439	1.7	W	1537	1.7
	2017	0.9		2117	0.7
13	0240	1.9	**28**	0344	1.9
	0903	0.7		1006	0.6
W	1521	1.6	TH	1627	1.7
	2059	0.9	☽	2218	0.8
14	0326	1.7	**29**	0443	1.7
	0949	0.7		1115	0.8
TH	1609	1.6	F	1727	1.6
☽	2151	0.9		2346	0.9
15	0418	1.7	**30**	0556	1.7
	1045	0.7		1234	0.9
F	1704	1.6	SA	1838	1.6
	2301	0.9			
			31	0112	0.9
				0718	1.6
			SU	1343	0.9
				1946	1.7

AUGUST

	Time	m		Time	m
1	0220	0.8	**16**	0121	0.9
	0829	1.6		0734	1.7
M	1439	0.9	TU	1350	0.9
	2045	1.8		1956	1.8
2	0313	0.8	**17**	0228	0.7
	0925	1.7		0847	1.9
TU	1525	0.9	W	1451	0.8
	2133	1.9		2057	2.0
3	0356	0.7	**18**	0324	0.5
	1009	1.8		0946	2.0
W	1604	0.9	TH	1543	0.7
	2214	2.0		2151	2.1
4	0433	0.6	**19**	0414	0.3
	1048	1.8		1038	2.1
TH	1639	0.8	F	1629	0.6
	2252	2.0	○	2239	2.3
5	0507	0.5	**20**	0459	0.2
	1123	1.9		1126	2.1
F	1711	0.7	SA	1712	0.5
●	2326	2.1		2326	2.4
6	0539	0.5	**21**	0542	0.1
	1156	1.9		1210	2.2
SA	1740	0.7	SU	1753	0.6
	2358	2.1			
7	0610	0.4	**22**	0010	2.4
	1227	1.9		0624	0.1
SU	1810	0.7	M	1253	2.1
				1833	0.4
8	0028	2.1	**23**	0054	2.4
	0640	0.4		0706	0.2
M	1257	1.9	TU	1333	2.0
	1839	0.7		1914	0.5
9	0059	2.0	**24**	0138	2.3
	0712	0.5		0748	0.4
TU	1328	1.8	W	1413	1.9
	1911	0.7		1956	0.6
10	0130	2.0	**25**	0222	2.1
	0746	0.6		0831	0.6
W	1400	1.8	TH	1455	1.8
	1944	0.7		2041	0.7
11	0205	1.9	**26**	0310	1.9
	0822	0.6		0918	0.8
TH	1438	1.8	F	1540	1.7
	2023	0.7	☽	2139	0.9
12	0246	1.9	**27**	0405	1.7
	0903	0.7		1019	1.0
F	1522	1.7	SA	1635	1.7
	2109	0.9		2317	1.1
13	0337	1.8	**28**	0520	1.6
	0954	0.8		1159	1.1
SA	1617	1.7	SU	1756	1.6
☽	2213	1.0			
14	0442	1.7	**29**	0058	1.0
	1103	0.8		0706	1.6
SU	1722	1.7	M	1325	1.1
	2349	0.9		1924	1.7
15	0603	1.7	**30**	0209	0.9
	1234	0.9		0825	1.6
M	1841	1.7	TU	1426	1.1
				2027	1.8
			31	0259	0.8
				0913	1.7
			W	1510	1.0
				2114	1.9

Chart Datum: 1·22 metres below Ordnance Datum (Local)

》》 **FREE** monthly updates from 《《
www.reedsalmanac.co.uk

TIME ZONE (UT) For Summer Time add ONE hour in **non-shaded areas**

SCOTLAND – LERWICK
LAT 60°09'N   LONG 1°08'W
TIMES AND HEIGHTS OF HIGH AND LOW WATERS

YEAR 2005

SEPTEMBER				OCTOBER				NOVEMBER				DECEMBER			
Time	m	Time	m	Time	m	Time	m	Time	m	Time	m	Time	m	Time	m
1 0338 0951 TH 1546 2153	0.7 1.8 0.9 2.0	**16** 0312 0935 F 1528 2135	0.5 2.0 0.7 2.2	**1** 0339 0953 SA 1547 2158	0.6 1.9 0.8 2.1	**16** 0335 0956 SU 1547 2159	0.3 2.1 0.6 2.3	**1** 0400 1016 TU 1614 2229	0.6 2.1 0.7 2.2	**16** 0428 1045 W 1646 ○2304	0.6 2.2 0.6 2.2	**1** 0405 1020 TH 1628 ●2244	0.7 2.2 0.7 2.2	**16** 0450 1105 F 1719 2338	0.8 2.2 0.7 2.1
2 0411 1025 F 1617 2229	0.6 1.9 0.8 2.1	**17** 0357 1021 SA 1610 2221	0.3 2.2 0.6 2.3	**2** 0408 1023 SU 1615 2229	0.5 2.0 0.7 2.1	**17** 0414 1036 M 1625 ○2241	0.3 2.2 0.5 2.4	**2** 0433 1048 W 1648 ●2304	0.5 2.2 0.6 2.2	**17** 0506 1121 TH 1727 2346	0.6 2.2 0.6 2.2	**2** 0445 1058 F 1710 2329	0.7 2.3 0.6 2.2	**17** 0528 1143 SA 1800	0.9 2.2 0.7
3 0441 1057 SA 1646 ●2301	0.5 1.9 0.7 2.1	**18** 0438 1103 SU 1649 ○2305	0.2 2.2 0.5 2.4	**3** 0436 1053 M 1643 ●2300	0.5 2.1 0.6 2.2	**18** 0452 1112 TU 1704 2322	0.2 2.2 0.5 2.4	**3** 0507 1121 TH 1724 2341	0.6 2.2 0.6 2.2	**18** 0543 1157 F 1809	0.8 2.2 0.6	**3** 0527 1138 SA 1754	0.8 2.3 0.6	**18** 0018 0604 SU 1220 1840	2.0 0.9 2.2 0.7
4 0510 1127 SU 1713 2331	0.5 2.0 0.6 2.1	**19** 0518 1143 M 1728 2346	0.1 2.2 0.4 2.4	**4** 0505 1121 TU 1714 2330	0.4 2.1 0.6 2.2	**19** 0530 1148 W 1744	0.4 2.2 0.5	**4** 0543 1155 F 1803	0.6 2.2 0.6	**19** 0028 0619 SA 1234 1851	2.1 0.9 2.2 0.7	**4** 0017 0610 SU 1221 1841	2.2 0.8 2.3 0.6	**19** 0058 0640 M 1257 1920	2.0 1.0 2.2 0.7
5 0539 1156 M 1742	0.4 2.0 0.6	**20** 0557 1221 TU 1807	0.2 2.2 0.4	**5** 0536 1150 W 1746	0.5 2.1 0.6	**20** 0003 0607 TH 1223 1824	2.3 0.5 2.2 0.6	**5** 0021 0621 SA 1231 1845	2.2 0.7 2.2 0.7	**20** 0111 0656 SU 1312 1936	2.0 1.0 2.1 0.8	**5** 0110 0657 M 1307 1933	2.1 0.9 2.2 0.6	**20** 0137 0714 TU 1334 2000	1.9 1.0 2.1 0.8
6 0000 0608 TU 1224 1811	2.2 0.4 2.0 0.6	**21** 0027 0636 W 1257 1846	2.4 0.3 2.1 0.5	**6** 0002 0608 TH 1220 1819	2.2 0.5 2.1 0.6	**21** 0045 0643 F 1259 1906	2.2 0.7 2.1 0.7	**6** 0107 0704 SU 1311 1934	2.1 0.8 2.1 0.7	**21** 0155 0733 M 1353 2026	1.9 1.1 2.0 0.9	**6** 0206 0748 TU 1359 2030	2.0 0.9 2.1 0.6	**21** 0216 0750 W 1413 2042	1.8 1.1 2.0 0.9
7 0029 0639 W 1252 1843	2.1 0.5 2.0 0.6	**22** 0109 0714 TH 1334 1928	2.2 0.5 2.0 0.6	**7** 0036 0642 F 1252 1857	2.2 0.6 2.1 0.7	**22** 0128 0720 SA 1336 1951	2.0 0.9 1.9 0.8	**7** 0201 0753 M 1400 2033	2.0 1.0 2.0 0.8	**22** 0242 0816 TU 1439 2125	1.8 1.2 1.9 0.9	**7** 0304 0843 W 1459 2133	1.9 1.0 2.1 0.7	**22** 0257 0831 TH 1456 2130	1.7 1.2 1.9 0.9
8 0100 0711 TH 1323 1917	2.1 0.5 1.9 0.7	**23** 0152 0753 F 1412 2013	2.1 0.7 1.9 0.8	**8** 0114 0720 SA 1328 1940	2.1 0.7 2.0 0.8	**23** 0214 0757 SU 1418 2048	1.9 1.1 1.9 0.9	**8** 0307 0853 TU 1504 2147	1.9 1.1 1.9 0.8	**23** 0334 0916 W 1533 ○2232	1.7 1.3 1.8 1.0	**8** 0406 0947 TH 1603 ○2247	1.8 1.1 2.0 0.7	**23** 0343 0920 F 1545 ○2225	1.7 1.2 1.8 0.9
9 0135 0747 F 1358 1956	2.0 0.7 1.9 0.8	**24** 0239 0833 SA 1454 2109	1.9 1.0 1.8 0.9	**9** 0200 0803 SU 1412 2033	2.0 0.9 1.9 0.9	**24** 0306 0843 M 1509 2209	1.7 1.2 1.8 1.0	**9** 0421 1014 W 1620 ○2322	1.8 1.2 1.9 0.8	**24** 0436 1042 TH 1636 2339	1.6 1.3 1.8 1.0	**9** 0514 1104 F 1714	1.8 1.1 2.0	**24** 0435 1026 SA 1641 2328	1.7 1.2 1.8 0.9
10 0216 0827 SA 1440 2044	1.9 0.8 1.8 0.9	**25** 0333 0925 SU 1547 ◐2248	1.7 1.2 1.7 1.0	**10** 0301 0900 M 1511 ◐2146	1.8 1.1 1.8 0.9	**25** 0410 1017 TU 1613 ◐2338	1.6 1.3 1.7 1.0	**10** 0547 1150 TH 1744	1.8 1.1 1.9	**25** 0558 1201 F 1758	1.6 1.2 1.7	**10** 0003 0622 SA 1222 1827	0.7 1.8 1.2 2.0	**25** 0536 1151 SU 1745	1.7 1.2 1.9
11 0309 0919 SU 1536 ◐2150	1.8 1.0 1.8 1.0	**26** 0445 1116 M 1702	1.6 1.3 1.7	**11** 0421 1024 TU 1630 2339	1.7 1.2 1.8 0.9	**26** 0554 1200 W 1755	1.6 1.3 1.7	**11** 0038 0702 F 1301 1900	0.7 1.8 1.0 2.0	**26** 0039 0704 SA 1303 1909	0.9 1.7 1.1 1.8	**11** 0108 0723 SU 1326 1932	0.7 1.8 1.0 2.0	**26** 0029 0643 M 1259 1857	0.9 1.7 1.1 1.8
12 0422 1034 M 1649 2339	1.7 1.1 1.7 1.0	**27** 0031 0649 TU 1257 1854	1.0 1.6 1.2 1.7	**12** 0559 1218 W 1805	1.7 1.1 1.8	**27** 0051 0714 TH 1313 1915	1.0 1.6 1.1 1.8	**12** 0139 0759 SA 1356 2000	0.6 1.9 0.9 2.1	**27** 0129 0751 SU 1352 1959	0.9 1.7 1.1 1.9	**12** 0202 0816 M 1421 2030	0.7 1.8 0.9 2.0	**27** 0124 0740 TU 1354 1959	0.9 1.7 1.0 1.9
13 0555 1226 TU 1819	1.7 1.1 1.7	**28** 0143 0804 W 1401 1959	0.9 1.7 1.1 1.8	**13** 0103 0729 TH 1329 1927	0.8 1.8 1.0 1.9	**28** 0145 0802 F 1402 2005	0.9 1.7 1.1 1.9	**13** 0228 0846 SU 1442 2051	0.5 2.0 0.8 2.1	**28** 0211 0830 M 1432 2041	0.8 1.8 0.9 2.0	**13** 0249 0903 TU 1509 2122	0.7 1.8 0.8 2.1	**28** 0212 0828 W 1442 2052	0.8 1.9 0.9 2.0
14 0115 0736 W 1344 1944	0.9 1.8 1.0 1.8	**29** 0231 0846 TH 1443 2045	0.7 1.8 1.0 1.9	**14** 0204 0827 F 1422 2026	0.7 1.9 0.9 2.1	**29** 0225 0840 SA 1439 2045	0.8 1.8 1.0 1.9	**14** 0311 0929 M 1525 2138	0.5 2.0 0.7 2.1	**29** 0249 0906 TU 1510 2121	0.7 1.9 0.8 2.1	**14** 0331 0946 W 1554 2211	0.8 1.9 0.7 2.1	**29** 0259 0914 TH 1528 2143	0.8 2.0 0.7 2.1
15 0220 0843 TH 1442 2045	0.7 1.9 0.8 2.0	**30** 0308 0920 F 1517 2123	0.6 1.8 0.9 2.0	**15** 0252 0914 SA 1506 2115	0.5 2.0 0.7 2.2	**30** 0258 0914 SU 1511 2121	0.7 1.9 0.9 2.0	**15** 0350 1008 TU 1605 2222	0.5 2.1 0.6 2.3	**30** 0327 0942 W 1548 2202	0.7 2.1 0.8 2.1	**15** 0411 1026 TH 1637 ○2255	0.8 2.0 0.7 2.1	**30** 0346 0958 F 1615 2233	0.8 2.2 0.7 2.1
						31 0329 0945 M 1542 2155	0.6 2.0 0.8 2.1							**31** 0432 1043 SA 1702 ●2324	0.7 2.3 0.5 2.2

Chart Datum: 1·22 metres below Ordnance Datum (Local)

》》 **FREE** monthly updates from 《《
www.reedsalmanac.co.uk

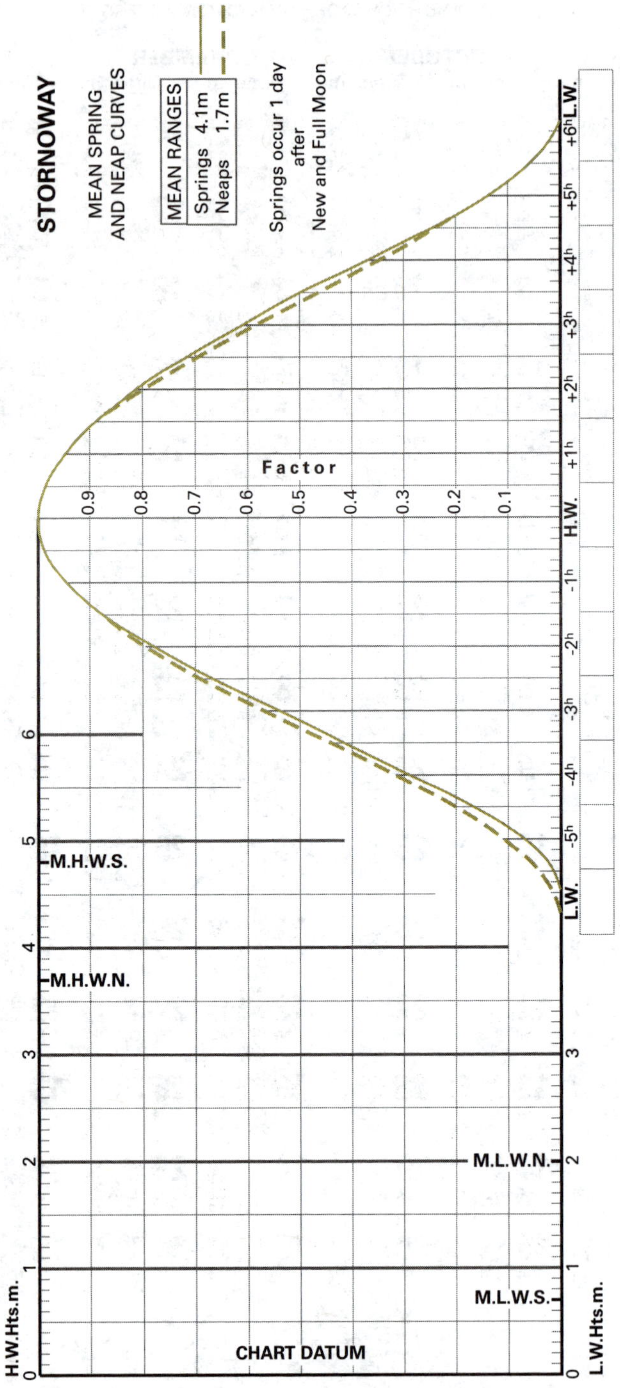
STORNOWAY
MEAN SPRING
AND NEAP CURVES
MEAN RANGES
Springs 4.1m
Neaps 1.7m
Springs occur 1 day
after
New and Full Moon
Factor
0.9
0.8
0.7
0.6
0.5
0.4
0.3
0.2
0.1
L.W.
-5h
-4h
-3h
-2h
-1h
H.W.
+1h
+2h
+3h
+4h
+5h
+6h
L.W.
M.H.W.S.
M.H.W.N.
M.L.W.N.
M.L.W.S.
CHART DATUM
H.W.Hts.m.
L.W.Hts.m.
0
1
2
3
4
5
6

| TIME ZONE (UT) For Summer Time add ONE hour in **non-shaded areas** | SCOTLAND – STORNOWAY LAT 58°12′N LONG 6°23′W TIMES AND HEIGHTS OF HIGH AND LOW WATERS | | YEAR **2005** |

SCOTLAND – STORNOWAY
LAT 58°12′N   LONG 6°23′W
TIMES AND HEIGHTS OF HIGH AND LOW WATERS

YEAR 2005

TIME ZONE (UT) — For Summer Time add ONE hour in **non-shaded areas**

	JANUARY			FEBRUARY			MARCH			APRIL	
	Time m	Time m		Time m	Time m		Time m	Time m		Time m	Time m
1 SA	0404 1.6 1009 4.1 1650 1.5 2251 3.7	**16** SU	0458 1.4 1116 4.5 1738 1.2 2358 3.7	**1** TU	0456 1.5 1049 4.0 1741 1.4 2344 3.6	**16** W	0600 1.8 1238 3.7 1830 1.9 ●	**1** TU	0346 0.9 0927 4.3 1619 1.0 2159 4.0	**16** W	0435 1.4 1032 3.9 1653 1.6 2245 3.6	**1** F	0451 1.4 1114 3.7 1724 1.7	**16** SA	0555 2.1 1254 3.3 1757 2.4 ●
2 SU	0447 1.7 1056 3.9 1737 1.6 2347 3.6	**17** M	0551 1.5 1219 4.2 1831 1.5 ☾	**2** W	0544 1.6 1153 3.8 1834 1.6 ○	**17** TH	0137 3.4 0710 2.1 1411 3.4 1944 2.2	**2** W	0424 1.2 1010 4.0 1700 1.3 2251 3.8	**17** TH	0521 1.8 1143 3.5 1738 2.0 ☾	**2** SA	0006 3.7 0557 1.7 1307 3.5 1846 2.0	**17** SU	0127 3.5 0741 2.3 1425 3.3 1952 2.5
3 M	0537 1.9 1152 3.9 1829 1.8 ○	**18** TU	0111 3.5 0652 1.9 1330 3.9 1932 1.8	**3** TH	0055 3.6 0644 1.8 1314 3.7 1941 1.9	**18** F	0304 3.4 0904 2.2 1532 3.4 2131 2.2	**3** TH	0509 1.4 1114 3.7 1751 1.6 ○	**18** F	0029 3.4 0623 2.2 1339 3.3 1840 2.4	**3** SU	0140 3.6 0753 1.9 1445 3.5 2050 2.0	**18** M	0248 3.5 0928 2.1 1535 3.4 2135 2.3
4 TU	0048 3.6 0634 2.0 1254 3.8 1927 1.7	**19** W	0229 3.5 0808 2.0 1443 3.7 2046 1.9	**4** F	0211 3.6 0801 1.9 1439 3.7 2103 1.7	**19** SA	0411 3.6 1033 2.0 1636 3.5 2242 2.0	**4** F	0015 3.6 0608 1.7 1257 3.5 1902 1.9	**19** SA	0223 3.4 0833 2.3 1506 3.3 2058 2.4	**4** M	0303 3.8 0941 1.6 1601 3.8 2210 1.7	**19** TU	0348 3.7 1022 1.8 1624 3.7 2227 2.0
5 W	0151 3.7 0738 2.0 1358 3.9 2031 1.6	**20** TH	0338 3.5 0932 2.0 1551 3.7 2159 1.9	**5** SA	0326 3.8 0935 1.8 1601 3.9 2224 1.6	**20** SU	0501 3.8 1127 1.7 1723 3.7 2330 1.7	**5** SA	0149 3.5 0739 1.9 1440 3.5 2051 1.9	**20** SU	0338 3.5 1015 2.1 1614 3.4 2219 2.2	**5** TU	0409 4.2 1045 1.2 1655 4.1 2303 1.4	**20** W	0433 3.9 1101 1.5 1700 3.9 2305 1.7
6 TH	0252 3.8 0846 1.9 1505 4.0 2136 1.5	**21** F	0434 3.7 1041 1.9 1648 3.7 2256 1.8	**6** SU	0431 4.1 1056 1.5 1708 4.1 2327 1.3	**21** M	0540 4.0 1208 1.5 1800 3.8	**6** SU	0314 3.7 0941 1.7 1605 3.7 2222 1.7	**21** M	0433 3.7 1105 1.8 1700 3.6 2306 1.9	**6** W	0501 4.5 1133 0.8 1738 4.4 2347 1.0	**21** TH	0507 4.2 1135 1.2 1729 4.2 2338 1.4
7 F	0351 4.0 0954 1.7 1609 4.1 2237 1.4	**22** SA	0518 3.9 1135 1.7 1734 3.8 2342 1.6	**7** M	0527 4.5 1157 1.1 1803 4.4	**22** TU	0009 1.4 0613 4.2 1243 1.2 1830 4.0	**7** M	0423 4.1 1057 1.3 1706 4.1 2320 1.3	**22** TU	0513 4.0 1142 1.5 1735 3.9 2344 1.6	**7** TH	0543 4.8 1214 0.5 1814 4.6	**22** F	0537 4.4 1205 1.0 1757 4.4
8 SA	0445 4.3 1059 1.5 1709 4.3 2333 1.2	**23** SU	0556 4.1 1219 1.5 1813 3.9	**8** TU	0019 1.0 0616 4.8 1249 0.7 1849 4.6 ●	**23** W	0044 1.2 0642 4.4 1314 0.9 1859 4.2	**8** TU	0517 4.5 1151 0.8 1754 4.4	**23** W	0546 4.2 1214 1.2 1804 4.1	**8** F	0027 0.7 0621 5.0 1252 0.4 1846 4.7 ●	**23** SA	0010 1.1 0605 4.6 1236 0.7 1825 4.6
9 SU	0536 4.6 1158 1.2 1805 4.5	**24** M	0022 1.4 0629 4.3 1258 1.3 1847 4.0	**9** W	0105 0.7 0701 5.1 1335 0.4 1931 4.7	**24** TH	0115 1.0 0708 4.6 1343 0.7 1926 4.4	**9** W	0007 1.0 0602 4.9 1236 0.4 1834 4.6	**24** TH	0016 1.3 0613 4.4 1244 0.9 1830 4.4	**9** SA	0105 0.5 0656 5.1 1327 0.3 1917 4.7	**24** SU	0042 0.9 0634 4.7 1307 0.6 1855 4.8
10 M	0024 1.0 0624 4.9 1253 0.9 1856 4.7 ●	**25** TU	0059 1.2 0701 4.4 1333 1.1 1919 4.1	**10** TH	0147 0.6 0742 5.3 1417 0.2 2010 4.8	**25** F	0144 0.8 0733 4.6 1411 0.6 1953 4.4	**10** TH	0050 0.7 0643 5.2 1316 0.2 1910 4.8	**25** F	0047 1.0 0639 4.6 1311 0.7 1856 4.6	**10** SU	0141 0.6 0729 5.0 1400 0.4 1947 4.7	**25** M	0116 0.7 0705 4.8 1340 0.5 1927 4.8
11 TU	0113 0.9 0712 5.1 1344 0.6 1945 4.7	**26** W	0133 1.1 0730 4.5 1406 1.0 1950 4.2	**11** F	0227 0.5 0822 5.3 1457 0.2 2048 4.6	**26** SA	0213 0.7 0759 4.6 1440 0.6 2020 4.4	**11** F	0129 0.5 0720 5.3 1354 0.1 1944 4.8	**26** SA	0115 0.8 0704 4.7 1340 0.5 1923 4.7	**11** M	0217 0.6 0803 4.8 1434 0.7 2018 4.5	**26** TU	0151 0.7 0739 4.8 1415 0.6 2001 4.7
12 W	0159 0.8 0758 5.2 1432 0.5 2031 4.7	**27** TH	0204 1.0 0759 4.5 1437 0.9 2020 4.1	**12** SA	0306 0.6 0902 5.1 1536 0.5 2126 4.4	**27** SU	0242 0.7 0825 4.6 1511 0.6 2049 4.3	**12** SA	0206 0.6 0756 5.1 1430 0.2 2017 4.7	**27** SU	0145 0.6 0730 4.7 1409 0.5 1951 4.7	**12** TU	0253 0.8 0838 4.6 1507 1.0 2050 4.3	**27** W	0228 0.7 0818 4.6 1452 0.8 2041 4.6
13 TH	0243 0.8 0844 5.1 1517 0.5 2117 4.5	**28** F	0236 1.0 0827 4.5 1508 0.9 2052 4.1	**13** SU	0345 0.8 0942 4.8 1615 0.9 2205 4.1	**28** M	0313 0.8 0854 4.5 1544 0.8 2121 4.2	**13** SU	0243 0.8 0831 4.8 1505 0.6 2049 4.5	**28** M	0215 0.6 0758 4.7 1441 0.5 2021 4.6	**13** W	0330 1.1 0916 4.2 1541 1.3 2126 4.1	**28** TH	0309 0.9 0905 4.4 1533 1.1 2129 4.3
14 F	0327 0.9 0931 5.0 1603 0.6 2204 4.3	**29** SA	0307 1.0 0856 4.4 1541 0.9 2124 4.1	**14** M	0425 1.1 1027 4.5 1655 1.1 2251 3.8			**14** M	0318 1.0 0907 4.5 1540 0.8 2122 4.2	**29** TU	0248 0.7 0830 4.7 1514 0.7 2054 4.4	**14** TH	0409 1.5 1003 3.8 1617 1.7 2213 3.8	**29** F	0355 1.1 1006 4.2 1617 1.5 2238 4.3
15 SA	0411 1.1 1021 4.8 1649 0.9 2256 4.0	**30** SU	0340 1.0 0927 4.3 1617 1.0 2201 4.0	**15** TU	0509 1.5 1121 4.0 1739 1.5 2355 3.5			**15** TU	0355 1.3 0945 4.1 1615 1.2 2159 3.9	**30** W	0323 0.9 0907 4.3 1550 1.0 2134 4.1	**15** F	0452 1.8 1110 3.5 1659 2.1 2333 3.6	**30** SA	0452 1.4 1135 3.7 1716 1.8
		31 M	0415 1.3 1003 4.1 1656 1.2 2245 3.8						**31** TH	0403 1.1 0956 4.0 1632 1.4 2231 3.9				

Chart Datum: 2·71 metres below Ordnance Datum (Newlyn)

》》 **FREE** monthly updates from 《《
www.reedsalmanac.co.uk

TIDES

TIME ZONE (UT)
For Summer Time add ONE hour in **non-shaded areas**

SCOTLAND – STORNOWAY
LAT 58°12′N LONG 6°23′W
TIMES AND HEIGHTS OF HIGH AND LOW WATERS

YEAR 2005

	MAY			JUNE			JULY			AUGUST		
	Time m	Time m		Time m	Time m		Time m	Time m		Time m	Time m
1 SU	0005 3.9 0612 1.6 1307 3.5 ☽ 1847 2.0	**16** M	0020 3.6 0644 2.0 1320 3.3 ☾ 1844 2.3	**1** W	0211 4.1 0837 1.3 1511 3.7 2103 1.7	**16** TH	0123 3.7 0754 1.7 1417 3.6 2003 2.1	**1** F	0241 4.0 0855 1.5 1535 3.6 2129 1.8	**16** SA	0122 3.7 0751 1.7 1416 3.6 2006 1.9	**1** M	0430 3.6 1039 1.9 1701 3.8 2321 1.7	**16** TU	0332 3.7 0952 1.8 1601 4.0 2226 1.6
2 M	0127 3.9 0753 1.6 1432 3.6 2029 2.0	**17** TU	0135 3.6 0809 2.0 1433 3.4 2015 2.3	**2** TH	0315 4.1 0940 1.3 1607 3.8 2202 1.6	**17** F	0221 3.7 0853 1.6 1512 3.7 2104 1.9	**2** SA	0344 3.9 0959 1.5 1629 3.8 2232 1.6	**17** SU	0229 3.7 0858 1.7 1518 3.8 2118 1.8	**2** TU	0521 3.7 1130 1.7 1740 4.0	**17** W	0444 4.0 1101 1.5 1700 4.4 2330 1.2
3 TU	0242 4.0 0918 1.4 1543 3.8 2142 1.7	**18** W	0241 3.7 0918 1.8 1530 3.6 2123 2.1	**3** F	0410 4.2 1033 1.2 1651 4.0 2253 1.4	**18** SA	0318 3.9 0949 1.5 1600 4.0 2200 1.7	**3** SU	0439 3.9 1054 1.5 1712 3.9 2325 1.5	**18** M	0339 3.8 1007 1.6 1617 4.0 2229 1.6	**3** W	0008 1.5 0602 3.8 1212 1.5 1815 4.2	**18** TH	0540 4.3 1155 1.2 1751 4.8
4 W	0346 4.2 1019 1.1 1635 4.0 2235 1.4	**19** TH	0335 3.8 1006 1.6 1612 3.8 2210 1.9	**4** SA	0456 4.3 1118 1.1 1728 4.1 2339 1.3	**19** SU	0410 4.0 1040 1.3 1645 4.2 2252 1.5	**4** M	0527 3.9 1140 1.4 1750 4.1	**19** TU	0446 4.0 1109 1.4 1711 4.3 2333 1.3	**4** TH	0048 1.3 0637 3.9 1249 1.5 1847 4.4	**19** F	0022 0.8 0628 4.6 1242 0.9 ○ 1835 5.1
5 TH	0437 4.4 1106 0.9 1716 4.1 2321 1.2	**20** F	0417 4.0 1045 1.4 1647 4.1 2250 1.6	**5** SU	0538 4.3 1158 1.1 1802 4.2	**20** M	0501 4.2 1128 1.2 1729 4.4 2344 1.2	**5** TU	0013 1.4 0609 3.9 1222 1.4 1825 4.2	**20** W	0545 4.2 1204 1.2 1801 4.6	**5** F	0123 1.1 0710 4.1 1323 1.2 ● 1917 4.5	**20** SA	0109 0.5 0710 4.8 1325 0.7 1917 5.4
6 F	0520 4.6 1146 0.8 1750 4.4	**21** SA	0454 4.3 1122 1.1 1721 4.4 2329 1.3	**6** M	0022 1.2 0616 4.3 1236 1.1 ● 1835 4.3	**21** TU	0550 4.4 1215 1.0 1813 4.7	**6** W	0057 1.3 0648 4.0 1301 1.3 ● 1900 4.3	**21** TH	0029 1.0 0637 4.5 1254 1.0 ○ 1848 4.9	**6** SA	0154 1.0 0740 4.2 1355 1.0 1945 4.5	**21** SU	0152 0.2 0750 4.9 1405 0.5 1957 5.4
7 SA	0002 1.0 0557 4.7 1224 0.7 1821 4.5	**22** SU	0530 4.5 1159 0.9 1755 4.6	**7** TU	0104 1.1 0654 4.2 1313 1.1 1909 4.4	**22** W	0035 1.0 0640 4.5 1302 0.9 ○ 1858 4.8	**7** TH	0136 1.2 0725 4.0 1337 1.2 1934 4.4	**22** F	0122 0.7 0726 4.6 1340 0.8 1934 5.1	**7** SU	0224 0.9 0809 4.2 1425 1.0 2012 4.5	**22** M	0232 0.2 0829 4.8 1445 0.6 2037 5.3
8 SU	0041 0.9 0633 4.7 1259 0.7 ● 1852 4.6	**23** M	0009 1.1 0607 4.6 1238 0.8 ○ 1830 4.7	**8** W	0144 1.1 0732 4.1 1348 1.2 1943 4.4	**23** TH	0126 0.8 0730 4.5 1348 0.9 1944 4.9	**8** F	0213 1.1 0800 4.0 1412 1.2 2007 4.4	**23** SA	0209 0.4 0811 4.7 1424 0.7 2019 5.2	**8** M	0254 0.9 0839 4.2 1454 1.0 2040 4.4	**23** TU	0312 0.3 0908 4.6 1524 0.7 2119 5.0
9 M	0119 0.8 0707 4.6 1333 0.8 1923 4.5	**24** TU	0051 0.9 0647 4.7 1317 0.7 1909 4.8	**9** TH	0222 1.2 0811 4.0 1424 1.3 2020 4.3	**24** F	0216 0.7 0821 4.5 1433 0.9 2033 4.9	**9** SA	0248 1.1 0835 4.0 1445 1.2 2040 4.3	**24** SU	0255 0.3 0856 4.6 1506 0.7 2105 5.1	**9** TU	0324 0.9 0911 4.1 1525 1.1 2108 4.3	**24** W	0351 0.6 0949 4.4 1604 1.0 2204 4.6
10 TU	0156 0.9 0742 4.5 1407 0.9 1955 4.5	**25** W	0134 0.9 0731 4.6 1357 0.8 1951 4.8	**10** F	0301 1.2 0851 3.9 1459 1.4 2100 4.2	**25** SA	0306 0.6 0913 4.4 1519 1.0 2125 4.8	**10** SU	0322 1.1 0911 3.9 1519 1.3 2115 4.3	**25** M	0339 0.4 0941 4.4 1549 0.9 2152 4.9	**10** W	0357 1.0 0945 4.0 1557 1.1 2139 4.1	**25** TH	0432 1.0 1036 4.0 1648 1.4 2301 4.2
11 W	0234 1.1 0819 4.3 1441 1.2 2030 4.3	**26** TH	0218 0.8 0819 4.5 1439 0.9 2038 4.7	**11** SA	0340 1.4 0935 3.8 1536 1.5 2144 4.1	**26** SU	0357 0.7 1007 4.2 1608 1.1 2221 4.6	**11** M	0357 1.2 0949 3.8 1553 1.4 2152 4.1	**26** TU	0424 0.6 1030 4.1 1634 1.1 2245 4.6	**11** TH	0433 1.2 1024 3.8 1634 1.5 2217 3.9	**26** F	0515 1.5 1143 3.7 ☾ 1738 1.9
12 TH	0312 1.3 0901 4.0 1515 1.4 2111 4.1	**27** F	0306 0.8 0914 4.3 1524 1.1 2133 4.5	**12** SU	0422 1.5 1023 3.6 1616 1.7 2233 3.9	**27** M	0450 0.8 1106 4.0 1701 1.4 2323 4.4	**12** TU	0434 1.3 1032 3.7 1632 1.6 2233 3.9	**27** W	0510 0.9 1125 3.9 1723 1.4 2346 4.3	**12** F	0514 1.4 1116 3.5 1718 1.7 2314 3.8	**27** SA	0022 3.8 1313 3.5 1848 2.2
13 F	0353 1.5 0949 3.8 1552 1.7 2200 3.9	**28** SA	0359 1.0 1018 4.0 1614 1.4 2239 4.3	**13** M	0508 1.6 1117 3.5 1703 1.8 2328 3.8	**28** TU	0546 1.0 1210 3.8 1800 1.6 ☽	**13** W	0516 1.4 1120 3.6 1714 1.7 2322 3.8	**28** TH	0600 1.2 1232 3.7 1820 1.7 ☽	**13** SA	0602 1.6 1222 3.7 1812 1.9	**28** SU	0151 3.6 0715 2.1 1438 3.5 2049 2.3
14 SA	0439 1.7 1050 3.5 1635 2.0 2306 3.7	**29** SU	0501 1.2 1131 3.8 1716 1.7 2351 4.2	**14** TU	0559 1.7 1215 3.4 1758 2.0	**29** W	0027 4.2 0644 1.2 1319 3.6 1906 1.7	**14** TH	0601 1.5 1215 3.5 1804 1.9	**29** F	0057 4.0 0656 1.6 1349 3.5 1932 2.0	**14** SU	0036 3.6 0702 1.9 1336 3.6 1922 2.0	**29** M	0312 3.5 0911 2.2 1551 3.7 2222 2.1
15 SU	0534 1.8 1202 3.4 1729 2.2	**30** M	0611 1.3 1245 3.7 1832 1.8	**15** W	0025 3.7 0654 1.8 1316 3.5 ☾ 1859 2.1	**30** TH	0134 4.0 0748 1.4 1430 3.6 2018 1.8	**15** F	0019 3.7 0652 1.6 1314 3.6 1901 1.9	**30** SA	0213 3.7 0807 1.9 1506 3.5 2103 2.1	**15** M	0205 3.7 0821 1.9 1451 3.7 2056 1.9	**30** TU	0421 3.7 1028 2.1 1645 3.9 2314 1.8
		31 TU	0102 4.1 0724 1.4 1401 3.6 1951 1.9							**31** SU	0326 3.6 0931 1.9 1611 3.7 2223 1.9				

Chart Datum: 2·71 metres below Ordnance Datum (Newlyn)

》》 **FREE** monthly updates from 《《
www.reedsalmanac.co.uk

TIME ZONE (UT)
For Summer Time add ONE hour in **non-shaded areas**

SCOTLAND – STORNOWAY
LAT 58°12′N LONG 6°23′W
TIMES AND HEIGHTS OF HIGH AND LOW WATERS

YEAR 2005

SEPTEMBER		OCTOBER		NOVEMBER		DECEMBER	
Time m	Time m	Time m	Time m	Time m	Time m	Time m	Time m
1 0547 3.9 / 1154 1.6 / TH 1757 4.3	**16** 0529 4.4 / 1140 1.2 / F 1736 5.0	**1** 0549 4.3 / 1200 1.5 / SA 1757 4.6	**16** 0549 4.8 / 1200 1.0 / SU 1756 5.2	**1** 0015 1.0 / 0609 4.7 / TU 1224 1.2 / 1816 4.8	**16** 0033 0.9 / 0635 4.8 / W 1257 1.0 / ○ 1849 4.8	**1** 0017 1.1 / 0613 4.8 / TH 1233 1.2 / ● 1829 4.7	**16** 0054 1.2 / 0658 4.6 / F 1329 1.2 / 1919 4.3
2 0027 1.3 / 0617 4.1 / F 1229 1.4 / 1825 4.5	**17** 0007 0.7 / 0611 4.7 / SA 1224 0.9 / 1817 5.3	**2** 0025 1.1 / 0615 4.5 / SU 1230 1.2 / 1822 4.7	**17** 0022 0.5 / 0624 4.9 / M 1239 0.8 / ○ 1832 5.3	**2** 0046 0.9 / 0637 4.8 / W 1257 1.1 / ● 1845 4.8	**17** 0110 1.0 / 0709 4.8 / TH 1337 1.1 / 1926 4.7	**2** 0055 1.0 / 0650 4.9 / F 1315 1.1 / 1910 4.7	**17** 0132 1.2 / 0734 4.6 / SA 1409 1.2 / 1957 4.2
3 0058 1.1 / 0645 4.3 / SA 1301 1.1 / ● 1852 4.6	**18** 0048 0.4 / 0649 4.9 / SU 1304 0.7 / ○ 1855 5.5	**3** 0052 0.9 / 0641 4.6 / M 1258 1.0 / ● 1846 4.8	**18** 0059 0.5 / 0658 5.0 / TU 1317 0.8 / 1908 5.3	**3** 0118 0.8 / 0708 4.9 / TH 1331 1.0 / 1917 4.8	**18** 0146 1.1 / 0744 4.7 / F 1417 1.2 / 2005 4.5	**3** 0135 1.0 / 0731 4.9 / SA 1358 1.0 / 1955 4.6	**18** 0209 1.3 / 0811 4.6 / SU 1448 1.2 / 2036 4.1
4 0126 0.9 / 0712 4.4 / SU 1329 1.0 / 1917 4.7	**19** 0127 0.2 / 0724 5.0 / M 1342 0.6 / 1932 5.5	**4** 0119 0.8 / 0706 4.7 / TU 1326 0.9 / 1911 4.9	**19** 0135 0.6 / 0730 4.9 / W 1355 0.8 / 1944 5.1	**4** 0152 0.9 / 0741 4.8 / F 1407 1.0 / 1954 4.7	**19** 0222 1.3 / 0821 4.6 / SA 1457 1.4 / 2048 4.2	**4** 0216 1.1 / 0815 4.8 / SU 1444 1.0 / 2045 4.4	**19** 0245 1.4 / 0849 4.5 / M 1527 1.3 / 2117 4.0
5 0153 0.8 / 0738 4.5 / M 1357 0.9 / 1941 4.7	**20** 0204 0.3 / 0759 5.0 / TU 1419 0.6 / 2009 5.3	**5** 0147 0.7 / 0733 4.8 / W 1356 0.9 / 1937 4.9	**20** 0210 0.8 / 0804 4.8 / TH 1433 1.0 / 2021 4.8	**5** 0228 1.0 / 0819 4.7 / SA 1446 1.1 / 2037 4.4	**20** 0259 1.5 / 0903 4.4 / SU 1539 1.6 / 2136 4.0	**5** 0259 1.2 / 0906 4.7 / M 1533 1.1 / 2143 4.2	**20** 0322 1.5 / 0929 4.3 / TU 1607 1.5 / 2200 3.9
6 0221 0.7 / 0805 4.5 / TU 1425 0.9 / 2005 4.6	**21** 0241 0.5 / 0834 4.8 / W 1457 0.8 / 2047 5.0	**6** 0218 0.8 / 0802 4.7 / TH 1427 1.0 / 2006 4.7	**21** 0246 1.1 / 0839 4.6 / F 1512 1.3 / 2102 4.4	**6** 0306 1.3 / 0904 4.5 / SU 1530 1.3 / 2133 4.1	**21** 0337 1.8 / 0953 4.2 / M 1625 1.8 / 2236 3.7	**6** 0347 1.4 / 1005 4.5 / TU 1629 1.2 / 2251 4.0	**21** 0401 1.7 / 1014 4.1 / W 1649 1.6 / 2249 3.7
7 0250 0.8 / 0833 4.4 / W 1454 1.0 / 2031 4.5	**22** 0317 0.8 / 0910 4.5 / TH 1535 1.1 / 2128 4.6	**7** 0250 0.9 / 0833 4.5 / F 1501 1.1 / 2039 4.4	**22** 0322 1.5 / 0919 4.3 / SA 1553 1.7 / 2152 4.0	**7** 0350 1.6 / 1008 4.2 / M 1623 1.6 / 2259 3.8	**22** 0420 2.1 / 1056 4.0 / TU 1720 2.0 / 2345 3.6	**7** 0442 1.7 / 1113 4.4 / W 1732 1.4	**22** 0444 1.9 / 1104 4.0 / TH 1736 1.8 / 2345 3.6
8 0321 0.9 / 0902 4.3 / TH 1526 1.2 / 2100 4.3	**23** 0354 1.2 / 0951 4.2 / F 1616 1.5 / 2219 4.1	**8** 0325 1.2 / 0910 4.3 / SA 1539 1.4 / 2123 4.1	**23** 0400 1.9 / 1014 4.0 / SU 1641 2.0 / 2311 3.7	**8** 0445 1.9 / 1132 4.1 / TU 1735 1.8	**23** 0514 2.3 / 1206 3.9 / W 1827 2.2 / ◐	**8** 0004 3.8 / 0548 1.9 / TH 1222 4.3 / ● 1840 1.5	**23** 0534 2.1 / 1158 3.8 / F 1828 1.9
9 0355 1.1 / 0937 4.1 / F 1601 1.4 / 2137 4.1	**24** 0434 1.7 / 1050 3.9 / SA 1704 2.0 / 2348 3.7	**9** 0405 1.5 / 1004 4.0 / SU 1624 1.6 / 2235 3.8	**24** 0444 2.2 / 1146 3.8 / M 1745 2.3	**9** 0031 3.7 / 0604 2.2 / W 1251 4.1 / ◐ 1909 1.8	**24** 0059 3.5 / 0624 2.4 / TH 1315 3.8 / 1946 2.2	**9** 0117 3.8 / 0704 1.9 / F 1330 4.2 / 1952 1.5	**24** 0046 3.5 / 0631 2.2 / SA 1257 3.8 / 1925 1.9
10 0434 1.4 / 1025 3.9 / SA 1643 1.6 / 2234 3.8	**25** 0520 2.1 / 1235 3.7 / SU 1812 2.3 / ◐	**10** 0454 1.9 / 1137 3.8 / M 1726 1.9 / ◐	**25** 0044 3.5 / 0544 2.5 / TU 1313 3.7 / ◐ 1935 2.4	**10** 0152 3.7 / 0745 2.2 / TH 1404 4.2 / 2037 1.6	**25** 0211 3.6 / 0751 2.4 / F 1421 3.8 / 2057 2.0	**10** 0228 3.8 / 0820 1.9 / SA 1436 4.2 / 2100 1.4	**25** 0150 3.6 / 0735 2.2 / SU 1356 3.8 / 2027 1.9
11 0521 1.7 / 1146 3.7 / SU 1738 1.9 / ◐	**26** 0125 3.5 / 0624 2.5 / M 1403 3.6 / 2031 2.4	**11** 0035 3.6 / 0607 2.2 / TU 1307 3.8 / 1910 2.1	**26** 0205 3.5 / 0739 2.6 / W 1427 3.8 / 2113 2.2	**11** 0305 3.9 / 0905 1.9 / F 1510 4.4 / 2143 1.4	**26** 0312 3.7 / 0904 2.3 / SA 1518 3.9 / 2147 1.8	**11** 0331 3.9 / 0927 1.7 / SU 1537 4.3 / 2159 1.4	**26** 0250 3.7 / 0839 2.1 / M 1456 3.8 / 2127 1.8
12 0023 3.6 / 0624 2.0 / M 1316 3.7 / 1900 2.1	**27** 0248 3.5 / 0843 2.6 / TU 1518 3.7 / 2204 2.2	**12** 0210 3.6 / 0807 2.3 / W 1427 4.0 / 2105 1.8	**27** 0315 3.6 / 0916 2.5 / TH 1529 3.9 / 2205 2.0	**12** 0403 4.1 / 1003 1.7 / SA 1606 4.6 / 2233 1.1	**27** 0357 3.9 / 0954 2.1 / SU 1602 4.1 / 2228 1.6	**12** 0423 4.1 / 1025 1.6 / TU 1630 4.3 / 2249 1.3	**27** 0343 3.9 / 0941 1.9 / TU 1553 3.9 / 2221 1.6
13 0209 3.6 / 0806 2.3 / TU 1439 3.8 / 2105 2.0	**28** 0359 3.6 / 1004 2.3 / W 1615 3.9 / 2250 1.9	**13** 0328 3.9 / 0937 1.9 / TH 1536 4.3 / 2213 1.4	**28** 0407 3.8 / 1009 2.2 / F 1615 4.1 / 2243 1.7	**13** 0448 4.4 / 1052 1.4 / SU 1653 4.8 / 2316 1.0	**28** 0433 4.2 / 1035 1.8 / M 1640 4.3 / 2304 1.5	**13** 0507 4.2 / 1116 1.4 / W 1717 4.4 / 2334 1.2	**28** 0429 4.1 / 1037 1.7 / TH 1646 4.1 / 2310 1.4
14 0336 3.7 / 0950 2.0 / W 1552 4.1 / 2227 1.6	**29** 0446 3.8 / 1049 2.0 / TH 1656 4.2 / 2325 1.6	**14** 0426 4.1 / 1033 1.6 / F 1631 4.7 / 2302 1.0	**29** 0444 4.1 / 1048 1.9 / SA 1652 4.3 / 2316 1.5	**14** 0527 4.5 / 1135 1.2 / M 1734 4.9 / 2355 0.9	**29** 0506 4.4 / 1114 1.4 / TU 1715 4.4 / 2340 1.2	**14** 0545 4.4 / 1202 1.3 / TH 1759 4.4	**29** 0513 4.4 / 1129 1.3 / F 1735 4.4 / 2357 1.3
15 0440 4.1 / 1052 1.6 / TH 1649 4.6 / 2321 1.1	**30** 0520 4.0 / 1126 1.7 / F 1729 4.4 / 2356 1.3	**15** 0511 4.5 / 1118 1.3 / SA 1716 5.0 / 2344 0.7	**30** 0515 4.3 / 1122 1.6 / SU 1722 4.5 / 2346 1.3	**15** 0602 4.7 / 1217 1.1 / TU 1812 4.9	**30** 0539 4.6 / 1153 1.1 / W 1751 4.6	**15** 0014 1.2 / 0622 4.5 / F 1247 1.2 / ○ 1839 4.4	**30** 0556 4.7 / 1219 1.1 / SA 1823 4.4
			31 0542 4.5 / 1153 1.4 / M 1749 4.7				**31** 0042 1.1 / 0640 4.8 / SA 1309 1.0 / ● 1910 4.6

Chart Datum: 2·71 metres below Ordnance Datum (Newlyn)

»» **FREE** monthly updates from ««
www.reedsalmanac.co.uk

Chapter 5

301

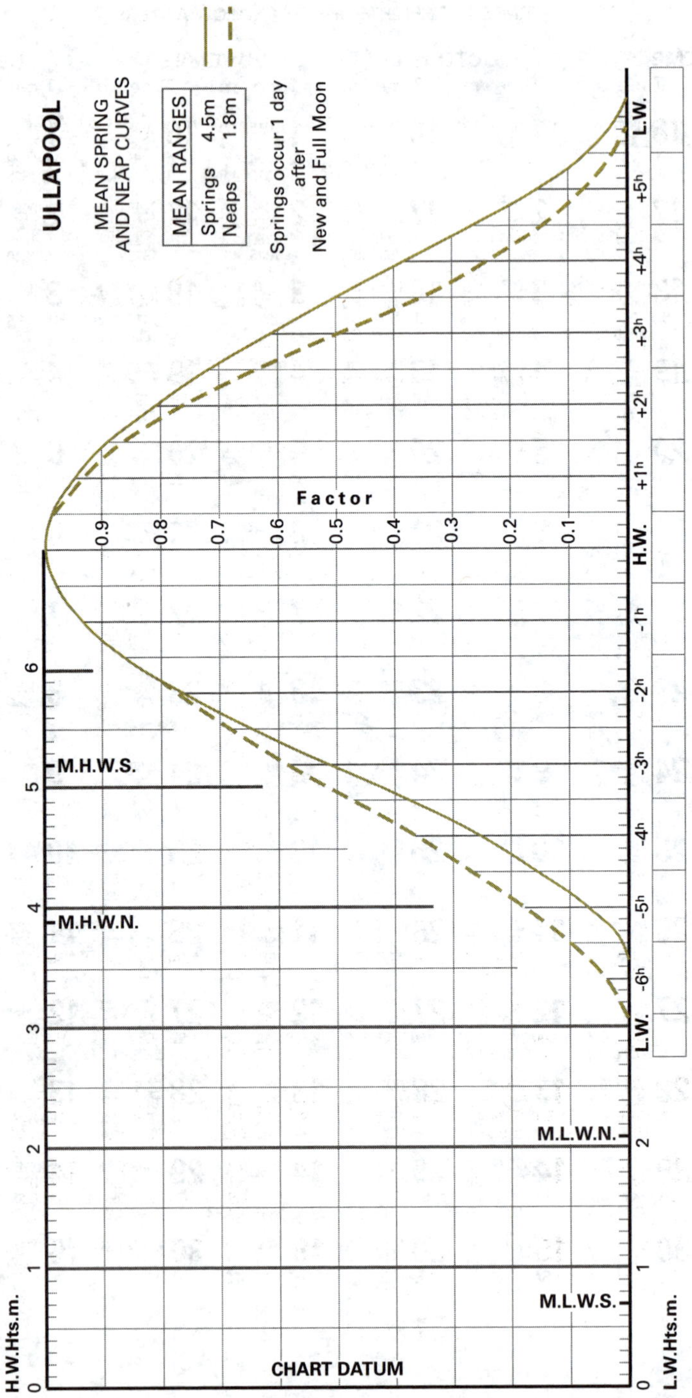
ULLAPOOL
MEAN SPRING AND NEAP CURVES
MEAN RANGES
Springs 4.5m
Neaps 1.8m
Springs occur 1 day after New and Full Moon
Factor
0.9
0.8
0.7
0.6
0.5
0.4
0.3
0.2
0.1
L.W.
-6h
-5h
-4h
-3h
-2h
-1h
H.W.
+1h
+2h
+3h
+4h
+5h
L.W.
H.W.Hts.m.
0
1
2
3
4
5
6
M.H.W.S.
M.H.W.N.
CHART DATUM
M.L.W.S.
M.L.W.N.
L.W.Hts.m.

TIME ZONE (UT)
For Summer Time add ONE hour in **non-shaded areas**

SCOTLAND – ULLAPOOL
LAT 57°54'N   LONG 5°10'W
TIMES AND HEIGHTS OF HIGH AND LOW WATERS

YEAR 2005

JANUARY | FEBRUARY | MARCH | APRIL

Day	JAN Time m	JAN Time m	FEB Time m	FEB Time m	MAR Time m	MAR Time m	APR Time m	APR Time m
1 / 16	**1** 0409 1.8 / 1005 4.6 / SA 1650 1.8 / 2250 4.3	**16** 0511 1.5 / 1122 4.8 / SU 1745 1.4	**1** 0503 1.7 / 1056 4.5 / TU 1738 1.7 / 2348 4.2	**16** 0005 4.0 / 0610 2.1 / W 1241 4.0 / ◐ 1834 2.1	**1** 0356 1.2 / 0941 4.8 / TU 1623 1.2 / 2214 4.5	**16** 0444 1.5 / 1044 4.2 / W 1659 1.7 / 2255 4.0	**1** 0503 1.6 / 1119 4.1 / F 1729 1.9	**16** 0558 2.2 / 1250 3.5 / SA 1803 2.4 ◐
2 / 17	**2** 0451 2.0 / 1051 4.5 / SU 1735 1.9 / 2345 4.1	**17** 0006 4.3 / 0602 1.9 / M 1225 4.5 / ◐ 1837 1.8	**2** 0552 1.9 / 1153 4.3 / W 1831 1.9	**17** 0131 3.8 / 0720 2.4 / TH 1409 3.8 / 1947 2.4	**2** 0434 1.4 / 1023 4.5 / W 1702 1.5 / 2305 4.3	**17** 0529 2.0 / 1154 3.8 / TH 1742 2.1 ◐	**2** 0007 4.0 / 0608 1.9 / SA 1305 3.8 / ◐ 1852 2.3	**17** 0113 3.6 / 0738 2.4 / SU 1416 3.5 / 1957 2.6
3 / 18	**3** 0540 2.1 / 1146 4.3 / M 1827 2.0 ◐	**18** 0114 4.1 / 0703 2.1 / TU 1335 4.2 / 1938 2.1	**3** 0101 4.1 / 0653 2.2 / TH 1314 4.1 / 1942 2.1	**18** 0307 3.8 / 0909 2.5 / F 1538 3.8 / 2138 2.5	**3** 0520 1.7 / 1120 4.2 / TH 1751 1.9 ◐	**18** 0021 3.7 / 0630 2.3 / F 1329 3.6 / 1844 2.5	**3** 0143 3.9 / 0755 2.1 / SU 1446 3.8 / 2059 2.2	**18** 0246 3.7 / 0926 2.2 / M 1532 3.7 / 2142 2.4
4 / 19	**4** 0049 4.1 / 0638 2.2 / TU 1254 4.2 / 1928 2.0	**19** 0231 4.0 / 0818 2.3 / W 1450 4.1 / 2052 2.2	**4** 0221 4.1 / 0815 2.2 / F 1445 4.1 / 2112 2.1	**19** 0421 3.9 / 1041 2.3 / SA 1645 3.9 / 2254 2.3	**4** 0020 4.0 / 0619 2.0 / F 1253 3.9 / 1904 2.2	**19** 0215 3.6 / 0830 2.5 / SA 1505 3.6 / 2101 2.6	**4** 0309 4.1 / 0943 1.8 / M 1607 4.1 / 2219 1.9	**19** 0352 3.8 / 1024 1.9 / TU 1625 3.9 / 2234 2.0
5 / 20	**5** 0157 4.1 / 0747 2.3 / W 1404 4.3 / 2037 2.0	**20** 0345 4.0 / 0941 2.3 / TH 1601 4.1 / 2207 2.0	**5** 0337 4.2 / 0948 2.1 / SA 1610 4.3 / 2234 1.9	**20** 0512 4.2 / 1134 2.0 / SU 1733 4.1 / 2341 2.0	**5** 0155 4.0 / 0752 2.2 / SA 1442 3.9 / 2100 2.3	**20** 0345 3.7 / 1018 2.3 / SU 1619 3.8 / 2231 2.4	**5** 0416 4.4 / 1049 1.3 / TU 1702 4.4 / 2311 1.4	**20** 0437 4.1 / 1105 1.6 / W 1703 4.2 / 2312 1.7
6 / 21	**6** 0302 4.2 / 0900 2.2 / TH 1512 4.4 / 2145 1.8	**21** 0443 4.2 / 1052 2.2 / F 1659 4.2 / 2307 1.9	**6** 0443 4.6 / 1103 1.7 / SU 1718 4.6 / 2335 1.6	**21** 0550 4.4 / 1214 1.7 / M 1809 4.4	**6** 0323 4.1 / 0946 2.0 / SU 1614 4.1 / 2231 2.0	**21** 0442 4.0 / 1109 1.9 / M 1707 4.0 / 2316 2.0	**6** 0506 4.8 / 1137 0.9 / W 1744 4.8 / 2355 1.0	**21** 0510 4.3 / 1139 1.3 / TH 1734 4.4 / 2347 1.4
7 / 22	**7** 0401 4.5 / 1009 2.0 / F 1617 4.5 / 2247 1.6	**22** 0529 4.4 / 1144 2.0 / SA 1745 4.3 / 2353 1.9	**7** 0537 4.9 / 1202 1.3 / M 1812 4.9	**22** 0018 1.8 / 0620 4.6 / TU 1249 1.5 / 1839 4.6	**7** 0433 4.4 / 1102 1.6 / M 1717 4.5 / 2329 1.5	**22** 0521 4.3 / 1146 1.6 / TU 1742 4.3 / 2352 1.7	**7** 0548 5.1 / 1219 0.6 / TH 1819 5.0	**22** 0539 4.5 / 1211 1.0 / F 1802 4.7
8 / 23	**8** 0455 4.8 / 1110 1.7 / SA 1716 4.8 / 2341 1.4	**23** 0606 4.6 / 1227 1.8 / SU 1824 4.5	**8** 0026 1.2 / 0623 5.3 / TU 1254 0.9 / ● 1857 5.2	**23** 0052 1.7 / 0648 4.8 / W 1320 1.2 / 1908 4.8	**8** 0526 4.9 / 1156 1.1 / TU 1803 4.9	**23** 0551 4.5 / 1219 1.3 / W 1811 4.5	**8** 0035 0.7 / 0625 5.3 / F 1258 0.4 / ● 1852 5.1	**23** 0019 1.1 / 0607 4.8 / SA 1243 0.8 / 1831 4.9
9 / 24	**9** 0544 5.1 / 1205 1.3 / SU 1811 5.0	**24** 0032 1.8 / 0638 4.8 / M 1305 1.6 / 1858 4.6	**9** 0113 0.9 / 0707 5.6 / W 1340 0.5 / 1939 5.3	**24** 0123 1.3 / 0714 5.0 / TH 1351 1.0 / ○ 1935 4.9	**9** 0015 1.1 / 0609 5.2 / W 1242 0.6 / 1841 5.1	**24** 0024 1.4 / 0617 4.7 / TH 1250 1.0 / 1837 4.8	**9** 0114 0.5 / 0701 5.4 / SA 1334 0.3 / 1924 5.2	**24** 0052 0.9 / 0637 5.0 / SU 1315 0.6 / ○ 1901 5.1
10 / 25	**10** 0032 1.2 / 0631 5.3 / M 1258 1.0 / ● 1902 5.2	**25** 0108 1.6 / 0707 4.9 / TU 1340 1.4 / ○ 1929 4.8	**10** 0156 0.7 / 0748 5.7 / TH 1424 0.4 / 2019 5.3	**25** 0152 1.1 / 0739 5.1 / F 1419 0.9 / 2002 4.9	**10** 0058 0.8 / 0648 5.5 / TH 1323 0.3 / ● 1918 5.3	**25** 0055 1.1 / 0643 4.9 / F 1319 0.8 / ○ 1904 4.9	**10** 0150 0.5 / 0736 5.3 / SU 1408 0.4 / 1956 5.1	**25** 0126 0.7 / 0709 5.1 / M 1348 0.6 / 1934 5.1
11 / 26	**11** 0120 1.0 / 0718 5.6 / TU 1348 0.8 / 1951 5.3	**26** 0141 1.5 / 0736 5.0 / W 1412 1.3 / 1959 4.8	**11** 0237 0.6 / 0829 5.7 / F 1505 0.4 / 2059 5.2	**26** 0221 1.0 / 0806 5.1 / SA 1448 0.8 / 2030 4.9	**11** 0137 0.5 / 0726 5.7 / F 1401 0.2 / 1952 5.3	**26** 0124 0.9 / 0709 5.0 / SA 1348 0.6 / 1931 5.0	**11** 0226 0.6 / 0812 5.1 / M 1442 0.6 / 2027 4.9	**26** 0201 0.7 / 0746 5.1 / TU 1422 0.6 / 2010 5.0
12 / 27	**12** 0207 1.0 / 0804 5.6 / W 1437 0.7 / 2039 5.2	**27** 0212 1.4 / 0803 5.0 / TH 1444 1.2 / 2029 4.8	**12** 0317 0.7 / 0910 5.5 / SA 1544 0.6 / 2138 4.9	**27** 0251 0.9 / 0834 5.1 / SU 1517 0.8 / 2100 4.9	**12** 0215 0.4 / 0803 5.4 / SA 1438 0.3 / 2027 5.2	**27** 0154 0.7 / 0736 5.1 / SU 1417 0.6 / 2000 5.1	**12** 0302 1.0 / 0849 4.8 / TU 1515 1.0 / 2100 4.6	**27** 0238 0.7 / 0826 4.9 / W 1459 0.8 / 2050 4.9
13 / 28	**13** 0253 1.1 / 0850 5.6 / TH 1524 0.7 / 2127 5.1	**28** 0243 1.5 / 0832 5.0 / F 1515 1.2 / 2100 4.7	**13** 0357 0.9 / 0952 5.2 / SU 1623 0.9 / 2219 4.6	**28** 0322 0.9 / 0905 5.0 / M 1548 1.0 / 2134 4.7	**13** 0252 0.5 / 0839 5.4 / SU 1513 0.5 / 2100 5.0	**28** 0225 0.7 / 0807 5.1 / M 1448 0.6 / 2032 5.0	**13** 0338 1.3 / 0929 4.4 / W 1548 1.3 / 2134 4.4	**28** 0319 0.8 / 0915 4.6 / TH 1539 1.2 / 2139 4.6
14 / 29	**14** 0338 1.1 / 0938 5.4 / F 1610 0.8 / 2215 4.9	**29** 0315 1.5 / 0902 5.0 / SA 1546 1.2 / 2132 4.6	**14** 0437 1.2 / 1036 4.8 / M 1702 1.3 / 2304 4.3		**14** 0328 0.8 / 0917 5.1 / M 1547 0.8 / 2134 4.7	**29** 0258 0.8 / 0841 5.0 / TU 1520 0.8 / 2107 4.8	**14** 0416 1.5 / 1017 4.1 / TH 1626 1.6 / 2216 4.1	**29** 0405 1.0 / 1017 4.3 / F 1626 1.4 / 2244 4.4
15 / 30	**15** 0424 1.3 / 1028 5.2 / SA 1657 1.1 / 2307 4.5	**30** 0347 1.4 / 0935 4.9 / SU 1619 1.3 / 2209 4.5	**15** 0520 1.6 / 1130 4.4 / TU 1744 1.7		**15** 0405 1.1 / 0957 4.6 / TU 1622 1.2 / 2210 4.3	**30** 0334 1.0 / 0920 4.8 / W 1556 1.1 / 2149 4.6	**15** 0500 1.9 / 1124 3.8 / F 1705 2.1 / 2324 3.8	**30** 0501 1.5 / 1141 4.0 / SA 1727 1.9
31		**31** 0423 1.5 / 1012 4.7 / M 1656 1.5 / 2253 4.4				**31** 0414 1.2 / 1008 4.4 / TH 1637 1.5 / 2243 4.3		

Chart Datum: 2·75 metres below Ordnance Datum (Newlyn)

》》 **FREE** monthly updates from 《《
www.reedsalmanac.co.uk

TIDES

TIME ZONE (UT)
For Summer Time add ONE hour in **non-shaded areas**

SCOTLAND – ULLAPOOL
LAT 57°54'N LONG 5°10'W
TIMES AND HEIGHTS OF HIGH AND LOW WATERS

YEAR 2005

	MAY			JUNE			JULY			AUGUST	
	Time m	Time m		Time m	Time m		Time m	Time m		Time m	Time m
1	0007 4.2 / 0615 1.7 / SU 1309 3.9 / ◐ 1857 2.2	**16** 0014 3.8 / 0646 2.1 / M 1318 3.6 / ◑ 1852 2.4	**1**	0216 4.3 / 0841 1.5 / W 1511 4.1 / 2110 1.7	**16** 0129 3.9 / 0801 1.9 / TH 1422 3.8 / 2016 2.1	**1**	0247 4.2 / 0900 1.7 / F 1537 4.1 / 2136 1.8	**16** 0128 4.0 / 0756 1.9 / SA 1428 3.9 / 2022 2.1	**1**	0440 4.0 / 1045 2.0 / M 1709 4.2 / 2328 1.9	**16** 0341 4.0 / 1003 2.0 / TU 1615 4.3 / 2236 1.8
2	0130 4.1 / 0754 1.8 / M 1433 3.9 / 2038 2.1	**17** 0134 3.7 / 0810 2.1 / TU 1427 3.6 / 2024 2.3	**2**	0320 4.4 / 0944 1.4 / TH 1608 4.2 / 2210 1.6	**17** 0229 4.0 / 0902 1.8 / F 1518 4.0 / 2120 2.0	**2**	0351 4.2 / 1004 1.7 / SA 1633 4.2 / 2240 1.7	**17** 0239 4.0 / 0908 1.9 / SU 1531 4.1 / 2136 2.0	**2**	0531 4.1 / 1137 1.9 / TU 1751 4.4	**17** 0453 4.3 / 1110 1.7 / W 1712 4.7 / 2337 1.3
3	0246 4.2 / 0920 1.5 / TU 1545 4.1 / 2150 1.8	**18** 0242 3.8 / 0919 1.9 / W 1527 3.8 / 2132 2.1	**3**	0415 4.5 / 1037 1.3 / F 1654 4.4 / 2302 1.4	**18** 0324 4.1 / 0958 1.6 / SA 1607 4.2 / 2216 1.7	**3**	0448 4.2 / 1100 1.6 / SU 1719 4.3 / 2334 1.6	**18** 0348 4.1 / 1017 1.7 / M 1629 4.4 / 2243 1.7	**3**	0014 1.6 / 0612 4.3 / W 1220 1.7 / 1825 4.6	**18** 0548 4.7 / 1202 1.3 / TH 1759 5.1
4	0351 4.4 / 1021 1.2 / W 1638 4.4 / 2243 1.4	**19** 0336 4.0 / 1009 1.6 / TH 1613 4.1 / 2221 1.8	**4**	0502 4.5 / 1123 1.2 / SA 1734 4.5 / 2348 1.3	**19** 0416 4.3 / 1048 1.4 / SU 1653 4.5 / 2307 1.5	**4**	0537 4.3 / 1147 1.6 / M 1800 4.5	**19** 0453 4.3 / 1117 1.5 / TU 1721 4.7 / 2342 1.4	**4**	0054 1.4 / 0646 4.5 / TH 1257 1.5 / 1855 4.7	**19** 0029 1.0 / 0633 5.0 / F 1249 1.0 / ◯ 1842 5.4
5	0441 4.7 / 1110 1.0 / TH 1719 4.6 / 2329 1.1	**20** 0419 4.2 / 1051 1.4 / F 1651 4.3 / 2302 1.5	**5**	0545 4.6 / 1205 1.1 / SU 1810 4.7	**20** 0505 4.5 / 1135 1.2 / M 1736 4.7 / 2356 1.2	**5**	0021 1.5 / 0619 4.4 / TU 1230 1.5 / 1835 4.6	**20** 0550 4.6 / 1210 1.3 / W 1810 5.0	**5**	0129 1.2 / 0718 4.6 / F 1330 1.4 / ● 1923 4.8	**20** 0116 0.5 / 0715 5.2 / SA 1333 0.7 / 1923 5.7
6	0524 4.9 / 1152 0.8 / F 1755 4.8	**21** 0456 4.4 / 1129 1.1 / SA 1726 4.6 / 2341 1.2	**6**	0031 1.2 / 0625 4.6 / M 1244 1.1 / ● 1843 4.7	**21** 0554 4.7 / 1221 1.0 / TU 1820 5.0	**6**	0104 1.4 / 0658 4.4 / W 1308 1.5 / ● 1908 4.7	**21** 0036 1.0 / 0641 4.9 / TH 1300 1.0 / ◯ 1856 5.2	**6**	0202 1.1 / 0747 4.7 / SA 1402 1.3 / 1950 4.9	**21** 0200 0.2 / 0755 5.3 / SU 1414 0.5 / 2004 5.7
7	0010 0.9 / 0602 5.0 / SA 1231 0.7 / 1828 4.9	**22** 0532 4.7 / 1206 0.9 / SU 1800 4.8	**7**	0112 1.1 / 0704 4.6 / TU 1320 1.2 / 1917 4.7	**22** 0044 1.0 / 0643 4.8 / W 1308 0.9 / ◯ 1904 5.1	**7**	0142 1.3 / 0734 4.5 / TH 1344 1.4 / 1940 4.7	**22** 0127 0.7 / 0730 5.0 / F 1347 0.8 / 1941 5.4	**7**	0233 1.0 / 0816 4.7 / SU 1433 1.2 / 2018 4.9	**22** 0241 0.2 / 0835 5.2 / M 1455 0.5 / 2045 5.6
8	0050 0.8 / 0639 5.0 / SU 1307 0.7 / ● 1900 4.9	**23** 0020 1.0 / 0610 4.8 / M 1244 0.8 / ◯ 1836 5.0	**8**	0150 1.1 / 0743 4.5 / W 1356 1.3 / 1950 4.7	**23** 0133 0.8 / 0734 4.9 / TH 1354 0.9 / 1951 5.2	**8**	0218 1.2 / 0809 4.5 / F 1418 1.4 / 2012 4.7	**23** 0215 0.5 / 0817 5.1 / SA 1432 0.8 / 2027 5.5	**8**	0303 1.0 / 0845 4.6 / M 1503 1.2 / 2046 4.9	**23** 0321 0.3 / 0915 5.0 / TU 1535 0.7 / 2128 5.3
9	0128 0.8 / 0715 4.9 / M 1341 0.8 / 1931 4.9	**24** 0101 0.8 / 0650 4.9 / TU 1323 0.7 / 1915 5.1	**9**	0228 1.2 / 0822 4.4 / TH 1431 1.4 / 2024 4.6	**24** 0222 0.7 / 0827 4.9 / F 1441 0.9 / 2041 5.2	**9**	0253 1.2 / 0843 4.5 / SA 1452 1.4 / 2043 4.7	**24** 0302 0.4 / 0903 5.0 / SU 1517 0.8 / 2113 5.4	**9**	0333 1.1 / 0916 4.6 / TU 1534 1.3 / 2117 4.7	**24** 0401 0.6 / 0957 4.7 / W 1616 1.0 / 2214 4.9
10	0205 0.9 / 0752 4.8 / TU 1415 1.0 / 2003 4.8	**25** 0143 0.7 / 0735 4.9 / W 1404 0.8 / 1957 5.1	**10**	0305 1.3 / 0902 4.3 / F 1506 1.5 / 2101 4.5	**25** 0312 0.7 / 0922 4.8 / SA 1530 1.1 / 2133 5.1	**10**	0327 1.2 / 0918 4.4 / SU 1526 1.5 / 2116 4.6	**25** 0348 0.5 / 0950 4.8 / M 1602 0.9 / 2202 5.2	**10**	0403 1.2 / 0950 4.4 / W 1607 1.4 / 2151 4.6	**25** 0440 1.0 / 1044 4.4 / TH 1700 1.4 / 2310 4.4
11	0241 1.0 / 0831 4.5 / W 1448 1.2 / 2037 4.6	**26** 0227 0.7 / 0826 4.8 / TH 1447 1.0 / 2045 5.0	**11**	0344 1.4 / 0944 4.2 / SA 1544 1.7 / 2140 4.3	**26** 0403 0.8 / 1018 4.6 / SU 1620 1.2 / 2230 4.9	**11**	0402 1.3 / 0954 4.3 / M 1601 1.6 / 2152 4.5	**26** 0433 0.7 / 1040 4.6 / TU 1647 1.1 / 2255 4.9	**11**	0437 1.3 / 1029 4.3 / TH 1644 1.6 / 2231 4.4	**26** 0523 1.4 / 1146 4.1 / F 1750 1.9 / ◐
12	0318 1.3 / 0913 4.3 / TH 1523 1.5 / 2113 4.4	**27** 0314 0.9 / 0923 4.6 / F 1533 1.2 / 2140 4.8	**12**	0425 1.6 / 1030 4.0 / SU 1624 1.8 / 2226 4.2	**27** 0457 0.9 / 1117 4.4 / M 1714 1.4 / 2330 4.7	**12**	0438 1.4 / 1034 4.2 / TU 1639 1.6 / 2233 4.3	**27** 0518 1.0 / 1136 4.4 / W 1736 1.4 / 2354 4.5	**12**	0515 1.5 / 1119 4.1 / F 1728 1.8 / 2322 4.2	**27** 0024 4.0 / 0611 2.0 / SA 1310 3.8 / 1858 2.2
13	0357 1.5 / 1002 4.0 / F 1600 1.7 / 2157 4.2	**28** 0406 1.0 / 1029 4.4 / SA 1626 1.5 / 2245 4.6	**13**	0509 1.7 / 1122 3.9 / M 1709 2.0 / 2320 4.0	**28** 0552 1.1 / 1221 4.2 / TU 1813 1.6 / ◐	**13**	0517 1.5 / 1121 4.0 / W 1721 1.8 / 2320 4.2	**28** 0607 1.4 / 1239 4.0 / TH 1832 1.8 / ◐	**13**	0601 1.8 / 1239 3.8 / SA 1823 2.0 / ◑	**28** 0152 3.8 / 0721 2.4 / SU 1443 3.8 / 2045 2.4
14	0441 1.8 / 1101 3.8 / SA 1642 2.0 / 2255 3.9	**29** 0505 1.3 / 1140 4.2 / SU 1728 1.7 / 2355 4.4	**14**	0600 1.8 / 1220 3.8 / TU 1803 2.1	**29** 0034 4.5 / 0651 1.4 / W 1325 4.1 / 1916 1.8	**14**	0601 1.7 / 1220 3.9 / TH 1811 1.9 / ◐	**29** 0102 4.2 / 0702 1.8 / F 1353 3.9 / 1941 2.0	**14**	0037 4.0 / 0702 2.0 / SU 1348 3.9 / 1938 2.2	**29** 0320 3.9 / 0912 2.2 / M 1600 3.9 / 2224 2.2
15	0535 2.0 / 1208 3.7 / SU 1736 2.3	**30** 0614 1.4 / 1251 4.0 / M 1843 1.9 / ◐	**15**	0023 3.9 / 0658 1.9 / W 1322 3.7 / ◐ 1907 2.1	**30** 0140 4.3 / 0754 1.5 / TH 1433 4.0 / 2026 1.9	**15**	0019 4.0 / 0653 1.8 / F 1323 3.9 / 1911 2.0	**30** 0218 4.0 / 0812 2.1 / SA 1510 3.9 / 2107 2.2	**15**	0212 3.9 / 0830 2.1 / M 1506 4.0 / 2113 2.1	**30** 0429 4.1 / 1036 2.1 / TU 1654 4.2 / 2318 1.9
					31 0106 4.3 / 0729 1.5 / TU 1404 4.0 / 2000 1.9				**31** 0334 3.9 / 0935 2.1 / SU 1617 4.0 / 2229 2.1			**31** 0518 4.1 / 1125 1.9 / W 1733 4.4 / 2359 1.6

Chart Datum: 2·75 metres below Ordnance Datum (Newlyn)

》》 **FREE** monthly updates from 《《
www.reedsalmanac.co.uk

TIME ZONE (UT)
For Summer Time add ONE hour in **non-shaded areas**

SCOTLAND – ULLAPOOL
LAT 57°54'N   LONG 5°10'W
TIMES AND HEIGHTS OF HIGH AND LOW WATERS

YEAR 2005

SEPTEMBER

Day	Time m	Time m
1 TH	0555 4.3 / 1203 1.8 / 1805 4.6	**16** F 0536 4.8 / 1148 1.3 / 1742 5.2
2 F	0033 1.4 / 0625 4.6 / 1237 1.5 / 1832 4.8	**17** SA 0014 0.7 / 0616 5.1 / 1231 0.9 / 1821 5.6
3 SA	0105 1.1 / 0652 4.7 / 1308 1.3 / 1857 5.0	**18** SU 0056 0.4 / 0652 5.3 / 1311 0.6 / 1900 5.8
4 SU	0135 1.0 / 0719 4.8 / 1337 1.1 / 1922 5.1	**19** M 0136 0.2 / 0728 5.4 / 1350 0.5 / 1937 5.8
5 M	0204 0.9 / 0745 4.9 / 1406 1.0 / 1947 5.1	**20** TU 0214 0.2 / 0803 5.3 / 1429 0.5 / 2016 5.6
6 TU	0232 0.8 / 0811 4.9 / 1435 1.0 / 2014 5.1	**21** W 0250 0.4 / 0838 5.1 / 1507 0.7 / 2055 5.2
7 W	0300 0.9 / 0840 4.8 / 1505 1.1 / 2044 4.9	**22** TH 0327 0.8 / 0915 4.8 / 1546 1.1 / 2138 4.8
8 TH	0329 1.0 / 0911 4.7 / 1537 1.2 / 2116 4.8	**23** F 0403 1.2 / 0954 4.5 / 1627 1.5 / 2230 4.3
9 F	0401 1.2 / 0948 4.5 / 1613 1.5 / 2155 4.5	**24** SA 0442 1.7 / 1045 4.1 / 1715 2.0 / 2348 3.9
10 SA	0437 1.5 / 1035 4.3 / 1656 1.7 / 2248 4.2	**25** SU 0526 2.2 / 1220 3.9 / 1821 2.4 ◐
11 SU	0522 1.9 / 1146 4.1 / 1751 2.1 ◐	**26** M 0122 3.7 / 0632 2.6 / 1406 3.8 / 2020 2.5
12 M	0018 3.9 / 0626 2.2 / 1325 4.0 / 1915 2.3	**27** TU 0254 3.7 / 0843 2.7 / 1530 3.9 / 2202 2.3
13 TU	0211 3.8 / 0816 2.4 / 1452 4.1 / 2112 2.2	**28** W 0405 3.9 / 1013 2.4 / 1626 4.1 / 2252 2.0
14 W	0344 4.0 / 1000 2.1 / 1604 4.4 / 2233 1.7	**29** TH 0452 4.1 / 1059 2.1 / 1704 4.4 / 2329 1.7
15 TH	0449 4.0 / 1101 1.7 / 1658 4.8 / 2328 1.2	**30** F 0526 4.4 / 1135 1.8 / 1735 4.6

OCTOBER

Day	Time m	Time m
1 SA	0002 1.4 / 0555 4.6 / 1207 1.5 / 1801 4.8	**16** SU 0554 5.2 / 1208 0.9 / 1759 5.5
2 SU	0033 1.1 / 0621 4.8 / 1237 1.3 / 1826 5.0	**17** M 0031 0.5 / 0628 5.3 / 1248 0.7 / 1836 5.6
3 M	0102 0.9 / 0647 5.0 / 1307 1.1 / 1851 5.2	**18** TU 0109 0.4 / 0701 5.4 / 1326 0.6 / 1913 5.6
4 TU	0130 0.8 / 0712 5.1 / 1336 1.0 / 1917 5.2	**19** W 0145 0.5 / 0734 5.3 / 1404 0.7 / 1951 5.4
5 W	0158 0.8 / 0740 5.1 / 1406 1.0 / 1945 5.2	**20** TH 0221 0.8 / 0808 5.2 / 1442 1.0 / 2030 5.1
6 TH	0227 0.9 / 0809 5.1 / 1438 1.0 / 2017 5.0	**21** F 0256 1.1 / 0842 4.9 / 1521 1.3 / 2112 4.7
7 F	0258 1.0 / 0842 4.9 / 1512 1.2 / 2053 4.8	**22** SA 0331 1.5 / 0920 4.6 / 1602 1.7 / 2204 4.3
8 SA	0332 1.3 / 0921 4.7 / 1551 1.4 / 2135 4.5	**23** SU 0409 1.9 / 1005 4.3 / 1649 2.0 / 2315 3.9
9 SU	0411 1.6 / 1011 4.4 / 1637 1.8 / 2243 4.2	**24** M 0453 2.3 / 1120 4.0 / 1751 2.4
10 M	0500 2.0 / 1131 4.2 / 1738 2.1 ◐	**25** TU 0041 3.7 / 0552 2.6 / 1307 3.9 / 1929 2.5
11 TU	0031 3.9 / 0612 2.4 / 1312 4.1 / 1915 2.2	**26** W 0206 3.7 / 0742 2.8 / 1436 3.9 / 2110 2.3
12 W	0211 3.9 / 0806 2.4 / 1436 4.2 / 2107 2.0	**27** TH 0319 3.9 / 0922 2.6 / 1539 4.1 / 2207 2.1
13 TH	0334 4.2 / 0946 2.1 / 1545 4.5 / 2217 1.6	**28** F 0411 4.1 / 1016 2.3 / 1623 4.3 / 2248 1.8
14 F	0433 4.5 / 1041 1.7 / 1637 4.9 / 2308 1.1	**29** SA 0449 4.3 / 1055 1.9 / 1656 4.5 / 2323 1.5
15 SA	0516 4.8 / 1126 1.3 / 1720 5.3 / 2351 0.8	**30** SU 0520 4.6 / 1129 1.6 / 1725 4.8 / 2354 1.3
		31 M 0548 4.8 / 1202 1.4 / 1752 5.0

NOVEMBER

Day	Time m	Time m
1 TU	0025 1.1 / 0615 5.0 / 1234 1.2 / 1820 5.1	**16** W 0044 0.9 / 0640 5.2 / 1306 1.0 / 1856 5.3 ○
2 W	0056 1.0 / 0643 5.2 / 1307 1.1 / 1851 5.2 ●	**17** TH 0121 1.0 / 0714 5.2 / 1346 1.1 / 1935 5.1
3 TH	0128 0.9 / 0714 5.2 / 1341 1.0 / 1924 5.2	**18** F 0157 1.1 / 0748 5.1 / 1425 1.2 / 2016 4.9
4 F	0201 1.0 / 0747 5.2 / 1417 1.1 / 2002 5.0	**19** SA 0232 1.4 / 0824 5.0 / 1504 1.4 / 2059 4.6
5 SA	0236 1.1 / 0825 5.1 / 1456 1.2 / 2047 4.8	**20** SU 0309 1.7 / 0901 4.7 / 1545 1.7 / 2146 4.3
6 SU	0315 1.4 / 0910 4.9 / 1540 1.4 / 2143 4.5	**21** M 0347 1.9 / 0944 4.5 / 1630 1.9 / 2242 4.1
7 M	0359 1.7 / 1009 4.6 / 1633 1.7 / 2300 4.3	**22** TU 0429 2.2 / 1038 4.3 / 1723 2.2 / 2347 3.9
8 TU	0454 2.1 / 1128 4.4 / 1740 1.9	**23** W 0521 2.5 / 1152 4.1 / 1830 2.3 ◐
9 W	0030 4.1 / 0612 2.3 / 1253 4.3 / 1911 2.0 ◐	**24** TH 0057 3.8 / 0631 2.6 / 1314 4.0 / 1948 2.3
10 TH	0154 4.1 / 0753 2.3 / 1410 4.4 / 2040 1.8	**25** F 0209 3.9 / 0758 2.6 / 1426 4.0 / 2058 2.2
11 F	0309 4.3 / 0912 2.1 / 1517 4.6 / 2147 1.5	**26** SA 0311 4.0 / 0909 2.4 / 1522 4.2 / 2152 2.0
12 SA	0407 4.5 / 1011 1.7 / 1611 4.9 / 2239 1.3	**27** SU 0400 4.2 / 1002 2.1 / 1607 4.4 / 2235 1.7
13 SU	0452 4.8 / 1059 1.5 / 1657 5.1 / 2324 1.0	**28** M 0439 4.5 / 1046 1.9 / 1644 4.6 / 2313 1.5
14 M	0531 5.0 / 1144 1.2 / 1739 5.3 / 2350 1.3	**29** TU 0513 4.7 / 1125 1.7 / 1720 4.8 / 2350 1.3
15 TU	0005 0.9 / 0606 5.2 / 1226 1.0 / 1818 5.3	**30** W 0546 4.9 / 1203 1.5 / 1755 4.9

DECEMBER

Day	Time m	Time m
1 TH	0026 1.2 / 0620 5.1 / 1243 1.3 / 1833 5.1 ●	**16** F 0105 1.4 / 0705 5.1 / 1336 1.3 / 1930 4.9
2 F	0104 1.1 / 0657 5.3 / 1323 1.1 / 1915 5.1	**17** SA 0142 1.4 / 0740 5.1 / 1416 1.4 / 2009 4.8
3 SA	0143 1.1 / 0736 5.3 / 1405 1.1 / 2001 5.0	**18** SU 0218 1.5 / 0814 5.0 / 1454 1.4 / 2047 4.7
4 SU	0224 1.2 / 0820 5.3 / 1450 1.1 / 2053 4.9	**19** M 0254 1.6 / 0849 4.9 / 1532 1.6 / 2126 4.5
5 M	0308 1.4 / 0910 5.1 / 1539 1.3 / 2151 4.7	**20** TU 0331 1.8 / 0925 4.7 / 1611 1.7 / 2207 4.3
6 TU	0357 1.6 / 1007 4.9 / 1634 1.4 / 2257 4.4	**21** W 0409 1.9 / 1004 4.6 / 1653 1.8 / 2252 4.2
7 W	0453 1.9 / 1113 4.8 / 1736 1.6	**22** TH 0450 2.1 / 1051 4.4 / 1738 2.0 / 2347 4.0
8 TH	0007 4.3 / 0559 2.0 / 1224 4.6 / 1845 1.7 ◐	**23** F 0538 2.2 / 1148 4.2 / 1831 2.1 ◐
9 F	0120 4.3 / 0714 2.1 / 1334 4.6 / 1958 1.7	**24** SA 0050 3.9 / 0635 2.4 / 1256 4.1 / 1931 2.2
10 SA	0231 4.3 / 0828 2.1 / 1442 4.6 / 2106 1.8	**25** SU 0157 3.9 / 0743 2.4 / 1405 4.1 / 2036 2.2
11 SU	0335 4.4 / 0935 1.9 / 1544 4.6 / 2206 1.6	**26** M 0259 4.1 / 0853 2.4 / 1506 4.1 / 2138 2.0
12 M	0428 4.6 / 1033 1.8 / 1638 4.8 / 2258 1.5	**27** TU 0353 4.3 / 0956 2.2 / 1602 4.3 / 2232 1.9
13 TU	0513 4.8 / 1125 1.6 / 1726 4.8 / 2344 1.4	**28** W 0440 4.5 / 1051 1.9 / 1653 4.5 / 2320 1.7
14 W	0553 4.9 / 1212 1.4 / 1809 4.9	**29** TH 0524 4.8 / 1140 1.6 / 1741 4.7
15 TH	0026 1.4 / 0630 5.0 / 1256 1.4 / 1850 4.9 ○	**30** F 0005 1.5 / 0605 5.0 / 1227 1.4 / 1827 4.9
		31 SA 0050 1.3 / 0647 5.3 / 1314 1.1 / 1914 5.1

Chart Datum: 2·75 metres below Ordnance Datum (Newlyn)

》》 **FREE** monthly updates from 《《
www.reedsalmanac.co.uk

TIDES

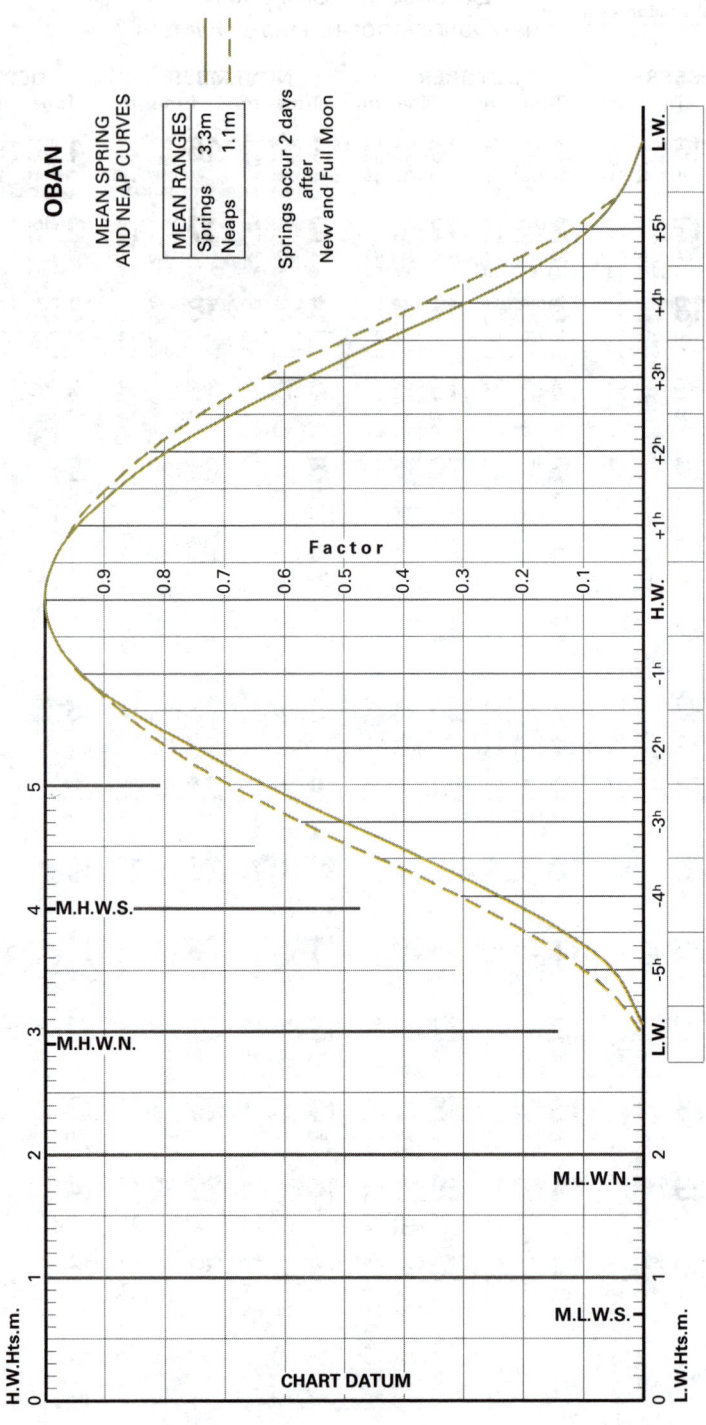

TIME ZONE (UT)
For Summer Time add ONE hour in **non-shaded areas**

SCOTLAND – OBAN
LAT 56°25'N   LONG 5°29'W
TIMES AND HEIGHTS OF HIGH AND LOW WATERS

YEAR 2005

JANUARY		FEBRUARY		MARCH		APRIL	
Time m	Time m	Time m	Time m	Time m	Time m	Time m	Time m
1 0254 1.5 0850 3.6 SA 1531 1.9 2115 3.3	**16** 0352 1.0 0954 3.6 SU 1627 1.4 2159 3.2	**1** 0335 1.3 0932 3.5 TU 1601 1.7 2159 3.2	**16** 0448 1.5 1036 3.0 W 1718 1.7 ☾ 2232 2.9	**1** 0228 0.9 0825 3.7 TU 1446 1.3 2045 3.5	**16** 0327 1.2 0908 3.2 W 1547 1.4 2108 3.2	**1** 0345 1.3 0927 3.1 F 1610 1.5 2207 3.0	**16** 0444 2.0 1012 2.6 SA 1710 1.8 ☾ 2229 2.8
2 0332 1.6 0928 3.5 SU 1611 1.9 2157 3.2	**17** 0441 1.2 1046 3.3 M 1717 1.6 ☾ 2249 3.0	**2** 0424 1.5 1020 3.3 W 1701 1.8 ☾ 2254 3.1	**17** 0545 1.8 1154 2.7 TH 1821 1.9	**2** 0306 1.1 0900 3.5 W 1526 1.4 2125 3.3	**17** 0411 1.6 0945 2.9 TH 1638 1.7 ☾ 2149 3.0	**2** 0504 1.5 1045 2.7 SA 1743 1.7 ◐	**17** 0612 2.1 1338 2.6 SU 1823 1.9
3 0416 1.6 1014 3.4 M 1705 2.0 ◐ 2248 3.1	**18** 0536 1.5 1154 3.1 TU 1813 1.8	**3** 0527 1.6 1126 3.1 TH 1824 1.9	**18** 0003 2.7 0707 2.0 F 1449 2.7 1938 1.9	**3** 0354 1.3 0944 3.2 TH 1622 1.6 ◐ 2218 3.1	**18** 0508 1.9 1042 2.6 F 1742 1.9 2252 2.7	**3** 0002 2.9 0640 1.6 SU 1353 2.7 1919 1.6	**18** 0126 2.7 0907 2.0 M 1443 2.7 1944 1.8
4 0509 1.7 1111 3.3 TU 1812 2.0 2355 3.0	**19** 0002 2.9 0641 1.7 W 1328 3.0 1916 1.9	**4** 0019 3.0 0648 1.7 F 1317 3.0 1951 1.8	**19** 0227 2.8 0947 2.0 SA 1601 2.9 2108 1.8	**4** 0502 1.6 1049 2.9 F 1752 1.8 2351 2.9	**19** 0633 2.1 1426 2.6 SA 1901 1.9	**4** 0221 3.1 0822 1.5 M 1513 2.9 2045 1.4	**19** 0247 2.9 0947 1.7 TU 1522 2.9 2054 1.6
5 0613 1.7 1226 3.3 W 1922 1.9	**20** 0134 2.9 0807 1.8 TH 1452 3.0 2025 1.9	**5** 0228 3.1 0816 1.6 SA 1510 3.2 2109 1.6	**20** 0342 3.0 1040 1.8 SU 1632 3.1 2210 1.6	**5** 0638 1.7 1326 2.8 SA 1933 1.8	**20** 0219 2.7 0944 2.0 SU 1533 2.8 2037 1.8	**5** 0323 3.4 0936 1.2 TU 1603 3.2 2147 1.0	**20** 0324 3.1 1014 1.5 W 1554 3.3 2141 1.3
6 0124 3.1 0722 1.6 TH 1356 3.4 2028 1.7	**21** 0247 3.0 0938 1.8 F 1550 3.1 2130 1.7	**6** 0345 3.4 0939 1.4 SU 1616 3.4 2213 1.3	**21** 0422 3.2 1117 1.5 M 1657 3.3 2253 1.3	**6** 0234 3.0 0818 1.6 SU 1525 3.0 2100 1.5	**21** 0333 2.9 1025 1.7 M 1606 3.0 2145 1.6	**6** 0409 3.7 1026 0.9 W 1639 3.5 2235 0.7	**21** 0357 3.4 1039 1.3 TH 1625 3.4 2218 1.1
7 0244 3.2 0833 1.5 F 1508 3.5 2127 1.5	**22** 0342 3.2 1037 1.7 SA 1629 3.3 2220 1.6	**7** 0438 3.7 1046 1.1 M 1704 3.6 2306 0.9	**22** 0458 3.5 1148 1.4 TU 1726 3.5 2328 1.1	**7** 0343 3.4 0945 1.3 M 1620 3.3 2205 1.2	**22** 0403 3.2 1055 1.5 TU 1631 3.2 2226 1.3	**7** 0448 4.0 1107 0.7 TH 1709 3.7 2318 0.5	**22** 0430 3.6 1105 1.0 F 1656 3.6 2251 0.9
8 0344 3.5 0941 1.3 SA 1605 3.7 2221 1.2	**23** 0427 3.4 1121 1.6 SU 1703 3.4 2303 1.4	**8** 0523 4.0 1139 0.8 TU 1745 3.8 ● 2353 0.6	**23** 0532 3.7 1216 1.2 W 1758 3.7	**8** 0431 3.7 1043 1.0 TU 1700 3.5 2255 0.8	**23** 0434 3.4 1121 1.2 W 1700 3.5 2301 1.0	**8** 0524 4.1 1144 0.6 F 1739 3.8 ● 2358 0.4	**23** 0503 3.8 1131 0.9 SA 1725 3.7 2324 0.7
9 0435 3.8 1043 1.1 SU 1656 3.9 2311 1.0	**24** 0508 3.6 1158 1.5 M 1738 3.6 2342 1.2	**9** 0605 4.2 1226 0.6 W 1823 3.9	**24** 0001 0.9 0605 3.8 TH 1243 1.1 ○ 1829 3.8	**9** 0511 4.0 1129 0.7 W 1734 3.8 2339 0.5	**24** 0506 3.7 1146 1.0 TH 1731 3.7 2332 0.8	**9** 0559 4.2 1219 0.5 SA 1809 3.9	**24** 0533 3.9 1158 0.7 SU 1752 3.8 ○ 2359 0.6
10 0522 4.0 1139 0.9 M 1743 3.9 ○ 2358 0.8	**25** 0546 3.7 1231 1.4 TU 1814 3.7 ○	**10** 0037 0.4 0644 4.3 TH 1309 0.5 1859 3.9	**25** 0033 0.8 0636 3.9 F 1310 1.0 1857 3.8	**10** 0549 4.2 1210 0.5 TH 1806 3.9 ●	**25** 0538 3.8 1210 0.9 F 1800 3.8	**10** 0037 0.4 0631 4.1 SU 1253 0.6 1839 3.9	**25** 0603 4.0 1227 0.7 M 1820 3.9
11 0608 4.1 1230 0.7 TU 1827 3.9	**26** 0019 1.1 0621 3.8 W 1303 1.3 1848 3.8	**11** 0120 0.4 0723 4.3 F 1350 0.6 1934 3.9	**26** 0101 0.7 0703 4.0 SA 1335 1.0 1921 3.8	**11** 0020 0.3 0624 4.3 F 1248 0.4 1837 4.0	**26** 0001 0.7 0607 4.0 SA 1236 0.8 1826 3.9	**11** 0114 0.5 0702 4.0 M 1325 0.7 1908 3.9	**26** 0035 0.5 0634 3.9 TU 1259 0.7 1852 3.8
12 0045 0.6 0653 4.2 W 1320 0.7 1910 3.9	**27** 0055 1.0 0655 3.9 TH 1334 1.3 1920 3.8	**12** 0201 0.4 0801 4.2 SA 1428 0.7 2008 3.7	**27** 0128 0.7 0728 3.9 SU 1356 1.0 1944 3.7	**12** 0100 0.3 0659 4.3 SA 1323 0.5 1908 3.9	**27** 0030 0.6 0633 4.0 SU 1301 0.8 1849 3.9	**12** 0149 0.8 0733 3.8 TU 1359 0.9 1937 3.7	**27** 0115 0.6 0710 3.8 W 1336 0.8 1930 3.7
13 0132 0.6 0738 4.2 TH 1407 0.8 1952 3.7	**28** 0127 1.0 0726 3.9 F 1403 1.3 1948 3.7	**13** 0241 0.6 0837 3.9 SU 1506 0.9 2041 3.5	**28** 0156 0.8 0754 3.9 M 1416 1.1 2012 3.6	**13** 0139 0.3 0732 4.1 SU 1357 0.6 1938 3.8	**28** 0100 0.6 0659 3.9 M 1324 0.8 1915 3.8	**13** 0224 1.1 0804 3.5 W 1435 1.1 2008 3.5	**28** 0159 0.8 0749 3.6 TH 1418 1.0 2014 3.6
14 0218 0.6 0822 4.0 F 1454 0.9 2034 3.6	**29** 0156 1.1 0755 3.8 SA 1429 1.4 2014 3.6	**14** 0321 0.9 0913 3.6 M 1544 1.2 2112 3.3		**14** 0215 0.6 0804 3.8 M 1431 0.9 2006 3.7	**29** 0132 0.7 0728 3.9 TU 1352 0.9 1947 3.7	**14** 0300 1.3 0838 3.2 TH 1517 1.4 2044 3.3	**29** 0250 1.0 0835 3.3 F 1509 1.2 2106 3.3
15 0304 0.7 0907 3.8 SA 1540 1.1 2116 3.4	**30** 0224 1.1 0823 3.8 SU 1449 1.5 2043 3.5	**15** 0402 1.2 0951 3.3 TU 1627 1.5 2147 3.1		**15** 0250 0.9 0835 3.6 TU 1506 1.1 2035 3.5	**30** 0208 0.8 0802 3.7 W 1426 1.1 2023 3.5	**15** 0344 1.7 0915 2.9 F 1608 1.6 2126 3.0	**30** 0353 1.2 0933 2.9 SA 1614 1.4 2215 3.1
	31 0256 1.2 0854 3.6 M 1518 1.6 2117 3.4				**31** 0250 1.0 0840 3.4 TH 1509 1.3 2107 3.3		

Chart Datum: 2·10 metres below Ordnance Datum (Newlyn)

》》 **FREE** monthly updates from 《《
www.reedsalmanac.co.uk

TIDES

TIME ZONE (UT)
For Summer Time add ONE hour in **non-shaded areas**

SCOTLAND – OBAN
LAT 56°25'N   LONG 5°29'W

TIMES AND HEIGHTS OF HIGH AND LOW WATERS

YEAR 2005

Day	MAY Time m	Time m	JUNE Time m	Time m	JULY Time m	Time m	AUGUST Time m	Time m
1	0509 1.4 / 1102 2.7 / SU 1734 1.5 ○	**16** 0539 2.1 / 1147 2.7 / M 1737 1.8 / ● 2335 2.9	0112 3.2 / 0728 1.4 / W 1357 2.9 / 1941 1.3	**16** 0656 1.9 / 1301 2.9 / TH 1834 1.7	0133 3.1 / 0743 1.5 / F 1359 2.9 / 2007 1.5	**16** 0643 1.8 / 1238 2.9 / SA 1844 1.7	0343 2.9 / 0913 1.7 / M 1536 3.0 / 2223 1.7	**16** 0241 3.0 / 0844 1.6 / TU 1529 3.3 / 2107 1.5
2	0012 3.0 / 0636 1.5 / M 1330 2.7 / 1859 1.5	**17** 0715 2.0 / 1338 2.7 / TU 1841 1.8	0217 3.3 / 0832 1.3 / TH 1451 3.0 / 2046 1.2	**17** 0052 3.1 / 0755 1.7 / F 1405 3.0 / 1932 1.6	0239 3.1 / 0844 1.5 / SA 1455 3.0 / 2117 1.5	**17** 0057 3.1 / 0753 1.7 / SU 1414 3.0 / 1955 1.6	0429 3.1 / 1010 1.5 / TU 1620 3.2 / 2310 1.6	**17** 0356 3.2 / 0951 1.3 / W 1621 3.6 / 2220 1.2
3	0152 3.2 / 0805 1.4 / TU 1444 2.9 / 2018 1.3	**18** 0120 2.9 / 0830 1.8 / W 1428 2.9 / 1943 1.7	0309 3.4 / 0923 1.2 / F 1531 3.2 / 2142 1.1	**18** 0204 3.2 / 0846 1.6 / SA 1455 3.1 / 2031 1.4	0335 3.2 / 0936 1.5 / SU 1542 3.2 / 2216 1.4	**18** 0233 3.2 / 0859 1.5 / M 1524 3.2 / 2108 1.4	0500 3.2 / 1053 1.3 / W 1658 3.5 / 2348 1.4	**18** 0446 3.5 / 1045 1.0 / TH 1705 3.9 / 2315 0.8
4	0253 3.4 / 0910 1.2 / W 1533 3.1 / 2119 1.0	**19** 0224 3.1 / 0912 1.6 / TH 1508 3.1 / 2037 1.5	0354 3.5 / 1006 1.2 / SA 1606 3.4 / 2230 1.1	**19** 0303 3.4 / 0933 1.4 / SU 1541 3.3 / 2129 1.2	0421 3.3 / 1021 1.4 / M 1624 3.3 / 2306 1.4	**19** 0343 3.4 / 0958 1.3 / TU 1619 3.5 / 2215 1.2	0532 3.4 / 1132 1.1 / TH 1735 3.6	**19** 0527 3.7 / 1131 0.6 / F 1746 4.2 ○
5	0340 3.6 / 0958 1.0 / TH 1608 3.4 / 2209 0.8	**20** 0308 3.3 / 0946 1.4 / F 1543 3.3 / 2124 1.2	0433 3.6 / 1044 1.1 / SU 1642 3.5 / 2314 1.1	**20** 0354 3.5 / 1017 1.2 / M 1625 3.5 / 2224 1.0	0500 3.4 / 1102 1.3 / TU 1704 3.5 / 2349 1.4	**20** 0440 3.5 / 1050 1.0 / W 1707 3.8 / 2315 0.9	0021 1.3 / 0604 3.6 / F 1209 1.0 / ● 1810 3.8	**20** 0002 0.6 / 0605 3.9 / SA 1215 0.4 / 1824 4.3
6	0420 3.8 / 1038 0.9 / F 1638 3.6 / 2253 0.7	**21** 0347 3.5 / 1018 1.2 / SA 1616 3.5 / 2207 1.0	0509 3.6 / 1121 1.1 / M 1717 3.7 / ● 2355 1.1	**21** 0442 3.7 / 1101 1.0 / TU 1709 3.7 / 2318 0.8	0538 3.4 / 1142 1.2 / W 1743 3.6 ●	**21** 0529 3.7 / 1139 0.7 / TH 1753 4.0 ○	0053 1.2 / 0638 3.7 / SA 1244 0.9 / 1844 3.9	**21** 0046 0.4 / 0641 3.9 / SU 1257 0.3 / 1903 4.4
7	0457 3.9 / 1114 0.8 / SA 1709 3.7 / 2334 0.7	**22** 0425 3.7 / 1050 1.0 / SU 1649 3.6 / 2249 0.8	0545 3.6 / 1157 1.0 / TU 1753 3.7	**22** 0528 3.7 / 1146 0.8 / W 1753 3.9 ○	0028 1.4 / 0614 3.5 / TH 1222 1.1 / 1821 3.7	**22** 0009 0.7 / 0613 3.8 / F 1226 0.5 / 1837 4.1	0123 1.2 / 0711 3.7 / SU 1316 0.9 / 1915 3.9	**22** 0127 0.4 / 0716 3.9 / M 1339 0.3 / 1941 4.3
8	0531 3.9 / 1148 0.8 / SU 1741 3.8 ●	**23** 0502 3.8 / 1124 0.8 / M 1723 3.8 / ○ 2333 0.7	0034 1.2 / 0620 3.6 / W 1236 1.1 / 1829 3.7	**23** 0010 0.7 / 0614 3.8 / TH 1232 0.7 / 1839 3.9	0105 1.4 / 0651 3.6 / F 1300 1.1 / 1857 3.7	**23** 0059 0.6 / 0656 3.8 / SA 1311 0.4 / 1921 4.2	0153 1.2 / 0740 3.7 / M 1346 1.0 / 1944 3.8	**23** 0206 0.5 / 0751 3.8 / TU 1420 0.4 / 2017 4.0
9	0013 0.7 / 0604 3.9 / M 1222 0.8 / 1812 3.9	**24** 0540 3.9 / 1201 0.7 / TU 1800 3.9	0113 1.3 / 0657 3.5 / TH 1314 1.1 / 1905 3.7	**24** 0103 0.7 / 0700 3.7 / F 1320 0.6 / 1926 3.9	0141 1.4 / 0727 3.5 / SA 1337 1.1 / 1933 3.7	**24** 0146 0.5 / 0738 3.7 / SU 1357 0.7 / 2004 4.1	0221 1.3 / 0806 3.6 / TU 1413 1.1 / 2010 3.8	**24** 0245 0.7 / 0825 3.6 / W 1500 0.7 / 2054 3.7
10	0051 0.9 / 0636 3.8 / TU 1257 0.9 / 1844 3.8	**25** 0018 0.6 / 0619 3.8 / W 1242 0.7 / 1840 3.9	0151 1.4 / 0735 3.4 / F 1354 1.2 / 1943 3.6	**25** 0155 0.7 / 0747 3.6 / SA 1408 0.6 / 2014 3.9	0217 1.4 / 0803 3.5 / SU 1412 1.2 / 2007 3.7	**25** 0232 0.6 / 0819 3.6 / M 1442 0.5 / 2047 3.9	0243 1.4 / 0831 3.5 / W 1441 1.2 / 2038 3.6	**25** 0324 1.0 / 0859 3.4 / TH 1543 1.0 / 2132 3.4
11	0127 1.1 / 0710 3.6 / W 1333 1.0 / 1917 3.7	**26** 0106 0.7 / 0701 3.7 / TH 1327 0.7 / 1925 3.8	0231 1.6 / 0814 3.3 / SA 1434 1.3 / 2022 3.5	**26** 0247 0.8 / 0836 3.4 / SU 1459 0.7 / 2105 3.7	0252 1.5 / 0836 3.4 / M 1446 1.3 / 2040 3.6	**26** 0317 0.8 / 0901 3.4 / TU 1528 0.7 / 2131 3.7	0304 1.5 / 0901 3.3 / TH 1515 1.3 / 2109 3.5	**26** 0408 1.3 / 0935 3.1 / F 1630 1.4 / ◐ 2215 3.0
12	0203 1.3 / 0744 3.4 / TH 1412 1.2 / 1952 3.6	**27** 0157 0.8 / 0747 3.5 / F 1415 0.8 / 2014 3.7	0313 1.7 / 0856 3.1 / SU 1515 1.5 / 2102 3.4	**27** 0341 1.0 / 0927 3.2 / M 1551 0.9 / 2201 3.5	0325 1.6 / 0909 3.2 / TU 1519 1.4 / 2114 3.4	**27** 0403 1.0 / 0943 3.2 / W 1616 1.0 / 2219 3.4	0338 1.6 / 0939 3.2 / F 1558 1.5 / 2149 3.3	**27** 0459 1.6 / 1022 2.7 / SA 1727 1.7 / 2326 2.7
13	0242 1.6 / 0822 3.2 / F 1454 1.4 / 2031 3.4	**28** 0252 0.9 / 0838 3.3 / SA 1508 1.0 / 2110 3.5	0400 1.8 / 0941 3.0 / M 1559 1.6 / 2147 3.2	**28** 0437 1.1 / 1025 3.0 / TU 1648 1.1 / ◐ 2304 3.3	0358 1.7 / 0944 3.1 / W 1557 1.5 / 2151 3.3	**28** 0451 1.3 / 1031 2.9 / TH 1708 1.3 / ◐ 2315 3.1	0429 1.7 / 1027 3.0 / SA 1655 1.6 / 2243 3.1	**28** 0602 1.8 / 1215 2.5 / SU 1850 1.9
14	0328 1.8 / 0905 3.0 / SA 1542 1.6 / 2115 3.2	**29** 0353 1.1 / 0938 3.0 / SU 1608 1.1 / 2216 3.3	0453 1.9 / 1034 2.9 / TU 1646 1.7 / 2237 3.1	**29** 0536 1.3 / 1134 2.9 / W 1749 1.2	0438 1.8 / 1027 3.0 / TH 1642 1.6 / ◐ 2237 3.2	**29** 0545 1.6 / 1136 2.8 / F 1808 1.5	0549 1.8 / 1141 2.9 / SU 1813 1.8	**29** 0226 2.7 / 0721 1.9 / M 1532 2.7 / 2131 2.0
15	0425 2.0 / 1002 2.8 / SU 1636 1.7 / 2212 3.0	**30** 0501 1.3 / 1056 2.8 / M 1715 1.3 / ◐ 2345 3.2	0553 1.9 / 1141 2.8 / W 1738 1.7 / ◐ 2338 3.1	**30** 0018 3.2 / 0639 1.4 / TH 1251 2.8 / 1855 1.4	0534 1.8 / 1121 2.9 / F 1738 1.6 / 2335 3.2	**30** 0039 2.9 / 0647 1.7 / SA 1308 2.8 / 1924 1.7	0013 3.0 / 0721 1.8 / M 1410 3.0 / 1940 1.7	**30** 0352 2.8 / 0857 1.7 / TU 1620 3.0 / 2227 1.7
16		**31** 0615 1.4 / 1240 2.8 / TU 1828 1.3				**31** 0220 2.8 / 0759 1.7 / SU 1432 2.9 / 2111 1.8		**31** 0426 3.0 / 0958 1.5 / W 1617 3.3 / 2302 1.4

Chart Datum: 2·10 metres below Ordnance Datum (Newlyn)

》》 **FREE** monthly updates from 《《
www.reedsalmanac.co.uk

SCOTLAND – OBAN
LAT 56°25′N LONG 5°29′W

TIME ZONE (UT) For Summer Time add ONE hour in **non-shaded areas**

TIMES AND HEIGHTS OF HIGH AND LOW WATERS

YEAR **2005**

SEPTEMBER		OCTOBER		NOVEMBER		DECEMBER	
Time m	Time m	Time m	Time m	Time m	Time m	Time m	Time m
1 0446 3.3 / 1040 1.3 / TH 1645 3.5 / 2332 1.4	**16** 0437 3.5 / 1031 0.9 / F 1648 4.1 / 2302 0.8	**1** 0442 3.5 / 1046 1.1 / SA 1648 3.8 / 2327 1.4	**16** 0445 3.8 / 1052 0.6 / SU 1700 4.3 / 2317 0.7	**1** 0508 3.8 / 1109 1.0 / TU 1715 4.0 / 2341 1.0	**16** 0519 4.0 / 1152 0.9 / W 1743 4.1 / ○	**1** 0508 3.8 / 1114 1.1 / TH 1721 4.0 / ● 2342 1.0	**16** 0538 3.9 / 1221 1.3 / F 1805 3.8
2 0512 3.5 / 1115 1.1 / F 1717 3.7	**17** 0512 3.8 / 1114 0.5 / SA 1726 4.3 / 2343 0.5	**2** 0512 3.7 / 1117 0.9 / SU 1719 4.0 / 2352 1.0	**17** 0515 3.9 / 1133 0.5 / M 1734 4.4 / ○ 2353 0.6	**2** 0536 3.9 / 1142 0.9 / W 1744 4.1 / ●	**17** 0000 0.9 / 0553 4.0 / TH 1232 1.2 / 1816 4.0	**2** 0543 3.9 / 1157 1.0 / F 1758 4.0	**17** 0018 1.1 / 0616 3.9 / SA 1302 1.4 / 1841 3.7
3 0000 1.2 / 0542 3.7 / SA 1149 0.9 / ● 1748 3.9	**18** 0543 3.9 / 1156 0.3 / SU 1802 4.4 / ○	**3** 0542 3.9 / 1147 0.8 / M 1748 4.1 / ●	**18** 0546 4.1 / 1213 0.5 / TU 1808 4.3	**3** 0009 0.9 / 0602 4.0 / TH 1216 0.9 / 1813 4.0	**18** 0037 1.0 / 0627 4.0 / F 1311 1.2 / 1850 3.8	**3** 0021 1.0 / 0621 4.0 / SA 1243 1.0 / 1837 3.9	**18** 0059 1.2 / 0653 3.9 / SU 1341 1.5 / 1918 3.7
4 0027 1.1 / 0614 3.8 / SU 1220 0.8 / 1819 4.0	**19** 0022 0.4 / 0615 4.0 / M 1237 0.3 / 1836 4.4	**4** 0018 0.9 / 0609 3.9 / TU 1215 0.8 / 1815 4.1	**19** 0028 0.6 / 0618 4.1 / W 1252 0.6 / 1840 4.2	**4** 0040 0.9 / 0633 3.9 / F 1253 0.9 / 1846 3.9	**19** 0115 1.1 / 0702 3.9 / SA 1350 1.4 / 1926 3.6	**4** 0103 0.9 / 0703 3.9 / SU 1331 1.5 / 1920 3.7	**19** 0139 1.2 / 0731 3.8 / M 1420 1.7 / 1956 3.5
5 0054 1.0 / 0643 3.9 / M 1248 0.8 / 1848 4.0	**20** 0059 0.5 / 0647 4.0 / TU 1316 0.3 / 1910 4.3	**5** 0044 0.9 / 0633 3.9 / W 1243 0.8 / 1840 4.1	**20** 0103 0.7 / 0649 4.0 / TH 1330 0.9 / 1912 4.0	**5** 0114 1.0 / 0708 3.9 / SA 1334 1.1 / 1923 3.7	**20** 0155 1.3 / 0739 3.8 / SU 1431 1.7 / 2004 3.4	**5** 0148 1.0 / 0749 3.9 / M 1423 1.2 / 2006 3.5	**20** 0219 1.3 / 0809 3.7 / TU 1500 1.8 / 2034 3.4
6 0121 1.0 / 0708 3.9 / TU 1315 0.8 / 1913 4.0	**21** 0135 0.6 / 0719 3.9 / W 1354 0.5 / 1943 4.0	**6** 0108 1.0 / 0657 3.9 / TH 1312 0.9 / 1907 3.9	**21** 0139 0.9 / 0721 3.9 / F 1408 1.2 / 1945 3.7	**6** 0153 1.2 / 0749 3.7 / SU 1422 1.3 / 2005 3.5	**21** 0238 1.4 / 0819 3.6 / M 1517 1.9 / 2046 3.2	**6** 0238 1.1 / 0841 3.7 / TU 1520 1.3 / 2059 3.3	**21** 0300 1.5 / 0848 3.6 / W 1543 1.9 / 2115 3.3
7 0144 1.1 / 0730 3.8 / W 1340 0.9 / 1937 3.9	**22** 0210 0.8 / 0750 3.8 / TH 1432 0.9 / 2016 3.7	**7** 0133 1.1 / 0726 3.8 / F 1345 1.1 / 1937 3.8	**22** 0217 1.2 / 0754 3.7 / SA 1447 1.5 / 2019 3.4	**7** 0240 1.3 / 0839 3.6 / M 1520 1.5 / 2056 3.2	**22** 0326 1.6 / 0905 3.4 / TU 1613 2.1 / 2138 3.0	**7** 0333 1.2 / 0941 3.6 / W 1622 1.5 / 2200 3.1	**22** 0342 1.6 / 0930 3.4 / TH 1630 2.0 / 2201 3.1
8 0203 1.2 / 0755 3.6 / TH 1409 1.1 / 2003 3.8	**23** 0248 1.1 / 0821 3.5 / F 1512 1.2 / 2049 3.4	**8** 0203 1.2 / 0801 3.6 / SA 1425 1.3 / 2011 3.5	**23** 0300 1.4 / 0831 3.4 / SU 1534 1.9 / 2058 3.1	**8** 0340 1.5 / 0943 3.3 / TU 1634 1.7 / 2208 2.9	**23** 0419 1.8 / 1002 3.2 / W 1723 2.2 / ● 2259 2.8	**8** 0436 1.4 / 1056 3.4 / TH 1731 1.6 / ● 2320 3.0	**23** 0426 1.7 / 1016 3.3 / F 1725 2.1 / ● 2255 3.0
9 0227 1.5 / 0826 3.5 / F 1443 1.2 / 2034 3.6	**24** 0330 1.4 / 0855 3.3 / SA 1558 1.6 / 2127 3.0	**9** 0243 1.4 / 0842 3.4 / SU 1515 1.5 / 2053 3.2	**24** 0352 1.7 / 0917 3.2 / M 1635 2.1 / 2154 2.8	**9** 0456 1.6 / 1127 3.2 / W 1759 1.7 / ○	**24** 0519 1.9 / 1123 3.1 / TH 1855 2.2	**9** 0546 1.4 / 1232 3.4 / F 1844 1.6	**24** 0515 1.8 / 1112 3.2 / SA 1825 2.1
10 0302 1.5 / 0903 3.3 / SA 1527 1.5 / 2112 3.3	**25** 0422 1.7 / 0938 3.0 / SU 1657 2.0 / ○ 2224 2.7	**10** 0337 1.6 / 0939 3.2 / M 1630 1.8 / ● 2156 2.9	**25** 0454 1.9 / 1030 3.0 / TU 1811 2.3 / ○	**10** 0036 2.8 / 0620 1.6 / TH 1326 3.4 / 1925 1.6	**25** 0114 2.9 / 0622 1.9 / F 1319 3.1 / 2013 2.1	**10** 0102 3.0 / 0659 1.4 / SA 1346 3.5 / 1951 1.6	**25** 0009 3.0 / 0609 1.9 / SU 1225 3.2 / 1927 2.0
11 0350 1.7 / 0952 3.1 / SU 1629 1.7 / ● 2205 3.0	**26** 0526 1.9 / 1103 2.8 / M 1833 2.2	**11** 0507 1.8 / 1125 3.0 / TU 1808 1.9	**26** 0122 2.7 / 0607 2.0 / W 1348 3.0 / 2049 2.1	**11** 0209 3.0 / 0741 1.5 / F 1427 3.6 / 2035 1.4	**26** 0210 3.0 / 0726 1.9 / SA 1416 3.3 / 2058 1.9	**11** 0214 3.1 / 0811 1.4 / SU 1444 3.6 / 2050 1.5	**26** 0135 3.0 / 0708 1.8 / M 1347 3.2 / 2024 1.9
12 0517 1.9 / 1116 2.9 / M 1804 1.9	**27** 0209 2.6 / 0647 2.0 / TU 1504 2.9 / 2130 2.0	**12** 0115 2.7 / 0647 1.9 / W 1401 3.2 / 1947 1.7	**27** 0227 2.9 / 0731 1.9 / TH 1443 3.1 / 2129 1.9	**12** 0303 3.2 / 0848 1.3 / SA 1515 3.8 / 2127 1.2	**27** 0251 3.2 / 0823 1.7 / SU 1456 3.4 / 2132 1.7	**12** 0304 3.3 / 0913 1.4 / M 1533 3.7 / 2138 1.4	**27** 0237 3.1 / 0810 1.7 / TU 1450 3.3 / 2115 1.7
13 0010 2.8 / 0704 1.9 / TU 1419 3.0 / 1945 1.8	**28** 0320 2.8 / 0827 1.8 / W 1540 3.1 / 2209 1.8	**13** 0243 3.0 / 0814 1.4 / TH 1459 3.5 / 2104 1.4	**28** 0307 3.1 / 0842 1.8 / F 1515 3.3 / 2158 1.7	**13** 0342 3.5 / 0941 1.1 / SU 1556 4.0 / 2209 1.1	**28** 0327 3.4 / 0910 1.6 / M 1533 3.6 / 2203 1.5	**13** 0345 3.5 / 1007 1.3 / TU 1615 3.7 / 2221 1.3	**28** 0327 3.3 / 0910 1.6 / W 1542 3.5 / 2200 1.5
14 0258 2.9 / 0834 1.6 / W 1522 3.4 / 2115 1.5	**29** 0353 3.1 / 0930 1.6 / TH 1554 3.3 / 2237 1.6	**14** 0335 3.3 / 0918 1.2 / F 1544 3.9 / 2156 1.1	**29** 0338 3.3 / 0929 1.5 / SA 1543 3.6 / 2223 1.5	**14** 0414 3.7 / 1028 1.0 / M 1634 4.1 / 2248 1.1	**28** 0401 3.5 / 0952 1.4 / TU 1609 3.8 / 2235 1.4	**14** 0423 3.6 / 1055 1.3 / W 1653 3.8 / 2300 1.2	**29** 0412 3.5 / 1006 1.5 / TH 1628 3.7 / 2243 1.3
15 0355 3.2 / 0941 1.3 / TH 1608 3.8 / 2216 1.1	**30** 0416 3.3 / 1012 1.3 / F 1619 3.6 / 2303 1.3	**15** 0413 3.6 / 1008 0.9 / SA 1623 4.1 / 2238 0.8	**30** 0407 3.5 / 1006 1.3 / SU 1613 3.8 / 2248 1.3	**15** 0446 3.8 / 1111 0.8 / TU 1709 4.1 / 2324 0.9	**30** 0435 3.7 / 1033 1.2 / W 1645 3.9 / 2307 1.2	**15** 0501 3.7 / 1140 1.2 / TH 1729 3.8 / ○ 2339 1.2	**30** 0501 3.7 / 1059 1.3 / F 1712 3.8 / 2326 1.0
			31 0438 3.7 / 1038 1.1 / M 1644 3.9 / 2314 1.1				**31** 0537 3.9 / 1150 1.0 / SA 1754 3.9

Chart Datum: 2·10 metres below Ordnance Datum (Newlyn)

FREE monthly updates from www.reedsalmanac.co.uk

TIDES

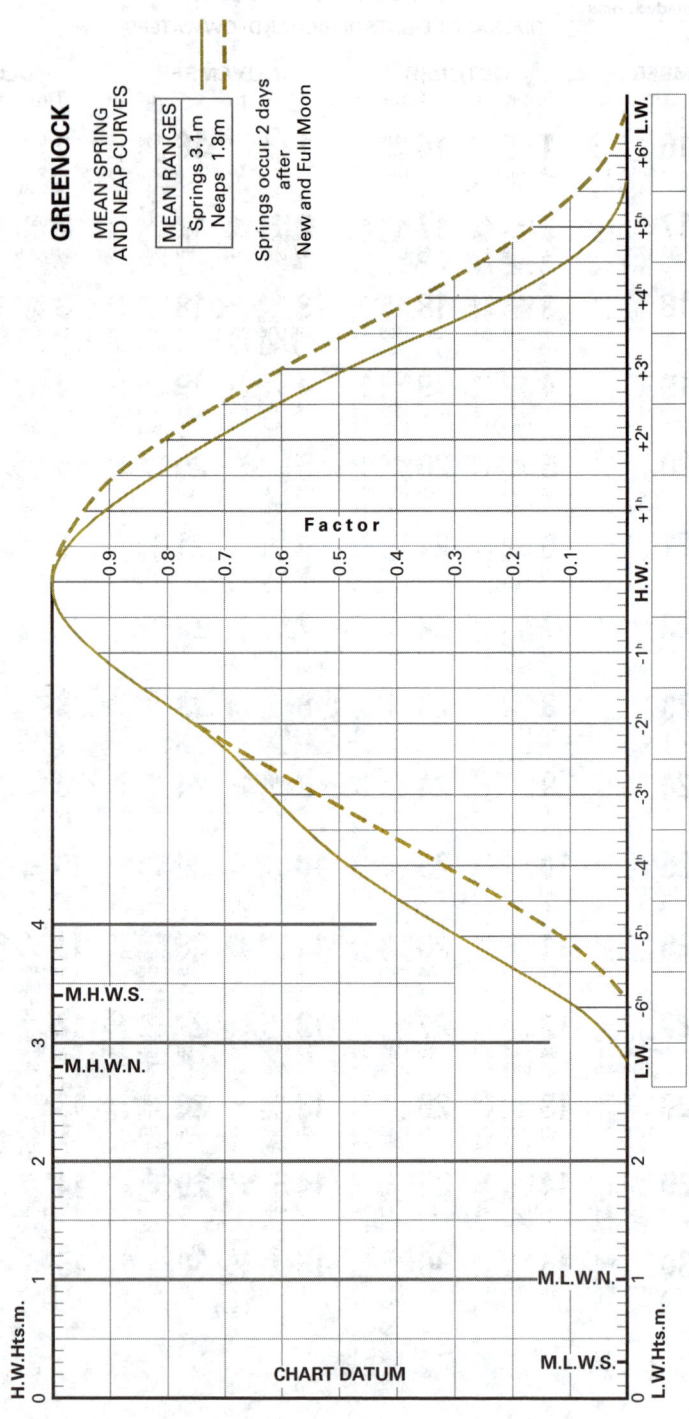

SCOTLAND – GREENOCK

LAT 55°57'N   LONG 4°46'W

TIMES AND HEIGHTS OF HIGH AND LOW WATERS

YEAR 2005

TIME ZONE (UT) For Summer Time add ONE hour in **non-shaded areas**

JANUARY

#	Time	m	#	Time	m
1 SA	0358 / 0921 / 1552 / 2135	3.0 / 0.9 / 3.4 / 0.5	**16** SU	0444 / 1006 / 1649 / 2247	3.3 / 0.8 / 3.6 / 0.5
2 SU	0441 / 1006 / 1633 / 2223	3.0 / 1.0 / 3.4 / 0.7	**17** M	0528 / 1100 / 1737 / ☽ 2349	3.2 / 1.0 / 3.5 / 0.7
3 M	0527 / 1057 / 1718 / ☽ 2318	2.9 / 1.0 / 3.3 / 0.7	**18** TU	0613 / 1203 / 1829	3.1 / 1.1 / 3.2
4 TU	0616 / 1154 / 1809	2.8 / 1.1 / 3.2	**19** W	0056 / 0702 / 1316 / 1930	0.8 / 3.0 / 1.2 / 3.0
5 W	0018 / 0710 / 1256 / 1908	0.8 / 2.8 / 1.1 / 3.1	**20** TH	0201 / 0803 / 1431 / 2108	0.9 / 2.9 / 1.2 / 2.9
6 TH	0119 / 0817 / 1400 / 2019	0.8 / 2.8 / 1.0 / 3.1	**21** F	0301 / 0931 / 1534 / 2228	0.9 / 2.9 / 1.0 / 2.9
7 F	0220 / 0934 / 1503 / 2137	0.7 / 2.9 / 0.9 / 3.1	**22** SA	0355 / 1036 / 1625 / 2322	3.1 / 0.9 / 3.0 / 0.9 (order: 0.8 / 3.1 / 0.9 / 3.0)
8 SA	0319 / 1037 / 1602 / 2243	0.7 / 3.1 / 0.7 / 3.2	**23** SU	0442 / 1124 / 1708	0.8 / 3.2 / 0.7
9 SU	0415 / 1129 / 1655 / 2342	0.6 / 3.3 / 0.5 / 3.3	**24** M	0008 / 0523 / 1206 / 1745	0.8 / 0.8 / 3.3 / 0.6
10 M	0508 / 1216 / 1745	0.6 / 3.5 / 0.3	**25** TU	0049 / 0601 / 1242 / ○ 1818	3.0 / 0.7 / 3.4 / 0.6
11 TU	0038 / 0559 / 1303 / 1833	3.4 / 0.6 / 3.6 / 0.3	**26** W	0126 / 0634 / 1314 / 1848	3.0 / 0.6 / 3.4 / 0.5
12 W	0133 / 0649 / 1349 / 1922	3.4 / 0.6 / 3.8 / 0.1	**27** TH	0159 / 0706 / 1345 / 1918	3.0 / 0.7 / 3.5 / 0.5
13 TH	0225 / 0739 / 1434 / 2011	3.4 / 0.6 / 3.8 / 0.1	**28** F	0229 / 0739 / 1418 / 1950	3.0 / 0.6 / 3.5 / 0.4
14 F	0314 / 0828 / 1518 / 2100	3.4 / 0.6 / 3.8 / 0.2	**29** SA	0300 / 0814 / 1452 / 2025	3.0 / 0.6 / 3.5 / 0.4
15 SA	0400 / 0916 / 1603 / 2151	3.3 / 0.7 / 3.8 / 0.3	**30** SU	0332 / 0851 / 1529 / 2103	3.0 / 0.6 / 3.5 / 0.4
			31 M	0406 / 0931 / 1606 / 2146	2.9 / 0.6 / 3.4 / 0.4

FEBRUARY

#	Time	m	#	Time	m
1 TU	0441 / 1016 / 1645 / 2236	3.0 / 0.7 / 3.3 / 0.5	**16** W	0522 / 1105 / 1742 / ●	3.1 / 1.0 / 3.1
2 W	0520 / 1108 / 1729 / ☽ 2333	2.9 / 0.9 / 3.2 / 0.7	**17** TH	0007 / 0605 / 1220 / 1831	1.0 / 3.0 / 1.2 / 2.9
3 TH	0605 / 1210 / 1822	2.8 / 1.0 / 3.0	**18** F	0129 / 0658 / 1403 / 1938	1.1 / 2.8 / 1.2 / 2.6
4 F	0036 / 0706 / 1320 / 1930	0.8 / 2.7 / 1.0 / 2.9	**19** SA	0238 / 0811 / 1513 / 2220	1.1 / 2.8 / 1.1 / 2.6
5 SA	0145 / 0850 / 1438 / 2110	0.9 / 2.7 / 0.9 / 2.9	**20** SU	0336 / 1012 / 1606 / 2312	1.0 / 2.9 / 0.9 / 2.8
6 SU	0258 / 1019 / 1551 / 2336	0.9 / 2.9 / 0.7 / 3.0	**21** M	0424 / 1106 / 1649 / 2354	0.9 / 3.1 / 0.7 / 2.9
7 M	0405 / 1116 / 1647	0.8 / 3.2 / 0.4	**22** TU	0505 / 1147 / 1724	0.7 / 3.2 / 0.5
8 TU	0501 / 1205 / 1736 / ●	0.6 / 3.4 / 0.2	**23** W	0033 / 0540 / 1223 / 1755	3.0 / 0.6 / 3.3 / 0.4
9 W	0035 / 0550 / 1253 / 1821	3.2 / 0.5 / 3.6 / 0.0	**24** TH	0109 / 0611 / 1253 / ○ 1824	3.0 / 0.5 / 3.3 / 0.4
10 TH	0127 / 0635 / 1338 / 1905	3.3 / 0.4 / 3.8 / 0.0	**25** F	0140 / 0640 / 1322 / 1851	3.0 / 0.5 / 3.4 / 0.3
11 F	0214 / 0720 / 1421 / 1949	3.4 / 0.4 / 3.8 / 0.0	**26** SA	0207 / 0710 / 1354 / 1921	3.0 / 0.4 / 3.4 / 0.3
12 SA	0255 / 0803 / 1502 / 2032	3.4 / 0.4 / 3.9 / 0.1	**27** SU	0232 / 0743 / 1429 / 1954	3.0 / 0.4 / 3.4 / 0.2
13 SU	0332 / 0846 / 1542 / 2117	3.4 / 0.5 / 3.8 / 0.3	**28** M	0300 / 0818 / 1504 / 2032	3.1 / 0.4 / 3.5 / 0.2
14 M	0407 / 0929 / 1620 / 2204	3.3 / 0.6 / 3.7 / 0.5			
15 TU	0443 / 1013 / 1700 / 2257	3.3 / 0.8 / 3.4 / 0.8			

MARCH

#	Time	m	#	Time	m
1 TU	0330 / 0857 / 1540 / 2114	3.1 / 0.4 / 3.4 / 0.3	**16** W	0404 / 0931 / 1628 / 2206	3.3 / 0.6 / 3.3 / 0.8
2 W	0402 / 0941 / 1617 / 2201	3.0 / 0.5 / 3.3 / 0.4	**17** TH	0440 / 1015 / 1708 / ☽ 2301	3.2 / 0.8 / 3.0 / 1.1
3 TH	0437 / 1033 / 1659 / ☽ 2257	2.9 / 0.7 / 3.1 / 0.7	**18** F	0523 / 1113 / 1756	3.0 / 1.1 / 2.7
4 F	0520 / 1138 / 1751	2.8 / 0.8 / 2.9	**19** SA	0046 / 0614 / 1328 / 1900	1.3 / 2.8 / 1.2 / 2.5
5 SA	0003 / 0619 / 1255 / 1900	0.9 / 2.7 / 0.9 / 2.7	**20** SU	0208 / 0722 / 1442 / 2200	1.3 / 2.7 / 1.1 / 2.5
6 SU	0121 / 0816 / 1429 / 2111	1.0 / 2.6 / 0.8 / 2.7	**21** M	0309 / 0933 / 1535 / 2248	1.1 / 2.7 / 0.9 / 2.7
7 M	0251 / 1006 / 1544 / 2239	1.0 / 2.9 / 0.5 / 2.9	**22** TU	0357 / 1036 / 1617 / 2328	0.9 / 2.9 / 0.6 / 2.9
8 TU	0400 / 1103 / 1636 / 2336	0.8 / 3.1 / 0.3 / 3.1	**23** W	0437 / 1117 / 1653	0.7 / 3.1 / 0.5
9 W	0451 / 1151 / 1721	0.6 / 3.4 / 0.0	**24** TH	0005 / 0510 / 1152 / 1723	2.9 / 0.6 / 3.2 / 0.4
10 TH	0026 / 0535 / 1237 / ● 1801	3.2 / 0.4 / 3.6 / -0.1	**25** F	0039 / 0540 / 1221 / ○ 1751	3.0 / 0.4 / 3.3 / 0.3
11 F	0111 / 0616 / 1321 / 1842	3.3 / 0.3 / 3.7 / -0.1	**26** SA	0109 / 0609 / 1253 / 1819	3.0 / 0.4 / 3.3 / 0.2
12 SA	0151 / 0655 / 1402 / 1921	3.3 / 0.3 / 3.8 / 0.0	**27** SU	0134 / 0639 / 1327 / 1851	3.0 / 0.3 / 3.3 / 0.1
13 SU	0226 / 0734 / 1440 / 2001	3.4 / 0.3 / 3.8 / 0.1	**28** M	0200 / 0713 / 1404 / 1926	3.1 / 0.2 / 3.4 / 0.1
14 M	0258 / 0812 / 1516 / 2041	3.4 / 0.3 / 3.7 / 0.3	**29** TU	0228 / 0750 / 1441 / 2006	3.1 / 0.2 / 3.4 / 0.1
15 TU	0330 / 0851 / 1551 / 2122	3.3 / 0.4 / 3.5 / 0.5	**30** W	0259 / 0831 / 1518 / 2050	3.2 / 0.2 / 3.4 / 0.3
			31 TH	0332 / 0918 / 1557 / 2138	3.2 / 0.4 / 3.2 / 0.5

APRIL

#	Time	m	#	Time	m
1 F	0409 / 1013 / 1641 / 2235	3.0 / 0.6 / 3.0 / 0.8	**16** SA	0448 / 1037 / 1735 / ☽ 2335	3.0 / 1.0 / 2.6 / 1.3
2 SA	0454 / 1122 / 1737 / ☽ 2345	2.9 / 0.7 / 2.8 / 1.0	**17** SU	0541 / 1218 / 1841	2.8 / 1.1 / 2.5
3 SU	0600 / 1249 / 1903	2.7 / 0.8 / 2.6	**18** M	0118 / 0647 / 1356 / 2031	1.3 / 2.7 / 1.0 / 2.4
4 M	0113 / 0816 / 1423 / 2121	1.1 / 2.6 / 0.6 / 2.6	**19** TU	0226 / 0811 / 1451 / 2204	1.2 / 2.7 / 0.8 / 2.6
5 TU	0244 / 0948 / 1527 / 2230	1.0 / 2.9 / 0.4 / 2.9	**20** W	0317 / 0941 / 1536 / 2248	1.0 / 2.8 / 0.6 / 2.8
6 W	0347 / 1043 / 1616 / 2321	0.8 / 3.2 / 0.1 / 3.1	**21** TH	0359 / 1029 / 1613 / 2325	0.8 / 3.0 / 0.5 / 2.9
7 TH	0435 / 1130 / 1659 / ●	0.5 / 3.4 / 0.0	**22** F	0435 / 1106 / 1646 / ●	0.6 / 3.1 / 0.3
8 F	0005 / 0515 / 1215 / 1738	3.2 / 0.4 / 3.5 / -0.1	**23** SA	0000 / 0506 / 1142 / 1716	3.0 / 0.4 / 3.2 / 0.3
9 SA	0045 / 0553 / 1258 / 1816	3.2 / 0.3 / 3.6 / 0.0	**24** SU	0031 / 0538 / 1220 / ○ 1748	3.0 / 0.3 / 3.3 / 0.1
10 SU	0121 / 0629 / 1338 / 1853	3.3 / 0.2 / 3.6 / 0.1	**25** M	0101 / 0612 / 1300 / 1824	3.1 / 0.2 / 3.3 / 0.1
11 M	0153 / 0705 / 1415 / 1931	3.3 / 0.2 / 3.5 / 0.2	**26** TU	0131 / 0649 / 1341 / 1904	3.2 / 0.1 / 3.3 / 0.1
12 TU	0225 / 0742 / 1450 / 2010	3.4 / 0.3 / 3.5 / 0.4	**27** W	0203 / 0730 / 1422 / 1948	3.3 / 0.1 / 3.3 / 0.2
13 W	0257 / 0819 / 1525 / 2049	3.4 / 0.4 / 3.3 / 0.6	**28** TH	0238 / 0815 / 1503 / 2036	3.3 / 0.2 / 3.3 / 0.4
14 TH	0331 / 0858 / 1602 / 2132	3.4 / 0.5 / 3.1 / 0.9	**29** F	0314 / 0907 / 1547 / 2128	3.2 / 0.4 / 3.1 / 0.6
15 F	0407 / 0942 / 1644 / 2222	3.2 / 0.7 / 2.9 / 1.1	**30** SA	0355 / 1008 / 1639 / 2229	3.1 / 0.6 / 2.9 / 0.8

Chart Datum: 1·62 metres below Ordnance Datum (Newlyn)

》》 **FREE** monthly updates from 《《
www.reedsalmanac.co.uk

Chapter 5

311

TIDES

TIME ZONE (UT)
For Summer Time add ONE hour in **non-shaded areas**

SCOTLAND – GREENOCK
LAT 55°57'N   LONG 4°46'W
TIMES AND HEIGHTS OF HIGH AND LOW WATERS

YEAR 2005

MAY				JUNE				JULY				AUGUST			
Time	m	Time	m	Time	m	Time	m	Time	m	Time	m	Time	m	Time	m
1 0446 3.0 1122 0.6 SU 1750 2.7 ☾ 2341 1.0		**16** 0511 2.9 1125 0.9 M 1821 2.6 ☽		**1** 0038 0.9 0730 3.0 W 1332 0.3 2024 2.8		**16** 0013 1.0 0631 2.9 TH 1245 0.7 1937 2.6		**1** 0112 0.9 0801 3.0 F 1401 0.5 2032 2.8		**16** 0021 0.9 0641 2.9 SA 1250 0.7 1936 2.6		**1** 0310 0.9 1011 2.8 M 1535 0.8 2211 2.9		**16** 0202 0.9 0840 2.7 TU 1429 0.9 2144 2.8	
2 0604 2.8 1247 0.6 M 1929 2.6		**17** 0007 1.2 0611 2.8 TU 1247 0.9 1928 2.5		**2** 0148 0.9 0845 3.1 TH 1431 0.3 2126 2.9		**17** 0113 1.0 0731 2.8 F 1342 0.6 2037 2.7		**2** 0222 0.9 0915 3.0 SA 1457 0.5 2138 2.9		**17** 0123 0.9 0748 2.8 SU 1351 0.7 2049 2.7		**2** 0408 0.8 1108 2.8 TU 1626 0.8 2306 3.0		**17** 0325 0.7 1010 2.9 W 1540 0.8 2250 3.0	
3 0102 1.1 0801 2.8 TU 1402 0.4 2103 2.7		**18** 0118 1.2 0719 2.8 W 1352 0.8 2042 2.6		**3** 0253 0.8 0946 3.2 F 1523 0.3 2218 3.0		**18** 0213 0.9 0836 2.9 SA 1435 0.5 2141 2.7		**3** 0326 0.8 1018 3.0 SU 1550 0.5 2235 2.9		**18** 0231 0.8 0904 2.9 M 1452 0.6 2205 2.8		**3** 0455 0.6 1155 2.9 W 1710 0.7 2351 3.2		**18** 0426 0.4 1115 3.1 TH 1638 0.7 2341 3.3	
4 0221 1.0 0921 3.0 W 1501 0.3 2205 2.9		**19** 0219 1.0 0828 2.8 TH 1442 0.6 2147 2.7		**4** 0348 0.6 1039 3.2 SA 1610 0.3 2304 3.0		**19** 0310 0.7 0939 3.0 SU 1525 0.4 2237 2.9		**4** 0420 0.6 1112 3.0 M 1638 0.6 2323 3.0		**19** 0338 0.7 1015 3.0 TU 1552 0.6 2304 3.0		**4** 0534 0.5 1237 2.9 TH 1750 0.7		**19** 0515 0.1 1210 3.2 F 1727 0.5 ○	
5 0323 0.8 1016 3.2 TH 1550 0.1 2253 3.0		**20** 0310 0.8 0929 2.9 F 1525 0.5 2236 2.8		**5** 0434 0.5 1127 3.2 SU 1653 0.3 2346 3.1		**20** 0402 0.6 1035 3.1 M 1613 0.4 2325 3.0		**5** 0506 0.5 1200 3.0 TU 1723 0.6		**20** 0436 0.4 1116 3.1 W 1647 0.5 2354 3.2		**5** 0030 3.2 0608 0.4 F 1317 2.9 ● 1825 0.6		**20** 0028 3.5 0559 0.0 SA 1302 3.3 1813 0.4	
6 0412 0.6 1105 3.3 F 1634 0.1 2336 3.1		**21** 0353 0.7 1020 3.0 SA 1604 0.3 2317 2.9		**6** 0516 0.4 1212 3.1 M 1734 0.4 ●		**21** 0450 0.4 1128 3.2 TU 1701 0.3		**6** 0005 3.2 0546 0.5 W 1245 2.9 ● 1804 0.6		**21** 0526 0.2 1213 3.1 TH 1739 0.5 ○		**6** 0105 3.3 0638 0.4 SA 1352 2.9 1857 0.6		**21** 0114 3.7 0642 -0.1 SU 1350 3.3 1857 0.4	
7 0454 0.4 1150 3.4 SA 1714 0.1		**22** 0433 0.5 1105 3.1 SU 1642 0.2 2354 3.0		**7** 0024 3.2 0553 0.4 TU 1254 3.1 1814 0.5		**22** 0010 3.2 0535 0.2 W 1220 3.2 ○ 1749 0.4		**7** 0044 3.2 0622 0.4 TH 1326 2.9 1843 0.6		**22** 0042 3.4 0614 0.0 F 1310 3.2 1829 0.4		**7** 0135 3.3 0707 0.4 SU 1423 2.9 1928 0.6		**22** 0158 3.8 0725 -0.1 M 1434 3.4 1941 0.4	
8 0014 3.2 0531 0.3 SU 1233 3.4 ● 1752 0.2		**23** 0511 0.3 1150 3.2 M 1722 0.2 ○		**8** 0100 3.3 0629 0.4 W 1334 3.0 1853 0.6		**23** 0054 3.3 0623 0.1 TH 1313 3.2 1839 0.4		**8** 0120 3.3 0656 0.4 F 1404 2.9 1920 0.6		**23** 0128 3.5 0701 -0.1 SA 1404 3.2 1919 0.4		**8** 0205 3.3 0736 0.4 M 1452 2.9 2001 0.5		**23** 0240 3.8 0808 0.0 TU 1512 3.4 2024 0.4	
9 0050 3.2 0607 0.3 M 1313 3.3 1830 0.3		**24** 0031 3.1 0550 0.2 TU 1236 3.3 1803 0.2		**9** 0135 3.3 0705 0.4 TH 1412 3.0 1933 0.7		**24** 0137 3.4 0712 0.0 F 1407 3.2 1932 0.4		**9** 0153 3.3 0729 0.4 SA 1440 2.9 1956 0.6		**24** 0214 3.6 0748 -0.1 SU 1455 3.2 2007 0.4		**9** 0237 3.3 0808 0.5 TU 1521 2.9 2036 0.5		**24** 0319 3.8 0852 0.2 W 1548 3.4 2107 0.5	
10 0124 3.3 0643 0.3 TU 1351 3.3 1908 0.5		**25** 0109 3.2 0633 0.1 W 1323 3.3 1849 0.3		**10** 0210 3.4 0742 0.5 F 1450 2.9 2014 0.7		**25** 0221 3.5 0803 0.0 SA 1502 3.2 2024 0.5		**10** 0227 3.3 0804 0.5 SU 1516 2.8 2032 0.6		**25** 0258 3.7 0836 0.0 M 1542 3.2 2054 0.4		**10** 0311 3.3 0842 0.4 W 1553 3.0 2113 0.5		**25** 0358 3.7 0940 0.4 TH 1623 3.3 2152 0.6	
11 0157 3.4 0719 0.3 W 1428 3.2 1947 0.6		**26** 0147 3.3 0718 0.1 TH 1410 3.3 1938 0.4		**11** 0245 3.4 0822 0.5 SA 1530 2.9 2056 0.7		**26** 0306 3.5 0856 0.1 SU 1556 3.1 2116 0.5		**11** 0301 3.3 0840 0.5 M 1553 2.8 2110 0.6		**26** 0341 3.7 0926 0.1 TU 1625 3.2 2142 0.5		**11** 0347 3.3 0922 0.4 TH 1627 2.9 2154 0.6		**26** 0437 3.5 1033 0.7 F 1701 3.2 ☾ 2242 0.9	
12 0231 3.4 0756 0.4 TH 1504 3.1 2028 0.7		**27** 0226 3.4 0809 0.1 F 1459 3.2 2031 0.5		**12** 0321 3.3 0904 0.6 SU 1614 2.8 2139 0.8		**27** 0354 3.5 0952 0.1 M 1650 3.1 2210 0.6		**12** 0337 3.3 0919 0.5 TU 1631 2.8 2151 0.7		**27** 0425 3.6 1020 0.3 W 1706 3.2 2232 0.6		**12** 0424 3.2 1008 0.5 F 1703 2.9 2242 0.7		**27** 0520 3.1 1146 1.0 SA 1744 3.1 2349 1.1	
13 0305 3.4 0837 0.5 F 1543 3.0 2112 0.8		**28** 0308 3.4 0904 0.2 SA 1552 3.1 2126 0.6		**13** 0400 3.2 0951 0.7 M 1701 2.7 2226 0.9		**28** 0446 3.4 1053 0.2 TU 1744 3.0 ☾ 2305 0.7		**13** 0416 3.2 1003 0.6 W 1712 2.8 2235 0.7		**28** 0511 3.4 1120 0.6 TH 1748 3.1 ☾ 2328 0.9		**13** 0506 3.1 1103 0.7 SA 1745 2.8 ☾ 2338 0.9		**28** 0610 2.8 1309 1.2 SU 1833 2.9	
14 0341 3.3 0922 0.7 SA 1628 2.8 2200 1.0		**29** 0354 3.3 1006 0.3 SU 1653 2.9 2226 0.8		**14** 0444 3.1 1045 0.7 TU 1752 2.7 2317 0.9		**29** 0544 3.2 1157 0.3 W 1836 2.9		**14** 0458 3.1 1054 0.7 TH 1755 2.7 ☾ 2325 0.8		**29** 0602 3.2 1207 0.8 F 1833 2.9		**14** 0557 2.8 1207 0.8 SU 1839 2.7		**29** 0134 1.2 0721 2.6 M 1418 1.1 1938 2.8	
15 0422 3.1 1015 0.8 SU 1720 2.7 2258 1.1		**30** 0452 3.1 1115 0.4 M 1802 2.8 ☾ 2330 0.9		**15** 0534 2.9 1144 0.7 W 1843 2.7 ☽		**30** 0006 0.9 0648 3.1 TH 1301 0.4 1930 2.9		**15** 0546 3.0 1151 0.6 F 1841 2.7		**30** 0034 1.0 0700 2.9 SA 1334 0.8 1924 2.8		**15** 0044 1.0 0705 2.6 M 1315 0.9 2000 2.6		**30** 0252 1.1 1009 2.7 TU 1517 1.1 2149 2.9	
						31 0605 1.0 1226 0.4 TU 1914 2.8						**31** 0156 1.0 0836 2.7 SU 1437 0.8 2041 2.8				**31** 0349 0.9 1100 2.9 W 1607 0.9 2248 3.1	

Chart Datum: 1·62 metres below Ordnance Datum (Newlyn)

》》 **FREE** monthly updates from 《《
www.reedsalmanac.co.uk

| TIME ZONE (UT) For Summer Time add ONE hour in **non-shaded areas** | SCOTLAND – GREENOCK
LAT 55°57′N   LONG 4°46′W
TIMES AND HEIGHTS OF HIGH AND LOW WATERS | | YEAR **2005** |

SEPTEMBER

Time	m	Time	m
1 0434 1141 1650 2332	0.7 3.0 0.8 3.2 TH	**16** 0412 1111 1625 2324	0.4 3.1 0.7 3.4 F
2 0511 1218 1726	0.5 3.0 0.7 F	**17** 0457 1159 1710	0.1 3.3 0.6 SA
3 0009 0542 1255 1758	3.3 0.4 3.0 0.6 SA	**18** 0010 0537 1244 1751	3.6 0.0 3.4 0.4 SU
4 0042 0611 1327 1827	3.3 0.4 3.0 0.6 SU	**19** 0054 0617 1325 1831	3.8 0.0 3.4 0.4 M
5 0110 0637 1355 1855	3.3 0.4 3.0 0.6 M	**20** 0137 0657 1403 1911	3.8 0.0 3.5 0.4 TU
6 0139 0703 1419 1926	3.4 0.4 3.1 0.5 TU	**21** 0216 0737 1437 1951	3.8 0.2 3.5 0.4 W
7 0210 0733 1445 1959	3.4 0.3 3.1 0.5 W	**22** 0254 0817 1510 2031	3.8 0.4 3.5 0.5 TH
8 0244 0807 1514 2037	3.4 0.3 3.1 0.5 TH	**23** 0330 0900 1545 2113	3.6 0.7 3.5 0.7 F
9 0319 0846 1546 2118	3.4 0.4 3.1 0.6 F	**24** 0407 0946 1622 2159	3.4 1.0 3.4 0.9 SA
10 0355 0930 1620 2207	3.3 0.6 3.0 0.7 SA	**25** 0447 1048 1704 2259	3.1 1.3 3.2 1.2 SU
11 0434 1025 1659 2307	3.1 0.8 2.9 0.9 SU	**26** 0537 1237 1755	2.8 1.5 3.0 M
12 0524 1133 1754	2.9 1.1 2.8 M	**27** 0106 0647 1350 1900	1.3 2.6 1.5 2.9
13 0020 0636 1251 1926	1.0 2.7 1.2 2.7 TU	**28** 0222 0952 1449 2106	1.2 2.7 1.3 2.9
14 0152 0840 1420 2131	1.0 2.7 1.2 2.9 W	**29** 0317 1036 1539 2218	1.0 2.9 1.1 3.1 TH
15 0317 1014 1533 2234	0.7 2.9 1.0 3.2 TH	**30** 0401 1113 1620 2302	0.6 3.1 0.9 3.2 F

OCTOBER

Time	m	Time	m
1 0438 1149 1656 2338	0.6 3.1 0.8 3.3 SA	**16** 0433 1137 1648 2347	0.2 3.4 0.6 3.7 SU
2 0510 1222 1726	0.5 3.2 0.7 SU	**17** 0513 1217 1728	0.1 3.5 0.5 M ○
3 0008 0537 1254 1754	3.3 0.4 3.2 0.6 M	**18** 0030 0551 1255 1806	3.8 0.1 3.5 0.3 TU
4 0038 0603 1320 1822	3.4 0.4 3.2 0.6 TU	**19** 0113 0629 1330 1844	3.8 0.3 3.6 0.5 W
5 0109 0630 1344 1854	3.4 0.4 3.2 0.5 W	**20** 0152 0708 1404 1922	3.7 0.4 3.6 0.5 TH
6 0143 0702 1412 1929	3.4 0.4 3.3 0.5 TH	**21** 0229 0748 1438 2002	3.7 0.7 3.7 0.6 F
7 0219 0739 1442 2008	3.5 0.5 3.3 0.5 F	**22** 0305 0829 1514 2043	3.5 0.9 3.6 0.8 SA
8 0256 0820 1515 2053	3.4 0.5 3.3 0.6 SA	**23** 0343 0914 1551 2129	3.3 1.1 3.5 1.0 SU
9 0333 0907 1550 2145	3.3 0.8 3.2 0.8 SU	**24** 0425 1008 1633 2227	3.1 1.4 3.4 1.2 M
10 0415 1003 1632 2251	3.1 1.0 3.1 1.0 M ◐	**25** 0517 1140 1724	2.8 1.6 3.2 TU ○
11 0508 1114 1731	2.9 1.3 2.9 TU	**26** 0010 0628 1305 1827	1.3 2.6 1.6 3.0 W
12 0011 0635 1241 1919	1.0 2.7 1.4 2.8 W	**27** 0136 0856 1407 2049	1.3 2.7 1.5 3.0 TH
13 0146 0847 1409 2111	0.9 2.8 1.3 3.0 TH	**28** 0233 0952 1459 2122	1.1 2.9 1.3 3.1 F
14 0257 1003 1515 2212	0.6 3.0 1.1 3.3 F	**29** 0319 1033 1543 2215	0.9 3.1 1.1 3.2 SA
15 0349 1053 1606 2301	0.4 3.2 0.8 3.6 SA	**30** 0358 1110 1620 2254	0.7 3.2 0.9 3.3 SU
		31 0431 1145 1652 2329	0.6 3.3 0.8 3.3 M

NOVEMBER

Time	m	Time	m
1 0501 1216 1723	0.5 3.3 0.7 TU	**16** 0008 0528 1226 1746	3.6 0.4 3.5 0.6 W ○
2 0003 0530 1245 1754	3.4 0.5 3.3 0.6 W ●	**17** 0051 0608 1302 1824	3.6 0.5 3.6 0.6 TH
3 0041 0602 1314 1829	3.4 0.5 3.4 0.5 TH	**18** 0131 0647 1338 1902	3.5 0.7 3.7 0.6 F
4 0120 0639 1346 1908	3.5 0.5 3.5 0.5 F	**19** 0210 0728 1414 1942	3.5 0.8 3.7 0.7 SA
5 0200 0720 1420 1951	3.5 0.6 3.5 0.5 SA	**20** 0247 0810 1450 2024	3.3 1.0 3.7 0.9 SU
6 0240 0806 1456 2041	3.4 0.7 3.5 0.6 SU	**21** 0327 0855 1528 2110	3.2 1.2 3.6 0.9 M
7 0322 0857 1535 2138	3.3 0.9 3.4 0.7 M	**22** 0411 0945 1609 2202	3.1 1.3 3.5 1.1 TU
8 0411 0956 1622 2246	3.1 1.1 3.3 0.9 TU	**23** 0503 1045 1656 2308	2.9 1.4 3.3 1.2 W ◐
9 0515 1107 1729	2.9 1.3 3.1 W ◐	**24** 0604 1156 1752	2.8 1.5 3.1 TH
10 0005 0648 1217 1908	0.9 2.8 1.4 3.1 TH	**25** 0026 0711 1311 1854	1.2 2.8 1.5 3.1 F
11 0123 0825 1328 2039	0.8 2.9 1.3 3.2 F	**26** 0132 0827 1415 2001	1.1 2.8 1.4 3.1 SA
12 0227 0933 1429 2143	0.6 3.1 1.1 3.4 SA	**27** 0225 0933 1455 2107	1.0 3.0 1.2 3.1 SU
13 0320 1024 1541 2235	0.4 3.2 1.0 3.5 SU	**28** 0310 1023 1539 2202	0.8 3.1 1.0 3.2 M
14 0406 1108 1627 2323	0.3 3.4 0.7 3.6 M	**29** 0349 1104 1618 2249	0.7 3.2 0.9 3.3 TU
15 0449 1148 1708	0.3 3.5 0.6 TU	**30** 0426 1140 1655 2333	0.5 3.3 0.7 3.3 W

DECEMBER

Time	m	Time	m
1 0503 1215 1733	0.6 3.4 0.6 TH ●	**16** 0037 0555 1242 1814	3.3 0.7 3.6 0.6 F
2 0017 0541 1251 1813	3.4 0.6 3.5 0.5 F	**17** 0120 0636 1320 1852	3.3 0.8 3.6 0.6 SA
3 0102 0624 1328 1856	3.4 0.6 3.6 0.4 SA	**18** 0200 0717 1356 1931	3.2 0.9 3.7 0.7 SU
4 0148 0710 1407 1944	3.4 0.7 3.6 0.4 SU	**19** 0238 0757 1433 2010	3.2 1.0 3.7 0.7 M
5 0234 0800 1448 2036	3.4 0.8 3.6 0.5 M	**20** 0317 0838 1510 2051	3.1 1.0 3.6 0.8 TU
6 0323 0854 1532 2133	3.3 0.9 3.5 0.5 TU	**21** 0357 0920 1548 2134	3.1 1.1 3.5 0.8 W
7 0418 0951 1624 2236	3.1 1.0 3.4 0.6 W	**22** 0441 1005 1629 2222	3.0 1.2 3.3 0.9 TH
8 0521 1053 1726 2343	3.0 1.1 3.4 0.8 TH ◐	**23** 0528 1055 1714 2316	2.9 1.3 3.3 1.0 F
9 0630 1201 1839	3.0 1.2 3.3 F	**24** 0618 1151 1804	2.9 1.3 3.2 SA
10 0051 0740 1310 1957	0.9 3.0 1.2 3.3 SA	**25** 0015 0711 1252 1859	1.2 2.9 1.3 3.1 SU
11 0154 0848 1417 2109	0.8 3.1 1.1 3.4 SU	**26** 0116 0812 1354 2001	1.1 2.8 1.3 3.0 M
12 0251 0948 1517 2210	0.6 3.2 0.9 3.4 M	**27** 0212 0921 1453 2110	0.9 2.9 1.1 3.0 TU
13 0342 1038 1608 2303	0.6 3.3 0.8 3.4 TU	**28** 0305 1021 1545 2214	0.9 3.1 0.9 3.1 W
14 0429 1123 1654 2351	0.6 3.4 0.6 3.4 W	**29** 0354 1110 1633 2309	0.8 3.2 0.7 3.2 TH
15 0513 1203 1735	0.7 3.5 0.5 TH ○	**30** 0441 1153 1718 2357	0.7 3.4 0.5 3.2 F
		31 0001 0527 1235 1803	3.3 0.6 3.5 0.4 SA ●

Chart Datum: 1·62 metres below Ordnance Datum (Newlyn)

》》 **FREE** monthly updates from 《《
www.reedsalmanac.co.uk

Chapter 5

TIDES

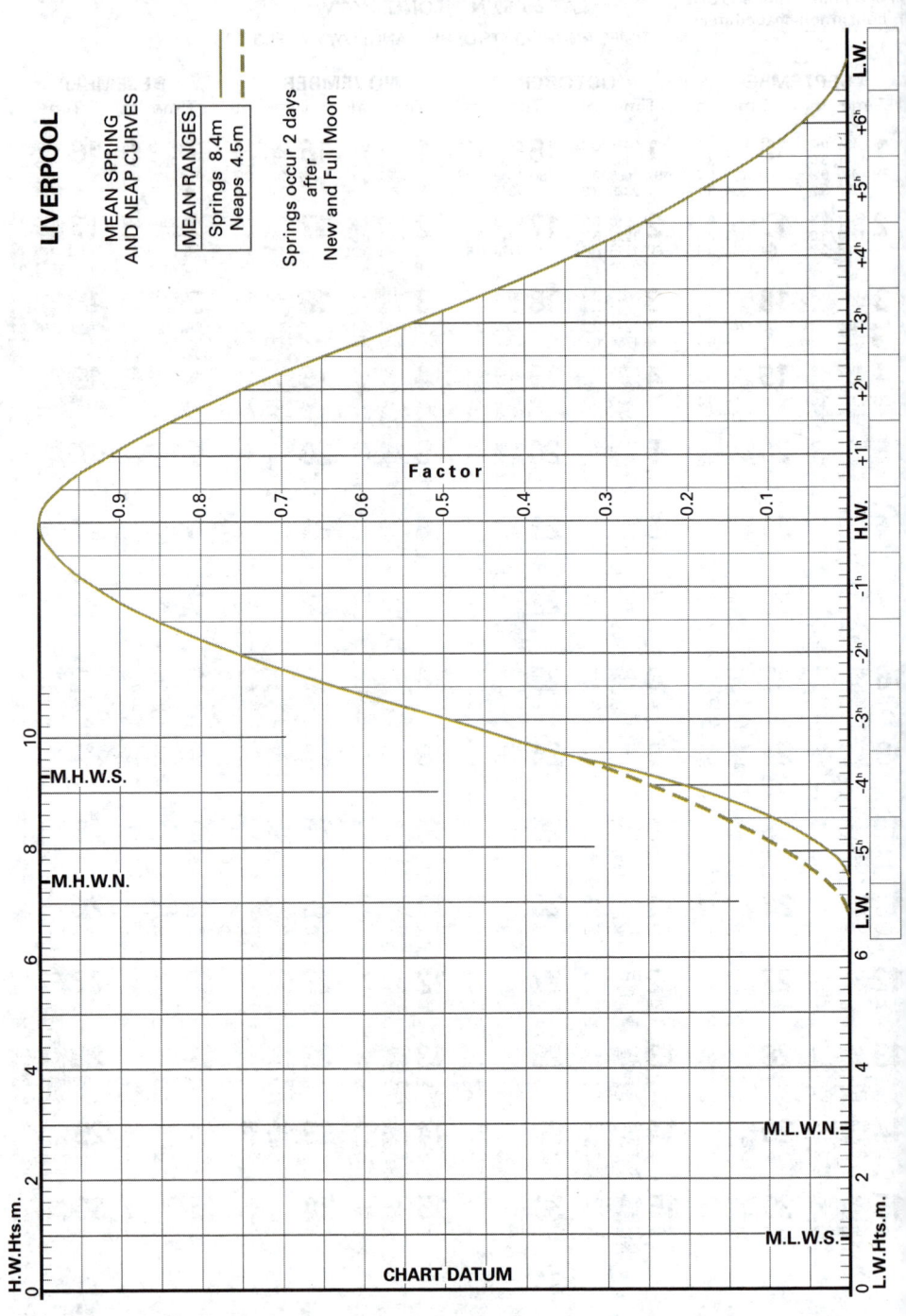

TIME ZONE (UT)
For Summer Time add ONE hour in **non-shaded areas**

ENGLAND – LIVERPOOL (ALFRED DK)
LAT 53°24′N   LONG 3°01′W
TIMES AND HEIGHTS OF HIGH AND LOW WATERS

YEAR 2005

JANUARY		FEBRUARY		MARCH		APRIL	
Time m	Time m	Time m	Time m	Time m	Time m	Time m	Time m
1 0219 8.3 / 0839 2.5 / SA 1436 8.5 / 2119 2.4	**16** 0319 8.7 / 0953 1.9 / SU 1539 9.0 / 2226 1.7	**1** 0310 8.3 / 0933 2.3 / TU 1530 8.5 / 2204 2.4	**16** 0406 7.8 / 1045 2.7 / W 1634 7.7 / ☾ 2311 3.0	**1** 0203 8.9 / 0829 1.6 / TU 1421 9.0 / 2052 1.8	**16** 0243 8.4 / 0921 2.0 / W 1507 8.2 / 2134 2.4	**1** 0304 8.2 / 0934 2.3 / F 1536 7.9 / 2200 2.8	**16** 0332 7.4 / 1024 3.1 / SA 1613 6.9 / ☾ 2235 3.6
2 0301 8.0 / 0922 2.7 / SU 1519 8.3 / 2202 2.6	**17** 0407 8.2 / 1040 2.4 / M 1629 8.4 / ☾ 2313 2.3	**2** 0357 8.0 / 1019 2.7 / W 1622 8.1 / ☾ 2256 2.8	**17** 0501 7.2 / 1146 3.3 / TH 1741 7.1	**2** 0239 8.6 / 0904 1.9 / W 1501 8.6 / 2128 2.2	**17** 0321 7.9 / 1001 2.7 / TH 1550 7.5 / ☾ 2215 3.1	**2** 0405 7.7 / 1041 2.8 / SA 1650 7.3 / ☾ 2322 3.3	**17** 0438 6.9 / 1143 3.4 / SU 1748 6.6
3 0347 7.8 / 1010 2.9 / M 1608 8.1 / ☾ 2253 2.7	**18** 0501 7.7 / 1133 2.8 / TU 1727 7.9	**3** 0457 7.7 / 1121 3.0 / TH 1728 7.8	**18** 0015 3.5 / 0623 6.9 / F 1303 3.5 / 1913 6.9	**3** 0323 8.2 / 0948 2.4 / TH 1551 8.1 / ☾ 2217 2.8	**18** 0409 7.3 / 1100 3.3 / F 1652 6.9 / 2321 3.7	**3** 0532 7.3 / 1219 3.0 / SU 1828 7.1	**18** 0001 3.8 / 0628 6.8 / M 1306 3.3 / 1920 6.8
4 0442 7.6 / 1107 3.1 / TU 1705 7.9 / 2355 2.8	**19** 0007 2.8 / 0605 7.4 / W 1237 3.1 / 1836 7.6	**4** 0011 3.0 / 0611 7.5 / F 1243 3.1 / 1844 7.7	**19** 0132 3.6 / 0757 7.1 / SA 1432 3.3 / 2033 7.2	**4** 0421 7.7 / 1049 2.9 / F 1659 7.5 / 2333 3.3	**19** 0527 6.8 / 1223 3.6 / SA 1836 6.6	**4** 0115 3.2 / 0708 7.5 / M 1404 2.6 / 1958 7.6	**19** 0126 3.6 / 0745 7.2 / TU 1421 2.9 / 2020 7.3
5 0546 7.6 / 1212 3.1 / W 1810 7.9	**20** 0111 3.1 / 0720 7.3 / TH 1349 3.2 / 1950 7.5	**5** 0142 3.0 / 0731 7.7 / SA 1414 2.9 / 2005 7.9	**20** 0254 3.3 / 0901 7.6 / SU 1546 2.8 / 2129 7.7	**5** 0542 7.3 / 1220 3.2 / SA 1828 7.3	**20** 0048 3.8 / 0719 6.8 / SU 1356 3.4 / 2004 6.9	**5** 0242 2.6 / 0823 8.1 / TU 1519 1.8 / 2102 8.3	**20** 0238 3.1 / 0838 7.7 / W 1518 2.3 / 2105 7.9
6 0104 2.8 / 0654 7.7 / TH 1325 2.9 / 1917 8.1	**21** 0220 3.1 / 0828 7.6 / F 1503 3.0 / 2054 7.7	**6** 0302 2.6 / 0846 8.2 / SU 1533 2.3 / 2118 8.4	**21** 0357 2.9 / 0949 8.1 / M 1635 2.3 / 2213 8.1	**6** 0122 3.3 / 0716 7.4 / SU 1407 2.9 / 2003 7.6	**21** 0219 3.6 / 0830 7.3 / M 1515 2.9 / 2101 7.5	**6** 0343 1.9 / 0920 8.8 / W 1614 1.1 / 2151 8.9	**21** 0330 2.5 / 0921 8.2 / TH 1601 1.8 / 2144 8.3
7 0215 2.5 / 0800 8.1 / F 1437 2.6 / 2023 8.4	**22** 0324 2.9 / 0922 7.9 / SA 1602 2.6 / 2146 8.0	**7** 0408 2.0 / 0947 8.9 / M 1638 1.6 / 2218 9.0	**22** 0442 2.4 / 1029 8.5 / TU 1714 1.9 / 2251 8.5	**7** 0254 2.7 / 0838 8.1 / M 1530 2.1 / 2116 8.2	**22** 0330 3.0 / 0920 7.9 / TU 1606 2.3 / 2145 8.0	**7** 0434 1.2 / 1007 9.4 / TH 1701 0.6 / 2235 9.3	**22** 0412 2.0 / 0958 8.6 / F 1639 1.4 / 2219 8.7
8 0320 2.1 / 0901 8.6 / SA 1543 2.1 / 2126 8.8	**23** 0413 2.6 / 1007 8.3 / SU 1648 2.3 / 2230 8.3	**8** 0504 1.4 / 1040 9.4 / TU 1734 0.9 / ● 2310 9.4	**23** 0520 2.0 / 1105 8.8 / W 1750 1.6 / 2325 8.7	**8** 0400 2.0 / 0938 8.8 / TU 1632 1.3 / 2210 8.9	**23** 0416 2.4 / 1001 8.4 / W 1645 1.8 / 2222 8.4	**8** 0518 0.8 / 1051 9.7 / F 1744 0.3 / ● 2315 9.5	**23** 0449 1.6 / 1033 8.9 / SA 1716 1.1 / 2253 8.9
9 0417 1.7 / 0956 9.1 / SU 1643 1.6 / 2223 9.1	**24** 0455 2.3 / 1047 8.6 / M 1729 2.0 / 2308 8.5	**9** 0554 1.0 / 1129 9.9 / W 1825 0.5 / ○ 2358 9.6	**24** 0554 1.7 / 1138 9.0 / TH 1824 1.4 / ○ 2357 8.8	**9** 0453 1.3 / 1027 9.5 / W 1723 0.6 / 2256 9.4	**24** 0454 1.9 / 1037 8.7 / TH 1720 1.4 / 2256 8.7	**9** 0600 0.5 / 1131 9.8 / SA 1822 0.3 / 2352 9.5	**24** 0526 1.2 / 1108 9.1 / SU 1751 1.0 / ○ 2327 9.1
10 0510 1.4 / 1048 9.5 / M 1739 1.1 / 2317 9.4	**25** 0533 2.1 / 1123 8.8 / TU 1807 1.9 / ○ 2344 8.6	**10** 0641 0.7 / 1215 10.1 / TH 1912 0.2	**25** 0626 1.5 / 1210 9.1 / F 1856 1.3	**10** 0540 0.8 / 1113 9.9 / TH 1808 0.2 / ● 2339 9.7	**25** 0528 1.6 / 1110 9.0 / F 1753 1.2 / 2328 8.9	**10** 0638 0.5 / 1210 9.7 / SU 1857 0.5	**25** 0603 1.0 / 1144 9.2 / M 1826 0.9
11 0601 1.1 / 1139 9.7 / TU 1833 0.8	**26** 0608 1.9 / 1157 8.9 / W 1843 1.7	**11** 0042 9.7 / 0725 0.6 / F 1300 10.1 / 1954 0.2	**26** 0028 8.9 / 0656 1.4 / SA 1241 9.2 / 1925 1.3	**11** 0624 0.5 / 1155 10.1 / F 1850 0.1	**26** 0600 1.3 / 1141 9.1 / SA 1825 1.0 / 2359 9.1	**11** 0028 9.3 / 0713 0.7 / M 1247 9.5 / 1928 0.9	**26** 0003 9.2 / 0640 0.9 / TU 1223 9.1 / 1900 1.0
12 0008 9.5 / 0650 1.0 / W 1229 9.9 / 1923 0.6	**27** 0017 8.7 / 0641 1.8 / TH 1231 9.0 / 1917 1.7	**12** 0125 9.6 / 0726 1.4 / SA 1342 10.0 / 2034 0.5	**27** 0059 9.0 / 0726 1.4 / SU 1313 9.2 / 1953 1.3	**12** 0019 9.7 / 0704 0.4 / SA 1236 10.0 / 1928 0.2	**27** 0631 1.1 / 1213 9.2 / SU 1856 1.0	**12** 0102 9.1 / 0746 1.1 / TU 1323 9.1 / 1956 1.4	**27** 0041 9.2 / 0717 1.0 / W 1304 9.1 / 1935 1.3
13 0059 9.5 / 0738 1.0 / TH 1318 9.9 / 2012 0.6	**28** 0050 8.7 / 0714 1.8 / F 1304 9.0 / 1949 1.7	**13** 0206 9.3 / 0844 1.0 / SU 1423 9.6 / 2111 1.0	**28** 0131 9.0 / 0757 1.4 / M 1345 9.1 / 2021 1.5	**13** 0058 9.6 / 0741 0.6 / SU 1315 9.8 / 2003 0.6	**28** 0031 9.1 / 0702 1.0 / M 1247 9.3 / 1925 1.1	**13** 0136 8.8 / 0817 1.5 / W 1358 8.6 / 2023 1.9	**28** 0122 9.1 / 0757 1.1 / TH 1348 8.8 / 2014 1.7
14 0147 9.4 / 0824 1.2 / F 1405 9.7 / 2057 0.8	**29** 0123 8.7 / 0746 1.8 / SA 1337 9.0 / 2020 1.7	**14** 0244 8.9 / 0921 1.5 / M 1504 9.1 / 2146 1.6		**14** 0134 9.3 / 0816 0.9 / M 1353 9.4 / 2035 1.1	**29** 0104 9.1 / 0735 1.1 / TU 1322 9.2 / 1955 1.3	**14** 0209 8.4 / 0849 1.8 / TH 1434 8.1 / 2052 2.5	**29** 0207 8.7 / 0842 1.6 / F 1437 8.4 / 2100 2.2
15 0233 9.1 / 0908 1.5 / SA 1452 9.4 / 2142 1.2	**30** 0157 8.7 / 0819 1.9 / SU 1412 8.9 / 2051 1.9	**15** 0323 8.4 / 1000 2.1 / TU 1545 8.4 / 2224 2.3		**15** 0209 9.1 / 0848 1.4 / TU 1429 8.9 / 2104 1.7	**30** 0139 9.0 / 0809 1.3 / W 1400 9.0 / 2027 1.7	**15** 0246 7.9 / 0928 2.6 / F 1517 7.4 / 2133 3.1	**30** 0259 8.3 / 0936 2.1 / SA 1536 7.8 / 2200 2.7
	31 0232 8.5 / 0854 2.1 / M 1448 8.7 / 2124 2.1				**31** 0218 8.7 / 0846 1.7 / TH 1443 8.5 / 2107 2.2		

Chart Datum: 4·93 metres below Ordnance Datum (Newlyn)

》》 **FREE** monthly updates from 《《
www.reedsalmanac.co.uk

Chapter 5

TIDES

TIME ZONE (UT)
For Summer Time add ONE hour in **non-shaded areas**

ENGLAND – LIVERPOOL (ALFRED DK)
LAT 53°24′N   LONG 3°01′W
TIMES AND HEIGHTS OF HIGH AND LOW WATERS

YEAR 2005

MAY

Day	Time	m	Time	m	Day	Time	m	Time	m
1 SU	0405 1048 1652 2323	7.9 2.5 7.4 3.0	**16** M	0403 1102 1651 2313	7.3 3.1 6.9 3.5
2 M	0528 1218 1820	7.6 2.5 7.4	**17** TU	0518 1210 1815	7.1 3.1 6.9
3 TU	0058 0649 1344 1936	2.9 7.8 2.2 7.8	**18** W	0025 0638 1316 1922	3.4 7.2 2.8 7.2
4 W	0216 0757 1453 2035	2.4 8.3 1.7 8.3	**19** TH	0131 0740 1415 2014	3.1 7.6 2.4 7.7
5 TH	0316 0853 1548 2125	1.9 8.8 1.2 8.7	**20** F	0230 0829 1508 2058	2.6 8.0 2.0 8.2
6 F	0407 0942 1634 2208	1.4 9.1 0.9 9.0	**21** SA	0322 0913 1555 2139	2.1 8.4 1.6 8.6
7 SA	0452 1026 1714 2248	1.1 9.3 0.8 9.1	**22** SU	0409 0955 1638 2218	1.7 8.7 1.3 8.9
8 SU	0533 1107 1751 2325	0.9 9.3 0.9 9.1	**23** M	0454 1037 1720 2258	1.4 9.0 1.1 9.1
9 M	0611 1145 1824	1.0 9.2 1.1	**24** TU	0538 1120 1801 2340	1.1 9.1 1.0 9.1
10 TU	0000 0646 1222 1854	9.0 1.1 9.0 1.4	**25** W	0622 1205 1842	1.0 9.2 1.1
11 W	0034 0719 1257 1922	8.9 1.4 8.7 1.7	**26** TH	0025 0707 1253 1924	9.3 1.0 9.1 1.3
12 TH	0108 0752 1332 1950	8.7 1.7 8.4 2.1	**27** F	0113 0755 1344 2010	9.1 1.1 8.8 1.6
13 F	0143 0826 1410 2023	8.4 2.1 8.0 2.5	**28** SA	0204 0847 1437 2102	8.9 1.4 8.5 2.0
14 SA	0222 0900 1453 2104	8.0 2.5 7.6 2.9	**29** SU	0300 0944 1536 2202	8.6 1.7 8.1 2.4
15 SU	0307 0958 1544 2201	7.6 2.9 7.1 3.3	**30** M	0402 1048 1643 2311	8.3 1.9 7.8 2.6
			31 TU	0510 1157 1754	8.2 2.0 7.7

JUNE

Day	Time	m	Time	m	Day	Time	m	Time	m
1 W	0025 0619 1309 1902	2.6 8.1 2.0 7.8	**16** TH	0527 1217 1810	7.5 2.7 7.3
2 TH	0138 0724 1417 2002	2.4 8.2 1.9 8.0	**17** F	0033 0629 1319 1912	3.0 7.6 2.6 7.6
3 F	0242 0823 1514 2055	2.1 8.4 1.7 8.3	**18** SA	0136 0730 1419 2009	2.8 7.9 2.3 8.0
4 SA	0336 0915 1602 2141	1.8 8.6 1.6 8.5	**19** SU	0237 0826 1515 2100	2.4 8.2 1.9 8.4
5 SU	0424 1002 1644 2223	1.6 8.7 1.5 8.7	**20** M	0334 0920 1607 2149	2.0 8.5 1.6 8.8
6 M	0506 1045 1720 2301	1.5 8.7 1.5 8.8	**21** TU	0428 1012 1656 2236	1.6 8.8 1.4 9.1
7 TU	0546 1124 1754 2337	1.5 8.7 1.6 8.7	**22** W	0521 1104 1744 2325	1.3 9.0 1.2 9.3
8 W	0623 1202 1826	1.6 8.6 1.8	**23** TH	0613 1155 1832	1.0 9.1 1.2
9 TH	0012 0659 1238 1857	8.7 1.7 8.5 2.0	**24** F	0015 0705 1247 1920	9.4 0.9 9.1 1.2
10 F	0048 0735 1314 1929	8.6 1.9 8.3 2.2	**25** SA	0106 0757 1339 2009	9.4 0.8 9.1 1.4
11 SA	0125 0811 1352 2004	8.4 2.1 8.1 2.4	**26** SU	0158 0848 1431 2059	9.4 0.9 8.9 1.6
12 SU	0204 0850 1432 2044	8.2 2.3 7.9 2.6	**27** M	0250 0938 1523 2150	9.2 1.1 8.6 1.9
13 M	0246 0933 1516 2132	8.0 2.5 7.6 2.9	**28** TU	0344 1030 1617 2245	8.9 1.4 8.2 2.2
14 TU	0333 1022 1606 2227	7.8 2.7 7.4 3.1	**29** W	0440 1124 1716 2344	8.5 1.8 7.9 2.4
15 W	0426 1118 1705 2329	7.6 2.8 7.3 3.1	**30** TH	0541 1222 1821	8.2 2.1 7.7

JULY

Day	Time	m	Time	m	Day	Time	m	Time	m
1 F	0049 0646 1327 1925	2.6 8.0 2.4 7.7	**16** SA	0535 1225 1816	7.7 2.8 7.5
2 SA	0200 0750 1432 2025	2.6 7.9 2.4 7.8	**17** SU	0049 0641 1336 1924	3.0 7.7 2.7 7.7
3 SU	0305 0850 1529 2118	2.4 8.0 2.3 8.1	**18** M	0202 0750 1445 2030	2.7 7.9 2.4 8.1
4 M	0400 0943 1615 2204	2.2 8.2 2.2 8.3	**19** TU	0311 0857 1546 2129	2.3 8.2 2.0 8.6
5 TU	0447 1029 1655 2245	2.0 8.3 2.1 8.5	**20** W	0414 0958 1642 2223	1.8 8.6 1.6 9.1
6 W	0529 1111 1732 2322	1.9 8.3 2.1 8.6	**21** TH	0512 1054 1735 2314	1.3 8.8 1.3 9.5
7 TH	0609 1149 1808 2358	1.8 8.4 2.0 8.7	**22** F	0608 1147 1826	0.9 9.2 1.1
8 F	0647 1224 1842	1.8 8.4 2.0	**23** SA	0004 0700 1238 1914	9.7 0.7 9.4 0.9
9 SA	0033 0723 1259 1914	8.7 1.8 8.3 2.1	**24** SU	0054 0749 1326 2000	9.8 0.7 9.4 1.0
10 SU	0109 0757 1334 1948	8.6 1.9 8.3 2.1	**25** M	0142 0835 1412 2044	9.8 0.5 9.2 1.1
11 M	0145 0831 1410 2024	8.5 2.0 8.1 2.2	**26** TU	0229 0918 1457 2127	9.6 0.7 9.0 1.5
12 TU	0222 0905 1447 2103	8.4 2.2 8.1 2.3	**27** W	0316 1001 1543 2212	9.2 1.1 8.5 1.9
13 W	0301 0942 1527 2146	8.2 2.3 7.9 2.6	**28** TH	0404 1045 1632 2303	8.7 1.6 8.0 2.4
14 TH	0344 1027 1614 2237	8.1 2.4 7.7 2.7	**29** F	0458 1136 1730	8.1 2.0 7.5
15 F	0435 1120 1710 2338	7.9 2.7 7.5 3.0	**30** SA	0004 0603 1236 1843	2.9 7.6 2.9 7.3
			31 SU	0118 0719 1346 1958	3.1 7.4 3.1 7.4

AUGUST

Day	Time	m	Time	m	Day	Time	m	Time	m
1 M	0239 0831 1459 2059	3.0 7.5 3.0 7.7	**16** TU	0140 0730 1426 2012	3.0 7.6 2.8 7.9
2 TU	0346 0928 1557 2149	2.6 7.7 2.7 8.1	**17** W	0301 0849 1536 2118	2.4 8.0 2.3 8.6
3 W	0437 1016 1641 2232	2.3 8.1 2.4 8.5	**18** TH	0408 0952 1634 2213	1.7 8.6 1.7 9.3
4 TH	0519 1058 1720 2309	2.0 8.3 2.1 8.7	**19** F	0506 1045 1726 2302	1.0 9.1 1.1 9.7
5 F	0557 1134 1756 2344	1.8 8.5 1.9 8.8	**20** SA	0558 1134 1814 2349	0.5 9.4 0.6 10.0
6 SA	0633 1208 1829	1.7 8.5 1.9	**21** SU	0646 1219 1859	0.2 9.6 0.6
7 SU	0017 0705 1240 1859	8.9 1.6 8.6 1.8	**22** M	0034 0730 1303 1941	10.1 0.3 9.6 0.6
8 M	0049 0736 1311 1929	8.8 1.6 8.6 1.8	**23** TU	0118 0810 1345 2020	10.0 0.5 9.4 0.9
9 TU	0121 0805 1342 2000	8.7 1.7 8.5 1.9	**24** W	0201 0849 1425 2058	9.7 0.7 9.1 1.3
10 W	0153 0834 1414 2034	8.7 1.8 8.4 2.0	**25** TH	0242 0925 1504 2138	9.2 1.2 8.5 1.9
11 TH	0227 0905 1449 2110	8.6 2.0 8.3 2.3	**26** F	0325 1004 1547 2223	8.5 1.9 8.0 2.5
12 F	0305 0940 1531 2152	8.4 2.3 8.0 2.6	**27** SA	0414 1050 1638 2324	7.8 2.7 7.4 3.1
13 SA	0353 1025 1623 2248	8.0 2.7 7.7 3.0	**28** SU	0519 1151 1757	7.2 3.3 7.0
14 SU	0454 1132 1732	7.7 3.1 7.4	**29** M	0653 1309 1933	7.1 3.6 7.1
15 M	0009 0607 1302 1853	3.2 7.5 3.2 7.5	**30** TU	0221 0814 1437 2041	3.3 7.4 3.4 7.6
			31 W	0335 0911 1543 2131	2.8 7.8 2.8 8.2

Chart Datum: 4·93 metres below Ordnance Datum (Newlyn)

》》 **FREE** monthly updates from 《《
www.reedsalmanac.co.uk

316

TIME ZONE (UT)
For Summer Time add ONE hour in **non-shaded areas**

ENGLAND – LIVERPOOL (ALFRED DK)
LAT 53°24′N   LONG 3°01′W
TIMES AND HEIGHTS OF HIGH AND LOW WATERS

YEAR 2005

SEPTEMBER				OCTOBER				NOVEMBER				DECEMBER			
Time	m	Time	m	Time	m	Time	m	Time	m	Time	m	Time	m	Time	m
1 0422 2.3 0957 8.0 TH 1628 2.5 2212 8.5		**16** 0400 1.5 0941 8.8 F 1622 1.5 2158 9.4		**1** 0430 1.8 1006 8.5 SA 1638 2.1 2219 8.8		**16** 0431 0.7 1007 9.3 SU 1649 0.9 2222 9.8		**1** 0456 1.4 1036 8.9 TU 1706 1.6 2247 9.1		**16** 0527 0.9 1103 9.3 W 1747 1.1 ○ 2322 9.4		**1** 0500 1.5 1040 9.1 TH 1718 1.5 ● 2258 9.1		**16** 0540 1.7 1123 9.0 F 1810 1.6 2345 8.8	
2 0501 1.9 1036 8.4 F 1706 2.1 2249 8.8		**17** 0453 0.7 1029 9.3 SA 1711 0.9 2244 9.9		**2** 0503 1.5 1040 8.7 SU 1710 1.7 2252 9.0		**17** 0515 0.4 1048 9.6 M 1731 0.7 ○ 2304 10.0		**2** 0530 1.2 1108 9.1 W 1742 1.4 ● 2321 9.2		**17** 0603 1.1 1140 9.3 TH 1826 1.2		**2** 0541 1.4 1120 9.2 F 1802 1.4 2341 9.2		**17** 0616 1.8 1200 9.0 SA 1850 1.7	
3 0536 1.6 1111 8.6 SA 1739 1.8 ● 2322 9.0		**18** 0539 0.3 1113 9.6 SU 1755 0.6 ○ 2327 10.2		**3** 0535 1.3 1111 8.9 M 1740 1.5 ● 2321 9.1		**18** 0555 0.3 1128 9.6 TU 1812 0.6 2344 9.9		**3** 0605 1.2 1141 9.2 TH 1818 1.3 2357 9.2		**18** 0000 9.2 0637 1.4 F 1216 9.1 1903 1.5		**3** 0622 1.4 1202 9.3 SA 1846 1.3		**18** 0023 8.7 0651 2.0 SU 1237 8.9 1928 1.9	
4 0609 1.4 1143 8.7 SU 1809 1.7 2353 9.0		**19** 0623 0.1 1155 9.7 M 1837 0.4		**4** 0605 1.2 1141 9.0 TU 1810 1.4 2351 9.1		**19** 0633 0.5 1205 9.5 W 1850 0.8		**4** 0639 1.4 1217 9.1 F 1855 1.4		**19** 0038 8.9 0710 1.8 SA 1252 8.9 1940 1.8		**4** 0026 9.1 0704 1.6 SU 1248 9.3 1932 1.4		**19** 0100 8.5 0725 2.2 M 1314 8.8 2005 2.1	
5 0639 1.4 1213 8.8 M 1837 1.6		**20** 0009 10.2 0703 0.1 TU 1235 9.6 1916 0.6		**5** 0635 1.2 1210 9.0 W 1841 1.3		**20** 0023 9.6 0707 0.9 TH 1242 9.3 1925 1.1		**5** 0036 9.1 0714 1.6 SA 1257 9.0 1933 1.6		**20** 0115 8.6 0742 2.2 SU 1329 8.6 2017 2.2		**5** 0115 8.9 0748 1.8 M 1337 9.1 2021 1.6		**20** 0138 8.3 0758 2.4 TU 1352 8.6 2042 2.3	
6 0022 9.0 0707 1.0 TU 1242 8.8 1905 1.5		**21** 0051 9.9 0740 0.5 W 1313 9.4 1952 0.9		**6** 0021 9.1 0704 1.3 TH 1241 9.0 1912 1.4		**21** 0101 9.2 0739 1.4 F 1317 8.9 2000 1.6		**6** 0119 8.8 0751 1.9 SU 1341 8.8 2016 1.9		**21** 0154 8.2 0816 2.6 M 1409 8.3 2058 2.6		**6** 0206 8.7 0837 2.1 TU 1429 8.9 2114 1.9		**21** 0217 8.1 0834 2.7 W 1432 8.3 2120 2.5	
7 0051 9.0 0734 1.4 W 1311 8.8 1935 1.6		**22** 0130 9.5 0814 1.0 TH 1350 9.0 2028 1.4		**7** 0055 9.0 0734 1.6 F 1315 8.9 1945 1.6		**22** 0138 8.7 0810 2.0 SA 1353 8.5 2036 2.1		**7** 0207 8.4 0835 2.4 M 1430 8.4 2107 2.3		**22** 0237 7.7 0855 3.1 TU 1453 7.9 2148 3.0		**7** 0301 8.4 0931 2.4 W 1526 8.7 2213 2.0		**22** 0258 7.6 0915 2.9 TH 1515 8.1 2203 2.8	
8 0122 8.9 0802 1.6 TH 1342 8.7 2006 1.8		**23** 0208 9.0 0847 1.7 F 1426 8.5 2104 2.0		**8** 0132 8.8 0805 1.9 SA 1352 8.6 2021 2.0		**23** 0217 8.1 0843 2.6 SU 1431 8.0 2117 2.7		**8** 0303 8.0 0930 2.8 TU 1531 8.1 2214 2.6		**23** 0327 7.3 0947 3.4 W 1547 7.5 ○ 2248 3.2		**8** 0402 8.1 1032 2.6 TH 1628 8.4 2316 2.2		**23** 0344 7.6 1004 3.1 F 1603 7.8 ○ 2253 2.9	
9 0155 8.8 0831 1.9 F 1416 8.5 2040 2.1		**24** 0248 8.3 0921 2.4 SA 1504 8.0 2146 2.7		**9** 0214 8.4 0842 2.4 SU 1436 8.2 2104 2.5		**24** 0301 7.5 0924 3.2 M 1517 7.5 2215 3.3		**9** 0413 7.6 1045 3.2 W 1645 7.8 ● 2338 2.7		**24** 0432 7.0 1054 3.7 TH 1655 7.3 2353 3.3		**9** 0510 7.8 1140 2.7 F 1735 8.3		**24** 0438 7.3 1100 3.3 SA 1659 7.6 2351 3.0	
10 0233 8.5 0904 2.3 SA 1456 8.2 2120 2.5		**25** 0333 7.6 1003 3.1 SU 1552 7.4 ● 2247 3.3		**10** 0305 7.9 0930 2.9 M 1534 7.8 ● 2207 3.0		**25** 0359 6.9 1025 3.7 TU 1623 7.1 ● 2333 3.5		**10** 0538 7.4 1213 3.1 TH 1808 7.9		**25** 0553 6.9 1205 3.6 F 1815 7.3		**10** 0025 2.3 0621 7.8 SA 1252 2.7 1844 8.3		**25** 0541 7.2 1204 3.4 SU 1801 7.5	
11 0321 8.0 0947 2.7 SU 1550 7.7 ○ 2215 3.0		**26** 0437 6.9 1107 3.7 M 1710 6.9		**11** 0415 7.3 1046 3.4 TU 1652 7.4 2344 3.2		**26** 0538 6.6 1148 4.0 W 1811 7.0		**11** 0103 2.5 0658 7.7 F 1335 2.8 1920 8.3		**26** 0058 3.1 0704 7.2 SA 1311 3.4 1920 7.6		**11** 0136 2.2 0728 8.0 SU 1403 2.5 1948 8.5		**26** 0054 3.0 0647 7.4 M 1310 3.2 1905 7.7	
12 0425 7.5 1048 3.3 M 1704 7.3 2347 3.3		**27** 0013 3.6 0625 6.6 TU 1234 3.9 1902 6.9		**12** 0548 7.1 1234 3.6 W 1828 7.5		**27** 0057 3.4 0705 6.9 TH 1314 3.7 1927 7.3		**12** 0216 2.0 0803 8.2 SA 1441 2.2 2020 8.8		**27** 0158 2.7 0758 7.6 SU 1411 3.0 2011 7.9		**12** 0241 2.0 0827 8.3 M 1505 2.2 2046 8.7		**27** 0157 2.8 0749 7.7 TU 1415 2.9 2005 8.0	
13 0551 7.2 1243 3.5 TU 1837 7.3		**28** 0153 3.4 0748 7.0 W 1409 3.6 2012 7.4		**13** 0126 2.8 0722 7.5 TH 1404 2.9 1948 8.1		**28** 0212 3.0 0803 7.4 F 1426 3.3 2021 7.8		**13** 0315 1.5 0856 8.7 SU 1536 1.7 2112 9.2		**28** 0251 2.3 0843 8.1 M 1506 2.6 2055 8.3		**13** 0335 1.8 0918 8.6 TU 1559 2.0 2138 8.8		**28** 0256 2.4 0843 8.1 W 1515 2.6 2101 8.3	
14 0133 3.1 0727 7.4 W 1418 3.0 2004 7.9		**29** 0306 2.8 0844 7.5 TH 1517 3.1 2102 8.0		**14** 0244 2.2 0830 8.2 F 1509 2.1 2048 8.8		**29** 0305 2.5 0849 7.9 SA 1516 2.7 2104 8.3		**14** 0404 1.1 0941 9.1 M 1623 1.3 2158 9.4		**29** 0337 2.1 0923 8.5 TU 1551 2.1 2136 8.7		**14** 0422 1.7 1003 8.8 W 1646 1.7 2224 8.9		**29** 0349 2.1 0932 8.5 TH 1610 2.1 2152 8.7	
15 0257 2.3 0845 8.0 TH 1527 2.2 2107 8.7		**30** 0306 2.8 0928 8.0 F 1601 2.5 2143 8.5		**15** 0342 1.5 0922 8.9 SA 1602 1.5 2137 9.4		**30** 0346 2.1 0928 8.4 SU 1556 2.2 2141 8.6		**15** 0448 0.9 1023 9.3 TU 1707 1.1 ○ 2241 9.5		**30** 0419 1.8 1001 8.8 W 1635 1.8 2216 8.9		**15** 0502 1.8 1044 9.0 TH 1729 1.6 ○ 2306 8.9		**30** 0438 1.8 1019 8.8 F 1702 1.7 2242 9.0	
						31 0422 1.6 1003 8.7 M 1631 1.8 2215 8.9								**31** 0526 1.5 1106 9.1 SA 1753 1.3 ● 2332 9.2	

Chart Datum: 4·93 metres below Ordnance Datum (Newlyn)

》》 **FREE** monthly updates from 《《
www.reedsalmanac.co.uk

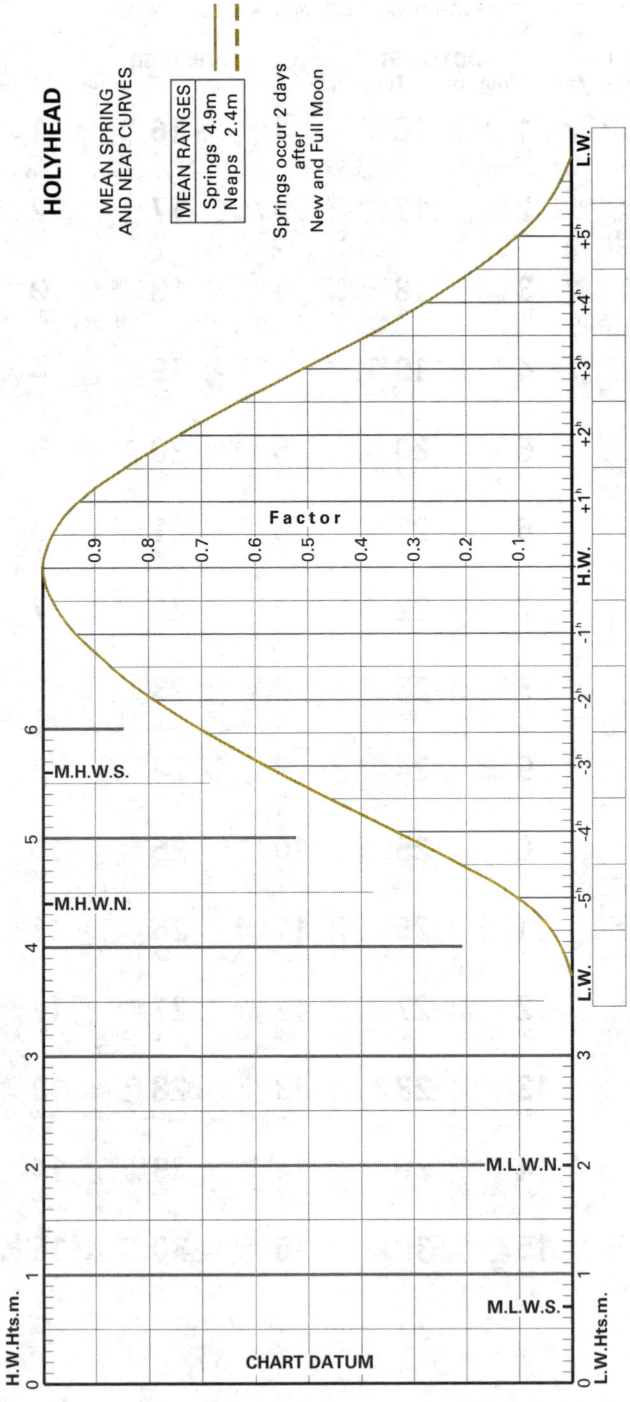
HOLYHEAD
MEAN SPRING AND NEAP CURVES
MEAN RANGES
Springs 4.9m
Neaps 2.4m
Springs occur 2 days after New and Full Moon
Factor
0.9
0.8
0.7
0.6
0.5
0.4
0.3
0.2
0.1
L.W.
-5h
-4h
-3h
-2h
-1h
H.W.
+1h
+2h
+3h
+4h
+5h
L.W.
H.W.Hts.m.
0
1
2
3
4
5
6
M.H.W.S.
M.H.W.N.
M.L.W.N.
M.L.W.S.
CHART DATUM
L.W.Hts.m.

| TIME ZONE (UT) For Summer Time add ONE hour in **non-shaded areas** | **WALES – HOLYHEAD** LAT 53°19'N LONG 4°37'W TIMES AND HEIGHTS OF HIGH AND LOW WATERS | | **YEAR 2005** |

WALES – HOLYHEAD
LAT 53°19'N LONG 4°37'W
TIMES AND HEIGHTS OF HIGH AND LOW WATERS

JANUARY		FEBRUARY		MARCH		APRIL	
Time m	Time m	Time m	Time m	Time m	Time m	Time m	Time m
1 0128 4.8 / 0724 1.7 / SA 1340 5.1 / 2002 1.6	**16** 0230 5.0 / 0828 1.4 / SU 1444 5.4 / 2107 1.3	**1** 0216 4.8 / 0816 1.6 / TU 1430 5.0 / 2051 1.5	**16** 0323 4.5 / 0935 1.9 / W 1550 4.6 / ◐ 2209 2.1	**1** 0105 5.2 / 0704 1.1 / TU 1319 5.3 / 1931 1.1	**16** 0149 4.9 / 0800 1.4 / W 1413 4.8 / 2021 1.7	**1** 0207 4.9 / 0821 1.5 / F 1439 4.7 / 2055 1.8	**16** 0247 4.4 / 0925 2.1 / SA 1540 4.1 / ◐ 2141 2.5
2 0211 4.7 / 0808 1.9 / SU 1423 5.0 / 2048 1.7	**17** 0324 4.7 / 0924 1.7 / M 1540 5.1 / ◐ 2205 1.6	**2** 0304 4.7 / 0907 1.8 / W 1521 4.8 / ◐ 2148 1.7	**17** 0429 4.3 / 1051 2.2 / TH 1706 4.3 / 2328 2.3	**2** 0142 5.0 / 0745 1.3 / W 1359 5.1 / 2015 1.4	**17** 0231 4.6 / 0852 1.8 / TH 1504 4.4 / ◐ 2113 2.2	**2** 0312 4.6 / 0937 1.8 / SA 1605 4.4 / ◐ 2224 2.1	**17** 0403 4.2 / 1053 2.2 / SU 1720 4.0 / 2319 2.6
3 0259 4.6 / 0857 2.0 / M 1513 4.9 / ◐ 2141 1.8	**18** 0425 4.5 / 1028 2.0 / TU 1643 4.8 / 2309 1.9	**3** 0405 4.5 / 1013 2.0 / TH 1630 4.7 / 2301 1.9	**18** 0557 4.2 / 1220 2.3 / F 1844 4.2	**3** 0227 4.8 / 0835 1.6 / TH 1450 4.8 / ◐ 2111 1.7	**18** 0328 4.3 / 1003 2.2 / F 1619 4.1 / 2231 2.5	**3** 0444 4.4 / 1115 1.8 / SU 1757 4.4	**18** 0541 4.2 / 1218 2.1 / M 1849 4.1
4 0357 4.5 / 0956 2.1 / TU 1612 4.8 / 2242 1.8	**19** 0535 4.4 / 1140 2.1 / W 1755 4.6	**4** 0525 4.5 / 1135 2.0 / F 1759 4.5	**19** 0053 2.3 / 0724 4.4 / SA 1341 2.1 / 2001 4.3	**4** 0327 4.6 / 0943 1.9 / F 1604 4.5 / 2232 2.0	**19** 0457 4.1 / 1141 2.3 / SA 1811 4.0	**4** 0001 2.1 / 0619 4.6 / M 1244 1.6 / 1920 4.6	**19** 0042 2.4 / 0657 4.4 / TU 1320 1.8 / 1944 4.4
5 0504 4.5 / 1102 2.1 / W 1720 4.8 / 2348 1.7	**20** 0017 2.0 / 0647 4.5 / TH 1253 2.1 / 1909 4.5	**5** 0023 1.9 / 0647 4.6 / SA 1257 1.8 / 1924 4.8	**20** 0203 2.2 / 0824 4.6 / SU 1438 1.8 / 2053 4.6	**5** 0454 4.4 / 1117 2.0 / SA 1751 4.4	**20** 0015 2.5 / 0643 4.2 / SU 1310 2.1 / 1938 4.2	**5** 0118 1.7 / 0730 4.9 / TU 1350 1.2 / 2018 5.0	**20** 0137 2.0 / 0748 4.6 / W 1405 1.5 / 2022 4.7
6 0612 4.6 / 1211 1.9 / TH 1831 4.9	**21** 0123 2.0 / 0750 4.6 / F 1359 2.0 / 2012 4.6	**6** 0137 1.7 / 0756 4.9 / SU 1408 1.4 / 2032 5.0	**21** 0252 1.9 / 0906 4.9 / M 1519 1.5 / 2130 4.8	**6** 0009 2.0 / 0631 4.5 / SU 1251 1.8 / 1925 4.6	**21** 0135 2.3 / 0752 4.5 / M 1409 1.8 / 2028 4.5	**6** 0214 1.3 / 0824 5.3 / W 1442 0.8 / 2103 5.2	**21** 0217 1.7 / 0827 4.9 / TH 1440 1.2 / 2054 4.9
7 0052 1.6 / 0715 4.9 / F 1317 1.7 / 1936 5.0	**22** 0220 1.9 / 0841 4.8 / SA 1453 1.8 / 2102 4.8	**7** 0238 1.3 / 0853 5.3 / M 1507 1.0 / 2127 5.3	**22** 0328 1.6 / 0940 5.1 / TU 1553 1.3 / 2202 5.0	**7** 0130 1.8 / 0746 4.9 / M 1403 1.3 / 2030 5.0	**22** 0224 2.0 / 0836 4.8 / TU 1449 1.5 / 2104 4.8	**7** 0300 1.0 / 0909 5.6 / TH 1524 0.5 / 2141 5.4	**22** 0250 1.4 / 0901 5.1 / F 1513 1.0 / 2124 5.1
8 0151 1.4 / 0811 5.1 / SA 1416 1.4 / 2035 5.2	**23** 0305 1.8 / 0922 5.0 / SU 1535 1.5 / 2143 4.9	**8** 0330 1.0 / 0943 5.6 / TU 1558 0.6 / ● 2216 5.6	**23** 0358 1.3 / 1010 5.3 / W 1623 1.0 / 2230 5.1	**8** 0231 1.4 / 0842 5.3 / TU 1459 0.9 / 2120 5.3	**23** 0259 1.6 / 0910 5.2 / W 1522 1.2 / 2133 5.0	**8** 0340 0.7 / 0919 5.8 / F 1603 0.4 / ● 2217 5.5	**23** 0322 1.1 / 0933 5.3 / SA 1544 0.8 / 2155 5.3
9 0246 1.2 / 0902 5.4 / SU 1512 1.1 / 2130 5.5	**24** 0343 1.6 / 0958 5.2 / M 1612 1.4 / 2218 5.0	**9** 0417 0.8 / 1029 5.9 / W 1645 0.4 / 2301 5.7	**24** 0427 1.1 / 1039 5.4 / TH 1652 0.9 / ○ 2258 5.3	**9** 0319 1.0 / 0929 5.6 / W 1545 0.5 / 2202 5.5	**24** 0329 1.3 / 0940 5.2 / TH 1552 0.9 / 2200 5.2	**9** 0418 0.5 / 1029 5.9 / SA 1641 0.4 / 2253 5.6	**24** 0355 0.8 / 1007 5.5 / SU 1617 0.6 / ○ 2228 5.4
10 0337 1.0 / 0951 5.7 / M 1604 0.8 / 2222 5.6	**25** 0416 1.4 / 1030 5.3 / TU 1645 1.3 / ○ 2250 5.1	**10** 0501 0.6 / 1113 6.1 / TH 1730 0.2 / 2344 5.7	**25** 0456 1.0 / 1108 5.5 / F 1721 0.8 / 2327 5.3	**10** 0401 0.7 / 1011 5.9 / TH 1627 0.3 / ● 2242 5.7	**25** 0358 1.0 / 1009 5.4 / F 1620 0.7 / ○ 2228 5.3	**10** 0456 0.5 / 1108 5.8 / SU 1717 0.5 / 2329 5.5	**25** 0429 0.7 / 1042 5.6 / M 1651 0.6 / 2303 5.4
11 0426 0.9 / 1038 5.9 / TU 1655 0.6 / 2312 5.7	**26** 0447 1.3 / 1101 5.4 / W 1716 1.1 / 2321 5.2	**11** 0544 0.5 / 1157 6.1 / F 1813 0.3	**26** 0526 0.9 / 1139 5.6 / SA 1751 0.8 / 2358 5.3	**11** 0441 0.5 / 1053 6.1 / F 1707 0.2 / 2320 5.7	**26** 0427 0.8 / 1039 5.5 / SA 1650 0.6 / 2258 5.4	**11** 0533 0.6 / 1147 5.6 / M 1753 0.7	**26** 0505 0.7 / 1120 5.6 / TU 1728 0.7 / 2340 5.5
12 0514 0.8 / 1127 6.0 / W 1745 0.5	**27** 0519 1.2 / 1132 5.4 / TH 1748 1.1 / 2353 5.2	**12** 0026 5.6 / 0625 0.7 / SA 1240 6.0 / 1855 0.5	**27** 0557 0.9 / 1211 5.5 / SU 1822 0.9	**12** 0520 0.4 / 1133 6.0 / SA 1746 0.3 / 2358 5.6	**27** 0457 0.7 / 1110 5.6 / SU 1720 0.6 / 2329 5.4	**12** 0005 5.4 / 0611 0.9 / TU 1225 5.4 / 1828 1.0	**27** 0545 0.7 / 1201 5.4 / W 1808 0.9
13 0001 5.6 / 0601 0.9 / TH 1216 6.0 / 1834 0.5	**28** 0550 1.2 / 1204 5.5 / F 1820 1.1	**13** 0108 5.4 / 0708 1.0 / SU 1323 5.7 / 1938 0.8	**28** 0030 5.3 / 0629 0.9 / M 1244 5.5 / 1854 0.9	**13** 0559 0.5 / 1213 5.9 / SU 1824 0.5	**28** 0529 0.7 / 1143 5.6 / M 1752 0.7	**13** 0040 5.2 / 0650 1.2 / W 1303 5.1 / 1904 1.4	**28** 0021 5.4 / 0629 0.9 / TH 1247 5.2 / 1853 1.2
14 0051 5.3 / 0649 0.9 / F 1304 5.9 / 1923 0.7	**29** 0026 5.1 / 0623 1.2 / SA 1238 5.4 / 1853 1.1	**14** 0150 5.1 / 0751 1.1 / M 1406 5.4 / 2022 1.2		**14** 0035 5.4 / 0637 0.7 / M 1253 5.6 / 1901 0.9	**28** 0003 5.4 / 0603 0.7 / TU 1219 5.5 / 1827 0.8	**14** 0116 5.0 / 0732 1.5 / TH 1343 4.7 / 1944 1.8	**29** 0107 5.2 / 0721 1.2 / F 1339 4.9 / 1946 1.5
15 0140 5.3 / 0738 1.1 / SA 1353 5.7 / 2014 0.9	**30** 0100 5.1 / 0657 1.3 / SU 1312 5.3 / 1927 1.2	**15** 0233 4.8 / 0838 1.5 / TU 1453 5.0 / 2110 1.7		**15** 0112 5.2 / 0717 1.0 / TU 1332 5.2 / 1939 1.3	**29** 0039 5.3 / 0642 0.9 / W 1257 5.3 / 1906 1.1	**15** 0156 4.7 / 0821 1.8 / F 1431 4.4 / 2033 2.2	**30** 0202 5.0 / 0824 1.5 / SA 1446 4.6 / 2055 1.8
	31 0136 5.0 / 0734 1.4 / M 1348 5.2 / 2006 1.3				**31** 0119 5.1 / 0726 1.2 / TH 1342 5.0 / 1953 1.4		

TIME ZONE (UT) For Summer Time add ONE hour in **non-shaded areas**

Chart Datum: 3·05 metres below Ordnance Datum (Newlyn)

》 **FREE** monthly updates from 《
www.reedsalmanac.co.uk

Chapter 5

319

TIDES

TIME ZONE (UT)
For Summer Time add ONE hour in **non-shaded areas**

WALES – HOLYHEAD
LAT 53°19'N   LONG 4°37'W
TIMES AND HEIGHTS OF HIGH AND LOW WATERS

YEAR 2005

	MAY			JUNE			JULY			AUGUST	
	Time m	Time m		Time m	Time m		Time m	Time m		Time m	Time m
1 SU	0311 4.8 / 0942 1.6 / 1615 4.4 / ◐ 2219 2.0	**16** M	0321 4.4 / 1001 2.0 / 1622 4.1 / ◐ 2216 2.4	**1** W	0528 4.9 / 1154 1.3 / 1826 4.7	**16** TH	0441 4.5 / 1110 1.8 / 1733 4.3 / 2327 2.1	**1** F	0557 4.8 / 1219 1.5 / 1847 4.6	**16** SA	0443 4.6 / 1111 1.8 / 1734 4.4 / 2336 2.0	**1** M	0134 1.9 / 0751 4.5 / 1358 1.9 / 2021 4.7	**16** TU	0025 1.9 / 0652 4.6 / 1306 1.8 / 1927 4.8
2 M	0437 4.7 / 1108 1.6 / 1747 4.5 / 2344 1.9	**17** TU	0437 4.3 / 1114 2.0 / 1739 4.2 / 2332 2.3	**2** TH	0019 1.6 / 0633 5.0 / 1255 1.2 / 1922 4.8	**17** F	0544 4.6 / 1208 1.6 / 1831 4.5	**2** SA	0047 1.7 / 0702 4.8 / 1318 1.6 / 1943 4.7	**17** SU	0555 4.6 / 1218 1.7 / 1843 4.6	**2** TU	0235 1.7 / 0848 4.6 / 1449 1.8 / 2107 4.9	**17** W	0140 1.6 / 0805 4.9 / 1411 1.5 / 2026 5.1
3 TU	0559 4.8 / 1224 1.4 / 1900 4.7	**18** W	0549 4.4 / 1218 1.8 / 1841 4.3	**3** F	0118 1.5 / 0730 5.1 / 1347 1.2 / 2010 4.9	**18** SA	0027 1.9 / 0643 4.7 / 1302 1.5 / 1923 4.7	**3** SU	0148 1.6 / 0801 4.8 / 1412 1.6 / 2033 4.9	**18** M	0046 1.8 / 0706 4.7 / 1323 1.6 / 1944 4.8	**3** W	0322 1.5 / 0932 4.8 / 1531 1.6 / 2145 5.1	**18** TH	0241 1.2 / 0902 5.2 / 1504 1.2 / 2117 5.5
4 W	0052 1.7 / 0705 5.0 / 1326 1.1 / 1954 4.9	**19** TH	0034 2.1 / 0648 4.6 / 1309 1.6 / 1929 4.6	**4** SA	0209 1.3 / 0819 5.1 / 1433 1.1 / 2052 5.1	**19** SU	0122 1.7 / 0737 4.9 / 1352 1.3 / 2011 4.9	**4** M	0242 1.5 / 0852 4.8 / 1459 1.5 / 2117 5.0	**19** TU	0150 1.5 / 0810 4.9 / 1421 1.4 / 2038 5.1	**4** TH	0400 1.3 / 1008 4.9 / 1605 1.5 / 2218 5.2	**19** F	0333 0.7 / 0951 5.4 / 1551 0.8 / ○ 2202 5.8
5 TH	0148 1.4 / 0759 5.2 / 1416 0.9 / 2038 5.1	**20** F	0124 1.8 / 0736 4.8 / 1352 1.3 / 2009 4.8	**5** SU	0255 1.2 / 0905 5.2 / 1515 1.1 / 2131 5.2	**20** M	0213 1.4 / 0828 5.0 / 1440 1.1 / 2056 5.2	**5** TU	0329 1.4 / 0937 4.9 / 1540 1.4 / 2156 5.1	**20** W	0248 1.2 / 0907 5.1 / 1514 1.1 / 2128 5.4	**5** F	0434 1.2 / 1040 5.0 / 1636 1.3 / ● 2249 5.3	**20** SA	0419 0.4 / 1036 5.6 / 1635 0.6 / 2247 6.1
6 F	0235 1.1 / 0844 5.4 / 1459 0.7 / 2116 5.3	**21** SA	0206 1.5 / 0818 5.0 / 1431 1.1 / 2046 5.0	**6** M	0338 1.1 / 0947 5.2 / 1554 1.1 / ● 2209 5.2	**21** TU	0301 1.1 / 0917 5.2 / 1526 1.0 / 2141 5.4	**6** W	0411 1.3 / 1018 4.9 / 1618 1.4 / ● 2232 5.2	**21** TH	0342 0.9 / 1000 5.3 / 1604 0.9 / ○ 2216 5.7	**6** SA	0505 1.1 / 1110 5.1 / 1706 1.2 / 2319 5.4	**21** SU	0504 0.2 / 1119 5.7 / 1718 0.5 / 2331 6.1
7 SA	0316 0.9 / 0925 5.5 / 1538 0.7 / 2152 5.4	**22** SU	0245 1.2 / 0858 5.2 / 1509 0.9 / 2123 5.3	**7** TU	0419 1.1 / 1028 5.1 / 1631 1.2 / 2246 5.3	**22** W	0350 0.9 / 1006 5.4 / 1613 0.9 / ○ 2227 5.5	**7** TH	0449 1.2 / 1055 5.0 / 1652 1.4 / 2307 5.2	**22** F	0432 0.6 / 1051 5.5 / 1651 0.7 / 2304 5.8	**7** SU	0535 1.0 / 1140 5.1 / 1737 1.2 / 2350 5.4	**22** M	0547 0.2 / 1201 5.6 / 1801 0.5
8 SU	0355 0.8 / 1006 5.6 / 1615 0.7 / ● 2228 5.4	**23** M	0324 1.0 / 0938 5.4 / 1547 0.8 / ○ 2201 5.4	**8** W	0459 1.1 / 1107 5.1 / 1707 1.3 / 2322 5.2	**23** TH	0440 0.7 / 1056 5.4 / 1701 0.8 / 2315 5.7	**8** F	0524 1.2 / 1130 5.0 / 1726 1.3 / 2341 5.2	**23** SA	0521 0.4 / 1138 5.5 / 1738 0.7 / 2351 5.9	**8** M	0606 1.0 / 1211 5.1 / 1808 1.2	**23** TU	0015 6.1 / 0630 0.4 / 1244 5.5 / 1843 0.7
9 M	0434 0.8 / 1045 5.5 / 1651 0.8 / 2304 5.4	**24** TU	0405 1.0 / 1020 5.5 / 1628 0.7 / 2241 5.5	**9** TH	0537 1.2 / 1145 5.0 / 1742 1.4 / 2357 5.1	**24** F	0531 0.6 / 1148 5.4 / 1751 0.9	**9** SA	0559 1.2 / 1205 4.9 / 1801 1.4	**24** SU	0610 0.3 / 1226 5.4 / 1825 0.7	**9** TU	0022 5.3 / 0637 1.1 / 1244 5.0 / 1841 1.4	**24** W	0059 5.9 / 0713 0.7 / 1327 5.2 / 1928 1.0
10 TU	0513 0.8 / 1124 5.3 / 1726 1.0 / 2340 5.3	**25** W	0449 0.7 / 1104 5.5 / 1711 0.8 / 2325 5.6	**10** F	0615 1.3 / 1223 4.8 / 1819 1.5	**25** SA	0004 5.7 / 0623 0.6 / 1241 5.3 / 1841 1.0	**10** SU	0015 5.2 / 0633 1.2 / 1240 4.9 / 1835 1.4	**25** M	0039 5.9 / 0658 0.4 / 1314 5.3 / 1912 0.8	**10** W	0055 5.3 / 0710 1.2 / 1318 4.9 / 1915 1.4	**25** TH	0144 5.5 / 0758 1.1 / 1411 5.0 / 2016 1.4
11 W	0551 1.0 / 1202 5.1 / 1802 1.2	**26** TH	0536 0.7 / 1152 5.4 / 1758 0.9	**11** SA	0034 5.1 / 0654 1.4 / 1302 4.7 / 1858 1.7	**26** SU	0056 5.6 / 0717 0.6 / 1335 5.2 / 1935 1.1	**11** M	0050 5.1 / 0709 1.3 / 1317 4.8 / 1912 1.5	**26** TU	0127 5.8 / 0747 0.6 / 1402 5.1 / 2001 1.1	**11** TH	0129 5.1 / 0745 1.3 / 1355 4.8 / 1954 1.5	**26** F	0232 5.1 / 0847 1.4 / 1501 4.7 / ◑ 2113 1.8
12 TH	0015 5.2 / 0630 1.2 / 1241 4.9 / 1838 1.5	**27** F	0012 5.5 / 0626 0.7 / 1245 5.2 / 1848 1.2	**12** SU	0113 4.9 / 0736 1.5 / 1345 4.6 / 1940 1.8	**27** M	0150 5.5 / 0813 0.8 / 1433 5.0 / 2031 1.3	**12** TU	0127 5.0 / 0747 1.4 / 1355 4.7 / 1952 1.6	**27** W	0217 5.5 / 0837 0.9 / 1453 4.9 / 2054 1.4	**12** F	0207 5.0 / 0825 1.5 / 1438 4.7 / 2040 1.8	**27** SA	0329 4.7 / 0945 1.7 / 1605 4.4 / 2228 2.1
13 F	0052 5.0 / 0712 1.5 / 1321 4.7 / 1918 1.8	**28** SA	0103 5.4 / 0723 0.8 / 1343 5.0 / 1945 1.4	**13** M	0155 4.8 / 0822 1.6 / 1432 4.4 / 2028 2.0	**28** TU	0246 5.3 / 0911 1.1 / 1534 4.8 / 2131 1.5	**13** W	0206 4.9 / 0828 1.5 / 1438 4.6 / 2035 1.8	**28** TH	0310 5.2 / 0932 1.3 / 1550 4.6 / ◑ 2154 1.8	**13** SA	0253 4.8 / 0916 1.6 / 1532 4.5 / 2140 2.0	**28** SU	0445 4.3 / 1102 2.3 / 1732 4.2 / 2357 2.2
14 SA	0132 4.8 / 0758 1.7 / 1408 4.4 / 2005 2.1	**29** SU	0200 5.2 / 0826 1.1 / 1449 4.8 / 2050 1.6	**14** TU	0244 4.7 / 0913 1.7 / 1527 4.3 / 2122 2.1	**29** W	0347 5.1 / 1013 1.3 / 1638 4.6 / ◑ 2235 1.7	**14** TH	0249 4.7 / 0914 1.6 / 1527 4.5 / 2126 1.9	**29** F	0410 4.9 / 1033 1.6 / 1656 4.5 / 2304 1.9	**14** SU	0354 4.5 / 1023 1.9 / 1646 4.4 / 2259 2.1	**29** M	0623 4.3 / 1229 2.2 / 1902 4.4
15 SU	0220 4.6 / 0854 1.9 / 1506 4.2 / 2103 2.3	**30** M	0306 5.1 / 0935 1.2 / 1604 4.6 / ◑ 2201 1.8	**15** W	0339 4.6 / 1010 1.8 / 1629 4.3 / ◐ 2223 2.1	**30** TH	0451 5.0 / 1116 1.4 / 1744 4.6 / 2342 1.7	**15** F	0339 4.5 / 1010 1.7 / 1629 4.3 / ◐ 2223 2.1	**30** SA	0521 4.6 / 1141 1.9 / 1811 4.4	**15** M	0521 4.3 / 1146 2.0 / 1813 4.5	**30** TU	0121 2.1 / 0745 4.5 / 1344 2.2 / 2005 4.7
		31 TU	0417 5.0 / 1046 1.3 / 1719 4.6 / 2313 1.8						**31** SU	0020 2.0 / 0639 4.5 / 1253 2.0 / 1922 4.5			**31** W	0222 1.8 / 0839 4.8 / 1435 2.0 / 2050 4.9

Chart Datum: 3·05 metres below Ordnance Datum (Newlyn)

》》 **FREE** monthly updates from 《《
www.reedsalmanac.co.uk

TIME ZONE (UT)
For Summer Time add ONE hour in **non-shaded areas**

WALES – HOLYHEAD
LAT 53°19'N LONG 4°37'W
TIMES AND HEIGHTS OF HIGH AND LOW WATERS

YEAR 2005

SEPTEMBER

Time m	Time m
1 0305 1.5 / 0917 4.8 / TH 1513 1.7 / 2125 5.1	**16** 0230 1.0 / 0852 5.3 / F 1450 1.1 / 2100 5.7
2 0339 1.3 / 0948 5.0 / F 1544 1.4 / 2155 5.3	**17** 0317 0.6 / 0935 5.5 / SA 1533 0.8 / 2143 6.0
3 0409 1.1 / 1016 5.1 / SA 1612 1.2 / ● 2223 5.4	**18** 0359 0.3 / 1015 5.7 / SU 1614 0.6 / ○ 2225 6.2
4 0437 1.0 / 1042 5.2 / SU 1639 1.1 / 2251 5.5	**19** 0440 0.2 / 1054 5.8 / M 1654 0.5 / 2306 6.2
5 0505 0.9 / 1110 5.2 / M 1708 1.0 / 2321 5.5	**20** 0520 0.3 / 1133 5.7 / TU 1734 0.5 / 2348 6.1
6 0533 0.9 / 1140 5.3 / TU 1738 1.0 / 2351 5.5	**21** 0600 0.5 / 1212 5.6 / W 1815 0.7
7 0603 0.9 / 1211 5.3 / W 1809 1.1	**22** 0030 5.8 / 0639 0.9 / TH 1252 5.3 / 1857 1.1
8 0023 5.4 / 0633 1.1 / TH 1244 5.2 / 1842 1.2	**23** 0112 5.4 / 0719 1.3 / F 1332 5.1 / 1943 1.5
9 0056 5.3 / 0707 1.3 / F 1320 5.0 / 1921 1.4	**24** 0157 5.0 / 0804 1.8 / SA 1418 4.8 / 2038 1.9
10 0134 5.1 / 0748 1.5 / SA 1402 4.8 / 2008 1.7	**25** 0251 4.5 / 0858 2.2 / SU 1517 4.5 / ◐ 2152 2.3
11 0221 4.8 / 0839 1.8 / SU 1457 4.6 / ◐ 2112 2.0	**26** 0410 4.2 / 1017 2.6 / M 1646 4.3 / 2329 2.4
12 0329 4.5 / 0954 2.1 / M 1618 4.5 / 2242 2.1	**27** 0600 4.1 / 1158 2.6 / TU 1828 4.4
13 0513 4.4 / 1132 2.2 / TU 1757 4.5	**28** 0054 2.2 / 0723 4.3 / W 1316 2.4 / 1935 4.6
14 0018 1.9 / 0653 4.6 / W 1257 2.0 / 1915 4.9	**29** 0153 1.9 / 0813 4.6 / TH 1407 2.1 / 2019 4.9
15 0133 1.5 / 0801 4.9 / TH 1400 1.6 / 2013 5.3	**30** 0234 1.6 / 0848 4.8 / F 1443 1.8 / 2053 5.1

OCTOBER

Time m	Time m
1 0307 1.3 / 0918 5.1 / SA 1513 1.5 / 2123 5.3	**16** 0255 0.7 / 0913 5.6 / SU 1511 0.9 / 2120 6.0
2 0336 1.1 / 0944 5.2 / SU 1540 1.2 / 2151 5.5	**17** 0336 0.5 / 0951 5.7 / M 1550 0.7 / ○ 2201 6.1
3 0403 0.9 / 1011 5.4 / M 1608 1.1 / ● 2220 5.6	**18** 0414 0.5 / 1028 5.8 / TU 1630 0.6 / 2242 6.0
4 0431 0.9 / 1039 5.4 / TU 1638 1.0 / 2250 5.6	**19** 0452 0.6 / 1106 5.7 / W 1710 0.7 / 2323 5.9
5 0500 0.9 / 1109 5.5 / W 1709 1.0 / 2322 5.6	**20** 0530 0.8 / 1144 5.6 / TH 1751 0.9
6 0531 0.9 / 1141 5.5 / TH 1742 1.0 / 2355 5.5	**21** 0004 5.6 / 0608 1.1 / F 1222 5.4 / 1832 1.2
7 0604 1.1 / 1216 5.4 / F 1818 1.2	**22** 0046 5.2 / 0647 1.5 / SA 1301 5.2 / 1917 1.6
8 0032 5.3 / 0640 1.3 / SA 1255 5.2 / 1900 1.4	**23** 0129 4.9 / 0729 1.9 / SU 1344 4.9 / 2010 2.0
9 0115 5.1 / 0725 1.6 / SU 1341 5.0 / 1953 1.7	**24** 0220 4.5 / 0819 2.3 / M 1437 4.6 / 2117 2.2
10 0209 4.8 / 0822 2.0 / M 1442 4.7 / ◐ 2105 2.0	**25** 0332 4.2 / 0929 2.6 / TU 1555 4.4 / ◐ 2243 2.4
11 0328 4.5 / 0945 2.3 / TU 1608 4.6 / 2240 2.0	**26** 0510 4.1 / 1104 2.7 / W 1727 4.4
12 0518 4.4 / 1123 2.3 / W 1744 4.7	**27** 0004 2.2 / 0634 4.3 / TH 1225 2.5 / 1841 4.6
13 0009 1.8 / 0646 4.7 / TH 1242 2.0 / 1857 5.1	**28** 0105 2.0 / 0728 4.5 / F 1320 2.2 / 1932 4.8
14 0118 1.4 / 0747 5.0 / F 1341 1.6 / 1952 5.4	**29** 0149 1.7 / 0807 4.8 / SA 1401 1.9 / 2011 5.1
15 0211 1.0 / 0833 5.3 / SA 1429 1.2 / 2038 5.7	**30** 0225 1.4 / 0839 5.0 / SU 1434 1.6 / 2044 5.3
	31 0257 1.2 / 0909 5.2 / M 1505 1.4 / 2116 5.4

NOVEMBER

Time m	Time m
1 0327 1.0 / 0938 5.4 / TU 1537 1.2 / 2148 5.5	**16** 0351 0.9 / 1006 5.6 / W 1612 0.9 / ○ 2223 5.7
2 0358 1.0 / 1009 5.5 / W 1610 1.0 / ● 2222 5.6	**17** 0429 1.0 / 1044 5.6 / TH 1653 1.0 / 2304 5.6
3 0431 0.9 / 1042 5.6 / TH 1645 1.0 / 2258 5.6	**18** 0507 1.1 / 1122 5.6 / F 1734 1.1 / 2345 5.4
4 0505 1.0 / 1118 5.6 / F 1723 1.0 / 2337 5.5	**19** 0545 1.4 / 1200 5.4 / SA 1816 1.4
5 0543 1.1 / 1157 5.5 / SA 1806 1.2	**20** 0026 5.1 / 0623 1.6 / SU 1239 5.2 / 1859 1.6
6 0020 5.3 / 0626 1.4 / SU 1242 5.4 / 1854 1.4	**21** 0108 4.8 / 0704 1.9 / M 1319 5.0 / 1946 1.8
7 0111 5.1 / 0716 1.7 / M 1334 5.2 / 1953 1.6	**22** 0155 4.6 / 0750 2.2 / TU 1406 4.8 / 2041 2.0
8 0212 4.8 / 0819 2.0 / IU 1438 5.0 / 2107 1.8	**23** 0251 4.4 / 0846 2.4 / W 1505 4.6 / ◐ 2145 2.2
9 0334 4.6 / 0939 2.2 / W 1558 4.9 / ◐ 2230 1.8	**24** 0403 4.2 / 0955 2.6 / TH 1616 4.5 / 2256 2.2
10 0506 4.6 / 1103 2.1 / TH 1720 5.0 / 2347 1.6	**25** 0518 4.3 / 1110 2.5 / F 1728 4.5
11 0623 4.8 / 1215 1.9 / F 1830 5.2	**26** 0000 2.0 / 0622 4.4 / SA 1215 2.4 / 1829 4.7
12 0051 1.3 / 0724 5.1 / SA 1314 1.6 / 1926 5.4	**27** 0053 1.8 / 0713 4.7 / SU 1307 2.1 / 1919 4.9
13 0145 1.1 / 0808 5.3 / SU 1404 1.3 / 2014 5.6	**28** 0137 1.6 / 0755 4.9 / M 1350 1.8 / 2003 5.1
14 0231 0.9 / 0849 5.4 / M 1448 1.1 / 2058 5.8	**29** 0216 1.4 / 0832 5.1 / TU 1430 1.6 / 2042 5.2
15 0312 0.8 / 0928 5.5 / TU 1530 0.9 / 2141 5.8	**30** 0253 1.3 / 0908 5.3 / W 1509 1.3 / 2121 5.4

DECEMBER

Time m	Time m
1 0330 1.1 / 0944 5.5 / TH 1548 1.2 / ● 2201 5.5	**16** 0415 1.3 / 1030 5.5 / F 1644 1.2 / 2253 5.3
2 0409 1.1 / 1022 5.6 / F 1629 1.0 / 2243 5.5	**17** 0453 1.4 / 1108 5.5 / SA 1724 1.2 / 2332 5.2
3 0449 1.1 / 1103 5.7 / SA 1714 1.0 / 2329 5.5	**18** 0529 1.4 / 1145 5.4 / SU 1803 1.3
4 0533 1.1 / 1148 5.7 / SU 1802 1.0	**19** 0010 5.1 / 0605 1.6 / M 1221 5.3 / 1841 1.4
5 0017 5.4 / 0621 1.3 / M 1236 5.6 / 1854 1.1	**20** 0049 4.9 / 0643 1.7 / TU 1258 5.2 / 1921 1.6
6 0112 5.2 / 0714 1.5 / TU 1330 5.4 / 1952 1.2	**21** 0128 4.8 / 0723 1.9 / W 1338 5.0 / 2004 1.7
7 0211 5.0 / 0813 1.7 / W 1429 5.3 / 2056 1.4	**22** 0211 4.6 / 0807 2.0 / TH 1422 4.9 / 2051 1.8
8 0320 4.8 / 0919 1.9 / TH 1536 5.2 / ◐ 2205 1.5	**23** 0301 4.5 / 0857 2.2 / F 1513 4.7 / ◐ 2144 1.9
9 0434 4.7 / 1030 1.9 / F 1647 5.1 / 2314 1.6	**24** 0359 4.4 / 0954 2.3 / SA 1612 4.6 / 2243 2.0
10 0545 4.8 / 1139 1.9 / SA 1755 5.1	**25** 0504 4.4 / 1058 2.3 / SU 1718 4.6 / 2345 2.0
11 0018 1.4 / 0647 4.9 / SU 1243 1.7 / 1856 5.2	**26** 0609 4.5 / 1204 2.2 / M 1822 4.6
12 0116 1.4 / 0741 5.1 / M 1339 1.6 / 1952 5.3	**27** 0043 1.9 / 0706 4.6 / TU 1304 2.0 / 1921 4.8
13 0207 1.3 / 0828 5.2 / TU 1431 1.4 / 2042 5.4	**28** 0136 1.8 / 0757 4.8 / W 1358 1.8 / 2014 5.0
14 0253 1.3 / 0911 5.3 / W 1518 1.3 / 2128 5.4	**29** 0225 1.5 / 0842 5.1 / TH 1447 1.5 / 2102 5.2
15 0335 1.3 / 0951 5.4 / TH 1602 1.2 / ○ 2212 5.4	**30** 0310 1.3 / 0926 5.3 / F 1534 1.2 / 2149 5.4
	31 0355 1.1 / 1009 5.5 / SA 1621 0.9 / ● 2236 5.5

Chart Datum: 3·05 metres below Ordnance Datum (Newlyn)

》》**FREE** monthly updates from 《《
www.reedsalmanac.co.uk

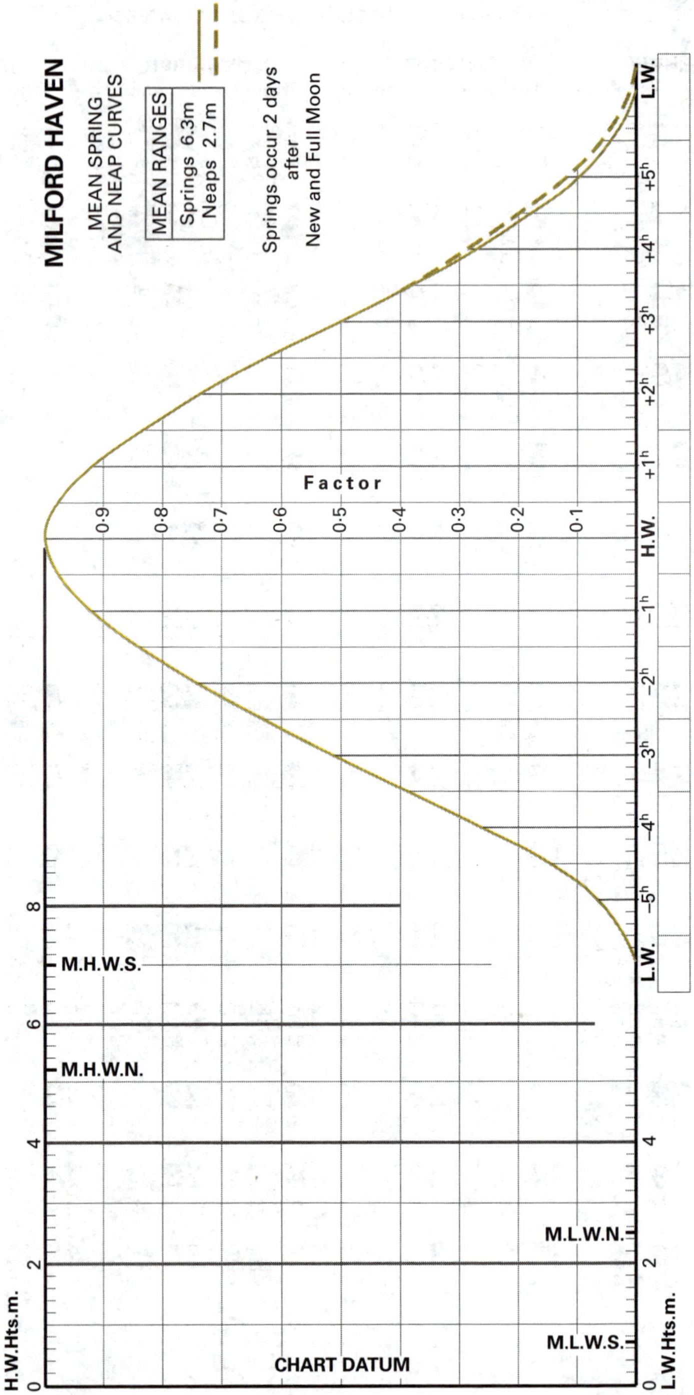
MILFORD HAVEN
MEAN SPRING AND NEAP CURVES
MEAN RANGES
Springs 6.3m
Neaps 2.7m
Springs occur 2 days after New and Full Moon
Factor
0·9
0·8
0·7
0·6
0·5
0·4
0·3
0·2
0·1
L.W.
−5h
−4h
−3h
−2h
−1h
H.W.
+1h
+2h
+3h
+4h
+5h
L.W.
H.W.Hts.m.
0
2
4
6
8
M.H.W.S.
M.H.W.N.
CHART DATUM
M.L.W.N.
M.L.W.S.
L.W.Hts.m.

| TIME ZONE (UT) For Summer Time add ONE hour in **non-shaded areas** | WALES – MILFORD HAVEN LAT 51°42'N   LONG 5°03'W TIMES AND HEIGHTS OF HIGH AND LOW WATERS | | YEAR 2005 |

WALES – MILFORD HAVEN
LAT 51°42'N   LONG 5°03'W
TIMES AND HEIGHTS OF HIGH AND LOW WATERS

TIME ZONE (UT) – For Summer Time add ONE hour in **non-shaded areas**

YEAR 2005

JANUARY		FEBRUARY		MARCH		APRIL	
Time m	Time m	Time m	Time m	Time m	Time m	Time m	Time m
1 0318 1.8 / 0925 6.1 / SA 1546 1.9 / 2149 5.8	**16** 0425 1.4 / 1033 6.5 / SU 1656 1.5 / 2255 6.0	**1** 0408 1.7 / 1016 6.1 / TU 1633 1.8 / 2240 5.7	**16** 0508 2.1 / 1121 5.5 / W 1735 2.3 / ◐ 2343 5.2	**1** 0306 1.1 / 0910 6.6 / TU 1525 1.3 / 2128 6.3	**16** 0347 1.6 / 0955 6.0 / W 1603 1.8 / 2208 5.7	**1** 0406 1.7 / 1014 5.8 / F 1628 2.1 / 2244 5.6	**16** 0437 2.5 / 1050 4.9 / SA 1655 2.7 / ◐ 2316 4.9
2 0357 2.0 / 1006 5.9 / SU 1628 2.0 / 2233 5.6	**17** 0513 1.8 / 1122 6.1 / M 1745 1.9 / ◐ 2346 5.6	**2** 0451 2.0 / 1103 5.8 / W 1721 2.1 / 2334 5.5	**17** 0605 2.6 / 1221 5.1 / TH 1841 2.7	**2** 0340 1.4 / 0946 6.3 / W 1600 1.6 / 2207 5.9	**17** 0422 2.1 / 1034 5.4 / TH 1640 2.4 / ◐ 2251 5.2	**2** 0508 2.2 / 1122 5.3 / SA 1743 2.5 / ◐	**17** 0557 2.8 / 1211 4.6 / SU 1835 3.0
3 0443 2.2 / 1053 5.8 / M 1716 2.2 / ◐ 2324 5.4	**18** 0608 2.2 / 1217 5.7 / TU 1842 2.3	**3** 0548 2.2 / 1204 5.5 / TH 1828 2.3	**18** 0100 4.9 / 0736 2.8 / F 1353 4.8 / 2020 2.8	**3** 0420 1.8 / 1030 5.9 / TH 1645 2.0 / ◐ 2258 5.6	**18** 0510 2.6 / 1126 4.9 / F 1737 2.8 / 2358 4.8	**3** 0007 5.3 / 0647 2.4 / SU 1302 5.0 / 1940 2.5	**18** 0101 4.8 / 0749 2.8 / M 1406 4.7 / 2019 2.8
4 0537 2.3 / 1149 5.6 / TU 1816 2.3	**19** 0048 5.3 / 0713 2.4 / W 1324 5.4 / 1950 2.4	**4** 0046 5.3 / 0710 2.4 / F 1326 5.4 / 2001 2.4	**19** 0242 5.0 / 0919 2.7 / SA 1525 5.0 / 2144 2.6	**4** 0516 2.2 / 1131 5.4 / F 1751 2.4	**19** 0641 2.9 / 1303 4.6 / SA 1929 3.0	**4** 0153 5.3 / 0833 2.1 / M 1445 5.3 / 2112 2.1	**19** 0237 5.0 / 0908 2.4 / TU 1516 5.1 / 2126 2.4
5 0026 5.4 / 0644 2.4 / W 1255 5.6 / 1927 2.3	**20** 0201 5.2 / 0831 2.5 / TH 1436 5.5 / 2104 2.4	**5** 0215 5.4 / 0845 2.2 / SA 1455 5.5 / 2129 2.1	**20** 0358 5.3 / 1025 2.3 / SU 1627 5.4 / 2239 2.2	**5** 0014 5.2 / 0644 2.4 / SA 1304 5.1 / 1942 2.6	**20** 0202 4.7 / 0847 2.8 / SU 1457 4.8 / 2113 2.7	**5** 0317 5.8 / 0948 1.6 / TU 1556 5.9 / 2215 1.5	**20** 0334 5.5 / 0959 2.0 / W 1602 5.5 / 2212 1.9
6 0137 5.4 / 0759 2.3 / TH 1407 5.7 / 2040 2.1	**21** 0314 5.3 / 0943 2.4 / F 1545 5.4 / 2206 2.2	**6** 0335 5.8 / 1004 1.8 / SU 1611 5.9 / 2237 1.6	**21** 0448 5.7 / 1111 1.9 / M 1711 5.8 / 2321 1.8	**6** 0158 5.2 / 0837 2.3 / SU 1449 5.3 / 2122 2.2	**21** 0328 5.1 / 0957 2.4 / M 1601 5.2 / 2212 2.3	**6** 0417 6.4 / 1043 1.0 / W 1647 6.4 / 2305 1.0	**21** 0416 5.9 / 1038 1.6 / TH 1639 6.0 / 2250 1.5
7 0248 5.7 / 0911 2.0 / F 1517 5.9 / 2147 1.8	**22** 0416 5.6 / 1039 2.1 / SA 1642 5.7 / 2256 2.0	**7** 0441 6.3 / 1108 1.3 / M 1713 6.4 / 2334 1.1	**22** 0528 6.1 / 1149 1.5 / TU 1748 6.1 / 2358 1.4	**7** 0329 5.7 / 1000 1.7 / M 1609 5.8 / 2231 1.5	**22** 0419 5.6 / 1043 1.9 / TU 1644 5.7 / 2254 1.9	**7** 0506 6.9 / 1130 0.6 / TH 1731 6.8 / 2348 0.6	**22** 0453 6.3 / 1114 1.2 / F 1714 6.4 / 2326 1.2
8 0351 6.1 / 1015 1.6 / SA 1620 6.3 / 2247 1.5	**23** 0505 5.9 / 1126 1.9 / SU 1727 5.9 / 2338 1.7	**8** 0537 6.8 / 1203 0.8 / TU 1806 6.8 / ●	**23** 0602 6.4 / 1222 1.3 / W 1821 6.4	**8** 0434 6.3 / 1101 1.1 / TU 1706 6.4 / 2324 1.0	**23** 0458 6.0 / 1120 1.5 / W 1719 6.1 / 2329 1.5	**8** 0549 7.2 / 1210 0.4 / F 1811 7.1 / ●	**23** 0527 6.6 / 1148 0.9 / SA 1747 6.7
9 0449 6.5 / 1114 1.2 / SU 1718 6.6 / 2341 1.1	**24** 0545 6.2 / 1205 1.6 / M 1806 6.1	**9** 0024 0.7 / 0627 7.3 / W 1252 0.4 / 1853 7.1	**24** 0030 1.2 / 0634 6.6 / TH 1253 1.0 / ○ 1852 6.6	**9** 0526 6.9 / 1151 0.6 / W 1753 6.9	**24** 0532 6.4 / 1153 1.2 / TH 1752 6.4	**9** 0027 0.4 / 0628 7.3 / SA 1248 0.4 / 1847 7.1	**24** 0001 0.9 / 0602 6.8 / SU 1223 0.8 / ○ 1821 6.9
10 0544 6.9 / 1209 0.9 / M 1812 6.9 / ●	**25** 0015 1.5 / 0621 6.4 / TU 1241 1.4 / ○ 1841 6.3	**10** 0111 0.5 / 0713 7.5 / TH 1338 0.2 / 1937 7.2	**25** 0102 1.1 / 0705 6.8 / F 1323 0.9 / 1922 6.7	**10** 0010 0.6 / 0611 7.3 / TH 1236 0.2 / ● 1835 7.2	**25** 0002 1.1 / 0604 6.7 / F 1224 0.9 / ○ 1822 6.7	**10** 0105 0.4 / 0705 7.3 / SU 1323 0.4 / 1922 7.1	**25** 0037 0.7 / 0637 7.0 / M 1258 0.7 / 1856 7.0
11 0032 0.9 / 0635 7.2 / TU 1301 0.6 / 1903 7.0	**26** 0050 1.4 / 0655 6.6 / W 1314 1.3 / 1914 6.4	**11** 0154 0.4 / 0757 7.5 / F 1420 0.2 / 2018 7.2	**26** 0132 0.9 / 0735 6.9 / SA 1353 0.8 / 1952 6.7	**11** 0053 0.3 / 0653 7.5 / F 1316 0.1 / 1914 7.3	**26** 0034 0.8 / 0635 6.9 / SA 1254 0.7 / 1853 6.8	**11** 0139 0.5 / 0741 7.1 / M 1356 0.7 / 1955 6.9	**26** 0114 0.7 / 0714 7.1 / TU 1333 0.7 / 1933 6.9
12 0122 0.7 / 0725 7.3 / W 1351 0.5 / 1952 7.1	**27** 0122 1.3 / 0727 6.6 / TH 1345 1.2 / 1946 6.4	**12** 0235 0.5 / 0838 7.4 / SA 1459 0.5 / 2057 7.0	**27** 0203 0.8 / 0806 6.9 / SU 1423 0.9 / 2023 6.7	**12** 0132 0.2 / 0733 7.5 / SA 1353 0.2 / 1951 7.2	**27** 0106 0.7 / 0707 7.0 / SU 1325 0.7 / 1924 6.9	**12** 0213 0.8 / 0815 6.8 / TU 1428 1.0 / 2027 6.6	**27** 0151 0.8 / 0752 7.0 / W 1410 0.9 / 2012 6.8
13 0209 0.7 / 0813 7.3 / TH 1439 0.6 / 2039 6.9	**28** 0154 1.2 / 0758 6.6 / F 1416 1.2 / 2017 6.3	**13** 0313 0.7 / 0918 7.0 / SU 1536 0.9 / 2135 6.6	**28** 0234 0.9 / 0837 6.8 / M 1454 1.0 / 2054 6.5	**13** 0208 0.3 / 0810 7.4 / SU 1428 0.4 / 2026 7.0	**28** 0138 0.7 / 0739 7.0 / M 1357 0.7 / 1956 6.9	**13** 0245 1.2 / 0848 6.3 / W 1458 1.4 / 2100 6.2	**28** 0231 1.0 / 0833 6.8 / TH 1449 1.2 / 2054 6.5
14 0255 0.8 / 0900 7.2 / F 1525 0.8 / 2124 6.7	**29** 0225 1.3 / 0830 6.6 / SA 1448 1.2 / 2049 6.3	**14** 0350 1.1 / 0956 6.5 / M 1613 1.3 / 2212 6.1		**14** 0242 0.6 / 0846 7.0 / M 1501 0.8 / 2100 6.6	**29** 0211 0.8 / 0812 6.8 / TU 1429 0.9 / 2029 6.7	**14** 0316 1.6 / 0922 5.8 / TH 1528 1.9 / 2134 5.8	**29** 0315 1.3 / 0919 6.1 / F 1534 1.6 / 2144 6.1
15 0340 1.1 / 0946 6.9 / SA 1610 1.1 / 2209 6.3	**30** 0258 1.3 / 0903 6.5 / SU 1521 1.4 / 2122 6.2	**15** 0427 1.6 / 1036 6.0 / TU 1650 1.9 / 2253 5.7		**15** 0315 1.1 / 0920 6.5 / TU 1532 1.3 / 2132 6.2	**30** 0244 1.1 / 0847 6.6 / W 1502 1.2 / 2105 6.3	**15** 0351 2.1 / 1000 5.4 / F 1603 2.3 / 2216 5.3	**30** 0408 1.7 / 1015 5.4 / SA 1630 2.0 / 2248 5.7
	31 0332 1.5 / 0937 6.3 / M 1555 1.6 / 2158 6.0			**31** 0321 1.3 / 0926 6.2 / TH 1540 1.6 / 2148 6.0			

Chart Datum: 3·71 metres below Ordnance Datum (Newlyn)

》》 **FREE** monthly updates from 《《
www.reedsalmanac.co.uk

TIDES

TIME ZONE (UT)
For Summer Time add ONE hour in **non-shaded areas**

WALES – MILFORD HAVEN
LAT 51°42'N   LONG 5°03'W
TIMES AND HEIGHTS OF HIGH AND LOW WATERS

YEAR 2005

	MAY			JUNE			JULY			AUGUST	
	Time m	Time m		Time m	Time m		Time m	Time m		Time m	Time m
1 SU ☽	0517 2.0 1128 5.3 1751 2.3	**16** M	0520 2.6 1129 4.8 1744 2.7 2359 5.0	**1** W	0107 5.9 0741 1.7 1346 5.6 2011 1.9	**16** TH ☾	0012 5.3 0645 2.3 1251 5.1 1910 2.4	**1** F	0133 5.8 0801 1.9 1407 5.5 2033 2.0	**16** SA	0015 5.5 0642 2.2 1255 5.3 1915 2.3	**1** M	0317 5.3 0939 2.3 1551 5.5 2218 2.2	**16** TU	0216 5.3 0851 2.3 1501 5.6 2131 2.0
2 M	0009 5.5 0649 2.1 1258 5.2 1929 2.3	**17** TU	0642 2.6 1250 4.8 1910 2.7	**2** TH	0215 6.0 0845 1.6 1450 5.8 2113 1.7	**17** F	0117 5.4 0749 2.2 1357 5.3 2014 2.2	**2** SA	0237 5.7 0903 1.9 1510 5.6 2135 2.0	**17** SU	0125 5.4 0757 2.2 1408 5.4 2031 2.2	**2** TU	0421 5.5 1035 2.1 1646 5.8 2309 1.9	**17** W	0339 5.7 1005 1.8 1611 6.1 2238 1.5
3 TU	0137 5.6 0814 1.9 1423 5.5 2048 1.9	**18** W	0122 5.1 0757 2.4 1409 5.0 2020 2.4	**3** F	0315 6.1 0941 1.5 1545 6.0 2206 1.5	**18** SA	0221 5.6 0850 2.0 1457 5.6 2114 1.9	**3** SU	0338 5.8 0910 2.0 1607 5.8 2230 1.8	**18** M	0240 5.6 0910 2.0 1518 5.7 2142 1.9	**3** W	0511 5.8 1121 1.8 1730 6.1 2351 1.6	**18** TH	0444 6.2 1104 1.3 1709 6.7 2334 0.9
4 W	0251 6.0 0922 1.5 1528 5.9 2148 1.5	**19** TH	0230 5.4 0857 2.1 1505 5.4 2116 2.1	**4** SA	0407 6.3 1029 1.4 1633 6.2 2253 1.4	**19** SU	0319 5.9 0945 1.7 1550 6.0 2209 1.6	**4** M	0433 5.9 1050 1.7 1657 6.0 2318 1.7	**19** TU	0348 5.9 1015 1.7 1620 6.1 2245 1.4	**4** TH	0552 6.0 1200 1.6 1808 6.3	**19** F ○	0538 6.7 1156 0.9 1800 7.1
5 TH	0350 6.4 1016 1.2 1619 6.3 2238 1.1	**20** F	0322 5.7 0946 1.8 1550 5.8 2203 1.8	**5** SU	0454 6.4 1112 1.3 1716 6.4 2335 1.3	**20** M	0412 6.2 1040 1.5 1640 6.3 2301 1.3	**5** TU	0521 6.0 1133 1.6 1741 6.2	**20** W	0450 6.2 1113 1.3 1717 6.6 2342 1.0	**5** F ●	0027 1.4 0627 6.2 1235 1.4 1841 6.5	**20** SA	0024 0.5 0626 7.1 1244 0.5 1846 7.5
6 F	0438 6.7 1101 0.9 1703 6.6 2321 0.9	**21** SA	0406 6.1 1029 1.4 1631 6.2 2246 1.4	**6** M ●	0537 6.4 1152 1.2 1756 6.4	**21** TU	0504 6.4 1127 1.1 1730 6.6 2352 1.0	**6** W ●	0001 1.6 0603 6.1 1214 1.5 1820 6.3	**21** TH ○	0546 6.6 1206 1.0 1810 6.9	**6** SA	0101 1.3 0700 6.3 1308 1.3 1913 6.5	**21** SU	0111 0.2 0711 7.2 1328 0.3 1931 7.6
7 SA	0522 6.9 1141 0.8 1743 6.8	**22** SU	0448 6.4 1111 1.1 1711 6.5 2328 1.1	**7** TU	0015 1.3 0617 6.4 1230 1.3 1833 6.5	**22** W	0555 6.7 1216 1.0 1819 6.9	**7** TH	0041 1.5 0642 6.1 1251 1.4 1857 6.3	**22** F	0035 0.7 0638 6.8 1256 0.7 1900 7.2	**7** SU	0132 1.2 0732 6.4 1339 1.2 1944 6.6	**22** M	0154 0.2 0753 7.2 1410 0.4 2013 7.5
8 SU ●	0000 0.8 0601 6.9 1219 0.8 1819 6.8	**23** M	0530 6.7 1152 0.9 1752 6.8	**8** W	0053 1.3 0655 6.3 1306 1.3 1909 6.4	**23** TH	0043 0.8 0645 6.8 1305 0.9 1908 7.0	**8** F	0117 1.4 0718 6.2 1326 1.4 1932 6.3	**23** SA	0126 0.5 0727 7.0 1345 0.6 1949 7.3	**8** M	0202 1.2 0802 6.4 1410 1.2 2015 6.5	**23** TU	0235 0.3 0834 7.1 1450 0.6 2054 7.2
9 M	0038 0.8 0638 6.8 1254 0.8 1854 6.8	**24** TU	0011 0.9 0612 6.8 1234 0.8 1833 6.9	**9** TH	0130 1.4 0731 6.2 1341 1.4 1945 6.3	**24** F	0133 0.7 0736 6.8 1354 0.7 1958 7.0	**9** SA	0151 1.4 0752 6.1 1359 1.4 2005 6.2	**24** SU	0214 0.4 0814 7.0 1431 0.6 2036 7.3	**9** TU	0232 1.2 0832 6.3 1441 1.3 2045 6.4	**24** W	0314 0.7 0913 6.7 1528 0.9 2134 6.8
10 TU	0113 0.9 0714 6.7 1328 1.0 1928 6.6	**25** W	0055 0.8 0656 6.9 1316 0.8 1917 6.9	**10** F	0205 1.5 0807 6.0 1415 1.6 2020 6.2	**25** SA	0224 0.7 0826 6.7 1443 0.8 2049 6.9	**10** SU	0224 1.4 0826 6.1 1432 1.5 2039 6.2	**25** M	0300 0.5 0900 6.8 1516 0.8 2122 7.1	**10** W	0302 1.3 0903 6.2 1513 1.4 2117 6.3	**25** TH	0351 1.2 0951 6.3 1607 1.4 2215 6.5
11 W	0148 1.1 0749 6.4 1400 1.3 2002 6.4	**26** TH	0140 0.8 0741 6.7 1359 1.0 2003 6.8	**11** SA	0241 1.6 0843 5.8 1449 1.7 2057 6.0	**26** SU	0315 0.8 0917 6.5 1533 1.1 2141 6.7	**11** M	0258 1.5 0900 5.9 1506 1.5 2114 6.1	**26** TU	0345 0.7 0944 6.6 1601 1.0 2207 6.7	**11** TH	0334 1.5 0936 6.0 1546 1.7 2152 6.1	**26** F ☾	0429 1.7 1032 5.8 1649 2.0 2259 5.7
12 TH	0221 1.4 0823 6.1 1432 1.6 2036 6.1	**27** F	0226 0.9 0829 6.5 1446 1.2 2052 6.6	**12** SU	0317 1.8 0921 5.6 1527 2.0 2137 5.8	**27** M	0407 1.0 1008 6.2 1625 1.4 2234 6.5	**12** TU	0332 1.6 0935 5.8 1543 1.7 2150 6.0	**27** W	0429 1.1 1029 6.2 1646 1.4 2254 6.3	**12** F	0408 1.8 1014 5.8 1624 1.9 2233 5.8	**27** SA	0513 2.2 1115 5.5 1744 2.5 2357 5.2
13 F	0255 1.7 0859 5.8 1505 1.9 2112 5.8	**28** SA	0317 1.0 0921 6.2 1536 1.5 2147 6.3	**13** M	0358 2.0 1003 5.4 1609 2.2 2221 5.6	**28** TU	0501 1.3 1101 5.9 1721 1.6 ☾ 2329 6.2	**13** W	0409 1.8 1013 5.6 1622 1.9 2231 5.8	**28** TH	0515 1.6 1117 5.8 1736 1.8 ☾ 2345 5.9	**13** SA	0450 2.1 1100 5.5 1714 2.2 2327 5.5	**28** SU	0616 2.6 1233 5.0 1913 2.7
14 SA	0332 2.0 0938 5.4 1542 2.2 2154 5.5	**29** SU	0413 1.2 1019 5.9 1635 1.7 2248 6.1	**14** TU	0445 2.2 1051 5.2 1701 2.3 2313 5.4	**29** W	0558 1.6 1159 5.7 1822 1.8	**14** TH	0451 2.0 1057 5.5 1708 2.1 ☾ 2318 5.6	**29** F	0607 2.1 1212 5.4 1836 2.2	**14** SU	0547 2.3 1205 5.4 1826 2.4	**29** M	0125 4.8 0754 2.6 1417 5.0 2059 2.4
15 SU	0417 2.3 1026 5.1 1631 2.5 2248 5.2	**30** M	0519 1.7 1123 5.6 1746 1.9 ☾ 2356 5.9	**15** W	0541 2.3 1146 5.1 1803 2.4 ☽	**30** TH	0029 6.0 0657 1.8 1302 5.6 1926 1.9	**15** F	0540 2.1 1149 5.3 1804 2.3	**30** SA	0047 5.5 0710 2.3 1322 5.2 1952 2.4	**15** M	0042 5.3 0714 2.5 1333 5.2 2005 2.4	**30** TU	0303 5.0 0924 2.4 1539 5.4 2208 2.4
		31 TU	0631 1.8 1234 5.5 1901 2.0						**31** SU	0201 5.2 0827 2.4 1440 5.2 2113 2.4			**31** W	0410 5.4 1022 2.2 1631 5.8 2255 2.0

Chart Datum: 3·71 metres below Ordnance Datum (Newlyn)

» **FREE** monthly updates from «
www.reedsalmanac.co.uk

TIME ZONE (UT)
For Summer Time add ONE hour in **non-shaded areas**

WALES – MILFORD HAVEN
LAT 51°42'N   LONG 5°03'W
TIMES AND HEIGHTS OF HIGH AND LOW WATERS

YEAR 2005

SEPTEMBER

Time	m	Time	m
1 TH 0455 1105 1712 2333	5.8 1.8 6.1 1.6	**16** F 0435 1054 1656 2321	6.3 1.2 6.9 0.8
2 F 0532 1141 1746	6.1 1.5 6.4	**17** SA 0524 1141 1743	6.9 0.7 7.4
3 SA 0006 0605 1214 1818	1.3 6.4 1.3 6.6	**18** SU 0006 0607 1224 1826	0.4 7.2 0.4 7.6
4 SU 0037 0635 1244 1848	1.1 6.5 1.1 6.8	**19** M 0049 0648 1305 1907	0.2 7.4 0.3 7.7
5 M 0105 0705 1314 1917	1.0 6.6 1.0 6.8	**20** TU 0128 0726 1343 1946	0.2 7.4 0.4 7.5
6 TU 0134 0733 1343 1946	1.0 6.7 1.0 6.8	**21** W 0205 0803 1420 2024	0.4 7.1 0.6 7.2
7 W 0203 0802 1413 2015	1.0 6.6 1.1 6.7	**22** TH 0240 0839 1456 2100	0.8 6.8 1.1 6.7
8 TH 0232 0832 1444 2046	1.2 6.5 1.5 6.5	**23** F 0314 0914 1531 2137	1.3 6.4 1.6 6.1
9 F 0302 0904 1516 2120	1.4 6.3 1.8 6.2	**24** SA 0348 0951 1608 2218	1.9 5.9 2.2 5.5
10 SA 0334 0940 1553 2200	1.7 6.0 1.9 5.9	**25** SU 0426 1036 1659 2312	2.4 5.3 2.7 5.0
11 SU 0414 1026 1643 2255	2.1 5.6 2.3 5.4	**26** M 0524 1146 1834	2.9 4.9 3.0
12 M 0513 1135 1803	2.5 5.3 2.6	**27** TU 0049 0717 1348 2037	4.6 3.1 4.9 2.9
13 TU 0020 0656 1318 2000	5.1 2.7 5.2 2.5	**28** W 0242 0900 1513 2144	4.8 2.8 5.3 2.5
14 W 0211 0847 1455 2127	5.2 2.4 5.6 2.0	**29** TH 0346 0956 1604 2228	5.3 2.4 5.7 2.0
15 TH 0336 0959 1603 2230	5.7 1.8 6.3 1.3	**30** F 0428 1037 1642 2304	5.8 1.9 6.2 1.6

OCTOBER

Time	m	Time	m
1 SA 0503 1112 1716 2335	6.2 1.5 6.5 1.3	**16** SU 0502 1119 1721 2343	6.9 0.8 7.3 0.5
2 SU 0535 1144 1747	6.5 1.2 6.7	**17** M 0543 1200 1802	7.2 0.6 7.5
3 M 0005 0604 1215 1817	1.1 6.7 1.0 6.9	**18** TU 0022 0622 1240 1841	0.4 7.3 0.5 7.5
4 TU 0035 0634 1245 1847	1.0 6.8 0.9 7.0	**19** W 0100 0659 1317 1919	0.5 7.2 0.6 7.3
5 W 0105 0703 1316 1917	0.9 6.8 0.9 7.0	**20** TH 0135 0734 1353 1955	0.8 7.1 0.9 6.9
6 TH 0135 0734 1348 1949	1.0 6.8 1.0 6.8	**21** F 0209 0809 1428 2031	1.1 6.7 1.3 6.5
7 F 0205 0806 1421 2022	1.1 6.7 1.2 6.6	**22** SA 0242 0844 1503 2107	1.6 6.3 1.8 6.0
8 SA 0237 0840 1456 2059	1.4 6.4 1.6 6.3	**23** SU 0315 0921 1541 2148	2.0 5.9 2.3 5.5
9 SU 0313 0920 1538 2144	1.8 6.1 1.9 5.8	**24** M 0352 1005 1629 2240	2.5 5.4 2.7 5.0
10 M 0358 1012 1636 2246	2.2 5.7 2.3 5.4	**25** TU 0446 1108 1752	2.9 5.1 3.0
11 TU 0506 1130 1808	2.6 5.3 2.6	**26** W 0002 0625 1252 1942	4.7 3.1 4.9 2.9
12 W 0020 0700 1314 1958	5.1 2.7 5.4 2.4	**27** TH 0151 0807 1423 2057	4.8 2.9 5.2 2.6
13 TH 0208 0837 1443 2115	5.3 2.3 5.8 1.8	**28** F 0301 0912 1519 2145	5.2 2.5 5.6 2.2
14 F 0323 0943 1546 2212	5.9 1.8 6.4 1.3	**29** SA 0347 0957 1601 2224	5.6 2.1 6.0 1.8
15 SA 0417 1034 1636 2300	6.4 1.2 7.0 0.8	**30** SU 0424 1035 1637 2258	6.0 1.7 6.4 1.5
		31 M 0458 1109 1711 2331	6.4 1.4 6.6 1.2

NOVEMBER

Time	m	Time	m
1 TU 0530 1143 1744	6.7 1.2 6.8	**16** W 0558 1216 1818	7.0 0.9 7.0
2 W 0003 0602 1217 1817	1.1 6.9 1.0 6.9	**17** TH 0034 0635 1255 1856	1.0 7.0 1.0 6.9
3 TH 0037 0636 1252 1852	1.0 6.9 1.0 6.9	**18** F 0111 0712 1332 1934	1.1 6.8 1.2 6.6
4 F 0111 0711 1329 1929	1.0 6.9 1.1 6.8	**19** SA 0146 0748 1409 2011	1.4 6.6 1.5 6.3
5 SA 0147 0748 1407 2008	1.2 6.8 1.2 6.6	**20** SU 0220 0824 1445 2048	1.7 6.3 1.8 6.0
6 SU 0225 0829 1450 2052	1.5 6.6 1.5 6.3	**21** M 0255 0902 1524 2128	2.0 6.0 2.2 5.6
7 M 0308 0916 1540 2145	1.8 6.2 1.9 5.8	**22** TU 0332 0945 1608 2215	2.3 5.7 2.5 5.3
8 TU 0401 1016 1644 2253	2.2 5.9 2.2 5.5	**23** W 0420 1037 1708 2314	2.6 5.4 2.7 5.0
9 W 0513 1132 1811	2.5 5.7 2.3	**24** TH 0527 1143 1825	2.9 5.2 2.7
10 TH 0017 0649 1259 1938	5.3 2.5 5.7 2.1	**25** F 0031 0650 1304 1940	4.9 2.9 5.2 2.7
11 F 0144 0812 1416 2048	5.5 2.2 6.0 1.8	**26** SA 0150 0802 1414 2042	5.1 2.7 5.4 2.4
12 SA 0254 0916 1518 2145	5.9 1.7 6.4 1.4	**27** SU 0249 0901 1507 2132	5.4 2.3 5.7 2.1
13 SU 0349 1008 1609 2233	6.3 1.3 6.8 1.1	**28** M 0336 0948 1552 2215	5.8 2.0 6.0 1.8
14 M 0436 1054 1656 2316	6.7 1.1 7.0 0.9	**29** TU 0417 1031 1633 2255	6.1 1.7 6.3 1.5
15 TU 0518 1136 1738 2356	6.9 0.9 7.1 0.9	**30** W 0456 1112 1713 2334	6.5 1.4 6.6 1.3

DECEMBER

Time	m	Time	m
1 TH 0535 1153 1754	6.7 1.2 6.8	**16** F 0016 0621 1242 1843	1.4 6.6 1.4 6.5
2 F 0014 0615 1235 1835	1.1 6.9 1.1 6.8	**17** SA 0055 0659 1320 1921	1.4 6.6 1.4 6.4
3 SA 0055 0656 1318 1919	1.1 7.0 1.0 6.8	**18** SU 0131 0736 1357 1958	1.5 6.5 1.5 6.3
4 SU 0137 0740 1404 2005	1.2 6.9 1.1 6.6	**19** M 0206 0812 1433 2034	1.6 6.4 1.7 6.1
5 M 0222 0828 1452 2055	1.3 6.7 1.3 6.4	**20** TU 0240 0848 1508 2111	1.8 6.2 1.8 5.9
6 TU 0310 0919 1544 2149	1.5 6.5 1.5 6.1	**21** W 0315 0925 1545 2149	2.0 6.0 2.0 5.6
7 W 0404 1017 1644 2248	1.7 6.3 1.7 5.9	**22** TH 0354 1006 1627 2232	2.2 5.8 2.2 5.4
8 TH 0508 1120 1752 2354	2.0 6.1 1.9 5.7	**23** F 0439 1052 1717 2322	2.4 5.6 2.3 5.2
9 F 0620 1228 1903	2.1 6.0 1.9	**24** SA 0534 1145 1817	2.6 5.4 2.5
10 SA 0105 0732 1338 2010	5.7 2.1 6.0 1.9	**25** SU 0021 0641 1249 1924	5.1 2.6 5.3 2.5
11 SU 0214 0839 1442 2111	5.8 1.9 6.2 1.7	**26** M 0131 0751 1357 2030	5.2 2.6 5.4 2.3
12 M 0315 0938 1540 2205	6.0 1.7 6.3 1.6	**27** TU 0237 0856 1501 2130	5.3 2.3 5.5 2.1
13 TU 0409 1031 1632 2253	6.2 1.6 6.4 1.5	**28** W 0334 0954 1557 2223	5.6 2.0 5.9 1.8
14 W 0457 1118 1720 2336	6.4 1.4 6.5 1.4	**29** TH 0425 1047 1648 2312	6.1 1.7 6.3 1.5
15 TH 0540 1201 1803	6.6 1.4 6.5	**30** F 0514 1136 1738 2359	6.5 1.3 6.7 1.2
		31 SA 0601 1225 1827	7.0 1.0 6.8

Chart Datum: 3·71 metres below Ordnance Datum (Newlyn)

FREE monthly updates from www.reedsalmanac.co.uk

TIDES

AVONMOUTH
MEAN SPRING AND NEAP CURVES

MEAN RANGES
Springs 12.2m
Neaps 6.0m

Springs occur 2 days after New and Full Moon

ENGLAND – AVONMOUTH

LAT 51°30′N LONG 2°44′W

TIMES AND HEIGHTS OF HIGH AND LOW WATERS

TIME ZONE (UT)
For Summer Time add ONE hour in **non-shaded areas**

YEAR 2005

	JANUARY			FEBRUARY			MARCH			APRIL	
	Time m	Time m		Time m	Time m		Time m	Time m		Time m	Time m
1 SA	0422 2.6 1015 11.4 1644 2.7 2238 11.1	**16** SU	0531 2.0 1124 12.4 1754 2.0 2344 11.7	**1** TU	0515 2.3 1110 11.7 1735 2.5 2333 11.2	**16** W	0552 2.7 1159 10.8 1816 3.0 ◐	**1** TU	0422 1.9 1009 12.4 1634 2.0 2227 12.1	**16** W	0446 2.0 1042 11.7 1700 2.2 2251 11.3	**1** F	0505 2.3 1111 11.2 1720 2.8 2333 10.7	**16** SA	0511 3.2 1113 9.6 1731 3.6 ◐ 2329 9.5
2 SU	0458 2.7 1052 11.2 1722 2.8 2318 10.8	**17** M	0603 2.5 1209 11.6 1829 2.5 ◐	**2** W	0554 2.6 1156 11.2 1817 2.9 ◐	**17** TH	0013 10.3 0630 3.4 1250 9.8 1903 3.8	**2** W	0450 1.9 1045 12.0 1705 2.2 2305 11.6	**17** TH	0510 2.5 1112 10.7 1729 2.9 ◐ 2323 10.4	**2** SA	0550 3.1 1209 10.1 1812 3.8 ◐	**17** SU	0600 4.0 1218 8.8 1836 4.4
3 M	0539 2.9 1138 11.0 1806 3.0 ◐	**18** TU	0027 11.0 0640 3.0 1302 10.8 1910 3.1	**3** TH	0023 10.7 0642 3.2 1255 10.6 1910 3.5	**18** F	0113 9.5 0729 4.2 1418 9.2 2014 4.3	**3** TH	0525 2.3 1128 11.3 1742 2.7 ◐ 2352 10.8	**18** F	0544 3.3 1151 9.6 1809 3.8	**3** SU	0043 9.8 0702 4.0 1342 9.5 1953 4.5	**18** M	0104 8.9 0733 4.5 1431 8.8 2026 4.6
4 TU	0006 10.6 0628 3.2 1233 10.7 1858 3.3	**19** W	0123 10.3 0728 3.6 1408 10.3 2004 3.6	**4** F	0129 10.2 0750 3.7 1412 10.2 2030 3.9	**19** SA	0258 9.2 0858 4.5 1552 9.4 2151 4.2	**4** F	0608 3.1 1224 10.4 1832 3.6	**19** SA	0010 9.4 0637 4.2 1310 8.7 1922 4.6	**4** M	0244 9.7 0934 3.8 1538 10.0 2221 3.6	**19** TU	0306 9.3 0915 4.2 1548 9.6 2202 3.9
5 W	0106 10.3 0728 3.5 1340 10.6 2003 3.6	**20** TH	0235 9.9 0834 4.0 1518 10.1 2117 3.8	**5** SA	0259 10.1 0940 3.8 1547 10.4 2234 3.7	**20** SU	0420 9.8 1049 3.9 1659 10.1 2316 3.4	**5** SA	0056 10.0 0712 3.9 1345 9.7 1950 4.3	**20** SU	0207 8.8 0814 4.7 1519 8.9 2111 4.5	**5** TU	0414 10.7 1055 2.7 1650 11.2 2326 2.4	**20** W	0410 10.2 1044 3.3 1643 10.6 2310 2.9
6 TH	0219 10.3 0847 3.6 1456 10.7 2132 3.5	**21** F	0347 10.1 1004 3.9 1624 10.3 2239 3.5	**6** SU	0431 10.7 1114 3.1 1708 11.1 2352 2.8	**21** M	0521 10.7 1154 3.0 1752 11.0	**6** SU	0239 9.6 0930 4.1 1541 9.9 2230 3.9	**21** M	0349 9.4 1017 4.1 1631 9.7 2251 3.6	**6** W	0515 11.9 1155 1.6 1744 12.3	**21** TH	0501 11.1 1141 2.5 1729 11.4
7 F	0340 10.7 1016 3.3 1613 11.1 2258 3.1	**22** SA	0449 10.5 1118 3.4 1721 10.8 2342 2.9	**7** M	0540 11.7 1224 2.2 1811 12.1	**22** TU	0014 2.6 0608 11.5 1246 2.3 1836 11.7	**7** M	0425 10.4 1110 3.1 1704 11.0 2345 2.7	**22** TU	0452 10.4 1130 3.1 1724 10.8 2350 2.7	**7** TH	0021 1.4 0605 13.0 1248 0.8 1830 13.2	**22** F	0002 2.3 0545 11.8 1231 2.0 1810 12.1
8 SA	0451 11.4 1129 2.7 1719 11.8	**23** SU	0542 11.2 1214 2.8 1811 11.3	**8** TU	0056 2.0 0636 12.8 1326 1.4 ● 1905 13.0	**23** W	0106 2.0 0651 12.1 1335 1.9 1916 12.1	**8** TU	0533 11.7 1216 2.0 1803 12.2	**23** W	0540 11.3 1221 2.3 1807 11.6	**8** F	0112 0.7 0650 13.7 1337 0.3 ● 1912 13.7	**23** SA	0051 1.8 0625 12.4 1317 1.7 1849 12.6
9 SU	0004 2.4 0550 12.2 1232 2.0 1817 12.5	**24** M	0035 2.4 0628 11.8 1304 2.3 1855 11.7	**9** W	0154 1.3 0727 13.6 1422 0.8 1955 13.6	**24** TH	0154 1.7 0729 12.5 1421 1.8 ○ 1953 12.3	**9** W	0045 1.7 0626 12.9 1313 1.0 1853 13.2	**24** TH	0040 2.0 0622 12.1 1309 1.8 1846 12.2	**9** SA	0159 0.4 0732 14.0 1421 0.2 1951 13.8	**24** SU	0136 1.6 0704 12.7 1400 1.6 ○ 1926 12.9
10 M	0104 1.9 0642 12.9 1331 1.5 ● 1912 13.0	**25** TU	0124 2.0 0710 12.1 1351 2.1 ○ 1936 12.0	**10** TH	0246 0.7 0815 14.0 1512 0.4 2040 13.8	**25** F	0238 1.7 0806 12.6 1502 1.8 2027 12.4	**10** TH	0139 0.9 0713 13.8 1405 0.4 ● 1938 13.8	**25** F	0128 1.7 0701 12.5 1355 1.6 ○ 1923 12.6	**10** SU	0241 0.4 0810 13.9 1500 0.4 2027 13.6	**25** M	0216 1.5 0742 12.9 1437 1.6 2002 13.0
11 TU	0200 1.5 0735 13.5 1427 1.2 2004 13.3	**26** W	0210 1.9 0749 12.3 1436 2.1 2014 12.0	**11** F	0332 0.5 0859 14.2 1554 0.3 2122 13.8	**26** SA	0315 1.7 0839 12.7 1535 1.9 2058 12.4	**11** F	0228 0.3 0757 14.2 1451 0.0 ● 2019 14.1	**26** SA	0212 1.5 0737 12.7 1436 1.6 1958 12.7	**11** M	0317 0.7 0845 13.5 1531 0.9 2059 13.2	**26** TU	0251 1.4 0819 13.0 1507 1.7 2038 13.0
12 W	0253 1.2 0825 13.8 1519 0.9 2053 13.4	**27** TH	0252 1.9 0826 12.3 1515 2.2 2048 12.0	**12** SA	0410 0.6 0940 14.0 1630 0.5 2200 13.5	**27** SU	0343 1.9 0907 12.5 1557 2.1 2126 12.4	**12** SA	0311 0.2 0837 14.3 1531 0.1 2057 14.0	**27** SU	0250 1.6 0811 12.8 1510 1.7 2030 12.7	**12** TU	0343 1.2 0917 12.8 1551 1.5 2127 12.6	**27** W	0322 1.4 0857 12.9 1534 1.8 2114 12.8
13 TH	0340 1.3 0913 13.7 1606 0.9 2139 13.3	**28** F	0327 2.1 0859 12.2 1547 2.3 2120 11.9	**13** SU	0441 1.1 1016 13.5 1657 1.1 2233 12.9			**13** SU	0347 0.4 0914 14.0 1603 0.5 2131 13.5	**28** M	0320 1.7 0843 12.9 1534 1.8 2101 12.7	**13** W	0359 1.7 0944 12.2 1606 1.9 2151 12.0	**28** TH	0351 1.5 0936 12.6 1601 1.9 2154 12.3
14 F	0422 1.7 0958 13.5 1646 1.0 2223 13.0	**29** SA	0353 2.2 0929 12.1 1610 2.4 2149 11.9	**14** M	0503 1.5 1050 13.0 1718 1.7 2303 12.3			**14** M	0414 0.9 0947 13.4 1625 1.1 2159 12.9	**28** TU	0341 1.8 0915 12.8 1550 1.8 2132 12.7	**14** TH	0414 2.1 1010 11.4 1626 2.3 2217 11.6	**29** F	0424 2.3 1019 11.9 1634 2.3 2237 11.6
15 SA	0459 1.5 1042 13.1 1722 1.4 2303 12.4	**30** SU	0415 2.2 0959 12.1 1632 2.3 2219 11.8	**15** TU	0524 2.1 1122 11.8 1743 2.3 2334 11.2			**15** TU	0431 1.5 1015 12.6 1641 1.7 2225 12.2	**30** W	0403 1.7 0949 12.6 1612 1.9 2206 12.2	**15** F	0439 2.5 1037 10.5 1653 2.9 2246 10.4	**30** SA	0503 3.0 1108 11.1 1716 3.0 2331 10.7
		31 M	0442 2.2 1032 11.9 1700 2.3 2252 11.6						**31** TH	0430 1.8 1027 12.0 1642 2.2 2245 11.6			

Chart Datum: 6·50 metres below Ordnance Datum (Newlyn)

» **FREE** monthly updates from «
www.reedsalmanac.co.uk

TIDES

TIME ZONE (UT) For Summer Time add ONE hour in **non-shaded areas**

ENGLAND – AVONMOUTH
LAT 51°30'N   LONG 2°44'W
TIMES AND HEIGHTS OF HIGH AND LOW WATERS

YEAR 2005

Day	MAY Time m	Time m	JUNE Time m	Time m	JULY Time m	Time m	AUGUST Time m	Time m
1 / 16	**1** 0556 3.1 / 1211 10.2 / SU 1817 3.8 ○	**16** 0543 3.6 / 1153 9.4 / M 1808 3.9	**1** 0205 10.9 / 0832 2.7 / W 1438 10.7 / 2108 3.0	**16** 0050 10.1 / 0721 3.4 / TH 1329 9.9 / 1954 3.6	**1** 0228 10.9 / 0841 2.9 / F 1455 10.6 / 2118 3.2	**16** 0104 10.4 / 0730 3.3 / SA 1340 10.2 / 2008 3.6	**1** 0358 10.0 / 1011 3.8 / M 1625 10.2 / 2300 3.6	**16** 0307 10.0 / 0950 3.9 / TU 1557 10.3 / 2242 3.4
2 / 17	**2** 0050 10.1 / 0727 3.6 / M 1347 9.9 / 2023 4.0	**17** 0019 9.4 / 0654 4.0 / TU 1317 9.2 / 1932 4.2	**2** 0311 11.2 / 0939 2.5 / TH 1541 11.1 / 2212 2.6	**17** 0200 10.2 / 0829 3.4 / F 1440 10.2 / 2108 3.4	**2** 0329 10.9 / 0948 3.0 / SA 1556 10.7 / 2228 3.1	**17** 0215 10.4 / 0844 3.5 / SU 1457 10.3 / 2135 3.5	**2** 0500 10.4 / 1123 3.2 / TU 1723 10.9 / 2359 2.9	**17** 0436 10.7 / 1120 3.1 / W 1711 11.4 / 2356 2.4
3 / 18	**3** 0235 10.2 / 0912 3.2 / TU 1516 10.4 / 2152 3.2	**18** 0157 9.5 / 0816 3.9 / W 1444 9.6 / 2056 3.9	**3** 0409 11.6 / 1039 2.2 / F 1637 11.6 / 2309 2.1	**18** 0309 10.6 / 0942 3.2 / SA 1548 10.7 / 2220 3.0	**3** 0427 11.0 / 1053 2.9 / SU 1653 11.0 / 2327 2.8	**18** 0333 10.6 / 1015 3.3 / M 1616 10.8 / 2255 2.9	**3** 0554 11.0 / 1219 2.6 / W 1813 11.5	**18** 0543 11.7 / 1228 2.2 / TH 1811 12.5
4 / 19	**4** 0348 11.0 / 1023 2.4 / W 1621 11.3 / 2254 2.3	**19** 0312 10.0 / 0932 3.4 / TH 1549 10.3 / 2209 3.3	**4** 0502 12.0 / 1134 1.9 / SA 1726 12.0	**19** 0413 11.1 / 1054 2.8 / SU 1649 11.4 / 2325 2.4	**4** 0522 11.2 / 1150 2.5 / M 1744 11.4	**19** 0446 11.2 / 1130 2.8 / TU 1722 11.6	**4** 0051 2.4 / 0641 11.5 / TH 1311 2.1 / 1857 12.0	**19** 0059 1.5 / 0639 12.7 / F 1329 1.5 / ○ 1902 13.4
5 / 20	**5** 0446 11.9 / 1121 1.7 / TH 1714 12.1 / 2347 1.5	**20** 0410 10.8 / 1042 2.9 / F 1643 11.1 / 2311 2.6	**5** 0001 1.8 / 0549 12.2 / SU 1225 1.7 / 1810 12.3	**20** 0512 11.7 / 1156 2.3 / M 1743 12.1	**5** 0020 2.4 / 0610 11.5 / TU 1242 2.2 / 1829 11.8	**20** 0002 2.3 / 0549 11.8 / W 1235 2.2 / 1818 12.4	**5** 0140 2.1 / 0723 11.8 / F 1359 1.9 / ● 1937 12.2	**20** 0157 0.8 / 0730 13.4 / SA 1423 0.8 / 1951 14.0
6 / 21	**6** 0536 12.7 / 1213 1.1 / F 1801 12.8	**21** 0501 11.5 / 1142 2.4 / SA 1730 11.8	**6** 0050 1.6 / 0634 12.3 / M 1311 1.6 / ● 1852 12.4	**21** 0022 1.9 / 0605 12.2 / TU 1252 1.9 / 1833 12.6	**6** 0109 2.2 / 0656 11.6 / W 1329 2.0 / ○ 1912 12.0	**21** 0105 1.7 / 0647 12.5 / TH 1335 1.7 / ○ 1912 13.1	**6** 0227 2.0 / 0802 11.9 / SA 1443 1.9 / 2015 12.3	**21** 0249 0.3 / 0817 13.8 / SU 1512 0.5 / 2036 14.3
7 / 22	**7** 0037 1.0 / 0621 13.2 / SA 1301 0.8 / 1842 13.2	**22** 0006 2.1 / 0547 12.1 / SU 1234 2.0 / 1814 12.4	**7** 0135 1.6 / 0716 12.3 / TU 1354 1.6 / 1931 12.4	**22** 0117 1.6 / 0657 12.7 / W 1345 1.6 / ○ 1922 13.0	**7** 0155 2.1 / 0739 11.7 / TH 1413 2.1 / 1953 12.0	**22** 0204 1.2 / 0741 13.0 / F 1432 1.3 / 2003 13.5	**7** 0308 2.0 / 0838 11.9 / SU 1521 2.0 / 2049 12.2	**22** 0335 0.1 / 0900 13.9 / M 1553 0.6 / 2118 14.2
8 / 23	**8** 0124 0.9 / 0702 13.3 / SU 1346 0.8 / ● 1921 13.2	**23** 0056 1.7 / 0632 12.6 / M 1322 1.7 / ○ 1856 12.8	**8** 0216 1.8 / 0755 12.1 / W 1432 1.8 / 2008 12.2	**23** 0210 1.3 / 0749 12.9 / TH 1436 1.4 / 2011 13.2	**8** 0239 2.2 / 0819 11.7 / F 1453 2.1 / 2030 11.9	**23** 0300 0.8 / 0832 13.3 / SA 1523 1.0 / 2052 13.7	**8** 0342 2.2 / 0910 11.8 / M 1551 2.2 / 2119 12.0	**23** 0414 0.6 / 0940 13.7 / TU 1628 0.7 / 2157 13.8
9 / 24	**9** 0207 0.9 / 0741 13.1 / M 1426 1.0 / 1957 13.0	**24** 0142 1.4 / 0716 12.8 / TU 1406 1.5 / 1938 13.0	**9** 0252 2.0 / 0832 11.8 / TH 1503 2.1 / 2042 11.9	**24** 0302 1.2 / 0839 12.9 / F 1524 1.4 / 2100 13.2	**9** 0316 2.3 / 0855 11.6 / SA 1527 2.3 / 2105 11.8	**24** 0349 0.6 / 0919 13.4 / SU 1608 0.9 / 2138 13.7	**9** 0407 2.4 / 0933 11.7 / TU 1610 2.3 / 2146 11.9	**24** 0445 0.8 / 1016 13.2 / W 1654 1.3 / 2233 13.0
10 / 25	**10** 0245 1.2 / 0818 12.8 / TU 1458 1.5 / 2030 12.7	**25** 0226 1.3 / 0800 12.9 / W 1447 1.5 / 2021 13.1	**10** 0321 2.3 / 0907 11.4 / F 1530 2.3 / 2115 11.6	**25** 0351 1.1 / 0929 12.9 / SA 1609 1.5 / 2149 13.0	**10** 0348 2.5 / 0929 11.4 / SU 1555 2.4 / 2135 11.6	**25** 0432 0.6 / 1004 13.3 / M 1647 1.0 / 2222 13.4	**10** 0424 2.4 / 1005 11.6 / W 1630 2.3 / 2214 11.7	**25** 0509 1.5 / 1049 12.4 / TH 1714 2.1 / 2306 12.0
11 / 26	**11** 0314 1.7 / 0851 12.3 / W 1523 1.8 / 2100 12.2	**26** 0308 1.3 / 0846 12.9 / TH 1525 1.6 / 2105 12.9	**11** 0346 2.5 / 0939 11.1 / SA 1556 2.5 / 2147 11.2	**26** 0437 1.2 / 1017 12.6 / SU 1652 1.7 / 2237 12.7	**11** 0414 2.6 / 1000 11.3 / M 1620 2.5 / 2208 11.4	**26** 0509 0.9 / 1045 12.9 / TU 1720 1.4 / 2304 12.9	**11** 0445 2.5 / 1034 11.4 / TH 1657 2.7 / 2247 11.5	**26** 0530 2.2 / 1120 11.3 / F 1737 2.7 / ◐ 2341 10.9
12 / 27	**12** 0334 2.0 / 0921 11.7 / TH 1542 2.1 / 2128 11.7	**27** 0349 1.4 / 0932 12.5 / F 1603 1.8 / 2151 12.5	**12** 0414 2.7 / 1012 10.5 / SU 1626 2.7 / 2220 10.9	**27** 0521 1.4 / 1105 12.1 / M 1735 2.0 / 2327 12.2	**12** 0440 2.6 / 1030 11.1 / TU 1650 2.5 / 2240 11.2	**27** 0542 1.4 / 1125 12.0 / W 1751 2.0 / 2346 12.1	**12** 0515 2.5 / 1110 11.1 / F 1732 2.9 / 2328 11.1	**27** 0559 3.0 / 1155 10.7 / SA 1811 3.3
13 / 28	**13** 0353 2.3 / 0949 11.1 / F 1605 2.4 / 2155 11.1	**28** 0430 1.7 / 1019 12.1 / SA 1643 2.2 / 2240 11.9	**13** 0448 2.8 / 1048 10.8 / M 1703 2.9 / 2259 10.5	**28** 0605 1.8 / 1154 11.7 / TU 1820 2.4 / ◐	**13** 0511 2.6 / 1104 10.9 / W 1725 2.7 / 2317 11.0	**28** 0613 2.0 / 1206 11.2 / TH 1823 2.6 / ◐	**13** 0552 2.8 / 1155 10.7 / SA 1814 3.2	**28** 0029 9.8 / 0640 3.8 / SU 1256 9.5 / 1904 4.3
14 / 29	**14** 0420 2.6 / 1019 10.5 / SA 1634 2.8 / 2228 10.5	**29** 0517 2.1 / 1111 11.5 / SU 1731 2.7 / 2336 11.3	**14** 0530 3.0 / 1131 10.1 / TU 1748 3.2 / 2348 10.2	**29** 0022 11.7 / 0651 2.7 / W 1250 11.2 / 1910 2.8 / ◐	**14** 0549 2.7 / 1145 10.7 / TH 1807 2.9 / ◐	**29** 0034 11.2 / 0649 2.7 / F 1255 10.7 / 1905 3.3	**14** 0021 10.5 / 0639 3.4 / SU 1255 10.1 / 1914 3.8	**29** 0203 9.1 / 0748 4.6 / M 1443 9.2 / 2039 4.8
15 / 30	**15** 0455 3.0 / 1057 9.9 / SU 1712 3.3 / 2312 9.9	**30** 0613 2.7 / 1212 10.9 / M 1833 2.9	**15** 0621 3.0 / 1224 10.0 / W 1845 3.5 / ◐	**30** 0124 11.2 / 0742 2.6 / TH 1351 10.8 / 2009 3.1	**15** 0005 10.7 / 0634 3.0 / F 1236 10.4 / 1859 3.3	**30** 0134 10.0 / 0737 3.4 / SA 1401 10.0 / 2004 3.9	**15** 0133 10.0 / 0750 3.9 / M 1419 9.9 / 2058 4.0	**30** 0336 9.2 / 0922 4.6 / TU 1603 9.7 / 2246 4.1
31					**31** 0047 10.9 / 0720 2.8 / TU 1326 10.6 / 1953 3.3		**31** 0248 9.9 / 0843 3.8 / SU 1516 9.9 / 2135 4.1		**31** 0442 10.2 / 1105 3.5 / W 1704 10.6 / 2344 3.1

Chart Datum: 6·50 metres below Ordnance Datum (Newlyn)

》》 **FREE** monthly updates from 《《
www.reedsalmanac.co.uk

ENGLAND – AVONMOUTH
LAT 51°30'N   LONG 2°44'W

TIME ZONE (UT) For Summer Time add ONE hour in **non-shaded areas**

TIMES AND HEIGHTS OF HIGH AND LOW WATERS

YEAR **2005**

SEPTEMBER

Time m	Time m
1 0536 10.9 / 1201 2.6 / TH 1754 11.5	**16** 0535 11.9 / 1217 1.9 / F 1759 12.8
2 0033 2.2 / 0620 11.6 / F 1251 2.0 / 1836 12.2	**17** 0046 1.2 / 0625 13.0 / SA 1312 1.1 / 1846 13.8
3 0120 1.8 / 0700 12.1 / SA 1339 1.7 / ● 1915 12.5	**18** 0139 0.5 / 0711 13.7 / SU 1403 0.5 / ○ 1931 14.3
4 0206 1.6 / 0737 12.3 / SU 1423 1.6 / 1951 12.6	**19** 0227 0.1 / 0754 14.1 / M 1448 0.3 / 2013 14.5
5 0248 1.7 / 0811 12.3 / M 1502 1.8 / 2023 12.5	**20** 0310 0.1 / 0834 14.0 / TU 1528 0.4 / 2052 14.2
6 0323 1.9 / 0842 12.2 / TU 1533 2.0 / 2052 12.4	**21** 0346 0.4 / 0910 13.7 / W 1600 0.9 / 2128 13.6
7 0348 2.2 / 0910 12.1 / W 1551 2.2 / 2119 12.2	**22** 0413 1.1 / 0943 13.1 / TH 1622 1.6 / 2159 12.8
8 0400 2.4 / 0936 12.2 / TH 1606 2.3 / 2147 12.1	**23** 0431 1.8 / 1011 12.2 / F 1636 2.2 / 2228 11.8
9 0416 2.4 / 1005 11.8 / F 1630 2.3 / 2220 11.8	**24** 0448 2.5 / 1039 11.3 / SA 1657 2.9 / 2257 10.6
10 0443 2.5 / 1040 11.4 / SA 1701 2.6 / 2259 11.2	**25** 0514 3.2 / 1110 10.3 / SU 1727 3.6 / ◐ 2334 9.5
11 0516 2.9 / 1124 10.7 / SU 1740 3.2 / ◐ 2351 10.3	**26** 0551 4.0 / 1158 9.3 / M 1816 4.5
12 0601 3.6 / 1224 9.9 / M 1837 4.0	**27** 0104 8.6 / 0659 4.8 / TU 1415 8.8 / 1957 5.1
13 0106 9.6 / 0710 4.4 / TU 1359 9.5 / 2047 4.4	**28** 0312 8.8 / 0903 4.8 / W 1538 9.5 / 2228 4.3
14 0304 9.6 / 0954 4.2 / W 1553 10.2 / 2243 3.4	**29** 0416 9.8 / 1044 3.8 / TH 1637 10.5 / 2320 3.1
15 0443 9.7 / 1117 3.0 / TH 1704 11.5 / 2350 2.2	**30** 0507 10.8 / 1136 2.7 / F 1725 11.5

OCTOBER

Time m	Time m
1 0006 2.2 / 0550 11.7 / SA 1224 2.0 / 1806 12.2	**16** 0020 1.0 / 0602 13.1 / SU 1245 1.0 / 1823 13.8
2 0052 1.7 / 0629 12.3 / SU 1310 1.6 / 1844 12.6	**17** 0110 0.5 / 0645 13.7 / M 1333 0.6 / ○ 1905 14.2
3 0136 1.6 / 0705 12.6 / M 1353 1.6 / ● 1920 12.8	**18** 0156 0.3 / 0726 13.9 / TU 1417 0.5 / 1946 14.1
4 0217 1.6 / 0739 12.6 / TU 1432 1.7 / 1953 12.7	**19** 0238 0.5 / 0804 13.8 / W 1457 0.8 / 2024 13.3
5 0252 1.8 / 0811 12.5 / W 1504 1.9 / 2023 12.6	**20** 0313 0.9 / 0839 13.4 / TH 1528 1.3 / 2059 12.6
6 0318 2.1 / 0840 12.4 / TH 1526 2.1 / 2053 12.5	**21** 0339 1.5 / 0911 12.7 / F 1550 2.0 / 2130 12.3
7 0334 2.3 / 0909 12.3 / F 1544 2.2 / 2124 12.3	**22** 0357 2.1 / 0939 12.0 / SA 1605 2.5 / 2158 11.4
8 0352 2.3 / 0942 12.0 / SA 1609 2.3 / 2200 11.8	**23** 0416 2.6 / 1006 11.2 / SU 1627 3.0 / 2226 10.5
9 0420 2.5 / 1020 11.5 / SU 1641 2.7 / 2242 11.1	**24** 0442 3.2 / 1037 10.3 / M 1658 3.6 / 2301 9.6
10 0455 3.0 / 1106 10.7 / M 1722 3.3 / ◐ 2336 10.2	**25** 0517 3.9 / 1121 9.4 / TU 1744 4.4 / ◐
11 0541 3.8 / 1210 9.8 / TU 1825 4.2	**26** 0007 8.7 / 0617 4.7 / W 1321 8.9 / 1914 4.9
12 0058 9.4 / 0658 4.6 / W 1405 9.6 / 2058 4.3	**27** 0228 8.8 / 0806 4.9 / TH 1458 9.4 / 2114 4.6
13 0304 9.8 / 0949 4.0 / TH 1542 10.6 / 2227 3.1	**28** 0335 9.6 / 0953 4.1 / F 1557 10.3 / 2237 3.6
14 0419 10.9 / 1058 2.8 / F 1645 11.8 / 2327 1.9	**29** 0428 10.5 / 1056 3.2 / SA 1646 11.2 / 2327 2.7
15 0515 12.5 / 1153 1.7 / SA 1737 13.0	**30** 0512 11.4 / 1145 2.4 / SU 1729 11.9
	31 0013 2.1 / 0552 12.1 / M 1231 2.0 / 1808 12.4

NOVEMBER

Time m	Time m
1 0057 1.8 / 0630 12.5 / TU 1314 1.8 / 1846 12.7	**16** 0122 0.9 / 0657 13.3 / W 1344 1.1 / ○ 1919 13.4
2 0139 1.7 / 0706 12.7 / W 1355 1.7 / ● 1922 12.8	**17** 0204 1.1 / 0736 13.2 / TH 1425 1.4 / 1959 13.1
3 0216 1.8 / 0741 12.8 / TH 1431 1.8 / 1957 12.8	**18** 0242 1.4 / 0813 12.9 / F 1500 1.8 / 2036 12.6
4 0248 1.9 / 0815 12.7 / F 1502 1.9 / 2033 12.7	**19** 0311 1.9 / 0847 12.4 / SA 1527 2.3 / 2110 11.9
5 0314 2.0 / 0851 12.6 / SA 1531 2.0 / 2111 12.4	**20** 0334 2.3 / 0919 11.9 / SU 1547 2.7 / 2141 11.3
6 0341 2.2 / 0929 12.2 / SU 1603 2.2 / 2153 11.9	**21** 0357 2.7 / 0949 11.2 / M 1612 3.0 / 2212 10.6
7 0413 2.5 / 1012 11.6 / M 1640 2.7 / 2239 11.2	**22** 0425 3.1 / 1023 10.6 / TU 1646 3.4 / 2248 10.0
8 0452 2.9 / 1103 10.9 / TU 1728 3.3 / 2336 10.4	**23** 0501 3.5 / 1105 10.0 / W 1730 3.9 / ◐ 2338 9.5
9 0545 3.8 / 1212 10.3 / W 1843 3.8	**24** 0552 4.1 / 1209 9.5 / TH 1833 4.2
10 0058 9.9 / 0720 4.2 / TH 1355 10.3 / 2033 3.7	**25** 0056 9.2 / 0705 4.4 / F 1344 9.5 / 1951 4.3
11 0239 10.2 / 0915 3.7 / F 1514 11.0 / 2151 2.9	**26** 0226 9.4 / 0828 4.2 / SA 1457 10.0 / 2109 3.9
12 0348 11.1 / 1023 2.7 / SA 1615 11.9 / 2252 2.1	**27** 0331 10.1 / 0944 3.7 / SU 1553 10.6 / 2222 3.4
13 0444 12.0 / 1119 1.9 / SU 1708 12.7 / 2346 1.4	**28** 0424 10.8 / 1049 3.1 / M 1644 11.3 / 2322 2.8
14 0533 12.7 / 1211 1.4 / M 1755 13.2	**29** 0511 11.5 / 1143 2.6 / TU 1730 11.9
15 0036 1.1 / 0616 13.2 / TU 1259 1.1 / 1838 13.5	**30** 0013 2.3 / 0554 12.2 / W 1233 2.1 / 1813 12.4

DECEMBER

Time m	Time m
1 0100 1.9 / 0636 12.6 / TH 1319 1.8 / ● 1856 12.7	**16** 0136 1.7 / 0715 12.6 / F 1401 1.9 / 1941 12.4
2 0143 1.7 / 0717 12.9 / F 1403 1.7 / 1939 12.8	**17** 0218 1.8 / 0755 12.5 / SA 1441 2.1 / 2021 12.1
3 0225 1.7 / 0759 12.9 / SA 1446 1.7 / 2023 12.8	**18** 0254 2.1 / 0833 12.2 / SU 1516 2.4 / 2058 11.8
4 0304 1.8 / 0842 12.9 / SU 1528 1.7 / 2108 12.6	**19** 0324 2.3 / 0908 11.9 / M 1543 2.7 / 2131 11.5
5 0342 2.0 / 0927 12.6 / M 1609 1.9 / 2154 12.3	**20** 0351 2.6 / 0941 11.6 / TU 1609 2.8 / 2203 11.1
6 0422 2.3 / 1014 12.2 / TU 1653 2.2 / 2242 11.8	**21** 0418 2.7 / 1014 11.4 / W 1639 3.0 / 2236 10.7
7 0505 2.7 / 1105 11.7 / W 1742 2.6 / 2335 11.2	**22** 0450 2.9 / 1049 10.9 / TH 1715 3.1 / 2313 10.4
8 0557 3.1 / 1201 11.0 / TH 1842 2.9	**23** 0529 3.2 / 1130 10.6 / F 1758 3.4 / ◑ 2358 10.1
9 0039 10.8 / 0704 3.4 / F 1321 11.0 / 1950 3.0	**24** 0617 3.5 / 1222 10.2 / SA 1850 3.6
10 0156 10.7 / 0823 3.4 / SA 1431 11.1 / 2101 3.1	**25** 0055 9.8 / 0717 3.8 / SU 1328 10.0 / 1953 3.8
11 0306 10.9 / 0936 3.1 / SU 1537 11.5 / 2207 2.7	**26** 0206 9.8 / 0830 3.9 / M 1440 10.0 / 2109 3.8
12 0407 11.3 / 1040 2.7 / M 1634 11.9 / 2308 2.4	**27** 0320 10.2 / 0948 3.6 / TU 1549 10.6 / 2226 3.4
13 0501 11.8 / 1136 2.3 / TU 1726 12.2 / 2332 2.3	**28** 0426 10.8 / 1058 3.0 / W 1651 11.2 / 2332 2.8
14 0001 2.0 / 0548 12.2 / W 1228 2.0 / 1813 12.4	**29** 0522 11.6 / 1158 2.2 / TH 1746 11.9
15 0051 1.8 / 0631 12.5 / TH 1316 1.9 / ○ 1858 12.5	**30** 0028 2.3 / 0612 12.3 / F 1253 2.0 / ○ 1837 12.4
	31 0121 1.9 / 0701 12.8 / SA 1346 1.6 / ● 1927 12.8

Chart Datum: 6·50 metres below Ordnance Datum (Newlyn)

》》 **FREE** monthly updates from 《《
www.reedsalmanac.co.uk

TIDES

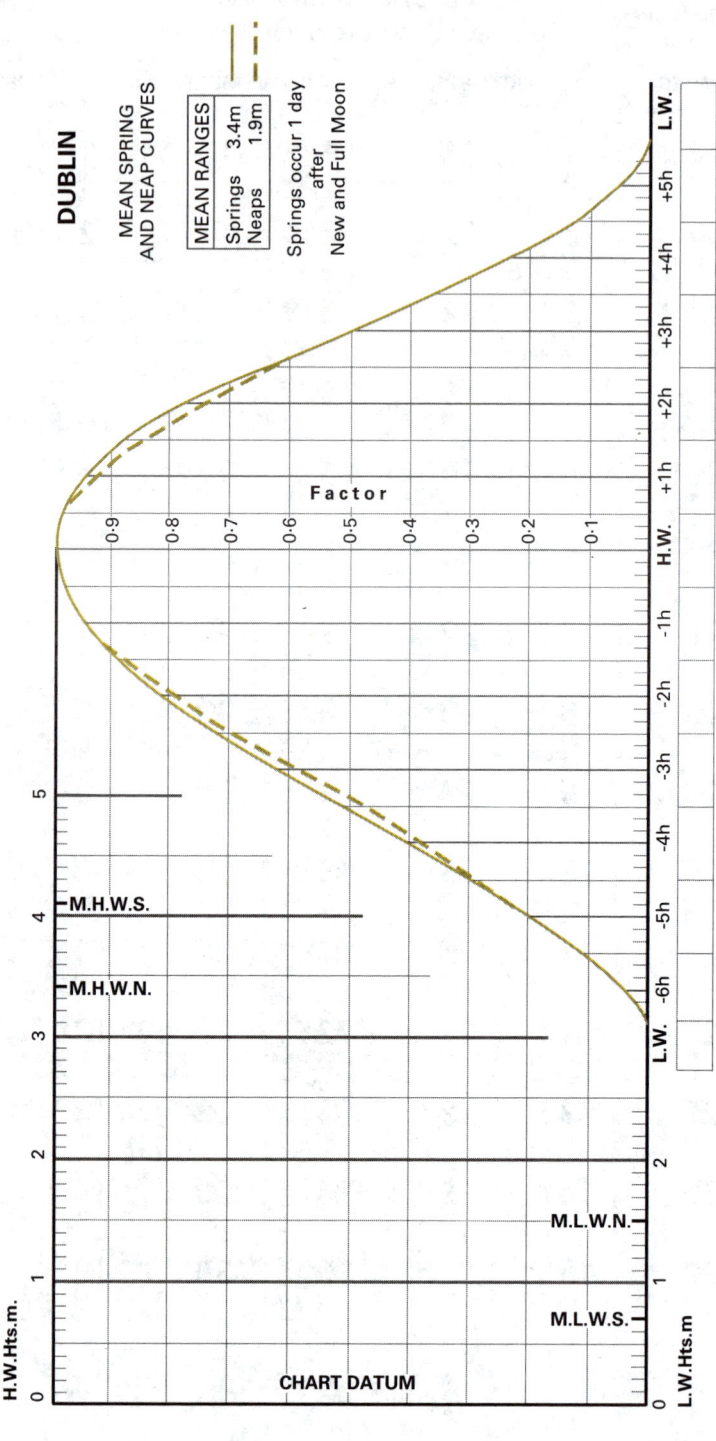

TIME ZONE (UT)
For Summer Time add ONE hour in **non-shaded areas**

IRELAND – DUBLIN (NORTH WALL)
LAT 53°21'N   LONG 6°13'W
TIMES AND HEIGHTS OF HIGH AND LOW WATERS

YEAR 2005

JANUARY		FEBRUARY		MARCH		APRIL	
Time m	Time m	Time m	Time m	Time m	Time m	Time m	Time m
1 0253 3.5 / 0822 1.3 / SA 1509 3.8 / 2103 1.1	**16** 0357 3.6 / 0920 1.1 / SU 1606 4.0 / 2202 0.9	**1** 0346 3.6 / 0915 1.1 / TU 1605 3.7 / 2154 1.0	**16** 0459 3.3 / 1038 1.3 / W 1723 3.4 / ☾ 2309 1.5	**1** 0224 3.8 / 0757 0.8 / TU 1447 3.9 / 2031 0.7	**16** 0311 3.5 / 0905 1.0 / W 1541 3.5 / 2127 1.2	**1** 0334 3.6 / 0924 1.0 / F 1617 3.5 / 2201 1.3	**16** 0426 3.3 / 1042 1.3 / SA 1726 3.0 / ☾ 2257 1.7
2 0340 3.5 / 0908 1.4 / SU 1555 3.7 / 2150 1.1	**17** 0456 3.5 / 1019 1.3 / M 1705 3.8 / ☾ 2300 1.1	**2** 0437 3.5 / 1007 1.3 / W 1657 3.6 / ☽ 2250 1.2	**17** 0608 3.2 / 1147 1.5 / TH 1838 3.2	**2** 0308 3.7 / 0843 0.9 / W 1534 3.7 / 2119 1.0	**17** 0402 3.3 / 1003 1.2 / TH 1641 3.3 / ☽ 2223 1.5	**2** 0438 3.4 / 1041 1.2 / SA 1736 3.3 / ☽ 2321 1.5	**17** 0552 3.1 / 1154 1.4 / SU 1846 3.0
3 0431 3.4 / 1000 1.5 / M 1645 3.6 / ☾ 2243 1.2	**18** 0557 3.4 / 1122 1.5 / TU 1810 3.6	**3** 0536 3.4 / 1111 1.4 / TH 1801 3.5 / 2359 1.3	**18** 0021 1.7 / 0718 3.2 / F 1313 1.6 / 1953 3.2	**3** 0358 3.5 / 0936 1.1 / TH 1629 3.5 / ☾ 2216 1.2	**18** 0512 3.2 / 1110 1.4 / F 1801 3.1 / 2333 1.8	**3** 0602 3.3 / 1213 1.2 / SU 1911 3.3	**18** 0016 1.8 / 0710 3.2 / M 1314 1.3 / 1956 3.1
4 0527 3.4 / 1058 1.5 / TU 1740 3.6 / 2342 1.2	**19** 0004 1.3 / 0700 3.4 / W 1232 1.5 / 1917 3.5	**4** 0647 3.4 / 1230 1.4 / F 1920 3.4	**19** 0202 1.7 / 0826 3.3 / SA 1439 1.5 / 2103 3.2	**4** 0459 3.4 / 1044 1.3 / F 1738 3.3 / 2331 1.4	**19** 0636 3.1 / 1232 1.5 / SA 1922 3.0	**4** 0053 1.5 / 0730 3.4 / M 1341 1.0 / 2031 3.4	**19** 0142 1.7 / 0813 3.3 / TU 1416 1.2 / 2052 3.3
5 0627 3.4 / 1202 1.5 / W 1841 3.6	**20** 0118 1.5 / 0803 3.4 / TH 1348 1.5 / 2024 3.4	**5** 0118 1.3 / 0801 3.5 / SA 1352 1.3 / 2039 3.5	**20** 0309 1.6 / 0926 3.5 / SU 1534 1.3 / 2200 3.3	**5** 0616 3.3 / 1214 1.4 / SA 1911 3.1	**20** 0111 1.8 / 0750 3.2 / SU 1408 1.4 / 2036 3.1	**5** 0212 1.3 / 0842 3.6 / TU 1447 0.8 / 2134 3.6	**20** 0238 1.4 / 0904 3.5 / W 1459 1.0 / 2134 3.4
6 0045 1.2 / 0729 3.5 / TH 1309 1.4 / 1947 3.6	**21** 0229 1.5 / 0901 3.5 / F 1456 1.4 / 2126 3.5	**6** 0232 1.2 / 0907 3.7 / SU 1503 1.0 / 2146 3.7	**21** 0353 1.4 / 1013 3.7 / M 1614 1.1 / 2241 3.5	**6** 0103 1.5 / 0744 3.4 / SU 1347 1.2 / 2036 3.4	**21** 0240 1.6 / 0854 3.4 / M 1504 1.2 / 2133 3.3	**6** 0309 1.0 / 0940 3.9 / W 1538 0.5 / 2224 3.8	**21** 0315 1.2 / 0945 3.6 / TH 1533 0.8 / 2208 3.6
7 0148 1.1 / 0828 3.6 / F 1411 1.3 / 2052 3.7	**22** 0325 1.4 / 0953 3.7 / SA 1550 1.3 / 2218 3.5	**7** 0333 1.0 / 1003 3.9 / M 1601 0.7 / 2242 3.9	**22** 0426 1.2 / 1051 3.8 / TU 1647 0.9 / 2313 3.6	**7** 0226 1.3 / 0856 3.6 / M 1500 0.9 / 2144 3.6	**22** 0325 1.4 / 0944 3.5 / TU 1544 1.0 / 2213 3.4	**7** 0354 0.8 / 1029 4.0 / TH 1621 0.3 / 2306 3.9	**22** 0345 1.0 / 1018 3.7 / F 1603 0.6 / 2235 3.7
8 0246 1.0 / 0923 3.8 / SA 1509 1.0 / 2152 3.9	**23** 0409 1.3 / 1036 3.8 / SU 1632 1.2 / 2259 3.6	**8** 0422 0.8 / 1053 4.1 / TU 1650 0.4 / ● 2331 4.0	**23** 0455 1.1 / 1123 3.9 / W 1716 0.8 / 2341 3.6	**8** 0326 1.0 / 0954 3.9 / TU 1555 0.6 / 2237 3.8	**23** 0358 1.2 / 1023 3.7 / W 1615 0.8 / 2245 3.6	**8** 0434 0.6 / 1111 4.1 / F 1700 0.2 / ● 2341 3.9	**23** 0412 0.8 / 1048 3.8 / SA 1631 0.5 / 2301 3.8
9 0339 0.9 / 1014 4.0 / SU 1603 0.8 / 2247 4.0	**24** 0444 1.2 / 1113 3.9 / M 1708 1.0 / 2333 3.6	**9** 0506 0.6 / 1139 4.3 / W 1735 0.3	**24** 0520 0.9 / 1151 3.9 / TH 1742 0.7 / O	**9** 0413 0.7 / 1043 4.1 / W 1639 0.3 / 2321 3.9	**24** 0425 1.0 / 1055 3.8 / TH 1642 0.6 / 2312 3.7	**9** 0511 0.5 / 1148 4.1 / SA 1737 0.3	**24** 0440 0.6 / 1119 3.8 / SU 1702 0.4 / O 2331 3.9
10 0428 0.8 / 1103 4.2 / M 1654 0.6 / ● 2338 4.1	**25** 0515 1.2 / 1145 3.9 / TU 1741 1.0 / O	**10** 0016 4.0 / 0546 0.5 / TH 1223 4.4 / 1817 0.2	**25** 0007 3.7 / 0543 0.8 / F 1219 3.9 / 1807 0.6	**10** 0453 0.6 / 1126 4.2 / TH 1720 0.2 / ●	**25** 0449 0.8 / 1122 3.9 / F 1707 0.5 / O 2335 3.8	**10** 0012 3.9 / 0547 0.4 / SU 1224 4.1 / 1812 0.4	**25** 0512 0.4 / 1155 4.0 / M 1737 0.4
11 0514 0.7 / 1150 4.3 / TU 1743 0.4	**26** 0004 3.6 / 0543 1.1 / W 1216 3.9 / 1811 0.9	**11** 0100 4.0 / 0627 0.5 / F 1307 4.3 / 1901 0.2	**26** 0034 3.8 / 0609 0.6 / SA 1250 4.0 / 1836 0.6	**11** 0000 4.0 / 0530 0.4 / F 1206 4.3 / 1758 0.1	**26** 0513 0.7 / 1149 3.9 / SA 1734 0.4	**11** 0043 3.8 / 0625 0.5 / M 1302 4.0 / 1848 0.6	**26** 0007 4.0 / 0549 0.5 / TU 1237 3.9 / 1815 0.5
12 0028 4.1 / 0559 0.7 / W 1238 4.4 / 1832 0.4	**27** 0034 3.7 / 0610 1.0 / TH 1246 3.9 / 1840 0.8	**12** 0142 3.9 / 0710 0.6 / SA 1351 4.2 / 1945 0.4	**27** 0106 3.8 / 0640 0.7 / SU 1326 4.0 / 1910 0.7	**12** 0036 4.0 / 0607 0.4 / SA 1244 4.2 / 1836 0.2	**27** 0001 3.8 / 0539 0.5 / SU 1221 4.0 / 1804 0.4	**12** 0118 3.8 / 0706 0.6 / TU 1342 3.8 / 1926 0.8	**27** 0048 4.0 / 0631 0.5 / W 1323 3.9 / 1859 0.7
13 0118 4.0 / 0645 0.7 / TH 1327 4.3 / 1922 0.4	**28** 0105 3.7 / 0638 1.0 / F 1320 3.9 / 1910 0.8	**13** 0226 3.8 / 0755 0.7 / SU 1437 4.1 / 2031 0.6	**28** 0143 3.8 / 0716 0.7 / M 1405 3.9 / 1948 0.8	**13** 0111 3.9 / 0646 0.5 / SU 1324 4.1 / 1915 0.4	**28** 0034 3.9 / 0612 0.5 / M 1258 4.0 / 1839 0.5	**13** 0156 3.7 / 0751 0.7 / W 1426 3.7 / 2007 1.0	**28** 0134 3.9 / 0721 0.6 / TH 1414 3.8 / 1949 0.9
14 0210 4.0 / 0734 0.8 / F 1417 4.3 / 2014 0.5	**29** 0140 3.6 / 0710 1.0 / SA 1356 3.9 / 1944 0.8	**14** 0311 3.6 / 0844 0.9 / M 1526 3.9 / 2119 0.9		**14** 0148 3.8 / 0727 0.6 / M 1406 3.9 / 1956 0.6	**29** 0112 3.9 / 0650 0.5 / TU 1339 3.9 / 1919 0.6	**14** 0237 3.6 / 0841 0.9 / TH 1514 3.4 / 2053 1.3	**29** 0226 3.8 / 0819 0.7 / F 1511 3.6 / 2048 1.1
15 0302 3.8 / 0825 1.0 / SA 1510 4.1 / 2107 0.7	**30** 0218 3.6 / 0747 1.0 / SU 1436 3.9 / 2023 0.9	**15** 0401 3.5 / 0938 1.1 / TU 1619 3.7 / 2210 1.2		**15** 0228 3.7 / 0813 0.7 / TU 1451 3.8 / 2039 0.8	**30** 0154 3.8 / 0733 0.6 / W 1425 3.8 / 2005 0.8	**15** 0324 3.4 / 0938 1.1 / F 1611 3.2 / 2149 1.5	**30** 0324 3.7 / 0928 1.1 / SA 1619 3.5 / 2156 1.3
	31 0300 3.6 / 0829 1.0 / M 1519 3.8 / 2106 0.9				**31** 0241 3.7 / 0824 0.8 / TH 1516 3.7 / 2057 1.0		

Chart Datum: 0·20 metres above Ordnance Datum (Dublin)

》》 **FREE** monthly updates from 《《
www.reedsalmanac.co.uk

Chapter 5

331

TIDES

TIME ZONE (UT)
For Summer Time add ONE hour in **non-shaded areas**

IRELAND – DUBLIN (NORTH WALL)
LAT 53°21′N   LONG 6°13′W
TIMES AND HEIGHTS OF HIGH AND LOW WATERS

YEAR 2005

MAY

Day	Time	m	Day	Time	m
1 SU ☽	0432 / 1045 / 1739 / 2313	3.6 / 1.0 / 3.4 / 1.4	16 M ☾	0502 / 1115 / 1758 / 2330	3.3 / 1.3 / 3.1 / 1.7
2 M	0553 / 1205 / 1901	3.5 / 1.0 / 3.4	17 TU	0616 / 1217 / 1905	3.2 / 1.3 / 3.1
3 TU	0032 / 0712 / 1320 / 2012	1.4 / 3.6 / 0.9 / 3.5	18 W	0036 / 0720 / 1316 / 2000	1.6 / 3.3 / 1.2 / 3.2
4 W	0143 / 0821 / 1422 / 2112	1.3 / 3.7 / 0.7 / 3.6	19 TH	0134 / 0813 / 1404 / 2045	1.5 / 3.4 / 1.0 / 3.4
5 TH	0241 / 0919 / 1514 / 2202	1.1 / 3.9 / 0.6 / 3.7	20 F	0220 / 0857 / 1445 / 2122	1.3 / 3.6 / 0.9 / 3.6
6 F	0329 / 1010 / 1558 / 2245	0.9 / 4.0 / 0.5 / 3.8	21 SA	0258 / 0936 / 1522 / 2155	1.1 / 3.7 / 0.7 / 3.7
7 SA	0412 / 1053 / 1639 / 2320	0.7 / 4.0 / 0.5 / 3.8	22 SU	0334 / 1014 / 1558 / 2229	0.9 / 3.8 / 0.6 / 3.9
8 SU ●	0452 / 1132 / 1716 / 2351	0.7 / 4.0 / 0.6 / 3.8	23 M	0410 / 1054 / 1635 / ○ 2306	0.7 / 3.9 / 0.5 / 4.0
9 M	0531 / 1207 / 1751	0.6 / 3.9 / 0.7	24 TU	0450 / 1137 / 1715 / 2347	0.6 / 3.9 / 0.5 / 4.0
10 TU	0021 / 0609 / 1244 / 1825	3.8 / 0.7 / 3.8 / 0.8	25 W	0534 / 1223 / 1759	0.5 / 4.0 / 0.6
11 W	0055 / 0651 / 1324 / 1902	3.8 / 0.7 / 3.7 / 1.0	26 TH	0032 / 0622 / 1315 / 1846	4.1 / 0.5 / 3.9 / 0.8
12 TH	0133 / 0735 / 1406 / 1942	3.7 / 0.8 / 3.6 / 1.1	27 F	0123 / 0717 / 1410 / 1940	4.0 / 0.6 / 3.8 / 0.9
13 F	0214 / 0823 / 1453 / 2027	3.7 / 1.0 / 3.4 / 1.3	28 SA	0218 / 0819 / 1511 / 2040	4.0 / 0.7 / 3.7 / 1.1
14 SA	0300 / 0916 / 1545 / 2120	3.5 / 1.1 / 3.3 / 1.5	29 SU	0318 / 0926 / 1616 / 2145	3.9 / 0.8 / 3.6 / 1.2
15 SU ☾	0354 / 1014 / 1647 / 2222	3.4 / 1.2 / 3.1 / 1.6	30 M	0425 / 1035 / 1726 / ☽ 2253	3.8 / 0.8 / 3.5 / 1.3
			31 TU	0537 / 1144 / 1837	3.8 / 0.9 / 3.5

JUNE

Day	Time	m	Day	Time	m
1 W	0001 / 0647 / 1250 / 1942	1.3 / 3.8 / 0.9 / 3.5	16 TH	0610 / 1216 / 1854	3.4 / 1.2 / 3.3
2 TH	0108 / 0752 / 1352 / 2041	1.3 / 3.8 / 0.8 / 3.6	17 F	0030 / 0709 / 1309 / 1947	1.5 / 3.4 / 1.1 / 3.4
3 F	0209 / 0853 / 1446 / 2134	1.2 / 3.8 / 0.8 / 3.7	18 SA	0123 / 0805 / 1358 / 2035	1.4 / 3.5 / 1.0 / 3.5
4 SA	0303 / 0947 / 1535 / 2219	1.1 / 3.8 / 0.8 / 3.7	19 SU	0213 / 0857 / 1445 / 2120	1.2 / 3.6 / 0.9 / 3.7
5 SU	0352 / 1035 / 1618 / 2258	1.0 / 3.8 / 0.9 / 3.8	20 M	0301 / 0947 / 1531 / 2205	1.0 / 3.8 / 0.8 / 3.9
6 M ●	0436 / 1116 / 1657 / 2332	0.9 / 3.8 / 0.9 / 3.8	21 TU	0348 / 1037 / 1616 / 2249	0.8 / 3.9 / 0.7 / 4.0
7 TU	0518 / 1153 / 1733	0.9 / 3.7 / 1.0	22 W	0436 / 1126 / 1701 / ○ 2334	0.7 / 4.0 / 0.7 / 4.1
8 W	0003 / 0558 / 1229 / 1807	3.8 / 0.9 / 3.7 / 1.0	23 TH	0525 / 1216 / 1747	0.5 / 4.0 / 0.7
9 TH	0037 / 0638 / 1306 / 1843	3.8 / 0.9 / 3.6 / 1.1	24 F	0022 / 0616 / 1308 / 1835	4.2 / 0.5 / 4.0 / 0.8
10 F	0114 / 0720 / 1346 / 1920	3.8 / 0.9 / 3.5 / 1.2	25 SA	0113 / 0711 / 1402 / 1927	4.2 / 0.5 / 3.9 / 0.9
11 SA	0153 / 0804 / 1429 / 2001	3.8 / 1.0 / 3.5 / 1.3	26 SU	0207 / 0809 / 1459 / 2023	4.2 / 0.5 / 3.8 / 1.0
12 SU	0236 / 0850 / 1514 / 2046	3.7 / 1.1 / 3.4 / 1.4	27 M	0304 / 0910 / 1558 / 2122	4.1 / 0.6 / 3.7 / 1.1
13 M	0323 / 0939 / 1603 / 2137	3.6 / 1.1 / 3.3 / 1.5	28 TU	0405 / 1011 / 1659 / ☽ 2222	4.0 / 0.7 / 3.6 / 1.2
14 TU	0414 / 1030 / 1658 / 2234	3.5 / 1.2 / 3.2 / 1.5	29 W	0509 / 1112 / 1803 / 2325	3.9 / 0.9 / 3.5 / 1.3
15 W ☾	0510 / 1123 / 1756 / ☽ 2333	3.4 / 1.2 / 3.2 / 1.5	30 TH	0616 / 1215 / 1906	3.8 / 1.0 / 3.5

JULY

Day	Time	m	Day	Time	m
1 F	0030 / 0721 / 1318 / 2006	1.4 / 3.7 / 1.1 / 3.5	16 SA	0614 / 1215 / 1854	3.4 / 1.2 / 3.4
2 SA	0137 / 0825 / 1419 / 2103	1.4 / 3.7 / 1.2 / 3.6	17 SU	0030 / 0722 / 1317 / 1957	1.4 / 3.5 / 1.2 / 3.5
3 SU	0240 / 0924 / 1514 / 2154	1.3 / 3.7 / 1.2 / 3.7	18 M	0137 / 0830 / 1417 / 2055	1.3 / 3.6 / 1.1 / 3.6
4 M	0337 / 1017 / 1601 / 2237	1.2 / 3.6 / 1.2 / 3.7	19 TU	0239 / 0931 / 1513 / 2148	1.1 / 3.7 / 1.0 / 3.8
5 TU	0425 / 1102 / 1642 / 2313	1.1 / 3.6 / 1.2 / 3.8	20 W	0336 / 1026 / 1603 / 2236	0.9 / 3.9 / 0.9 / 4.0
6 W ●	0507 / 1139 / 1718 / ● 2346	1.0 / 3.6 / 1.1 / 3.8	21 TH	0429 / 1117 / 1650 / ○ 2323	0.6 / 4.0 / 0.7 / 4.2
7 TH	0546 / 1212 / 1751	1.0 / 3.6 / 1.1	22 F	0518 / 1206 / 1735	0.4 / 4.0 / 0.6
8 F	0018 / 0623 / 1246 / 1822	3.9 / 0.9 / 3.6 / 1.1	23 SA	0009 / 0606 / 1254 / 1820	4.3 / 0.3 / 4.0 / 0.6
9 SA	0052 / 0659 / 1321 / 1855	3.9 / 0.9 / 3.6 / 1.1	24 SU	0056 / 0656 / 1343 / 1907	4.3 / 0.3 / 4.0 / 0.7
10 SU	0128 / 0735 / 1358 / 1929	3.9 / 0.9 / 3.6 / 1.1	25 M	0146 / 0748 / 1434 / 1957	4.3 / 0.4 / 3.9 / 0.8
11 M	0207 / 0812 / 1438 / 2007	3.8 / 0.9 / 3.5 / 1.2	26 TU	0238 / 0842 / 1526 / 2050	4.2 / 0.5 / 3.7 / 1.0
12 TU	0248 / 0851 / 1520 / 2049	3.7 / 1.0 / 3.5 / 1.2	27 W	0332 / 0937 / 1621 / 2146	4.1 / 0.7 / 3.6 / 1.1
13 W	0332 / 0934 / 1606 / 2135	3.7 / 1.0 / 3.4 / 1.3	28 TH	0432 / 1033 / 1720 / ☽ 2247	3.9 / 1.0 / 3.5 / 1.3
14 TH	0420 / 1022 / 1656 / ☽ 2226	3.6 / 1.1 / 3.4 / 1.4	29 F	0538 / 1133 / 1824 / 2353	3.7 / 1.2 / 3.4 / 1.4
15 F	0513 / 1115 / 1752 / 2325	3.5 / 1.1 / 3.3 / 1.5	30 SA	0649 / 1240 / 1930	3.5 / 1.4 / 3.4
			31 SU	0108 / 0759 / 1354 / 2032	1.5 / 3.5 / 1.5 / 3.5

AUGUST

Day	Time	m	Day	Time	m
1 M	0226 / 0906 / 1458 / 2129	1.4 / 3.5 / 1.5 / 3.6	16 TU	0118 / 0816 / 1402 / 2038	1.4 / 3.4 / 1.3 / 3.6
2 TU	0328 / 1004 / 1547 / 2217	1.3 / 3.5 / 1.4 / 3.7	17 W	0232 / 0923 / 1504 / 2135	1.2 / 3.6 / 1.1 / 3.9
3 W	0416 / 1049 / 1627 / 2255	1.2 / 3.5 / 1.3 / 3.8	18 TH	0333 / 1019 / 1555 / 2224	0.8 / 3.8 / 0.8 / 4.1
4 TH	0454 / 1123 / 1700 / 2327	1.0 / 3.6 / 1.2 / 3.9	19 F	0423 / 1107 / 1639 / ○ 2309	0.5 / 4.0 / 0.7 / 4.3
5 F ●	0528 / 1153 / 1731 / ● 2357	0.9 / 3.6 / 1.1 / 3.9	20 SA	0508 / 1151 / 1720 / 2352	0.3 / 4.1 / 0.5 / 4.4
6 SA	0600 / 1222 / 1758	0.9 / 3.6 / 1.0	21 SU	0551 / 1234 / 1801	0.2 / 4.1 / 0.5
7 SU	0027 / 0628 / 1252 / 1825	3.9 / 0.8 / 3.6 / 1.0	22 M	0034 / 0634 / 1317 / 1843	4.4 / 0.2 / 4.0 / 0.5
8 M	0059 / 0657 / 1325 / 1855	3.9 / 0.8 / 3.7 / 1.0	23 TU	0119 / 0719 / 1401 / 1927	4.3 / 0.3 / 3.9 / 0.7
9 TU	0134 / 0728 / 1401 / 1929	3.9 / 0.8 / 3.7 / 1.0	24 W	0205 / 0807 / 1446 / 2016	4.2 / 0.5 / 3.7 / 0.8
10 W	0213 / 0804 / 1440 / 2008	3.9 / 0.9 / 3.6 / 1.0	25 TH	0255 / 0857 / 1535 / 2110	4.0 / 0.8 / 3.6 / 1.1
11 TH	0254 / 0846 / 1523 / 2051	3.8 / 1.0 / 3.6 / 1.1	26 F	0350 / 0950 / 1630 / ☽ 2210	3.8 / 1.1 / 3.5 / 1.3
12 F	0339 / 0932 / 1610 / 2140	3.7 / 1.1 / 3.5 / 1.3	27 SA	0457 / 1048 / 1738 / 2318	3.5 / 1.4 / 3.3 / 1.5
13 SA	0430 / 1025 / 1705 / ☽ 2238	3.5 / 1.3 / 3.4 / 1.4	28 SU	0617 / 1157 / 1851	3.3 / 1.6 / 3.3
14 SU	0533 / 1130 / 1812 / 2353	3.4 / 1.4 / 3.3 / 1.5	29 M	0041 / 0735 / 1328 / 2002	1.6 / 3.2 / 1.7 / 3.4
15 M	0654 / 1247 / 1929	3.3 / 1.4 / 3.4	30 TU	0214 / 0851 / 1441 / 2105	1.5 / 3.3 / 1.6 / 3.6
			31 W	0315 / 0950 / 1530 / 2155	1.3 / 3.4 / 1.5 / 3.7

Chart Datum: 0·20 metres above Ordnance Datum (Dublin)

》 **FREE** monthly updates from 《
www.reedsalmanac.co.uk

IRELAND – DUBLIN (NORTH WALL)

LAT 53°21′N LONG 6°13′W

YEAR 2005

TIMES AND HEIGHTS OF HIGH AND LOW WATERS

TIME ZONE (UT) For Summer Time add ONE hour in **non-shaded areas**

SEPTEMBER		OCTOBER		NOVEMBER		DECEMBER	
Time m	Time m	Time m	Time m	Time m	Time m	Time m	Time m
1 0358 1.1 / 1032 3.5 / TH 1607 1.3 / 2234 3.9	**16** 0326 0.7 / 1010 3.9 / F 1543 0.9 / 2210 4.2	**1** 0402 0.9 / 1034 3.7 / SA 1609 1.1 / 2238 3.9	**16** 0353 0.4 / 1038 4.0 / SU 1605 0.7 / 2237 4.3	**1** 0419 0.7 / 1053 3.9 / TU 1629 0.9 / 2302 4.0	**16** 0453 0.6 / 1133 4.0 / W 1709 0.7 / ○ 2342 4.1	**1** 0419 0.8 / 1055 4.0 / TH 1637 0.9 / ● 2317 4.0	**16** 0518 1.0 / 1154 4.0 / F 1742 0.9
2 0433 0.9 / 1103 3.6 / F 1638 1.1 / 2305 3.9	**17** 0412 0.4 / 1055 4.0 / SA 1624 0.6 / 2253 4.3	**2** 0430 0.7 / 1102 3.8 / SU 1636 0.9 / 2305 4.0	**17** 0434 0.3 / 1116 4.1 / M 1644 0.6 / ○ 2316 4.3	**2** 0446 0.7 / 1120 4.0 / W 1658 0.8 / ● 2334 4.0	**17** 0530 0.7 / 1207 4.0 / TH 1750 0.7	**2** 0456 0.7 / 1133 4.1 / F 1717 0.8	**17** 0013 3.8 / 0553 1.1 / SA 1229 4.0 / 1822 0.9
3 0502 0.8 / 1130 3.7 / SA 1705 1.0 / ● 2333 4.0	**18** 0453 0.2 / 1135 4.1 / SU 1702 0.5 / ○ 2333 4.4	**3** 0455 0.7 / 1126 3.8 / M 1700 0.8 / ● 2330 4.0	**18** 0511 0.3 / 1151 4.1 / TU 1722 0.5 / 2354 4.3	**3** 0517 0.7 / 1152 4.0 / TH 1732 0.8	**18** 0021 4.0 / 0606 0.9 / F 1243 4.0 / 1831 0.8	**3** 0000 4.0 / 0536 0.8 / SA 1215 4.1 / 1801 0.7	**18** 0050 3.7 / 0628 1.1 / SU 1305 4.0 / 1903 0.9
4 0529 0.7 / 1156 3.7 / SU 1730 0.9 / 2359 4.0	**19** 0532 0.1 / 1212 4.1 / M 1740 0.4	**4** 0519 0.6 / 1149 3.9 / TU 1725 0.8 / 2359 4.0	**19** 0548 0.4 / 1224 4.0 / W 1801 0.6	**4** 0012 4.0 / 0552 0.7 / F 1231 4.0 / 1810 0.8	**19** 0103 3.9 / 0644 1.0 / SA 1321 4.0 / 1916 0.9	**4** 0048 4.0 / 0621 0.9 / SU 1302 4.1 / 1851 0.7	**19** 0129 3.7 / 0705 1.2 / M 1343 3.9 / 1945 1.0
5 0554 0.7 / 1221 3.8 / M 1754 0.8	**20** 0012 4.4 / 0610 0.2 / TU 1249 4.0 / 1819 0.5	**5** 0545 0.6 / 1219 3.9 / W 1754 0.7	**20** 0034 4.2 / 0625 0.6 / TH 1301 4.0 / 1843 0.7	**5** 0055 4.0 / 0633 0.9 / SA 1315 4.0 / 1856 0.8	**20** 0146 3.7 / 0725 1.2 / SU 1404 3.9 / 2004 1.0	**5** 0140 3.9 / 0710 1.0 / M 1353 4.1 / 1946 0.8	**20** 0211 3.6 / 0745 1.3 / TU 1424 3.9 / 2028 1.1
6 0028 4.0 / 0619 0.7 / TU 1251 3.8 / 1822 0.8	**21** 0053 4.3 / 0650 0.4 / W 1328 3.9 / 1901 0.6	**6** 0033 4.0 / 0617 0.7 / TH 1255 3.9 / 1828 0.8	**21** 0116 4.0 / 0704 0.8 / F 1341 3.9 / 1929 0.8	**6** 0144 3.8 / 0720 1.1 / SU 1404 3.9 / 1949 1.0	**21** 0234 3.6 / 0811 1.4 / M 1450 3.8 / 2056 1.2	**6** 0237 3.8 / 0806 1.2 / TU 1449 4.0 / 2048 0.9	**21** 0255 3.5 / 0829 1.4 / W 1508 3.7 / 2114 1.1
7 0102 4.0 / 0649 0.7 / W 1326 3.8 / 1856 0.8	**22** 0137 4.1 / 0732 0.7 / TH 1409 3.8 / 1948 0.8	**7** 0112 4.0 / 0654 0.8 / F 1335 3.9 / 1909 0.8	**22** 0202 3.8 / 0747 1.1 / SA 1425 3.7 / 2020 1.0	**7** 0240 3.7 / 0816 1.3 / M 1459 3.8 / 2053 1.1	**22** 0328 3.4 / 0905 1.6 / TU 1543 3.6 / 2152 1.3	**7** 0339 3.7 / 0909 1.3 / W 1549 4.0 / 2153 0.9	**22** 0343 3.4 / 0918 1.5 / TH 1555 3.6 / 2202 1.2
8 0139 3.9 / 0725 1.0 / TH 1405 3.8 / 1934 0.9	**23** 0224 3.9 / 0818 1.0 / F 1454 3.7 / 2041 1.0	**8** 0156 3.8 / 0738 1.0 / SA 1420 3.8 / 1956 1.0	**23** 0253 3.6 / 0837 1.4 / SU 1515 3.6 / 2117 1.2	**8** 0346 3.5 / 0924 1.5 / TU 1601 3.7 / 2206 1.2	**23** 0432 3.2 / 1006 1.7 / W 1646 3.5 / ○ 2252 1.4	**8** 0447 3.6 / 1016 1.4 / TH 1654 3.9 / ○ 2301 1.0	**23** 0436 3.3 / 1013 1.6 / F 1646 3.5 / ○ 2254 1.3
9 0221 3.8 / 0807 1.2 / F 1447 3.7 / 2017 1.1	**24** 0316 3.6 / 0909 1.3 / SA 1546 3.5 / 2140 1.3	**9** 0247 3.7 / 0829 1.2 / SU 1511 3.7 / 2054 1.2	**24** 0355 3.3 / 0935 1.6 / M 1616 3.5 / 2222 1.4	**9** 0503 3.5 / 1040 1.6 / W 1714 3.7 / ○ 2326 1.2	**24** 0542 3.2 / 1113 1.8 / TH 1754 3.4 / 2356 1.4	**9** 0557 3.6 / 1125 1.5 / F 1802 3.9	**24** 0535 3.3 / 1113 1.7 / SA 1743 3.4 / 2350 1.4
10 0307 3.7 / 0854 1.5 / SA 1535 3.6 / 2108 1.2	**25** 0421 3.4 / 1008 1.6 / SU 1653 3.4 / ○ 2248 1.5	**10** 0347 3.5 / 0932 1.4 / M 1611 3.5 / ○ 2207 1.4	**25** 0511 3.2 / 1043 1.8 / TU 1733 3.4 / ○ 2334 1.5	**10** 0625 3.5 / 1158 1.6 / TH 1830 3.7	**25** 0648 3.2 / 1220 1.8 / F 1859 3.4	**10** 0010 1.0 / 0704 3.6 / SA 1233 1.4 / 1908 3.9	**25** 0637 3.3 / 1213 1.7 / SU 1844 3.4
11 0400 3.5 / 0951 1.3 / SU 1631 3.4 / ○ 2212 1.4	**26** 0544 3.2 / 1118 1.8 / M 1813 3.3	**11** 0504 3.3 / 1052 1.6 / TU 1726 3.5 / 2337 1.4	**26** 0631 3.1 / 1201 1.9 / W 1848 3.4	**11** 0043 1.1 / 0737 3.6 / F 1309 1.4 / 1939 3.8	**26** 0058 1.4 / 0745 3.3 / SA 1321 1.7 / 1954 3.5	**11** 0116 1.0 / 0806 3.7 / SU 1337 1.3 / 2013 3.9	**26** 0046 1.4 / 0733 3.4 / M 1310 1.6 / 1944 3.4
12 0509 3.3 / 1104 1.5 / M 1742 3.3 / 2339 1.5	**27** 0011 1.6 / 0708 3.1 / TU 1250 1.9 / 1928 3.4	**12** 0640 3.3 / 1213 1.6 / W 1852 3.5	**27** 0057 1.5 / 0743 3.2 / TH 1324 1.8 / 1952 3.5	**12** 0149 0.9 / 0839 3.7 / SA 1408 1.2 / 2040 4.0	**27** 0151 1.2 / 0834 3.5 / SU 1410 1.5 / 2041 3.6	**12** 0217 1.0 / 0903 3.8 / M 1436 1.2 / 2113 3.9	**27** 0140 1.3 / 0824 3.5 / TU 1403 1.5 / 2040 3.5
13 0643 3.3 / 1232 1.6 / TU 1910 3.4	**28** 0148 1.5 / 0828 3.2 / W 1413 1.7 / 2035 3.5	**13** 0106 1.2 / 0801 3.5 / TH 1337 1.4 / 2005 3.7	**28** 0203 1.3 / 0840 3.4 / F 1420 1.6 / 2046 3.6	**13** 0244 0.7 / 0931 3.9 / SU 1459 1.1 / 2134 4.1	**28** 0234 1.1 / 0914 3.6 / M 1450 1.4 / 2123 3.7	**13** 0310 1.0 / 0954 3.9 / TU 1529 1.1 / 2207 3.9	**28** 0230 1.2 / 0910 3.7 / W 1451 1.3 / 2132 3.7
14 0113 1.4 / 0811 3.4 / W 1353 1.4 / 2023 3.6	**29** 0248 1.3 / 0925 3.4 / TH 1502 1.5 / 2126 3.7	**14** 0216 0.9 / 0904 3.7 / F 1436 1.2 / 2104 4.0	**29** 0248 1.1 / 0923 3.6 / SA 1501 1.4 / 2128 3.8	**14** 0332 0.6 / 1017 4.0 / M 1545 1.0 / 2221 4.1	**29** 0311 1.0 / 0949 3.8 / TU 1525 1.2 / 2200 3.8	**14** 0358 1.0 / 1039 3.9 / W 1617 1.0 / 2254 3.9	**29** 0316 1.1 / 0954 3.8 / TH 1537 1.1 / 2220 3.8
15 0230 1.1 / 0918 3.6 / TH 1455 1.2 / 2122 3.9	**30** 0329 1.1 / 1003 3.6 / F 1539 1.3 / 2205 3.8	**15** 0309 0.6 / 0955 3.9 / SA 1523 0.9 / 2154 4.2	**30** 0323 0.9 / 0958 3.7 / SU 1533 1.2 / 2204 3.9	**15** 0414 0.6 / 1057 4.0 / TU 1628 0.8 / 2303 4.1	**30** 0345 0.9 / 1021 3.9 / W 1600 1.0 / 2238 3.9	**15** 0440 1.0 / 1119 3.9 / TH 1701 0.9 / ○ 2335 3.9	**30** 0400 1.0 / 1036 4.0 / F 1623 0.9 / 2307 3.9
			31 0352 0.8 / 1028 3.8 / M 1602 1.0 / 2234 3.9				**31** 0443 0.9 / 1119 4.1 / SA 1708 0.7 / ● 2353 4.0

Chart Datum: 0·20 metres above Ordnance Datum (Dublin)

>> FREE monthly updates from <<
www.reedsalmanac.co.uk

333

TIDES

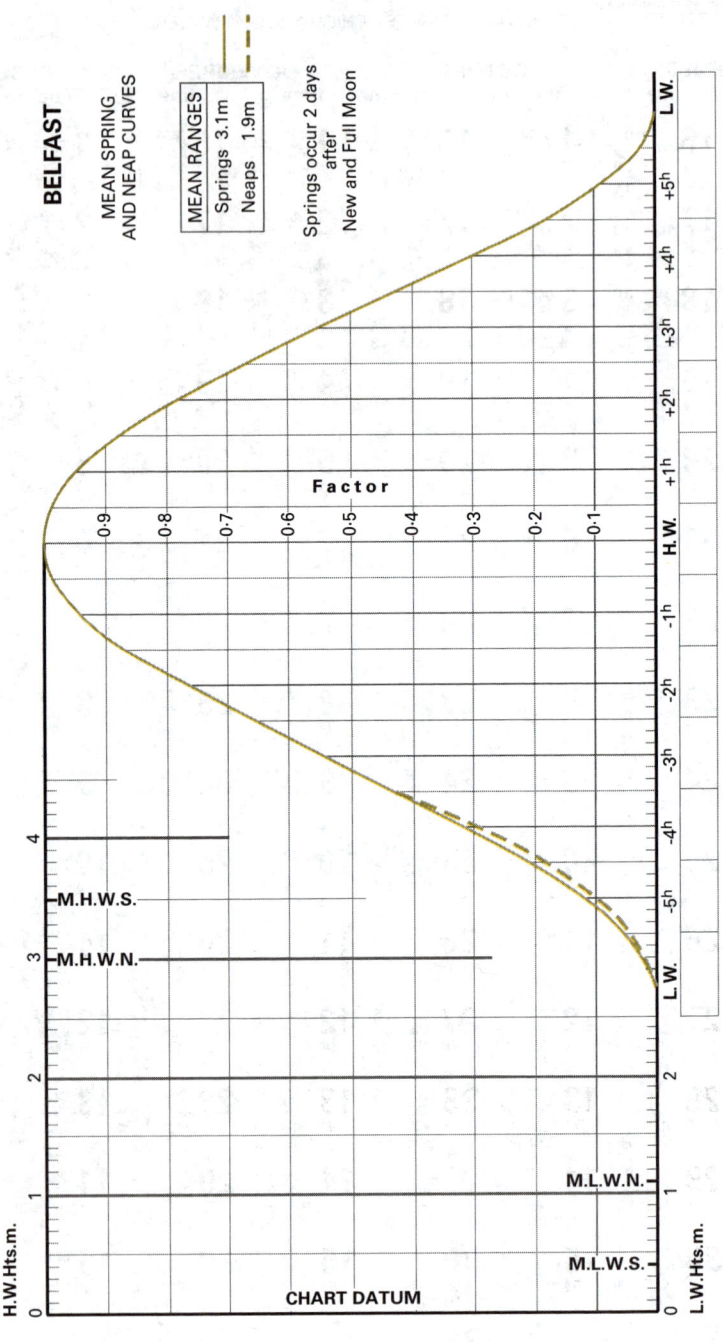

TIME ZONE (UT)
For Summer Time add ONE hour in **non-shaded areas**

NORTHERN IRELAND – BELFAST
LAT 54°36'N   LONG 5°55'W
TIMES AND HEIGHTS OF HIGH AND LOW WATERS

YEAR 2005

JANUARY

Time	m	Time	m
1 SA 0211 0817 1431 2040	3.0 1.0 3.4 0.8	**16** SU 0328 0910 1536 2158	3.1 0.8 3.5 0.5
2 SU 0255 0901 1513 2126	2.9 1.1 3.3 0.8	**17** M 0420 1003 1629 ☽2256	3.0 0.9 3.4 0.7
3 M 0346 0949 1602 ☾2220	2.9 1.1 3.3 0.9	**18** TU 0513 1104 1726 2359	3.0 1.0 3.2 0.9
4 TU 0442 1045 1659 2320	2.9 1.2 3.2 0.9	**19** W 0611 1212 1833	2.9 1.1 3.0
5 W 0542 1149 1803	2.9 1.2 3.2	**20** TH 0104 0715 1324 1947	1.0 2.9 1.2 3.0
6 TH 0024 0644 1301 1908	0.9 2.9 1.2 3.2	**21** F 0205 0818 1432 2053	1.0 3.0 1.1 3.0
7 F 0129 0747 1408 2012	0.8 3.1 1.0 3.3	**22** SA 0259 0914 1529 2145	1.0 3.1 1.0 3.0
8 SA 0227 0847 1506 2112	0.8 3.2 0.9 3.3	**23** SU 0344 1001 1613 2229	1.0 3.3 0.9 3.1
9 SU 0320 0942 1559 2208	0.7 3.3 0.7 3.4	**24** M 0422 1042 1649 2307	0.9 3.4 0.8 3.1
10 M 0411 1035 1651 ●2303	0.7 3.5 0.5 3.4	**25** TU 0457 1119 1720 ☉2340	0.9 3.5 0.8 3.1
11 TU 0501 1126 1742 2356	0.7 3.6 0.4 3.4	**26** W 0530 1153 1752	0.8 3.5 0.7
12 W 0552 1216 1832	0.7 3.7 0.3	**27** TH 0011 0604 1225 1824	3.1 0.8 3.5 0.7
13 TH 0050 0641 1307 1922	3.3 0.7 3.7 0.3	**28** F 0037 0637 1253 1856	3.0 0.8 3.5 0.6
14 F 0143 0731 1356 2012	3.3 0.7 3.7 0.3	**29** SA 0103 0711 1323 1930	3.0 0.8 3.5 0.6
15 SA 0236 0820 1446 2104	3.2 0.7 3.6 0.4	**30** SU 0136 0746 1358 2006	3.0 0.8 3.5 0.6
		31 M 0214 0824 1438 2047	3.0 0.8 3.4 0.6

FEBRUARY

Time	m	Time	m
1 TU 0259 0907 1524 2136	3.0 0.9 3.3 0.7	**16** W 0421 1015 1642 ●2308	3.0 0.9 3.0 1.0
2 W 0350 0959 1619 2234	2.9 1.0 3.2 0.9	**17** TH 0514 1128 1745	2.9 1.1 2.8
3 TH 0450 1104 1726 2344	2.9 1.1 3.1 1.0	**18** F 0021 0623 1249 1921	1.2 2.8 1.2 2.7
4 F 0600 1230 1840	2.8 1.2 3.0	**19** SA 0132 0749 1403 2039	1.2 2.9 1.1 2.8
5 SA 0105 0716 1355 1954	1.0 2.9 1.0 3.1	**20** SU 0233 0853 1507 2132	1.1 3.0 0.9 2.9
6 SU 0216 0829 1459 2103	0.9 3.1 0.8 3.2	**21** M 0322 0941 1551 2214	1.0 3.2 0.8 3.0
7 M 0314 0931 1554 2202	0.8 3.3 0.6 3.3	**22** TU 0401 1022 1626 2250	0.9 3.3 0.7 3.0
8 TU 0405 1024 1645 2254	0.7 3.4 0.4 3.3	**23** W 0436 1057 1657 2321	0.8 3.3 0.6 3.0
9 W 0454 1114 1733 2345	0.6 3.6 0.2 3.3	**24** TH 0509 1128 1729 ◯2346	0.7 3.4 0.5 3.0
10 TH 0540 1202 1819	0.6 3.6 0.2	**25** F 0542 1153 1800	0.7 3.4 0.5
11 F 0034 0625 1250 1903	3.3 0.6 3.7 0.2	**26** SA 0005 0613 1220 1829	3.0 0.6 3.4 0.5
12 SA 0122 0709 1336 1946	3.3 0.5 3.7 0.2	**27** SU 0030 0643 1252 1900	3.1 0.6 3.5 0.4
13 SU 0207 0751 1421 2029	3.2 0.6 3.6 0.4	**28** M 0103 0715 1328 1935	3.1 0.6 3.5 0.5
14 M 0251 0834 1505 2113	3.1 0.6 3.5 0.6		
15 TU 0334 0921 1550 2204	3.1 0.8 3.3 0.8		

MARCH

Time	m	Time	m
1 TU 0141 0752 1409 2014	3.1 0.6 3.4 0.6	**16** W 0252 0844 1515 2117	3.2 0.7 3.1 0.9
2 W 0223 0834 1456 2101	3.1 0.7 3.3 0.7	**17** TH 0336 0936 1604 ☽2216	3.1 0.9 2.9 1.1
3 TH 0312 0926 1552 2158	3.0 0.9 3.1 0.9	**18** F 0427 1049 1704 2338	2.9 1.1 2.7 1.3
4 F 0412 1033 1703 2311	2.9 1.1 2.9 1.1	**19** SA 0529 1214 1847	2.8 1.1 2.5
5 SA 0528 1220 1824	2.8 1.2 2.9	**20** SU 0054 0700 1327 2017	1.3 2.8 1.0 2.6
6 SU 0053 0656 1349 1948	1.1 2.8 0.9 2.9	**21** M 0159 0821 1430 2108	1.2 2.9 0.9 2.8
7 M 0211 0819 1452 2100	1.0 3.0 0.6 3.0	**22** TU 0252 0911 1517 2147	1.0 3.0 0.7 2.9
8 TU 0308 0921 1546 2154	0.8 3.2 0.4 3.2	**23** W 0334 0950 1554 2221	0.9 3.2 0.6 2.9
9 W 0357 1010 1633 2241	0.7 3.4 0.2 3.2	**24** TH 0410 1022 1627 2249	0.7 3.2 0.5 3.0
10 TH 0442 1057 1717 ●2326	0.5 3.5 0.1 3.3	**25** F 0444 1049 1659 ☉2310	0.7 3.3 0.4 3.0
11 F 0524 1142 1759	0.5 3.6 0.1	**26** SA 0516 1115 1730 2332	0.6 3.3 0.4 3.1
12 SA 0010 0546 1147 1759	3.3 0.5 3.4 0.4	**27** SU 0546 1147 1759	0.6 3.4 0.4
13 SU 0053 0643 1310 1915	3.3 0.5 3.6 0.3	**28** M 0001 0615 1223 1831	3.2 0.5 3.5 0.4
14 M 0133 0721 1351 1952	3.3 0.6 3.5 0.5	**29** TU 0036 0649 1304 1907	3.2 0.5 3.5 0.5
15 SA 0212 0801 1432 2031	3.2 0.6 3.4 0.7	**30** W 0115 0728 1348 1949	3.0 0.5 3.4 0.7
		31 TH 0159 0812 1438 2038	3.2 0.6 3.2 0.8

APRIL

Time	m	Time	m
1 F 0248 0907 1540 2137	3.1 0.8 3.0 1.0	**16** SA 0351 1016 1632 ●2256	3.0 1.0 2.6 1.3
2 SA 0351 1023 1656 ☽2254	2.9 1.0 2.8 1.2	**17** SU 0450 1137 1743	2.9 1.0 2.5
3 SU 0513 1219 1819	2.8 1.0 2.8	**18** M 0012 0557 1246 1932	1.3 2.8 1.0 2.6
4 M 0044 0646 1338 1946	1.2 2.9 0.7 2.9	**19** TU 0117 0716 1345 2026	1.2 2.8 0.9 2.7
5 TU 0158 0807 1440 2049	1.0 3.1 0.5 3.0	**20** W 0212 0818 1434 2104	1.1 2.9 0.7 2.8
6 W 0255 0904 1530 2137	0.8 3.3 0.3 3.2	**21** TH 0258 0900 1515 2136	0.9 3.1 0.6 2.9
7 TH 0343 0951 1615 2221	0.7 3.4 0.2 3.2	**22** F 0338 0935 1551 2204	0.8 3.2 0.5 3.0
8 F 0425 1035 1656 ●2303	0.6 3.5 0.2 3.3	**23** SA 0413 1008 1624 2232	0.7 3.2 0.4 3.1
9 SA 0504 1118 1734 2343	0.5 3.5 0.3 3.3	**24** SU 0446 1043 1656 ◯2303	0.6 3.4 0.4 3.2
10 SU 0542 1200 1809	0.5 3.5 0.4	**25** M 0518 1121 1740 2338	0.6 3.4 0.4 3.3
11 M 0022 0617 1242 1844	3.3 0.5 3.4 0.5	**26** TU 0552 1202 1807	0.5 3.5 0.5
12 TU 0101 0654 1322 1920	3.3 0.5 3.4 0.6	**27** W 0018 0630 1249 1848	3.3 0.5 3.4 0.6
13 W 0139 0733 1402 1958	3.3 0.5 3.3 0.8	**28** TH 0101 0714 1338 1935	3.4 0.5 3.3 0.7
14 TH 0218 0816 1445 2042	3.3 0.7 3.0 1.0	**29** F 0148 0804 1435 2028	3.3 0.6 3.2 0.9
15 F 0302 0906 1535 2138	3.2 0.9 2.8 1.2	**30** SA 0241 0906 1540 2131	3.2 0.8 3.0 1.1

Chart Datum: 2·01 metres below Ordnance Datum (Belfast)

FREE monthly updates from
www.reedsalmanac.co.uk

Chapter 5

TIDES

TIME ZONE (UT)
For Summer Time add ONE hour in **non-shaded areas**

NORTHERN IRELAND – BELFAST
LAT 54°36′N   LONG 5°55′W
TIMES AND HEIGHTS OF HIGH AND LOW WATERS

YEAR 2005

	MAY			JUNE			JULY			AUGUST	
	Time m	Time m		Time m	Time m		Time m	Time m		Time m	Time m
1 SU 0346 3.0 / 1032 0.8 / 1654 2.8 / ☽ 2250 1.2		**16** M 0415 3.0 / 1047 1.0 / 1703 2.6 / ☾ 2316 1.3	**1** W 0607 3.2 / 1245 0.5 / 1857 2.9		**16** TH 0523 3.0 / 1146 0.8 / 1811 2.8	**1** F 0017 1.0 / 0638 3.2 / 1310 0.7 / 1917 3.0		**16** SA 0531 3.1 / 1151 0.9 / 1812 2.9	**1** M 0205 1.0 / 0830 2.9 / 1436 1.0 / 2045 3.1		**16** TU 0124 1.1 / 0723 3.0 / 1347 1.0 / 1951 3.0
2 M 0506 3.0 / 1204 0.7 / 1815 2.8		**17** TU 0514 2.9 / 1153 0.9 / 1807 2.6	**2** TH 0055 1.0 / 0713 3.2 / 1345 0.5 / 1953 3.0		**17** F 0012 1.2 / 0621 3.0 / 1244 0.8 / 1904 2.9	**2** SA 0124 1.0 / 0743 3.1 / 1407 0.8 / 2013 3.0		**17** SU 0026 1.1 / 0637 3.1 / 1259 0.9 / 1913 3.0	**2** TU 0310 0.9 / 0927 3.0 / 1526 1.0 / 2135 3.2		**17** W 0234 0.9 / 0834 3.0 / 1448 0.9 / 2054 3.2
3 TU 0020 1.1 / 0632 3.0 / 1317 0.6 / 1927 2.9		**18** W 0022 1.2 / 0615 2.9 / 1253 0.9 / 1908 2.7	**3** F 0158 0.9 / 0812 3.3 / 1438 0.5 / 2043 3.1		**18** SA 0115 1.1 / 0719 3.1 / 1339 0.7 / 1955 3.0	**3** SU 0228 0.9 / 0844 3.1 / 1459 0.8 / 2105 3.1		**18** M 0140 1.1 / 0744 3.1 / 1402 0.8 / 2014 3.1	**3** W 0402 0.8 / 1013 3.0 / 1608 1.0 / 2218 3.3		**18** TH 0331 0.6 / 0934 3.2 / 1540 0.8 / 2148 3.4
4 W 0133 1.0 / 0744 3.1 / 1417 0.4 / 2024 3.1		**19** TH 0121 1.2 / 0714 3.0 / 1344 0.8 / 1959 2.8	**4** SA 0254 0.8 / 0905 3.3 / 1524 0.5 / 2129 3.2		**19** SU 0212 1.0 / 0815 3.2 / 1429 0.7 / 2045 3.1	**4** M 0325 0.9 / 0937 3.1 / 1545 0.8 / 2152 3.3		**19** TU 0244 0.9 / 0847 3.2 / 1458 0.7 / 2110 3.2	**4** TH 0442 0.8 / 1051 3.0 / 1643 0.9 / 2257 3.4		**19** F 0421 0.4 / 1026 3.3 / 1626 0.7 / ○ 2238 3.5
5 TH 0231 0.9 / 0840 3.3 / 1507 0.3 / 2112 3.1		**20** F 0212 1.0 / 0806 3.1 / 1429 0.6 / 2042 3.0	**5** SU 0343 0.8 / 0952 3.3 / 1606 0.6 / 2212 3.3		**20** M 0304 0.9 / 0907 3.3 / 1517 0.6 / 2132 3.2	**5** TU 0413 0.8 / 1023 3.1 / 1626 0.9 / 2235 3.3		**20** W 0340 0.7 / 0944 3.3 / 1550 0.7 / 2203 3.4	**5** F 0513 0.7 / 1126 3.0 / 1716 0.9 / ● 2331 3.4		**20** SA 0509 0.5 / 1115 3.3 / 1714 0.6 / 2326 3.6
6 F 0321 0.7 / 0928 3.4 / 1551 0.3 / 2156 3.2		**21** SA 0257 0.9 / 0852 3.2 / 1509 0.6 / 2122 3.1	**6** M 0427 0.7 / 1036 3.3 / 1645 0.7 / ● 2253 3.3		**21** TU 0353 0.7 / 0958 3.4 / 1603 0.6 / 2220 3.3	**6** W 0456 0.8 / 1103 3.1 / 1703 0.9 / ● 2314 3.4		**21** TH 0431 0.5 / 1037 3.3 / 1640 0.7 / ○ 2254 3.5	**6** SA 0541 0.7 / 1156 3.0 / 1749 0.9		**21** SU 0554 0.5 / 1203 3.3 / 1759 0.6
7 SA 0404 0.6 / 1013 3.5 / 1630 0.4 / 2237 3.3		**22** SU 0337 0.8 / 0934 3.3 / 1546 0.5 / 2200 3.2	**7** TU 0507 0.7 / 1117 3.2 / 1722 0.9 / 2332 3.4		**22** W 0440 0.6 / 1049 3.4 / 1650 0.6 / ○ 2309 3.4	**7** TH 0532 0.8 / 1141 3.1 / 1738 0.9 / 2352 3.4		**22** F 0521 0.4 / 1129 3.3 / 1729 0.6 / 2344 3.5	**7** SU 0003 3.4 / 0610 0.7 / 1223 3.0 / 1821 0.8		**22** M 0014 3.7 / 0637 0.2 / 1251 3.2 / 1842 0.6
8 SU 0444 0.6 / 1055 3.4 / 1708 0.5 / ● 2317 3.3		**23** M 0415 0.7 / 1017 3.4 / 1625 0.5 / ○ 2240 3.3	**8** W 0545 0.7 / 1156 3.2 / 1758 0.9		**23** TH 0529 0.5 / 1140 3.4 / 1740 0.6 / 2358 3.5	**8** F 0604 0.7 / 1216 3.0 / 1813 0.9		**23** SA 0610 0.3 / 1222 3.3 / 1818 0.6	**8** M 0033 3.4 / 0640 0.6 / 1248 3.0 / 1854 0.8		**23** TU 0103 3.7 / 0720 0.2 / 1338 3.2 / 1926 0.6
9 M 0522 0.6 / 1136 3.4 / 1743 0.6 / 2356 3.4		**24** TU 0455 0.6 / 1102 3.4 / 1706 0.5 / 2323 3.4	**9** TH 0011 3.4 / 0620 0.8 / 1234 3.1 / 1834 1.0		**24** F 0619 0.4 / 1234 3.3 / 1831 0.7	**9** SA 0029 3.5 / 0635 0.7 / 1251 3.0 / 1848 0.9		**24** SU 0035 3.6 / 0659 0.2 / 1315 3.3 / 1907 0.6	**9** TU 0102 3.4 / 0711 0.6 / 1318 3.0 / 1928 0.8		**24** W 0149 3.6 / 0802 0.2 / 1423 3.2 / 2010 0.6
10 TU 0558 0.6 / 1216 3.3 / 1818 0.7		**25** W 0537 0.5 / 1150 3.4 / 1750 0.6	**10** F 0050 3.5 / 0656 0.8 / 1314 3.0 / 1912 1.0		**25** SA 0049 3.5 / 0710 0.3 / 1329 3.3 / 1923 0.7	**10** SU 0105 3.4 / 0709 0.7 / 1325 2.9 / 1925 0.9		**25** M 0126 3.6 / 0747 0.2 / 1407 3.2 / 1955 0.6	**10** W 0136 3.4 / 0745 0.6 / 1354 3.0 / 2004 0.8		**25** TH 0235 3.5 / 0845 0.3 / 1508 3.2 / 2056 0.7
11 W 0033 3.4 / 0634 0.7 / 1256 3.2 / 1854 0.9		**26** TH 0008 3.4 / 0622 0.5 / 1242 3.4 / 1838 0.7	**11** SA 0130 3.4 / 0734 0.8 / 1355 2.9 / 1953 1.0		**26** SU 0140 3.5 / 0804 0.3 / 1426 3.2 / 2016 0.8	**11** M 0139 3.4 / 0744 0.7 / 1402 2.9 / 2003 0.9		**26** TU 0215 3.6 / 0836 0.3 / 1458 3.2 / 2044 0.7	**11** TH 0213 3.4 / 0822 0.6 / 1436 3.0 / 2045 0.9		**26** F 0322 3.3 / 0935 0.6 / 1554 3.0 / ☽ 2150 0.9
12 TH 0112 3.4 / 0711 0.7 / 1336 3.1 / 1934 1.0		**27** F 0056 3.4 / 0711 0.5 / 1336 3.3 / 1929 0.8	**12** SU 0210 3.4 / 0815 0.8 / 1439 2.9 / 2037 1.0		**27** M 0234 3.5 / 0901 0.4 / 1525 3.1 / 2112 0.8	**12** TU 0214 3.4 / 0822 0.7 / 1441 2.9 / 2044 0.9		**27** W 0305 3.5 / 0927 0.3 / 1549 3.1 / 2135 0.8	**12** F 0256 3.3 / 0907 0.7 / 1524 2.9 / 2133 1.0		**27** SA 0414 3.1 / 1037 1.0 / 1647 2.9 / 2300 1.1
13 F 0152 3.4 / 0754 0.8 / 1420 3.0 / 2018 1.1		**28** SA 0146 3.4 / 0807 0.6 / 1434 3.1 / 2025 0.9	**13** M 0251 3.3 / 0901 0.9 / 1529 2.8 / 2124 1.1		**28** TU 0330 3.4 / 1002 0.4 / 1624 3.0 / ☽ 2210 0.9	**13** W 0252 3.4 / 0904 0.7 / 1527 2.9 / 2128 0.9		**28** TH 0357 3.4 / 1023 0.5 / 1641 3.0 / ☽ 2232 0.9	**13** SA 0348 3.2 / 1000 0.9 / 1621 2.9 / ☽ 2231 1.1		**28** SU 0516 2.9 / 1153 1.2 / 1751 2.9
14 SA 0235 3.3 / 0842 0.8 / 1508 2.8 / 2108 1.2		**29** SU 0241 3.3 / 0912 0.7 / 1538 3.0 / 2127 1.0	**14** TU 0336 3.2 / 0951 0.9 / 1622 2.8 / 2215 1.1		**29** W 0430 3.3 / 1104 0.5 / 1722 2.9 / 2311 0.9	**14** TH 0337 3.3 / 0953 0.8 / 1618 2.9 / ☾ 2218 1.1		**28** F 0453 3.2 / 1126 0.7 / 1736 3.0 / 2339 1.0	**14** SU 0452 3.1 / 1105 1.0 / 1728 2.9 / 2349 1.2		**29** M 0021 1.1 / 0652 2.9 / 1307 1.0 / 1914 3.0
15 SU 0322 3.2 / 0939 0.9 / 1603 2.7 / 2208 1.2		**30** M 0343 3.2 / 1025 0.6 / 1646 2.9 / ☽ 2236 1.0	**15** W 0427 3.1 / 1047 0.9 / 1717 2.8 / ☾ 2311 1.2		**30** TH 0533 3.2 / 1207 0.6 / 1820 3.0	**15** F 0427 3.2 / 1047 0.9 / 1713 2.8 / ☾ 2316 1.1		**30** SA 0558 3.0 / 1233 1.1 / 1840 2.9	**15** M 0607 3.0 / 1225 1.1 / 1840 2.9		**30** TU 0140 1.1 / 0819 3.0 / 1412 1.0 / 2024 3.1
		31 TU 0454 3.2 / 1138 0.6 / 1755 2.9 / 2347 1.0						**31** SU 0052 1.1 / 0715 2.9 / 1338 1.0 / 1944 3.0			**31** W 0252 1.0 / 0913 3.1 / 1505 1.1 / 2115 3.2

Chart Datum: 2·01 metres below Ordnance Datum (Belfast)

》》 **FREE** monthly updates from 《《
www.reedsalmanac.co.uk

TIME ZONE (UT)
For Summer Time add ONE hour in **non-shaded areas**

NORTHERN IRELAND – BELFAST
LAT 54°36'N   LONG 5°55'W
TIMES AND HEIGHTS OF HIGH AND LOW WATERS

YEAR 2005

SEPTEMBER

Day	Time m	Time m	Day	Time m	Time m
1 TH	0342 0.8 / 0956 3.0 / 1546 1.0 / 2157 3.3		16 F	0319 0.5 / 0924 3.2 / 1528 0.8 / 2133 3.5	
2 F	0417 0.7 / 1032 3.0 / 1620 0.9 / 2233 3.4		17 SA	0406 0.3 / 1011 3.3 / 1612 0.7 / 2220 3.6	
3 SA	0445 0.7 / 1103 3.0 / 1652 0.8 / ● 2303 3.4		18 SU	0450 0.2 / 1055 3.4 / 1654 0.6 / ○ 2306 3.7	
4 SU	0513 0.6 / 1129 3.0 / 1723 0.8 / 2329 3.4		19 M	0531 0.2 / 1139 3.4 / 1735 0.6 / 2351 3.7	
5 M	0541 0.6 / 1149 3.1 / 1753 0.8 / 2355 3.5		20 TU	0610 0.3 / 1223 3.4 / 1815 0.6	
6 TU	0609 0.6 / 1211 3.1 / 1823 0.8		21 W	0037 3.7 / 0647 0.4 / 1306 3.4 / 1855 0.6	
7 W	0026 3.5 / 0637 0.6 / 1242 3.2 / 1853 0.7		22 TH	0121 3.6 / 0726 0.6 / 1347 3.4 / 1937 0.7	
8 TH	0102 3.5 / 0709 0.6 / 1318 3.2 / 1929 0.8		23 F	0205 3.4 / 0806 0.8 / 1429 3.3 / 2022 0.8	
9 F	0141 3.5 / 0747 0.7 / 1358 3.2 / 2010 0.8		24 SA	0250 3.2 / 0852 1.0 / 1513 3.2 / 2114 0.9	
10 SA	0225 3.3 / 0831 0.8 / 1444 3.1 / 2058 1.0		25 SU	0341 3.0 / 0949 1.2 / 1604 3.1 / ◐ 2225 1.1	
11 SU	0317 3.2 / 0925 1.0 / 1541 3.0 / ◐ 2159 1.1		26 M	0441 2.8 / 1112 1.4 / 1706 2.9 / 2349 1.2	
12 M	0427 3.0 / 1031 1.2 / 1654 2.9 / 2327 1.2		27 TU	0622 2.6 / 1230 1.4 / 1827 2.9	
13 TU	0549 2.9 / 1201 1.3 / 1818 2.9		28 W	0104 1.1 / 0756 2.7 / 1338 1.3 / 1952 3.0	
14 W	0116 1.1 / 0712 2.9 / 1338 1.2 / 1937 3.0		29 TH	0213 1.0 / 0848 2.8 / 1434 1.2 / 2045 3.1	
15 TH	0224 0.9 / 0829 3.0 / 1439 1.0 / 2042 3.3		30 F	0304 0.9 / 0929 2.9 / 1517 1.0 / 2126 3.2	

OCTOBER

Day	Time m	Time m	Day	Time m	Time m
1 SA	0340 0.7 / 1003 3.0 / 1553 0.9 / 2200 3.3		16 SU	0345 0.4 / 0950 3.4 / 1553 0.7 / 2201 3.6	
2 SU	0411 0.7 / 1032 3.1 / 1625 0.9 / 2228 3.4		17 M	0426 0.4 / 1033 3.4 / 1632 0.7 / ○ 2245 3.7	
3 M	0441 0.6 / 1055 3.1 / 1655 0.8 / 2254 3.4		18 TU	0504 0.4 / 1114 3.5 / 1711 0.6 / 2329 3.7	
4 TU	0508 0.6 / 1116 3.2 / 1724 0.8 / 2323 3.5		19 W	0541 0.5 / 1156 3.5 / 1750 0.6	
5 W	0535 0.6 / 1142 3.3 / 1753 0.7 / 2357 3.5		20 TH	0013 3.6 / 0617 0.7 / 1237 3.5 / 1829 0.7	
6 TH	0605 0.6 / 1214 3.3 / 1825 0.7		21 F	0056 3.5 / 0655 0.8 / 1317 3.5 / 1911 0.7	
7 F	0035 3.5 / 0640 0.7 / 1251 3.4 / 1902 0.8		22 SA	0139 3.3 / 0736 1.0 / 1358 3.5 / 1956 0.8	
8 SA	0118 3.5 / 0720 0.8 / 1332 3.3 / 1945 0.8		23 SU	0224 3.2 / 0821 1.1 / 1442 3.4 / 2048 1.0	
9 SU	0205 3.4 / 0807 0.9 / 1420 3.2 / 2037 1.0		24 M	0314 3.0 / 0916 1.3 / 1532 3.2 / 2154 1.1	
10 M	0303 3.1 / 0902 1.1 / 1518 3.1 / ◐ 2144 1.1		25 TU	0412 2.8 / 1031 1.5 / 1629 3.1 / 2311 1.2	
11 TU	0419 2.9 / 1012 1.3 / 1635 3.0 / 2326 1.1		26 W	0523 2.6 / 1147 1.5 / 1736 3.0	
12 W	0541 2.8 / 1146 1.4 / 1803 3.0		27 TH	0020 1.1 / 0710 2.7 / 1253 1.4 / 1851 3.0	
13 TH	0101 1.0 / 0706 2.9 / 1321 1.2 / 1924 3.1		28 F	0122 1.0 / 0806 2.8 / 1351 1.3 / 1955 3.1	
14 F	0207 0.7 / 0815 3.1 / 1421 1.0 / 2026 3.3		29 SA	0214 0.9 / 0847 2.9 / 1439 1.2 / 2041 3.2	
15 SA	0259 0.5 / 0906 3.2 / 1510 0.9 / 2116 3.5		30 SU	0256 0.8 / 0922 3.1 / 1518 1.0 / 2119 3.3	
			31 M	0332 0.7 / 0952 3.2 / 1553 0.9 / 2152 3.4	

NOVEMBER

Day	Time m	Time m	Day	Time m	Time m
1 TU	0404 0.7 / 1021 3.3 / 1625 0.9 / 2225 3.5		16 W	0439 0.6 / 1052 3.5 / 1653 0.7 / ○ 2311 3.6	
2 W	0434 0.7 / 1050 3.3 / 1656 0.8 / ● 2300 3.5		17 TH	0517 0.8 / 1133 3.6 / 1733 0.7 / 2354 3.5	
3 TH	0506 0.7 / 1121 3.4 / 1730 0.8 / 2339 3.5		18 F	0555 0.9 / 1214 3.6 / 1813 0.8	
4 F	0541 0.7 / 1157 3.5 / 1807 0.7		19 SA	0036 3.4 / 0634 1.0 / 1255 3.6 / 1854 0.8	
5 SA	0021 3.5 / 0621 0.8 / 1238 3.5 / 1848 0.7		20 SU	0118 3.2 / 0715 1.1 / 1336 3.6 / 1938 0.9	
6 SU	0108 3.4 / 0705 0.9 / 1322 3.5 / 1936 0.8		21 M	0202 3.1 / 0759 1.2 / 1419 3.5 / 2025 1.0	
7 M	0201 3.3 / 0756 1.0 / 1412 3.3 / 2032 0.9		22 TU	0250 3.0 / 0848 1.3 / 1505 3.3 / 2119 1.0	
8 TU	0303 3.1 / 0854 1.2 / 1512 3.2 / 2144 1.0		23 W	0343 2.8 / 0944 1.4 / 1557 3.2 / ◐ 2220 1.1	
9 W	0405 3.0 / 1004 1.3 / 1625 3.1 / ● 2314 1.0		24 TH	0442 2.7 / 1047 1.4 / 1654 3.1 / 2323 1.1	
10 TH	0533 2.9 / 1126 1.3 / 1748 3.1		25 F	0546 2.7 / 1153 1.4 / 1755 3.0	
11 F	0033 0.9 / 0647 3.0 / 1247 1.2 / 1902 3.2		26 SA	0023 1.1 / 0649 2.8 / 1254 1.4 / 1854 3.0	
12 SA	0138 0.7 / 0749 3.1 / 1351 1.1 / 2003 3.4		27 SU	0118 1.0 / 0745 2.9 / 1348 1.3 / 1949 3.1	
13 SU	0232 0.6 / 0841 3.3 / 1444 0.9 / 2055 3.5		28 M	0206 0.9 / 0831 3.0 / 1436 1.1 / 2037 3.2	
14 M	0318 0.6 / 0927 3.4 / 1530 0.8 / 2143 3.6		29 TU	0248 0.8 / 0913 3.2 / 1518 1.0 / 2121 3.3	
15 TU	0400 0.6 / 1010 3.5 / 1612 0.8 / 2227 3.6		30 W	0327 0.8 / 0951 3.3 / 1557 0.9 / 2202 3.4	

DECEMBER

Day	Time m	Time m	Day	Time m	Time m
1 TH	0405 0.8 / 1029 3.4 / 1636 0.8 / ● 2244 3.5		16 F	0502 0.9 / 1118 3.6 / 1725 0.8 / 2341 3.3	
2 F	0445 0.8 / 1108 3.5 / 1717 0.7 / 2329 3.5		17 SA	0541 1.0 / 1158 3.6 / 1805 0.8	
3 SA	0527 0.8 / 1149 3.5 / 1800 0.7 / 2342 3.6		18 SU	0021 3.2 / 0619 1.0 / 1238 3.6 / 1842 0.8	
4 SU	0016 3.5 / 0612 0.8 / 1234 3.5 / 1846 0.6		19 M	0101 3.1 / 0657 1.1 / 1318 3.6 / 1920 0.8	
5 M	0106 3.4 / 0700 0.9 / 1320 3.6 / 1937 0.6		20 TU	0141 3.0 / 0736 1.1 / 1357 3.5 / 1959 0.8	
6 TU	0201 3.3 / 0753 1.0 / 1411 3.5 / 2033 0.7		21 W	0223 3.0 / 0817 1.1 / 1438 3.5 / 2042 0.9	
7 W	0300 3.1 / 0849 1.1 / 1507 3.4 / 2138 0.7		22 TH	0309 2.9 / 0901 1.2 / 1521 3.4 / 2128 1.0	
8 TH	0405 3.0 / 0950 1.1 / 1613 3.3 / ◐ 2248 0.7		23 F	0359 2.6 / 0949 1.2 / 1608 3.2 / ◐ 2219 1.0	
9 F	0513 3.0 / 1057 1.1 / 1724 3.3 / 2358 0.7		24 SA	0452 2.8 / 1043 1.3 / 1701 3.1 / 2316 1.0	
10 SA	0618 3.0 / 1207 1.1 / 1833 3.3		25 SU	0547 2.8 / 1144 1.3 / 1758 3.1	
11 SU	0103 0.7 / 0718 3.1 / 1315 1.1 / 1936 3.3		26 M	0016 1.0 / 0644 2.9 / 1250 1.3 / 1857 3.1	
12 M	0201 0.7 / 0813 3.3 / 1417 1.0 / 2034 3.4		27 TU	0116 1.0 / 0741 3.0 / 1352 1.2 / 1957 3.1	
13 TU	0253 0.7 / 0904 3.4 / 1511 0.9 / 2126 3.4		28 W	0211 0.9 / 0836 3.1 / 1447 1.1 / 2052 3.2	
14 W	0339 0.8 / 0951 3.5 / 1559 0.8 / 2214 3.4		29 TH	0301 0.8 / 0925 3.2 / 1537 1.0 / 2143 3.3	
15 TH	0422 0.8 / 1036 3.5 / 1644 0.8 / ○ 2259 3.4		30 F	0347 0.8 / 1011 3.3 / 1623 0.8 / 2231 3.4	
			31 SA	0433 0.8 / 1055 3.4 / 1709 0.6 / ● 2320 3.4	

Chart Datum: 2·01 metres below Ordnance Datum (Belfast)

》 **FREE** monthly updates from 《
www.reedsalmanac.co.uk

TIDES

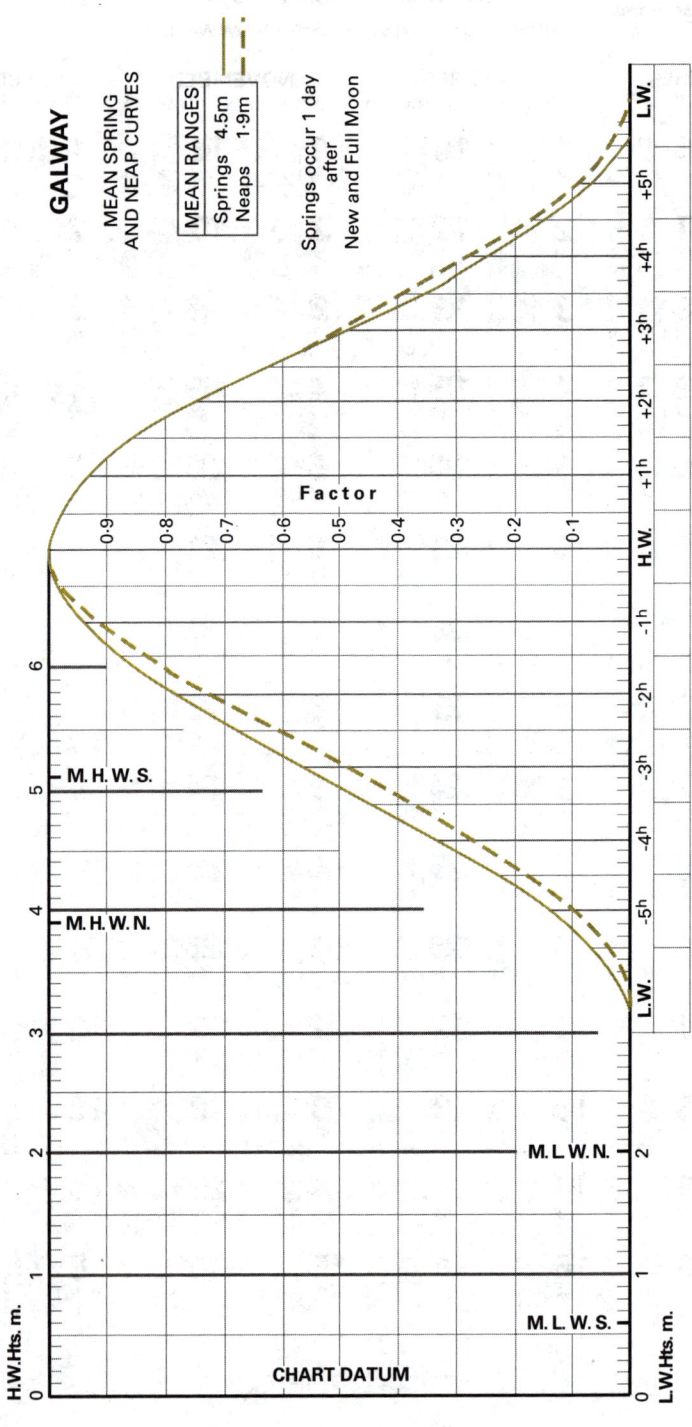

TIME ZONE (UT)
For Summer Time add ONE hour in **non-shaded areas**

IRELAND – GALWAY
LAT 53°16'N LONG 9°03'W
TIMES AND HEIGHTS OF HIGH AND LOW WATERS

YEAR 2005

JANUARY		FEBRUARY		MARCH		APRIL	
Time m	Time m	Time m	Time m	Time m	Time m	Time m	Time m
1 0202 1.7 0833 4.4 SA 1431 1.4 2112 4.2	**16** 0251 1.3 0926 4.6 SU 1514 1.1 2204 4.2	**1** 0258 1.5 0915 4.3 TU 1521 1.4 2201 4.1	**16** 0403 1.7 1032 3.9 W 1616 1.9 ◐ 2310 3.7	**1** 0148 0.9 0805 4.6 TU 1407 1.0 2028 4.4	**16** 0231 1.3 0902 4.2 W 1439 1.5 2119 4.0	**1** 0255 1.4 0924 4.0 F 1515 1.8 2157 3.9	**16** 0418 2.0 1022 3.5 SA 1622 2.4 ◐ 2243 3.5
2 0246 1.8 0913 4.3 SU 1514 1.5 2200 4.1	**17** 0348 1.6 1022 4.3 M 1609 1.5 ◐ 2304 4.0	**2** 0348 1.7 1008 4.2 W 1613 1.6 ◐ 2259 4.0	**17** 0521 2.0 1138 3.6 TH 1739 2.2	**2** 0228 1.2 0840 4.4 W 1448 1.3 2112 4.1	**17** 0322 1.7 0949 3.8 TH 1525 2.0 2212 3.7	**2** 0359 1.7 1045 3.8 SA 1629 2.1 ◐ 2323 3.8	**17** 0541 2.0 1154 3.4 SU 1807 2.4
3 0335 1.9 1000 4.2 M 1603 1.7 ◐ 2252 4.0	**18** 0455 1.8 1122 4.0 TU 1715 1.8	**3** 0448 1.9 1113 4.0 TH 1716 1.8	**18** 0031 3.5 0646 2.1 F 1311 3.5 1920 2.2	**3** 0316 1.5 0933 4.1 TH 1538 1.7 ◐ 2218 3.9	**18** 0445 2.0 1052 3.5 F 1657 2.3 2329 3.4	**3** 0535 1.8 1217 3.7 SU 1851 2.1	**18** 0058 3.5 0648 1.9 M 1344 3.5 1915 2.1
4 0433 2.0 1052 4.2 TU 1701 1.7 2347 4.1	**19** 0007 3.9 0609 2.0 W 1228 3.9 1837 2.0	**4** 0005 3.9 0603 1.9 F 1229 3.9 1845 1.9	**19** 0210 3.6 0807 2.0 SA 1441 3.6 2034 2.0	**4** 0416 1.8 1049 3.8 F 1644 2.0 2336 3.8	**19** 0614 2.1 1243 3.3 SA 1845 2.3	**4** 0058 3.9 0726 1.6 M 1356 4.0 2002 1.7	**19** 0208 3.7 0747 1.7 TU 1437 3.8 2008 1.8
5 0539 2.0 1151 4.1 W 1810 1.8	**20** 0118 3.9 0722 2.0 TH 1342 3.8 1954 2.0	**5** 0121 4.0 0738 1.8 SA 1358 4.0 2019 1.7	**20** 0310 3.9 0906 1.7 SU 1533 3.9 2118 1.5	**5** 0537 1.9 1216 3.7 SA 1840 2.1	**20** 0148 3.5 0734 2.0 SU 1425 3.5 2004 2.1	**5** 0216 4.3 0828 1.2 TU 1456 4.4 2052 1.3	**20** 0252 3.9 0834 1.4 W 1514 4.1 2050 1.5
6 0047 4.2 0651 1.9 TH 1300 4.2 1926 1.7	**21** 0226 4.0 0826 1.8 F 1449 3.9 2049 1.8	**6** 0235 4.3 0850 1.4 SU 1512 4.3 2117 1.3	**21** 0352 4.1 0947 1.4 M 1613 4.1 2154 1.4	**6** 0106 3.9 0736 1.7 SU 1401 3.9 2018 1.7	**21** 0248 3.7 0838 1.7 M 1513 3.8 2051 1.8	**6** 0310 4.7 0915 0.8 W 1541 4.7 2134 0.9	**21** 0329 4.2 0913 1.1 TH 1548 4.4 2128 1.1
7 0151 4.3 0759 1.6 F 1414 4.3 2029 1.4	**22** 0319 4.1 0917 1.7 SA 1540 4.0 2131 1.7	**7** 0334 4.6 0944 0.9 M 1608 4.6 2206 0.9	**22** 0429 4.3 1021 1.1 TU 1649 4.3 2229 1.1	**7** 0230 4.2 0846 1.3 M 1511 4.3 2111 1.3	**22** 0329 4.0 0917 1.3 TU 1549 4.1 2127 1.4	**7** 0355 5.0 0956 0.5 TH 1622 5.0 2214 0.5	**22** 0403 4.4 0949 0.8 F 1620 4.6 2203 0.9
8 0249 4.6 0856 1.3 SA 1517 4.5 2121 1.2	**23** 0402 4.2 1001 1.4 SU 1624 4.2 2209 1.5	**8** 0426 5.0 1032 0.5 TU 1657 4.9 ● 2251 0.6	**23** 0505 4.5 1055 0.8 W 1723 4.5 2303 0.9	**8** 0327 4.6 0936 0.8 TU 1600 4.6 2154 0.9	**23** 0405 4.3 0951 1.0 W 1623 4.4 2202 1.1	**8** 0438 5.2 1035 0.3 F 1702 5.1 ● 2253 0.4	**23** 0436 4.6 1023 0.7 SA 1651 4.8 2238 0.7
9 0342 4.9 0948 1.0 SU 1612 4.8 2210 1.0	**24** 0441 4.4 1040 1.2 M 1703 4.3 2246 1.3	**9** 0515 5.2 1116 0.2 W 1744 5.1 2334 0.4	**24** 0539 4.7 TH 1757 4.7 ○ 2337 0.7	**9** 0415 5.0 1018 0.4 W 1644 4.9 2235 0.5	**24** 0439 4.5 1024 0.7 TH 1656 4.6 2236 0.8	**9** 0520 5.3 1112 0.3 SA 1740 5.2 2332 0.3	**24** 0509 4.8 1055 0.6 SU 1723 5.0 ○ 2311 0.5
10 0432 5.1 1037 0.7 M 1704 5.0 ● 2258 0.8	**25** 0518 4.5 1117 1.0 TU 1741 4.5 ○ 2322 1.2	**10** 0601 5.4 1158 0.1 TH 1828 5.1	**25** 0611 4.8 1159 0.5 F 1830 4.7	**10** 0500 5.2 1058 0.2 TH 1726 5.1 ● 2316 0.3	**25** 0512 4.7 1057 0.5 F 1729 4.8 ○ 2309 0.6	**10** 0601 5.2 1148 0.4 SU 1818 5.1	**25** 0543 4.9 1128 0.5 M 1755 5.0 2346 0.5
11 0523 5.3 1126 0.6 TU 1754 5.1 2345 0.7	**26** 0555 4.6 1152 0.9 W 1817 4.5 2357 1.1	**11** 0016 0.3 0645 5.4 F 1239 0.1 1910 5.1	**26** 0009 0.7 0642 4.8 SA 1230 0.5 1900 4.7	**11** 0543 5.4 1137 0.0 F 1807 5.2 2355 0.2	**26** 0544 4.8 1129 0.4 SA 1759 4.9 2341 0.4	**11** 0010 0.4 0639 5.1 M 1223 0.6 1853 4.9	**26** 0618 4.9 1202 0.6 TU 1830 5.0
12 0612 5.3 1212 0.3 W 1843 5.1	**27** 0630 4.7 1225 0.8 TH 1853 4.6	**12** 0057 0.4 0728 5.2 SA 1318 0.2 1952 4.9	**27** 0040 0.7 0711 4.8 SU 1259 0.6 1929 4.7	**12** 0625 5.4 1214 0.1 SA 1846 5.1	**27** 0614 4.9 1159 0.4 SU 1829 4.9	**12** 0048 0.7 0717 4.8 TU 1256 0.9 1929 4.7	**27** 0025 0.6 0655 4.8 W 1240 0.8 1907 4.9
13 0031 0.7 0700 5.3 TH 1257 0.3 1929 5.0	**28** 0031 1.0 0704 4.7 F 1257 0.8 1927 4.6	**13** 0138 0.6 0810 5.0 SU 1356 0.6 2034 4.6	**28** 0113 0.7 0738 4.7 M 1331 0.7 1957 4.5	**13** 0034 0.2 0704 5.2 SU 1251 0.3 1923 4.9	**28** 0013 0.5 0643 4.9 M 1229 0.5 1857 4.8	**13** 0125 1.0 0755 4.5 W 1330 1.2 2005 4.5	**28** 0107 0.7 0737 4.6 TH 1321 1.1 1949 4.6
14 0117 0.8 0747 5.2 F 1341 0.4 2017 4.8	**29** 0105 1.0 0736 4.7 SA 1328 0.8 2001 4.5	**14** 0220 1.0 0853 4.6 M 1437 1.0 2119 4.3		**14** 0112 0.5 0743 5.0 TU 1325 0.6 1959 4.7	**29** 0047 0.6 0713 4.8 TU 1303 0.7 1926 4.7	**14** 0206 1.3 0835 4.2 TH 1407 1.6 2047 4.1	**29** 0153 1.0 0825 4.4 F 1408 1.4 2042 4.4
15 0202 1.0 0835 4.9 SA 1426 0.7 2108 4.5	**30** 0139 1.1 0806 4.6 SU 1401 1.0 2035 4.4	**15** 0306 1.4 0939 4.2 TU 1521 1.4 2209 3.9		**15** 0150 0.8 0821 4.6 W 1340 1.0 2037 4.3	**30** 0124 0.8 0745 4.6 W 1340 1.0 2000 4.5	**15** 0255 1.7 0922 3.8 F 1450 2.0 2138 3.8	**30** 0246 1.3 0927 4.1 SA 1506 1.8 2154 4.1
	31 0216 1.3 0836 4.5 M 1438 1.2 2112 4.2				**31** 0206 1.1 0825 4.3 TH 1422 1.4 2046 4.2		

Chart Datum: 0·20 metres above Ordnance Datum (Dublin)

》》 **FREE** monthly updates from 《《
www.reedsalmanac.co.uk

TIDES

TIME ZONE (UT)
For Summer Time add ONE hour in **non-shaded areas**

IRELAND – GALWAY
LAT 53°16′N   LONG 9°03′W
TIMES AND HEIGHTS OF HIGH AND LOW WATERS

YEAR 2005

	MAY			JUNE			JULY			AUGUST	
	Time m	Time m		Time m	Time m		Time m	Time m		Time m	Time m
1 SU	0355 1.6 1044 3.9 1632 2.0 ☽ 2317 4.0	**16** M	0458 1.9 1100 3.6 1717 2.3 ☾ 2316 3.7	**1** W	0010 4.3 0623 1.4 1254 4.2 1901 1.6	**16** TH	0550 1.7 1204 3.9 1819 2.0	**1** F	0039 4.2 0645 1.5 1318 4.1 1927 1.6	**16** SA	0532 1.7 1205 4.0 1814 1.9	**1** M	0227 3.8 0820 1.9 1459 4.0 2103 1.5	**16** TU	0125 3.8 0746 1.8 1357 4.1 2028 1.5
2 M	0534 1.6 1209 3.9 1829 1.9	**17** TU	0600 1.9 1216 3.6 1824 2.2	**2** TH	0116 4.4 0727 1.3 1356 4.4 1957 1.4	**17** F	0017 3.9 0647 1.7 1304 4.0 1917 1.8	**2** SA	0143 4.1 0748 1.6 1419 4.2 2024 1.5	**17** SU	0031 3.9 0643 1.8 1310 4.1 1931 1.7	**2** TU	0324 3.9 0909 1.7 1546 4.2 2146 1.3	**17** W	0246 4.1 0851 1.5 1505 4.5 2122 1.0
3 TU	0040 4.1 0700 1.4 1331 4.1 1935 1.6	**18** W	0040 3.7 0655 1.7 1331 3.8 1919 1.9	**3** F	0214 4.5 0820 1.2 1447 4.5 2045 1.2	**18** SA	0121 4.0 0742 1.5 1402 4.2 2010 1.5	**3** SU	0242 4.2 0841 1.6 1510 4.3 2112 1.4	**18** M	0144 4.0 0759 1.6 1417 4.3 2035 1.4	**3** W	0409 4.1 0951 1.5 1626 4.4 2224 1.1	**18** TH	0345 4.4 0940 1.1 1558 4.8 2208 0.6
4 W	0150 4.4 0801 1.2 1430 4.5 2026 1.3	**19** TH	0150 3.8 0746 1.5 1421 4.1 2008 1.6	**4** SA	0305 4.6 0905 1.2 1531 4.7 2128 1.1	**19** SU	0224 4.1 0832 1.4 1451 4.4 2057 1.2	**4** M	0333 4.2 0925 1.5 1554 4.4 2156 1.2	**19** TU	0254 4.2 0858 1.4 1515 4.5 2128 1.0	**4** TH	0451 4.2 1029 1.3 1703 4.5 2301 0.9	**19** F	0434 4.7 1025 0.7 1647 5.1 ○ 2252 0.2
5 TH	0244 4.7 0849 0.9 1516 4.7 2109 1.0	**20** F	0237 4.1 0831 1.3 1501 4.3 2050 1.3	**5** SU	0350 4.6 0945 1.1 1611 4.7 2210 1.0	**20** M	0317 4.3 0917 1.2 1537 4.7 2142 1.0	**5** TU	0419 4.3 1006 1.4 1634 4.5 2238 1.1	**20** W	0352 4.4 0949 1.1 1607 4.8 2218 0.7	**5** F	0529 4.4 1105 1.2 1740 4.6 ● 2337 0.8	**20** SA	0521 5.0 1108 0.4 1733 5.3 2334 0.0
6 F	0331 4.9 0930 0.8 1556 4.9 2150 0.8	**21** SA	0317 4.3 0911 1.1 1536 4.6 2129 1.1	**6** M	0434 4.6 1024 1.1 1649 4.7 ● 2252 1.0	**21** TU	0407 4.6 1001 1.0 1622 4.9 2227 0.7	**6** W	0502 4.3 1045 1.4 1713 4.5 ● 2320 1.0	**21** TH	0445 4.7 1037 0.8 1658 5.0 ○ 2306 0.4	**6** SA	0606 4.5 1140 1.0 1815 4.7	**21** SU	0605 5.1 1150 0.3 1818 5.4
7 SA	0414 5.0 1009 0.7 1635 5.0 2230 0.6	**22** SU	0354 4.5 0948 0.9 1611 4.8 2206 0.8	**7** TU	0516 4.6 1100 1.2 1727 4.7 2333 1.0	**22** W	0456 4.7 1046 0.8 1709 5.0 ○ 2314 0.5	**7** TH	0544 4.4 1122 1.3 1752 4.6 2359 1.0	**22** F	0535 4.9 1123 0.6 1747 5.2 2352 0.2	**7** SU	0011 0.7 0641 4.5 1215 1.0 1848 4.7	**22** M	0015 -0.1 0647 5.1 1231 0.3 1901 5.3
8 SU	0456 5.0 1046 0.7 1713 5.0 ○ 2310 0.7	**23** M	0433 4.7 1024 0.8 1648 5.0 ○ 2245 0.6	**8** W	0557 4.5 1136 1.3 1806 4.7	**23** TH	0546 4.8 1132 0.7 1758 5.1	**8** F	0623 4.4 1159 1.3 1831 4.6	**23** SA	0623 5.0 1208 0.5 1835 5.2	**8** M	0043 0.7 0716 4.5 1247 1.0 1920 4.6	**23** TU	0056 0.1 0728 5.0 1312 0.5 1944 5.1
9 M	0536 5.0 1122 0.8 1750 5.0 2349 0.7	**24** TU	0515 4.8 1102 0.7 1728 5.1 2326 0.5	**9** TH	0013 1.1 0637 4.4 1213 1.3 1844 4.6	**24** F	0002 0.4 0634 4.9 1219 0.7 1846 5.1	**9** SA	0036 1.0 0701 4.4 1236 1.3 1908 4.5	**24** SU	0037 0.1 0709 5.0 1252 0.5 1922 5.2	**9** TU	0115 0.9 0748 4.5 1319 1.1 1950 4.5	**24** W	0136 0.4 0809 4.8 1353 0.8 2027 4.7
10 TU	0616 4.8 1156 1.0 1827 4.8	**25** W	0559 4.9 1142 0.7 1811 5.1	**10** F	0054 1.2 0717 4.3 1251 1.4 1924 4.4	**25** SA	0050 0.4 0723 4.8 1306 0.8 1936 5.0	**10** SU	0112 1.0 0739 4.4 1312 1.4 1945 4.4	**25** M	0121 0.2 0754 4.9 1336 0.7 2009 5.0	**10** W	0146 0.9 0819 4.4 1353 1.2 2019 4.4	**25** TH	0217 0.8 0851 4.5 1437 1.2 2116 4.3
11 W	0027 0.9 0655 4.6 1231 1.2 1904 4.6	**26** TH	0010 0.5 0644 4.7 1226 0.8 1855 5.0	**11** SA	0134 1.3 0758 4.2 1330 1.6 2006 4.3	**26** SU	0138 0.5 0812 4.7 1354 1.0 2029 4.8	**11** M	0147 1.1 0817 4.3 1348 1.4 2022 4.3	**26** TU	0205 0.4 0840 4.6 1422 1.0 2100 4.7	**11** TH	0221 1.1 0851 4.3 1431 1.4 2054 4.2	**26** F	0302 1.2 0938 4.1 1530 1.6 ☽ 2213 3.9
12 TH	0107 1.1 0734 4.4 1306 1.5 1942 4.4	**27** F	0057 0.6 0731 4.7 1312 1.1 1944 4.8	**12** SU	0216 1.4 0841 4.1 1412 1.8 2050 4.1	**27** M	0228 0.7 0906 4.5 1447 1.3 2128 4.6	**12** TU	0223 1.2 0856 4.2 1426 1.5 2101 4.2	**27** W	0251 0.8 0931 4.3 1512 1.3 2156 4.4	**12** F	0300 1.4 0929 4.1 1516 1.6 2145 4.0	**27** SA	0358 1.8 1034 3.8 1650 1.9 2324 3.6
13 F	0149 1.4 0815 4.1 1345 1.7 2025 4.2	**28** SA	0147 0.7 0822 4.5 1403 1.3 2040 4.6	**13** M	0302 1.6 0928 3.9 1500 1.9 2138 4.0	**28** TU	0323 1.0 1005 4.3 1549 1.5 ☽ 2232 4.4	**13** W	0302 1.4 0936 4.1 1509 1.7 2144 4.1	**28** TH	0343 1.3 1026 4.1 1615 1.6 ☽ 2257 4.1	**13** SA	0346 1.6 1020 4.0 1612 1.9 ● 2250 3.8	**28** SU	0519 2.1 1154 3.6 1828 2.1
14 SA	0238 1.6 0902 3.9 1430 2.0 2113 3.9	**29** SU	0241 0.9 0922 4.3 1502 1.6 2147 4.3	**14** TU	0355 1.8 1018 3.9 1601 2.0 2229 3.9	**29** W	0426 1.2 1108 4.1 1704 1.7 2335 4.2	**14** TH	0345 1.5 1020 4.0 1601 1.8 2235 3.9	**29** F	0444 1.7 1127 3.9 1734 1.8	**14** SU	0444 1.9 1122 3.9 1724 2.0 2359 3.7	**29** M	0052 3.5 0647 2.1 1342 3.7 2001 1.9
15 SU	0344 1.7 0956 3.7 1538 2.2 2211 3.8	**30** M	0347 1.3 1031 4.1 1621 1.8 ☽ 2304 4.2	**15** W	0453 1.7 1110 3.8 1712 2.1 ☽ 2322 3.9	**30** TH	0535 1.4 1212 4.1 1821 1.7	**15** F	0434 1.6 1109 4.0 1701 1.9 ☽ 2322 3.9	**30** SA	0002 3.9 0557 1.8 1237 3.8 1857 1.8	**15** M	0559 2.0 1234 3.9 1909 1.8	**30** TU	0220 3.7 0800 1.9 1448 3.9 2116 1.6
		31 TU	0507 1.4 1143 4.1 1752 1.8						**31** SU	0115 3.8 0715 1.9 1356 3.8 2009 1.7			**31** W	0313 3.9 0851 1.8 1533 4.2 2131 1.3

Chart Datum: 0·20 metres above Ordnance Datum (Dublin)

》 **FREE** monthly updates from 《
www.reedsalmanac.co.uk

TIME ZONE (UT)
For Summer Time add ONE hour in **non-shaded areas**

IRELAND – GALWAY
LAT 53°16′N   LONG 9°03′W
TIMES AND HEIGHTS OF HIGH AND LOW WATERS

YEAR 2005

SEPTEMBER

	Time	m		Time	m
1 TH	0354 0931 1610 2202	4.1 1.5 4.4 1.0	**16** F	0333 0925 1545 2151	4.6 1.1 5.0 0.5
2 F	0431 1007 1645 2235	4.4 1.2 4.6 0.8	**17** SA	0417 1007 1630 2231	4.9 0.7 5.3 0.2
3 SA	0507 1041 1719 ● 2308	4.5 1.0 4.7 0.6	**18** SU	0459 1047 1713 ○ 2310	5.2 0.4 5.5 0.0
4 SU	0541 1117 1752 2340	4.7 0.8 4.8 0.6	**19** M	0541 1127 1755 2349	5.3 0.3 5.5 0.1
5 M	0615 1147 1823	4.7 0.8 4.8	**20** TU	0621 1207 1837	5.3 0.3 5.4
6 TU	0011 0646 1218 1850	0.6 4.7 0.8 4.8	**21** W	0027 0659 1246 1916	0.3 5.1 0.5 5.1
7 W	0041 0715 1249 1915	0.7 4.7 0.9 4.7	**22** TH	0105 0737 1325 1957	0.6 4.9 0.8 4.8
8 TH	0111 0741 1322 1940	0.9 4.6 1.0 4.5	**23** F	0143 0815 1405 2040	1.1 4.6 1.3 4.3
9 F	0144 0808 1359 2013	1.1 4.4 1.3 4.3	**24** SA	0224 0856 1454 2134	1.6 4.2 1.7 3.9
10 SA	0223 0843 1443 2104	1.4 4.2 1.6 4.0	**25** SU	0317 0947 1615 ◐ 2248	2.0 3.9 2.1 3.6
11 SU	0310 0937 1538 ◐ 2224	1.8 4.0 1.9 3.8	**26** M	0451 1100 1759	2.4 3.6 2.2
12 M	0412 1052 1655 2347	2.1 3.9 2.1 3.7	**27** TU	0034 0621 1319 1935	3.5 2.4 3.6 2.0
13 TU	0546 1213 1913	2.2 3.9 1.9	**28** W	0202 0730 1425 2034	3.7 2.2 3.9 1.7
14 W	0122 0743 1350 2021	3.8 1.9 4.1 1.4	**29** TH	0251 0822 1508 2101	4.0 1.9 4.2 1.4
15 TH	0242 0839 1457 2109	4.1 1.5 4.6 0.9	**30** F	0329 0902 1545 2131	4.3 1.6 4.4 1.1

OCTOBER

	Time	m		Time	m
1 SA	0403 0938 1618 2203	4.5 1.2 4.6 0.9	**16** SU	0353 0944 1608 2207	5.1 0.7 5.4 0.4
2 SU	0437 1013 1650 2235	4.7 1.0 4.9 0.7	**17** M	0434 1024 1650 ○ 2245	5.3 0.5 5.5 0.4
3 M	0509 1046 1721 ● 2307	4.8 0.8 4.9 0.6	**18** TU	0513 1104 1731 2322	5.3 0.5 5.5 0.5
4 TU	0541 1117 1750 2336	4.9 0.7 4.9 0.7	**19** W	0553 1143 1812	5.3 0.5 5.3
5 W	0611 1148 1818	4.9 0.7 4.9	**20** TH	0000 0630 1222 1851	0.7 5.2 0.7 5.1
6 TH	0006 0639 1220 1846	0.8 4.9 0.8 4.8	**21** F	0037 0708 1301 1932	1.0 4.9 1.0 4.7
7 F	0039 0708 1256 1917	1.0 4.9 1.0 4.6	**22** SA	0114 0746 1342 2015	1.4 4.6 1.4 4.3
8 SA	0115 0739 1335 1956	1.2 4.6 1.2 4.4	**23** SU	0155 0828 1430 2106	1.8 4.3 1.8 4.0
9 SU	0157 0819 1422 2053	1.6 4.4 1.5 4.1	**24** M	0246 0917 1543 2215	2.2 4.0 2.1 3.7
10 M	0247 0917 1519 ◐ 2216	1.9 4.1 1.9 3.9	**25** TU	0419 1020 1719 ◐ 2353	2.5 3.8 2.2 3.6
11 TU	0356 1038 1643 2342	2.2 4.0 2.0 3.8	**26** W	0546 1222 1833	2.5 3.7 2.1
12 W	0610 1204 1859	2.3 4.0 1.8	**27** TH	0119 0649 1342 1933	3.8 2.3 3.9 1.9
13 TH	0116 0725 1335 2000	4.0 1.9 4.3 1.4	**28** F	0213 0742 1431 2017	4.0 2.0 4.1 1.6
14 F	0224 0818 1437 2047	4.4 1.5 4.7 1.0	**29** SA	0253 0826 1509 2053	4.3 1.7 4.3 1.3
15 SA	0311 0903 1525 2128	4.8 1.1 5.1 0.6	**30** SU	0327 0905 1543 2128	4.5 1.4 4.5 1.1
			31 M	0400 0941 1615 2201	4.7 1.2 4.7 0.9

NOVEMBER

	Time	m		Time	m
1 TU	0432 1015 1645 2233	4.9 1.0 4.9 0.9	**16** W	0448 1044 1709 ○ 2259	5.2 0.8 5.2 0.9
2 W	0503 1048 1716 ● 2304	5.0 0.9 4.9 0.9	**17** TH	0527 1124 1750 2336	5.2 0.9 5.1 1.1
3 TH	0535 1121 1751 2337	5.0 0.8 4.9 0.9	**18** F	0607 1205 1832	5.0 1.0 4.9
4 F	0610 1158 1828	5.0 0.8 4.9	**19** SA	0014 0646 1245 1913	1.3 4.9 1.2 4.6
5 SA	0014 0646 1238 1908	1.1 4.9 0.9 4.7	**20** SU	0054 0726 1327 1957	1.6 4.7 1.4 4.3
6 SU	0056 0726 1322 1956	1.2 4.8 1.1 4.5	**21** M	0136 0808 1413 2045	1.9 4.4 1.7 4.1
7 M	0143 0813 1412 2056	1.6 4.6 1.4 4.2	**22** TU	0224 0854 1508 2143	2.1 4.2 1.9 3.9
8 TU	0238 0914 1512 2210	2.0 4.4 1.7 4.1	**23** W	0331 0947 1621 2251	2.3 4.0 2.0 3.8
9 W	0352 1029 1635 ◐ 2331	2.2 4.2 1.8 4.1	**24** TH	0453 1048 1732	2.4 3.9 2.0
10 TH	0547 1148 1826	2.1 4.3 1.7	**25** F	0002 0557 1200 1831	3.8 2.3 3.8 2.0
11 F	0050 0657 1306 1930	4.3 1.9 4.5 1.4	**26** SA	0107 0653 1318 1924	4.0 2.2 3.9 1.9
12 SA	0155 0752 1404 2021	4.6 1.5 4.8 1.1	**27** SU	0159 0744 1414 2010	4.2 1.9 4.1 1.6
13 SU	0245 0839 1452 2104	4.8 1.2 5.0 0.9	**28** M	0241 0828 1456 2051	4.4 1.7 4.3 1.4
14 M	0328 0922 1533 2143	5.1 0.9 5.2 0.7	**29** TU	0317 0908 1533 2128	4.6 1.4 4.5 1.2
15 TU	0408 1003 1611 2221	5.2 0.8 5.2 0.8	**30** W	0353 0946 1610 2203	4.8 1.2 4.7 1.1

DECEMBER

	Time	m		Time	m
1 TH	0429 1024 1650 ● 2240	5.0 1.0 4.8 1.0	**16** F	0510 1113 1736 2321	5.0 1.1 4.7 1.3
2 F	0508 1103 1732 2320	5.1 0.8 4.9 1.0	**17** SA	0551 1154 1818	4.9 1.1 4.6
3 SA	0550 1146 1817	5.1 0.8 4.9	**18** SU	0000 0631 1235 1859	1.4 4.8 1.2 4.5
4 SU	0003 0634 1231 1904	1.1 5.1 0.8 4.8	**19** M	0040 0711 1313 1941	1.5 4.7 1.3 4.4
5 M	0049 0720 1317 1953	1.2 5.0 0.9 4.7	**20** TU	0120 0751 1352 2024	1.6 4.6 1.4 4.2
6 TU	0138 0810 1407 2050	1.4 4.8 1.1 4.5	**21** W	0202 0832 1434 2110	1.7 4.4 1.5 4.1
7 W	0233 0907 1503 2155	1.7 4.6 1.3 4.3	**22** TH	0247 0914 1519 2200	1.9 4.2 1.7 4.0
8 TH	0339 1013 1611 ◐ 2305	1.9 4.5 1.5 4.2	**23** F	0340 1000 1612 2253	2.1 4.1 1.8 4.0
9 F	0503 1122 1735	1.9 4.4 1.6	**24** SA	0442 1048 1711 2346	2.2 4.0 1.9 3.9
10 SA	0014 0619 1232 1853	4.3 1.8 4.5 1.5	**25** SU	0547 1140 1815	2.2 3.9 1.9
11 SU	0120 0722 1337 1952	4.4 1.7 4.6 1.4	**26** M	0043 0649 1241 1918	4.0 2.1 3.9 1.9
12 M	0217 0816 1435 2041	4.6 1.4 4.7 1.3	**27** TU	0141 0747 1353 2013	4.1 1.9 3.9 1.7
13 TU	0305 0903 1524 2124	4.8 1.3 4.8 1.3	**28** W	0234 0838 1454 2100	4.3 1.7 4.0 1.5
14 W	0348 0948 1610 2204	4.9 1.2 4.8 1.3	**29** TH	0320 0925 1545 2144	4.6 1.4 4.3 1.3
15 TH	0429 1031 1653 ○ 2243	4.9 1.1 4.8 1.3	**30** F	0406 1010 1634 2228	4.8 1.2 4.5 1.1
			31 SA	0452 1055 1722 ● 2313	4.7 0.8 4.9 0.9

Chart Datum: 0.20 metres above Ordnance Datum (Dublin)

)) **FREE** monthly updates from ((
www.reedsalmanac.co.uk

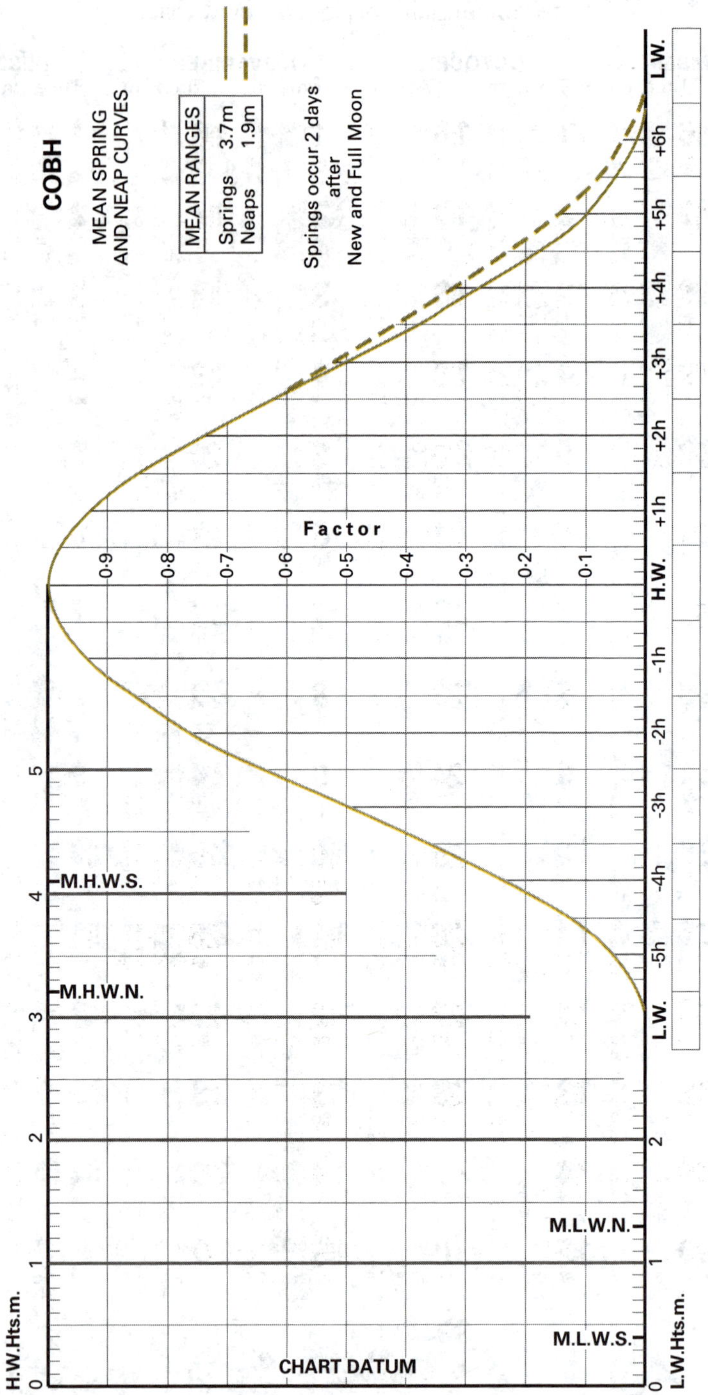

COBH
MEAN SPRING AND NEAP CURVES
MEAN RANGES
Springs 3.7m
Neaps 1.9m
Springs occur 2 days after New and Full Moon
Factor
0·9
0·8
0·7
0·6
0·5
0·4
0·3
0·2
0·1
L.W.
-5h
-4h
-3h
-2h
-1h
H.W.
+1h
+2h
+3h
+4h
+5h
+6h
L.W.
H.W.Hts.m.
0
1
2
3
4
5
M.H.W.S.
M.H.W.N.
CHART DATUM
L.W.Hts.m.
M.L.W.S.
M.L.W.N.

TIME ZONE (UT)
For Summer Time add ONE hour in **non-shaded areas**

IRELAND – COBH
LAT 51°51′N   LONG 8°18′W
TIMES AND HEIGHTS OF HIGH AND LOW WATERS

YEAR 2005

	JANUARY		FEBRUARY		MARCH		APRIL	
	Time m	Time m	Time m	Time m	Time m	Time m	Time m	Time m
1	0240 1.1 0844 3.8 SA 1510 1.2 2057 3.7	**16** 0353 0.7 0947 3.9 SU 1618 0.8 2203 3.6	**1** 0337 1.0 0936 3.8 TU 1600 1.2 2154 3.7	**16** 0446 1.0 1035 3.4 W 1707 1.2 ◐ 2252 3.3	**1** 0226 0.7 0822 3.9 TU 1446 0.8 2037 3.8	**16** 0322 0.7 0909 3.6 W 1537 0.9 2123 3.5	**1** 0337 0.9 0930 3.5 F 1600 1.1 2157 3.5	**16** 0422 1.3 1001 3.1 SA 1643 1.4 ◐ 2232 3.1
2	0325 1.2 0927 3.7 SU 1556 1.3 2144 3.6	**17** 0443 0.8 1036 3.7 M 1708 1.0 ◐ 2253 3.5	**2** 0425 1.1 1024 3.6 W 1650 1.3 ● 2248 3.6	**17** 0541 1.3 1130 3.2 TH 1807 1.4 2358 3.1	**2** 0306 0.8 0901 3.8 W 1525 1.0 2119 3.7	**17** 0404 1.0 0949 3.4 TH 1620 1.2 ◐ 2207 3.3	**2** 0439 1.1 1034 3.2 SA 1712 1.3 ◐ 2312 3.3	**17** 0529 1.4 1107 2.9 SU 1800 1.5 2359 2.9
3	0414 1.2 1015 3.7 M 1646 1.3 ◐ 2236 3.6	**18** 0538 1.0 1129 3.5 TU 1804 1.2 2350 3.3	**3** 0524 1.3 1123 3.5 TH 1758 1.4 2355 3.4	**18** 0649 1.4 1247 3.0 F 1923 1.5	**3** 0352 1.0 0948 3.6 TH 1614 1.2 ◐ 2213 3.5	**18** 0456 1.3 1038 3.1 F 1719 1.4 2308 3.0	**3** 0559 1.3 1159 3.1 SU 1843 1.3	**18** 0647 1.4 1251 2.9 M 1922 1.4
4	0510 1.3 1109 3.6 TU 1746 1.4 2335 3.5	**19** 0638 1.2 1230 3.4 W 1906 1.3	**4** 0639 1.4 1236 3.4 F 1922 1.4	**19** 0131 3.1 0808 1.4 SA 1412 3.1 2044 1.4	**4** 0452 1.2 1049 3.3 F 1722 1.4 2323 3.3	**19** 0605 1.5 1153 2.9 SA 1840 1.5	**4** 0049 3.2 0732 1.2 M 1337 3.1 2014 1.1	**19** 0141 3.0 0801 1.3 TU 1412 3.1 2031 1.2
5	0614 1.3 1210 3.6 W 1853 1.4	**20** 0058 3.3 0743 1.3 TH 1337 3.3 2012 1.3	**5** 0114 3.4 0801 1.3 SA 1356 3.4 2043 1.2	**20** 0251 3.2 0927 1.3 SU 1520 3.3 2154 1.2	**5** 0610 1.4 1209 3.1 SA 1854 1.4	**20** 0052 2.9 0728 1.5 SU 1342 2.9 2007 1.4	**5** 0221 3.4 0857 0.9 TU 1456 3.4 2127 0.7	**20** 0242 3.3 0901 1.1 W 1505 3.3 2124 1.0
6	0041 3.5 0721 1.3 TH 1316 3.6 2000 1.3	**21** 0209 3.3 0850 1.3 F 1441 3.4 2116 1.3	**6** 0236 3.5 0921 1.1 SU 1514 3.5 2154 0.9	**21** 0350 3.5 1025 1.0 M 1612 3.5 2243 0.9	**6** 0053 3.2 0741 1.3 SU 1343 3.2 2026 1.2	**21** 0225 3.1 0852 1.3 M 1455 3.1 2123 1.2	**6** 0326 3.7 0959 0.6 W 1553 3.7 2222 0.4	**21** 0327 3.5 0948 0.8 TH 1547 3.6 2205 0.7
7	0148 3.6 0829 1.2 F 1422 3.7 2106 1.1	**22** 0314 3.5 0951 1.2 SA 1539 3.5 2213 1.1	**7** 0350 3.8 1028 0.8 M 1620 3.8 2253 0.6	**22** 0436 3.7 1107 0.8 TU 1654 3.7 2320 0.7	**7** 0229 3.4 0910 1.0 M 1508 3.4 2142 0.9	**22** 0324 3.4 0954 1.0 TU 1546 3.4 2214 0.9	**7** 0417 4.0 1048 0.3 TH 1640 4.0 2308 0.2	**22** 0406 3.7 1027 0.7 F 1625 3.7 2240 0.6
8	0255 3.8 0935 1.0 SA 1526 3.8 2207 0.9	**23** 0408 3.6 1042 1.0 SU 1629 3.7 2258 1.0	**8** 0449 4.0 1123 0.5 TU 1714 4.0 ● 2344 0.3	**23** 0515 3.9 1140 0.7 W 1731 3.8 2349 0.6	**8** 0342 3.7 1018 0.7 TU 1611 3.7 2241 0.5	**23** 0408 3.6 1036 0.8 W 1628 3.6 2250 0.7	**8** 0501 4.2 1130 0.2 F 1722 4.1 ● 2349 0.1	**23** 0441 3.8 1103 0.5 SA 1659 3.9 2314 0.5
9	0359 3.9 1037 0.8 SU 1627 3.9 2303 0.7	**24** 0454 3.8 1123 0.9 M 1711 3.8 2335 0.8	**9** 0539 4.2 1211 0.3 W 1801 4.1	**24** 0549 4.0 1208 0.6 TH 1803 3.9 ○	**9** 0437 4.0 1109 0.4 W 1701 4.0 2329 0.2	**24** 0446 3.8 1110 0.6 TH 1703 3.8 2320 0.6	**9** 0541 4.2 1209 0.1 SA 1800 4.2	**24** 0514 3.9 1138 0.5 SU 1733 3.9 ○ 2349 0.4
10	0457 4.1 1132 0.6 M 1722 4.1 ● 2354 0.5	**25** 0534 3.9 1157 0.8 TU 1748 3.9 ○	**10** 0029 0.2 0624 4.3 TH 1255 0.2 1844 4.2	**25** 0015 0.6 0619 4.0 F 1237 0.6 1832 3.9	**10** 0523 4.2 1153 0.1 TH 1744 4.2 ●	**25** 0519 3.9 1139 0.5 F 1735 3.9 ○ 2347 0.5	**10** 0027 0.1 0617 4.2 SU 1246 0.2 1834 4.1	**25** 0548 4.0 1214 0.4 M 1808 4.0
11	0550 4.2 1222 0.4 TU 1812 4.1	**26** 0007 0.8 0609 4.0 W 1228 0.8 1821 3.9	**11** 0113 0.1 0707 4.3 F 1337 0.2 1925 4.2	**26** 0044 0.6 0647 4.1 SA 1307 0.6 1900 3.9	**11** 0011 0.1 0604 4.3 F 1234 0.1 1823 4.2	**26** 0549 4.0 1208 0.4 SA 1804 3.9	**11** 0103 0.2 0652 4.1 M 1320 0.3 1907 4.0	**26** 0026 0.4 0624 4.0 TU 1251 0.5 1843 4.0
12	0042 0.4 0638 4.3 W 1310 0.4 1859 4.1	**27** 0036 0.7 0641 4.0 TH 1259 0.8 1852 3.9	**12** 0156 0.2 0749 4.2 SA 1418 0.3 2005 4.1	**27** 0115 0.6 0716 4.0 SU 1338 0.7 1929 3.9	**12** 0051 0.0 0643 4.3 SA 1312 0.1 1900 4.2	**27** 0016 0.4 0617 4.0 SU 1239 0.5 1833 4.0	**12** 0138 0.4 0726 3.9 TU 1355 0.5 1940 3.9	**27** 0107 0.4 0703 3.9 W 1331 0.5 1923 4.0
13	0130 0.3 0726 4.3 TH 1357 0.4 1945 4.1	**28** 0107 0.7 0712 4.0 F 1331 0.8 1923 3.9	**13** 0237 0.3 0830 4.0 SU 1458 0.5 2044 3.9	**28** 0149 0.6 0748 4.0 M 1411 0.7 2001 3.9	**13** 0129 0.1 0721 4.2 SU 1349 0.2 1936 4.1	**28** 0049 0.4 0647 4.0 M 1312 0.5 1904 4.0	**13** 0213 0.6 0759 3.7 W 1429 0.7 2014 3.7	**28** 0151 0.5 0745 3.8 TH 1415 0.6 2007 3.9
14	0217 0.4 0813 4.2 F 1443 0.5 2031 3.9	**29** 0140 0.8 0744 3.9 SA 1405 0.9 1955 3.8	**14** 0318 0.5 0910 3.9 M 1538 0.7 2123 3.7		**14** 0207 0.3 0757 4.0 M 1425 0.4 2010 3.9	**29** 0124 0.4 0721 3.9 TU 1346 0.6 1937 3.9	**14** 0250 0.9 0835 3.6 TH 1504 0.9 2052 3.5	**29** 0239 0.7 0833 3.6 F 1504 0.8 2058 3.7
15	0305 0.5 0900 4.0 SA 1530 0.7 2117 3.8	**30** 0216 0.8 0818 3.9 SU 1441 1.0 2030 3.8	**15** 0400 0.7 0950 3.7 TU 1619 0.9 2204 3.5		**15** 0244 0.5 0832 3.9 TU 1500 0.6 2045 3.8	**30** 0203 0.5 0758 3.9 W 1424 0.7 2016 3.8	**15** 0331 1.1 0914 3.3 F 1546 1.2 2136 3.3	**30** 0334 0.9 0928 3.5 SA 1603 1.0 2158 3.5
16		**31** 0255 0.9 0855 3.8 M 1519 1.0 2109 3.8				**31** 0246 0.7 0840 3.7 TH 1507 0.9 2101 3.7		

Chart Datum: 0·13 metres above Ordnance Datum (Dublin)

》》 **FREE** monthly updates from 《《
www.reedsalmanac.co.uk

TIDES

TIME ZONE (UT)
For Summer Time add ONE hour in **non-shaded areas**

IRELAND – COBH
LAT 51°51′N   LONG 8°18′W
TIMES AND HEIGHTS OF HIGH AND LOW WATERS

YEAR **2005**

	MAY			JUNE			JULY			AUGUST	
	Time m	Time m		Time m	Time m		Time m	Time m		Time m	Time m
1 SU	0438 1.0 1035 3.2 1714 1.1 ◐ 2313 3.3	**16** M	0454 1.3 1034 3.1 1719 1.3 ◐ 2311 3.1	**1** W	0017 3.5 0655 0.9 1249 3.4 1928 0.8	**16** TH	0612 1.2 1158 3.3 1835 1.2	**1** F	0043 3.5 0719 0.9 1311 3.4 1952 0.9	**16** SA	0615 1.2 1207 3.4 1842 1.2	**1** M	0212 3.2 0848 1.2 1447 3.3 2126 1.1	**16** TU	0116 3.3 0806 1.3 1401 3.4 2041 1.1
2 M	0555 1.1 1155 3.2 1836 1.1	**17** TU	0602 1.4 1146 3.0 1830 1.3	**2** TH	0125 3.3 0800 0.9 1353 3.5 2030 0.7	**17** F	0028 3.4 0712 1.2 1300 3.4 1934 1.1	**2** SA	0145 3.5 0819 1.0 1412 3.4 2052 0.9	**17** SU	0038 3.4 0723 1.2 1314 3.4 1951 1.1	**2** TU	0315 3.3 0953 1.1 1547 3.5 2224 1.0	**17** W	0237 3.4 0920 1.0 1517 3.6 2152 0.8
3 TU	0041 3.3 0720 1.0 1320 3.3 1956 0.9	**18** W	0029 3.1 0707 1.3 1303 3.1 1933 1.2	**3** F	0224 3.6 0857 0.7 1451 3.6 2125 0.6	**18** SA	0129 3.5 0808 1.1 1359 3.5 2030 1.0	**3** SU	0243 3.5 0917 0.9 1511 3.5 2148 0.9	**18** M	0145 3.5 0831 1.1 1421 3.5 2100 1.0	**3** W	0409 3.5 1046 0.9 1636 3.6 2309 0.9	**18** TH	0347 3.6 1023 0.7 1619 3.9 2250 0.5
4 W	0159 3.5 0833 0.8 1430 3.5 2102 0.6	**19** TH	0137 3.3 0805 1.1 1404 3.3 2027 1.0	**4** SA	0317 3.7 0949 0.7 1542 3.7 2215 0.6	**19** SU	0225 3.6 0904 0.9 1455 3.6 2126 0.8	**4** M	0337 3.5 1012 0.9 1605 3.6 2239 0.7	**19** TU	0253 3.6 0937 0.9 1528 3.7 2204 0.8	**4** TH	0455 3.6 1127 0.8 1718 3.8 2344 0.8	**19** F	0444 3.9 1116 0.4 1711 4.1 ○ 2340 0.3
5 TH	0259 3.7 0931 0.6 1526 3.7 2156 0.4	**20** F	0230 3.5 0856 0.9 1454 3.5 2115 0.8	**5** SU	0405 3.8 1037 0.6 1629 3.8 2300 0.5	**20** M	0320 3.7 0959 0.8 1550 3.8 2221 0.7	**5** TU	0427 3.6 1100 0.8 1652 3.7 2322 0.7	**20** W	0357 3.7 1037 0.7 1629 3.9 2302 0.6	**5** F	0534 3.7 1200 0.7 1755 3.9 ●	**20** SA	0533 4.1 1203 0.2 1758 4.3
6 F	0350 3.9 1020 0.4 1613 3.9 2243 0.3	**21** SA	0315 3.6 0943 0.8 1539 3.7 2200 0.7	**6** M	0449 3.8 1119 0.6 1711 3.8 ● 2341 0.6	**21** TU	0415 3.8 1052 0.6 1643 3.9 2313 0.5	**6** W	0511 3.7 1141 0.8 1734 3.8 ● 2359 0.7	**21** TH	0456 3.9 1131 0.5 1724 4.1 ○ 2354 0.4	**6** SA	0014 0.7 0609 3.8 1229 0.7 1827 3.9	**21** SU	0025 0.1 0618 4.2 1248 0.1 1841 4.3
7 SA	0434 4.0 1104 0.3 1656 4.0 2325 0.3	**22** SU	0358 3.8 1028 0.6 1622 3.8 2244 0.6	**7** TU	0530 3.8 1158 0.6 1750 3.8	**22** W	0507 3.9 1142 0.5 1734 4.0 ○	**7** TH	0550 3.7 1216 0.8 1811 3.8	**22** F	0548 4.0 1220 0.3 1814 4.2	**7** SU	0043 0.7 0640 3.8 1256 0.7 1857 3.9	**22** M	0109 0.1 0701 4.2 1331 0.1 1923 4.3
8 SU	0515 4.0 1144 0.2 1735 4.0 ●	**23** M	0441 3.9 1112 0.5 1705 3.9 ○ 2328 0.5	**8** W	0017 0.7 0606 3.8 1234 0.7 1825 3.8	**23** TH	0003 0.4 0557 3.9 1232 0.4 1823 4.1	**8** F	0032 0.8 0626 3.7 1249 0.8 1845 3.8	**23** SA	0043 0.3 0636 4.0 1308 0.2 1901 4.2	**8** M	0113 0.8 0711 3.8 1326 0.7 1927 3.8	**23** TU	0151 0.2 0743 4.1 1413 0.2 2005 4.1
9 M	0003 0.3 0552 4.0 1221 0.4 1810 4.0	**24** TU	0524 3.9 1155 0.5 1748 4.0	**9** TH	0051 0.8 0640 3.7 1308 0.8 1859 3.8	**24** F	0053 0.4 0647 3.9 1320 0.4 1913 4.1	**9** SA	0105 0.8 0700 3.7 1321 0.8 1919 3.8	**24** SU	0130 0.2 0724 4.0 1355 0.2 1948 4.2	**9** TU	0146 0.8 0742 3.7 1359 0.8 1958 3.8	**24** W	0233 0.3 0824 3.9 1455 0.4 2046 3.9
10 TU	0039 0.4 0627 3.9 1255 0.5 1843 3.9	**25** W	0012 0.4 0608 3.9 1240 0.5 1831 4.0	**10** F	0125 0.8 0715 3.7 1342 0.8 1935 3.7	**25** SA	0143 0.7 0737 3.9 1410 0.4 2003 4.0	**10** SU	0139 0.9 0734 3.7 1354 0.8 1953 3.7	**25** M	0217 0.3 0810 4.0 1441 0.3 2034 4.1	**10** W	0220 0.9 0815 3.7 1435 0.8 2033 3.8	**25** TH	0314 0.6 0905 3.8 1538 0.6 2127 3.7
11 W	0113 0.6 0700 3.8 1329 0.6 1916 3.8	**26** TH	0058 0.4 0653 3.9 1326 0.5 1917 4.0	**11** SA	0201 0.9 0751 3.6 1418 0.9 2013 3.6	**26** SU	0234 0.4 0828 3.8 1501 0.4 2055 3.9	**11** M	0215 0.9 0809 3.7 1430 0.9 2030 3.7	**26** TU	0304 0.4 0856 3.9 1528 0.4 2121 3.9	**11** TH	0257 1.0 0851 3.7 1513 0.9 2111 3.7	**26** F	0357 0.8 0947 3.6 1622 0.9 ◐ 2211 3.5
12 TH	0147 0.7 0733 3.7 1403 0.8 1951 3.7	**27** F	0147 0.5 0742 3.8 1415 0.6 2007 3.9	**12** SU	0241 1.0 0830 3.5 1458 1.0 2054 3.5	**27** M	0326 0.5 0920 3.7 1554 0.5 2148 3.8	**12** TU	0255 1.0 0848 3.6 1510 1.0 2109 3.6	**27** W	0351 0.6 0942 3.7 1616 0.6 2207 3.7	**12** F	0336 1.1 0932 3.6 1556 1.1 2155 3.6	**27** SA	0445 1.1 1035 3.4 1715 1.1 2304 3.2
13 F	0224 0.9 0809 3.5 1439 1.0 2030 3.5	**28** SA	0239 0.6 0834 3.8 1507 0.7 2101 3.8	**13** M	0326 1.1 0914 3.4 1543 1.1 2140 3.4	**28** TU	0420 0.6 1013 3.6 1649 0.8 ◐ 2243 3.7	**13** W	0336 1.1 0929 3.5 1553 1.1 2151 3.6	**28** TH	0439 0.7 1029 3.6 1706 0.8 ◐ 2258 3.5	**13** SA	0421 1.2 1021 3.5 1649 1.2 ◐ 2249 3.5	**28** SU	0544 1.3 1134 3.1 1821 1.4
14 SA	0305 1.1 0849 3.4 1521 1.1 2114 3.4	**29** SU	0335 0.7 0930 3.7 1605 0.8 2201 3.6	**14** TU	0416 1.1 1003 3.3 1635 1.2 2231 3.4	**29** W	0518 0.8 1108 3.5 1748 0.8 2341 3.6	**14** TH	0421 1.1 1015 3.5 1641 1.1 ◐ 2239 3.5	**29** F	0531 1.0 1122 3.4 1802 1.0 2355 3.3	**14** SU	0521 1.3 1123 3.3 1758 1.3 2357 3.3	**29** M	0019 3.0 0659 1.4 1310 3.0 1943 1.4
15 SU	0354 1.2 0936 3.2 1613 1.3 2206 3.2	**30** M	0436 0.8 1031 3.6 1709 0.8 ◐ 2307 3.5	**15** W	0512 1.2 1058 3.3 1733 1.2 ◐ 2328 3.4	**30** TH	0618 0.9 1208 3.4 1850 0.8	**15** F	0513 1.3 1107 3.3 1737 1.2 ◐ 2334 3.5	**30** SA	0631 1.2 1224 3.3 1907 1.2	**15** M	0642 1.4 1239 3.3 1920 1.3	**30** TU	0149 3.0 0824 1.3 1431 3.1 2108 1.3
		31 TU	0544 0.9 1139 3.4 1819 0.9						**31** SU	0102 3.2 0738 1.2 1337 3.2 2017 1.2			**31** W	0258 3.2 0938 1.1 1531 3.4 2208 1.1

Chart Datum: 0·13 metres above Ordnance Datum (Dublin)

FREE monthly updates from
www.reedsalmanac.co.uk

344

IRELAND – COBH

LAT 51°51'N   LONG 8°18'W

TIMES AND HEIGHTS OF HIGH AND LOW WATERS

TIME ZONE (UT) For Summer Time add ONE hour in **non-shaded areas**

YEAR 2005

	SEPTEMBER		OCTOBER		NOVEMBER		DECEMBER	
	Time m	Time m	Time m	Time m	Time m	Time m	Time m	Time m
1	0352 3.5 / 1030 0.9 / TH 1618 3.7 / 2250 0.9	**16** 0337 3.7 / 1008 0.6 / F 1606 4.0 / 2235 0.5	**1** 0407 3.7 / 1035 0.8 / SA 1628 3.8 / 2250 0.7	**16** 0408 4.1 / 1037 0.3 / SU 1632 4.3 / 2258 0.3	**1** 0440 3.9 / 1056 0.7 / TU 1656 4.0 / 2315 0.7	**16** 0511 4.2 / 1141 0.5 / W 1730 4.2 / ○ 2356 0.5	**1** 0446 4.0 / 1111 0.7 / TH 1704 4.0 / ● 2333 0.7	**16** 0535 4.0 / 1205 0.8 / F 1751 3.9
2	0435 3.7 / 1108 0.7 / F 1657 3.8 / 2323 0.7	**17** 0429 4.0 / 1058 0.3 / SA 1653 4.2 / 2321 0.2	**2** 0443 3.8 / 1104 0.7 / SU 1701 4.0 / 2318 0.7	**17** 0452 4.2 / 1121 0.2 / M 1713 4.3 / ○ 2339 0.2	**2** 0513 4.0 / 1129 0.6 / W 1727 4.0 / ● 2349 0.7	**17** 0550 4.1 / 1220 0.6 / TH 1807 4.1	**2** 0529 4.1 / 1153 0.7 / F 1746 4.0	**17** 0017 0.8 / 0613 4.0 / SA 1242 0.9 / 1826 3.9
3	0513 3.8 / 1137 0.6 / SA 1732 3.9 / ● 2350 0.7	**18** 0514 4.2 / 1143 0.1 / SU 1737 4.4 / ○	**3** 0515 3.9 / 1129 0.6 / M 1730 4.0 / ● 2344 0.6	**18** 0532 4.3 / 1201 0.2 / TU 1752 4.3	**3** 0547 4.1 / 1205 0.6 / TH 1801 4.1	**18** 0033 0.6 / 0626 4.1 / F 1257 0.7 / 1842 4.0	**3** 0015 0.7 / 0611 4.1 / SA 1237 0.7 / 1828 4.0	**18** 0052 0.8 / 0649 4.0 / SU 1316 1.0 / 1900 3.8
4	0546 3.9 / 1202 0.6 / SU 1802 4.0	**19** 0003 0.1 / 0555 4.3 / M 1225 0.0 / 1817 4.4	**4** 0544 3.9 / 1155 0.6 / TU 1757 4.0	**19** 0017 0.3 / 0610 4.2 / W 1240 0.3 / 1829 4.2	**4** 0025 0.7 / 0622 4.1 / F 1243 0.7 / 1837 4.0	**19** 0109 0.8 / 0702 4.0 / SA 1333 0.9 / 1916 3.8	**4** 0059 0.7 / 0656 4.1 / SU 1323 0.7 / 1914 4.0	**19** 0126 0.9 / 0725 3.9 / M 1351 1.1 / 1935 3.7
5	0015 0.6 / 0615 3.9 / M 1226 0.6 / 1829 4.0	**20** 0043 0.1 / 0635 4.2 / TU 1305 0.1 / 1855 4.3	**5** 0013 0.6 / 0612 0.6 / W 1226 0.6 / 1825 4.0	**20** 0055 0.4 / 0647 4.1 / TH 1318 0.5 / 1904 4.1	**5** 0104 0.7 / 0700 4.0 / SA 1325 0.8 / 1917 3.9	**20** 0145 0.9 / 0739 3.8 / SU 1410 1.1 / 1951 3.7	**5** 0146 0.7 / 0743 4.0 / M 1412 0.8 / 2003 3.8	**20** 0201 1.0 / 0802 3.8 / TU 1427 1.2 / 2012 3.7
6	0043 0.7 / 0642 3.9 / TU 1254 0.7 / 1855 3.9	**21** 0122 0.2 / 0714 4.1 / W 1344 0.3 / 1933 4.1	**6** 0046 0.7 / 0642 4.0 / TH 1300 0.7 / 1856 4.0	**21** 0132 0.6 / 0723 4.0 / F 1355 0.7 / 1939 3.9	**6** 0147 0.8 / 0743 3.9 / SU 1411 0.9 / 2003 3.8	**21** 0223 1.1 / 0819 3.7 / M 1450 1.2 / 2031 3.5	**6** 0236 0.8 / 0835 3.9 / TU 1504 0.9 / 2056 3.7	**21** 0239 1.1 / 0842 3.7 / W 1508 1.3 / 2053 3.6
7	0114 0.7 / 0710 3.8 / W 1327 0.7 / 1925 3.9	**22** 0201 0.4 / 0751 4.0 / TH 1423 0.5 / 2010 3.9	**7** 0120 0.8 / 0714 3.9 / F 1337 0.8 / 1931 3.9	**22** 0209 0.8 / 0759 3.8 / SA 1433 0.9 / 2015 3.7	**7** 0236 1.0 / 0833 3.8 / M 1504 1.1 / 2056 3.6	**22** 0306 1.2 / 0903 3.5 / TU 1537 1.4 / 2116 3.4	**7** 0332 0.9 / 0932 3.8 / W 1601 1.0 / 2154 3.6	**22** 0322 1.2 / 0925 3.6 / TH 1554 1.4 / 2138 3.5
8	0147 0.8 / 0741 3.8 / TH 1402 0.8 / 1957 3.9	**23** 0240 0.6 / 0829 3.8 / F 1503 0.7 / 2048 3.7	**8** 0157 0.9 / 0752 3.8 / SA 1419 0.9 / 2011 3.8	**23** 0249 1.0 / 0839 3.6 / SU 1515 1.2 / 2055 3.4	**8** 0333 1.1 / 0932 3.6 / TU 1605 1.2 / 2159 3.4	**23** 0358 1.4 / 0955 3.3 / W 1634 1.5 / ◐ 2211 3.2	**8** 0432 1.0 / 1033 3.7 / TH 1704 1.1 / ◐ 2257 3.5	**23** 0411 1.3 / 1012 3.5 / F 1645 1.4 / ◐ 2230 3.4
9	0221 0.9 / 0815 3.8 / F 1440 0.9 / 2034 3.8	**24** 0320 0.9 / 0909 3.5 / SA 1545 1.0 / 2129 3.4	**9** 0239 1.0 / 0836 3.7 / SU 1507 1.1 / 2059 3.6	**24** 0333 1.3 / 0925 3.3 / M 1605 1.4 / 2142 3.2	**9** 0441 1.2 / 1042 3.5 / W 1717 1.3 / ◐ 2313 3.3	**24** 0502 1.5 / 1058 3.2 / TH 1740 1.6 / 2320 3.2	**9** 0539 1.0 / 1139 3.6 / F 1814 1.1	**24** 0507 1.4 / 1104 3.5 / SA 1744 1.5 / 2328 3.4
10	0300 1.0 / 0856 3.7 / SA 1524 1.1 / 2118 3.6	**25** 0406 1.2 / 0955 3.3 / SU 1636 1.3 / ◐ 2218 3.1	**10** 0332 1.2 / 0932 3.5 / M 1606 1.3 / ◐ 2200 3.4	**25** 0432 1.5 / 1024 3.1 / TU 1710 1.6 / 2248 3.0	**10** 0600 1.2 / 1204 3.5 / TH 1840 1.2	**25** 0612 1.5 / 1213 3.3 / F 1847 1.5	**10** 0005 3.5 / 0649 1.0 / SA 1247 3.7 / 1922 1.1	**25** 0609 1.4 / 1203 3.4 / SU 1846 1.4
11	0346 1.2 / 0946 3.5 / SU 1618 1.2 / ◐ 2215 3.4	**26** 0505 1.4 / 1058 3.1 / M 1744 1.5 / 2332 2.9	**11** 0442 1.4 / 1043 3.3 / TU 1722 1.4 / 2319 3.2	**26** 0548 1.6 / 1156 3.0 / W 1830 1.6	**11** 0037 3.4 / 0719 1.1 / F 1323 3.6 / 1955 1.0	**26** 0038 3.2 / 0717 1.4 / SA 1321 3.4 / 1947 1.4	**11** 0114 3.6 / 0756 1.0 / SU 1351 3.7 / 2025 1.0	**26** 0031 3.4 / 0712 1.4 / M 1305 3.5 / 1947 1.4
12	0450 1.4 / 1053 3.3 / M 1731 1.4 / 2330 3.2	**27** 0625 1.5 / 1243 3.0 / TU 1911 1.6	**12** 0609 1.4 / 1213 3.3 / W 1852 1.3	**27** 0030 3.0 / 0711 1.5 / TH 1328 3.2 / 1947 1.5	**12** 0152 3.6 / 0827 0.9 / SA 1427 3.8 / 2057 0.8	**27** 0143 3.4 / 0812 1.2 / SU 1414 3.5 / 2038 1.2	**12** 0217 3.7 / 0856 0.9 / M 1448 3.8 / 2121 0.9	**27** 0135 3.5 / 0812 1.2 / TU 1405 3.6 / 2045 1.2
13	0618 1.4 / 1219 3.3 / TU 1901 1.4	**28** 0123 2.9 / 0756 1.4 / W 1410 3.1 / 2039 1.4	**13** 0053 3.2 / 0737 1.3 / TH 1346 3.5 / 2017 1.1	**28** 0153 3.2 / 0819 1.3 / F 1426 3.4 / 2046 1.2	**13** 0252 3.8 / 0924 0.6 / SU 1520 4.0 / 2148 0.5	**28** 0235 3.6 / 0900 1.0 / M 1500 3.7 / 2125 1.0	**13** 0314 3.8 / 0951 0.8 / TU 1541 3.9 / 2212 0.8	**28** 0236 3.6 / 0910 1.1 / W 1503 3.7 / 2141 1.1
14	0101 3.2 / 0750 1.3 / W 1354 3.4 / 2029 1.1	**29** 0236 3.2 / 0910 1.2 / TH 1506 3.4 / 2137 1.1	**14** 0218 3.5 / 0851 0.9 / F 1453 3.8 / 2122 0.7	**29** 0246 3.4 / 0910 1.1 / SA 1511 3.6 / 2130 1.0	**14** 0343 4.0 / 1014 0.5 / M 1607 4.1 / 2234 0.5	**29** 0320 3.8 / 0945 0.9 / TU 1542 3.8 / 2209 0.9	**14** 0406 3.9 / 1040 0.8 / W 1629 3.9 / 2258 0.8	**29** 0333 3.8 / 1006 1.0 / TH 1557 3.8 / 2233 0.9
15	0230 3.4 / 0907 1.0 / TH 1509 3.7 / 2140 0.8	**30** 0326 3.4 / 0959 0.9 / F 1550 3.7 / 2218 0.9	**15** 0319 3.8 / 0948 0.5 / SA 1546 4.1 / 2213 0.5	**30** 0328 3.6 / 0950 0.9 / SU 1549 3.8 / 2208 0.9	**15** 0428 4.1 / 1059 0.5 / TU 1650 4.2 / 2317 0.5	**30** 0404 3.9 / 1028 0.8 / W 1623 4.0 / 2251 0.8	**15** 0453 4.0 / 1125 0.8 / TH 1712 3.9 / ○ 2339 0.8	**30** 0427 3.9 / 1058 0.9 / F 1649 3.9 / 2322 0.8
				31 0405 3.7 / 1024 0.8 / M 1624 3.9 / 2242 0.7				**31** 0517 4.1 / 1147 0.9 / SA 1737 4.0 / ●

Chart Datum: 0·13 metres above Ordnance Datum (Dublin)

》》 **FREE** monthly updates from 《《
www.reedsalmanac.co.uk

TIDES

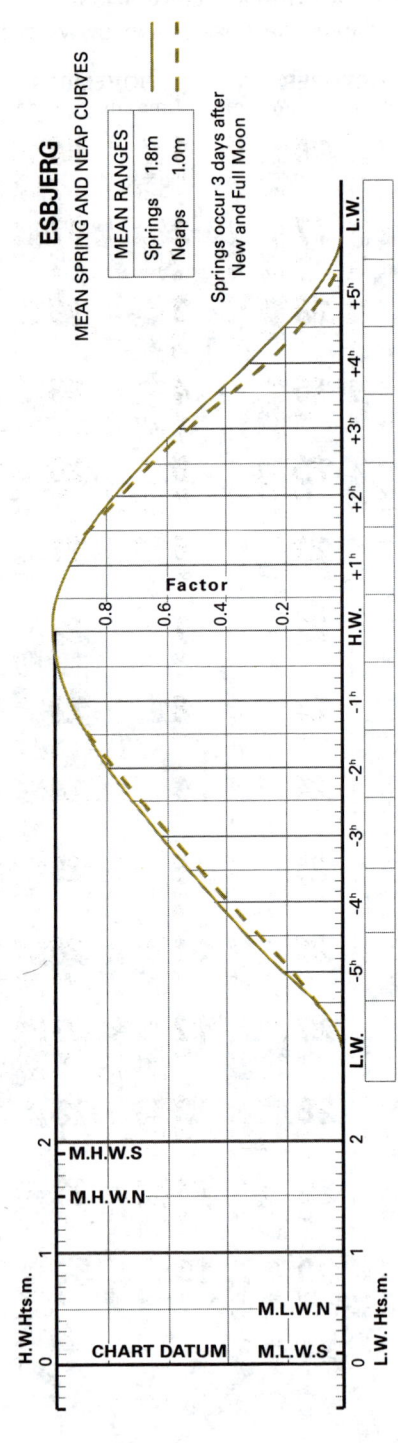

TIME ZONE -0100 (Danish Standard Time) Subtract 1 hour for UT	DENMARK – ESBJERG	YEAR 2005
For Danish Summer Time add ONE hour in **non-shaded areas**	LAT 55°28'N LONG 8°27'E TIMES AND HEIGHTS OF HIGH AND LOW WATERS	

JANUARY

Time	m	Time	m
1 0545 SA 1208 1815	1.8 0.1 1.5	**16** 0023 SU 0658 1305 1936	0.1 1.8 0.0 1.4
2 0013 SU 0622 1249 1857	0.2 1.8 0.1 1.5	**17** 0112 M 0749 1356 2027	0.1 1.8 0.1 1.4
3 0057 M 0707 1335 ☾ 1945	0.2 1.8 0.1 1.5	**18** 0204 TU 0845 1451 2123	0.1 1.7 0.2 1.4
4 0147 TU 0759 1427 2041	0.2 1.8 0.1 1.5	**19** 0303 W 0948 1553 2224	0.2 1.7 0.2 1.4
5 0242 W 0857 1524 2145	0.2 1.7 0.2 1.5	**20** 0411 TH 1053 1700 2325	0.2 1.6 0.2 1.5
6 0342 TH 1006 1627 2254	0.2 1.7 0.2 1.5	**21** 0525 F 1157 1804	0.2 1.6 0.2
7 0451 F 1121 1734	0.2 1.6 0.2	**22** 0025 SA 0633 1257 1900	1.5 0.2 1.5 0.2
8 0006 SA 0601 1236 1839	1.5 0.2 1.6 0.2	**23** 0121 SU 0730 1351 1949	1.6 0.1 1.5 0.2
9 0111 SU 0708 1344 1937	1.6 0.1 1.6 0.2	**24** 0210 M 0820 1438 2031	1.6 0.1 1.5 0.2
10 0209 M 0807 1445 ● 2030	1.6 0.1 1.6 0.1	**25** 0254 TU 0902 1520 ○ 2107	1.7 0.1 1.5 0.2
11 0303 TU 0902 1539 2119	1.7 0.0 1.6 0.1	**26** 0333 W 0938 1556 2139	1.7 0.1 1.5 0.1
12 0352 W 0953 1630 2206	1.7 -0.1 1.6 0.1	**27** 0405 TH 1009 1627 2209	1.7 0.1 1.4 0.1
13 0439 TH 1041 1718 2251	1.8 -0.1 1.5 0.1	**28** 0433 F 1039 1654 2241	1.7 0.1 1.4 0.1
14 0524 F 1129 1803 2337	1.8 -0.1 1.5 0.1	**29** 0459 SA 1110 1723 2315	1.7 0.0 1.5 0.0
15 0610 SA 1216 1848	1.8 -0.1 1.5	**30** 0528 SU 1145 1754 2352	1.7 0.0 1.4 0.0
		31 0602 M 1223 1830	1.7 0.0 1.5

FEBRUARY

Time	m	Time	m
1 0033 TU 0642 1305 1911	0.0 1.7 0.1 1.5	**16** 0128 W 0805 1403 ☾ 2028	0.0 1.6 0.1 1.4
2 0118 W 0729 1352 2000	0.0 1.7 0.1 1.4	**17** 0221 TH 0902 1458 2127	0.1 1.5 0.2 1.4
3 0209 TH 0824 1445 2057	0.0 1.6 0.1 1.4	**18** 0326 F 1009 1609 2237	0.1 1.4 0.3 1.4
4 0308 F 0931 1548 2209	0.1 1.5 0.2 1.4	**19** 0452 SA 1121 1729 2346	0.2 1.3 0.3 1.4
5 0418 SA 1055 1700 2333	0.2 1.4 0.3 1.4	**20** 0611 SU 1225 1833	0.2 1.3 0.2
6 0539 SU 1221 1817	0.2 1.4 0.2	**21** 0048 M 0711 1323 1925	1.5 0.1 1.4 0.1
7 0049 M 0656 1335 1922	1.4 0.1 1.4 0.2	**22** 0142 TU 0759 1412 2007	1.5 0.0 1.4 0.1
8 0154 TU 0758 1436 ● 2016	1.5 0.0 1.5 0.1	**23** 0228 W 0839 1456 2044	1.6 0.0 1.4 0.0
9 0249 W 0851 1529 2105	1.6 -0.2 1.5 0.0	**24** 0308 TH 0913 1533 ○ 2116	1.6 -0.1 1.4 0.0
10 0339 TH 0939 1615 2150	1.7 -0.2 1.6 -0.1	**25** 0342 F 0944 1605 2147	1.6 -0.1 1.4 0.1
11 0424 F 1024 1657 2233	1.8 -0.2 1.5 -0.1	**26** 0412 SA 1014 1633 2219	1.6 -0.1 1.4 0.1
12 0507 SA 1108 1737 2315	1.8 -0.2 1.5 -0.2	**27** 0440 SU 1045 1702 2253	1.6 -0.2 1.4 0.1
13 0549 SU 1150 1815 2358	1.8 -0.2 1.4 -0.1	**28** 0509 M 1119 1731 2330	1.6 -0.2 1.4 0.1
14 0631 M 1233 1855	1.7 -0.1 1.4		
15 0042 TU 0715 1316 1938	-0.1 1.7 0.0 1.4		

MARCH

Time	m	Time	m
1 0542 TU 1157 1803	1.6 -0.2 1.4	**16** 0012 W 0639 1236 ☾ 1851	-0.2 1.5 0.0 1.4
2 0009 W 0621 1237 1842	-0.2 1.6 -0.1 1.4	**17** 0054 TH 0722 1317 ☾ 1934	-0.1 1.4 0.1 1.3
3 0054 TH 0706 1323 ☾ 1927	-0.2 1.5 0.0 1.4	**18** 0142 F 0813 1403 2027	0.0 1.3 0.2 1.3
4 0144 F 0802 1415 2022	-0.1 1.4 0.1 1.4	**19** 0240 SA 0919 1504 2139	0.1 1.2 0.3 1.3
5 0243 SA 0912 1518 2136	0.0 1.3 0.2 1.3	**20** 0409 SU 1037 1636 2259	0.2 1.1 0.3 1.3
6 0359 SU 1047 1638 2312	0.1 1.3 0.3 1.3	**21** 0540 M 1148 1756	0.1 1.2 0.2
7 0530 M 1216 1802	0.1 1.3 0.1	**22** 0008 TU 0640 1248 1851	1.3 0.1 1.2 0.1
8 0034 TU 0647 1325 1906	1.4 0.0 1.3 0.1	**23** 0105 W 0727 1339 1934	1.4 0.0 1.3 0.0
9 0139 W 0745 1423 2000	1.5 -0.2 1.4 0.0	**24** 0154 TH 0806 1424 2012	1.5 -0.1 1.4 0.0
10 0233 TH 0836 1511 ● 2046	1.6 -0.3 1.5 -0.2	**25** 0236 F 0841 1503 ○ 2046	1.5 -0.2 1.4 -0.1
11 0321 F 0920 1554 2130	1.7 -0.4 1.5 -0.2	**26** 0312 SA 0912 1537 2120	1.6 -0.2 1.4 -0.1
12 0405 SA 1002 1632 2211	1.7 -0.4 1.5 -0.3	**27** 0345 SU 0945 1609 2154	1.6 -0.2 1.4 -0.2
13 0445 SU 1042 1707 2251	1.7 -0.4 1.5 -0.3	**28** 0418 M 1018 1639 2230	1.6 -0.3 1.4 -0.3
14 0523 M 1120 1741 2331	1.7 -0.4 1.4 -0.2	**29** 0451 TU 1054 1709 2308	1.6 -0.3 1.4 -0.3
15 0600 TU 1158 1815	1.6 -0.2 1.4	**30** 0526 W 1132 1742 2349	1.5 -0.2 1.4 -0.3
		31 0606 TH 1213 1819	1.5 -0.2 1.4

APRIL

Time	m	Time	m
1 0035 F 0654 1259 1905	-0.2 1.4 0.0 1.3	**16** 0108 SA 0727 1318 ☾ 1937	0.0 1.1 0.1 1.3
2 0127 SA 0753 1352 ☾ 2003	-0.1 1.3 0.1 1.3	**17** 0200 SU 0826 1410 2039	0.1 1.1 0.2 1.3
3 0230 SU 0913 1459 2126	0.0 1.2 0.2 1.3	**18** 0314 M 0943 1524 2158	0.1 1.1 0.3 1.3
4 0354 M 1048 1624 2301	0.1 1.1 0.3 1.3	**19** 0447 TU 1100 1654 2315	0.1 1.1 0.2 1.3
5 0524 TU 1206 1745	0.0 1.2 0.1	**20** 0553 W 1204 1800	0.0 1.2 0.1
6 0018 W 0632 1309 1846	1.4 -0.2 1.3 0.0	**21** 0018 TH 0642 1259 1851	1.4 -0.1 1.3 0.0
7 0119 TH 0726 1402 1937	1.5 -0.3 1.4 -0.2	**22** 0111 F 0724 1346 1933	1.4 -0.2 1.3 -0.1
8 0212 F 0813 1447 ● 2024	1.6 -0.4 1.5 -0.3	**23** 0157 SA 0003 1429 2012	1.5 -0.2 1.4 -0.2
9 0300 SA 0857 1527 2106	1.7 -0.4 1.5 -0.3	**24** 0239 SU 0839 1507 ○ 2051	1.5 -0.3 1.4 -0.2
10 0342 SU 0936 1603 2148	1.6 -0.4 1.5 -0.4	**25** 0318 M 0915 1542 2129	1.5 -0.3 1.4 -0.3
11 0421 M 1014 1637 2227	1.6 -0.3 1.4 -0.3	**26** 0356 TU 0951 1617 2209	1.5 -0.3 1.4 -0.3
12 0457 TU 1050 1709 2306	1.5 -0.3 1.4 -0.3	**27** 0434 W 1030 1651 2250	1.5 -0.3 1.4 -0.3
13 0531 W 1124 1739 2344	1.5 -0.1 1.4 -0.3	**28** 0515 TH 1111 1727 2334	1.5 -0.2 1.4 -0.3
14 0606 TH 1200 1811	1.4 0.0 1.4	**29** 0600 F 1154 1807	1.5 -0.1 1.4
15 0024 F 0642 1236 1849	-0.1 1.2 0.1 1.3	**30** 0024 SA 0652 1242 1857	-0.2 1.2 0.0 1.4

Chart Datum: 0·69 metres below Dansk Normal Null

FREE monthly updates from www.reedsalmanac.co.uk

Chapter 5

347

TIDES

TIME ZONE -0100
(Danish Standard Time)
Subtract 1 hour for UT
For Danish Summer Time add ONE hour in **non-shaded areas**

DENMARK – ESBJERG
LAT 55°28'N LONG 8°27'E
TIMES AND HEIGHTS OF HIGH AND LOW WATERS

YEAR 2005

MAY

Day	Time	m	Day	Time	m
1 SU	0119 / 0757 / 1339 / 2002	-0.2 / 1.1 / 0.1 / 1.3	16 M	0128 / 0742 / 1333 / 1953	0.0 / 1.1 / 0.1 / 1.3
2 M	0227 / 0917 / 1447 / 2123	-0.1 / 1.1 / 0.2 / 1.3	17 TU	0225 / 0846 / 1432 / 2057	0.1 / 1.1 / 0.2 / 1.3
3 TU	0348 / 1037 / 1606 / 2245	-0.1 / 1.1 / 0.1 / 1.4	18 W	0334 / 1000 / 1543 / 2210	0.1 / 1.1 / 0.2 / 1.3
4 W	0506 / 1145 / 1719 / 2355	-0.1 / 1.2 / 0.1 / 1.5	19 TH	0445 / 1109 / 1655 / 2320	0.0 / 1.2 / 0.1 / 1.4
5 TH	0608 / 1244 / 1820	-0.2 / 1.3 / -0.1	20 F	0545 / 1210 / 1757	0.0 / 1.2 / 0.0
6 F	0055 / 0701 / 1335 / 1912	1.5 / -0.3 / 1.3 / -0.2	21 SA	0021 / 0636 / 1303 / 1850	1.4 / -0.1 / 1.3 / 0.0
7 SA	0148 / 0748 / 1420 / 2000	1.6 / -0.3 / 1.4 / -0.3	22 SU	0116 / 0722 / 1352 / 1937	1.4 / -0.2 / 1.4 / -0.1
8 SU	0236 / 0831 / 1500 / 2045	1.6 / -0.3 / 1.4 / -0.3	23 M	0206 / 0805 / 1436 / 2023	1.5 / -0.2 / 1.4 / -0.2
9 M	0320 / 0911 / 1538 / 2127	1.6 / -0.3 / 1.4 / -0.3	24 TU	0254 / 0847 / 1518 / 2107	1.5 / -0.2 / 1.4 / -0.2
10 TU	0359 / 0948 / 1612 / 2206	1.5 / -0.2 / 1.4 / -0.3	25 W	0339 / 0929 / 1558 / 2152	1.4 / -0.2 / 1.4 / -0.3
11 W	0434 / 1023 / 1642 / 2245	1.4 / -0.1 / 1.4 / -0.2	26 TH	0424 / 1012 / 1638 / 2238	1.4 / -0.2 / 1.4 / -0.3
12 TH	0506 / 1056 / 1711 / 2322	1.3 / -0.1 / 1.4 / -0.2	27 F	0510 / 1055 / 1719 / 2326	1.3 / -0.1 / 1.4 / -0.3
13 F	0538 / 1129 / 1741	1.2 / 0.0 / 1.4	28 SA	0600 / 1142 / 1805	1.3 / -0.1 / 1.4
14 SA	0000 / 0611 / 1204 / 1816	-0.1 / 1.1 / 0.1 / 1.4	29 SU	0018 / 0654 / 1232 / 1858	-0.2 / 1.2 / 0.0 / 1.4
15 SU	0041 / 0651 / 1245 / 1900	0.0 / 1.1 / 0.1 / 1.4	30 M	0115 / 0756 / 1327 / 2000	-0.2 / 1.2 / 0.1 / 1.4
			31 TU	0218 / 0903 / 1430 / 2110	-0.1 / 1.1 / 0.1 / 1.4

JUNE

Day	Time	m	Day	Time	m
1 W	0327 / 1011 / 1539 / 2221	-0.1 / 1.2 / 0.1 / 1.5	16 TH	0240 / 0900 / 1452 / 2112	0.0 / 1.2 / 0.1 / 1.4
2 TH	0436 / 1114 / 1648 / 2327	-0.1 / 1.2 / 0.0 / 1.5	17 F	0339 / 1006 / 1555 / 2220	0.0 / 1.2 / 0.1 / 1.4
3 F	0538 / 1212 / 1751	-0.2 / 1.3 / -0.1	18 SA	0443 / 1114 / 1702 / 2330	0.0 / 1.3 / 0.1 / 1.4
4 SA	0028 / 0633 / 1303 / 1847	1.5 / -0.2 / 1.4 / -0.2	19 SU	0545 / 1217 / 1806	0.0 / 1.3 / 0.0
5 SU	0124 / 0722 / 1351 / 1939	1.6 / -0.2 / 1.4 / -0.2	20 M	0036 / 0642 / 1315 / 1906	1.4 / 0.0 / 1.4 / 0.0
6 M	0214 / 0808 / 1436 / 2027	1.5 / -0.2 / 1.5 / -0.2	21 TU	0138 / 0735 / 1408 / 2000	1.4 / -0.1 / 1.4 / -0.1
7 TU	0300 / 0849 / 1516 / 2112	1.5 / -0.2 / 1.5 / -0.2	22 W	0234 / 0824 / 1457 / 2051	1.4 / -0.1 / 1.5 / -0.2
8 W	0341 / 0927 / 1552 / 2152	1.4 / -0.1 / 1.5 / -0.2	23 TH	0327 / 0912 / 1544 / 2141	1.4 / -0.1 / 1.5 / -0.2
9 TH	0417 / 1002 / 1624 / 2230	1.3 / 0.0 / 1.5 / -0.1	24 F	0418 / 0957 / 1629 / 2230	1.4 / -0.1 / 1.5 / -0.2
10 F	0449 / 1035 / 1654 / 2306	1.2 / 0.0 / 1.4 / -0.1	25 SA	0506 / 1044 / 1714 / 2318	1.4 / -0.1 / 1.6 / -0.2
11 SA	0518 / 1106 / 1721 / 2341	1.2 / 0.0 / 1.4 / 0.0	26 SU	0556 / 1130 / 1801	1.3 / -0.1 / 1.6
12 SU	0548 / 1141 / 1753	1.2 / 0.0 / 1.5	27 M	0009 / 0645 / 1218 / 1851	-0.2 / 1.3 / 0.0 / 1.6
13 M	0018 / 0623 / 1220 / 1831	0.0 / 1.2 / 0.0 / 1.5	28 TU	0101 / 0738 / 1309 / 1946	-0.2 / 1.3 / 0.0 / 1.6
14 TU	0100 / 0707 / 1304 / 1918	0.0 / 1.2 / 0.0 / 1.5	29 W	0157 / 0834 / 1405 / 2046	-0.1 / 1.3 / 0.0 / 1.6
15 SU	0146 / 0759 / 1354 / 2011	0.0 / 1.2 / 0.1 / 1.5	30 TH	0256 / 0933 / 1506 / 2151	-0.1 / 1.3 / 0.0 / 1.6

JULY

Day	Time	m	Day	Time	m
1 F	0359 / 1034 / 1612 / 2256	0.0 / 1.3 / 0.0 / 1.5	16 SA	0251 / 0908 / 1509 / 2130	0.0 / 1.3 / 0.1 / 1.5
2 SA	0503 / 1134 / 1720 / 2359	0.0 / 1.3 / 0.0 / 1.5	17 SU	0351 / 1015 / 1615 / 2245	0.1 / 1.3 / 0.1 / 1.5
3 SU	0603 / 1231 / 1824	0.0 / 1.4 / 0.0	18 M	0458 / 1130 / 1728	0.1 / 1.3 / 0.1
4 M	0059 / 0658 / 1324 / 1922	1.5 / 0.0 / 1.5 / -0.1	19 TU	0004 / 0608 / 1242 / 1840	1.4 / 0.1 / 1.4 / 0.1
5 TU	0153 / 0748 / 1413 / 2015	1.5 / 0.0 / 1.5 / -0.1	20 W	0118 / 0712 / 1345 / 1945	1.4 / 0.1 / 1.5 / 0.0
6 W	0242 / 0832 / 1458 / 2101	1.4 / 0.0 / 1.5 / -0.1	21 TH	0221 / 0807 / 1440 / 2040	1.5 / 0.1 / 1.5 / -0.1
7 TH	0325 / 0912 / 1537 / 2142	1.4 / 0.0 / 1.5 / -0.1	22 F	0318 / 0857 / 1531 / 2131	1.5 / 0.0 / 1.6 / -0.2
8 F	0403 / 0946 / 1611 / 2218	1.3 / 0.1 / 1.5 / 0.0	23 SA	0409 / 0945 / 1618 / 2219	1.5 / 0.0 / 1.7 / -0.2
9 SA	0435 / 1018 / 1640 / 2251	1.2 / 0.1 / 1.5 / 0.0	24 SU	0455 / 1030 / 1703 / 2305	1.5 / 0.0 / 1.7 / -0.1
10 SU	0503 / 1049 / 1706 / 2321	1.3 / 0.1 / 1.5 / 0.0	25 M	0539 / 1114 / 1748 / 2351	1.5 / -0.1 / 1.8 / 0.0
11 M	0530 / 1121 / 1734 / 2354	1.3 / 0.1 / 1.6 / 0.0	26 TU	0623 / 1159 / 1833	1.4 / -0.1 / 1.8
12 TU	0600 / 1157 / 1807	1.3 / 0.1 / 1.6	27 W	0037 / 0707 / 1245 / 1921	-0.2 / 1.4 / -0.1 / 1.7
13 W	0030 / 0636 / 1237 / 1847	0.0 / 1.3 / 0.1 / 1.6	28 TH	0126 / 0755 / 1336 / 2015	-0.1 / 1.3 / 0.0 / 1.7
14 TH	0112 / 0720 / 1322 / 1934	-0.1 / 1.3 / 0.1 / 1.6	29 F	0218 / 0848 / 1430 / 2115	0.0 / 1.3 / 0.0 / 1.6
15 F	0159 / 0810 / 1412 / 2027	0.0 / 1.3 / 0.1 / 1.6	30 SA	0315 / 0948 / 1535 / 2221	0.1 / 1.3 / 0.1 / 1.5
			31 SU	0423 / 1054 / 1651 / 2330	0.2 / 1.4 / 0.1 / 1.5

AUGUST

Day	Time	m	Day	Time	m
1 M	0533 / 1157 / 1806	0.2 / 1.5 / 0.1	16 TU	0420 / 1049 / 1702 / 2346	0.3 / 1.4 / 0.2 / 1.4
2 TU	0033 / 0636 / 1257 / 1909	1.5 / 0.2 / 1.5 / 0.1	17 W	0542 / 1215 / 1826	0.3 / 1.5 / 0.0
3 W	0131 / 0730 / 1351 / 2002	1.5 / 0.2 / 1.6 / 0.0	18 TH	0106 / 0654 / 1325 / 1933	1.5 / 0.2 / 1.6 / 0.1
4 TH	0223 / 0815 / 1439 / 2048	1.5 / 0.1 / 1.6 / 0.0	19 F	0209 / 0751 / 1424 / 2027	1.6 / 0.0 / 1.7 / -0.1
5 F	0307 / 0854 / 1520 / 2127	1.5 / 0.1 / 1.7 / 0.0	20 SA	0304 / 0842 / 1515 / 2116	1.6 / -0.1 / 1.8 / -0.2
6 SA	0345 / 0929 / 1554 / 2200	1.4 / 0.1 / 1.7 / 0.0	21 SU	0352 / 0927 / 1601 / 2201	1.6 / -0.1 / 1.9 / -0.3
7 SU	0416 / 0959 / 1623 / 2228	1.4 / 0.1 / 1.7 / 0.0	22 M	0434 / 1010 / 1645 / 2244	1.6 / -0.1 / 1.9 / -0.3
8 M	0444 / 1029 / 1648 / 2257	1.4 / 0.1 / 1.7 / 0.0	23 TU	0514 / 1052 / 1727 / 2326	1.6 / -0.1 / 1.9 / -0.3
9 TU	0509 / 1100 / 1715 / 2327	1.4 / 0.0 / 1.7 / 0.0	24 W	0553 / 1135 / 1809	1.5 / -0.1 / 1.9
10 W	0536 / 1133 / 1744	1.5 / 0.0 / 1.7	25 TH	0008 / 0631 / 1218 / 1852	-0.3 / 1.5 / 0.0 / 1.8
11 TH	0002 / 0607 / 1212 / 1820	0.0 / 1.5 / 0.0 / 1.7	26 F	0051 / 0710 / 1304 / 1940	-0.2 / 1.4 / 0.0 / 1.7
12 F	0040 / 0645 / 1254 / 1903	0.0 / 1.5 / 0.0 / 1.7	27 SA	0136 / 0755 / 1355 / 2036	-0.2 / 1.4 / 0.0 / 1.6
13 SA	0124 / 0730 / 1341 / 1954	0.0 / 1.4 / 0.0 / 1.6	28 SU	0229 / 0857 / 1457 / 2143	-0.1 / 1.3 / 0.0 / 1.5
14 SU	0213 / 0822 / 1435 / 2055	0.1 / 1.4 / 0.1 / 1.6	29 M	0335 / 1007 / 1621 / 2257	0.1 / 1.3 / 0.0 / 1.5
15 M	0310 / 0926 / 1540 / 2213	0.2 / 1.4 / 0.2 / 1.5	30 TU	0459 / 1121 / 1748	0.3 / 1.4 / 0.3
			31 W	0006 / 0611 / 1227 / 1851	1.5 / 0.2 / 1.6 / 0.2

Chart Datum: 0·69 metres below Dansk Normal Null

FREE monthly updates from www.reedsalmanac.co.uk

TIME ZONE -0100
(Danish Standard Time)
Subtract 1 hour for UT
For Danish Summer Time add ONE hour in **non-shaded areas**

DENMARK – ESBJERG
LAT 55°28'N LONG 8°27'E
TIMES AND HEIGHTS OF HIGH AND LOW WATERS

YEAR 2005

SEPTEMBER		OCTOBER		NOVEMBER		DECEMBER	
Time m	Time m	Time m	Time m	Time m	Time m	Time m	Time m
1 0106 1.5 / 0706 0.3 / TH 1323 1.7 / 1942 0.2	**16** 0053 1.5 / 0636 0.4 / F 1306 1.7 / 1918 0.1	**1** 0123 1.6 / 0718 0.3 / SA 1337 1.8 / 1951 0.2	**16** 0130 1.7 / 0707 0.2 / SU 1341 1.9 / 1945 0.0	**1** 0211 1.7 / 0757 0.3 / TU 1423 1.8 / 2022 0.2	**16** 0235 1.8 / 0820 0.1 / W 1455 1.9 / ○ 2048 0.1	**1** 0218 1.7 / 0805 0.2 / TH 1435 1.8 / ● 2028 0.2	**16** 0255 1.8 / 0852 0.1 / F 1524 1.7 / 2109 0.2
2 0157 1.5 / 0751 0.2 / F 1412 1.7 / 2025 0.1	**17** 0154 1.6 / 0732 0.2 / SA 1404 1.8 / 2009 0.0	**2** 0209 1.6 / 0758 0.3 / SU 1421 1.8 / 2027 0.1	**17** 0218 1.7 / 0756 0.1 / M 1431 2.0 / ○ 2030 0.0	**2** 0251 1.7 / 0834 0.2 / W 1502 1.8 / ● 2057 0.1	**17** 0315 1.8 / 0905 0.0 / TH 1539 1.8 / 2127 0.2	**2** 0300 1.7 / 0849 0.2 / F 1521 1.7 / 2109 0.2	**17** 0336 1.8 / 0937 0.1 / SA 1604 1.6 / 2148 0.2
3 0242 1.6 / 0830 0.2 / SA 1454 1.8 / ● 2101 0.1	**18** 0244 1.7 / 0821 0.1 / SU 1454 1.9 / ○ 2054 -0.1	**3** 0248 1.7 / 0833 0.2 / M 1458 1.8 / ● 2058 0.1	**18** 0301 1.8 / 0842 0.0 / TU 1517 2.0 / 2112 0.0	**3** 0326 1.8 / 0912 0.2 / TH 1539 1.8 / 2133 0.1	**18** 0353 1.8 / 0948 0.1 / F 1618 1.8 / 2206 0.2	**3** 0341 1.7 / 0933 0.1 / SA 1606 1.7 / 2151 0.2	**18** 0412 1.8 / 1018 0.1 / SU 1640 1.5 / 2224 0.3
4 0319 1.6 / 0904 0.2 / SU 1530 1.8 / 2132 0.1	**19** 0328 1.7 / 0905 0.0 / M 1540 1.9 / 2137 -0.1	**4** 0322 1.7 / 0905 0.2 / TU 1531 1.8 / 2128 0.1	**19** 0340 1.8 / 0924 0.0 / W 1559 2.0 / 2151 0.0	**4** 0400 1.8 / 0950 0.1 / F 1617 1.8 / 2209 0.2	**19** 0428 1.8 / 1030 0.1 / SA 1655 1.7 / 2242 0.3	**4** 0420 1.8 / 1018 0.1 / SU 1651 1.7 / 2234 0.2	**19** 0445 1.7 / 1057 0.2 / M 1712 1.5 / 2258 0.3
5 0352 1.6 / 0934 0.1 / M 1600 1.8 / 2200 0.1	**20** 0408 1.7 / 0948 -0.1 / TU 1622 2.0 / 2218 -0.1	**5** 0353 1.7 / 0937 0.1 / W 1602 1.8 / 2200 0.1	**20** 0417 1.8 / 1006 0.0 / TH 1638 1.9 / 2230 0.1	**5** 0433 1.8 / 1030 0.1 / SA 1655 1.7 / 2248 0.2	**20** 0500 1.8 / 1110 0.2 / SU 1730 1.6 / 2318 0.3	**5** 0500 1.8 / 1105 0.1 / M 1738 1.6 / 2319 0.2	**20** 0516 1.7 / 1133 0.2 / TU 1743 1.4 / 2332 0.3
6 0420 1.6 / 1004 0.1 / TU 1627 1.8 / 2228 0.1	**21** 0445 1.7 / 1029 -0.1 / W 1702 1.9 / 2257 0.0	**6** 0422 1.7 / 1012 0.1 / TH 1633 1.8 / 2233 0.1	**21** 0451 1.8 / 1047 0.0 / F 1715 1.8 / 2306 0.2	**6** 0506 1.8 / 1113 0.1 / SU 1737 1.7 / 2331 0.3	**21** 0533 1.8 / 1151 0.3 / M 1805 1.5 / 2354 0.4	**6** 0543 1.8 / 1154 0.1 / TU 1828 1.6	**21** 0546 1.7 / 1210 0.3 / W 1815 1.4
7 0446 1.6 / 1036 0.1 / W 1653 1.8 / 2300 0.0	**22** 0520 1.7 / 1109 -0.1 / TH 1741 1.9 / 2336 0.1	**7** 0450 1.7 / 1048 0.1 / F 1706 1.8 / 2309 0.1	**22** 0524 1.7 / 1128 0.1 / SA 1753 1.7 / 2343 0.3	**7** 0545 1.8 / 1200 0.1 / M 1826 1.6	**22** 0607 1.7 / 1233 0.3 / TU 1844 1.5	**7** 0007 0.3 / 0632 1.8 / W 1247 0.1 / 1923 1.5	**22** 0009 0.3 / 0621 1.7 / TH 1248 0.3 / 1853 1.4
8 0512 1.6 / 1109 0.0 / TH 1723 1.8 / 2334 0.0	**23** 0555 1.7 / 1151 0.0 / F 1821 1.8	**8** 0521 1.7 / 1127 0.1 / SA 1743 1.8 / 2348 0.2	**23** 0557 1.7 / 1210 0.2 / SU 1832 1.6	**8** 0017 0.3 / 0631 1.7 / TU 1253 0.2 / 1924 1.5	**23** 0033 0.4 / 0649 1.7 / W 1319 0.4 / ● 1931 1.4	**8** 0059 0.3 / 0727 1.8 / TH 1345 0.1 / ● 2024 1.5	**23** 0049 0.3 / 0703 1.7 / F 1330 0.3 / ● 1939 1.4
9 0542 1.6 / 1148 0.0 / F 1758 1.8	**24** 0015 0.2 / 0632 1.7 / SA 1235 0.1 / 1905 1.7	**9** 0555 1.7 / 1210 0.1 / SU 1827 1.7	**24** 0021 0.4 / 0636 1.7 / M 1256 0.3 / 1917 1.5	**9** 0109 0.4 / 0727 1.7 / W 1354 0.2 / ● 2034 1.5	**24** 0120 0.5 / 0739 1.7 / TH 1413 0.4 / 2030 1.4	**9** 0155 0.3 / 0830 1.8 / F 1447 0.2 / 2128 1.5	**24** 0136 0.3 / 0751 1.7 / SA 1418 0.3 / 2034 1.5
10 0012 0.1 / 0616 1.6 / SA 1229 0.0 / 1840 1.7	**25** 0057 0.3 / 0714 1.6 / SU 1323 0.2 / ◐ 1955 1.6	**10** 0032 0.3 / 0637 1.7 / M 1300 0.2 / ◐ 1921 1.6	**25** 0104 0.5 / 0723 1.7 / TU 1350 0.4 / ◐ 2014 1.4	**10** 0211 0.5 / 0839 1.7 / TH 1506 0.3 / 2153 1.5	**25** 0215 0.5 / 0839 1.7 / F 1515 0.4 / 2137 1.4	**10** 0258 0.2 / 0938 1.8 / SA 1553 0.2 / 2233 1.5	**25** 0228 0.3 / 0848 1.7 / SU 1512 0.3 / 2136 1.5
11 0054 0.2 / 0657 1.6 / SU 1316 0.1 / ◐ 1930 1.6	**26** 0143 0.4 / 0806 1.6 / M 1421 0.3 / 2100 1.5	**11** 0122 0.4 / 0730 1.7 / TU 1358 0.3 / 2031 1.5	**26** 0156 0.6 / 0823 1.7 / W 1501 0.5 / 2127 1.4	**11** 0322 0.5 / 1000 1.7 / F 1622 0.3 / 2305 1.5	**26** 0321 0.5 / 0948 1.7 / SA 1622 0.4 / 2245 1.5	**11** 0405 0.3 / 1047 1.8 / SU 1658 0.2 / 2333 1.6	**26** 0327 0.4 / 0951 1.6 / M 1612 0.3 / 2243 1.5
12 0143 0.3 / 0748 1.6 / M 1411 0.2 / 2034 1.5	**27** 0242 0.5 / 0915 1.6 / TU 1547 0.4 / 2218 1.4	**12** 0222 0.5 / 0840 1.6 / W 1512 0.4 / 2202 1.5	**27** 0306 0.6 / 0939 1.7 / TH 1628 0.5 / 2241 1.5	**12** 0437 0.4 / 1114 1.8 / SA 1730 0.2 /	**27** 0430 0.5 / 1057 1.7 / SU 1723 0.4 / 2346 1.6	**12** 0512 0.3 / 1151 1.8 / M 1758 0.2 /	**27** 0432 0.4 / 1101 1.6 / TU 1716 0.3 / 2350 1.5
13 0240 0.4 / 0853 1.5 / TU 1520 0.3 / 2201 1.5	**28** 0410 0.6 / 1036 1.6 / W 1719 0.4 / 2330 1.4	**13** 0339 0.5 / 1012 1.6 / TH 1641 0.3 / 2327 1.5	**28** 0433 0.6 / 1054 1.7 / F 1735 0.4 / 2345 1.5	**13** 0007 1.6 / 0543 0.3 / SU 1218 1.9 / 1828 0.1	**28** 0534 0.4 / 1159 1.7 / M 1815 0.3 /	**13** 0030 1.6 / 0614 0.3 / TU 1252 1.8 / 1852 0.1	**28** 0539 0.3 / 1211 1.6 / W 1817 0.3
14 0354 0.5 / 1024 1.5 / W 1650 0.3 / 2338 1.5	**29** 0534 0.5 / 1147 1.6 / TH 1821 0.3	**14** 0503 0.5 / 1137 1.7 / F 1757 0.2	**29** 0541 0.5 / 1158 1.7 / SA 1826 0.3	**14** 0101 1.7 / 0640 0.2 / M 1316 1.9 / 1918 0.1	**29** 0042 1.6 / 0629 0.4 / TU 1255 1.7 / 1903 0.3	**14** 0122 1.7 / 0711 0.2 / W 1347 1.8 / 1942 0.1	**29** 0051 1.6 / 0642 0.2 / TH 1315 1.6 / 1913 0.2
15 0523 0.5 / 1156 1.6 / TH 1815 0.2	**30** 0030 1.5 / 0632 0.4 / F 1246 1.7 / 1910 0.2	**15** 0034 1.6 / 0612 0.3 / SA 1244 1.8 / 1855 0.1	**30** 0039 1.6 / 0633 0.4 / SU 1252 1.8 / 1909 0.2	**15** 0151 1.7 / 0732 0.1 / TU 1408 1.9 / 2005 0.1	**30** 0132 1.7 / 0718 0.3 / W 1347 1.7 / 1946 0.2	**15** 0211 1.7 / 0803 0.2 / TH 1438 1.8 / ○ 2027 0.2	**30** 0147 1.6 / 0740 0.2 / F 1413 1.6 / 2004 0.2
			31 0128 1.7 / 0717 0.3 / M 1339 1.8 / 1947 0.2				**31** 0238 1.7 / 0833 0.1 / SA 1507 1.6 / ● 2052 0.2

Chart Datum: 0·69 metres below Dansk Normal Null

》》 **FREE** monthly updates from 《《
www.reedsalmanac.co.uk

TIDES

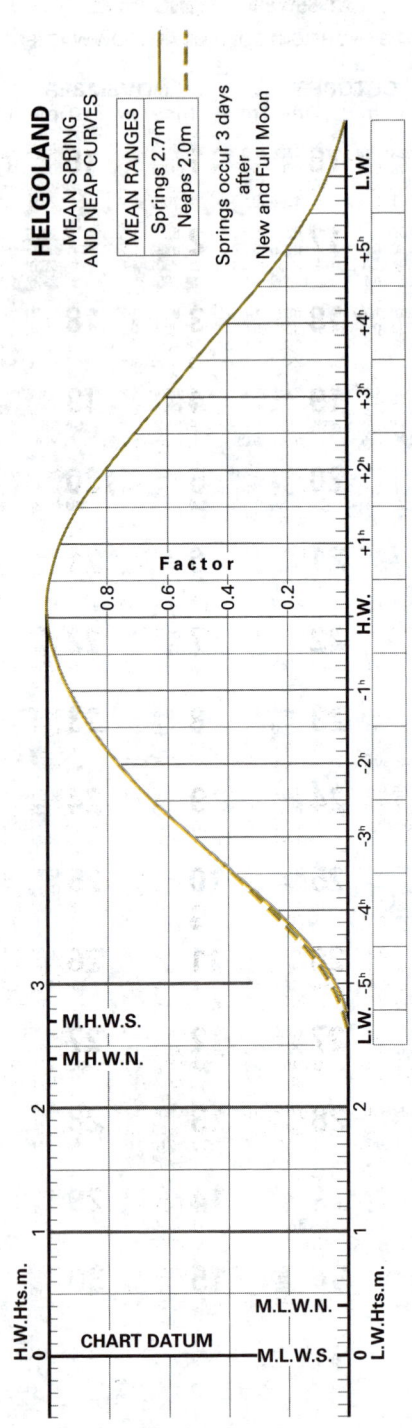

TIME ZONE -0100
(German Standard Time)
Subtract 1 hour for UT
For German Summer Time add
ONE hour in **non-shaded areas**

GERMANY – HELGOLAND
LAT 54°11′N   LONG 7°53′E
TIMES AND HEIGHTS OF HIGH AND LOW WATERS

YEAR 2005

JANUARY		FEBRUARY		MARCH		APRIL	
Time m	Time m	Time m	Time m	Time m	Time m	Time m	Time m
1 0255 3.2 / 0943 0.6 / SA 1523 2.9 / 2149 0.7	**16** 0352 3.3 / 1049 0.5 / SU 1623 2.9 / 2252 0.6	**1** 0344 3.1 / 1032 0.4 / TU 1612 2.8 / 2241 0.6	**16** 0442 3.1 / 1120 0.7 / W 1702 2.8 / ◑ 2338 0.7	**1** 0245 3.1 / 0935 0.3 / TU 1508 2.9 / 2148 0.3	**16** 0330 3.1 / 1007 0.5 / W 1544 3.0 / 2224 0.5	**1** 0338 2.9 / 1015 0.5 / F 1556 2.9 / 2243 0.4	**16** 0418 2.7 / 1041 0.8 / SA 1631 2.9 / ◑ 2320 0.7
2 0331 3.1 / 1021 0.6 / SU 1603 2.8 / 2229 0.7	**17** 0437 3.3 / 1130 0.6 / M 1707 2.8 / ◐ 2336 0.7	**2** 0418 3.0 / 1101 0.5 / W 1646 2.8 / ◐ 2317 0.7	**17** 0529 2.9 / 1204 0.9 / TH 1754 2.8	**2** 0318 3.1 / 1005 0.4 / W 1540 2.9 / 2216 0.4	**17** 0405 3.0 / 1035 0.7 / TH 1618 2.9 / ◐ 2259 0.6	**2** 0427 2.8 / 1103 0.7 / SA 1651 2.8 / ◐ 2345 0.5	**17** 0512 2.6 / 1138 0.9 / SU 1733 2.8
3 0410 3.1 / 1100 0.6 / M 1646 2.8 / ◐ 2311 0.8	**18** 0526 3.2 / 1213 0.7 / TU 1756 2.8	**3** 0500 3.0 / 1145 0.7 / TH 1735 2.7	**18** 0038 0.8 / 0633 2.7 / F 1312 1.0 / 1907 2.7	**3** 0351 3.0 / 1031 0.5 / TH 1612 2.8 / ◐ 2249 0.5	**18** 0447 2.8 / 1114 0.8 / F 1705 2.8 / 2352 0.8	**3** 0537 2.7 / 1219 0.8 / SU 1810 2.8	**18** 0030 0.8 / 0625 2.5 / M 1259 1.0 / 1854 2.8
4 0455 3.0 / 1143 0.7 / TU 1733 2.8	**19** 0028 0.8 / 0621 3.0 / W 1306 0.8 / 1855 2.7	**4** 0015 0.8 / 0604 2.9 / F 1254 0.8 / 1846 2.8	**19** 0202 0.9 / 0756 2.6 / SA 1439 1.0 / 2034 2.8	**4** 0431 2.9 / 1111 0.6 / F 1700 2.7 / 2346 0.6	**19** 0547 2.6 / 1219 1.0 / SA 1815 2.7	**4** 0117 0.5 / 0709 2.6 / M 1358 0.8 / 1945 2.9	**19** 0158 0.8 / 0751 2.5 / TU 1431 0.9 / 2020 2.8
5 0003 0.9 / 0550 3.0 / W 1240 0.8 / 1832 2.8	**20** 0135 0.9 / 0728 2.9 / TH 1415 0.9 / 2005 2.8	**5** 0139 0.8 / 0729 2.8 / SA 1421 0.9 / 2013 2.8	**20** 0332 0.9 / 0921 2.7 / SU 1602 1.0 / 2153 2.9	**5** 0537 2.7 / 1224 0.8 / SA 1817 2.7	**20** 0113 0.9 / 0709 2.5 / SU 1349 1.0 / 1945 2.7	**5** 0258 0.5 / 0845 2.7 / TU 1532 0.7 / 2113 3.0	**20** 0324 0.6 / 0909 2.7 / W 1548 0.8 / 2130 2.9
6 0110 1.0 / 0658 3.0 / TH 1350 0.8 / 1940 2.9	**21** 0254 0.9 / 0843 2.8 / F 1528 0.9 / 2118 2.9	**6** 0310 0.7 / 0859 2.9 / SU 1547 0.9 / 2135 3.0	**21** 0447 0.8 / 1030 2.8 / M 1705 0.8 / 2251 3.1	**6** 0117 0.7 / 0711 2.7 / SU 1402 0.9 / 1954 2.8	**21** 0249 0.8 / 0841 2.6 / M 1523 1.0 / 2113 2.9	**6** 0423 0.3 / 1004 2.7 / W 1644 0.5 / 2219 3.1	**21** 0427 0.5 / 1007 2.9 / TH 1643 0.7 / 2220 3.0
7 0224 0.9 / 0812 3.0 / F 1502 0.8 / 2049 2.9	**22** 0408 0.8 / 0954 2.9 / SA 1633 0.9 / 2221 3.0	**7** 0434 0.6 / 1018 3.0 / M 1703 0.7 / 2246 3.1	**22** 0540 0.7 / 1119 2.9 / TU 1753 0.7 / 2333 3.0	**7** 0300 0.6 / 0850 2.7 / M 1539 0.8 / 2125 3.0	**22** 0414 0.7 / 0958 2.7 / TU 1635 0.8 / 2218 3.0	**7** 0524 0.2 / 1100 2.8 / TH 1739 0.3 / 2311 3.1	**22** 0512 0.4 / 1048 2.9 / F 1727 0.6 / 2300 3.1
8 0337 0.8 / 0923 3.1 / SA 1610 0.8 / 2155 3.0	**23** 0508 0.8 / 1051 3.0 / SU 1725 0.9 / 2311 3.1	**8** 0545 0.4 / 1123 3.0 / TU 1806 0.6 / ● 2343 3.2	**23** 0622 0.6 / 1158 3.0 / W 1833 0.6	**8** 0430 0.4 / 1014 2.8 / TU 1657 0.6 / 2236 3.1	**23** 0513 0.6 / 1051 2.8 / W 1726 0.7 / 2303 3.1	**8** 0614 0.1 / 1146 2.9 / F 1826 0.2 / ● 2357 3.2	**23** 0550 0.3 / 1125 3.0 / SA 1807 0.5 / 2336 3.2
9 0446 0.7 / 1027 3.1 / SU 1713 0.8 / 2255 3.2	**24** 0557 0.7 / 1137 3.0 / M 1810 0.8 / 2352 3.2	**9** 0644 0.3 / 1218 3.0 / W 1900 0.4	**24** 0009 3.2 / 0658 0.5 / TH 1232 3.0 / ◯ 1909 0.5	**9** 0539 0.3 / 1117 2.9 / W 1758 0.4 / 2331 3.1	**24** 0554 0.4 / 1129 2.9 / TH 1806 0.5 / 2339 3.1	**9** 0659 0.1 / 1227 2.9 / SA 1909 0.2 / ◯	**24** 0626 0.3 / 1159 3.1 / SU 1843 0.4 / ◯
10 0549 0.6 / 1126 3.2 / M 1808 0.7 / ● 2349 3.2	**25** 0638 0.7 / 1217 3.0 / TU 1848 0.7 / ◯	**10** 0032 3.3 / 0736 0.2 / TH 1308 3.0 / 1948 0.4	**25** 0043 3.2 / 0732 0.4 / F 1303 3.0 / 1940 0.4	**10** 0635 0.2 / 1208 2.9 / TH 1848 0.3 / ●	**25** 0630 0.3 / 1203 3.0 / F 1843 0.4 / ◯	**10** 0040 3.2 / 0737 0.2 / SU 1304 3.0 / 1947 0.2	**25** 0010 3.2 / 0700 0.3 / M 1231 3.1 / 1916 0.3
11 0646 0.4 / 1221 3.1 / TU 1905 0.6	**26** 0029 3.3 / 0715 0.6 / W 1251 3.0 / 1923 0.6	**11** 0119 3.3 / 0824 0.2 / F 1355 3.0 / 2033 0.3	**26** 0115 3.2 / 0802 0.3 / SA 1332 3.0 / 2011 0.3	**11** 0018 3.2 / 0723 0.1 / F 1251 3.0 / 1932 0.2	**26** 0013 3.1 / 0702 0.3 / SA 1235 3.0 / 1915 0.3	**11** 0117 3.2 / 0809 0.3 / M 1336 3.1 / 2021 0.3	**26** 0044 3.2 / 0734 0.3 / TU 1303 3.1 / 1952 0.3
12 0040 3.3 / 0741 0.3 / W 1317 3.1 / 1958 0.5	**27** 0103 3.3 / 0750 0.5 / TH 1323 3.0 / 1957 0.6	**12** 0205 3.4 / 0908 0.2 / SA 1438 3.0 / 2113 0.3	**27** 0144 3.1 / 0832 0.3 / SU 1403 3.0 / 2041 0.3	**12** 0101 3.3 / 0804 0.2 / SA 1332 3.0 / 2012 0.2	**27** 0045 3.2 / 0733 0.3 / SU 1304 3.0 / 1946 0.3	**12** 0151 3.2 / 0838 0.3 / TU 1407 3.1 / 2054 0.3	**27** 0121 3.2 / 0811 0.3 / W 1340 3.1 / 2031 0.2
13 0131 3.4 / 0835 0.3 / TH 1411 3.0 / 2048 0.5	**28** 0136 3.2 / 0823 0.5 / F 1355 3.0 / 2028 0.5	**13** 0248 3.4 / 0945 0.3 / SU 1515 3.0 / 2148 0.4	**28** 0213 3.1 / 0903 0.3 / M 1435 2.9 / 2114 0.3	**13** 0142 3.3 / 0841 0.3 / SU 1409 3.0 / 2048 0.3	**28** 0115 3.2 / 0805 0.2 / M 1334 3.0 / 2017 0.2	**13** 0225 3.1 / 0904 0.4 / W 1439 3.0 / 2125 0.3	**28** 0202 3.1 / 0848 0.4 / TH 1420 3.0 / 2112 0.2
14 0221 3.4 / 0925 0.3 / F 1459 3.0 / 2131 0.5	**29** 0206 3.2 / 0854 0.4 / SA 1426 2.9 / 2059 0.4	**14** 0327 3.3 / 1018 0.5 / M 1549 3.0 / 2223 0.5		**14** 0220 3.2 / 0913 0.4 / M 1442 3.0 / 2122 0.3	**28** 0146 3.1 / 0837 0.4 / TU 1406 3.0 / 2051 0.2	**14** 0300 2.9 / 0932 0.5 / TH 1512 3.0 / 2157 0.4	**29** 0248 3.0 / 0928 0.5 / F 1504 3.0 / 2159 0.3
15 0308 3.4 / 1008 0.4 / SA 1541 2.9 / 2211 0.5	**30** 0236 3.1 / 0926 0.4 / SU 1501 2.9 / 2134 0.4	**15** 0404 3.2 / 1049 0.6 / TU 1624 2.9 / 2258 0.6		**15** 0256 3.2 / 0941 0.4 / TU 1513 3.0 / 2153 0.4	**30** 0220 3.1 / 0909 0.3 / W 1440 2.9 / 2125 0.2	**15** 0337 2.8 / 1003 0.7 / F 1547 3.0 / 2233 0.6	**30** 0339 2.9 / 1014 0.6 / SA 1553 3.0 / 2252 0.4
	31 0310 3.1 / 1000 0.4 / M 1537 2.9 / 2210 0.5				**31** 0258 3.0 / 0941 0.4 / TH 1515 2.9 / 2201 0.3		

Chart Datum: 1·68 metres below Normal Null (German reference level)

>> **FREE** monthly updates from <<
www.reedsalmanac.co.uk

Chapter 5

TIDES

TIME ZONE -0100
(German Standard Time)
Subtract 1 hour for UT
For German Summer Time add
ONE hour in **non-shaded areas**

GERMANY – HELGOLAND
LAT 54°11′N   LONG 7°53′E
TIMES AND HEIGHTS OF HIGH AND LOW WATERS

YEAR 2005

	MAY				JUNE				JULY				AUGUST			
	Time m		Time m		Time m		Time m		Time m		Time m		Time m		Time m	

1 SU 0436 2.7 / 1111 0.7 / 1654 2.9 / ☽ 2357 0.4
16 M 0445 2.7 / 1108 0.8 / 1659 2.9 / ☾ 2353 0.7
1 W 0108 0.4 / 0652 2.7 / 1328 0.6 / 1913 3.0
16 TH 0011 0.6 / 0600 2.7 / 1231 0.8 / 1816 2.9
1 F 0136 0.6 / 0719 2.8 / 1357 0.6 / 1944 3.0
16 SA 0010 0.7 / 0558 2.8 / 1235 0.8 / 1820 3.0
1 M 0300 0.9 / 0848 2.9 / 1544 0.8 / 2128 2.9
16 TU 0140 0.9 / 0733 2.9 / 1432 0.8 / 2022 2.9

2 M 0545 2.7 / 1223 0.7 / 1809 2.9
17 TU 0544 2.6 / 1212 0.9 / 1803 2.9
2 TH 0220 0.4 / 0802 2.7 / 1441 0.6 / 2023 3.1
17 F 0112 0.6 / 0701 2.8 / 1340 0.8 / 1923 3.0
2 SA 0239 0.6 / 0821 2.8 / 1506 0.6 / 2050 3.0
17 SU 0111 0.7 / 0659 2.8 / 1346 0.8 / 1931 3.0
2 TU 0411 0.9 / 0957 3.0 / 1651 0.7 / 2232 2.9
17 W 0310 0.9 / 0859 3.0 / 1600 0.7 / 2146 3.0

3 TU 0119 0.4 / 0707 2.6 / 1350 0.7 / 1934 2.9
18 W 0104 0.7 / 0655 2.6 / 1331 0.9 / 1918 2.9
3 F 0328 0.4 / 0905 2.7 / 1545 0.5 / 2124 3.1
18 SA 0218 0.6 / 0804 2.8 / 1446 0.8 / 2028 3.0
3 SU 0342 0.6 / 0922 2.9 / 1611 0.6 / 2151 3.0
18 M 0223 0.7 / 0809 2.9 / 1501 0.8 / 2046 3.0
3 W 0509 0.8 / 1053 3.2 / 1743 0.7 / 2322 3.0
18 TH 0431 0.8 / 1014 3.1 / 1715 0.5 / 2256 3.1

4 W 0248 0.4 / 0831 2.6 / 1514 0.6 / 2053 3.0
19 TH 0220 0.6 / 0808 2.7 / 1447 0.8 / 2029 2.9
4 SA 0422 0.3 / 0958 2.8 / 1639 0.4 / 2216 3.1
19 SU 0320 0.6 / 0902 2.9 / 1547 0.7 / 2127 3.1
4 M 0437 0.6 / 1018 3.0 / 1706 0.6 / 2245 3.0
19 TU 0335 0.7 / 0919 3.0 / 1614 0.7 / 2156 3.1
4 TH 0556 0.8 / 1137 3.2 / 1827 0.7
19 F 0540 0.7 / 1115 3.3 / 1818 0.4 / ○ 2353 3.1

5 TH 0403 0.2 / 0940 2.7 / 1620 0.4 / 2155 3.1
20 F 0327 0.5 / 0910 2.8 / 1548 0.7 / 2127 3.0
5 SU 0508 0.4 / 1045 2.9 / 1729 0.4 / 2305 3.1
20 M 0416 0.6 / 0954 3.0 / 1644 0.6 / 2221 3.2
5 TU 0527 0.7 / 1108 3.1 / 1756 0.6 / 2335 3.1
20 W 0443 0.7 / 1024 3.1 / 1722 0.6 / 2300 3.1
5 F 0004 3.1 / 0638 0.7 / 1216 3.3 / ● 1907 0.6
20 SA 0637 0.5 / 1207 3.4 / 1912 0.3

6 F 0457 0.2 / 1032 2.8 / 1710 0.3 / 2244 3.1
21 SA 0419 0.5 / 0958 2.9 / 1638 0.6 / 2214 3.1
6 M 0554 0.5 / 1130 3.1 / 1817 0.4 / ● 2353 3.1
21 TU 0509 0.6 / 1045 3.1 / 1739 0.6 / 2311 3.2
6 W 0612 0.7 / 1152 3.2 / 1841 0.6
21 TH 0546 0.7 / 1124 3.2 / 1824 0.5 / ○ 2357 3.1
6 SA 0041 3.0 / 0715 0.6 / 1252 3.3 / 1942 0.5
21 SU 0043 3.1 / 0726 0.4 / 1255 3.5 / 2000 0.3

7 SA 0543 0.2 / 1116 2.9 / 1757 0.3 / 2331 3.1
22 SU 0504 0.4 / 1040 3.0 / 1725 0.6 / 2257 3.2
7 TU 0636 0.5 / 1210 3.1 / 1858 0.4
22 W 0600 0.6 / 1135 3.2 / 1831 0.5 / ○
7 TH 0019 3.1 / 0652 0.7 / 1231 3.3 / 1920 0.6
22 F 0644 0.6 / 1217 3.3 / 1920 0.3
7 SU 0113 3.0 / 0748 0.6 / 1325 3.3 / 2014 0.5
22 M 0130 3.1 / 0811 0.4 / 1341 3.5 / 2045 0.3

8 SU 0627 0.3 / 1158 3.0 / 1843 0.3 / ●
23 M 0546 0.4 / 1120 3.1 / 1808 0.5 / ○ 2336 3.2
8 W 0033 3.1 / 0710 0.5 / 1245 3.2 / 1935 0.5
23 TH 0002 3.2 / 0651 0.5 / 1225 3.3 / 1924 0.4
8 F 0056 3.0 / 0728 0.6 / 1307 3.3 / 1958 0.6
23 SA 0053 3.1 / 0737 0.5 / 1308 3.4 / 2014 0.3
8 M 0143 3.1 / 0818 0.5 / 1354 3.3 / 2043 0.5
23 TU 0213 3.1 / 0852 0.4 / 1425 3.5 / 2124 0.4

9 M 0016 3.1 / 0706 0.3 / 1236 3.1 / 1921 0.3
24 TU 0626 0.4 / 1158 3.2 / 1848 0.4
9 TH 0109 3.0 / 0742 0.6 / 1319 3.2 / 2010 0.5
24 F 0057 3.2 / 0743 0.5 / 1316 3.3 / 2019 0.3
9 SA 0130 3.0 / 0802 0.6 / 1342 3.3 / 2033 0.6
24 SU 0146 3.1 / 0828 0.4 / 1358 3.4 / 2104 0.3
9 TU 0212 3.0 / 0847 0.5 / 1422 3.2 / 2112 0.5
24 W 0251 3.1 / 0929 0.4 / 1506 3.4 / 2159 0.5

10 TU 0053 3.1 / 0737 0.4 / 1307 3.1 / 1955 0.3
25 W 0017 3.2 / 0707 0.4 / 1239 3.2 / 1932 0.4
10 F 0144 3.0 / 0815 0.6 / 1355 3.2 / 2046 0.5
25 SA 0153 3.1 / 0836 0.5 / 1408 3.3 / 2112 0.2
10 SU 0204 3.0 / 0835 0.6 / 1415 3.3 / 2105 0.5
25 M 0234 3.0 / 0912 0.4 / 1445 3.4 / 2149 0.3
10 W 0244 3.0 / 0919 0.5 / 1454 3.2 / 2145 0.5
25 TH 0328 3.1 / 1005 0.5 / 1545 3.3 / 2232 0.7

11 W 0126 3.1 / 0805 0.5 / 1338 3.1 / 2028 0.4
26 TH 0104 3.2 / 0752 0.4 / 1324 3.2 / 2021 0.3
11 SA 0221 2.9 / 0849 0.6 / 1432 3.2 / 2122 0.5
26 SU 0246 3.0 / 0923 0.4 / 1457 3.3 / 2202 0.2
11 M 0237 2.9 / 0907 0.6 / 1448 3.2 / 2138 0.5
26 TU 0318 3.0 / 0952 0.4 / 1530 3.4 / 2231 0.4
11 TH 0319 3.0 / 0954 0.5 / 1529 3.1 / 2217 0.5
26 F 0405 2.9 / 1044 0.6 / 1626 3.2 / ☾ 2306 0.3

12 TH 0200 3.0 / 0835 0.5 / 1412 3.1 / 2102 0.4
27 F 0155 3.1 / 0839 0.5 / 1412 3.2 / 2111 0.2
12 SU 0259 2.9 / 0924 0.6 / 1509 3.2 / 2159 0.6
27 M 0336 2.9 / 1010 0.4 / 1547 3.3 / 2252 0.3
12 TU 0312 2.9 / 0942 0.6 / 1523 3.1 / 2214 0.5
27 W 0401 3.0 / 1035 0.5 / 1616 3.3 / 2313 0.5
12 F 0353 2.9 / 1026 0.6 / 1601 3.1 / 2244 0.6
27 SA 0447 2.9 / 1126 0.7 / 1713 3.1 / 2348 0.6

13 F 0238 2.9 / 0906 0.6 / 1449 3.1 / 2137 0.5
28 SA 0248 3.0 / 0926 0.6 / 1501 3.1 / 2203 0.3
13 M 0337 2.8 / 1002 0.6 / 1547 3.1 / 2238 0.6
28 TU 0427 2.8 / 1100 0.4 / 1640 3.2 / ☾ 2345 0.3
13 W 0350 2.9 / 1020 0.6 / 1600 3.1 / 2250 0.5
28 TH 0447 2.9 / 1120 0.6 / 1704 3.2 / ☾ 2355 0.7
13 SA 0425 2.9 / 1056 0.7 / 1637 3.1 / ☾ 2318 0.7
28 SU 0537 2.9 / 1222 0.7 / 1814 2.8

14 SA 0317 2.8 / 0941 0.7 / 1527 3.1 / 2215 0.6
29 SU 0342 2.8 / 1016 0.6 / 1553 3.1 / 2259 0.3
14 TU 0419 2.8 / 1044 0.6 / 1629 3.0 / 2321 0.6
29 W 0522 2.8 / 1154 0.4 / 1738 3.2
14 TH 0430 2.8 / 1057 0.6 / 1638 3.1 / ☾ 2325 0.6
29 F 0535 2.9 / 1209 0.7 / 1756 3.1
14 SU 0505 2.8 / 1144 0.8 / 1731 2.9 / ☾
29 M 0051 1.1 / 0647 2.8 / 1342 0.8 / 1934 2.7

15 SU 0358 2.7 / 1020 0.8 / 1608 3.0 / 2258 0.7
30 M 0439 2.7 / 1113 0.6 / 1653 3.1
15 W 0506 2.7 / 1132 0.6 / 1718 3.0
30 TH 0039 0.5 / 0620 2.8 / 1252 0.5 / 1839 3.1
15 F 0510 2.7 / 1132 0.6 / 1721 3.0 / ☾
30 SA 0042 0.8 / 0628 2.8 / 1309 0.8 / 1858 2.9
15 M 0016 0.9 / 0608 2.8 / 1300 0.8 / 1851 2.9
30 TU 0216 1.1 / 0812 2.8 / 1514 1.0 / 2102 2.8

16 M 0445 2.7 / 1108 0.8 / 1659 2.9 / ☾ 2353 0.7 (already listed)

31 TU 0000 0.4 / 0543 2.7 / 1217 0.6 / 1801 3.0
31 SU 0144 0.9 / 0734 2.8 / 1425 0.8 / 2012 2.9
31 W 0344 1.1 / 0934 3.0 / 1633 0.9 / 2216 2.9

Chart Datum: 1·68 metres below Normal Null (German reference level)

FREE monthly updates from
www.reedsalmanac.co.uk

352

TIME ZONE -0100
(German Standard Time)
Subtract 1 hour for UT
For German Summer Time add
ONE hour in non-shaded areas

GERMANY – HELGOLAND
LAT 54°11′N   LONG 7°53′E
TIMES AND HEIGHTS OF HIGH AND LOW WATERS

YEAR 2005

Chart Datum: 1·68 metres below Normal Null (German reference level)

	SEPTEMBER			OCTOBER			NOVEMBER			DECEMBER	
	Time m	Time m		Time m	Time m		Time m	Time m		Time m	Time m
1 TH	0452 0.9 / 1036 3.2 / 1729 0.7 / 2307 3.0	**16** F	0425 0.8 / 1005 3.2 / 1708 0.5 / 2249 3.0	**1** SA	0511 0.9 / 1049 3.2 / 1739 0.7 / 2315 3.1	**16** SU	0508 0.6 / 1042 3.3 / 1742 0.3 / 2319 3.0	**1** TU	0545 0.8 / 1119 3.3 / 1803 0.6 / 2340 3.2	**16** W	0616 0.5 / 1151 3.3 / 1839 0.6 / ○	**1** TH	0546 0.8 / 1120 3.3 / 1803 0.7 / ● 2339 3.3	**16** F	0640 0.7 / 1218 3.2 / 1853 0.8
2 F	0539 0.8 / 1119 3.2 / 1809 0.7 / 2344 3.1	**17** SA	0529 0.7 / 1102 3.3 / 1805 0.3 / 2341 3.0	**2** SU	0548 0.7 / 1123 3.2 / 1811 0.6 / 2346 3.1	**17** M	0557 0.5 / 1128 3.3 / 1828 0.4 / ○	**2** W	0621 0.7 / 1153 3.3 / 1837 0.6	**17** TH	0014 3.2 / 0658 0.6 / 1232 3.3 / 1914 0.7	**2** F	0627 0.7 / 1200 3.3 / 1843 0.7	**17** SA	0032 3.3 / 0719 0.7 / 1256 3.1 / 1927 0.8
3 SA	0618 0.7 / 1154 3.3 / 1844 0.6 / ●	**18** SU	0622 0.5 / 1151 3.3 / 1854 0.3 / ○	**3** M	0623 0.7 / 1156 3.2 / 1843 0.5 / ●	**18** TU	0001 3.1 / 0642 0.4 / 1213 3.3 / 1909 0.4	**3** TH	0011 3.2 / 0654 0.7 / 1226 3.3 / 1910 0.6	**18** F	0049 3.3 / 0736 0.6 / 1309 3.2 / 1946 0.7	**3** SA	0019 3.3 / 0710 0.7 / 1245 3.3 / 1928 0.8	**18** SU	0108 3.3 / 0757 0.7 / 1333 3.1 / 2002 0.8
4 SU	0017 3.1 / 0656 0.6 / 1228 3.3 / 1917 0.5	**19** M	0026 3.1 / 0707 0.4 / 1235 3.4 / 1937 0.3	**4** TU	0017 3.1 / 0656 0.6 / 1228 3.3 / 1913 0.5	**19** W	0040 3.2 / 0723 0.5 / 1253 3.4 / 1944 0.6	**4** F	0043 3.2 / 0728 0.6 / 1301 3.3 / 1946 0.7	**19** SA	0123 3.3 / 0812 0.7 / 1347 3.1 / 2019 0.8	**4** SU	0103 3.3 / 0757 0.6 / 1334 3.2 / 2015 0.8	**19** M	0145 3.3 / 0835 0.7 / 1411 3.0 / 2038 0.8
5 M	0048 3.1 / 0726 0.5 / 1300 3.3 / 1947 0.5	**20** TU	0107 3.1 / 0748 0.4 / 1318 3.5 / 2016 0.4	**5** W	0046 3.2 / 0726 0.6 / 1258 3.3 / 1943 0.5	**20** TH	0115 3.2 / 0800 0.5 / 1331 3.4 / 2016 0.6	**5** SA	0118 3.2 / 0806 0.6 / 1340 3.2 / 2022 0.7	**20** SU	0159 3.3 / 0849 0.7 / 1427 3.0 / 2053 0.8	**5** M	0150 3.3 / 0845 0.5 / 1424 3.1 / 2059 0.8	**20** TU	0222 3.3 / 0911 0.7 / 1448 3.0 / 2111 0.8
6 TU	0117 3.1 / 0755 0.5 / 1328 3.2 / 2014 0.5	**21** W	0145 3.2 / 0826 0.4 / 1358 3.5 / 2051 0.5	**6** TH	0114 3.2 / 0755 0.5 / 1326 3.3 / 2012 0.6	**21** F	0148 3.3 / 0835 0.6 / 1408 3.3 / 2047 0.7	**6** SU	0157 3.2 / 0846 0.6 / 1422 3.1 / 2100 0.8	**21** M	0236 3.2 / 0925 0.7 / 1507 2.9 / 2128 0.9	**6** TU	0236 3.3 / 0932 0.5 / 1511 3.0 / 2143 0.8	**21** W	0256 3.3 / 0944 0.7 / 1524 2.9 / 2145 0.8
7 W	0144 3.1 / 0823 0.5 / 1354 3.2 / 2042 0.5	**22** TH	0219 3.2 / 0902 0.5 / 1437 3.4 / 2122 0.6	**7** F	0143 3.1 / 0826 0.5 / 1356 3.2 / 2042 0.6	**22** SA	0221 3.2 / 0909 0.6 / 1446 3.1 / 2117 0.8	**7** M	0238 3.2 / 0929 0.6 / 1509 3.0 / 2142 0.9	**22** TU	0314 3.2 / 1003 0.8 / 1547 2.8 / 2206 1.0	**7** W	0323 3.3 / 1022 0.6 / 1603 2.9 / 2234 0.8	**22** TH	0331 3.2 / 1020 0.8 / 1602 2.9 / 2223 0.9
8 TH	0214 3.1 / 0853 0.5 / 1423 3.2 / 2112 0.5	**23** F	0252 3.2 / 0936 0.5 / 1513 3.2 / 2151 0.7	**8** SA	0215 3.1 / 0859 0.5 / 1432 3.1 / 2113 0.7	**23** SU	0256 3.2 / 0944 0.7 / 1526 2.9 / 2150 0.9	**8** TU	0324 3.1 / 1018 0.7 / 1603 2.9 / 2234 1.0	**23** W	0355 3.2 / 1045 0.9 / 1632 2.8 / ○ 2251 1.1	**8** TH	0417 3.2 / 1119 0.6 / 1701 2.8 / ○ 2332 0.9	**23** F	0408 3.1 / 1058 0.6 / 1644 2.8 / ○ 2305 1.0
9 F	0245 3.0 / 0925 0.5 / 1456 3.1 / 2142 0.6	**24** SA	0326 3.1 / 1010 0.6 / 1551 3.1 / 2222 0.9	**9** SU	0250 3.1 / 0934 0.6 / 1512 3.0 / 2148 0.8	**24** M	0335 3.1 / 1023 0.8 / 1609 2.8 / 2230 1.1	**9** W	0420 3.1 / 1118 0.7 / 1707 2.8 / ○ 2340 1.0	**24** TH	0443 3.1 / 1135 1.0 / 1727 2.7 / 2349 1.2	**9** F	0519 3.2 / 1221 0.7 / 1807 2.8	**24** SA	0452 3.0 / 1141 0.9 / 1732 2.8 / 2357 1.0
10 SA	0317 3.0 / 0956 0.6 / 1530 3.0 / 2209 0.7	**25** SU	0405 3.0 / 1050 0.7 / 1636 2.9 / ○ 2303 1.0	**10** M	0330 3.0 / 1015 0.7 / 1600 2.9 / ○ 2232 0.9	**25** TU	0421 3.0 / 1111 1.0 / 1703 2.7 / ○ 2324 1.2	**10** TH	0530 3.0 / 1233 0.7 / 1825 2.7	**25** F	0543 3.0 / 1239 1.0 / 1833 2.7	**10** SA	0038 0.9 / 0628 3.2 / 1330 0.7 / 1917 2.8	**25** SU	0546 3.0 / 1237 0.9 / 1830 2.8
11 SU	0349 2.9 / 1026 0.7 / 1609 2.9 / ○ 2244 0.8	**26** M	0454 2.9 / 1142 0.9 / 1735 2.7	**11** TU	0421 2.9 / 1111 0.8 / 1705 2.8 / 2340 1.0	**26** W	0521 2.9 / 1216 1.1 / 1812 2.6	**11** F	0102 1.0 / 0652 3.1 / 1353 0.7 / 1950 2.7	**26** SA	0101 1.2 / 0655 3.0 / 1353 1.0 / 1946 2.8	**11** SU	0152 0.8 / 0741 3.2 / 1442 0.7 / 2026 2.8	**26** M	0102 1.1 / 0652 3.0 / 1343 1.0 / 1935 2.9
12 M	0432 2.8 / 1115 0.8 / 1707 2.8 / 2346 1.0	**27** TU	0003 1.2 / 0602 2.9 / 1258 1.1 / 1854 2.6	**12** W	0534 2.9 / 1234 0.9 / 1831 2.7	**27** TH	0039 1.3 / 0639 2.9 / 1340 1.1 / 1934 2.7	**12** SA	0219 0.9 / 0814 3.1 / 1502 0.6 / 2105 2.8	**27** SU	0219 1.2 / 0807 3.1 / 1502 0.9 / 2051 2.9	**12** M	0304 0.8 / 0850 3.2 / 1546 0.7 / 2127 2.9	**27** TU	0213 1.1 / 0801 3.0 / 1450 0.9 / 2038 2.9
13 TU	0541 2.8 / 1249 0.9 / 1833 2.8	**28** W	0130 1.3 / 0730 2.9 / 1433 1.1 / 2025 2.7	**13** TH	0113 1.1 / 0705 2.9 / 1414 0.8 / 2007 2.8	**28** F	0208 1.2 / 0803 3.0 / 1505 1.0 / 2054 2.8	**13** SU	0343 0.8 / 0923 3.2 / 1624 0.5 / 2203 2.9	**28** M	0325 1.1 / 0909 3.1 / 1557 0.8 / 2141 3.0	**13** TU	0408 0.7 / 0950 3.3 / 1640 0.7 / 2220 3.0	**28** W	0320 0.9 / 0906 3.1 / 1550 0.9 / 2135 3.1
14 W	0120 1.1 / 0714 2.9 / 1420 0.8 / 2013 2.8	**29** TH	0305 1.0 / 0858 3.0 / 1601 0.9 / 2146 2.8	**14** F	0251 0.9 / 0836 3.1 / 1545 0.6 / 2130 2.9	**29** SA	0329 1.1 / 0915 3.1 / 1611 0.8 / 2154 2.9	**14** M	0439 0.6 / 1017 3.3 / 1712 0.5 / 2250 3.0	**29** TU	0416 1.0 / 0958 3.1 / 1642 0.8 / 2222 3.1	**14** W	0503 0.7 / 1043 3.3 / 1729 0.7 / 2309 3.1	**29** TH	0420 0.9 / 1003 3.2 / 1645 0.9 / 2227 3.2
15 TH	0300 0.9 / 0849 3.0 / 1555 0.6 / 2142 2.9	**30** F	0421 0.8 / 1006 3.1 / 1701 0.8 / 2240 2.9	**15** SA	0410 0.6 / 0949 3.2 / 1652 0.4 / 2232 3.0	**30** SU	0426 1.0 / 1006 3.2 / 1655 0.7 / 2234 3.0	**15** TU	0528 0.6 / 1105 3.3 / 1757 0.5 / 2333 3.1	**30** W	0502 0.9 / 1040 3.3 / 1723 0.8 / 2301 3.3	**15** TH	0554 0.8 / 1133 3.2 / 1814 0.8 / ○ 2353 3.3	**30** F	0517 0.8 / 1054 3.3 / 1737 0.8 / 2317 3.3
						31 M	0507 0.7 / 1044 3.2 / 1729 0.7 / 2307 3.2						**31** SA	0610 0.7 / 1145 3.2 / 1828 0.8 / ●

Chapter 5

>> FREE monthly updates from <<
www.reedsalmanac.co.uk

TIDES

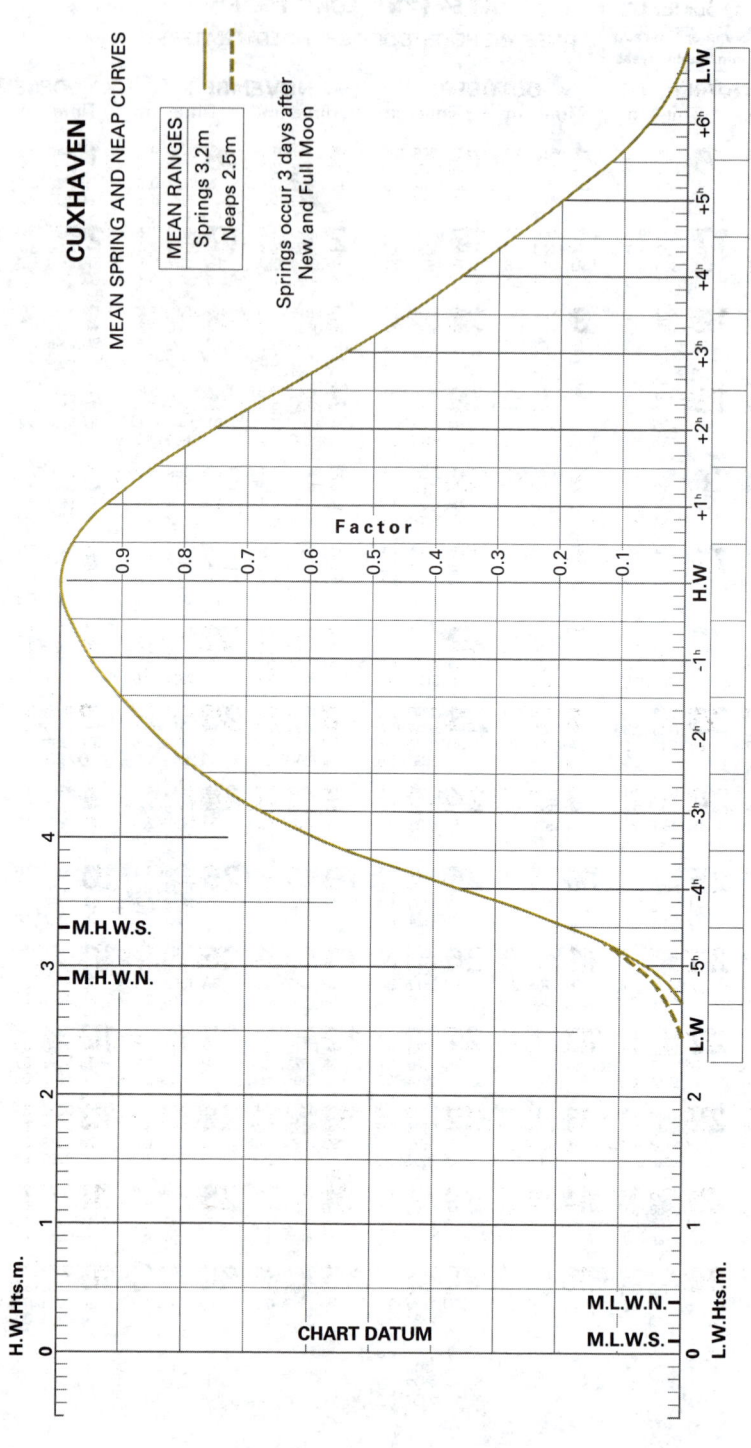

TIME ZONE -0100
(German Standard Time)
Subtract 1 hour for UT
For German Summer Time add
ONE hour in **non-shaded areas**

GERMANY – CUXHAVEN
LAT 53°52'N   LONG 8°43'E
TIMES AND HEIGHTS OF HIGH AND LOW WATERS

YEAR 2005

JANUARY				FEBRUARY				MARCH				APRIL			
Time	m	Time	m	Time	m	Time	m	Time	m	Time	m	Time	m	Time	m
1 0405 3.8 1105 0.6 SA 1637 3.4 2312 0.7		**16** 0500 3.9 1212 0.5 SU 1738 3.4		**1** 0457 3.7 1153 0.5 TU 1723 3.4		**16** 0015 0.6 0550 3.6 W 1240 0.7 ❶ 1811 3.4		**1** 0356 3.7 1056 0.3 TU 1620 3.5 2307 0.3		**16** 0439 3.7 1130 0.5 W 1654 3.5 2338 0.5		**1** 0450 3.5 1132 0.5 F 1707 3.5 2354 0.4		**16** 0527 3.3 1154 0.8 SA 1738 3.4 ❶	
2 0442 3.7 1141 0.6 SU 1716 3.3 2350 0.8		**17** 0014 0.7 0545 3.9 M 1252 0.6 ❶ 1820 3.4		**2** 0000 0.6 0530 3.6 W 1221 0.6 ❶ 1758 3.3		**17** 0050 0.7 0637 3.4 TH 1317 0.8 1902 3.2		**2** 0431 3.7 1125 0.4 W 1652 3.4 2333 0.4		**17** 0514 3.5 1154 0.7 TH 1726 3.4 ❶		**2** 0539 3.3 1216 0.7 SA 1801 3.3 ❶		**17** 0026 0.7 0621 3.1 SU 1245 0.9 1841 3.3	
3 0522 3.6 1219 0.7 M 1757 3.3 ❶		**18** 0055 0.7 0633 3.7 TU 1332 0.7 1906 3.3		**3** 0032 0.7 0611 3.5 TH 1301 0.7 1848 3.3		**18** 0145 0.8 0741 3.2 F 1421 1.0 2015 3.2		**3** 0503 3.6 1150 0.5 TH 1724 3.4 ❶		**18** 0008 0.6 0555 3.3 F 1226 0.8 1812 3.3		**3** 0052 0.5 0649 3.2 SU 1328 0.8 1919 3.3		**18** 0133 0.8 0735 3.0 M 1404 1.0 2003 3.3	
4 0029 0.8 0606 3.6 TU 1301 0.7 1845 3.3		**19** 0144 0.8 0729 3.5 W 1422 0.8 2004 3.2		**4** 0126 0.8 0714 3.4 F 1407 0.9 1959 3.3		**19** 0307 0.9 0905 3.2 SA 1548 1.0 2142 3.3		**4** 0002 0.5 0543 3.4 F 1226 0.7 1811 3.2		**19** 0056 0.8 0655 3.1 SA 1325 1.0 1923 3.2		**4** 0220 0.6 0821 3.2 M 1506 0.8 2054 3.4		**19** 0303 0.8 0902 3.1 TU 1539 0.9 2129 3.4	
5 0119 1.0 0700 3.5 W 1356 0.8 1945 3.3		**20** 0248 0.9 0837 3.4 TH 1529 0.9 2114 3.3		**5** 0247 0.9 0838 3.4 SA 1535 0.9 2124 3.4		**20** 0442 0.9 1031 3.2 SU 1716 1.0 2300 3.5		**5** 0054 0.6 0648 3.3 SA 1334 0.8 1928 3.2		**20** 0214 0.9 0818 3.0 SU 1454 1.0 2054 3.3		**5** 0403 0.5 0956 3.2 TU 1645 0.7 2221 3.6		**20** 0433 0.6 1021 3.2 W 1702 0.8 2239 3.5	
6 0224 1.0 0806 3.6 TH 1506 0.9 2054 3.4		**21** 0406 0.9 0953 3.4 F 1644 1.0 2227 3.4		**6** 0421 0.7 1008 3.5 SU 1706 0.9 2245 3.6		**21** 0603 0.8 1141 3.4 M 1826 0.8 2359 3.7		**6** 0222 0.7 0820 3.2 SU 1512 0.9 2102 3.4		**21** 0354 0.9 0951 3.1 M 1633 1.0 2221 3.4		**6** 0534 0.3 1115 3.3 W 1803 0.5 2329 3.7		**21** 0542 0.5 1119 3.4 TH 1801 0.6 2329 3.7	
7 0339 1.0 0919 3.6 F 1620 0.9 2204 3.5		**22** 0525 0.9 1104 3.4 SA 1753 0.9 2331 3.5		**7** 0549 0.6 1129 3.6 M 1826 0.7 2355 3.7		**22** 0700 0.7 1231 3.5 TU 1916 0.7		**7** 0407 0.6 1000 3.3 M 1655 0.8 2232 3.5		**22** 0526 0.7 1109 3.3 TU 1752 0.8 2326 3.6		**7** 0640 0.2 1213 3.4 TH 1900 0.3		**22** 0629 0.4 1201 3.5 F 1847 0.5	
8 0454 0.8 1032 3.7 SA 1732 0.8 2308 3.6		**23** 0628 0.8 1202 3.5 SU 1850 0.9		**8** 0704 0.4 1236 3.6 TU 1932 0.6 ●		**23** 0042 3.8 0742 0.6 W 1310 3.6 1957 0.6		**8** 0542 0.4 1124 3.4 TU 1818 0.6 2344 3.7		**23** 0630 0.5 1202 3.4 W 1846 0.6		**8** 0022 3.8 0732 0.1 F 1300 3.5 ● 1949 0.2		**23** 0009 3.8 0708 0.3 SA 1238 3.6 1927 0.5	
9 0606 0.7 1139 3.7 SU 1837 0.8		**24** 0020 3.7 0718 0.8 M 1248 3.6 1936 0.8		**9** 0053 3.8 0805 0.3 W 1333 3.6 2027 0.4		**24** 0118 3.8 0820 0.5 TH 1345 3.6 ○ 2033 0.5		**9** 0656 0.3 1230 3.5 W 1922 0.4		**24** 0012 3.7 0712 0.4 TH 1241 3.5 1928 0.5		**9** 0109 3.8 0818 0.1 SA 1343 3.6 2032 0.2		**24** 0046 3.8 0746 0.3 SU 1312 3.7 ○ 2004 0.4	
10 0007 3.8 0711 0.6 M 1240 3.7 ● 1936 0.7		**25** 0101 3.8 0801 0.7 TU 1327 3.6 ○ 2015 0.7		**10** 0144 3.9 0858 0.2 TH 1424 3.6 2115 0.3		**25** 0153 3.8 0855 0.4 F 1417 3.6 2106 0.4		**10** 0041 3.8 0754 0.2 TH 1322 3.6 ● 2013 0.3		**25** 0048 3.8 0749 0.3 F 1316 3.6 ○ 2005 0.4		**10** 0152 3.9 0858 0.2 SU 1420 3.7 2109 0.2		**25** 0121 3.9 0820 0.3 M 1344 3.8 2038 0.3	
11 0101 3.9 0809 0.4 TU 1337 3.7 2031 0.6		**26** 0138 3.9 0839 0.6 W 1403 3.6 2050 0.7		**11** 0232 4.0 0947 0.2 F 1511 3.6 2200 0.3		**26** 0224 3.8 0927 0.3 SA 1446 3.6 2136 0.3		**11** 0130 3.9 0843 0.1 F 1408 3.6 2057 0.2		**26** 0123 3.8 0824 0.3 SA 1348 3.6 2038 0.3		**11** 0230 3.9 0933 0.3 M 1451 3.7 2142 0.3		**26** 0155 3.9 0854 0.3 TU 1415 3.8 2112 0.3	
12 0153 3.9 0904 0.4 W 1433 3.7 2125 0.6		**27** 0212 3.9 0916 0.6 TH 1437 3.6 2124 0.6		**12** 0316 4.0 1033 0.2 SA 1553 3.6 2240 0.3		**27** 0252 3.8 0956 0.3 SU 1515 3.6 2205 0.3		**12** 0214 3.9 0926 0.2 SA 1448 3.6 2136 0.2		**27** 0154 3.8 0856 0.2 SU 1417 3.7 2109 0.3		**12** 0303 3.9 1002 0.4 TU 1520 3.7 2212 0.3		**27** 0232 3.8 0930 0.2 W 1451 3.7 2149 0.2	
13 0244 4.0 0959 0.4 TH 1526 3.7 2215 0.5		**28** 0245 3.9 0950 0.6 F 1509 3.6 2154 0.5		**13** 0357 4.0 1111 0.4 SU 1629 3.6 2313 0.4		**28** 0322 3.7 1025 0.3 M 1546 3.5 2235 0.3		**13** 0254 4.0 1006 0.2 SU 1524 3.7 2212 0.2		**28** 0224 3.8 0927 0.2 M 1445 3.7 2139 0.2		**13** 0336 3.7 1028 0.4 W 1549 3.7 2241 0.3		**28** 0314 3.7 1007 0.4 TH 1532 3.7 2229 0.3	
14 0333 4.0 1049 0.4 F 1614 3.6 2258 0.5		**29** 0315 3.9 1019 0.4 SA 1540 3.5 2224 0.4		**14** 0435 3.9 1143 0.5 M 1703 3.5 2344 0.5				**14** 0333 3.9 1039 0.4 M 1555 3.7 2244 0.3		**29** 0256 3.8 0957 0.3 TU 1517 3.6 2210 0.2		**14** 0410 3.6 1054 0.6 TH 1620 3.6 2310 0.4		**29** 0401 3.6 1046 0.5 F 1616 3.6 2313 0.3
15 0417 4.0 1132 0.4 SA 1657 3.5 2336 0.6		**30** 0346 3.7 1048 0.5 SU 1614 3.4 2256 0.6		**15** 0512 3.8 1212 0.6 TU 1735 3.5				**15** 0405 3.8 1106 0.4 TU 1624 3.6 2312 0.3		**30** 0331 3.7 1029 0.4 W 1551 3.5 2243 0.2		**15** 0446 3.4 1120 0.7 F 1655 3.5 2342 0.6		**30** 0452 3.4 1129 0.6 SA 1705 3.6	
		31 0421 3.7 1121 0.4 M 1650 3.4 2330 0.5								**31** 0410 3.6 1100 0.4 TH 1628 3.5 2316 0.3						

Chart Datum: 1·66 metres below Normal Null (German reference level)

FREE monthly updates from **www.reedsalmanac.co.uk**

TIDES

TIME ZONE -0100
(German Standard Time)
Subtract 1 hour for UT
For German Summer Time add ONE hour in **non-shaded areas**

GERMANY – CUXHAVEN
LAT 53°52′N LONG 8°43′E
TIMES AND HEIGHTS OF HIGH AND LOW WATERS

YEAR 2005

	MAY			JUNE			JULY			AUGUST	
	Time m	Time m		Time m	Time m		Time m	Time m		Time m	Time m
1 SU	0002 0.4 0549 3.3 1223 0.7 ☽1805 3.5	**16** M	0009 0.6 0556 3.2 1219 0.9 ☾1808 3.5	**1** W	0218 0.4 0807 3.2 1441 0.6 2023 3.7	**16** TH	0123 0.6 0714 3.3 1342 0.8 1930 3.5	**1** F	0251 0.6 0833 3.3 1512 0.7 2055 3.7	**16** SA	0124 0.7 0715 3.4 1346 0.9 1934 3.6	**1** M	0412 0.9 1002 3.5 1656 0.8 2243 3.5	**16** TU	0254 1.0 0850 3.4 1540 0.8 2136 3.5
2 M	0104 0.4 0658 3.2 1333 0.7 1919 3.5	**17** TU	0102 0.7 0655 3.1 1321 0.9 1914 3.4	**2** TH	0331 0.6 0916 3.3 1555 0.6 2134 3.7	**17** F	0223 0.7 0816 3.3 1450 0.9 2035 3.6	**2** SA	0353 0.6 0935 3.4 1621 0.6 2202 3.6	**17** SU	0223 0.8 0818 3.4 1455 0.9 2044 3.6	**2** TU	0527 0.9 1112 3.6 1808 0.7 2347 3.5	**17** W	0428 1.0 1014 3.6 1713 0.7 2301 3.6
3 TU	0224 0.4 0821 3.2 1459 0.7 2044 3.5	**18** W	0210 0.7 0807 3.1 1439 0.9 2029 3.5	**3** F	0440 0.4 1019 3.3 1702 0.5 2236 3.7	**18** SA	0330 0.6 0920 3.4 1558 0.8 2139 3.7	**3** SU	0457 0.6 1037 3.5 1727 0.6 2305 3.6	**18** M	0337 0.8 0928 3.5 1612 0.8 2159 3.6	**3** W	0630 0.8 1207 3.8 1903 0.7	**18** TH	0553 0.9 1128 3.8 1833 0.6
4 W	0355 0.4 0944 3.2 1627 0.6 2203 3.6	**19** TH	0329 0.6 0921 3.3 1558 0.8 2139 3.6	**4** SA	0537 0.3 1112 3.4 1757 0.4 2329 3.7	**19** SU	0435 0.6 1019 3.5 1701 0.7 2237 3.8	**4** M	0554 0.6 1133 3.6 1825 0.6	**19** TU	0452 0.8 1036 3.6 1728 0.7 2310 3.7	**4** TH	0038 3.6 0720 0.8 1251 3.9 1949 0.7	**19** F	0013 3.7 0705 0.7 1229 3.9 ○1939 0.4
5 TH	0514 0.3 1053 3.3 1736 0.4 2306 3.7	**20** F	0439 0.5 1023 3.4 1703 0.7 2236 3.7	**5** SU	0626 0.4 1159 3.6 1848 0.4	**20** M	0533 0.6 1112 3.7 1800 0.6 2333 3.8	**5** TU	0000 3.6 0647 0.7 1222 3.8 1917 0.6	**20** W	0604 0.8 1140 3.8 1839 0.6	**5** F	0119 3.7 0802 0.8 1329 4.0 ●2029 0.6	**20** SA	0111 3.7 0803 0.6 1322 4.0 2033 0.3
6 F	0613 0.2 1145 3.4 1830 0.3 2356 3.7	**21** SA	0535 0.4 1113 3.5 1756 0.6 2323 3.8	**6** M	0018 3.7 0713 0.5 1244 3.7 ●1938 0.4	**21** TU	0628 0.6 1202 3.8 1856 0.6	**6** W	0049 3.7 0735 0.7 1305 3.9 ●2002 0.6	**21** TH	0016 3.8 0709 0.7 1238 4.0 ○1942 0.5	**6** SA	0156 3.7 0839 0.7 1405 4.0 2106 0.6	**21** SU	0203 3.6 0853 0.4 1411 4.1 2123 0.3
7 SA	0700 0.2 1230 3.5 1918 0.3	**22** SU	0622 0.4 1155 3.7 1844 0.6	**7** TU	0105 3.7 0758 0.5 1324 3.8 2020 0.5	**22** W	0026 3.9 0720 0.6 1250 3.9 ○1949 0.5	**7** TH	0132 3.7 0816 0.7 1343 3.9 2042 0.6	**22** F	0115 3.8 0807 0.6 1331 4.0 2040 0.4	**7** SU	0230 3.7 0913 0.6 1438 4.0 2138 0.5	**22** M	0251 3.7 0938 0.4 1456 4.2 2209 0.3
8 SU	0043 3.8 0746 0.3 1313 3.6 ●2004 0.3	**23** M	0007 3.9 0705 0.4 1235 3.8 ○1927 0.5	**8** W	0146 3.7 0834 0.6 1358 3.9 2054 0.5	**23** TH	0119 3.9 0811 0.6 1339 4.0 2042 0.4	**8** F	0209 3.7 0852 0.7 1419 4.0 2119 0.6	**23** SA	0212 3.8 0901 0.5 1423 4.1 2135 0.3	**8** M	0301 3.7 0943 0.6 1507 3.9 2206 0.5	**23** TU	0333 3.8 1019 0.4 1538 4.2 2249 0.4
9 M	0128 3.8 0827 0.3 1350 3.7 2043 0.3	**24** TU	0049 3.9 0745 0.4 1313 3.8 2008 0.4	**9** TH	0221 3.7 0906 0.6 1431 3.9 2129 0.5	**24** F	0214 3.9 0904 0.5 1430 4.0 2138 0.4	**9** SA	0245 3.7 0926 0.6 1453 4.0 2154 0.6	**24** SU	0305 3.7 0952 0.5 1513 4.2 2226 0.3	**9** TU	0329 3.6 1010 0.5 1536 3.9 2233 0.5	**24** W	0411 3.7 1055 0.4 1618 4.1 2324 0.5
10 TU	0206 3.8 0900 0.4 1421 3.8 2114 0.4	**25** W	0131 3.9 0825 0.4 1352 3.9 2051 0.4	**10** F	0256 3.6 0939 0.6 1505 3.9 2204 0.5	**25** SA	0310 3.8 0957 0.5 1521 4.0 2230 0.3	**10** SU	0319 3.6 0958 0.6 1526 3.9 2226 0.5	**25** M	0354 3.7 1037 0.4 1558 4.1 2310 0.3	**10** W	0400 3.6 1040 0.5 1608 3.8 2305 0.5	**25** TH	0447 3.7 1129 0.5 1658 4.0 2356 0.7
11 W	0239 3.7 0929 0.4 1450 3.8 2145 0.4	**26** TH	0218 3.9 0911 0.4 1436 3.9 2139 0.3	**11** SA	0333 3.5 1011 0.6 1541 3.9 2240 0.5	**26** SU	0403 3.6 1045 0.6 1610 4.0 2319 0.3	**11** M	0353 3.6 1029 0.6 1559 3.9 2257 0.5	**26** TU	0438 3.6 1117 0.4 1643 4.1 2352 0.4	**11** TH	0435 3.6 1114 0.5 1644 3.8 2338 0.6	**26** F	0522 3.6 1204 0.7 1739 3.8 ◑
12 TH	0312 3.6 0958 0.5 1522 3.8 2218 0.4	**27** F	0310 3.7 0958 0.5 1524 3.8 2228 0.4	**12** SU	0411 3.5 1044 0.7 1617 3.8 2315 0.5	**27** M	0453 3.5 1130 0.7 1659 4.0	**12** TU	0428 3.5 1102 0.6 1635 3.8 2332 0.5	**27** W	0521 3.6 1157 0.5 1728 4.0	**12** F	0509 3.5 1145 0.6 1716 3.7	**27** SA	0028 0.8 0601 3.5 1241 0.9 1826 3.6
13 F	0348 3.5 1027 0.6 1557 3.7 2252 0.5	**28** SA	0403 3.6 1044 0.6 1614 3.8 2318 0.3	**13** M	0450 3.4 1120 0.7 1656 3.7 2353 0.6	**28** TU	0009 0.4 1545 0.6 1218 0.6 ☽1753 3.9	**13** W	0506 3.5 1139 0.7 1713 3.7 ☽1816 3.9	**28** TH	0034 0.6 0604 3.5 1240 0.7 ☽1752 3.6	**13** SA	0005 0.7 0541 3.5 1212 0.7 1752 3.6	**28** SU	0105 1.0 0649 3.4 1331 0.9 1927 3.3
14 SA	0427 3.4 1059 0.7 1634 3.7 2328 0.6	**29** SU	0457 3.4 1132 0.6 1706 3.8	**14** TU	0532 3.3 1159 0.8 1740 3.6	**29** W	0101 0.4 0639 3.4 1311 0.7 1849 3.8	**14** TH	0008 0.6 0544 3.4 1214 0.7 ☽1752 3.7	**29** F	0114 0.7 0649 3.5 1326 0.8 1908 3.7	**14** SU	0036 0.8 0622 3.4 1254 0.8 1846 3.5	**29** M	0203 1.1 0759 3.4 1448 1.0 2049 3.3
15 SU	0508 3.3 1135 0.8 1716 3.6	**30** M	0011 0.4 0555 3.4 1225 0.7 ☽1805 3.7	**15** W	0035 0.6 0619 3.3 1245 0.8 ☽1830 3.5	**30** TH	0154 0.4 0734 3.4 1408 0.7 1950 3.7	**15** F	0042 0.7 0625 3.4 1253 0.8 1836 3.6	**30** SA	0158 0.8 0741 3.4 1421 0.9 2011 3.5	**15** M	0130 0.9 0726 3.4 1407 0.9 2005 3.4	**30** TU	0327 1.2 0925 3.3 1612 1.0 2217 3.3
		31 TU	0111 0.4 0658 3.3 1330 0.7 1911 3.7					**31** SU	0258 0.9 0847 3.4 1535 0.8 2126 3.5	**31** W	0458 1.1 1048 3.6 1749 0.9 2332 3.4

Chart Datum: 1·66 metres below Normal Null (German reference level)

》》 **FREE** monthly updates from 《《
www.reedsalmanac.co.uk

TIME ZONE -0100
(German Standard Time)
Subtract 1 hour for UT
For German Summer Time add
ONE hour in non-shaded areas

GERMANY – CUXHAVEN
LAT 53°52′N   LONG 8°43′E
TIMES AND HEIGHTS OF HIGH AND LOW WATERS

YEAR 2005

	SEPTEMBER			OCTOBER			NOVEMBER			DECEMBER	
	Time m	Time m		Time m	Time m		Time m	Time m		Time m	Time m
1 TH	0612 1.0 / 1151 3.8 / 1849 0.8	**16** F	0547 0.9 / 1118 3.8 / 1827 0.5	**1** SA	0636 0.9 / 1204 3.8 / 1902 0.6	**16** SU	0634 0.6 / 1157 3.9 / 1906 0.4	**1** TU	0023 3.7 / 0711 0.7 / 1232 3.8 / 1929 0.6	**16** W	0050 3.7 / 0743 0.6 / 1306 3.8 / ○ 2007 0.6	**1** TH	0017 3.8 / 0711 0.8 / 1233 3.9 / ● 1928 0.8	**16** F	0107 3.8 / 0806 0.7 / 1331 3.7 / 2023 0.8
2 F	0023 3.6 / 0704 0.9 / 1234 3.8 / 1931 0.7	**17** SA	0006 3.6 / 0655 0.7 / 1217 3.9 / 1927 0.4	**2** SU	0031 3.6 / 0714 0.7 / 1237 3.8 / 1934 0.6	**17** M	0037 3.6 / 0723 0.5 / 1244 3.9 / ○ 1953 0.4	**2** W	0056 3.8 / 0748 0.7 / 1306 3.9 / ● 2003 0.6	**17** TH	0130 3.8 / 0826 0.6 / 1347 3.8 / 2044 0.7	**2** F	0055 3.8 / 0752 0.7 / 1315 3.9 / 2009 0.8	**17** SA	0144 3.9 / 0845 0.7 / 1408 3.7 / 2058 0.8
3 SA	0101 3.7 / 0744 0.7 / 1306 4.0 / ● 2007 0.6	**18** SU	0059 3.6 / 0749 0.5 / 1306 4.0 / ○ 2018 0.3	**3** M	0102 3.7 / 0749 0.6 / 1310 3.8 / ● 2008 0.5	**18** TU	0120 3.7 / 0810 0.4 / 1329 4.0 / 2036 0.4	**3** TH	0128 3.8 / 0821 0.7 / 1340 3.9 / 2036 0.6	**18** F	0205 3.9 / 0902 0.6 / 1424 3.8 / 2117 0.8	**3** SA	0134 3.9 / 0835 0.7 / 1400 3.9 / 2053 0.8	**18** SU	0219 3.9 / 0922 0.7 / 1445 3.6 / 2133 0.8
4 SU	0134 3.7 / 0819 0.6 / 1342 3.9 / 2042 0.5	**19** M	0146 3.7 / 0835 0.4 / 1352 4.1 / 2102 0.3	**4** TU	0133 3.7 / 0823 0.6 / 1342 3.9 / 2040 0.5	**19** W	0159 3.8 / 0850 0.5 / 1410 4.0 / 2113 0.6	**4** F	0159 3.8 / 0855 0.6 / 1415 3.9 / 2111 0.7	**19** SA	0238 3.9 / 0936 0.7 / 1500 3.7 / 2149 0.8	**4** SU	0217 3.9 / 0922 0.6 / 1449 3.8 / 2140 0.8	**19** M	0255 3.9 / 0959 0.7 / 1523 3.6 / 2206 0.8
5 M	0206 3.7 / 0852 0.6 / 1414 3.9 / 2113 0.5	**20** TU	0228 3.7 / 0915 0.4 / 1434 4.1 / 2143 0.4	**5** W	0202 3.8 / 0853 0.6 / 1411 3.9 / 2109 0.5	**20** TH	0233 3.8 / 0926 0.5 / 1447 4.0 / 2146 0.7	**5** SA	0232 3.8 / 0931 0.6 / 1455 3.8 / 2146 0.7	**20** SU	0312 3.9 / 1011 0.7 / 1539 3.6 / 2221 0.8	**5** M	0303 3.9 / 1009 0.6 / 1539 3.7 / 2223 0.8	**20** TU	0330 3.9 / 1035 0.7 / 1600 3.5 / 2237 0.8
6 TU	0235 3.7 / 0921 0.5 / 1441 3.9 / 2140 0.5	**21** W	0305 3.8 / 0953 0.5 / 1513 4.1 / 2219 0.6	**6** TH	0229 3.8 / 0922 0.6 / 1440 3.9 / 2137 0.6	**21** F	0305 3.9 / 0959 0.6 / 1523 3.9 / 2216 0.7	**6** SU	0310 3.8 / 1008 0.6 / 1539 3.7 / 2222 0.8	**21** M	0347 3.9 / 1046 0.7 / 1618 3.5 / 2252 0.8	**6** TU	0348 3.9 / 1054 0.6 / 1628 3.6 / 2305 0.8	**21** W	0405 3.8 / 1107 0.7 / 1637 3.4 / 2309 0.9
7 W	0301 3.7 / 0948 0.5 / 1508 3.9 / 2206 0.5	**22** TH	0338 3.8 / 1028 0.5 / 1550 4.0 / 2249 0.6	**7** F	0258 3.7 / 0950 0.5 / 1512 3.8 / 2205 0.6	**22** SA	0337 3.8 / 1031 0.6 / 1600 3.7 / 2244 0.8	**7** M	0352 3.7 / 1049 0.6 / 1626 3.5 / 2303 0.9	**22** TU	0424 3.7 / 1121 0.8 / 1659 3.3 / 2327 1.0	**7** W	0435 3.9 / 1142 0.6 / 1720 3.5 / 2353 0.9	**22** TH	0441 3.8 / 1140 0.7 / 1715 3.3 / 2344 0.9
8 TH	0329 3.7 / 1015 0.4 / 1539 3.8 / 2234 0.5	**23** F	0410 3.8 / 1058 0.5 / 1627 3.8 / 2317 0.7	**8** SA	0330 3.7 / 1020 0.5 / 1549 3.7 / 2235 0.7	**23** SU	0410 3.7 / 1102 0.6 / 1639 3.5 / 2313 0.9	**8** TU	0438 3.7 / 1136 0.7 / 1719 3.4 / 2352 1.0	**23** W	0505 3.7 / 1201 0.9 / 1745 3.2 / ◐	**8** TH	0528 3.8 / 1236 0.7 / 1817 3.4 / ◐	**23** F	0519 3.7 / 1216 0.8 / 1756 3.3 / ◐
9 F	0401 3.6 / 1046 0.5 / 1613 3.6 / 2304 0.6	**24** SA	0443 3.7 / 1129 0.6 / 1705 3.6 / 2345 0.9	**9** SU	0405 3.6 / 1054 0.6 / 1629 3.6 / 2308 0.8	**24** M	0447 3.6 / 1137 0.8 / 1722 3.3 / 2349 1.1	**9** W	0532 3.6 / 1232 0.8 / 1822 3.3 / ◐	**24** TH	0009 1.1 / 0553 3.6 / 1249 1.0 / 1840 3.1	**9** F	0051 0.9 / 0629 3.7 / 1338 0.7 / 1921 3.3	**24** SA	0024 1.0 / 0604 3.6 / 1258 0.9 / 1844 3.2
10 SA	0433 3.6 / 1115 0.6 / 1646 3.6 / 2331 0.7	**25** SU	0519 3.6 / 1203 0.8 / 1750 3.4 / ◐	**10** M	0444 3.6 / 1132 0.7 / 1715 3.4 / ◐ 2351 3.4	**25** TU	0531 3.5 / 1222 1.0 / 1815 3.2 / ◐	**10** TH	0057 1.0 / 0641 3.6 / 1346 0.8 / 1940 3.2	**25** F	0104 1.2 / 0654 3.5 / 1352 1.0 / 1946 3.1	**10** SA	0158 0.9 / 0738 3.7 / 1447 0.7 / 2030 3.3	**25** SU	0114 1.1 / 0658 3.5 / 1352 1.0 / 1943 3.3
11 SU	0505 3.5 / 1143 0.7 / 1724 3.5 / ◐	**26** M	0020 1.0 / 0605 3.4 / 1250 1.0 / 1848 3.2	**11** TU	0534 3.5 / 1224 0.8 / 1819 3.3	**26** W	0038 1.2 / 0631 3.4 / 1325 1.1 / 1925 3.1	**11** F	0219 1.0 / 0803 3.6 / 1514 0.7 / 2104 3.3	**26** SA	0217 1.2 / 0806 3.5 / 1507 1.0 / 2058 3.3	**11** SU	0312 0.9 / 0851 3.7 / 1601 0.7 / 2138 3.3	**26** M	0218 1.2 / 0802 3.5 / 1458 1.0 / 2048 3.4
12 M	0003 0.8 / 0548 3.4 / 1227 0.9 / 1822 3.3	**27** TU	0115 1.2 / 0713 3.4 / 1404 1.1 / 2008 3.1	**12** W	0055 1.1 / 0646 3.4 / 1343 0.8 / 1945 3.2	**27** TH	0151 1.3 / 0749 3.4 / 1449 1.1 / 2048 3.1	**12** SA	0348 1.0 / 0926 3.7 / 1639 0.6 / 2220 3.3	**27** SU	0336 1.2 / 0918 3.6 / 1620 0.9 / 2203 3.4	**12** M	0426 0.8 / 1001 3.7 / 1707 0.6 / 2240 3.4	**27** TU	0329 1.2 / 0910 3.5 / 1608 1.0 / 2152 3.5
13 TU	0101 1.0 / 0657 3.3 / 1345 0.9 / 1948 3.3	**28** W	0239 1.3 / 0841 3.4 / 1541 1.1 / 2140 3.2	**13** TH	0227 1.1 / 0818 3.5 / 1525 0.8 / 2122 3.3	**28** F	0322 1.3 / 0915 3.5 / 1619 1.0 / 2208 3.3	**13** SU	0505 0.8 / 1036 3.8 / 1746 0.5 / 2319 3.4	**28** M	0445 1.1 / 1018 3.7 / 1718 0.8 / 2255 3.5	**13** TU	0531 0.7 / 1102 3.8 / 1803 0.6 / 2334 3.5	**28** W	0438 1.0 / 1014 3.7 / 1711 0.9 / 2250 3.6
14 W	0233 1.1 / 0829 3.4 / 1528 0.8 / 2128 3.4	**29** TH	0418 1.3 / 1011 3.6 / 1715 1.0 / 2301 3.4	**14** F	0409 1.1 / 0949 3.6 / 1700 0.6 / 2246 3.5	**29** SA	0448 1.1 / 1027 3.6 / 1731 0.8 / 2308 3.5	**14** M	0604 0.7 / 1131 3.8 / 1837 0.5 / ○ 2338 3.6	**29** TU	0540 1.0 / 1108 3.7 / 1805 0.7 / 2338 3.7	**14** W	0627 0.7 / 1157 3.8 / 1855 0.7 /	**29** TH	0541 0.9 / 1113 3.8 / 1809 0.9 / 2342 3.7
15 TH	0418 1.0 / 1002 3.6 / 1708 0.7 / 2257 3.5	**30** F	0541 1.1 / 1119 3.7 / 1821 0.8 / 2356 3.5	**15** SA	0533 0.8 / 1102 3.7 / 1812 0.5 / 2348 3.5	**30** SU	0550 0.9 / 1118 3.7 / 1817 0.7 / 2349 3.6	**15** TU	0654 0.6 / 1219 3.8 / 1923 0.5	**30** W	0627 0.9 / 1151 3.8 / 1848 0.6	**15** TH	0023 3.7 / 0719 0.6 / 1247 3.7 / ○ 1942 0.8	**30** F	0639 0.8 / 1207 3.8 / 1902 0.9
						31 M	0633 0.8 / 1157 3.8 / 1853 0.6							**31** SA	0031 3.9 / 0733 0.7 / 1300 3.8 / ● 1954 0.8

Chart Datum: 1·66 metres below Normal Null (German reference level)

》》 **FREE** monthly updates from 《《
www.reedsalmanac.co.uk

TIDES

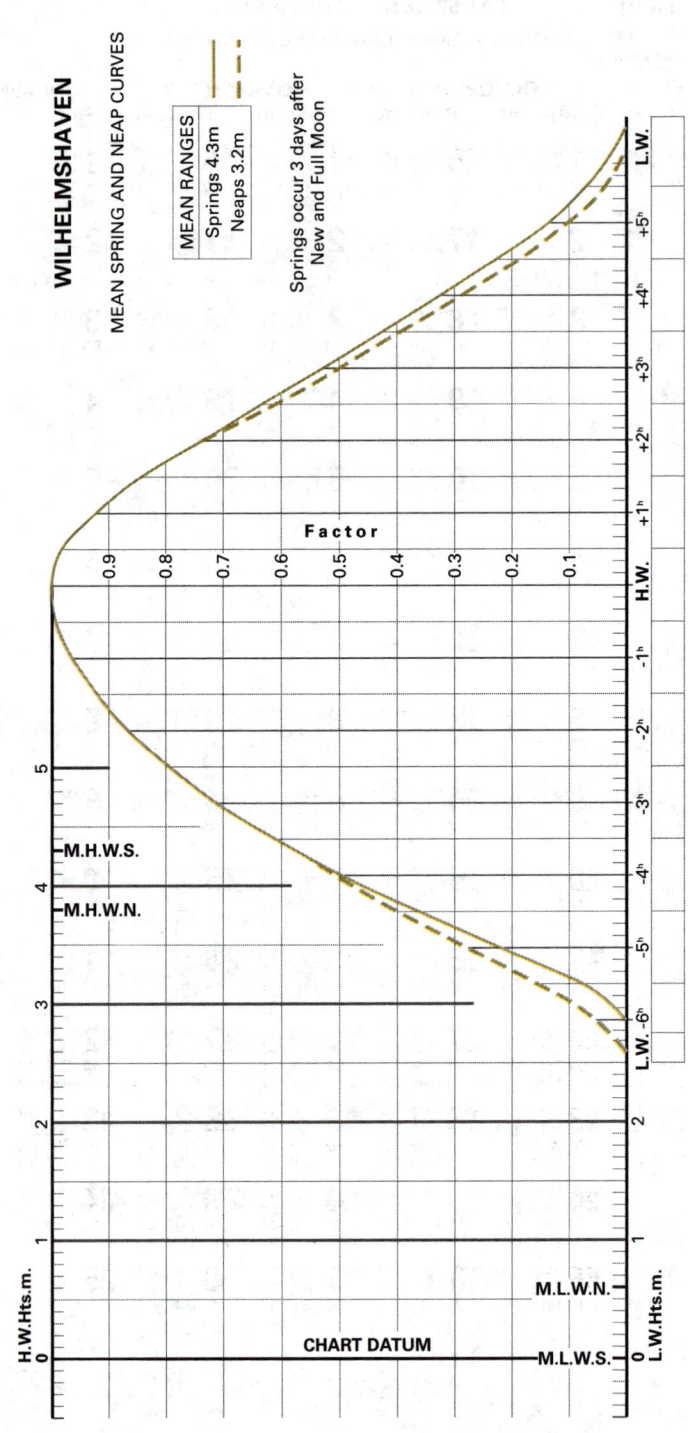

TIME ZONE -0100
(German Standard Time)
Subtract 1 hour for UT
For German Summer Time add
ONE hour in **non-shaded areas**

GERMANY – WILHELMSHAVEN
LAT 53°31′N   LONG 8°09′E
TIMES AND HEIGHTS OF HIGH AND LOW WATERS

YEAR 2005

JANUARY

#	Time	m	#	Time	m
1 SA	0351 1011 1620 2218	4.7 0.7 4.3 0.8	**16** SU	0452 1117 1726 2317	4.9 0.5 4.4 0.7
2 SU	0428 1047 1659 2255	4.6 0.7 4.4 0.9	**17** M	0535 1156 1806 ☽2357	4.8 0.7 4.3 0.8
3 M	0507 1123 1739 2334	4.6 0.7 4.4 0.9	**18** TU	0620 1236 1850	4.7 0.8 4.2
4 TU	0550 1204 1826	4.5 0.8 4.1	**19** W	0044 0714 1325 1946	0.9 4.5 1.0 4.1
5 W	0023 0642 1259 1925	1.1 4.5 1.0 4.2	**20** TH	0148 0821 1430 2056	1.0 4.3 1.1 4.2
6 TH	0126 0748 1407 2034	1.2 4.5 1.0 4.3	**21** F	0306 0937 1545 2209	1.1 4.3 1.2 4.3
7 F	0240 0902 1520 2145	1.1 4.5 1.0 4.4	**22** SA	0425 1048 1654 2312	1.0 4.3 1.1 4.5
8 SA	0356 1016 1633 2251	1.0 4.6 0.9 4.5	**23** SU	0531 1145 1752	0.9 4.4 1.0
9 SU	0508 1125 1742 2351	0.9 4.6 0.8 4.7	**24** M	0003 0624 1231 1840	4.6 0.9 4.5 0.9
10 M	0614 1228 1843 ●	0.7 4.7 0.7	**25** TU	0046 0707 1312 ○1920	4.7 0.8 4.5 0.8
11 TU	0047 0712 1326 1938	4.8 0.5 4.7 0.7	**26** W	0124 0746 1350 1957	4.8 0.7 4.5 0.7
12 W	0140 0807 1423 2032	4.9 0.4 4.6 0.6	**27** TH	0201 0822 1425 2032	4.8 0.6 4.5 0.6
13 TH	0233 0903 1518 2121	5.0 0.4 4.6 0.6	**28** F	0234 0856 1457 2102	4.8 0.6 4.5 0.6
14 F	0324 0954 1606 2203	5.0 0.4 4.5 0.5	**29** SA	0305 0925 1529 2130	4.8 0.5 4.5 0.5
15 SA	0409 1037 1647 2239	4.9 0.4 4.4 0.6	**30** SU	0337 0954 1603 2201	4.7 0.5 4.4 0.5
			31 M	0411 1027 1638 2235	4.7 0.5 4.4 0.6

FEBRUARY

#	Time	m	#	Time	m
1 TU	0445 1059 1709 2305	4.6 0.5 4.3 0.7	**16** W	0539 1146 1757 ☽2354	4.6 0.8 4.3 0.8
2 W	0517 1126 1741 2336	4.5 0.6 4.2 0.8	**17** TH	0622 1223 1845	4.3 1.0 4.1
3 TH	0556 1203 1829	4.4 0.8 4.2	**18** F	0047 0726 1325 1957	1.0 4.1 1.2 4.1
4 F	0028 0658 1307 1940	1.0 4.3 1.0 4.2	**19** SA	0208 0849 1450 2124	1.1 4.1 1.3 4.2
5 SA	0147 0822 1433 2106	1.0 4.3 1.1 4.3	**20** SU	0342 1015 1618 2243	1.1 4.1 1.2 4.4
6 SU	0319 0953 1605 2228	0.9 4.4 1.0 4.5	**21** M	0504 1124 1728 2344	0.9 4.3 1.0 4.6
7 M	0448 1116 1728 2339	0.7 4.5 0.7 4.7	**22** TU	0604 1215 1820	0.7 4.4 0.9
8 TU	0605 1226 1837 ●	0.6 4.6 0.5	**23** W	0029 0649 1256 1903	4.7 0.7 4.5 0.7
9 W	0041 0707 1325 1933	4.8 0.4 4.6 0.5	**24** TH	0107 0727 1335 ○1940	4.7 0.5 4.5 0.6
10 TH	0135 0801 1418 2021	4.9 0.3 4.6 0.4	**25** F	0143 0802 1408 2014	4.8 0.4 4.5 0.5
11 F	0225 0852 1505 2107	5.0 0.2 4.5 0.4	**26** SA	0216 0834 1438 2044	4.8 0.3 4.6 0.4
12 SA	0311 0939 1547 2146	5.0 0.3 4.5 0.4	**27** SU	0246 0903 1508 2112	4.8 0.3 4.5 0.4
13 SU	0352 1017 1622 2218	5.0 0.3 4.5 0.4	**28** M	0317 0932 1539 2141	4.7 0.3 4.5 0.3
14 M	0429 1049 1653 2249	4.9 0.4 4.4 0.5			
15 TU	0504 1118 1723 2319	4.8 0.6 4.4 0.6			

MARCH

#	Time	m	#	Time	m
1 TU	0350 1003 1612 2212	4.7 0.3 4.4 0.4	**16** W	0433 1037 1643 2244	4.6 0.5 4.5 0.5
2 W	0422 1032 1640 2239	4.7 0.3 4.4 0.4	**17** TH	0504 1101 1713 ☽2314	4.6 0.7 4.3 0.7
3 TH	0452 1056 1709 ☽2306	4.5 0.5 4.3 0.6	**18** F	0542 1133 1756	4.2 0.9 4.2
4 F	0530 1129 1755 2355	4.4 0.7 4.2 0.8	**19** SA	0000 0640 1230 1906	0.9 4.0 1.1 4.1
5 SA	0634 1234 1911	4.2 1.0 4.1	**20** SU	0116 0802 1357 2037	1.1 3.9 1.3 4.1
6 SU	0120 0806 1411 2047	0.9 4.1 1.1 4.3	**21** M	0255 0935 1534 2206	1.1 4.0 1.2 4.3
7 M	0304 0947 1553 2218	0.8 4.2 1.0 4.4	**22** TU	0427 1054 1654 2314	0.9 4.2 1.0 4.5
8 TU	0440 1114 1720 2332	0.6 4.3 0.8 4.6	**23** W	0532 1149 1750	0.7 4.3 0.9
9 W	0557 1222 1827 ●	0.4 4.5 0.6	**24** TH	0001 0618 1231 1834	4.6 0.5 4.5 0.6
10 TH	0033 0657 1317 ●1919	4.8 0.2 4.7 0.4	**25** F	0040 0656 1309 1912	4.7 0.4 4.6 0.5
11 F	0125 0748 1404 2004	4.9 0.1 4.7 0.2	**26** SA	0116 0732 1343 1947	4.7 0.3 4.6 0.3
12 SA	0211 0833 1444 2044	4.9 0.2 4.6 0.2	**27** SU	0149 0805 1412 2019	4.8 0.2 4.6 0.3
13 SU	0252 0913 1519 2120	5.0 0.2 4.6 0.3	**28** M	0221 0836 1441 2048	4.8 0.2 4.6 0.3
14 M	0328 0946 1549 2151	5.0 0.3 4.6 0.3	**29** TU	0253 0906 1512 2117	4.7 0.2 4.5 0.2
15 TU	0401 1013 1616 2218	4.8 0.4 4.6 0.4	**30** W	0327 0936 1545 2149	4.7 0.3 4.5 0.3
			31 TH	0404 1008 1618 2221	4.6 0.4 4.5 0.3

APRIL

#	Time	m	#	Time	m
1 F	0441 1040 1655 2257	4.5 0.6 4.4 0.5	**16** SA	0515 1102 1724 ☽2332	4.1 0.9 4.3 0.8
2 SA	0528 1121 1748 ☽2353	4.3 0.7 4.3 0.7	**17** SU	0606 1152 1826	4.0 1.1 4.2
3 SU	0637 1230 1907	4.1 0.9 4.2	**18** M	0037 0719 1309 1949	0.9 3.9 1.2 4.2
4 M	0119 0809 1406 2042	0.7 4.1 1.0 4.3	**19** TU	0206 0846 1442 2116	0.9 3.9 1.1 4.3
5 TU	0302 0947 1545 2212	0.6 4.2 0.9 4.5	**20** W	0336 1008 1605 2228	0.8 4.1 0.9 4.4
6 W	0433 1108 1704 2322	0.4 4.3 0.6 4.6	**21** TH	0445 1109 1706 2320	0.6 4.3 0.7 4.6
7 TH	0541 1208 1804	0.2 4.5 0.4	**22** F	0535 1154 1753	0.4 4.5 0.4
8 F	0017 0636 1257 ●1855	4.8 0.1 4.6 0.3	**23** SA	0002 0617 1233 1836	4.7 0.4 4.6 0.5
9 SA	0107 0724 1340 1939	4.8 0.1 4.7 0.2	**24** SU	0040 0656 1308 ○1914	4.7 0.3 4.6 0.3
10 SU	0151 0805 1416 2017	4.9 0.2 4.6 0.2	**25** M	0117 0731 1340 1948	4.8 0.2 4.7 0.3
11 M	0228 0840 1447 2051	4.9 0.2 4.7 0.3	**26** TU	0152 0805 1412 2022	4.8 0.2 4.7 0.3
12 TU	0300 0910 1514 2120	4.8 0.3 4.7 0.3	**27** W	0230 0840 1447 2057	4.8 0.2 4.7 0.2
13 W	0332 0935 1541 2147	4.7 0.3 4.6 0.3	**28** TH	0311 0916 1527 2135	4.7 0.2 4.6 0.2
14 TH	0404 1001 1610 2216	4.5 0.4 4.5 0.4	**29** F	0356 0954 1609 2217	4.5 0.3 4.6 0.3
15 F	0437 1028 1642 2249	4.3 0.7 4.4 0.6	**30** SA	0445 1037 1657 2305	4.4 0.4 4.5 0.4

Chart Datum: 2·26 metres below Normal Null (German reference level)

FREE monthly updates from
www.reedsalmanac.co.uk

Chapter 5

TIDES

TIME ZONE -0100
(German Standard Time)
Subtract 1 hour for UT
For German Summer Time add
ONE hour in **non-shaded areas**

GERMANY – WILHELMSHAVEN
LAT 53°31'N   LONG 8°09'E
TIMES AND HEIGHTS OF HIGH AND LOW WATERS

YEAR 2005

MAY

Time	m		Time	m
1 0540	4.2	**16**	0541	4.0
1129	0.8		1128	0.9
SU 1755	4.4	M	1755	4.4
2 0007	0.5	**17**	0008	0.8
0648	4.1		0640	3.9
M 1236	0.8	TU	1228	1.0
1910	4.4		1902	4.3
3 0126	0.5	**18**	0116	0.8
0811	4.1		0753	4.0
TU 1401	0.9	W	1345	1.0
2037	4.5		2017	4.3
4 0256	0.5	**19**	0234	0.7
0936	4.1		0909	4.1
W 1528	0.7	TH	1504	0.9
2157	4.6		2128	4.4
5 0415	0.3	**20**	0345	0.6
1047	4.2		1014	4.3
TH 1638	0.5	F	1610	0.8
2302	4.7		2227	4.6
6 0515	0.2	**21**	0441	0.5
1141	4.3		1105	4.4
F 1733	0.3	SA	1705	0.7
2354	4.7		2316	4.7
7 0605	0.2	**22**	0531	0.4
1227	4.4		1149	4.6
SA 1824	0.3	SU	1754	0.6
8 0042	4.7	**23**	0002	4.8
0653	0.3		0616	0.4
SU 1309	4.6	M	1230	4.7
● 1912	0.3	○	1838	0.5
9 0126	4.7	**24**	0045	4.8
0735	0.3		0657	0.4
M 1346	4.7	TU	1308	4.8
1951	0.3		1918	0.4
10 0203	4.7	**25**	0127	4.8
0808	0.4		0738	0.4
TU 1415	4.7	W	1348	4.8
2023	0.3		2001	0.3
11 0234	4.7	**26**	0215	4.8
0837	0.5		0822	0.4
W 1444	4.7	TH	1432	4.8
2053	0.4		2047	0.3
12 0307	4.5	**27**	0307	4.6
0905	0.5		0908	0.4
TH 1514	4.7	F	1520	4.8
2125	0.4		2134	0.2
13 0342	4.4	**28**	0359	4.5
0935	0.5		0953	0.5
F 1548	4.6	SA	1608	4.7
2159	0.5		2223	0.3
14 0418	4.3	**29**	0451	4.4
1007	0.7		1040	0.6
SA 1623	4.6	SU	1700	4.7
2236	0.6		2316	0.4
15 0456	4.2	**30**	0547	4.3
1044	0.8		1134	0.7
SU 1704	4.5	M	1759	4.6
2316	0.7	◐		
		31	0016	0.4
			0649	4.2
		TU	1234	0.7
			1905	4.6

JUNE

Time	m		Time	m
1 0123	0.4	**16**	0032	0.7
0757	4.1		0700	4.1
W 1344	0.7	TH	1251	0.9
2018	4.6		1918	4.4
2 0235	0.4	**17**	0132	0.7
0907	4.2		0803	4.2
TH 1457	0.6	F	1358	1.0
2129	4.6		2023	4.5
3 0344	0.4	**18**	0239	0.7
1012	4.3		0909	4.3
F 1604	0.5	SA	1507	0.9
2232	4.6		2128	4.6
4 0442	0.3	**19**	0342	0.6
1106	4.4		1010	4.4
SA 1701	0.4	SU	1610	0.8
2326	4.6		2229	4.6
5 0532	0.4	**20**	0441	0.6
1153	4.5		1104	4.6
SU 1754	0.4	M	1711	0.7
			2326	4.7
6 0015	4.7	**21**	0538	0.5
0621	0.5		1154	4.7
M 1238	4.6	TU	1806	0.6
◐ 1845	0.4			
7 0101	4.7	**22**	0020	4.8
0706	0.5		0632	0.5
TU 1317	4.7	W	1244	4.8
1928	0.4	○	1858	0.5
8 0140	4.6	**23**	0114	4.8
0743	0.5		0723	0.5
W 1351	4.8	TH	1333	4.9
2004	0.4		1951	0.4
9 0215	4.6	**24**	0210	4.8
0815	0.6		0816	0.5
TH 1424	4.9	F	1425	4.9
2038	0.5		2046	0.3
10 0250	4.5	**25**	0307	4.7
0848	0.6		0908	0.5
F 1458	4.8	SA	1517	4.9
2113	0.5		2139	0.2
11 0326	4.4	**26**	0400	4.5
0921	0.6		0954	0.4
SA 1533	4.8	SU	1606	4.9
2148	0.5		2227	0.2
12 0402	4.4	**27**	0450	4.4
0954	0.7		1038	0.5
SU 1609	4.7	M	1656	4.9
2225	0.5		2316	0.3
13 0440	4.3	**28**	0539	4.4
1030	0.7		1125	0.6
M 1647	4.7	TU	1748	4.8
2303	0.6	◐		
14 0520	4.2	**29**	0008	0.4
1109	0.8		0630	4.3
TU 1730	4.5	W	1217	0.7
2344	0.6		1844	4.8
15 0605	4.1	**30**	0101	0.5
1155	0.8		0723	4.2
W 1819	4.4	TH	1313	0.7
			1943	4.7

JULY

Time	m		Time	m
1 0157	0.6	**16**	0035	0.7
0821	4.2		0659	4.2
F 1416	0.7	SA	1256	0.9
2048	4.6		1920	4.5
2 0259	0.7	**17**	0133	0.8
0924	4.3		0803	4.3
SA 1525	0.7	SU	1404	1.0
2156	4.6		2031	4.5
3 0403	0.7	**18**	0243	0.9
1027	4.4		0915	4.3
SU 1631	0.6	M	1519	0.9
2258	4.5		2147	4.5
4 0502	0.7	**19**	0358	0.8
1123	4.5		1025	4.5
M 1731	0.6	TU	1636	0.7
2352	4.5		2300	4.6
5 0556	0.7	**20**	0512	0.8
1212	4.7		1129	4.7
TU 1826	0.6	W	1747	0.6
6 0040	4.6	**21**	0008	4.7
0645	0.7		0619	0.7
W 1256	4.8	TH	1229	4.8
● 1912	0.6	○	1851	0.5
7 0123	4.6	**22**	0110	4.7
0726	0.7		0719	0.6
TH 1335	4.9	F	1325	5.0
1952	0.6		1948	0.4
8 0201	4.6	**23**	0208	4.7
0803	0.7		0813	0.5
F 1411	4.9	SA	1418	5.0
2029	0.6		2044	0.3
9 0237	4.6	**24**	0302	4.7
0838	0.6		0904	0.4
SA 1446	4.9	SU	1509	5.1
2105	0.5		2136	0.2
10 0312	4.6	**25**	0351	4.6
0911	0.6		0947	0.4
SU 1519	4.9	M	1556	5.1
2137	0.5		2221	0.2
11 0345	4.5	**26**	0434	4.5
0941	0.6		1026	0.4
M 1552	4.9	TU	1640	5.0
2208	0.5		2302	0.3
12 0419	4.4	**27**	0514	4.5
1013	0.6		1105	0.5
TU 1627	4.9	W	1724	4.9
2243	0.5		2344	0.5
13 0456	4.4	**28**	0554	4.4
1049	0.7		1148	0.6
W 1704	4.8	TH	1809	4.8
2319	0.5	◐		
14 0532	4.3	**29**	0024	0.7
1125	0.7		0636	4.4
TH 1741	4.6	F	1232	0.7
◐ 2353	0.6		1858	4.6
15 0611	4.3	**30**	0107	0.8
1204	0.8		0726	4.3
F 1823	4.5	SA	1327	0.8
			2000	4.5
		31	0206	1.0
			0831	4.3
		SU	1440	0.9
			2116	4.4

AUGUST

Time	m		Time	m
1 0320	1.0	**16**	0158	1.1
0947	4.4		0833	4.3
M 1601	0.9	TU	1444	0.9
2232	4.4		2121	4.4
2 0434	1.0	**17**	0332	1.1
1058	4.5		1000	4.3
TU 1714	0.8	W	1617	0.8
2336	4.4		2249	4.5
3 0538	0.9	**18**	0459	0.9
1154	4.7		1115	4.7
W 1813	0.7	TH	1739	0.6
4 0025	4.5	**19**	0003	4.6
0630	0.9		0613	0.8
TH 1240	4.8	F	1219	4.9
1900	0.7	○	1846	0.4
5 0108	4.6	**20**	0105	4.7
0714	0.8		0713	0.6
F 1320	4.9	SA	1315	5.1
● 1940	0.6		1943	0.3
6 0147	4.6	**21**	0159	4.7
0752	0.7		0804	0.4
SA 1357	4.9	SU	1407	5.1
2017	0.6		2034	0.2
7 0222	4.6	**22**	0247	4.7
0827	0.6		0849	0.4
SU 1431	4.9	M	1454	5.2
2050	0.5		2121	0.2
8 0253	4.6	**23**	0330	4.7
0857	0.5		0930	0.3
M 1501	4.9	TU	1537	5.2
2118	0.5		2201	0.3
9 0322	4.6	**24**	0406	4.7
0923	0.5		1005	0.4
TU 1529	4.8	W	1615	5.0
2144	0.4		2236	0.4
10 0353	4.5	**25**	0439	4.6
0951	0.5		1038	0.5
W 1602	4.8	TH	1652	4.9
2216	0.5		2307	0.6
11 0426	4.5	**26**	0511	4.5
1025	0.6		1112	0.6
TH 1635	4.7	F	1730	4.7
2249	0.5	◐	2339	0.7
12 0457	4.4	**27**	0546	4.4
1055	0.6		1148	0.8
F 1706	4.6	SA	1813	4.6
2316	0.6			
13 0525	4.3	**28**	0015	1.0
1123	0.7		0632	4.3
SA 1738	4.5	SU	1237	1.0
◐ 2345	0.7		1912	4.2
14 0605	4.2	**29**	0111	1.2
1204	0.7		0739	4.3
SU 1830	4.4	M	1353	1.1
			2033	4.1
15 0038	1.0	**30**	0233	1.3
0708	4.2		0906	4.3
M 1314	1.0	TU	1527	1.1
1949	4.3		2202	4.2
		31	0404	1.3
			1031	4.5
		W	1655	1.0
			2316	4.3

Chart Datum: 2·26 metres below Normal Null (German reference level)

>> **FREE** monthly updates from <<
www.reedsalmanac.co.uk

TIME ZONE –0100
(German Standard Time)
Subtract 1 hour for UT
For German Summer Time add
ONE hour in non-shaded areas

GERMANY – WILHELMSHAVEN
LAT 53°31′N   LONG 8°09′E
TIMES AND HEIGHTS OF HIGH AND LOW WATERS

YEAR 2005

SEPTEMBER

Time m	Time m
1 0520 1.1 / 1135 4.6 / TH 1757 0.8	**16** 0451 1.0 / 1104 4.7 / F 1732 0.5 / 2355 4.5
2 0008 4.5 / 0614 0.9 / F 1221 4.8 / 1842 0.7	**17** 0602 0.8 / 1206 4.9 / SA 1835 0.4
3 0048 4.6 / 0655 0.8 / SA 1258 4.8 / ● 1918 0.6	**18** 0052 4.6 / 0657 0.6 / SU 1300 5.0 / ○ 1927 0.3
4 0124 4.6 / 0732 0.6 / SU 1333 4.8 / 1953 0.5	**19** 0140 4.6 / 0744 0.4 / M 1348 5.0 / 2013 0.3
5 0158 4.6 / 0805 0.5 / M 1406 4.8 / 2025 0.5	**20** 0222 4.7 / 0827 0.4 / TU 1431 5.1 / 2055 0.4
6 0227 4.7 / 0835 0.5 / TU 1434 4.9 / 2052 0.5	**21** 0259 4.7 / 0905 0.4 / W 1509 5.1 / 2131 0.5
7 0254 4.7 / 0901 0.5 / W 1502 4.8 / 2118 0.5	**22** 0331 4.8 / 0938 0.4 / TH 1545 4.9 / 2201 0.6
8 0321 4.6 / 0926 0.5 / TH 1532 4.8 / 2145 0.5	**23** 0400 4.7 / 1007 0.5 / F 1619 4.7 / 2227 0.7
9 0351 4.5 / 0956 0.5 / F 1604 4.7 / 2215 0.6	**24** 0430 4.6 / 1036 0.6 / SA 1653 4.5 / 2255 0.9
10 0420 4.5 / 1024 0.6 / SA 1634 4.6 / 2241 0.7	**25** 0502 4.5 / 1110 0.8 / SU 1734 4.3 / ◐ 2329 1.1
11 0449 4.4 / 1052 0.7 / SU 1709 4.4 / ◐ 2311 0.9	**26** 0546 4.3 / 1156 1.0 / M 1829 4.1
12 0529 4.3 / 1134 0.9 / M 1804 4.2	**27** 0023 1.3 / 0651 4.2 / TU 1308 1.2 / 1948 4.0
13 0007 1.1 / 0637 4.2 / TU 1249 1.0 / 1930 4.2	**28** 0145 1.5 / 0819 4.3 / W 1445 1.3 / 2120 4.1
14 0137 1.3 / 0810 4.3 / W 1430 1.0 / 2111 4.2	**29** 0323 1.5 / 0951 4.4 / TH 1619 1.1 / 2242 4.2
15 0320 1.2 / 0946 4.5 / TH 1610 0.8 / 2243 4.4	**30** 0446 1.2 / 1102 4.6 / F 1727 0.8 / 2338 4.4

OCTOBER

Time m	Time m
1 0543 1.0 / 1149 4.7 / SA 1810 0.7	**16** 0538 0.7 / 1146 4.8 / SU 1812 0.4
2 0017 4.6 / 0624 0.8 / SU 1225 4.7 / 1845 0.6	**17** 0027 4.5 / 0631 0.6 / M 1237 4.9 / ○ 1901 0.4
3 0051 4.6 / 0700 0.7 / M 1259 4.8 / ● 1919 0.6	**18** 0111 4.6 / 0718 0.5 / TU 1323 4.9 / 1945 0.4
4 0124 4.7 / 0735 0.6 / TU 1332 4.8 / 1952 0.5	**19** 0151 4.7 / 0759 0.5 / W 1404 4.9 / 2023 0.5
5 0153 4.7 / 0806 0.6 / W 1402 4.8 / 2022 0.5	**20** 0224 4.8 / 0836 0.5 / TH 1439 4.9 / 2056 0.6
6 0220 4.7 / 0834 0.6 / TH 1432 4.8 / 2049 0.5	**21** 0254 4.8 / 0908 0.6 / F 1514 4.8 / 2124 0.7
7 0248 4.7 / 0901 0.5 / F 1503 4.8 / 2116 0.6	**22** 0324 4.7 / 0938 0.6 / SA 1549 4.6 / 2152 0.8
8 0319 4.6 / 0929 0.5 / SA 1537 4.7 / 2145 0.7	**23** 0356 4.6 / 1008 0.7 / SU 1624 4.4 / 2221 0.9
9 0351 4.6 / 1001 0.6 / SU 1615 4.5 / 2218 0.9	**24** 0430 4.5 / 1043 0.8 / M 1704 4.2 / 2256 1.1
10 0428 4.5 / 1038 0.8 / M 1659 4.3 / ◐ 2258 1.0	**25** 0512 4.4 / 1127 1.0 / TU 1754 4.0 / ◐ 2345 1.3
11 0516 4.4 / 1128 0.9 / TU 1801 4.2 / 2359 1.2	**26** 0610 4.3 / 1228 1.2 / W 1901 3.9
12 0627 4.3 / 1245 1.0 / W 1927 4.1	**27** 0056 1.5 / 0727 4.3 / TH 1352 1.3 / 2025 4.0
13 0129 1.3 / 0759 4.4 / TH 1425 1.0 / 2104 4.2	**28** 0226 1.5 / 0854 4.4 / F 1523 1.2 / 2147 4.1
14 0310 1.2 / 0932 4.5 / F 1601 0.7 / 2230 4.3	**29** 0351 1.3 / 1008 4.5 / SA 1635 0.9 / 2249 4.4
15 0435 1.0 / 1048 4.7 / SA 1715 0.5 / 2336 4.4	**30** 0455 1.1 / 1101 4.6 / SU 1724 0.5 / 2333 4.5
	31 0541 0.9 / 1141 4.7 / M 1802 0.7

NOVEMBER

Time m	Time m
1 0009 4.6 / 0621 0.8 / TU 1218 4.8 / 1840 0.7	**16** 0038 4.5 / 0649 0.6 / W 1256 4.8 / ○ 1914 0.6
2 0043 4.7 / 0658 0.7 / W 1254 4.8 / ● 1915 0.6	**17** 0118 4.7 / 0733 0.6 / TH 1337 4.8 / 1952 0.7
3 0116 4.7 / 0733 0.7 / TH 1329 4.8 / 1948 0.6	**18** 0152 4.8 / 0809 0.6 / F 1412 4.7 / 2024 0.8
4 0147 4.8 / 0806 0.7 / F 1404 4.8 / 2022 0.7	**19** 0224 4.8 / 0843 0.7 / SA 1448 4.6 / 2056 0.8
5 0220 4.8 / 0840 0.6 / SA 1444 4.7 / 2056 0.7	**20** 0257 4.8 / 0917 0.7 / SU 1525 4.5 / 2127 0.8
6 0258 4.7 / 0916 0.6 / SU 1526 4.6 / 2131 0.8	**21** 0332 4.7 / 0951 0.7 / M 1602 4.3 / 2159 0.9
7 0338 4.7 / 0955 0.6 / M 1612 4.5 / 2211 1.0	**22** 0407 4.7 / 1027 0.8 / TU 1641 4.2 / 2234 1.1
8 0422 4.6 / 1040 0.7 / TU 1703 4.3 / 2258 1.2	**23** 0446 4.6 / 1106 1.0 / W 1723 4.1 / ◐ 2316 1.2
9 0516 4.5 / 1135 0.8 / W 1805 4.2 / ◐ 2359 1.2	**24** 0534 4.4 / 1153 1.1 / TH 1816 4.0
10 0624 4.3 / 1248 0.9 / TH 1922 4.1	**25** 0010 1.3 / 0634 4.3 / F 1255 1.2 / 1922 4.0
11 0119 1.2 / 0746 4.5 / F 1414 0.9 / 2046 4.1	**26** 0121 1.4 / 0745 4.4 / SA 1411 1.2 / 2035 4.1
12 0247 1.2 / 0910 4.6 / SA 1539 0.7 / 2203 4.2	**27** 0239 1.4 / 0857 4.5 / SU 1524 1.1 / 2142 4.3
13 0405 1.0 / 1021 4.6 / SU 1646 0.6 / 2304 4.5	**28** 0349 1.3 / 0959 4.6 / M 1624 0.9 / 2236 4.5
14 0506 0.7 / 1119 4.7 / M 1740 0.5 / 2353 4.5	**29** 0446 1.1 / 1050 4.7 / TU 1712 0.6 / 2320 4.6
15 0559 4.8 / 1209 4.8 / TU 1829 4.0	**30** 0535 1.0 / 1135 4.7 / W 1757 0.6

DECEMBER

Time m	Time m
1 0001 4.7 / 0620 0.9 / TH 1218 4.8 / ● 1839 0.8	**16** 0051 4.8 / 0712 0.8 / F 1316 4.6 / 1928 0.9
2 0040 4.8 / 0701 0.8 / F 1301 4.8 / 1919 0.8	**17** 0129 4.6 / 0751 0.7 / SA 1354 4.6 / 2003 0.9
3 0120 4.8 / 0743 0.7 / SA 1347 4.8 / 2004 0.8	**18** 0204 4.9 / 0828 0.8 / SU 1430 4.6 / 2039 0.9
4 0204 4.9 / 0829 0.7 / SU 1437 4.7 / 2049 0.8	**19** 0241 4.9 / 0905 0.8 / M 1508 4.5 / 2113 0.8
5 0249 4.9 / 0915 0.6 / M 1527 4.6 / 2131 0.8	**20** 0316 4.8 / 0940 0.7 / TU 1544 4.4 / 2145 0.8
6 0335 4.8 / 0959 0.5 / TU 1615 4.5 / 2212 0.8	**21** 0350 4.8 / 1013 0.7 / W 1619 4.3 / 2216 0.9
7 0422 4.8 / 1046 0.6 / W 1706 4.4 / 2258 0.9	**22** 0425 4.7 / 1046 0.8 / TH 1656 4.2 / 2251 0.9
8 0515 4.7 / 1140 0.6 / TH 1802 4.3 / ◑ 2353 1.0	**23** 0503 4.6 / 1122 0.9 / F 1735 4.1 / ◑ 2330 1.1
9 0615 4.7 / 1240 0.8 / F 1904 4.2	**24** 0546 4.5 / 1204 1.0 / SA 1822 4.1
10 0057 1.1 / 0723 4.6 / SA 1349 0.8 / 2013 4.2	**25** 0019 1.2 / 0638 4.4 / SU 1257 1.1 / 1920 4.1
11 0210 1.1 / 0835 4.6 / SU 1500 0.8 / 2121 4.2	**26** 0122 1.4 / 0741 4.4 / M 1404 1.1 / 2026 4.2
12 0324 1.0 / 0946 4.7 / M 1607 0.7 / 2223 4.4	**27** 0233 1.4 / 0849 4.5 / TU 1512 1.1 / 2131 4.4
13 0430 0.8 / 1048 4.6 / TU 1704 0.6 / 2318 4.5	**28** 0342 1.3 / 0959 4.6 / W 1615 1.0 / 2230 4.5
14 0529 0.8 / 1143 4.6 / W 1758 0.6	**29** 0445 1.1 / 1055 4.6 / TH 1714 1.0 / 2323 4.7
15 0007 4.6 / 0624 0.8 / TH 1233 4.7 / ○ 1847 0.8	**30** 0544 0.9 / 1152 4.7 / F 1810 0.7
	31 0014 4.7 / 0638 0.8 / SA 1246 4.7 / ● 1902 0.8

Chart Datum: 2·26 metres below Normal Null (German reference level)

》》 **FREE** monthly updates from 《《
www.reedsalmanac.co.uk

TIDES

HOEK VAN HOLLAND
MEAN SPRING AND NEAP CURVES

MEAN RANGES
Springs 1.9m
Neaps 1.5m

Springs occur 2 days after New and Full Moon

TIME ZONE -0100
(Dutch Standard Time)
Subtract 1 hour for UT
For Dutch Summer Time add ONE hour in **non-shaded areas**

NETHERLANDS – HOEK VAN HOLLAND
LAT 51°59′N   LONG 4°07′E
TIMES AND HEIGHTS OF HIGH AND LOW WATERS

YEAR 2005
Note - Double LWs often occur. The predictions are for the lower LW which is usually the first.

JANUARY

Day	Time	m	Day	Time	m
1 SA	0125 / 0606 / 1135 / 1825	0.4 / 1.9 / 0.1 / 2.0	**16** SU	0244 / 0659 / 1215 / 1925	0.5 / 1.9 / 0.0 / 2.1
2 SU	0200 / 0646 / 1215 / 1904	0.4 / 1.8 / 0.1 / 2.0	**17** M	0345 / 0755 / 1314 / 2030	0.5 / 1.9 / 0.0 / 2.0
3 M	0240 / 0736 / 1304 / ◑ 1954	0.5 / 1.8 / 0.1 / 2.0	**18** TU	0224 / 0844 / 1425 / 2125	0.5 / 1.8 / 0.1 / 1.9
4 TU	0247 / 0824 / 1404 / 2117	0.5 / 1.8 / 0.1 / 2.0	**19** W	0324 / 0955 / 1550 / 2250	0.5 / 1.8 / 0.2 / 1.8
5 W	0315 / 0935 / 1516 / 2216	0.5 / 1.8 / 0.2 / 1.8	**20** TH	0425 / 1110 / 1655 / 2355	0.5 / 1.7 / 0.3 / 1.8
6 TH	0405 / 1046 / 1604 / 2314	0.6 / 1.8 / 0.2 / 2.0	**21** F	0540 / 1215 / 1810	0.5 / 1.8 / 0.3
7 F	0504 / 1150 / 1705	0.4 / 1.9 / 0.2	**22** SA	0055 / 0615 / 1315 / 1855	1.8 / 0.4 / 1.8 / 0.4
8 SA	0025 / 0606 / 1246 / 1825	0.2 / 0.4 / 2.0 / 0.3	**23** SU	0149 / 0956 / 1405 / 1950	1.8 / 0.3 / 1.9 / 0.4
9 SU	0115 / 0634 / 1336 / 1905	2.0 / 0.3 / 2.1 / 0.4	**24** M	0240 / 0744 / 1435 / 2015	1.9 / 0.3 / 2.0 / 0.4
10 M	0205 / 0723 / 1426 / ● 1949	2.0 / 0.3 / 2.2 / 0.4	**25** TU	0326 / 0819 / 1512 / ○ 2110	1.9 / 0.3 / 2.1 / 0.5
11 TU	0255 / 0805 / 1515 / 2325	2.0 / 0.2 / 2.3 / 0.4	**26** W	0345 / 0850 / 1544 / 2237	1.9 / 0.2 / 2.1 / 0.5
12 W	0345 / 0849 / 1601	2.0 / 0.1 / 2.3	**27** TH	0405 / 0909 / 1626 / 2325	1.9 / 0.2 / 2.1 / 0.4
13 TH	0005 / 0435 / 0935 / 1648	0.4 / 2.0 / 0.1 / 2.3	**28** F	0446 / 0945 / 1655	2.0 / 0.1 / 2.1
14 F	0100 / 0518 / 1019 / 1739	0.4 / 2.0 / 0.0 / 2.3	**29** SA	0020 / 0516 / 1014 / 1725	0.4 / 1.9 / 0.1 / 2.1
15 SA	0145 / 0608 / 1116 / 1828	0.5 / 2.0 / 0.0 / 2.2	**30** SU	0054 / 0546 / 1045 / 1759	0.4 / 1.9 / 0.1 / 2.1
			31 M	0146 / 0615 / 1129 / 1835	0.4 / 1.9 / 0.0 / 2.1

FEBRUARY

Day	Time	m	Day	Time	m
1 TU	0155 / 0655 / 1215 / 1918	0.4 / 1.9 / 0.0 / 2.0	**16** W	0130 / 0805 / 1404 / ◑ 2035	0.4 / 1.9 / 0.1 / 1.7
2 W	0157 / 0746 / 1304 / ◑ 2014	0.4 / 1.9 / 0.0 / 2.0	**17** TH	0225 / 0854 / 1524 / 2144	0.4 / 1.8 / 0.2 / 1.6
3 TH	0235 / 0850 / 1446 / 2130	0.4 / 1.8 / 0.1 / 1.9	**18** F	0355 / 1026 / 1635 / 2336	0.4 / 1.6 / 0.3 / 1.5
4 F	0315 / 0954 / 1544 / 2246	0.4 / 1.8 / 0.2 / 1.8	**19** SA	0510 / 1150 / 1744	0.3 / 1.6 / 0.3
5 SA	0435 / 1126 / 1705	0.4 / 1.8 / 0.2	**20** SU	0035 / 0555 / 1300 / 1835	1.6 / 0.3 / 1.7 / 0.4
6 SU	0000 / 0534 / 1225 / 1804	1.8 / 0.3 / 1.9 / 0.3	**21** M	0135 / 0650 / 1343 / 2150	1.7 / 0.3 / 1.8 / 0.4
7 M	0106 / 0630 / 1325 / 2135	1.8 / 0.3 / 2.0 / 0.3	**22** TU	0219 / 0724 / 1425 / 2227	1.8 / 0.3 / 1.9 / 0.4
8 TU	0155 / 0709 / 1216 / ● 2215	1.9 / 0.2 / 2.2 / 0.3	**23** W	0256 / 0804 / 1455 / 2257	1.7 / 0.2 / 2.0 / 0.4
9 W	0245 / 0749 / 1500 / 2310	1.9 / 0.1 / 2.3 / 0.4	**24** TH	0319 / 0815 / 1525 / ○ 2300	1.9 / 0.2 / 2.1 / 0.4
10 TH	0331 / 0829 / 1547 / 2345	2.0 / 0.0 / 2.3 / 0.4	**25** F	0349 / 0846 / 1559 / 2320	2.0 / 0.1 / 2.2 / 0.4
11 F	0416 / 0915 / 1636	2.0 / 0.0 / 2.3	**26** SA	0419 / 0915 / 1625	0.5 / 0.1 / 2.2
12 SA	0034 / 0459 / 0955 / 1716	0.4 / 2.0 / 0.0 / 2.2	**27** SU	0006 / 0449 / 0945 / 1659	0.3 / 2.0 / 0.1 / 2.1
13 SU	0124 / 0541 / 1046 / 1806	0.4 / 2.0 / 0.0 / 2.2	**28** M	0040 / 0515 / 1015 / 1731	0.3 / 2.0 / 0.0 / 2.1
14 M	0225 / 0625 / 1139 / 1849	0.4 / 2.0 / 0.0 / 2.0			
15 TU	0305 / 0716 / 1250 / 1939	0.4 / 1.9 / 0.1 / 1.9			

MARCH

Day	Time	m	Day	Time	m
1 TU	0115 / 0549 / 1055 / 1807	0.3 / 2.0 / 0.0 / 2.1	**16** W	0220 / 0631 / 1300 / 1855	0.3 / 2.0 / 0.1 / 1.8
2 W	0145 / 0626 / 1134 / 1848	0.3 / 2.0 / 0.0 / 2.0	**17** TH	0040 / 0715 / 1400 / ◑ 1946	0.3 / 1.9 / 0.2 / 1.6
3 TH	0000 / 0709 / 1234 / ◑ 1946	0.3 / 2.0 / 0.0 / 1.9	**18** F	0140 / 0804 / 1510 / 2034	0.2 / 1.8 / 0.2 / 1.5
4 F	0105 / 0805 / 1425 / 2056	0.3 / 1.9 / 0.1 / 1.7	**19** SA	0340 / 0925 / 1626 / 2237	0.3 / 1.6 / 0.3 / 1.3
5 SA	0245 / 0936 / 1535 / 2214	0.3 / 1.8 / 0.2 / 1.6	**20** SU	0435 / 1114 / 1714	0.2 / 1.5 / 0.3
6 SU	0404 / 1106 / 1706 / 2350	0.3 / 1.7 / 0.3 / 1.6	**21** M	0004 / 0534 / 1225 / 1814	1.4 / 0.2 / 1.7 / 0.3
7 M	0520 / 1219 / 2007	0.3 / 1.9 / 0.3	**22** TU	0116 / 0630 / 1315 / 2116	1.6 / 0.2 / 1.8 / 0.3
8 TU	0054 / 0610 / 1319 / 2124	1.7 / 0.2 / 2.0 / 0.3	**23** W	0145 / 0714 / 1355 / 2200	1.7 / 0.2 / 2.0 / 0.3
9 W	0149 / 0644 / 1405 / 2155	1.8 / 0.1 / 2.1 / 0.3	**24** TH	0214 / 1000 / 1425 / 2246	1.8 / 0.2 / 2.0 / 0.3
10 TH	0231 / 0730 / 1446 / 2234	1.9 / 0.1 / 2.2 / 0.4	**25** F	0244 / 1030 / 1455 / ○ 2304	1.9 / 0.2 / 2.1 / 0.3
11 F	0315 / 0808 / 1527 / 2330	2.0 / 0.0 / 2.2 / 0.4	**26** SA	0315 / 0804 / 1525 / 2310	1.9 / 0.1 / 2.2 / 0.3
12 SA	0350 / 0848 / 1608	2.0 / 0.0 / 2.2	**27** SU	0345 / 0839 / 1558 / 2340	2.0 / 0.1 / 2.2 / 0.3
13 SU	0020 / 0435 / 0924 / 1651	0.4 / 2.1 / 0.0 / 2.1	**28** M	0418 / 0916 / 1629	2.0 / 0.1 / 2.2
14 M	0115 / 0516 / 1015 / 1731	0.3 / 2.1 / 0.0 / 2.1	**29** TU	0449 / 0949 / 1705 / 2215	2.1 / 0.1 / 2.1 / 0.3
15 TU	0155 / 0551 / 1405 / 1815	0.3 / 2.1 / 0.1 / 1.9	**30** W	0525 / 1036 / 1745 / 2251	2.1 / 0.1 / 2.1 / 0.3
			31 TH	0603 / 1119 / 1830 / 2345	2.1 / 0.1 / 1.9 / 0.1

APRIL

Day	Time	m	Day	Time	m
1 F	0648 / 1340 / 1919	2.1 / 0.1 / 1.8	**16** SA	0110 / 0736 / 1445 / ◑ 1950	0.1 / 1.8 / 0.3 / 1.5
2 SA	0110 / 0746 / 1424 / ◑ 2046	0.1 / 1.9 / 0.2 / 1.5	**17** SU	0320 / 0856 / 1544 / 2110	0.2 / 1.6 / 0.3 / 1.3
3 SU	0234 / 0914 / 1534 / 2215	0.2 / 1.8 / 0.3 / 1.4	**18** M	0426 / 1015 / 1655 / 2325	0.1 / 1.5 / 0.3 / 1.3
4 M	0344 / 1054 / 1834 / 2339	0.2 / 1.8 / 0.3 / 1.5	**19** TU	0515 / 1144 / 1744	0.1 / 1.7 / 0.3
5 TU	0445 / 1215 / 2010	0.2 / 1.9 / 0.3	**20** W	0026 / 0605 / 1240 / 2000	1.5 / 0.1 / 1.8 / 0.3
6 W	0044 / 0815 / 1305 / 2107	1.6 / 0.1 / 2.0 / 0.2	**21** TH	0106 / 0645 / 1315 / 2126	1.6 / 0.2 / 2.0 / 0.2
7 TH	0128 / 0914 / 1345 / 2135	1.7 / 0.1 / 2.1 / 0.3	**22** F	0135 / 0920 / 1350 / 2215	1.7 / 0.1 / 2.1 / 0.2
8 F	0208 / 0955 / 1428 / ● 2226	1.9 / 0.1 / 2.2 / 0.3	**23** SA	0205 / 0955 / 1419 / 2246	1.9 / 0.1 / 2.1 / 0.2
9 SA	0255 / 0745 / 1506 / 2254	1.9 / 0.0 / 2.2 / 0.3	**24** SU	0240 / 0735 / 1451 / ○ 2300	2.0 / 0.1 / 2.2 / 0.3
10 SU	0327 / 0825 / 1547 / 2356	2.0 / 0.1 / 2.2 / 0.3	**25** M	0315 / 0809 / 1526 / 2034	2.0 / 0.1 / 2.2 / 0.3
11 M	0405 / 1225 / 1626 / 2109	2.1 / 0.1 / 2.1 / 0.2	**26** TU	0347 / 0844 / 1621	2.1 / 0.1 / 2.1
12 TU	0035 / 0445 / 1305 / 1708	0.2 / 2.1 / 0.1 / 2.1	**27** W	0425 / 0935 / 1645 / 2156	2.1 / 0.1 / 2.1 / 0.2
13 W	0120 / 0526 / 1325 / 1745	0.2 / 2.1 / 0.1 / 1.8	**28** TH	0502 / 1014 / 1728 / 2235	2.2 / 0.2 / 2.0 / 0.1
14 TH	0150 / 0559 / 1340 / 1819	0.2 / 2.0 / 0.2 / 1.7	**29** F	0546 / 1320 / 1815 / 2344	2.1 / 0.2 / 1.8 / 0.1
15 F	0004 / 0646 / 1400 / 1900	0.2 / 1.9 / 0.2 / 1.6	**30** SA	0635 / 1350 / 1916	2.1 / 0.2 / 1.6

Chart Datum: 0·84 metres below NAP Datum

》》 **FREE** monthly updates from 《《
www.reedsalmanac.co.uk

TIDES

TIME ZONE -0100 (Dutch Standard Time) Subtract 1 hour for UT. For Dutch Summer Time add ONE hour in **non-shaded areas**

NETHERLANDS – HOEK VAN HOLLAND
LAT 51°59'N   LONG 4°07'E
TIMES AND HEIGHTS OF HIGH AND LOW WATERS

YEAR 2005

Note - Double LWs often occur. The predictions are for the lower LW which is usually the first.

MAY

Day	Time	m	Day	Time	m
1 SU	0104 / 0746 / 2045	0.0 / 1.9 / 0.2 / 1.5	16 M	0301 / 0805 / 1536 / 2024	0.1 / 1.7 / 0.3 / 1.4
2 M	0220 / 0926 / 1700 / 2206	0.0 / 1.8 / 0.3 / 1.4	17 TU	0344 / 0925 / 1636 / 2146	0.1 / 1.7 / 0.3 / 1.4
3 TU	0325 / 1044 / 1825 / 2314	0.1 / 1.9 / 0.3 / 1.5	18 W	0445 / 1034 / 1715 / 2316	0.1 / 1.7 / 0.3 / 1.4
4 W	0644 / 1155 / 1954	0.1 / 2.0 / 0.2	19 TH	0540 / 1146 / 1850	0.1 / 1.8 / 0.3
5 TH	0015 / 0805 / 1246 / 2050	1.6 / 0.0 / 2.1 / 0.2	20 F	0016 / 0640 / 1230 / 2035	1.6 / 0.2 / 2.0 / 0.2
6 F	0104 / 0844 / 1325 / 2115	1.8 / 0.0 / 2.1 / 0.3	21 SA	0050 / 0846 / 1305 / 2125	1.7 / 0.1 / 2.1 / 0.2
7 SA	0149 / 0940 / 1405 / 2145	1.9 / 0.1 / 2.1 / 0.3	22 SU	0128 / 0635 / 1346 / 2215	1.9 / 0.2 / 2.1 / 0.2
8 SU	0225 / 0730 / 1446 / 2225	1.9 / 0.1 / 2.1 / 0.1	23 M	0206 / 0716 / 1422 / 1946	2.0 / 0.1 / 2.2 / 0.3
9 M	0308 / 1047 / 1526 / 2314	2.0 / 0.2 / 2.1 / 0.2	24 TU	0246 / 0755 / 1506 / 2020	2.1 / 0.2 / 2.1 / 0.2
10 TU	0345 / 1135 / 1606	2.1 / 0.2 / 1.9	25 W	0322 / 0836 / 1545 / 2055	2.1 / 0.2 / 2.1 / 0.1
11 W	0016 / 0421 / 1235 / 1641	0.2 / 2.1 / 0.2 / 1.9	26 TH	0406 / 0919 / 1632 / 2146	2.2 / 0.2 / 2.0 / 0.1
12 TH	0044 / 0506 / 1257 / 1719	0.1 / 2.1 / 0.2 / 1.8	27 F	0449 / 1255 / 1716 / 2236	2.2 / 1.9 / 1.9 / 0.0
13 F	0125 / 0539 / 1317 / 1755	0.1 / 2.0 / 0.3 / 1.7	28 SA	0536 / 1330 / 1809 / 2335	2.1 / 0.2 / 1.7 / 0.0
14 SA	0130 / 0619 / 1350 / 1824	0.1 / 1.9 / 0.3 / 1.6	29 SU	0631 / 1420 / 1920	2.1 / 0.3 / 1.6
15 SU	0040 / 0710 / 1440 / 1925	0.1 / 1.8 / 0.3 / 1.5	30 M	0045 / 0750 / 1527 / 2036	0.0 / 2.0 / 0.3 / 1.6
			31 TU	0155 / 0916 / 1705 / 2134	0.0 / 2.0 / 0.3 / 1.6

JUNE

Day	Time	m	Day	Time	m
1 W	0254 / 1020 / 1805 / 2244	0.0 / 2.0 / 0.3 / 1.6	16 TH	0244 / 0935 / 1640 / 2154	0.1 / 1.8 / 0.3 / 1.6
2 TH	0624 / 1125 / 1915 / 2345	0.0 / 2.0 / 0.3 / 1.7	17 F	0340 / 1034 / 1717 / 2305	0.1 / 1.9 / 0.3 / 1.6
3 F	0725 / 1220 / 2020	1.9 / 2.0 / 0.3	18 SA	0424 / 1135 / 1800 / 2359	0.1 / 1.9 / 0.3 / 1.8
4 SA	0034 / 0815 / 1306 / 2100	1.8 / 0.1 / 2.1 / 0.3	19 SU	0525 / 1225 / 1820	0.2 / 2.0 / 0.3
5 SU	0126 / 0639 / 1345 / 2140	1.9 / 0.2 / 2.2 / 0.3	20 M	0052 / 0610 / 1316 / 1850	1.9 / 0.2 / 2.1 / 0.3
6 M	0208 / 0724 / 1435 / 1955	1.9 / 0.2 / 1.9 / 0.3	21 TU	0136 / 0655 / 1359 / 1926	2.0 / 0.2 / 2.1 / 0.2
7 TU	0249 / 0920 / 1515 / 2024	2.0 / 0.2 / 1.9 / 0.2	22 W	0226 / 0734 / 1446 / 1959	2.1 / 0.2 / 2.0 / 0.2
8 W	0329 / 1050 / 1555 / 2105	2.1 / 0.3 / 1.9 / 0.2	23 TH	0307 / 0826 / 1530 / 2046	2.2 / 0.3 / 2.0 / 0.1
9 TH	0405 / 1150 / 1624 / 2150	2.2 / 0.3 / 1.8 / 0.1	24 F	0351 / 1155 / 1618 / 2130	2.2 / 0.3 / 1.9 / 0.0
10 F	0446 / 1240 / 1705 / 2224	2.0 / 0.3 / 1.8 / 0.1	25 SA	0439 / 1256 / 1715 / 2214	2.2 / 0.3 / 1.8 / 0.0
11 SA	0526 / 1257 / 1734 / 2320	2.0 / 0.3 / 1.7 / 0.1	26 SU	0528 / 1334 / 1803 / 2316	2.2 / 0.3 / 1.8 / 0.0
12 SU	0606 / 1325 / 1813	1.9 / 0.3 / 1.7	27 M	0625 / 1355 / 1905	2.1 / 0.4 / 1.8
13 M	0155 / 0656 / 1414 / 1855	0.1 / 1.9 / 0.3 / 1.6	28 TU	0015 / 0729 / 1527 / 2005	0.0 / 2.1 / 0.4 / 1.7
14 TU	0055 / 0735 / 1500 / 1956	0.1 / 1.8 / 0.3 / 1.6	29 W	0114 / 0833 / 1640 / 2105	0.0 / 2.0 / 0.4 / 1.7
15 W	0200 / 0835 / 1550 / 2055	0.1 / 1.8 / 0.3 / 1.8	30 TH	0224 / 0939 / 1737 / 2210	0.0 / 2.0 / 0.4 / 1.7

JULY

Day	Time	m	Day	Time	m
1 F	0334 / 1043 / 1846 / 2316	0.1 / 1.9 / 0.4 / 1.7	16 SA	0244 / 0946 / 1545 / 2216	0.1 / 1.9 / 0.4 / 1.7
2 SA	0444 / 1144 / 1940	0.1 / 1.9 / 0.3	17 SU	0345 / 1056 / 1634 / 2314	0.1 / 1.9 / 0.4 / 1.8
3 SU	0004 / 0550 / 1250 / 2040	1.8 / 0.2 / 1.9 / 0.3	18 M	0455 / 1149 / 1735	0.2 / 1.9 / 0.3
4 M	0106 / 0644 / 1339 / 1855	1.8 / 0.2 / 1.9 / 0.3	19 TU	0019 / 0555 / 1256 / 1824	1.9 / 0.2 / 1.9 / 0.3
5 TU	0155 / 0724 / 1424 / 1935	1.9 / 0.3 / 1.9 / 0.3	20 W	0116 / 0644 / 1345 / 1904	2.0 / 0.3 / 2.0 / 0.2
6 W	0234 / 0815 / 1515 / 2014	1.9 / 0.4 / 1.9 / 0.2	21 TH	0205 / 0724 / 1435 / 1950	2.1 / 0.3 / 2.0 / 0.1
7 TH	0319 / 0904 / 1545 / 2055	2.0 / 0.4 / 1.8 / 0.2	22 F	0255 / 1110 / 1521 / 2025	2.2 / 0.4 / 2.0 / 0.1
8 F	0355 / 1120 / 1625 / 2124	2.0 / 0.3 / 1.8 / 0.1	23 SA	0338 / 1155 / 1608 / 2109	2.3 / 0.4 / 2.0 / 0.0
9 SA	0428 / 1210 / 1655 / 2205	2.2 / 0.4 / 1.8 / 0.1	24 SU	0427 / 1240 / 1657 / 2156	2.3 / 0.4 / 1.9 / 0.0
10 SU	0505 / 1240 / 1730 / 2239	2.0 / 0.4 / 1.8 / 0.1	25 M	0515 / 1336 / 1745 / 2246	2.3 / 0.4 / 1.9 / 0.0
11 M	0546 / 1314 / 1800 / 2319	2.0 / 0.4 / 1.8 / 0.1	26 TU	0605 / 1424 / 1835 / 2334	2.2 / 0.4 / 1.9 / 0.1
12 TU	0620 / 1355 / 1836	2.0 / 0.4 / 1.8	27 W	0659 / 1514 / 1925	2.1 / 0.4 / 1.9
13 W	0004 / 0655 / 1430 / 1904	0.1 / 2.0 / 0.4 / 1.7	28 TH	0044 / 0754 / 1610 / 2019	0.0 / 2.0 / 0.4 / 1.9
14 TH	0054 / 0734 / 1500 / 2005	0.1 / 1.9 / 0.4 / 1.7	29 F	0200 / 0854 / 1455 / 2119	0.0 / 1.9 / 0.4 / 1.9
15 F	0144 / 0845 / 1505 / 2110	0.1 / 1.9 / 0.4 / 1.7	30 SA	0305 / 1016 / 1555 / 2236	0.1 / 1.8 / 0.4 / 1.8
			31 SU	0430 / 1136 / 1705 / 2350	0.2 / 1.8 / 0.4 / 1.8

AUGUST

Day	Time	m	Day	Time	m
1 M	0524 / 1229 / 1759	0.3 / 1.8 / 0.3	16 TU	0434 / 1130 / 1705 / 2359	0.3 / 1.8 / 0.3 / 1.9
2 TU	0056 / 0624 / 1329 / 1844	1.8 / 0.3 / 1.8 / 0.3	17 W	0556 / 1235 / 1804	0.5 / 1.8 / 0.3
3 W	0145 / 0715 / 1414 / 1924	1.9 / 0.4 / 1.8 / 0.3	18 TH	0101 / 0634 / 1336 / 1844	2.0 / 0.4 / 1.9 / 0.3
4 TH	0235 / 0754 / 1506 / 2005	2.0 / 0.5 / 1.9 / 0.2	19 F	0155 / 1005 / 1426 / 1924	2.2 / 0.4 / 1.9 / 0.1
5 F	0304 / 0824 / 1540 / 2035	2.0 / 0.5 / 1.9 / 0.2	20 SA	0239 / 1035 / 1506 / 2008	2.3 / 0.4 / 1.9 / 0.1
6 SA	0334 / 1140 / 1605 / 2053	2.1 / 0.5 / 1.9 / 0.2	21 SU	0322 / 1125 / 1548 / 2045	2.3 / 0.5 / 1.9 / 0.0
7 SU	0408 / 1140 / 1635 / 2130	2.1 / 0.5 / 1.9 / 0.1	22 M	0405 / 1215 / 1636 / 2130	2.3 / 0.5 / 1.9 / 0.0
8 M	0448 / 1207 / 1705 / 2206	2.1 / 0.5 / 1.9 / 0.1	23 TU	0451 / 1310 / 1716 / 2215	2.3 / 0.5 / 2.1 / 0.0
9 TU	0515 / 1256 / 1736 / 2235	2.1 / 0.4 / 1.9 / 0.1	24 W	0535 / 1355 / 1759 / 2305	2.2 / 0.5 / 2.1 / 0.1
10 W	0548 / 1330 / 1806 / 2304	2.1 / 0.4 / 1.9 / 0.1	25 TH	0627 / 1435 / 1845	2.1 / 0.5 / 2.0
11 TH	0615 / 1400 / 1831 / 2345	2.1 / 0.4 / 1.9 / 0.1	26 F	0015 / 0715 / 1304 / 1936	0.1 / 2.0 / 0.5 / 2.0
12 F	0656 / 1410 / 1916	2.1 / 0.4 / 1.9	27 SA	0140 / 0804 / 1410 / 2029	0.2 / 1.8 / 0.4 / 1.9
13 SA	0034 / 0746 / 1400 / 2003	0.1 / 1.9 / 0.4 / 1.9	28 SU	0254 / 0919 / 1525 / 2144	0.2 / 1.7 / 0.4 / 1.7
14 SU	0216 / 0850 / 1500 / 2126	0.1 / 1.9 / 0.4 / 1.8	29 M	0415 / 1106 / 1656 / 2336	0.5 / 1.6 / 0.4 / 1.7
15 M	0325 / 1010 / 1616 / 2245	0.2 / 1.8 / 0.4 / 1.8	30 TU	0520 / 1216 / 1734	0.4 / 1.7 / 0.3
			31 W	0045 / 0626 / 1316 / 1830	1.8 / 0.4 / 1.8 / 0.3

Chart Datum: 0·84 metres below NAP Datum

》FREE monthly updates from《
www.reedsalmanac.co.uk

TIME ZONE -0100
(Dutch Standard Time)
Subtract 1 hour for UT
For Dutch Summer Time add ONE hour in **non-shaded areas**

NETHERLANDS – HOEK VAN HOLLAND
LAT 51°59'N LONG 4°07'E
TIMES AND HEIGHTS OF HIGH AND LOW WATERS

YEAR 2005

Note - Double LWs often occur. The predictions are for the lower LW which is usually the first.

SEPTEMBER

	Time	m		Time	m
1 TH	0135 0945 1406 1915	2.0 0.4 1.9 0.3	**16** F	0056 0850 1325 1825	2.1 0.4 1.8 0.2
2 F	0220 1025 1434 1956	2.0 0.4 1.9 0.3	**17** SA	0139 0944 1405 1905	2.2 0.4 2.0 0.2
3 SA	0243 1106 1504 2004	2.1 0.5 1.9 0.3	**18** SU	0218 1015 1445 1946	2.3 0.5 2.0 0.1
4 SU	0316 1120 1535 2025	2.2 0.5 1.9 0.2	**19** M	0306 1055 1525 2022	2.4 0.5 2.1 0.1
5 M	0346 1110 1606 2056	2.2 0.5 2.0 0.2	**20** TU	0346 1144 1605 2101	2.4 0.5 2.2 0.1
6 TU	0411 1140 1635 2126	2.2 0.5 2.0 0.2	**21** W	0427 1245 1647 2150	2.3 0.5 2.2 0.1
7 W	0440 1225 1659 2200	2.2 0.5 2.0 0.2	**22** TH	0509 1324 1729 2235	2.2 0.5 2.2 0.2
8 TH	0516 1306 1729 2236	2.2 0.5 2.1 0.1	**23** F	0556 1100 1809 2334	2.1 0.5 2.2 0.3
9 F	0546 1055 1806 2316	2.2 0.4 2.0 0.1	**24** SA	0638 1200 1855	1.9 0.4 2.1
10 SA	0622 1136 1841	2.1 0.3 2.1	**25**	0130 0726 1305 ◐ 1956	0.3 1.8 0.4 1.9
11 SU	0005 0709 1224 ◐ 1936	0.2 0.3 0.3 2.0	**26**	0240 0825 1507 2105	0.4 1.6 0.4 1.7
12 M	0200 0804 1420 2035	0.2 0.3 0.4 1.9	**27** TU	0345 1025 1625 2254	0.4 1.5 0.4 1.7
13 TU	0304 0946 1524 2215	0.3 1.7 0.4 1.8	**28** W	0506 1150 1714	0.5 1.6 0.3
14 W	0424 1105 1650 2350	1.8 1.6 0.3 0.4	**29** TH	0015 0555 1245 1804	1.8 0.5 1.7 0.2
15 TH	0535 1223 1734	0.4 1.7 0.3	**30** F	0110 0850 1336 1855	2.0 0.5 1.8 0.3

OCTOBER

	Time	m		Time	m
1 SA	0146 0944 1416 1924	2.1 0.4 1.9 0.3	**16** SU	0126 0915 1345 1834	2.3 0.4 2.0 0.2
2 SU	0216 1025 1435 1934	2.2 0.4 2.0 0.3	**17** M	0158 0955 1425 ○ 1914	2.3 0.5 2.1 0.2
3 M	0238 1045 1459 ● 1953	2.2 0.5 2.1 0.3	**18** TU	0241 1024 1505 1959	2.3 0.5 2.2 0.2
4 TU	0308 0825 1525 2025	2.3 0.5 2.1 0.2	**19** W	0326 0819 1542 2046	2.3 0.5 2.2 0.2
5 W	0341 0845 1559 2056	2.3 0.5 2.2 0.2	**20** TH	0406 0859 1625 2125	2.2 0.5 2.2 0.3
6 TH	0415 0915 1629 2124	2.3 0.5 2.2 0.2	**21** F	0446 0945 1701	2.1 0.4 2.3
7 F	0446 0949 1703 2205	2.3 0.4 2.2 0.2	**22** SA	0117 0526 1035 1746	0.3 2.0 0.4 2.2
8 SA	0522 1030 1738 2249	2.2 0.3 2.2 0.2	**23** SU	0144 0605 1130 1826	0.4 1.9 0.3 2.1
9 SU	0602 1116 1819 2344	2.1 0.3 2.2 0.3	**24** M	0130 0643 1235 1920	0.4 1.8 0.3 1.9
10	0650 1205 M 1909 ◐	2.0 0.3 2.1	**25** TU	0217 0735 1440 ◐ 2025	0.5 1.6 0.3 1.8
11	0210 1035 TU 1406 2030	0.4 1.4 0.3 1.9	**26** W	0325 0856 1606 2154	0.5 1.5 0.3 1.7
12	0304 0935 W 1510 2215	0.4 1.6 0.3 1.9	**27** TH	0435 1055 1656 2335	0.5 1.5 0.3 1.8
13 TH	0510 1106 1620 2335	1.3 1.6 1.6 2.0	**28** F	0525 1216 1734	0.5 1.6 0.3
14 F	0734 1209 1956	0.5 1.7 0.3	**29** SA	0026 0750 1255 1840	2.0 0.5 1.8 0.3
15 SA	0035 0844 1306 2055	2.1 0.4 1.8 0.2	**30** SU	0106 0906 1326 2055	2.2 0.4 1.9 0.3
31 M	0135 0934 1351 2140	2.2 0.4 2.0 0.3			

NOVEMBER

	Time	m		Time	m
1 TU	0206 1030 1421 1923	2.2 0.4 2.1 0.3	**16** W	0220 1010 1438 ○ 1944	2.2 0.5 2.2 0.3
2 W	0238 0755 1435 ● 2006	2.3 0.5 2.2 0.3	**17** TH	0306 0809 1521 2036	2.2 0.4 2.2 0.3
3 TH	0312 0826 1529 2029	2.3 0.4 2.2 0.3	**18** F	0348 0849 1601 2116	2.1 0.4 2.3 0.3
4 F	0346 0856 1605 2110	2.3 0.4 2.2 0.3	**19** SA	0004 0429 0935 1646	0.4 2.0 0.3 2.2
5 SA	0422 0931 1641 2156	2.2 0.3 2.3 0.3	**20** SU	0050 0510 1015 1725	0.5 2.0 0.3 2.2
6 SU	0505 1020 1721 2245	2.1 0.2 2.3 0.4	**21** M	0110 0545 1114 1806	0.5 1.9 0.2 2.1
7 M	0548 1109 1806	2.0 0.2 2.2	**22** TU	0120 0626 1205 1856	0.5 1.8 0.2 2.0
8 TU	0117 0640 1226 1906	0.4 1.9 0.2 2.1	**23** W	0157 0705 1320 ◐ 1945	0.5 1.7 0.3 1.9
9 W	0210 0744 1335 ◐ 2035	0.5 1.7 0.2 2.0	**24** TH	0257 0816 1515 2106	0.5 1.6 0.3 1.8
10 TH	0330 0920 1439 2153	0.5 1.6 0.2 2.0	**25** F	0354 0925 1626 2215	0.5 1.5 0.3 1.8
11 F	0550 1035 1544 2313	0.5 1.6 0.3 2.0	**26** SA	0500 1034 1720 2325	0.5 1.6 0.3 1.9
12 SA	0717 1145 1924	0.5 1.7 0.3	**27** SU	0554 1150 1820	0.5 1.7 0.3
13 SU	0015 0824 1240 2036	2.1 0.4 1.8 0.2	**28** M	0016 0815 1225 2010	2.0 0.4 1.8 0.3
14 M	0059 0857 1319 2105	2.2 0.4 2.0 0.2	**29** TU	0055 0916 1304 2116	2.1 0.4 1.9 0.3
15 TU	0138 0915 1401 1905	2.2 0.4 2.0 0.2	**30** W	0130 0956 1348 1859	2.2 0.4 2.0 0.3

DECEMBER

	Time	m		Time	m
1 TH	0205 0735 1425 ● 1933	2.2 0.4 2.2 0.3	**16** F	0255 0815 1509 2130	2.0 0.4 2.2 0.4
2 F	0245 0805 1506 2013	2.2 0.4 2.3 0.3	**17** SA	0345 0844 1544 2310	2.0 0.3 2.2 0.5
3 SA	0328 0845 1545 2059	2.2 0.3 2.3 0.3	**18** SU	0419 0930 1635	2.0 0.2 2.2
4 SU	0409 0914 1627 2150	2.1 0.3 2.3 0.4	**19** M	0020 0455 1005 1716	0.5 1.9 0.3 2.1
5 M	0455 1010 1715 2243	2.0 0.3 2.3 0.4	**20** TU	0050 0536 1044 1744	0.5 1.8 0.3 2.1
6 TU	0106 0545 1059 1805	0.4 1.9 0.1 2.2	**21** W	0110 0605 1134 1836	0.5 1.9 0.3 2.0
7 W	0144 0634 1206 1905	0.4 1.8 0.1 2.1	**22** TH	0140 0645 1225 1915	0.5 1.8 0.2 1.9
8 TH	0244 0745 1304 ◐ 2014	0.5 1.7 0.1 2.1	**23** F	0220 0729 1315 ◐ 2010	0.5 1.8 0.2 1.9
9 F	0400 0900 1415 2146	0.5 1.7 0.1 2.0	**24** SA	0310 0825 1414 2110	0.5 1.7 0.2 1.9
10 SA	0540 1006 1514 2245	0.5 1.7 0.2 2.0	**25** SU	0400 0935 1505 2210	0.5 1.7 0.3 1.9
11 SU	0654 1109 1854 2315	0.5 1.8 0.2 1.9	**26** M	0450 1046 1605 2315	0.5 1.7 0.3 1.9
12 M	0754 1205 2000	0.5 1.9 0.3	**27** TU	0540 1148 1710	0.5 1.8 0.4
13 TU	0040 0837 1258 2040	2.1 0.4 2.0 0.3	**28** W	0005 0837 1229 1754	2.0 0.4 1.9 0.4
14 W	0125 0910 1346 1855	2.1 0.4 2.0 0.3	**29** TH	0055 0635 1320 1855	2.1 0.4 2.0 0.3
15 TH	0216 0729 1430 ○ 1955	2.1 0.3 2.1 0.4	**30** F	0141 0704 1405 1925	2.1 0.4 2.1 0.3
31 SA	0225 0744 1448 ● 2010	2.1 0.3 2.2 0.4			

Chart Datum: 0·84 metres below NAP Datum

》 **FREE** monthly updates from 《
www.reedsalmanac.co.uk

TIDES

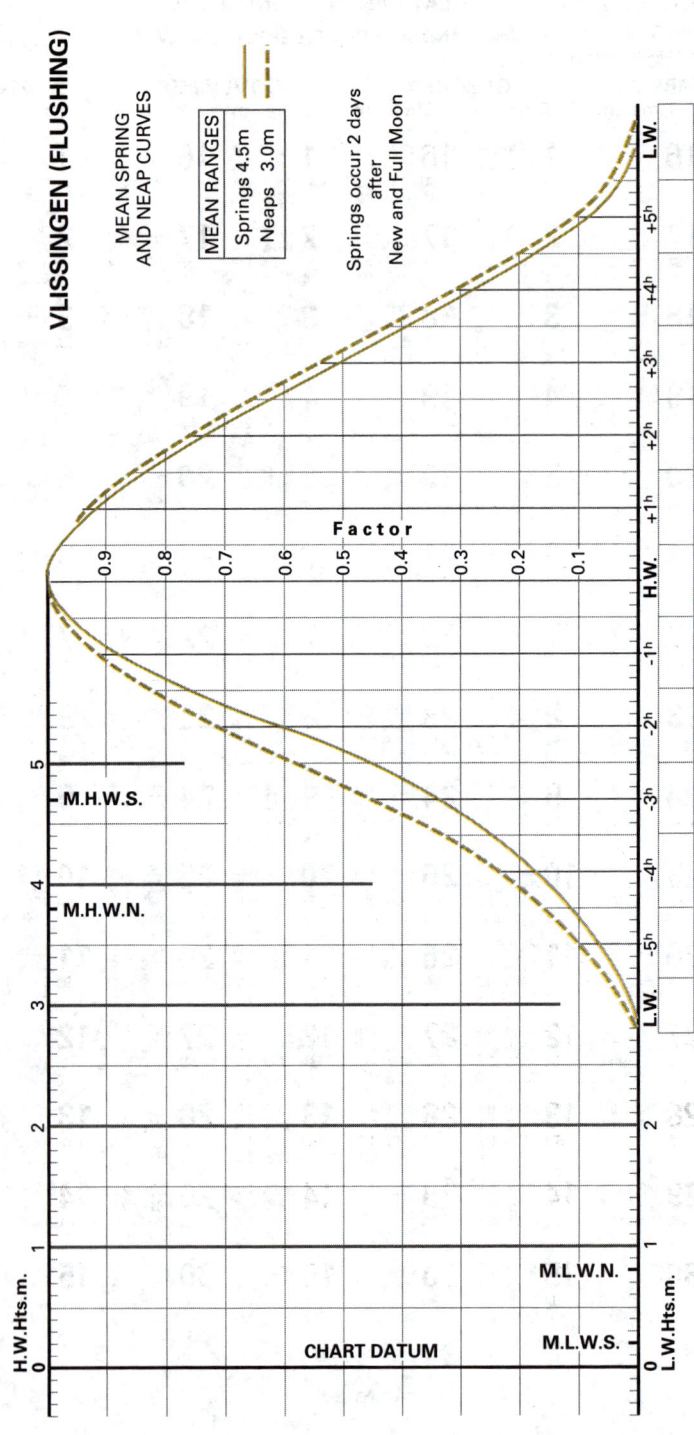

TIME ZONE -0100
(Dutch Standard Time)
Subtract 1 hour for UT
For Dutch Summer Time add
ONE hour in **non-shaded areas**

NETHERLANDS – VLISSINGEN

LAT 51°27'N   LONG 3°36'E

TIMES AND HEIGHTS OF HIGH AND LOW WATERS

YEAR 2005

	JANUARY			FEBRUARY			MARCH			APRIL	
	Time m	Time m		Time m	Time m		Time m	Time m		Time m	Time m
1 SA	0518 4.3 1145 0.5 1735 4.3 2346 0.9	**16** SU	0000 0.7 0609 4.5 1235 0.2 1839 4.5	**1** TU	0001 0.7 0606 4.4 1235 0.4 1828 4.4	**16** W	0055 0.8 0709 4.2 1330 0.6 ① 1945 3.9	**1** TU	0458 4.7 1132 0.2 1720 4.6 2336 0.5	**16** W	0541 4.5 1206 0.4 1806 4.2	**1** F	0000 0.4 0600 4.5 1236 0.5 1831 4.1	**16** SA	0025 0.8 0646 3.8 1254 1.0 ① 1859 3.5
2 SU	0558 4.2 1220 0.5 1819 4.3	**17** M	0045 0.8 0706 4.3 1331 0.3 ① 1938 4.3	**2** W	0040 0.7 0652 4.3 1321 0.5 ① 1928 4.2	**17** TH	0144 1.0 0810 3.9 1436 0.9 2056 3.6	**2** W	0537 4.6 1206 0.3 1759 4.5	**17** TH	0011 0.7 0625 4.2 1246 0.7 ① 1849 3.8	**2** SA	0056 0.5 0659 4.2 1331 0.7 ① 1945 3.7	**17** SU	0206 1.0 0744 3.5 1435 1.2 2015 3.2
3 M	0025 0.9 0642 4.1 1305 0.6 ① 1911 4.2	**18** TU	0145 0.9 0800 4.1 1414 0.6 2046 4.0	**3** TH	0129 0.8 0751 4.1 1415 0.6 2035 4.0	**18** F	0316 1.1 0936 3.6 1555 1.1 2224 3.4	**3** TH	0016 0.5 0617 4.5 1250 0.4 ① 1848 4.2	**18** F	0054 0.9 0716 3.8 1340 1.0 1946 3.5	**3** SU	0210 0.7 0835 3.9 1454 0.9 2120 3.6	**18** M	0325 1.0 0935 3.4 1606 1.1 2226 3.3
4 TU	0120 1.0 0740 4.0 1400 0.6 2021 4.1	**19** W	0245 1.1 0905 3.9 1523 0.8 2156 3.9	**4** F	0240 0.9 0912 4.0 1530 0.7 2155 3.9	**19** SA	0435 1.1 1106 3.6 1715 1.1 2346 3.6	**4** F	0106 0.6 0718 4.2 1356 0.6 2002 3.9	**19** SA	0225 1.1 0835 3.5 1520 1.2 2125 3.2	**4** M	0346 0.8 1010 3.9 1647 0.9 2245 3.7	**19** TU	0430 0.9 1106 3.7 1655 1.0 2331 3.6
5 W	0214 1.0 0846 3.9 1506 0.7 2125 4.1	**20** TH	0405 1.1 1026 3.8 1644 0.9 2306 3.8	**5** SA	0406 0.9 1030 4.0 1649 0.8 2309 4.0	**20** SU	0556 1.0 1215 3.8 1820 1.0	**5** SA	0215 0.8 0839 3.9 1516 0.9 2136 3.7	**20** SU	0353 1.1 1037 3.4 1633 1.2 2316 3.4	**5** TU	0526 0.6 1125 4.2 1756 0.7 2351 4.0	**20** W	0536 0.7 1149 4.0 1755 0.8
6 TH	0324 1.0 0956 4.0 1615 0.7 2236 4.2	**21** F	0526 1.1 1130 3.9 1749 0.9	**6** SU	0530 0.8 1139 4.2 1810 0.7	**21** M	0039 3.9 0644 0.8 1306 4.1 1905 0.8	**6** SU	0350 0.9 1016 3.9 1634 0.9 2259 3.7	**21** M	0516 1.0 1146 3.7 1746 1.0	**6** W	0625 0.3 1225 4.5 1848 0.5	**21** TH	0009 3.9 0625 0.5 1229 4.3 1839 0.6
7 F	0440 0.9 1058 4.2 1720 0.6 2331 4.3	**22** SA	0006 3.9 0619 0.9 1224 4.0 1846 0.8	**7** M	0018 4.2 0639 0.5 1241 4.5 1908 0.5	**22** TU	0126 4.1 0736 0.6 1339 4.3 1939 0.7	**7** M	0514 0.7 1135 4.1 1759 0.7	**22** TU	0009 3.7 0620 0.8 1236 4.0 1846 0.8	**7** TH	0041 4.3 0716 0.1 1305 4.7 1929 0.4	**22** F	0045 4.2 0708 0.3 1302 4.5 1915 0.5
8 SA	0551 0.8 1156 4.4 1825 0.5	**23** SU	0100 4.1 0709 0.8 1319 4.2 1925 0.8	**8** TU	0111 4.4 0738 0.3 1332 4.8 ● 1958 0.4	**23** W	0155 4.2 0816 0.5 1416 4.5 2015 0.6	**8** TU	0006 4.0 0636 0.4 1236 4.5 1900 0.5	**23** W	0056 4.0 0705 0.5 1309 4.3 1918 0.6	**8** F	0122 4.5 0756 0.0 1346 4.8 ● 2010 0.3	**23** SA	0115 4.4 0740 0.2 1336 4.7 1950 0.4
9 SU	0030 4.5 0656 0.6 1249 4.6 1921 0.4	**24** M	0146 4.2 0756 0.7 1400 4.3 1959 0.6	**9** W	0159 4.6 0830 0.1 1421 4.9 2045 0.4	**24** TH	0226 4.4 0846 0.3 1438 4.6 ○ 2045 0.5	**9** W	0058 4.3 0730 0.2 1322 4.7 1948 0.4	**24** TH	0126 4.2 0746 0.4 1341 4.5 1950 0.5	**9** SA	0202 4.7 0835 -0.1 1426 4.9 2045 0.3	**24** SU	0148 4.6 0815 0.1 1407 4.8 ○ 2026 0.3
10 M	0122 4.6 0749 0.4 1341 4.8 ● 2011 0.4	**25** TU	0215 4.3 0916 0.1 1435 4.4 ○ 2036 0.7	**10** TH	0243 4.8 0916 -0.1 1505 5.0 2128 0.4	**25** F	0255 4.6 0916 0.2 1511 4.7 2119 0.5	**10** TH	0142 4.6 0817 0.0 1406 4.9 ● 2030 0.4	**25** F	0156 4.4 0816 0.3 1412 4.7 ○ 2019 0.4	**10** SU	0239 4.8 0915 -0.1 1503 4.9 2126 0.3	**25** M	0222 4.8 0852 0.1 1443 4.9 2106 0.3
11 TU	0209 4.7 0838 0.4 1431 5.0 2058 0.4	**26** W	0248 4.4 0901 0.4 1506 4.5 2111 0.6	**11** F	0326 4.8 1002 -0.1 1549 5.0 2210 0.4	**26** SA	0325 4.6 0952 0.1 1541 4.8 2156 0.4	**11** F	0223 4.8 0858 -0.1 1447 5.0 2110 0.3	**26** SA	0222 4.6 0846 0.1 1439 4.8 2056 0.4	**11** M	0318 4.9 0952 0.0 1540 4.7 2206 0.3	**26** TU	0258 4.9 0930 0.1 1516 4.8 2146 0.2
12 W	0258 4.8 0928 0.2 1519 5.0 2146 0.4	**27** TH	0317 4.5 0940 0.2 1538 4.6 2142 0.6	**12** SA	0411 4.9 1045 -0.1 1632 5.0 2249 0.5	**27** SU	0355 4.7 1026 0.1 1613 4.8 2225 0.5	**12** SA	0303 4.9 0937 -0.2 1526 4.9 2148 0.3	**27** SU	0253 4.7 0922 0.1 1511 4.9 2131 0.3	**12** TU	0357 4.8 1026 0.2 1619 4.6 2241 0.5	**27** W	0336 4.9 1008 0.1 1556 4.7 2222 0.2
13 TH	0346 4.8 1015 0.2 1606 5.0 2228 0.5	**28** F	0348 4.5 1015 0.2 1606 4.6 2221 0.6	**13** SU	0452 4.8 1126 0.0 1717 4.8 2330 0.5	**28** M	0427 4.7 1101 0.1 1643 4.7 2300 0.4	**13** SU	0345 4.9 1018 -0.1 1606 4.9 2226 0.4	**28** M	0325 4.8 0955 0.1 1543 4.8 2206 0.3	**13** W	0436 4.7 1100 0.4 1656 4.3 2316 0.5	**28** TH	0413 4.8 1051 0.2 1639 4.6 2306 0.2
14 F	0432 4.7 1101 0.0 1657 4.9 2315 0.6	**29** SA	0420 4.5 1050 0.3 1639 4.6 2244 0.6	**14** M	0536 4.7 1206 0.1 1800 4.5			**14** M	0426 4.9 1057 0.1 1647 4.7 2306 0.4	**29** TU	0358 4.8 1032 0.1 1618 4.8 2235 0.3	**14** TH	0516 4.4 1129 0.6 1731 4.1 2351 0.6	**29** F	0456 4.7 1132 0.4 1728 4.3 2356 0.3
15 SA	0522 4.6 1156 0.1 1745 4.8	**30** SU	0455 4.5 1126 0.3 1711 4.6 2326 0.6	**15** TU	0010 0.6 0622 4.5 1246 0.4 1856 4.2			**15** TU	0502 4.7 1130 0.2 1725 4.5 2336 0.5	**29** W	0436 4.8 1105 0.2 1655 4.7 2315 0.3	**15** F	0555 4.2 1205 0.8 1816 3.8	**30** SA	0548 4.5 1227 0.6 1826 4.0
		31 M	0527 4.4 1156 0.3 1747 4.5							**31** TH	0513 4.7 1149 0.3 1737 4.4				

Chart Datum: 2·32 metres below NAP Datum
》 FREE monthly updates from **《**
www.reedsalmanac.co.uk

Chapter 5

367

TIDES

TIME ZONE -0100
(Dutch Standard Time)
Subtract 1 hour for UT
For Dutch Summer Time add
ONE hour in **non-shaded areas**

NETHERLANDS – VLISSINGEN
LAT 51°27'N   LONG 3°36'E
TIMES AND HEIGHTS OF HIGH AND LOW WATERS

YEAR 2005

	MAY				JUNE				JULY				AUGUST			
	Time	m	Time	m	Time	m	Time	m	Time	m	Time	m	Time	m	Time	m
1	0056 0701 SU 1324 ☽ 1948	0.4 4.2 0.8 3.8	**16** 0125 0714 M 1400 ☾ 1945	0.8 3.7 1.1 3.5	**1** 0320 0930 W 1606 2156	0.3 4.2 0.9 4.0	**16** 0246 0850 TH 1505 2116	0.7 3.9 1.0 3.7	**1** 0356 1002 F 1626 2226	0.4 4.2 0.9 4.1	**16** 0236 0855 SA 1500 2126	0.6 4.0 1.0 3.9	**1** 0530 1145 M 1800	0.8 4.0 0.9	**16** 0414 1040 TU 1706 2315	0.8 3.9 0.9 4.1
2	0215 0824 M 1454 2105	0.5 4.0 0.9 3.7	**17** 0234 0835 TU 1516 2106	0.8 3.6 1.1 3.4	**2** 0436 1038 TH 1705 2300	0.3 4.3 0.8 4.1	**17** 0334 0956 F 1603 2215	0.6 4.0 0.9 3.9	**2** 0506 1106 SA 1730 2321	0.5 4.2 0.8 4.1	**17** 0340 1006 SU 1605 2229	0.7 4.1 0.9 4.0	**2** 0016 0626 TU 1246 1855	4.1 0.8 4.1 0.7	**17** 0540 1152 W 1816	4.1 4.1 0.6
3	0334 0956 TU 1616 2230	0.5 4.1 0.9 3.8	**18** 0346 0956 W 1616 2214	0.8 3.7 1.0 3.6	**3** 0541 1136 F 1800 2351	0.3 4.4 0.7 4.2	**18** 0435 1049 SA 1706 2311	0.6 4.2 0.8 4.1	**3** 0555 1206 SU 1826	0.5 4.2 0.7	**18** 0444 1108 M 1725 2331	0.6 4.2 0.8 4.2	**3** 0105 0709 W 1329 1946	4.2 0.8 4.2 0.6	**18** 0017 0646 TH 1249 1915	4.4 0.6 4.4 0.4
4	0505 1110 W 1735 2329	0.4 4.3 0.7 4.1	**19** 0445 1101 TH 1710 2316	0.7 4.0 0.9 3.9	**4** 0625 1221 SA 1846	0.2 4.5 0.6	**19** 0536 1141 SU 1756	0.5 4.4 0.7	**4** 0019 0645 M 1251 1910	4.2 0.5 4.3 0.6	**19** 0558 1206 TU 1825	0.6 4.3 0.6	**4** 0149 0750 TH 1410 2014	4.4 0.8 4.3 0.5	**19** 0111 0735 F 1336 ○ 2008	4.7 0.5 4.6 0.1
5	0605 1206 TH 1831	0.2 4.5 0.6	**20** 0536 1146 F 1756 2358	0.5 4.3 0.7 4.2	**5** 0037 0711 SU 1305 1928	4.4 0.3 4.5 0.5	**20** 0002 0626 M 1230 1848	4.3 0.4 4.5 0.5	**5** 0116 0728 TU 1339 1952	4.3 0.6 4.3 0.5	**20** 0029 0656 W 1300 1926	4.5 0.5 4.5 0.4	**5** 0225 0825 F 1439 ● 2056	4.5 0.7 4.4 0.4	**20** 0158 0822 SA 1420 2056	4.9 0.4 4.8 0.0
6	0016 0656 F 1246 1905	4.3 0.1 4.6 0.5	**21** 0626 1226 SA 1836	0.4 4.5 0.6	**6** 0121 0748 M 1349 ● 2008	4.5 0.3 4.5 0.4	**21** 0047 0716 TU 1315 1935	4.5 0.3 4.7 0.4	**6** 0158 0806 W 1419 ● 2036	4.4 0.6 4.3 0.5	**21** 0121 0748 TH 1348 ○ 2018	4.7 0.4 4.6 0.2	**6** 0257 0901 SA 1512 2130	4.5 0.7 4.5 0.4	**21** 0242 0905 SU 1505 2140	5.1 0.4 4.9 -0.1
7	0058 0736 SA 1325 1946	4.5 0.1 4.7 0.4	**22** 0038 0702 SU 1259 1918	4.4 0.3 4.7 0.4	**7** 0205 0825 TU 1429 2046	4.5 0.4 4.5 0.4	**22** 0136 0806 W 1359 ○ 2028	4.7 0.3 4.7 0.2	**7** 0236 0839 TH 1455 2116	4.4 0.7 4.3 0.4	**22** 0209 0835 F 1436 2105	4.9 0.4 4.7 0.1	**7** 0328 0936 SU 1546 2205	4.6 0.7 4.5 0.3	**22** 0326 0950 M 1546 2223	5.1 0.5 4.9 -0.1
8	0138 0812 SU 1406 ● 2025	4.6 0.1 4.7 0.3	**23** 0116 0742 M 1336 ○ 1958	4.6 0.2 4.8 0.3	**8** 0240 0906 W 1506 2125	4.5 0.5 4.4 0.4	**23** 0219 0851 TH 1446 2116	4.8 0.3 4.7 0.1	**8** 0311 0921 F 1529 2150	4.5 0.7 4.4 0.4	**23** 0256 0926 SA 1526 2155	5.0 0.4 4.7 0.0	**8** 0359 1006 M 1615 2240	4.6 0.7 4.5 0.3	**23** 0409 1036 TU 1629 2307	5.0 0.5 4.9 0.0
9	0217 0850 M 1446 2105	4.7 0.1 4.7 0.3	**24** 0156 0826 TU 1416 2046	4.8 0.2 4.8 0.3	**9** 0326 0941 TH 1546 2206	4.5 0.6 4.3 0.5	**24** 0306 0936 F 1535 2208	4.9 0.4 4.7 0.1	**9** 0348 0955 SA 1606 2230	4.5 0.7 4.4 0.4	**24** 0345 1010 SU 1609 2246	5.0 0.5 4.7 -0.1	**9** 0429 1040 TU 1642 2316	4.6 0.7 4.5 0.3	**24** 0456 1111 W 1712 2346	4.7 0.6 4.8 0.2
10	0256 0926 TU 1521 2145	4.7 0.2 4.6 0.3	**25** 0236 0906 W 1459 2126	4.9 0.2 4.8 0.2	**10** 0359 1016 F 1618 2245	4.5 0.7 4.3 0.4	**25** 0356 1021 SA 1626 2256	4.9 0.4 4.6 0.0	**10** 0421 1030 SU 1638 2308	4.5 0.7 4.4 0.4	**25** 0435 1055 M 1657 2332	4.9 0.5 4.7 -0.1	**10** 0459 1110 W 1712 2339	4.5 0.7 4.4 0.4	**25** 0541 1156 TH 1757	4.7 0.7 4.6
11	0335 1006 W 1559 2214	4.7 0.4 4.4 0.4	**26** 0316 0948 TH 1543 2212	4.9 0.2 4.7 0.1	**11** 0436 1050 SA 1655 2326	4.4 0.8 4.1 0.5	**26** 0447 1111 SU 1718 2349	4.8 0.5 4.5 0.4	**11** 0456 1105 M 1708 2345	4.4 0.7 4.3 0.4	**26** 0520 1139 TU 1745	4.8 0.6 4.6	**11** 0532 1146 TH 1745	4.5 0.7 4.4	**26** 0028 0629 F 1241 ☽ 1848	0.3 4.4 0.8 4.4
12	0412 1037 TH 1635 2256	4.5 0.5 4.3 0.5	**27** 0403 1036 F 1631 2259	4.8 0.3 4.5 0.1	**12** 0520 1125 SU 1736	4.2 0.8 4.0	**27** 0542 1205 M 1811	4.7 0.5 4.4	**12** 0531 1146 TU 1748	4.3 0.8 4.2	**27** 0020 0616 W 1230 1838	0.0 4.7 0.7 4.5	**12** 0012 0610 F 1218 1826	0.4 4.5 0.8 4.5	**27** 0115 0721 SA 1336 1951	0.7 4.1 0.9 4.0
13	0451 1105 F 1709 2329	4.7 0.7 4.1 0.6	**28** 0452 1125 SA 1722 2355	4.7 0.4 4.3 0.2	**13** 0006 0600 M 1203 1816	0.5 4.1 0.9 3.9	**28** 0048 0648 TU 1305 ☽ 1912	0.1 4.6 0.7 4.3	**13** 0016 0609 W 1220 1825	0.5 4.3 0.7 4.1	**28** 0108 0715 TH 1315 ☽ 1932	0.5 4.4 0.8 4.3	**13** 0056 0655 SA 1305 1918	0.8 4.2 0.8 4.1	**28** 0209 0836 SU 1445 2105	0.9 3.7 1.1 3.7
14	0532 1146 SA 1750	4.2 0.9 3.9	**29** 0548 1220 SU 1828	4.1	**14** 0044 0650 TU 1255 1905	0.6 4.1 1.0 3.8	**29** 0145 0748 W 1406 2016	0.4 4.4 0.8 4.1	**14** 0044 0655 TH 1306 ☾ 1916	0.5 4.2 0.8 4.0	**29** 0206 0816 F 1414 2035	0.4 4.2 0.9 4.1	**14** 0146 0754 SU 1416 2036	0.6 4.0 1.0 4.0	**29** 0335 1011 M 1620 2239	1.1 3.6 1.1 3.7
15	0015 0620 SU 1235 1846	0.7 3.9 1.0 3.7	**30** 0106 0705 M 1326 ☽ 1935	0.2 4.4 0.8 4.2	**15** 0134 0751 W 1404 ☾ 2010	0.6 3.9 1.0 3.7	**30** 0246 0856 TH 1503 2116	0.3 4.3 0.9 4.1	**15** 0135 0756 F 1344 ○ 2016	0.6 4.1 0.9 4.0	**30** 0255 0914 SA 1529 2146	0.6 4.0 1.0 3.9	**15** 0300 0920 M 1530 2201	0.7 3.9 1.0 3.9	**30** 0500 1125 TU 1740 2356	1.2 3.7 1.0 3.8
			31 0206 0816 TU 1434 2045	0.3 4.3 0.9 4.1					**31** 0420 1038 SU 1656 2306	0.8 3.9 1.0 3.9					**31** 0605 1225 W 1840	1.1 4.0 0.8

Chart Datum: 2·32 metres below NAP Datum

)) **FREE** monthly updates from ((
www.reedsalmanac.co.uk

TIME ZONE -0100
(Dutch Standard Time)
Subtract 1 hour for UT
For Dutch Summer Time add
ONE hour in **non-shaded areas**

NETHERLANDS – VLISSINGEN
LAT 51°27'N   LONG 3°36'E
TIMES AND HEIGHTS OF HIGH AND LOW WATERS

YEAR 2005

SEPTEMBER
Time	m	Time	m
1 0049 TH 0656 1921	4.2 0.9 4.2 0.6	**16** 0009 F 0631 1236 1906	4.5 0.7 4.4 0.3
2 0129 F 0735 1348 1959	4.4 0.8 4.4 0.5	**17** 0055 SA 0726 1317 1956	4.8 0.6 4.8 0.1
3 0201 SA 0801 1415 ● 2032	4.5 0.7 4.5 0.4	**18** 0141 SU 0806 1358 ○ 2035	5.0 0.5 4.8 0.0
4 0236 SU 0835 1445 2102	4.6 0.7 4.6 0.3	**19** 0220 M 0845 1439 2116	5.1 0.4 4.9 0.0
5 0257 M 0908 1515 2135	4.7 0.6 4.7 0.3	**20** 0302 TU 0925 1518 2155	5.1 0.5 5.0 0.0
6 0327 TU 0935 1541 2211	4.8 0.5 4.7 0.3	**21** 0343 W 1006 1600 2235	5.0 0.5 5.0 0.2
7 0357 W 1010 1612 2240	4.7 0.6 4.7 0.3	**22** 0426 TH 1041 1640 2316	4.8 0.6 4.9 0.3
8 0426 TH 1040 1639 2310	4.7 0.6 4.7 0.4	**23** 0505 F 1126 1722 2345	4.6 0.7 4.7 0.6
9 0458 F 1110 1713 2346	4.7 0.6 4.6 0.4	**24** 0549 SA 1159 1806	4.3 0.8 4.4
10 0536 SA 1145 1756	4.6 0.7 4.5	**25** 0030 SU 0636 1245 1854	0.8 4.0 1.0 4.0
11 0026 SU 0619 1232 ◐ 1842	0.6 4.3 0.7 4.3	**26** 0125 M 0724 1426 2020	1.1 3.6 1.2 3.6
12 0116 M 0719 1346 1956	0.8 4.0 0.9 4.0	**27** 0306 TU 0925 1539 2216	1.3 3.4 1.2 3.6
13 0229 TU 0850 1504 2135	1.0 3.8 1.0 3.9	**28** 0419 W 1055 1700 2325	1.3 3.5 1.1 3.9
14 0406 W 1021 1645 2305	1.0 3.8 0.9 4.1	**29** 0536 TH 1156 1805	1.1 3.9 0.8
15 0535 TH 1140 1805	0.9 4.2 0.6	**30** 0019 F 0631 1239 1856	4.2 0.9 4.2 0.6

OCTOBER
Time	m	Time	m
1 0100 SA 0706 1316 1929	4.4 0.8 4.4 0.5	**16** 0037 SU 0706 1257 1935	4.8 0.6 4.6 0.1
2 0129 SU 0736 1341 2002	4.6 0.7 4.5 0.4	**17** 0119 M 0746 1335 ○ 2012	4.9 0.5 4.8 0.1
3 0157 M 0806 1409 2032	4.7 0.6 4.7 0.3	**18** 0159 TU 0826 1415 2052	5.0 0.5 5.0 0.1
4 0226 TU 0838 1437 2102	4.8 0.6 4.8 0.3	**19** 0239 W 0903 1456 2132	5.0 0.4 5.0 0.2
5 0256 W 0910 1508 2136	4.9 0.5 4.8 0.3	**20** 0319 TH 0946 1536 2208	4.9 0.5 5.0 0.3
6 0326 TH 0942 1540 2211	4.9 0.5 4.9 0.3	**21** 0359 F 1020 1616 2242	4.7 0.5 4.8 0.5
7 0359 F 1019 1613 2245	4.8 0.5 4.9 0.4	**22** 0439 SA 1101 1656 2316	4.5 0.6 4.6 0.7
8 0433 SA 1050 1650 2321	4.7 0.5 4.8 0.5	**23** 0518 SU 1135 1736 2356	4.2 0.8 4.3 1.0
9 0513 SU 1130 1731	4.6 0.6 4.7	**24** 0600 M 1219 1830	4.0 0.9 4.0
10 0006 M 0557 1226 ◐ 1823	0.7 4.3 0.7 4.3	**25** 0056 TU 0650 1345 1940	1.2 3.7 1.1 3.7
11 0106 TU 0705 1336 1950	0.9 3.9 0.9 4.0	**26** 0226 W 0755 1454 2115	1.4 3.4 1.1 3.5
12 0226 W 0841 1505 2125	1.1 3.7 0.9 3.9	**27** 0340 TH 1011 1615 2245	1.4 3.4 1.1 3.7
13 0354 TH 1005 1640 2255	1.1 3.7 0.8 4.2	**28** 0445 F 1116 1727 2341	1.2 3.7 0.9 4.1
14 0514 F 1119 1755 2355	1.0 4.0 0.5 4.5	**29** 0534 SA 1156 1815	1.0 4.0 0.7
15 0620 SA 1215 1851	0.8 4.4 0.3	**30** 0015 SU 0636 1232 1852	4.3 0.9 4.3 0.6
		31 0056 M 0659 1301 1925	4.5 0.7 4.5 0.5

NOVEMBER
Time	m	Time	m
1 0122 TU 0736 1333 1955	4.7 0.7 4.7 0.4	**16** 0139 W 0803 ○ 2028 1355	4.8 0.5 4.8 0.3
2 0151 W 0806 1405 ● 2030	4.8 0.6 4.8 0.3	**17** 0221 TH 0846 1435 2106	4.8 0.5 4.9 0.4
3 0225 TH 0842 1438 2109	4.9 0.5 4.9 0.3	**18** 0300 F 0925 1515 2142	4.7 0.4 4.8 0.5
4 0258 F 0921 1515 2146	4.9 0.5 5.0 0.4	**19** 0341 SA 1002 1558 2218	4.6 0.5 4.7 0.7
5 0336 SA 0958 1553 2222	4.8 0.4 4.9 0.4	**20** 0418 SU 1046 1636 2252	4.4 0.6 4.5 0.8
6 0415 SU 1041 1635 2306	4.7 0.4 4.8 0.6	**21** 0455 M 1126 1720 2330	4.2 0.7 4.3 1.0
7 0459 M 1125 1722 2356	4.5 0.5 4.6 0.7	**22** 0538 TU 1206 1806	4.0 0.8 4.1
8 0551 IU 1226 1822	1.2 4.3 0.6 4.3	**23** 0016 W 0626 1305 ◐ 1859	1.2 3.8 0.9 3.9
9 0056 W 0706 1335 ◐ 1951	1.0 3.9 0.9 4.1	**24** 0114 TH 0726 1415 2010	1.3 3.6 1.0 3.7
10 0205 TH 0825 1506 2116	1.1 3.8 0.7 4.1	**25** 0256 F 0824 1526 2125	1.3 3.5 1.0 3.7
11 0340 F 0946 1615 2230	1.1 3.8 0.7 4.2	**26** 0356 SA 1000 1620 2235	1.3 3.6 0.9 3.9
12 0500 SA 1055 1736 2329	1.0 3.8 0.5 4.3	**27** 0446 SU 1055 1715 2326	1.1 3.8 0.6 4.2
13 0600 SU 1146 1826	0.9 4.3 0.3	**28** 0540 M 1146 1806	1.0 4.1 0.7
14 0018 M 0645 1231 1911	4.7 0.7 4.5 0.2	**29** 0008 TU 0626 1219 1846	4.4 0.8 4.4 0.6
15 0059 TU 0721 1313 1947	4.8 0.6 4.7 0.2	**30** 0046 W 0701 1257 1926	4.6 0.7 4.6 0.5

DECEMBER
Time	m	Time	m
1 0119 TH 0736 1337 ● 2002	4.7 0.6 4.8 0.4	**16** 0211 F 0826 1426 2046	4.5 0.5 4.6 0.5
2 0159 F 0818 1416 2042	4.8 0.5 4.9 0.4	**17** 0251 SA 0908 1506 2119	4.5 0.4 4.7 0.6
3 0239 SA 0906 1455 2126	4.8 0.4 4.9 0.4	**18** 0329 SU 0950 1545 2156	4.5 0.4 4.6 0.7
4 0321 SU 0945 1539 2208	4.8 0.3 4.9 0.5	**19** 0408 M 1025 1625 2232	4.4 0.5 4.6 0.8
5 0405 M 1036 1625 2256	4.7 0.3 4.8 0.6	**20** 0446 TU 1111 1706 2304	4.3 0.5 4.4 0.9
6 0456 TU 1128 1717 2347	4.5 0.3 4.7 0.7	**21** 0519 W 1146 1746 2345	4.2 0.6 4.2 1.0
7 0548 W 1226 1825	4.3 0.4 4.5	**22** 0600 TH 1236 1831	4.1 0.7 4.1
8 0042 TH 0658 ◐ 1931 1330	0.9 4.1 0.6 4.3	**23** 0030 F 0646 ◐ 1915 1305	1.1 3.9 0.8 4.0
9 0144 F 0801 1436 2045	1.0 4.0 0.5 4.2	**24** 0125 SA 0740 ● 2015 1355	1.2 3.8 0.9 3.9
10 0305 SA 0916 1545 2156	1.1 4.0 0.6 4.2	**25** 0230 SU 0840 1515 2126	1.2 3.8 0.9 3.9
11 0420 SU 1015 1700 2300	1.1 4.1 0.5 4.3	**26** 0335 M 0951 1610 2221	1.2 3.8 0.8 4.0
12 0531 M 1118 1801 2356	1.0 4.4 0.4 4.4	**27** 0446 TU 1051 1716 2320	1.1 4.0 0.8 4.0
13 0621 TU 1209 1846	0.8 4.4 0.4	**28** 0529 W 1146 1806	1.0 4.2 0.7
14 0041 W 0706 1255 1928	4.5 0.7 4.5 0.4	**29** 0009 TH 0625 1229 1855	4.4 0.9 4.4 0.5
15 0127 TH 0748 ○ 2005 1340	4.6 0.6 4.6 0.5	**30** 0057 F 0715 1315 1940	4.6 0.6 4.5 0.5
		31 0141 SA 0806 ● 2026 1401	4.7 0.6 4.8 0.4

Chart Datum: 2·32 metres below NAP Datum

FREE monthly updates from
www.reedsalmanac.co.uk

TIDES

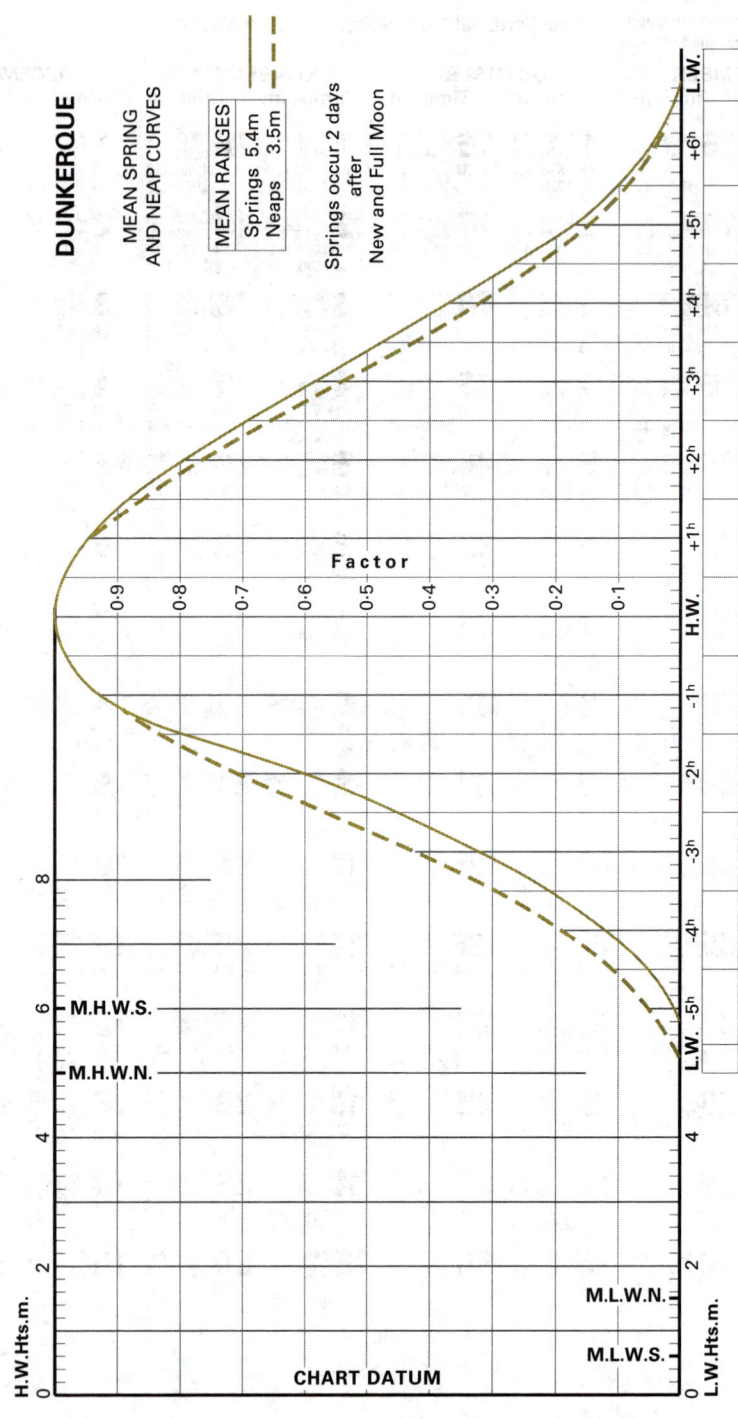

TIME ZONE -0100
(French Standard Time)
Subtract 1 hour for UT
For French Summer Time add
ONE hour in **non-shaded areas**

FRANCE – DUNKERQUE
LAT 51°03'N LONG 2°22'E
TIMES AND HEIGHTS OF HIGH AND LOW WATERS

YEAR 2005

JANUARY		FEBRUARY		MARCH		APRIL	
Time m	Time m	Time m	Time m	Time m	Time m	Time m	Time m
1 0355 5.4 / 1047 1.1 / SA 1620 5.4 / 2301 1.4	**16** 0447 5.6 / 1154 0.7 / SU 1726 5.5	**1** 0432 5.5 / 1136 0.9 / TU 1700 5.4 / 2349 1.3	**16** 0012 1.3 / 0542 5.3 / W 1244 1.3 / ☽ 1820 4.9	**1** 0325 5.8 / 1032 0.6 / TU 1546 5.7 / 2242 0.9	**16** 0418 5.6 / 1117 1.0 / W 1643 5.3 / 2329 1.2	**1** 0431 5.5 / 1130 1.1 / F 1702 5.1 / 2352 1.3	**16** 0524 4.8 / 1211 1.8 / SA 1755 4.5 / ☽
2 0433 5.2 / 1126 1.2 / SU 1703 5.2 / 2342 1.5	**17** 0012 1.3 / 0536 5.4 / M 1244 1.0 / ☽ 1821 5.2	**2** 0518 5.4 / 1221 1.1 / W 1754 5.2 / ☽	**17** 0104 1.6 / 0643 4.9 / TH 1342 1.7 / 1932 4.6	**2** 0400 5.4 / 1107 0.8 / W 1623 5.5 / 2319 1.1	**17** 0501 5.3 / 1156 1.4 / TH 1728 4.9 / ☽	**2** 0542 5.2 / 1234 1.5 / SA 1826 4.7 / ☽	**17** 0041 1.8 / 0636 4.5 / SU 1321 2.0 / 1917 4.3
3 0516 5.1 / 1211 1.3 / M 1753 5.1 / ☽	**18** 0104 1.5 / 0633 5.2 / TU 1339 1.2 / 1924 5.0	**3** 0040 1.5 / 0621 5.2 / TH 1318 1.3 / 1903 5.0	**18** 0212 1.9 / 0807 4.6 / F 1456 1.9 / 2058 4.4	**3** 0445 5.5 / 1148 1.0 / TH 1715 5.2 / ☽	**18** 0016 1.6 / 0555 4.8 / F 1249 1.8 / 1834 4.4	**3** 0111 1.6 / 0710 4.9 / SU 1409 1.7 / 2004 4.6	**18** 0159 1.9 / 0808 4.3 / M 1458 2.1 / 2054 4.3
4 0032 1.6 / 0611 5.0 / TU 1303 1.4 / 1851 5.0	**19** 0203 1.7 / 0742 5.0 / W 1440 1.5 / 2031 4.8	**4** 0149 1.7 / 0734 5.0 / F 1438 1.5 / 2022 4.9	**19** 0336 1.9 / 0933 4.6 / SA 1631 1.9 / 2219 4.6	**4** 0007 1.3 / 0547 5.2 / F 1245 1.3 / 1831 4.9	**19** 0120 1.9 / 0718 4.4 / SA 1407 2.1 / 2011 4.2	**4** 0253 1.6 / 0855 4.9 / M 1544 1.5 / 2139 4.8	**19** 0336 1.8 / 0935 4.6 / TU 1620 1.8 / 2202 4.7
5 0130 1.7 / 0713 5.0 / W 1409 1.4 / 1954 5.0	**20** 0308 1.8 / 0854 4.9 / TH 1549 1.6 / 2138 4.8	**5** 0317 1.7 / 0857 5.0 / SA 1603 1.4 / 2153 5.0	**20** 0509 1.7 / 1046 4.8 / SU 1743 1.6 / 2319 4.9	**5** 0118 1.6 / 0711 4.9 / SA 1412 1.6 / 2005 4.6	**20** 0249 2.0 / 0900 4.3 / SU 1550 2.0 / 2145 4.4	**5** 0426 1.3 / 1014 5.3 / TU 1702 1.2 / 2242 5.2	**20** 0446 1.4 / 1031 5.0 / W 1714 1.4 / 2250 5.0
6 0243 1.7 / 0818 5.1 / TH 1523 1.4 / 2101 5.1	**21** 0421 1.7 / 1001 4.9 / F 1703 1.6 / 2243 4.9	**6** 0442 1.5 / 1023 5.2 / SU 1721 1.2 / 2305 5.3	**21** 0607 1.4 / 1140 5.1 / M 1830 1.3	**6** 0256 1.7 / 0853 4.9 / SU 1550 1.5 / 2148 4.8	**21** 0432 1.8 / 1020 4.6 / M 1710 1.7 / 2248 4.7	**6** 0535 0.8 / 1110 5.6 / W 1759 0.9 / 2332 5.6	**21** 0533 1.1 / 1114 5.3 / TH 1755 1.1 / 2330 5.3
7 0358 1.6 / 0925 5.2 / F 1632 1.2 / 2209 5.3	**22** 0532 1.5 / 1102 5.1 / SA 1802 1.4 / 2337 5.1	**7** 0558 1.1 / 1129 5.6 / M 1827 0.9	**22** 0002 5.2 / 0648 1.1 / TU 1220 5.4 / 1906 1.1	**7** 0435 1.5 / 1023 5.2 / M 1715 1.2 / 2258 5.1	**22** 0536 1.4 / 1113 5.0 / TU 1759 1.4 / 2332 5.1	**7** 0626 0.5 / 1156 5.9 / TH 1844 0.7	**22** 0612 0.8 / 1149 5.5 / F 1829 0.9
8 0504 1.4 / 1030 5.4 / SA 1734 1.0 / 2311 5.5	**23** 0624 1.3 / 1153 5.2 / SU 1847 1.3	**8** 0001 5.6 / 0656 0.7 / TU 1223 5.9 / ● 1920 0.7	**23** 0036 5.4 / 0722 0.9 / W 1254 5.6 / 1936 1.0	**8** 0551 0.9 / 1124 5.6 / TU 1817 0.9 / 2351 5.5	**23** 0618 1.1 / 1153 5.3 / W 1836 1.1	**8** 0009 5.8 / 0710 0.1 / F 1236 6.0 / ● 1923 0.6	**23** 0002 5.6 / 0647 0.7 / SA 1220 5.7 / 1903 0.8
9 0605 1.1 / 1130 5.7 / SU 1832 0.9	**24** 0017 5.3 / 0705 1.1 / M 1235 5.4 / 1923 1.2	**9** 0045 5.8 / 0746 0.5 / W 1311 6.1 / 2006 0.6	**24** 0106 5.5 / 0753 0.7 / TH 1324 5.7 / ○ 2006 0.9	**9** 0645 0.5 / 1214 5.9 / W 1906 0.7	**24** 0007 5.4 / 0651 0.8 / TH 1227 5.6 / 1907 0.9	**9** 0045 5.9 / 0749 0.3 / SA 1312 6.0 / 2001 0.6	**24** 0028 5.7 / 0723 0.6 / SU 1248 5.7 / ○ 1937 0.7
10 0004 5.7 / 0701 0.9 / M 1224 6.0 / ● 1926 0.8	**25** 0054 5.5 / 0741 1.0 / TU 1311 5.6 / ○ 1956 1.1	**10** 0130 6.0 / 0833 0.3 / TH 1357 6.2 / 2050 0.6	**25** 0134 5.7 / 0825 0.6 / F 1352 5.8 / 2037 0.8	**10** 0030 5.8 / 0732 0.3 / TH 1256 6.1 / ● 1948 0.6	**25** 0038 5.6 / 0723 0.6 / F 1256 5.7 / ○ 1937 0.8	**10** 0121 6.0 / 0827 0.3 / SU 1347 6.0 / 2038 0.6	**25** 0058 5.9 / 0759 0.5 / M 1318 5.9 / 2013 0.6
11 0052 5.9 / 0753 0.6 / TU 1316 6.1 / 2016 0.7	**26** 0125 5.6 / 0815 0.8 / W 1343 5.7 / 2028 1.0	**11** 0212 6.1 / 1442 6.2 / F 1442 6.2 / 2132 0.6	**26** 0202 5.8 / 0858 0.6 / SA 1420 5.8 / 2109 0.7	**11** 0110 6.0 / 0814 0.2 / F 1338 6.2 / 2028 0.5	**26** 0105 5.8 / 0756 0.5 / SA 1323 5.8 / 2008 0.7	**11** 0158 6.0 / 0902 0.4 / M 1423 5.9 / 2113 0.6	**26** 0131 6.0 / 0836 0.4 / TU 1352 5.9 / 2051 0.6
12 0141 6.0 / 0843 0.5 / W 1407 6.2 / 2104 0.7	**27** 0155 5.7 / 0848 0.8 / TH 1413 5.7 / 2101 0.9	**12** 0253 6.1 / 0959 0.2 / SA 1525 6.1 / 2212 0.6	**27** 0229 5.8 / 0930 0.5 / SU 1448 5.8 / 2140 0.8	**12** 0148 6.1 / 0855 0.2 / SA 1417 6.1 / 2106 0.5	**27** 0131 5.9 / 0829 0.5 / SU 1349 5.9 / 2041 0.6	**12** 0234 6.0 / 0937 0.6 / TU 1459 5.8 / 2148 0.7	**27** 0208 6.0 / 0914 0.4 / W 1429 5.8 / 2129 0.6
13 0229 6.0 / 0932 0.4 / TH 1458 6.1 / 2151 0.7	**28** 0226 5.7 / 0921 0.7 / F 1444 5.7 / 2133 1.0	**13** 0334 6.0 / 1040 0.4 / SU 1605 5.8 / 2250 0.9	**28** 0256 5.8 / 1001 0.5 / M 1516 5.8 / 2210 0.8	**13** 0226 6.1 / 0932 0.3 / SU 1454 6.0 / 2142 0.6	**28** 0158 5.9 / 0903 0.5 / M 1418 5.9 / 2114 0.6	**13** 0311 5.8 / 1010 0.8 / W 1533 5.5 / 2223 0.9	**28** 0249 5.9 / 0953 0.7 / TH 1513 5.7 / 2210 0.8
14 0315 5.9 / 1020 0.4 / F 1548 6.0 / 2237 0.9	**29** 0257 5.7 / 0954 0.7 / SA 1517 5.7 / 2205 1.0	**14** 0413 5.8 / 1119 0.6 / M 1644 5.6 / 2329 1.1		**14** 0303 6.0 / 1008 0.4 / M 1530 5.8 / 2217 0.7	**29** 0228 6.0 / 0935 0.5 / TU 1448 5.9 / 2146 0.7	**14** 0349 5.6 / 1044 1.1 / TH 1610 5.2 / 2300 1.2	**29** 0338 5.7 / 1036 0.9 / F 1606 5.4 / 2257 1.0
15 0401 5.8 / 1107 0.5 / SA 1636 5.8 / 2323 1.1	**30** 0327 5.7 / 1026 0.8 / SU 1549 5.6 / 2236 1.1	**15** 0455 5.6 / 1158 0.8 / TU 1727 5.3		**15** 0340 5.9 / 1042 0.6 / TU 1606 5.6 / 2252 0.9	**30** 0302 6.0 / 1008 0.6 / W 1522 5.7 / 2221 0.7	**15** 0431 5.2 / 1121 1.5 / F 1654 4.9 / 2342 1.5	**30** 0439 5.4 / 1129 1.2 / SA 1714 5.1 / 2356 1.2
	31 0401 5.8 / 1107 0.5 / M 1621 5.5 / 2310 1.1				**31** 0341 5.8 / 1045 0.8 / TH 1604 5.5 / 2301 0.7		

Chart Datum: 2·69 metres below IGN Datum
》》 **FREE** monthly updates from 《《
www.reedsalmanac.co.uk

TIDES

TIME ZONE -0100
(French Standard Time)
Subtract 1 hour for UT
For French Summer Time add
ONE hour in **non-shaded areas**

FRANCE – DUNKERQUE
LAT 51°03′N   LONG 2°22′E
TIMES AND HEIGHTS OF HIGH AND LOW WATERS

YEAR 2005

MAY

Day	Time	m	Day	Time	m
1 SU	0549 / 1241 / 1826	5.2 / 1.5 / 4.8	16 M	0011 / 0603 / 1241 / 1831	1.6 / 4.7 / 1.9 / 4.5
2 M	0119 / 0710 / 1409 / 1956	1.4 / 5.0 / 1.6 / 4.7	17 TU	0114 / 0711 / 1355 / 1944	1.7 / 4.6 / 1.9 / 4.5
3 TU	0248 / 0843 / 1529 / 2118	1.3 / 5.1 / 1.4 / 5.0	18 W	0230 / 0825 / 1517 / 2058	1.6 / 4.7 / 1.8 / 4.7
4 W	0407 / 0953 / 1638 / 2216	1.0 / 5.3 / 1.2 / 5.3	19 TH	0344 / 0931 / 1618 / 2156	1.4 / 4.9 / 1.5 / 5.0
5 TH	0510 / 1046 / 1732 / 2304	0.8 / 5.6 / 1.0 / 5.5	20 F	0440 / 1022 / 1706 / 2241	1.2 / 5.2 / 1.3 / 5.2
6 F	0601 / 1131 / 1817 / 2345	0.6 / 5.7 / 0.9 / 5.7	21 SA	0527 / 1103 / 1749 / 2320	0.9 / 5.4 / 1.1 / 5.4
7 SA	0644 / 1210 / 1857	0.5 / 5.8 / 0.8	22 SU	0610 / 1138 / 1828 / 2356	0.8 / 5.6 / 0.9 / 5.6
8 SU	0019 / 0722 / 1246 / 1935	5.8 / 0.6 / 5.8 / 0.7	23 M	0651 / 1214 / 1909	0.7 / 5.7 / 0.8
9 M	0056 / 0759 / 1322 / 2012	5.8 / 0.6 / 5.6 / 0.7	24 TU	0030 / 0732 / 1252 / 1950	5.8 / 0.6 / 5.8 / 0.7
10 TU	0134 / 0835 / 1358 / 2049	5.9 / 0.7 / 5.7 / 0.9	25 W	0111 / 0815 / 1335 / 2034	6.0 / 0.6 / 5.9 / 0.6
11 W	0212 / 0910 / 1435 / 2125	5.8 / 0.8 / 5.6 / 0.8	26 TH	0157 / 0900 / 1423 / 2120	6.0 / 0.7 / 5.8 / 0.6
12 TH	0250 / 0945 / 1511 / 2202	5.7 / 1.0 / 5.5 / 0.9	27 F	0248 / 0948 / 1517 / 2209	5.9 / 0.8 / 5.7 / 0.7
13 F	0329 / 1020 / 1549 / 2239	5.5 / 1.2 / 5.2 / 1.1	28 SA	0344 / 1039 / 1614 / 2302	5.8 / 0.9 / 5.5 / 0.8
14 SA	0413 / 1059 / 1634 / 2320	5.2 / 1.5 / 5.0 / 1.4	29 SU	0443 / 1136 / 1712	5.6 / 1.1 / 5.3
15 SU	0504 / 1144 / 1728	4.9 / 1.7 / 4.7	30 M	0003 / 0544 / 1242 / 1816	0.9 / 5.4 / 1.3 / 5.1
			31 TU	0116 / 0657 / 1352 / 1932	1.0 / 5.2 / 1.4 / 5.0

JUNE

Day	Time	m	Day	Time	m
1 W	0228 / 0816 / 1500 / 2044	1.0 / 5.2 / 1.3 / 5.1	16 TH	0130 / 0720 / 1402 / 1946	1.4 / 4.9 / 1.7 / 4.8
2 TH	0336 / 0921 / 1604 / 2142	0.9 / 5.3 / 1.2 / 5.3	17 F	0237 / 0820 / 1513 / 2048	1.4 / 4.9 / 1.6 / 4.9
3 F	0438 / 1015 / 1700 / 2233	0.9 / 5.4 / 1.1 / 5.4	18 SA	0344 / 0919 / 1614 / 2146	1.3 / 5.1 / 1.4 / 5.1
4 SA	0532 / 1103 / 1749 / 2318	0.8 / 5.5 / 1.1 / 5.5	19 SU	0442 / 1013 / 1708 / 2238	1.1 / 5.3 / 1.3 / 5.3
5 SU	0618 / 1146 / 1833 / 2359	0.9 / 5.5 / 1.0 / 5.6	20 M	0534 / 1103 / 1758 / 2327	1.0 / 5.4 / 1.1 / 5.5
6 M	0659 / 1226 / 1914	0.9 / 5.6 / 0.9	21 TU	0624 / 1150 / 1847	0.9 / 5.6 / 0.9
7 TU	0039 / 0737 / 1305 / 1954	5.6 / 0.9 / 5.6 / 0.8	22 W	0012 / 0714 / 1238 / 1936	5.8 / 0.8 / 5.7 / 0.7
8 W	0120 / 0814 / 1344 / 2032	5.7 / 1.0 / 5.6 / 0.8	23 TH	0101 / 0803 / 1328 / 2025	5.9 / 0.7 / 5.8 / 0.6
9 TH	0158 / 0851 / 1421 / 2110	5.6 / 1.0 / 5.5 / 0.8	24 F	0153 / 0854 / 1420 / 2115	6.0 / 0.7 / 5.8 / 0.5
10 F	0237 / 0928 / 1457 / 2147	5.6 / 1.1 / 5.4 / 0.9	25 SA	0246 / 0944 / 1513 / 2206	6.0 / 0.7 / 5.8 / 0.5
11 SA	0316 / 1004 / 1535 / 2223	5.5 / 1.2 / 5.3 / 1.0	26 SU	0339 / 1035 / 1605 / 2258	6.0 / 0.8 / 5.7 / 0.5
12 SU	0357 / 1040 / 1616 / 2301	5.3 / 1.4 / 5.2 / 1.2	27 M	0433 / 1127 / 1656 / 2353	5.8 / 1.0 / 5.5 / 0.6
13 M	0442 / 1120 / 1701 / 2343	5.1 / 1.5 / 5.0 / 1.3	28 TU	0528 / 1222 / 1751	5.6 / 1.1 / 5.3
14 TU	0530 / 1205 / 1751	5.0 / 1.6 / 4.9	29 W	0055 / 0629 / 1320 / 1853	0.8 / 5.4 / 1.3 / 5.3
15 W	0033 / 0623 / 1258 / 1847	1.3 / 4.9 / 1.7 / 4.8	30 TH	0155 / 0736 / 1420 / 2000	1.1 / 5.3 / 1.4 / 5.2

JULY

Day	Time	m	Day	Time	m
1 F	0257 / 0841 / 1522 / 2103	1.0 / 5.2 / 1.4 / 5.1	16 SA	0136 / 0721 / 1405 / 1948	1.3 / 5.0 / 1.6 / 5.0
2 SA	0400 / 0941 / 1626 / 2202	1.1 / 5.1 / 1.4 / 5.2	17 SU	0247 / 0825 / 1522 / 2056	1.4 / 5.0 / 1.6 / 5.0
3 SU	0503 / 1037 / 1726 / 2258	1.2 / 5.2 / 1.3 / 5.2	18 M	0359 / 0934 / 1632 / 2208	1.3 / 5.1 / 1.5 / 5.2
4 M	0558 / 1130 / 1818 / 2350	1.2 / 5.2 / 1.2 / 5.4	19 TU	0506 / 1041 / 1736 / 2313	1.2 / 5.3 / 1.3 / 5.4
5 TU	0644 / 1217 / 1902	1.2 / 5.3 / 1.0	20 W	0609 / 1140 / 1835	1.0 / 5.5 / 0.9
6 W	0032 / 0724 / 1258 / 1943	5.5 / 1.1 / 5.4 / 0.9	21 TH	0007 / 0705 / 1233 / 1928	5.8 / 0.9 / 5.7 / 0.7
7 TH	0113 / 0801 / 1336 / 2021	5.5 / 1.1 / 5.5 / 0.8	22 F	0056 / 0756 / 1322 / 2018	6.0 / 0.8 / 5.8 / 0.5
8 F	0150 / 0837 / 1410 / 2057	5.6 / 1.1 / 5.5 / 0.8	23 SA	0145 / 0845 / 1410 / 2107	6.1 / 0.6 / 5.9 / 0.3
9 SA	0225 / 0912 / 1442 / 2131	5.6 / 1.1 / 5.5 / 0.8	24 SU	0235 / 0932 / 1457 / 2154	6.2 / 0.6 / 5.9 / 0.3
10 SU	0259 / 0946 / 1515 / 2205	5.5 / 1.1 / 5.4 / 0.9	25 M	0324 / 1018 / 1543 / 2241	6.1 / 0.7 / 5.9 / 0.3
11 M	0336 / 1019 / 1551 / 2239	5.5 / 1.2 / 5.4 / 0.9	26 TU	0412 / 1104 / 1628 / 2328	5.9 / 0.8 / 5.8 / 0.5
12 TU	0413 / 1053 / 1628 / 2314	5.4 / 1.2 / 5.3 / 1.0	27 W	0500 / 1149 / 1714	5.7 / 1.0 / 5.6
13 W	0451 / 1129 / 1707 / 2352	5.3 / 1.3 / 5.2 / 1.1	28 TH	0020 / 0551 / 1238 / 1807	0.7 / 5.4 / 1.2 / 5.4
14 TH	0533 / 1211 / 1753	5.1 / 1.4 / 5.1	29 F	0113 / 0649 / 1334 / 1910	1.0 / 5.2 / 1.5 / 5.1
15 F	0040 / 0623 / 1300 / 1847	1.2 / 5.0 / 1.5 / 5.0	30 SA	0212 / 0756 / 1438 / 2023	1.3 / 5.1 / 1.6 / 4.9
			31 SU	0320 / 0907 / 1552 / 2138	1.5 / 4.8 / 1.6 / 4.9

AUGUST

Day	Time	m	Day	Time	m
1 M	0438 / 1018 / 1709 / 2247	1.6 / 4.9 / 1.5 / 5.0	16 TU	0328 / 0913 / 1608 / 2158	1.6 / 4.9 / 1.6 / 5.1
2 TU	0545 / 1120 / 1807 / 2344	1.5 / 5.0 / 1.3 / 5.2	17 W	0451 / 1035 / 1726 / 2307	1.4 / 5.1 / 1.3 / 5.5
3 W	0634 / 1209 / 1852	1.3 / 5.2 / 1.1	18 TH	0602 / 1135 / 1828	1.1 / 5.5 / 0.9
4 TH	0025 / 0713 / 1247 / 1931	5.4 / 1.2 / 5.4 / 0.9	19 F	0001 / 0657 / 1224 / 1919	5.9 / 0.8 / 5.8 / 0.5
5 F	0103 / 0747 / 1321 / 2005	5.6 / 1.1 / 5.6 / 0.8	20 SA	0045 / 0745 / 1308 / 2006	6.1 / 0.7 / 6.0 / 0.3
6 SA	0135 / 0819 / 1352 / 2037	5.7 / 1.0 / 5.6 / 0.7	21 SU	0131 / 0829 / 1349 / 2050	6.3 / 0.5 / 6.0 / 0.2
7 SU	0205 / 0851 / 1420 / 2109	5.7 / 1.0 / 5.7 / 0.7	22 M	0215 / 0911 / 1430 / 2133	6.3 / 0.4 / 6.1 / 0.2
8 M	0236 / 0923 / 1448 / 2141	5.7 / 1.0 / 5.7 / 0.7	23 TU	0259 / 0952 / 1511 / 2215	6.2 / 0.5 / 6.1 / 0.3
9 TU	0306 / 0953 / 1518 / 2211	5.7 / 1.0 / 5.6 / 0.7	24 W	0342 / 1032 / 1555 / 2256	6.0 / 0.5 / 5.9 / 0.5
10 W	0336 / 1022 / 1546 / 2242	5.6 / 1.1 / 5.6 / 0.8	25 TH	0424 / 1112 / 1634 / 2337	5.7 / 1.0 / 5.7 / 0.8
11 TH	0404 / 1054 / 1614 / 2315	5.5 / 1.1 / 5.5 / 0.9	26 F	0509 / 1154 / 1722	5.5 / 1.3 / 5.4
12 F	0438 / 1129 / 1651 / 2355	5.4 / 1.2 / 5.4 / 1.1	27 SA	0025 / 0601 / 1245 / 1823	1.3 / 5.1 / 1.5 / 5.0
13 SA	0525 / 1213 / 1744	5.2 / 1.3 / 5.1	28 SU	0123 / 0710 / 1352 / 1944	1.7 / 4.7 / 1.7 / 4.7
14 SU	0047 / 0630 / 1312 / 1900	1.4 / 4.9 / 1.7 / 4.9	29 M	0239 / 0835 / 1519 / 2117	1.9 / 4.6 / 1.9 / 4.6
15 M	0159 / 0746 / 1438 / 2025	1.6 / 4.8 / 1.8 / 4.9	30 TU	0416 / 1000 / 1650 / 2236	1.9 / 4.6 / 1.7 / 4.8
			31 W	0529 / 1105 / 1750 / 2331	1.7 / 4.9 / 1.3 / 5.1

Chart Datum: 2·69 metres below IGN Datum
》》 **FREE** monthly updates from 《《
www.reedsalmanac.co.uk

TIME ZONE -0100
(French Standard Time)
Subtract 1 hour for UT
For French Summer Time add
ONE hour in **non-shaded areas**

FRANCE – DUNKERQUE
LAT 51°03'N   LONG 2°22'E
TIMES AND HEIGHTS OF HIGH AND LOW WATERS

YEAR **2005**

SEPTEMBER

Time	m	Time	m
1 0617 1.4		**16** 0552 1.1	
1151 5.2		1123 5.5	
TH 1835 1.0		F 1815 0.7	
		2349 6.0	
2 0010 5.5		**17** 0642 0.8	
0653 1.2		1207 5.9	
F 1226 5.5		SA 1903 0.4	
1910 0.9			
3 0043 5.7		**18** 0028 6.2	
0724 1.1		0725 0.7	
SA 1258 5.7		SU 1245 6.1	
● 1941 0.7		○ 1946 0.3	
4 0112 5.8		**19** 0109 6.3	
0753 1.0		0805 0.6	
SU 1325 5.8		M 1322 6.3	
2010 0.7		2027 0.2	
5 0139 5.8		**20** 0149 6.3	
0823 0.9		0844 0.7	
M 1350 5.8		TU 1359 6.2	
2041 0.6		2106 0.3	
6 0205 5.9		**21** 0229 6.2	
0854 0.9		0922 0.7	
TU 1415 5.8		W 1438 6.1	
2111 0.6		2145 0.5	
7 0231 5.9		**22** 0308 6.0	
0923 0.9		1000 0.9	
W 1440 5.8		TH 1517 6.0	
2141 0.7		2222 0.8	
8 0257 5.8		**23** 0347 5.7	
0951 1.0		1037 1.1	
TH 1505 5.8		F 1558 5.8	
2211 0.8		2259 1.1	
9 0324 5.7		**24** 0428 5.4	
1022 1.1		1116 1.3	
F 1534 5.7		SA 1644 5.4	
2243 1.0		2340 1.5	
10 0359 5.6		**25** 0516 5.0	
1056 1.2		1202 1.6	
SA 1611 5.5		SU 1742 5.0	
2321 1.2		☾	
11 0444 5.3		**26** 0035 1.9	
1140 1.5		0623 4.6	
SU 1703 5.2		M 1307 2.0	
☾		1906 4.6	
12 0013 1.5		**27** 0155 2.2	
0553 5.0		0757 4.4	
M 1241 1.7		TU 1441 2.1	
1831 4.9		2050 4.5	
13 0131 1.8		**28** 0343 2.2	
0725 4.7		0931 4.5	
TU 1415 1.9		W 1619 1.8	
2016 4.8		2210 4.8	
14 0312 1.8		**29** 0459 1.8	
0908 4.7		1034 4.9	
W 1556 1.6		TH 1721 1.4	
2153 5.1		2302 5.2	
15 0445 1.5		**30** 0547 1.5	
1028 5.1		1119 5.2	
TH 1717 1.2		F 1805 1.1	
2258 5.6		2341 5.5	

OCTOBER

Time	m	Time	m
1 0623 1.2		**16** 0619 0.9	
1155 5.5		1142 5.9	
SA 1839 0.9		SU 1841 0.5	
2 0013 5.7		**17** 0009 6.2	
0653 1.1		0701 0.8	
SU 1226 5.7		M 1218 6.1	
1908 0.8		○ 1922 0.4	
3 0041 5.8		**18** 0045 6.2	
0722 1.0		0739 0.8	
M 1253 5.8		TU 1254 6.2	
● 1938 0.7		2001 0.4	
4 0105 5.9		**19** 0122 6.2	
0752 0.9		0817 0.8	
TU 1316 5.9		W 1331 6.2	
2008 0.6		2039 0.6	
5 0130 6.0		**20** 0200 6.1	
0823 0.9		0854 0.8	
W 1340 5.9		TH 1410 6.1	
2040 0.6		2116 0.7	
6 0156 6.0		**21** 0238 5.9	
0854 0.9		0931 0.9	
TH 1407 6.0		F 1450 6.0	
2112 0.7		2152 1.0	
7 0226 5.9		**22** 0316 5.7	
0924 0.9		1008 1.1	
F 1437 5.9		SA 1530 5.7	
2144 0.9		2228 1.3	
8 0258 5.6		**23** 0355 5.4	
0957 1.0		1047 1.3	
SA 1511 5.8		SU 1615 5.3	
2218 1.0		2307 1.6	
9 0337 5.6		**24** 0442 5.0	
1035 1.2		1131 1.6	
SU 1553 5.5		M 1710 4.9	
2300 1.3		2356 2.0	
10 0427 5.3		**25** 0542 4.6	
1123 1.5		1228 1.9	
M 1654 5.2		TU 1823 4.6	
☾ 2356 1.6		☾	
11 0545 4.9		**26** 0107 2.2	
1231 1.7		0702 4.4	
TU 1833 4.9		W 1350 2.1	
		2001 4.5	
12 0124 1.9		**27** 0246 2.2	
0718 4.7		0838 4.5	
W 1410 1.8		TH 1525 1.9	
2014 4.9		2124 4.7	
13 0307 1.9		**28** 0407 2.0	
0859 4.8		0947 4.8	
TH 1545 1.5		F 1632 1.6	
2141 5.2		2217 5.1	
14 0431 1.5		**29** 0501 1.6	
1010 5.1		1035 5.1	
F 1659 1.0		SA 1720 1.2	
2241 5.7		2259 5.4	
15 0532 1.1		**30** 0541 1.3	
1101 5.6		1114 5.4	
SA 1755 0.7		SU 1758 1.0	
2330 6.0		2335 5.6	
		31 0615 1.2	
		1148 5.6	
		M 1831 0.9	

NOVEMBER

Time	m	Time	m
1 0004 5.8		**16** 0022 6.0	
0647 1.0		0715 0.9	
TU 1215 5.8		W 1231 6.0	
1903 0.8		○ 1937 0.7	
2 0029 5.9		**17** 0100 6.0	
0720 1.0		0754 0.9	
W 1241 5.9		TH 1311 6.0	
● 1937 0.8		2015 0.8	
3 0058 6.0		**18** 0138 5.9	
0754 0.9		0832 0.9	
TH 1310 6.0		F 1352 6.0	
2012 0.8		2053 1.0	
4 0130 6.0		**19** 0217 5.8	
0829 0.9		0910 0.9	
F 1344 6.0		SA 1432 5.8	
2049 0.8		2129 1.2	
5 0206 6.0		**20** 0255 5.6	
0902 0.8		0949 1.1	
SA 1421 6.0		SU 1514 5.6	
2126 0.9		2206 1.4	
6 0246 5.8		**21** 0334 5.4	
0945 1.0		1027 1.3	
SU 1505 5.8		M 1557 5.3	
2207 1.1		2244 1.6	
7 0334 5.6		**22** 0418 5.1	
1029 1.2		1108 1.5	
M 1559 5.5		TU 1645 5.1	
2255 1.4		2328 1.9	
8 0434 5.4		**23** 0509 4.9	
1124 1.4		1156 1.7	
TU 1712 5.3		W 1742 4.9	
2357 1.7		☾	
9 0546 5.0		**24** 0023 2.0	
1236 1.6		0609 4.7	
W 1830 5.1		TH 1254 1.8	
☾		1849 4.6	
10 0124 1.8		**25** 0132 2.1	
0704 4.8		0718 4.6	
TH 1403 1.5		F 1411 1.8	
2001 5.1		2008 4.7	
11 0251 1.7		**26** 0253 2.0	
0834 5.0		0833 4.7	
F 1525 1.3		SA 1524 1.6	
2118 5.3		2116 4.9	
12 0404 1.5		**27** 0358 1.7	
0941 5.3		0935 4.9	
SA 1633 1.0		SU 1622 1.4	
2216 5.6		2206 5.2	
13 0504 1.2		**28** 0448 1.5	
1032 5.6		1023 5.2	
SU 1729 0.8		M 1709 1.2	
2305 5.8		2249 5.4	
14 0553 1.1		**29** 0532 1.1	
1114 5.8		1103 5.4	
M 1816 0.7		TU 1751 1.0	
2348 5.9		2327 5.6	
15 0636 1.0		**30** 0612 1.2	
1153 5.9		1138 5.6	
TU 1858 0.7		W 1831 0.7	

DECEMBER

Time	m	Time	m
1 0001 5.7		**16** 0048 5.7	
0651 1.1		0740 1.0	
TH 1213 5.8		F 1303 5.8	
● 1910 0.9		2001 0.8	
2 0034 5.9		**17** 0128 5.7	
0732 0.9		0820 0.9	
F 1251 5.9		SA 1345 5.8	
1951 0.8		2038 1.1	
3 0114 5.9		**18** 0206 5.7	
0814 0.9		0858 0.9	
SA 1333 6.0		SU 1425 5.7	
2034 0.9		2115 1.2	
4 0158 5.9		**19** 0242 5.6	
0858 0.8		0935 1.0	
SU 1420 6.0		M 1503 5.6	
2119 0.9		2150 1.3	
5 0246 5.8		**20** 0318 5.5	
0945 0.9		1011 1.1	
M 1512 5.9		TU 1540 5.4	
2207 1.1		2225 1.4	
6 0337 5.6		**21** 0356 5.3	
1035 1.0		1047 1.2	
TU 1608 5.7		W 1620 5.3	
2259 1.3		2302 1.6	
7 0432 5.4		**22** 0437 5.2	
1130 1.1		1125 1.3	
W 1708 5.5		TH 1704 5.1	
2357 1.4		2342 1.7	
8 0531 5.3		**23** 0523 5.0	
1233 1.2		1208 1.4	
TH 1815 5.3		F 1753 5.0	
☾		☾	
9 0108 1.6		**24** 0031 1.8	
0637 5.1		0616 4.9	
F 1343 1.3		SA 1259 1.4	
1932 5.2		1849 4.9	
10 0219 1.6		**25** 0128 1.9	
0754 5.0		0714 4.8	
SA 1453 1.2		SU 1403 1.6	
2044 5.3		1951 4.8	
11 0326 1.5		**26** 0238 1.9	
0902 5.1		0817 4.9	
SU 1600 1.1		M 1514 1.6	
2145 5.4		2056 4.9	
12 0429 1.4		**27** 0347 1.8	
0959 5.4		0920 5.1	
M 1701 1.0		TU 1617 1.4	
2238 5.5		2157 5.1	
13 0526 1.3		**28** 0446 1.6	
1049 5.5		1018 5.2	
TU 1754 1.0		W 1712 1.3	
2327 5.6		2250 5.3	
14 0615 1.2		**29** 0540 1.4	
1136 5.6		1108 5.4	
W 1840 1.0		TH 1803 1.1	
		2339 5.5	
15 0008 5.6		**30** 0630 1.1	
0659 1.0		1156 5.7	
TH 1220 5.7		F 1852 1.0	
○ 1922 1.0			
		31 0021 5.7	
		0718 1.0	
		SA 1242 5.9	
		● 1940 0.8	

Chart Datum: 2·69 metres below IGN Datum

FREE monthly updates from
www.reedsalmanac.co.uk

TIDES

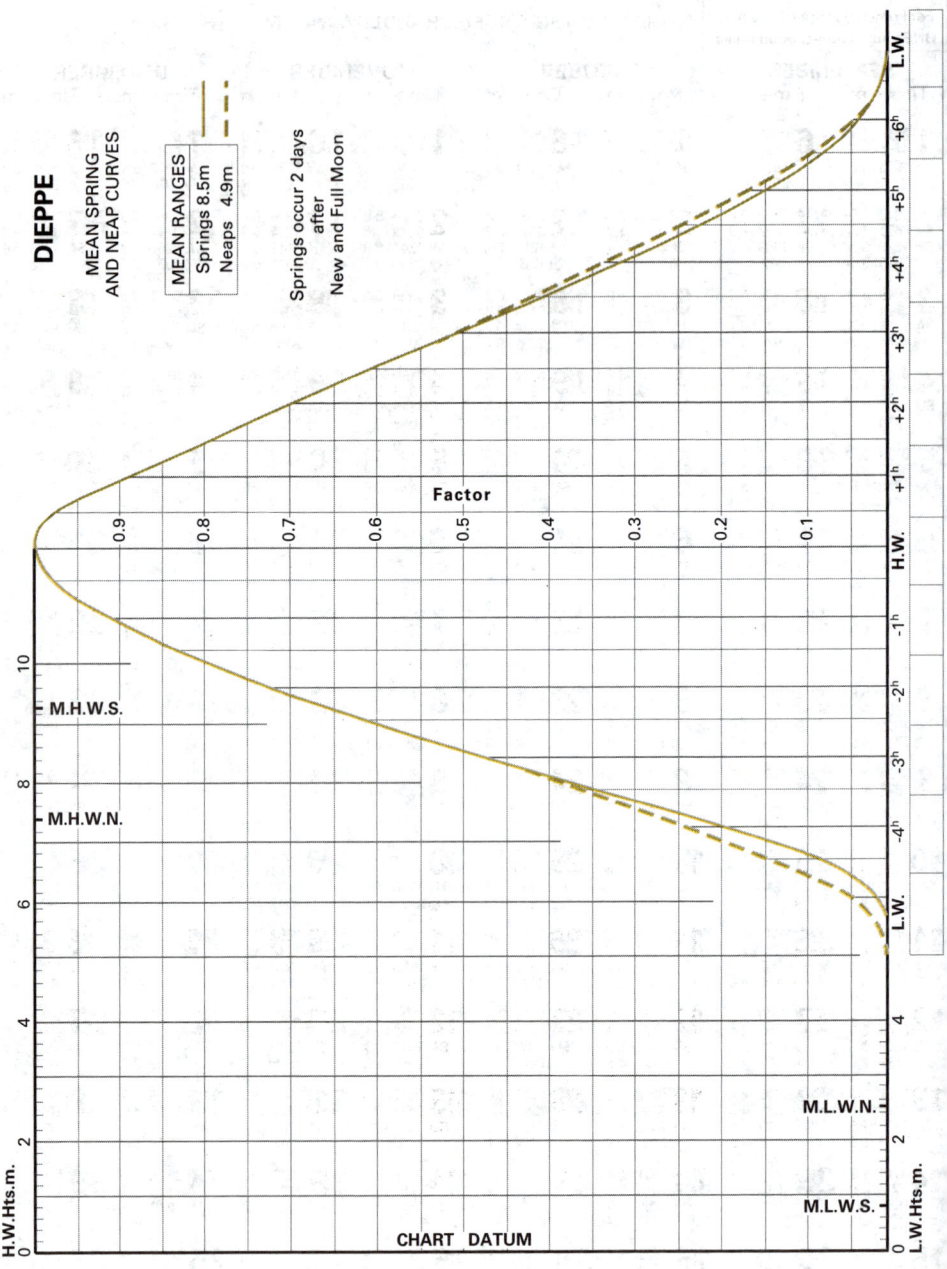

TIME ZONE -0100
(French Standard Time)
Subtract 1 hour for UT
For French Summer Time add
ONE hour in **non-shaded areas**

FRANCE – DIEPPE

LAT 49°56′N   LONG 1°05′E

TIMES AND HEIGHTS OF HIGH AND LOW WATERS

YEAR 2005

JANUARY

Time	m	Time	m
1 0247 / 0927 / SA 1500 / 2150	8.1 / 2.1 / 8.0 / 2.0	**16** 0348 / 1043 / SU 1608 / 2303	8.6 / 1.6 / 8.5 / 1.6
2 0325 / 1007 / SU 1540 / 2229	7.9 / 2.3 / 7.8 / 2.2	**17** 0433 / 1125 / M 1656 / ◐ 2345	8.2 / 2.0 / 8.0 / 2.1
3 0408 / 1052 / M 1626 / ◐ 2316	7.7 / 2.5 / 7.6 / 2.4	**18** 0523 / 1214 / TU 1751	7.7 / 2.4 / 7.4
4 0458 / 1145 / TU 1721	7.5 / 2.6 / 7.4	**19** 0034 / 0624 / W 1315 / 1859	2.5 / 7.3 / 2.7 / 7.1
5 0011 / 0559 / W 1248 / 1828	2.5 / 7.4 / 2.6 / 7.3	**20** 0140 / 0739 / TH 1429 / 2017	2.8 / 7.1 / 2.8 / 7.0
6 0117 / 0713 / TH 1400 / 1943	2.5 / 7.5 / 2.5 / 7.5	**21** 0257 / 0853 / F 1541 / 2125	2.9 / 7.3 / 2.6 / 7.3
7 0234 / 0824 / F 1515 / 2053	2.4 / 7.8 / 2.1 / 7.9	**22** 0406 / 0951 / SA 1640 / 2218	2.6 / 7.6 / 2.2 / 7.6
8 0348 / 0927 / SA 1622 / 2155	2.0 / 8.3 / 1.7 / 8.3	**23** 0500 / 1038 / SU 1728 / 2302	2.3 / 7.9 / 1.9 / 8.0
9 0451 / 1025 / SU 1722 / 2252	1.7 / 8.7 / 1.3 / 8.7	**24** 0545 / 1117 / M 1810 / 2339	2.0 / 8.2 / 1.6 / 8.3
10 0550 / 1119 / M 1820 / ● 2346	1.3 / 9.1 / 0.9 / 9.1	**25** 0626 / 1152 / TU 1848 / ○	1.8 / 8.5 / 1.4
11 0646 / 1211 / TU 1916	1.1 / 9.3 / 0.7	**26** 0015 / 0703 / W 1227 / 1925	8.5 / 1.6 / 8.6 / 1.3
12 0043 / 0741 / W 1302 / 2008	9.3 / 0.9 / 9.5 / 0.5	**27** 0049 / 0737 / TH 1301 / 1958	8.6 / 1.5 / 8.8 / 1.2
13 0132 / 0832 / TH 1351 / 2057	9.3 / 0.9 / 9.5 / 0.5	**28** 0122 / 0809 / F 1334 / 2030	8.7 / 1.4 / 8.8 / 1.2
14 0219 / 0919 / F 1437 / 2142	9.1 / 1.0 / 9.3 / 0.7	**29** 0155 / 0840 / SA 1406 / 2100	8.7 / 1.5 / 8.7 / 1.5
15 0304 / 1002 / SA 1522 / 2223	9.0 / 1.2 / 8.9 / 1.1	**30** 0227 / 0912 / SU 1439 / 2131	8.6 / 1.5 / 8.6 / 1.4
		31 0300 / 0944 / M 1513 / 2202	8.5 / 1.7 / 8.4 / 1.6

FEBRUARY

Time	m	Time	m
1 0334 / 1020 / TU 1550 / 2239	8.3 / 1.9 / 8.1 / 1.9	**16** 0428 / 1117 / W 1656 / ◐ 2334	7.7 / 2.4 / 7.3 / 2.7
2 0413 / 1103 / W 1636 / ◐ 2325	8.0 / 2.2 / 7.7 / 2.3	**17** 0518 / 1212 / TH 1801	7.1 / 2.9 / 6.7
3 0504 / 1159 / TH 1736	7.6 / 2.5 / 7.4	**18** 0037 / 0639 / F 1334 / 1937	3.2 / 6.6 / 3.2 / 6.4
4 0027 / 0618 / F 1313 / 1901	2.6 / 7.4 / 2.6 / 7.2	**19** 0214 / 0822 / SA 1508 / 2106	3.4 / 6.6 / 3.0 / 6.8
5 0151 / 0751 / SA 1444 / 2030	2.7 / 7.4 / 2.4 / 7.4	**20** 0343 / 0933 / SU 1619 / 2203	3.0 / 7.1 / 2.5 / 7.3
6 0324 / 0910 / SU 1603 / 2144	2.4 / 7.8 / 1.9 / 8.0	**21** 0445 / 1021 / M 1711 / 2245	2.5 / 7.6 / 2.0 / 7.9
7 0437 / 1016 / M 1711 / 2247	1.9 / 8.4 / 1.3 / 8.6	**22** 0531 / 1100 / TU 1754 / 2321	2.0 / 8.1 / 1.6 / 8.3
8 0543 / 1114 / TU 1814 / ● 2341	1.4 / 9.0 / 0.8 / 9.1	**23** 0610 / 1135 / W 1832 / 2354	1.6 / 8.5 / 1.3 / 8.6
9 0642 / 1205 / W 1910	1.0 / 9.4 / 0.5	**24** 0646 / 1208 / TH 1907 / ○	1.4 / 8.8 / 1.1
10 0034 / 0735 / TH 1252 / 1959	9.4 / 0.7 / 9.7 / 0.2	**25** 0029 / 0719 / F 1241 / 1940	8.9 / 1.2 / 9.0 / 0.9
11 0118 / 0821 / F 1335 / 2042	9.5 / 0.6 / 9.7 / 0.3	**26** 0100 / 0751 / SA 1313 / 2011	9.0 / 1.1 / 9.1 / 0.9
12 0159 / 0901 / SA 1416 / 2120	9.5 / 0.7 / 9.5 / 0.5	**27** 0131 / 0822 / SU 1344 / 2040	9.0 / 1.0 / 9.1 / 0.9
13 0238 / 0936 / SU 1455 / 2153	9.3 / 0.9 / 9.2 / 0.9	**28** 0202 / 0852 / M 1415 / 2108	9.0 / 1.1 / 9.0 / 1.1
14 0314 / 1007 / M 1532 / 2222	8.9 / 1.4 / 8.7 / 1.5		
15 0349 / 1038 / TU 1611 / 2253	8.3 / 1.9 / 8.0 / 2.0		

MARCH

Time	m	Time	m
1 0233 / 0921 / TU 1448 / 2137	8.9 / 1.3 / 8.7 / 1.4	**16** 0309 / 0958 / W 1531 / 2209	8.4 / 1.8 / 8.0 / 2.1
2 0305 / 0953 / W 1523 / 2210	8.6 / 1.6 / 8.4 / 1.7	**17** 0341 / 1032 / TH 1609 / 2246	7.8 / 2.4 / 7.3 / 2.8
3 0342 / 1034 / TH 1606 / ◐ 2254	8.2 / 2.0 / 7.9 / 2.2	**18** 0423 / 1120 / F 1706 / 2344	7.0 / 3.0 / 6.5 / 3.4
4 0430 / 1128 / F 1706 / 2357	7.7 / 2.4 / 7.3 / 2.7	**19** 0537 / 1238 / SA 1852	6.4 / 3.4 / 6.2
5 0546 / 1245 / SA 1841	7.1 / 2.7 / 6.9	**20** 0128 / 0741 / SU 1429 / 2036	3.7 / 6.3 / 3.3 / 6.5
6 0131 / 0736 / SU 1428 / 2025	2.9 / 7.1 / 2.5 / 7.2	**21** 0313 / 0904 / M 1548 / 2134	3.2 / 6.8 / 2.7 / 7.2
7 0315 / 0906 / M 1555 / 2143	2.5 / 7.7 / 1.9 / 7.9	**22** 0416 / 0953 / TU 1641 / 2215	2.5 / 7.5 / 2.1 / 7.8
8 0433 / 1012 / TU 1705 / 2241	1.8 / 8.4 / 1.2 / 8.6	**23** 0502 / 1032 / W 1724 / 2252	2.0 / 8.1 / 1.6 / 8.4
9 0537 / 1105 / W 1805 / 2329	1.1 / 9.0 / 0.7 / 9.2	**24** 0541 / 1107 / TH 1803 / 2326	1.5 / 8.5 / 1.2 / 8.7
10 0632 / 1151 / TH 1856 / ●	0.8 / 9.5 / 0.4	**25** 0618 / 1141 / F 1839 / ○ 2359	1.2 / 8.9 / 0.9 / 9.0
11 0016 / 0718 / F 1233 / 1939	9.5 / 0.6 / 9.7 / 0.2	**26** 0653 / 1214 / SA 1913	1.0 / 9.1 / 0.9
12 0056 / 0759 / SA 1312 / 2017	9.6 / 0.6 / 9.7 / 0.3	**27** 0032 / 0726 / SU 1246 / 1945	9.1 / 0.9 / 9.2 / 0.7
13 0132 / 0832 / SU 1349 / 2049	9.5 / 0.6 / 9.5 / 0.6	**28** 0104 / 0759 / M 1319 / 2015	9.2 / 0.8 / 9.2 / 0.8
14 0206 / 0904 / M 1424 / 2117	9.3 / 0.9 / 9.2 / 1.0	**29** 0136 / 0831 / TU 1352 / 2046	9.2 / 0.9 / 9.1 / 1.0
15 0238 / 0930 / TU 1457 / 2141	8.9 / 1.3 / 8.7 / 1.5	**30** 0209 / 0902 / W 1427 / 2117	9.0 / 1.1 / 8.9 / 1.3
		31 0243 / 0937 / TH 1506 / 2153	8.7 / 1.4 / 8.4 / 1.8

APRIL

Time	m	Time	m
1 0323 / 1019 / F 1552 / 2241	8.2 / 1.9 / 7.8 / 2.3	**16** 0347 / 1043 / SA 1630 / ◐ 2308	7.1 / 2.9 / 6.7 / 3.3
2 0416 / 1117 / SA 1659 / ◐ 2348	7.6 / 2.4 / 7.2 / 2.8	**17** 0453 / 1152 / SU 1801	6.4 / 3.3 / 6.3
3 0542 / 1240 / SU 1844	7.0 / 2.7 / 6.9	**18** 0038 / 0643 / M 1334 / 1941	3.6 / 6.3 / 3.3 / 6.5
4 0131 / 0734 / M 1424 / 2022	2.9 / 7.1 / 2.4 / 7.4	**19** 0219 / 0811 / TU 1455 / 2046	3.2 / 6.7 / 2.8 / 7.1
5 0310 / 0858 / TU 1546 / 2131	2.4 / 7.8 / 1.7 / 8.1	**20** 0325 / 0907 / W 1552 / 2132	2.6 / 7.3 / 2.2 / 7.7
6 0423 / 0958 / W 1652 / 2223	1.7 / 8.5 / 1.1 / 8.7	**21** 0415 / 0952 / TH 1639 / 2213	2.0 / 7.9 / 1.7 / 8.3
7 0521 / 1046 / TH 1746 / 2308	1.2 / 9.0 / 0.7 / 9.2	**22** 0459 / 1031 / F 1722 / 2250	1.6 / 8.4 / 1.3 / 8.7
8 0610 / 1129 / F 1832 / ● 2348	1.0 / 9.3 / 0.5 / 9.4	**23** 0540 / 1108 / SA 1802 / 2325	1.3 / 8.8 / 1.0 / 8.9
9 0653 / 1209 / SA 1911 / ○	0.9 / 9.5 / 0.5	**24** 0620 / 1144 / SU 1840 / ○	1.1 / 9.0 / 0.9
10 0028 / 0729 / SU 1245 / 1945	9.4 / 0.7 / 9.5 / 0.5	**25** 0000 / 0658 / M 1219 / 1917	9.1 / 0.9 / 9.1 / 0.8
11 0102 / 0802 / M 1320 / 2015	9.3 / 0.8 / 9.4 / 0.8	**26** 0037 / 0735 / TU 1255 / 1952	9.2 / 0.8 / 9.2 / 0.9
12 0134 / 0831 / TU 1354 / 2042	9.1 / 1.0 / 9.0 / 1.2	**27** 0113 / 0811 / W 1333 / 2027	9.2 / 0.8 / 9.1 / 1.0
13 0206 / 0858 / W 1427 / 2108	8.8 / 1.4 / 8.5 / 1.7	**28** 0150 / 0848 / TH 1414 / 2105	9.0 / 1.0 / 8.8 / 1.4
14 0236 / 0926 / TH 1500 / 2137	7.7 / 1.8 / 7.9 / 2.2	**29** 0231 / 0929 / F 1459 / 2148	8.7 / 1.3 / 8.4 / 1.8
15 0307 / 0959 / F 1537 / 2214	7.7 / 2.3 / 7.3 / 2.8	**30** 0318 / 1018 / SA 1553 / 2242	8.1 / 1.8 / 7.8 / 2.3

Chart Datum: 4·45 metres below IGN Datum

FREE monthly updates from
》》 www.reedsalmanac.co.uk 《《

TIDES

TIME ZONE -0100
(French Standard Time)
Subtract 1 hour for UT
For French Summer Time add
ONE hour in **non-shaded areas**

FRANCE – DIEPPE
LAT 49°56'N   LONG 1°05'E
TIMES AND HEIGHTS OF HIGH AND LOW WATERS

YEAR 2005

	MAY			JUNE			JULY			AUGUST	
	Time m	Time m		Time m	Time m		Time m	Time m		Time m	Time m
1 SU	0420 7.6 1120 2.2 1708 7.3 ◐ 2354 2.6	**16** M	0424 6.8 1117 2.9 1713 6.7 ◐ 2350 3.2	**1** W	0107 2.2 0648 7.7 1342 1.9 1923 7.8	**16** TH	0008 2.7 0551 7.1 1240 2.6 1830 7.2	**1** F	0132 2.1 0714 7.6 1402 2.1 1945 7.7	**16** SA	0013 2.5 0551 7.3 1242 2.5 1829 7.4	**1** M	0311 2.6 0907 7.2 1541 2.6 2130 7.4	**16** TU	0202 2.7 0758 7.2 1447 2.6 2033 7.5
2 M	0549 7.2 1244 2.3 1839 7.3	**17** TU	0542 6.6 1232 3.0 1832 6.8	**2** TH	0216 2.0 0757 7.9 1447 1.7 2027 8.0	**17** F	0111 2.6 0658 7.2 1344 2.4 1935 7.5	**2** SA	0237 2.2 0822 7.6 1506 2.2 2049 7.8	**17** SU	0119 2.5 0705 7.3 1354 2.5 1944 7.5	**2** TU	0418 2.3 1007 7.6 1642 2.3 2223 7.8	**17** W	0330 2.2 0918 7.7 1605 2.1 2144 8.1
3 TU	0129 2.6 0719 7.4 1412 2.1 2000 7.7	**18** W	0110 3.1 0702 6.8 1348 2.7 1942 7.1	**3** F	0319 1.8 0859 8.1 1547 1.6 2123 8.3	**18** SA	0216 2.4 0803 7.5 1449 2.2 2034 7.8	**3** SU	0340 2.1 0925 7.7 1606 2.1 2146 7.9	**18** M	0234 2.4 0823 7.5 1512 2.3 2053 7.8	**3** W	0512 2.0 1054 7.9 1732 2.0 2306 8.1	**18** TH	0441 1.6 1024 8.3 1710 1.5 2244 8.7
4 W	0251 2.1 0833 7.9 1524 1.6 2104 8.2	**19** TH	0220 2.7 0807 7.2 1451 2.3 2038 7.6	**4** SA	0416 1.6 0951 8.3 1640 1.5 2211 8.5	**19** SU	0319 2.1 0902 7.8 1550 1.9 2128 8.2	**4** M	0437 1.9 1018 7.9 1658 2.0 2234 8.1	**19** TU	0347 2.0 0930 7.9 1620 1.9 2154 8.2	**4** TH	0558 1.7 1132 8.3 1813 1.7 2342 8.4	**19** F	0546 1.1 1119 9.0 1811 1.0 ○ 2337 9.2
5 TH	0357 1.6 0932 8.4 1625 1.2 2156 8.6	**20** F	0318 2.2 0901 7.7 1546 1.9 2125 8.1	**5** SU	0506 1.5 1037 8.4 1726 1.5 2253 8.6	**20** M	0418 1.7 1001 8.1 1646 1.6 2217 8.5	**5** TU	0525 1.8 1104 8.1 1743 1.8 2316 8.3	**20** W	0452 1.6 1031 8.4 1720 1.5 2251 8.7	**5** F	0638 1.5 1207 8.5 1851 1.6 ●	**20** SA	0646 0.6 1209 9.4 1906 0.7
6 F	0452 1.3 1020 8.8 1716 1.0 2240 8.9	**21** SA	0409 1.8 0948 8.2 1636 1.5 2209 8.5	**6** M	0549 1.4 1119 8.5 1806 1.5 ● 2332 8.6	**21** TU	0513 1.4 1047 8.5 1739 1.4 2306 8.8	**6** W	0609 1.6 1144 8.3 1825 1.7 ● 2355 8.4	**21** TH	0553 1.2 1127 8.8 1819 1.2 ○ 2345 9.0	**6** SA	0018 8.6 0715 1.3 1240 8.6 1926 1.4	**21** SU	0029 9.6 0737 0.4 1306 9.6 1955 0.5
7 SA	0540 1.1 1103 9.0 1800 1.0 2320 9.0	**22** SU	0458 1.5 1031 8.5 1723 1.3 2250 8.8	**7** TU	0628 1.4 1157 8.5 1843 1.5	**22** W	0607 1.1 1137 8.8 1831 1.2 ○ 2354 9.0	**7** TH	0650 1.5 1221 8.4 1904 1.6	**22** F	0653 0.8 1220 9.1 1916 0.9	**7** SU	0051 8.7 0749 1.3 1312 8.7 1959 1.4	**22** M	0113 9.7 0822 0.3 1337 9.7 2039 0.5
8 SU	0621 1.0 1142 9.0 1838 1.0 ● 2357 9.1	**23** M	0545 1.2 1113 8.8 1807 1.1 ○ 2330 9.0	**8** W	0010 8.6 0706 1.3 1234 8.5 1919 1.5	**23** TH	0659 0.9 1226 9.0 1921 1.1	**8** F	0032 8.4 0729 1.4 1257 8.4 1941 1.6	**23** SA	0041 9.3 0749 0.6 1310 9.3 2009 0.8	**8** M	0123 8.7 0819 1.2 1344 8.7 2029 1.4	**23** TU	0155 9.5 0902 0.6 1417 9.5 2118 0.7
9 M	0657 1.0 1219 9.0 1911 1.1	**24** TU	0630 1.0 1154 9.0 1851 1.0	**9** TH	0046 8.6 0743 1.4 1311 8.5 1955 1.6	**24** F	0047 9.1 0751 0.8 1317 9.1 2012 1.0	**9** SA	0108 8.5 0805 1.4 1333 8.5 2017 1.6	**24** SU	0130 9.4 0839 0.4 1357 9.4 2057 0.7	**9** TU	0154 8.7 0848 1.3 1414 8.7 2058 1.5	**24** W	0235 9.3 0936 0.8 1455 9.3 2153 1.1
10 TU	0033 9.0 0731 1.1 1254 8.9 1943 1.2	**25** W	0013 9.1 0714 0.9 1237 9.1 1933 1.0	**10** F	0121 8.4 0818 1.5 1348 8.4 2030 1.8	**25** SA	0137 9.1 0843 0.8 1408 9.1 2103 1.1	**10** SU	0143 8.4 0838 1.5 1408 8.5 2049 1.7	**25** M	0217 9.4 0924 0.5 1442 9.3 2141 0.9	**10** W	0224 8.6 0916 1.4 1445 8.5 2127 1.6	**25** TH	0313 8.9 1007 1.3 1533 8.6 2226 1.6
11 W	0106 8.8 0804 1.2 1329 8.7 2014 1.5	**26** TH	0056 9.1 0757 0.9 1322 9.0 2016 1.1	**11** SA	0157 8.2 0851 1.7 1425 8.2 2103 2.1	**26** SU	0228 9.0 0933 0.8 1458 8.9 2153 1.2	**11** M	0217 8.3 0910 1.7 1442 8.2 2121 1.9	**26** TU	0302 9.2 1006 0.7 1526 9.0 2223 1.2	**11** TH	0255 8.4 0944 1.6 1516 8.3 2200 1.9	**26** F	0352 8.3 1040 2.0 1612 7.9 ◐ 2304 2.3
12 TH	0139 8.6 0835 1.5 1404 8.3 2045 1.8	**27** F	0140 9.0 0842 1.0 1409 8.8 2101 1.3	**12** SU	0233 7.9 0924 2.0 1503 7.8 2139 2.3	**27** M	0320 8.8 1023 1.0 1549 8.6 2244 1.5	**12** TU	0251 8.2 0941 1.8 1516 8.1 2155 2.0	**27** W	0346 8.8 1045 1.2 1609 8.6 2304 1.6	**12** F	0329 8.1 1016 1.9 1551 8.0 2238 2.1	**27** SA	0437 7.5 1124 2.6 1701 7.2 2355 2.8
13 F	0212 8.2 0905 1.8 1439 7.9 2117 2.2	**28** SA	0229 8.7 0930 1.2 1501 8.5 2151 1.6	**13** M	0312 7.7 1002 2.2 1544 7.5 2220 2.5	**28** TU	0412 8.5 1112 1.3 1642 8.3 2336 1.7	**13** W	0327 7.9 1016 1.9 1552 7.9 2233 2.1	**28** TH	0431 8.3 1124 1.8 1656 8.1 ◐ 2349 2.0	**13** SA	0409 7.8 1058 2.3 1635 7.7 ◐ 2327 2.5	**28** SU	0540 6.8 1222 3.1 1815 6.8
14 SA	0247 7.7 0938 2.2 1518 7.5 2154 2.6	**29** SU	0323 8.3 1023 1.5 1559 8.1 2248 2.0	**14** TU	0357 7.4 1047 2.4 1631 7.3 2310 2.7	**29** W	0508 8.1 1204 1.7 1737 8.0	**14** TH	0406 7.7 1056 2.1 1634 7.7 2318 2.4	**29** F	0523 7.7 1211 2.4 1751 7.6	**14** SU	0502 7.4 1154 2.7 1736 7.3	**29** M	0113 3.3 0718 6.5 1355 3.3 1957 6.7
15 SU	0328 7.3 1020 2.6 1607 7.0 2243 3.0	**30** M	0426 7.8 1125 1.8 1705 7.8 ◐ 2354 2.1	**15** W	0450 7.2 1140 2.5 1727 7.2 ◐	**30** TH	0031 2.0 0608 7.8 1300 1.9 1839 7.8	**15** F	0453 7.5 1144 2.4 1725 7.5	**30** SA	0043 2.5 0628 7.2 1312 2.6 1900 7.2	**15** M	0033 2.7 0620 7.1 1312 2.9 1905 7.2	**30** TU	0249 3.0 0854 6.7 1525 3.0 2117 7.1
		31 TU	0536 7.7 1233 1.9 1814 7.7							**31** SU	0154 2.7 0748 7.0 1427 2.8 2020 7.2			**31** W	0404 2.5 0953 7.0 1629 2.4 2208 7.5

Chart Datum: 4·45 metres below IGN Datum

》 **FREE** monthly updates from 《
www.reedsalmanac.co.uk

TIME ZONE -0100
(French Standard Time)
Subtract 1 hour for UT
For French Summer Time add
ONE hour in non-shaded areas

FRANCE – DIEPPE
LAT 49°56'N   LONG 1°05'E
TIMES AND HEIGHTS OF HIGH AND LOW WATERS

YEAR 2005

SEPTEMBER

Time	m		Time	m
1 0457	2.0	**16**	0434	1.5
1036	8.0		1014	8.6
TH 1716	1.9	F	1701	1.4
2247	8.1		2233	8.9
2 0540	1.6	**17**	0535	0.9
1111	8.4		1104	9.2
F 1755	1.6	SA	1758	0.9
2322	8.5		2321	9.4
3 0618	1.4	**18**	0629	0.5
1143	8.7		1149	9.6
SA 1830	1.4	SU	1848	0.6
● 2353	8.8	○		
4 0652	1.2	**19**	0006	9.7
1215	8.9		0715	0.4
SU 1903	1.3	M	1231	9.7
			1933	0.5
5 0026	8.9	**20**	0049	9.8
0724	1.1		0756	0.4
M 1245	9.0	TU	1310	9.7
1934	1.2		2012	0.6
6 0056	9.0	**21**	0128	9.6
0753	1.1		0831	0.6
TU 1315	9.0	W	1347	9.5
2003	1.2		2047	0.9
7 0126	9.0	**22**	0204	9.3
0821	1.1		0901	1.0
W 1344	9.0	TH	1422	9.1
2032	1.3		2118	1.3
8 0156	8.9	**23**	0240	8.8
0848	1.1		0928	1.6
TH 1413	8.8	F	1450	8.6
2100	1.4		2148	1.8
9 0226	8.7	**24**	0315	8.1
0914	1.6		0958	2.2
F 1444	8.6	SA	1531	7.9
2131	1.7		2222	2.4
10 0259	8.3	**25**	0356	7.4
0943	1.9		1037	2.8
SA 1518	8.2	SU	1615	7.2
2207	2.1	○	2310	3.0
11 0338	7.9	**26**	0456	6.7
1023	2.4		1138	3.5
SU 1602	7.7	M	1729	6.5
◐ 2256	2.5			
12 0432	7.3	**27**	0029	3.5
1123	2.9		0642	6.3
M 1705	7.1	TU	1322	3.7
			1925	6.4
13 0006	2.9	**28**	0219	3.3
0559	6.9		0827	6.7
TU 1251	3.1	W	1459	3.2
1848	6.9		2049	6.9
14 0148	2.8	**29**	0335	2.8
0752	7.1		0923	7.4
W 1438	2.8	TH	1600	2.5
2027	7.4		2138	7.5
15 0323	2.2	**30**	0426	2.1
0914	7.8		1004	8.0
TH 1557	2.0	F	1645	2.0
2137	8.2		2216	8.1

OCTOBER

Time	m		Time	m
1 0508	1.6	**16**	0514	0.9
1039	8.5		1042	9.3
SA 1723	1.6	SU	1736	0.9
2251	8.6		2258	9.4
2 0545	1.3	**17**	0603	0.7
1112	8.8		1124	9.5
SU 1759	1.3	M	1823	0.7
2323	8.9	○	2340	9.4
3 0620	1.2	**18**	0646	0.7
1143	9.0		1203	9.6
M 1833	1.2	TU	1905	0.7
● 2355	9.0			
4 0652	1.1	**19**	0022	9.5
1214	9.1		0723	0.8
TU 1905	1.1	W	1241	9.5
			1942	0.8
5 0027	9.1	**20**	0100	9.4
0723	1.1		0756	1.0
W 1244	9.2	TH	1316	9.3
1936	1.1		2015	1.1
6 0058	9.1	**21**	0136	9.1
0752	1.1		0826	1.3
TH 1314	9.1	F	1350	9.0
2007	1.2		2046	1.4
7 0129	9.0	**22**	0211	8.6
0821	1.3		0855	1.8
F 1345	9.0	SA	1424	8.5
2038	1.3		2117	1.9
8 0203	8.8	**23**	0246	8.0
0850	1.6		0926	2.4
SA 1419	8.7	SU	1459	7.9
2111	1.6		2150	2.4
9 0239	8.4	**24**	0326	7.4
0923	2.0		1005	2.9
SU 1457	8.2	M	1542	7.2
2150	2.1		2234	3.0
10 0322	7.8	**25**	0421	6.8
1008	2.5		1102	3.5
M 1545	7.6	TU	1648	6.6
◐ 2242	2.5	○	2342	3.4
11 0422	7.2	**26**	0551	6.4
1113	3.0		1233	3.7
TU 1657	7.1	W	1827	6.4
2356	2.9			
12 0602	6.9	**27**	0123	3.4
1249	3.1		0727	6.6
W 1846	7.0	TH	1407	3.3
			1953	6.7
13 0145	2.7	**28**	0242	2.9
0747	7.3		0832	7.2
TH 1432	2.6	F	1510	2.7
2016	7.6		2050	7.3
14 0313	2.1	**29**	0338	2.4
0859	8.1		0918	7.8
F 1544	1.9	SA	1558	2.2
2121	8.3		2133	7.9
15 0418	1.4	**30**	0423	1.9
0955	8.8		0957	8.3
SA 1644	1.3	SU	1641	1.7
2213	9.1		2212	8.4
		31	0504	1.5
			1034	8.7
		M	1721	1.4
			2248	8.7

NOVEMBER

Time	m		Time	m
1 0542	1.3	**16**	0613	1.1
1108	9.0		1137	9.2
TU 1758	1.3	W	1836	1.0
2322	8.9	○	2356	9.1
2 0618	1.2	**17**	0651	1.2
1142	9.1		1214	9.2
W 1834	1.2	TH	1913	1.1
● 2356	9.1			
3 0652	1.2	**18**	0036	9.0
1215	9.2		0726	1.3
TH 1910	1.1	F	1250	9.0
			1948	1.2
4 0033	9.1	**19**	0113	8.8
0727	1.2		0800	1.6
F 1249	9.1	SA	1326	8.8
1946	1.1		2022	1.5
5 0109	9.0	**20**	0149	8.5
0801	1.4		0833	1.9
SA 1325	9.0	SU	1402	8.4
2022	1.3		2055	1.9
6 0148	8.8	**21**	0227	8.1
0837	1.7		0906	2.3
SU 1405	8.7	M	1439	7.9
2102	1.6		2130	2.3
7 0231	8.4	**22**	0306	7.6
0919	2.0		0944	2.7
M 1450	8.3	TU	1521	7.4
2147	1.9		2209	2.7
8 0321	7.9	**23**	0354	7.2
1010	2.5		1032	3.1
TU 1545	7.7	W	1614	7.0
2243	2.3	◐	2301	3.0
9 0429	7.4	**24**	0456	6.9
1118	2.9		1135	3.3
W 1703	7.3	TH	1722	6.7
○ 2358	2.6			
10 0559	7.3	**25**	0009	3.2
1247	2.8		0610	6.8
TH 1832	7.4	F	1250	3.3
			1837	6.8
11 0131	2.4	**26**	0125	3.0
0723	7.6		0721	7.1
F 1412	2.4	SA	1400	2.9
1949	7.8		1944	7.1
12 0247	2.0	**27**	0231	2.7
0831	8.1		0820	7.5
SA 1519	1.8	SU	1459	2.5
2053	8.3		2039	7.6
13 0350	1.5	**28**	0327	2.3
0927	8.6		0909	7.9
SU 1618	1.4	M	1551	2.1
2146	8.8		2127	8.0
14 0445	1.3	**29**	0416	1.9
1014	9.0		0952	8.4
M 1709	1.1	TU	1639	1.7
2233	9.0		2210	8.4
15 0532	1.1	**30**	0502	1.7
1057	9.2		1033	8.7
TU 1755	1.0	W	1724	1.5
2316	9.2		2251	8.6

DECEMBER

Time	m		Time	m
1 0545	1.5	**16**	0627	1.6
1112	8.9		1156	8.8
TH 1807	1.3	F	1852	1.3
● 2331	8.9			
2 0626	1.4	**17**	0020	8.7
1151	9.1		0705	1.6
F 1849	1.1	SA	1233	8.8
			1929	1.4
3 0014	9.0	**18**	0058	8.6
0708	1.3		0743	1.7
SA 1232	9.1	SU	1310	8.7
1932	1.1		2006	1.6
4 0058	9.0	**19**	0135	8.5
0750	1.4		0819	1.8
SU 1315	9.1	M	1347	8.5
2016	1.1		2041	1.7
5 0143	8.9	**20**	0212	8.3
0835	1.5		0853	2.0
M 1402	8.9	TU	1423	8.2
2102	1.3		2115	1.9
6 0232	8.6	**21**	0248	8.0
0923	1.8		0926	2.3
TU 1453	8.5	W	1501	7.9
2152	1.5		2148	2.2
7 0327	8.3	**22**	0326	7.7
1017	2.0		1003	2.5
W 1550	8.2	TH	1540	7.6
2247	1.8		2226	2.4
8 0428	8.0	**23**	0407	7.5
1118	2.3		1047	2.7
TH 1653	7.9	F	1625	7.3
◐ 2349	2.0	◐	2310	2.6
9 0535	7.8	**24**	0457	7.3
1227	2.5		1139	2.9
F 1802	7.8	SA	1719	7.1
10 0058	2.1	**25**	0005	2.8
0645	7.8		0558	7.2
SA 1337	2.2	SU	1239	2.9
1912	7.8		1824	7.0
11 0208	2.1	**26**	0107	2.8
0753	8.0		0707	7.2
SU 1445	2.0	M	1346	2.8
2019	8.0		1934	7.2
12 0313	1.9	**27**	0217	2.7
0854	8.2		0813	7.5
M 1547	1.8	TU	1455	2.5
2118	8.2		2038	7.5
13 0412	1.8	**28**	0325	2.4
0947	8.5		0910	7.8
TU 1642	1.6	W	1557	2.1
2210	8.4		2134	7.9
14 0502	1.7	**29**	0425	2.1
1034	8.6		1001	8.1
W 1730	1.5	TH	1653	1.7
2256	8.6		2225	8.3
15 0546	1.6	**30**	0518	1.7
1117	8.7		1049	8.6
TH 1812	1.4	F	1745	1.4
○ 2339	8.6		2313	8.7
		31	0608	1.5
			1136	8.9
		SA	1836	1.1
		●		

Chart Datum: 4·45 metres below IGN Datum

FREE monthly updates from
www.reedsalmanac.co.uk

Chapter 5

377

TIDES

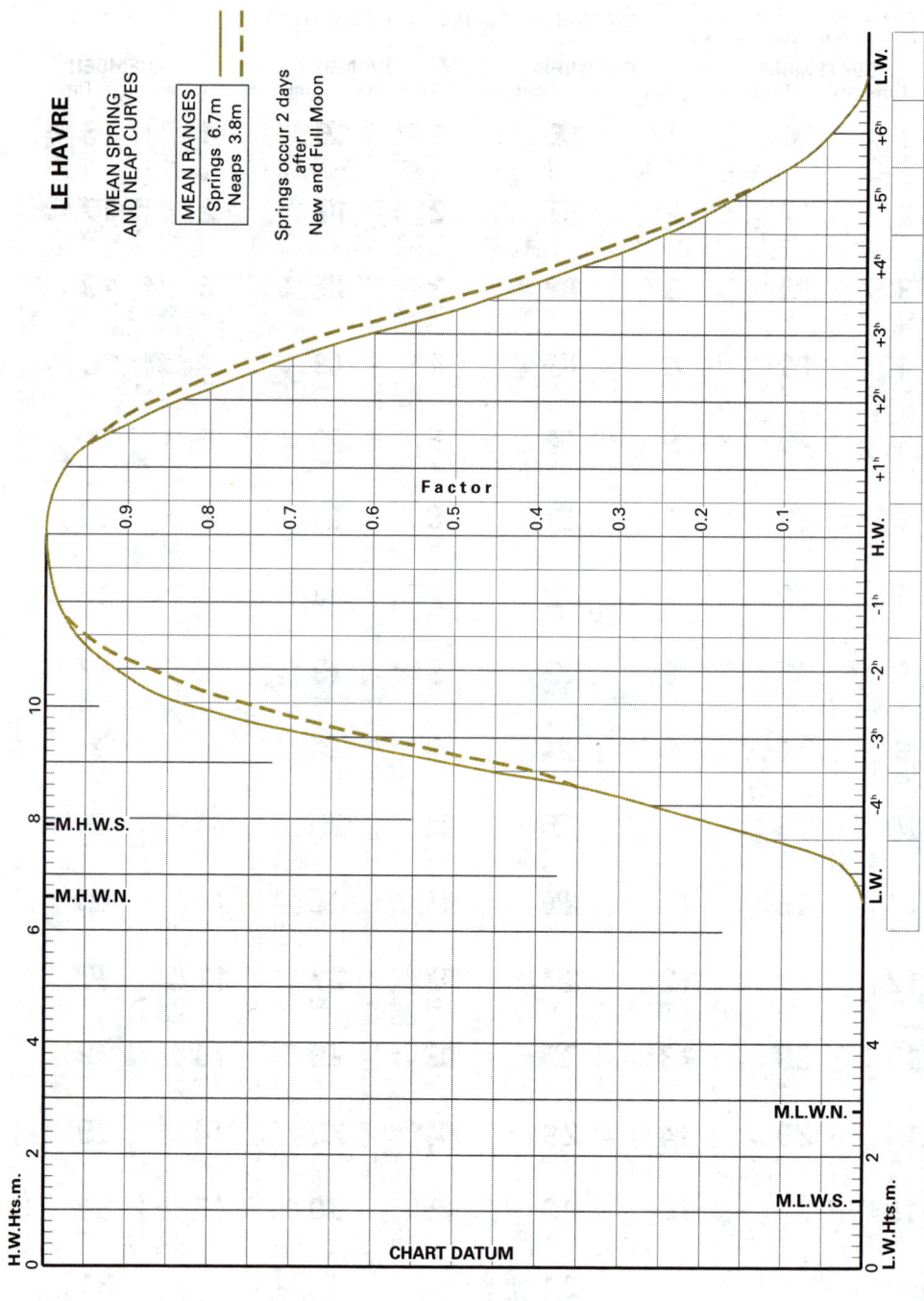

TIME ZONE -0100
(French Standard Time)
Subtract 1 hour for UT
For French Summer Time add ONE hour in **non-shaded areas**

FRANCE – LE HAVRE
LAT 49°29′N   LONG 0°07′E
TIMES AND HEIGHTS OF HIGH AND LOW WATERS

YEAR 2005

	JANUARY				FEBRUARY				MARCH				APRIL		
	Time m		Time m		Time m		Time m		Time m		Time m		Time m		Time m
1	0150 7.1 0836 2.5 SA 1357 7.1 2058 2.3	**16**	0253 7.4 0952 2.0 SU 1507 7.3 2211 1.9	**1**	0238 7.1 0928 2.3 TU 1448 7.1 2147 2.3	**16**	0332 6.8 1021 2.7 W 1558 6.6 ○ 2237 3.0	**1**	0136 7.5 0833 1.7 TU 1347 7.5 2049 1.7	**16**	0211 7.3 0906 2.1 W 1431 7.0 2113 2.5	**1**	0227 7.1 0926 2.2 F 1500 6.8 2146 2.6	**16**	0252 6.4 0944 3.1 SA 1544 6.0 ☾ 2210 3.5
2	0229 6.9 0914 2.7 SU 1438 7.0 2136 2.5	**17**	0339 7.1 1032 2.4 M 1556 7.0 ☾ 2251 2.4	**2**	0317 6.9 1009 2.6 W 1533 6.9 ☾ 2232 2.6	**17**	0425 6.4 1111 3.2 TH 1710 6.2 2338 3.5	**2**	0208 7.3 0905 2.0 W 1423 7.3 2120 2.1	**17**	0244 6.9 0935 2.7 TH 1513 6.5 ☾ 2148 3.1	**2**	0323 6.7 1020 2.7 SA 1614 6.4 ☾ 2254 3.1	**17**	0402 5.9 1055 3.4 SU 1726 5.9 2349 3.8
3	0313 6.8 0958 2.8 M 1525 6.8 ☾ 2222 2.7	**18**	0430 6.8 1119 2.8 TU 1654 6.7 2340 2.8	**3**	0408 6.8 1103 2.8 TH 1636 6.6 2333 2.9	**18**	0548 6.2 1232 3.5 F 1854 6.0	**3**	0244 7.1 0941 2.3 TH 1506 6.9 ☾ 2201 2.6	**18**	0328 6.4 1019 3.2 F 1620 6.0 2246 3.6	**3**	0457 6.4 1145 2.9 SU 1805 6.4	**18**	0553 5.8 1241 3.4 M 1852 6.1
4	0404 6.7 1050 2.9 TU 1620 6.7 2318 2.8	**19**	0532 6.6 1218 3.1 W 1807 6.4	**4**	0525 6.6 1217 3.0 F 1810 6.5	**19**	0117 3.6 0727 6.2 SA 1413 3.3 2018 6.2	**4**	0333 6.8 1033 2.7 F 1612 6.5 2303 3.0	**19**	0451 5.9 1136 3.6 SA 1813 5.8	**4**	0040 3.2 0640 6.5 M 1333 2.7 1933 6.7	**19**	0128 3.4 0712 6.1 TU 1401 3.0 1954 6.5
5	0507 6.7 1152 3.0 W 1729 6.6	**20**	0046 3.1 0647 6.5 TH 1335 3.1 1930 6.4	**5**	0059 3.0 0657 6.7 SA 1353 2.8 1941 6.7	**20**	0247 3.3 0837 6.4 SU 1525 2.9 2112 6.6	**5**	0457 6.4 1151 3.0 SA 1801 6.3	**20**	0032 3.8 0646 5.9 SU 1332 3.5 1946 6.1	**5**	0221 2.7 0756 6.9 TU 1457 2.1 2038 7.2	**20**	0234 2.9 0808 6.5 W 1500 2.5 2039 6.9
6	0024 2.8 0619 6.8 TH 1304 2.9 1847 6.7	**21**	0205 3.2 0800 6.6 F 1448 2.9 2038 6.5	**6**	0235 2.7 0814 7.0 SU 1516 2.3 2054 7.1	**21**	0351 2.9 0923 6.8 M 1620 2.4 2151 6.9	**6**	0039 3.2 0646 6.5 SU 1338 2.8 1938 6.6	**21**	0218 3.4 0804 6.3 M 1453 3.0 2042 6.5	**6**	0334 2.0 0854 7.3 W 1606 1.5 2127 7.6	**21**	0327 2.4 0851 6.9 TH 1549 2.0 2116 7.2
7	0141 2.7 0728 7.0 F 1424 2.6 1958 6.9	**22**	0311 2.9 0856 6.8 SA 1547 2.6 2128 6.8	**7**	0349 2.2 0918 7.4 M 1625 1.7 2155 7.5	**22**	0441 2.3 0959 7.1 TU 1705 2.0 2224 7.1	**7**	0226 2.8 0808 6.9 M 1507 2.3 2051 7.1	**22**	0324 2.8 0854 6.7 TU 1549 2.4 2121 6.9	**7**	0435 1.5 0942 7.7 TH 1701 1.1 2209 7.8	**22**	0412 2.0 0928 7.3 F 1633 1.7 2151 7.5
8	0258 2.4 0829 7.2 SA 1534 2.1 2101 7.2	**23**	0406 2.7 0941 6.9 SU 1636 2.3 2209 7.1	**8**	0455 1.7 1013 7.7 TU 1730 1.2 ● 2246 7.8	**23**	0522 2.0 1032 7.4 W 1744 1.6 2255 7.3	**8**	0345 2.2 0911 7.3 TU 1620 1.6 2146 7.6	**23**	0413 2.3 0930 7.1 W 1635 1.9 2154 7.3	**8**	0524 1.1 1024 7.9 F 1746 0.9 ● 2249 7.9	**23**	0453 1.6 1005 7.6 SA 1712 1.4 2226 7.7
9	0402 2.0 0925 7.5 SU 1635 1.7 2159 7.5	**24**	0453 2.4 1018 7.2 M 1719 2.0 2244 7.2	**9**	0556 1.3 1102 8.0 W 1826 0.8 2333 8.0	**24**	0559 1.7 1104 7.6 TH 1819 1.4 ○ 2327 7.6	**9**	0452 1.6 1001 7.7 W 1722 1.1 2232 7.9	**24**	0455 1.8 1004 7.4 TH 1715 1.6 2226 7.5	**9**	0606 0.7 1104 8.0 SA 1823 0.9 2326 7.8	**24**	0531 1.4 1041 7.7 SU 1749 1.3 ○ 2301 7.8
10	0501 1.7 1019 7.8 M 1733 1.4 ● 2253 7.8	**25**	0534 2.1 1051 7.4 TU 1759 1.7 ○ 2317 7.4	**10**	0648 1.0 1148 8.1 TH 1913 0.6	**25**	0631 1.5 1136 7.7 F 1850 1.3 2359 7.6	**10**	0546 1.1 1046 8.0 TH 1811 0.8 ● 2314 8.0	**25**	0531 1.6 1037 7.6 F 1750 1.4 ○ 2259 7.7	**10**	0641 1.0 1142 8.0 SU 1856 1.0	**25**	0608 1.2 1118 7.8 M 1826 1.2 2337 7.8
11	0559 1.4 1110 8.0 TU 1829 1.0 2344 7.9	**26**	0613 2.0 1124 7.5 W 1835 1.7 2350 7.4	**11**	0018 8.1 0732 0.8 F 1232 8.2 1954 0.6	**26**	0702 1.4 1208 7.8 SA 1920 1.2	**11**	0632 0.8 1128 8.1 F 1853 0.6 2354 8.1	**26**	0604 1.4 1110 7.7 SA 1822 1.2 2331 7.8	**11**	0002 7.9 0713 1.1 M 1219 7.9 1925 1.2	**26**	0645 1.1 1156 7.8 TU 1902 1.2
12	0653 1.3 1200 8.0 W 1922 0.8	**27**	0647 1.9 1157 7.6 TH 1908 1.6	**12**	0100 8.0 0811 1.0 SA 1313 8.1 2030 0.9	**27**	0031 7.7 0731 1.3 SU 1241 7.8 1950 1.3	**12**	0710 0.7 1208 8.2 SA 1928 0.7	**27**	0636 1.2 1143 7.8 SU 1853 1.1	**12**	0035 7.8 0742 1.4 TU 1255 7.6 1952 1.6	**27**	0014 7.8 0722 1.2 W 1236 7.7 1939 1.4
13	0034 7.9 0744 1.3 TH 1248 8.0 2010 0.9	**28**	0022 7.5 0719 1.9 F 1229 7.6 1940 1.6	**13**	0140 7.8 0846 1.3 SU 1352 7.8 2101 1.3	**28**	0103 7.6 0802 1.4 M 1314 7.7 2020 1.5	**13**	0032 8.0 0744 0.8 SU 1246 8.1 1959 0.9	**28**	0004 7.8 0708 1.2 M 1217 7.8 1925 1.2	**13**	0108 7.5 0809 1.7 W 1329 7.3 2015 2.0	**28**	0053 7.7 0759 1.4 TH 1319 7.5 2015 1.6
14	0122 7.9 0830 1.4 F 1335 7.9 2053 1.1	**29**	0055 7.4 0751 2.0 SA 1302 7.6 2011 1.6	**14**	0217 7.5 0917 1.7 M 1430 7.5 2129 1.8			**14**	0107 7.9 0814 1.2 M 1322 7.8 2026 1.4	**29**	0037 7.8 0741 1.2 TU 1253 7.7 1957 1.4	**14**	0139 7.2 0834 2.1 TH 1404 6.9 2041 2.5	**29**	0135 7.5 0837 1.7 F 1406 7.2 2055 2.1
15	0208 7.7 0912 1.6 SA 1421 7.6 2133 1.5	**30**	0128 7.4 0822 2.0 SU 1336 7.5 2041 1.8	**15**	0252 7.0 0947 2.2 TU 1509 7.0 2158 2.4			**15**	0140 7.6 0841 1.6 TU 1357 7.4 2049 1.9	**30**	0111 7.7 0813 1.5 W 1330 7.5 2029 1.7	**15**	0208 6.8 0903 2.6 F 1444 6.4 2115 3.1	**30**	0223 7.1 0922 2.1 SA 1503 6.8 2146 2.6
		31	0202 7.3 0854 2.1 M 1411 7.3 2112 2.0							**31**	0147 7.4 0847 1.8 TH 1410 7.2 2102 2.1				

Chart Datum: 4·38 metres below IGN Datum

》 **FREE** monthly updates from 《
www.reedsalmanac.co.uk

379

TIDES

TIME ZONE -0100
(French Standard Time)
Subtract 1 hour for UT
For French Summer Time add ONE hour in **non-shaded areas**

FRANCE – LE HAVRE
LAT 49°29′N   LONG 0°07′E
TIMES AND HEIGHTS OF HIGH AND LOW WATERS

YEAR 2005

MAY

#	Time	m	#	Time	m
1 SU	0327 / 1023 / 1625 / ☾2302	6.8 / 2.5 / 6.6 / 2.9	16 M	0326 / 1022 / 1630 / ☾2304	6.2 / 3.1 / 6.1 / 3.5
2 M	0457 / 1149 / 1756	6.6 / 2.6 / 6.6	17 TU	0447 / 1143 / 1751	6.1 / 3.2 / 6.2
3 TU	0039 / 0622 / 1319 / 1911	2.9 / 6.7 / 2.4 / 6.9	18 W	0024 / 0609 / 1256 / 1854	3.3 / 6.2 / 3.0 / 6.5
4 W	0201 / 0732 / 1432 / 2012	2.4 / 7.0 / 2.0 / 7.2	19 TH	0130 / 0711 / 1358 / 1946	3.0 / 6.5 / 2.6 / 6.8
5 TH	0307 / 0829 / 1535 / 2101	2.0 / 7.3 / 1.6 / 7.5	20 F	0227 / 0802 / 1453 / 2031	2.6 / 6.8 / 2.2 / 7.1
6 F	0404 / 0917 / 1628 / 2143	1.6 / 7.5 / 1.4 / 7.7	21 SA	0319 / 0847 / 1543 / 2112	2.2 / 7.1 / 1.9 / 7.4
7 SA	0453 / 1000 / 1712 / 2222	1.4 / 7.7 / 1.3 / 7.7	22 SU	0408 / 0929 / 1630 / 2152	1.9 / 7.4 / 1.7 / 7.6
8 SU	0534 / 1040 / 1749 / ●2259	1.3 / 7.7 / 1.3 / 7.7	23 M	0455 / 1011 / 1716 / ○2232	1.6 / 7.5 / 1.5 / 7.7
9 M	0609 / 1119 / 1822 / 2334	1.3 / 7.7 / 1.4 / 7.7	24 TU	0540 / 1054 / 1800 / 2313	1.3 / 7.6 / 1.4 / 7.8
10 TU	0643 / 1156 / 1853	1.4 / 7.6 / 1.6	25 W	0624 / 1139 / 1843 / 2356	1.2 / 7.7 / 1.4 / 7.8
11 W	0008 / 0714 / 1233 / 1923	7.6 / 1.5 / 7.4 / 1.9	26 TH	0708 / 1225 / 1927	1.2 / 7.6 / 1.5
12 TH	0042 / 0743 / 1309 / 1951	7.4 / 1.9 / 7.2 / 2.2	27 F	0041 / 0752 / 1314 / 2011	7.7 / 1.3 / 7.5 / 1.8
13 F	0115 / 0812 / 1346 / 2021	7.2 / 2.1 / 6.9 / 2.6	28 SA	0130 / 0838 / 1407 / 2100	7.5 / 1.5 / 7.3 / 2.1
14 SA	0150 / 0844 / 1426 / 2057	6.9 / 2.5 / 6.5 / 3.0	29 SU	0223 / 0930 / 1507 / 2157	7.3 / 1.8 / 7.0 / 2.3
15 SU	0231 / 0923 / 1516 / 2147	6.5 / 2.8 / 6.3 / 3.3	30 M	0327 / 1031 / 1618 / ☽2305	7.0 / 2.1 / 6.9 / 2.5
			31 TU	0440 / 1139 / 1729	6.8 / 2.2 / 6.9

JUNE

#	Time	m	#	Time	m
1 W	0016 / 0551 / 1248 / 1836	2.5 / 6.9 / 2.2 / 7.0	16 TH	0451 / 1146 / 1743	6.4 / 2.8 / 6.5
2 TH	0124 / 0658 / 1352 / 1937	2.4 / 7.0 / 2.1 / 7.1	17 F	0020 / 0600 / 1249 / 1845	3.0 / 6.5 / 2.7 / 6.7
3 F	0228 / 0758 / 1453 / 2030	2.2 / 7.1 / 2.0 / 7.3	18 SA	0124 / 0705 / 1353 / 1940	2.8 / 6.7 / 2.5 / 6.9
4 SA	0326 / 0851 / 1547 / 2116	2.0 / 7.2 / 1.9 / 7.4	19 SU	0227 / 0803 / 1456 / 2032	2.5 / 6.9 / 2.3 / 7.2
5 SU	0417 / 0938 / 1634 / 2157	1.9 / 7.3 / 1.9 / 7.5	20 M	0328 / 0856 / 1554 / 2120	2.1 / 7.1 / 2.0 / 7.4
6 M	0500 / 1021 / 1714 / ●2236	1.7 / 7.4 / 1.9 / 7.5	21 TU	0424 / 0948 / 1649 / 2208	1.8 / 7.3 / 1.7 / 7.6
7 TU	0539 / 1101 / 1752 / 2312	1.7 / 7.4 / 1.9 / 7.5	22 W	0518 / 1038 / 1741 / ○2257	1.5 / 7.5 / 1.6 / 7.7
8 W	0616 / 1139 / 1828 / 2347	1.7 / 7.4 / 1.9 / 7.4	23 TH	0610 / 1129 / 1833 / 2346	1.2 / 7.7 / 1.5 / 7.8
9 TH	0651 / 1216 / 1902	1.7 / 7.3 / 2.0	24 F	0702 / 1220 / 1924	1.1 / 7.7 / 1.4
10 F	0023 / 0725 / 1253 / 1936	7.3 / 1.8 / 7.1 / 2.2	25 SA	0035 / 0753 / 1311 / 2015	7.8 / 1.1 / 7.7 / 1.5
11 SA	0058 / 0758 / 1330 / 2010	7.2 / 2.0 / 7.0 / 2.4	26 SU	0126 / 0843 / 1403 / 2106	7.7 / 1.2 / 7.5 / 1.7
12 SU	0134 / 0832 / 1407 / 2045	7.0 / 2.2 / 6.8 / 2.7	27 M	0218 / 0932 / 1456 / 2155	7.5 / 1.4 / 7.4 / 1.9
13 M	0212 / 0909 / 1448 / 2127	6.8 / 2.5 / 6.6 / 2.9	28 TU	0312 / 1020 / 1551 / ☽2246	7.3 / 1.7 / 7.2 / 2.1
14 TU	0255 / 0952 / 1537 / 2218	6.5 / 2.7 / 6.3 / 3.0	29 W	0409 / 1110 / 1649 / 2340	7.1 / 2.0 / 7.0 / 2.4
15 SU (W)	0348 / 1046 / 1636 / ☽2317	6.5 / 2.8 / 6.5 / 3.0	30 TH	0511 / 1205 / 1751	6.9 / 2.3 / 6.9

JULY

#	Time	m	#	Time	m
1 F	0040 / 0617 / 1307 / 1856	2.5 / 6.8 / 2.5 / 6.9	16 SA	0452 / 1145 / 1737	6.6 / 2.8 / 6.6
2 SA	0146 / 0727 / 1411 / 1959	2.5 / 6.8 / 2.5 / 7.0	17 SU	0024 / 0607 / 1258 / 1851	2.9 / 6.5 / 2.8 / 6.7
3 SU	0249 / 0830 / 1510 / 2054	2.4 / 6.9 / 2.5 / 7.1	18 M	0143 / 0725 / 1419 / 1959	2.7 / 6.6 / 2.6 / 6.9
4 M	0344 / 0924 / 1602 / 2140	2.3 / 7.0 / 2.4 / 7.2	19 TU	0258 / 0834 / 1529 / 2059	2.3 / 6.9 / 2.3 / 7.2
5 TU	0433 / 1009 / 1648 / 2221	2.1 / 7.1 / 2.3 / 7.3	20 W	0403 / 0935 / 1631 / 2155	1.9 / 7.3 / 1.9 / 7.5
6 W	0517 / 1050 / ●1731 / 2258	2.0 / 7.2 / 2.1 / 7.4	21 TH	0503 / 1030 / 1731 / ○2247	1.5 / 7.5 / 1.6 / 7.8
7 TH	0557 / 1126 / 1811 / 2332	1.8 / 7.3 / 2.1 / 7.4	22 F	0604 / 1122 / 1830 / 2337	1.1 / 7.8 / 1.3 / 7.9
8 F	0636 / 1201 / 1849	1.8 / 7.3 / 2.0	23 SA	0700 / 1211 / 1923	0.9 / 7.9 / 1.1
9 SA	0007 / 0712 / 1235 / 1925	7.3 / 1.8 / 7.3 / 2.1	24 SU	0026 / 0749 / 1259 / 2010	8.0 / 0.7 / 8.0 / 1.1
10 SU	0041 / 0746 / 1310 / 1958	7.3 / 1.8 / 7.3 / 2.1	25 M	0113 / 0834 / 1345 / 2053	8.0 / 0.8 / 7.9 / 1.3
11 M	0114 / 0818 / 1343 / 2030	7.3 / 1.9 / 7.1 / 2.2	26 TU	0159 / 0914 / 1430 / 2133	7.8 / 1.1 / 7.6 / 1.6
12 TU	0148 / 0850 / 1418 / 2103	7.2 / 2.1 / 7.0 / 2.4	27 W	0244 / 0952 / 1514 / 2213	7.5 / 1.5 / 7.3 / 2.0
13 W	0225 / 0923 / 1456 / 2140	7.0 / 2.3 / 6.9 / 2.6	28 TH	0331 / 1030 / 1602 / ☽2256	7.2 / 2.0 / 7.0 / 2.4
14 TH	0306 / 1000 / 1539 / ☽2224	6.9 / 2.5 / 6.8 / 2.8	29 F	0425 / 1115 / 1658 / 2350	6.9 / 2.5 / 6.7 / 2.8
15 F	0353 / 1047 / 1631 / 2318	6.7 / 2.7 / 6.7 / 2.9	30 SA	0533 / 1215 / 1810	6.7 / 3.0 / 6.5
			31 SU	0103 / 0659 / 1333 / 1932	3.0 / 6.4 / 3.1 / 6.6

AUGUST

#	Time	m	#	Time	m
1 M	0218 / 0817 / 1444 / 2039	2.9 / 6.5 / 3.0 / 6.7	16 TU	0112 / 0707 / 1357 / 1942	3.0 / 6.5 / 3.0 / 6.8
2 TU	0322 / 0914 / 1543 / 2128	2.6 / 6.8 / 2.7 / 7.0	17 W	0242 / 0826 / 1516 / 2050	2.5 / 6.9 / 2.4 / 7.2
3 W	0416 / 0959 / 1635 / 2208	2.3 / 7.0 / 2.4 / 7.2	18 TH	0351 / 0928 / 1623 / 2146	1.9 / 7.3 / 1.8 / 7.6
4 TH	0503 / 1036 / 1721 / 2242	2.0 / 7.2 / 2.2 / 7.4	19 F	0457 / 1021 / 1726 / ○2237	1.4 / 7.7 / 1.4 / 7.9
5 F	0545 / 1108 / ●1801 / 2315	1.8 / 7.3 / 2.0 / 7.5	20 SA	0557 / 1109 / 1822 / 2323	0.9 / 8.0 / 1.1 / 8.1
6 SA	0623 / 1140 / 1837 / 2347	1.6 / 7.4 / 1.9 / 7.5	21 SU	0648 / 1154 / 1909	0.6 / 8.1 / 0.9
7 SU	0657 / 1212 / 1909	1.5 / 7.4 / 1.8	22 M	0008 / 0732 / 1237 / 1951	8.2 / 0.5 / 8.1 / 0.9
8 M	0019 / 0728 / 1244 / 1938	7.5 / 1.6 / 7.4 / 1.8	23 TU	0051 / 0811 / 1319 / 2028	8.2 / 0.7 / 8.0 / 1.1
9 TU	0050 / 0757 / 1315 / 2007	7.5 / 1.6 / 7.4 / 1.9	24 W	0132 / 0845 / 1358 / 2102	8.0 / 1.1 / 7.7 / 1.5
10 W	0121 / 0825 / 1347 / 2037	7.5 / 1.7 / 7.3 / 2.0	25 TH	0212 / 0916 / 1435 / 2134	7.7 / 1.6 / 7.3 / 2.0
11 TH	0154 / 0854 / 1420 / 2108	7.3 / 2.0 / 7.2 / 2.2	26 F	0253 / 0946 / 1515 / ☽2209	7.2 / 2.2 / 6.9 / 2.6
12 F	0229 / 0925 / 1456 / 2144	7.1 / 2.3 / 7.0 / 2.5	27 SA	0341 / 1023 / 1606 / 2257	6.7 / 2.8 / 6.6 / 3.1
13 SA	0310 / 1003 / 1540 / ☽2231	6.8 / 2.6 / 6.8 / 2.8	28 SU	0451 / 1122 / 1725	6.2 / 3.4 / 6.2
14 SU	0404 / 1055 / 1644 / 2337	6.5 / 2.9 / 6.6 / 2.9	29 M	0018 / 0636 / 1300 / 1909	3.4 / 6.0 / 3.6 / 6.2
15 M	0527 / 1214 / 1818	6.5 / 2.9 / 6.5	30 TU	0154 / 0804 / 1427 / 2024	3.3 / 6.3 / 3.3 / 6.5
			31 W	0306 / 0901 / 1532 / 2112	2.7 / 6.7 / 2.8 / 6.9

Chart Datum: 4·38 metres below IGN Datum

)) **FREE** monthly updates from ((
www.reedsalmanac.co.uk

TIME ZONE −0100
(French Standard Time)
Subtract 1 hour for UT
For French Summer Time add
ONE hour in **non-shaded areas**

FRANCE – LE HAVRE
LAT 49°29′N   LONG 0°07′E
TIMES AND HEIGHTS OF HIGH AND LOW WATERS

YEAR 2005

SEPTEMBER		OCTOBER		NOVEMBER		DECEMBER	
Time m	Time m	Time m	Time m	Time m	Time m	Time m	Time m
1 0402 2.4 / 0941 7.0 / TH 1623 2.4 / 2149 7.2	**16** 0343 1.8 / 0918 7.5 / F 1615 1.7 / 2133 7.7	**1** 0415 2.0 / 0940 7.4 / SA 1635 2.0 / 2149 7.5	**16** 0424 1.2 / 0942 7.9 / SU 1650 1.3 / 2157 8.0	**1** 0451 1.7 / 1007 7.7 / TU 1709 1.7 / 2221 7.7	**16** 0525 1.4 / 1037 7.9 / W 1748 1.4 / ○ 2258 7.9	**1** 0453 1.8 / 1010 7.7 / TH 1717 1.7 / ● 2233 7.6	**16** 0536 2.0 / 1058 7.6 / F 1802 1.7 / 2326 7.5
2 0447 2.0 / 1013 7.3 / F 1706 2.0 / 2220 7.4	**17** 0446 1.2 / 1005 7.9 / SA 1713 1.3 / 2219 8.1	**2** 0454 1.7 / 1010 7.6 / SU 1711 1.7 / 2220 7.7	**17** 0513 1.0 / 1023 8.1 / M 1736 1.1 / ○ 2238 8.2	**2** 0526 1.6 / 1040 7.8 / W 1744 1.5 / ● 2256 7.8	**17** 0602 1.5 / 1115 7.9 / TH 1824 1.4 / 2338 7.8	**2** 0536 1.7 / 1049 7.8 / F 1800 1.5 / 2315 7.7	**17** 0614 2.0 / 1135 7.6 / SA 1839 1.7
3 0526 1.7 / 1043 7.5 / SA 1742 1.8 / ● 2250 7.6	**18** 0540 0.8 / 1048 8.1 / SU 1803 0.9 / ○ 2302 8.2	**3** 0530 1.5 / 1041 7.7 / M 1744 1.6 / ● 2252 7.8	**18** 0556 0.9 / 1102 8.1 / TU 1817 1.0 / 2319 8.1	**3** 0601 1.5 / 1114 7.8 / TH 1820 1.5 / 2332 7.8	**18** 0637 1.7 / 1151 7.7 / F 1859 1.6	**3** 0618 1.7 / 1131 7.8 / SA 1843 1.4	**18** 0004 7.5 / 0651 2.1 / SU 1211 7.5 / 1915 1.8
4 0601 1.5 / 1113 7.6 / SU 1815 1.6 / 2321 7.7	**19** 0626 0.6 / 1130 8.2 / M 1846 0.8 / 2344 8.3	**4** 0601 1.4 / 1112 7.8 / TU 1814 1.5 / 2323 7.8	**19** 0634 1.0 / 1140 8.0 / W 1853 1.2 / 2359 8.0	**4** 0637 1.6 / 1148 7.8 / F 1857 1.5	**19** 0017 7.6 / 0709 2.0 / SA 1227 7.6 / 1932 1.8	**4** 0000 7.7 / 0702 1.7 / SU 1215 7.8 / 1927 1.5	**19** 0041 7.4 / 0727 2.2 / M 1247 7.4 / 1950 2.0
5 0633 1.4 / 1144 7.7 / M 1844 1.6 / 2352 7.8	**20** 0705 0.7 / 1210 8.1 / TU 1924 0.9	**5** 0631 1.4 / 1143 7.8 / W 1845 1.5 / 2355 7.8	**20** 0707 1.3 / 1216 7.9 / TH 1926 1.4	**5** 0010 7.7 / 0713 1.7 / SA 1226 7.7 / 1934 1.6	**20** 0056 7.3 / 0741 2.3 / SU 1303 7.3 / 2004 2.2	**5** 0046 7.6 / 0746 1.9 / M 1302 7.6 / 2012 1.6	**20** 0117 7.2 / 0802 2.4 / TU 1322 7.2 / 2024 2.2
6 0701 1.4 / 1214 7.7 / TU 1913 1.6	**21** 0025 8.2 / 0740 0.9 / W 1248 8.0 / 1957 1.2	**6** 0701 1.5 / 1214 7.7 / TH 1917 1.5	**21** 0037 7.8 / 0737 1.7 / F 1251 7.6 / 1956 1.8	**6** 0052 7.5 / 0749 2.0 / SU 1307 7.5 / 2012 1.9	**21** 0135 7.0 / 0814 2.7 / M 1340 7.0 / 2037 2.5	**6** 0137 7.4 / 0833 2.1 / TU 1352 7.4 / 2100 1.9	**21** 0154 7.0 / 0837 2.6 / W 1358 7.0 / 2058 2.5
7 0023 7.7 / 0730 1.4 / W 1245 7.6 / 1942 1.6	**22** 0103 7.9 / 0810 1.3 / TH 1323 7.7 / 2028 1.6	**7** 0029 7.7 / 0733 1.6 / F 1247 7.6 / 1950 1.7	**22** 0115 7.4 / 0805 2.2 / SA 1326 7.3 / 2025 2.2	**7** 0138 7.2 / 0828 2.4 / M 1354 7.2 / 2054 2.3	**22** 0217 6.7 / 0851 3.0 / TU 1422 6.7 / 2117 2.9	**7** 0232 7.2 / 0925 2.4 / W 1450 7.2 / 2151 2.1	**22** 0232 6.8 / 0913 2.9 / TH 1436 6.8 / 2135 2.7
8 0054 7.6 / 0758 1.6 / TH 1315 7.5 / 2012 1.8	**23** 0141 7.5 / 0837 1.9 / F 1357 7.4 / 2056 2.1	**8** 0104 7.5 / 0804 1.9 / SA 1321 7.4 / 2023 2.0	**23** 0153 7.0 / 0833 2.7 / SU 1402 6.9 / 2056 2.7	**8** 0232 6.9 / 0916 2.8 / TU 1452 6.9 / 2149 2.6	**23** 0307 6.4 / 0939 3.4 / W 1515 6.3 / ○ 2211 3.2	**8** 0336 7.0 / 1026 2.6 / TH 1557 7.0 / ○ 2258 2.3	**23** 0314 6.6 / 0955 3.1 / F 1522 6.6 / ○ 2219 2.9
9 0126 7.4 / 0827 1.9 / F 1347 7.3 / 2042 2.1	**24** 0219 7.1 / 0904 2.5 / SA 1433 7.0 / 2127 2.7	**9** 0144 7.2 / 0837 2.3 / SU 1400 7.1 / 2059 2.4	**24** 0238 6.5 / 0908 3.2 / M 1447 6.5 / 2139 3.2	**9** 0343 6.7 / 1022 3.1 / W 1613 6.7 / ○ 2307 2.7	**24** 0416 6.2 / 1046 3.6 / TH 1630 6.2 / 2323 3.3	**9** 0447 6.9 / 1133 2.7 / F 1709 6.9	**24** 0406 6.5 / 1046 3.2 / SA 1618 6.5 / 2312 3.0
10 0200 7.2 / 0856 2.3 / SA 1420 7.1 / 2116 2.4	**25** 0304 6.6 / 0938 3.1 / SU 1521 6.5 / ○ 2211 3.2	**10** 0231 6.8 / 0917 2.8 / M 1452 6.7 / ○ 2148 2.8	**25** 0342 6.2 / 1004 3.7 / TU 1600 6.1 / ○ 2250 3.5	**10** 0516 6.6 / 1155 3.1 / TH 1743 6.7	**25** 0531 6.3 / 1201 3.5 / F 1749 6.2	**10** 0005 2.4 / 0556 7.0 / SA 1243 2.6 / 1818 7.0	**25** 0510 6.5 / 1144 3.2 / SU 1726 6.4
11 0241 6.9 / 0932 2.7 / SU 1505 6.8 / ○ 2201 2.8	**26** 0414 6.1 / 1036 3.7 / M 1643 6.1 / 2332 3.6	**11** 0338 6.5 / 1017 3.2 / TU 1613 6.5 / 2304 3.1	**26** 0517 6.0 / 1141 3.9 / W 1741 6.0	**11** 0040 2.6 / 0634 6.9 / F 1322 2.7 / 1855 7.0	**26** 0035 3.2 / 0636 6.5 / SA 1309 3.2 / 1852 6.5	**11** 0115 2.4 / 0700 7.1 / SU 1353 2.5 / 1924 7.1	**26** 0013 3.1 / 0617 6.6 / M 1248 3.2 / 1838 6.5
12 0340 6.5 / 1026 3.1 / M 1617 6.4 / 2311 3.1	**27** 0605 5.9 / 1227 3.9 / TU 1835 6.0	**12** 0525 6.3 / 1155 3.4 / W 1802 6.5	**27** 0032 3.5 / 0640 6.2 / TH 1315 3.5 / 1900 6.2	**12** 0155 2.2 / 0740 7.3 / SA 1430 2.2 / 1956 7.3	**27** 0139 2.9 / 0728 6.8 / SU 1408 2.9 / 1944 6.8	**12** 0221 2.2 / 0759 7.3 / M 1456 2.2 / 2023 7.3	**27** 0121 3.0 / 0718 6.8 / TU 1359 2.9 / 1942 6.7
13 0518 6.3 / 1153 3.3 / TU 1807 6.4	**28** 0125 3.5 / 0736 6.2 / W 1404 3.5 / 1955 6.3	**13** 0056 2.9 / 0657 6.7 / TH 1345 2.9 / 1921 6.9	**28** 0148 3.1 / 0742 6.5 / F 1419 3.0 / 1955 6.6	**13** 0258 1.8 / 0830 7.6 / SU 1529 1.8 / 2048 7.6	**28** 0234 2.6 / 0813 7.1 / M 1501 2.5 / 2029 7.1	**13** 0320 2.1 / 0850 7.4 / TU 1552 2.0 / 2116 7.3	**28** 0231 2.7 / 0812 7.0 / W 1505 2.5 / 2038 7.0
14 0100 3.1 / 0705 6.5 / W 1351 2.9 / 1935 6.8	**29** 0238 2.9 / 0833 6.6 / TH 1505 2.9 / 2043 6.7	**14** 0221 2.3 / 0805 7.2 / F 1456 2.2 / 2023 7.4	**29** 0244 2.6 / 0825 6.9 / SA 1509 2.5 / 2036 7.0	**14** 0354 1.6 / 0915 7.8 / M 1621 1.5 / 2134 7.8	**29** 0325 2.3 / 0853 7.3 / TU 1549 2.2 / 2111 7.3	**14** 0412 2.0 / 0937 7.5 / W 1640 1.9 / 2203 7.5	**29** 0333 2.4 / 0901 7.3 / TH 1603 2.1 / 2129 7.3
15 0233 2.5 / 0820 7.0 / TH 1510 2.4 / 2041 7.3	**30** 0330 2.2 / 0910 7.0 / F 1553 2.4 / 2118 7.1	**15** 0326 1.7 / 0857 7.7 / SA 1556 1.7 / 2112 7.8	**30** 0331 2.2 / 0900 7.3 / SU 1553 2.1 / ○ 2112 7.4	**15** 0442 1.5 / 0957 7.9 / TU 1707 1.4 / 2217 7.9	**30** 0410 2.0 / 0932 7.5 / W 1633 1.9 / 2152 7.5	**15** 0456 2.0 / 1019 7.6 / TH 1723 1.8 / ○ 2246 7.6	**30** 0427 2.1 / 0948 7.5 / F 1656 1.8 / 2218 7.5
			31 0413 1.9 / 0933 7.6 / M 1633 1.9 / 2147 7.6				**31** 0519 1.7 / 1035 7.7 / SA 1747 1.5 / ● 2306 7.6

Chart Datum: 4·38 metres below IGN Datum

》 **FREE** monthly updates from 《
www.reedsalmanac.co.uk

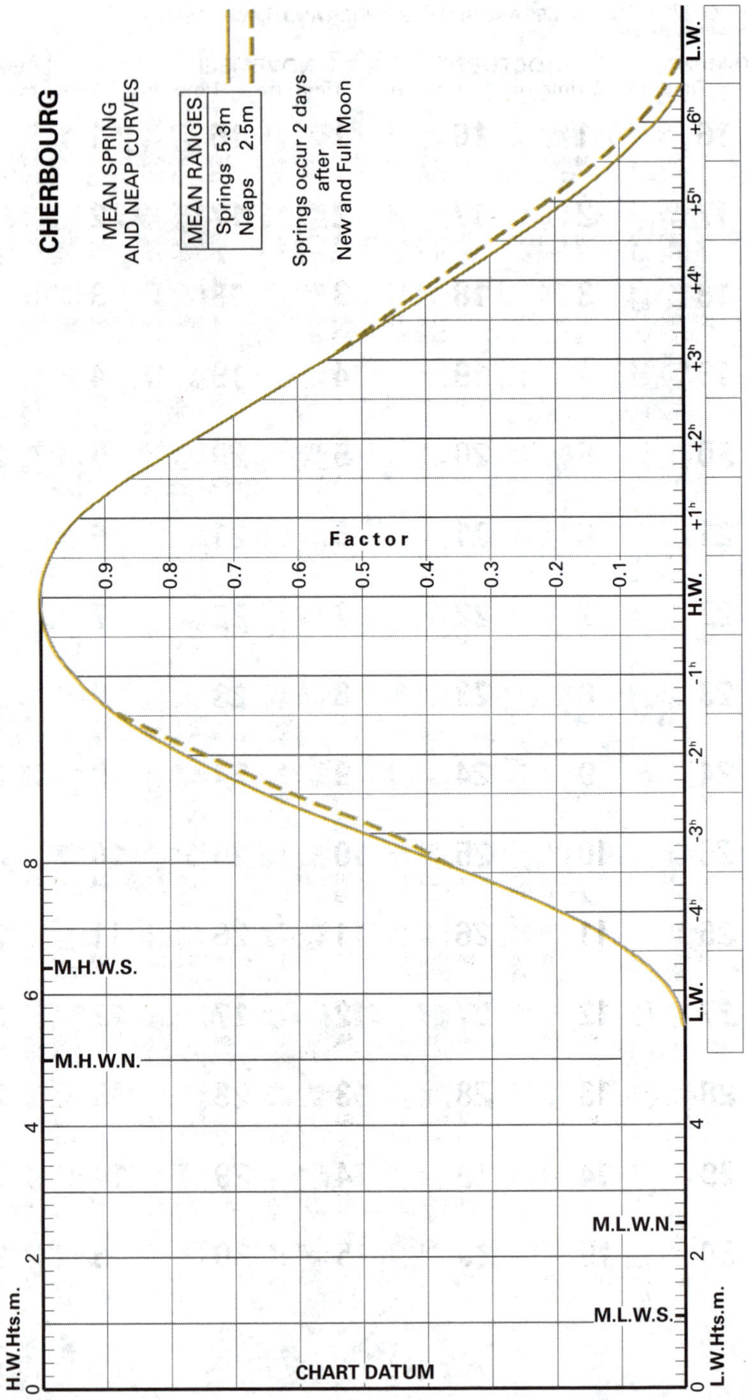
CHERBOURG
MEAN SPRING AND NEAP CURVES
MEAN RANGES
Springs 5.3m
Neaps 2.5m
Springs occur 2 days after New and Full Moon
Factor
0.9
0.8
0.7
0.6
0.5
0.4
0.3
0.2
0.1
L.W.
-4h
-3h
-2h
-1h
H.W.
+1h
+2h
+3h
+4h
+5h
+6h
L.W.
H.W.Hts.m.
0
2
4
6
8
M.H.W.S.
M.H.W.N.
CHART DATUM
M.L.W.N.
M.L.W.S.
L.W.Hts.m.
0
2
4

TIME ZONE -0100
(French Standard Time)
Subtract 1 hour for UT
For French Summer Time add
ONE hour in **non-shaded areas**

FRANCE – CHERBOURG
LAT 49°39′N   LONG 1°38′W
TIMES AND HEIGHTS OF HIGH AND LOW WATERS

YEAR 2005

JANUARY		FEBRUARY		MARCH		APRIL	
Time m	Time m	Time m	Time m	Time m	Time m	Time m	Time m
1 0628 2.2 / 1159 5.6 / SA 1852 2.0	**16** 0052 5.8 / 0738 1.9 / SU 1308 5.9 / 2000 1.7	**1** 0036 5.5 / 0721 2.0 / TU 1246 5.5 / 1941 2.0	**16** 0126 5.2 / 0820 2.4 / W 1351 5.0 / ☽ 2038 2.6	**1** 0617 1.5 / 1146 6.0 / TU 1835 1.5	**16** 0008 5.7 / 0658 1.9 / W 1227 5.4 / 1910 2.2	**1** 0023 5.6 / 0720 1.9 / F 1251 5.2 / 1942 2.3	**16** 0046 4.9 / 0751 2.6 / SA 1331 4.5 / ☽ 2015 3.0
2 0030 5.3 / 0708 2.3 / SU 1239 5.4 / 1933 2.1	**17** 0136 5.5 / 0825 2.2 / M 1355 5.5 / ☽ 2047 2.1	**2** 0115 5.3 / 0806 2.3 / W 1331 5.3 / ☽ 2030 2.2	**17** 0217 4.9 / 0918 2.8 / TH 1459 4.6 / 2144 3.0	**2** 0006 5.8 / 0653 1.7 / W 1218 5.7 / 1911 1.8	**17** 0038 5.3 / 0735 2.3 / TH 1304 4.9 / ☽ 1948 2.7	**2** 0118 5.2 / 0822 2.3 / SA 1404 4.8 / ☽ 2058 2.7	**17** 0153 4.6 / 0906 2.9 / SU 1529 4.4 / 2154 3.2
3 0115 5.2 / 0755 2.5 / M 1326 5.2 / ☽ 2021 2.3	**18** 0226 5.2 / 0919 2.5 / TU 1450 5.1 / 2143 2.5	**3** 0209 5.1 / 0906 2.5 / TH 1434 5.0 / 2137 2.5	**18** 0343 4.6 / 1050 3.0 / F 1648 4.5 / 2326 3.1	**3** 0040 5.5 / 0736 2.0 / TH 1300 5.3 / ☽ 1958 2.2	**18** 0119 4.9 / 0824 2.8 / F 1403 4.5 / 2048 3.1	**3** 0247 4.9 / 0952 2.5 / SU 1605 4.7 / 2245 2.8	**18** 0355 4.5 / 1053 2.9 / M 1709 4.5 / 2334 3.0
4 0207 5.1 / 0850 2.6 / TU 1422 5.1 / 2120 2.4	**19** 0328 5.0 / 1026 2.7 / W 1600 4.9 / 2252 2.7	**4** 0324 5.0 / 1024 2.6 / F 1604 4.9 / 2303 2.5	**19** 0525 4.7 / 1225 2.9 / SA 1820 4.7	**4** 0131 5.2 / 0833 2.4 / F 1403 4.9 / 2104 2.6	**19** 0237 4.5 / 0952 3.0 / SA 1618 4.3 / 2243 3.2	**4** 0441 4.9 / 1136 2.3 / M 1742 5.1	**19** 0519 4.7 / 1209 2.5 / TU 1804 4.9
5 0310 5.1 / 0957 2.6 / W 1530 5.1 / 2229 2.4	**20** 0442 4.9 / 1142 2.7 / TH 1720 4.8	**5** 0457 5.1 / 1152 2.4 / SA 1740 5.1	**20** 0056 2.8 / 0636 5.0 / SU 1330 2.4 / 1915 5.0	**5** 0250 4.9 / 0956 2.6 / SA 1553 4.7 / 2243 2.8	**20** 0451 4.5 / 1149 2.9 / SU 1758 4.6	**5** 0021 2.4 / 0601 5.4 / TU 1251 1.8 / 1844 5.5	**20** 0038 2.6 / 0613 5.0 / W 1301 2.1 / 1845 5.3
6 0420 5.2 / 1110 2.5 / TH 1644 5.2 / 2342 2.3	**21** 0007 2.7 / 0554 5.0 / F 1251 2.5 / 1832 5.0	**6** 0032 2.3 / 0616 5.4 / SU 1309 2.0 / 1855 5.5	**21** 0152 2.5 / 0725 5.3 / M 1417 2.1 / 1955 5.4	**6** 0444 4.9 / 1140 2.4 / SU 1743 5.0	**21** 0030 2.9 / 0609 4.8 / M 1301 2.5 / 1849 5.0	**6** 0125 1.9 / 0700 5.8 / W 1349 1.3 / 1934 6.0	**21** 0122 2.2 / 0656 5.4 / TH 1342 1.8 / 1923 5.6
7 0529 5.4 / 1220 2.2 / F 1756 5.4	**22** 0113 2.5 / 0653 5.3 / SA 1347 2.3 / 1927 5.2	**7** 0142 1.9 / 0720 5.8 / M 1413 1.5 / 1956 5.9	**22** 0235 2.1 / 0805 5.6 / TU 1456 1.7 / 2030 5.7	**7** 0027 2.5 / 0611 5.3 / M 1303 1.9 / 1855 5.4	**22** 0126 2.5 / 0658 5.2 / TU 1348 2.1 / 1927 5.3	**7** 0216 1.4 / 0750 6.2 / TH 1437 1.0 / 2018 6.3	**22** 0201 1.8 / 0735 5.8 / F 1419 1.5 / 1959 5.9
8 0052 2.0 / 0631 5.7 / SA 1323 1.8 / 1901 5.7	**23** 0205 2.3 / 0741 5.5 / SU 1433 2.0 / 2010 5.5	**8** 0242 1.5 / 0816 6.2 / TU 1509 1.0 / ● 2050 6.2	**23** 0310 1.8 / 0840 5.9 / W 1530 1.5 / 2104 5.9	**8** 0138 2.0 / 0715 5.8 / TU 1405 1.4 / 1951 5.9	**23** 0207 2.1 / 0737 5.6 / W 1426 1.7 / 2002 5.7	**8** 0301 1.1 / 0835 6.5 / F 1520 0.8 / ● 2058 6.4	**23** 0238 1.5 / 0813 6.0 / SA 1455 1.2 / 2034 6.2
9 0152 1.7 / 0728 6.0 / SU 1421 1.5 / 1959 6.0	**24** 0248 2.1 / 0821 5.7 / M 1512 1.8 / 2048 5.7	**9** 0334 1.2 / 0908 6.6 / W 1559 0.7 / 2139 6.5	**24** 0343 1.6 / 0913 6.1 / TH 1602 1.3 / ○ 2136 6.0	**9** 0234 1.5 / 0809 6.3 / W 1457 0.9 / 2039 6.3	**24** 0242 1.7 / 0813 5.9 / TH 1500 1.4 / 2035 6.0	**9** 0341 0.9 / 0915 6.6 / SA 1558 0.7 / 2134 6.5	**24** 0314 1.2 / 0849 6.2 / SU 1531 1.0 / ○ 2109 6.3
10 0247 1.5 / 0821 6.3 / M 1515 1.1 / ● 2054 6.2	**25** 0326 1.9 / 0857 5.9 / TU 1548 1.6 / ○ 2122 5.8	**10** 0422 1.0 / 0956 6.8 / TH 1645 0.5 / 2224 6.5	**25** 0414 1.4 / 0944 6.2 / F 1633 1.1 / 2206 6.1	**10** 0322 1.1 / 0856 6.6 / TH 1543 0.6 / ● 2123 6.5	**25** 0314 1.5 / 0847 6.1 / F 1532 1.2 / ○ 2108 6.1	**10** 0418 0.9 / 0951 6.6 / SU 1633 0.8 / 2208 6.4	**25** 0350 1.0 / 0925 6.3 / M 1607 1.0 / 2143 6.4
11 0340 1.3 / 0913 6.5 / TU 1607 0.9 / 2146 6.4	**26** 0400 1.8 / 0930 6.0 / W 1622 1.5 / 2155 5.9	**11** 0506 0.9 / 1040 6.8 / F 1728 0.6 / 2305 6.5	**26** 0444 1.3 / 1015 6.2 / SA 1703 1.1 / 2236 6.1	**11** 0405 0.8 / 0939 6.8 / F 1625 0.5 / 2202 6.6	**26** 0346 1.2 / 0919 6.2 / SA 1603 1.0 / 2140 6.3	**11** 0452 1.0 / 1025 6.4 / M 1705 1.1 / 2238 6.3	**26** 0427 1.0 / 1001 6.3 / TU 1643 1.0 / 2218 6.3
12 0431 1.2 / 1004 6.7 / W 1657 0.8 / 2236 6.4	**27** 0433 1.7 / 1002 6.1 / TH 1654 1.4 / 2227 5.9	**12** 0547 1.0 / 1121 6.7 / SA 1807 0.8 / 2343 6.3	**27** 0515 1.2 / 1046 6.2 / SU 1732 1.1 / 2306 6.1	**12** 0444 0.8 / 1018 6.8 / SA 1702 0.6 / 2238 6.5	**27** 0418 1.1 / 0951 6.4 / SU 1635 0.9 / 2210 6.3	**12** 0524 1.2 / 1057 6.1 / TU 1735 1.4 / 2307 6.0	**27** 0504 1.0 / 1038 6.2 / W 1720 1.2 / 2255 6.2
13 0520 1.2 / 1053 6.6 / TH 1745 0.8 / 2324 6.3	**28** 0505 1.6 / 1034 6.1 / F 1726 1.4 / 2258 5.9	**13** 0625 1.2 / 1157 6.4 / SU 1843 1.1	**28** 0545 1.3 / 1116 6.1 / M 1803 1.2 / 2336 6.0	**13** 0520 0.9 / 1054 6.6 / SU 1737 0.8 / 2311 6.3	**28** 0450 1.0 / 1023 6.4 / M 1706 1.0 / 2241 6.3	**13** 0555 1.5 / 1127 5.8 / W 1805 1.8 / 2335 5.7	**28** 0543 1.2 / 1118 6.0 / TH 1800 1.6 / 2335 5.9
14 0607 1.3 / 1139 6.5 / F 1831 1.0	**29** 0536 1.6 / 1106 6.1 / SA 1757 1.4 / 2331 5.8	**14** 0016 6.0 / 0701 1.6 / M 1232 6.0 / 1918 1.6		**14** 0554 1.1 / 1126 6.3 / M 1808 1.2 / 2341 6.1	**29** 0523 1.1 / 1055 6.3 / TU 1738 1.2 / 2312 6.1	**14** 0627 1.9 / 1159 5.4 / TH 1837 2.2	**29** 0626 1.5 / 1204 5.6 / F 1846 2.0
15 0010 6.1 / 0652 1.5 / SA 1224 6.2 / 1916 1.3	**30** 0608 1.7 / 1139 5.9 / SU 1828 1.5	**15** 0049 5.6 / 0738 2.0 / TU 1307 5.5 / 1954 2.1		**15** 0626 1.3 / 1157 5.9 / TU 1838 1.7	**30** 0556 1.3 / 1127 6.0 / W 1812 1.5 / 2345 5.9	**15** 0005 5.3 / 0704 2.3 / F 1235 4.9 / 1917 2.7	**30** 0022 5.6 / 0719 1.8 / SA 1259 5.2 / 1946 2.4
	31 0004 5.7 / 0642 1.8 / M 1211 5.8 / 1902 1.7				**31** 0634 1.6 / 1204 5.7 / TH 1852 1.9		

Chart Datum: 3·29 metres below IGN Datum
》》 **FREE** monthly updates from 《《
www.reedsalmanac.co.uk

Chapter 5

TIDES

TIME ZONE -0100
(French Standard Time)
Subtract 1 hour for UT
For French Summer Time add
ONE hour in non-shaded areas

FRANCE – CHERBOURG
LAT 49°39′N LONG 1°38′W
TIMES AND HEIGHTS OF HIGH AND LOW WATERS

YEAR 2005

MAY

	Time	m		Time	m
1 SU ☾	0123 0827 1419 2106	5.2 2.1 4.9 2.6	**16** M	0128 0831 1430 2105	4.8 2.6 4.6 3.0
2 M	0250 0953 1601 2239	5.0 2.2 4.9 2.5	**17** TU	0247 0948 1555 2226	4.6 2.7 4.6 2.9
3 TU	0424 1119 1720 2356	5.1 2.0 5.2 2.2	**18** W	0407 1101 1701 2332	4.7 2.5 4.9 2.6
4 W	0536 1226 1818	5.4 1.7 5.6	**19** TH	0510 1200 1751	5.0 2.2 5.2
5 TH	0059 0633 1322 1906	1.8 5.8 1.4 5.9	**20** F	0027 0602 1250 1836	2.3 5.3 1.9 5.5
6 F	0149 0723 1409 1949	1.5 6.0 1.2 6.1	**21** SA	0114 0650 1335 1917	1.9 5.6 1.6 5.8
7 SA	0234 0808 1451 2029	1.3 6.2 1.1 6.2	**22** SU	0159 0734 1418 1958	1.6 5.8 1.4 6.0
8 SU ●	0314 0848 1529 2105	1.2 6.2 1.1 6.2	**23** M	0242 0818 1500 2038	1.3 6.0 1.2 6.2
9 M	0351 0925 1603 2138	1.2 6.2 1.3 6.2	**24** TU	0325 0900 1542 2119	1.2 6.2 1.2 6.3
10 TU	0426 1000 1636 2210	1.2 6.1 1.4 6.1	**25** W	0407 0944 1625 2201	1.0 6.2 1.2 6.3
11 W	0459 1034 1709 2241	1.4 5.9 1.7 5.9	**26** TH	0451 1029 1709 2245	1.0 6.1 1.4 6.2
12 TH	0533 1107 1742 2313	1.6 5.6 2.0 5.7	**27** F	0537 1116 1757 2333	1.1 6.0 1.6 6.0
13 F	0607 1142 1817 2348	1.9 5.3 2.3 5.4	**28** SA	0628 1207 1850	1.3 5.7 1.9
14 SA	0645 1222 1858	2.1 5.0 2.6	**29** SU	0025 0724 1306 1952	5.8 1.6 5.4 2.1
15 SU	0030 0731 1314 1952	5.1 2.4 4.7 2.8	**30** M ☾	0126 0827 1416 2102	5.6 1.8 5.2 2.3
			31 TU	0238 0937 1532 2215	5.3 1.9 5.2 2.3

JUNE

	Time	m		Time	m
1 W	0352 1047 1641 2322	5.3 1.9 5.3 2.2	**16** TH	0255 0951 1545 2225	4.9 2.4 4.9 2.6
2 TH	0459 1151 1740	5.4 1.8 5.4	**17** F	0359 1055 1646 2328	4.9 2.3 5.1 2.4
3 F	0025 0559 1247 1832	2.0 5.5 1.7 5.6	**18** SA	0502 1156 1743	5.1 2.1 5.3
4 SA	0119 0653 1337 1919	1.8 5.7 1.5 5.8	**19** SU	0029 0602 1252 1836	2.1 5.3 1.9 5.6
5 SU	0207 0742 1422 2001	1.7 5.8 1.6 5.9	**20** M	0123 0659 1345 1926	1.8 5.6 1.7 5.9
6 M	0250 0826 1503 ● 2040	1.6 5.8 1.6 6.0	**21** TU	0215 0752 1436 2014	1.5 5.8 1.5 6.1
7 TU	0330 0906 1540 2116	1.5 5.8 1.7 6.0	**22** W	0305 0844 1525 ○ 2102	1.3 6.0 1.4 6.3
8 W	0407 0943 1616 2150	1.5 5.8 1.7 5.9	**23** TH	0355 0934 1615 2151	1.1 6.1 1.3 6.4
9 TH	0442 1019 1652 2225	1.5 5.7 1.8 5.8	**24** F	0445 1025 1705 2240	1.0 6.2 1.3 6.4
10 F	0518 1054 1727 2300	1.6 5.6 2.0 5.7	**25** SA	0535 1115 1756 2331	0.9 6.1 1.4 6.2
11 SA	0554 1130 1804 2337	1.8 5.4 2.2 5.5	**26** SU	0626 1206 1848	1.0 6.0 1.6
12 SU	0631 1208 1843	1.9 5.2 2.3	**27** M	0022 0717 1258 1942	6.1 1.2 5.7 1.8
13 M	0016 0711 1251 1927	5.3 2.1 5.0 2.5	**28** TU ☾	0114 0810 1352 2038	5.9 1.5 5.5 2.0
14 TU	0101 0756 1342 2019	5.1 2.3 4.9 2.6	**29** W	0209 0906 1449 2138	5.6 1.7 5.3 2.2
15 W ☾	0154 0850 1441 ● 2120	5.0 2.4 4.8 2.7	**30** TH	0309 1005 1551 2242	5.4 2.0 5.2 2.3

JULY

	Time	m		Time	m
1 F	0414 1108 1656 2347	5.2 2.1 5.2 2.3	**16** SA	0254 0953 1540 2233	5.0 2.4 5.0 2.5
2 SA	0522 1211 1758	5.2 2.2 5.3	**17** SU	0405 1106 1653 2346	5.0 2.4 5.1 2.4
3 SU	0050 0627 1309 1853	2.2 5.2 2.2 5.5	**18** M	0524 1218 1803	5.1 2.2 5.4
4 M	0144 0724 1400 1941	2.0 5.4 2.1 5.6	**19** TU	0056 0636 1322 1904	2.0 5.4 1.8 5.7
5 TU	0232 0812 1445 2024	1.9 5.5 2.0 5.7	**20** W	0157 0739 1421 1959	1.7 5.7 1.7 6.0
6 W	0315 0854 1526 ● 2102	1.7 5.6 1.9 5.8	**21** TH	0253 0835 1515 ○ 2052	1.3 6.0 1.4 6.3
7 TH	0354 0932 1604 2138	1.6 5.7 1.9 5.9	**22** F	0347 0929 1608 2144	1.0 6.2 1.2 6.5
8 F	0430 1007 1640 2213	1.6 5.7 1.8 5.9	**23** SA	0437 1019 1657 2233	0.8 6.3 1.1 6.6
9 SA	0505 1041 1714 2246	1.6 5.7 1.9 5.9	**24** SU	0526 1107 1745 2321	0.7 6.4 1.1 6.6
10 SU	0539 1114 1748 2320	1.6 5.6 1.9 5.8	**25** M	0612 1152 1831	0.7 6.2 1.2
11 M	0612 1148 1821 2354	1.7 5.5 2.0 5.6	**26** TU	0006 0656 1234 1917	6.4 1.0 6.0 1.5
12 TU	0645 1223 1857	1.8 5.3 2.1	**27** W	0049 0740 1316 2003	6.1 1.4 5.7 1.8
13 W	0030 0720 1300 1937	5.5 2.0 5.2 2.3	**28** TH	0133 0825 1400 ☾ 2054	5.7 1.8 5.4 2.2
14 TH	0109 0801 1343 ○ 2025	5.2 2.2 5.1 2.4	**29** F	0223 0916 1454 2156	5.3 2.2 5.1 2.5
15 F	0156 0851 1435 2123	5.0 2.3 5.0 2.5	**30** SA	0328 1021 1607 2311	4.9 2.6 4.9 2.6
			31 SU	0451 1137 1728	4.8 2.7 5.0

AUGUST

	Time	m		Time	m
1 M	0027 0613 1249 1837	2.5 4.9 2.6 5.2	**16** TU	0507 1157 1746	4.9 2.5 5.2
2 TU	0130 0716 1347 1929	2.3 5.1 2.4 5.4	**17** W	0041 0630 1311 1853	2.2 5.3 2.2 5.6
3 W	0221 0803 1435 2012	2.0 5.4 2.1 5.6	**18** TH	0147 0733 1412 1950	1.7 5.7 1.7 6.1
4 TH	0303 0843 1515 2049	1.8 5.6 1.9 5.8	**19** F	0244 0828 1506 ○ 2043	1.3 6.1 1.3 6.5
5 F ●	0340 0918 1551 2124	1.6 5.7 1.7 6.0	**20** SA	0335 0918 1555 2132	0.8 6.4 1.0 6.7
6 SA	0414 0950 1624 2156	1.4 5.8 1.7 6.0	**21** SU	0422 1004 1641 2217	0.6 6.5 0.9 6.8
7 SU	0446 1021 1654 2226	1.4 5.9 1.6 6.1	**22** M	0506 1046 1724 2300	0.5 6.4 0.9 6.7
8 M	0516 1050 1724 2256	1.4 5.9 1.7 6.0	**23** TU	0547 1125 1804 2340	0.6 6.4 1.0 6.4
9 TU	0545 1120 1754 2326	1.4 5.8 1.7 5.9	**24** W	0625 1201 1843	1.0 6.1 1.4
10 W	0614 1150 1825 2357	1.5 5.7 1.8 5.7	**25** TH	0016 0701 1235 1922	6.1 1.5 5.8 1.8
11 TH	0644 1221 1859	1.7 5.5 2.0	**26** F	0053 0739 1310 2006	5.6 1.9 5.4 2.2
12 F	0028 0716 1254 1940	5.5 1.9 5.4 2.2	**27** SA	0137 0823 1357 ☾ 2104	5.1 2.4 5.0 2.6
13 SA	0107 0802 1338 ☾ 2033	5.3 2.1 5.1 2.5	**28** SU	0242 0928 1516 2234	4.7 3.0 4.7 3.0
14 SU	0202 0901 1443 2146	5.0 2.5 5.0 2.6	**29** M	0431 1110 1707	4.5 3.1 4.7
15 M	0323 1021 1616 2317	4.9 2.7 4.9 2.6	**30** TU	0007 0608 1236 1825	2.8 4.7 2.8 5.0
			31 W	0116 0705 1335 1914	2.4 5.0 2.4 5.4

Chart Datum: 3·29 metres below IGN Datum

》 **FREE** monthly updates from 《
www.reedsalmanac.co.uk

TIME ZONE -0100
(French Standard Time)
Subtract 1 hour for UT
For French Summer Time add
ONE hour in **non-shaded areas**

FRANCE – CHERBOURG
LAT 49°39′N   LONG 1°38′W
TIMES AND HEIGHTS OF HIGH AND LOW WATERS

YEAR 2005

SEPTEMBER

Time	m	Time	m
1 0204 0746 1419 1953	2.1 5.4 2.1 5.7	**16** 0136 0724 1401 1938	1.6 5.9 1.6 6.2
2 0243 0820 1456 2028	1.8 5.7 1.9 5.9	**17** 0229 0813 1450 2026	1.1 6.3 1.2 6.6
3 0317 0853 SA 1528 ● 2100	1.5 5.9 1.7 6.1	**18** 0316 0858 SU 1536 ○ 2112	0.7 6.6 0.9 6.9
4 0349 0920 SU 1558 2131	1.3 6.1 1.5 6.2	**19** 0359 0939 M 1618 2154	0.6 6.7 0.8 6.9
5 0418 0953 M 1627 2200	1.2 6.1 1.4 6.3	**20** 0439 1017 TU 1657 2233	0.6 6.6 0.9 6.8
6 0447 1021 TU 1656 2228	1.2 6.1 1.4 6.2	**21** 0516 1052 W 1733 2309	0.8 6.5 1.1 6.5
7 0514 1049 W 1725 2256	1.3 6.1 1.5 6.1	**22** 0550 1123 TH 1808 2343	1.2 6.2 1.5 6.1
8 0542 1116 TH 1755 2325	1.4 5.9 1.6 5.9	**23** 0622 1153 F 1843	1.7 5.8 1.9
9 0612 1144 F 1827 2356	1.6 5.8 1.8 5.6	**24** 0015 0656 SA 1225 1921	5.5 2.2 5.4 2.4
10 0645 1214 SA 1906	2.0 5.5 2.1	**25** 0055 0736 SU 1307 ◐ 2014	5.0 2.8 5.0 2.8
11 0033 0727 SU 1257 ◐ 1958	5.3 2.3 5.2 2.5	**26** 0200 0839 M 1425 2150	4.6 3.2 4.6 3.1
12 0131 0828 M 1407 2117	4.9 2.7 4.9 2.7	**27** 0411 1041 TU 1639 2340	4.4 3.3 4.6 2.9
13 0308 1005 TU 1602 2303	4.7 2.9 4.8 2.6	**28** 0548 1213 W 1758	4.7 3.0 4.9
14 0511 1151 W 1739	4.9 2.7 5.2	**29** 0048 0638 TH 1308 1844	2.5 5.1 2.6 5.3
15 0034 0628 TH 1304 1844	2.1 5.3 2.2 5.7	**30** 0133 0714 F 1349 1921	2.1 5.4 2.2 5.6

OCTOBER

Time	m	Time	m
1 0210 0747 SA 1424 1956	1.8 5.8 1.9 5.9	**16** 0206 0749 SU 1428 2003	1.1 6.3 1.2 6.6
2 0244 0820 SU 1456 2028	1.5 6.0 1.6 6.2	**17** 0251 0831 M 1511 ○ 2046	0.9 6.5 1.0 6.8
3 0314 0851 M 1526 ● 2100	1.3 6.2 1.4 6.3	**18** 0332 0910 TU 1551 2126	0.8 6.6 0.9 6.7
4 0345 0920 TU 1556 2130	1.2 6.3 1.3 6.3	**19** 0409 0945 W 1629 2204	0.9 6.6 1.0 6.6
5 0415 0949 W 1627 2159	1.2 6.3 1.3 6.3	**20** 0444 1018 TH 1704 2239	1.2 6.4 1.3 6.3
6 0444 1017 TH 1658 2229	1.3 6.2 1.3 6.2	**21** 0517 1048 F 1738 2312	1.5 6.2 1.6 5.9
7 0514 1046 F 1730 2301	1.4 6.1 1.5 6.0	**22** 0550 1119 SA 1812 2347	1.9 5.8 2.0 5.5
8 0546 1117 SA 1805 2337	1.7 5.9 1.8 5.7	**23** 0624 1152 SU 1850	2.4 5.4 2.4
9 0623 1153 SU 1847	2.1 5.6 2.1	**24** 0026 0704 M 1234 1939	5.0 2.8 5.0 2.8
10 0020 0709 M 1243 ◐ 1944	5.3 2.5 5.3 2.5	**25** 0127 0804 TU 1344 2058	4.6 3.2 4.7 3.0
11 0127 0818 TU 1402 2110	4.9 2.9 4.9 2.7	**26** 0321 0948 W 1541 2245	4.5 3.3 4.6 3.0
12 0319 1005 W 1559 2257	4.7 3.0 4.9 2.6	**27** 0455 1124 TH 1704 2356	4.7 3.1 4.8 2.6
13 0508 1143 TH 1726	5.0 2.6 5.3	**28** 0550 1222 F 1757	5.1 2.7 5.1
14 0020 0613 F 1249 1826	2.0 5.5 2.1 5.8	**29** 0047 0630 SA 1306 1838	2.3 5.4 2.3 5.5
15 0117 0704 SA 1341 1917	1.5 6.0 1.6 6.3	**30** 0127 0706 SU 1343 1915	2.0 5.7 2.0 5.8
		31 0202 0740 M 1418 1951	1.7 6.0 1.7 6.1

NOVEMBER

Time	m	Time	m
1 0237 0814 TU 1452 2026	1.5 6.2 1.5 6.2	**16** 0305 0841 W 1527 ○ 2102	1.3 6.4 1.3 6.4
2 0311 0846 W 1527 ● 2100	1.3 6.3 1.3 6.3	**17** 0343 0916 TH 1605 2140	1.4 6.4 1.3 6.2
3 0345 0918 TH 1602 2134	1.3 6.4 1.3 6.3	**18** 0418 0950 F 1641 2216	1.5 6.3 1.5 6.0
4 0419 0951 F 1638 2210	1.4 6.3 1.3 6.2	**19** 0453 1024 SA 1716 2252	1.8 6.1 1.7 5.8
5 0454 1026 SA 1715 2249	1.5 6.2 1.5 6.0	**20** 0528 1058 SU 1752 2329	2.1 5.8 1.9 5.5
6 0532 1105 SU 1756 2333	1.8 6.0 1.7 5.7	**21** 0604 1134 M 1830	2.4 5.5 2.2
7 0616 1150 M 1845	2.1 5.7 2.0	**22** 0009 0645 TU 1216 1915	5.2 2.7 5.2 2.5
8 0026 0710 TU 1247 1947	5.4 2.5 5.4 2.3	**23** 0100 0736 W 1311 ◐ 2012	4.9 2.9 4.9 2.8
9 0137 0824 W 1405 2109	5.1 2.8 5.2 2.4	**24** 0211 0844 TH 1425 2126	4.7 3.1 4.8 2.8
10 0315 0957 TH 1541 2238	5.0 2.8 5.2 2.3	**25** 0332 1004 F 1543 2241	4.7 3.1 4.8 2.7
11 0442 1120 F 1658 2349	5.2 2.5 5.5 2.0	**26** 0439 1114 SA 1648 2342	4.9 2.8 5.0 2.5
12 0544 1221 SA 1758	5.6 2.1 5.8	**27** 0531 1209 SU 1742	5.2 2.5 5.2
13 0050 0635 SU 1316 1850	1.6 5.9 1.7 6.1	**28** 0033 0616 M 1256 1829	2.2 5.5 2.2 5.5
14 0139 0720 M 1404 1937	1.4 6.2 1.4 6.3	**29** 0118 0657 TU 1339 1913	2.0 5.8 1.9 5.7
15 0224 0802 TU 1447 2021	1.3 6.3 1.3 6.4	**30** 0159 0737 W 1420 1955	1.7 6.0 1.6 6.0

DECEMBER

Time	m	Time	m
1 0240 0815 TH 1501 ● 2036	1.5 6.2 1.4 6.2	**16** 0324 0858 F 1549 2126	1.7 6.1 1.5 5.9
2 0321 0854 F 1543 2118	1.5 6.3 1.3 6.2	**17** 0403 0934 SA 1627 2203	1.8 6.1 1.6 5.8
3 0402 0934 SA 1625 2201	1.5 6.4 1.3 6.2	**18** 0439 1010 SU 1703 2239	1.9 6.0 1.6 5.8
4 0445 1017 SU 1710 2246	1.5 6.3 1.3 6.1	**19** 0515 1046 M 1739 2315	2.0 5.9 1.8 5.6
5 0530 1102 M 1757 2336	1.7 6.2 1.4 5.9	**20** 0551 1122 TU 1815 2352	2.2 5.7 1.9 5.4
6 0619 1152 TU 1849	1.9 6.0 1.6	**21** 0628 1159 W 1852	2.3 5.5 2.1
7 0030 0715 W 1249 1947	5.6 2.2 5.7 1.9	**22** 0031 0707 TH 1238 1932	5.2 2.5 5.3 2.3
8 0133 0819 TH 1354 ◐ 2053	5.4 2.4 5.5 2.0	**23** 0116 0752 F 1325 ◐ 2019	5.0 2.7 5.1 2.5
9 0245 0931 F 1507 2204	5.3 2.4 5.4 2.1	**24** 0209 0846 SA 1421 2115	4.9 2.8 4.9 2.6
10 0358 1043 SA 1618 2312	5.3 2.4 5.4 2.0	**25** 0311 0950 SU 1525 2221	4.9 2.8 4.9 2.6
11 0503 1149 SU 1723	5.4 2.2 5.4	**26** 0416 1059 M 1633 2328	5.0 2.7 5.0 2.5
12 0017 0600 M 1248 1822	1.9 5.6 2.0 5.7	**27** 0518 1203 TU 1739	5.2 2.5 5.2
13 0111 0651 TU 1341 1915	1.8 5.8 1.8 5.8	**28** 0032 0614 W 1301 1837	2.3 5.5 2.2 5.4
14 0200 0738 W 1428 2003	1.7 6.0 1.7 5.9	**29** 0126 0705 TH 1353 1931	2.1 5.7 2.0 5.7
15 0244 0819 TH 1510 ○ 2046	1.6 6.1 1.6 6.0	**30** 0217 0753 F 1443 2020	1.9 6.0 1.7 6.0
		31 0305 0839 SA 1531 ● 2108	1.6 6.3 1.3 6.2

Chart Datum: 3·29 metres below IGN Datum

》》 **FREE** monthly updates from 《《
www.reedsalmanac.co.uk

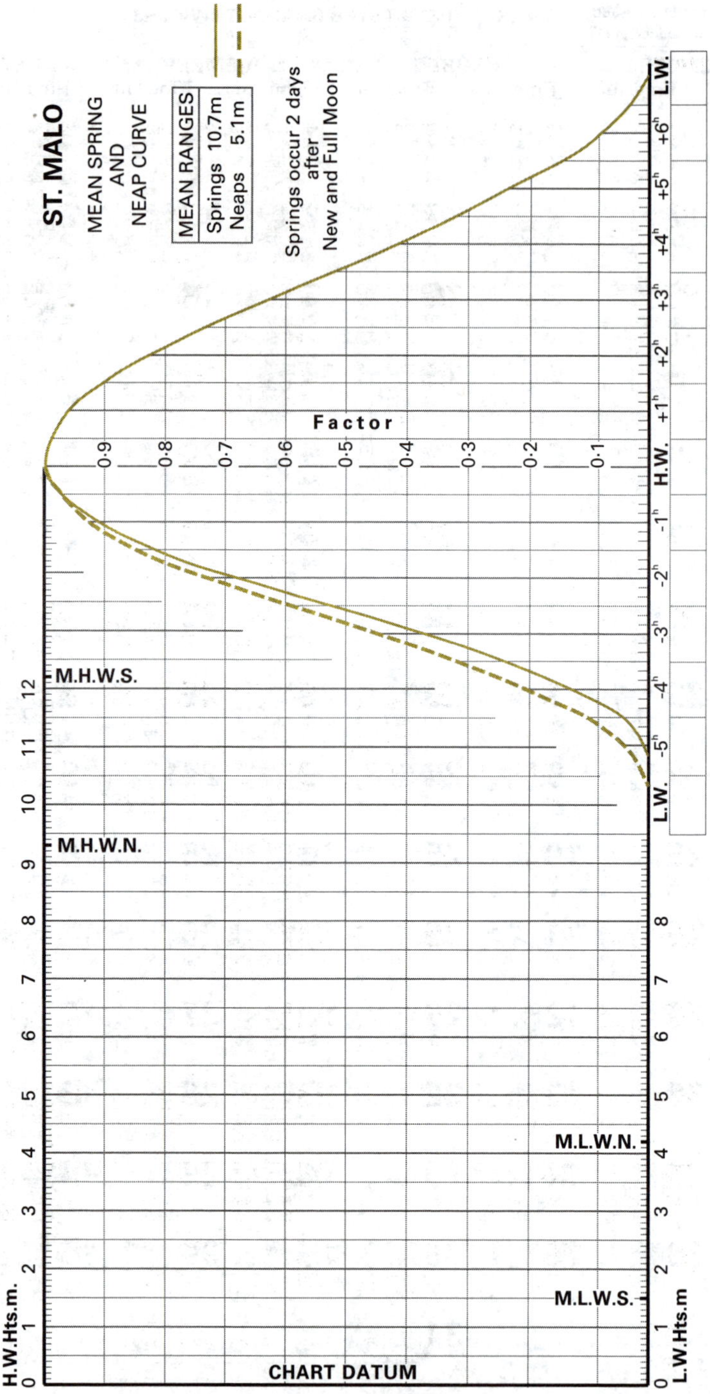

ST. MALO
MEAN SPRING AND NEAP CURVE
MEAN RANGES
Springs 10.7m
Neaps 5.1m
Springs occur 2 days after New and Full Moon
Factor
0·9
0·8
0·7
0·6
0·5
0·4
0·3
0·2
0·1
L.W. -5h -4h -3h -2h -1h H.W. +1h +2h +3h +4h +5h +6h L.W.
M.H.W.S.
M.H.W.N.
M.L.W.N.
M.L.W.S.
CHART DATUM
H.W.Hts.m.
L.W.Hts.m
0 1 2 3 4 5 6 7 8 9 10 11 12
0 1 2 3 4 5 6 7 8

TIME ZONE -0100
(French Standard Time)
Subtract 1 hour for UT
For French Summer Time add
ONE hour in **non-shaded areas**

FRANCE – ST MALO
LAT 48°38'N   LONG 2°02'W
TIMES AND HEIGHTS OF HIGH AND LOW WATERS

YEAR 2005

JANUARY

Time	m	Time	m
1 0442 3.4 SA 1011 10.4 1705 3.3 2236 9.9		**16** 0558 2.7 SU 1123 11.0 1823 2.7 2345 10.3	
2 0519 3.7 SU 1049 10.1 1744 3.6 2315 9.5		**17** 0638 3.3 M 1208 10.2 1904 3.4	
3 0601 4.0 M 1132 9.7 1829 3.9 ◐		**18** 0032 9.7 TU 0724 4.0 1301 9.5 1952 4.0	
4 0003 9.2 TU 0653 4.2 1227 9.4 1925 4.1		**19** 0130 9.2 W 0823 4.4 1410 9.0 2054 4.4	
5 0109 9.1 W 0757 4.3 1337 9.3 2033 4.1		**20** 0247 8.9 TH 0936 4.5 1532 8.9 2206 4.4	
6 0226 9.2 TH 0913 4.1 1456 9.5 2150 3.9		**21** 0405 9.1 F 1049 4.3 1644 9.2 2313 4.1	
7 0342 9.6 F 1029 3.6 1610 9.9 2302 3.3		**22** 0507 9.6 SA 1150 3.8 1739 9.6	
8 0448 10.3 SA 1137 2.9 1716 10.5		**23** 0010 3.7 SU 0555 10.1 1240 3.3 1824 10.1	
9 0009 2.7 SU 0548 11.1 1240 2.3 1817 11.2		**24** 0058 3.3 M 0635 10.6 1323 2.9 1902 10.5	
10 0111 2.2 M 0646 11.7 1340 1.7 ● 1913 11.7		**25** 0139 2.9 TU 0712 10.9 1403 2.6 ○ 1937 10.8	
11 0207 1.7 TU 0736 12.2 1436 1.3 2005 12.0		**26** 0217 2.6 W 0747 11.2 1440 2.4 2011 11.0	
12 0300 1.5 W 0825 12.4 1528 1.0 2053 12.1		**27** 0252 2.4 TH 0820 11.4 1514 2.2 2043 11.1	
13 0349 1.5 TH 0912 12.4 1616 1.1 2139 12.0		**28** 0326 2.3 F 0852 11.5 1547 2.2 2115 11.1	
14 0435 1.6 F 0957 12.2 1701 1.4 2222 11.6		**29** 0359 2.3 SA 0923 11.4 1619 2.2 2145 10.9	
15 0517 2.1 SA 1041 11.6 1743 2.0 2303 11.0		**30** 0430 2.5 SU 0955 11.2 1651 2.5 2215 10.7	
		31 0502 2.8 M 1026 10.8 1722 2.8 2247 10.3	

FEBRUARY

Time	m	Time	m
1 0535 3.2 TU 1101 10.4 1757 3.3 2323 9.9		**16** 0627 3.8 W 1202 9.4 1849 4.1 ◐	
2 0615 3.6 W 1142 9.9 1839 3.7 ◐		**17** 0022 9.1 TH 0713 4.6 1258 8.6 1944 4.9	
3 0011 9.4 TH 0707 4.0 1241 9.4 1939 4.2		**18** 0135 8.5 F 0832 5.0 1444 8.2 2114 5.1	
4 0125 9.1 F 0822 4.3 1408 9.0 2103 4.3		**19** 0327 8.4 SA 1014 4.9 1625 8.5 2247 4.8	
5 0304 9.1 SA 0955 4.0 1547 9.3 2235 3.9		**20** 0447 9.0 SU 1129 4.3 1725 9.2 2352 4.1	
6 0433 9.8 SU 1119 3.3 1709 10.0 2353 3.1		**21** 0538 9.7 M 1223 3.6 1808 9.9	
7 0542 10.7 M 1231 2.4 1814 10.9		**22** 0043 3.4 TU 0618 10.4 1307 2.9 1845 10.5	
8 0105 2.3 TU 0639 11.6 1334 1.6 ● 1909 11.6		**23** 0125 2.8 W 0655 11.0 1347 2.4 1919 11.0	
9 0203 1.6 W 0730 12.3 1430 0.9 1957 12.2		**24** 0202 2.3 TH 0729 11.4 1424 2.0 ○ 1952 11.4	
10 0254 1.1 TH 0816 12.7 1520 0.6 2041 12.5		**25** 0238 2.0 F 0803 11.7 1459 1.7 2024 11.6	
11 0340 0.9 F 0900 12.8 1603 0.5 2121 12.4		**26** 0311 1.7 SA 0834 11.9 1531 1.5 2055 11.7	
12 0420 1.0 SA 0939 12.6 1642 0.9 2158 12.1		**27** 0342 1.7 SU 0904 11.9 1601 1.6 2124 11.6	
13 0456 1.5 SU 1015 12.1 1716 1.5 2232 11.5		**28** 0413 1.8 M 0934 11.7 1630 1.9 2152 11.3	
14 0527 2.3 M 1050 11.3 1746 2.3 2305 10.7			
15 0556 3.0 TU 1124 10.4 1814 3.3 2339 9.9			

MARCH

Time	m	Time	m
1 0442 2.2 TU 1004 11.4 1659 2.4 2221 10.9		**16** 0515 2.9 W 1044 10.4 1727 3.3 2255 10.2	
2 0512 2.7 W 1036 10.8 1729 3.0 2254 10.3		**17** 0540 3.8 TH 1115 9.4 1755 4.2 ◐ 2329 9.3	
3 0547 3.3 TH 1114 10.1 1806 3.7 ◐ 2336 9.7		**18** 0617 4.6 F 1158 8.5 1841 5.1	
4 0636 3.9 F 1207 9.3 1903 4.3		**19** 0029 8.4 SA 0726 5.3 1349 7.8 2018 5.6	
5 0049 9.0 SA 0752 4.4 1345 8.7 2036 4.7		**20** 0242 8.1 SU 0934 5.3 1556 8.2 2218 5.2	
6 0251 8.9 SU 0939 4.4 1546 9.0 2226 4.3		**21** 0416 8.6 M 1102 4.6 1658 9.0 2326 4.4	
7 0429 9.6 M 1113 3.4 1708 9.9 2349 3.2		**22** 0508 9.5 TU 1155 3.7 1739 9.8	
8 0535 10.7 TU 1225 2.4 1806 10.9		**23** 0016 3.5 W 0549 10.3 1239 2.9 1816 10.5	
9 0058 2.2 W 0629 11.7 1325 1.4 1856 11.8		**24** 0057 2.8 TH 0627 10.9 1319 2.3 1851 11.2	
10 0151 1.4 TH 0715 12.5 1416 0.8 ● 1940 12.4		**25** 0135 2.2 F 0703 11.4 1357 1.8 ○ 1925 11.6	
11 0238 0.8 F 0758 13.0 1500 0.4 2019 12.6		**26** 0212 1.8 SA 0737 11.7 1432 1.5 1958 11.9	
12 0319 0.7 SA 0837 13.0 1539 0.5 2056 12.1		**27** 0246 1.5 SU 0810 11.9 1506 1.3 2029 12.1	
13 0355 0.9 SU 0913 12.7 1612 1.2 2128 12.2		**28** 0320 1.4 M 0841 12.3 1537 1.4 2059 12.0	
14 0426 1.3 M 0945 12.1 1641 1.6 2159 11.8		**29** 0352 1.5 TU 0912 12.1 1607 1.7 2129 11.8	
15 0452 2.1 TU 1016 11.3 1705 2.4 2227 11.0		**30** 0423 1.9 W 0944 11.6 1637 2.1 2200 11.3	
		31 0454 2.5 TH 1019 11.0 1709 3.0 2235 10.6	

APRIL

Time	m	Time	m
1 0532 3.2 F 1100 10.1 1749 3.8 2322 9.8		**16** 0543 4.5 SA 1125 8.6 1803 5.1 ◐ 2347 8.6	
2 0623 4.0 SA 1202 9.2 1850 4.6 ◐		**17** 0641 5.2 SU 1254 8.0 1925 5.6	
3 0048 9.0 SU 0745 4.4 1354 8.7 2035 4.8		**18** 0143 8.2 M 0832 5.3 1502 8.2 2126 5.4	
4 0251 9.0 M 0937 4.2 1543 9.2 2223 4.2		**19** 0322 8.5 TU 1011 4.8 1611 8.8 2239 4.6	
5 0417 9.8 TU 1105 3.3 1654 10.1 2337 3.1		**20** 0422 9.3 W 1109 3.9 1657 9.6 2329 3.7	
6 0518 10.9 W 1210 2.3 1747 11.1		**21** 0508 10.1 TH 1156 3.2 1736 10.4	
7 0039 2.2 TH 0608 11.7 1304 1.5 1833 11.8		**22** 0015 3.0 F 0549 10.8 1239 2.5 1814 11.1	
8 0129 1.5 F 0653 12.3 1351 1.0 ● 1914 12.3		**23** 0058 2.3 SA 0628 11.5 1321 1.9 1851 11.6	
9 0212 1.1 SA 0732 12.6 1432 0.9 1951 12.5		**24** 0138 1.9 SU 0706 12.0 1400 1.6 ○ 1926 12.0	
10 0250 1.1 SU 0810 12.6 1507 1.1 2025 12.4		**25** 0217 1.5 M 0742 12.4 1437 1.5 2001 12.2	
11 0323 1.2 M 0843 12.3 1537 1.4 2056 12.2		**26** 0255 1.4 TU 0817 12.5 1512 1.5 2034 12.2	
12 0352 1.6 TU 0915 11.8 1603 1.9 2125 11.7		**27** 0332 1.6 W 0853 12.1 1547 1.8 2109 12.1	
13 0417 2.1 W 0944 11.1 1627 2.4 2153 11.0		**28** 0408 1.9 TH 0931 11.6 1622 2.4 2147 11.4	
14 0441 3.0 TH 1012 10.3 1650 3.5 2221 10.3		**29** 0446 2.5 F 1013 10.9 1701 3.1 2232 10.7	
15 0508 3.7 F 1043 9.5 1720 4.3 2255 9.4		**30** 0530 3.2 SA 1105 10.1 1749 3.9 2330 9.9	

Chart Datum: 6·29 metres below IGN Datum

》》 **FREE** monthly updates from 《《
www.reedsalmanac.co.uk

TIDES

TIME ZONE -0100
(French Standard Time)
Subtract 1 hour for UT
For French Summer Time add ONE hour in **non-shaded areas**

FRANCE – ST MALO
LAT 48°38'N   LONG 2°02'W
TIMES AND HEIGHTS OF HIGH AND LOW WATERS

YEAR 2005

	MAY			JUNE			JULY			AUGUST	
	Time m	Time m		Time m	Time m		Time m	Time m		Time m	Time m
1 SU ◐	0628 3.8 1217 9.4 1859 4.5	**16** M	0616 4.7 1214 8.5 1848 5.2	**1** W	0205 10.0 0856 3.6 1443 9.8 2129 3.7	**16** TH	0100 9.1 0750 4.3 1344 9.0 2023 4.5	**1** F	0229 9.9 0916 3.7 1502 9.7 2151 3.8	**16** SA	0102 9.4 0754 4.2 1342 9.1 2032 4.4	**1** M	0420 9.1 1050 4.3 1647 9.6 2330 4.0	**16** TU	0310 9.1 0958 4.4 1557 9.1 2244 3.9
2 M	0100 9.4 0751 4.1 1353 9.1 2037 4.5	**17** TU	0044 8.6 0731 4.9 1344 8.4 2015 5.2	**2** TH	0315 10.1 1003 3.3 1549 10.1 2233 3.4	**17** F	0208 9.2 0858 4.2 1452 9.2 2131 4.2	**2** SA	0337 9.8 1019 3.7 1607 9.9 2254 3.7	**17** SU	0216 9.3 0907 4.2 1500 9.3 2149 4.1	**2** TU	0524 9.6 1153 3.9 1742 10.1	**17** W	0438 9.7 1123 3.7 1712 10.3 2358 2.9
3 TU	0236 9.5 0926 3.9 1521 9.5 2204 3.9	**18** W	0210 8.7 0858 4.7 1502 8.8 2133 4.7	**3** F	0416 10.5 1103 3.0 1644 10.5 2330 3.0	**18** SA	0314 9.6 1005 3.8 1553 9.7 2234 3.7	**3** SU	0440 9.9 1118 3.6 1705 10.2 2350 3.4	**18** M	0333 9.5 0612 10.1 1614 9.8 2302 3.5	**3** W	0026 3.5 0612 10.1 1244 3.5 1826 10.6	**18** TH	0546 10.6 1232 2.8 1812 11.3
4 W	0352 10.1 1041 3.2 1627 10.3 2310 3.1	**19** TH	0319 9.2 1007 4.1 1600 9.4 2232 4.0	**4** SA	0509 10.8 1156 2.7 1732 10.9	**19** SU	0415 10.1 1106 3.3 1649 10.3 2333 3.1	**4** M	0535 10.1 1211 3.4 1754 10.5	**19** TU	0445 10.1 1136 3.3 1719 10.5	**4** TH	0112 3.1 0653 10.5 1328 3.1 1903 11.0	**19** F ○	0107 2.0 0643 11.5 1333 1.9 1904 12.2
5 TH	0451 10.8 1142 2.5 1711 11.0	**20** F	0414 9.8 1102 3.5 1648 10.1 2324 3.3	**5** SU	0022 2.7 0556 11.0 1242 2.6 1815 11.2	**20** M	0511 10.6 1204 2.8 1741 10.9	**5** TU	0041 3.1 0623 10.4 1258 3.2 1837 10.8	**20** W	0009 2.8 0550 10.7 1240 2.7 1818 11.3	**5** F ●	0153 2.7 0729 10.8 1407 2.8 1938 11.2	**20** SA	0205 1.3 0733 12.2 1428 1.3 1952 12.6
6 F	0007 2.4 0540 11.4 1233 2.0 1804 11.5	**21** SA	0503 10.5 1153 2.8 1732 10.8	**6** M	0107 2.5 0639 11.1 1323 2.5 ● 1854 11.3	**21** TU	0032 2.5 0605 11.1 1258 2.4 1830 11.5	**6** W ●	0125 2.9 0705 10.6 1339 3.0 1916 11.0	**21** TH ○	0113 2.2 0649 11.3 1340 2.2 1912 11.9	**6** SA	0231 2.5 0803 11.0 1444 2.5 2011 11.4	**21** SU	0257 0.7 0819 12.6 1516 0.9 2036 13.1
7 SA	0057 2.0 0625 11.8 1318 1.7 1844 11.8	**22** SU	0015 2.7 0549 11.1 1241 2.3 1814 11.3	**7** TU	0146 2.4 0719 11.1 1359 2.5 1930 11.4	**22** W ○	0126 2.1 0657 11.5 1350 2.1 1919 11.9	**7** TH	0204 2.8 0743 10.7 1418 2.9 1952 11.1	**22** F	0212 1.6 0743 11.8 1436 1.7 2003 12.4	**7** SU	0305 2.3 0835 11.1 1517 2.4 2042 11.5	**22** M	0343 0.6 0901 12.7 1559 0.9 2117 13.0
8 SU ●	0140 1.8 0705 11.9 1357 1.7 1921 12.0	**23** M	0103 2.2 0632 11.6 1326 2.0 ○ 1855 11.8	**8** W	0222 2.4 0755 11.0 1434 2.6 2004 11.4	**23** TH	0219 1.7 0748 11.8 1440 1.9 2008 12.1	**8** F	0242 2.7 0818 10.8 1455 2.8 2026 11.2	**23** SA	0307 1.2 0833 12.2 1528 1.4 2051 12.6	**8** M	0337 2.2 0905 11.2 1548 2.4 2112 11.5	**23** TU	0423 0.8 0940 12.4 1638 1.2 2156 12.6
9 M	0217 1.8 0742 11.9 1431 1.8 1954 12.0	**24** TU	0149 1.8 0715 11.9 1410 1.8 1935 12.1	**9** TH	0256 2.5 0830 10.9 1507 2.7 2038 11.2	**24** F	0310 1.6 0838 11.9 1530 1.9 2057 12.2	**9** SA	0318 2.6 0852 10.8 1530 2.8 2100 11.1	**24** SU	0357 1.0 0920 12.2 1615 1.4 2137 12.6	**9** TU	0407 2.3 0934 11.1 1617 2.5 2142 11.3	**24** W	0459 1.4 1016 11.9 1713 1.9 2232 11.8
10 TU	0250 1.9 0816 11.7 1501 2.1 2026 11.8	**25** W	0233 1.6 0758 12.0 1452 1.8 2016 12.1	**10** F	0329 2.7 0904 10.7 1541 3.0 2112 10.9	**25** SA	0401 1.6 0928 11.8 1619 2.1 2146 12.0	**10** SU	0352 2.7 0925 10.7 1604 2.9 2133 10.9	**25** M	0443 1.1 1004 12.0 1659 1.6 2221 12.2	**10** W	0436 2.5 1002 10.8 1647 2.8 2211 11.0	**25** TH	0530 2.2 1050 11.0 1745 2.8 2307 10.9
11 W	0320 2.1 0848 11.3 1530 2.4 2057 11.5	**26** TH	0317 1.6 0841 11.9 1534 2.0 2059 12.0	**11** SA	0402 3.0 0938 10.3 1614 3.4 2147 10.5	**26** SU	0450 1.8 1017 11.5 1708 2.3 2236 11.6	**11** M	0425 2.8 0958 10.5 1637 3.2 2206 10.7	**26** TU	0525 1.5 1046 11.6 1741 2.1 2303 11.6	**11** TH	0504 2.8 1031 10.5 1717 3.2 2241 10.5	**26** F ◐	0600 3.1 1124 10.4 1818 3.7 2346 9.9
12 TH	0350 2.5 0919 10.9 1558 2.9 2127 11.0	**27** F	0401 1.9 0927 11.6 1617 2.4 2146 11.6	**12** SU	0437 3.3 1014 10.0 1650 3.8 2224 10.1	**27** M	0539 2.1 1106 11.0 1758 2.7 2327 11.1	**12** TU	0458 3.1 1031 10.3 1711 3.4 2240 10.3	**27** W	0605 2.2 1126 11.0 1821 2.8 2346 10.9	**12** F	0535 3.3 1102 10.1 1752 3.7 2317 10.0	**27** SA	0634 4.1 1206 9.5 1902 4.5
13 F	0417 3.0 0951 10.3 1627 3.5 2200 10.3	**28** SA	0447 2.3 1017 11.1 1704 2.9 2238 11.0	**13** M	0514 3.7 1054 9.5 1730 4.2 2306 9.6	**28** TU	0629 2.5 1157 10.5 1849 3.2	**13** W	0532 3.4 1105 9.9 1748 3.7 2317 10.0	**28** TH	0644 3.0 1209 10.3 1904 3.5	**13** SA	0611 3.8 1141 9.6 1837 4.2	**28** SU ◐	0043 8.9 0726 5.0 1313 8.8 2017 5.1
14 SA	0448 3.6 1025 9.6 1700 4.2 2237 9.6	**29** SU	0537 2.8 1113 10.5 1759 3.5 2338 10.5	**14** TU	0556 4.0 1140 9.2 1818 4.5	**29** W	0023 10.6 0720 3.1 1252 10.1 1945 3.6	**14** TH ◐	0610 3.7 1145 9.5 1831 4.1	**29** F	0036 10.0 0728 3.7 1300 9.7 1957 4.1	**14** SU	0005 9.5 0702 4.3 1234 9.1 1942 4.6	**29** M	0223 8.5 0855 5.3 1507 9.0 2159 5.0
15 SU	0525 4.2 1109 9.0 1744 4.8 2327 9.0	**30** M	0636 3.3 1217 9.9 1904 3.9 ◑	**15** W	0648 4.3 1236 9.0 1917 4.6	**30** TH	0123 10.1 0816 3.5 1354 9.8 2046 3.8	**15** F	0002 9.6 0656 4.0 1235 9.2 1924 4.3	**30** SA	0137 9.4 0824 4.3 1409 9.2 2106 4.5	**15** M	0126 9.0 0818 4.6 1419 9.0 2114 4.5	**30** TU	0408 8.6 1033 5.0 1634 9.1 2316 4.1
		31 TU	0050 10.0 0745 3.6 1329 9.7 2018 4.0							**31** SU	0258 9.0 0936 4.5 1534 9.2 2223 4.4			**31** W	0512 9.3 1140 4.2 1727 9.9

Chart Datum: 6·29 metres below IGN Datum

FREE monthly updates from
www.reedsalmanac.co.uk

TIME ZONE −0100
(French Standard Time)
Subtract 1 hour for UT
For French Summer Time add
ONE hour in non-shaded areas

FRANCE – ST MALO
LAT 48°38′N   LONG 2°02′W
TIMES AND HEIGHTS OF HIGH AND LOW WATERS

YEAR 2005

SEPTEMBER

Time m	Time m
1 0011 3.7 / 0555 10.0 / TH 1229 3.5 / 1807 10.5	**16** 0537 10.9 / 1224 2.6 / F 1759 11.6
2 0056 3.0 / 0632 10.6 / F 1311 3.0 / 1842 11.1	**17** 0055 1.8 / 0628 11.8 / SA 1320 1.6 / 1848 12.5
3 0134 2.6 / 0706 11.1 / SA 1348 2.5 / ● 1916 11.5	**18** 0148 1.0 / 0714 12.5 / SU 1410 1.0 / ○ 1932 13.0
4 0210 2.2 / 0738 11.4 / SU 1423 2.2 / 1948 11.8	**19** 0235 0.6 / 0756 12.8 / M 1454 0.8 / 2013 13.2
5 0243 2.0 / 0809 11.6 / M 1454 2.1 / 2018 11.9	**20** 0317 0.6 / 0834 12.8 / TU 1534 0.9 / 2051 13.0
6 0313 1.9 / 0838 11.7 / TU 1524 2.0 / 2047 11.9	**21** 0353 1.0 / 0909 12.5 / W 1608 1.3 / 2126 12.5
7 0342 2.0 / 0905 11.6 / W 1553 2.1 / 2114 11.7	**22** 0424 1.6 / 0941 12.0 / TH 1639 2.1 / 2158 11.7
8 0409 2.2 / 0932 11.4 / TH 1621 2.5 / 2142 11.4	**23** 0450 2.5 / 1012 11.3 / F 1705 2.9 / 2230 10.7
9 0435 2.6 / 0958 11.0 / F 1649 2.9 / 2211 10.9	**24** 0514 3.4 / 1042 10.4 / SA 1732 3.9 / 2303 9.7
10 0502 3.2 / 1027 10.5 / SA 1721 3.5 / 2244 10.2	**25** 0543 4.4 / 1117 9.5 / SU 1809 4.8 / ◐ 2350 8.7
11 0536 3.8 / 1104 9.8 / SU 1804 4.2 / ◐ 2331 9.4	**26** 0630 5.3 / 1218 8.6 / M 1919 5.5
12 0626 4.5 / 1203 9.1 / M 1911 4.7	**27** 0146 8.0 / 0809 5.8 / TU 1435 8.3 / 2130 5.5
13 0101 8.7 / 0749 5.0 / TU 1404 8.8 / 2057 4.7	**28** 0345 8.4 / 1012 5.3 / W 1607 8.9 / 2253 4.7
14 0310 8.9 / 0950 4.7 / W 1554 9.4 / 2238 3.9	**29** 0445 9.2 / 1116 4.5 / TH 1658 9.7 / 2342 3.3
15 0436 9.8 / 1119 3.7 / TH 1704 10.5 / 2350 2.8	**30** 0526 10.0 / 1201 3.6 / F 1736 10.5

OCTOBER

Time m	Time m
1 0025 3.1 / 0601 10.7 / SA 1240 2.9 / 1811 11.1	**16** 0034 1.8 / 0605 11.9 / SU 1257 1.7 / 1824 12.4
2 0103 2.5 / 0634 11.2 / SU 1317 2.4 / 1845 11.6	**17** 0123 1.2 / 0648 12.4 / M 1344 1.2 / ○ 1907 12.8
3 0138 2.1 / 0707 11.6 / M 1352 2.1 / ● 1918 11.9	**18** 0206 1.0 / 0727 12.6 / TU 1426 1.1 / 1946 12.8
4 0211 1.9 / 0738 11.9 / TU 1425 1.9 / 1949 12.1	**19** 0245 1.1 / 0803 12.6 / W 1503 1.3 / 2022 12.6
5 0243 1.8 / 0807 12.0 / W 1456 1.8 / 2019 12.1	**20** 0318 1.5 / 0837 12.3 / TH 1535 1.7 / 2056 12.1
6 0313 1.9 / 0835 11.9 / TH 1527 2.0 / 2048 12.0	**21** 0347 2.1 / 0908 11.9 / F 1604 2.3 / 2127 11.3
7 0342 2.2 / 0903 11.7 / F 1557 2.3 / 2117 11.6	**22** 0412 2.8 / 0938 11.2 / SA 1631 3.1 / 2158 10.5
8 0410 2.6 / 0933 11.3 / SA 1629 2.8 / 2149 11.0	**23** 0438 3.6 / 1008 10.4 / SU 1659 3.9 / 2231 9.6
9 0439 3.3 / 1006 10.7 / SU 1704 3.5 / 2227 10.2	**24** 0508 4.5 / 1043 9.5 / M 1734 4.7 / 2315 8.7
10 0516 4.0 / 1048 10.0 / M 1750 4.2 / ◐ 2321 9.3	**25** 0552 5.3 / 1137 8.7 / TU 1833 5.4 / ◐
11 0612 4.7 / 1158 9.2 / TU 1903 4.7	**26** 0049 8.1 / 0714 5.8 / W 1334 8.3 / 2024 5.5
12 0110 8.7 / 0806 5.1 / W 1407 9.0 / 2054 4.6	**27** 0251 8.3 / 0916 5.5 / TH 1513 8.6 / 2201 5.0
13 0306 9.1 / 0947 4.6 / TH 1541 9.7 / 2228 3.8	**28** 0358 8.9 / 1028 4.8 / F 1611 9.4 / 2256 4.2
14 0421 10.0 / 1105 3.5 / F 1646 10.7 / 2334 2.7	**29** 0442 9.7 / 1116 3.9 / SA 1653 10.1 / 2339 3.4
15 0517 11.1 / 1205 2.5 / SA 1738 11.7	**30** 0520 10.5 / 1157 3.2 / SU 1732 10.8
	31 0021 2.8 / 0556 11.1 / M 1237 2.6 / 1809 11.4

NOVEMBER

Time m	Time m
1 0100 2.3 / 0631 11.5 / TU 1316 2.2 / 1845 11.8	**16** 0134 1.7 / 0659 12.1 / W 1356 1.7 / ○ 1921 12.0
2 0137 2.0 / 0705 11.9 / W 1353 2.0 / ● 1919 12.0	**17** 0211 1.8 / 0735 12.1 / TH 1433 1.9 / 1957 11.8
3 0212 1.9 / 0737 12.0 / TH 1429 1.9 / 1953 12.1	**18** 0245 2.1 / 0809 11.9 / F 1506 2.1 / 2032 11.5
4 0247 2.0 / 0809 12.1 / F 1505 2.0 / 2027 11.9	**19** 0316 2.5 / 0842 11.6 / SA 1537 2.5 / 2105 11.0
5 0320 2.2 / 0843 11.9 / SA 1541 2.2 / 2102 11.6	**20** 0346 3.0 / 0914 11.1 / SU 1608 3.1 / 2139 10.4
6 0354 2.7 / 0919 11.5 / SU 1619 2.7 / 2142 11.0	**21** 0416 3.6 / 0948 10.5 / M 1639 3.7 / 2214 9.7
7 0431 3.3 / 1001 10.9 / M 1701 3.3 / 2230 10.2	**22** 0440 4.2 / 1025 9.8 / TU 1716 4.3 / 2256 9.1
8 0516 3.9 / 1054 10.1 / TU 1755 3.9 / 2335 9.5	**23** 0532 4.8 / 1111 9.1 / W 1804 4.8 / ◐ 2355 8.6
9 0619 4.5 / 1213 9.5 / W 1909 4.3 / ◐	**24** 0630 5.2 / 1219 8.7 / TH 1911 5.1
10 0110 9.2 / 0750 4.7 / TH 1351 9.4 / 2042 4.2	**25** 0120 8.4 / 0751 5.3 / F 1347 8.6 / 2034 4.9
11 0242 9.4 / 0926 4.3 / F 1514 10.0 / 2202 3.6	**26** 0242 8.7 / 0911 4.9 / SA 1500 9.0 / 2145 4.5
12 0353 10.1 / 1037 3.5 / SA 1618 10.7 / 2306 2.8	**27** 0342 9.2 / 1014 4.3 / SU 1557 9.6 / 2242 3.9
13 0448 10.9 / 1136 2.7 / SU 1710 11.4 / 2332 3.3	**28** 0430 9.9 / 1106 3.7 / M 1645 10.2 / 2332 3.3
14 0001 2.2 / 0536 11.5 / M 1228 2.1 / 1758 11.9	**29** 0513 10.5 / 1154 3.1 / TU 1729 10.8
15 0052 1.8 / 0619 11.9 / TU 1314 1.8 / 1841 12.1	**30** 0020 2.7 / 0554 11.1 / W 1239 2.6 / 1812 11.3

DECEMBER

Time m	Time m
1 0104 2.4 / 0634 11.6 / TH 1324 2.2 / ● 1853 11.6	**16** 0145 2.5 / 0716 11.5 / F 1409 2.3 / 1942 11.2
2 0146 2.1 / 0713 11.9 / F 1408 1.9 / 1934 11.8	**17** 0222 2.5 / 0752 11.5 / SA 1446 2.4 / 2018 11.1
3 0227 2.1 / 0752 12.0 / SA 1451 1.9 / 2016 11.8	**18** 0257 2.6 / 0828 11.3 / SU 1521 2.5 / 2053 10.8
4 0309 2.2 / 0834 12.0 / SU 1535 2.0 / 2059 11.6	**19** 0331 2.9 / 0902 11.1 / M 1555 2.8 / 2128 10.5
5 0352 2.5 / 0919 11.7 / M 1620 2.3 / 2147 11.2	**20** 0405 3.2 / 0936 10.7 / TU 1628 3.2 / 2202 10.1
6 0437 2.9 / 1008 11.2 / TU 1709 2.7 / 2238 10.6	**21** 0439 3.6 / 1011 10.3 / W 1702 3.6 / 2237 9.7
7 0527 3.4 / 1103 10.7 / W 1803 3.2 / 2337 10.1	**22** 0514 4.0 / 1047 9.8 / TH 1739 3.9 / 2316 9.3
8 0626 3.8 / 1207 10.2 / TH 1906 3.5	**23** 0556 4.3 / 1130 9.4 / F 1823 4.3 / ◐
9 0047 9.7 / 0735 4.0 / F 1319 9.7 / 2014 3.7	**24** 0002 9.0 / 0646 4.6 / SA 1223 9.1 / 1916 4.5
10 0201 9.6 / 0849 4.0 / SA 1434 10.0 / 2124 3.5	**25** 0107 8.8 / 0747 4.7 / SU 1331 8.9 / 2021 4.5
11 0312 9.9 / 0958 3.8 / SU 1541 10.2 / 2229 3.2	**26** 0221 8.8 / 0858 4.6 / M 1445 9.1 / 2133 4.3
12 0414 10.3 / 1101 3.4 / M 1640 10.6 / 2327 2.9	**27** 0330 9.2 / 1008 4.3 / TU 1552 9.5 / 2240 3.9
13 0507 10.7 / 1157 3.0 / TU 1733 10.9 / 2339 3.3	**28** 0429 9.8 / 1111 3.6 / W 1651 10.0 / 2339 3.3
14 0020 2.7 / 0554 11.1 / W 1247 2.6 / 1820 11.1	**29** 0522 10.5 / 1208 2.9 / TH 1745 10.6
15 0105 2.6 / 0637 11.3 / TH 1330 2.4 / ○ 1903 11.2	**30** 0036 2.8 / 0611 11.1 / F 1302 2.4 / 1836 11.1
	31 0128 2.3 / 0659 11.6 / SA 1354 1.9 / ● 1925 11.5

Chart Datum: 6·29 metres below IGN Datum

》》 **FREE** monthly updates from 《《
www.reedsalmanac.co.uk

Chapter 5

TIDES

ST. PETER PORT
MEAN SPRING AND NEAP CURVES

MEAN RANGES
Springs 7.9m
Neaps 3.4m

Springs occur 2 days after New and Full Moon

TIME ZONE (UT)
For Summer Time add ONE hour in **non-shaded areas**

CHANNEL ISLES – ST PETER PORT
LAT 49°27'N   LONG 2°31'W
TIMES AND HEIGHTS OF HIGH AND LOW WATERS

YEAR 2005

JANUARY		FEBRUARY		MARCH		APRIL	
Time m	Time m	Time m	Time m	Time m	Time m	Time m	Time m
1 0337 2.9 / 0938 7.9 / SA 1604 2.8 / 2204 7.5	**16** 0448 2.1 / 1046 8.5 / SU 1716 2.1 / 2310 7.9	**1** 0429 2.7 / 1032 7.9 / TU 1653 2.7 / 2255 7.6	**16** 0525 3.1 / 1127 7.1 / W 1748 3.4 / ◐ 2345 6.9	**1** 0330 1.8 / 0929 8.5 / TU 1548 2.0 / 2146 8.2	**16** 0408 2.3 / 1006 7.8 / W 1622 2.7 / 2216 7.6	**1** 0425 2.6 / 1031 7.5 / F 1647 3.1 / 2254 7.4	**16** 0442 3.6 / 1055 6.5 / SA 1700 4.0 / ◐ 2309 6.5
2 0415 3.1 / 1018 7.7 / SU 1643 3.0 / 2246 7.4	**17** 0533 2.7 / 1133 7.8 / M 1801 2.7 / ◐ 2358 7.4	**2** 0512 3.0 / 1119 7.5 / W 1739 3.1 / ◐ 2347 7.3	**17** 0616 3.7 / 1224 6.5 / TH 1846 4.0	**2** 0402 2.2 / 1004 8.1 / W 1622 2.5 / 2223 7.8	**17** 0437 3.0 / 1039 7.1 / TH 1652 3.4 / ◐ 2250 6.9	**2** 0525 3.2 / 1139 6.9 / SA 1757 3.7 / ◐	**17** 0600 4.1 / 1219 6.1 / SU 1836 4.4
3 0500 3.3 / 1105 7.5 / M 1730 3.2 / ◐ 2336 7.2	**18** 0624 3.2 / 1227 7.3 / TU 1853 3.3	**3** 0610 3.3 / 1220 7.2 / TH 1843 3.4	**18** 0055 6.4 / 0736 4.1 / F 1401 6.2 / 2012 4.2	**3** 0441 2.7 / 1047 7.6 / TH 1705 3.0 / ◐ 2312 7.3	**18** 0517 3.7 / 1126 6.4 / F 1739 4.1 / 2345 6.4	**3** 0015 6.9 / 0704 3.6 / SU 1325 6.6 / 1952 3.8	**18** 0046 6.2 / 0749 4.1 / M 1423 6.2 / 2020 4.2
4 0555 3.5 / 1201 7.3 / TU 1828 3.3	**19** 0058 7.0 / 0728 3.6 / W 1336 6.9 / 1959 3.6	**4** 0059 7.1 / 0731 3.5 / F 1344 7.0 / 2012 3.5	**19** 0245 6.4 / 0930 4.0 / SA 1541 6.4 / 2154 3.9	**4** 0537 3.2 / 1149 7.0 / F 1809 3.5	**19** 0642 4.2 / 1303 5.9 / SA 1921 4.4	**4** 0213 6.9 / 0859 3.2 / M 1514 7.1 / 2135 3.3	**19** 0242 6.5 / 0919 3.7 / TU 1534 6.9 / 2138 3.6
5 0038 7.1 / 0702 3.5 / W 1308 7.3 / 1938 3.3	**20** 0213 6.8 / 0848 3.7 / TH 1453 6.8 / 2114 3.7	**5** 0232 7.1 / 0909 3.2 / SA 1517 7.2 / 2146 3.2	**20** 0406 6.8 / 1044 3.5 / SU 1641 6.9 / 2258 3.4	**5** 0025 6.9 / 0705 3.6 / SA 1324 6.7 / 1952 3.8	**20** 0147 6.1 / 0841 4.2 / SU 1517 6.2 / 2117 4.2	**5** 0340 7.6 / 1013 2.4 / TU 1619 7.8 / 2238 2.5	**20** 0346 7.1 / 1015 3.0 / W 1620 7.3 / 2229 3.0
6 0151 7.2 / 0821 3.3 / TH 1423 7.4 / 2055 3.1	**21** 0326 6.9 / 1001 3.5 / F 1600 6.9 / 2220 3.5	**6** 0356 7.5 / 1029 2.7 / SU 1634 7.7 / 2259 2.6	**21** 0457 7.4 / 1131 2.9 / M 1726 7.4 / 2342 2.8	**6** 0217 6.9 / 0902 3.4 / SU 1517 6.9 / 2142 3.4	**21** 0338 6.6 / 1017 3.6 / M 1617 6.8 / 2231 3.5	**6** 0438 8.4 / 1107 1.7 / W 1709 8.5 / 2329 1.7	**21** 0432 7.6 / 1058 2.4 / TH 1701 7.9 / 2312 2.4
7 0305 7.6 / 0935 2.9 / F 1535 7.7 / 2205 2.7	**22** 0425 7.3 / 1058 3.2 / SA 1654 7.3 / 2312 3.1	**7** 0503 8.3 / 1135 2.0 / M 1737 8.3	**22** 0540 7.9 / 1210 2.5 / TU 1806 8.0	**7** 0352 7.5 / 1026 2.6 / M 1633 7.6 / 2254 2.5	**22** 0431 7.2 / 1103 2.9 / TU 1701 7.4 / 2315 2.9	**7** 0526 9.0 / 1154 1.0 / TH 1753 9.1	**22** 0513 8.2 / 1137 1.9 / F 1739 8.4 / 2351 1.8
8 0411 8.0 / 1040 2.4 / SA 1641 8.1 / 2308 2.3	**23** 0513 7.7 / 1144 2.8 / SU 1741 7.6 / 2356 2.8	**8** 0000 1.9 / 0559 8.9 / TU 1232 1.3 / 1831 8.9	**23** 0020 2.3 / 0618 8.4 / W 1247 1.9 / 1843 8.4	**8** 0456 8.3 / 1127 1.8 / TU 1730 8.4 / 2350 1.8	**23** 0513 7.8 / 1142 2.3 / W 1739 8.0 / 2352 2.2	**8** 0014 1.1 / 0610 9.5 / F 1237 0.6 / ◯ 1833 9.6	**23** 0551 8.6 / 1214 1.5 / SA 1815 8.8
9 0510 8.5 / 1140 1.9 / SU 1741 8.5	**24** 0555 8.1 / 1225 2.5 / M 1822 8.0	**9** 0053 1.3 / 0650 9.5 / W 1322 0.7 / 1919 9.4	**24** 0056 1.9 / 0654 8.7 / TH 1321 1.6 / ◯ 1918 8.7	**9** 0548 9.0 / 1218 1.0 / W 1817 9.1	**24** 0551 8.4 / 1217 1.8 / TH 1816 8.5	**9** 0056 0.7 / 0651 9.7 / SA 1317 0.5 / 1911 9.6	**24** 0029 1.4 / 0628 9.0 / SU 1251 1.2 / ◯ 1849 9.1
10 0005 1.9 / 0605 9.0 / M 1237 1.4 / ◯ 1836 8.9	**25** 0035 2.4 / 0634 8.4 / TU 1303 2.2 / ◯ 1900 8.2	**10** 0141 0.8 / 0736 9.9 / TH 1407 0.4 / 2002 9.6	**25** 0129 1.6 / 0728 9.0 / F 1352 1.4 / 1950 8.8	**10** 0038 1.1 / 0634 9.6 / TH 1304 0.4 / ● 1900 9.5	**25** 0028 1.7 / 0627 8.8 / F 1251 1.4 / ◯ 1850 8.8	**10** 0134 0.6 / 0729 9.7 / SU 1353 0.6 / 1946 9.6	**25** 0106 1.1 / 0704 9.2 / M 1326 1.1 / 1923 9.2
11 0059 1.5 / 0657 9.4 / TU 1330 1.0 / 1927 9.2	**26** 0111 2.2 / 0711 8.6 / W 1338 2.0 / 1936 8.4	**11** 0224 0.6 / 0819 10.0 / F 1449 0.3 / 2043 9.6	**26** 0200 1.4 / 0759 9.0 / SA 1422 1.3 / 2019 8.8	**11** 0122 0.6 / 0716 9.9 / F 1345 0.2 / 1940 9.8	**26** 0102 1.4 / 0701 9.1 / SA 1324 1.1 / 1922 9.0	**11** 0209 0.8 / 0804 9.5 / M 1426 0.9 / 2018 9.3	**26** 0142 1.0 / 0740 9.2 / TU 1400 1.2 / 1957 9.2
12 0150 1.2 / 0746 9.7 / W 1419 0.8 / 2015 9.3	**27** 0145 2.0 / 0746 8.7 / TH 1411 1.8 / 2010 8.4	**12** 0304 0.7 / 0859 9.8 / SA 1527 0.6 / 2120 9.3	**27** 0231 1.4 / 0828 9.0 / SU 1450 1.4 / 2046 8.7	**12** 0202 0.4 / 0756 10.0 / SA 1423 0.2 / 2016 9.7	**27** 0135 1.1 / 0733 9.2 / SU 1355 1.0 / 1952 9.1	**12** 0240 1.1 / 0835 9.0 / TU 1455 1.5 / 2047 8.8	**27** 0218 1.2 / 0816 9.0 / W 1435 1.4 / 2032 9.0
13 0237 1.1 / 0833 9.7 / TH 1506 0.8 / 2101 9.2	**28** 0218 1.9 / 0818 8.7 / F 1442 1.9 / 2040 8.4	**13** 0341 0.8 / 0936 9.3 / SU 1603 1.1 / 2155 8.8	**28** 0301 1.4 / 0857 8.8 / M 1519 1.6 / 2115 8.5	**13** 0238 0.5 / 0832 9.7 / SU 1458 0.6 / 2050 9.4	**28** 0207 1.1 / 0805 9.2 / M 1425 1.1 / 2021 9.0	**13** 0309 1.7 / 0905 8.4 / W 1521 2.1 / 2115 8.3	**28** 0255 1.5 / 0854 8.7 / TH 1512 1.9 / 2111 8.6
14 0322 1.3 / 0919 9.5 / F 1550 1.0 / 2144 8.9	**29** 0250 2.0 / 0848 8.6 / SA 1513 2.0 / 2110 8.3	**14** 0415 1.7 / 1011 8.7 / M 1636 1.9 / 2228 8.1		**14** 0311 0.8 / 0905 9.3 / M 1529 1.2 / 2120 8.8	**29** 0238 1.2 / 0835 9.0 / TU 1455 1.4 / 2051 8.8	**14** 0336 2.3 / 0935 7.8 / TH 1547 2.7 / 2143 7.7	**29** 0335 2.0 / 0938 8.1 / F 1554 2.5 / 2157 8.1
15 0405 1.6 / 1002 9.1 / SA 1633 1.5 / 2227 8.5	**30** 0322 2.2 / 0920 8.4 / SU 1543 2.1 / 2140 8.1	**15** 0448 2.4 / 1047 7.9 / TU 1709 2.7 / 2302 7.5		**15** 0340 1.5 / 0936 8.6 / TU 1556 1.9 / 2148 8.3	**30** 0309 1.6 / 0907 8.7 / W 1526 1.9 / 2124 8.5	**15** 0404 3.0 / 1009 7.1 / F 1616 3.4 / 2217 7.1	**30** 0425 2.5 / 1032 7.5 / SA 1647 3.1 / 2255 7.5
	31 0354 2.4 / 0953 8.2 / M 1616 2.4 / 2214 7.8				**31** 0343 2.0 / 0945 8.1 / TH 1601 2.4 / 2202 7.9		

Chart Datum: 5·06 metres below Ordnance Datum (Local)

》 **FREE** monthly updates from 《
www.reedsalmanac.co.uk

TIDES

TIME ZONE (UT)
For Summer Time add ONE hour in non-shaded areas

CHANNEL ISLES – ST PETER PORT
LAT 49°27′N LONG 2°31′W
TIMES AND HEIGHTS OF HIGH AND LOW WATERS

YEAR 2005

MAY

Day	Time	m	Time	m
1 SU ☽	0533 / 1143 / 1803	3.0 / 7.0 / 3.5	**16** M	0529 / 1143 / 1754 / 2358	3.8 / 6.4 / 4.1 / 6.6
2 M	0015 / 0705 / 1320 / 1945	7.2 / 3.2 / 6.9 / 3.5	**17** TU	0656 / 1307 / 1922	3.8 / 6.4 / 4.0
3 TU	0155 / 0838 / 1448 / 2110	7.3 / 2.9 / 7.3 / 3.0	**18** W	0124 / 0812 / 1425 / 2035	6.6 / 3.6 / 6.7 / 3.7
4 W	0311 / 0944 / 1549 / 2210	7.7 / 2.3 / 7.9 / 2.4	**19** TH	0239 / 0913 / 1523 / 2134	7.0 / 3.2 / 7.2 / 3.1
5 TH	0408 / 1037 / 1638 / 2300	8.3 / 1.8 / 8.4 / 1.9	**20** F	0336 / 1005 / 1610 / 2224	7.4 / 2.7 / 7.7 / 2.6
6 F	0457 / 1123 / 1722 / 2345	8.7 / 1.4 / 8.8 / 1.5	**21** SA	0425 / 1051 / 1654 / 2310	7.9 / 2.2 / 8.2 / 2.1
7 SA	0541 / 1206 / 1803	9.0 / 1.2 / 9.1	**22** SU	0510 / 1135 / 1736 / 2355	8.2 / 1.8 / 8.6 / 1.6
8 SU ●	0026 / 0622 / 1246 / 1841	1.2 / 9.2 / 1.1 / 9.2	**23** M	0554 / 1218 / 1818 ○	8.7 / 1.5 / 8.9
9 M	0105 / 0701 / 1323 / 1917	1.2 / 9.1 / 1.2 / 9.1	**24** TU	0038 / 0637 / 1300 / 1858	1.3 / 8.9 / 1.3 / 9.1
10 TU	0141 / 0737 / 1356 / 1949	1.3 / 8.9 / 1.5 / 9.0	**25** W	0122 / 0721 / 1342 / 1940	1.2 / 9.0 / 1.5 / 9.2
11 W	0213 / 0810 / 1426 / 2020	1.6 / 8.6 / 1.9 / 8.6	**26** TH	0205 / 0805 / 1425 / 2023	1.2 / 8.9 / 1.5 / 9.1
12 TH	0243 / 0842 / 1455 / 2051	2.0 / 8.2 / 2.4 / 8.2	**27** F	0250 / 0851 / 1509 / 2108	1.4 / 8.7 / 1.8 / 8.8
13 F	0313 / 0916 / 1524 / 2122	2.5 / 7.7 / 2.9 / 7.8	**28** SA	0338 / 0940 / 1557 / 2159	1.7 / 8.3 / 2.3 / 8.4
14 SA	0346 / 0952 / 1558 / 2159	3.0 / 7.2 / 3.4 / 7.3	**29** SU	0432 / 1035 / 1653 / 2257	2.1 / 7.9 / 2.7 / 8.0
15 SU	0427 / 1039 / 1643 / 2249	3.4 / 6.7 / 3.8 / 6.9	**30** M	0535 / 1139 / 1800 ☾	2.5 / 7.5 / 3.0
			31 TU	0005 / 0647 / 1254 / 1917	7.7 / 2.7 / 7.7 / 3.1

JUNE

Day	Time	m	Time	m
1 W	0121 / 0801 / 1407 / 2033	7.6 / 2.7 / 7.5 / 3.0	**16** TH	0018 / 0701 / 1307 / 1926	7.0 / 3.4 / 6.9 / 3.6
2 TH	0233 / 0907 / 1510 / 2135	7.7 / 2.5 / 7.7 / 2.6	**17** F	0125 / 0808 / 1413 / 2034	7.1 / 3.3 / 7.1 / 3.3
3 F	0333 / 1002 / 1603 / 2228	7.9 / 2.3 / 8.0 / 2.3	**18** SA	0233 / 0909 / 1514 / 2135	7.3 / 3.0 / 7.5 / 2.9
4 SA	0426 / 1051 / 1650 / 2315	8.2 / 2.1 / 8.3 / 2.1	**19** SU	0335 / 1006 / 1610 / 2232	7.6 / 2.6 / 7.9 / 2.4
5 SU	0513 / 1136 / 1734 / 2359	8.3 / 2.0 / 8.5 / 1.9	**20** M	0433 / 1100 / 1702 / 2326	8.0 / 2.2 / 8.3 / 2.0
6 M	0557 / 1218 / 1814 ●	8.4 / 1.9 / 8.6	**21** TU	0527 / 1152 / 1753	8.4 / 1.9 / 8.7
7 TU	0039 / 0638 / 1257 / 1852	1.8 / 8.5 / 1.9 / 8.7	**22** W	0018 / 0619 / 1243 / 1842 ○	1.6 / 8.7 / 1.6 / 9.1
8 W	0117 / 0716 / 1332 / 1927	1.9 / 8.4 / 2.0 / 8.6	**23** TH	0110 / 0710 / 1333 / 1930	1.3 / 8.9 / 1.4 / 9.3
9 TH	0152 / 0753 / 1406 / 2002	2.0 / 8.2 / 2.2 / 8.4	**24** F	0200 / 0800 / 1421 / 2018	1.1 / 9.0 / 1.4 / 9.3
10 F	0226 / 0828 / 1438 / 2035	2.2 / 8.0 / 2.5 / 8.2	**25** SA	0249 / 0849 / 1509 / 2106	1.1 / 8.9 / 1.5 / 9.2
11 SA	0300 / 0903 / 1511 / 2109	2.5 / 7.7 / 2.8 / 7.9	**26** SU	0338 / 0937 / 1557 / 2155	1.2 / 8.7 / 1.7 / 8.9
12 SU	0335 / 0940 / 1547 / 2146	2.8 / 7.4 / 3.1 / 7.6	**27** M	0428 / 1028 / 1646 / 2245	1.5 / 8.4 / 2.1 / 8.5
13 M	0414 / 1021 / 1627 / 2228	3.1 / 7.2 / 3.4 / 7.3	**28** TU	0520 / 1120 / 1739 / 2340 ☾	1.9 / 8.0 / 2.5 / 8.1
14 TU	0459 / 1107 / 1716 / 2318	3.3 / 6.9 / 3.6 / 7.1	**29** W	0615 / 1216 / 1838	2.4 / 7.7 / 2.9
15 W	0555 / 1203 / 1817 ☽	3.4 / 6.8 / 3.7	**30** TH	0040 / 0715 / 1320 / 1945	7.7 / 2.7 / 7.4 / 3.1

JULY

Day	Time	m	Time	m
1 F	0149 / 0821 / 1426 / 2054	7.4 / 2.9 / 7.3 / 3.1	**16** SA	0026 / 0657 / 1308 / 1931	7.2 / 3.3 / 7.1 / 3.4
2 SA	0256 / 0925 / 1528 / 2157	7.4 / 3.0 / 7.4 / 3.0	**17** SU	0137 / 0814 / 1423 / 2052	7.2 / 3.3 / 7.2 / 3.2
3 SU	0357 / 1021 / 1622 / 2251	7.5 / 2.9 / 7.7 / 2.8	**18** M	0256 / 0929 / 1536 / 2204	7.3 / 3.0 / 7.6 / 2.8
4 M	0451 / 1112 / 1711 / 2339	7.6 / 2.7 / 7.9 / 2.6	**19** TU	0408 / 1037 / 1641 / 2308	7.7 / 2.6 / 8.1 / 2.2
5 TU	0539 / 1157 / 1755 ●	7.8 / 2.5 / 8.1	**20** W	0512 / 1138 / 1739	8.1 / 2.2 / 8.6
6 W	0022 / 0622 / 1239 / 1835	2.5 / 8.0 / 2.4 / 8.3	**21** TH	0008 / 0611 / 1235 / 1833 ○	1.7 / 8.6 / 1.7 / 9.1
7 TH	0102 / 0703 / 1317 / 1913	2.2 / 8.1 / 2.3 / 8.4	**22** F	0103 / 0704 / 1327 / 1923	1.1 / 9.0 / 1.2 / 9.5
8 F	0139 / 0741 / 1352 / 1949	2.1 / 8.2 / 2.2 / 8.4	**23** SA	0154 / 0754 / 1415 / 2011	0.8 / 9.3 / 1.0 / 9.7
9 SA	0214 / 0817 / 1426 / 2023	2.1 / 8.1 / 2.3 / 8.4	**24** SU	0242 / 0840 / 1501 / 2056	0.6 / 9.4 / 0.9 / 9.7
10 SU	0248 / 0850 / 1458 / 2055	2.2 / 8.0 / 2.4 / 8.2	**25** M	0327 / 0924 / 1544 / 2139	0.7 / 9.3 / 1.1 / 9.4
11 M	0320 / 0923 / 1531 / 2128	2.4 / 7.9 / 2.6 / 8.0	**26** TU	0409 / 1006 / 1625 / 2222	1.1 / 8.9 / 1.6 / 8.9
12 TU	0353 / 0955 / 1605 / 2202	2.6 / 7.8 / 2.8 / 7.8	**27** W	0451 / 1048 / 1707 / 2306	1.6 / 8.4 / 2.2 / 8.3
13 W	0428 / 1031 / 1642 / 2241	2.8 / 7.5 / 3.0 / 7.6	**28** TH	0535 / 1133 / 1753 / 2355 ☾	2.3 / 7.8 / 2.8 / 7.6
14 TH	0507 / 1113 / 1726 / 2328	3.0 / 7.3 / 3.2 / 7.3	**29** F	0625 / 1226 / 1849	3.0 / 7.3 / 3.4
15 F	0555 / 1204 / 1821 ☽	3.2 / 7.1 / 3.4	**30** SA	0057 / 0726 / 1336 / 2003	7.0 / 3.5 / 6.9 / 3.7
			31 SU	0219 / 0845 / 1456 / 2132	6.7 / 3.7 / 6.8 / 3.7

AUGUST

Day	Time	m	Time	m
1 M	0338 / 1000 / 1604 / 2238	6.8 / 3.6 / 7.1 / 3.3	**16** TU	0235 / 0910 / 1520 / 2153	7.0 / 3.5 / 7.3 / 3.0
2 TU	0439 / 1059 / 1657 / 2329	7.1 / 3.2 / 7.5 / 2.9	**17** W	0401 / 1028 / 1633 / 2303	7.5 / 2.9 / 8.0 / 2.3
3 W	0528 / 1146 / 1742	7.5 / 2.9 / 7.9	**18** TH	0509 / 1131 / 1732	8.1 / 2.2 / 8.7
4 TH ●	0012 / 0610 / 1227 / 1822	2.6 / 7.8 / 2.5 / 8.3	**19** F ○	0001 / 0604 / 1226 / 1823	1.5 / 8.8 / 1.5 / 9.4
5 F	0051 / 0649 / 1304 / 1900	2.2 / 8.2 / 2.2 / 8.5	**20** SA	0053 / 0653 / 1315 / 1911	0.9 / 9.3 / 0.9 / 9.9
6 SA	0126 / 0726 / 1338 / 1934	2.0 / 8.4 / 2.0 / 8.7	**21** SU	0140 / 0738 / 1400 / 1954	0.4 / 9.6 / 0.6 / 10.1
7 SU	0159 / 0759 / 1409 / 2006	1.9 / 8.5 / 1.9 / 8.7	**22** M	0224 / 0820 / 1442 / 2036	0.2 / 9.8 / 0.5 / 10.1
8 M	0229 / 0830 / 1439 / 2036	1.8 / 8.4 / 2.0 / 8.6	**23** TU	0304 / 0859 / 1520 / 2114	0.4 / 9.6 / 0.8 / 9.7
9 TU	0258 / 0858 / 1509 / 2104	1.9 / 8.3 / 2.1 / 8.5	**24** W	0341 / 0936 / 1556 / 2151	0.9 / 9.1 / 1.4 / 9.0
10 W	0326 / 0925 / 1538 / 2133	2.1 / 8.1 / 2.3 / 8.2	**25** TH	0416 / 1011 / 1631 / 2227	1.6 / 8.5 / 2.1 / 8.2
11 TH	0355 / 0955 / 1609 / 2207	2.4 / 7.9 / 2.6 / 7.9	**26** F	0451 / 1047 / 1707 / 2306 ☾	2.5 / 7.7 / 2.9 / 7.4
12 F	0427 / 1030 / 1645 / 2247	2.8 / 7.6 / 3.0 / 7.5	**27** SA	0532 / 1130 / 1754 / 2359	3.3 / 6.9 / 3.7 / 6.7
13 SA	0508 / 1116 / 1733 / 2341	3.1 / 7.3 / 3.3 / 7.0	**28** SU	0630 / 1237 / 1911	4.0 / 6.5 / 4.2
14 SU	0605 / 1219 / 1844 ☽	3.5 / 6.9 / 3.6	**29** M	0140 / 0803 / 1430 / 2119	6.2 / 4.3 / 6.5 / 4.1
15 M	0056 / 0730 / 1348 / 2024	6.5 / 3.7 / 6.7 / 3.5	**30** TU	0330 / 0951 / 1552 / 2231	6.5 / 4.0 / 7.0 / 3.5
			31 W	0429 / 1048 / 1643 / 2317	7.0 / 3.5 / 7.4 / 3.1

Chart Datum: 5·06 metres below Ordnance Datum (Local)

》》 **FREE** monthly updates from 《《
www.reedsalmanac.co.uk

TIME ZONE (UT)
For Summer Time add ONE hour in **non-shaded areas**

CHANNEL ISLES – ST PETER PORT
LAT 49°27'N   LONG 2°31'W
TIMES AND HEIGHTS OF HIGH AND LOW WATERS

YEAR 2005

SEPTEMBER				OCTOBER				NOVEMBER				DECEMBER			
Time m		Time m		Time m		Time m		Time m		Time m		Time m		Time m	
1 0513 7.5 / 1131 2.9 / TH 1725 7.9 / 2356 2.5		**16** 0500 8.4 / 1120 2.0 / F 1719 9.0 / 2347 1.3		**1** 0522 8.1 / 1139 2.4 / SA 1734 8.4		**16** 0524 9.2 / 1146 1.3 / SU 1742 9.6		**1** 0554 8.8 / 1210 1.8 / TU 1808 8.9		**16** 0022 1.4 / 0618 9.3 / W 1246 1.3 / ○ 1840 9.3		**1** 0556 8.8 / 1219 1.8 / TH 1817 8.8 ●		**16** 0042 2.1 / 0637 8.8 / F 1308 2.0 / 1903 8.5	
2 0552 8.0 / 1209 2.4 / F 1803 8.4		**17** 0549 9.1 / 1210 1.3 / SA 1806 9.6		**2** 0000 2.0 / 0557 8.6 / SU 1213 1.9 / 1808 8.8		**17** 0008 0.9 / 0606 9.6 / M 1230 0.9 / ○ 1824 9.9		**2** 0028 1.6 / 0627 9.0 / W 1246 1.6 / ● 1842 9.1		**17** 0102 1.4 / 0657 9.3 / TH 1325 1.4 / 1919 9.1		**2** 0037 1.8 / 0636 9.0 / F 1302 1.6 / 1858 8.9		**17** 0120 2.1 / 0716 8.8 / SA 1346 2.0 / 1942 8.4	
3 0031 2.1 / 0627 8.4 / SA 1244 2.0 / ● 1838 8.8		**18** 0034 0.7 / 0633 9.6 / SU 1255 0.7 / ○ 1850 10.1		**3** 0032 1.7 / 0630 8.9 / M 1245 1.6 / ● 1842 9.1		**18** 0050 0.7 / 0646 9.8 / TU 1311 0.7 / 1904 9.9		**3** 0102 1.5 / 0700 9.2 / TH 1321 1.5 / 1917 9.1		**18** 0138 1.7 / 0733 9.1 / F 1401 1.7 / 1955 8.8		**3** 0119 1.7 / 0717 9.2 / SA 1344 1.5 / 1941 8.9		**18** 0156 2.3 / 0752 8.7 / SU 1422 2.2 / 2018 8.2	
4 0104 1.7 / 0702 8.7 / SU 1315 1.7 / 1912 9.0		**19** 0117 0.4 / 0714 9.9 / M 1337 0.5 / 1931 10.2		**4** 0103 1.5 / 0702 9.1 / TU 1316 1.4 / 1913 9.2		**19** 0129 0.7 / 0723 9.8 / W 1349 0.9 / 1942 9.7		**4** 0136 1.6 / 0733 9.1 / F 1356 1.6 / 1952 9.0		**19** 0212 2.0 / 0807 8.8 / SA 1435 2.1 / 2029 8.4		**4** 0200 1.8 / 0759 9.1 / SU 1428 1.6 / 2026 8.8		**19** 0230 2.5 / 0827 8.4 / M 1457 2.4 / 2053 8.0	
5 0134 1.6 / 0733 8.9 / M 1346 1.6 / 1942 9.1		**20** 0157 0.3 / 0753 9.9 / TU 1416 0.5 / 2009 10.1		**5** 0132 1.4 / 0731 9.1 / W 1347 1.4 / 1942 9.2		**20** 0205 1.1 / 0758 9.5 / TH 1424 1.2 / 2017 9.2		**5** 0210 1.8 / 0808 9.0 / SA 1432 1.8 / 2028 8.7		**20** 0243 2.5 / 0839 8.4 / SU 1508 2.6 / 2104 7.9		**5** 0244 2.0 / 0844 8.9 / M 1514 1.8 / 2112 8.5		**20** 0302 2.7 / 0901 8.1 / TU 1530 2.7 / 2128 7.7	
6 0203 1.5 / 0802 8.8 / TU 1415 1.6 / 2010 9.0		**21** 0235 0.6 / 0829 9.7 / W 1452 0.9 / 2045 9.6		**6** 0201 1.5 / 0758 9.0 / TH 1417 1.6 / 2011 9.0		**21** 0237 1.6 / 0831 9.1 / F 1456 1.8 / 2049 8.6		**6** 0245 2.2 / 0845 8.6 / SU 1511 2.2 / 2110 8.3		**21** 0314 3.0 / 0914 7.9 / M 1542 3.1 / 2141 7.4		**6** 0330 2.3 / 0933 8.6 / TU 1605 2.2 / 2204 8.1		**21** 0336 3.0 / 0937 7.8 / W 1605 3.0 / 2205 7.4	
7 0230 1.6 / 0828 8.7 / W 1443 1.7 / 2037 8.8		**22** 0308 1.1 / 0902 9.2 / TH 1524 1.5 / 2118 8.9		**7** 0230 1.8 / 0827 8.8 / F 1447 1.9 / 2042 8.7		**22** 0307 2.3 / 0901 8.5 / SA 1526 2.5 / 2121 8.0		**7** 0325 2.7 / 0930 8.2 / M 1557 2.7 / 2200 7.8		**22** 0348 3.5 / 0952 7.4 / TU 1622 3.5 / 2225 7.0		**7** 0423 2.7 / 1027 8.3 / W 1701 2.5 / 2302 7.8		**22** 0413 3.4 / 1016 7.5 / TH 1644 3.3 / 2245 7.1	
8 0257 1.9 / 0854 8.5 / TH 1510 2.0 / 2105 8.6		**23** 0339 1.9 / 0933 8.5 / F 1555 2.3 / 2150 8.1		**8** 0259 2.2 / 0858 8.5 / SA 1518 2.3 / 2116 8.3		**23** 0335 3.0 / 0932 7.8 / SU 1557 3.2 / 2156 7.3		**8** 0416 3.2 / 1026 7.7 / TU 1658 3.2 / 2305 7.3		**23** 0433 4.0 / 1041 7.0 / W 1718 3.9 / ◐ 2324 6.6		**8** 0524 3.1 / 1130 7.9 / TH 1805 2.8 / ◐		**23** 0456 3.7 / 1101 7.2 / F 1729 3.5 / ◐ 2334 6.9	
9 0324 2.2 / 0923 8.2 / F 1539 2.4 / 2137 8.2		**24** 0409 2.8 / 1004 7.8 / SA 1626 3.1 / 2224 7.3		**9** 0332 2.7 / 0934 8.0 / SU 1556 2.9 / 2159 7.7		**24** 0406 3.7 / 1009 7.2 / M 1637 3.8 / 2243 6.6		**9** 0527 3.7 / 1140 7.4 / W 1821 3.4 ●		**24** 0542 4.3 / 1148 6.7 / TH 1834 4.1		**9** 0008 7.5 / 0636 3.2 / F 1241 7.7 / 1917 2.9		**24** 0550 3.8 / 1154 7.0 / SA 1826 3.7	
10 0354 2.7 / 0956 7.8 / SA 1613 2.8 / 2215 7.7		**25** 0441 3.6 / 1041 7.1 / SU 1707 3.8 / ◐ 2311 6.5		**10** 0414 3.3 / 1024 7.5 / M 1650 3.6 / ● 2300 7.1		**25** 0453 4.3 / 1106 6.6 / TU 1753 4.3 ◐		**10** 0031 7.1 / 0705 3.8 / TH 1313 7.4 / 1955 3.2		**25** 0045 6.5 / 0708 4.3 / F 1310 6.7 / 1950 3.9		**10** 0124 7.5 / 0755 3.2 / SA 1354 7.8 / 2028 2.8		**25** 0033 6.8 / 0658 3.9 / SU 1259 6.9 / 1934 3.6	
11 0432 3.2 / 1041 7.4 / SU 1701 3.6 / ◐ 2309 7.1		**26** 0534 4.3 / 1141 6.4 / M 1828 4.4		**11** 0520 3.9 / 1140 7.0 / TU 1818 3.8		**26** 0007 6.2 / 0636 4.6 / W 1248 6.4 / 1939 4.4		**11** 0208 7.3 / 0836 3.3 / F 1435 7.8 / 2109 2.7		**26** 0206 6.7 / 0822 4.0 / SA 1422 7.0 / 2054 3.6		**11** 0235 7.7 / 0904 2.9 / SU 1501 7.9 / 2131 2.6		**26** 0144 6.9 / 0810 3.7 / M 1409 7.0 / 2041 3.5	
12 0531 3.7 / 1148 6.9 / M 1818 3.8		**27** 0042 6.2 / 0722 4.6 / TU 1352 6.2 / 2055 4.4		**12** 0035 6.7 / 0714 4.1 / W 1330 7.0 / 2017 3.6		**27** 0219 6.3 / 0828 4.4 / TH 1436 6.6 / 2113 3.9		**12** 0316 7.9 / 0927 2.7 / SA 1536 8.3 / 2206 2.2		**27** 0305 7.2 / 0920 3.5 / SU 1519 7.4 / 2146 3.1		**12** 0334 8.0 / 1003 2.6 / M 1558 8.1 / 2225 2.4		**27** 0251 7.2 / 0915 3.3 / TU 1514 7.3 / 2142 3.1	
13 0036 6.7 / 0712 4.0 / TU 1334 6.8 / 2019 3.7		**28** 0311 6.4 / 0930 4.3 / W 1528 6.7 / 2208 3.8		**13** 0236 7.1 / 0902 3.4 / TH 1505 7.6 / 2138 2.8		**28** 0323 6.9 / 0937 3.8 / F 1533 7.2 / 2203 3.3		**13** 0409 8.4 / 1032 2.1 / SU 1628 8.8 / 2255 1.7		**28** 0352 7.6 / 1009 3.0 / M 1607 7.8 / 2231 2.7		**13** 0426 8.3 / 1054 2.2 / TU 1650 8.3 / 2314 2.2		**28** 0349 7.6 / 1013 2.9 / W 1613 7.6 / 2238 2.7	
14 0236 6.9 / 0909 3.6 / W 1517 7.4 / 2151 3.0		**29** 0406 7.0 / 1024 3.6 / TH 1618 7.3 / 2250 3.1		**14** 0347 7.8 / 1008 2.5 / F 1606 8.4 / 2235 2.0		**29** 0406 7.5 / 1020 3.1 / SA 1616 7.7 / 2243 2.8		**14** 0455 8.9 / 1119 1.7 / M 1715 9.1 / 2340 1.5		**29** 0435 8.1 / 1053 2.5 / TU 1651 8.2 / 2314 2.3		**14** 0513 8.5 / 1142 2.2 / W 1738 8.4		**29** 0442 8.1 / 1108 2.4 / TH 1708 8.0 / 2330 2.3	
15 0402 7.6 / 1024 2.9 / TH 1626 8.2 / 2255 2.2		**30** 0446 7.6 / 1104 3.0 / F 1658 7.9 / 2326 2.5		**15** 0439 8.6 / 1100 1.9 / SA 1656 9.0 / 2323 1.4		**30** 0443 8.0 / 1058 2.6 / SU 1655 8.2 / 2319 2.3		**15** 0538 9.1 / 1204 1.4 / TU 1759 9.3		**30** 0516 8.5 / 1136 2.1 / W 1734 8.5 / ○ 1822 8.5		**15** 0000 2.2 / 0556 8.7 / TH 1227 2.0 / ○ 1822 8.5		**30** 0533 8.5 / 1200 2.0 / F 1800 8.5	
						31 0519 8.5 / 1134 2.1 / M 1732 8.6 / 2354 1.9								**31** 0021 1.9 / 0621 8.8 / SA 1251 1.6 / ● 1849 8.8	

Chart Datum: 5·06 metres below Ordnance Datum (Local)
》》 **FREE** monthly updates from 《《
www.reedsalmanac.co.uk

Chapter 5

TIDES

ST. HELIER

MEAN SPRING AND NEAP CURVES

MEAN RANGES
Springs 9.6m
Neaps 4.1m

Springs occur 2 days after New and Full Moon

TIME ZONE (UT)
For Summer Time add ONE hour in **non-shaded areas**

CHANNEL ISLES – ST HELIER
LAT 49°11′N LONG 2°07′W
TIMES AND HEIGHTS OF HIGH AND LOW WATERS

YEAR 2005

JANUARY		FEBRUARY		MARCH		APRIL	
Time m	Time m	Time m	Time m	Time m	Time m	Time m	Time m
1 0343 3.0 / 0927 9.4 / SA 1607 3.0 / 2154 8.9	**16** 0500 2.3 / 1037 10.0 / SU 1726 2.4 / 2301 9.4	**1** 0436 2.9 / 1018 9.4 / TU 1655 3.0 / 2242 8.9	**16** 0529 3.4 / 1115 8.5 / W 1749 3.8 / ◐ 2336 8.2	**1** 0342 1.9 / 0920 10.2 / TU 1558 2.2 / 2137 9.8	**16** 0417 2.6 / 0957 9.3 / W 1628 3.0 / 2207 9.0	**1** 0435 2.9 / 1017 8.9 / F 1653 3.4 / 2240 8.7	**16** 0449 4.0 / 1039 7.6 / SA 1709 4.5 / ◐ 2259 7.6
2 0421 3.3 / 1006 9.1 / SU 1646 3.3 / 2235 8.6	**17** 0542 2.9 / 1121 9.3 / M 1808 3.0 / ◐ 2346 8.8	**2** 0516 3.3 / 1101 8.9 / W 1738 3.5 / ◐ 2332 8.5	**17** 0615 4.1 / 1211 7.7 / TH 1845 4.4	**2** 0413 2.4 / 0952 9.7 / W 1628 2.7 / 2211 9.3	**17** 0443 3.4 / 1028 8.4 / TH 1657 3.8 / ◐ 2242 8.2	**2** 0530 3.6 / 1121 8.1 / SA 1800 4.1 / ◐	**17** 0553 4.6 / 1215 7.0 / SU 1832 4.9
3 0504 3.6 / 1050 8.8 / M 1732 3.6 / ◐ 2324 8.4	**18** 0628 3.5 / 1213 8.6 / TU 1858 3.6	**3** 0610 3.7 / 1201 8.4 / TH 1841 3.9	**18** 0047 7.6 / 0734 4.6 / F 1352 7.3 / 2022 4.7	**3** 0449 3.0 / 1031 9.0 / TH 1706 3.4 / ◐ 2255 8.6	**18** 0520 4.1 / 1113 7.5 / F 1744 4.6 / 2341 7.4	**3** 0003 8.0 / 0658 4.0 / SU 1310 7.8 / 1950 4.3	**18** 0058 7.2 / 0738 4.7 / M 1420 7.2 / 2028 4.8
4 0557 3.9 / 1146 8.5 / TU 1829 3.8	**19** 0043 8.3 / 0728 4.0 / W 1320 8.1 / 2002 4.0	**4** 0044 8.2 / 0729 4.0 / F 1325 8.2 / 2014 4.0	**19** 0234 7.5 / 0922 4.5 / SA 1533 7.6 / 2159 4.3	**4** 0539 3.6 / 1128 8.3 / F 1807 4.0	**19** 0632 4.7 / 1303 7.0 / SA 1921 5.0	**4** 0205 8.1 / 0848 3.6 / M 1501 8.3 / 2134 3.6	**19** 0242 7.6 / 0918 4.2 / TU 1527 7.9 / 2147 4.0
5 0028 8.2 / 0703 4.0 / W 1255 8.4 / 1940 3.8	**20** 0157 8.1 / 0842 4.1 / TH 1440 8.0 / 2116 4.0	**5** 0219 8.3 / 0905 3.7 / SA 1503 8.4 / 2148 3.6	**20** 0413 7.8 / 1041 3.9 / SU 1638 8.2 / 2303 3.7	**5** 0008 8.1 / 0701 4.0 / SA 1303 7.8 / 1951 4.3	**20** 0154 7.2 / 0839 4.7 / SU 1509 7.3 / 2127 4.7	**5** 0333 8.9 / 1012 2.8 / TU 1611 9.2 / 2244 2.6	**20** 0341 8.3 / 1017 3.4 / W 1613 8.6 / 2238 3.3
6 0142 8.4 / 0820 3.8 / TH 1412 8.6 / 2058 3.5	**21** 0313 8.2 / 0957 3.9 / F 1553 8.2 / 2224 3.8	**6** 0347 8.9 / 1028 3.0 / SU 1626 9.1 / 2305 2.8	**21** 0453 8.7 / 1133 3.2 / M 1724 8.9 / 2349 3.0	**6** 0203 8.0 / 0852 3.8 / SU 1503 8.1 / 2142 3.8	**21** 0331 7.7 / 1013 4.1 / M 1613 8.0 / 2236 3.9	**6** 0433 9.8 / 1113 1.9 / W 1704 10.1 / 2339 1.8	**21** 0425 9.0 / 1103 2.7 / TH 1653 9.3 / 2322 2.6
7 0256 8.8 / 0936 3.3 / F 1526 9.0 / 2210 3.1	**22** 0417 8.6 / 1059 3.5 / SA 1651 8.6 / 2319 3.3	**7** 0457 9.7 / 1138 2.2 / M 1731 9.9	**22** 0535 9.3 / 1215 2.6 / TU 1802 9.4	**7** 0343 8.7 / 1024 3.1 / M 1625 9.0 / 2300 2.8	**22** 0426 8.5 / 1105 3.3 / TU 1657 8.8 / 2322 3.1	**7** 0523 10.6 / 1205 1.2 / TH 1749 10.7	**22** 0505 9.6 / 1145 2.1 / F 1729 9.9
8 0403 9.4 / 1043 2.7 / SA 1633 9.6 / 2315 2.5	**23** 0508 9.0 / 1148 3.0 / SU 1738 9.1	**8** 0008 2.0 / 0554 10.5 / TU 1239 1.4 / ● 1825 10.6	**23** 0029 2.5 / 0612 9.8 / W 1254 2.1 / 1836 9.8	**8** 0450 9.7 / 1132 2.0 / TU 1723 10.0 / 2359 1.9	**23** 0507 9.2 / 1147 2.6 / W 1734 9.4	**8** 0027 1.2 / 0606 11.2 / F 1251 0.8 / ● 1829 11.1	**23** 0003 2.0 / 0542 10.2 / SA 1226 1.7 / 1805 10.4
9 0504 10.0 / 1145 2.1 / SU 1734 10.1	**24** 0004 2.9 / 0550 9.5 / M 1226 2.4 / 1818 9.4	**9** 0104 1.4 / 0645 11.2 / W 1333 0.8 / 1913 11.2	**24** 0107 2.1 / 0646 10.2 / TH 1329 1.8 / ○ 1908 10.2	**9** 0543 10.6 / 1227 1.1 / W 1812 10.8	**24** 0002 2.4 / 0544 9.8 / TH 1226 2.0 / 1807 10.0	**9** 0110 0.9 / 0646 11.4 / SA 1331 0.7 / 1906 11.3	**24** 0043 1.6 / 0618 10.6 / SU 1304 1.4 / ○ 1840 10.7
10 0014 2.0 / 0559 10.6 / M 1244 1.4 / ● 1830 10.6	**25** 0045 2.6 / 0628 9.8 / TU 1309 2.3 / ○ 1854 9.7	**10** 0154 0.9 / 0731 11.6 / TH 1421 0.5 / 1957 11.4	**25** 0140 1.8 / 0718 10.5 / F 1402 1.6 / 1939 10.4	**10** 0050 1.1 / 0630 11.3 / TH 1317 0.6 / ● 1855 11.3	**25** 0040 1.9 / 0618 10.3 / F 1302 1.6 / ○ 1840 10.4	**10** 0148 0.8 / 0723 11.4 / SU 1406 0.8 / 1940 11.2	**25** 0120 1.3 / 0655 10.9 / M 1339 1.3 / 1915 10.9
11 0110 1.6 / 0652 11.1 / TU 1339 1.1 / 1922 10.9	**26** 0121 2.3 / 0703 10.1 / W 1345 2.1 / 1928 9.9	**11** 0239 0.7 / 0814 11.8 / F 1504 0.4 / 2037 11.3	**26** 0212 1.6 / 0749 10.7 / SA 1432 1.5 / 2009 10.5	**11** 0136 0.7 / 0712 11.7 / F 1400 0.3 / 1934 11.5	**26** 0115 1.6 / 0651 10.7 / SA 1336 1.3 / 1911 10.7	**11** 0222 1.0 / 0757 11.1 / M 1437 1.1 / 2011 10.9	**26** 0157 1.2 / 0732 10.9 / TU 1414 1.3 / 1950 10.9
12 0202 1.3 / 0742 11.3 / W 1431 0.9 / 2010 11.0	**27** 0155 2.2 / 0736 10.2 / TH 1418 2.0 / 2000 10.0	**12** 0319 0.8 / 0853 11.5 / SA 1542 0.7 / 2114 11.0	**27** 0242 1.5 / 0819 10.8 / SU 1501 1.5 / 2039 10.5	**12** 0217 0.5 / 0751 11.8 / SA 1438 0.4 / 2010 11.4	**27** 0149 1.3 / 0723 10.9 / SU 1408 1.2 / 1943 10.8	**12** 0251 1.4 / 0829 10.6 / TU 1504 1.7 / 2039 10.4	**27** 0232 1.3 / 0809 10.9 / W 1449 1.6 / 2026 10.6
13 0251 1.3 / 0829 11.4 / TH 1519 1.0 / 2056 10.9	**28** 0228 2.1 / 0808 10.3 / F 1449 2.0 / 2031 10.0	**13** 0355 1.2 / 0929 11.0 / SU 1616 1.3 / 2147 10.4	**28** 0312 1.6 / 0850 10.6 / M 1529 1.7 / 2108 10.2	**13** 0253 0.7 / 0827 11.5 / SU 1511 0.7 / 2043 11.1	**28** 0221 1.2 / 0755 10.9 / M 1438 1.3 / 2014 10.8	**13** 0318 1.9 / 0857 9.9 / W 1529 2.3 / 2105 9.8	**28** 0309 1.6 / 0848 10.3 / TH 1524 2.1 / 2105 10.1
14 0336 1.4 / 0913 11.1 / F 1604 1.2 / 2139 10.5	**29** 0259 2.1 / 0840 10.3 / SA 1520 2.1 / 2102 9.9	**14** 0427 1.9 / 1003 10.2 / M 1646 2.1 / 2219 9.7		**14** 0324 1.1 / 0859 11.0 / M 1540 1.4 / 2112 10.5	**29** 0252 1.4 / 0827 10.8 / TU 1507 1.5 / 2044 10.5	**14** 0344 2.6 / 0925 9.1 / TH 1554 3.1 / 2132 9.0	**29** 0349 2.1 / 0930 9.6 / F 1605 2.7 / 2149 9.5
15 0419 1.7 / 0956 10.6 / SA 1646 1.7 / 2220 10.0	**30** 0330 2.3 / 0911 10.1 / SU 1550 2.3 / 2132 9.7	**15** 0457 2.6 / 1037 9.4 / TU 1715 3.0 / 2253 8.9		**15** 0352 1.8 / 0929 10.2 / TU 1605 2.1 / 2140 9.8	**30** 0323 1.8 / 0900 10.4 / W 1537 2.0 / 2116 10.1	**15** 0411 3.3 / 0956 8.3 / F 1623 3.8 / 2205 8.3	**30** 0436 2.8 / 1023 8.9 / SA 1656 3.4 / 2248 8.8
	31 0402 2.5 / 0943 9.8 / M 1621 2.6 / 2205 9.3			**31** 0356 2.2 / 0934 9.7 / TH 1610 2.7 / 2152 9.4			

Chart Datum: 5·88 metres below Ordnance Datum (Local)

》》 **FREE** monthly updates from 《《
www.reedsalmanac.co.uk

TIDES

TIME ZONE (UT)
For Summer Time add ONE hour in **non-shaded areas**

CHANNEL ISLES – ST HELIER
LAT 49°11'N LONG 2°07'W
TIMES AND HEIGHTS OF HIGH AND LOW WATERS

YEAR 2005

MAY

Day	Time m	Time m	Day	Time m	Time m
1 SU ☽	0538 3.3 / 1135 8.3 / 1810 3.9		**16** M	0527 4.2 / 1133 7.4 / 1754 4.5 / 2356 7.6	
2 M	0012 8.4 / 0703 3.5 / 1311 8.1 / 1945 3.8		**17** TU	0641 4.3 / 1306 7.4 / 1917 4.5	
3 TU	0150 8.5 / 0832 3.2 / 1437 8.6 / 2110 3.3		**18** W	0129 7.7 / 0804 4.1 / 1421 7.8 / 2038 4.1	
4 W	0306 9.1 / 0944 2.6 / 1542 9.3 / 2215 2.6		**19** TH	0238 8.1 / 0913 3.6 / 1516 8.4 / 2140 3.5	
5 TH	0404 9.8 / 1043 2.0 / 1634 9.9 / 2309 1.9		**20** F	0331 8.7 / 1008 3.0 / 1602 9.0 / 2232 2.9	
6 F	0454 10.3 / 1133 1.6 / 1719 10.4 / 2357 1.6		**21** SA	0418 9.3 / 1058 2.5 / 1646 9.7 / 2320 2.3	
7 SA	0538 10.6 / 1218 1.4 / 1759 10.6		**22** SU	0502 9.9 / 1145 2.0 / 1728 10.2	
8 SU ●	0039 1.4 / 0618 10.7 / 1258 1.4 / 1835 10.7		**23** M	0007 1.8 / 0546 10.3 / 1230 1.7 / 1809 10.6	
9 M	0117 1.4 / 0655 10.7 / 1332 1.5 / 1909 10.7		**24** TU	0052 1.5 / 0629 10.6 / 1313 1.5 / 1851 10.8	
10 TU	0151 1.5 / 0730 10.5 / 1404 1.7 / 1941 10.5		**25** W	0136 1.3 / 0714 10.7 / 1355 1.5 / 1934 10.8	
11 W	0222 1.8 / 0803 10.1 / 1433 2.1 / 2011 10.1		**26** TH	0219 1.4 / 0759 10.6 / 1438 1.7 / 2018 10.7	
12 TH	0251 2.2 / 0834 9.6 / 1502 2.6 / 2041 9.6		**27** F	0304 1.6 / 0846 10.2 / 1522 2.1 / 2104 10.3	
13 F	0321 2.7 / 0905 9.0 / 1532 3.1 / 2112 9.1		**28** SA	0351 1.9 / 0936 9.8 / 1610 2.5 / 2156 9.8	
14 SA	0353 3.3 / 0940 8.4 / 1605 3.7 / 2148 8.5		**29** SU	0444 2.4 / 1031 9.2 / 1705 3.0 / 2254 9.3	
15 SU ☾	0432 3.8 / 1025 7.8 / 1650 4.2 / 2238 7.9		**30** M ◐	0544 2.7 / 1134 8.8 / 1810 3.3	
			31 TU	0002 9.0 / 0651 2.9 / 1246 8.7 / 1922 3.3	

JUNE

Day	Time m	Time m	Day	Time m	Time m
1 W	0117 8.9 / 0801 2.9 / 1357 8.8 / 2033 3.2		**16** TH	0013 8.1 / 0655 3.8 / 1301 8.0 / 1927 4.0	
2 TH	0226 9.1 / 0906 2.7 / 1501 9.1 / 2137 2.8		**17** F	0123 8.2 / 0802 3.7 / 1408 8.3 / 2036 3.7	
3 F	0327 9.3 / 1005 2.5 / 1556 9.4 / 2233 2.5		**18** SA	0229 8.5 / 0909 3.4 / 1507 8.7 / 2141 3.2	
4 SA	0421 9.6 / 1057 2.3 / 1645 9.7 / 2324 2.3		**19** SU	0329 9.0 / 1011 2.9 / 1602 9.3 / 2240 2.7	
5 SU	0509 9.8 / 1144 2.2 / 1729 10.0		**20** M	0425 9.5 / 1108 2.5 / 1655 9.9 / 2335 2.2	
6 M ●	0009 2.2 / 0552 9.9 / 1226 2.1 / 1808 10.1		**21** TU	0520 10.0 / 1202 2.1 / 1746 10.3	
7 TU	0050 2.1 / 0632 9.9 / 1304 2.2 / 1845 10.1		**22** W	0029 1.7 / 0612 10.3 / 1254 1.8 / 1836 10.7	
8 W	0126 2.1 / 0710 9.9 / 1339 2.3 / 1920 10.1		**23** TH	0122 1.4 / 0704 10.6 / 1345 1.6 / 1926 10.9	
9 TH	0200 2.2 / 0745 9.7 / 1412 2.4 / 1953 9.9		**24** F	0213 1.2 / 0755 10.6 / 1434 1.6 / 2015 10.9	
10 F	0234 2.4 / 0820 9.4 / 1445 2.7 / 2026 9.6		**25** SA	0304 1.2 / 0845 10.5 / 1523 1.7 / 2104 10.8	
11 SA	0307 2.6 / 0854 9.1 / 1518 3.0 / 2100 9.3		**26** SU	0353 1.4 / 0934 10.3 / 1612 1.9 / 2153 10.5	
12 SU	0341 3.0 / 0929 8.8 / 1553 3.3 / 2137 8.9		**27** M	0442 1.7 / 1023 9.9 / 1701 2.3 / 2243 10.0	
13 M	0419 3.3 / 1009 8.4 / 1633 3.6 / 2219 8.5		**28** TU	0532 2.1 / 1113 9.4 / 1752 2.7 / ◐ 2335 9.5	
14 TU	0502 3.6 / 1056 8.1 / 1721 3.9 / 2311 8.2		**29** W	0624 2.5 / 1206 9.0 / 1847 3.0	
15 W ◯	0554 3.9 / 1154 7.9 / 1820 4.0		**30** TH	0033 9.1 / 0719 2.9 / 1307 8.7 / 1948 3.3	

JULY

Day	Time m	Time m	Day	Time m	Time m
1 F	0138 8.8 / 0820 3.2 / 1412 8.6 / 2053 3.4		**16** SA	0016 8.3 / 0657 3.8 / 1259 8.2 / 1937 3.9	
2 SA	0245 8.6 / 0922 3.2 / 1516 8.8 / 2157 3.3		**17** SU	0129 8.3 / 0812 3.7 / 1415 8.4 / 2055 3.6	
3 SU	0349 8.7 / 1023 3.1 / 1614 9.0 / 2256 3.0		**18** M	0247 8.5 / 0931 3.4 / 1528 8.9 / 2209 3.1	
4 M	0445 9.0 / 1117 2.9 / 1705 9.3 / 2347 2.7		**19** TU	0400 9.0 / 1042 2.9 / 1634 9.5 / 2315 2.4	
5 TU	0534 9.2 / 1204 2.7 / 1749 9.6		**20** W	0506 9.7 / 1144 2.4 / 1734 10.2	
6 W ●	0031 2.5 / 0617 9.4 / 1246 2.6 / ◯ 1829 9.8		**21** TH	0017 1.8 / 0605 10.3 / 1245 1.8 / 1828 10.8	
7 TH	0111 2.4 / 0657 9.6 / 1323 2.5 / 1906 9.9		**22** F	0115 1.2 / 0659 10.7 / 1339 1.4 / 1919 11.2	
8 F	0148 2.3 / 0733 9.6 / 1359 2.5 / 1941 9.9		**23** SA	0209 0.9 / 0749 11.0 / 1430 1.1 / 2007 11.4	
9 SA	0222 2.3 / 0807 9.6 / 1432 2.5 / 2015 9.9		**24** SU	0258 0.7 / 0835 11.1 / 1516 1.1 / 2053 11.4	
10 SU	0255 2.4 / 0840 9.5 / 1505 2.6 / 2047 9.7		**25** M	0344 0.8 / 0919 10.9 / 1600 1.3 / 2136 11.1	
11 M	0328 2.5 / 0912 9.3 / 1538 2.7 / 2120 9.5		**26** TU	0426 1.1 / 1000 10.4 / 1641 1.7 / 2217 10.5	
12 TU	0401 2.7 / 0945 9.0 / 1612 3.0 / 2155 9.0		**27** W	0506 1.8 / 1040 9.7 / 1721 2.3 / 2259 9.7	
13 W	0435 3.0 / 1021 8.8 / 1650 3.3 / ◐ 2345 9.0		**28** TH	0546 2.5 / 1122 9.0 / 1804 3.0 / ◐ 2345 9.0	
14 TH	0513 3.6 / 1101 8.5 / 1733 3.6 / ◐ 2318 8.6		**29** F	0629 3.1 / 1212 8.6 / 1856 3.6	
15 F	0559 3.8 / 1153 8.3 / 1828 3.8		**30** SA	0044 8.3 / 0725 3.8 / 1318 8.1 / 2005 4.0	
			31 SU	0203 7.9 / 0840 4.1 / 1439 8.1 / 2126 4.0	

AUGUST

Day	Time m	Time m	Day	Time m	Time m
1 M	0326 8.0 / 0956 3.9 / 1553 8.4 / 2238 3.6		**16** TU	0224 8.1 / 0909 3.9 / 1512 8.5 / 2153 3.3	
2 TU	0432 8.4 / 1100 3.5 / 1651 8.9 / 2334 3.1		**17** W	0354 8.7 / 1031 3.2 / 1627 9.4 / 2307 2.3	
3 W	0524 8.9 / 1151 3.1 / 1737 9.3		**18** TH	0503 9.6 / 1138 2.3 / 1727 10.3	
4 TH	0020 2.7 / 0606 9.3 / 1233 2.7 / 1816 9.7		**19** F	0009 1.6 / 0558 10.5 / 1236 1.6 / 1818 11.1	
5 F ●	0059 2.4 / 0643 9.6 / 1311 2.4 / ● 1852 10.0		**20** SA	0106 0.9 / 0648 11.1 / 1328 1.0 / 1906 11.7	
6 SA	0135 2.2 / 0717 9.8 / 1345 2.2 / 1925 10.2		**21** SU	0156 0.5 / 0733 11.5 / 1415 0.7 / 1951 11.9	
7 SU	0208 2.0 / 0749 10.0 / 1418 2.1 / 1957 10.3		**22** M	0241 0.3 / 0815 11.5 / 1458 0.7 / 2032 11.8	
8 M	0239 2.0 / 0819 10.0 / 1448 2.1 / 2027 10.3		**23** TU	0322 0.5 / 0853 11.3 / 1536 1.0 / 2110 11.3	
9 TU	0309 2.0 / 0848 9.9 / 1518 2.2 / 2057 10.1		**24** W	0358 1.0 / 0929 10.7 / 1612 1.5 / 2146 10.7	
10 W	0338 2.2 / 0917 9.7 / 1549 2.4 / 2127 9.8		**25** TH	0431 1.8 / 1002 10.0 / 1644 2.4 / 2220 9.7	
11 TH	0406 2.5 / 0946 9.4 / 1620 2.8 / 2158 9.4		**26** F	0502 2.7 / 1036 9.1 / 1717 3.2 / ◐ 2257 8.7	
12 F	0437 3.0 / 1018 9.0 / 1655 3.3 / ◐ 2234 8.9		**27** SA	0535 3.6 / 1116 8.2 / 1800 4.0 / 2349 7.8	
13 SA	0513 3.4 / 1100 8.6 / 1741 3.7 / ◐ 2325 8.4		**28** SU	0626 4.4 / 1221 7.7 / 1914 4.6	
14 SU	0606 3.9 / 1203 8.2 / 1851 4.1		**29** M	0125 7.3 / 0757 4.8 / 1411 7.5 / 2104 4.6	
15 M	0042 8.0 / 0729 4.2 / 1336 8.1 / 2024 4.0		**30** TU	0316 7.7 / 0940 4.5 / 1541 8.0 / 2228 4.0	
			31 W	0423 8.2 / 1048 3.9 / 1638 8.7 / 2320 3.3	

Chart Datum: 5·88 metres below Ordnance Datum (Local)

》 **FREE** monthly updates from 《
www.reedsalmanac.co.uk

TIME ZONE (UT)
For Summer Time add ONE hour in **non-shaded areas**

CHANNEL ISLES – ST HELIER
LAT 49°11'N   LONG 2°07'W
TIMES AND HEIGHTS OF HIGH AND LOW WATERS

YEAR 2005

SEPTEMBER

Time m	Time m
1 0509 8.9 / 1135 3.1 / TH 1721 9.3	**16** 0454 9.9 / 1127 2.1 / F 1715 10.6 / 2356 1.4
2 0002 2.7 / 0547 9.5 / F 1215 2.6 / 1757 9.9	**17** 0544 10.7 / 1219 1.3 / SA 1802 11.4
3 0039 2.2 / 0621 9.9 / SA 1251 2.2 / ● 1831 10.2	**18** 0047 0.7 / 0628 11.3 / SU 1308 0.8 / ○ 1846 11.8
4 0113 1.9 / 0653 10.2 / SU 1324 1.9 / 1902 10.5	**19** 0133 0.4 / 0709 11.6 / M 1351 0.6 / 1927 12.0
5 0146 1.7 / 0723 10.4 / M 1355 1.8 / 1932 10.7	**20** 0214 0.4 / 0747 11.6 / TU 1430 0.7 / 2005 11.8
6 0215 1.5 / 0752 10.5 / TU 1425 1.7 / 2001 10.7	**21** 0251 0.7 / 0822 11.3 / W 1506 1.1 / 2040 11.2
7 0244 1.7 / 0820 10.4 / W 1454 1.8 / 2030 10.5	**22** 0323 1.3 / 0854 10.8 / TH 1537 1.7 / 2112 10.4
8 0311 1.9 / 0847 10.2 / TH 1523 2.1 / 2058 10.2	**23** 0352 2.1 / 0924 10.0 / F 1605 2.6 / 2142 9.5
9 0338 2.3 / 0915 9.8 / F 1553 2.6 / 2128 9.7	**24** 0418 3.0 / 0953 9.2 / SA 1634 3.5 / 2215 8.5
10 0406 2.9 / 0944 9.3 / SA 1626 3.2 / 2202 9.0	**25** 0447 3.9 / 1027 8.3 / SU 1712 4.3 / ☾ 2301 7.6
11 0441 3.5 / 1023 8.7 / SU 1711 3.8 / ☾ 2252 8.3	**26** 0533 4.7 / 1126 7.5 / M 1825 4.9
12 0534 4.1 / 1126 8.2 / M 1826 4.2	**27** 0053 7.0 / 0713 5.2 / TU 1344 7.3 / 2037 4.9
13 0019 7.8 / 0709 4.5 / TU 1321 7.8 / 2014 4.1	**28** 0258 7.4 / 0918 4.8 / W 1520 7.8 / 2204 4.2
14 0226 7.9 / 0904 4.1 / W 1512 8.5 / 2149 3.3	**29** 0359 8.1 / 1024 4.0 / TH 1613 8.6 / 2252 3.4
15 0354 8.8 / 1026 3.1 / TH 1621 9.6 / 2258 2.3	**30** 0442 8.9 / 1107 3.2 / F 1653 9.3 / 2330 2.7

OCTOBER

Time m	Time m
1 0517 9.5 / 1144 2.6 / SA 1728 9.9	**16** 0520 10.8 / 1155 1.4 / SU 1739 11.3
2 0007 2.2 / 0550 10.0 / SU 1220 2.1 / 1800 10.3	**17** 0020 1.0 / 0602 11.2 / M 1241 1.0 / ○ 1820 11.6
3 0042 1.8 / 0621 10.4 / M 1255 1.8 / ● 1832 10.7	**18** 0104 0.8 / 0641 11.4 / TU 1322 0.9 / 1900 11.6
4 0115 1.6 / 0652 10.6 / TU 1328 1.6 / 1903 10.8	**19** 0142 0.9 / 0717 11.4 / W 1400 1.1 / 1936 11.3
5 0146 1.6 / 0722 10.7 / W 1359 1.6 / 1934 10.9	**20** 0216 1.3 / 0751 11.1 / TH 1433 1.5 / 2011 10.8
6 0216 1.6 / 0751 10.7 / TH 1430 1.7 / 2004 10.7	**21** 0247 1.8 / 0822 10.6 / F 1504 2.1 / 2042 10.1
7 0245 1.9 / 0820 10.5 / F 1500 2.0 / 2035 10.3	**22** 0315 2.5 / 0851 9.9 / SA 1532 2.8 / 2113 9.3
8 0314 2.3 / 0850 10.1 / SA 1532 2.5 / 2107 9.7	**23** 0342 3.3 / 0920 9.2 / SU 1601 3.6 / 2145 8.4
9 0345 2.9 / 0923 9.5 / SU 1609 3.1 / 2147 9.0	**24** 0413 4.1 / 0954 8.4 / M 1640 4.3 / 2231 7.6
10 0425 3.6 / 1007 8.8 / M 1701 3.8 / ☾ 2244 8.2	**25** 0459 4.7 / 1049 7.7 / TU 1746 4.8 / ○
11 0527 4.3 / 1121 8.1 / TU 1824 4.2	**26** 0007 7.1 / 0623 5.1 / W 1248 7.3 / 1938 4.9
12 0026 7.8 / 0710 4.5 / W 1325 8.0 / 2011 4.0	**27** 0209 7.3 / 0822 4.9 / TH 1432 7.7 / 2111 4.4
13 0226 8.2 / 0857 3.9 / TH 1501 8.8 / 2137 3.1	**28** 0315 8.0 / 0935 4.2 / F 1529 8.4 / 2205 3.6
14 0340 9.1 / 1010 3.0 / F 1603 9.8 / 2240 2.2	**29** 0400 8.7 / 1023 3.5 / SA 1612 9.1 / 2247 3.0
15 0434 10.0 / 1106 2.0 / SA 1654 10.6 / 2333 1.4	**30** 0437 9.3 / 1104 2.8 / SU 1649 9.7 / 2326 2.4
	31 0512 9.9 / 1142 2.3 / M 1724 10.1

NOVEMBER

Time m	Time m
1 0004 2.0 / 0546 10.3 / TU 1221 1.9 / 1759 10.5	**16** 0032 1.5 / 0613 10.9 / W 1254 1.6 / ○ 1834 10.8
2 0041 1.8 / 0619 10.6 / W 1257 1.7 / ● 1833 10.7	**17** 0111 1.6 / 0650 10.9 / TH 1332 1.7 / 1912 10.7
3 0116 1.7 / 0652 10.8 / TH 1333 1.6 / 1908 10.8	**18** 0146 1.9 / 0724 10.7 / F 1406 1.9 / 1948 10.3
4 0150 1.8 / 0726 10.8 / F 1408 1.7 / 1944 10.6	**19** 0219 2.2 / 0757 10.3 / SA 1439 2.3 / 2022 9.8
5 0224 2.0 / 0801 10.6 / SA 1444 2.0 / 2022 10.3	**20** 0249 2.7 / 0829 9.8 / SU 1510 2.9 / 2055 9.2
6 0259 2.4 / 0838 10.2 / SU 1522 2.4 / 2103 9.7	**21** 0320 3.3 / 0902 9.3 / M 1543 3.4 / 2131 8.6
7 0338 2.9 / 0920 9.6 / M 1608 3.0 / 2152 9.1	**22** 0354 3.8 / 0938 8.7 / TU 1622 3.9 / 2214 8.0
8 0427 3.5 / 1015 9.0 / TU 1706 3.5 / 2257 8.5	**23** 0437 4.3 / 1026 8.1 / W 1714 4.4 / ○ 2316 7.6
9 0534 4.0 / 1131 8.5 / W 1826 3.7 / ○	**24** 0538 4.7 / 1137 7.7 / TH 1826 4.6
10 0027 8.2 / 0704 4.1 / TH 1308 8.5 / 1954 3.5	**25** 0043 7.5 / 0659 4.7 / F 1308 7.7 / 1948 4.4
11 0159 8.5 / 0832 3.6 / F 1430 9.0 / 2109 3.0	**26** 0203 7.8 / 0820 4.4 / SA 1421 8.1 / 2058 4.0
12 0309 9.2 / 0940 2.9 / SA 1533 9.7 / 2210 2.3	**27** 0301 8.3 / 0924 3.9 / SU 1516 8.6 / 2152 3.5
13 0404 9.8 / 1037 2.3 / SU 1625 10.3 / 2303 1.8	**28** 0347 8.9 / 1015 3.3 / M 1602 9.1 / 2240 2.9
14 0451 10.4 / 1127 1.8 / M 1712 10.7 / 2350 1.6	**29** 0429 9.4 / 1101 2.7 / TU 1644 9.7 / 2325 2.5
15 0534 10.7 / 1212 1.6 / TU 1755 10.9	**30** 0509 10.0 / 1146 2.3 / W 1726 10.1

DECEMBER

Time m	Time m
1 0008 2.1 / 0548 10.4 / TH 1230 1.9 / ● 1808 10.4	**16** 0049 2.3 / 0631 10.3 / F 1314 2.2 / 1857 10.0
2 0050 1.9 / 0629 10.7 / F 1312 1.7 / 1851 10.6	**17** 0127 2.3 / 0708 10.3 / SA 1350 2.2 / 1935 9.9
3 0131 1.9 / 0710 10.8 / SA 1355 1.7 / 1934 10.6	**18** 0202 2.5 / 0744 10.1 / SU 1425 2.4 / 2011 9.7
4 0213 2.0 / 0753 10.7 / SU 1438 1.8 / 2020 10.4	**19** 0235 2.7 / 0818 9.9 / M 1458 2.7 / 2045 9.4
5 0255 2.2 / 0838 10.5 / M 1524 2.0 / 2108 10.0	**20** 0308 3.0 / 0851 9.6 / TU 1531 3.0 / 2119 9.1
6 0342 2.5 / 0927 10.1 / TU 1614 2.4 / 2200 9.6	**21** 0341 3.3 / 0926 9.2 / W 1606 3.3 / 2155 8.7
7 0433 2.9 / 1021 9.7 / W 1710 2.8 / 2257 9.1	**22** 0417 3.6 / 1003 8.8 / TH 1644 3.6 / 2235 8.3
8 0533 3.3 / 1123 9.3 / TH 1813 3.0 / ○	**23** 0459 3.9 / 1047 8.4 / F 1730 3.9 / ○ 2324 8.0
9 0002 8.8 / 0640 3.5 / F 1233 9.0 / 1921 3.1	**24** 0552 4.2 / 1142 8.1 / SA 1826 4.1
10 0114 8.8 / 0752 3.4 / SA 1346 9.0 / 2029 2.9	**25** 0027 7.9 / 0655 4.3 / SU 1249 8.0 / 1933 4.2
11 0224 8.9 / 0901 3.2 / SU 1453 9.2 / 2132 2.8	**26** 0138 7.9 / 0809 4.2 / M 1401 8.1 / 2045 4.0
12 0326 9.3 / 1003 2.8 / M 1553 9.5 / 2230 2.6	**27** 0245 8.3 / 0919 3.8 / TU 1507 8.5 / 2150 3.5
13 0420 9.6 / 1058 2.6 / TU 1646 9.7 / 2321 2.4	**28** 0343 8.8 / 1020 3.3 / W 1605 9.0 / 2248 3.0
14 0508 9.9 / 1148 2.4 / W 1734 9.9	**29** 0435 9.3 / 1116 2.7 / TH 1700 9.6 / 2342 2.5
15 0007 2.3 / 0551 10.2 / TH 1233 2.2 / ○ 1817 10.0	**30** 0526 10.0 / 1208 2.1 / F 1752 10.1
	31 0033 2.1 / 0615 10.5 / SA 1300 1.7 / ● 1842 10.5

Chart Datum: 5·88 metres below Ordnance Datum (Local)

》 **FREE** monthly updates from 《《
www.reedsalmanac.co.uk

TIDES

BREST

MEAN SPRING AND NEAP CURVES

MEAN RANGES
Springs 5.9m
Neaps 2.8m

Springs occur 2 days after New and Full Moon

TIME ZONE -0100
(French Standard Time)
Subtract 1 hour for UT
For French Summer Time add
ONE hour in **non-shaded areas**

FRANCE – BREST
LAT 48°23'N   LONG 4°30'W
TIMES AND HEIGHTS OF HIGH AND LOW WATERS

YEAR 2005

JANUARY		FEBRUARY		MARCH		APRIL	
Time m	Time m	Time m	Time m	Time m	Time m	Time m	Time m
1 0211 2.2 / 0809 6.0 / SA 1438 2.2 / 2035 5.7	**16** 0320 1.7 / 0919 6.3 / SU 1545 1.8 / 2142 5.8	**1** 0304 2.1 / 0859 6.0 / TU 1528 2.1 / 2126 5.7	**16** 0413 2.5 / 1006 5.4 / W 1636 2.7 / ◐ 2232 5.2	**1** 0158 1.5 / 0752 6.5 / TU 1418 1.6 / 2012 6.2	**16** 0248 2.0 / 0837 5.9 / W 1503 2.3 / 2050 5.6	**1** 0308 2.1 / 0902 5.7 / F 1531 2.4 / 2133 5.6	**16** 0352 2.9 / 0948 4.9 / SA 1612 3.1 / ◐ 2218 4.9
2 0252 2.3 / 0850 5.8 / SU 1520 2.3 / 2120 5.5	**17** 0409 2.1 / 1009 5.9 / M 1635 2.2 / ◐ 2234 5.5	**2** 0351 2.3 / 0947 5.7 / W 1619 2.4 / ◐ 2222 5.5	**17** 0513 2.9 / 1113 5.0 / TH 1742 3.1 / 2354 4.9	**2** 0237 1.8 / 0830 6.1 / W 1458 2.0 / 2053 5.9	**17** 0330 2.5 / 0918 5.3 / TH 1548 2.8 / ◐ 2138 5.2	**2** 0411 2.4 / 1016 5.2 / SA 1644 2.8 / ◐ 2300 5.3	**17** 0504 3.1 / 1121 4.7 / SU 1735 3.3 / 2358 4.9
3 0339 2.5 / 0939 5.6 / M 1609 2.5 / ◐ 2214 5.4	**18** 0505 2.5 / 1105 5.5 / TU 1732 2.6 / 2337 5.3	**3** 0450 2.5 / 1051 5.4 / TH 1724 2.6 / 2335 5.3	**18** 0635 3.1 / 1251 4.8 / F 1912 3.1	**3** 0323 2.1 / 0916 5.7 / TH 1547 2.4 / ◐ 2146 5.5	**18** 0426 2.9 / 1021 4.8 / F 1651 3.2 / 2259 4.8	**3** 0537 2.6 / 1201 5.1 / SU 1820 2.8	**18** 0638 3.0 / 1301 4.8 / M 1908 3.1
4 0434 2.6 / 1036 5.5 / TU 1708 2.6 / 2318 5.4	**19** 0609 2.7 / 1214 5.3 / W 1839 2.8	**4** 0604 2.6 / 1214 5.3 / F 1844 2.6	**19** 0140 5.0 / 0810 2.9 / SA 1422 5.0 / 2034 2.9	**4** 0421 2.5 / 1020 5.3 / F 1653 2.7 / 2304 5.3	**19** 0547 3.2 / 1208 4.6 / SA 1825 3.3	**4** 0049 5.4 / 0714 2.4 / M 1338 5.4 / 1952 2.4	**19** 0125 5.1 / 0753 2.7 / TU 1403 5.2 / 2011 2.7
5 0538 2.6 / 1144 5.5 / W 1815 2.6	**20** 0055 5.2 / 0723 2.8 / TH 1330 5.2 / 1952 2.7	**5** 0106 5.5 / 0728 2.5 / SA 1344 5.5 / 2006 2.4	**20** 0249 5.3 / 0913 2.6 / SU 1517 5.4 / 2127 2.5	**5** 0540 2.7 / 1156 5.1 / SA 1823 2.8	**20** 0059 4.8 / 0736 3.1 / SU 1356 4.9 / 2003 3.0	**5** 0208 5.9 / 0830 1.9 / TU 1443 5.9 / 2056 1.9	**20** 0219 5.5 / 0842 2.3 / W 1446 5.6 / 2056 2.2
6 0031 5.5 / 0648 2.5 / TH 1256 5.6 / 1924 2.4	**21** 0208 5.3 / 0833 2.6 / F 1438 5.4 / 2055 2.6	**6** 0225 5.8 / 0846 2.0 / SU 1459 5.9 / 2116 2.0	**21** 0335 5.7 / 0957 2.2 / M 1557 5.7 / 2208 2.2	**6** 0052 5.3 / 0717 2.5 / SU 1341 5.3 / 1959 2.5	**21** 0219 5.2 / 0844 2.7 / M 1450 5.3 / 2059 2.6	**6** 0305 6.4 / 0926 1.4 / W 1533 6.4 / 2147 1.3	**21** 0301 5.9 / 0922 1.9 / TH 1523 6.0 / 2135 1.8
7 0138 5.7 / 0756 2.2 / F 1405 5.9 / 2028 2.1	**22** 0305 5.6 / 0929 2.4 / SA 1530 5.6 / 2144 2.3	**7** 0330 6.4 / 0950 1.5 / M 1559 6.4 / 2214 1.5	**22** 0412 6.0 / 1034 1.9 / TU 1632 6.1 / 2243 1.8	**7** 0219 5.8 / 0841 2.0 / M 1456 5.9 / 2110 2.0	**22** 0305 5.6 / 0927 2.2 / TU 1529 5.7 / 2139 2.2	**7** 0353 6.9 / 1014 1.1 / TH 1616 6.8 / 2233 1.0	**22** 0338 6.3 / 0959 1.5 / F 1559 6.4 / 2212 1.5
8 0241 6.1 / 0900 1.9 / SA 1507 6.2 / 2127 1.7	**23** 0350 5.9 / 1014 2.1 / SU 1613 5.8 / 2226 2.1	**8** 0425 6.8 / 1045 1.0 / TU 1651 6.8 / ● 2306 1.1	**23** 0445 6.3 / 1107 1.6 / W 1704 6.3 / 2316 1.6	**8** 0322 6.0 / 0942 1.4 / TU 1551 6.4 / 2205 1.4	**23** 0342 6.0 / 1004 1.8 / W 1602 6.1 / 2214 1.8	**8** 0436 7.2 / 1056 0.7 / F 1656 7.0 / ● 2314 0.8	**23** 0414 6.6 / 1035 1.3 / SA 1633 6.7 / 2248 1.2
9 0338 6.5 / 0958 1.4 / SU 1604 6.5 / 2222 1.4	**24** 0429 6.1 / 1053 1.9 / M 1650 6.0 / 2302 1.9	**9** 0514 7.2 / 1135 0.6 / W 1738 7.1 / 2354 0.8	**24** 0517 6.6 / 1139 1.4 / TH 1735 6.5 / ○ 2348 1.4	**9** 0413 6.9 / 1033 0.9 / W 1638 6.9 / 2253 0.9	**24** 0416 6.4 / 1037 1.5 / TH 1635 6.4 / 2248 1.5	**9** 0515 7.3 / 1135 0.7 / SA 1732 7.1 / 2353 0.8	**24** 0449 6.8 / 1110 1.1 / SU 1707 6.9 / ○ 2324 1.0
10 0431 6.9 / 1053 1.1 / M 1658 6.8 / ● 2314 1.2	**25** 0504 6.3 / 1128 1.7 / TU 1724 6.2 / ○ 2336 1.7	**10** 0600 7.5 / 1221 0.5 / TH 1822 7.1	**25** 0548 6.8 / 1210 1.2 / F 1805 6.6	**10** 0458 7.3 / 1119 0.6 / TH 1720 7.1 / ● 2337 0.7	**25** 0448 6.7 / 1110 1.2 / F 1706 6.7 / ○ 2320 1.2	**10** 0551 7.2 / 1212 0.8 / SU 1806 7.0	**25** 0523 6.9 / 1145 1.0 / M 1741 7.0
11 0523 7.1 / 1145 1.0 / TU 1748 6.9	**26** 0537 6.5 / 1201 1.6 / W 1756 6.3	**11** 0042 0.7 / 0643 7.5 / F 1305 0.5 / 1903 7.1	**26** 0020 1.2 / 0618 6.8 / SA 1241 1.2 / 1835 6.7	**11** 0540 7.5 / 1201 0.5 / F 1759 7.2	**26** 0520 6.9 / 1141 1.1 / SA 1737 6.8 / 2353 1.1	**11** 0031 0.9 / 0625 7.0 / M 1246 1.1 / 1838 6.8	**26** 0001 1.0 / 0559 6.9 / TU 1221 1.1 / 1817 6.9
12 0005 1.0 / 0612 7.3 / W 1235 0.7 / 1837 6.9	**27** 0010 1.6 / 0609 6.6 / TH 1234 1.5 / 1828 6.3	**12** 0124 0.8 / 0723 7.2 / SA 1346 0.8 / 1941 6.8	**27** 0052 1.2 / 0648 6.8 / SU 1311 1.2 / 1905 6.6	**12** 0020 0.6 / 0619 7.5 / SA 1240 0.5 / 1835 7.1	**27** 0551 7.0 / 1213 1.0 / SU 1807 6.9	**12** 0106 1.2 / 0658 6.7 / TU 1320 1.5 / 1910 6.5	**27** 0042 1.1 / 0637 6.8 / W 1300 1.3 / 1856 6.7
13 0058 1.0 / 0700 7.3 / TH 1323 0.8 / 1924 6.8	**28** 0043 1.6 / 0641 6.6 / F 1305 1.5 / 1900 6.3	**13** 0205 1.1 / 0802 6.9 / SU 1426 1.2 / 2018 6.4	**28** 0124 1.3 / 0719 6.7 / M 1343 1.4 / 1937 6.5	**13** 0058 0.7 / 0655 7.3 / SU 1317 0.8 / 1909 6.9	**28** 0027 1.1 / 0622 7.0 / M 1245 1.1 / 1839 6.9	**13** 0141 1.6 / 0731 6.2 / W 1353 1.9 / 1943 6.1	**28** 0124 1.3 / 0719 6.5 / TH 1343 1.6 / 1940 6.4
14 0145 1.1 / 0747 7.1 / F 1411 1.1 / 2010 6.6	**29** 0115 1.6 / 0713 6.5 / SA 1337 1.6 / 1932 6.3	**14** 0245 1.5 / 0839 6.4 / M 1505 1.7 / 2056 6.0		**14** 0135 1.1 / 0728 6.9 / M 1352 1.3 / 1941 6.5	**29** 0101 1.1 / 0655 6.8 / TU 1318 1.3 / 1913 6.7	**14** 0218 2.0 / 0806 5.7 / TH 1430 2.4 / 2019 5.7	**29** 0211 1.6 / 0808 6.1 / F 1432 2.0 / 2032 6.0
15 0232 1.4 / 0833 6.8 / SA 1458 1.4 / 2055 6.2	**30** 0148 1.7 / 0745 6.4 / SU 1410 1.7 / 2005 6.1	**15** 0326 2.0 / 0919 5.9 / TU 1547 2.2 / 2137 5.6		**15** 0211 1.5 / 0802 6.4 / TU 1426 1.8 / 2014 6.1	**30** 0137 1.3 / 0731 6.5 / W 1355 1.6 / 1950 6.4	**15** 0259 2.5 / 0848 5.3 / F 1513 2.8 / 2106 5.2	**30** 0306 2.0 / 0907 5.6 / SA 1531 2.4 / 2139 5.7
	31 0224 1.8 / 0820 6.2 / M 1446 1.9 / 2042 5.9				**31** 0219 1.7 / 0812 6.1 / TH 1438 2.0 / 2034 6.0		

Chart Datum: 3·64 metres below IGN Datum

》》 **FREE** monthly updates from 《《
www.reedsalmanac.co.uk

TIDES

TIME ZONE -0100 (French Standard Time)
Subtract 1 hour for UT
For French Summer Time add ONE hour in **non-shaded areas**

FRANCE – BREST
LAT 48°23′N   LONG 4°30′W
TIMES AND HEIGHTS OF HIGH AND LOW WATERS

YEAR 2005

MAY

Day	Time	m	Time	m	Day	Time	m	Time	m
1	0414	2.3			16	0424	2.8		
	1026	5.3				1033	4.9		
SU	1646	2.6			M	1647	3.0		
☽	2303	5.5				2259	5.0		
2	0536	2.4			17	0535	2.9		
	1157	5.3				1151	4.9		
M	1813	2.6			TU	1801	2.9		
3	0033	5.7			18	0016	5.2		
	0658	2.2				0646	2.7		
TU	1316	5.6			W	1258	5.2		
	1930	2.2				1908	2.7		
4	0143	6.0			19	0119	5.4		
	0806	1.8				0745	2.4		
W	1417	6.0			TH	1352	5.5		
	2031	1.8				2003	2.4		
5	0239	6.3			20	0210	5.7		
	0901	1.5				0833	2.1		
TH	1506	6.3			F	1437	5.9		
	2122	1.5				2050	2.0		
6	0327	6.6			21	0255	6.1		
	0948	1.2				0917	1.7		
F	1549	6.6			SA	1519	6.2		
	2208	1.2				2134	1.6		
7	0410	6.8			22	0337	6.4		
	1030	1.1				0958	1.5		
SA	1629	6.7			SU	1559	6.5		
	2249	1.1				2216	1.4		
8	0449	6.8			23	0418	6.6		
	1108	1.1				1039	1.3		
SU	1705	6.8			M	1639	6.8		
●	2328	1.1			○	2258	1.2		
9	0525	6.8			24	0500	6.7		
	1144	1.3				1121	1.2		
M	1739	6.7			TU	1719	6.9		
						2341	1.0		
10	0005	1.3			25	0543	6.8		
	0600	6.6				1204	1.2		
TU	1219	1.4			W	1802	6.9		
	1813	6.6							
11	0042	1.5			26	0030	1.1		
	0634	6.3				0628	6.7		
W	1253	1.7			TH	1249	1.3		
	1847	6.4				1849	6.8		
12	0118	1.7			27	0118	1.2		
	0710	6.0				0718	6.4		
TH	1329	2.0			F	1338	1.5		
	1922	6.1				1940	6.6		
13	0156	2.0			28	0210	1.4		
	0747	5.7				0812	6.1		
F	1406	2.3			SA	1431	1.8		
	2000	5.7				2036	6.3		
14	0237	2.4			29	0308	1.7		
	0830	5.3				0912	5.8		
SA	1449	2.6			SU	1531	2.1		
	2046	5.4				2140	6.0		
15	0325	2.7			30	0411	1.9		
	0923	5.0				1020	5.6		
SU	1541	2.9			M	1638	2.3		
	2145	5.2			☽	2248	5.9		
					31	0519	2.0		
						1132	5.5		
					TU	1749	2.3		
						2358	5.8		

JUNE

Day	Time	m	Day	Time	m
1	0628 2.0 / 1240 5.6 / W 1857 2.2		16	0538 2.6 / 1149 5.2 / TH 1802 2.6	
2	0108 5.9 / 0732 1.9 / TH 1342 5.8 / 1959 2.0		17	0011 5.4 / 0641 2.5 / F 1251 5.4 / 1905 2.5	
3	0207 6.1 / 0829 1.8 / F 1435 6.0 / 2054 1.8		18	0114 5.6 / 0740 2.3 / SA 1347 5.7 / 2002 2.2	
4	0258 6.2 / 0919 1.7 / SA 1521 6.1 / 2142 1.6		19	0210 5.8 / 0834 2.0 / SU 1439 6.0 / 2056 1.9	
5	0344 6.3 / 1003 1.6 / SU 1604 6.3 / 2226 1.6		20	0303 6.1 / 0925 1.7 / M 1529 6.3 / 2148 1.6	
6	0426 6.3 / 1044 1.6 / M 1642 6.4 / ● 2307 1.5		21	0354 6.3 / 1014 1.5 / TU 1617 6.6 / 2238 1.3	
7	0504 6.3 / 1122 1.6 / TU 1719 6.4 / 2345 1.6		22	0444 6.5 / 1103 1.3 / W 1705 6.8 / ○ 2328 1.1	
8	0542 6.2 / 1158 1.7 / W 1755 6.4		23	0534 6.7 / 1152 1.2 / TH 1755 6.9	
9	0024 1.7 / 0618 6.1 / TH 1234 1.8 / 1831 6.2		24	0022 0.9 / 0624 6.7 / F 1242 1.2 / 1845 6.9	
10	0101 1.8 / 0655 5.9 / F 1310 2.0 / 1907 6.1		25	0113 0.9 / 0715 6.6 / SA 1333 1.3 / 1936 6.9	
11	0138 2.0 / 0732 5.7 / SA 1347 2.2 / 1945 5.9		26	0205 1.1 / 0807 6.4 / SU 1425 1.4 / 2029 6.7	
12	0216 2.1 / 0811 5.5 / SU 1426 2.4 / 2026 5.7		27	0258 1.3 / 0900 6.1 / M 1519 1.7 / 2123 6.4	
13	0257 2.3 / 0855 5.3 / M 1510 2.5 / 2111 5.5		28	0352 1.6 / 0955 5.9 / TU 1615 1.9 / ☽ 2219 6.1	
14	0344 2.5 / 0946 5.2 / TU 1601 2.7 / 2205 5.4		29	0449 1.9 / 1053 5.7 / W 1715 2.1 / 2319 5.8	
15	0437 2.6 / 1046 5.1 / W 1659 2.7 / ☽ 2306 5.3		30	0549 2.1 / 1156 5.5 / TH 1818 2.2	

JULY

Day	Time	m	Day	Time	m
1	0026 5.7 / 0651 2.2 / F 1301 5.5 / 1923 2.3		16	0539 2.5 / 1150 5.3 / SA 1808 2.6	
2	0131 5.6 / 0754 2.3 / SA 1403 5.6 / 2026 2.2		17	0018 5.4 / 0648 2.5 / SU 1300 5.5 / 1919 2.4	
3	0232 5.7 / 0852 2.2 / SU 1458 5.8 / 2121 2.1		18	0132 5.5 / 0757 2.3 / M 1407 5.7 / 2027 2.1	
4	0325 5.8 / 0942 2.1 / M 1546 6.0 / 2210 1.9		19	0240 5.8 / 0900 2.0 / TU 1508 6.1 / 2129 1.7	
5	0411 5.9 / 1026 2.0 / TU 1628 6.1 / 2253 1.8		20	0341 6.2 / 0958 1.6 / W 1604 6.5 / 2225 1.3	
6	0451 6.0 / 1106 1.9 / W 1706 6.2 / ● 2332 1.7		21	0436 6.5 / 1052 1.3 / TH 1657 6.9 / ○ 2318 0.9	
7	0529 6.1 / 1143 1.8 / TH 1742 6.3		22	0527 6.7 / 1143 1.0 / F 1747 7.1	
8	0009 1.7 / 0604 6.1 / F 1218 1.8 / 1817 6.3		23	0011 0.7 / 0616 6.9 / SA 1232 0.9 / 1835 7.3	
9	0044 1.7 / 0639 6.0 / SA 1252 1.8 / 1851 6.3		24	0102 0.6 / 0703 6.9 / SU 1320 0.9 / 1922 7.2	
10	0118 1.7 / 0713 6.0 / SU 1326 1.9 / 1925 6.2		25	0149 0.7 / 0748 6.7 / M 1407 1.1 / 2008 7.0	
11	0152 1.8 / 0747 5.9 / M 1401 2.0 / 1959 6.1		26	0235 1.0 / 0833 6.4 / TU 1454 1.4 / 2054 6.6	
12	0226 2.0 / 0822 5.7 / TU 1437 2.1 / 2035 5.9		27	0322 1.4 / 0919 6.1 / W 1543 1.7 / 2142 6.2	
13	0304 2.2 / 0901 5.6 / W 1518 2.3 / 2117 5.7		28	0410 1.9 / 1008 5.7 / TH 1636 2.1 / ☽ 2235 5.7	
14	0347 2.5 / 0948 5.4 / TH 1606 2.5 / ☽ 2206 5.5		29	0504 2.3 / 1106 5.4 / F 1736 2.5 / 2338 5.3	
15	0438 2.6 / 1044 5.3 / F 1702 2.6 / 2306 5.3		30	0607 2.6 / 1218 5.2 / SA 1847 2.7	
			31	0058 5.2 / 0721 2.7 / SU 1337 5.3 / 2003 2.6	

AUGUST

Day	Time	m	Day	Time	m
1	0215 5.3 / 0832 2.6 / M 1444 5.5 / 2108 2.4		16	0110 5.3 / 0734 2.6 / TU 1349 5.6 / 2011 2.3	
2	0315 5.5 / 0928 2.4 / TU 1535 5.8 / 2158 2.1		17	0231 5.7 / 0848 2.2 / W 1458 6.1 / 2119 1.7	
3	0401 5.7 / 1013 2.1 / W 1617 6.0 / 2240 1.9		18	0334 6.2 / 0948 1.6 / TH 1554 6.6 / 2216 1.2	
4	0439 5.9 / 1051 1.9 / TH 1653 6.2 / 2316 1.7		19	0427 6.6 / 1041 1.2 / F 1645 7.1 / ○ 2307 0.7	
5	0513 6.1 / 1126 1.8 / F 1726 6.4 / ● 2350 1.6		20	0514 7.0 / 1129 0.8 / SA 1733 7.4 / 2354 0.5	
6	0546 6.2 / 1158 1.6 / SA 1757 6.5		21	0559 7.2 / 1215 0.6 / SU 1817 7.5	
7	0022 1.5 / 0616 6.3 / SU 1230 1.6 / 1828 6.5		22	0042 0.4 / 0641 7.1 / M 1259 0.7 / 1859 7.4	
8	0053 1.5 / 0647 6.3 / M 1301 1.6 / 1858 6.5		23	0124 0.6 / 0720 7.0 / TU 1342 0.9 / 1940 7.1	
9	0123 1.5 / 0717 6.2 / TU 1332 1.7 / 1928 6.4		24	0205 1.0 / 0759 6.7 / W 1424 1.4 / 2019 6.7	
10	0154 1.7 / 0748 6.1 / W 1405 1.8 / 2000 6.2		25	0246 1.5 / 0837 6.2 / TH 1507 1.8 / 2100 6.1	
11	0227 1.9 / 0821 5.9 / TH 1441 2.1 / 2036 5.9		26	0329 2.1 / 0920 5.7 / F 1555 2.3 / ☽ 2148 5.5	
12	0305 2.1 / 0901 5.7 / F 1524 2.3 / 2118 5.7		27	0418 2.6 / 1015 5.1 / SA 1654 2.8 / 2253 5.1	
13	0351 2.4 / 0952 5.4 / SA 1617 2.5 / ☽ 2215 5.4		28	0523 3.0 / 1136 4.8 / SU 1813 3.0	
14	0451 2.6 / 1100 5.3 / SU 1725 2.6 / 2332 5.3		29	0031 4.9 / 0652 3.1 / M 1317 5.0 / 1947 3.0	
15	0608 2.7 / 1225 5.3 / M 1848 2.6 / 2055 2.5		30	0206 5.1 / 0817 2.9 / TU 1432 5.5 / 2055 2.5	
			31	0303 5.5 / 0913 2.5 / W 1520 5.7 / 2141 2.1	

Chart Datum: 3·64 metres below IGN Datum

FREE monthly updates from www.reedsalmanac.co.uk

TIME ZONE -0100
(French Standard Time)
Subtract 1 hour for UT
For French Summer Time add
ONE hour in **non-shaded areas**

FRANCE – BREST
LAT 48°23′N   LONG 4°30′W
TIMES AND HEIGHTS OF HIGH AND LOW WATERS

YEAR 2005

SEPTEMBER

Time	m		Time	m
1 TH	0344 5.7 / 0954 2.2 / 1558 6.1 / 2219 1.8	**16** F	0323 6.3 / 0936 1.5 / 1541 6.8 / 2202 1.0
2 F	0418 6.0 / 1030 1.9 / 1631 6.3 / 2253 1.6	**17** SA	0411 6.8 / 1025 1.0 / 1628 7.3 / 2249 0.6
3 SA ●	0450 6.3 / 1102 1.6 / 1701 6.5 / 2324 1.4	**18** SU ○	0454 7.1 / 1110 0.7 / 1712 7.6 / 2333 0.4
4 SU	0519 6.5 / 1133 1.5 / 1731 6.7 / 2354 1.3	**19** M	0535 7.3 / 1153 0.6 / 1753 7.6
5 M	0549 6.6 / 1203 1.4 / 1800 6.8	**20** TU	0016 0.5 / 0613 7.2 / 1234 0.7 / 1831 7.4
6 TU	0024 1.3 / 0617 6.6 / 1233 1.4 / 1829 6.7	**21** W	0055 0.8 / 0649 7.0 / 1313 1.0 / 1908 7.0
7 W	0052 1.4 / 0646 6.6 / 1303 1.4 / 1858 6.6	**22** TH	0133 1.2 / 0723 6.7 / 1352 1.4 / 1944 6.5
8 TH	0122 1.5 / 0715 6.4 / 1335 1.6 / 1928 6.4	**23** F	0210 1.7 / 0758 6.2 / 1433 1.9 / 2022 6.0
9 F	0155 1.7 / 0748 6.2 / 1411 1.9 / 2003 6.1	**24** SA	0249 2.3 / 0837 5.7 / 1518 2.5 / 2107 5.4
10 SA	0232 2.1 / 0826 5.9 / 1454 2.2 / 2045 5.7	**25** SU ◐	0336 2.8 / 0929 5.2 / 1616 2.9 / 2213 4.9
11 SU ◐	0318 2.4 / 0917 5.5 / 1548 2.6 / 2144 5.3	**26** M	0442 3.2 / 1055 4.9 / 1739 3.2 / 2359 4.7
12 M	0420 2.8 / 1031 5.2 / 1701 2.8 / 2313 5.0	**27** TU	0618 3.3 / 1250 5.0 / 1923 3.0
13 TU	0547 2.9 / 1211 5.2 / 1836 2.7	**28** W	0144 5.0 / 0750 3.0 / 1405 5.3 / 2029 2.6
14 W	0109 5.2 / 0726 2.7 / 1343 5.7 / 2005 2.3	**29** TH	0236 5.4 / 0844 2.6 / 1451 5.7 / 2112 2.2
15 TH	0227 5.7 / 0840 2.1 / 1448 6.3 / 2109 1.6	**30** F	0314 5.8 / 0924 2.2 / 1527 6.1 / 2148 1.9

OCTOBER

Time	m		Time	m
1 SA	0347 6.1 / 0958 1.9 / 1559 6.4 / 2220 1.6	**16** SU	0348 6.9 / 1004 1.1 / 1606 7.3 / 2226 0.8
2 SU	0418 6.4 / 1031 1.6 / 1630 6.6 / 2252 1.4	**17** M ○	0430 7.1 / 1048 0.8 / 1648 7.4 / 2308 0.7
3 M	0448 6.6 / 1103 1.4 / 1701 6.8 / 2322 1.3	**18** TU	0508 7.2 / 1129 0.8 / 1727 7.4 / 2347 0.8
4 TU	0518 6.8 / 1134 1.3 / 1730 6.9 / 2352 1.2	**19** W	0545 7.1 / 1208 0.9 / 1804 7.1
5 W	0547 6.8 / 1205 1.3 / 1800 6.9	**20** TH	0026 1.1 / 0619 6.9 / 1246 1.2 / 1840 6.8
6 TH	0023 1.3 / 0617 6.8 / 1237 1.4 / 1831 6.7	**21** F	0102 1.5 / 0653 6.6 / 1325 1.6 / 1915 6.3
7 F	0055 1.5 / 0649 6.6 / 1311 1.5 / 1904 6.5	**22** SA	0139 1.9 / 0729 6.2 / 1404 2.0 / 1953 5.8
8 SA	0130 1.8 / 0724 6.4 / 1351 1.8 / 1942 6.1	**23** SU ◐	0217 2.4 / 0808 5.8 / 1449 2.5 / 2038 5.4
9 SU	0211 2.1 / 0806 6.0 / 1437 2.2 / 2029 5.7	**24** M	0303 2.8 / 0858 5.3 / 1543 2.9 / 2141 4.9
10 M	0301 2.5 / 0902 5.6 / 1536 2.6 / 2136 5.2	**25** TU ◐	0404 3.2 / 1013 5.0 / 1657 3.2 / 2313 4.8
11 TU	0409 2.9 / 1025 5.3 / 1655 2.8 / 2316 5.1	**26** W	0527 3.3 / 1152 5.0 / 1829 3.1
12 W	0544 3.0 / 1208 5.4 / 1833 2.6	**27** TH	0050 4.9 / 0656 3.1 / 1312 5.2 / 1940 2.8
13 TH	0104 5.4 / 0717 2.6 / 1330 5.8 / 1953 2.2	**28** F	0149 5.3 / 0757 2.7 / 1404 5.6 / 2028 2.4
14 F	0212 5.9 / 0824 2.0 / 1430 6.4 / 2052 1.5	**29** SA	0231 5.7 / 0841 2.3 / 1444 5.9 / 2106 2.0
15 SA	0303 6.5 / 0917 1.5 / 1520 6.9 / 2141 1.1	**30** SU	0307 6.1 / 0919 2.0 / 1521 6.3 / 2142 1.7
		31 M	0342 6.4 / 0955 1.7 / 1555 6.5 / 2216 1.5

NOVEMBER

Time	m		Time	m
1 TU	0415 6.6 / 1030 1.5 / 1629 6.7 / 2250 1.3	**16** W ○	0444 6.9 / 1107 1.2 / 1704 6.9 / 2322 1.2
2 W ●	0447 6.8 / 1105 1.3 / 1702 6.8 / 2323 1.3	**17** TH	0521 6.9 / 1147 1.3 / 1742 6.8
3 TH	0520 6.9 / 1140 1.3 / 1736 6.8 / 2358 1.3	**18** F	0000 1.4 / 0557 6.7 / 1225 1.4 / 1819 6.5
4 F	0555 6.9 / 1217 1.3 / 1812 6.7	**19** SA	0039 1.7 / 0633 6.5 / 1304 1.7 / 1856 6.2
5 SA	0036 1.5 / 0632 6.7 / 1257 1.5 / 1852 6.5	**20** SU	0116 2.0 / 0710 6.2 / 1343 2.0 / 1935 5.8
6 SU	0117 1.8 / 0714 6.5 / 1342 1.8 / 1937 6.1	**21** M	0154 2.3 / 0750 5.9 / 1425 2.4 / 2018 5.5
7 M	0203 2.1 / 0803 6.1 / 1434 2.1 / 2032 5.7	**22** TU	0237 2.7 / 0835 5.6 / 1513 2.7 / 2110 5.2
8 TU	0259 2.5 / 0906 5.8 / 1536 2.4 / 2143 5.4	**23** W ◐	0328 2.9 / 0931 5.3 / 1609 2.9 / 2215 5.0
9 W	0410 2.7 / 1026 5.6 / 1653 2.5 / 2312 5.3	**24** TH	0430 3.1 / 1041 5.1 / 1716 3.0 / 2330 5.0
10 TH	0535 2.7 / 1151 5.7 / 1816 2.3	**25** F	0542 3.1 / 1155 5.2 / 1827 2.9
11 F	0040 5.6 / 0655 2.4 / 1304 6.0 / 1927 2.0	**26** SA	0041 5.2 / 0650 2.9 / 1259 5.4 / 1927 2.6
12 SA	0145 5.9 / 0746 2.0 / 1404 6.4 / 2026 1.7	**27** SU	0136 5.5 / 0746 2.6 / 1352 5.7 / 2016 2.3
13 SU	0237 6.3 / 0833 1.6 / 1455 6.7 / 2116 1.4	**28** M	0221 5.8 / 0834 2.2 / 1437 6.0 / 2059 2.0
14 M	0323 6.6 / 0941 1.4 / 1542 6.9 / 2201 1.2	**29** TU	0303 6.1 / 0917 1.9 / 1519 6.3 / 2140 1.8
15 TU	0405 6.8 / 1025 1.2 / 1624 7.0 / 2243 1.2	**30** W	0342 6.4 / 0959 1.7 / 1559 6.5 / 2219 1.6

DECEMBER

Time	m		Time	m
1 TH ●	0421 6.7 / 1040 1.4 / 1639 6.6 / 2259 1.4	**16** F	0506 6.6 / 1132 1.5 / 1728 6.4 / 2344 1.7
2 F	0500 6.8 / 1122 1.3 / 1720 6.7 / 2340 1.4	**17** SA	0544 6.6 / 1211 1.6 / 1806 6.3
3 SA	0541 6.9 / 1205 1.3 / 1803 6.7	**18** SU	0022 1.8 / 0620 6.5 / 1249 1.7 / 1843 6.2
4 SU	0026 1.5 / 0626 6.8 / 1251 1.5 / 1849 6.5	**19** M	0059 1.9 / 0657 6.3 / 1326 1.9 / 1919 6.0
5 M	0113 1.6 / 0714 6.7 / 1340 1.5 / 1940 6.3	**20** TU	0135 2.1 / 0733 6.1 / 1403 2.1 / 1957 5.8
6 TU	0203 1.8 / 0807 6.4 / 1433 1.7 / 2035 6.0	**21** W	0213 2.3 / 0811 5.9 / 1441 2.3 / 2036 5.5
7 W	0259 2.1 / 0905 6.1 / 1532 1.9 / 2137 5.8	**22** TH	0253 2.5 / 0851 5.7 / 1523 2.5 / 2121 5.3
8 TH	0401 2.2 / 1010 6.0 / 1636 2.1 / 2246 5.6	**23** F ○	0338 2.7 / 0938 5.5 / 1610 2.7 / 2214 5.1
9 F	0510 2.2 / 1119 5.9 / 1744 2.2 / 2357 5.6	**24** SA	0431 2.8 / 1034 5.3 / 1707 2.8 / 2317 5.0
10 SA	0620 2.3 / 1228 5.9 / 1852 2.1	**25** SU	0532 2.9 / 1139 5.3 / 1811 2.8
11 SU	0108 5.8 / 0726 2.2 / 1332 6.0 / 1954 2.0	**26** M	0025 5.3 / 0639 2.8 / 1247 5.4 / 1915 2.6
12 M	0206 6.0 / 0826 2.0 / 1429 6.2 / 2049 1.8	**27** TU	0127 5.5 / 0742 2.6 / 1349 5.6 / 2013 2.4
13 TU	0258 6.2 / 0919 1.8 / 1520 6.3 / 2139 1.7	**28** W	0223 5.8 / 0839 2.3 / 1444 5.9 / 2106 2.1
14 W	0344 6.4 / 1007 1.6 / 1606 6.4 / 2224 1.7	**29** TH	0313 6.1 / 0931 1.9 / 1536 6.2 / 2155 1.8
15 TH	0426 6.5 / 1051 1.6 / 1649 6.4 / 2305 1.6	**30** F	0401 6.5 / 1021 1.5 / 1624 6.6 / 2242 1.5
		31 SA ●	0448 6.7 / 1110 1.2 / 1712 6.6 / 2329 1.3

Chart Datum: 3·64 metres below IGN Datum

》》 **FREE** monthly updates from 《《
www.reedsalmanac.co.uk

Chapter 5

401

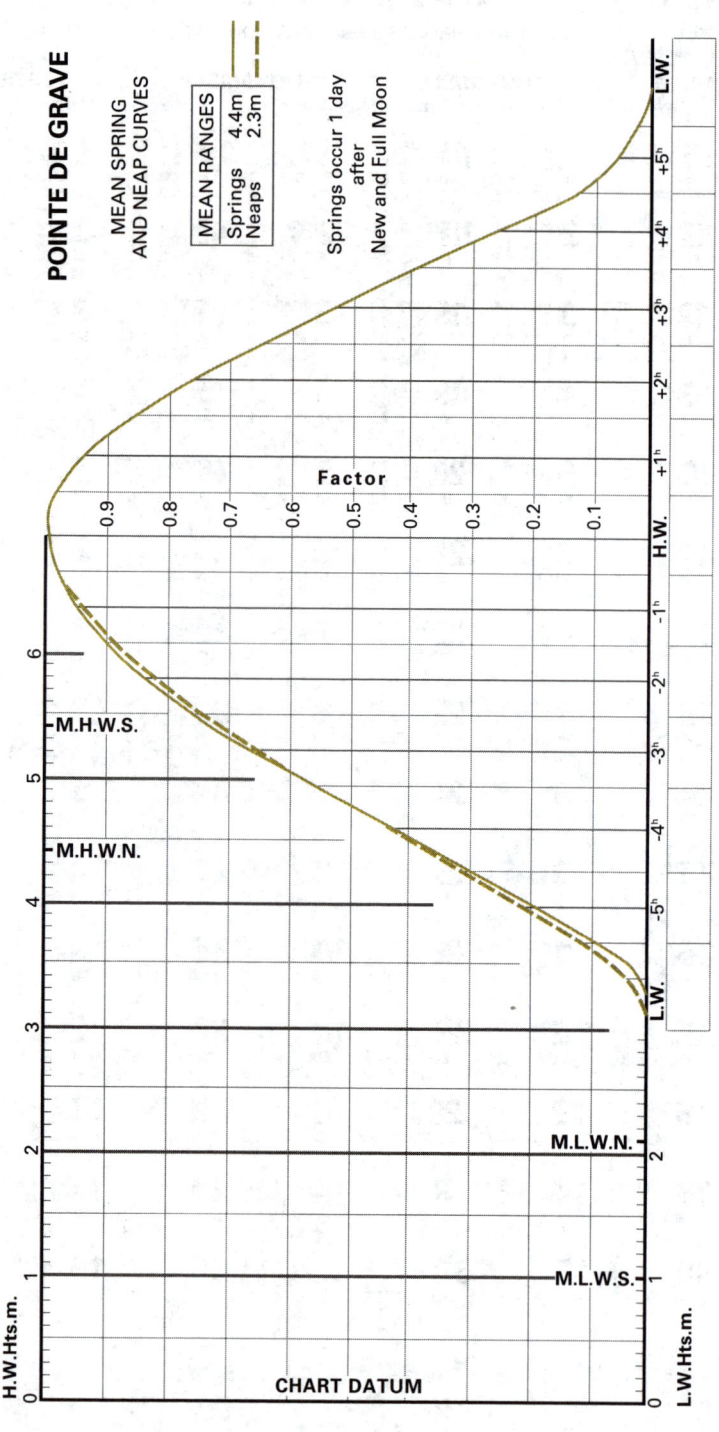

TIME ZONE -0100
(French Standard Time)
Subtract 1 hour for UT
For French Summer Time add
ONE hour in **non-shaded areas**

FRANCE – POINTE DE GRAVE
LAT 45°34'N   LONG 1°04'W
TIMES AND HEIGHTS OF HIGH AND LOW WATERS

YEAR 2005

JANUARY		FEBRUARY		MARCH		APRIL	
Time m	Time m	Time m	Time m	Time m	Time m	Time m	Time m
1 0200 1.8 / 0813 4.8 / SA 1429 1.8 / 2043 4.5	**16** 0307 1.5 / 0934 5.1 / SU 1532 1.6 / 2205 4.6	**1** 0253 1.7 / 0906 4.8 / TU 1518 1.7 / 2139 4.5	**16** 0409 2.0 / 1022 4.4 / W 1631 2.2 / ◐ 2300 4.2	**1** 0147 1.3 / 0754 5.1 / TU 1407 1.4 / 2015 4.9	**16** 0240 1.6 / 0840 4.7 / W 1454 1.9 / 2051 4.5	**1** 0253 1.6 / 0919 4.5 / F 1516 2.0 / 2153 4.5	**16** 0344 2.3 / 1012 4.0 / SA 1606 2.5 / ◐ 2242 4.1
2 0242 1.9 / 0857 4.7 / SU 1512 1.9 / 2133 4.4	**17** 0358 1.8 / 1026 4.8 / M 1624 1.9 / ◐ 2306 4.4	**2** 0341 1.8 / 1002 4.6 / W 1610 1.9 / ◐ 2245 4.4	**17** 0514 2.3 / 1148 4.1 / TH 1743 2.5	**2** 0225 1.4 / 0835 4.9 / W 1446 1.6 / 2101 4.7	**17** 0324 2.0 / 0929 4.3 / TH 1542 2.2 / ◐ 2150 4.2	**2** 0356 1.9 / 1052 4.3 / SA 1630 2.3 / ◐ 2331 4.4	**17** 0505 2.5 / 1201 3.9 / SU 1735 2.6
3 0330 2.0 / 0950 4.6 / M 1601 2.0 / ◐ 2234 4.4	**18** 0456 2.0 / 1130 4.5 / TU 1724 2.1	**3** 0441 2.0 / 1118 4.4 / TH 1717 2.1	**18** 0042 4.1 / 0638 2.4 / F 1326 4.1 / 1910 2.5	**3** 0310 1.7 / 0929 4.6 / TH 1535 1.9 / ◐ 2205 4.4	**18** 0425 2.3 / 1053 4.0 / F 1651 2.6 / 2342 4.0	**3** 0526 2.1 / 1239 4.3 / SU 1809 2.3	**18** 0029 4.1 / 0635 2.4 / M 1322 4.1 / 1857 2.5
4 0425 2.1 / 1053 4.5 / TU 1701 2.1 / 2342 4.4	**19** 0018 4.3 / 0604 2.2 / W 1245 4.4 / 1834 2.2	**4** 0009 4.4 / 0557 2.1 / F 1249 4.4 / 1837 2.1	**19** 0203 4.2 / 0757 2.3 / SA 1439 4.3 / 2022 2.3	**4** 0409 1.9 / 1051 4.3 / F 1642 2.2 / 2339 4.3	**19** 0554 2.5 / 1251 4.0 / SA 1828 2.6	**4** 0108 4.6 / 0704 1.9 / M 1359 4.6 / 1939 2.0	**19** 0141 4.3 / 0742 2.2 / TU 1416 4.4 / 1956 2.2
5 0529 2.1 / 1205 4.5 / W 1808 2.1	**20** 0129 4.3 / 0716 2.2 / TH 1357 4.4 / 1943 2.2	**5** 0132 4.5 / 0717 2.0 / SA 1412 4.6 / 1955 2.0	**20** 0300 4.5 / 0858 2.1 / SU 1530 4.5 / 2114 2.1	**5** 0532 2.1 / 1240 4.3 / SA 1815 2.3	**20** 0126 4.1 / 0726 2.4 / SU 1409 4.2 / 1950 2.5	**5** 0219 4.9 / 0819 1.6 / TU 1459 4.9 / 2043 1.7	**20** 0231 4.6 / 0832 1.9 / W 1457 4.7 / 2043 1.9
6 0053 4.5 / 0636 2.0 / TH 1318 4.6 / 1914 1.9	**21** 0229 4.5 / 0821 2.1 / F 1456 4.5 / 2043 2.1	**6** 0241 4.8 / 0833 1.7 / SU 1519 4.9 / 2105 1.7	**21** 0344 4.7 / 0944 1.8 / M 1608 4.7 / 2155 1.8	**6** 0119 4.5 / 0707 2.0 / SU 1407 4.5 / 1948 2.1	**21** 0230 4.4 / 0829 2.2 / M 1501 4.4 / 2044 2.2	**6** 0315 5.2 / 0915 1.3 / W 1548 5.2 / 2135 1.3	**21** 0311 4.8 / 0912 1.6 / TH 1532 4.9 / 2123 1.6
7 0156 4.7 / 0743 1.8 / F 1425 4.8 / 2017 1.8	**22** 0318 4.6 / 0916 2.0 / SA 1544 4.6 / 2131 1.9	**7** 0341 5.2 / 0940 1.4 / M 1616 5.2 / 2204 1.4	**22** 0419 4.9 / 1023 1.6 / TU 1641 4.9 / 2231 1.6	**7** 0230 4.8 / 0830 1.7 / M 1513 4.9 / 2059 1.7	**22** 0315 4.6 / 0915 1.9 / TU 1539 4.7 / 2126 1.9	**7** 0402 5.5 / 1003 1.0 / TH 1629 5.4 / 2221 1.1	**22** 0346 5.1 / 0950 1.4 / F 1605 5.1 / 2201 1.4
8 0253 5.0 / 0846 1.6 / SA 1525 5.0 / 2115 1.6	**23** 0359 4.8 / 1002 1.8 / SU 1624 4.8 / 2213 1.8	**8** 0434 5.5 / 1037 1.1 / TU 1706 5.4 / ● 2256 1.1	**23** 0451 5.1 / 1058 1.4 / W 1711 5.1 / 2305 1.4	**8** 0332 5.2 / 0933 1.3 / TU 1606 5.2 / 2154 1.3	**23** 0351 4.9 / 0953 1.6 / W 1611 4.9 / 2202 1.6	**8** 0443 5.7 / 1045 0.9 / F 1706 5.5 / ● 2303 0.9	**23** 0420 5.2 / 1026 1.2 / SA 1638 5.3 / 2238 1.2
9 0348 5.3 / 0946 1.4 / SU 1621 5.3 / 2211 1.4	**24** 0436 5.0 / 1041 1.7 / M 1659 4.9 / 2250 1.7	**9** 0523 5.8 / 1127 0.8 / W 1752 5.6 / 2344 1.0	**24** 0521 5.3 / 1131 1.3 / TH 1740 5.2 / ○ 2338 1.3	**9** 0422 5.6 / 1024 1.0 / W 1651 5.4 / 2242 1.0	**24** 0423 5.1 / 1028 1.4 / TH 1641 5.1 / 2237 1.4	**9** 0521 5.7 / 1125 0.9 / SA 1741 5.5 / 2343 0.9	**24** 0453 5.4 / 1101 1.1 / SU 1711 5.4 / ○ 2315 1.1
10 0440 5.5 / 1043 1.1 / M 1713 5.4 / ● 2304 1.2	**25** 0509 5.1 / 1118 1.5 / TU 1732 5.0 / ○ 2324 1.6	**10** 0608 5.9 / 1213 0.7 / TH 1835 5.6	**25** 0550 5.4 / 1203 1.2 / F 1809 5.2	**10** 0506 5.8 / 1110 0.8 / TH 1732 5.6 / ● 2326 0.9	**25** 0453 5.3 / 1101 1.2 / F 1711 5.2 / ○ 2311 1.2	**10** 0556 5.6 / 1201 1.0 / SU 1813 5.4	**25** 0528 5.4 / 1137 1.1 / M 1746 5.4 / 2352 1.0
11 0532 5.7 / 1137 1.0 / TU 1804 5.5 / 2354 1.1	**26** 0541 5.2 / 1152 1.4 / W 1803 5.0 / 2358 1.5	**11** 0032 0.9 / 0652 5.9 / F 1256 0.7 / 1915 5.5	**26** 0011 1.2 / 0619 5.4 / SA 1234 1.2 / 1837 5.2	**11** 0547 5.9 / 1152 0.7 / F 1810 5.6	**26** 0523 5.4 / 1134 1.1 / SA 1740 5.4 / 2344 1.1	**11** 0021 1.0 / 0630 5.5 / M 1235 1.1 / 1843 5.3	**26** 0605 5.4 / 1212 1.1 / TU 1823 5.4
12 0622 5.8 / 1227 0.9 / W 1853 5.5	**27** 0612 5.2 / 1225 1.4 / TH 1833 5.0	**12** 0114 0.9 / 0732 5.7 / SA 1336 0.9 / 1953 5.3	**27** 0042 1.2 / 0649 5.4 / SU 1304 1.2 / 1907 5.2	**12** 0009 0.8 / 0625 5.8 / SA 1231 0.8 / 1845 5.5	**27** 0553 5.5 / 1206 1.1 / SU 1810 5.4	**12** 0056 1.1 / 0701 5.2 / TU 1308 1.3 / 1912 5.1	**27** 0032 1.0 / 0644 5.2 / W 1249 1.2 / 1903 5.3
13 0046 1.1 / 0711 5.7 / TH 1314 0.9 / 1940 5.3	**28** 0032 1.4 / 0642 5.2 / F 1258 1.4 / 1903 5.0	**13** 0154 1.1 / 0810 5.4 / SU 1415 1.2 / 2028 5.0	**28** 0114 1.2 / 0720 5.3 / M 1334 1.3 / 1939 5.1	**13** 0049 0.9 / 0702 5.6 / SU 1307 0.9 / 1916 5.3	**28** 0018 1.0 / 0624 5.6 / M 1237 1.1 / 1842 5.3	**13** 0131 1.3 / 0733 4.9 / W 1342 1.6 / 1943 4.8	**28** 0112 1.1 / 0728 5.1 / TH 1329 1.4 / 1949 5.1
14 0133 1.2 / 0759 5.6 / F 1400 1.1 / 2027 5.1	**29** 0104 1.4 / 0713 5.2 / SA 1329 1.4 / 1934 4.9	**14** 0234 1.2 / 0847 5.1 / M 1454 1.5 / 2102 4.7		**14** 0125 1.0 / 0733 5.4 / M 1341 1.2 / 1945 5.1	**29** 0051 1.1 / 0658 5.3 / TU 1309 1.2 / 1916 5.2	**14** 0207 1.6 / 0810 4.6 / TH 1418 1.9 / 2022 4.6	**29** 0156 1.2 / 0820 4.8 / F 1415 1.7 / 2045 4.8
15 0219 1.4 / 0846 5.4 / SA 1445 1.3 / 2114 4.9	**30** 0138 1.5 / 0746 5.1 / SU 1402 1.5 / 2009 4.8	**15** 0318 1.6 / 0927 4.7 / TU 1538 1.8 / 2146 4.4		**15** 0201 1.3 / 0805 5.0 / TU 1416 1.5 / 2014 4.8	**30** 0126 1.2 / 0735 5.1 / W 1343 1.4 / 1954 5.0	**15** 0249 2.0 / 0857 4.3 / F 1503 2.2 / 2115 4.3	**30** 0249 1.5 / 0928 4.5 / SA 1513 2.0 / 2157 4.7
	31 0213 1.5 / 0823 5.0 / M 1437 1.6 / 2049 4.7				**31** 0205 1.3 / 0819 4.8 / TH 1424 1.6 / 2043 4.8		

Chart Datum: 2·83 metres below IGN Datum
》 **FREE** monthly updates from 《
www.reedsalmanac.co.uk

Chapter 5

403

TIDES

TIME ZONE -0100
(French Standard Time)
Subtract 1 hour for UT
For French Summer Time add
ONE hour in **non-shaded areas**

FRANCE – POINTE DE GRAVE
LAT 45°34′N   LONG 1°04′W
TIMES AND HEIGHTS OF HIGH AND LOW WATERS

YEAR 2005

	MAY				JUNE				JULY				AUGUST			
	Time m		Time m		Time m		Time m		Time m		Time m		Time m		Time m	

1 0358 1.8 / 1059 4.4 / SU 1631 2.2 / ☽ 2325 4.6
16 0417 2.3 / 1058 4.0 / M 1640 2.4 / ● 2316 4.2
1 0020 4.8 / 0614 1.7 / W 1309 4.6 / 1842 1.8
16 0532 2.0 / 1207 4.3 / TH 1752 2.1
1 0047 4.6 / 0641 1.8 / F 1333 4.5 / 1912 1.8
16 0532 2.0 / 1212 4.3 / SA 1800 2.0
1 0234 4.3 / 0821 2.0 / M 1504 4.5 / 2055 1.9
16 0135 4.3 / 0722 2.0 / TU 1408 4.6 / 1958 1.8

2 0523 1.9 / 1229 4.4 / M 1758 2.1
17 0531 2.3 / 1217 4.1 / TU 1753 2.4
2 0125 4.8 / 0720 1.6 / TH 1406 4.7 / 1945 1.7
17 0023 4.4 / 0633 2.0 / F 1307 4.4 / 1853 2.0
2 0151 4.5 / 0744 1.8 / SA 1429 4.6 / 2014 1.8
17 0037 4.3 / 0641 1.9 / SU 1321 4.4 / 1908 1.9
2 0330 4.4 / 0916 1.9 / TU 1549 4.7 / 2146 1.7
17 0248 4.6 / 0836 1.8 / W 1510 5.0 / 2107 1.5

3 0049 4.7 / 0646 1.8 / TU 1339 4.7 / 1915 1.9
18 0031 4.3 / 0639 2.2 / W 1317 4.3 / 1855 2.2
3 0222 4.9 / 0817 1.5 / F 1455 4.8 / 2040 1.5
18 0125 4.5 / 0731 1.8 / SA 1401 4.6 / 1949 1.8
3 0249 4.6 / 0841 1.8 / SU 1517 4.7 / 2109 1.7
18 0150 4.5 / 0747 1.8 / M 1424 4.7 / 2014 1.7
3 0413 4.6 / 1001 1.7 / W 1626 4.8 / 2228 1.6
18 0349 4.9 / 0937 1.4 / TH 1605 5.3 / 2206 1.1

4 0156 4.9 / 0754 1.6 / W 1436 4.9 / 2017 1.6
19 0131 4.5 / 0736 1.9 / TH 1405 4.6 / 1949 2.0
4 0311 4.9 / 0907 1.5 / SA 1537 4.9 / 2129 1.4
19 0222 4.7 / 0824 1.6 / SU 1450 4.8 / 2043 1.6
4 0338 4.6 / 0930 1.7 / M 1559 4.8 / 2158 1.6
19 0257 4.7 / 0849 1.6 / TU 1521 4.9 / 2116 1.5
4 0449 4.7 / 1039 1.6 / TH 1700 5.0 / 2306 1.5
19 0441 5.2 / 1031 1.1 / F 1655 5.6 / ○ 2259 0.9

5 0251 5.1 / 0849 1.4 / TH 1523 5.1 / 2109 1.4
20 0220 4.7 / 0823 1.7 / F 1447 4.8 / 2037 1.7
5 0354 5.0 / 0951 1.4 / SU 1615 5.0 / 2214 1.4
20 0316 4.9 / 0915 1.5 / M 1539 5.0 / 2136 1.4
5 0422 4.7 / 1014 1.6 / TU 1637 4.9 / 2241 1.5
20 0356 4.9 / 0947 1.4 / W 1615 5.2 / 2215 1.2
5 0522 4.8 / 1114 1.5 / F 1731 5.0 / ● 2340 1.4
20 0528 5.4 / 1120 0.9 / SA 1741 5.8 / 2346 0.7

6 0337 5.3 / 0935 1.2 / F 1603 5.2 / 2155 1.2
21 0304 4.9 / 0907 1.5 / SA 1526 5.0 / 2121 1.5
6 0434 5.0 / 1031 1.4 / M 1651 5.1 / ● 2256 1.4
21 0407 5.0 / 1004 1.3 / TU 1627 5.2 / 2227 1.2
6 0501 4.8 / 1053 1.6 / W 1714 5.0 / ● 2321 1.5
21 0451 5.1 / 1042 1.2 / TH 1707 5.4 / ○ 2310 1.0
6 0553 4.9 / 1147 1.4 / SA 1801 5.1
21 0612 5.5 / 1206 0.8 / SU 1826 5.8

7 0418 5.4 / 1018 1.1 / SA 1639 5.3 / 2238 1.1
22 0345 5.1 / 0949 1.3 / SU 1605 5.2 / 2205 1.3
7 0512 5.0 / 1109 1.4 / TU 1726 5.1 / 2335 1.4
22 0458 5.2 / 1053 1.2 / W 1716 5.4 / ○ 2319 1.1
7 0538 4.8 / 1129 1.5 / TH 1749 5.0 / 2357 1.4
22 0542 5.3 / 1134 1.1 / F 1757 5.6
7 0014 1.3 / 0621 4.9 / SU 1219 1.4 / 1830 5.1
22 0034 0.7 / 0653 5.4 / M 1249 0.8 / 1910 5.7

8 0455 5.4 / 1056 1.1 / SU 1712 5.3 / ● 2317 1.1
23 0427 5.2 / 1030 1.2 / M 1645 5.3 / ○ 2248 1.1
8 0549 4.9 / 1144 1.5 / W 1802 5.0
23 0549 5.2 / 1142 1.2 / TH 1806 5.5
8 0613 4.8 / 1204 1.5 / F 1822 5.0
23 0002 0.8 / 0631 5.3 / SA 1223 1.0 / 1847 5.7
8 0045 1.3 / 0650 4.9 / M 1250 1.4 / 1859 5.0
23 0115 0.8 / 0733 5.3 / TU 1331 0.9 / 1951 5.5

9 0531 5.3 / 1132 1.2 / M 1745 5.3 / 2355 1.2
24 0509 5.3 / 1111 1.1 / TU 1727 5.4 / 2332 1.1
9 0012 1.4 / 0625 4.8 / TH 1219 1.6 / 1837 5.0
24 0012 1.0 / 0640 5.2 / F 1231 1.2 / 1857 5.5
9 0033 1.4 / 0645 4.8 / SA 1239 1.5 / 1855 4.9
24 0054 0.8 / 0718 5.3 / SU 1309 1.0 / 1935 5.6
9 0115 1.4 / 0719 4.8 / TU 1321 1.4 / 1930 4.9
24 0154 1.0 / 0810 5.0 / W 1412 1.2 / 2032 5.1

10 0605 5.2 / 1206 1.3 / TU 1818 5.2
25 0554 5.3 / 1153 1.2 / W 1812 5.4
10 0048 1.5 / 0701 4.7 / F 1255 1.7 / 1913 4.9
25 0103 1.0 / 0731 5.1 / SA 1321 1.2 / 1950 5.4
10 0108 1.5 / 0718 4.7 / SU 1313 1.6 / 1928 4.9
25 0139 0.9 / 0804 5.2 / M 1355 1.1 / 2022 5.4
10 0145 1.4 / 0750 4.7 / W 1353 1.5 / 2002 4.8
25 0234 1.3 / 0846 4.7 / TH 1455 1.5 / 2115 4.7

11 0031 1.3 / 0639 5.0 / W 1240 1.5 / 1851 5.0
26 0019 1.0 / 0641 5.2 / TH 1237 1.3 / 1900 5.3
11 0125 1.6 / 0738 4.6 / SA 1332 1.8 / 1950 4.7
26 0153 1.1 / 0824 5.0 / SU 1411 1.4 / 2044 5.3
11 0142 1.5 / 0751 4.6 / M 1349 1.6 / 2003 4.8
26 0223 1.0 / 0849 4.9 / TU 1441 1.2 / 2109 5.2
11 0217 1.5 / 0826 4.6 / TH 1429 1.6 / 2041 4.6
26 0317 1.7 / 0930 4.4 / F 1545 1.8 / ☽ 2208 4.3

12 0106 1.5 / 0714 4.8 / TH 1314 1.7 / 1926 4.8
27 0106 1.1 / 0731 5.0 / F 1324 1.4 / 1952 5.2
12 0204 1.7 / 0818 4.4 / SU 1413 1.9 / 2032 4.6
27 0244 1.2 / 0919 4.8 / M 1504 1.5 / 2139 5.1
12 0217 1.6 / 0828 4.5 / TU 1426 1.7 / 2041 4.6
27 0308 1.3 / 0935 4.7 / W 1529 1.5 / 2159 4.8
12 0254 1.7 / 0909 4.4 / F 1511 1.8 / 2129 4.4
27 0409 2.1 / 1039 4.2 / SA 1649 2.2 / 2329 4.1

13 0143 1.7 / 0752 4.6 / F 1352 1.9 / 2006 4.6
28 0156 1.3 / 0828 4.8 / SA 1415 1.6 / 2050 5.0
13 0246 1.9 / 0905 4.3 / M 1459 2.0 / 2120 4.5
28 0337 1.4 / 1018 4.6 / TU 1559 1.6 / ☽ 2238 4.9
13 0255 1.7 / 0910 4.4 / W 1507 1.7 / 2125 4.5
28 0357 1.6 / 1030 4.5 / TH 1624 1.7 / ☽ 2257 4.5
13 0339 1.8 / 1008 4.3 / SA 1604 1.9 / ☽ 2236 4.3
28 0518 2.3 / 1223 4.1 / SU 1812 2.3

14 0224 1.9 / 0838 4.3 / SA 1436 2.1 / 2055 4.4
29 0252 1.5 / 0933 4.6 / SU 1515 1.8 / 2156 4.9
14 0335 2.0 / 1000 4.2 / TU 1551 2.1 / 2215 4.4
29 0433 1.5 / 1123 4.5 / W 1700 1.7 / 2342 4.7
14 0338 1.8 / 1001 4.3 / TH 1556 1.9 / ☽ 2219 4.4
29 0453 1.9 / 1139 4.3 / F 1728 2.0
14 0440 2.0 / 1127 4.2 / SU 1715 2.1 / 1938 2.2
29 0105 4.0 / 0646 2.4 / M 1348 4.2 / 1938 2.2

15 0313 2.1 / 0939 4.1 / SU 1531 2.3 / 2158 4.3
30 0355 1.6 / 1048 4.5 / M 1622 1.8 / ☽ 2308 4.8
15 0430 2.0 / 1103 4.2 / W 1650 2.2 / 2318 4.3
30 0535 1.7 / 1230 4.5 / TH 1806 1.8
15 0429 1.9 / 1103 4.2 / F 1653 2.0 / 2322 4.3
30 0008 4.3 / 0600 2.1 / SA 1259 4.2 / 1841 2.1
15 0003 4.3 / 0600 2.1 / M 1253 4.3 / 1839 2.0
30 0222 4.2 / 0804 2.2 / TU 1448 4.4 / 2041 2.0

| | | **31** 0504 1.7 / 1203 4.5 / TU 1733 1.9 | | | | | **31** 0125 4.2 / 0714 2.1 / SU 1408 4.3 / 1954 2.0 | | **31** 0315 4.4 / 0859 2.0 / W 1532 4.7 / 2129 1.8 |

Chart Datum: 2·83 metres below IGN Datum
FREE monthly updates from
www.reedsalmanac.co.uk

404

TIME ZONE -0100
(French Standard Time)
Subtract 1 hour for UT
For French Summer Time add
ONE hour in **non-shaded areas**

FRANCE – POINTE DE GRAVE
LAT 45°34′N   LONG 1°04′W
TIMES AND HEIGHTS OF HIGH AND LOW WATERS

YEAR 2005

SEPTEMBER		OCTOBER		NOVEMBER		DECEMBER	
Time m	Time m	Time m	Time m	Time m	Time m	Time m	Time m
1 0354 4.6 / 0941 1.8 / TH 1606 4.9 / 2207 1.6	**16** 0335 5.0 / 0924 1.4 / F 1550 5.5 / 2152 1.1	**1** 0353 4.9 / 0946 1.6 / SA 1606 5.1 / 2210 1.4	**16** 0358 5.3 / 0952 1.1 / SU 1614 5.7 / 2214 1.0	**1** 0415 5.2 / 1019 1.4 / TU 1632 5.3 / 2239 1.3	**16** 0449 5.4 / 1056 1.2 / W 1711 5.4 / ○ 2309 1.3	**1** 0423 5.3 / 1029 1.4 / TH 1646 5.3 / ● 2248 1.4	**16** 0512 5.2 / 1121 1.4 / F 1736 5.1 / 2330 1.5
2 0427 4.8 / 1018 1.6 / F 1637 5.0 / 2242 1.4	**17** 0422 5.3 / 1015 1.1 / SA 1636 5.7 / 2239 0.8	**2** 0422 5.0 / 1019 1.5 / SU 1634 5.2 / 2242 1.3	**17** 0438 5.5 / 1037 1.0 / M 1654 5.8 / ○ 2256 0.9	**2** 0447 5.3 / 1055 1.3 / W 1704 5.4 / ● 2313 1.3	**17** 0525 5.4 / 1136 1.2 / TH 1748 5.3 / 2347 1.4	**2** 0503 5.4 / 1112 1.3 / F 1728 5.3 / 2329 1.4	**17** 0549 5.2 / 1200 1.5 / SA 1813 5.0
3 0456 4.9 / 1051 1.4 / SA 1658 5.2 / ● 2315 1.3	**18** 0505 5.5 / 1101 0.9 / SU 1719 5.9 / ○ 2323 0.7	**3** 0450 5.2 / 1052 1.3 / M 1702 5.3 / ● 2313 1.2	**18** 0515 5.5 / 1119 0.9 / TU 1733 5.7 / 2336 1.0	**3** 0520 5.4 / 1131 1.2 / TH 1739 5.3 / 2347 1.3	**18** 0601 5.3 / 1214 1.4 / F 1825 5.1	**3** 0546 5.4 / 1155 1.2 / SA 1813 5.2	**18** 0007 1.6 / 0625 5.2 / SU 1237 1.5 / 1849 4.9
4 0524 5.0 / 1123 1.3 / SU 1734 5.2 / 2345 1.2	**19** 0545 5.5 / 1144 0.8 / M 1800 5.8	**4** 0517 5.2 / 1124 1.2 / TU 1730 5.3 / 2343 1.2	**19** 0550 5.4 / 1158 1.0 / W 1810 5.5	**4** 0556 5.3 / 1207 1.3 / F 1816 5.2	**19** 0024 1.6 / 0637 5.1 / SA 1251 1.5 / 1902 4.9	**4** 0013 1.4 / 0632 5.4 / SU 1240 1.3 / 1901 5.1	**19** 0044 1.7 / 0700 5.1 / M 1313 1.6 / 1925 4.8
5 0551 5.1 / 1153 1.3 / M 1801 5.2	**20** 0005 0.8 / 0622 5.5 / TU 1224 0.8 / 1839 5.7	**5** 0546 5.3 / 1156 1.2 / W 1800 5.3	**20** 0014 1.2 / 0624 5.3 / TH 1236 1.2 / 1846 5.3	**5** 0025 1.4 / 0634 5.2 / SA 1245 1.4 / 1857 5.0	**20** 0101 1.7 / 0713 5.0 / SU 1330 1.7 / 1941 4.6	**5** 0059 1.5 / 0722 5.3 / M 1328 1.4 / 1954 5.0	**20** 0122 1.8 / 0736 4.9 / TU 1351 1.8 / 2003 4.6
6 0016 1.2 / 0618 5.1 / TU 1223 1.2 / 1828 5.2	**21** 0045 0.9 / 0657 5.3 / W 1303 1.0 / 1917 5.4	**6** 0014 1.3 / 0616 5.2 / TH 1227 1.2 / 1831 5.2	**21** 0050 1.4 / 0656 5.1 / F 1313 1.4 / 1921 4.9	**6** 0103 1.6 / 0718 5.1 / SU 1327 1.5 / 1947 4.8	**21** 0140 2.0 / 0754 4.7 / M 1411 2.0 / 2027 4.4	**6** 0149 1.7 / 0818 5.2 / TU 1420 1.5 / 2055 4.8	**21** 0201 1.9 / 0815 4.8 / W 1431 1.9 / 2045 4.5
7 0045 1.3 / 0646 5.0 / W 1253 1.3 / 1857 5.1	**22** 0122 1.2 / 0729 5.1 / TH 1341 1.2 / 1953 5.1	**7** 0045 1.3 / 0648 5.1 / F 1300 1.3 / 1905 5.0	**22** 0126 1.7 / 0730 4.9 / SA 1352 1.7 / 2000 4.6	**7** 0148 1.8 / 0813 4.9 / M 1417 1.7 / 2051 4.5	**22** 0225 2.2 / 0843 4.5 / TU 1500 2.2 / 2127 4.2	**7** 0244 1.8 / 0920 5.0 / W 1518 1.7 / 2204 4.6	**22** 0243 2.1 / 0859 4.6 / TH 1515 2.1 / 2135 4.3
8 0113 1.1 / 0715 4.9 / TH 1324 1.4 / 1928 4.9	**23** 0159 1.5 / 0801 4.8 / F 1421 1.6 / 2031 4.6	**8** 0118 1.5 / 0724 4.9 / SA 1337 1.5 / 1945 4.8	**23** 0205 2.0 / 0811 4.6 / SU 1435 2.0 / 2050 4.3	**8** 0242 2.0 / 0923 4.7 / TU 1519 2.0 / 2215 4.4	**23** 0318 2.4 / 0947 4.4 / W 1600 2.4 / ● 2244 4.1	**8** 0347 1.9 / 1029 4.9 / TH 1622 1.8 / ● 2317 4.6	**23** 0330 2.2 / 0950 4.5 / F 1606 2.2 / ○ 2236 4.2
9 0144 1.4 / 0748 4.8 / F 1358 1.5 / 2005 4.7	**24** 0238 1.9 / 0840 4.5 / SA 1507 2.0 / 2123 4.3	**9** 0157 1.7 / 0810 4.7 / SU 1420 1.7 / 2041 4.5	**24** 0252 2.3 / 0910 4.3 / M 1531 2.4 / 2211 4.0	**9** 0354 2.2 / 1048 4.6 / W 1639 2.1 / ○ 2345 4.4	**24** 0422 2.5 / 1103 4.3 / TH 1712 2.4 / 2359 4.2	**9** 0455 2.0 / 1141 4.9 / F 1730 1.9	**24** 0425 2.3 / 1051 4.4 / SA 1704 2.3 / 2342 4.3
10 0220 1.6 / 0829 4.6 / SA 1439 1.7 / 2054 4.5	**25** 0326 2.2 / 0945 4.2 / SU 1608 2.3 / ○ 2251 4.0	**10** 0245 2.0 / 0917 4.5 / M 1517 2.0 / ○ 2208 4.2	**25** 0355 2.6 / 1044 4.2 / TU 1651 2.6 / ○ 2352 4.0	**10** 0518 2.2 / 1210 4.6 / TH 1803 2.0	**25** 0532 2.5 / 1217 4.4 / F 1821 2.3	**10** 0029 4.6 / 0604 2.0 / SA 1248 4.9 / 1839 1.8	**25** 0526 2.3 / 1159 4.4 / SU 1808 2.3
11 0304 1.9 / 0929 4.4 / SU 1532 2.0 / ○ 2209 4.2	**26** 0435 2.5 / 1140 4.1 / M 1739 2.5	**11** 0352 2.3 / 1053 4.3 / TU 1640 2.2 / 2355 4.2	**26** 0520 2.7 / 1220 4.2 / W 1822 2.5	**11** 0101 4.6 / 0637 2.0 / F 1319 5.0 / 1915 1.8	**26** 0059 4.3 / 0636 2.4 / SA 1317 4.5 / 1918 2.2	**11** 0131 4.7 / 0711 1.8 / SU 1350 5.0 / 1941 1.7	**26** 0046 4.4 / 0629 2.2 / M 1306 4.5 / 1909 2.1
12 0405 2.2 / 1100 4.2 / M 1647 2.2 / 2353 4.1	**27** 0039 3.9 / 0612 2.6 / TU 1315 4.2 / 1913 2.4	**12** 0529 2.4 / 1229 4.4 / W 1822 2.1	**27** 0107 4.2 / 0641 2.5 / TH 1328 4.4 / 1929 2.3	**12** 0200 4.9 / 0742 1.8 / SA 1417 5.2 / 2013 1.5	**27** 0147 4.5 / 0731 2.2 / SU 1405 4.7 / 2006 2.0	**12** 0224 4.9 / 0811 1.7 / M 1445 5.0 / 2036 1.6	**27** 0142 4.5 / 0730 2.0 / TU 1405 4.6 / 2004 2.0
13 0536 2.3 / 1239 4.3 / TU 1826 2.1	**28** 0154 4.1 / 0734 2.2 / W 1418 4.4 / 2015 2.1	**13** 0122 4.5 / 0700 2.2 / TH 1342 4.9 / 1942 1.8	**28** 0159 4.4 / 0740 2.3 / F 1417 4.6 / 2016 2.0	**13** 0250 5.1 / 0838 1.5 / SU 1507 5.4 / 2103 1.3	**28** 0228 4.8 / 0819 1.9 / M 1447 4.9 / 2048 1.8	**13** 0311 5.0 / 0905 1.6 / TU 1534 5.1 / 2125 1.6	**28** 0233 4.8 / 0826 1.9 / W 1458 4.8 / 2054 1.8
14 0131 4.3 / 0711 2.1 / W 1357 4.7 / 1953 1.8	**29** 0245 4.4 / 0829 2.2 / TH 1502 4.7 / 2059 1.9	**14** 0224 4.8 / 0809 1.9 / F 1440 5.2 / 2040 1.4	**29** 0239 4.7 / 0826 2.0 / SA 1455 4.9 / 2055 1.8	**14** 0333 5.2 / 0928 1.4 / M 1551 5.5 / 2148 1.2	**29** 0307 5.0 / 0903 1.7 / TU 1527 5.0 / 2128 1.6	**14** 0354 5.1 / 0955 1.5 / W 1617 5.1 / 2210 1.5	**29** 0320 5.0 / 0918 1.7 / TH 1548 5.0 / 2143 1.6
15 0240 4.7 / 0826 1.8 / TH 1458 5.1 / 2059 1.4	**30** 0322 4.7 / 0910 1.9 / F 1536 4.9 / 2136 1.6	**15** 0315 5.1 / 0904 1.4 / SA 1530 5.5 / 2130 1.1	**30** 0313 4.9 / 0905 1.8 / SU 1529 5.1 / 2131 1.5	**15** 0412 5.3 / 1013 1.3 / TU 1632 5.5 / 2230 1.2	**30** 0344 5.2 / 0946 1.5 / W 1606 5.2 / 2208 1.5	**15** 0433 5.2 / 1040 1.4 / TH 1658 5.1 / ○ 2251 1.5	**30** 0407 5.2 / 1010 1.5 / F 1636 5.1 / 2231 1.5
			31 0344 5.1 / 0943 1.6 / M 1600 5.2 / 2205 1.4				**31** 0454 5.3 / 1100 1.3 / SA 1724 5.3 / ● 2318 1.3

Chart Datum: 2·83 metres below IGN Datum

》 **FREE** monthly updates from 《
www.reedsalmanac.co.uk

TIDES

LISBOA

MEAN SPRING AND NEAP CURVES

MEAN RANGES	
Springs	3.2m
Neaps	1.5m

Springs occur 1 day after New and Full Moon

PORTUGAL – LISBOA
LAT 38°43'N   LONG 9°07'W
TIMES AND HEIGHTS OF HIGH AND LOW WATERS

TIME ZONE (UT) For Summer Time add ONE hour in **non-shaded areas**

YEAR 2005

JANUARY

Time	m	Time	m
1 0624 1226 SA 1852	3.3 1.0 3.0	**16** 0058 0737 SU 1332 2007	0.9 3.4 0.9 3.1
2 0034 0708 SU 1312 1941	1.2 3.2 1.1 2.9	**17** 0150 0830 M 1426 ◐ 2104	1.1 3.2 1.1 3.0
3 0124 0800 M 1406 ◐ 2039	1.3 3.1 1.2 2.9	**18** 0252 0932 TU 1528 2211	1.3 3.0 1.3 2.9
4 0225 0902 TU 1509 2147	1.3 3.0 1.3 2.9	**19** 0405 1043 W 1640 2322	1.4 2.8 1.4 2.9
5 0334 1011 W 1617 2255	1.3 3.0 1.2 3.0	**20** 0523 1153 TH 1748	1.4 2.8 1.3
6 0446 1121 TH 1722 2358	1.2 3.1 1.1 3.2	**21** 0025 0631 F 1254 1846	3.0 1.3 2.9 1.2
7 0552 1225 F 1823	1.1 3.2 0.9	**22** 0118 0723 SA 1345 1932	3.1 1.1 3.0 1.1
8 0056 0654 SA 1326 1918	3.4 0.9 3.4 0.8	**23** 0203 0805 SU 1427 2011	3.2 1.0 3.1 1.0
9 0152 0750 SU 1423 2011	3.6 0.6 3.5 0.6	**24** 0241 0841 M 1504 2045	3.3 0.9 3.2 0.9
10 0246 0844 M 1518 ● 2102	3.8 0.4 3.6 0.5	**25** 0316 0914 TU 1538 ○ 2118	3.4 0.8 3.2 0.9
11 0338 0935 TU 1609 2151	3.9 0.3 3.7 0.5	**26** 0349 0946 W 1610 2150	3.5 0.7 3.3 0.8
12 0427 1024 W 1658 2238	4.0 0.3 3.7 0.5	**27** 0421 1017 TH 1642 2222	3.6 0.7 3.3 0.8
13 0515 1111 TH 1745 2324	4.0 0.3 3.6 0.6	**28** 0454 1049 F 1714 2255	3.6 0.7 3.3 0.8
14 0602 1157 F 1830	3.9 0.5 3.5	**29** 0528 1122 SA 1748 2329	3.5 0.7 3.3 0.8
15 0010 0648 SA 1244 1917	0.7 3.7 0.7 3.3	**30** 0603 1156 SU 1824	3.5 0.8 3.2
		31 0005 0640 M 1233 1904	0.9 3.3 0.9 3.1

FEBRUARY

Time	m	Time	m
1 0046 0721 TU 1317 1951	1.0 3.2 1.0 3.0	**16** 0159 0834 W 1427 ◐ 2109	1.3 2.9 1.4 2.8
2 0136 0813 W 1412 2052	1.2 3.0 1.2 2.9	**17** 0313 0949 TH 1546 2235	1.5 2.7 1.6 2.7
3 0242 0922 TH 1524 2208	1.3 2.9 1.3 2.9	**18** 0452 1124 F 1719	1.5 2.6 1.6
4 0406 1046 F 1648 2329	1.3 2.9 1.2 3.0	**19** 0000 0616 SA 1240 1829	2.8 1.4 2.7 1.4
5 0532 1209 SA 1805	1.1 3.0 1.1	**20** 0100 0710 SU 1331 1917	3.0 1.2 2.9 1.3
6 0041 0645 SU 1320 1910	3.3 0.9 3.2 0.9	**21** 0145 0749 M 1411 1954	3.2 1.0 3.1 1.1
7 0144 0746 M 1419 2005	3.5 0.6 3.5 0.7	**22** 0222 0822 TU 1445 2028	3.4 0.9 3.3 0.9
8 0238 0838 TU 1510 2054	3.8 0.4 3.7 0.5	**23** 0256 0853 W 1517 2059	3.5 0.7 3.4 0.8
9 0328 0925 W 1557 2139	4.0 0.2 3.8 0.4	**24** 0328 0924 TH 1548 ○ 2130	3.7 0.6 3.5 0.7
10 0414 1009 TH 1640 2222	4.1 0.2 3.8 0.3	**25** 0401 0954 F 1619 2201	3.7 0.6 3.6 0.6
11 0457 1050 F 1721 2302	4.1 0.2 3.8 0.4	**26** 0434 1024 SA 1651 2233	3.8 0.6 3.6 0.6
12 0538 1129 SA 1800 2342	4.0 0.4 3.6 0.5	**27** 0506 1055 SU 1724 2305	3.7 0.6 3.5 0.7
13 0618 1208 SU 1839	3.8 0.6 3.4	**28** 0539 1127 M 1757 2339	3.6 0.7 3.4 0.8
14 0022 0658 M 1247 1919	0.8 3.5 0.9 3.2		
15 0106 0741 TU 1331 2006	1.0 3.2 1.2 3.0		

MARCH

Time	m	Time	m
1 0614 1201 TU 1834	3.5 0.8 3.3	**16** 0029 0658 W 1244 1916	1.1 3.1 1.3 3.1
2 0018 0653 W 1242 1918	0.9 3.3 1.0 3.2	**17** 0117 0743 TH 1333 ◐ 2008	1.4 2.8 1.5 2.8
3 0106 0743 TH 1335 ◐ 2017	1.1 3.1 1.2 3.0	**18** 0227 0852 F 1451 2136	1.6 2.6 1.8 2.7
4 0213 0855 F 1452 2140	1.3 2.9 1.4 3.0	**19** 0416 1050 SA 1643 2323	1.7 2.6 1.8 2.8
5 0349 1035 SA 1632 2315	1.4 2.8 1.4 3.1	**20** 0547 1215 SU 1801	1.5 2.7 1.6
6 0528 1208 SU 1759	1.2 3.0 1.3	**21** 0030 0641 M 1305 1850	3.0 1.3 3.0 1.4
7 0034 0642 M 1316 1904	3.3 0.9 3.3 1.0	**22** 0115 0719 TU 1342 1927	3.2 1.1 3.2 1.2
8 0135 0730 TU 1409 1955	3.6 0.6 3.6 0.7	**23** 0152 0752 W 1415 2000	3.4 0.9 3.4 1.0
9 0226 0825 W 1455 2039	3.9 0.4 3.8 0.5	**24** 0227 0824 TH 1448 2032	3.6 0.8 3.6 0.8
10 0311 0907 TH 1537 ● 2120	4.1 0.3 3.9 0.4	**25** 0301 0855 F 1520 ○ 2104	3.8 0.6 3.7 0.7
11 0353 0945 F 1616 2159	4.2 0.3 3.9 0.3	**26** 0335 0926 SA 1553 2136	3.9 0.6 3.8 0.6
12 0433 1020 SA 1653 2236	4.1 0.3 3.9 0.4	**27** 0408 0957 SU 1626 2208	3.9 0.6 3.8 0.6
13 0511 1057 SU 1728 2313	4.0 0.5 3.8 0.6	**28** 0442 1028 M 1659 2242	3.8 0.6 3.7 0.6
14 0546 1132 M 1802 2349	3.8 0.6 3.5 0.8	**29** 0517 1101 TU 1735 2319	3.7 0.7 3.6 0.7
15 0621 1206 TU 1837	3.5 0.9 3.3	**30** 0554 1137 W 1814	3.6 0.9 3.5
		31 0001 0637 TH 1220 1900	0.9 3.3 1.1 3.3

APRIL

Time	m	Time	m
1 0053 0733 F 1318 2003	1.1 3.1 1.4 3.1	**16** 0149 0808 SA 1404 ◐ 2036	1.6 2.7 1.8 2.8
2 0208 0854 SA 1444 2133	1.4 2.9 1.5 3.1	**17** 0325 0955 SU 1549 2221	1.7 2.6 1.9 2.8
3 0350 1039 SU 1629 2309	1.4 2.9 1.5 3.2	**18** 0454 1127 M 1712 2339	1.6 2.8 1.7 3.0
4 0524 1202 M 1751	1.2 3.2 1.3	**19** 0553 1221 TU 1806	1.4 3.0 1.5
5 0022 0630 TU 1302 1849	3.5 0.9 3.4 1.0	**20** 0031 0637 W 1302 1848	3.2 1.2 3.2 1.3
6 0118 0720 W 1349 1936	3.7 0.7 3.7 0.8	**21** 0113 0714 TH 1338 1925	3.4 1.0 3.4 1.0
7 0206 0803 TH 1432 2018	4.0 0.4 3.9 0.6	**22** 0151 0748 F 1413 2000	3.6 0.8 3.6 0.9
8 0249 0841 F 1511 ● 2057	4.1 0.4 4.0 0.5	**23** 0228 0821 SA 1448 2034	3.8 0.7 3.7 0.7
9 0329 0918 SA 1548 2134	4.1 0.4 4.0 0.5	**24** 0305 0854 SU 1523 ○ 2109	3.8 0.6 3.8 0.6
10 0407 0953 SU 1624 2210	4.0 0.5 3.9 0.6	**25** 0342 0928 M 1600 2146	3.9 0.6 3.9 0.6
11 0443 1026 M 1658 2246	3.8 0.7 3.8 0.7	**26** 0420 1004 TU 1638 2224	3.8 0.7 3.8 0.6
12 0517 1059 TU 1731 2322	3.6 0.9 3.6 0.9	**27** 0500 1041 W 1718 2307	3.7 0.8 3.8 0.8
13 0550 1132 W 1803 2356	3.4 1.1 3.6 0.9	**28** 0543 1123 TH 1803 2356	3.5 0.9 3.6 0.9
14 0625 1207 TH 1839	3.1 1.4 3.2	**29** 0634 1213 F 1856	3.3 1.1 3.4
15 0045 0706 F 1252 1924	1.4 2.9 1.6 3.0	**30** 0056 0737 SA 1318 2004	1.1 3.1 1.4 3.3

Chapter 5

FREE monthly updates from
www.reedsalmanac.co.uk

407

TIDES

TIME ZONE (UT)
For Summer Time add ONE hour in **non-shaded areas**

PORTUGAL – LISBOA
LAT 38°43'N   LONG 9°07'W
TIMES AND HEIGHTS OF HIGH AND LOW WATERS

YEAR **2005**

	MAY			JUNE			JULY			AUGUST	
	Time m	Time m		Time m	Time m		Time m	Time m		Time m	Time m
1 SU ☽	0215 1.3 / 0900 3.0 / 1445 1.5 / 2129 3.2	**16** M	0230 1.6 / 0853 2.7 / 1447 1.8 / 2113 2.9	**1** W	0430 1.1 / 1107 3.2 / 1654 1.3 / 2327 3.4	**16** TH	0344 1.4 / 1015 2.9 / 1604 1.5 / 2233 3.1	**1** F	0449 1.2 / 1127 3.2 / 1720 1.2 / 2352 3.2	**16** SA	0341 1.3 / 1018 3.0 / 1610 1.4 / 2242 3.0	**1** M	0033 2.9 / 0624 1.3 / 1259 3.2 / 1906 1.2	**16** TU	0530 1.3 / 1207 3.3 / 1813 1.1
2 M	0346 1.3 / 1030 3.0 / 1616 1.5 / 2252 3.3	**17** TU	0347 1.5 / 1017 2.8 / 1607 1.7 / 2233 3.0	**2** TH	0530 1.0 / 1203 3.3 / 1753 1.1	**17** F	0444 1.3 / 1115 3.0 / 1704 1.3 / 2333 3.2	**2** SA	0548 1.2 / 1224 3.2 / 1821 1.1	**17** SU	0447 1.2 / 1123 3.1 / 1720 1.2 / 2350 3.1	**2** TU	0129 3.3 / 0715 1.2 / 1348 3.3 / 1952 1.1	**17** W	0047 3.5 / 0638 1.1 / 1313 3.5 / 1917 0.8
3 TU	0505 1.2 / 1141 3.2 / 1728 1.3 / 2359 3.5	**18** W	0452 1.4 / 1122 3.0 / 1709 1.5 / 2336 3.2	**3** F	0023 3.5 / 0621 1.0 / 1253 3.5 / 1844 1.0	**18** SA	0537 1.1 / 1208 3.2 / 1759 1.2	**3** SU	0049 3.2 / 0641 1.1 / 1315 3.3 / 1914 1.1	**18** M	0551 1.1 / 1225 3.3 / 1824 1.0	**3** W	0214 3.1 / 0757 1.1 / 1429 3.4 / 2030 1.0	**18** TH	0149 3.5 / 0736 0.8 / 1410 3.8 / 2010 0.6
4 W	0605 1.0 / 1236 3.5 / 1824 1.1	**19** TH	0544 1.3 / 1212 3.2 / 1759 1.3	**4** SA	0113 3.5 / 0706 0.9 / 1338 3.6 / 1930 0.9	**19** SU	0027 3.3 / 0626 1.0 / 1257 3.4 / 1850 1.0	**4** M	0140 3.2 / 0727 1.1 / 1402 3.4 / 2001 1.0	**19** TU	0055 3.2 / 0649 0.9 / 1324 3.5 / 1924 0.8	**4** TH	0253 3.2 / 0833 1.0 / 1505 3.5 / 2103 0.9	**19** F	0242 3.5 / 0827 0.6 / 1501 4.0 / ○ 2059 0.4
5 TH	0053 3.7 / 0653 0.8 / 1323 3.6 / 1911 0.9	**20** F	0026 3.3 / 0628 1.1 / 1254 3.3 / 1843 1.1	**5** SU	0158 3.5 / 0747 0.9 / 1420 3.6 / 2013 0.9	**20** M	0119 3.4 / 0713 0.9 / 1345 3.5 / 1939 0.8	**5** TU	0226 3.1 / 0809 1.0 / 1444 3.5 / 2042 0.9	**20** W	0156 3.4 / 0745 0.8 / 1420 3.7 / 2019 0.6	**5** F ●	0327 3.3 / 0906 0.9 / 1538 3.6 / 2134 0.8	**20** SA	0331 3.5 / 0913 0.5 / 1548 4.1 / 2143 0.3
6 F	0140 3.8 / 0735 0.7 / 1405 3.8 / 1953 0.7	**21** SA	0110 3.5 / 0707 0.9 / 1335 3.5 / 1924 0.9	**6** M ●	0241 3.5 / 0826 0.9 / 1500 3.6 / 2053 0.9	**21** TU	0210 3.5 / 0759 0.8 / 1433 3.7 / 2028 0.7	**6** W ●	0307 3.2 / 0847 1.0 / 1522 3.5 / 2119 0.9	**21** TH ○	0252 3.6 / 0837 0.6 / 1513 3.9 / 2111 0.4	**6** SA	0359 3.4 / 0938 0.9 / 1610 3.6 / 2205 0.8	**21** SU	0415 3.5 / 0957 0.4 / 1633 4.2 / 2226 0.3
7 SA	0223 3.9 / 0814 0.7 / 1444 3.8 / 2033 0.7	**22** SU	0152 3.6 / 0746 0.8 / 1415 3.7 / 2004 0.8	**7** TU	0321 3.4 / 0902 0.9 / 1538 3.6 / 2132 0.9	**22** W ○	0301 3.6 / 0847 0.7 / 1523 3.8 / 2118 0.6	**7** TH	0345 3.2 / 0922 1.0 / 1557 3.5 / 2154 0.9	**22** F	0344 3.7 / 0927 0.6 / 1603 4.0 / 2200 0.3	**7** SU	0430 3.4 / 1009 0.8 / 1641 3.6 / 2236 0.8	**22** M	0458 3.5 / 1039 0.4 / 1716 4.2 / 2307 0.4
8 SU ●	0303 3.7 / 0850 0.7 / 1522 3.8 / 2111 0.7	**23** M	0234 3.7 / 0824 0.7 / 1456 3.8 / ○ 2045 0.7	**8** W	0359 3.3 / 0938 1.0 / 1613 3.5 / 2208 0.9	**23** TH	0352 3.6 / 0935 0.6 / 1613 3.9 / 2208 0.5	**8** F	0419 3.2 / 0956 1.0 / 1630 3.5 / 2227 0.9	**23** SA	0434 3.7 / 1014 0.5 / 1652 4.1 / 2247 0.3	**8** M	0501 3.4 / 1041 0.8 / 1713 3.6 / 2307 0.8	**23** TU	0539 3.5 / 1120 0.5 / 1758 4.0 / 2347 0.6
9 M	0341 3.7 / 0925 0.8 / 1558 3.8 / 2148 0.8	**24** TU	0318 3.7 / 0904 0.7 / 1538 3.8 / 2128 0.6	**9** TH	0435 3.3 / 1012 1.0 / 1646 3.5 / 2244 1.0	**24** F	0444 3.6 / 1024 0.7 / 1703 3.9 / 2300 0.5	**9** SA	0452 3.2 / 1030 1.0 / 1702 3.5 / 2301 0.9	**24** SU	0521 3.7 / 1101 0.5 / 1739 4.0 / 2334 0.4	**9** TU	0533 3.4 / 1113 0.9 / 1747 3.5 / 2340 0.9	**24** W	0619 3.6 / 1202 0.7 / 1840 3.7
10 TU	0418 3.6 / 0959 0.9 / 1632 3.7 / 2224 0.9	**25** W	0402 3.7 / 0946 0.7 / 1622 3.8 / 2214 0.6	**10** F	0509 3.2 / 1046 1.1 / 1719 3.4 / 2321 1.1	**25** SA	0535 3.6 / 1114 0.8 / 1754 3.8 / 2352 0.6	**10** SU	0525 3.2 / 1104 1.0 / 1736 3.4 / 2336 0.9	**25** M	0607 3.6 / 1147 0.6 / 1825 3.9	**10** W	0607 3.3 / 1147 1.0 / 1821 3.4	**25** TH	0028 0.9 / 0701 3.4 / 1247 1.0 / 1924 3.4
11 W	0452 3.4 / 1032 1.0 / 1705 3.5 / 2300 1.0	**26** TH	0450 3.6 / 1030 0.8 / 1709 3.8 / 2303 0.7	**11** SA	0544 3.1 / 1123 1.2 / 1754 3.3	**26** SU	0628 3.5 / 1206 0.9 / 1846 3.7	**11** M	0600 3.2 / 1140 1.1 / 1812 3.4	**26** TU	0020 0.6 / 0653 3.5 / 1234 0.8 / 1912 3.7	**11** TH	0014 1.0 / 0644 3.2 / 1225 1.1 / 1900 3.3	**26** F ☽	0113 1.2 / 0749 3.2 / 1341 1.3 / 2018 3.1
12 TH	0526 3.3 / 1105 1.2 / 1738 3.4 / 2339 1.2	**27** F	0540 3.5 / 1119 0.9 / 1800 3.7 / 2357 0.8	**12** SU	0001 1.2 / 0623 3.0 / 1204 1.3 / 1835 3.2	**27** M	0046 0.7 / 0721 3.3 / 1301 1.0 / 1941 3.6	**12** TU	0013 1.0 / 0638 3.1 / 1220 1.2 / 1852 3.3	**27** W	0107 0.8 / 0741 3.3 / 1324 1.0 / 2003 3.4	**12** F	0053 1.1 / 0726 3.1 / 1310 1.2 / 1946 3.1	**27** SA	0208 1.4 / 0851 3.0 / 1453 1.4 / 2131 2.8
13 F	0601 3.1 / 1142 1.4 / 1813 3.2	**28** SA	0635 3.4 / 1213 1.1 / 1856 3.6	**13** M	0046 1.3 / 0708 2.9 / 1253 1.4 / 1923 3.1	**28** TU	0142 0.9 / 0819 3.2 / 1401 1.1 / 2040 3.4	**13** W	0055 1.1 / 0721 3.0 / 1304 1.3 / 1937 3.2	**28** TH	0158 1.0 / 0835 3.1 / 1422 1.2 / ☽ 2101 3.2	**13** SA ☽	0142 1.3 / 0821 3.0 / 1409 1.4 / 2046 3.0	**28** SU	0325 1.6 / 1014 2.9 / 1632 1.4 / 2304 2.7
14 SA	0022 1.4 / 0642 2.9 / 1226 1.5 / 1856 3.1	**29** SU	0058 1.0 / 0738 3.2 / 1317 1.3 / 2000 3.4	**14** TU	0139 1.4 / 0803 2.8 / 1351 1.5 / 2021 3.0	**29** W	0243 1.1 / 0921 3.1 / 1505 1.2 / 2144 3.3	**14** TH	0142 1.2 / 0812 2.9 / 1357 1.4 / ☽ 2031 3.1	**29** F	0257 1.3 / 0939 3.0 / 1532 1.4 / 2210 3.0	**14** SU	0247 1.4 / 0930 2.9 / 1528 1.4 / 2205 2.9	**29** M	0459 1.6 / 1140 3.0 / 1758 1.3
15 SU ☽	0117 1.5 / 0737 2.8 / 1326 1.7 / 1955 3.0	**30** M	0208 1.1 / 0848 3.1 / 1431 1.4 / 2111 3.3	**15** W	0240 1.5 / 0908 2.8 / 1458 1.5 / 2127 3.0	**30** TH	0346 1.3 / 1025 3.0 / 1613 1.3 / 2250 3.2	**15** F ☽	0240 1.4 / 0912 2.9 / 1500 1.4 / 2134 3.0	**30** SA	0407 1.4 / 1050 3.0 / 1652 1.4 / 2325 2.9	**15** M	0409 1.4 / 1050 3.0 / 1656 1.3 / 2331 3.0	**30** TU	0022 2.8 / 0612 1.4 / 1243 3.1 / 1854 1.1
		31 TU	0321 1.1 / 1001 3.1 / 1546 1.4 / 2223 3.3						**31** SU	0520 1.4 / 1200 3.0 / 1807 1.3			**31** W	0115 3.0 / 0701 1.2 / 1330 3.3 / 1934 1.1

>> FREE monthly updates from <<
www.reedsalmanac.co.uk

TIME ZONE (UT)
For Summer Time add ONE hour in **non-shaded areas**

PORTUGAL – LISBOA
LAT 38°43'N   LONG 9°07'W
TIMES AND HEIGHTS OF HIGH AND LOW WATERS

YEAR 2005

SEPTEMBER		OCTOBER		NOVEMBER		DECEMBER	
Time m	Time m	Time m	Time m	Time m	Time m	Time m	Time m
1 0156 3.2 / 0740 1.2 / TH 1408 3.5 / 2008 1.0	**16** 0138 3.6 / 0725 0.9 / F 1356 4.0 / 1956 0.6	**1** 0159 3.5 / 0744 1.1 / SA 1410 3.7 / 2007 0.9	**16** 0204 3.9 / 0750 0.7 / SU 1421 4.2 / 2015 0.5	**1** 0229 3.7 / 0816 0.8 / TU 1444 3.8 / 2036 0.8	**16** 0301 3.9 / 0851 0.6 / W 1522 3.8 / ○ 2107 0.7	**1** 0235 3.7 / 0826 0.8 / TH 1456 3.6 / ● 2044 0.7	**16** 0324 3.6 / 0919 0.8 / F 1548 3.4 / 2127 0.9
2 0230 3.3 / 0813 1.0 / F 1441 3.6 / 2038 0.9	**17** 0226 3.9 / 0811 0.6 / SA 1443 4.2 / 2039 0.4	**2** 0230 3.6 / 0815 0.9 / SU 1443 3.8 / 2037 0.8	**17** 0245 4.0 / 0831 0.5 / M 1503 4.2 / ○ 2054 0.5	**2** 0303 3.8 / 0850 0.8 / W 1520 3.8 / ● 2108 0.7	**17** 0340 3.9 / 0930 0.7 / TH 1602 3.7 / 2143 0.8	**2** 0316 3.8 / 0907 0.7 / F 1539 3.6 / 2123 0.7	**17** 0403 3.6 / 0957 0.9 / SA 1625 3.3 / 2202 0.9
3 0301 3.5 / 0844 0.9 / SA 1513 3.7 / ● 2108 0.8	**18** 0310 4.0 / 0854 0.5 / SU 1527 4.3 / ○ 2120 0.3	**3** 0301 3.7 / 0846 0.8 / M 1515 3.9 / ● 2107 0.7	**18** 0324 4.1 / 0911 0.5 / TU 1544 4.2 / 2131 0.5	**3** 0338 3.8 / 0924 0.7 / TH 1556 3.8 / 2141 0.8	**18** 0418 3.8 / 1009 0.8 / F 1640 3.5 / 2218 1.0	**3** 0358 3.8 / 0950 0.6 / SA 1624 3.6 / 2205 0.8	**18** 0438 3.5 / 1034 0.9 / SU 1701 3.2 / 2237 1.0
4 0332 3.6 / 0914 0.8 / SU 1544 3.8 / 2138 0.7	**19** 0351 4.1 / 0934 0.4 / M 1609 4.3 / 2159 0.4	**4** 0333 3.8 / 0917 0.7 / TU 1548 3.9 / 2137 0.7	**19** 0403 4.0 / 0949 0.6 / W 1623 4.0 / 2207 0.7	**4** 0414 3.8 / 1001 0.8 / F 1635 3.7 / 2217 0.9	**19** 0454 3.6 / 1048 1.0 / SA 1717 3.3 / 2254 1.1	**4** 0443 3.8 / 1037 0.7 / SU 1712 3.5 / 2251 0.9	**19** 0511 3.3 / 1110 1.0 / M 1734 3.1 / 2313 1.1
5 0402 3.6 / 0944 0.8 / M 1616 3.8 / 2207 0.7	**20** 0430 4.1 / 1014 0.4 / TU 1649 4.2 / 2236 0.5	**5** 0405 3.8 / 0948 0.7 / W 1621 3.9 / 2207 0.8	**20** 0440 3.9 / 1028 0.7 / TH 1701 3.8 / 2242 0.9	**5** 0453 3.8 / 1041 0.8 / SA 1716 3.5 / 2256 1.0	**20** 0529 3.5 / 1128 1.1 / SU 1754 3.1 / 2331 1.3	**5** 0532 3.7 / 1127 0.8 / M 1804 3.4 / 2342 1.0	**20** 0544 3.3 / 1147 1.0 / TU 1810 3.0 / 2351 1.2
6 0433 3.6 / 1015 0.8 / TU 1648 3.8 / 2237 0.8	**21** 0508 3.9 / 1052 0.6 / W 1728 3.9 / 2313 0.7	**6** 0437 3.8 / 1020 0.8 / TH 1654 3.8 / 2238 0.9	**21** 0516 3.7 / 1107 0.9 / F 1738 3.5 / 2318 1.1	**6** 0536 3.6 / 1127 1.0 / SU 1804 3.4 / 2342 1.2	**21** 0605 3.3 / 1211 1.3 / M 1834 2.9	**6** 0624 3.6 / 1223 0.9 / TU 1901 3.2	**21** 0620 3.2 / 1228 1.1 / W 1850 2.9
7 0504 3.6 / 1046 0.8 / W 1720 3.7 / 2307 0.8	**22** 0546 3.7 / 1132 0.8 / TH 1807 3.6 / 2350 1.0	**7** 0511 3.7 / 1055 0.9 / F 1730 3.6 / 2312 1.0	**22** 0553 3.5 / 1148 1.2 / SA 1817 3.2 / 2356 1.4	**7** 0625 3.5 / 1222 1.2 / M 1902 3.2	**22** 0015 1.5 / 0647 3.1 / TU 1304 1.5 / 1926 2.8	**7** 0040 1.2 / 0723 3.5 / W 1326 1.0 / 2006 3.1	**22** 0034 1.3 / 0703 3.1 / TH 1315 1.3 / 1938 2.8
8 0537 3.5 / 1118 0.9 / TH 1753 3.5 / 2339 1.0	**23** 0624 3.5 / 1214 1.1 / F 1848 3.3	**8** 0548 3.5 / 1134 1.0 / SA 1810 3.4 / 2351 1.2	**23** 0632 3.3 / 1235 1.5 / SU 1902 2.9	**8** 0041 1.4 / 0728 3.3 / TU 1333 1.3 / 2018 3.0	**23** 0111 1.7 / 0742 3.0 / W 1411 1.5 / ☾ 2036 2.7	**8** 0147 1.3 / 0830 3.3 / TH 1437 1.1 / ☾ 2118 3.1	**23** 0126 1.4 / 0755 3.0 / F 1412 1.3 / ☾ 2038 2.8
9 0612 3.4 / 1154 1.0 / F 1829 3.4	**24** 0031 1.3 / 0707 3.2 / SA 1305 1.4 / 1937 3.0	**9** 0632 3.4 / 1222 1.2 / SU 1901 3.2	**24** 0043 1.7 / 0720 3.0 / M 1341 1.7 / 2008 2.7	**9** 0200 1.5 / 0848 3.2 / W 1501 1.4 / ☾ 2147 3.0	**24** 0227 1.7 / 0856 2.9 / TH 1526 1.5 / 2157 2.8	**9** 0301 1.3 / 0942 3.3 / F 1549 1.1 / 2228 3.1	**24** 0229 1.5 / 0858 2.9 / SA 1516 1.4 / 2146 2.8
10 0016 1.1 / 0652 3.3 / SA 1238 1.2 / 1915 3.2	**25** 0121 1.6 / 0803 3.0 / SU 1418 1.7 / ☾ 2051 2.7	**10** 0043 1.4 / 0730 3.2 / M 1330 1.4 / ☾ 2014 3.0	**25** 0155 1.9 / 0835 2.9 / TU 1516 1.7 / 2150 2.7	**10** 0333 1.5 / 1013 3.3 / TH 1625 1.3 / 2304 3.2	**25** 0346 1.7 / 1015 3.0 / F 1634 1.5 / 2304 2.9	**10** 0414 1.3 / 1052 3.3 / SA 1655 1.1 / 2331 3.3	**25** 0337 1.5 / 1007 2.9 / SU 1620 1.3 / 2251 2.9
11 0103 1.3 / 0746 3.1 / SU 1339 1.4 / ☾ 2019 3.0	**26** 0242 1.8 / 0932 2.9 / M 1607 1.7 / 2240 2.7	**11** 0201 1.6 / 0852 3.1 / TU 1507 1.5 / 2155 3.0	**26** 0338 1.9 / 1014 2.9 / W 1641 1.6 / 2313 2.8	**11** 0451 1.4 / 1124 3.5 / F 1731 1.1 / 2355 3.1	**26** 0452 1.5 / 1118 3.1 / SA 1728 1.3 / 2355 3.1	**11** 0520 1.1 / 1153 3.4 / SU 1753 1.0	**26** 0443 1.4 / 1111 3.0 / M 1718 1.2 / 2347 3.0
12 0213 1.5 / 0901 3.0 / M 1508 1.5 / 2151 2.9	**27** 0432 1.8 / 1110 2.9 / TU 1733 1.6	**12** 0347 1.6 / 1029 3.2 / W 1646 1.4 / 2326 3.2	**27** 0458 1.8 / 1126 3.1 / TH 1739 1.5	**12** 0004 3.4 / 0544 1.1 / SA 1222 3.7 / 1824 0.9	**27** 0544 1.4 / 1209 3.3 / SU 1813 1.1	**12** 0025 3.4 / 0617 0.9 / M 1248 3.5 / 1843 0.9	**27** 0541 1.3 / 1208 3.1 / TU 1809 1.1
13 0351 1.6 / 1036 3.0 / TU 1650 1.4 / 2330 3.0	**28** 0000 2.9 / 0547 1.7 / W 1215 3.1 / 1825 1.4	**13** 0515 1.5 / 1147 3.5 / TH 1756 1.1	**28** 0006 3.0 / 0552 1.6 / F 1216 3.3 / 1822 1.3	**13** 0054 3.6 / 0642 0.8 / SU 1312 3.8 / 1909 0.8	**28** 0038 3.3 / 0628 1.2 / M 1253 3.4 / 1852 1.0	**13** 0114 3.5 / 0708 0.8 / TU 1337 3.5 / 1928 0.9	**28** 0038 3.2 / 0633 1.1 / W 1300 3.3 / 1856 1.0
14 0523 1.4 / 1159 3.3 / W 1809 1.1	**29** 0049 3.1 / 0634 1.5 / TH 1300 3.3 / 1904 1.2	**14** 0029 3.3 / 0617 1.2 / F 1247 3.8 / 1849 0.8	**29** 0046 3.3 / 0633 1.3 / SA 1257 3.5 / 1858 1.1	**14** 0138 3.8 / 0727 0.7 / M 1358 3.9 / 1950 0.7	**29** 0117 3.4 / 0708 1.0 / TU 1334 3.5 / 1929 0.9	**14** 0200 3.6 / 0755 0.7 / W 1423 3.5 / 2010 0.8	**29** 0126 3.4 / 0721 1.0 / TH 1350 3.3 / 1942 0.8
15 0043 3.3 / 0632 1.1 / TH 1303 3.7 / 1907 0.8	**30** 0126 3.3 / 0711 1.3 / F 1336 3.5 / 1936 1.0	**15** 0119 3.7 / 0706 0.9 / SA 1336 4.0 / 1934 0.6	**30** 0121 3.5 / 0706 1.1 / SU 1334 3.6 / 1932 0.9	**15** 0220 3.9 / 0810 0.6 / TU 1441 3.9 / 2029 0.7	**30** 0156 3.6 / 0747 0.9 / W 1414 3.6 / 2006 0.8	**15** 0243 3.7 / 0838 0.8 / TH 1507 3.5 / ○ 2049 0.8	**30** 0213 3.5 / 0810 0.7 / F 1440 3.5 / 2027 0.7
			31 0155 3.6 / 0743 0.9 / M 1409 3.8 / 2004 0.8				**31** 0301 3.7 / 0857 0.6 / SA 1530 3.5 / ● 2113 0.6

Chapter 5

>> FREE monthly updates from <<
www.reedsalmanac.co.uk

409

TIDES

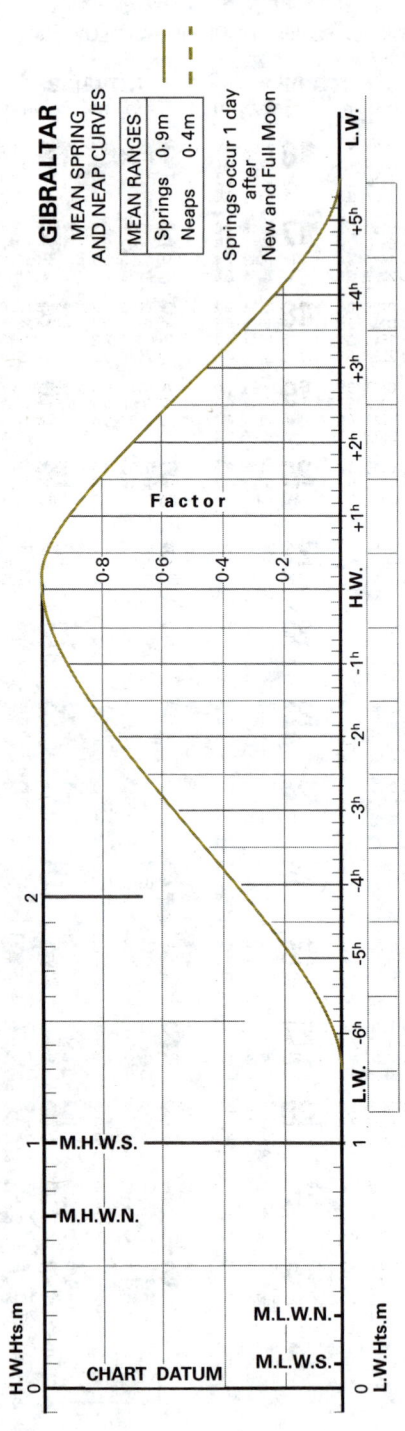

TIME ZONE -0100
(Gibraltar Standard Time)
Subtract 1 hour for UT
For Gibraltar Summer Time add
ONE hour in **non-shaded areas**

GIBRALTAR

LAT 36°08′N   LONG 5°21′W

TIMES AND HEIGHTS OF HIGH AND LOW WATERS

YEAR 2005

JANUARY

Time m	Time m
1 0627 0.8 / 1210 0.3 / SA 1844 0.8	**16** 0048 0.1 / 0737 0.9 / SU 1320 0.2 / 2006 0.8
2 0020 0.2 / 0712 0.8 / SU 1301 0.3 / 1932 0.7	**17** 0140 0.2 / 0832 0.8 / M 1420 0.2 / ☾ 2103 0.7
3 0110 0.3 / 0805 0.8 / M 1403 0.3 / ☽ 2028 0.7	**18** 0242 0.3 / 0931 0.8 / TU 1529 0.3 / 2210 0.7
4 0213 0.3 / 0905 0.7 / TU 1511 0.3 / 2133 0.7	**19** 0358 0.3 / 1038 0.7 / W 1655 0.3 / 2329 0.7
5 0328 0.3 / 1013 0.8 / W 1624 0.3 / 2248 0.7	**20** 0520 0.3 / 1146 0.7 / TH 1807 0.3
6 0446 0.3 / 1122 0.8 / TH 1733 0.3 / 2359 0.7	**21** 0039 0.7 / 0621 0.3 / F 1246 0.7 / 1856 0.3
7 0551 0.2 / 1223 0.8 / F 1831 0.1	**22** 0133 0.7 / 0706 0.2 / SA 1335 0.8 / 1937 0.3
8 0059 0.8 / 0644 0.0 / SA 1319 0.9 / 1922 0.1	**23** 0216 0.8 / 0746 0.2 / SU 1417 0.8 / 2014 0.1
9 0153 0.9 / 0733 0.1 / SU 1412 0.9 / 2011 0.0	**24** 0254 0.8 / 0823 0.2 / M 1456 0.8 / 2049 0.1
10 0245 0.9 / 0823 0.1 / M 1505 1.0 / ● 2100 0.0	**25** 0327 0.8 / 0858 0.1 / TU 1532 0.8 / ○ 2122 0.1
11 0335 1.0 / 0912 0.1 / TU 1556 1.0 / 2147 0.0	**26** 0357 0.8 / 0932 0.1 / W 1605 0.9 / 2152 0.1
12 0423 1.0 / 1001 0.1 / W 1645 1.0 / 2232 0.0	**27** 0426 0.9 / 1004 0.1 / TH 1637 0.9 / 2221 0.1
13 0510 1.0 / 1048 0.1 / TH 1733 0.8 / 2316 0.0	**28** 0455 0.9 / 1036 0.1 / F 1709 0.8 / 2250 0.1
14 0557 1.0 / 1136 0.1 / F 1822 0.9	**29** 0526 0.9 / 1108 0.1 / SA 1742 0.8 / 2319 0.1
15 0000 0.1 / 0645 0.9 / SA 1227 0.1 / 1913 0.8	**30** 0600 0.8 / 1143 0.1 / SU 1818 0.8 / 2351 0.1
	31 0639 0.8 / 1222 0.2 / M 1901 0.8

FEBRUARY

Time m	Time m
1 0028 0.2 / 0724 0.8 / TU 1312 0.2 / 1951 0.7	**16** 0142 0.2 / 0842 0.7 / W 1426 0.3 / ☾ 2121 0.6
2 0116 0.2 / 0820 0.7 / W 1416 0.2 / ☽ 2053 0.7	**17** 0255 0.3 / 0947 0.6 / TH 1609 0.3 / 2245 0.6
3 0225 0.3 / 0928 0.7 / TH 1543 0.2 / 2210 0.6	**18** 0454 0.3 / 1115 0.6 / F 1757 0.3
4 0407 0.3 / 1051 0.7 / F 1721 0.2 / 2339 0.7	**19** 0022 0.6 / 0612 0.3 / SA 1234 0.7 / 1849 0.2
5 0543 0.2 / 1210 0.8 / SA 1831 0.1	**20** 0123 0.7 / 0658 0.2 / SU 1327 0.7 / 1927 0.2
6 0051 0.7 / 0645 0.2 / SU 1314 0.8 / 1924 0.1	**21** 0204 0.7 / 0735 0.2 / M 1407 0.8 / 2001 0.1
7 0149 0.8 / 0736 0.1 / M 1409 0.9 / 2013 0.1	**22** 0237 0.8 / 0809 0.1 / TU 1442 0.8 / 2032 0.1
8 0240 0.9 / 0824 0.0 / TU 1501 0.9 / ● 2058 0.0	**23** 0307 0.8 / 0841 0.1 / W 1515 0.8 / 2102 0.1
9 0327 1.0 / 0911 0.0 / W 1548 1.0 / 2140 -0.1	**24** 0335 0.9 / 0913 0.1 / TH 1546 0.9 / ○ 2131 0.1
10 0412 1.0 / 0955 0.0 / TH 1634 1.0 / 2220 -0.1	**25** 0403 0.9 / 0944 0.1 / F 1617 0.9 / 2159 0.0
11 0454 1.0 / 1036 0.0 / F 1718 1.0 / 2257 0.0	**26** 0432 0.9 / 1014 0.1 / SA 1648 0.9 / 2226 0.1
12 0536 1.0 / 1117 0.0 / SA 1801 0.9 / 2334 0.0	**27** 0502 0.9 / 1045 0.1 / SU 1721 0.9 / 2255 0.1
13 0619 0.9 / 1156 0.1 / SU 1846 0.8	**28** 0535 0.9 / 1118 0.1 / M 1757 0.8 / 2326 0.1
14 0011 0.1 / 0702 0.9 / M 1238 0.1 / 1931 0.8	
15 0053 0.2 / 0749 0.8 / TU 1325 0.2 / 2022 0.7	

MARCH

Time m	Time m
1 0612 0.9 / 1154 0.1 / TU 1839 0.8	**16** 0012 0.2 / 0708 0.7 / W 1238 0.2 / 1944 0.7
2 0001 0.2 / 0655 0.8 / W 1239 0.2 / 1928 0.7	**17** 0055 0.3 / 0757 0.7 / TH 1328 0.3 / ☽ 2040 0.6
3 0045 0.2 / 0750 0.7 / TH 1340 0.2 / ☽ 2029 0.7	**18** 0200 0.3 / 0859 0.6 / F 1508 0.3 / 2156 0.6
4 0151 0.3 / 0901 0.7 / F 1523 0.3 / 2149 0.6	**19** 0417 0.4 / 1032 0.6 / SA 1726 0.3 / 2346 0.6
5 0358 0.3 / 1036 0.7 / SA 1723 0.2 / 2329 0.7	**20** 0551 0.3 / 1209 0.6 / SU 1821 0.3
6 0548 0.2 / 1207 0.7 / SU 1831 0.1	**21** 0051 0.7 / 0635 0.3 / M 1303 0.7 / 1858 0.1
7 0046 0.7 / 0647 0.2 / M 1312 0.8 / 1920 0.1	**22** 0131 0.7 / 0710 0.2 / TU 1341 0.8 / 1930 0.2
8 0141 0.8 / 0734 0.1 / TU 1403 0.9 / 2003 0.0	**23** 0202 0.8 / 0743 0.1 / W 1414 0.8 / 2001 0.1
9 0228 0.9 / 0818 0.0 / W 1450 0.9 / 2044 0.0	**24** 0232 0.8 / 0814 0.1 / TH 1447 0.9 / 2030 0.1
10 0311 1.0 / 0859 0.0 / TH 1534 1.0 / ● 2122 -0.1	**25** 0302 0.9 / 0846 0.1 / F 1519 0.9 / ○ 2059 0.1
11 0352 1.0 / 0938 -0.1 / F 1615 1.0 / 2157 -0.1	**26** 0333 0.9 / 0917 0.0 / SA 1552 0.9 / 2129 0.1
12 0431 1.0 / 1015 -0.1 / SA 1656 1.0 / 2231 0.0	**27** 0405 1.0 / 0949 0.0 / SU 1626 0.9 / 2159 0.1
13 0509 1.0 / 1051 0.0 / SU 1736 0.9 / 2304 0.0	**28** 0438 1.0 / 1022 0.0 / M 1701 0.9 / 2231 0.1
14 0547 0.9 / 1125 0.0 / M 1816 0.8 / 2337 0.1	**29** 0513 0.9 / 1056 0.1 / TU 1739 0.9 / 2305 0.1
15 0626 0.8 / 1159 0.1 / TU 1858 0.8	**30** 0552 0.9 / 1134 0.1 / W 1823 0.8 / 2343 0.2
	31 0637 0.8 / 1219 0.2 / TH 1915 0.8

APRIL

Time m	Time m
1 0030 0.3 / 0734 0.7 / F 1326 0.3 / 2019 0.7	**16** 0127 0.4 / 0822 0.6 / SA 1422 0.3 / ☽ 2115 0.6
2 0148 0.3 / 0850 0.7 / SA 1526 0.3 / ☽ 2141 0.7	**17** 0322 0.4 / 0941 0.6 / SU 1624 0.3 / 2240 0.6
3 0407 0.3 / 1031 0.7 / SU 1712 0.2 / 2319 0.7	**18** 0502 0.3 / 1116 0.6 / M 1730 0.3 / 2354 0.7
4 0542 0.2 / 1201 0.7 / M 1813 0.2	**19** 0554 0.3 / 1218 0.7 / TU 1813 0.3
5 0031 0.8 / 0636 0.2 / TU 1300 0.7 / 1859 0.1	**20** 0039 0.7 / 0632 0.2 / W 1300 0.7 / 1847 0.2
6 0122 0.9 / 0719 0.1 / W 1347 0.9 / 1939 0.0	**21** 0115 0.8 / 0706 0.2 / TH 1336 0.8 / 1918 0.2
7 0205 0.9 / 0759 0.0 / TH 1430 0.9 / 2017 0.0	**22** 0149 0.9 / 0739 0.1 / F 1411 0.9 / 1950 0.1
8 0246 1.0 / 0838 0.0 / F 1511 0.9 / ● 2053 0.0	**23** 0223 0.9 / 0813 0.1 / SA 1446 0.9 / 2022 0.1
9 0325 1.0 / 0914 0.0 / SA 1551 0.9 / 2128 0.0	**24** 0259 1.0 / 0847 0.0 / SU 1523 0.9 / ○ 2056 0.1
10 0403 0.9 / 0949 0.0 / SU 1630 0.9 / 2201 0.0	**25** 0336 1.0 / 0923 0.0 / M 1602 0.9 / 2132 0.1
11 0440 0.9 / 1022 0.1 / M 1708 0.9 / 2234 0.1	**26** 0415 1.0 / 1000 0.0 / TU 1642 0.9 / 2209 0.1
12 0516 0.9 / 1055 0.1 / TU 1747 0.8 / 2307 0.1	**27** 0455 0.9 / 1039 0.0 / W 1725 0.9 / 2248 0.1
13 0553 0.8 / 1127 0.1 / W 1828 0.8 / 2342 0.2	**28** 0538 0.9 / 1121 0.1 / TH 1813 0.9 / 2333 0.2
14 0633 0.7 / 1203 0.2 / TH 1914 0.7	**29** 0629 0.8 / 1212 0.2 / F 1909 0.8
15 0024 0.3 / 0721 0.3 / F 1251 0.3 / 2008 0.7	**30** 0030 0.3 / 0730 0.7 / SA 1328 0.2 / 2015 0.8

Chart Datum: 0·25 metres below Alicante Datum (Mean Sea Level, Alicante)

》》 **FREE** monthly updates from 《《
www.reedsalmanac.co.uk

Chapter 5

411

TIDES

TIME ZONE -0100
(Gibraltar Standard Time)
Subtract 1 hour for UT
For Gibraltar Summer Time add ONE hour in non-shaded areas

GIBRALTAR
LAT 36°08′N   LONG 5°21′W
TIMES AND HEIGHTS OF HIGH AND LOW WATERS

YEAR 2005

	MAY			JUNE			JULY			AUGUST	
	Time m	Time m		Time m	Time m		Time m	Time m		Time m	Time m
1 SU	0158 0.3 / 0846 0.7 / 1512 0.3 / ☽ 2132 0.7	**16** M	0225 0.4 / 0853 0.6 / 1510 0.3 / ☾ 2137 0.7	**1** W	0428 0.3 / 1100 0.8 / 1654 0.2 / 2322 0.8	**16** TH	0334 0.3 / 1003 0.7 / 1557 0.3 / 2231 0.8	**1** F	0452 0.3 / 1128 0.8 / 1711 0.3 / 2342 0.8	**16** SA	0335 0.3 / 1014 0.7 / 1557 0.3 / 2238 0.8	**1** M	0019 0.8 / 0642 0.3 / 1313 0.8 / 1846 0.3	**16** TU	0559 0.2 / 1220 0.8 / 1813 0.3
2 M	0350 0.3 / 1016 0.7 / 1638 0.3 / 2254 0.8	**17** TU	0347 0.3 / 1005 0.6 / 1620 0.3 / 2242 0.7	**2** TH	0533 0.2 / 1202 0.8 / 1748 0.2	**17** F	0438 0.3 / 1109 0.7 / 1656 0.3 / 2329 0.8	**2** SA	0600 0.2 / 1228 0.8 / 1809 0.3	**17** SU	0456 0.3 / 1128 0.7 / 1715 0.3 / 2347 0.8	**2** TU	0116 0.8 / 0724 0.2 / 1400 0.8 / 1929 0.3	**17** W	0039 0.8 / 0654 0.2 / 1320 0.9 / 1906 0.2
3 TU	0514 0.2 / 1137 0.7 / 1739 0.2	**18** W	0452 0.3 / 1114 0.7 / 1713 0.3 / 2337 0.7	**3** F	0016 0.9 / 0624 0.2 / 1253 0.8 / 1834 0.2	**18** SA	0536 0.2 / 1206 0.8 / 1749 0.2	**3** SU	0036 0.8 / 0651 0.2 / 1321 0.8 / 1857 0.2	**18** M	0605 0.2 / 1233 0.8 / 1818 0.2	**3** W	0202 0.8 / 0800 0.2 / 1440 0.9 / 2006 0.2	**18** TH	0138 0.9 / 0742 0.1 / 1411 1.0 / 1955 0.1
4 W	0001 0.8 / 0609 0.2 / 1235 0.8 / 1826 0.2	**19** TH	0542 0.2 / 1207 0.7 / 1755 0.2	**4** SA	0103 0.9 / 0708 0.1 / 1339 0.8 / 1916 0.2	**19** SU	0022 0.8 / 0626 0.2 / 1258 0.8 / 1835 0.2	**4** M	0126 0.8 / 0734 0.2 / 1409 0.8 / 1940 0.2	**19** TU	0049 0.9 / 0700 0.1 / 1330 0.9 / 1910 0.2	**4** TH	0242 0.8 / 0834 0.2 / 1515 0.9 / 2042 0.2	**19** F	0230 1.0 / 0826 0.0 / 1459 1.0 / ○ 2041 0.1
5 TH	0051 0.9 / 0654 0.1 / 1322 0.9 / 1907 0.1	**20** F	0023 0.8 / 0622 0.2 / 1251 0.8 / 1832 0.2	**5** SU	0146 0.9 / 0748 0.1 / 1422 0.9 / 1955 0.2	**20** M	0111 0.9 / 0713 0.1 / 1347 0.9 / 1921 0.2	**5** TU	0211 0.8 / 0814 0.2 / 1452 0.8 / 2020 0.2	**20** W	0146 0.9 / 0750 0.1 / 1423 0.9 / 2001 0.1	**5** F	0318 0.9 / 0906 0.2 / 1545 0.9 / ● 2117 0.2	**20** SA	0319 1.0 / 0908 0.0 / 1543 1.1 / 2126 0.0
6 F	0135 0.9 / 0733 0.1 / 1404 0.9 / 1944 0.1	**21** SA	0104 0.9 / 0701 0.1 / 1332 0.8 / 1909 0.2	**6** M	0228 0.9 / 0827 0.1 / 1504 0.9 / ● 2034 0.2	**21** TU	0201 0.9 / 0759 0.1 / 1436 0.9 / 2008 0.1	**6** W	0254 0.8 / 0851 0.2 / 1532 0.8 / ● 2059 0.2	**21** TH	0240 1.0 / 0838 0.0 / 1513 1.0 / ○ 2050 0.1	**6** SA	0350 0.9 / 0936 0.1 / 1614 0.9 / 2150 0.2	**21** SU	0405 1.1 / 0949 0.0 / 1627 1.1 / 2209 0.0
7 SA	0215 0.9 / 0811 0.0 / 1445 0.9 / 2021 0.1	**22** SU	0145 0.9 / 0739 0.1 / 1413 0.9 / 1946 0.2	**7** TU	0309 0.9 / 0904 0.1 / 1545 0.8 / 2113 0.2	**22** W	0251 1.0 / 0846 0.1 / 1525 0.9 / ○ 2056 0.1	**7** TH	0334 0.8 / 0926 0.1 / 1608 0.9 / 2136 0.2	**22** F	0332 1.0 / 0925 0.0 / 1601 1.0 / 2139 0.1	**7** SU	0421 0.9 / 1005 0.1 / 1642 0.9 / 2221 0.2	**22** M	0449 1.1 / 1028 0.0 / 1709 1.1 / 2249 0.0
8 SU	0255 0.9 / 0848 0.0 / 1525 0.9 / ● 2057 0.1	**23** M	0226 0.9 / 0819 0.1 / 1456 0.9 / ○ 2027 0.1	**8** W	0349 0.9 / 0940 0.1 / 1624 0.8 / 2150 0.2	**23** TH	0342 1.0 / 0934 0.1 / 1614 1.0 / 2146 0.1	**8** F	0411 0.8 / 1000 0.1 / 1642 0.9 / 2212 0.2	**23** SA	0421 1.0 / 1009 0.0 / 1648 1.1 / 2227 0.1	**8** M	0452 0.9 / 1033 0.2 / 1710 0.9 / 2252 0.2	**23** TU	0533 1.0 / 1105 0.1 / 1751 1.1 / 2329 0.1
9 M	0333 0.9 / 0923 0.0 / 1604 0.9 / 2133 0.1	**24** TU	0310 1.0 / 0901 0.1 / 1541 0.9 / 2109 0.1	**9** TH	0428 0.8 / 1015 0.1 / 1702 0.8 / 2228 0.2	**24** F	0432 1.0 / 1021 0.1 / 1703 1.0 / 2236 0.1	**9** SA	0446 0.8 / 1032 0.1 / 1713 0.8 / 2247 0.2	**24** SU	0509 1.0 / 1053 0.0 / 1734 1.0 / 2313 0.1	**9** TU	0522 0.9 / 1101 0.2 / 1740 0.9 / 2324 0.2	**24** W	0617 1.0 / 1143 0.1 / 1834 1.0
10 TU	0411 0.9 / 0957 0.1 / 1643 0.9 / 2208 0.1	**25** W	0355 1.0 / 0944 0.1 / 1626 0.9 / 2153 0.1	**10** F	0506 0.8 / 1050 0.2 / 1740 0.8 / 2306 0.2	**25** SA	0522 1.0 / 1109 0.1 / 1753 1.0 / 2327 0.2	**10** SU	0520 0.8 / 1103 0.2 / 1745 0.8 / 2322 0.2	**25** M	0557 1.0 / 1136 0.1 / 1821 1.0 / 2359 0.1	**10** W	0556 0.9 / 1131 0.2 / 1814 0.9 / 2359 0.2	**25** TH	0009 0.2 / 0704 0.9 / 1224 0.2 / 1919 0.9
11 W	0448 0.8 / 1031 0.1 / 1722 0.8 / 2244 0.2	**26** TH	0441 1.0 / 1028 0.1 / 1713 0.9 / 2240 0.2	**11** SA	0545 0.8 / 1126 0.2 / 1820 0.8 / 2347 0.3	**26** SU	0615 0.9 / 1159 0.1 / 1845 0.9	**11** M	0555 0.8 / 1135 0.2 / 1819 0.8 / 2358 0.2	**26** TU	0647 0.9 / 1220 0.1 / 1910 1.0	**11** TH	0636 0.9 / 1204 0.2 / 1854 0.9	**26** F	0054 0.3 / 0757 0.8 / 1311 0.3 / ☽ 2009 0.8
12 TH	0526 0.8 / 1105 0.2 / 1803 0.8 / 2321 0.2	**27** F	0530 0.9 / 1116 0.2 / 1804 0.9 / 2331 0.2	**12** SU	0627 0.7 / 1206 0.2 / 1903 0.7	**27** M	0022 0.2 / 0710 0.8 / 1254 0.2 / 1940 0.9	**12** TU	0633 0.8 / 1209 0.2 / 1858 0.8	**27** W	0048 0.2 / 0739 0.9 / 1308 0.2 / 2000 0.9	**12** F	0039 0.2 / 0723 0.8 / 1246 0.3 / 1942 0.8	**27** SA	0148 0.3 / 0858 0.7 / 1417 0.4 / 2110 0.8
13 F	0607 0.7 / 1143 0.2 / 1848 0.7	**28** SA	0624 0.9 / 1211 0.2 / 1901 0.9	**13** M	0033 0.3 / 0713 0.7 / 1255 0.3 / 1949 0.7	**28** TU	0123 0.2 / 0810 0.8 / 1354 0.2 / ☽ 2038 0.9	**13** W	0039 0.2 / 0715 0.8 / 1249 0.3 / 1941 0.8	**28** TH	0141 0.2 / 0836 0.8 / 1403 0.3 / ☽ 2055 0.8	**13** SA	0133 0.3 / 0822 0.7 / 1344 0.4 / ☽ 2042 0.8	**28** SU	0315 0.4 / 1018 0.7 / 1606 0.4 / 2233 0.7
14 SA	0005 0.3 / 0654 0.7 / 1230 0.3 / 1939 0.7	**29** SU	0033 0.3 / 0725 0.8 / 1320 0.2 / 2003 0.8	**14** TU	0129 0.3 / 0804 0.7 / 1353 0.3 / 2038 0.7	**29** W	0227 0.2 / 0912 0.7 / 1456 0.3 / 2137 0.8	**14** TH	0128 0.3 / 0806 0.7 / 1339 0.3 / ☽ 2031 0.8	**29** F	0243 0.3 / 0938 0.7 / 1511 0.3 / 2156 0.8	**14** SU	0248 0.3 / 0935 0.7 / 1514 0.4 / 2158 0.8	**29** M	0530 0.4 / 1156 0.7 / 1742 0.4
15 SU	0104 0.3 / 0750 0.7 / 1342 0.3 / 2036 0.7	**30** M	0149 0.3 / 0834 0.8 / 1437 0.3 / ☽ 2110 0.8	**15** W	0231 0.3 / 0901 0.7 / 1456 0.3 / ☽ 2132 0.7	**30** TH	0336 0.3 / 1019 0.6 / 1603 0.3 / 2240 0.8	**15** F	0225 0.3 / 0905 0.7 / 1441 0.3 / 2130 0.8	**30** SA	0407 0.3 / 1054 0.7 / 1637 0.4 / 2308 0.8	**15** M	0435 0.3 / 1102 0.7 / 1702 0.3 / 2326 0.8	**30** TU	0007 0.7 / 0627 0.3 / 1300 0.8 / 1832 0.4
		31 TU	0311 0.3 / 0947 0.8 / 1549 0.2 / 2218 0.8						**31** SU	0544 0.3 / 1211 0.7 / 1754 0.3			**31** W	0106 0.8 / 0704 0.3 / 1342 0.8 / 1910 0.3

Chart Datum: 0·25 metres below Alicante Datum (Mean Sea Level, Alicante)
》 **FREE** monthly updates from 《
www.reedsalmanac.co.uk

TIME ZONE −0100
(Gibraltar Standard Time)
Subtract 1 hour for UT
For Gibraltar Summer Time add ONE hour in **non-shaded areas**

GIBRALTAR
LAT 36°08′N LONG 5°21′W
TIMES AND HEIGHTS OF HIGH AND LOW WATERS

YEAR 2005

SEPTEMBER				OCTOBER				NOVEMBER				DECEMBER			
Time m		Time m		Time m		Time m		Time m		Time m		Time m		Time m	

SEPTEMBER

1 0147 0.8 / 0736 0.2 / TH 1416 0.9 / 1944 0.2
16 0129 0.9 / 0726 0.1 / F 1354 1.0 / 1941 0.1

2 0221 0.9 / 0806 0.2 / F 1445 0.9 / 2017 0.2
17 0216 1.0 / 0806 0.1 / SA 1438 1.1 / 2023 0.1

3 0252 0.9 / 0836 0.2 / SA 1513 1.0 / ● 2049 0.2
18 0300 1.1 / 0844 0.0 / SU 1519 1.1 / ○ 2104 0.0

4 0322 1.0 / 0905 0.2 / SU 1540 1.0 / 2121 0.1
19 0342 1.1 / 0922 0.0 / M 1600 1.1 / 2143 0.0

5 0352 1.0 / 0933 0.1 / M 1608 1.0 / 2151 0.1
20 0423 1.1 / 0958 0.1 / TU 1639 1.1 / 2220 0.1

6 0422 1.0 / 1000 0.2 / TU 1637 1.0 / 2222 0.1
21 0503 1.0 / 1033 0.1 / W 1717 1.1 / 2256 0.1

7 0453 1.0 / 1029 0.2 / W 1707 1.0 / 2253 0.2
22 0544 1.0 / 1107 0.2 / TH 1756 1.0 / 2331 0.2

8 0527 0.9 / 1058 0.2 / TH 1741 1.0 / 2326 0.2
23 0628 0.9 / 1144 0.3 / F 1838 0.9

9 0605 0.9 / 1131 0.3 / F 1820 0.9
24 0008 0.3 / 0716 0.8 / SA 1227 0.4 / 1925 0.8

10 0004 0.2 / 0653 0.8 / SA 1212 0.4 / 1908 0.9
25 0055 0.4 / 0816 0.7 / SU 1330 0.5 / ☽ 2025 0.7

11 0055 0.3 / 0754 0.8 / SU 1310 0.4 / ☽ 2012 0.8
26 0222 0.5 / 0936 0.7 / M 1532 0.5 / 2151 0.7

12 0222 0.4 / 0911 0.7 / M 1501 0.4 / 2136 0.8
27 0453 0.4 / 1123 0.7 / TU 1714 0.4 / 2343 0.7

13 0436 0.3 / 1048 0.8 / TU 1703 0.4 / 2319 0.8
28 0555 0.4 / 1228 0.8 / W 1805 0.4

14 0554 0.3 / 1211 0.8 / W 1809 0.3
29 0041 0.8 / 0631 0.3 / TH 1307 0.9 / 1841 0.3

15 0034 0.9 / 0643 0.2 / TH 1308 0.9 / 1857 0.2
30 0118 0.9 / 0702 0.3 / F 1338 0.9 / 1913 0.2

OCTOBER

1 0150 0.9 / 0732 0.2 / SA 1407 1.0 / 1945 0.2
16 0155 1.0 / 0739 0.1 / SU 1411 1.1 / 1959 0.1

2 0220 1.0 / 0801 0.2 / SU 1436 1.0 / 2017 0.2
17 0236 1.1 / 0816 0.1 / M 1451 1.1 / ○ 2037 0.1

3 0250 1.0 / 0830 0.2 / M 1505 1.0 / ● 2048 0.1
18 0316 1.1 / 0852 0.1 / TU 1530 1.1 / 2114 0.1

4 0321 1.0 / 0859 0.2 / TU 1536 1.1 / 2120 0.1
19 0355 1.0 / 0927 0.1 / W 1608 1.1 / 2150 0.1

5 0353 1.0 / 0929 0.2 / W 1608 1.1 / 2152 0.1
20 0434 1.0 / 1002 0.2 / TH 1646 1.0 / 2225 0.2

6 0427 1.0 / 0959 0.2 / TH 1641 1.0 / 2225 0.2
21 0513 0.9 / 1037 0.2 / F 1723 0.9 / 2259 0.2

7 0503 1.0 / 1032 0.2 / F 1717 1.0 / 2300 0.2
22 0553 0.9 / 1114 0.3 / SA 1803 0.9 / 2334 0.3

8 0544 0.9 / 1108 0.3 / SA 1758 0.9 / 2339 0.3
23 0640 0.8 / 1167 0.4 / SU 1851 0.8

9 0634 0.9 / 1152 0.4 / SU 1850 0.9
24 0018 0.4 / 0738 0.8 / M 1301 0.4 / 1951 0.7

10 0033 0.4 / 0737 0.8 / M 1259 0.4 / ☽ 1958 0.8
25 0139 0.5 / 0852 0.7 / TU 1450 0.5 / 2107 0.7

11 0219 0.4 / 0857 0.8 / TU 1508 0.4 / 2128 0.8
26 0350 0.5 / 1020 0.7 / W 1625 0.4 / 2245 0.7

12 0426 0.4 / 1034 0.8 / W 1652 0.4 / 2312 0.8
27 0504 0.4 / 1133 0.8 / TH 1722 0.4 / 2355 0.7

13 0534 0.3 / 1152 0.9 / TH 1753 0.3
28 0549 0.4 / 1218 0.8 / F 1803 0.3

14 0022 0.9 / 0621 0.2 / F 1246 1.0 / 1838 0.2
29 0038 0.8 / 0623 0.3 / SA 1254 0.9 / 1837 0.3

15 0111 1.0 / 0702 0.1 / SA 1330 1.0 / 1919 0.1
30 0112 0.9 / 0655 0.3 / SU 1325 1.0 / 1911 0.2

31 0144 1.0 / 0725 0.2 / M 1357 1.0 / 1944 0.2

NOVEMBER

1 0217 1.0 / 0755 0.2 / TU 1431 1.0 / 2017 0.1
16 0252 1.0 / 0826 0.1 / W 1503 1.0 / ○ 2051 0.1

2 0251 1.0 / 0827 0.2 / W 1506 1.1 / ● 2052 0.1
17 0332 1.0 / 0903 0.2 / TH 1543 1.0 / 2128 0.1

3 0328 1.0 / 0901 0.2 / TH 1543 1.1 / 2128 0.1
18 0411 0.9 / 0940 0.2 / F 1622 0.9 / 2203 0.2

4 0406 1.0 / 0936 0.2 / F 1622 1.0 / 2204 0.2
19 0450 0.9 / 1018 0.2 / SA 1701 0.9 / 2239 0.2

5 0446 1.0 / 1014 0.2 / SA 1703 1.0 / 2244 0.2
20 0530 0.9 / 1057 0.3 / SU 1742 0.8 / 2316 0.3

6 0531 1.0 / 1057 0.3 / SU 1749 0.9 / 2328 0.3
21 0614 0.8 / 1141 0.3 / M 1828 0.8

7 0623 0.9 / 1149 0.4 / M 1844 0.9
22 0000 0.3 / 0706 0.8 / TU 1239 0.4 / 1921 0.7

8 0029 0.3 / 0727 0.9 / TU 1307 0.4 / 1953 0.8
23 0104 0.4 / 0806 0.7 / W 1400 0.4 / ☽ 2023 0.7

9 0212 0.4 / 0843 0.8 / W 1456 0.4 / ☽ 2117 0.8
24 0236 0.4 / 0912 0.7 / TH 1521 0.4 / 2131 0.7

10 0352 0.4 / 1007 0.8 / TH 1623 0.3 / 2248 0.8
25 0355 0.4 / 1019 0.7 / F 1625 0.4 / 2245 0.7

11 0500 0.3 / 1121 0.9 / F 1725 0.3 / 2357 0.9
26 0454 0.4 / 1118 0.8 / SA 1716 0.3 / 2345 0.8

12 0551 0.2 / 1216 1.0 / SA 1813 0.2
27 0539 0.3 / 1204 0.8 / SU 1759 0.3

13 0047 0.9 / 0634 1.0 / SU 1302 1.0 / 1856 0.1
28 0029 0.8 / 0617 0.3 / M 1244 0.9 / 1838 0.2

14 0131 1.0 / 0712 0.1 / M 1343 1.0 / 1935 0.1
29 0107 0.9 / 0651 0.2 / TU 1322 0.9 / 1915 0.2

15 0212 1.0 / 0750 0.1 / TU 1423 1.0 / 2014 0.1
30 0148 0.9 / 0726 0.2 / W 1402 1.0 / 1953 0.1

DECEMBER

1 0228 1.0 / 0803 0.2 / TH 1443 1.0 / ● 2032 0.1
16 0321 0.9 / 0852 0.2 / F 1529 0.9 / 2119 0.1

2 0310 1.0 / 0842 0.2 / F 1527 1.0 / 2113 0.1
17 0400 0.9 / 0931 0.2 / SA 1610 0.9 / 2155 0.1

3 0353 1.0 / 0923 0.2 / SA 1611 1.0 / 2155 0.1
18 0438 0.9 / 1009 0.2 / SU 1649 0.8 / 2231 0.2

4 0438 1.0 / 1008 0.2 / SU 1658 1.0 / 2240 0.2
19 0515 0.8 / 1048 0.2 / M 1728 0.8 / 2306 0.2

5 0525 1.0 / 1057 0.2 / M 1747 0.9 / 2329 0.2
20 0553 0.8 / 1128 0.3 / TU 1808 0.8 / 2344 0.2

6 0617 0.9 / 1153 0.3 / TU 1842 0.9
21 0634 0.8 / 1212 0.3 / W 1850 0.7

7 0028 0.3 / 0716 0.9 / W 1304 0.3 / 1944 0.8
22 0026 0.3 / 0719 0.7 / TH 1306 0.3 / 1936 0.7

8 0143 0.3 / 0822 0.9 / TH 1425 0.3 / ☽ 2054 0.8
23 0119 0.3 / 0809 0.7 / F 1407 0.3 / ☽ 2029 0.7

9 0302 0.3 / 0932 0.9 / F 1541 0.3 / 2210 0.8
24 0223 0.3 / 0905 0.7 / SA 1511 0.3 / 2128 0.7

10 0414 0.3 / 1042 0.9 / SA 1650 0.2 / 2323 0.8
25 0333 0.3 / 1005 0.7 / SU 1617 0.3 / 2236 0.7

11 0516 0.3 / 1144 0.9 / SU 1749 0.2
26 0441 0.3 / 1108 0.8 / M 1718 0.3 / 2342 0.7

12 0022 0.8 / 0608 0.2 / M 1235 0.9 / 1837 0.2
27 0537 0.3 / 1203 0.8 / TU 1810 0.2

13 0112 0.9 / 0652 0.2 / TU 1321 0.9 / 1921 0.2
28 0037 0.8 / 0624 0.2 / W 1254 0.8 / 1855 0.2

14 0156 0.9 / 0733 0.2 / W 1405 0.9 / 2001 0.1
29 0126 0.8 / 0707 0.2 / TH 1342 0.9 / 1939 0.1

15 0239 0.9 / 0813 0.2 / TH 1447 0.9 / ○ 2041 0.1
30 0213 0.9 / 0749 0.2 / F 1430 0.9 / 2024 0.1

31 0300 0.9 / 0834 0.1 / SA 1519 1.0 / ● 2109 0.1

Chart Datum: 0·25 metres below Alicante Datum (Mean Sea Level, Alicante)

》》 **FREE** monthly updates from 《《
www.reedsalmanac.co.uk

INDEX

Admiralty chart symbols	back cover
Selected lights, buoys and waypoints	
1 SW England	9
2 S Central England	11
3 SE England	13
4 East England	14
5 East Scotland	17
6 NW Scotland	20
7 SW Scotland	22
8 NW England, Wales and E Ireland	24
9 SW England, S Wales and S Ireland	26
10 Ireland	28
11 W Denmark	31
12 Germany	33
13 Netherlands and Belgium	35
14 N France	38
15 N Central France and Channel Isles	40
16 N & S Brittany	42
17 W France and NE Spain	45
18 N & NW Spain	47
19 Portugal	49
20 SW Spain & Gibraltar	51
BBC Radio 4 Broadcasts	70
Beaufort Scale	67
Belgium CRS weather forecasts	86
Brest tidal coefficients	143
Channel Is weather forecasts	81
Coast Radio Stations, VHF	112
Communications chapter	94
Contents	4
Conversion Tables	65
Danish CRS weather forecasts	83
Danish Shipping Forecast Areas	83
Distance from Dipping Lights Table	64
Distress	front cover
Dover tidal ranges	142
First Aid	120
Essential information	120
General medical information	121
First Aid Kit	123
Flags - International Code	inside front cover
French Shipping Forecast Areas	88
French weather forecasts	86
German CRS weather forecasts	84
Gibraltar weather forecasts	92
GMDSS	139
Helicopter rescue	119
IALA Buoyage	inside front cover
Irish CRS weather forecasts	82
Light Recognition	inside back cover
Lights for small craft	inside front cover
Marinas	53
Marinecall	75
MAYDAY	118
Medical help	119
Morse Code	inside front cover
Moonrise & moonset	61, 62
Military exercise areas	135
Navigation chapter	8
Navtex	73
Netherlands CG weather forecasts	85
Netherlands local radio weather forecasts	86
Port Radio Stations	
South coast of England	99
East coast of England	100
Scotland	101
West coast of England and Wales	102
Ireland	102
Denmark	103
Germany	103
Netherlands	104
Belgium	105
North France	106
Channel Islands	106
West France	106
Spain	107
Portugal	107
Gibraltar	107
Portuguese weather forecasts	91
Portuguese Shipping Forecast Areas	91
Radio data	97
Short, medium & long range radio comms	97
The marine VHF band	97
Medium range MF/RT	98
Traffic lists	98
Silence periods	98
Long range HF radio	98
Radio operation	95
Phonetic alphabet	95
Phonetic numerals	95
Prowords	96
Safety chapter	116
Safety, Think about	117
Secondary Ports & Tidal Differences	152
Shipping forecast record	69
Sounds signals & Shapes	115
SMS (Short Message Service)	77
Spanish CG MRCC/MRSC weather forecasts	89
Spanish & Portuguese CRS map	90
Spanish Shipping Forecast Areas	89
Special tidal instructions for places between Bournemouth & Selsey Bill	148
Speed, Time & Distance Table	63
Sunrise & sunset	59, 60
Telephone & Fax Weather Forecasts	75
Tides chapter	141
Tidal calculations	144
Tidal curves - Bournemouth to Selsey Bill	150
Tidal gates	
Southern England	171

Scotland	174
Irish Sea	177
Menai Strait	178

Tidal streams

English Channel & S Brittany	180
Portland	186
Isle of Wight	188
Channel Islands	194
North Sea	200
Scotland	206
West UK & Ireland	212

Tide Tables - Standard Ports

Aberdeen curves & predictions	286
Aberdeen secondary port data	156
Avonmouth curves & predictions	326
Avonmouth secondary port data	161
Belfast curves & predictions	334
Belfast secondary port data	162
Brest curves & predictions	398
Brest secondary port data	167
Burnham-on-Crouch curves & predictions	264
Cherbourg curves & predictions	382
Cherbourg secondary port data	167
Cobh curves & predictions	342
Cobh secondary port data	163
Cuxhaven curves & predictions	354
Cuxhaven secondary port data	164
Dartmouth curves & predictions	226
Dieppe curves & predictions	374
Dieppe secondary port data	166
Dover curves & predictions	250
Dover secondary port data	153
Dublin curves & predictions	330
Dublin secondary port data	162
Dunkerque curves & predictions	370
Dunkerque secondary port data	166
Esbjerg curves & predictions	346
Esbjerg secondary port data	164
Falmouth curves & predictions	218
Galway curves & predictions	338
Galway secondary port data	163
Gibraltar curves & predictions	410
Gibraltar secondary port data	170
Greenock curves & predictions	310
Greenock secondary port data	159
Helgoland curves & predictions	350
Helgoland secondary port data	164
Holyhead curves & predictions	318
Holyhead secondary port data	160
Hoek van Holland curves & predictions	362
Immingham curves & predictions	274
Immingham secondary port data	155
Le Havre curves & predictions	378
Le Havre secondary port data	166
Leith curves & predictions	282
Leith secondary port data	155
Lerwick curves & predictions	294
Lerwick secondary port data	157
Lisboa curves & predictions	406
Lisboa secondary port data	169
Liverpool curves & predictions	314
Liverpool secondary port data	159
London Bridge curves & predictions	258
London Bridge secondary port data	154
Lowestoft curves & predictions	270
Lowestoft secondary port data	155
Milford Haven curves & predictions	322
Milford Haven secondary port data	160
Oban curves & predictions	306
Oban secondary port data	158
Plymouth curves & predictions	222
Plymouth secondary port data	152
Pointe de Grave curves & predictions	402
Pointe de Grave secondary port data	168
Poole curves & predictions	234
Portland curves & predictions	230
Portland secondary port data	152
Portsmouth curves & predictions	242
Portsmouth secondary port data	152
River Tyne curves & predictions	278
River Tyne secondary port data	155
St Helier curves & predictions	394
St Helier secondary port data	167
St Malo curves & predictions	386
St Malo secondary port data	167
St Peter Port curves & predictions	390
Sheerness curves & predictions	254
Sheerness secondary port data	153
Shoreham curves & predictions	246
Shoreham secondary port data	153
Southampton curves & predictions	238
Southampton secondary port data	153
Stornoway curves & predictions	298
Stornoway secondary port data	157
Ullapool curves & predictions	302
Ullapool secondary port data	157
Vlissingen curves & predictions	366
Vlissingen secondary port data	165
Walton-on-the-Naze curves & predictions	266
Walton-on-the-Naze secondary port data	154
Wick curves & predictions	290
Wick secondary port data	156
Wilhelmshaven curves & predictions	358
Wilhelmshaven secondary port data	165
UK Shipping Forecast Areas	68
Vessel Traffic Service Charts	108
VHF Direction Finding Services	132
Weather chapter	66
Weather forecasts from HMCG	70
Weather forecasts - Local Radio Stations	71
Weather information, sources	78
Weather terms defined	67
Weather terms in five languages	92

415

Adlard Coles Nautical
THE BEST SAILING BOOKS

Practical

Fitting Out Your Boat
Micheal Naujok
£18.99
0713668067

12 Volt Bible
Miner Brotherton
£14.99
0713667036

Practical Boat Owner' Electrics Afloat
Alastair Garrod
£19.99
0713661496

Practical Books from
Adlard Coles Nautica

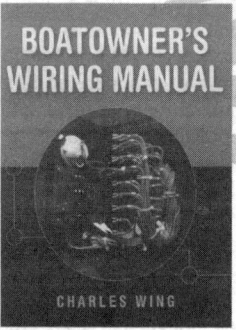

Boatowner's Wiring Manual
Charles Wing
£25.00
0713668660

The Rigging Handbook
Brion Toss
£30.00
0713669187

Boatowner's Practica and Technical Cruisin Manual
Nigel Calder
£39.99
0713661275

TO ORDER
Available from chandlers & bookshops or order direct from:
MDL, Houndmills, Basingstoke RG21 6XS
Tel: 01256 302692 email: mdl@macmillan.co.uk or www.adlardcoles.com